Research Methods in Anthropology

Tom Leatherman

Research Methods in Anthropology

Qualitative and Quantitative Approaches

FIFTH EDITION

H. RUSSELL BERNARD

ALTAMIRA
PRESS

A division of
ROWMAN & LITTLEFIELD PUBLISHERS, INC.
Lanham • New York • Toronto • Plymouth, UK

Published by AltaMira Press
A division of Rowman & Littlefield Publishers, Inc.
A wholly owned subsidiary of The Rowman & Littlefield Publishing Group, Inc.
4501 Forbes Boulevard, Suite 200, Lanham, Maryland 20706
http://www.altamirapress.com

Estover Road, Plymouth PL6 7PY, United Kingdom

British Library Cataloguing in Publication Information Available

Library of Congress Cataloging-in-Publication Data
Bernard, H. Russell (Harvey Russell), 1940–
    Research methods in anthropology : qualitative and quantitative approaches / H. Russell
Bernard.—5th ed.
        p.   cm.
    Includes bibliographical references and index.
    ISBN 978-0-7591-1241-4 (cloth : alk. paper)
    ISBN 978-0-7591-1242-1 (pbk. : alk. paper)
    ISBN 978-0-7591-1243-8 (electronic)
    1. Ethnology—Methodology.   I. Title.
GN345.B36   2011
301.072′1—dc22   2010047454

Printed in the United States of America

Contents

Preface to the Fifth Edition

Since 1988, when I wrote the first edition of this book, I've heard from many colleagues that their departments are offering courses in research methods. This is wonderful. Anthropologists of my generation, trained in the 1950s and 1960s, were hard-pressed to find courses we could take on how to do research. There was something rather mystical about the how-to of fieldwork; it seemed inappropriate to make the experience too methodical.

The mystique is still there. Anthropological fieldwork is fascinating and dangerous. Seriously, read Nancy Howell's (1990) book on the physical hazards of fieldwork if you think this is a joke. But many anthropologists have found that participant observation loses none of its allure when they collect data systematically and according to a research design. Instead, they learn that having lots of reliable data when they return from fieldwork makes the experience all the more magical.

I wrote this book to make it easier for students to collect and analyze reliable data beginning with their first fieldwork experience. We properly challenge one another's explanations for why Hindus don't eat their cattle and why, in some cultures, mothers are more likely than fathers are to abuse their children. That's how knowledge grows. Whatever our theories, though, all of us need data on which to test those theories. The methods for collecting and analyzing data belong to all of us.

WHAT'S IN THIS BOOK

The book begins with a chapter about where I think anthropology fits in the social sciences. With one foot planted squarely in the humanities and the other in the sciences, there has always been a certain tension in the discipline between those who would make anthropology a quantitative science and those whose goal it is to produce documents that convey the richness—indeed, the uniqueness—of human thought and experience.

Students of cultural anthropology and archeology may be asked early in their training to take a stand for qualitative *or* quantitative research. Readers of this textbook will find no support for this pernicious distinction. I lay out my support for positivism in chapter 1, but I also make clear that positivism is not a synonym for quantitative. As you read chapter 1, think about your own position. You don't have to agree with my ideas on epistemological issues to profit from the later chapters on how to select informants, how to choose a sample, how to do questionnaire surveys, how to write and manage field notes, and so on.

Chapter 2 introduces the vocabulary of social research. There's a lot of jargon, but it's the good kind. Important concepts deserve words of their own, and chapter 2 is full of important concepts like reliability, validity, levels of measurement, operationism, and covariation.

Whenever I introduce a new term, like **positivism**, **hermeneutics**, or whatever, I put it in boldface type. If you aren't sure what a **factorial design** is (while you're reading about focus groups in chapter 8, on unstructured and semistructured interviewing), the index will tell you that there are other examples of that piece of jargon in chapter 4 (on experiments), in chapter 9 (on questionnaires), and in chapter 19 (on analytic induction).

Chapter 3 is about preparing for research: choosing research topics and showing how your research question contributes to theory. We always want our research to be theoretically important, but what does that mean? After you study this chapter, you should know what theory is and how to tell if your research is likely to contribute to theory or not. It may seem incongruous to spend a lot of time talking about theory in a textbook about methods, but it isn't. Theory is about answering research questions . . . and so is method. I don't like the bogus distinction between method and theory any more than I like the one between qualitative and quantitative.

Part of preparing for research is covering the literature. In the old days, before the Internet, you could get away with starting a research paper or a grant proposal with the phrase "little is known about . . ." and filling in the blank. Now, with online databases, you simply can't do that. Chapter 3 is also one of several places in the book where I deal with ethics. I don't have a separate chapter on ethics. The topic is important in every phase of research, even in the beginning phase of choosing a problem to study.

Chapter 4 is about research design and the experimental method. You should come away from chapter 4 with a tendency to see the world as a series of natural experiments waiting for your evaluation.

Chapters 5, 6, and 7 are about sampling. Chapter 5 is an introduction to the basics: why we need samples and how samples of individual data and cultural data are different. Chapter 6 is about sampling theory—where we deal with the question: "How big should my sample be?" If you've had a course in statistics, the concepts in chapter 6 will be familiar to you. If you haven't had any stats before, read the chapter anyway. Trust me. There is almost no math in chapter 6. The formula for calculating the standard error of the mean has a square root sign. That's as hard as it gets. If you don't understand what the standard error is, you have two choices. You can ignore it and concentrate on the concepts that underlie good sampling or you can study chapter 20 on univariate statistics and return to chapter 6 later. Chapter 7 is about nonprobability sampling and about choosing informants.

I've placed the sampling chapters early in the book because the concepts in these chapters are so important. The validity of research findings depends crucially on measurement, but your ability to generalize from valid findings depends crucially on sampling.

Chapters 8–14 are about methods for collecting data. Chapter 8 is on unstructured and semistructured interviewing. All data gathering in fieldwork boils down to two broad kinds of activities: watching and listening. You can observe people and the environment and you can talk to people and get them to tell you things. Most data collection in anthropology is done by just talking to people. This chapter is about how to do that effectively.

Chapter 9 is devoted entirely to questionnaires—how to write good questions, how to train interviewers, the merits of face-to-face interviews versus self-administered and telephone interviews, minimizing response effects, and so on.

Chapter 10 is about structured interviewing for cultural domain analysis: pile sorts, triad tests, free listing, frame eliciting, ratings, rankings, and paired comparisons.

Chapter 11 is about how to build and use scales to measure concepts. This chapter has a long section on Likert-like scales, the most common scaling device in social research, but it also covers Guttman scaling, semantic differential scaling, and other methods.

Chapter 12 is about participant observation, the core method in cultural anthropology. Participant observation is what produces rapport, and rapport is what makes it possible for anthropologists to do all kinds of otherwise unthinkably intrusive things—watch people bury their dead, accompany fishermen for weeks at a time at sea, ask women how long they breast-feed, go into people's homes at random times and weigh their food, watch people apply poultices to open sores. . . .

Lone fieldworkers don't have time—even in a year—to interview hundreds and hundreds of people, so our work tends to be less reliable than that of our colleagues in some other disciplines. But participant observation lends validity to our work, and this is a very precious commodity. (More about the difference between reliability and validity in chapter 2.)

Participant observation fieldwork produces field notes—lots of them. Chapter 13 describes how to write and manage field notes.

Chapter 14 is about watching. There are two kinds of watching: the direct, obtrusive kind (standing around with a stopwatch and a note pad) and the indirect, unobtrusive kind (lurking out of sight). Direct observation includes continuous monitoring and spot sampling, and the latter is the method used in time allocation research. Unobtrusive observation poses serious ethical problems, which I treat in some detail in this chapter. One kind of unobtrusive observation poses hardly any ethical problems: research on the physical traces of behavior. You may be surprised at how much you can learn from studying phone bills, marriage contracts, office memos, and other traces of behavior. Your credit rating, after all, is based on other people's evaluation of the traces of your behavior.

Chapters 15–22 are about data analysis. Chapter 15 is a general introduction to the fundamentals of analysis. Data do not "speak for themselves." You have to process data, pore over them, sort them out, and produce an analysis. The canons of science that govern data analysis and the development of explanations apply equally to qualitative and quantitative data.

Chapters 16 and 17 are about analyzing data in cognitive anthropology. Chapter 16 focuses on analyzing the data from methods on interviewing introduced in chapter 10: free lists, pile sorts, and so on. This involves multidimensional scaling, cluster analysis, and cultural consensus analysis, so these methods of analysis are explained here, rather than in the chapter on multivariate statistics, as in previous editions. Chapter 17 is about ethnographic decision tree modeling, taxonomies, and componential analysis.

Chapters 18 and 19 cover text analysis. Chapter 18 is about methods that treat whole texts as the unit of interest, while chapter 19 is about methods that involve coding for themes, either inductively or a priori.

Finally, chapters 20, 21, and 22 are an introduction to the basics of statistical reasoning and data analysis—methods that are used across the social sciences. Chapter 20 deals with univariate statistics—that is, statistics that describe a *single variable*, without making any comparisons among variables. Chapters 21 and 22 are discussions of bivariate and multivariate statistics—statistics that describe *relationships among variables* and let you test hypotheses about what causes what.

If you want to become comfortable with statistical analysis, you need more than a basic course; you need a course in regression and applied multivariate analysis and a course (or a lot of hands-on practice) in the use of one of the major statistical packages, like SPSS®, SAS®, STATA®, and SYSTAT®. Neither the material in this book nor a course in the use of statistical packages is a replacement for taking statistics from professional instructors of that subject. Nevertheless, after working through the materials in chapters 20–22, you will be able to use basic statistics to describe your data and be able to take your data to a professional statistical consultant and understand what she or he suggests.

I don't provide exercises at the end of chapters. Instead, throughout the book, you'll find dozens of examples of real research that you can replicate. One of the best ways to learn about research is to repeat someone else's successful project. The best thing about replicating previous research is that *whatever* you find out has to be significant. Whether you corroborate or falsify someone else's findings, you've made a serious contribution to the store of knowledge. If you repeat any of the research projects described in this book, write and tell me about what you found.

WHAT'S NEW IN THIS EDITION?

There is now a section labeled **Further Reading** at the end of each chapter and pointers within the chapters to chunks of that further reading. The result is that the bibliography is about 40% larger than in the last edition. People ask me why there are so many references to really, really old stuff. The reason is that I want students to know that the literature on research methods is very rich and I want them to know about many of the classics. Many examples have been updated, including, when available, new information about classics.

The separate chapter on searching the literature is gone from this edition because students are universally aware of the databases. I've retained the information, however, about the databases that I think are most important for students to control and instructions on how to use the databases effectively.

Sampling takes up three chapters in this edition, up from two in the last one. In earlier editions, I treated consensus analysis in the chapter on nonprobability sampling and choosing informants. Consensus analysis has been moved to chapter 16, on cultural domain analysis.

Interviewing takes up three chapters in this edition. In chapter 8, on unstructured and semistructured interviewing, the sections on recording equipment and on voice recognition software (VRS) have been updated, and examples have been added or updated. Chapters 9 and 10 are on two very different kinds of structured interviewing. Chapter 9 focuses on questionnaires and surveys. I've updated the material on computer-based methods and on Internet-based surveys and added material on the list experiment. Chapter 10 introduces methods used in cognitive anthropology, including free lists, pile sorts, triad tests, and paired comparisons. Methods for analyzing these data are in chapter 16. In chapter 11, on scaling, I've added material on an instrument called the happiness stick. In chapter 12, on participant observation, I've updated several examples and added bibliography. In chapter 13, on taking and managing field notes, I've updated or added examples, and added information on using word processors as text managers. In chapter 14, the bibliography has been updated.

Chapter 15 is essentially unchanged. Chapter 16 contains new material on analyzing data from the systematic ethnographic methods described in chapter 10: free lists, pile sorts, and so on. Multidimensional scaling and cluster analysis are described in chapter 16, as is cultural consensus analysis and cultural consonance analysis. Chapter 17 continues with other methods associated with cognitive anthropology. The chapter on text analysis in the previous edition is now two chapters. The work in these two chapters owes much to my work with Gery Ryan (Bernard and Ryan 2010; Ryan and Bernard 2000, 2003). Chapter 18 focuses on methods for analyzing whole texts; chapter 19 deals with methods that involve finding themes in texts and analyzing the distribution of themes.

Chapters 20, 21, and 22 have been updated, but are essentially the same as chapters 19, 20, and 21 in the 4th edition.

A word about some things that are *not* in this book. Visual anthropology is developing quickly with the advent of easy-to-carry, easy-to-use cameras that produce high-quality still and moving images and synchronized sound as well as software for analyzing video as text (see appendix E). For more on visual anthropology, see El Guindi (2004).

Those interested in geospatial analysis should consult De Smith et al. (2007) and various online tutorials (e.g., http://www.spatialanalysisonline.com).

For methods in the study of online communities, see Hine (2000) and Kozinets (2010).

And finally, network analysis. Anthropologists contributed in the 1950s and '60s to the development of this field but, with a few exceptions, abandoned it after the 1970s. Interest by anthropologists has picked up recently with the development of software for collecting and analyzing network data (Borgatti et al. 2002) and especially personal network data (McCarty et al. 2010). Key work on analyzing personal, or egocentric, networks is by McCarty (2002) and Wellman (2007) (and see the entire May 2007 issue of *Field Methods*). For an introduction to the field of network analysis, see the online text by Hanneman and Riddle (2005): http://faculty.ucr.edu/~hanneman.

ACKNOWLEDGMENTS

My debt to colleagues, students, and friends is enormous. Colleagues and students who use this book continue to share their ideas with me on the teaching of research methods or to point out errors. My thanks to Susan Andreatta, Michael Chibnik, Bonnie Dixson, Kerry Feldman, Penn Handwerker, Margo-Lea Hurwicz, Paul James, Robert Van Kemper, Carmella Moore, John Poggie (and his student, Timothy Campbell), Paula Sabloff (and her student, Shimul Melwani), and David Zeitlyn. I'm grateful—and very pleased to know that the book is read so carefully and that students are learning from my mistakes.

I can not thank my students enough for the help I've received from them over the years, particularly Clarence Gravlee, Christopher McCarty, and Gery Ryan. Continuing discussions with Gravlee and McCarty have sharpened my focus on the methods for analyzing relational data. Ryan's influence will be evident in chapters 17, 18, and 19 in the discussions about ethnographic decision models, conversation analysis, and coding themes. He is also the coauthor with me of a book on analyzing qualitative data (Bernard and Ryan 2010).

Students at the University of Florida have been keen critics of my writing over the years. Domenick Dellino, Michael Evans, Camilla Harshbarger, Fred Hay, Shepherd Iverson, Christopher McCarty, and David Price were very helpful as I wrote the first edition. Holly Williams, Gery Ryan, Gene Ann Shelley, Barbara Marriott, Kenneth Adams, Susan Stans, Bryan Byrne, and Louis Forline gave me the benefit of their advice for the second edition. Discussions with Nanette Barkey, Clarence Gravlee, Harold Green, Scott Hill, David Kennedy, George Mbeh, Isaac Nyamongo, Jorge Rocha, Amanda Stronza, and Kenneth Sturrock helped me with the third edition, as did discussions with Oliver Kortendick, Julia Pauli, and Michael Schnegg at the University of Cologne during 1994–95. For the fourth and fifth editions, I have benefited from the continuing input of many former students, as well as from discussions with Aryeh Jacobsohn, Stacey Giroux, Mark House, Adam Kiš, Mason Mathews, Chad Maxwell, Rosalyn Negron, Fatma Soud, Eri Sugita, Tracy Van Holt, and Amber Wutich. All gave freely of their time to talk to me about research methods and about how to teach research methods.

Over 45 years of teaching research methods, I have benefited from the many textbooks on the subject in psychology (e.g., Kerlinger 1973; Murphy et al. 1937), sociology (e.g.,

Babbie 1983; Goode and Hatt 1952; Lundberg 1964; Nachmias and Nachmias 1976), and anthropology (e.g., Brim and Spain 1974; A. Johnson 1978; Pelto and Pelto 1978). The scholars whose works most influenced my thinking about research methods were Paul Lazarsfeld (1954, 1982; Lazarsfeld and Rosenberg 1955; Lazarsfeld et al. 1972) and Donald Campbell (1957, 1974, 1975; Campbell and Stanley 1966; Cook and Campbell 1979).

Over those same 45 years, I've profited from discussions about research methods with Michael Agar, Stephen Borgatti, James Boster, Devon Brewer, Michael Burton, Joel Cohen, Ronald Cohen, Roy D'Andrade, Don Dillman, William Dressler, Carol Ember, the late Melvin Ember, Michael Fischer, Linton Freeman, Sue Freeman, John Gatewood, Christina Gladwin, Ricardo Godoy, Raymond Hames, the late Marvin Harris, Penn Handwerker, Jeffrey Johnson, Hartmut Lang, Gary Martin, Michael Paolisso, Pertti Pelto, the late Jack Roberts, A. Kimball Romney, Lee Sailer, the late Thomas Schweizer, J. Richard Stepp, Susan Weller, Douglas White, and Oswald Werner. Other colleagues who have influenced on my thinking about research methods include Ronald Burt, Patrick Doreian, Linda Garro, Theodore Graves, Eugene Hammel, Allen Johnson, Charles Kadushin, Conrad Kottak, Maxine Margolis, Stuart Plattner, Ronald Rice, the late Peter Rossi, James Short, Harry Triandis, the late Charles Wagley, Eben Weitzman, Harry Wolcott, and Alvin Wolfe. Most of them knew that they were helping me talk and think through the issues presented in this book, but some may not have, so I take this opportunity to thank them all.

Time is a gift we all cherish. The first edition of this book was written in 1985–86 during a year of research leave from the University of Florida, for which I thank Charles Sidman, then dean of the College of Liberal Arts and Sciences. I had the opportunity to read widely about research methods and to begin writing the second edition when I was a guest professor at the Museum of Ethnology in Osaka, Japan, from March to June, 1991. My deep appreciation to Kazuko Matsuzawa for that opportunity. A year at the University of Cologne, in 1994–95, as a von Humboldt scholar, gave me the time to continue reading about research methods, across the social and behavioral sciences. Alas, my colleague and host for that year, Thomas Schweizer, died in 1999. The University of Florida granted me a sabbatical to bring out the fourth edition. Since 2007, I've been on a permanent sabbatical—that is, retired from full-time teaching.

In 1987, Pertti Pelto, Lee Sailer, and I taught the first National Science Foundation Summer Institute on Research Methods in Cultural Anthropology. Stephen Borgatti joined the team in 1988 (when Sailer left), and the three of us taught together for 8 years, from 1988 to 1995. My intellectual debt to those two colleagues is profound. Pelto, wrote the pioneering methods text in cultural anthropology (1970), and I've long been influenced by his sensible combination of ethnographic and numerical data in field research. Borgatti's influence is evident in my discussion of domain analysis. He is the author of ANTHROPAC, an antique DOS program that is still the only software I know that supports the collection and analysis of free lists, triad tests, pile sorts, and paired comparisons. The manual that Borgatti wrote for ANTHROPAC is an underground treasure (see appendix E). Teachers of these methods will want to consult that manual as well as Borgatti's web pages and his chapter in the *Ethnographer's Tool Kit* (Borgatti 1999).

When the original methods camp ended in 1995, Jeffrey Johnson initiated a new, NSF-supported program, the Summer Institute on Research Design in Cultural Anthropology (the SIRD)—this one for Ph.D. students. Johnson invited Susan Weller and me to join him in that program and I've benefited every year since then from long discussions with these colleagues—and the more than 200 students who have participated—about the pedagogy of research methods.

In 2005, we initiated another program, the Short Courses on Research Methods in Cultural Anthropology (the SCRM)—again, supported by NSF. These 5-day courses run in parallel to the SIRD at the Duke University Marine Laboratories, in Beaufort, North Carolina. And here again I have benefited from the wisdom of the faculty who teach in this program, including Christopher McCarty, Amber Wutich, Clarence Gravlee, Jeffrey Johnson, J. Richard Stepp, Gary Martin, Raymond Hames, Michael Paolisso, Elizabeth Cartwright, and Jerome Crowder.

My closest colleague, and the one to whom I am most intellectually indebted, was Peter Killworth, with whom I worked from 1972 until his death in 2008. Peter was a geophysicist at the University of Southampton and was accustomed to working with data that had been collected by deep-sea current meters, satellite weather scanners, and the like. He shared my vision of an effective science of humanity and he showed an appreciation for the difficulties a naturalist like me encounters in collecting real-life data, in the field, about human behavior and thought. Most importantly, he helped me see the possibilities for overcoming those difficulties through the application of scientific research practices. The results are never perfect, but the process of trying is always exhilarating. That's the central lesson of this book, and I hope it comes through.

Mitch Allen commissioned the first four editions of this book and is a treasured friend and critic. My editors for this edition, Jack Meinhardt and Marissa Parks, have continued this tradition of support. I thank the production staff at Rowman & Littlefield for their thoroughly professional work. It's so important to have really good production people on your side.

Finally, my enduring thanks to Carole Bernard for editing my work and for all her support over the years. Every writer needs an editor. Few are blessed with an editor who is a life partner.

H. R. B.
March 15, 2010
Gainesville, Florida

Anthropology and the Social Sciences

THE CRAFT OF RESEARCH

This book is about research methods in anthropology—methods for designing research, methods for sampling, methods for collecting data, and methods for analyzing data. And in anthropology, this all has to be done twice—once for qualitative data and once for quantitative data.

No one is expert in all the methods for research. But by the time you get through this book, you'll know about the range of methods used in anthropology and you'll know which kinds of research problems are best addressed by which methods.

Research is a craft. I'm not talking *analogy* here. Research isn't *like* a craft. It *is* a craft. If you know what people have to go through to become skilled carpenters or makers of clothes, you have some idea of what it takes to learn the skills for doing research. It takes practice, practice, and more practice.

Have you ever known a professional seamstress? My wife and I were doing fieldwork in Ixmiquilpan, a small town in the state of Hidalgo, Mexico, in 1962 when we met Florencia. She made dresses for little girls—Communion dresses, mostly. Mothers would bring their girls to Florencia's house. Florencia would look at the girls and say "turn around . . . turn again . . . OK," and that was that. The mother and daughter would leave, and Florencia would start making a dress. No pattern, no elaborate measurement. There would be one fitting to make some adjustments, and that was it.

We were amazed at Florencia's ability to pick up a scissors and start cutting fabric without a pattern. Then, 2 years later, in 1964, we went to Greece and met Irini. She made dresses for women on the island of Kalymnos where I did my doctoral fieldwork. Women would bring Irini a catalog or a picture—from Sears or from some Paris fashion show—and Irini would make the dresses. Irini was more cautious than Florencia was. She made lots of measurements and took notes. But there were no patterns. She just looked at her clients, made the measurements, and started cutting fabric.

How do people learn that much? With lots of practice. And that's the way it is with research. Don't expect to do perfect research the first time out. In fact, don't ever expect to do perfect research. Just expect that each time you do a research project, you will bring more and more experience to the effort and that your abilities to gather and analyze data and write up the results will get better and better.

METHODS BELONG TO ALL OF US

As you go through this book, you'll learn about methods that were developed in other fields as well as methods that were developed in anthropology. In my view, there are no anthropological or sociological or psychological methods. The questions we ask about the human condition may differ across the social sciences, but methods belong to all of us.

Truth is, from the earliest days of the discipline, right up to the present, anthropologists have been prodigious inventors, consumers, and adapters of research methods. Anthropologists developed some of the widely used methods for finding patterns in text, for studying how people use their time, and for learning how people make decisions. Those methods are up for grabs by everyone. The questionnaire survey has been developed mostly by sociologists, but that method is now everyone's. Psychologists make the most consistent use of the experiment, and historians of archives, but anthropologists use and contribute to the improvement of those methods, too.

Anthropologists make the most consistent use of participant observation, but that method turns up in political science, nursing, criminology, and education. The boundaries between the social science disciplines remain strong, but those boundaries are less and less about methods and even less and less about content. These days, anthropologists are just as likely as sociologists are to study the values of working-class Americans in Pennsylvania and New York (Durrenberger and Doukas 2008), or environmental degradation in Arizona (West and Vásquez-León 2008), or how women are socialized to become modern mothers in Greece (Paxon 2004).

In fact, the differences *within* anthropology and sociology with regard to methods are more important than the differences *between* those disciplines. There is an irreducible difference, for example, between those of us in any of the social sciences for whom the first principle of inquiry is that reality is constructed uniquely by each person (the **constructivist** view) and those of us who start from the principle that external reality awaits our discovery through a series of increasingly good approximations to the truth (the **positivist** view). There is also an important (but not incompatible) difference between those of us who seek to *understand* people's beliefs—the grand interpretivist tradition in the social sciences—and those of us who seek to *explain* what causes those beliefs and action and what those beliefs and actions cause—the equally grand scientific tradition.

Whatever our epistemological differences, though, the actual methods for collecting and analyzing data belong to everyone (Bernard 1993).

EPISTEMOLOGY: WAYS OF KNOWING

The problem with trying to write a book about research methods (besides the fact that there are so *many* of them) is that the word "method" has at least three meanings. At the most general level, it means **epistemology**, or the study of how we know things. At a still-pretty-general level, it's about strategic choices, like whether to do participant observation fieldwork, dig up information from libraries and archives, do a survey, or run an experiment. These are **strategic methods**, which means that they comprise lots of methods at once. (For a review of epistemological issues in anthropology, see Schweizer 1998.)

At the specific level, method is about choice of technique—whether to stratify a sample or not, whether to do face-to-face interviews or use the telephone or the Internet, whether to use a Solomon four-group design or a static-group comparison design in running an experiment, and so on. (We'll get to all these things as we go along—experimental designs in chapter 4, sampling in chapters 5, 6, and 7, personal and telephone interview formats in chapters 8 and 9).

When it comes to epistemology, there are several key questions. One is whether you subscribe to the philosophical principles of **rationalism** or **empiricism**. Another is whether you buy the assumptions of the scientific method, often called **positivism** in the social sciences, or favor the competing method, often called **humanism** or **interpretivism**. These are tough questions, with no easy answers. I discuss them in turn.

RATIONALISM, EMPIRICISM, AND KANT

The virtues and dangers of rationalism versus empiricism have been debated for centuries. Rationalism is the idea that human beings achieve knowledge because of their capacity to reason. From the rationalist perspective, there are a priori truths, which, if we just prepare our minds adequately, will become evident to us. From this perspective, progress of the human intellect over the centuries has resulted from reason. Many great thinkers, from Plato (428 327 BCE) to Leibnitz (Gottfried Wilhelm Baron von Leibniz, 1646–1716) subscribed to the rationalist principle of knowledge. "We hold these truths to be self-evident" is an example of assuming a priori truths.

The competing epistemology is empiricism. For empiricists, like John Locke (1632–1704), human beings are born **tabula rasa**—with a "clean slate." What we come to know is the result of our experience written on that slate. David Hume (1711–1776) elaborated the empiricist philosophy of knowledge: We see and hear and taste things, and, as we accumulate experience, we make generalizations. We come, in other words, to understand what is true from what we are exposed to.

This means, Hume held, that we can never be absolutely sure that what we know is true. (By contrast, if we reason our way to a priori truths, we can be certain of whatever knowledge we have gained.) Hume's brand of **skepticism** is a fundamental principle of modern science. The scientific method, as it's understood today, involves making incremental improvements in what we know, edging toward truth but never quite getting there—and always being ready to have yesterday's truths overturned by today's empirical findings.

Immanuel Kant (1724–1804) proposed a way out, an alternative to either rationalism or empiricism. A priori truths exist, he said, but if we see those truths it's because of the way our brains are structured. The human mind, said Kant, has a built-in capacity for ordering and organizing sensory experience. This was a powerful idea that led many scholars to look to the human mind itself for clues about how human behavior is ordered.

Noam Chomsky, for example, proposed that any human can learn any language because we have a universal grammar already built into our minds. This would account, he said, for the fact that material from one language can be translated into any other language. A competing theory was proposed by B. F. Skinner, a radical behaviorist. Humans learn their language, Skinner said, the way all animals learn everything, by operant conditioning, or reinforced learning. Babies learn the sounds of their language, for example, because people who speak the language reward babies for making the "right" sounds. A famous debate between Chomsky (1957, 1959) and Skinner (1957) that began over 50 years ago has been a hot topic for partisans on both sides ever since (**Further Reading:** the Chomsky-Skinner debate).

RATIONALISM, EMPIRICISM, AND MORALITY

The intellectual clash between empiricism and rationalism creates a dilemma for all social scientists. Empiricism holds that people learn their values and that values are therefore relative. I consider myself an empiricist, but I accept the rationalist idea that there are universal truths about right and wrong.

I'm not in the least interested, for example, in transcending my disgust with, or taking a value-neutral stance about genocide in Germany of the 1940s, or in Cambodia of the

1970s, or in Bosnia and Rwanda of the 1990s, or in Sudan in 2010. I can never say that the Aztec practice of sacrificing thousands of captured prisoners was just another religious practice that one has to tolerate to be a good cultural relativist. No one has ever found a satisfactory way out of this rationalist-empiricist dilemma. As a practical matter, I recognize that both rationalism and empiricism have contributed to our current understanding of the diversity of human behavior.

Modern social science has its roots in the empiricists of the French and Scottish Enlightenment. The early empiricists of the period, like David Hume, looked outside the human mind, to human behavior and experience, for answers to questions about human differences. They made the idea of a mechanistic science of humanity as plausible as the idea of a mechanistic science of other natural phenomena.

In the rest of this chapter, I outline the assumptions of the scientific method and how they apply to the study of human thought and behavior in the social sciences today.

THE NORMS OF SCIENCE
The norms of science are clear. Science is "an objective, logical, and systematic method of analysis of phenomena, devised to permit the accumulation of reliable knowledge" (Lastrucci 1963:6). Three words in Lastrucci's definition—"objective," "method," and "reliable"—are especially important.

1. **Objective**. The idea of truly objective inquiry has long been understood to be a delusion. Scientists do hold, however, that *striving* for objectivity is useful. In practice, this means being explicit about our measurements (whether we make them in words or in numbers), so that others can more easily find the errors we make. We constantly try to improve measurement, to make it more precise and more accurate, and we submit our findings to peer review—what Robert Merton called the "organized skepticism" of our colleagues (1938:334–36).
2. **Method**. Each scientific discipline has developed a set of techniques for gathering and handling data, but there is, in general, a single scientific method. The method is based on three assumptions: (1) that reality is "out there" to be discovered; (2) that direct observation is the way to discover it; and (3) that material explanations for observable phenomena are always sufficient and metaphysical explanations are never needed. Direct observation can be done with the naked eye or enhanced with various instruments (like microscopes); and human beings can be improved by training as instruments of observation. (I'll say more about that in chapters 12 and 14 on participant observation and direct observation.)

Metaphysics refers to explanations of phenomena by any nonmaterial force, such as the mind or spirit or a deity—things that, by definition, cannot be investigated by the methods of science. This does not deny the existence of metaphysical knowledge, but scientific and metaphysical knowledge are quite different. There are time-honored traditions of metaphysical knowledge—knowledge that comes from introspection, self-denial, and spiritual revelation—in cultures across the world.

In fact, science does not reject metaphysical knowledge—though individual scientists may do so—only the use of metaphysics to explain natural phenomena. The great insights about the nature of existence, expressed throughout the ages by poets, theologians, philosophers, historians, and other humanists may one day be understood as biophysical phenomena, but so far, they remain tantalizingly metaphysical.

3. **Reliable**. Something that is true in Detroit is just as true in Vladivostok and Nairobi. Knowledge can be kept secret by nations, but there can never be such a thing as "Venezuelan physics," "American chemistry," or "Kenyan geology."

Not that it hasn't been tried. From around 1935–1965, T. D. Lysenko, with the early help of Josef Stalin, succeeded in gaining absolute power over biology in what was then the Soviet Union. Lysenko developed a Lamarckian theory of genetics, in which human-induced changes in seeds would, he claimed, become inherited. Despite public rebuke from the entire non-Soviet scientific world, Lysenko's "Russian genetics" became official Soviet policy—a policy that nearly ruined agriculture in the Soviet Union and its European satellites well into the 1960s (Joravsky 1970; Soifer 1994) (**Further Reading:** the norms of science).

THE DEVELOPMENT OF SCIENCE: FROM DEMOCRITUS TO NEWTON

The scientific method is barely 400 years old, and its systematic application to human thought and behavior is less than half that. Aristotle insisted that knowledge should be based on experience and that conclusions about general cases should be based on the observation of more limited ones. But Aristotle did not advocate disinterested, objective accumulation of reliable knowledge. Moreover, like Aristotle, all scholars until the 17th century relied on metaphysical concepts, like the soul, to explain observable phenomena. Even in the 19th century, biologists still talked about "vital forces" as a way of explaining the existence of life.

Early Greek philosophers, like Democritus (460–370 BCE), who developed the atomic theory of matter, were certainly materialists, but one ancient scholar stands out for the kind of thinking that would eventually divorce science from studies of mystical phenomena. In his single surviving work, a poem entitled *On the Nature of the Universe* (1998), Titus Lucretius Carus (98–55 BCE) suggested that everything that existed in the world had to be made of some material substance. Consequently, if the soul and the gods were real, they had to be material, too (see Minadeo 1969). Lucretius' work did not have much impact on the way knowledge was pursued, and his work is little appreciated in the social sciences (but see Harris [1968] for an exception).

EXPLORATION, PRINTING, AND MODERN SCIENCE

Skip to around 1400, when a series of revolutionary changes began in Europe—some of which are still going on—that transformed Western society and other societies around the world. In 1413, the first Spanish ships began raiding the coast of West Africa, hijacking cargo and capturing slaves from local traders. New tools of navigation (the compass and the sextant) made it possible for adventurous plunderers to go farther and farther from European shores in search of booty.

These breakthroughs were like those in architecture and astronomy by the ancient Mayans and Egyptians. They were based on systematic observation of the natural world, but they were not generated by the social and philosophical enterprise we call science. That required several other revolutions.

Johannes Gutenberg (1397–1468) completed the first edition of the Bible on his newly invented printing press in 1455. (Printing presses had been used earlier in China, Japan, and Korea, but lacked movable type.) By the end of the 15th century, every major city in Europe had a press. Printed books provided a means for the accumulation and distribution of knowledge. Eventually, printing would make organized science possible, but it did not by itself guarantee the objective pursuit of reliable knowledge, any more than the invention of writing had done four millennia before (N. Z. Davis 1981; Eisenstein 1979).

Martin Luther (1483–1546) was born just 15 years after Gutenberg died. No historical figure is more associated with the Protestant Reformation, which began in 1517, and the Reformation added much to the history of modern science. It challenged the authority of the Roman Catholic Church to be the sole interpreter and disseminator of theological doctrine.

The Protestant affirmation of every person's right to interpret scripture required literacy on the part of everyone, not just the clergy. The printing press made it possible for every family of some means to own and read its own Bible. This promoted widespread literacy, in Europe and later in the United States, and this, in turn, helped make possible the development of science as an organized activity.

Galileo

The direct philosophical antecedents of modern science came at the end of the 16th century. If I had to pick one single figure on whom to bestow the honor of founding modern science, it would have to be Galileo Galilei (1564–1642). His best-known achievement was his thorough refutation of the Ptolemaic geocentric (Earth-centered) theory of the heavens. But he did more than just insist that scholars *observe* things rather than rely on metaphysical dogma to explain them. He developed the idea of the experiment by causing things to happen (rolling balls down differently inclined planes, for example, to see how fast they go) and measuring the results.

Galileo became professor of mathematics at the University of Padua in 1592 when he was just 28. He developed a new method for making lenses and used the new technology to study the motions of the planets. He concluded that the sun (as Copernicus claimed), not the Earth (as the ancient scholar Ptolemy had claimed) was at the center of the solar system.

This was one more threat to their authority that Roman church leaders didn't need at the time. They already had their hands full, what with breakaway factions in the Reformation and other political problems. The church reaffirmed its official support for the Ptolemaic theory, and in 1616 Galileo was ordered not to espouse either his refutation of it or his support for the Copernican heliocentric (sun-centered) theory of the heavens.

Galileo waited 16 years and published the book that established science as an effective method for seeking knowledge. The book's title was *Dialogue Concerning the Two Chief World Systems, Ptolemaic and Copernican*, and it still makes fascinating reading (Galilei 1967 [1632], 1997 [1632]). Between the direct observational evidence that he had gathered with his telescopes and the mathematical analyses that he developed for making sense of his data, Galileo hardly had to espouse anything. The Ptolemaic theory was simply rendered obsolete.

In 1633, Galileo was convicted by the Inquisition for heresy and disobedience. He was ordered to recant his sinful teachings and was confined to house arrest until his death in 1642. He nearly published *and* perished. For the record, in 1992, Pope John Paul II reversed the Roman Catholic Church's 1616 ban on teaching the Copernican theory and apologized for its condemnation of Galileo.

Bacon and Descartes

Two other figures are often cited as founders of modern scientific thinking: Francis Bacon (1561–1626) and René Descartes (1596–1650). Bacon is known for his emphasis on **induction**, the use of direct observation to confirm ideas and the linking together of observed facts to form theories or explanations of how natural phenomena work. Bacon correctly never told us how to get ideas or how to accomplish the linkage of empirical facts. Those activities remain essentially humanistic—you think hard (box 1.1).

BOX 1.1

ON INDUCTION AND DEDUCTION

There are two great epistemological approaches in all research: **induction** and **deduction**. In its idealized form, inductive research involves the search for pattern from observation and the development of explanations—theories—for those patterns through a series of hypotheses. The hypotheses are tested against new cases, modified, retested against yet more cases, and so on, until saturation occurs—that is, new cases stop requiring more testing. In its idealized form, deductive research starts with theories (derived from common sense, from observation, or from the literature) and hypotheses derived from theories, and then moves on to observations—which either confirm or falsify the hypotheses.

Real research is never purely inductive or purely deductive. In general, the less we know about a research problem, the more inductive we'll be—the more we let observation be our guide—and the more we know about a problem, the more deductive we'll be. **Exploratory research** is, therefore, likely to be pretty inductive, while **confirmatory research** is likely to be deductive.

When I started working with the Ñähñu of central Mexico, for example, I wondered why so many parents wanted their children *not* to learn how to read and write Ñähñu in school. As I became aware of the issue, I started asking everyone I talked to about it. With each new interview, pieces of the puzzle fell into place. This was a really, really inductive approach. After a while, as I came to understand the problem (it's a long, sad story, repeated across the world by indigenous people who have learned to devalue their own cultures) I started right off by asking people about my hunches. In other words, I switched to a really, really deductive approach.

It's messy, but this paradigm for building knowledge—the continual combination of inductive and deductive research—is used by scholars across the humanities and the sciences alike and has proved itself, over thousands of years. If we know anything about how and why stars explode or about how HIV is transmitted or about why women lower their fertility when they enter the labor market, it's because of this combination of effort. Human experience—the way real people experience real events—is endlessly interesting because it is endlessly unique, and so, in a way, the study of human experience is always exploratory, and is best done inductively. On the other hand, we also know that human experience is patterned. A migrant from Mexico who crosses the U.S. border one step ahead of the authorities lives through a unique experience and has a unique story to tell, but 20 such stories will almost certainly reveal similarities.

To Bacon goes the dubious honor of being the first "martyr of empiricism." In March 1626, at the age of 65, Bacon was driving through a rural area north of London. He had noticed earlier that both cold and fire impeded putrefaction (Bacon 1902 [1620]:137). To test his observation, he stopped his carriage, bought a hen from a local resident, killed the hen, and stuffed it with snow. Bacon was right—the cold snow did keep the bird from rotting—but he himself caught bronchitis and died a month later (Lea 1980).

Descartes didn't make any systematic, direct observations—he did neither fieldwork nor experiments—but in his *Discourse on Method* (1960 [1637]) and particularly in his monumental *Meditations* (1993 [1641]), he distinguished between the mind and all external material phenomena—matter—and argued for what is called **dualism** in philosophy, or the independent existence of the physical and the mental world. Descartes also outlined clearly his vision of a universal science of nature based on direct experience and the application of reason—that is, observation and theory.

Newton

Isaac Newton (1643–1727) pressed the scientific revolution at Cambridge University. He invented calculus and used it to develop celestial mechanics and other areas of physics. Just as important, he devised the **hypothetico-deductive model of science** that combines both **induction** (empirical observation) and **deduction** (reason) into a single, unified method (Toulmin 1980).

In this model, which more accurately reflects how scientists actually conduct their work, it makes no difference where you get an idea: from data, from a conversation with your brother-in-law, or from just plain, hard, reflexive thinking. What matters is whether you can *test* your idea against data in the real world. This model seems rudimentary to us now, but it is of fundamental importance and was quite revolutionary in the late 17th century (**Further Reading:** history of science).

SCIENCE, MONEY, AND WAR

The scientific approach to knowledge was established just as Europe began to experience the growth of industry and the development of large cities. Those cities were filled with uneducated factory laborers. This created a need for increased productivity in agriculture among those not engaged in industrial work.

Optimism for science ran high, as it became obvious that the new method for acquiring knowledge about natural phenomena promised bigger crops, more productive industry, and more successful military campaigns. The Royal Society in England has its roots in meetings among a group of philosophers in London in 1644 who did experiments (much like a club . . . they paid dues for the experiments).

One of the leaders of that group was John Wilkins. In 1648, he published *Mathematicall Magick*, a book about the benefit of science in developing new technology, "particularly for such Gentlemen as employ their Estates in those chargeable Adventures of Draining Mines, Coalpits, etc." The organizing mandate for the French Academy of Science in 1666 included a modest proposal to study "the explosive force of gunpowder enclosed (in small amounts) in an iron or very thick copper box" (Easlea 1980:207, 216).

As the potential benefits of science became evident, political support increased across Europe. More scientists were produced; more university posts were created for them to work in. More laboratories were established at academic centers. Journals and learned societies developed as scientists sought more outlets for publishing their work. Sharing knowledge through journals made it easier for scientists to do their own work and to advance through the university ranks. Publishing and sharing knowledge became a material benefit, and the behaviors were soon supported by a value, a norm.

The norm was so strong that European nations at war allowed enemy scientists to cross their borders freely in pursuit of knowledge. In 1780, Reverend Samuel Williams of Harvard University applied for and received a grant from the Massachusetts legislature to observe a total eclipse of the sun predicted for October 27. The perfect spot, he said, was an island off the coast of Massachusetts.

Unfortunately, Williams and his party would have to cross Penobscot Bay. The American Revolutionary War was still on, and the bay was controlled by the British. The speaker of the Massachusetts House of Representatives, John Hancock, wrote a letter to the commander of the British forces, saying "Though we are politically enemies, yet with regard to Science it is presumable we shall not dissent from the practice of civilized people in promoting it" (Rothschild 1981, quoted in Bermant 1982:126). The appeal of one "civilized" person to another worked. Williams got his free passage (box 1.2).

BOX 1.2

CAPTAIN STANLEY GETS INSTRUCTIONS

In 1846, the great naturalist Thomas Huxley set sail from Plymouth, England, to Australia on Her Majesty's ship, *Rattlesnake*. The expedition, to map the Torres Straits and to report on discoveries of scientific interest, would be gone for 4 years. The Admiralty Commission gave the captain of the ship, Owen Stanley, strict instructions to:

> refrain from any act of aggression towards the vessels or settlements of any nation with which we may be at war, as expeditions employed on behalf of discovery and science have always been considered by all civilised communities as acting under a general safeguard. [quoted in Mitchell 1913:14]

THE DEVELOPMENT OF SOCIAL SCIENCE: FROM NEWTON TO ROUSSEAU

It is fashionable these days to say that social science should not imitate physics. As it turns out, physics and social science were developed at about the same time, and on the same philosophical basis, by two friends, Isaac Newton and John Locke (1632–1704). It would not be until the 19th century that a formal program of applying the scientific method to the study of humanity would be proposed by Auguste Comte, Claude-Henri de Saint-Simon, Adolphe Quételet, and John Stuart Mill (more about them in a bit). But Locke understood that the rules of science applied equally to the study of celestial bodies (what Newton was interested in) and to human behavior (what Locke was interested in).

In his *An Essay Concerning Human Understanding* (1996 [1690]), Locke reasoned that because we cannot see everything and because we cannot even record perfectly what we do see, some knowledge will be closer to the truth than will other knowledge. Prediction of the behavior of planets might be more accurate than prediction of human behavior, but both predictions should be based on better and better observation, measurement, and reason (see Nisbet 1980; Woolhouse 1996).

Voltaire, Condorcet, and Rousseau

The legacy of Descartes, Galileo, and Locke was crucial to the 18th-century **Enlightenment** and to the development of social science. Voltaire (François Marie Arouet, 1694–1778) was an outspoken proponent of Newton's nonreligious approach to the study of all natural phenomena, including human behavior (Voltaire 1967 [1738]). In several essays, Voltaire introduced the idea of a science to uncover the laws of history. This was to be a science that could be applied to human affairs and *enlightened* those who governed so that they might govern better.

Other Enlightenment figures had quite specific ideas about the progress of humanity. Marie Jean de Condorcet (1743–1794) described all of human history in 10 stages, beginning with hunting and gathering, and moving up through pastoralism, agriculture, and several stages of Western states. The ninth stage, he reckoned, began with Descartes and ended with the French Revolution and the founding of the republic. The last stage was the future, reckoned as beginning with the French Revolution.

Jean-Jacques Rousseau (1712–1778), by contrast, believed that humanity had started out in a state of grace, characterized by equality of relations, but that civilization, with its agriculture and commerce, had corrupted humanity and led to slavery, taxation, and other inequalities. Rousseau was not, however, a raving romantic, as is sometimes supposed. He did not advocate that modern people abandon civilization and return to hunt their food in the forests. Rousseau held that the state embodied humanity's efforts, through a **social contract**, to control the evils brought about by civilization. In his classic work *On the Social Contract*, Rousseau (1988 [1762]) laid out a plan for a state-level society based on equality and agreement between the governed and those who govern.

The Enlightenment philosophers, from Bacon to Rousseau, produced a philosophy that focused on the use of knowledge in service to the improvement of humanity, or, if that weren't possible, at least to the amelioration of its pain. The idea that science and reason could lead humanity toward perfection may seem naive to some people these days, but the ideas of John Locke, Jean Jacques Rousseau, and other Enlightenment figures were built into the writings of Thomas Paine (1737–1809) and Thomas Jefferson (1743–1826), and were incorporated into the rhetoric surrounding rather sophisticated events—like the American and French Revolutions (**Further Reading:** history of social science).

EARLY POSITIVISM: QUÉTELET, SAINT-SIMON, COMTE

The person most responsible for laying out a program of mechanistic social science was Auguste Comte (1798–1857). In 1824, he wrote: "I believe that I shall succeed in having it recognized . . . that there are laws as well defined for the development of the human species as for the fall of a stone" (quoted in Sarton 1935:10).

Comte could not be bothered with the empirical research required to uncover the Newtonian laws of social evolution that he believed existed. He was content to deduce the social laws and to leave "the verification and development of them to the public" (1875–1877, III:xi; quoted in Harris 1968).

Not so Adolphe Quételet (1796–1874), a Belgian astronomer who turned his skills to both fundamental and applied social research. He developed life expectancy tables for insurance companies and, in his book *A Treatise on Man* (1969 [1842]), he presented statistics on crime and mortality in Europe. The first edition of that book (1835) carried the audacious subtitle "Social Physics," and, indeed, Quételet extracted some very strong generalizations from his data. He showed that, for the Paris of his day, it was easier to predict the proportion of men of a given age who would be in prison than the proportion of those same men who would die in a given year. "Each age [cohort]" said Quételet, "paid a more uniform and constant tribute to the jail than to the tomb" (1969 [1842]:viii).

Despite Quételet's superior empirical efforts, he did not succeed in building a following around his ideas for social science. But Claude-Henri de Saint-Simon (1760–1825) did, and he was apparently quite a figure. He fought in the American Revolution, became wealthy in land speculation in France, was imprisoned by Robespierre during the French Revolution, studied science after his release, and went bankrupt living flamboyantly.

Saint-Simon's arrogance must have been something. He proposed that scientists become priests of a new religion that would further the emerging industrial society and would distribute wealth equitably. Saint-Simon's narcissistic ideas were taken up by industrialists after his death in 1825, but the movement broke up in the early 1830s, partly because its treasury was impoverished by paying for some monumental parties (see Durkheim 1958).

Saint-Simon may have been the originator of the **positivist school** of social science, but it was Comte who developed the idea in a series of major books. Comte tried to forge a synthesis of the great ideas of the Enlightenment—the ideas of Kant, Hume, and Voltaire—and he hoped that the new science he envisioned would help to alleviate human suffering. Between 1830 and 1842, Comte published a six-volume work on what he called positive philosophy, in which he proposed his famous "law of three stages" through which knowledge developed (see Comte 1877, 1974).

In the first stage of human knowledge, said Comte, phenomena are explained by invoking the existence of capricious gods whose whims can't be predicted by human beings. Comte and his contemporaries proposed that religion itself evolved, beginning with the worship of inanimate objects (fetishism) and moving up through polytheism to monotheism. But any reliance on supernatural forces as explanations for phenomena, said Comte, even a modern belief in a single deity, represented a primitive and ineffectual stage of human knowledge.

Next came the metaphysical stage, in which explanations for observed phenomena are given in terms of "essences," like the "vital forces" commonly invoked by biologists of the time. The so-called positive stage of human knowledge is reached when people come to rely on empirical data, reason, and the development of scientific laws to explain phenomena. Comte's program of positivism, and his development of a new science he called "sociology," is contained in his four-volume work *System of Positive Polity* (1875–1877).

I share many of the sentiments expressed by the word "positivism," but I've never liked the word itself. I suppose we're stuck with it. Here is John Stuart Mill (1866) explaining the sentiments of the word to an English-speaking audience: "Whoever regards all events as parts of a constant order, each one being the invariable consequent of some antecedent condition, or combination of conditions, accepts fully the Positive mode of thought" (p. 15) and "All theories in which the ultimate standard of institutions and rules of actions was the happiness of mankind, and observation and experience the guides . . . are entitled to the name Positive" (p. 69).

Mill thought that the word "positive" was not really suited to English and would have preferred to use "phenomenal" or "experiential" in his translation of Comte. I wish Mill had trusted his gut on that one.

Comte's Excesses

Comte wanted to call the new positivistic science of humanity "social physiology," but Saint-Simon had used that term. Comte tried out the term "social physics," but apparently dropped it when he found that Quételet was using it, too. The term "sociology" became somewhat controversial; language puritans tried for a time to expunge it from the literature on the grounds that it was a bastardization—a mixture of both Latin (*societas*) and Greek (*logo*) roots. Despite the dispute over the name, Comte's vision of a scientific discipline that both focused on and served society found wide support.

Unfortunately, Comte, like Saint-Simon, had more in mind than just the pursuit of knowledge for the betterment of humankind. Comte envisioned a class of philosophers who, with support from the state, would direct all education. They would advise the government, which would be composed of capitalists "whose dignity and authority," explained John Stuart Mill, "are to be in the ratio of the degree of generality of their conceptions and operations—bankers at the summit, merchants next, then manufacturers, and agriculturalists at the bottom" (1866:122).

It got worse. Comte proposed his own religion; condemned the study of planets that were not visible to the naked eye; and advocated burning most books except for a hundred or so of the ones that people needed to become best educated. "As his thoughts grew more extravagant," Mill tells us, Comte's "self-confidence grew more outrageous. The height it ultimately attained," Mill continued, "must be seen, in his writings, to be believed" (p. 130).

Comte attracted a coterie of admirers who wanted to implement the master's plans. Mercifully, they are gone (we hope), but for many scholars, the word "positivism" still carries the taint of Comte's outrageous ego.

The Activist Legacy of Comte's Positivism

Despite Comte's excesses, there were three fundamental ideas in his brand of positivism that captured the imagination of many scholars in the 19th century and continue to motivate many social scientists, including me. The first is the idea that the scientific method is the surest way to produce knowledge about the natural world. The second is that scientifically produced knowledge is effective—it lets us control nature, whether we're talking about the weather, or disease, or our own fears, or buying habits. And the third is that effective knowledge can be used to improve human lives. As far as I'm concerned, those ideas haven't lost any of their luster.

Some people are very uncomfortable with this "mastery over nature" metaphor. When all is said and done, though, few people—not even the most outspoken critics of science— would give up the material benefits of science. For example, one of science's great triumphs over nature is antibiotics. We know that overprescription of those drugs eventually sets the stage for new strains of drug-resistant bacteria, but we also know perfectly well that we're not going to stop using antibiotics. We'll rely (we hope) on *more* science to come up with better bacteria fighters.

Air conditioning is another of science's triumphs over nature. In Florida, where I live, there is constant criticism of overdevelopment. But try getting middle-class people in my state to give up air conditioning for even a day in the summer and you'll find out in a hurry about the weakness of ideology compared to the power of creature comforts. If running air conditioners pollutes the air or uses up fossil fuel, we'll rely (we hope) on *more* science to solve those problems, too.

TECHNOLOGY AND SCIENCE

We are accustomed to thinking about the success of the physical and biological sciences, but not about the success of the social sciences. Ask 500 people, as I did in a telephone survey, to list "the major contributions that science has made to humanity" and there is strong consensus: Cures for diseases, space exploration, computers, nuclear power, satellite telecommunications, television, automobiles, artificial limbs, and transplant surgery head the list. Not one person—not one—mentioned the discovery of the dual helix structure of DNA or Einstein's theory of relativity.

In other words, the contributions of science are, in the public imagination, technologies—the things that provide the mastery over nature I mentioned.

Ask those same people to list "the major contributions that the social and behavioral sciences have made to humanity" and you get a long silence on the phone, followed by a raggedy list, with no consensus.

I want you to know, right off the bat, that social science is serious business and that it has been a roaring success, contributing mightily to humanity's global effort to control nature. Everyone in science today, from astronomy to zoology, uses probability theory and the array of statistical tools that have developed from that theory. It is all but forgotten that probability theory was applied social science from the start. It was developed in the 17th century by mathematicians Pierre Fermat (1601–1665) and Blaise Pascal (1623–1662) to help people do better in games of chance, and it was well established a century later when two other mathematicians, Daniel Bernoulli (1700–1782) and Jean D'Alambert (1717–1783), debated publicly the pros and cons of large-scale inoculations in Paris against smallpox.

In those days (before Edward Jenner's breakthrough in 1798), inoculations against smallpox involved injecting small doses of the live disease. There was a substantial risk of death from the inoculation (about 1-in-200), but the disease was ravaging cities in Europe and killing people by the thousands. The problem was to assess the probability of dying from smallpox versus dying from the vaccine.

This is one of the earliest uses of I have found of social science and probability theory in the making of state policy, but there were soon to be many more. One of them is state lotteries—taxes on people who are bad at math. Another is social security.

In 1889, Otto von Bismarck came up with a pension plan for retired German workers. Based on sound social science data, Bismarck's minister suggested that 70 would be just the right age for retirement. At that time, the average life expectancy in Germany was closer to 50, and just 30% of children born then could expect to live to 70. Germany lowered the retirement age to 65 in 1916, by which time, life expectancy had edged up a bit—to around 55 (Max-Planck Institute 2002). In 1935, when the Social Security system was signed into law in the United States, Germany's magic number 65 was adopted as the age of retirement. White children born that year in the United States had an average life expectancy of about 63; for black children it was about 51 (SAUS 1947:table 88).

Today, life expectancy in the highly industrialized nations is close to 80—fully 30 years longer than it was 100 years ago—and social science data are being used more than ever in the development of public policy. How much leisure time should we have? What kinds of tax structures are needed to support a medical system that caters to the needs of 80-somethings, when birthrates are low and there are fewer working adults to support the retirement of the elderly?

The success of social science is not all about probability theory and risk assessment. Fundamental breakthroughs by psychologists in understanding the stimulus-response mechanism in humans have made possible the treatment and management of phobias, bringing comfort to untold millions of people. Unfortunately, the same breakthroughs have brought us wildly successful attack ads in politics and millions of adolescents becoming hooked on cigarettes. I never said you'd *like* all the successes of social science.

And speaking of great successes that are easy not to like. . . . In 1895, Frederick Winslow Taylor read a paper before the American Society of Mechanical Engineers, entitled "A piece-rate system." This was the start of scientific management, which brought spectacular gains in productivity and profits—and spectacular gains in worker alienation as well. In 1911, F. B. Gilbreth studied bricklayers. He looked at things like where masons set up their pile of bricks and how far they had to reach to retrieve each brick. From these studies, he made recommendations on how to lessen worker fatigue, increase morale, and raise productivity through conservation of motion.

The method was an instant hit—at least among people who hired bricklayers. Before Gilbreth, the standard in the trade was 120 bricks per hour. After Gilbreth published, the standard reached 350 bricks per hour (Niebel 1982:24). Bricklayers, of course, were less enthusiastic about the new standards.

Just as in the physical and biological sciences, the application of social science knowledge can result in great benefits or great damage to humankind.

SOCIAL SCIENCE FAILURES

If the list of successes in the social sciences is long, so is the list of failures. School busing to achieve racial integration was based on scientific findings in a report by James Coleman (1966). Those findings were achieved in the best tradition of careful scholarship. They just happened to be wrong because the scientists involved in the study couldn't anticipate "white flight"—a phenomenon in which Whites abandoned cities for suburbs, taking much of the urban tax base with them and driving the inner cities further into poverty.

On the other hand, the list of failures in the physical and biological sciences is impressive. In the Middle Ages, alchemists tried everything they could to turn lead into gold. They had lots of people investing in them, but it just didn't work. Cold fusion is still a dream that attracts a few hardy souls. And no one who saw the explosion of the space shuttle *Challenger* on live television in January 1986 will ever forget it.

There are some really important lessons from all this. (1) Science isn't perfect but it isn't going away because it's just too successful at doing what people everywhere want it to do. (2) The sciences of human thought and human behavior are much, much more powerful than most people understand them to be. (3) The power of social science, like that of the physical and biological sciences, comes from the same source: the scientific method in which ideas, based on hunches or on formal theories, are put forward, tested publicly, and replaced by ideas that produce better results. (4) Social science knowledge, like that of any science, can be used to enhance our lives or to degrade them.

THE VARIETIES OF POSITIVISM

These days, positivism is often linked to support for whatever power relations happen to be in place. It's an astonishing turnabout, because historically, positivism was linked to social activism. In *The Subjection of Women* (1869), John Stuart Mill advocated full equality for women, and Adolphe Quételet, the Belgian astronomer whose study of demography and criminology carried the audacious title *Social Physics* (1969 [1835]), was a committed social reformer.

The legacy of positivism as a vehicle for social activism is clear in Jane Addams's work with destitute immigrants at Chicago's Hull House (1926), in Sidney and Beatrice Webb's attack on the abuses of the British medical system (1910), in Charles Booth's account of the living conditions of the poor in London (1902), and in Florence Nightingale's (1871) assessment of death rates in maternity hospitals. (See McDonald [1993] for an extended account of Nightingale's long-ignored research.)

The central position of positivism is that experience is the foundation of knowledge. We record what we experience—what we see others do, what we hear others say, what we feel others feel. The quality of the recording, then, becomes the key to knowledge. Can we, in fact, record what others do, say, and feel? Yes, of course we can. Are there pitfalls in doing so? Yes, of course there are. To some social researchers, these pitfalls are evidence of natural limits to a science of humanity; to others, like me, they are a challenge to extend the current limits by improving measurement. The fact that knowledge is tentative is something we all learn to live with.

LATER POSITIVISM: THE VIENNA CIRCLE

Positivism has taken some interesting turns. Ernst Mach (1838–1916), an Austrian physicist, took an arch-empiricist stance further than even Hume might have done himself: If you could not verify something, Mach insisted, you should question its existence. If you can't see it, it isn't there. This stance led Mach to reject the atomic theory of physics because, at the time, atoms could not be seen.

Discussion of Mach's ideas was the basis of a seminar group that met in Vienna and Berlin during the 1920s and 1930s. The group, composed of mathematicians, philosophers, and physicists, came to be known as the **Vienna Circle of logical positivists**. They were also known as logical empiricists, and when social scientists today discuss positivism, it is often this particular brand that they have in mind (see Mach 1976).

The term **logical empiricism** better reflects the philosophy of knowledge of the members of the Vienna Circle than does **logical positivism**. Unfortunately, Herbert Feigl and Albert Blumberg used "logical positivism" in the title of their 1931 article in the *Journal of Philosophy* in which they laid out the program of their movement, and the name "positivism" stuck—again (L. D. Smith 1986).

The fundamental principles of the Vienna Circle were that knowledge is based on experience and that metaphysical explanations of phenomena were incompatible with science. Science and philosophy, they said, should attempt to answer only scientifically answerable questions. A question like "Was Mozart or Brahms the better composer?" can only be addressed by metaphysics and should be left to artists.

In fact, the logical positivists of the Vienna Circle did not see art—painting, sculpture, poetry, music, literature, and literary criticism—as being in conflict with science. The arts, they said, allow people to express personal visions and emotions and are legitimate unto themselves. Because poets do not claim that their ideas are testable expressions of reality, their ideas can be judged on their own merits as either evocative and insightful, or not. Therefore, any source of wisdom (like poetry) that generates ideas, and science, which tests ideas, are mutually supportive and compatible (Feigl 1980).

I find this eminently sensible. Sometimes, when I read a really great line of poetry, like Robert Frost's line from *The Mending Wall*, "Good fences make good neighbors," I think "How could I *test* that? Do good fences *always* make good neighbors?" When sheepherders fenced off grazing lands across the western United States in the 19th century, keeping cattle out of certain regions, it started range wars.

Listen to what Frost had to say about this in the same poem: "Before I built a wall I'd ask to know / What I was walling in or walling out, / And to whom I was like to give offence." The way I see it, the search for understanding is a human activity, no matter who does it and no matter what epistemological assumptions they follow.

Understanding begins with questions and with ideas about how things work. When do fences make good neighbors? Why do women earn less, on average, for the same work as men in most industrialized countries? Why is Barbados's birthrate falling faster than Saudi

Arabia's? Why is there such a high rate of alcoholism on Native American reservations? Why do nation states, from Italy to Kenya, almost universally discourage people from maintaining minority languages? Why do public housing programs often wind up as slums? If advertising can get children hooked on cigarettes, why is public service advertising so ineffective in lowering the incidence of high-risk sex among adolescents?

INSTRUMENTAL POSITIVISM

The practice that many researchers today love to hate, however, is neither the positivism of Auguste Comte nor that of the Vienna Circle. It is, instead, what Christopher Bryant (1985:137) called **instrumental positivism**.

In his 1929 presidential address to the American Sociological Society, William F. Ogburn laid out the rules. In turning sociology into a science, he said, "it will be necessary to crush out emotion." Further, "it will be desirable to taboo ethics and values (except in choosing problems); and it will be inevitable that we shall have to spend most of our time doing hard, dull, tedious, and routine tasks" (Ogburn 1930:10). Eventually, he said, there would be no need for a separate field of statistics because "all sociologists will be statisticians" (p. 6).

THE REACTION AGAINST POSITIVISM

That kind of rhetoric just begged to be reviled. In *The Counter-Revolution of Science*, Friedrich von Hayek (1952) laid out the case against the possibility of what Ogburn imagined would be a science of humanity. In the social sciences, Hayek said, we deal with mental phenomena, not with material facts. The data of the social sciences, Hayek insisted, are not susceptible to treatment as if they were data from the natural world. To pretend that they are is what he called "scientism."

Furthermore, said Hayek, scientism is more than just foolish. It is evil. The ideas of Comte and of Marx, said Hayek, gave people the false idea that governments and economies could be managed scientifically and this, he concluded, had encouraged the development of the communism and totalitarianism that seemed to be sweeping the world when he was writing in the 1950s (Hayek 1952:110, 206).

I have long appreciated Hayek's impassioned and articulate caution about the need to protect liberty, but he was wrong about positivism, and even about scientism. Science did not cause Nazi or Soviet tyranny any more than religion caused the tyranny of the Crusades or the burning of witches in 17th-century Salem, Massachusetts. Tyrants of every generation have used any means, including any convenient epistemology or cosmology, to justify and further their despicable behavior. Whether tyrants seek to justify their power by claiming that they speak to the gods or to scientists, the awful result is the same. But the *explanation* for tyranny is surely neither religion nor science.

It is also apparent that an effective science of human behavior exists, no matter whether it's called positivism or scientism or human engineering or anything else. However distasteful it may be to some, John Stuart Mill's simple formula for a science applied to the study of human phenomena has been very successful in helping us understand (and control) human thought and behavior. Whether we like the outcomes is a matter of conscience, but no amount of moralizing diminishes the fact of success.

Today's truths are tomorrow's rubbish, in anthropology just as in physics, and no epistemological tradition has a patent on interesting questions or on good ideas about the answers to such questions. Several competing traditions offer alternatives to positivism in the social sciences. These include humanism, hermeneutics, and phenomenology (**Further Reading:** positivism).

Humanism

Humanism is an intellectual tradition that traces its roots to Protagoras' (485–410 BC) famous dictum that "Man is the measure of all things," which means that truth is not absolute but is decided by individual human judgment. Humanism has been historically at odds with the philosophy of knowledge represented by science.

Ferdinand C. S. Schiller (1864–1937), for example, was a leader of the European humanist revolt against positivism. He argued that as the method and contents of science are the products of human thought, reality and truth could not be "out there" to be found, as positivists assume, but must be made up by human beings (Schiller 1969 [1903]).

Wilhelm Dilthey (1833–1911) was another leader of the revolt against positivism in the social sciences. He argued that the methods of the physical sciences, although undeniably effective for the study of inanimate objects, were inappropriate for the study of human beings. There were, he insisted, two distinct kinds of sciences: the **Geisteswissenschaften** and the **Naturwissenschaften**—that is, the human sciences and the natural sciences. Human beings live in a web of meanings that they spin themselves. To study humans, he argued, we need to understand those meanings (Dilthey 1989 [1883]) (**Further Reading:** Dilthey).

Humanists, then, do not deny the effectiveness of science for the study of nonhuman objects, but emphasize the uniqueness of humanity and the need for a different (that is, nonscientific) method for studying human beings. Similarly, scientists do not deny the inherent value of humanistic knowledge. To explore whether King Lear is to be pitied as a pathetic leader or admired as a successful one is an exercise in seeking humanistic knowledge. The answer to the question cannot possibly be achieved by the scientific method.

In any event, finding *the* answer to the question is not important. Carefully *examining* the question of Lear, however, and producing many possible answers, leads to insight about the human condition. And that *is* important (box 1.3).

Hermeneutics

The ancient Greek god, Hermes (known as Mercury in the Roman pantheon—he of the winged hat), had the job of delivering and interpreting for humans the messages of the other gods. From this came the Greek word *hermeneus*, or interpreter, and from that comes our word **hermeneutics**, the continual interpretation and reinterpretation of texts.

Modern hermeneutics in social science is an outgrowth of the Western tradition of biblical exegesis. In that tradition, the Old and New Testaments are assumed to contain eternal truths, put there by an omnipotent creator through some emissaries—prophets, writers of the gospels, and the like. The idea is to continually interpret the words of those texts to understand their original meaning and their directives for living in the present (box 1.4).

The hermeneutic tradition has come into the social sciences with the close and careful study of all free-flowing texts. In anthropology, the texts may be myths or folk tales. The hermeneutic approach would stress that: (1) The myths contain some underlying meaning, at least for the people who tell the myths; and (2) It is our job to discover that meaning, knowing that the meaning can change over time and can also be different for subgroups within a society. Think, for example, of the stories taught in U.S. schools about Columbus's voyages. The meaning of those stories may be quite different for Navajos, urban African Americans, Chicanos, and Americans of northern and central European descent.

BOX 1.3

THE MANY KINDS OF HUMANISM

Just as there are many competing definitions of positivism, so there are for humanism as well. Humanism is often used as a synonym for humanitarian or compassionate values and a commitment to the amelioration of suffering. The problem is that died-in-the-wool positivists can also be committed to humanitarian values. Counting the dead *accurately* in Darfur is a really good way to preserve outrage. We need more, not less, science, lots and lots more, and more humanistically informed science, to contribute more to the amelioration of suffering and the weakening of false ideologies—racism, sexism, ethnic nationalism—in the world.

Humanism sometimes means a commitment to subjectivity—that is, to using our own feelings, values, and beliefs to achieve insight into the nature of human experience. In fact, **trained subjectivity** is the foundation of clinical disciplines, like psychology, as well as the foundation of participant observation ethnography. It isn't something apart from social science. (See Berg and Smith [1988] for a review of clinical methods in social research.)

Humanism sometimes means an appreciation of the unique in human experience. Writing a story about the thrill or the pain of giving birth, about surviving hand-to-hand combat, about living with AIDS, about winning or losing a long struggle with illness—or writing someone else's story for them, as ethnographers often do—are not activities *opposed* to a natural science of experience. They *are* the activities of a natural science of experience.

The hermeneutic approach—the discovery of the meaning of texts through constant interpretation and reinterpretation—is easily extended to the study of any body of texts: sets of political speeches, letters from soldiers in battle to their families at home, transcriptions of doctor-patient interactions. The idea that culture is "an assemblage of texts" is the basis for the interpretive anthropology of Clifford Geertz (1973). And Paul Ricoeur, arguing that action, like the written word, has meaning to actors, extended the hermeneutic approach even to free-flowing behavior itself (1981, 2007). In fact, portable camcorders make it easy to capture the natural behavior of people dancing, singing, interacting over meals, telling stories, and participating in events. In chapter 18, we'll look at how anthropologists apply the hermeneutic model to the study of culture (**Further Reading:** hermeneutics).

Phenomenology

Phenomenology is a branch of philosophy that emphasizes the direct experience of phenomena to determine their essences, the things that make them what they are. Gold, for example, has been a universal currency for centuries, but variations in its price are accidents of history, and do not reflect its essence. This distinction between essential and accidental properties of things was first made by Aristotle in his *Metaphysics* (especially Book VII) and has influenced philosophy ever since.

The philosophical foundations of phenomenology were developed by Edmund Husserl

BOX 1.4

BIBLICAL HERMENEUTICS

Rules for reconciling contradictions in scripture were developed by early Talmudic scholars, about a hundred years after the death of Jesus of Nazareth. For example, one of the rules was that "the meaning of a passage can be derived either from its context or from a statement later on in the same passage" (Jacobs 1995:236). Another was that "when two verses appear to contradict one another, a third verse can be discovered which reconciles them" (Jacobs 1995:236). Today, the 13 Talmudic rules for interpreting scripture remain part of the morning service among Orthodox Jews.

Scholars of the New Testament have used hermeneutic reasoning since the time of Augustine (354–430) to determine the order in which the three synoptic gospels (Mark, Mathew, and Luke) were written. They are called synoptic gospels because they are all synopses of the same events and can be lined up and compared for details. Whenever there is a discrepancy about the order of events, Mark and Mathew agree or Mark and Luke agree, but Mathew and Luke almost never agree against Mark. There are many theories about what caused this—including some that involve one or more of the gospels being derived from an undiscovered source. Research on this problem continues to this day (for a review, see Stein 1987).

Today, in the United States, constitutional law is a form of biblical hermeneutics. Jurists take it as their task to consider what the writers of each phrase in the U.S. Constitution meant when they wrote the phrase, and to interpret that meaning in light of current circumstances. It is exegesis on the U.S. Constitution that has produced entirely different interpretations across time about the legality of slavery, abortion, women's right to vote, the government's ability to tax income, and so on.

Although they have not influenced Western social science, there are long exegetical traditions in Islam (Abdul-Rahman 2003; Calder 1993), Hinduism (Sherma and Sharma 2008; Timm 1992), and other religions.

(1859–1938), who argued that the scientific method, appropriate for the study of physical phenomena, was inappropriate for the study of human thought and action (see Husserl 1964 [1907], 1999). Husserl was no antipositivist. What was needed, he said, was an approach that, like positivism, respects the data that we acquire through our senses but that is appropriate for understanding how human beings experience the world (Spiegelberg 1980:210). To do this requires putting aside—or **bracketing**—our biases so that we don't filter other people's experiences through our own cultural lens and can understand experiences as others experience them (Giorgi 1986; McNamara 2005:697; Moustakas 1994).

Husserl's ideas were elaborated by Alfred Schutz, and Schutz's version of phenomenology has had a major impact in social science, particularly in psychology but also in anthropology. When you study molecules, Schutz said, you don't have to worry about what the world "means" to the molecules (1962:59). But when you try to understand the reality of a human being, it's a different matter entirely. The only way to understand social reality, said Schutz, was through the meanings that people give to that reality. In a phenomeno-logical study, the researcher tries to see reality through another person's eyes.

Phenomenologists try to produce convincing descriptions of what they experience rather than explanations and causes. Good ethnography—a narrative that describes a culture or a part of a culture—is usually good phenomenology, and there is still no substi-tute for a good story, well told, especially if you're trying to make people understand how the people you've studied think and feel about their lives (**Further Reading:** phenome-nology).

ABOUT NUMBERS AND WORDS: THE QUALITATIVE/ QUANTITATIVE SPLIT

The split between the positivistic approach and the interpretive-phenomenological approach pervades the human sciences. In psychology and social psychology, most *research* is in the positivistic tradition, but much *clinical* work is in the interpretivist tradition because, as its practitioners cogently point out, it works. In sociology, there is a growing tradition of interpretive research, but most sociology is done from the positivist perspective.

In anthropology, the situation is a bit more complicated. Most anthropological *data collection* is done by fieldworkers who go out and stay out, watch and listen, take notes, and bring it all home. This makes anthropology a thoroughly empirical enterprise. But much of anthropological *data analysis* is done in the interpretivist tradition; some empiri-cal anthropologists reject the positivist epistemological tradition, and other empirical anthropologists (like me) identify with that tradition.

Notice in the last two paragraphs the use of words like "approach," "perspective," "tradition," and "epistemology." Not once did I say that "research in X is mostly quanti-tative" or that "research in Y is mostly qualitative." That's because a commitment to an interpretivist or a positivist epistemology is independent of any commitment to, or skill for, quantification. Searching the Bible for statistical evidence to support the subjugation of women doesn't turn the enterprise into science.

By the same token, at the early stages of its development, any science relies primarily on qualitative data. Long before the application of mathematics to describe the dynamics of avian flight, qualitative, fieldworking ornithologists did systematic observation and recorded (in words) data about such things as wing movements, perching stance, hovering patterns, and so on. Qualitative description is a kind of measurement, an integral part of the complex whole that comprises scientific research.

As sciences mature, they come inevitably to depend more and more on quantitative data and on quantitative tests of qualitatively described relations. But this never, ever lessens the need for or the importance of qualitative research in any science.

For example, qualitative research might lead us to say that "most of the land in Popot-lán is controlled by a minority." Later, quantitative research might result in our saying "76% of the land in Popotlán is controlled by 14% of the inhabitants." The first statement is not wrong, but its sentiment is confirmed and made stronger by the second statement. If it turned out that "54% of the land is controlled by 41% of the inhabitants," then the first part of the qualitative statement would still be true—more than 50% of the land is owned by less than 50% of the people, so most of the land is, indeed controlled by a minority—but the sentiment of the qualitative assertion would be rendered weak by the quantitative observations.

For anthropologists whose work is in the humanistic, phenomenological tradition, quantification is inappropriate. And for those whose work is in the positivist tradition, it is important to remember that numbers do not automatically make any inquiry scientific. In chapters 18 and 19, I'll discuss how texts—words and pictures—can be collected and analyzed by scholars who identify with either the positivist or the interpretivist tradition.

In the rest of this book, you'll read about methods for describing individuals and groups of people. Some of those methods involve library work, some involve controlled experiments, and some involve fieldwork. Some methods result in words, others in numbers. Never use the distinction between quantitative and qualitative as cover for talking about the difference between science and humanism. Lots of scientists do their work without numbers, and many scientists whose work is highly quantitative consider themselves humanists.

ETHICS AND SOCIAL SCIENCE

The biggest problem in conducting a science of human behavior is not selecting the right sample size or making the right measurement. It's doing those things ethically, so you can live with the consequences of your actions. I'm not exaggerating about this. Ethics is part of method in science, just as it is in medicine, business, or any other part of life. For although philosophers discuss the fine points of whether a true science of human behavior is really possible, effective social science is being done all the time, and with rather spectacular, if sometimes disturbing, success.

In the mid-19th century, when Quételet and Comte were laying down the program for a science of human affairs, no one could predict the outcome of elections, or help people through crippling phobias with behavior modification, or engineer the increased consumption of a particular brand of cigarettes. We may question the wisdom of engineering cigarette purchases in the first place, but the fact remains, we *can* do these things, we *are* doing these things, and we're getting better and better at it all the time.

It hardly needs to be pointed out that the increasing effectiveness of science over the past few centuries has also given human beings the ability to cause greater environmental degradation, to spread tyranny, and even to cause the ultimate, planetary catastrophe through nuclear war. This makes a science of humanity even more important now than it has ever been before.

Consider this: Marketers in a midwestern city, using the latest supercomputers, found that if someone bought disposable diapers at 5 P.M., the next thing he or she was likely to buy was a six-pack of beer. So they set up a display of chips next to the disposable diapers and increased snack sales by 17% (Wilke 1992). At the time, 20 years ago, that was a breakthrough in the monitoring of consumer behavior. Today, every time you buy something on the Internet or download a computer program or a piece of music, you leave a trail of information about yourself and your consumer preferences. By tracking your purchases over time, and by sharing information about your buying behavior across websites, market researchers develop ads that are targeted just for you.

We need to turn our skills in the production of such effective knowledge to solving the problems of hunger, disease, poverty, war, environmental pollution, family and ethnic violence, and racism, among others. Social scientists, including anthropologists, can play an important role in social change by predicting the consequences of ethically mandated programs and by refuting false notions (such as various forms of racism) that are inherent in most popular ethical systems. This has been a hallmark of anthropology since Franz Boas's devastating critique, a century ago, of racial theories about why some ethnic minorities in the United States were taller and healthier than others (Boas 1910b; Gravlee et al. 2003a, 2003b).

Don't get me wrong. The people who discovered that fact about the six-packs and the diapers were good scientists, as are the people who design all those automated data-collection mechanisms for monitoring your behavior on the Internet. I'm not calling for rules to make all those scientists work on problems that I think are important. Scientists choose to study the things that industry and government pay for, and those things change from country to country and from time to time in the same country. Science has to earn its support by producing useful knowledge. What "useful" means, however, changes from time to time even in the same society, depending on all sorts of historical circumstances.

Suppose we agreed that "useful" means to save lives. AIDS is a terrible disease, but over three times as many people died in motor vehicle accidents in the United States in 2005 as died of AIDS—about 45,000 and 13,000 respectively (SAUS 2009:table 118). Should we spend three times more money teaching safe driving than we do teaching safe sex?

I think the answer is pretty clear. In a democracy, researchers and activists want the freedom to put their skills and energies to work on what they think is important. Fortunately, that's just how it is, and, personally, I hope it stays just that way.

FURTHER READING

The Chomsky-Skinner debate: Chomsky (1969, 1972, 1977); MacCorquodale (1970); Palmer (2006); Stemmer (1990, 2004); Virués-Ortega (2006).
The norms of sciences: Ben-David and Sullivan (1975); Jasanoff et al. (1995); Merton (1970, 1973); Resnik (2007); Storer (1966).
The history of science: Porter (2003–2006). For the early history of science, see Sarton (1952–1959). See Drake (1978) and Finocchiaro (2005) for more on Galileo; see Cottingham (1999), Hausman and Hausman (1997), Markie (1986), Schuster (1977), and M. D. Wilson (1991) on Descartes.
The history of social science: S. Gordon (1991); McDonald (1994); Olson (1993); R. Smith (1997); Wagner (2001); Znaniecki (1963 [1952]).
Positivism: Bryant (1985). See Goldman (2002) on social science and policy in 19th-century Britain and see O'Connor (2001) on social science and poverty in the United States. See Turner (1986) on the history of methods in the social sciences.
Dilthey: Hodges (1952); Makkreel (1975).
Hermeneutics: Hoffman et al. (2005); Sherratt (2006); Zigon (2009).
Phenomenology: Elliott (2005); Moran (2000); Sokolowski (2000); Zahavi (2003).

2

The Foundations of Social Research

THE LANGUAGE OF SOCIAL RESEARCH

This chapter is about the fundamental concepts of social research: **variables**, **measurement**, **validity**, **reliability**, **cause and effect**, and **theory**. When you finish this chapter, you should understand the crucial role of measurement in science and the mutually supportive roles of data and ideas in the development of theory.

You should also have a new skill: You should be able to **operationalize** any complex human phenomenon, like "machismo" or "anomie" or "alienation" or "acculturation." You should, in other words, be able to reduce any complex variable to a set of measurable traits.

By the end of this chapter, though, you should also become very critical of your new ability at operationalizing. Just because you *can* make up measurements doesn't guarantee that they'll be useful or meaningful. The better you get at concocting clever measurements for complex things, the more critical you'll become of your own concoctions and those of others.

VARIABLES

A **variable** is something that can take more than one value. The *values can be words or numbers*. If you ask a woman how old she was at her first pregnancy, the answer will be a number (16 or 40, or whatever), but if you ask her about her religion, the answer will be a word ("Muslim" or "Methodist").

Social research is based on defining variables, looking for associations among them, and trying to understand whether—and how—variation in one thing causes variation in another. Some common variables that you'll find in social research are age, sex, ethnicity, race, education, income, marital status, and occupation.

A few of the hundreds of variables you'll see in anthropological research include number of children by each of several wives in a polygynous household, distance from a clinic or a market or a source of clean water, blood pressure, and level of support for various causes (the distribution of clean needles to drug addicts, the new farmer's co-op, rebels fighting in Eritrea, etc.).

Variables Have Dimensions

Variables can be **unidimensional** or **multidimensional**. The distance from Chicago to Albuquerque can be expressed in driving time or in miles, but no matter how you measure it, distance is expressed as a straight line and straight lines are one dimensional. You can see this in figure 2.1.

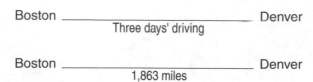

FIGURE 2.1.
Two ways to measure distance.

If we add Miami, we have three distances: Chicago-Miami, Chicago-Albuquerque, Albuquerque-Miami. One dimension isn't enough to express the relation among three cities. We have to use two dimensions. Look at figure 2.2.

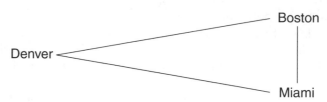

FIGURE 2.2.
Three points create two dimensions.

The two dimensions in figure 2.2 are up-down and right-left, or North-South and East-West. If we add Nairobi to the exercise, we'd either have to add a third dimension (straight through the paper at a slight downward angle from Albuquerque), or do what Gerardus Mercator (1512–1594) did to force a three-dimensional object (the Earth) into a two-dimensional picture. Mercator was able to project a sphere in two dimensions, but at the cost of distortion at the edges. This is why, on a map of the world, Greenland (an island of 840,000 square miles), looks the same size as China (a land mass of about 3.7 *million* square miles).

Height, weight, birth order, age, and marital status are unidimensional variables and are relatively easy to measure. By contrast, political orientation (being conservative or liberal) is multidimensional and is, therefore, a lot more difficult to measure. We often talk about political orientation as if it were unidimensional, with people lying somewhere along a line between strictly conservative and strictly liberal. But if you think about it, people can be liberal about some dimensions of life and conservative about others. For example, you might agree strongly with the statement that "men and women should get equal pay for equal work" and also with the statement that "a strong military is necessary to defend freedom in America." These statements test political orientation about domestic economic policy and foreign policy—two of the many dimensions of political orientation.

Even something as seemingly straightforward as income is multidimensional. To measure the annual income of retired Americans in Florida, for example, you have to account for social security benefits, private pension funds, gifts from children and other kin, gambling winnings, tax credits, interest on savings, wages paid entirely in cash (including tips), food stamps. . . .

And don't think it's easier in out-of-the-way communities around the world. If you think it's tough assessing the amount that a waitress earns from tips, try assessing the amount a family in Haiti gets from people who are working in Miami and sending money home.

In chapter 11, I'll discuss the building of scales and how to test for the unidimensionality of variables.

Simplifying Variables: Race and Gender

In the United States, at least, race is treated (by academics as well as by people in general) as a **dichotomous variable**, with two values: black and white. This makes race easy to measure and, in fact, we've learned a lot by making the measurement simple. For example, any man in the United States who is labeled "black" is about seven times more likely to be the victim of homicide than is any man labeled "white." Black babies are about two-and-a-half times more likely to die in infancy than are white babies, and people labeled "black" are two-and-a-half times more likely as people labeled "white" to be poor (which meant $20,614 for a family of four in 2006) (SAUS 2009: tables 100, 111, 689).

Still, we know that there are gradations of skin color besides black and white, so it's reasonable to ask whether people who are *more* black are *more* likely to be a victim of homicide, to die in infancy, to be poor, etc. Around 1970, medical researchers began to find a relation in the United States between darkness of skin color and blood pressure among people labeled "Blacks" (see Boyle 1970; Harburg et al. 1978). The darker the skin, the higher the blood pressure was likely to be.

Later, researchers began to find that education and social class were more important predictors of high blood pressure among Blacks than was darkness of skin color (see Keil, Sandifer et al. 1981; Keil, Tyroler et al. 1977). This meant that darker-skinned people were more likely to be the victims of discrimination and, as a consequence, uneducated and poor. Poverty causes stress and poor diet, both of which are direct causes of high blood pressure.

But suppose we treated skin color as the continuous variable it really is rather than as a dichotomous variable? Clarence Gravlee (2002b; Gravlee et al. 2005) did this in his study of race and blood pressure in Puerto Rico. He measured skin color in two ways. First, he showed people a line with nine numbers on it and asked them to rate themselves from light to dark by telling him which number best described their skin color. Then he measured the color of people's inner arm with a photospectrometer. The first measure is emic (what people think, themselves, about their color) and the second is etic (an objective, external measurement that doesn't depend on what people think).

Now, etic skin color—the amount of melanin that people have in their skin, as measured by a photospectrometer—by itself doesn't account for variation in blood pressure. But the *difference* between etic skin color and what people *say* their color is strongly associated with people's blood pressure (Gravlee 2002b:182). The relationship between these variables is anything but simple. Poor people who rate themselves as having darker skin than they really have are likely to have higher blood pressure. For middle-class people, it's the other way around: They are likely to have lower blood pressure when they rate their skin color as darker than it really is. The puzzle requires a lot more work, but this much is clear: Variation in blood pressure is not caused by melanin (Gravlee and Dressler 2005) (box 2.1).

Gender is another dichotomous variable (male and female) that is more complex than it seems. We usually measure gender according to the presence of male or female sexual characteristics. Then we look at the relation between the presence of those characteristics and things like income, level of education, amount of labor migration, attitudes to various social issues, aptitude for math, success in certain jobs, and so on. But if you think about it, we're not interested in whether differences in human anatomy predict any of these things. What we really want to know is how being *more* male or *more* female (socially and

BOX 2.1

EVERY RESEARCH QUESTION HAS AN ETHICAL COMPONENT

It may not be possible for everyone who uses skin color as an independent variable to measure it with a photospectrometer (the gadgets are very expensive), but if we did this, we could assess whether white schoolteachers react more negatively to darker-skinned black children than they do to lighter-skinned black children, and if so, by how much. This would help us account for some of the variation in black children's school scores as a function of teacher reaction to skin color. This, in turn, would show *how* skin color leads to discrimination in education, *how* discrimination in education leads to poverty, and *how* all this leads to lowered life expectancy.

We already know that Whites live longer than Blacks do. Making skin color a continuous variable would help us learn how racism actually works, not just its consequences. If the benefits of such research are attractive, though, consider the risks. Racists might claim that our findings support their despicable ideas about the genetic inferiority of African Americans. Life insurance companies might start charging premiums based on amount of skin pigmentation. Even if the Supreme Court ruled against this practice, how many people would be hurt before the matter was adjudicated? As you can see, every research question has an ethical component.

psychologically) predicts attitudes about social issues, success in various jobs, and many other things—like the ability to secure agricultural credit, the ability to cope with widowhood, or health status in old age.

Sandra Bem (1974, 1979) developed a scale called the BSRI (Bem Sex Role Inventory) to measure sex-role identity. The scale consists of 60 words or phrases: 20 that represent what Americans in the early 1970s generally thought of as masculine traits (like independent and assertive); 20 that represented generally accepted feminine traits (like affectionate and sympathetic); and 20 that represented generally accepted gender-neutral traits (like tactful and happy). Respondents rate themselves on a scale of 1 to 7 on how much they think each trait applies to them. Depending on your score, you are either "sex typed" (displaying stereotyped feminine traits or masculine traits) or androgynous (getting a high score on both feminine and masculine traits) or undifferentiated (getting a low score on both feminine and masculine traits).

The BSRI has been used in hundreds of studies across many societies and, although ideas about typically masculine or feminine traits have changed in four decades, the work has produced many interesting results. In Finland, Sundvik and Lindeman (1993) applied the BSRI to 257 managers (159 men and 98 women) of a government-controlled transportation company. Each manager had rated a subordinate on 30 dimensions—things like the ability to get along with others, independence in getting the job done, willingness to implement innovations, and so on. The sex-typed female managers (the women who scored high on femaleness, according to the BSRI) rated their male subordinates more favorably than they rated their female subordinates. Similarly, the sex-typed male managers rated their female subordinates more favorably than they rated their male subordinates.

The bottom line, according to Sundvik and Lindeman: "Among persons whose self-concepts are formed on the basis of gender, both the queen bee and the king ape syndromes are alive and well" (1993:8). Sex-typed managers discriminate against subordinates of the same sex.

Of course, traits thought to be masculine in one culture might be thought of as feminine in another. Aggressiveness is a trait widely viewed across many cultures to be desirable for men and boys and undesirable for women and girls. In Zimbabwe, however, 488 schoolteachers, half of whom were men, gave this trait their lowest desirability rating of the 20 masculine items in the BSRI (Wilson et al. 1990).

In Japan, Katsurada and Sugihara (1999) found that all 20 masculine traits in the BSRI were culturally appropriate, but that three of the classically 20 feminine traits in the scale ("sensitive to the needs of others," "understanding," and "loyal") were inappropriate. (Loyalty, for example, is seen as a highly desirable trait for everyone in Japan, so it can't be used in a test to distinguish between men and women.) Based on tests with 300 college students, Katsurada and Sugihara recommend substituting "conscientious," "tactful," and "happy" in the list of feminine adjectives when the BSRI is used in Japan. After nearly 40 years of research with the BSRI, we've learned a lot about the differences between men and women.

One thing we've learned is that those differences are much more complex than a biological dichotomy would make them appear to be. We've also learned that gender role differences are even more complex than Bem imagined. Choi and Fuqua (2003) looked at 23 validation studies of the BSRI and found that Bem's inventory doesn't fully capture the complexity of masculinity and femininity. But that just means that we're learning more with each generation of researchers—exactly what we expect from a cumulative science (**Further Reading:** measuring gender across cultures).

Dependent and Independent Variables

Beginning in the 1840s, breakthroughs in sociology and anthropology produced insights into the impact of economic and political forces on demography. One practical result of all this work was life insurance. The way life insurance works is that you bet the company that you'll die within 365 days. You answer a few questions (How old are you? Do you smoke? What do you do for a living? Do you fly a small plane?), and the company sets the odds—say, your $235 against the company's promise to pay your heirs $100,000 if you win the bet and die within 365 days. But if you *lose* the bet and stay alive, they keep your $235, and next year you go through all this again, except that now the odds are raised against you to, say, your $300 against the company's promise to pay your heirs a lot of money.

For insurance companies to turn a profit, they have to win more bets than they lose. They can make mistakes at the individual level, but in the aggregate (that is, averaging over all people) they have to predict longevity from things they can measure.

Longevity, then, is the **dependent variable**, because it *depends on* sex, education, occupation, etc. These latter are called **independent variables** because they are logically prior to, and therefore independent of, the dependent variable of longevity. How long you live doesn't have any effect on your sex. In our earlier example, blood pressure was the dependent variable. There is no way skin color depends on a person's blood pressure.

It's not always easy to tell whether a variable is independent or dependent. Does high female infant mortality among Amazonian tribal people depend on high levels of warfare, or is it the other way around? Does high income depend on having a lot of land, or vice versa? Do inner-city adolescent girls get pregnant because they are poor, or . . .? Does the need for litigation stimulate the production of attorneys, or . . . ?

Failure to understand which of two variables depends on the other is the source of endless shenanigans. One of my teachers, Oscar Lewis (1961, 1965), described what he called a "culture of poverty" among slum dwellers in cities around the world. People who live in a culture of poverty, said Lewis, are not very future oriented. This plays out, he said, in their shopping for food every day and in never buying large economy sizes of anything. Lewis's point was that truly poor people can't invest in soap futures by buying large boxes of it. He saw a low level of expressed orientation toward the future, then, as the dependent variable and poverty as the independent variable.

Many people interpreted Lewis's work as meaning exactly the opposite: that poverty is caused by a low level of future orientation. According to this topsy-turvy, victim-blaming reasoning, if poor people everywhere would just learn to save their money and invest in the future, then they could break the poverty cycle. Such reasoning may serve to create pointless programs to teach poor people how to save money they don't have, but it doesn't do much else.

In rural West Virginia, for example, there is a lot of teen pregnancy and many adolescents drop out of high school. Since the 1960s, according to Bickel et al. (1997), state policymakers in West Virginia have blamed these behaviors on the culture of poverty. The behaviors that state policymakers want so much to change, however, are caused by the continuing deterioration of economic and social conditions in rural communities. No amount of "educating" poor people about their bad habits will change the material circumstances that cause the so-called culture of poverty (box 2.2).

MEASUREMENT AND CONCEPTS

Variables are measured by their **indicators**, and indicators are defined by their **values**. Some variables, and their indicators, are easily observed and measured. Others are more conceptual. The difference is important.

Consider the variables race and gender again. If skin color can take one of two values (black or white), then to *measure* race you simply look at a person and decide which value to record. If you use secondary sexual characteristics as an indicator of gender, then to *measure* gender you look at a person and decide whether they are female or male.

In other words, *measurement is deciding which value to record*. That decision is prone to error. Some people whom you classify as white or black might be classified as black or white by another observer. And gender is even worse. Many people, both men and women, have ambiguous secondary sexual characteristics and many women wear what were once considered to be men's clothes. Is Pat a man's name or a woman's? What about Chris? Leslie? Any of these indicators may lead you into making the wrong measurement—marking down a man or boy as a woman or girl, or vice versa.

Improving measurement in science means lowering the probability of and the amount of error. Light-skinned African Americans who cease to identify themselves ethnically as black persons count on those errors for what they hope will be upward economic mobility. Dark-skinned "Whites," like some Americans of Mediterranean descent, sometimes complain that they are being "mistaken for" Blacks and discriminated against.

Race and gender are concepts or constructs. We have to make them up to study them. All variables are concepts, but some concepts, like height and weight, are easy to measure; other concepts like religious intensity, jealousy, compassion, willingness to accept new

BOX 2.2

THE EDUCATIONAL MODEL OF SOCIAL CHANGE

This **educational model of social change** is a lesson in confusion about dependent and independent variables. The model is based on the attractive idea that, because the last thing that happens before an action is a thought, if you want to create better actions then you need to create better thoughts. In other words, if you want to change people's behavior, you have to change how they think: Teach women in India the value of small families so they'll use birth control to prevent unwanted pregnancies; teach Kenyans why it's important to use bed nets to prevent malaria; teach farmers across the world the importance of washing their hands after handling manure and before preparing or eating food.

The educational model is the basis for one of the world's biggest industries—social change and development—but the model is mostly ineffective because behavioral change (the supposed dependent variable) doesn't usually depend on education (the supposed independent variable). In fact, across the developing world, when women have access to well-paying jobs outside the home, they tend to lower their fertility. Once that happens, they encourage their daughters to stay in school longer (Handwerker 1989). Education doesn't just cause jobs to happen. Instead, jobs for women in one generation cause education in the next. (I'll have more to say on fertility control and the educational model of behavioral change in chapter 3, when I discuss the role of theory in the development of research questions.)

agricultural technologies, and tolerance for foreign fieldwork are complex and difficult to measure.

We are led to defining constructs by our experience: Some people just seem more religiously intense than others, more jealous than others, more tolerant of foreign fieldwork than others, etc. We verify our intuition about conceptual variables by measuring them, or by measuring their results.

Suppose you put an ad in the paper that says: "Roommate wanted. Easy-going, non-smoker preferred." When people answer the ad you can look at their fingers and smell their clothes to see if they smoke. But you have to ask people a series of indicator *questions* to gauge their easy-goingness.

Similarly, if you are doing fieldwork in a Peruvian highland village and you want to predict who among the villagers is predisposed to migrate to the coast in search of work, you will want to measure that predisposition with a series of indicators. In this case, the indicators can be answers to questions ("Have you ever thought about migrating?"). Or they might be observable facts (Does a person have a close relative who has already migrated?). Or they might be a combination of these.

It may be easier to measure some concepts than others, but all measurement is difficult. People have worked for centuries to develop good instruments for measuring things like temperature. And if it's difficult to measure temperature (a concept, after all, backed up by time-tested theories), how do you measure future orientation or machismo? Measuring variables like these is one of our biggest challenges because these variables are mostly what we're interested in.

One of the most famous variables in all of social science is "socioeconomic status" (SES). Measuring it is no easy task. You can use income as one indicator, but there are many wealthy people who have low SES (the so-called nouveau riche), and many relatively low-income people who have high SES (think of those down-at-the-heels nobles in England who have to open their castles to tourists to make ends meet).

You can add "level of education" to income as an indicator, but that still won't be enough in most societies of the world to get at something as multidimensional as SES. You can add occupation, father's occupation, number of generations in a community, and so on, depending on the group you are studying, and you still might wind up dissatisfied with the result if your measure fails to predict some dependent variable of interest.

And, as you saw with the Bem androgyny scale earlier, indicators of any concept may vary from culture to culture. This doesn't mean that measurement is impossible. *It means that you have to test (and, if necessary, adapt) every measure of every variable in every new culture where you want to use it.*

CONCEPTUAL AND OPERATIONAL DEFINITIONS

Although most of the interesting variables in social science are concepts, some of our most important concepts are not variables. The concept of "positivism" is *not* a variable, but the concept of "philosophies of science" *is* a variable, and positivism is one member of the list of those philosophies. The concept of "love" is not a variable, but the concept of "being in love or not" *is* one. The concept of "culture" is not a variable, but the concept of "intensity of feeling of belonging to a particular culture" *is* one. The concept of "attitude" is not a variable, but the concept of "attitude toward clitoridectomy as a violation of human rights" implies a variable with at least two attributes, support and nonsupport.

CONCEPTUAL DEFINITIONS

There are two ways to define variables—conceptually and operationally. **Conceptual definitions** are abstractions, articulated in words, that facilitate understanding. They are the sort of definitions we see in dictionaries, and we use them in everyday conversation to tell people what we mean by some term or phrase. **Operational definitions** consist of a set of instructions on how to measure a variable that has been conceptually defined.

Suppose I tell you that "Alice and Fred just moved to a spacious house." Nice concept. You ask: "What do you mean by 'spacious'?" and I say: "You know, big rooms, high ceilings."

If that isn't enough for you, we'll have to move from a conceptual definition of "spacious" to an operational one. We'll have to agree on what to measure: Do we count the screened-in porch and the garage or just the interior living space? Do we count the square footage or the cubic footage? That is, do we get a measure of the living surface, or some measure of the "feeling of spaciousness" that comes from high ceilings? Do we measure the square footage of open space before or after the furniture and appliances go in? If we had to agree on things like this for every concept, ordinary human discourse would come to a grinding halt.

Science is not ordinary human discourse, however, and this, in my view, is the most important difference between the humanistic and the scientific (positivistic) approaches to social science. Humanistic researchers seek to maintain the essential feel of human discourse. Positivists focus more on specific measurement. I do not see these two styles as inimical to one another, but as complementary.

To get a feel for how complementary the two styles can be, ask some 50 year olds and some 20 year olds—men and women of both ages—to tell you how old you have to be in order to be middle aged. You'll see immediately how volatile the conceptual definition of "middle age" is. If you ask people about what it *means* to "be middle aged," you'll get plenty of material for an interesting paper on the subject. If you want to *measure* the differences between men and women and between older and younger people on this variable, you'll have to do more than just ask them. Figure 2.3 shows an instrument for measuring this variable.

| 1 | 5 | 10 | 15 | 20 | 25 | 30 | 35 | 40 | 45 | 50 | 55 | 60 | 65 | 70 | 75 | 80 | 85 | 90 | 95 | 100 |

Here is a line that represents age. Obviously, a person 1 year of age is a baby, and a person 100 years of age is old. Put a mark on the line where you think middle age begins and another mark where you think middle age ends.

FIGURE 2.3.
An instrument for measuring what people think "middle age" means.

Many concepts that we use in anthropology have volatile definitions: "power," "social class," "machismo," "alienation," "willingness to change," and "fear of retribution." If we are to talk sensibly about such things, we need clear, **intersubjective** definitions of them. In other words, although there can be no objective definition of middle age, we can at least agree on what we mean by "middle age" for a particular study and on how to measure the concept.

Complex variables are conceptually defined by reducing them to a series of simpler variables. Saying that "the people in this village are highly acculturated" can be interpreted in many ways. But if you state clearly that you include "being bilingual," "working in the national economy," and "going to school" in your conceptual definition of acculturation, then at least others will understand what you're talking about when you say that people are "highly acculturated."

Similarly, "machismo" might be characterized by "a general feeling of male superiority," accompanied by "insecure behavior in relationships with women." Intelligence might be conceptually defined as "the ability to think in abstractions and to generalize from cases." These definitions have something important in common: They have no external reality against which to test their truth value.

Conceptual definitions are at their most powerful when they are linked together to build theories that explain research results. When the United Nations was founded in 1945, the hope was that trade between industrialized and nonindustrialized countries of the world would result in economic development for everyone. The economies of the developed countries would expand and the benefits of an expanding economy would be seen in the underdeveloped countries. A decade later, it was obvious that this wasn't what was happening. The rich countries were getting richer and the poor countries were getting poorer.

Raul Prebisch, an Argentinian economist who worked at the UN, argued that under colonialism, rich countries were importing raw materials from poor countries to produce manufactured goods and that poor countries had come to depend economically on the rich countries. Prebisch's "dependency theory" links the concept of "control of capital" with those of "mutual security" and "economic dependency," and the linkage helps explain why economic development often results in some groups winding up with less access to capital than they had before a development program (Prebisch 1984, 1994).

Conceptual definitions are at their weakest in the conduct of research itself, because concepts are abstractions—we have to make them up to study them.

There is nothing wrong with this. There are three things one wants to do in any science: (1) describe a phenomenon of interest; (2) explain what causes it; and (3) predict what it causes. The existence of a conceptual variable is inferred from what it predicts—how well it makes theoretical sense out of a lot of data.

The Concept of Intelligence

The classic example of a conceptual variable is intelligence. Intelligence is anything we say it is. There is no way to tell whether it is: (1) the ability to think in abstractions and to generalize from cases; (2) the ability to remember long strings of unconnected facts; or (3) the ability to recite all of Shakespeare from memory. In the last analysis, the value of the concept of intelligence is that it allows us to predict, *with varying success*, things like job success, grade-point average, likelihood of having healthy children, and likelihood of being arrested for a felony.

The key to understanding the last statement is the phrase "with varying success." It is by now well known that measures of intelligence are culture bound; the standard U.S. intelligence tests are biased in favor of Whites and against African Americans because of differences in access to education and differences in life experiences. Further afield, intelligence tests that are designed for Americans may not have any meaning at all to people in radically different cultures.

There is an apocryphal story about some American researchers who were determined to develop a culture-free intelligence test based on manipulating and matching shapes and colors. With an interpreter along for guidance, they administered the test to a group of Bushmen in the Kalahari Desert of South Africa. The first Bushman they tested listened politely to the instructions about matching the colors and shapes and then excused himself.

He returned in a few minutes with half a dozen others, and they began an animated discussion about the test. The researchers asked the interpreter to explain that each man had to take the test himself. The Bushmen responded by saying how silly that was; they solve problems together, and they would solve this one, too. So, although the content of the test might have been culture free, the testing procedure itself was not.

This critique of intelligence *testing* in no way lessens the importance or usefulness of the *concept* of intelligence. The concept is useful, in certain contexts, because its measurement allows us to predict other things we want to know. And it is to actual measurement that we now turn.

OPERATIONAL DEFINITIONS

Conceptual definitions are limited because, although they point us toward measurement, they don't really give us any recipe for measurement. Without measurement, we cannot make useful comparisons. We cannot tell whether Spaniards are more flamboyant than the British, or whether Catholicism is more authoritarian than Buddhism. We cannot evaluate the level of anger in an urban community over perceived abuses by the police of their authority, or compare the level of that anger to the anger found in another community in another city.

Operational definitions specify exactly what you have to do to measure something that has been defined conceptually. Here are four examples of operational definitions:

1. Intelligence: Take the Wechsler Adults Intelligence Scale (WAIS) and administer it to a person. Count up the score. Whatever score the person gets is his or her intelligence.

2. Machismo: Ask a man if he approves of women working outside the home, assuming the family doesn't need the money; if he says "no," then give him a score of 1, and if he says "yes," score him 0. Ask him if he thinks women and men should have the same sexual freedom before marriage; if he says "no," score 1 and score 0 for "yes." Ask him if a man should be punished for killing his wife and her lover; if he says "no," score 1; score 0 for "yes." Add the scores. A man who scores 3 has more machismo than a man who scores 2, and a man who scores 2 has more machismo than a man who scores 1.

3. Tribal identity: Ask American Indians if they speak the language of their ancestors fluently. If "yes," score 1. If "no," score 0. Ask them if they attend at least one tribal pow-wow each year. Score 1 for "yes," and 0 for "no." Ask them eight other questions of this type, and give them a score of 1 for each answer that signifies self-identification with their tribal heritage. Anyone who scores at least 6 out of 10 is an "identifier." Five or less is a "rejecter" of tribal heritage or identity.

4. Support for trade barriers against China: Ask workers in a textile factory to complete the Support of Trade Barriers against China Scale. Add the four parts of the scale together to produce a single score. Record that score.

These definitions sound pretty boring, but think about this: If you and I use the same definitions for variables, *and if we stick to those definitions in making measurements*, then our data are strictly comparable:

> We can tell if children in city A have higher intelligence scores than do children in city B.
> We can tell if older men in Huehuetenango have higher machismo scores than do younger men in that same village.
> We can tell if people in tribe A have higher cultural identity scores than do people in tribe B.
> We can tell whether the average scores indicating level of support for trade barriers against China is greater among workers in the factory you studied than among workers in the factory I studied.

I find the ability to make such comparisons exciting and not at all boring. But did you notice that I *never* said anything in those comparisons about ethnic identity per se, or intelligence per se, or machismo per se, or support for trade barriers per se. In each case, all I said was that we could tell if the *scores* were bigger or smaller.

What's So Good about Operationism?

Operational definitions are *strictly limited to the content of the operations specified.* That's why I also didn't say anything about whether it was a good idea or a bad one to make any of these measurements or comparisons. *If the content of an operational definition is bad, then so are all conclusions you draw from using it to measure something.*

This is *not* an argument against operationism in science. Just the opposite. Operationism is the best way to expose bad measurement. By defining measurements operationally, we can tell if one measurement is better than another. If the operational measurement of, say, machismo, seems silly or offensive, it may be because the concept is not very useful to begin with. No amount of measurement or operationism bails out bad concepts. The act of trying, though, usually *exposes* bad concepts and helps you jettison them.

Adhering to bad measurements is bad science and can have some bad consequences for people. In the 1960s, I was a consultant on a project that was supposed to help Chicano high schoolers develop good career aspirations. Studies had been conducted in which Chicano and Anglo high schoolers were asked what they wanted to be when they reached 30 years of age. Chicanos expressed, on average, a lower occupational aspiration than did Anglos. This led some social scientists to advise policymakers that Chicano youth needed reinforcement of career aspirations at home. (There's that educational model again.)

Contrary to survey findings, ethnographic research showed that Chicano parents had very high aspirations for their children. The parents were frustrated by two things: (1) despair over the cost of sending their children to college; and (2) high school counselors who systematically encouraged Chicana girls to become housewives and Chicano boys to learn a trade or go into the armed services.

The presumed relation between the dependent variable (level of career aspiration among adolescents) and the independent variable (level of aspiration by parents for the careers of their children) was backward. The parents' level of career aspiration for their children didn't cause the children to have low aspirations. The children were driven to low aspirations by structural features of their environment. The parents of those children reflected this reality *in order*—they said explicitly to interviewers who bothered to ask—not to give their children false hopes.

The operational definition of the variable "parents' career aspirations for their children" was useless. Here's the operational definition that should have been used in the study of Chicano parents' aspirations for their children's careers:

Go to the homes of the respondents. Using the native language of the respondents (Spanish or English as the case may be), talk to parents about what they want their high school-age children to be doing in 10 years. Explore each answer in depth and find out why parents give each answer.

Ask specifically if the parents are telling you what they think their children *will* be doing or what they *want* their children to be doing. If parents hesitate, say: "Suppose nothing stood in the way of your [son] [daughter] becoming anything they wanted to be. What would you like them to be doing 10 years from now?"

Write down what the parents say and code it for the following possible scores: 1 = unambivalently in favor of children going into high-status occupations; 2 = ambivalent about children going into high-status occupations; 3 = unambivalently in favor of children going into low- or middle-status occupations.

Use the Nam-Powers-Boyd occupation scale (Nam and Boyd 2004) to decide whether the occupations selected by parents as fitting for their children are high, middle, or low status. Be sure to take and keep notes on what parents say are the reasons for their selections of occupations.

Notice that taking an ethnographic—a so-called qualitative—approach did not stop us from being operational.

Operationism is often crude, but that, too, can be a strength. Robert Wuthnow (1976) operationalized the concept of religiosity in 43 countries using UNESCO data on the number of books published in those countries and the fraction of those books classified as religious literature. Now *that's* crude. Still, Wuthnow's measure of "average religiosity" correlates with seven out of eight indicators of modernity. For example, the higher the literacy rate in 1952, the lower the religiosity in 1972.

I have no idea what that means, but I think following up Wuthnow's work with more refined measurements—to test hypotheses about the societal conditions that support or weaken religiosity—is a lot more exciting than dismissing it because it was so audaciously crude.

The Problem with Operationism

Strict operationism creates a knotty philosophical problem. We make up concepts and measurement turns these abstractions into reality. Because there are many ways to measure the same abstraction, the reality of any concept hinges on the device you use to measure it. So, sea temperature is different if you measure it from a satellite (you get an answer based on radiation) or with a thermometer (you get an answer based on a column of mercury). Intelligence is different if you measure it with a Stanford-Binet test or the Wechsler scales. If you ask a person in any of the industrialized nations "How old are you?" or "How many birthdays have you had?" you will probably retrieve the same number. But the very concept of age in the two cases is different because different "instruments" (queries are instruments) were used to measure it.

This principle was articulated in 1927 by Percy Bridgman in *The Logic of Modern Physics* and has become the source of an enduring controversy. The bottom line on strict operational definitions is this: No matter how much you insist that intelligence is really more than what is measured by an intelligence test, that's all it can ever be. Whatever you think intelligence is, it is exactly and only what you measure with an intelligence test and nothing more.

If you don't like the results of your measurement, then build a better test, where "better" means that the outcomes are more useful in building theory, in making predictions, and in engineering behavior.

I see no reason to waffle about this, or to look for philosophically palatable ways to soften the principle here. The science that emerges from a strict operational approach to understanding variables is much too powerful to water down with backpedaling. It is obvious that "future orientation" is more than my asking someone "Do you buy large or small boxes of soap?" The problem is, *you* might not include that question in your interview of the same respondent unless I specify that I asked that question in that particular way (box 2.3).

LEVELS OF MEASUREMENT

Whenever you define a variable operationally, you do so at some **level of measurement**. Most social scientists recognize the following four levels of measurement, in ascending order: nominal, ordinal, interval, and ratio. The general principle in research is: Always use the highest level of measurement that you can. (This principle will be clear by the time you get through the next couple of pages.)

Nominal Variables

A variable is something that can take more than one value. The values of a **nominal variable** comprise a list of names (from the Latin *nomen* for name). You can list religions, occupations, and ethnic groups; and you can list fruits, emotions, body parts, things to do on the weekend, baseball teams, rock stars . . . the list of things you can list is endless.

All of the following questions produce nominal data: In what country were you born? Are you healthy? On the whole, do you think the economy is in good shape? Is Bangladesh a poor country? Is Switzerland a rich country? What is your sex?

For sex, you can assign the numeral 1 to men and 2 to women, but gender will still be a qualitative, nominal variable. The number 2 happens to be twice as big as the number 1,

BOX 2.3

OPERATIONAL DEFINITIONS PERMIT SCIENTISTS
TO TALK TO ONE ANOTHER USING THE SAME
LANGUAGE

Operational definitions permit replication of research and the accumulation of
knowledge. The Attitudes Toward Women Scale (AWS), for example, was developed by Janet Spence and Robert Helmreich in 1972 (Spence and Helmreich
1972, 1978) and has been used in about 400 studies since then, including some
70 dissertations. Many of those studies involved American college students and,
as you'd guess, attitudes toward women have became more liberal/feminist
over the years.

By 1990, men's average score on the AWS was about the same as women's
average score in 1975 (Twenge 1997). In other words, men's attitudes changed
but lagged those of women by 15 years. (These data, remember, reflect the
attitudes of college students—the quarter of the population whom we expect to
be at the vanguard of social change.)

Some of the items on the AWS seem pretty old-fashioned today. For example, in one item, people are asked how much they agree or disagree with the
idea that "women should worry less about their rights and more about becoming good wives and mothers." You probably wouldn't use that item if you were
building an attitudes-toward-women scale today, but keeping the original, 1972
AWS intact over all this time lets us track attitudes toward women over time.
(For an assessment of the AWS, see Loo and Thorpe 1998, 2005.)

but this fact is meaningless with nominal variables. You can't add up all the 1s and 2s and
calculate the "average sex" any more than you can add up all the telephone numbers in
the Chicago phone book and get the average phone number.

Assigning numbers to things does make it easier to do certain kinds of statistical analysis on qualitative data—more on this in chapters 19 (on coding text) and 21 (on regression).

The following survey item is an operationalization of the nominal variable called "religious affiliation":

26a. Do you identify with any religion? (check one)
      ☐ Yes
      ☐ No
If you checked "yes," then please answer question 26b.

26b. What is your religion (check one):
      ☐ Protestant
      ☐ Catholic
      ☐ Jewish
      ☐ Moslem
      ☐ Other religion

This operationalization of the variable "religious affiliation" has two important characteristics: It is *exhaustive* and *mutually exclusive*. The famous "other" category in nominal
variables makes the list exhaustive—that is, all possible categories have been named in
the list—and the instruction to "check one" makes the list mutually exclusive. (More on
this in chapter 9 when we discuss questionnaire design.)

"Mutually exclusive" means that things can't belong to more than one category of a
nominal variable at a time. We assume, for example, that people who say they are Catholic
generally don't say they are Moslem. I say "generally" because life is complicated and
variables that seem mutually exclusive may not be. Some citizens of Lebanon have one
Catholic and one Moslem parent and may think of themselves as both Moslem and Catholic.

Most people think of themselves as either male or female, but not everyone does. The
prevalence of transsexuals in human populations is not known precisely, but worldwide,
it is likely to be between one in ten thousand and one in a hundred thousand for male-
to-female transsexuals (biological males whose gender identity is female) and between
one in a hundred thousand and one in four hundred thousand for female-to-male transsexuals (Cohen-Kettenis and Gooren 1999).

Most people think of themselves as a member of one so-called race or another, but
more and more people think of themselves as belonging to two or more races. In 2000,
the U.S. Census offered people the opportunity to check off more than one so-called race
from six choices: White, Black or African American, American Indian or Alaska Native,
Asian, Native Hawaiian and other Pacific islander, and Other. Nearly seven million people
(2.4% of the 281 million in the United States in 2000) checked more than one of the six
options (Grieco and Cassidy 2001).

And when it comes to ethnicity, the requirement for mutual exclusivity is just hopeless.
There are Chicano African Americans, Chinese Cuban Americans, Filipino Cherokees,
and so on. This just reflects the complexity of real life, but it does make analyzing data
more complicated because each *combination of attributes* has to be treated as a separate
category of the variable "ethnicity" or collapsed into one of the larger categories. More
about this in chapters 20 and 21 when we get to data analysis.

Occupation is a nominal variable, but lots of people have more than one occupation.
People can be peasant farmers and makers of fireworks displays for festivals; they can be
herbalists and jewelers; or they can be pediatric oncology nurses and antique car salespeople at the same time. A list of occupations is a measuring instrument at the nominal
level: You hold each person up against the list and see which occupation(s) he or she has
(have).

Ordinal Variables

Like nominal-level variables, **ordinal variables** are generally exhaustive and mutually
exclusive, but they have one additional property: Their values can be rank ordered. Any
variable measured as high, medium, or low, like socioeconomic class, is ordinal. The three
classes are, in theory, mutually exclusive and exhaustive. In addition, a person who is
labeled "middle class" is lower in the social class hierarchy than someone labeled "high
class" and higher in the same hierarchy than someone labeled "lower class." What ordinal
variables do not tell us is *how much* more.

Scales of opinion—like the familiar "strongly agree," "agree," "neutral," "disagree,"
"strongly disagree" found on so many surveys—are ordinal measures. They measure an
internal state, agreement, in terms of *less* and *more*, but not in terms of *how much* more.

This is the most important characteristic of ordinal measures: There is no way to tell how far apart the attributes are from one another. A person who is middle class might be twice as wealthy and three times as educated as a person who is lower class. Or he or she might be three times as wealthy and four times as educated. A person who "agrees strongly" with a statement may agree twice as much as someone who says they "agree"—or eight times as much, or half again as much. There is no way to tell.

Interval and Ratio Variables

Interval variables have all the properties of nominal and ordinal variables. They are an exhaustive and mutually exclusive list of attributes, and the attributes have a rank-order structure. They have one additional property as well: The distances between the attributes are meaningful. Interval variables, then, involve true **quantitative measurement**.

The difference between 30 and 40 Celsius is the same 10 as the difference between 70 and 80, and the difference between an IQ score of 90 and 100 is (assumed to be) the same as the difference between one of 130 and 140. On the other hand, 80 Fahrenheit is not twice as hot as 40, and a person who has an IQ of 150 is not 50% smarter than a person who has an IQ of 100.

Ratio variables are interval variables that have a true **zero point**—that is, a 0 that measures the absence of the phenomenon being measured. The Kelvin scale of temperature has a true zero: It identifies the absence of molecular movement, or heat.

The consequence of a true zero point is that measures have ratio properties. A person who is 40 years old is 10 years older than a person who is 30, and a person who is 20 is 10 years older than a person who is 10. The 10-year intervals between the attributes (years are the attributes of age) are identical. That much is true of an interval variable. In addition, however, a person who is 20 is twice as old as a person who is 10; and a person who is 40 is twice as old as a person who is 20. These, then, are true ratios.

Although temperature (in Fahrenheit or Celsius) and IQ are nonratio interval variables, most interval-level variables in the social sciences are also ratio variables. In fact, it has become common practice in the social sciences to refer to ratio-level variables as interval variables and vice versa. This is not technically pure, but the confusion of the terms "interval" and "ratio" doesn't cause much real damage.

Some examples of ratio variables include: age, number of times a person has changed residence, income in dollars or other currency, years married, years spent migrating, population size, distance in meters from a house to a well, number of hospital beds per hundred thousand population, number of months since last employment, number of kilograms of fish caught per week, number of hours per week spent in food preparation activities. Number of years of education is usually treated as a ratio variable, even though a year of grade school is hardly worth the same as a year of graduate school.

In general, **concepts** (like alienation, political orientation, level of assimilation) are measured at the ordinal level. People get a high score for being "very assimilated," a low score for being "unassimilated," and a medium score for being "somewhat assimilated." When a concept variable like intelligence is measured at the interval level, it is likely to be the focus of a lot of controversy regarding the validity of the measuring instrument.

Concrete **observables**—things you can actually see—are often measured at the interval level. But not always. Observing whether a woman has a job outside her home is nominal, qualitative measurement based on direct observation.

A Rule about Measurement

Remember this rule: Always measure things at the highest level of measurement possible. Don't measure things at the ordinal level if you can measure them as ratio variables.

If you really want to know the price that people paid for their homes, then ask the price. Don't ask them whether they paid "less than a million pesos, between a million and five million, or more than five million." If you really want to know how much education people have had, ask them how many years they went to school. Don't ask: "Have you completed grade school, high school, some college, four years of college?"

This kind of packaging just throws away information by turning interval-level variables into ordinal ones. As we'll see in chapter 9, survey questions are pretested before going into a questionnaire. If people won't give you straight answers to straight questions, you can back off and try an ordinal scale. But why start out crippling a perfectly good interval-scale question by making it ordinal when you don't know that you have to?

During data analysis you can lump interval level data together into ordinal or nominal categories. If you know the ages of your respondents on a survey, you can divide them into "old" and "young"; if you know the number of calories consumed per week for each family in a study, you can divide the data into low, medium, and high. But you cannot do this the other way around. If you collect data on income by asking people whether they earn "up to a million pesos per year" or "more than a million per year," you cannot go back and assign actual numbers of pesos to each informant.

Notice that "up to a million" and "more than a million" is an ordinal variable that *looks like* a nominal variable because there are only two attributes. If the attributes are rankable, then the variable is ordinal. "A lot of fish" is more than "a small amount of fish," and "highly educated" is greater than "poorly educated." Ordinal variables can have any number of ranks. For purposes of statistical analysis, though, ordinal scales with five or more ranks are often treated as if they were interval-level variables. More about this in chapter 21 on bivariate data analysis.

UNITS OF ANALYSIS

One of the very first things to do in any research project is decide on the **unit of analysis**. In a case study, there is exactly one unit of analysis—the village, the school, the hospital, the organization. Research designed to test hypotheses requires a sample of units of analysis from a population. How many? That depends on several things, which we'll get to in chapter 6 on sampling theory and in chapter 16 on cultural domain analysis. Here's a hint, though: Good research samples can be much smaller than you might think (peek at table 16.13).

Although most research in social science is about populations of people, many other things can be the units of analysis. You can focus on farms instead of farmers, or on unions instead of union members, or on wars instead of warriors. You can study marriage contracts; folk tales, songs, and myths; and countries, cultures, and cities.

Paul Doughty (1979), for example, surveyed demographic data on 134 countries to make a list of "primate cities." Geographers say that a country has a primate city if its most populous city is at least twice the size of its second-most populous city (Jefferson 1939). Doughty, an anthropologist who had worked in Peru, looked at the population of the three largest cities in each country and coded whether the largest city was at least three times greater than the second and third cities combined. He discovered that this extreme form of population concentration was associated with Latin America more than with any other region of the world at the time.

Holly Mathews (1987, 1992) did a study of how men and women in a Mexican village tell a famous folk tale differently. The tale is called *La Llorona* (The Weeping Woman) and is known all over Mexico. Mathews's research has to do with the problem of intracultural variation—different people telling the same story in different ways. She studied a sample of the population of *La Llorona* stories in a community where she was working. Each story, as told by a different person, had characteristics that could be compared across the sample of stories. One of the characteristics was whether the story was told by a man or by a woman, and this turned out to be the most important variable associated with the stories, which were the units of analysis. (See the section on schema analysis in chapter 19 for more about Mathews's study of the *La Llorona* tales.)

You can have more than one unit of analysis in a study. When Mathews looked for similarities and differences in tellings of the story, then the stories were the units of analysis. But when she looked at patterns in the tellers of the stories, then people were her units of analysis.

Robert Aunger (2004:145–62) asked 424 people in four ethnic groups (Sudanic, Efe, Bantu, and Tswa) in the Ituri Forest (Democratic Republic of Congo) about food taboos. For each of 145 animals, Aunger asked each informant if it was edible, and, if so, if there were any times when it should not be eaten. For example, some animals were said to be off limits to pregnant women or to children; some animals required permission from an elder to eat; some animals should not be eaten by members of this or that clan; and so on. When Aunger analyzes looks at which animals have similar patterns of avoidance, the 145 animals are the units of analysis. But when he looks at differences in food taboos across people—like patterns of food taboos in the four ethnic groups—then people are the units of analysis.

A Rule about Units of Analysis

Remember this rule: No matter what you are studying, always collect data on the lowest level unit of analysis possible.

Household economics can only be understood by studying . . . households (Wilk 1990). Collect data, though, on individuals within households. You can always package your data about individuals into data about households during analysis, but if you want to examine the association between female income and child spacing and you collect income data on households in the first place, then you are locked out. You can always **aggregate** data collected on individuals, but you can never **disaggregate** data collected on groups.

This rule applies whether you're studying people or countries. If you are studying relations among trading blocs in major world regions, then collect trade data on countries and pairs of countries, not on regions of the world.

Sometimes, though, *the smallest unit of analysis is a collective*, like a household or a region. For example, each person in a household consumes a certain number of grams of protein per week. But you can't just add up what individuals consume and get the number of grams of protein that comes into a household. Some grams are lost to waste, some to pets, some to fertilizer, some to fuel. After you add up all the grams, you get a single number for the household. If you are testing whether this number predicts the number of days per year that people in the household are sick, then the household is your unit of analysis.

The Ecological Fallacy

Once you select your unit of analysis, remember it as you go through data analysis, or you're likely to commit the dreaded "ecological fallacy." This fallacy (also known as the Nosnibor effect, after W. S. Robinson [1950], who described it) comes from drawing conclusions about the wrong units of analysis—making generalizations about people, for example, from data about groups or places. For example, in 1930, 11% of foreign-born people in the United States were illiterate, compared with 3% of those born in the United States. The correlation between these two variables was .118. In other words, across 97 million people (the population of the United States at the time), being foreign born was a moderately strong predictor of being illiterate. But when Robinson looked at the data for the (then) 48 states in the United States, he got an entirely different result. The correlation between the percent illiterate and the percent of foreign-born people was −.526. That minus sign means that the more foreign born, the *less* illiteracy.

What's going on? Well, as Jargowsky (2005) observes, immigrants went mostly to the big industrial states where they were more likely to find jobs. Those northern and midwestern states had better schools and, of course, higher literacy—along with a lot of immigrants, many of whom were illiterate. And that was Robinson's point: If you only looked at the state-by-state averages (the aggregated units of analysis) instead of at the individual data, you'd draw the wrong conclusion about the relationship between the two variables (**Further Reading:** the ecological inference problem).

This is an important issue for anthropologists. Suppose you do a survey of villages in a region of southern India. For each village, you have data on such things as the number of people, the average age of men and women, and the monetary value of a list of various consumer goods in each village. That is, when you went through each village, you noted how many refrigerators and kerosene lanterns and radios there were, but you do not have these data for each person or household in the village because you were not interested in that when you designed your study. (You were interested in characteristics of villages as units of analysis.)

In your analysis, you notice that the villages with the population having the lowest average age also have the highest average dollar value of modern consumer goods. You are tempted to conclude that young people are more interested in (and purchase) modern consumer goods more frequently than do older people.

But you might be wrong. Villages with greater employment resources (land and industry) will have lower levels of labor migration by young people. Because more young people stay there, this will lower the average age of wealthier villages. Though *everyone* wants household consumer goods, only older people can afford them, having had more time to accumulate the funds.

It might turn out that the wealthy villages with low average age simply have wealthier older people than villages with higher average age. It is not valid to take data gathered about villa*ges* and draw conclusions about villa*gers*, and this brings us to the crucial issue of validity.

VALIDITY, RELIABILITY, ACCURACY, AND PRECISION

Validity refers to the accuracy and trustworthiness of instruments, data, and findings in research. Nothing in research is more important than validity.

The Validity of Instruments and Data

Are the instruments that were used to measure something valid? Are SAT and GRE scores, for example, valid instruments for measuring the ability of students to get good grades? If they are, then are grades a valid measure of how smart students are? Is the question "Do you practice polytheistic fetishism?" a valid instrument for measuring religious practices? No, it isn't, because the concept of "polytheistic fetishism" is something that is meaningful only to specialists in the comparative study of religion.

Asking people that question is asking them to think in categories that are alien to their culture. Is the instrument "How long does it take you to drive to work each day?" a valid one for measuring the amount of time it takes people to drive to work each day? That depends on how accurate you want the data to be. If you want the data to be accurate to within, say, 20 minutes on, say 70% of occasions, then the instrument is probably valid. If you want the data to be accurate to, say, within 5 minutes on, say, 90% of occasions, then the instrument is probably not valid because people just can't dredge up the information you want at that level of accuracy.

The validity of data is tied to the validity of instruments. If questions asking people to recall their behavior are not valid instruments for tapping into informants' past behavior, then the data retrieved by those instruments are not valid either.

The Validity of Findings

Assuming, however, that the instruments and data are valid, we can ask whether the findings and conclusions derived from the data are valid. Asian Americans get higher average scores on the math part of the SATs (scholastic aptitude tests) than do other ethnic groups in the United States—581 versus 515 for all ethnic groups combined (College Board 2008). Suppose that the SAT math test is a valid instrument for measuring the general math ability of 18 year olds in the United States. Is it valid to conclude that "Asians are better at math" than other people are? No, it isn't. That conclusion can only be reached by invoking an unfounded, racist assumption about the influence of certain genes—particularly genes responsible for epicanthic eye folds—on the ability of people to do math.

Reliability

Reliability refers to whether or not you get the same answer by using an instrument to measure something more than once. If you insert a thermometer into boiling water at sea level, it should register 212 Fahrenheit each and every time. "Instruments" can be things like thermometers and scales, or they can be questions that you ask people.

Like all other kinds of instruments, some questions are more reliable for retrieving information than others. If you ask 10 people "Do the ancestors take revenge on people who don't worship them?" don't expect to get the same answer from everyone. "How many brothers and sisters do you have?" is a pretty reliable instrument (you almost always get the same response when you ask a person that question a second time as you get the first time), but "How much is your parents' house worth?" is much less reliable. And "How old were you when you were toilet trained?" is just futile.

Precision

Precision is about the number of decimal points in a measurement. When you stand on an old-fashioned scale, the spring is compressed. As the spring compresses, it moves a pointer to a number that signifies how much weight is being put on the scale. Let's say that you really, truly weigh 156.625 pounds, to the nearest thousandth of a pound.

If you have a predigital bathroom scale like mine, there are five little marks between each pound reading; that is, the scale registers weight in fifths of a pound. In terms of precision, then, your scale is somewhat limited. The best it could possibly do would be to announce that you weigh "somewhere between 156.6 and 156.8 pounds, and closer to the former figure than to the latter." In this case, you might not be too concerned about the error introduced by lack of precision.

Whether you care or not depends on the needs you have for the data. If you are concerned about losing weight, then you're probably not going to worry too much about the fact that your scale is only precise to the nearest fifth of a pound. But if you're measuring the weights of pharmaceuticals, and someone's life depends on your getting the precise amounts into a compound, that's another matter.

Accuracy

Finally, **accuracy**. Assume that you are satisfied with the level of precision of the scale. What if the spring was not calibrated correctly (there was an error at the factory where the scale was built, or last week your overweight house guest bent the spring a little too much) and the scale was off? Now we have the following interesting situation: The data from this instrument are valid (it has already been determined that the scale is measuring weight—exactly what you think it's measuring); they are reliable (you get the same answer every time you step on it); and they are precise enough for your purposes. But they are not *accurate*. What next?

You could see if the scale were always inaccurate in the same way. You could stand on it 10 times in a row, without eating or doing exercise in between. That way, you'd be measuring the same thing 10 different times with the same instrument. If the reading was always the same, then the instrument would at least be reliable, even though it wasn't accurate. Suppose it turned out that your scale was always incorrectly lower by 5 pounds. This is called **systematic bias**. Then, a simple correction formula would be all you'd need to feel confident that the data from the instrument were pretty close to the truth. The formula would be:

$$\text{true weight} = \text{your scale weight} + 5 \text{ pounds}$$

The scale might be off in more complicated ways, however. It might be that for every 10 pounds of weight put on the scale, an additional half-pound correction has to be made. Then the **recalibration** formula would be

$$\text{true weight} = (\text{your scale weight}) + (\text{scale weight}/10)(.5)$$

or

$$(\text{your scale weight})(1.05)$$

That is, take the scale weight, divide by 10, multiply by half a pound, and add the result to the reading on your scale.

If an instrument is not precise enough for what you want to do with the data, then you simply have to build a more precise one. There is no way out. If it is precise enough for your research and reliable, but inaccurate in known ways, then a formula can be applied to correct for the inaccuracy.

The real problem is when instruments are inaccurate in unknown ways. The bad news is that this happens a lot. If you ask people how long it takes them to drive to work, they'll tell you. If you ask people what they ate for breakfast, they'll tell you that, too. Answers to both questions may be dead on target, or they may bear no useful resemblance to the truth. The good news is that informant accuracy is one of the methodological questions that social scientists have been investigating for years and on which real progress continues to be made (**Further Reading:** informant accuracy).

DETERMINING VALIDITY

You may have noticed a few paragraphs back that I casually slipped in the statement that some scale had *already been determined* to be a valid instrument. How do we know that the scale is measuring weight? Maybe it's measuring something else. How can we be sure? We have to make concepts up to study them, so there is no direct way to evaluate the validity of an instrument for measuring a concept. Ultimately, we are left to decide, on the basis of our best judgment, whether an instrument is valid or not.

We are helped in making that judgment by some tests for **face validity**, **content validity**, **construct validity**, and **criterion validity**.

Face Validity

Establishing **face validity** involves simply looking at the operational indicators of a concept and deciding whether or not, *on the face of it*, the indicators make sense. On the face of it, asking people "How old were you when you were toilet trained?" is not a valid way to get at this kind of information. A paper-and-pencil test about the rules of the road is not, on the face of it, a valid indicator of whether someone knows how to drive a car. But the paper-and-pencil test is probably a valid test for determining if an applicant for a driver's license can read road signs. These different instruments—the road test and the paper-and-pencil test—have face validity for measuring different things.

Boster (1985) studied how well the women of the Aguaruna Jívaro in Peru understood the differences among manioc plants. He planted some fields with different varieties of manioc and asked women to identify the varieties. This technique, or instrument, for measuring cultural competence has great face validity; most researchers would agree that being able to identify more varieties of manioc is a valid indicator of cultural competence in this domain.

Boster might have simply asked women to list as many varieties of manioc as they could. This instrument would not have been as valid, on the face of it, as having them identify actual plants that were growing in the field. There are just too many things that could interfere with a person's memory of manioc names, even if they were really competent about planting roots, harvesting them, cooking them, trading them, and so on.

Face validity is based on consensus among researchers: If everyone agrees that asking people "How old are you" is a valid instrument for measuring age, then, until proven otherwise, that question is a valid instrument for measuring age.

Content Validity

Content validity is achieved when an instrument has appropriate content for measuring a complex concept, or construct. If you walk out of a test and feel that it was unfair because it tapped too narrow a band of knowledge, your complaint is that the test lacked content validity.

Content validity is very, very tough to achieve, particularly for complex, multidimensional constructs. Consider, for example, what's involved in measuring a concept like strength of ethnic identity among, say, second-generation Mexican Americans. Any scale to assess this has to have components that deal with religion, language, socioeconomic status, sense of history, and gastronomy.

Religion: Mexican Americans tend to be mostly Roman Catholic, but a growing number of Mexicans are now Protestants. The migration of a few million of these converts to the United States over the next decade will have an impact on ethnic politics—and ethnic identity—within the Mexican American population.

Language: Some second-generation Mexican Americans speak almost no Spanish; others are completely bilingual. Some use Spanish only in the home; others use it with their friends and business associates.

Socioeconomic status: Many Mexican Americans are poor (about 31% of Hispanic households in the United States have incomes below $25,000 a year), but many others are well off (about 20% have incomes above $75,000 a year) (SAUS 2010:table 674). People with radically different incomes tend to have different political and economic values.

Sense of history: Some so-called Mexican Americans have roots that go back to before the British Pilgrims landed at Plymouth Rock. The Hispanos (as they are known) of New Mexico were Spaniards who came north from the Spanish colony of Mexico. Their self-described ethnic identity is quite different from recent immigrants from Mexico.

Gastronomy: The last refuge of ethnicity is food. When language is gone (Spanish, Yiddish, Polish, Gaelic, Greek, Chinese . . .), and when ties to the "old country" are gone, burritos, bagels, pirogis, corned beef, mousaka, and lo mein remain. For some second-generation Mexican Americans, cuisine is practically synonymous with identity; for others it's just part of a much larger complex of traits.

A valid measure of ethnic identity, then, has to get at all these areas. People's use of Spanish inside and outside the home and their preference for Mexican or Mexican American foods are good measures of *some* of the content of Mexican American ethnicity. But if these are the only questions you ask, then your measure of ethnicity has low content validity. (See Cabassa [2003] and Cruz et al. [2008] on acculturation scales for Hispanics in the United States.)

"Life satisfaction" is another very complex variable, composed of several concepts—like "having sufficient income," "a general feeling of well-being," and "satisfaction with level of personal control over one's life." In fact, most of the really interesting things that social scientists study are complex constructs, things like "quality of life," "socioeconomic class," "ability of teenagers to resist peer pressure to smoke," and so on.

Construct Validity

An instrument has high **construct validity** if there is a close fit between the construct it supposedly measures and actual observations made with the instrument. An instrument has high construct validity, in other words, if it allows you to infer that a unit of analysis (a person, a country, whatever) has a particular complex trait and if it supports predictions that are made from theory.

Scholars have offered various definitions of the construct of ethnicity, based on different theoretical perspectives. Does a particular measure of Mexican American ethnicity have construct validity? Does it somehow "get at," or measure, the components of this complex idea?

Asking people "How old are you?" has so much face validity that you hardly need to ask whether the instrument gets at the construct of chronological age. Giving people an IQ test, by contrast, is controversial because there is so much disagreement about what the construct of intelligence is. In fact, lots of constructs in which we're interested—intelligence, ethnicity, machismo, alienation, acculturation—are controversial and so are the measures for them. Getting people to agree that a particular *measure* has high construct validity requires that they agree that the construct is valid in the first place.

Criterion Validity—The Gold Standard

An instrument has high **criterion validity** if there is a close fit between the measures it produces and the measures produced by some other instrument that is known to be valid. This is the gold standard test.

A tape measure, for example, is known to be an excellent instrument for measuring height. If you knew that a man in the United States wore shirts with 35″ sleeves, and pants with 34″ cuffs, you could bet that he was over 6′ tall and be right more than 95% of the time. On the other hand, you might ask: "Why should I measure his cuff length and sleeve length in order to know *most of the time, in general,* how tall he is, when I could use a tape measure and know *all of the time, precisely* how tall he is?"

Indeed. If you want to measure someone's height, use a tape measure. Don't substitute a lot of fuzzy proxy variables for something that's directly measurable by known, valid indicators. But if you want to measure things like acculturation or quality of life or socio-economic class—things that don't have universally accepted, valid indicators—then a complex measure will just have to do until something simpler comes along (box 2.4).

BOX 2.4

THE PRINCIPLE OF OCKHAM'S RAZOR

The preference in science for simpler explanations and measures over more complicated ones is called the principle of **parsimony**. It is also known as **Ockham's razor**, after William of Ockham (1285–1349), a medieval philosopher who argued *Pluralitas non est ponenda sine necessitate*, or "Don't make things more complicated than they need to be."

You can tap the power of criterion validity for complex constructs with the **known group comparison** technique. If you develop a scale to measure political ideology, you might try it out on members of the American Civil Liberties Union and on members of the Christian Coalition of America. Members of the ACLU should get high "left" scores, and members of the CCA should get high "right" scores. If they don't, there's probably something wrong with the scale. In other words, the known-group scores are the criteria for the validity of your instrument.

A particularly strong form of criterion validity is **predictive validity**—whether an instrument lets you predict accurately something else you're interested in. "Stress" is a complex construct. It occurs when people interpret events as threatening to their lives. Some people interpret a bad grade on an exam as a threat to their whole life, and others just blow it off. Now, stress is widely thought to produce a lowered immune response and increase the chances of getting sick. A really good *measure* of stress, then, ought to predict the likelihood of getting sick.

Remember the life insurance problem? You want to predict whether someone is likely to die in the next 365 days to know how much to charge them in premiums. Age and sex tell you a lot. But if you know their weight, whether they smoke, whether they exercise regularly, what their blood pressure is, whether they have ever had any one of a list of diseases, and whether they test-fly experimental aircraft for a living, then you can predict—with a higher and higher degree of accuracy—whether they will die within the next 365 days. Each piece of data—each component of a construct you might call "life-style"—adds to your ability to predict something of interest.

The Bottom Line

The bottom line on all this is that although various forms of validity can be demonstrated, Truth, with a capital T, is never final. We are never dead sure of anything in science. We try to get closer and closer to the truth by better and better measurement. All of science relies on concepts whose existence must ultimately be demonstrated by their effects. You can ram a car against a cement wall at 50 miles an hour and account for the amount of crumpling done to the radiator by referring to a concept called "force." You can't see force, but you can sure see its effects. The greater the force, the more crumpled the radiator. You demonstrate the existence of intelligence by showing how it predicts school achievement or monetary success (**Further Reading:** validity).

The Problem with Validity

If you suspect that there is something deeply, desperately wrong with all this, you're right. The whole argument for the validity (indeed, the very existence) of something like intelligence is, frankly, circular: How do you know that intelligence exists? Because you see its effects in achievement. And how do you account for achievement? By saying that someone has achieved highly because they're intelligent. How do you know machismo exists? Because men dominate women in some societies. And how do you account for dominance behavior, like wife beating? By saying that wife beaters are acting out their machismo.

In the hierarchy of construct reality, then, force ranks way up there (after all, it's got several hundred years of theory and experimentation behind it), and things like intelligence and machismo are pretty weak by comparison. And yet, as I made clear in chapter 1, the social and behavioral sciences are roaring successes, on a par with the physical sciences in terms of the effects they have on our lives every day. This is possible because social scientists have refined and tested many useful concepts and measurements for those concepts.

Ultimately, the validity of any concept—force in physics, the self in psychology, modernization in sociology and political science, acculturation in anthropology—depends on two things: (1) the utility of the device that measures it; and (2) the collective judgment of the scientific community that a concept and its measure are valid. In the end, we are left to deal with the effects of our judgments, which is just as it should be. Valid measurement makes valid data, but validity itself depends on the collective opinion of researchers.

CAUSE AND EFFECT

Cause and effect is among the most highly debated issues in the philosophy of knowledge. (See Hollis [1996] for a review.) We can never be absolutely certain that variation in one thing causes variation in another. Still, if measurements of two variables are valid, you can be reasonably confident that one variable causes another if four conditions are met.

1. The two variables **co-vary**—that is, as scores for one variable increase or decrease, scores for the other variable increase of decrease as well.
2. The covariation between the two variables is not **spurious**.
3. There is a **logical time order** to the variables. The presumed causal variable must always precede the other in time.
4. A mechanism is available that explains *how* an independent variable causes a dependent variable. There must, in other words, be a **theory**.

Condition 1: Covariation

When two variables are related they are said to **co-vary**. Covariation is also called **correlation** or, simply, **association**.

Association is a necessary but insufficient condition for claiming a causal relation between two variables. Whatever else is needed to establish cause and effect, you can't claim that one thing causes another if they aren't related in the first place.

Here are a few interesting covariations:

1. Sexual freedom for women tends to increase with the amount that women contribute to subsistence (Schlegel and Barry 1986).
2. Ground-floor, corner apartments occupied by students at big universities have a much higher chance of being burglarized than other units in the same apartment bloc (M. B. Robinson and C. E. Robinson 1997).
3. When married men and women are both employed full time, they spend the same amount of time in the various rooms of their house—except for the kitchen (Ahrentzen et al. 1989).

You might think that to establish cause, independent variables would have to be strongly related to the dependent variable. Not always. People all over the world make decisions about whether or not to use (or demand the use of) a condom as a part of sexual relations. These decisions are based on many factors, all of which may be weakly but causally related to the ultimate decision. These factors include: the education level of one or both partners; the level of income of one or both partners; the availability and cost of condoms; the amount of time that partners have been together; the amount of previous sexual experience of one or both partners; whether either or both partners know anyone personally who has died of AIDS; and so on.

Each independent variable may contribute only a little to the outcome of the dependent variable (the decision that is finally made), but the contribution may be quite direct and causal.

Condition 2: Lack of Spuriousness

Just as weak correlations can be causal, strong correlations can turn out not to be. When this happens, the original correlation is said to be **spurious**. There is a correlation between the number of firefighters at a fire and the amount of damage done: the more firefighters, the higher the insurance claim. You could easily conclude that firefighters cause fire damage.

We know better: Both the amount of damage and the number of firefighters is caused by the size of the blaze. We need to **control for** this third variable—the size of the blaze—to understand what's really going on.

Dellino (1984) found an inverse relation between perceived quality of life and involvement with the tourism industry on the island of Exuma in the Bahamas. When he controlled for the size of the community (he studied several on the island), the original correlation disappeared. People in the more congested areas were more likely to score low on the perceived-quality-of-life index whether or not they were involved with tourism, and those in the small, outlying communities were more likely to score high on the index. People in the congested areas were also more likely to be involved in tourism-related activities, because that's where the tourists go.

Mwango (1986) found that illiterates in Malawi were much more likely than literates to brew beer for sale from part of their maize crop. The covariation vanished when he controlled for wealth, which causes both greater education (hence, literacy) and the purchase, rather than the brewing, of maize beer.

The list of spurious relations is endless, and it is not always easy to detect them for the frauds that they are. A higher percentage of men than women get lung cancer, but when you control for the length of time that people have smoked, the gender difference in lung cancer vanishes. Pretty consistently, young people accept new technologies more readily than older people, but in many societies, the relation between age and readiness to adopt innovations disappears when you control for level of education. Urban migrants from tribal groups often give up polygyny in Africa and Asia, but both migration *and* abandonment of polygyny are likely to be caused by a third factor: lack of wealth.

Your only defense against spurious covariations is vigilance. No matter how obvious a covariation may appear, discuss it with disinterested colleagues—people who have no stake at all in telling you what you want to hear. Present your initial findings in class seminars at your university or where you work. Beg people to find potentially spurious relations in your work. You'll thank them for it if they do.

Condition 3: Precedence, or Time Order

Besides a nonspurious association, something else is required to establish a cause-and-effect relation between two variables: a **logical time order**. Firefighters don't cause fires—they show up *after* the blaze starts. African Americans have higher blood pressure, on average, than Whites do, but high blood pressure does not cause people to be African American.

Unfortunately, things are not always clear-cut. Does adoption of new technologies cause wealth, or is it the other way around? Does urban migration cause dissatisfaction with rural life, or the reverse? Does consumer demand cause new products to appear, or vice versa? Does the growth in the number of lawsuits cause more people to study law so that they can cash in, or does overproduction of lawyers cause more lawsuits?

What about the increase in elective surgery in the United States? Does the increased supply of surgeons cause an increase in elective surgery, or does the demand for surgery create a surfeit of surgeons? Or are both caused by external variables, like an increase in discretionary income in the upper middle class or the fact that insurance companies pay more and more of Americans' medical bills?

Figure 2.4 shows three kinds of time order between two variables. Read figure 2.4a as "*a* is **antecedent** to *b*." Read figure 2.4b as "*a* and *b* are antecedent to *c*." And read figure 2.4c as "*a* is antecedent to *b*, which is an **intervening variable** antecedent to *c*." A lot of data analysis is about understanding and controlling for antecedent and intervening variables—about which much more in chapter 21.

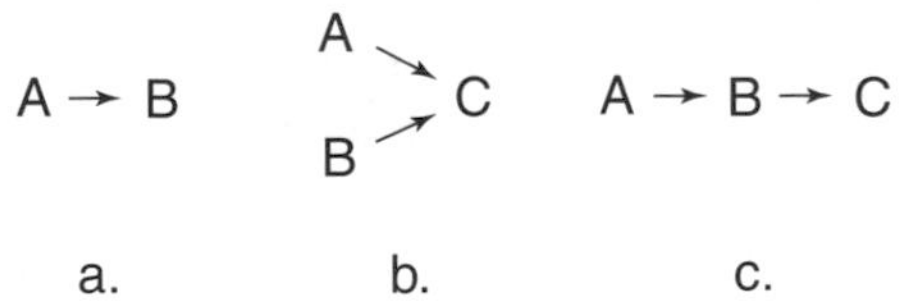

$$A \rightarrow B \qquad \begin{matrix} A \\ \searrow \\ \end{matrix} C \qquad A \rightarrow B \rightarrow C$$
$$\qquad\qquad B \nearrow$$

a.   b.   c.

FIGURE 2.4.
Time order between two or three variables.

Condition 4: Theory

Finally, even when you have established nonspurious, consistent, strong covariation, as well as a logical time sequence for two or more variables, you need a **theory**—a mechanism—that *explains* the association. Theories are ideas about how things work. Good theories are good ideas about how things work—that is, ideas that have held up against challenges and that explain new cases of things as they come up.

One of my favorites is called **cognitive dissonance** theory (Festinger 1957). It's based on the insight that: (1) People can tell when their beliefs about what *ought* to be don't match their perception of how things really are; and (2) This causes an uncomfortable feeling. The feeling is called cognitive dissonance. People then have a choice: They can live with the dissonance (be uncomfortable); change the external reality (fight city hall); or change their beliefs (usually the path of least resistance, but not necessarily the easy way out).

Cognitive dissonance theory helps explain why some people accept new technologies that they initially reject out of fear for their jobs: Once a technology is entrenched, and there is no chance of getting rid of it, it's easier to change your ideas about what's good and what's bad than it is to live with dissonance (Bernard and Pelto 1987). Dissonance theory helps explain why men in countries across the world are increasingly accepting of women working outside the home: When economic necessity drives women into the workforce, it's painful to hold on to the idea that that's the wrong thing for women to do.

On the other hand, some people do actually quit their jobs rather than accept new technologies, and some men continue to argue against women working outside the home, even when those men depend on their wives' income to make ends meet. This is an example of a general theory that fails to predict local phenomena. It leads us to seek more data and more understanding to predict when cognitive dissonance theory is insufficient as an explanation.

Many theories are developed to explain a purely local phenomenon and then turn out to have wider applicability. Many observers have noticed, for example, that when men from polygynous African societies move to cities, they often give up polygyny (Clignet 1970; Dorjahn 1977, 1988; Jacoby 1995). This consistent covariation is explained by the fact that men who move away from tribal territories in search of wage labor must abandon their land, their houses, and the shared labor of their kinsmen. Under those conditions, they simply cannot afford to provide for more than one wife, much less the children that multiple wives produce. The relation between urbanization and changes in marriage customs is explained by antecedent and intervening variables.

If you read the literature across the social sciences, you'll see references to something called "contagion theory." This one invokes a copycat mechanism to explain why suicides are more likely to come in batches when one of them is widely publicized in the press (Jamieson et al. 2003) and why more women candidates stand for election in districts that already have women legislators in office (Matland and Studlar 1996).

"Relative deprivation theory" is based on the insight that people compare themselves to specific peer groups, not to the world at large (Martin 1981; Stouffer et al. 1949). It explains why anthropology professors don't feel all that badly about engineering professors earning a lot of money, but hate it if sociologists in their university get significantly higher salaries than they do.

Theories start with one or two **primitive axioms**—things that are simply defined and that you have to take at face value. The definition of cognitive dissonance is an example: When people have inconsistent beliefs, or when they perceive things in the real world to be out of whack with their ideas of how things *should* be, they feel discomfort. This discomfort leads people to strive naturally toward cognitive consonance. Neither the fact of dissonance, nor the discomfort it produces, nor the desire for consonance are ever explained. They are primitive axioms. *How* people deal with dissonance and *how* they try to achieve consonance are areas for empirical research. As empirical research accumulates, the theory is tested and refined (box 2.5).

BOX 2.5

CULTURAL CONSONANCE THEORY

William Dressler developed his theory of cultural consonance based on cognitive dissonance theory. Cultural consonance is the degree to which people's lives mirror a widely shared set of beliefs about what lives should look like. What's a successful life? This differs from culture to culture, but in many cultures, the list of things that indicate success is widely shared. Dressler and his colleagues have found that people who have more of these things (whose lives are in consonance with the cultural model) have lower stress and fewer blood pressure problems than do people whose lives lack cultural consonance (Dressler et al. 1997, 2002, 2007; Dressler, Ribeiro et al. 2004, and see chapter 16 on measuring cultural consensus).

In relative deprivation theory, the fact that people have reference groups to which they compare themselves doesn't get explained, either. It, too, is a primitive axiom, an assumption, from which you deduce some results. The results are predictions, or hypotheses, that you then go out and test. The ideal in science is to deduce a prediction from theory and to test the prediction. That's the culture of science. The way social science really works much of the time is that you don't predict results, you **postdict** them. You analyze your data, come up with findings, and explain the findings after the fact.

There is nothing wrong with this. Knowledge and understanding can come from good ideas before you collect data or after collect data. You must admit, though, there's a certain panache in making a prediction, sealing it in an envelope, and testing it. Later, when you take the prediction out of the envelope and it matches your empirical findings, you get a lot of points (**Further Reading:** causal analysis in the social sciences).

THE KALYMNIAN CASE

Here's an example of explaining findings after the fact. In my experience, it's pretty typical of how social scientists develop, refine, and change their minds about theories.

In my fieldwork in 1964–1965 on the island of Kalymnos, Greece, I noticed that young sponge divers (in their 20s) were more likely to get the bends than were older divers (those over 30). (The bends is a crippling malady that affects divers who come up too quickly after a long time in deep water.) I also noticed that younger divers were more productive than very old divers (those over 45), but not more productive than those in their middle years (30–40).

As it turned out, younger divers were subject to much greater social stress to demonstrate their daring and to take risks with their lives—risks that men over 30 had already put behind them. The younger divers worked longer under water (gathering more sponges), but they came up faster and were consequently at higher risk of bends. The middle group of divers made up in experience for the shortened time they spent in the water, so they maintained their high productivity at lower risk of bends. The older divers were feeling the effects of infirmity brought on by years of deep diving, hence their productivity was lowered, along with their risk of death or injury from bends.

The real question was: What *caused* the young Kalymnian divers to engage in acts that placed them at greater risk?

My first attempt at explaining all this was pretty lame. I noticed that the men who took the most chances with their lives had a certain rhetoric and swagger. They were called *levédhis* (Greek for a brave young man) by other divers and by their captains. I concluded that somehow these men had more *levedhiá* (the quality of being brave and young) and that this made them higher risk takers. In fact, this is what many of my informants told me. Young men, they said, feel the need to show their manhood, and that's why they take risks by staying down too long and coming up too fast.

The problem with this cultural explanation was that it just didn't explain anything. Yes, the high risk takers swaggered and exhibited something we could label machismo or *levedhiá*. But what good did it do to say that lots of machismo caused people to dive deep and come up quickly? Where did young men get this feeling, I asked? "That's just how young men are," my informants told me. I reckoned that there might be something to this testosterone-poisoning theory, but it didn't seem adequate.

Eventually, I saw that the swaggering behavior and the values voiced about manliness were cultural ways to ratify, not explain, the high-risk diving behavior. Both the diving behavior and the ratifying behavior were the product of a third factor, an economic distribution system called *plátika*.

Divers traditionally took their entire season's expected earnings in advance, before shipping out in April for the 6-month sponge fishing expedition in North Africa. By taking their money (*plátika*) in advance, they placed themselves in debt to the boat captains. Just before they shipped out, the divers would pay off the debts that their families had accumulated during the preceding year. By the time they went to sea, the divers were nearly broke and their families started going into debt again for food and other necessities.

In the late 1950s, synthetic sponges began to take over the world markets, and young men on Kalymnos left for overseas jobs rather than go into sponge fishing. As divers left the island, the remaining divers demanded higher and higher *plátika*. They said that it was to compensate them for increases in the cost of living, but their demand for more money was a pure response by the divers to the increasing scarcity of their labor. The price of sponges, however, was dropping over the long term, due to competition with synthetics, so the higher *plátika* for the divers meant that the boat captains were losing profits. The captains put more and more pressure on the divers to produce more sponges, to stay down longer, and to take greater risks. This resulted in more accidents on the job (Bernard 1967, 1987).

Note that in all the examples of theory I've just given, the predictions and the post hoc explanations, I didn't have to quote a single statistic—not even a percentage score. That's because theories are qualitative. Ideas about cause and effect are based on insight; they are derived from either qualitative or quantitative observations and are initially expressed in words. *Testing* causal statements—finding out how *much* they explain rather than *whether* they seem to be plausible explanations—requires quantitative observations. But theory construction—explanation itself—is the quintessential qualitative act.

FURTHER READING

Measuring gender across cultures: Auster and Ohm (2000); Isaac and Shah (2004); Norvilitis and Reid (2002); Öngen (2007); Özkan and Lajunen (2006); Peng (2006); Sugihara and Katsurada

(2000); Sugihara and Warner (1999); Zhang et al. (2001). For a version of the BSRI tested for use in Mexico, see Lara-Cantú and Navarro-Arias (1987). For a version of the BSRI for use in China, see Qin and Yianjie (2003).

The ecological inference problem: Freedman (2001); Jargowsky (2005); King (1997).

Informant accuracy: Adams and Moody (2007); Bernard, Killworth et al. (1984); Calahan (1968); Dressler, Borges et al. (2005); Freeman et al. (1987); Godoy et al. (2008); Lapham et al. (2004); McPhee et al. (2002); Patten et al. (2002); Pescosolido and Wright (2003); Rocha (2005); Romney et al. (1986); Schwarz (1999); Sudman et al. (1996); Vadez et al. (2003); Woodside and Wilson (2002); Zimmerman et al. (2002).

Validity: Adams (1950); Hardesty and Bearden (2004); McKenzie et al. (1999); Mosier (1947); Nevo (1985); Sireci (1998).

Causal analysis in the social sciences: Blalock (1964, 1971); Lagnado et al. (2007); Marini and Singer (1988); Maxwell (2004); Rafferty (1998).

Preparing for Research

SETTING THINGS UP

This chapter is about the things that go on *before* data are collected and analyzed. I'll take you through the ideal research process and compare that to how research really gets done. Then I'll discuss the problem of choosing problems—how do I know what to study?—and I'll give you some pointers on how to scour the literature so you can benefit from the work of others when you start a research project.

I'll have a lot more to say about the ethics of social research in this chapter—choosing a research problem involves decisions that can have serious ethical consequences—and a lot more about theory, too. Method and theory, it turns out, are closely related.

THE IDEAL RESEARCH PROCESS

Despite all the myths about how research is done, it's actually a messy process that's cleaned up in the reporting of results. Figure 3.1 shows how the research process is supposed to work in the ideal world:

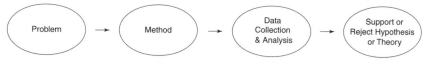

FIGURE 3.1.
How research is supposed to work.

1. First, a theoretical problem is formulated;
2. Next, an appropriate site and method are selected;
3. Then, data are collected and analyzed;
4. Finally, the theoretical proposition with which the research was launched is either challenged or supported.

In fact, all kinds of practical and intellectual issues get in the way of this neat scheme. In the end, research papers are written so that the chaotic aspects of research are not emphasized, and the orderly inputs and outcomes are.

I see nothing wrong with this. It would be a monumental waste of precious space in books and journals to describe the *real* research process for every project that's reported. Besides, every seasoned researcher knows just how messy it all is, anyway. You shouldn't have to become a highly experienced researcher before you're let into the secret of how it's really done.

A REALISTIC APPROACH

There are five questions to ask yourself about every research question you are thinking about pursuing. Most of these can also be asked about potential research sites and research methods. If you answer these questions honestly (at least to yourself), chances are you'll do good research every time. If you cheat on this test, even a teeny bit, chances are you'll regret it. Here are the five questions:

1. Does this topic (or research site, or data collection method) really interest me?
2. Is this a problem that is amenable to scientific inquiry?
3. Are adequate resources available to investigate this topic? To study this population at this particular research site? To use this particular data collection method?
4. Will my research question, or the methods I want to use, lead to unresolvable ethical problems?
5. Is the topic of theoretical and/or practical interest?

Personal Interest

The first thing to ask about any research question is: Am I really excited about this? Researchers do their best work when they are genuinely having fun, so don't do boring research when you can choose any topic you like.

Of course, you can't always choose any topic you like. In contract research, you sometimes have to take on a research question that a client finds interesting but that you find deadly dull. The most boring research I've ever done was on a contract where my coworkers and I combined ethnographic and survey research of rural homeowners' knowledge of fire prevention and their attitudes toward volunteer fire departments. This was in 1973. I had young children at home and the research contract paid me a summer salary. It was honest work and I delivered a solid product to the agency that supported the project. But I never wrote up the results for publication.

By comparison, that same year I did some contract research on the effects of co-ed prisons on homosexuality among male and female inmates. I was very interested in that study and it was much easier to spend the extra time and effort polishing the contract reports for publication (Killworth and Bernard 1974).

I've seen many students doing research for term projects, M.A. theses, and even doctoral dissertations simply out of convenience and with no enthusiasm for the topic. If you are not interested in a research question, then no matter how important other people tell you it is, don't bother with it. If others are so sure that it's a dynamite topic of great theoretical significance, let *them* study it.

The same goes for people and places. Agricultural credit unions and brokerage houses are both complex organizations. But they are very different kinds of places to spend time in, so if you are going to study a complex organization, check your gut first and make sure you're excited about where you're going. It's really hard to conduct penetrating, in-depth interviews over a period of a several weeks to a year if you aren't interested in the lives of the people you're studying.

You don't need any justification for your interest in studying a particular group of people or a particular topic. Personal interest is . . . personal. So ask yourself: Will my interest be sustained there? If the answer is "no," then reconsider. Accessibility of a research site or the availability of funds for the conduct of a survey are pluses, but by themselves they're not enough to make good research happen.

Science Versus Nonscience

The next question is: Is this a topic that can be studied by the methods of science? If the answer is "no," then no matter how much fun it is, and no matter how important it seems, don't even try to make a scientific study of it. Either let someone else do it, or use a different approach.

Consider this empirical question: How often do derogatory references to women occur in the Old Testament? If you can come up with a good, operational definition of "derogatory," then you can answer this question by looking through the corpus of data and counting the instances that turn up. Pretty straightforward, descriptive science.

But consider this question: Does the Old Testament offer support for unequal pay for women today? This is simply not answerable by the scientific method. It is no more answerable than the question: Is Rachmaninoff's music better than Tchaikovsky's? Or this: Should the remaining hunting-and-gathering bands of the world be preserved just the way they are and kept from being spoiled by modern civilization? Whether or not a study is a scientific one depends first on the nature of the question being asked and *then* on the methods used.

I can't stress too often or too strongly that when I talk about using the scientific method I'm *not* talking about numbers. In science, whenever a research problem can be investigated with quantitative measurement, numbers are more than just desirable; they're required. On the other hand, there are many intellectual problems for which quantitative measures are not yet available. Those problems require qualitative measurement.

Descriptions of processes (skinning a goat, building a fireworks tower, putting on makeup, setting the table for Thanksgiving), or of events (funerals, Little League games, parades), or of systems of nomenclature (kinship terms, disease terms, ways to avoid getting AIDS) require words, not numbers. Dorothy Holland and Debra Skinner (1987) asked some university women to list the kinds of guys there are. They got a list of words like "creep," "hunk," "nerd," "jerk," "sweetie pie," and so on. Then they asked some women, for each kind: "Is this someone you'd like to date?" The yes-no answers are nominal—that is, qualitative—measurement.

We'll get back to this kind of systematic, qualitative data collection in chapters 16 and 17 on cultural domain analysis.

Resources

The next question to ask is whether adequate resources are available for you to conduct your study. There are three major kinds of resources: time, money, and people. What may be adequate for some projects may be inadequate for others. Be totally honest with yourself about this issue.

Time

Some research projects take a few weeks or months; others take years. It takes a year or more to do an ethnographic study of a culture that is very different from your own, but a lot of focused ethnography can be done much more quickly. Gwendolyn Dordick (1996) spent 3 months studying a homeless shelter for 700 men in New York City. She visited the shelter four times a week for 3 hours or more each time, and spent 4 days at the shelter from morning until lights-out at 10 P.M. This was enough time for her to understand a great deal about life in the shelter, including how a group of just 15 men had coalesced into a ruling elite and how some men had formed faux marriages (that could, but did not necessarily, involve sex) to protect themselves and their few possessions from violence and thievery.

Much of today's applied anthropological research is done in weeks or months, using **rapid assessment methods**. Rapid assessment methods are the same ones that everyone else uses but they are done quickly. (I'll lay out some rapid assessment methods in chapter 12 on participant observation.) If you are doing research for a term project, the topic has to be something you can look at in a matter of a few months—and squeezing the research into a schedule of other classes, at that. It makes no sense to choose a topic that demands two semesters' work when you have one semester in which to do the research. The effort to cram 10 gallons of water into a 5-gallon can is futile and quite common. Don't do it.

Money

Many things come under the umbrella of money. Equipment is essentially a money issue, as is salary or subsistence for you and other people involved in the research. Funds for assistants, supplies, and travel have to be calculated before you can actually conduct a major research project. No matter how interesting it is to you, and no matter how important it may seem theoretically, if you haven't got the resources to use the right methods, skip it for now.

Naturally, most people do not have the money it takes to mount a major research effort. That's why there are granting agencies. Writing proposals is a special craft. It pays to learn it early. Research grants for M.A. research are typically between $1,000 and $5,000. Grants for doctoral research are typically between $10,000 and $30,000. If you spend 100 hours working on a grant proposal that brings you $10,000 to do your research, that's $100 an hour for your time. If you get turned down and spend another 100 hours rewriting the proposal, that's still $50 an hour for your time if you're successful. Pretty good pay for interesting work.

If your research requires comparison of two groups over a period of 12 months, and you only have money for 6 months of research, can you accomplish your research goal by studying one group? Can you accomplish it by studying two groups for 3 months each? Ask yourself whether it's worthwhile pursuing your research if it has to be scaled down to fit available resources. If the answer is "no," then consider other topics.

Does the research require access to a particular village? Can you gain access to that village? Will the research require that you interview elite members of the society you are studying—like village elders, shamans, medical malpractice lawyers, Lutheran priests? Will you be able to gain their cooperation? Or will they tell you to get lost or, even worse, lead you on with a lot of clichés about their culture? It's better not to do the study in the first place than to wind up with useless data.

People

"People" includes you and others involved in the research as well as those whom you are studying. Does the research require that you speak Papiamento? If so, are you willing to put in the time and effort to learn that language? Can the research be done effectively with interpreters? If so, are such people available at a cost that you can handle? Does the research require that you personally do multiple regression? If it does, are you prepared to acquire that skill?

ETHICS

I wish I could give you a list of criteria against which you could measure the "ethicalness" of every research idea you ever come up with. Unfortunately, it's not so simple. What's popularly ethical today may become popularly unethical tomorrow, and vice versa. (This does *not* mean that all ethics are relative. But more on that later.) During World War II, lots of anthropologists worked for what would today be called the Department of Defense, and they were applauded as patriots for lending their expertise to the war effort (Mead 1979). In the 1960s, anthropologists took part in Project Camelot, a project by the U.S. Army to study counterinsurgency in Latin America (Horowitz 1965). This caused a huge outpouring of criticism, and the American Anthropological Association (AAA) produced its first statement on ethics—not a formal code, but a statement—in 1967, rejecting quite specifically the use of the word "anthropology" as a disguise for spying (Fluehr-Lobban 1998:175).

During the Vietnam War, some anthropologists did clandestine work for the Department of Defense. There was a strong reaction against this behavior, and in 1971 the AAA promulgated a formal code of ethics, titled *Principles of Professional Responsibility* (American Anthropological Association 1991). That document specifically forbade anthropologists from doing any secret research and asserted the AAA's right to investigate allegations of behavior by anthropologists that hurts people who are studied, students, or colleagues (Fluehr-Lobban 1998:177). More recently, anthropologists have participated in U.S. military programs for studying local culture in battle zones and this, too, has produced intense debate within the discipline about the proper role, if any, of anthropologists in military and intelligence operations (Rohde 2007) (**Further Reading:** anthropology in the military and in intelligence).

Despite the rhetoric, though, no anthropologists have been expelled from the AAA because of unethical conduct. One reason is that, when push comes to shove, everyone recognizes that there are conflicting, legitimate interests. In applied anthropology, for example, you have a serious obligation to those who pay for research. This obligation may conflict with your obligation to those whom you are studying. And when this happens, where do you stand? The Society for Applied Anthropology has maintained that the first obligation is to those whom we study. But the National Association of Practicing Anthropologists has promulgated a statement of professional responsibilities that recognizes how complex this issue can be (http://practicinganthropology.org/ethical -guidelines).

We are a long, long way from finding the answers to these questions (Caplan 2003; Fluehr-Lobban 2002). Today, anthropologists are once again working for the Department of Defense. Is this simply because that's where the jobs are? (box 3.1).

Perhaps. Times and popular ethics change. Whether you are subject to those changes is a matter for your own conscience, but it's because popular ethics change that Stanley Milgram was able to conduct his famous experiment on obedience in the 1960s.

Milgram's Obedience Experiment

Milgram (1963, 1965) duped people into thinking that they were taking part in an experiment on how well human beings learn under conditions of punishment. The subjects in the experiment were "teachers." The "learners" were Milgram's accomplices. The idea was to see how obedient people would be—how much electrical shock they would administer to a "learner" when told to do so by someone in authority, like an experimenter in a lab coat.

Milgram varied the conditions in his experiments to test for gender differences, for differences in locale (the Yale University campus vs. a run-down building in downtown Bridgeport, Connecticut), and for differences the proximity of the experimenter and the victim to the subject (in the same room, in different rooms), but in all the experiments, the basics were the same. The subjects sat at a panel of 30 switches, labeled from 15 volts

BOX 3.1

WHERE THE JOBS ARE

In 1961, when I entered graduate school, there were 39 departments of anthropology in the United States and fewer than 100 Ph.D. degrees awarded—in all four fields of anthropology. Today, there are 105 Ph.D.-granting departments of anthropology in the United States awarding about 500 Ph.D.s per year (Rudd et al. 2008:3). As of 2005, about 22% of Ph.D. anthropologists went into nonacademic jobs (Rudd et al. 2008:4). This is only a part of the story, though. Counting all anthropologists, including those without the Ph.D., there were more working outside academe in 1986 than in it (Fluehr-Lobban 2002:xii). The growth in nonacademic jobs for anthropologists has increased steadily since then. In 2009, there were over 1,500 registered members of the anthrodesign listerv (devoted to an anthropological approach to product design and marketing) on Yahoo.com.

to 450 volts. Each switch supposedly delivered 15 more volts than the last, and the panel had labels every four switches (that is, every 60 volts), from "Slight Shock" (15 volts) all the way up to "Danger: Severe Shock" (375 volts) and "XXX" (435 volts and 450 volts). Each time the learner made a mistake on a word-recall test, the subject was told to give the learner a bigger shock.

Milgram paid each participant $4.50 up front (about $32 in 2010 dollars) to make them feel obligated to go through with the experiment. He also gave them a little test shock—45 volts (the second lever on the 30-lever panel)—to make them believe that the punishment they'd be delivering to the so-called learners was for real.

In many of the experiments, the learner grunted at 75 volts. The reaction escalated as the putative voltage increased. At 150 volts, learners began pleading to be let out of the experiment. And at 285 volts, the learner's response, as Milgram reported it, could "only be described as an agonizing scream" (1974:4). All those reactions by the learners were actually played back from tape so that subjects would hear exactly the same things. The experimenter, in a gray lab coat, kept telling the subject to administer the shocks—saying things like: "You have no choice. You must go on." In the original experiment (where, by the way, the learner didn't complain until the subject supposedly gave him a 300-volt shock, and then pounded on the wall of the room separating him from the subject), 65% of Milgrams's subjects obeyed orders and administered what they thought were shocks beyond the XXX level. Many subjects protested but were convinced by the researchers that it was all right to follow orders.

Until Milgram did his experiments, it had been easy to scoff at Nazi war criminals whose defense was that they were "just following orders." In 1979, Milgram was asked on CBS's show, *Sixty Minutes*, if that sort of thing could happen again. His answer: "Having observed a thousand people in the experiment . . . if a system of death camps were set up in the United States of the sort we had seen in Nazi Germany, one would be able to find sufficient personnel for those camps in any medium-sized American town" (quoted in Blass 1999:955) (box 3.2).

BOX 3.2

SOME QUESTIONS ABOUT MILGRAM'S EXPERIMENTS ON OBEDIENCE

Are Milgram's findings still important? When people hear about Milgram's study they typically say that they wouldn't be as blindly obedient to authority as Milgram's subjects were. Most of those who dropped out of Milgram's experiments did so after administering 150-volt shocks. Milgram's full experiment wouldn't get by any Human Subjects Review Board now, but Jerry Burger (2009) was able to replicate Milgram's original experiment up to that crucial 150-volt limit. The bottom line: Twenty-eight of Burger's 40 subjects agreed to continue after the 150-volt limit.

Were Milgram's experiments unethical? Did Milgram cause his subjects emotional harm when they thought about what they'd done? If you were among Milgram's subjects who obeyed to the end, would you be haunted by this? The literature on this is mixed (see Murray [1980] and Herrera [2001] for contrasting views), but we do know this: Milgram's make-believe experiment was less costly, and more ethical, than the natural experiments carried out at My Lai, or Chatila, or Srebenica—the Vietnamese village (in 1968) and the Lebanese refugee camp (in 1982), and the Bosnian village (1995)—whose civilian inhabitants were wiped out by American and Lebanese and Serbian soldiers, respectively, "under orders." Those experiments, too, showed what ordinary people are capable of doing—except that in those cases, real people really got killed.

What Does It All Mean?

Just because times, and ethics, seem to change, does not mean that anything goes. Everyone agrees that scholars have ethical responsibilities, but not everyone agrees on what those responsibilities are. All the major scholarly societies have published their own code of ethics—all variations on the same theme, but all variations nonetheless. I've listed the Internet addresses for several of these codes of ethics in appendix E.

These documents are not perfect, but they cover a lot of ground and are based on the accumulated experience of thousands of researchers who have grappled with ethical dilemmas over the past 60 years. Look at those codes of ethics regularly during the course of any research project, both to get some of the wisdom that has gone into them and to develop your own ideas about how the documents might be improved.

Don't get trapped into nihilistic relativism. Cultural relativism (the unassailable fact that people's ideas about what is good and beautiful are shaped by their culture) is a great antidote for overdeveloped ethnocentrism. But, as Merrilee Salmon makes clear (1997), ethical relativism (that all ethical systems are equally good since they are all cultural products) is something else entirely.

Can you imagine defending the human rights violations of Nazi Germany as just another expression of the richness of culture? Would you feel comfortable defending, on the basis of cultural relativism, the so-called ethnic cleansing in the 1990s of Bosnians and Kosovar Albanians by Serbs in the former Yugoslavia? Or the slaughter of Tutsis by Hutus in Rwanda? Or of American Indians by immigrant Europeans in the 19th century?

There is no value-free science. Everything that interests you as a potential research focus comes fully equipped with risks to you and to the people you study. Should anthropologists do social marketing for a state lottery, knowing that poor people will be squandering their meager resources on false hopes of sudden riches? Or is social marketing only for getting people to use condoms and to wash their hands before preparing food? Should anthropologists work on projects that raise worker productivity in developing nations if that means some workers will become redundant? In each case, all you can do (and *must* do) is assess the potential human costs and the potential benefits. And when I say "potential benefits," I mean not just to humanity in the abstract, but also to you personally.

Don't hide from the fact that you are interested in your own glory, your own career, your own advancement. It's a safe bet that your colleagues are interested in their career advancement, too. We have all heard of cases in which a scientist put her or his career above the health and well-being of others. This is devastating to science, and to scientists, but it happens when otherwise good, ethical people (1) convince themselves that they are doing something noble for humanity, rather than for themselves, and (2) consequently fool themselves into thinking that *that* justifies their hurting others. (See Hudson [2004] for more on fraud in science.) When you make these assessments of costs and benefits, be prepared to come to decisions that may not be shared by all your colleagues. Remember the problem of the relation between darkness of skin color and measures of life success, like wealth and longevity? Would you, personally, be willing to participate in a study of this problem?

Suppose the study was likely to show that a statistically significant percentage of the variation in earning power in the United States is predictable from (*not* caused by) darkness of skin color. Some would argue that this would be useful evidence in the fight against racism and would jump at the chance to do the investigation. Others would argue that the evidence would be used by racists to do further damage in our society, so the study should simply not be done lest the information it produces fall into the wrong hands.

There is no answer to this dilemma. Above all, be honest with yourself. Ask yourself: Is this ethical? If the answer is "no," then skip it; find another topic. Once again, there are plenty of interesting research questions that won't put you into a moral bind (**Further Reading:** ethical issues in anthropology).

THEORY—EXPLANATION AND PREDICTION

All research is specific. Whether you conduct ethnographic or questionnaire research, the first thing you do is *describe a process* or *investigate a relation* among some variables in a population. Description is essential, but to get from description to theory is a big leap. It involves asking: "What causes the phenomenon to exist in the first place?" and "What does this phenomenon cause?" Theory, then, is about explaining and predicting things.

It may seem odd to talk about theory in a book about methods, but you can't design research until you choose a research question, and research questions depend crucially on theory. A good way to understand what theory is about is to pick something that begs to be explained and to look at competing explanations for it. See which explanation you like best. Do that for a few phenomena and you'll quickly discover which paradigm you identify with. That will make it easier to pick research problems and to develop hypotheses that you can go off and test.

Here is an example of something that begs to be explained: Everywhere in the world, there is a very small chance that children will be killed or maimed by their parents. However, the chance that a child is killed by a parent is much higher if a child has one or more nonbiological parents than if the child has two biological parents (Daly and Wilson 1988, 1998; Lightcap et al. 1982). This "Cinderella effect," as it's known, means that those evil-step-parent folk tales are based on more than fantasy. Or are they? A lot depends on the paradigm you start with.

Alternative Paradigms for Building Theories

One explanation is that this is all biological—in the genes. After all, male gorillas are known to kill off the offspring of new females they bring into their harem. Humans, the reasoning goes, have a bit of that instinct in them, too. They mostly fight and overcome the impulse, but over millions of cases, it's bound to come out once in a while. Culture usually trumps biology, but sometimes, biology is just stronger. This is an explanation based on assumptions from **sociobiology** or **evolutionary psychology** or **evolutionary anthropology**.

Another explanation is that it's cultural. Yes, it seems like it's more common for children to be killed by nonbiological than by biological parents, but this kind of mayhem is more common in some cultures than in others. Also, the deaths of some children at the hand of their biological parents may go unnoticed and unreported simply because we don't expect that, while the deaths of children at the hands of nonbiological parents get more notice simply because we're on the lookout for it (Crume et al. 2002). And, although killing children is rare everywhere, in some cultures mothers are more likely to kill their children; in other cultures, fathers are more likely to be the culprits. This is because women and men learn different gender roles in different societies. So, the reasoning goes, we have to look at cultural differences for a true explanation of the phenomenon. This is called an **idealist**, or a cultural, theory because it is based on what people think—on their ideas.

Yet another explanation is that when adult men and women bring children to a second marriage, they know that their assets are going to be diluted by the claims the spouse's children have on those assets—immediate claims and later claims of inheritance. This leads some of those people to harm their spouse's children from the former marriage. In a few cases, this causes death. This is a **materialist** theory, as is the idea that women who have children from a previous marriage may, on average, be forced to marry men who carry a higher risk of being abusive.

Sociobiology, idealism, and materialism are not theories. They are **paradigms** or **theoretical perspectives**. They contain a few basic *rules for finding theories* that explain observed events. Sociobiology stresses the primacy of evolutionary, biological features of humans as the basis for human behavior. Idealism stresses the importance of internal states—attitudes, preferences, ideas, beliefs, values—as the basis for human behavior. And materialism stresses structural and infrastructural forces—like the economy, the technology of production and reproduction, demography, and environmental conditions—as causes of human behavior.

When you want to explain a specific phenomenon, you apply the principles of your favorite paradigm and come up with a specific explanation—a theory.

Why do women everywhere in the world tend to have nurturing roles? If you think that biology rules here, then you'll be inclined to support evolutionary theories about other phenomena as well. If you think economic and political forces cause values and behavior, then you'll be inclined to apply the materialist perspective in your search for explanations in general. If you think that culture—people's values—is of paramount importance, then you'll tend to apply the idealist perspective to come up with explanations. The different paradigms are not so much in competition as they are complementary, for different **levels of analysis**. The evolutionary explanation for the battering of nonbiological children is appealing for aggregate, evolutionary phenomena—the big, big picture. An evolutionary explanation addresses the question: What is the reproductive advantage of this behavior happening at all?

But we know that the behavior of hurting or killing step-children is not inevitable, so an evolutionary explanation can't account for why some step-parents hurt their children and others don't. A materialist explanation is more productive for addressing this question. Some step-parents who bring a lot of resources to a second marriage become personally frustrated by the possibility of having their wealth raided and diluted by their new spouse's children. The reaction would be strongest for step-parents who have competing obligations to support their biological children who are living with yet another family. These frustrations will cause *some* people to become violent, but not others.

But even this doesn't explain why a particular step-parent is supportive or unsupportive of his or her nonbiological children. At this level of analysis, we need a processual and psychological explanation, one that takes into account the particular historical facts of the case. Whatever paradigm they follow, all empirical anthropologists rely on ethnography to test their theories.

Handwerker (1996b), for example, found that step-parents in Barbados were, overall, no more likely to treat children violently than were biological parents. But the presence of a *step-father* increased the likelihood that women battered their daughters and decreased the likelihood that women battered their sons. In homes with step-parents, women saw their daughters as potential competitors for resources available from their partner and they saw sons as potential sources of physical protection and income.

And there was more. Powerful women (those who had their own sources of income) protected their children from violence, treated them affectionately, and elicited affection for them from their man. The probability that a son experienced an affectionate relationship with a biological father rose with the length of time the two lived together, but only for sons who had powerful mothers. Men battered powerless women and the children of powerless women, and powerless women battered their own children.

Is there any evolutionary basis for powerful spouses to batter powerless ones? Or is this all something that gets stimulated by material conditions, like poverty? A lot of research is being done on this now but this much is clear: Different paradigms produce different, interesting answers to the same question.

Idiographic and Nomothetic Theory

Theory comes in two basic sizes: elemental, or **idiographic** theory and generalizing or **nomothetic** theory. An idiographic theory accounts for the facts in a single case. A nomothetic theory accounts for the facts in many cases. The more cases that a theory accounts for, the more nomothetic it is.

The distinction was first made by Wilhelm Windelband, a philosopher of science, in 1894. By the late 1800s, Wilhelm Dilthey's distinction between the **Naturwissenschaften** and **Geisteswissenschaften**—the sciences of nature and the sciences of the mind—had become quite popular. The problem with Dilthey's distinction, said Windelband, was that it couldn't accommodate the then brand-new science of psychology. The subject matter made psychology a Geisteswissenchaft, but the discipline relied on the experimental method, and this made it a Naturwissenschaft.

What to do? Yes, said Windelband, the search for reliable knowledge is, indeed, of two kinds: the sciences of law and the sciences of events, or, in a memorable turn of phrase, "the study of what always is and the study of what once was." Windelband coined the terms **idiographic** and **nomothetic** to replace Dilthey's Natur- and Geisteswissenschaften.

Organic evolution is governed by laws, Windelband observed, but the sequence of organisms on this planet is an event that is not likely to be repeated on any other planet. Languages are governed by laws, but any given language at any one time is an event in human linguistic life. The goal of the idiographic, or historical sciences, then, is to deliver "portraits of humans and human life with all the richness of their unique forms" (Windelband 1998 [1894]:16).

Windelband went further. Every causal explanation of an event—every idiographic analysis, in other words—requires some idea of how things happen at all. No matter how vague the idea, there must be nomothetic principles guiding idiographic analysis.

Windelband's formulation is a perfect description of what all natural scientists—vulcanologists, ornithologists, astronomers, ethnographers—do all the time. They describe things; they develop deep understanding of the cases they study; and they produce explanations for individual cases based on nomothetic rules. The study of *a* volcanic eruption, of *a* species' nesting habits, of *a* star's death is no more likely to produce new nomothetic knowledge than is the study of *a* culture's adaptation to new circumstances. But the idiographic effort, based on the application of nomothetic rules, is required equally across all the sciences if induction is to be applied and greater nomothetic knowledge achieved.

Those efforts in psychology are well known: Sigmund Freud based his theory of psychosexual development on just a few cases. Jean Piaget did the same in developing his universal theory of cognitive development, as did B. F. Skinner in developing the theory of operant conditioning.

In anthropology, Lewis Henry Morgan (1877) and others made a brave, if ill-fated effort in the 19th century to create nomothetic theories about the evolution of culture from the study of cases at hand. The unilineal evolutionary theories they advanced were wrong, but the effort to produce nomothetic theory was *not* wrong. Franz Boas and his students made clear the importance of paying careful attention to the particulars of each culture, but Leslie White (1959) and Julian Steward (1949, 1955) did not reject the idea that cultures evolve. Instead, they advanced more nuanced theories about how the process works.

Steward (1955) chose just a handful of cases when he developed his theory of cultural evolution. Over time, data from Tehuacán, Mexico, and Ali Kosh, Iran—6,000 miles and several thousand years apart—support Steward's nomothetic formulation about the multistage transition from hunting and gathering to agriculture. (The sequences appear to be similar responses to the retreat of the last glacier of the Paleolithic.) As we get more comparisons, the big picture will either become more and more nomothetic or it will be challenged.

And the effort goes on. Wittfogel (1957) developed his so-called hydraulic theory of cultural evolution—that complex civilizations, in Mexico, India, China, Egypt, and Mesopotamia developed out of the need to organize the distribution of water for irrigation—based on idiographic knowledge of a handful of cases. David Price (1995) studied a modern, bureaucratically organized water supply system in the Fayoum area of Egypt. The further downstream a farmer's plot is from an irrigation pump, the less water he is likely to get because farmers upstream divert more water than the system allows them legally to have. Price's in-depth, idiographic analysis of the Fayoum irrigation system lends support to Wittfogel's long neglected theory because, says Price, it shows "how farmers try to optimize the disadvantaged position in which the state has placed them"

(1995:107–108). Susan Lees (1986) showed how farmers in Israel, Kenya, and Sudan got around bureaucratic limitations on the water they were allotted. We need much more idiographic analysis, more explanations of cases, to test the limitations of Wittfogel's theory. (See Harrower [2009] for recent archeological work in southern Arabia on the role of irrigation systems in state formation.)

Idiographic Theory

As in all sciences, most theory in anthropology is idiographic. Here are three examples:

1. In 1977, the New Delhi police reported 311 deaths by kitchen fires of women, mostly young brides who were killed because their families had not delivered a promised dowry to the groom's family (Claiborne 1984). By 1987, the government of India reported 1,912 such "dowry deaths" of young women, and by 1997 the number was 6,975—over 19 per day (Dugger 2000; and see Shenk 2007; Srinivasan 2005; Van Willigen and Chana 1991). How to explain this?

Gross (1992) theorized that the phenomenon is a consequence of female hypergamy (marrying up) and dowry. Families that can raise a large dowry in India can marry off their daughter to someone of a higher caste and greater means. This has created a bidding war, as the families of wealthier sons demand more and more for the privilege of marrying those sons (and see S. Anderson 2003).

Apparently, many families of daughters in India have gone into debt to accumulate the dowries. When they can't pay off the debt, some of the families of grooms have murdered the brides in faked "kitchen accidents," where kerosene stoves purportedly blow up. This gives the grooms' families a chance to get another bride whose families can deliver.

2. Next, consider the case of fraternal polyandry, where two or more brothers marry one woman. This phenomenon has been the subject of investigation by anthropologists for generations (Petros 1963). In 1971, Goldstein observed that the custom was practiced in Tibet only among a class of serfs, known as tre-ba, who held title to their land but who also had major tax and corvée obligations to their lord. In order not to break up the land, Goldstein concluded, brothers would take a single bride into one household.

3. Finally, consider an idiographic theory derived entirely from ethnography. When Anthony Paredes began his study of the Poarch Band of Creek Indians in Alabama the group was a remnant of an earlier group. They had lost the use of the Creek language, were not recognized by the U.S. government as a tribe, and had little contact with other Indians for decades. Yet, the Poarch Creek Indians had somehow maintained their identity.

Paredes wanted to know how the Indians had managed this. He did what he called "old-fashioned ethnography," including key-informant interviewing and learned about a cultural revitalization movement that had been going on since the 1940s. That movement was led by some key people whose efforts over the years had made a difference. Paredes's description of how the Poarch Creek Indians held their cultural identity in the face of such odds is an excellent example of elemental, idiographic theory. As you read his account you feel you understand how it worked (see Paredes 1974, 1992).

So What's Wrong?

Nothing's wrong. Gross's explanation for the kitchen fires in India rings true, but it doesn't explain why other societies that have escalating dowry don't have kitchen fires. Nor does it tell us why dowry persists in India despite being outlawed since 1961, or why dowry—which, after all, only occurs in 7.5% of the world's societies—exists in the first place. But Gross's theory is a first-class example of theory at the local level—where research begins.

Goldstein's theory is attractive for understanding the Tibetan case of fraternal polyandry, but it doesn't say anything about other cases of polyandry, like the one studied by Hiatt in Sri Lanka (1980). Over the years, other case studies of polyandry, in Tibet and elswhere, have either supported or not supported Goldstein's theory (Levine 1988; Levine and Silk 1997). As the idiographic studies build, we'll gain better and better understanding of the nomothetic principles, if any, at work. In the meantime, E. A. Smith (1998) and others have applied an an evolutionary perspective to understanding polyandry and other scholars have tested the effects of structural changes on polyandry.

Paredes's theory helps us understand how the Poarch Creeks maintained their cultural identity, but it doesn't tell us how other Native American groups managed to do this or why some groups did *not* manage it. Nor does it tell us anything about why other ethnic groups maintain or fail to maintain their identity in the United States or why ethnicity persists at all in the face of pressure from states on ethnic groups to assimilate. Others can try to make the theory more nomothetic.

In any science, much of the best work is at the idiographic level of theory making.

Nomothetic Theory

Nomothetic theories address questions like "So, what *does* account for the existence of dowry?"

Several theorists have tried to answer this question. Esther Boserup (1970) hypothesized that dowry should occur in societies where a woman's role in subsistence production is low. She was right, but many societies where women's productive effort is of low value do *not* have dowry.

Gaulin and Boster (1990) offered a sociobiological theory that predicts dowry in stratified societies that have monogamous or polyandrous marriage. They tested their theory on Murdock and White's (1969) Standard Cross-Cultural Sample of 186 societies. The Gaulin-Boster theory works better than Boserup's—it misclassifies fewer societies. That's how nomothetic theory grows, though the Gaulin-Boster theory still makes some mistakes. Fully 77% of dowry societies are, in fact, stratified and have monogamous marriage, but 63% of all monogamous, stratified societies do *not* have dowry. We need more good ideas and more tests to make the theory more inclusive—more nomothetic (box 3.3).

One More: The Second Demographic Transition

Let's do one more—the second demographic transition. The first demographic transition happened at the end of the Paleolithic when people swapped agriculture for hunting and gathering as the main means of production. During the Paleolithic, population growth was very, very slow. But across the world, as people switched from hunting and gathering to agriculture, as they settled down and accumulated surplus, their populations exploded.

The second demographic transition began in the late 18th century in Europe with industrialization and has been spreading around the world ever since. Today, Japan, Germany, Italy, and other highly industrialized countries have **total fertility rates** (the aver-

BOX 3.3

COMPARATIVE RESEARCH AND TESTING THEORY

If an idiographic theory accounts for some data in say, India, Japan, or England, then an obvious next step is to see how far the theory extends. Alice Schlegel and Herbert Barry (1986), for example, looked at the consequences of female contribution to subsistence. Their nomothetic theory predicts that women will be more respected in societies where they contribute a lot to subsistence than in societies where their contribution is low.

Whether their theory is supported depends crucially on how Schlegel and Barry operationalize the concept of *respect*. In societies where women contribute a lot to subsistence, say Schlegel and Barry, women will be spared some of the burden of pregnancy "through the attempt to space children" more evenly (Schlegel and Barry 1986:146). In such societies, women will be subjected to rape less often; they will have greater sexual freedom; they will be worth more in bride wealth; and they will have greater choice in selection of a spouse. Schlegel and Barry coded the 186 societies in the Standard Cross-Cultural Sample for each of those indicators of respect—and their predictions were supported.

age number of children born to women during their reproductive years), or TFRs, in the neighborhood of 1.5 to 1.2—that's 29% to 43% below the 2.1 TFR needed in those countries just to replace the current population. In the past 40 years, some previously high TFR countries, like Barbados, Mauritius, and Mexico, have been through a major demographic transition.

Explaining why women in Barbados are having fewer children is idiographic; predicting the conditions under which women in *any* underdeveloped country will start lowering their fertility rate is nomothetic. Handwerker's theory (1989) is that women in low-wage jobs encourage their daughters to get more education. And when women get sufficiently educated, their participation in the labor market becomes more effective (they earn more), freeing them from dependency on men (sons and husbands). As this dependency diminishes, women lower their fertility.

Handwerker's theory is nomothetic and materialist. It relies on material conditions forces to explain how preferences develop for fewer children and it does not rely on preferences (culture, ideas, values) to explain the level of a country's TFR.

The Consequences of Paradigm

Differences in theoretical paradigms have profound consequences. If you think that beliefs and attitudes are what make people behave as they do, then if you want to change people's behavior, the obvious thing to do is change their attitudes. This is the basis of the **educational model of social change** I mentioned in chapter 2—the runaway bestseller model for change in our society.

Want to get women in developing nations to have fewer children? Educate them about the importance of small families. Want to lower the rate of infectious disease in developing countries? Educate people about the importance of good hygiene. Want to get adolescents in Boston or Seattle or wherever to stop having high-risk sex? Educate them about the importance of abstinence or, if that fails, about how to take protective measures against sexually transmitted disease. Want to get people in the United States to use their cars less? Educate them about car pooling.

These kinds of programs rarely work—but they do work sometimes. You *can* educate people (through commercial advertising) about why they should switch from, say, a Honda to a Toyota, or from a Toyota to a Ford, but you can't get people to give up their cars. You *can* educate people (through social advertising) to use the pill rather than less-effective methods of birth control, once they have decided to lower their fertility, but educational rhetoric doesn't influence the number of children that people want in the first place.

The closer a behavior is to the culture (or **superstructure**) of society, the easier it is to intervene culturally. Brand preferences are often superstructural, so advertising works to get people to switch brands—to change their behavior. But if people's behavior is rooted in the **structure** or **infrastructure** of society, then forget about changing their behavior by educating them to have better attitudes.

Eri Sugita (2006) studied 50 women in rural Uganda who had children under 5 years of age in their care. Over 14 months of fieldwork, Sugita found that the number of liters of water available per person in each household did a better job of predicting whether the women washed their hands before preparing or serving food than did the women's education or knowledge of hygiene. Women and children fetched all the water, so those who lived near a well were able to make more trips and get more water—unless they had a bicycle. Men, however, monopolized the bicycle in families that could afford one. Teaching people more about hygiene wouldn't do nearly as much for public health in that village as giving women bicycles would.

In poor countries, having many children may be the only security people have in their old age. Under those circumstances, no amount of rhetoric about the advantages of small families is going to change anyone's mind about the number of children they want to have. If you need a car because the only affordable housing is 30 miles from your job, no amount of rhetoric will convince you to take the bus. Demographic transition theory is highly nomothetic. It accounts for why Japan, a fully industrialized nation, has such a low TFR. But it doesn't predict what the consequences of that low TFR will be. For the time being, at least (until even bigger nomothetic theories are developed), we still need an idiographic theory for this.

Japan has about 126 million people—about 40% of the population of the United States—living in an area the size of Montana. Japan has the world's second largest economy and the Japanese enjoy a per capita income of about $34,000 in 2008 (IMF 2009). This is based on manufacturing products for export. The oil to run the factories that produce all those exports has to be imported. So does a lot of food to feed all those people who are working in the factories. The TFR of 1.3 in Japan makes it easy to predict that Japan's industries need to find lots of new workers to maintain productivity—and the lifestyle supported by that productivity.

Belgium and Italy—two other countries with low TFRs—solved this problem by opening their borders to people from the formerly communist countries of eastern Europe and by increasing female participation in the labor force. In 1991, there was strong resistance to these solutions. By 2000, there were over 700,000 foreign workers in Japan (about 1% of the labor force), including about 230,000 illegals (Ducanes and Abella 2008:18).

How will lower TFR in the developed countries of the world affect world migration? This is one of my current favorite topics to think about because it illustrates how important theory is in developing research questions and it showcases the contributions of idealist and materialist perspectives as well as the importance of idiographic and nomothetic theory.

There is no list of research questions. You have to use your imagination and your curiosity about how things work, and follow your hunches. Above all, never take anything at face value. Every time you read an article, ask yourself: "What would a study look like that would test whether the major assertions and conclusions of this article were really correct?" If someone says: "The only things students care about are sex, drugs, and twitter," the proper response is: "We can test that."

A GUIDE TO RESEARCH TOPICS, ANYWAY

There may not be a list of research topics, but there are some useful guidelines. First of all, there are very few big-theory issues—I call them research *arenas*—in all of social science. Here are four of them: (1) the nature-nurture problem, (2) the evolution problem, (3) the internal-external problem, and (4) the social facts or emergent properties problem.

1. **The nature-nurture problem**. This is an age-old question: How much of our personality and behavior is determined by our genes and how much by our exposure to different environments? Many diseases (cystic fibrosis, Tay-Sachs, sickle-cell anemia) are highly determined by our genes, but others (heart disease, diabetes, asthma) are at least partly the result of our cultural and physical environment.

   Schizophrenia is a genetically inherited disease, but its expression is heavily influenced by our cultural environment. Hallucinations are commonly associated with schizophrenia, but when Robert Edgerton (1966) asked over 500 people in four East African tribes to list the behavior of people who are severely mentally ill, less than 1% of them mentioned hallucinations (see also Edgerton and Cohen 1994; Jenkins and Barrett 2004).

   Research on the extent to which differences in cognitive functions of men and women are the consequence of environmental factors (nurture) or genetic factors (nature) or the interaction between those factors is part of this research arena (Caplan et al. 1997). So are studies of human response to signs of illness across cultures (Hielscher and Sommerfeld 1985; Kleinman 1980).

2. **The evolution problem**. Studies of how groups change through time from one *kind* of thing to another kind of thing are in this arena. Societies change very slowly through time, but at some point we say that a village has changed into a town or a town into a city or that a society has changed from a feudal to an industrial economy. All studies of the differences between small societies—**Gemeinschaften**—and big societies—**Gesellschaften**—are in this arena. So are studies of inexorable bureaucratization as organizations grow.

3. **The internal-external problem**. Studies of the way in which behavior is influenced by values and by environmental conditions are in this arena. Studies of **response effects** (how people respond differently to the same question asked by a woman or by a man, for example) are in this arena, too. So are studies of the difference between what people say they do and what they actually do.

4. **The social facts, or emergent properties problem**. The name for this problem comes from Emile Durkheim's (1933 [1893]) argument that social facts exist outside of individuals and are not reducible to psychological facts. A great deal of social research is

based on the assumption that people are influenced by social forces that *emerge* from the interaction of humans but that transcend individuals. Many studies of social networks and social support, for example, are in this arena, as are studies that test the influence of organizational forms on human thought and behavior.

Generating of Types of Studies

Now look at table 3.1. I have divided research topics (not arenas) into classes, based on the relation among kinds of variables.

Table 3.1 Types of Studies

	Internal States	External States	Reported Behavior	Observed Behavior	Artifacts	Environment
Internal states	I	II	IIIa	IIIb	IV	V
External states		VI	VIIa	VIIb	VIII	IX
Reported behavior			Xa	Xb	XIa	XIIa
Observed behavior				Xc	XIb	XIIb
Artifacts					XIII	XIV
Environment						XV

The five major kinds of variables are:

1. **Internal states.** These include attitudes, beliefs, values, and perceptions. Cognition is an internal state.
2. **External states.** These include characteristics of people, such as age, wealth, health status, height, weight, gender, and so on.
3. **Behavior.** This covers what people eat, who they communicate with, how much they work and play—in short, everything that people do and much of what social scientists are interested in understanding.
4. **Artifacts.** This includes all physical residue from human behavior—radioactive waste, tomato slices, sneakers, arrowheads, computer disks, Viagra, skyscrapers—everything.
5. **Environment.** This includes physical and social environmental characteristics. The amount of rainfall, the amount of biomass per square kilometer, location on a river or ocean front—these are physical features that influence human thought and behavior. Humans also live in a social environment. Living under a democratic versus an authoritarian régime or working in an organization that tolerates or does not tolerate sexual harassment are examples of social environments that have consequences for what people think and how they behave.

Keep in mind that category (3) includes both reported behavior and actual behavior. A great deal of research has shown that about a third to a half of everything people report about their behavior is not true (Bernard, Killworth et al. 1984). If you want to know what people eat, for example, asking them is not a good way to find out (Basiotis et al. 1987; R. K. Johnson et al. 1996). If you ask people how many times a year they go to church, you're likely to get highly exaggerated data (Hadaway et al. 1993, 1998).

Some of the difference between what people say they do and what they actually do is the result of out-and-out lying. Most of the difference, though, is the result of the fact that people can't hang on to the level of detail about their behavior that is called for when they are confronted by social scientists asking them how many times they did this or that in the last month. What people *think* about their behavior may be what you're interested in, but that's a different matter.

Most social research focuses on internal states and on reported behavior. But the study of humanity can be much richer, once you get the hang of putting together these five kinds of variables and conjuring up potential relations. Here are some examples of studies for each of the cells in table 3.1.

Cell I:

The interaction of internal states, like perceptions, attitudes, beliefs, values, and moods.

Religious beliefs, authoritarianism, and prejudice against homosexuals (Tsang and Rowatt 2007).

Perceived gender role and attitudes about rape in Turkey (Gölge et al. 2003).

American Indians' beliefs about ethnic identity and their perceptions about the beliefs their parents hold regarding education (Okaqaki et al. 2009).

This cell is also filled with studies that compare internal states across groups. For example, Cooke's (2004) study of attitudes toward gun control among American, British, and Australian youth and Yarrow et al.'s (2006) study comparing the early development of implicit racial prejudice in rural Japan and urban United States.

Cell II:

The interaction of internal states (perceptions, beliefs, moods, etc.) and external states (completed education, health status, organizational conditions).

Health status and hopefulness about the future (Vieth et al. 1997).

The relation between racial attitudes and the political context in different cities (Glaser and Gilens 1997).

Cell IIIa:

The interaction between *reported* behavior and internal states.

The relation, among adolescent girls in New Hampshire, between feeling that it's important to contribute to their community and self-reports of taking up smoking (Dinapoli 2009).

Attitudes toward the environment and reported environment-friendly behavior (Minton and Rose 1997).

Cell IIIb:

The interaction between *observed* behavior and internal states.

Attitudes and beliefs about resources and actual behavior in the control of a household thermostat (Kempton 1987).

Mexicans report being less talkative (feeling less sociable) than Americans but are behaviorally more social (more talkative) than Americans (Ramírez-Esparza et al. 2009).

Cell IV:

The interaction of material artifacts and internal states.

The effects on Holocaust Museum staff in Washington, DC, of working with the physical reminders of the Holocaust (McCarroll et al. 1995).

The ideas and values that brides and grooms in the United States share (or don't share) about the kinds of ritual artifacts that are supposed to be used in a wedding (Lowrey and Otnes 1994).

How children learn that domestic artifacts are considered feminine and artifacts associated with nondomestic production are considered masculine (Crabb and Bielawski 1994).

Cell V:

The interaction of social and physical environmental factors and internal states.

How culture influences the course of schizophrenia (Edgerton and Cohen 1994).

The extent to which adopted children and biological children raised in the same household develop similar personalities (Loehlin et al. 2009).

Cell VI:

How the interaction among external states relates to outcomes, like longevity or financial success.

The effects of age, sex, race, marital status, education, income, employment status, and health status on the risk of dying from the abuse of illegal drugs (Kallan 1998).

The impact of a person's race, age, and gender, along with community crime rate, unemployment rate, and voting patterns on the length of received prison sentences (Helms and Jacobs 2002).

The effect of skin color on acculturation among Mexican Americans (Montalvo and Codina 2001; Vasquez et al. 1997).

Cell VIIa:

The relation between external states and *reported* behavior.

The likelihood that baby-boomers will report attending church as they get older (Miller and Nakamura 1996).

The effect of age, income, and season on how much leisure time Tawahka Indian spouses spend with each other (Godoy 2002).

Gender differences in self-reported marijuana use (Warner et al. 1999) and suicidal behavior (Vannatta 1996) among adolescents.

Cell VIIb:

The relation between external states and *observed* behavior.

The relation between the importance of gender-specific subsistence activities and the amount of time in childhood allocated to playing (and and learning) those activities (Bock and Johnson 2004).

Observed recycling behavior among Mexican housewives is better predicted by their observed competencies than by their beliefs about recycling (Corral-Verdugo 1997).

Cell VIII:

The relation of physical artifacts and external states.

How age and gender differences relate to cherished possessions among children and adolescents from 6 to 18 years of age (Dyl and Wapner 1996).

How engineering drawings and machines delineate boundaries and facilitate interaction among engineers, technicians, and assemblers in a firm that manufactures computer chips (Bechky 2003).

Cell IX:

The relation of external states and environmental conditions.

How the work environment contributes to heart disease (Kasl 1996).

The different effects, for older men and women in the United States, of neighborhood characteristics on the likelihood of obesity (Grafova et al. 2008).

How proximity to a supermarket affects the nutrition of pregnant women (Laraia et al. 2004).

Cell Xa:

The relation between behaviors, as *reported* by people to researchers.

The relation of self-reported level of church attendance and self-reported level of environmental activism among African Americans in Louisiana (Arp and Boeckelman 1997).

The relation of reported changes in fertility practices to reported changes in actions to avoid HIV infection among women in rural Zimbabwe (Gregson et al. 1998).

Cell Xb:

The relation between reported and *observed* behavior.

Assessing the accuracy of reports by Tsimane Indians in Bolivia about the size of forest plots they've cleared in the past year by comparing those reports to a direct physical measure of the plots (Vadez et al. 2003).

The relation of reports about recycling behavior and actual recyling behavior (Corral-Verdugo 1997).

Cell Xc

The relation between observed behaviors

Slower eating reduces the amount of food that men actually eat, but not on how much women eat (C. Martin et al. 2007).

Cell XIa:

The relation of *observed* behavior to specific physical artifacts.

The number of incidents of smoking in movies was the same in 2002 as it was in 1950, even though the incidence of smoking had declined by half in that time (Glantz et al. 2004).

Cell XIb:

The relation of *reported* behavior to specific physical artifacts.

People who are employed view prized possessions as symbols of their own personal history, whereas people who are unemployed see prized possessions as having utilitarian value (Ditmar 1991).

Cell XIIa:

The relation of *reported* behavior to factors in the social or physical environment.

The relation of compulsive consumer behavior in young adults and whether they were raised in intact or disrupted families (Rindfleisch et al. 1997).

The relation of social support and independent daily functioning (bathing, eating, etc.) in elder Navajos (Fitzpatrick et al. 2008).

Cell XIIb:

The relation of *observed* behavior to factors in the social or physical environment.

People are willing to wait longer when music is playing than when there is silence (North and Hargreaves 1999).

How environmental features of gay bathhouses facilitate sexual activity (Tewksbury 2002).

Cell XIII:

The association of physical artifacts to one another and what this predicts about human thought or behavior.

The research on how to arrange products in stores to maximize sales is in this cell. Comparing the favorite possessions of urban Indians (in India) and Indian immigrants to the United States to see whether certain sets of possessions remain meaningful among immigrants (Mehta and Belk 1991). This is also an example of Cell IV. Note the difference between expressed *preferences* across artifacts and the coexistence of artifacts across places or times.

Cell XIV:

The probability that certain artifacts (relating, for example, to subsistence) will be found in certain physical or social environments (rain forests, deserts, shoreline communities). In anthropology, this area of research is mostly the province of archeology.

Cell XV:

How features of the social and physical environment interact and affect human behavioral and cognitive outcomes.

Social and physical environmental features of retail stores interact to affect the buying behavior of consumers (Baker et al. 1992).

Social and physical environmental features of communities interact to affect people's physical activity (Transportation Research Board and Institute of Medicine 2005).

The above list is only meant to give you an idea of how to think about potential covariations and, consequently, about potential research topics. Always keep in mind that *covariation does not mean cause.* Covariation can be the result of an antecedent or an intervening variable, or even just an accident. (Refer to chapter 2 for a discussion of causality, spurious relations, and antecedent variables.)

And keep in mind that many of the examples in the list above are statements about possible **bivariate correlations**—that is, about possible covariation between two things. Social phenomena being the complex sorts of things they are, a lot of research involves **multivariate relations**—that is, covariation among three or more things at the same time.

For example, it's well known that people who call themselves religious conservatives in the United States are likely to support the National Rifle Association's policy on gun control (Cell I). But the association between the two variables (religious beliefs and attitudes toward gun control) is by no means perfect and is affected by many intervening variables.

I'll tell you about testing for bivariate relations in chapter 21 and about testing for multivariate relations in chapter 22. As in so many other things, you crawl before you run and you run before you fly.

THE LITERATURE SEARCH

The first thing to do after you get an idea for a piece of research is to find out what has already been done on it. Don't neglect this part of the research process. You need to make a heroic effort to uncover sources. People will know it if you don't, and without that effort you risk wasting a lot of time going over already-covered ground. Even worse, you risk having your colleagues ignore your work because you didn't do your homework. Fortunately, heroic efforts are pretty easy, what with all the resources available for scouring the literature.

Begin by looking through volumes of the *Annual Review*. There are *Annual Review* volumes for psychology (every year since 1950), anthropology (every 2 years from 1959–1971 and every year since 1972), sociology (since 1975), public health (since 1997), and political science (since 1998). Authors who are invited to publish in these volumes are experts in their fields; they have digested a lot of information and have packaged it in a way that gets you right into the middle of a topic in a hurry.

Also contact people on listservs and networking groups that deal with your research topic. If there are central figures in the field, contact them by e-mail and request a time when you can call them on the phone. Yes, by phone. E-mail may be convenient for *you*, but most scholars are just too busy to respond to requests for lists of articles and books. On the other hand, many scholars *will* talk to you on the phone if they think they can really help.

All you need is a few key references to get started. Don't worry about the key references being out of date. The *ISI Web of Knowledge* eliminates the problem of obsolescence in bibliographies.

The *ISI Web of Knowledge*

The Thompson Reuters corporation produces the *ISI Web of Knowledge*, which contains the *Science Citation Index Expanded*, the *Social Sciences Citation Index*, and the *Arts and Humanities Citation Index*. These indexes are available online at most university libraries, and in many small college libraries. I used the paper versions of these indexes for 30 years before they went online. If the online versions vanished, I'd go back to the paper ones in a minute. They're that good.

At the *ISI Web of Knowledge* headquarters in Philadelphia, hundreds of people pore over thousands of journals each year—about 8,000 in the sciences, about 2,700 in the social sciences, and about 1,500 in the arts and humanities. (Some journals are indexed in more than one database, but that still means about 10,000 journals every year.) The staff at ISI enter the title, author, journal, year, page numbers for each article and, where available, the e-mail address of the corresponding author—that is, the author to whom you would write if you had a question about something in an article.

The most important part though is this: The staff enters all the references cited by each author of each article in each journal surveyed. Some articles have a handful of references, but review articles, like the ones in the *Annual Review* series, can have hundreds of citations. All those citations go into the *Web of Knowledge* databases. So, if you know the name of just one author whose work *should* be cited by anyone working in a particular field, you can find out, for any given year, who cited that author, and where. In other words, you can search the literature *forward* in time, and this means that older bibliographies, like those in the *Annual Review* series, are never out of date.

Suppose you are interested in the sociolinguistics of African American Vernacular English, also known as Black English. If you ask anyone who has worked on this topic (a sociolinguist in your department, for example) you'll run right into William Labov's *Lan-*

guage in the Inner City: Studies in the Black English Vernacular, published in 1972. Look up the subject heading of Black English in your library's catalog and you'll also find *Spoken Soul: The Story of Black English*, by John and Russell Rickford (2000) and *Black Street Speech* by John Baugh (1983). You'll find Labov's book mentioned prominently in both of the latter books, so right away, you know that Labov's book is a pioneering work and is going to be mentioned by scholars who come later to the topic.

If you are starting a search today of the literature about Black English, you'd want to know who has cited Labov's work, as well as the works of Baugh and the Rickfords. That's where the *Web of Knowledge* comes in. The *Social Science Citation Index* alone indexes about 150,000 articles a year. Okay, so 150,000 *sources* is only a good-sized fraction of the social science papers published in the world each year, but the *authors* of those articles read—and cited—about 3 *million* citations to references to the literature (Web of Science Databases. http://tinyurl.com/nltbhy). That's 3 million citations every year, for decades and decades. Now *that's* a database.

That classic book by Labov on Black English? As of January 2009, some 1,500 researcher articles had cited the book across the sciences and the humanities. Of those, the *Web of Knowledge* shows you the full citation for about 1,100 (that is, articles that are in its own database). You can take any of *those* citations and clip it into another search window and keep the search going. And going and going.

Don't get overwhelmed by this. You'll be surprised at how quickly you can scan through a thousand hits and pick out things you really need to take a closer look at. As you read some articles and books, you'll find yourself running into the same key literature again and again. That's when you know you're getting to the edges of the world on a particular topic. That's what you want when you're doing research—you want to be working at the edges so as to push the frontiers of knowledge back a bit (box 3.4).

BOX 3.4

GETTING ARTICLE TITLES RIGHT

A word of caution to new scholars who are writing for publication: Online literature searches make it easy for people to find articles only if the articles (or their abstracts) contain descriptive words. Cute titles on scientific articles hide them from people who want to find them in the indexing tools. If you write an article about illegal Mexican labor migration to the United States and call it something like "Whither Juan? Mexicans on the Road," it's a sure bet to get lost immediately, unless (1) you happen to publish it in one of the most widely read journals and (2) it happens to be a blockbuster piece of work that everyone talks about and is cited in articles that *do* have descriptive titles.

Because most scientific writing is not of the blockbuster variety, you're better off putting words into the titles of your articles that describe what the articles are about. It may seem awfully dull, but descriptive, unimaginative titles are terrific for helping your colleagues find and cite your work.

I use the *Web of Knowledge* regularly to keep current with the literature on several topics. I've studied bilingualism in Mexico, for example, particularly the development of bilingual education among the Ñähñu of the Mezquital Valley. The Ñähñu are widely known in the literature as the Otomí, so I scan the *Web of Knowledge* and look for every-thing with the word "Otomí" in the title or abstract. Doing this even once a year makes a big difference in your ability to keep up with the expanding literature in every field.

ANTHROPOLOGY DATABASES

Besides the *Web of Knowledge,* important resources for anthropologists include *Anthro-Source, JSTOR,* and *Anthropology Plus.*

AnthroSource and JSTOR

AnthroSource is a service of the American Anthropological Association and is available to all members of the association. The database covers 32 journals in anthropology. *JSTOR* is a full-text database that covers over 1,000 journals in humanities, social sciences, and sciences. Journals available through *JSTOR,* including many covered by *AnthroSource,* have a 3 to 5 year lag. Members of the AAA, however, can access all years of the journals covered by *AnthroSource.*

Anthropology Plus

Anthropology Plus combines two databases, *Anthropological Index* Online (which is free) and *Anthropological Literature* (by subscription). AIO is published by the Royal Anthropological Institute in London and indexes the periodicals in Museum of Mankind library of the British Museum. Besides the major journals for cultural anthropology and archeology, AIO covers small journals from developing nations and Eastern Europe. You'll find articles in AIO from journals like the *Annals of the Náprstek Museum* in Prague, the *Quarterly Journal of the Mythic Society,* in Bangalore, and the *Hong Kong Anthropology Bulletin. Anthropological Literature* is the index for the books and articles at the Tozzer Library at Harvard University. The Tozzer is the largest collection of anthropological literature in the world, and *Anthropological Literature* grows by about 10,000 citations every year. It is particularly good for finding older materials on North American, Middle American, and South American archeology and ethnology.

If your library doesn't subscribe to *Anthropology Plus,* you can use *Anthropological Index Online* free, here: http://aio.anthropology.org.uk/aio.

FREE DATABASES OF RELEVANCE TO ANTHROPOLOGY

ERIC

The Educational Resources Information Center, or ERIC, indexes nearly 1,000 journals of interest to researchers in education. ERIC is free at http://www.eric.ed.gov. With over a million citations, it's a treasure, but the unique advantage of ERIC is the access it gives you to the gray literature—over 200,000, full-text research reports on research funded by government agencies and by private foundations. (The database is updated weekly and grows by about 34,000 documents every year.)

For example, I follow the efforts of indigenous peoples around the world to keep their languages alive. I found a report in ERIC by Marion Blue Arm, published in a conference proceeding, on attitudes by Indians, Whites, and mixed families toward the teaching of Lakota in the schools on the Cheyenne River Sioux Reservation in South Dakota. ERIC is filled with useful material like that.

NTIS

NTIS, the National Technical Information Service, indexes and abstracts federally funded research reports in all areas of science. Many technical reports eventually get published as articles, which means you can find them through all the other databases. But many research reports just get filed and shelved—and lost. A major reason that technical reports don't get published is that they contain data—huge tables of the stuff—which journals don't have room for.

The NTIS has technical reports from archeological digs, from focus groups on attitudes about unprotected sex, from development projects on giant clam mariculture in the Solomon Islands, from natural experiments to test how long people can stay in a submerged submarine without going crazy—if the federal government has funded it under contract, there's probably a technical report of it. The NTIS is available free at http://www.gov.

MEDLINE

MEDLINE is a product of the National Library of Medicine and the National Institutes of Health. It covers over 5,200 journals in the life sciences—including the medical social sciences—going back to 1949. MEDLINE is free through PUBMED at http://www.ncbi .nlm.nih.gov/pubmed. If you are working on anything that has to do with health care, MEDLINE, with its 16 million citations (and growing at around 700,000 citations a year) is a must.

OTHER DATABASES

There are dozens of subscription databases that are useful for work in anthropology. Here are just a few, to give you an idea of what's out there.

PsycINFO, from the American Psychological Association, is a Jurassic database, covering some 2,500 journals in the behavioral and social sciences back to the 1800s. Cambridge Scientific Abstracts (CSA) is portal to databases in science, social science, and the humanities. CSA's *Sociological Abstracts* covers about 1,800 journals, with nearly a million records going back to 1952. PsycINFO and *Sociological Abstracts* have excellent coverage of research methods, the sociology of language, occupations and professions, health, family violence, poverty, and social control. They cover the sociology of knowledge and the sociology of science, as well as the sociology of the arts, religion, and education. CSA's *Linguistics and Language Behavior Abstracts* covers 1,500 journals, back to 1973.

Lexis/Nexis (http://www.lexisnexis.com) provides access to about five billion documents including hundreds of newspapers and the documents from the Congressional Information Service (CIS). The CIS indexes U.S. House and Senate hearings, reports entered into public access by submission to Congress, and testimony before congressional committees. You can get access to public documents published by the U.S. Congress at http://thomas.loc.gov (the "thomas" refers to Thomas Jefferson), but if you have access to Lexis-Nexis, it's easier to use that service to find things in the CIS. There are congressional reports on many topics of interest to anthropologists, including reports on current social issues (housing, nutrition, cultural conservation, rural transportation). The proceedings for recognizing American Indian tribes are published in the Congressional Record and are available through CIS, as are reports on the demographics of American ethnic groups.

WorldCat is a product of OCLC (http://www.oclc.org), the Online Computer Library Center. *WorldCat* contains the catalogs of 71,000 libraries in over a hundred countries. If you find a book or article in the *Web of Science* or PsycINFO, etc., and your library doesn't have it, then *WorldCat* will tell you which library *does* have it. Interlibrary loans depend on this database.

WEBSITES

In addition to library databases, many super information resources of interest to anthropologists are available through the Internet pages of international organizations. A good place to start is the University of Michigan Document Center's page, "International Organizations and Related Information" at http://www.lib.umich.edu/govdocs/intl.html. This page will point you to the portals for thousands of intergovernmental and nongovernmental organizations, like the Union of International Associations' guide to IGOs and NGOs at http://www.uia.org/website.htm. The Michigan site will also point you directly to international agency sites, like the Food and Agriculture Organization of the UN, with many full-text reports on its projects since 1986. Interested in "shrimp aquaculture"? Go to FAO's archiving site at http://www.fao.org/documents and type that phrase into the search engine to find reports on local farming practices. Go to the site of the United Nations High Commission on Refugees (UNHCR) at http://www.unhcr.ch for the latest statistics on the refugees around the world. Go to the site of the Pan American Health Organization (PAHO) at http://www.paho.org for the latest statistics on health indicators for countries in North and South America.

There is a world of high-quality documents available on the Internet. The Anthropology Review Database at http://wings.buffalo.edu/ARD provides an expanding list of reviews of books, articles, and software of interest to anthropologists. The Scout Report, at http://scout.cs.wisc.edu, is an expanding database of Internet sites. Search the site for "anthropology" and you'll find lots of useful, full-text resources, like the one at http://www.nativetech.org, devoted to Native American technology and art.

To find general information about particular countries of the world, start with the Yahoo server http://dir.yahoo.com/Regional/Countries and also consult the CIA Factbook at https://www.cia.gov/library/publications/the-world-factbook. Going to the Manu'a Islands to do fieldwork? Detailed maps for just about every country and region of the world (including the Manu'a Islands) are available online at http://www.lib.utexas.edu/maps/index.html. For websites developed and maintained by particular countries, start with http://www.library.northwestern.edu/govinfo/resource/internat/foreign.html. All government statistical reports are subject to error. Use with caution (box 3.5).

The logic of Boolean operators is used in database management—about which, more at the end of chapter 13 on field notes.

META-ANALYSIS

Meta-analysis involves piling up all the quantitative studies ever done on a particular topic to assess quantitatively what is known about the size of the effect. The pioneering work on meta-analysis (M. L. Smith and Glass 1977) addressed the question: Does psychotherapy make a difference? That is, do people who get psychotherapy benefit, compared to people who have the same problems and who don't get psychotherapy? Since then, there have been thousands of meta-analyses, but most of them are in fields like psychology and medicine, where data from experiments lend themselves to direct comparison.

A few anthropologists, though, have done important meta-analyses. Until the 1970s, conventional wisdom had it that hunters and gatherers lived a precarious existence, searching all the time for food, never knowing where their next meal was coming from.

BOX 3.5

TIPS FOR SEARCHING ONLINE DATABASES

1. Get the spelling right. Some databases have intelligent spell checkers (if you ask for information on "New Guinae," they'll ask if you really meant "New Guinea"), but many don't. If you ask for references on "apropriate technology" and the database comes back, incongruously, with "nothing found," check the spelling with your word processor's spell check or with an online dictionary.

2. If there are two or more ways to spell a word, then search with all spellings. Use both Koran and Qur'an (and several other spelling variants) in your searches; behavior and behaviour; Chanukah and Hanukah (and several other spelling variants); Rom and Roma (both are used to refer to Gypsies); Thessaloniki and Salonika; Mumbai and Bombay; Beijing and Peking; and so on.

3. Use wildcards liberally. Search for "behav* measur*" rather than "behavior measurement." That way, you'll capture "behaviour measurement," "behavioral measurement," "behavioral measures," and so on. I asked *MEDLINE* for articles from 1990 until June 2009 on (child* diarrhea) OR (infant* diarrhea) and got 11,541 hits. I used the wildcard asterisk to indicate that I wanted any records with the words "children's" or "childhood" and any records with the words "infant's" or "infantile." Then I remembered that the British spelling of "diarrhea" is "diarrhoea" so I changed the parameters to (child* diarrh*) OR (infant* diarrh*) and got another 4,061 hits.

4. Become really facile with the Boolean operators (AND, OR, NOT) to narrow your searches. Changing the MEDLINE search to [(child* diarrh*) OR (infant* diarrh*) AND (cultural factors)] reduced the number of hits from over 15,000 to 5. I asked *MEDLINE* for all articles from 1977 to 2009 on (regimen compliance AND malaria). That search brought back abstracts for 81 articles. When I restricted the search to [(regimen compliance AND malaria) NOT Africa], I got back 57 abstracts. The parentheses and brackets in Boolean searches work just like equations in algebra. So, that last search I did fetched all the items that had "regimen compliance" and "malaria" in their titles or abstract. Then, the items were sorted and any of those items that contained the word "Africa" was dropped.

In 1970, Esther Boserup made the important observation that plow agriculture takes more time than does hoe agriculture. And in 1972, Marshall Sahlins generalized this observation, arguing that hunter-gatherer societies had more leisure than anyone else and that people have to work more and more as societies become more complex.

In 1996, Ross Sackett did a meta-analysis of 102 cases of time allocation studies and 207 energy-expenditure studies to test Sahlins's (1972) primitive-affluence hypothesis. Sackett found that, indeed, adults in foraging and horticultural societies work, on average, about 6.5 hours a day, while people in agricultural and industrial societies work about 8.8 hours a day. The difference, by the way, is statistically very significant (Sackett 1996:231, 547).

Meta-analysis can be delightfully subversive. Morrison and Morrison (1995), for example, found that only 6.3% of the variance in graduate-level GPA is predicted by performance on the GRE quantitative and verbal exams. And White (1980) found that across a hundred studies up to 1979, socioeconomic status explained, on average, an identical 6.3% of the variance in school achievement. The raw correlation across those hundred studies, ranged from −.14 (yes, *minus* .14) to .97.

Meta-analyses are becoming more and more common as electronic databases, including databases of ethnography, develop. Meta-analysis gives us the tools to see if we are making progress on important question. It is, as Hunt (1997) says, the way science takes stock.

FURTHER READING

Anthropology in the military and in intelligence: For contrasting takes on the activities of anthropologists in Thailand during the Vietnam War, see Wolf and Jorgensen (1970) and Hinton (2002). For an exhaustive historical account of the issue, see Wakin (1992). For opposing views of anthropologists' involvement in the wars in Iraq and Afgahanistan, see Price (2003) and McFate (2005); see also González (2007) and Kilcullen (2007). For a summary of this debate, see Fluehr-Lobban (2008).

Ethical issues in anthropology: Anspach and Mizrachi (2006); Borofsky (2005); Cantwell et al. (2000); Caplan (2003); Carrithers (2005); Cassell and Jacobs (1987); Cushman (2004); Edel and Edel (1968); Einarsdóttir (2006); Feinberg (2007); Fluehr-Lobban (2002); D. Gordon (1991); E. Harrison (2006); F. V. Harrison (1997); Kemper (1997); MacClancy (2002); Montgomery (2007); Pels (2008); Posey (2004); Rynkiewick and Spradley (1976); Silverman (2004).

4

Research Design: Experiments and Experimental Thinking

Early in the 20th century, F. C. Bartlett, the pioneering psychologist who developed schema theory, went to Cambridge University to study with W.H.R. Rivers—an experimental psychologist who became one of the pioneers of modern anthropology. In 1899, Rivers had been invited to join the Torres Straits Expedition and saw the opportunity to do comparative psychology studies of non-Western people (Tooker 1997:xiv). When Bartlett got to Cambridge, he asked Rivers for some advice. Bartlett expected a quick lecture on how to go out and stay out, about the rigors of fieldwork, and so on. Instead, Rivers told him: "The best training you can possibly have is a thorough drilling in the experimental methods of the psychological laboratory" (Bartlett 1937:416).

Bartlett found himself spending hours in the lab, "lifting weights, judging the brightness of lights, learning nonsense syllables, and engaging in a number of similarly abstract occupations" that seemed to be "particularly distant from the lives of normal human beings." In the end, though, Bartlett concluded that Rivers was right. Training in the **experimental method**, said Bartlett, gives one "a sense of evidence, a realization of the difficulties of human observation, and a kind of scientific conscience which no other field of study can impart so well" (Bartlett 1937:417).

I agree. Most anthropologists don't do experiments, but a solid grounding in the **logic of experiments** is one of the keys to good research skills, no matter what kind of research you're doing. At the end of this chapter, you should understand the variety of **research designs**. You should also understand the concept of **threats to validity** and how we can respond to those threats.

EXPERIMENTS

Experiments can be done in the laboratory or in the field, but the logic is the same, no matter where they are done. There are, of course, differences in experiments with people versus experiments with rocks or pigeons or plants. But these differences involve ethical issues—like deception, informed consent, and withholding of treatment—not logic. More on these ethical issues later.

The Logic of True Experiments

There are five steps in a **classic experiment**:

1. Formulate a hypothesis.
2. Randomly assign participants to the intervention group or to the control group.

3. Measure the dependent variable(s) in one or both groups. This is called O_1 or "observation at time 1."
4. Introduce the treatment or intervention.
5. Measure the dependent variable(s) again. This is called O_2 or "observation at time 2."

Later, I'll walk you through some variations on this five-step formula, including one very important variation that does not involve Step 3 at all. But first, the basics.

Step 1. Before you can do an experiment, you need a clear hypothesis about the relation between some independent variable (or variables) and some dependent variable (or variables). Experiments thus tend to be based on **confirmatory** rather than **exploratory research** questions (see box 1.1).

The testing of new drugs can be a simple case of one independent and one dependent variable. The independent variable might be, say, "taking vs. not taking" a drug. The dependent variable might be "getting better vs. not getting better." The independent and dependent variables can be much more subtle. "Taking vs. not taking" a drug might be "taking more of, or less of" a drug, and "getting better vs. not getting better" might be "the level of improvement in high-density lipoprotein" (the so-called good cholesterol).

Move this logic to agriculture: *ceteris paribus* (holding everything else—like amount of sunlight, amount of water, amount of weeding—constant), some corn plants get a new fertilizer and some don't. Then, the dependent variable might be the number of ears per corn stalk or the number of days it takes for the cobs to mature, or the number of kernels per cob.

Now move this same logic to human thought and human behavior: *Ceteris paribus*, people in Nairobi who take this course in AIDS awareness will report fewer high-risk sex practices than will people who don't take this course. *Ceteris paribus* here means that people in both groups—the treatment group and the control group—start with the same amount of reported high-risk sexual activity.

Things get more complicated when there are multiple independent (or dependent) variables. You might want to test two different courses, with different content, on people who come from three different tribal backgrounds. But the underlying logic for setting up experiments and for analyzing the results is the same across the sciences. When it comes to experiments, everything starts with a clear hypothesis.

Step 2. You need at least two groups, called the **treatment group** (or the **intervention group** or the **stimulus group**) and the **control group**. One group gets the intervention (the new drug, the new teaching program) and the other group doesn't. The treatment group (or groups) and the control group(s) are involved in different **experimental conditions**.

In true experiments, people are **randomly assigned** to either the intervention group or to the control group. This ensures that any differences between the groups are the consequence of chance and not of **systematic bias**. Some people in a population may be more religious, or more wealthy, or less sickly, or more prejudiced than others, but random assignment ensures that those traits are randomly distributed through all the groups in an experiment.

Random assignment doesn't eliminate selection bias. It makes differences between experimental conditions (groups) due solely to chance by taking the decision of who goes in what group out of your hands. The principle behind random assignment will become clearer after you work through chapter 6 on probability sampling, but the bottom line is this: Whenever you *can* assign participants randomly in an experiment, do it.

Step 3. One or both groups are measured on one or more dependent variables. This is called the **pretest**.

Dependent variables in people can be physical things like weight, height, systolic blood pressure, or resistance to malaria. They can also be attitudes, moods, knowledge, or mental and physical achievements. For example, in weight-loss programs, you might measure the ratio of body fat to body mass as the dependent variable. If you are trying to raise women's understanding of the benefits of breast-feeding by exposing them to a multimedia presentation on this topic, then a preliminary test of women's attitudes about breast-feeding before they see the presentation is an appropriate pretest for your experiment.

You don't always need a pretest. More on this in a bit, when we discuss threats to validity in experiments.

Step 4. The intervention (the independent variable) is introduced.

Step 5. The dependent variables are measured again. This is the **posttest**.

A Walkthrough

Here's a made-up example of a true experiment: Take 100 college women (18–22 years of age) and randomly assign 50 of them to each of two groups. Bring each woman to the lab and show her a series of flash cards. Let each card contain a single, three-digit random number. Measure how many three-digit numbers each woman can remember. Repeat the task, but let the members of one group hear the most popular rock song of the week playing in the background as they take the test. Let the other group hear nothing. Measure how many three-digit numbers people can remember and whether rock music improves or worsens performance on the task.

Do you think this is a frivolous experiment? Many college students study while listening to rock music, which drives their parents crazy. I'll bet that more than one reader of this book has been asked something like: "How can you learn anything with all that noise?" The experiment I've outlined here is designed to test whether students can, in fact, "learn anything with all that noise."

Now, this experiment is very limited. Only women are involved. There are no graduate students or high school students. There's no test of whether classic rock helps or hinders learning more than, say, hip-hop, or country music, or Beethoven. And the learning task is artificial. What we know at the end of this experiment is whether college-age women at one school learn to memorize more or fewer three-digit numbers when the learning is accompanied by a single rock tune.

But a lot of what's really powerful about the experimental method is embodied in this example. Suppose that the rock-music group does better on the task. We can be pretty sure this outcome is not because of the participants' sex, age, or education, but because of the music. Just sticking in more independent variables (like expanding the group to include men, graduate students, or high school students; or playing different tunes; or making the learning task more realistic), without modifying the experiment's design to control for all those variables, creates what are called **confounds**. They *confound* the experiment and make it impossible to tell if the intervention is what really caused any observed differences in the dependent variable.

Good experiments test narrowly defined questions. This is what gives them knowledge-making power. When you do a good experiment, you *know* something at the end of it. In this case, you know that women students at one school memorize or do not memorize three-digit numbers better when they listen to a particular rock tune.

This may not seem like much, but you really know it. You can repeat the experiment at the same school to verify or refute this little bit of knowledge. You can repeat the experiment at another school to see if the knowledge holds up.

Suppose you don't get the same answer at another school, holding all the other elements of the experiment—age, sex, type of music—constant. The new finding demands an explanation. Perhaps there is something about the student selection process at the two schools that produces the different results? Perhaps students at one school come primarily from working-class families and students from the other school come from upper-middle-class families. Perhaps students from different socioeconomic classes grow up with different study habits or prefer different kinds of music.

Conduct the experiment again but include men this time. Conduct it again and include two music conditions: a rock tune and a classical piece. Take the experiment on the road and run it all over again at different-sized schools in different regions of the country. Then, on to Paraguay . . . (box 4.1).

BOX 4.1

EXPERIMENTS AND VALIDITY

True experiments, with randomized assignment and full control by the researcher, produce knowledge that has high **internal validity**. This means that changes in the dependent variables were probably *caused by*—not merely related to or correlated with—the treatment. Continual replication produces **cumulative knowledge** with high **external validity**—that is, knowledge that you can generalize to people who were not part of your experiment.

Replication of knowledge is every bit as important as its production in the first place. In fact, in terms of usefulness, replicated knowledge is exactly what we're after.

KINDS OF CONFOUNDS: THREATS TO VALIDITY

It's pointless to ask questions about external validity until you establish internal validity. In a series of influential publications, Donald Campbell and his colleagues identified the threats to internal validity of experiments (see Campbell 1957, 1979; Campbell and Stanley 1966; Cook and Campbell 1979). Here are seven of the most important confounds:

1. History

The **history confound** refers to any independent variable, other than the treatment, that (1) occurs between the pretest and the posttest in an experiment and (2) affects the experimental groups differently. Suppose you are doing a laboratory experiment with two groups (experimental and control) and there is a power failure in the building. So long as the lights go out for both groups, there is no problem. But if the lights go out for one group and not the other, it's difficult to tell whether it was the treatment or the power failure that causes changes in the dependent variable.

In a laboratory experiment, history is controlled by isolating participants as much as possible from outside influences. When we do experiments outside the laboratory, it is almost impossible to keep new independent variables from creeping in and confounding things.

Here's an example of an experiment outside the lab. Suppose you run an experiment to test whether monetary incentives help third graders do better in arithmetic. Kids in the treatment classes get a penny for each right answer on their tests; kids in the control classes get nothing. Now, right in the middle of the school term, while you're running this experiment, the Governor's Task Force on Education issues its long-awaited report, with a recommendation that arithmetic skills be emphasized during the early school years. Furthermore, it says, teachers whose classes make exceptional progress in this area should be rewarded with 10% salary bonuses.

The governor accepts the recommendation and announces a request for a special legislative appropriation. Elementary teachers all over the state start paying extra attention to arithmetic skills. Even supposing that the students in the treatment classes do better than those in the control classes in your experiment, we can't tell if the magnitude of the difference would not have been greater had this historical confound not occurred. That's just the breaks of experimenting in real life without being able to control everything.

2. Maturation

The **maturation confound** refers to the fact that people in any experiment grow older or get more experienced while you are trying to conduct an experiment. Consider the following experiment: Start with a group of teenagers on a Native American reservation and follow them for the next 60 years. Some of them will move to cities; some will go to small towns; and some will stay on the reservation. Periodically, test them on a variety of dependent variables (their political opinions, their wealth, their health, their family size, and so on). See how the experimental treatments (city vs. reservation vs. town living) affect these variables.

Here is where the maturation confound enters the picture. The people you are studying get older. Older people in many societies become more politically conservative. They are usually wealthier than younger people. Eventually, they come to be more illness prone than younger people. Some of the changes you measure in your dependent variables will be the result of the various treatments—and some of them may just be the result of maturation.

Maturation is not just about people getting older. Social service delivery programs "mature" by working out bugs in their administration. People "mature" through practice with experimental conditions and they become fatigued. We see this all the time in new social programs where people start out being really enthusiastic about innovations in organizations and eventually get bored or disenchanted.

3. Testing and Instrumentation

The **testing confound** happens when people change their responses in reaction to being constantly examined. Asking people the same questions again and again in a longitudinal study, or even in an ethnographic study done over 6 months or more, can have this effect.

The **instrumentation confound** results from changing measurement instruments. Changing the wording of questions in a survey is essentially changing instruments. Which responses do you trust: the ones to the earlier wording or the ones to the later wording? If you do a set of observations in the field and later send in someone else to continue the observations you have changed instruments. Which observations do you trust as closer to the truth: yours or those of the substitute instrument (the new field researcher)?

In multi-researcher projects, this problem is usually dealt with by training all investigators to see and record things in more or less the same way. This is called increasing **interrater reliability**. (More on this in chapter 19 in the section on **Cohen's kappa**.)

4. Regression to the Mean

Regression to the mean is a confound that can occur when you study groups that have extreme scores on a dependent variable. No matter what the intervention is, the extreme scores are likely to become more moderate just because there's nowhere else for them to go.

If men who are taller than 6'7" marry women who are taller than 6'3", then their children are likely to be (1) taller than average and (2) closer to average height than either of their parents are. There are two independent variables (the height of each of the parents) and one dependent variable (the height of the children). We expect the dependent variable to "regress toward the mean," since it really can't get more extreme than the height of the parents.

I put that phrase "regress toward the mean" in quotes because it's easy to misinterpret this phenomenon—to think that the "regressing" toward the mean of an dependent variable is caused by the extreme scores on the independent variables. It isn't, and here's how you can tell that it isn't: Very, very tall children are likely to have parents whose height is more like the mean. One thing we know for sure is that the height of children doesn't cause the height of their parents. Regression to the mean is a statistical phenomenon—it happens in the aggregate and is not something that happens to individuals (box 4.2).

BOX 4.2

THE PROBLEM OF EXTREME VALUES

Many social intervention programs make the mistake of using people with extreme values on dependent variables as subjects. Run some irrigation canals through the most destitute villages in a region of a Third World country and watch the average income of villagers rise. But understand that income might have risen anyway, if you'd done nothing, because it couldn't have gone down. Test a reading program on the kids in a school district who score in the bottom 10% of all kids on reading skills and watch their test scores rise. But understand that their scores might have risen anyway.

---

5. Selection of Participants

Selection bias in choosing participants is a major confound to validity. In true experiments, you assign participants at random, from a single population, to treatment groups and control groups. This distributes any differences among individuals in the population throughout the groups, making the groups equivalent.

This reduces the possibility that differences among the groups will cause differences in outcomes on the dependent variables. Random assignment in true experiments, in other words, maximizes the chance for valid outcomes—outcomes that are not clobbered by hidden factors.

In natural experiments, however, we have *no control* over assignment of individuals to groups.

Question: Do victims of violent crime have less stable marriages than people who have not been victims? Obviously, researchers cannot randomly assign participants to the treatment (violent crime). It could turn out that people who are victims of this treatment are more likely to have unstable marriages anyway.

Question: Do migrants to cities from villages in developing nations engage in more entrepreneurial activities than stay-at-homes? If we could assign rural people randomly to the treatment group (those engaging in urban migration), we'd have a better chance of finding out. But we can't, so selection is a threat to the internal validity of the experiment. Suppose that the answer to question at the top of this paragraph was "yes." We still don't know the direction of the causal arrow: Does the treatment (migration) cause the outcome (greater entrepreneurial activity)? Or does having an entrepreneurial personality cause migration?

6. Mortality

The **mortality confound** refers to the fact that people may not complete their participation in an experiment. Suppose we follow two sets of Mexican villagers—some who receive irrigation and some who do not—for 5 years. During the 1st year of the experiment, we have 200 villagers in each group. By the 5th year, 170 remain in the treatment group, and only 120 remain in the control group. One conclusion is that lack of irrigation caused those in the control group to leave their village at a faster rate than those in the treatment group.

But what about those 30 people in the treatment group who left? It could be that they moved to another community where they acquired even more irrigated land, or they may have abandoned farming altogether to become labor migrants. These two outcomes would affect the results of the experiment quite differently. Mortality can be a serious problem in natural experiments if it gets to be a large fraction of the group(s) under study.

Mortality also affects panel surveys. That's where you interview the same people more than once to track something about their lives. (More about panel studies in chapter 9.)

7. Diffusion of Treatments

The **diffusion of treatments** threat to validity occurs when a control group cannot be prevented from receiving the treatment in an experiment. This is particularly likely in quasi-experiments where the independent variable is an information program.

In a project with which I was associated, a group of African Americans were given instruction on modifying their diet and exercise behavior to lower their blood pressure. Another group was randomly assigned from the population to act as controls—that is, they would not receive instruction. The evaluation team measured blood pressure in the treatment group and in the control group before the program was implemented. But when they went back after the program was completed, they found that control group members had also been changing their behavior. They had learned of the new diet and exercises from the members of the treatment group.

CONTROLLING FOR THREATS TO VALIDITY

In what follows, I want to show you how the power of experimental logic is applied to real research problems. The major experimental designs are shown in figure 4.1. The notation is pretty standard. The letter **X** stands for some intervention—a stimulus or a

	Time 1		Time 2	
	Assignment	Pretest	Intervention	Posttest
Group 1	R	O_1	X	O_2
Group 2	R	O_3		O_4
a.	The Classic Design: Two-Group Pretest-Posttest			
Group 1	R	O_1	X	O_2
Group 2	R	O_3		O_4
Group 3	R		X	O_5
Group 4	R			O_6
b.	The Solomon Four-Group Design			
Group 1		O_1	X	O_2
Group 2		O_3		O_4
c.	The Classic Design Without Randomization			
Group 1	R		X	O_1
Group 2	R			O_2
d.	The Campbell and Stanley Posttest-Only Design			
			X	O
e.	The One-Shot Case Study Design			
		O_1	X	O_2
f.	The One-Group Pretest-Posttest Design			
			X	O_1
				O_2
g.	Two-Group Posttest Only: Static Group Comparison Design			
		O O O	X	O O O
h.	The Interrupted Time Series Design			

FIGURE 4.1.
Some research designs.

treatment. **R** means that participants are randomly assigned to experimental conditions—either to the intervention group that gets the treatment, or to the control group that doesn't. Several designs include random assignment and several don't. **O** stands for "observation." O_1 means that some observation is made at Time 1, O_2 means that some observation is made at Time 2, and so on.

"Observation" means "measurement of some dependent variable," but as you already know, the idea of measurement is pretty broad. It can be taking someone's temperature or testing their reading skill. It can also be just writing down whether they were successful at hunting game that day.

The Classic Two-Group Pretest-Posttest Design with Random Assignment

Figure 4.1a shows the classic experimental design: the **two-group pretest-posttest** with random assignment. From a population of potential participants, some participants have

	Time 1		Time 2	
	Assignment	Pretest	Intervention	Posttest
Group 1	R	O_1	X	O_2
Group 2	R	O_3		O_4

FIGURE 4.1a.
The classic design: Two-group pretest-posttest.

been assigned randomly to a treatment group and a control group. Read across the top row of the figure. An observation (measurement) of some dependent variable or variables is made at time 1 on the members of group 1. That is O_1. Then an intervention is made (the group is exposed to some treatment, X). Then, another observation is made at time 2. That is O_2.

Now look at the second row of figure 4.1a. A second group of people are observed, also at time 1. Measurements are made of the same dependent variable(s) that were made for the first group. The observation is labeled O_3. There is no X on this row, which means that no intervention is made on this group of people. They remain unexposed to the treatment or intervention in the experiment. Later, at time 2, after the first group has been exposed to the intervention, the second group is observed again. That's O_4.

Random assignment of participants ensures equivalent groups, and the second group, without the intervention, ensures that several threats to internal validity are taken care of. Most importantly, you can tell how often (how many times out of a hundred, for example) any differences between the pretest and posttest scores for the first group might have occurred anyway, even if the intervention hadn't taken place.

Patricia Chapman (Chapman et al. 1997) wanted to educate young female athletes about sports nutrition. She and her colleagues worked with an eight-team girl's high school softball league in California. There were nine 14–18 years olds on each team, and Chapman et al. assigned each of the 72 players randomly to one of two groups. In the treatment group, the girls got two, 45-minute lectures a week for 6 weeks about dehydration, weight loss, vitamin and mineral supplements, energy sources, and so on. The control group got no instruction.

Before the program started, Chapman et al. asked each participant to complete the Nutrition Knowledge and Attitude Questionnaire (Werblow et al. 1978) and to list the foods they'd eaten in the previous 24 hours. The nutrition knowledge-attitude test and the 24-hour dietary recall test were the **pretests** in this experiment. Six weeks later, when the program was over, Chapman et al. gave the participants the same two tests. These were the **posttests**. By comparing the data from the pretests and the posttests, Chapman et al. hoped to test whether the nutrition education program had made a difference.

The education intervention did make a difference—in knowledge, but not in reported behavior. Both groups scored about the same in the pretest on knowledge and attitudes about nutrition, but the girls who went through the lecture series scored about 18 points more (out of 200 possible points) in the posttest than did those in the control group.

However, the program had no effect on what the girls reported eating. After 6 weeks of lectures, the girls in the treatment group reported consuming 1,892 calories in the previous 24 hours, while the girls in the control group reported 1,793 calories. A statistical dead heat. This is not nearly enough for young female athletes, and the results confirmed for Chapman what other studies had already shown—that for many adolescent females, the attraction of competitive sports is the possibility of losing weight.

This classic experimental design is used widely to evaluate educational programs. Kunovich and Rashid (1992) used this design to test their program for training freshman dental students in how to handle a mirror in a patient's mouth (think about it; it's not easy—everything you see is backward) (**Further Reading:** the classic experimental design and evaluation research).

The Solomon Four-Group Design

The classic design has one important flaw—it's subject to testing bias. Differences between variable measurements at time 1 and time 2 might be the result of the intervention, but they also might be the result of people getting savvy about being watched and measured. Pretesting can, after all, sensitize people to the purpose of an experiment, and this, in turn, can change people's behavior. The **Solomon four-group design**, shown in figure 4.1b, controls for this. Since there are no measurements at time 1 for groups 3 and 4, this problem is controlled for.

	Time 1		Time 2	
	Assignment	Pretest	Intervention	Posttest
Group 1	R	O_1	X	O_2
Group 2	R	O_3		O_4
Group 3	R		X	O_5
Group 4	R			O_6

FIGURE 4.1b.
The Solomon four-group design.

Larry Leith (1988) used the Solomon four-group design to study a phenomenon known to all sports fans as the "choke." That's when an athlete plays well during practice and then loses it during the real game, or plays well all game long and folds in the clutch when it really counts. It's not pretty.

Leith assigned 20 male students randomly to each of the four conditions in the Solomon 4-group design. The pretest and the posttest were the same: Each participant shot 25 free throws on a basketball court. The dependent variable was the number of successful free throws out of 25 shots in the posttest. The independent variable—the treatment—was giving or not giving the following little pep talk to each participant just before he made those 25 free throws for the posttest:

Research has shown that some people have a tendency to choke at the free-throw line when shooting free throws. No one knows why some people tend to choking behavior. However, don't let that bother you. Go ahead and shoot your free throws. (Leith 1988:61)

What a wonderfully simple, utterly diabolic experiment. You can guess the result: There was a significantly greater probability of choking if you were among the groups that got that little pep talk, irrespective of whether they'd been given the warm-up pretest (**Further Reading:** the Solomon four-group design).

The Two-Group Pretest-Posttest without Random Assignment

Figure 4.1c shows the design for a **quasi-experiment**—an experiment in which participants are *not* assigned randomly to the control and the experimental condition. This compromise with design purity is often the best we can do.

	Time 1		Time 2	
	Assignment	*Pretest*	*Intervention*	*Posttest*
Group 1		O_1	X	O_2
Group 2		O_3		O_4

FIGURE 4.1c.
The classical design without randomization: The quasi-experiment.

Program evaluation research is usually quasi-experimental. Consider a program in rural Kenya in which women farmers are offered instruction on applying for bank credit to buy fertilizer. The idea is to increase corn production.

You select two villages in the district—one that gets the program, and one that doesn't. Before the program starts, you measure the amount of credit, on average, that women in each village have applied for in the past 12 months. A year later, you measure again and find that, on average, women in the program village have applied for more agricultural credit than have their counterparts in the control village.

Campbell and Boruch (1975) show how this research design leads to problems. Suppose that the women in the program village have, on average, more land than the women in the control village have. Would you (or the agency you're working for) be willing to bet, say, $300,000 on implementing the program across the district, in, say, 30 villages? Would you bet that it was the intervention and not some confound, like the difference in land holdings, that caused the difference in outcome between the two villages?

The way around this is to assign each woman randomly to one of the two conditions in the experiment. Then the confound would disappear—not because land holding stops being a factor in how well women respond to the opportunity to get agricultural credits, but because women who have varying amounts of land would be equally likely to be in the treatment group or in the control group. Any bias that the amount of land causes in interpreting the results of the experiment would be distributed randomly and would be equally distributed across the groups.

But people come packaged in villages, and you can't give just some women in a small village instruction about applying for credit and not give it to others. So evaluation of these kinds of interventions are usually quasi-experiments because they have to be (**Further Reading:** quasi-experiments).

The Posttest-Only Design with Random Assignment

Look carefully at figure 4.1d. It is the second half of the Solomon four-group design and is called the **Campbell and Stanley posttest-only design**. This design has a lot going for it. It retains the random assignment of participants in the classical design and in the Solomon four-group design, but it *eliminates pretesting*—and the possibility of a confound

	Time 1		Time 2	
	Assignment	Pretest	Intervention	Posttest
Group 1	R		X	O_1
Group 2	R			O_2

FIGURE 4.1d.
The Campbell and Stanley posttest-only design.

from pretest sensitization. When participants are assigned randomly to experimental conditions (control or treatment group), a significant difference on O_1 and O_2 in the posttest-only design means that we can have a lot of confidence that the intervention, X, caused that difference (Cook and Campbell 1979).

Another advantage is the huge saving in time and money. There are no pretests in this design and there are only two posttests instead of the four in the Solomon four-group design.

Here's an example of this elegant design. McDonald and Bridge (1991) asked 160 female nurses to read an information packet about a surgery patient whom they would be attending within the next 8 hours. The nurses were assigned randomly to one of eight experimental conditions: (1) The patient was named Mary B. or Robert B. This produced *two patient-gender conditions*. (2) Half the nurses read only a synopsis of the condition of Mary B. or Robert B., and half read the same synopsis as the fourth one in a series of seven. This produced *two memory-load conditions*. (3) Finally, half the nurses read that the temperature of Mary B. or Robert B. had just spiked unexpectedly to 102°, and half did not. This produced *two patient stability conditions*. The three binary conditions combined to form eight experimental conditions in a **factorial design** (more on factorial designs at the end of this chapter).

Next, McDonald and Bridge asked nurses to estimate, to the nearest minute, how much time they would plan for each of several important nursing actions. Irrespective of the memory load, nurses planned significantly more time for giving the patient analgesics, for helping the patient to walk around, and for giving the patient emotional support when the patient was a man (box 4.3).

The One-Shot Case Study

The **one-shot case study design** is shown in figure 4.1e. It is also called the **ex post facto design** because a single group of people is measured on some dependent variable *after* an intervention has taken place. This is the most common research design in culture change studies, where it is obviously impossible to manipulate the dependent variable. You arrive in a community and notice that something important has taken place. A clinic or a school has been built. You try to evaluate the experiment by interviewing people (O) and assessing the impact of the intervention (X).

With neither a pretest nor a control group, you can't be sure that what you observe is the result of some particular intervention. Despite this apparent weakness, however, the intuitive appeal of findings produced by one-shot case studies can be formidable.

In the 1950s, physicians began general use of the Pap Test, a simple office procedure for determining the presence of cervical cancer. Figure 4.2 shows that since 1950, the death rate from cervical cancer in the United States has dropped steadily, from about 18

BOX 4.3

POSTTEST ONLY: THE UNDERAPPRECIATED DESIGN

The posttest-only design, with random assignment, is not used as much as I think it should be, despite its elegance and its low cost. In June 2009, a search of PsycINFO turned up 1,110 examples of studies that used the pretest-posttest design, compared to 133 for studies that used the posttest-only design (with or without random assignment). This preference for the classic design is due partly to the appealing-but-mistaken idea that matching participants in experiments on key independent variables (age, ethnicity, etc.) is somehow better than randomly assigning participant to groups, and partly to the nagging suspicion that pretests are essential to the experimental method. That nagging suspicion (that we can do better than trust the outcome of events to randomness) has been the focus of a lot of research since a paper by Gilovich et al. in 1985 titled: "The hot hand in basketball—on the misperception of random sequences." The hot-hand phenomenon—the belief that streaks (in sports and in money management, for example) are the result of nonrandom forces—is hard to break. By the same token, so is the belief that small samples, if drawn randomly, are sufficient to warrant generalizing to a population. On this one, see the 600 + citations to Tversky and Kahneman (1971) and chapters 6 and 7 on representative and nonrepresentative sampling (**Further Reading:** the posttest-only design).

Time 1		Time 2	
Assignment	Pretest	Intervention	Posttest
		X	O

FIGURE 4.1e.
The one-shot case study design.

per 100,000 women to about 11 in 1970, to about 8.3 in 1980, to about 6.5 in 1995 and to about 2.4 in 2005. If you look only at the data *after* the intervention (the one-shot case study X O design), you could easily conclude that the intervention (the Pap Test) was the sole cause of this drop in cervical cancer deaths. There is no doubt that the continued decline of cervical cancer deaths is due largely to the early detection provided by the Pap Test, but by 1950, the death rate had already declined by 36% from 28 per 100,000 in 1930 (B. Williams 1978:16).

Never use a design of less logical power when one of greater power is feasible. If pretest data are available, use them. On the other hand, a one-shot case study is often the best you can do. Virtually all ethnography falls in this category, and, as I have said before, nothing beats a good story, well told (**Further Reading:** case study methods).

The One-Group Pretest-Posttest

The **one-group pretest-posttest** design is shown in figure 4.1f. Some variables are measured (observed), then the intervention takes place, and then the variables are mea-

Time 1		Time 2	
Assignment	Pretest	Intervention	Posttest
	O_1	X	O_2

FIGURE 4.1f.
The one-group pretest-posttest design.

sured again. This takes care of some of the problems associated with the one-shot case study, but it doesn't eliminate the threats of history, testing, maturation, selection, and mortality. Most importantly, if there is a significant difference in the pretest and posttest measurements, we can't tell if the intervention made that difference happen.

The one-group pretest-posttest design is commonly used in evaluating training programs. The question asked is: Did the people who were exposed to this skill-building program (midwives, coal miners, kindergarten teachers, etc., etc.) get any effect from the program?

M. Peterson and Johnstone (1995) studied the effects on 43 women inmates of a U.S. federal prison of an education program about drug abuse. The participants all had a history of drug abuse, so there is no random assignment here. Peterson and Johnstone measured the participants' health status and perceived well-being before the program began and after the program had been running for 9 months. They found that physical fitness measures were improved for the participants as were self-esteem, health awareness, and health-promoting attitudes (**Further Reading:** one-group pretest-posttest design).

The Two-Group Posttest-Only Design without Random Assignment

The **two-group posttest-only design without random assignment** design is shown in figure 4.1g. This design, also known as the **static group comparison**, improves on the

Time 1		Time 2	
Assignment	Pretest	Intervention	Posttest
		X	O_1
			O_2

FIGURE 4.1g.
Two-group posttest only design without random assignment: Static group comparison design.

one-shot *ex post facto* design by adding an untreated control group—an independent case that is evaluated only at time 2. The relation between smoking cigarettes (the intervention) and getting lung cancer (the dependent variable) is easily seen by applying the humble *ex post facto* design with a control group for a second posttest.

In 1965, when the American Cancer Society did its first big Cancer Prevention Study, men who smoked (that is, those who were subject to the intervention) were about 12 times more likely than nonsmokers (the control group) to die of lung cancer. At that time, relatively few women smoked, and those who did had not been smoking very long. Their risk was just 2.7 times that for women nonsmokers of dying from lung cancer.

By 1988, things had changed dramatically. Male smokers were then about 23 times more likely than nonsmokers to die of lung cancer, and female smokers were 12.8 times more likely than female nonsmokers to die of lung cancer. Men's risk had doubled (from about 12 to about 23), but women's risk had more than quadrupled (from 2.7 to about 13) (National Cancer Institute 1997). The death rate for lung cancer has continued to fall among men in the United States, while the death rate for women has increased (http://apps.nccd.cdc.gov/uscs).

In true experiments run with the posttest-only design, participants are assigned at random to either the intervention or the control group. In the static group comparison design, the researcher has no control over assignment of participants. This leaves the static-group comparison design open to an unresolvable validity threat. There is no way to tell whether the two groups were comparable at time 1, before the intervention, even with a comparison of observations 1 and 3. Therefore, you can only guess whether the intervention caused any differences in the groups at time 2.

Despite this, the static-group comparison design is useful for evaluating natural experiments, where you have no control over the assignment of participants anyway (**Further Reading:** static group comparison design) (box 4.4).

BOX 4.4

MIGRATION AND GENDER ROLES: A STATIC-GROUP COMPARISON DESIGN

Lambros Comitas and I wanted to find out if the experience abroad of Greek labor migrants had any influence on men's and women's attitudes toward gender roles when they returned to Greece. The best design would have been to survey a group before they went abroad, then again while they were away, and again when they returned to Greece. Since this was not possible, we studied one group of persons who had been abroad and another group of persons who had never left Greece. We treated these two groups as if they were part of a static-group comparison design (Bernard and Comitas 1978).

From a series of life histories with migrants and nonmigrants, we learned that the custom of giving dowry was under severe stress (Bernard and Ashton-Vouyoucalos 1976). Our survey confirmed this: Those who had worked abroad were far less enthusiastic about providing expensive dowries for their daughters than were those who had never left Greece. We concluded that this was in some measure due to the experiences of migrants in what was then West Germany.

There were threats to the validity of this conclusion: Perhaps migrants were a self-selected bunch of people who held the dowry and other traditional Greek customs in low esteem to begin with. But we had those life histories to back up our conclusion. Surveys are weak compared to true experiments, but their power is improved if they are conceptualized in terms of testing natural experiments and if their results are backed up with data from open-ended interviews.

Interrupted Time Series Design

The interrupted time series design, shown in figure 4.1h, can be very persuasive. It involves making a series of observation before and after an intervention. Figure 4.3 shows

	Time 1		Time 2	
Assignment	Pretest	Intervention		Posttest
	O O O	X		O O O

FIGURE 4.1h.
The interrupted time series design.

the rate of alcohol deaths, per 100,000 population, in Russia, from 1956 to 2002 (Pridemore et al. 2007:281). The year 1992 marks the formal shift in Russia to a market economy from a centrally planned economy. As it turns out, homicide and suicide rates show very similar patterns—something that Pridemore et al. interpret as outcomes that are predictable from Durkheim's (1933 [1893], 1951 [1897]) theory of anomie (**Further Reading:** interrupted time series).

THOUGHT EXPERIMENTS

As you can see, it is next to impossible to eliminate threats to validity in natural experiments. However, there is a way to understand those threats and to keep them as low as possible: Think about research questions as if it were possible to test them in *true* experiments. These are called **thought experiments**.

This wonderful device is part of the everyday culture in the physical sciences. In 1972, I did an ethnographic study of scientists at Scripps Institution of Oceanography. Here's a snippet from a conversation I heard among some physicists there. "If we could only get rid of clouds, we could capture more of the sun's energy to run stuff on Earth," one person said. "Well," said another, "there are no clouds above the Earth's atmosphere. The sun's energy would be lots easier to capture out there."

"Yeah," said the first, "so suppose we send up a satellite, with solar panels to convert sunlight to electricity, and we attach a really long extension cord so the satellite was tethered to the Earth. Would that work?" The discussion got weirder from there (if you can imagine), but it led to a lot of really useful ideas for research.

Suppose you wanted to know if small farms can produce organically grown food on a

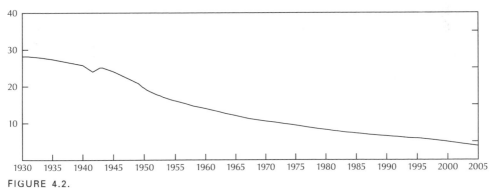

FIGURE 4.2.
Death rate from cervical cancer, 1930–2005.
SOURCE: Adapted from B. Williams, *A Sampler on Sampling.* Figure 2.1, p. 17. © 1978, Lucent Technologies. Used by permission of John Wiley & Sons.

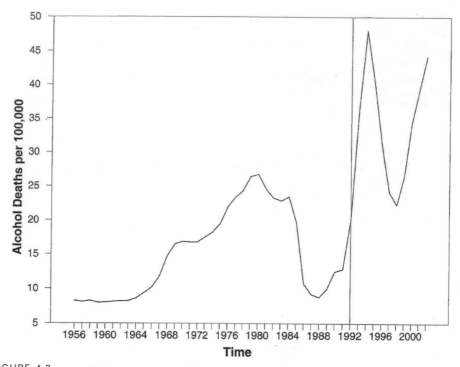

FIGURE 4.3.

Alcohol deaths in Russia, 1956–2002.

SOURCE: W. A. Pridemore, M. B. Chamlin, and J. K. Cochran, "An Interrupted Time-Series Analysis of Durk-heim's Social Deregulation Thesis: The Case of the Russian Federation." *Justice Quarterly* Vol. 24, pp. 272–90, 2007. Reprinted by permission.

scale sufficiently large to be profitable. What would a true experiment to test this question look like? You might select some smallish farms with similar acreage and assign half of them randomly to grow vegetables organically. You'd assign the other half of the farms to grow the same vegetables using all usual technology (pesticides, fungicides, chemical fertilizers, and so on). Then, after a while, you'd measure some things about the farms' productivity and profitability and see which of them did better.

How could you be sure that organic or nonorganic methods of farming made the difference in profitability? Perhaps you'd need to control for access to the kinds of market populations that are friendly toward organically produced food (like university towns) or for differences in the characteristics of soils and weather patterns. Obviously, you can't do a true experiment on this topic, randomly assigning farmers to use organic or high-tech methods, but you *can* evaluate the experiments that real farmers are conducting every day in their choice of farming practices.

So, after you've itemized the possible threats to validity in your thought experiment, go out and look for natural experiments—societies, voluntary associations, organiza-tions—that conform most closely to your ideal experiment. Then evaluate those natural experiments.

That's what Karen Davis and Susan Weller (1999) did in their study of the efficacy of condoms in preventing the transmission of HIV among heterosexuals. Here's the experi-ment you'd have to conduct. First, get a thousand heterosexual couples. Make each couple randomly serodiscordant. That is, for each couple, randomly assign the man or the woman to be HIV-positive. Assign each couple randomly to one of three conditions: (1) They use condoms for each sexual act; (2) They sometimes use condoms; or (3) They don't use condoms at all. Let the experiment run a few years. Then see how many of the couples in which condoms are always used remain serodiscordant and how many become seroconcordant—that is, they are both HIV-positive. Compare across conditions and see how much difference it makes to always use a condom.

Clearly, no one could conduct this experiment. But Davis and Weller scoured the literature on condom efficacy and found 25 studies that met three criteria: (1) The focus was on serodiscordant heterosexual couples who said they regularly had penetrative sexual intercourse; (2) The HIV status of the participants in each study had been determined by a blood test; and (3) There was information on the use of condoms. The 25 studies involved thousands of participants, and from this **meta-analysis** Davis and Weller established that consistent use of condoms reduced the rate of HIV transmission by over 85%.

TRUE EXPERIMENTS IN THE LAB

Laboratory experiments to test theories about how things work in the real world is the preeminent method in social psychology. Cognitive dissonance theory, for example, predicts that people who come out of a tough initiation experience (marine recruits at boot camp, prisoners of war, girls and boys who go through genital mutilation, etc.) wind up as supporters of their tormentors. In a classic experiment, Elliot Aronson and Judson Mills (1959) recruited 63 college women for a discussion group that ostensibly was being formed to talk about psychological aspects of sex. To make sure that only mature people— people who could discuss sex openly—would make it into this group, some of the women would have to go through a screening test. Well, that's what they were *told*.

A third of the women were assigned randomly to a group that had to read a list of obscene words and some sexually explicit passages from some novels—aloud, in front of a man who was running the experiment. (It may be hard to imagine now, but those women who went through this in the 1950s must have been very uncomfortable.) Another third were assigned randomly to a group that had to recite some nonobscene words that had to do with sex and a third group went through no screening at all.

Then, each participant was given headphones to listen in on a discussion that was supposedly going on among the members of the group she was joining. The "discussion" was actually a tape and it was, as Aronson and Mills said, "one of the most worthless and uninteresting discussions imaginable" (Aronson and Mills 1959:179). The women rated the discussion, on a scale of 0–15, on things like dull-interesting, intelligent-unintelligent, and so on.

Those in the tough initiation condition rated the discussion higher than did the women the women in either the control group or the mild initiation group. Since all the women were assigned randomly to participate in one of the groups, the outcome was unlikely to have occurred by chance. Well, the women in the tough initiation condition had gone through a lot to join the discussion. When they discovered how boringly nonprurient it was, what did they do? They convinced themselves that the group was worth joining.

Aaronson and Mills's findings were corroborated by Gerard and Mathewson (1966) in an independent experiment. Those findings from the laboratory can now be the basis for a field test, across cultures, of the original hypothesis.

Conversely, events in the real world can stimulate laboratory experiments. In 1963, in Queens, New York, Kitty Genovese was stabbed to death in the street one night. According to a local news report, there were supposedly 38 eyewitnesses who saw the whole grisly episode from their apartment windows but did not call called the police. The news stories called the episode an example of "apathy," but Bibb Latané and John Darley had a different explanation. They called it **diffusion of responsibility** and they did an experiment to test their idea (1968).

Latané and Darley invited ordinary people to participate in a "psychology experiment." While the participants were waiting in an anteroom to be called for the experiment, the room filled with smoke. If there was a single participant in the room, 75% reported the smoke right away. If there were three or more participants waiting together, they reported the smoke only 38% of the time. People in groups just couldn't figure out whose responsibility it was to do something. So they did nothing.

As it turns out, there probably weren't 38 witnesses; none of the witnesses could have seen the whole episode; and some of the witnesses did call the police (Manning et al. 2007). Nevertheless, hundreds of studies on what's known as the bystander effect have been published since Latané and Darley did their pioneering work. A real event gave two scientists an idea that they tested in an experiment, and that experiment opened a whole area of research.

TRUE EXPERIMENTS IN THE FIELD

When experiments are done outside the lab, they are called **field experiments**. Several researchers have been studying the effect of being touched on consumers' spending. In one experiment (Hornik 1992), as lone shoppers (no couples) entered a large bookstore, an "employee" came up and handed them a catalog. Alternating between customers, the employee-experimenter touched about half the shoppers lightly on the upper arm. The results? Across 286 shoppers, those who were touched spent an average of $15.03; those who were not touched spent just $12.23. (That's $25 vs. $20 in 2010 dollars.) The difference was across the board, no matter what the sex of the toucher or the shopper.

In another of his experiments, Hornik enlisted the help of eight servers—four waiters and four waitresses—at a large restaurant. At the end of the meal, the servers asked each of 248 couples (men and women) how the meal was. Right then, for half the couples, the servers touched the arm of either the male or the female in the couple for one second. The servers didn't know it, but they had been selected out of 27 waiters and waitresses in the restaurant to represent two ends of a physical attractiveness scale. The results? Men and women alike left bigger tips when they were touched, but the effect was stronger for women patrons than it was for men. Overall, couples left about a 19% tip when the woman was touched, but only 16.5% when the man was touched.

Field experiments like these can produce powerful evidence for applications projects, but to be really useful, you need to back up results with ethnography so that you understand the process. How did all this tipping behavior play out? Did women who were touched suggest a bigger tip when the time came to pay the bill, or did the men suggest the tip? Or did it all happen without any discussion? Rich ethnographic data are needed here.

Field experiments are rare in anthropology, but not unprecedented. Marvin Harris and his colleagues (Byrne et al. 1995; Harris et al. 1993) ran an experiment in Brazil to test the effect of substituting one word in the question that deals with race on the Brazilian census. The demographers who designed the census had decided that the term *parda* was a more reliable gloss than the term *morena* for what English speakers call "brown," despite overwhelming evidence that Brazilians prefer the term *morena*.

In the town of Rio de Contas, Harris et al. assigned 505 houses randomly to one of two groups and interviewed one adult in each house. All respondents were asked to say what *cor* (color) they thought they were. This was the "free-choice option." Then they were asked to choose one of four terms that best described their *cor*. One group (with 252 respondents) was asked to select among *branca* (white), *parda* (brown), *preta* (black), and *amerela* (yellow). This was the "*parda* option"—the one used on the Brazilian census. The other group (with 253 respondents) was asked to select among *branca*, *morena* (brown), *preta*, and *amerela*. This was the "*morena* option," and is the intervention, or treatment in Harris's experiment.

Among the 252 people given the *parda* option, 131 (52%) identified themselves as *morena* in the free-choice option (when simply asked to say what color they were). But when given the *parda* option, only 80 of those people said they were *parda* and 41 said they were *branca* (the rest chose the other two categories). Presumably, those 41 people would have labeled themselves *morena* if they'd had the chance; not wanting to be labeled *parda*, they said they were *branca*. The *parda* option, then, produces more Whites (*brancas*) in the Brazilian census and fewer Browns (*pardas*).

Of the 253 people who responded to the *morena* option, 160 (63%) said they were *morena*. Of those 160, only 122 had chosen to call themselves *morena* in the free-choice option. So, giving people the *morena* option actually increases the number of Browns (*morenas*) and decreases the number of Whites (*brancas*) in the Brazilian census.

Does this difference make a difference? Demographers who study the Brazilian census have found that those who are labeled Whites live about 7 years longer than do those labeled non-Whites in that country. If 31% of self-described *morenas* say they are Whites when there is no *morena* label on a survey and are forced to label themselves *parda*, what does this do to all the social and economic statistics about racial groups in Brazil? (Harris et al. 1993) (**Further Research:** field experiments) (box 4.5).

NATURAL EXPERIMENTS

True experiments and quasi-experiments are *conducted* and the results are *evaluated* later. **Natural experiments**, by contrast, are going on around us all the time. They are not conducted by researchers at all—they are simply evaluated.

Here are four examples of common natural experiments: (1) Some people choose to migrate from villages to cities; others stay put. (2) Some villages in a region are provided with electricity, some are not. (3) Some middle-class Chicano students go to college, some do not. (4) Some cultures practice female infanticide, some do not.

Each of these situations is a natural experiment that tests *something* about human behavior and thought. The trick is to ask: "What hypothesis is being tested by what's going on here?"

To evaluate natural experiments—that is, to figure out what hypothesis is being tested—you need to be alert to the possibilities and collect the right data. There's a really important natural experiment going in an area of Mexico where I've worked over the years. A major irrigation system has been installed over the last 50 years in parts of the Mezquital, a high desert valley. Some of the villages affected by the irrigation system are populated entirely by Ñähñu (Otomí) Indians; other villages are entirely mestizo (as the majority population of Mexico is called).

Some of the Indian villages in the area are too high up the valley slope for the irrigation system to reach. I could not have decided to run this multimillion-dollar system through certain villages and bypass others, but the instant the decision was made by others, a natural experiment on the effects of a particular intervention was set in motion. There is a treatment (irrigation), there are treatment groups (villages full of people who get the irrigation), and there are control groups (villages full of people who are left out).

BOX 4.5

ECONOMIC GAMES

In classical economic theory, it is assumed that *Homo economicus* is pro-grammed to maximize gain in any bargaining situation. In 1982, however, econ-omists in Germany found evidence that challenged this assumption (Güth et al. 1982). In what the researchers called the ultimatum game, there are two players who never see each other or find out the other's identity. Player 1 gets a sum of money, x, and offers some fraction of it, $x-p$, to player 2 through an intermedi-ary. If player 2 accepts, the money is split according to the terms of player 1. If player 2 rejects the offer, then neither player gets anything. Economic theory predicts that player 1 should offer next to nothing and that player 2 should accept anything player 1 offers. As Thaler put it, "the data are inconsistent with both of these predictions" (1988:197). For player 2, it costs nothing to reject very small offers—and to punish player 1—but as the fraction of the offer goes up, player 2 has to weigh the joy of teaching the other player a lesson with the loss of real money. If you're player 1, the trick is to figure out how much to offer so that you don't wind up with nothing but you still get what you can.

By the late 1990s, there were hundreds of studies using economics games in developed countries. Then, Joseph Henrich and colleagues (2005) ran the ultimatum game in 15 small-scale societies around the world—from foragers to farmers—as well as with American university students. "The selfishness axiom," they conclude "was violated in some way in every society we studied" (p. 803). And the violations weren't random. The more integrated people were into a market economy, the more prosocial behavior they exhibited in the games (p. 795) (**Further Reading**: economic games in anthropology).

Unfortunately, I can't evaluate the experiment because I simply failed to see the possi-bilities early enough. Finkler (1974) saw the possibilities; her ethnographic study of the effects of irrigation on an Indian village in the same area shows that the intervention is having profound effects. But neither she nor I measured (pretested) things like average village wealth, average personal wealth, migration rates, alcoholism, and so on that I believe have been affected by the coming of irrigation.

Had anyone done so—if we had **baseline data**—we would be in a better position to ask: "What hypotheses about human behavior are being tested by this experiment?" I can't reconstruct variables from 20 or 30 years ago. The logical power of the experimental model for establishing cause and effect between the intervention and the dependent vari-ables is destroyed.

Some natural experiments, though, produce terrific data all by themselves for evalua-tion. In 1955, the governor of Connecticut ordered strict enforcement of speeding laws in the state. Anyone caught speeding had his or her driver's license suspended for at least 30 days. Traffic deaths fell from 324 in 1955 to 284 in 1956. A lot of people had been inconvenienced with speeding tickets and suspension of driving privileges, but 40 lives had been saved.

Did the crackdown cause the decline in traffic deaths? Campbell and Ross (1968) used the available data to find out. They plotted the traffic deaths from 1951 to 1959 in Connecticut, Massachusetts, New York, New Jersey, and Rhode Island. Four of the five states showed an increase in highway deaths in 1955, and all five states showed a decline in traffic deaths the following year, 1956. If that were all you knew, you couldn't be sure about the cause of the decline. However, traffic deaths continued to decline steadily in Connecticut for the next 3 years (1957, 1958, 1959). In Rhode Island and Massachusetts, they went up; in New Jersey, they went down a bit and then up again; and in New York, they remained about the same.

Connecticut was the only state that showed a consistent reduction in highway deaths for 4 years after the stiff penalties were introduced. Campbell and Ross treated these data as a series of natural experiments, and the results were convincing: Stiff penalties for speeders saves lives.

Natural Experiments Are Everywhere

If you think like an experimentalist, you eventually come to see the unlimited possibilities for research going on all around you. Across the United States, school boards set rigid cutoff dates for children who are starting school. Suppose the cutoff is August 1. Children born at the end of July start kindergarten at age 5. Children born at the beginning of August start at age 6. Since children from 5 to 7 are going through an intense period of cognitive development, Morrison et al. (1996) treat this situation as a natural experiment and ask: Are there short- and long-term impacts on cognitive skills of just missing or just making the cutoff?

Ever notice how people like to tell stories about the time they found themselves sitting next to a famous person on a plane? It's called BIRGing in social psychology—basking in reflected glory. Cialdini et al. (1976) evaluated the natural BIRGing experiment that is conducted on most big university campuses every weekend during football season. Over a period of 8 weeks, professors at Arizona State, Louisiana State, Ohio State, Notre Dame, Michigan, the University of Pittsburgh, and the University of Southern California recorded the percentage of students in their introductory psychology classes who wore school insignias (buttons, hats, t-shirts, etc.) on the Monday after Saturday football games. For 177 students per week, on average, over 8 weeks, 63% wore some school insignia after wins in football versus 44% after losses or ties. The difference was statistically significant and the finding opened up a whole area of research that continues (Madrigal and Chen 2008).

Here's another one. On January 1, 2002, 12 of the then-15 members of the European Union gave up their individual currencies and adopted the euro (there are now 16 countries in the eurozone out of 27 in the European Union). Greece was one of the 12, Denmark wasn't. Some researchers noticed that many of the euro coins were smaller than the Greek drachma coins they'd replaced and thought that this might create a choking hazard for small children (Papadopoulos et al. 2004). The researchers compared the number of choking incidents reported in Danish and Greek hospitals in January through March from 1996 through 2002. Sure enough, there was no increase in the rate of those incidents in Denmark (which hadn't converted to the euro), but the rate in Greece suddenly more than doubled in 2002 (box 4.6).

TURNING A CONFOUND INTO A NATURAL EXPERIMENT

If you think like an experimentalist you can do what Kathy Oths did—turn what could have been a killer history confound into a research opportunity. From July 1 to December 15, 1988, Oths visited each of the 166 households in Chugurpampa, Peru, several times

BOX 4.6

CASE CONTROL AND NATURAL EXPERIMENTS

In a case control design, you compare naturally occurring cases of a criterion (like having a certain illness or injury, or attempting suicide, or being homeless) with people who match the cases on many criteria, but *not* on the case criterion.

This method is widely used in public health research, and in fact, the classic case-control study in anthropology was done by Art Rubel and colleagues (1984) on the Latin American folk illness known as *susto*. Among Indian people, the symptoms of *susto*—anxiety, diarrhea, difficulty breathing, and others—are often said to result from a loss of soul, while among mestizo people the symptoms are often attributed to having experiences some fright (from the verb *asustarse*, to become frightened). Rubel and his colleagues compared people in two Indian villages and one mestizo village in Mexico, all of whom suffered from *susto* (the **index cases**) with people in the same villages who did not (the **control cases**). There were no statistically significant differences between the 47 index cases and the 48 controls on tests of psychiatric symptoms. Seven years after the study was completed, however, 17% of the index cases had died—and *none* of the control cases had died. The design in this study makes it thoroughly convincing (**Further Reading**: case control).

to collect illness histories—what kinds of illnesses people came down with and what they did about them (Oths 1994). When she began the project, the harvest season had just ended in the high Andes and the farmers in Chugurpampa had collected most of the money they would have for the year. But in August, a month into her work, catastrophic inflation hit Peru and the local currency, the Peruvian inti, which was at 40 to the U.S. dollar, was crushed. It hit 683 by November.

Oths continued her household visits. As the hard times dragged on, the people of Chugurpampa continued to report the same number of illnesses (between seven and eight per household per month) but they defined a larger percentage of their illnesses as mild (requiring only home remedies) and a smaller percentage as moderate or severe (requiring visits to doctors or to the hospital). In other words, they spent what little money they had on cases that they thought needed biomedical intervention and stopped spending money on traditional healers (**Further Reading**: natural experiments).

NATURALISTIC EXPERIMENTS

In a **naturalistic** experiment, you *contrive* to collect experimental data under natural conditions. You make the data happen, out in the natural world (not in the lab), and you evaluate the results.

In a memorable experiment, elegant in its simplicity of design, Doob and Gross (1968) had a car stop at a red light and wait for 15 seconds after the light turned green before moving again. In one experimental condition, they used a new car and a well-dressed driver. In another condition, they used an old, beat-up car and a shabbily dressed driver. They repeated the experiment many times and measured the time it took for people in the car behind the experimental car to start honking their horns. It won't surprise you to learn that people were quicker to vent their frustration at apparently low-status cars and drivers.

Piliavin et al. (1969) did a famous naturalistic experiment to test the "good Samaritan" problem. Students in New York City rode a particular subway train that had a 7.5-minute run at one point. At 70 seconds into the run, a researcher pitched forward and collapsed. The team used four experimental conditions: The "stricken" person was either black or white and was either carrying a cane or a liquor bottle. Observers noted how long it took for people in the subway car to come to the aid of the supposedly stricken person, the total population of the car, whether bystanders were black or white, and so on. You can conjure up the results. There were no surprises.

Harari et al. (1985) recruited drama majors to test whether men on a college campus would come to the aid of a woman being raped. They staged realistic-sounding rape scenes and found that there was a significant difference in the helping reaction of male passersby if those men were alone or in groups.

And Walker (2006) rode his bicycle 200 miles through Bristol and Salisbury, England during regular working hours dressed as an ordinary commuter—sometimes wearing a helmet, sometimes not; sometimes wearing a woman's long-haired wig, sometimes not. Walker outfitted his bike with a hidden distance sensor and a tiny camera and then, systematically varying his distance from the curb, he measured how close cars came as they passed him. The farther from the edge he rode, the closer drivers came; drivers stayed farther from him when he appeared to be a woman; and drivers came closer to him when he wasn't wearing a helmet than when he was. Fortunately, both times he got hit doing this experiment, he was wearing the helmet (**Further Reading:** naturalistic experiments).

The Small-World Experiment

Consider this: You're having coffee near the Trevi Fountain in Rome. You overhear two Americans chatting next to you and you ask where they're from. One of them says she's from Sioux City, Iowa. You say you've got a friend from Sioux City and it turns out to be your new acquaintance's cousin. The culturally appropriate reaction at this point is for everyone to say, "Wow, what a small world!"

Stanley Milgram (1967) invented an experiment to test how small the world really is. He asked a group of people in the midwestern United States to send a folder to a divinity student at Harvard University, but only if the participant *knew* the divinity student personally. Otherwise, Milgram asked people to send the folders to an acquaintance whom they thought had a chance of knowing the "target" at Harvard.

The folders got sent around from acquaintance to acquaintance until they wound up in the hands of someone who actually knew the target—at which point the folders were sent, as per the instructions in the game, to the target. The average number of *links* between all the "starters" and the target was about five. It really *is* a small world.

No one expects this experiment to actually happen in real life. It's contrived as can be and it lacks control. But it's compelling because it says *something* about how the natural world works. The finding was so compelling that it was the basis for the Broadway play "Six Degrees of Separation," as well as the movie of the same name that followed and the game "Six Degrees of Kevin Bacon." It also provoked research, first by social scientists and then by physicists and mathematicians, on the structure of relations in everything from people to corporations to nations to neurons to sites on the Internet. Looking for the structure of relations is another way of saying "network analysis."

The Lost-Letter Technique

Another of Milgram's contributions is a method for doing unobtrusive surveys of political opinion. The method is called the "lost-letter technique" and consists of "losing" a lot of letters that have addresses and stamps on them (Milgram et al. 1965).

The technique is based on two assumptions. First, people in many societies believe that they ought to mail a letter if they find one, especially if it has a stamp on it. Second, people will be less likely to drop a lost letter in the mail if it is addressed to someone or some organization that they don't like.

Milgram et al. (1965) tested this in New Haven, Connecticut. They lost 400 letters in ten districts of the city. They dropped the letters on the street; they left them in phone booths; they left them on counters at shops; and they tucked them under windshield wipers (after penciling "found near car" on the back of the envelope). Over 70% of the letters addressed to an individual or to a medical research company were returned. Only 25% of the letters addressed to either "Friends of the Communist Party" or "Friends of the Nazi Party" were returned. (The addresses were all the same post box that had been rented for the experiment.)

By losing letters in a sample of communities, then, and by counting the differential rates at which they are returned, you can test variations in sentiment. Two of Milgram's students distributed anti-Nazi letters in Munich. The letters did not come back as much from some neighborhoods as from others, and they were thus able to pinpoint the areas of strongest neo-Nazi sentiment (Milgram 1969:68). The lost-letter technique has sampling problems and validity problems galore associated with it. But it's still an interesting way to infer public opinion about emotionally charged issues, and you can see just how intuitively powerful the results can be (**Further Reading:** the lost-letter technique).

COMPARATIVE FIELD EXPERIMENTS

Naturalistic field experiments appeal to me because they are excellent for comparative research, and comparison is so important for developing theory. Feldman (1968) did five field experiments in Paris, Boston, and Athens to test whether people in those cities respond more kindly to foreigners or to members of their own culture.

In one experiment, the researchers simply asked for directions and measured whether foreigners or natives got better treatment. Parisians and Athenians gave help significantly more often to fellow citizens than to foreigners. In Boston, there was no difference.

In the second experiment, foreigners and natives stood at major metro stops and asked total strangers to do them a favor. They explained that they were waiting for a friend, couldn't leave the spot they were on, and had to mail a letter. They asked people to mail the letters for them (the letters were addressed to the experiment headquarters) and simply counted how many letters they got back from the different metro stops in each city. Half the letters were unstamped.

In Boston and Paris, between 32% and 35% of the people refused to mail a letter for a fellow citizen. In Athens, 93% refused. Parisians treated Americans significantly better than Bostonians treated Frenchmen on this task. In fact, in cases where Parisians were asked to mail a letter that was stamped, they treated Americans significantly better than they treated other Parisians! (So much for *that* stereotype.)

In the third experiment, researchers approached informants and said: "Excuse me, sir. Did you just drop this dollar bill?" (or other currency, depending on the city). It was easy to measure whether or not people falsely claimed the money more from foreigners than from natives. This experiment yielded meager results.

In the fourth experiment, foreigners and natives went to pastry shops in the three cities, bought a small item and gave the clerk 25% more than the item cost. Then they left the shop and recorded whether the clerk had offered to return the overpayment. This experiment also showed little difference among the cities or between the way foreigners and locals are treated.

And in the fifth experiment, researchers took taxis from the same beginning points to the same destinations in all three cities. They measured whether foreigners or natives were charged more. In neither Boston nor Athens was a foreigner overcharged more than a local. In Paris, however, Feldman found that "the American foreigner was overcharged significantly more often than the French compatriot in a variety of ingenious ways" (1968:11).

Feldman collected data on more than 3,000 interactions and was able to draw conclusions about cultural differences in how various peoples respond to foreigners as opposed to other natives. Some stereotypes were confirmed; others were crushed. Since Feldman's pioneering work, dozens of studies have been done on cross-cultural differences in helping strangers (see Levine et al. [2001], for example).

Bochner did a series of interesting experiments on the nature of Aboriginal-white relations in urban Australia (see Bochner [1980:335–40] for a review). These experiments are clever, inexpensive, and illuminating, and Bochner's self-conscious critique of the limitations of his own work is a model for field experimentalists to follow. In one experiment, Bochner put two classified ads in a Sydney paper:

> Young couple, no children, want to rent small unfurnished flat up to $25 per week. Saturday only. 759–6000.
>   Young Aboriginal couple, no children, want to rent small unfurnished flat up to $25 per week. Saturday only. 759–6161. (Bochner 1972:335)

Different people were assigned to answer the two phones, to ensure that callers who responded to both ads would not hear the same voice. Note that the ads were identical in every respect, except for the fact that in one of the ads the ethnicity of the couple was identified and in the other it was not. There were 14 responses to the ethnically nonspecific ad and two responses to the ethnically specific ad (three additional people responded to both ads).

In another experiment, Bochner exploited what he calls the "Fifi effect" (Bochner 1980:336). The Fifi effect refers to the fact that urbanites acknowledge the presence of strangers who pass by while walking a dog and ignore others. Bochner sent a white woman and an Aboriginal woman, both in their early 20s, and similarly dressed, to a public park in Sydney. He had them walk a small dog through randomly assigned sectors of the park, for 10 minutes in each sector.

Each woman was followed by two observers, who gave the impression that they were just out for a stroll. The two observers *independently* recorded the interaction of the women with passersby. The observers recorded the frequency of smiles offered to the women; the number of times anyone said anything to the women; and the number of nonverbal recognition nods the women received. The white woman received 50 approaches; the Aboriginal woman received only 18 (Bochner 1971:111).

There are many elegant touches in this experiment. Note how the age and dress of the experimenters were controlled, so that only their ethnic identity remained as a dependent variable. Note how the time for each experimental trial (10 minutes in each sector) was controlled to ensure an equal opportunity for each woman to receive the same treatment by strangers. Bochner did preliminary observation in the park and divided it into sectors that had the same population density, so that the chance for interaction with strangers would be about equal in each run of the experiment, and he used two independent observer-recorders.

As Bochner points out, however, there were still design flaws that threatened the internal validity of the experiment (1980:337). As it happens, the interrater reliability of the two observers in this experiment was nearly perfect. But suppose the two observers shared the same cultural expectations about Aboriginal-white relations in urban Australia. They might have quite reliably misrecorded the cues that they were observing.

Reactive and unobtrusive observations alike tell you *what* happened, not *why*. It is tempting to conclude that the Aboriginal woman was ignored because of active prejudice. But, says Bochner, "perhaps passersby ignored the Aboriginal . . . because they felt a personal approach might be misconstrued as patronizing" (Bochner 1980:338).

In Bochner's third study, a young white or Aboriginal woman walked into a butcher's shop and asked for 10 cents' worth of bones for her pet dog. The dependent variables in the experiment were the weight and quality of the bones. (An independent dog fancier rated the bones on a 3-point scale, without knowing how the bones were obtained, or why.) Each woman visited seven shops in a single middle-class shopping district.

In both amount and quality of bones received, the white woman did better than the Aboriginal, but the differences were not statistically significant—the sample was just too small so no conclusions could be drawn from that study alone. *Taken all together*, though, the three studies done by Bochner and his students comprise a powerful set of information about Aboriginal-white relations in Sydney. Naturalistic experiments like these have their limitations, but they often produce intuitively compelling results. And since Bochner's work, nearly 40 years ago, dozens of other field studies have been done testing for discrimination in housing, lending, and hiring (Ahmed and Hammarstedt 2008; Sharpe 1998).

ARE FIELD EXPERIMENTS ETHICAL?

Field experiments come in a range of ethical varieties, from innocuous to borderline to downright ugly. I see no ethical problems with the lost-letter technique. When people mail one of the lost letters, they don't know that they are taking part in an experiment, but that doesn't bother me. Personally, I see no harm in the experiment to test whether people vent their anger by honking their car horns more quickly at people they think are lower socioeconomic class. These days, however, with road rage an increasing problem, I don't recommend repeating Doob and Gross's experiment.

Randomized field experiments, used mostly in evaluation research, can be problematic. Suppose you wanted to know whether fines or jail sentences are better at changing the behavior of drunk drivers. One way to do that would be to randomly assign people who were convicted of the offense to one or the other condition and watch the results. Suppose one of the participants whom you didn't put in jail kills an innocent person?

The classic experimental design in drug testing requires that some people get the new drug, that some people get a placebo (a sugar pill that has no effect), and that neither the patients nor the doctors administering the drugs know which is which. This double-blind placebo design is responsible for great advances in medicine and the saving of many lives. But suppose that, in the middle of a double-blind trial of a drug you find out that the drug really works. Do you press on and complete the study? Or do you stop right there and make sure that you aren't withholding treatment from people whose lives could be saved? The ethical problems associated with **withholding of treatment** are under increasing scrutiny (Storosum et al. 2003; Walther 2005; Wertz 1987).

There is a long history of debate about the ethics of **deception** in psychology and social psychology (see Hertwig and Ortmann [2008] for a review). My own view is that, on balance, some deception is clearly necessary—certain types of research just can't be done without it. When you use deception, though, you run all kinds of risks—not just to research participants, but to the research itself. These days, college students (who are the participants for most social psych experiments) are very savvy about all this and are on the lookout for clues as to the "real" reason for an experiment the minute they walk in the door.

If you don't absolutely need deception in true behavioral experiments, that's one less problem you have to deal with. If you decide that deception is required, then understand that the responsibility for any bad outcomes is yours and yours alone.

The experiments by Piliavin et al. (1969) and Harari et al. (1985) on whether people will come to the aid of a stricken person, or a woman being raped, present real ethical problems. Some of the participants (who neither volunteered to be in an experiment nor were paid for their services) might still be wondering what happened to that poor guy on the subway whom they stepped over in their hurry to get away from an uncomfortable situation—or that woman whose screams they ignored. In laboratory experiments, at least, participants are debriefed—told what the real purpose of the study was—to reduce emotional distress. In the guerrilla theater type of field experiment, though, no debriefing is possible.

Even debriefing has its dark side. People don't like to find out that they have been duped into being part of an experiment, and some may suffer a terrible loss of self-esteem if they do find out and conclude that they acted badly. How would *you* feel if you were one of the people who failed to respond to a rape victim and then were told that you were just part of an experiment—that no real rape ever took place, and thank you very much for your help? (**Further Reading:** deception and debriefing).

If you think some of *these* cases are borderline, consider the study by West et al. (1975) on whether there is a little larceny in us all.

THE WATERGATE EXPERIMENT

In the Watergate affair of 1974, men loyal to then President Richard Nixon broke into the headquarters of the Democratic Party at the Watergate Hotel in Washington, DC, to photograph documents pertinent to the 1972 election campaign. Their bungling of the job, and the subsequent cover-up by Nixon and his staff at the White House, led to the unprecedented resignation of the president of the United States from office in 1974. Soon thereafter, West et al. conducted their experiment.

They confronted 80 different students with a proposition to burglarize a local advertising firm. Participants were randomly assigned to one of four conditions. In the first condition, participants were told that the job was to be done for the Internal Revenue Service. The IRS, it seemed, needed to get the goods on this company to bring them to trial for tax evasion. If the participants were caught in the act, then the government would guarantee immunity from prosecution. In the second condition, participants were told that there was no immunity from prosecution.

In the third condition, participants were told that another advertising agency had paid $8,000 for the job, and that they (the participants) would get $2,000 for their part in it. (Remember, that was $2,000 in 1979—about $6,000 today.) Finally, in the fourth condition, participants were told that the burglary was being committed just to see if the plan would work. Nothing would be taken from the office.

Understand that this was not a "let's pretend" exercise. Participants were not brought into a laboratory and told to imagine that they were being asked to commit a crime. This was for real. Participants met the experimenter at his home or at a restaurant. They were all criminology students at a university and knew the experimenter to be an actual local private investigator. The private eye arranged an elaborate and convincing plan for the burglary, including data on the comings and goings of police patrol cars, aerial photographs, blueprints of the building—the works.

The participants really believed that they were being solicited to commit a crime. Just as predicted by the researchers, a lot of them agreed to do it in the first condition, when they thought the crime was for a government agency and that they'd be free of danger from prosecution if caught. What do you suppose would happen to *your* sense of self-worth when you were finally debriefed and told that you were one of the 36 out of 80 (45%) who agreed to participate in the burglary in the first condition? (See Cook [1975] for a critical comment on the ethics of this experiment.) (box 4.7).

FACTORIAL DESIGNS: MAIN EFFECTS AND INTERACTION EFFECTS

Most experiments involve analyzing the effects of several independent variables at once. A **factorial design** lays out all the combinations of all the categories of the independent variables. That way you know how many participants you need, how many to assign to each condition, and how to run the analysis when the data are in.

It is widely believed that a good laugh has healing power. Rotton and Shats (1996) developed an experimental design to test this. They recruited 39 men and 39 women who were scheduled for orthopedic surgery. The patients were assigned randomly to one of nine groups—eight experimental groups and one control group. The patients in the eight treatment groups got to watch a movie in their room the day after their surgery.

There were three variables: choice, humor, and expectancy. The participants in the high-choice group got a list of 20 movies from which they chose 4. The participants in the low-choice group watched a movie that one of the people in the high-choice group had selected. Half the participants watched humorous movies and half watched action or adventure movies. Before watching their movie, half the participants read an article about the benefits of humor and half read an article about the healthful benefits of exciting movies.

Figure 4.4 is a branching tree diagram that shows how these three variables, each with two attributes, create the eight logical groups for Rotton and Shats's experiment. Table 4.1 shows the same eight-group design, but in a format that is more common. The eight nodes at the bottom of the tree in figure 4.4 and the sets of numbers in the eight boxes of table 4.1 are called conditions.

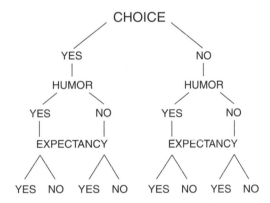

FIGURE 4.4.
The eight conditions in Rotton and Shats's 2 × 2 × 2 design.
SOURCE: J. Rotton and M. Shats, "Effects of State Humor, Expectancies, and Choice on Postsurgical Mood and Self-Medication: A Field Experiment," *Journal of Applied Social Psychology*, Vol. 26, pp. 1775–94, 1996. Copyright © 1996 by V. H. Winston & Son, Inc. Reprinted with permission.

The dependent variables in this study included a self-report by patients on the amount of pain they had and a direct measure of the amount of pain medication they took. All the patients had an access device that let them administer more or less of the analgesics that are used for controlling pain after orthopedic surgery.

In assessing the results of a factorial experiment, researchers look for **main effects** and **interaction effects**. Main effects are the effects of each independent variable on each dependent variable. Interaction effects are effects on dependent variables that occur as a result of *interaction* between two or more independent variables. In this case, Rotton and Shats wanted to know the effects of humor on postoperative pain, but they wanted to know the effect *in different contexts*: in the context of choosing the vehicle of humor or not, in the context of being led to believe that humor has healing benefits or not, and so on.

As it turned out, being able to choose their own movie had no effect when patients saw action films. But patients who saw humorous films and who had not been able to make their own choice of film gave themselves more pain killer than did patients who

Table 4.1   Three-Way, 2 × 2 × 2, Factorial Design

			Variable 3	
		Variable 2	Attribute 1	Attribute 2
Variable 1	Attribute 1	Attribute 1	1,1,1 Condition 1	1,1,2 Condition 2
		Attribute 2	1,2,1 Condition 3	1,2,2 Condition 4
	Attribute 2	Attribute 1	2,1,1 Condition 5	2,1,2 Condition 6
		Attribute 2	2,2,1 Condition 7	2,2,2 Condition 8

saw humorous films and had been able to make the selection themselves (Rotton and Shats 1996).

We'll look at how to measure these effects when we take up ANOVA, or analysis of variance, in chapter 21.

FURTHER READING

The classic experimental design and evaluation research: Cotton and Byrd-Bredbenner (2007); R. Jones (2008); Klass and Cothers (2000); Mishra et al. (1999).

Solomon four-group design: Holmes and Keffer (1995); Jorgensen et al. (1985); Probst (2003).

Quasi-experiments: Coleman (1999); Rotton et al. (1990); Shadish and Cook (2008); Yildirim et al. (2007).

Posttest-only design: Goodall and Appiah (2008); Ortberg et al. (2001); J. A. Robinson (1996); Trockel et al. (2008).

Case study methods: Gerring (2007); Merriam (2009); Naumes and Naumes (2006); Wolcott (2001, 2005); Yin (2008).

One group pretest posttest design: Chan et al. (2007); D'Eramo-Melkus et al. (2004); Derrick et al. (2008).

Static group comparison design: Coast (2002); Marlanai (2008); Pinkleton et al. (2008).

Interrupted time series design: Gorman and Huber (2007); Ramirez and Crano (2003); Villaveces et al. (2000).

Field experiments: Banerjee et al. (2009); Knecht and Martinez (2009); Scheerer et al. (2009).

Economic games in anthropology: Alvard (2004); Cronk (2007); Gil-White (2004); Lesorogol (2007); Wiessner (2009).

Case control: Beautrais et al. (1998); Pfeiffer et al. (2001).

Natural experiments: Becker et al. (2002); Morrison and Clements (1997); Zhu et al. (2007).

Naturalistic experiments: Guéguen et al. (2008); Keating et al. (2003); Levine et al. (2001); Walters and Curran (1996).

Lost-letter technique: Bridges and Coady (1996); Bridges et al. (2002); Hedge and Yousif (1992); Keating et al. (2003); D. S. Wilson et al. (2009).

Ethics of deception and debriefing: Barchard and Williams (2008); Korn (1997); Riach and Rich (2004).

5

Sampling I: The Basics

WHAT ARE SAMPLES AND WHY DO WE NEED THEM?

Informant accuracy, data validity, and ethical questions—like whether it's alright to deceive people in conducting experiments—are all measurement problems in research. The other big class of problems involves sampling: Given that your measurements are credible, how much of the world do they represent? How far can you generalize the results of your research?

The answer depends, first of all, on the kind of data in which you're interested. There are two kinds of data of interest to social scientists: **individual attribute data** and **cultural data**. These two kinds require different approaches to sampling.

Individual data are about *attributes of individuals in a population*. Each person has an age, for example; each person has an income; and each person has preferences for things like characteristics of a mate. If the idea to estimate the average age, or income, or preference in a population—that is, to estimate some **population parameters**—then a scientifically drawn, unbiased sample is a must.

By "scientifically drawn," I mean random selection of cases so that *every unit of analysis has an equal chance of being chosen for study*.

Cultural data are different. We expect cultural facts to be shared, so cultural data require experts. If you want to understand a process—like breast-feeding, or the making up of a guest list for a wedding, or a shaman's treatment of a sick person—then you want people who can offer expert explanations about the cultural norm and about variations on that norm (Handwerker et al. 1997). It's one thing to ask: "How many cows did *you* give to your in-laws as bride price when you got married?" It's quite another thing to ask: "Why do men who get married around here deliver cows to their in-laws? . . . And how many do men usually give?"

Individual attribute data require **probability sampling**; cultural data require **nonprobability sampling**. This chapter is about the basics of probability sampling, which will take us into a discussion of probability theory, variance, and distributions in chapter 6. We'll get to nonprobability sampling in chapter 7.

WHY THE UNITED STATES STILL HAS A CENSUS

If samples were just easier and cheaper to study but failed to produce useful data, there wouldn't be much to say for them. A study based on a random sample, however, is often *better* than one based on the whole population.

Since 1790, the United States has conducted a census once every 10 years in which every person in the country is supposed to be counted in order to apportion seats in the House of Representatives to the states. Lots of things can go wrong with counting. Heads of households are responsible for filling out and returning the census forms, but in 1990, only 63% of the mailed forms were returned, and that was down from 78% in 1970. The Bureau of the Census had to hire and train half a million people to track down all the people who had not been enumerated in the mailed-back forms. Even then, there were problems with the final numbers. Some college students were counted twice: Their parents had counted them on the mailed-back census form and then, on census day, some of those same students were tracked down again by enumerators who canvassed the dorms. Meanwhile, lots of other people (like illegal immigrants and people living in places to which the census takers would rather not go) were not being counted at all.

In 1997, the Bureau of the Census asked the U.S. Congress to allow sampling instead of counting for at least some parts of the 2000 Census. This caused a serious political problem: If sampling produced more accurate (and, presumably, higher) estimates of the number of citizens who are, say, homeless or who are migrant farm workers, this would benefit only certain states and might benefit the Democratic Party over the Republican Party. So, Congress rejected the proposal, citing the Article 1, Section 2 of the Constitution, which refer to the Census as an "actual Enumeration" (with a capital E, no less).

No getting around it: Actually enumerating means counting, not estimating, and the U.S. Supreme Court agreed, in 1999. To deal with the inaccuracies of a head count, the Bureau of the Census publishes adjustment tables, based on samples. In 2000, for example, the bureau determined that it had undercounted American Indians who live off reservations by about 53,000 (see U.S. Bureau of the Census n.d.).

IT PAYS TO TAKE SAMPLES AND TO STICK WITH THEM

If you are doing all the work yourself, it's next to impossible to interview more than a few hundred people. Even in a community of just 1,000 households, you'd need several interviewers to reach everyone. Interviewers may not use the same wording of questions; they may not probe equally well on subjects that require sensitive interviewing; they may not be equally careful in recording data on field instruments and in coding data for analysis. The more personnel there are on any project, the greater the instrumentation threat and the more risk to the validity of the data.

Most important, you have no idea how much error is introduced by these problems. A well-chosen sample, interviewed by people who have similarly high skills in getting data, has a known chance of being incorrect on any variable. (Careful, though: If you have a project that requires multiple interviewers and you try to skimp on personnel, you run a big risk. Overworked or poorly trained interviewers will cut corners; see chapter 8.)

Furthermore, studying an entire population may pose a history threat to the internal validity of your data. If you *don't* add interviewers, it may take you so long to complete your research that events intervene that make it impossible to interpret your data.

For example, suppose you are interested in how people in a community feel about being relocated in anticipation of a new dam coming on line and their land being flooded. You decide to interview *all* 210 adults in the community. It's difficult to get some people at home, but you figure that you'll just do the survey, a little at a time, while you're doing other things during your year in the field.

About 6 months into your fieldwork, you've gotten 160 interviews on the topic—only 50 to go. Just about that time, the courts adjudicate a particularly sore point that has been in dispute for a decade regarding access to a particular sacred site. All of a sudden, the picture changes. Your "sample" of 160 is biased toward those people whom it was easy to find, and you have no idea what *that* means. And even if you could now get those remaining 50 informants, their opinions may have been radically changed by the court judgment. The opinions of the 160 informants who already talked to you may have also changed.

Now you're really stuck. You can't simply throw together the 50 and the 160, because you have no idea what that will do to your results. Nor can you compare the 160 and the 50 as representing the community's attitudes before and after the judgment. Neither sample is representative of the community.

If you had taken a representative sample of 60 people in a single week early in your fieldwork, you'd now be in much better shape because you'd know the potential sampling error in your study. (I'll discuss how you know this later on in this chapter.) When historical circumstances (the surprise court judgment, for example) require it, you could interview the same sample of 60 again (in what is known as a **panel study**), or take another representative sample of the same size and see what differences there are before and after the critical event.

In either case, *you are better off with the sample than with the whole population.* By the way, there is no guarantee that a week is quick enough to avoid the problem described here. It's just less likely to be a problem.

SAMPLING FRAMES

If you can get it, the first thing you need for a good sample is a good **sampling frame**. (I say, "If you can get it," because a lot of social research is done on populations for which no sampling frame exists. More on this at the end of this chapter.) A sampling frame is a list of units of analysis *from which* you take a sample and *to which* you generalize.

A sampling frame may be a telephone directory, or the tax rolls of a community, or a census of a community that you do yourself. In the United States, the city directories (published by R. L. Polk and Company) are available for many towns and cities at the local library or Chamber of Commerce. Professional survey researchers in the United States often purchase samples from firms that keep up-to-date databases just for this purpose.

For many projects, though, especially projects that involve field research, you have to get your own census of the population you are studying. Whether you work in a village or a hospital, a census gives you a sampling frame from which to take many samples during a research project. It also gives you a basis for comparison if you go back to the same community later.

SIMPLE RANDOM SAMPLES

To get a **simple random sample** of 200 out of 640 people in a village, you number each individual from 1 to 640 and then take a random grab of 200 out of the numbers from 1 to 640. Most packages for statistical analysis have built in random-number generators (Internet addresses for several programs are given in appendix E), and you can create random samples by using one of the random-number generators on the Internet—like the one at http://www.randomizer.org/form.htm.

When you have your list of random numbers, then whoever goes with each one is in the sample. Period. If there are 1,230 people in the population and your list of random numbers says that you have to interview person #212, then do it. No fair leaving out some people because they are members of the elite and probably wouldn't want to give you the time of day. No fair leaving out people you don't like or don't want to work with. None of that.

In the real world of research, of course, random samples are tampered with all the time. (And no snickering here about the "real world" of research. Social research—in universities, in marketing firms, in polling firms, in the military—is a multibillion-dollar-a-year industry in the United States alone—and that's real enough for most people.) A common form of meddling with samples is when door-to-door interviewers find a sample selectee not at home and go to the nearest house for a replacement. This can have dramatically bad results.

Suppose you go out to interview between 10 A.M. and 4 P.M. People who are home during these hours tend to be old, or sick, or mothers with small children. Those same people are home in the evening, too, but now they're joined by all the single people home from work, so the average family size goes down.

Telephone survey researchers call back from three to 10 times before replacing a member of a sample. When survey researchers suspect (from prior work) that, say, 25% of a sample won't be reachable, even after call-backs, they increase their original sample size by 25% so the final sample will be both the right size and representative.

SYSTEMATIC RANDOM SAMPLING

If you have a big, unnumbered sampling frame, like the 51,413 students at the University of Florida in 2008, then simple random sampling is nearly impossible. You would have to number all those names first. Instead, you can do **systematic random sampling**. For this, you need a **random start** and a **sampling interval**, N. You enter the sampling frame at the random start and take every Nth person (or item) in the frame. If you have a printout of 51,413 names, listed 400 to a page, select a single random number between 1 and 51,413. If the random number is 9,857, the listing will be 257 names down from the top of page 25.

The sampling interval depends on the size of the population and the number of units in your sample. If there are 51,413 people in the population, and you are sampling 400 of them, then after you enter the sampling frame (the list of 51,413 names) you need to take every 128th person (400 × 128 = 51,200) to ensure that every person has *at least one chance* of being chosen. If there are 640 people in a population, and you are sampling 200 of them, then you would take every 4th person. If you get to the end of the list and you are at number 2 in an interval of 4, just go to the top of the list, start at 3, and keep on going (box 5.1).

Sampling from a Telephone Book

Systematic sampling is fine if you know that the sampling frame has 51,413 elements. What do you do when the size of the sampling frame is unknown? A big telephone book is an unnumbered sampling frame of unknown size. To use this kind of sampling frame, first determine the number of pages that actually contain listings. To do this, jot down the number of the first and last pages on which listings appear. Most phone books begin with a lot of pages that do not contain listings.

Suppose the listings begin on page 30 and end on page 520. Subtract 30 from 520 and add 1 (520 − 30 + 1 = 491) to calculate the number of pages that carry listings.

Then note the number of columns per page and the number of lines per column (count all the lines in a column, even the blank ones).

Suppose the phone book has three columns and 96 lines per column (this is quite typical). To take a random sample of 200 nonbusiness listings from this phone book, take a random sample of 400 page numbers (yes, 400) out of the 491 page numbers between 30 and 520. Just think of the pages as a numbered sampling frame of 491 elements. Next,

BOX 5.1

PERIODICITY AND SYSTEMATIC SAMPLING

Systematic sampling *usually* produces a representative sample, but be aware of the **periodicity** problem. Suppose you're studying a big retirement community in South Florida. The development has 30 identical buildings. Each has six floors, with 10 apartments on each floor, for a total of 1,800 apartments. Now suppose that each floor has one big corner apartment that costs more than the others and attracts a slightly more affluent group of buyers. If you do a systematic sample of every 10th apartment, then, depending on where you entered the list of apartments, you'd have a sample of 180 corner apartments or no corner apartments at all.

David and Mary Hatch (1947) studied the Sunday society pages of the *New York Times* for the years 1932–1942. They found only stories about weddings of Protestants and concluded that the elite of New York must therefore be Protestant. Cahnman (1948) pointed out that the Hatches had studied only June issues of the *Times*. It seemed reasonable. After all, aren't most society weddings in June? Well, yes. Protestant weddings. Upper-class Jews married in other months. The *Times* covered those weddings, but the Hatches missed them.

You can avoid the periodicity problem by doing simple random sampling, but if that's not possible, another solution is to make two systematic passes through the population using different sampling intervals. Then you can compare the two samples one a few independent variables, like age or years of education. Any differences should be attributable to sampling error. If they're not, then you might have a periodicity problem.

take a sample of 400 column numbers. Since there are three columns, you want 400 random choices of the numbers 1, 2, 3. Finally, take a sample of 400 line numbers. Since there are 96 lines, you want 400 random numbers between 1 and 96.

Match up the three sets of numbers and pick the sample of listings in the phone book. If the first random number between 30 and 520 is 116, go to page 116. If the first random number between 1 and 3 is 3, go to column 3. If the first random number between 1 and 96 is 43, count down 43 lines. Decide if the listing is eligible. It may be a blank line or a business. That's why you generate 400 sets of numbers to get 200 good listings.

Telephone books don't actually make good sampling frames—too many people have unlisted numbers (which is why we have random digit dialing—see chapter 9). But because everyone knows what a phone book looks like, it makes a good example for learning how to sample big, unnumbered lists of things, like the list of Catholic priests in Paraguay or the list of orthopedic surgeons in California.

STRATIFIED SAMPLING

Stratified random sampling ensures that key subpopulations are included in your sample. You divide a population (a sampling frame) into subpopulations (subframes), based on key independent variables and then take a random (unbiased), sample from each of those subpopulations. You might divide the population into men and women, or into rural and urban subframes—or into key age groups (18–34, 35–49, etc.) or key income groups. As the main sampling frame gets divided by key *independent* variables, the subframes presumably get more and more homogeneous with regard to the key *dependent* variable in the study.

In 2009, for example, the Quinnipiac University Poll asked a representative sample of 2,041 registered voters in the United States the following question: Do you think abortion should be legal in all cases, legal in most cases, illegal in most cases or illegal in all cases? Across all voters, 52% said that abortion should be legal in all (15%) or most (37%) cases and 41% said it should be illegal in all (14%) or most (27%) cases. (The remaining 7% had no opinion.)

These facts hide some important differences across religious, political, and other subgroups. Among Catholic voters, 50% said that abortion should be legal in all (8%) or most (42%) cases; among Jewish voters, 86% said that abortion should be legal in all (33%) or most (53%) cases. Among registered Democrats, 66% favored legal abortion in all or most cases; among registered Republicans, 30% took that position (Quinnipiac University 2009). Sampling from smaller chunks (by age, gender, and so on) ensures not only that you capture the variation, but that you also wind up understanding how that variation is distributed.

This is called **maximizing the between-group variance** and **minimizing the within-group variance** for the independent variables in a study. *It's what you want to do in building a sample* because it reduces sampling error and thus makes samples more precise.

This sounds like a great thing to do, but you have to *know what the key independent variables are*. Shoe size is almost certainly not related to what people think is the ideal number of children to have. Gender and generation, however, seem like plausible variables on which to stratify a sample. So, if you are taking a poll to find out the ideal number of children, you might divide the adult population into, say, four generations: 15–29, 30–44, 45–59, and over 59.

With two genders, this creates a **sampling design** with eight strata: men 15–29, 30–44, 45–59, and over 59; women 15–29, 30–44, 45–59, and over 59. Then you take a random sample of people from each of the eight strata and run your poll. If your hunch about the importance of gender and generation is correct, you'll find the attitudes of men and the attitudes of women more homogeneous than the attitudes of men and women thrown together.

Table 5.1 shows the distribution of gender and **age cohorts** for St. Lucia in 2001. The numbers in parentheses are percentages of the total population 15 and older (106,479), not percentages of the column totals.

Table 5.1   Estimated Population by Sex and Age Groups for St. Lucia, 2001

Age cohort	Males	Females	Total
15–29	21,097 (19.8%)	22,177 (20.8%)	43,274 (40.6%)
30–44	15,858 (14.9%)	16,763 (15.7%)	32,621 (30.6%)
45–59	8,269 (7.8%)	8,351 (7.8%)	16,620 (15.6%)
>59	7,407 (7%)	6,557 (6.2%)	13,964 (13.1%)
Total	52,631 (49.5%)	53,848 (50.5%)	106,479 (100%)

SOURCE: Govt. Statistics, St. Lucia. http://www.stats.gov.lc/cen2001.htm.

A **proportionate stratified random sample** of 800 respondents would include 112 men between the ages of 30 and 44 (14% of 800 = 112), but 120 women between the ages of 30 and 44 (15% of 800 = 120), and so on.

Watch out, though. We're asking people about their ideal family size and thinking about stratifying by gender because we're accustomed to thinking in terms of gender on questions about family size. But gender-associated preferences are changing rapidly in late industrial societies, and we might be way off base in our thinking. Separating the population into gender strata might just be creating unnecessary work. Worse, it might introduce unknown error. If your guess about age and gender being related to desired number of children is wrong, then using table 5.1 to create a sampling design will just make it harder for you to discover your error (box 5.2).

BOX 5.2

THE RULES ON STRATIFYING SAMPLES

Here are the rules on stratification: (1) If differences on a dependent variable are large across strata like age, sex, ethnic group, and so on, then stratifying a sample is a great idea. (2) If differences are small, then stratifying just adds unnecessary work. (3) If you are uncertain about the independent variables that could be at work in affecting your dependent variable, then leave well enough alone and don't stratify the sample. *You can always stratify the data* you collect and test various stratification schemes in the analysis instead of in the sampling.

Disproportionate Sampling

Disproportionate stratified random sampling is appropriate whenever an important subpopulation is likely to be underrepresented in a simple random sample or in a stratified random sample. Suppose you are doing a study of factors affecting grade-point averages among college students. You suspect that the independent variable called "race" is, in some way, associated with the dependent variable.

Suppose further that 5% of the student population is African American and that you have time and money to interview 400 students out of the population of 8,000. If you took 10,000 samples of 400 each from the population (replacing the 400 each time), then the average number of African Americans in all the samples would approach 20—that is, 5% of the sample.

But you are going to take *one* sample of 400. It might contain exactly 20 (5%) African Americans; on the other hand, it might contain just 5 (1.25%) African Americans. To ensure that you have enough data on African American students and on white students, you put the African Americans and the Whites into separate *strata* and draw two random samples of 200 each. The African Americans are disproportionately sampled by a factor of 10 (200 instead of the expected 20).

Native Americans comprise just 1.3% of the population of the United States. If you take 1,000 samples of 1,000 Americans at random, you expect to run into about 13 Native Americans, on average, across all the samples. (Some samples will have no Native Americans and some may have 20, but on average you'll get about 13.) Without disproportionate sampling, Native Americans would be underrepresented in any national survey in the United States. When Sugarman et al. (1994) ran the National Maternal and Infant Health Survey in 1988, they used birth certificates dated July 1–December 31, 1988, from 35

Native American health centers as their sampling frame and selected 1,480 eligible mothers for the study of maternal and infant health in that population.

Weighting Results

One popular method for collecting data about daily activities is called **experience sampling** (Csikszentmihalyi and Larson 1987; Hektner et al. 2007). You give a sample of people a beeper or a cell phone. They carry it around and you beep or call them at random times during the day. They fill out a little form (either on paper or on a PDA) about what they're doing at the time. (We'll look more closely at this method in chapter 14.)

Suppose you want to contrast what people do on weekends with what they do during the week. If you beep people, say, eight times during each day, you'll wind up with 40 reports for each person for the 5-day workweek but only 16 forms for each person for each 2-day weekend because you've sampled the two strata—weekdays and weekends—proportionately.

If you want more data points for the weekend, you might beep people 12 times on Saturday and 12 times on Sunday. That gives you 24 data points, but you've disproportionately sampled one stratum. The weekend represents 2/7, or 28.6% of the week, but you've got 64 data points and 24 of them, or 37.5%, are about the weekend. Before comparing any data across the strata, you need to make the weekend data and the weekday data statistically comparable.

This is where **weighting** comes in. Multiply each weekday data point by 1.50 so that the 40 data points become worth 60 and the 24 weekend data points are again worth exactly 2/7 of the total.

You should also weight your data when you have unequal response rates in a stratified sample. Suppose you sample 200 farmers and 200 townspeople in a rural African district where 60% of the families are farmers and 40% are residents of the local town. Of the 400 potential informants, 178 farmers and 163 townspeople respond to your questions. If you compare the answers of farmers and townspeople on a variable, you'll need to weight each farmer's data by 178/163 = 1.09 times each herder's data on that variable. That takes care of the unequal response rates.

Then, you'll need to weight each farmer's data as counting 1.5 times each townsperson's data on the variable. That takes care of the fact that there are half again as many farmers as there are people living in town. Weighting is a simple procedure available in all major statistical analysis packages.

CLUSTER SAMPLING AND COMPLEX SAMPLING DESIGNS

Cluster sampling is based on the fact that people act out their lives in more or less natural groups, or "clusters," like geographic areas (counties, precincts, states), and institutions (like schools, churches, brotherhoods, credit unions, and so on). By sampling from these clusters, we narrow the sampling field from large, heterogeneous chunks to small, homogeneous ones that are relatively easy to find. This minimizes travel time in reaching scattered units of data collection. It also lets you sample populations for which there are no convenient lists or frames.

For example, there are no lists of schoolchildren in large cities, but children cluster in schools. There *are* lists of schools, so you can take a sample of them, and then sample children within each school selected.

Laurent et al. (2003) wanted to assess the rate of sexually transmitted diseases among unregistered female sex workers in Dakar, Senegal. By definition, unregistered means no list, so the researchers used a two-stage cluster sample. They created a sampling frame of all registered and all clandestine bars in Dakar, plus all the unregistered brothels, and all the nightclubs. They did this over a period of several months with the help of some women prostitutes, some local physicians who had treated those women, and two social workers, each of whom had worked with female sex workers for over 25 years. Laurent et al. calculated that they needed 94 establishments, so they chose a simple random of places from the list of 183. Then they went in teams to each of the 94 places and interviewed all the unregistered prostitutes who were there at the time of the visit.

Anthony and Suely Anderson (1983) wanted to compare people in Bacabal County, Brazil, who exploited the babassu palm with those who didn't. There was no list of households, but they managed to get a list of the 344 named hamlets in the county. They divided the hamlets into those that supplied whole babassu fruits to new industries in the area and those that did not. Only 10.5% of the 344 hamlets supplied fruits to the industries, so the Andersons selected 10 hamlets randomly from each group for their survey. In other words, in the first stage of the process they stratified the clusters and took a disproportionate random sample from one of the clusters.

Next, they did a census of the 20 hamlets, collecting information on every household and particularly whether the household had land or was landless. At this stage, then, they created a sampling frame (the census) and stratified the frame into landowning and landless households. Finally, they selected 89 landless households randomly for interviewing. This was 25% of the stratum of landless peasants. Since there were only 61 landowners, they decided to interview the entire population of this stratum.

PROBABILITY PROPORTIONATE TO SIZE

The best estimates of a parameter are produced in samples taken from clusters of equal size. When clusters are not equal in size, then samples should be taken **PPS**—with **probability proportionate to size**.

Suppose you had money and time to do 800 household interviews in a city of 50,000 households. You intend to select 40 blocks, out of a total of 280, and do 20 interviews in each block. You want each of the 800 households in the final sample to have exactly the same probability of being selected.

Should each block be equally likely to be chosen for your sample? No, because census blocks never contribute equally to the total population from which you will take your final sample. A block that has 100 households in it *should* have twice the chance of being chosen for 20 interviews as a block that has 50 households and half the chance of a block that has 200 households.

When you get down to the block level, each household on a block with 100 residences has a 20% (20/100) chance of being selected for the sample; each household on a block with 300 residences has only a 6.7% (20/300) chance of being selected.

Lené Levy-Storms wanted to talk to older Samoan women in Los Angeles County about mammography. The problem was not that women were reticent to talk about the subject. The problem was how do you find a representative sample of older Samoan women in Los Angeles County?

From prior ethnographic research, Levy-Storms knew that Samoan women regularly attend churches where the minister is Samoan. She went to the president of the Samoan Federation of America in Carson, California, and he suggested nine cities in L.A. County where Samoans were concentrated. There were 60 churches with Samoan ministers in the nine cities, representing nine denominations. Levy-Storms asked each of the ministers to estimate the number of female church members who were over 50 years old. Based on these estimates, she chose a PPS sample of 40 churches (so that churches with more or fewer older women were properly represented). This gave her a sample of 299 Samoan women over 50. This clever sampling strategy really worked: Levy-Storms contacted the 299 women and wound up with 290 interviews—a 97% cooperation rate (Levy-Storms and Wallace 2003).

PPS sampling is called for under three conditions: (1) when you are dealing with large, unevenly distributed populations (such as cities that have high-rise and single-family neighborhoods); (2) when your sample is large enough to withstand being broken up into a lot of pieces (clusters) without substantially increasing the sampling error; and (3) when you have data on the population of many small blocks in a population and can calculate their respective proportionate contributions to the total population.

PPS Samples in the Field

What do you do when you don't have neat clusters and neat sampling frames printed out on a computer by a reliable government agency? The answer is to place your trust in randomness and *create* maximally heterogeneous clusters from which to take a random sample.

Draw or get a map of the area you are studying. Place 100 numbered dots around the edge of the map. Try to space the numbers equidistant from one another, but don't worry if they are not. Select a pair of numbers at random and draw a line between them. Now select another pair of numbers (be sure to replace the first pair before selecting the second) and draw a line between them. In the unlikely event that you choose the same pair twice, simply choose a third pair. Keep doing this, replacing the numbers each time. After you've drawn about 50 lines, you can begin sampling.

Notice that the lines drawn across the map in figure 5.1 create a lot of wildly uneven spaces. Because you don't know the distribution of population density in the area you are studying, this technique maximizes the chance that you will properly survey the popula-

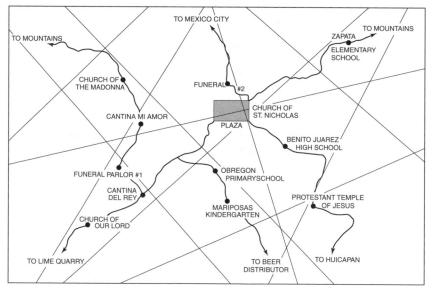

FIGURE 5.1.
Creating maximally heterogeneous sampling clusters in the field.

tion, more or less PPS. By creating a series of (essentially) random chunks of different sizes, you distribute the error you might introduce by not knowing the density, and that distribution lowers the possible error.

Number the uneven spaces created by the lines and choose some of them at random. Go to those spaces, number the households, and select an appropriate number at random. Remember, you want to have the same number of households from *each* made-up geographic cluster, no matter what its size. If you are doing 400 interviews, you would select 20 geographic chunks and do 20 interviews or behavioral observations in each.

My colleagues and I used this method in 1986 to find out how many people in Mexico City knew someone who died in that city's monster earthquake the year before (Bernard et al. 1989). Instead of selecting households, though, my interview team went to each geographic chunk we'd selected and stopped the first 10 people they ran into on the street at each point. This is called a **street-intercept survey** (box 5.3).

BOX 5.3

STREET- AND MALL-INTERCEPT SAMPLING

K. W. Miller et al. (1997) sampled blocks of streets in a city and did a street-intercept survey of African American men. They compared the results to a random-digit dialing telephone survey in the same city. The street-intercept survey did a better job of representing the population than did the telephone survey. For one thing, the response rate for the street intercept survey was over 80%. Compare that to the typical telephone survey, where half or more of the respondents may refuse to be interviewed. Also, with telephone surveys, the socioeconomic profile of respondents is generally higher than in the population (partly because more affluent people agree more often to be interviewed on the telephone). A variant of this method is mall-intercept sampling, used widely in marketing (**Further Reading**: street and mall intercept surveys).

Handwerker (1993) used a map-sampling method in his study of sexual behavior on Barbados. In his variation of map sampling, you generate 10 random numbers between 0 and 360 (the degrees on a compass). Next, put a dot in the center of a map that you will use for the sampling exercise, and use a protractor to identify the 10 randomly chosen compass points. You then draw lines from the dot in the center of the map through all 10 points to the edge of the map and interview people (or observe houses, or whatever) along those lines. (See Duranleau [1999] for an empirical test of the power of map sampling.)

If you use this technique, you may want to establish a sampling interval (like every fifth case, beginning with the third case). If you finish interviewing along the lines and don't have enough cases, you can take another random start, with the same or a different interval and start again. Be careful of periodicity, though (box 5.4).

Camilla Harshbarger (1995) used another variation of map sampling in her study of farmers in North West Province, Cameroon (1995). To create a sample of 400 farmers, she took a map of a rural community and drew 100 dots around the perimeter. She used a random number table to select 50 pairs of dots and drew lines between them. She numbered the points created by the crossing of lines, and chose 80 of those points at

BOX 5.4

COMBINING MAP SAMPLING AND CLUSTER
SAMPLING

In chapter 4, I mentioned a study in which Lambros Comitas and I compared
Greeks who had returned from what was then West Germany as labor migrants
with Greeks who had never left their country (Bernard and Comitas 1978). There
were no lists of returned migrants, but we thought we could do a cluster sample
by locating the children of returned migrants in the Athens schools and then
use the children to select a sample of their parents.

The problem was, we couldn't even get a list of schools in Athens. So we
took a map of the city and divided it into small bits by laying a grid over it. Then
we took a random sample of the bits and sent interviewers to find the school
nearest each bit selected. The interviewers asked the principal of each school to
identify the children of returned labor migrants. (It was easy for the principal to
do, by the way. The principal said that all the returned migrant children spoke
Greek with a German accent.) That way, we were able to make up two lists for
each school: one of children who had been abroad, and one of children who
had not. By sampling children randomly from those lists at each school, we
were able to select a representative sample of parents.

random. Then, Harshbarger and her field assistants interviewed one farmer in each of the
five compounds they found closest to each of the 80 selected dots. (If you use this dot
technique, remember to include the points along the edges of the map in your sample or
you'll miss households on those edges.)

There are times when a random, representative sample is out of the question. After
Harshbarger did those interviews with 400 randomly selected farmers in North West
Province, Cameroon, she set out to interview Fulani cattle herders in the same area. Here's
what Harshbarger wrote about her experience in trying to interview the herders:

> It was rainy season in Wum and the roads were a nightmare. The grazers lived very far
> out of town and quite honestly, my research assistants were not willing to trek to the
> compounds because it would have taken too much time and we would never have
> finished the job. I consulted X and he agreed to call selected people to designated school
> houses on certain days. We each took a room and administered the survey with each
> individual grazer.
>
> Not everyone who was called came for the interview, so we ended up taking who we
> could get. Therefore, the Wum grazer sample was not representative and initially that
> was extremely difficult for me to accept. Our team had just finished the 400-farmer
> survey of Wum that *was* representative, and after all that work it hit me hard that the
> grazer survey would not be. To get a representative sample, I would have needed a four-
> wheel drive vehicle, a driver, and more money to pay research assistants for a lengthy
> stay in the field. Eventually, I forgave myself for the imperfection. (personal communi-
> cation)

The lessons here are clear: (1) If you are ever in Harshbarger's situation, you, too, can forgive yourself for having a nonrepresentative sample. (2) Even then, like Harshbarger, you should feel badly about it (**Further Reading:** space sampling).

Maximizing Between-Group Variance: The Wichita Study

Whenever you do multistage cluster sampling, be sure to take as large a sample as possible from the largest, most heterogeneous clusters. The larger the cluster, the larger the **between-group variance**; the smaller the cluster, the smaller the between-group variance. Counties in the same state in the United States are more like each other for many variables—such as average income, distribution of racial and ethnic groups, average age, etc.—than states are. Towns within a county are more like each other than counties are; neighborhoods in a town are more like each other than towns are. And blocks within a neighborhood are more like each other than neighborhoods are. In sampling, the rule is: *maximize between-group variance.*

What does this mean in practice? Following is an actual example of multistage sampling from John Hartman's study of Wichita, Kansas (Hartman 1978; Hartman and Hedblom 1979:160). At the time of the study, in the mid-1970s, Wichita had a population of about 193,000 persons over the age of 16. This was the population to which the study team wanted to generalize. The team decided that they could afford only 500 interviews. There are 82 census tracts in Wichita from which they randomly selected 20. These 20 tracts then became the actual population of their study. We'll see in a moment how well their actual study population simulated (represented) the study population to which they wanted to generalize.

Hartman and Hedblom added up the total population in the 20 tracts and divided the population of *each tract* by the total. This gave the percentage of people that each tract, or cluster, contributed to the new population total. The researchers were going to do 500 interviews, so each tract was assigned that percentage of the interviews. If there were 50,000 people in the 20 tracts, and one of the tracts had a population of 5,000, or 10% of the total, then 50 interviews (10% of the 500) would be done in that tract.

Next, the team numbered the blocks in each tract and selected blocks at random until they had enough for the number of interviews that were to be conducted in that tract. When a block was selected it stayed in the pool, so in some cases more than one interview was to be conducted in a single block. This did not happen very often, and the team wisely left it up to chance to determine this.

This study team made some excellent decisions that maximized the heterogeneity (and hence the representativeness) of their sample. As clusters get smaller and smaller (as you go from tract to block to household, or from village to neighborhood to household), the homogeneity of the units of analysis within the clusters gets greater and greater. People in one census tract or village are more like each other than people in different tracts or villages. People in one census block or barrio are more like each other than people across blocks or barrios. And people in households are more like each other than people in households across the street or over the hill.

This is very important. Most researchers would have no difficulty with the idea that they should only interview one person in a household because, for example, husbands and wives often have similar ideas about things and report similar behavior with regard to kinship, visiting, health care, child care, and consumption of goods and services. Somehow, the lesson becomes less clear when new researchers move into clusters that are larger than households.

But the rule stands: Maximize heterogeneity of the sample by taking as many of the biggest clusters in your sample as you can, and as many of the next biggest, and so on, always at the expense of the number of clusters at the bottom where homogeneity is greatest. Take more tracts or villages and fewer blocks per tract or barrios per village. Take more blocks per tract or barrios per village and fewer households per block or barrio. Take more households and fewer persons per household.

Many survey researchers say that, as a rule, you should have no fewer than five households in a census block. The Wichita group did not follow this rule but only had enough money and person power to do 500 interviews and they wanted to maximize the likelihood that their sample would represent faithfully the characteristics of the 193,000 adults in their city.

The Wichita team drew two samples—one main sample and one alternate sample. Whenever they could not get someone on the main sample, they took the alternate. That way, they maximized the representativeness of their sample because the alternates were chosen with the same randomized procedure as the main respondents in their survey. They were not forced to take "next door-neighbors" when a main respondent wasn't home. (This kind of winging it in survey research has a tendency to clobber the representativeness of samples. In the United States, at least, interviewing only people who are at home during the day produces results that represent women with small children, shut-ins, telecommuters, and the elderly—and not much else.)

Next, the Wichita team randomly selected the households for interview within each block. This was the third stage in this multistage cluster design. The fourth stage consisted of flipping a coin to decide whether to interview a man or a woman in households with both. Whoever came to the door was asked to provide a list of those in the household over 16 years of age. If there was more than one eligible person in the household, the interviewer selected one at random, conforming to the decision made earlier on sex of respondent.

Table 5.2 shows how well the Wichita team did. All in all, they did very well. In addition to the variables shown in the table here, the Wichita sample was a fair representation of marital status and occupation, though it was off a bit on education. For example, at the time, 8% of the population of Wichita had less than 8 years of schooling, but only 4% of the sample had this characteristic. Only 14% of the general population had completed from 1 to 2 years of college, but 22% of the sample had that much education.

Table 5.2   Comparison of Survey Results and Population Parameters for the Wichita Study by Hartman and Hedblom

	Wichita in 1973	Hartman and Hedblom's Sample for 1973
White	86.8%	82.8%
African	9.7%	10.8%
Chicano	2.5%	2.6%
Other	1.0%	2.8%
Male	46.6%	46.9%
Female	53.4%	53.1%
Median age	38.5	39.5

SOURCE: *Methods for the Social Sciences: A Handbook for Students and Non-Specialists*, by J. J. Hartman and J. H. Hedblom, 1979, p. 165. Reproduced with permission of Greenwood Publishing Group.

All things considered, though, the sampling procedure followed in the Wichita study was a model of technique, and the results show it. Whatever they found out about the

500 people they interviewed, the researchers could be very confident that the results were generalizable to the 193,000 adults in Wichita.

In sum: If you don't have a sampling frame for a population, try to do a multistage cluster sample, narrowing down to natural clusters that do have lists. Sample heavier at the higher levels in a multistage sample and lighter at the lower stages (box 5.5).

BOX 5.5

MULTISTAGE CLUSTER SAMPLING IN THE FIELD

Just in case you're wondering if you can do this under difficult field conditions, Oyuela-Cacedo and Vieco-Albarracín (1999) studied the social organization of the Ticuna Indians of the Colombian Amazon. Most of the 9,500 Ticuna in Colombia are in 32 hamlets, along the Amazon, the Loreta Yacu, the Cotuhé, and the Putumayo Rivers. The Ticuna live in large houses that comprise from one to three families, including grandparents, unmarried children, and married sons with their wives and children. To get a representative sample of the Ticuna, Oyuela-Cacedo and Vieco-Albarracín selected six of the 32 hamlets along the four rivers and made a list of the household heads in those hamlets. Then, they numbered the household heads and randomly selected 50 women and 58 men. Oyuela-Cacedo and Vieco-Albarracín had to visit some of the selected houses several times to secure an interview, but they wound up interviewing all the members of their sample.

Is the sample representative? We can't know for sure, but take a look at figure 5.2. Figure 5.2a shows the distribution of the ages of the household heads in the sample; figure 5.2b shows the distribution of the number of children in the households of the sample. Both curves look very normal—just what we expect from variables like age and number of children (more about normal distributions in chapter 6). If the sample of Ticuna household heads represents what we expect from age and number of children, then any other variables the research team measured are likely (not guaranteed, just likely) to be representative, too.

HOW BIG SHOULD A SAMPLE BE?

There are two things you can do to get good samples. (1) You can ensure **sample accuracy** by making sure that every element in the population has an equal chance of being selected—that is, you can make sure the sample is unbiased. (2) You can ensure **sample precision** by increasing the size of unbiased samples. We've already discussed the importance of how to make samples unbiased. The next step is to decide how big a sample needs to be.

Sample size depends on: (1) the heterogeneity of the population or chunks of population (strata or clusters) from which you choose the elements; (2) how many population subgroups (that is, independent variables) you want to deal with simultaneously in your analysis; (3) the size of the phenomenon that you're trying to detect; and (4) how precise you want your **sample statistics** (or **parameter estimators**) to be.

1. **Heterogeneity of the population.** When all elements of a population have the same score on some measure, a sample of 1 will do. Ask a lot of people to tell you how many

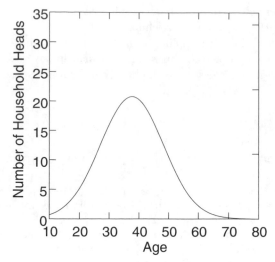

FIGURE 5.2a.

Distribution of the ages of Ticuna household heads.

SOURCE: Adapted from data in A. Oyuela-Cacedo and J. J. Vieco Albarracín, "Approximación cuantitativa a la organización social de los Ticuna del trapecio amazónico colombiano," *Revista Colombiana de Antropología*, Vol. 35, pp. 146–79, figure 1, p. 157, 1999.

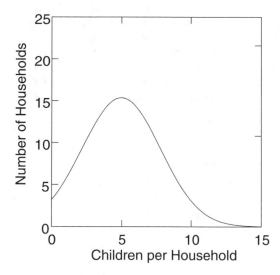

FIGURE 5.2b.

Distribution of the number of children in Ticuna households.

SOURCE: Adapted from data in A. Oyuela-Cacedo and J. J. Vieco Albarracín, "Approximación cuantitativa a la organización social de los Ticuna del trapecio amazónico colombiano," *Revista Colombiana de Antropología*, Vol. 35, pp. 146–79, table 6, p. 159, 1999.

days there are in a week and you'll soon understand that a big sample isn't going to uncover a lot of heterogeneity. But if you want to know what the average ideal family size is, you may need to cover a lot of social ground. People of different ethnicities, religions, incomes, genders, and ages may have very different ideas about this. (In fact, these independent variables may interact in complex ways. Multivariate analysis tells you about this interaction. We'll get to this in chapter 22.)

2. **The number of subgroups in the analysis**. Remember the **factorial design** problem in chapter 4 on experiments? We had three independent variables, each with two attributes, so we needed eight groups ($2^3 = 8$). It wouldn't do you much good to have, say, one experimental subject in each of those eight groups. If you're going to analyze all eight of the conditions in the experiment, you've got to fill each of the conditions with some reasonable number of subjects. If you have only 15 people in each of the eight conditions, then you need a sample of 120.

The same principle holds when you're trying to figure out how big a sample you need for a survey. If you have four age groups and two genders, you wind up with an eight-cell sampling design.

If all you want to know is a single proportion—like what percentage of people in a population approve or disapprove of something—then you need about 100 respondents to be 95% confident, within plus or minus 3 points, that your sample estimate is within 2 standard deviations of the population parameter (more about confidence limits, normal distributions, standard deviations, and parameters in a minute). But if you want to know whether women factory workers in Rio de Janeiro who earn less than $300 per month have different opinions than, say, middle-class women in Rio whose family income is more than $600 per month, then you'll need a bigger sample.

3. **The size of the subgroup**. If the population you are trying to study is rare and hard to find, and if you have to rely on a simple random sample of the entire population, you'll need a very large initial sample. A needs assessment survey of people over 75 in Florida took 72,000 phone calls to get 1,647 interviews—about 44 calls per interview (Henry 1990:88). This is because only 6.5% of Florida's population was over 75 at the time of the survey. By contrast, the monthly Florida survey of 600 representative consumers takes about 5,000 calls (about eight per interview). That's because just about everyone in the state 18 and older is a consumer and is eligible for the survey. [Christopher McCarty, personal communication]

The smaller the difference on any measure between two populations, the bigger the sample you need to detect that difference. Suppose you suspect that Blacks and Whites in a prison system have received different sentences for the same crime. Henry (1990:121) shows that a difference of 16 months in sentence length for the same crime would be detected with a sample of just 30 in each racial group (if the members of the sample were selected randomly, of course). To detect a difference of 3 months, however, you need 775 in each group.

4. **Precision**. This one takes us into sampling theory.

FURTHER READING

Street intercept surveys: Ross et al. (2006); Waltermaurer et al. (2003).
Mall-intercept survey: Bruwer and Haydam (1996); Bush and Hair (1985); Gates and Solomon (1982); Hornik and Ellis (1988); Wang and Heitmeyer (2006).
Space sampling: Daley et al. (2001); Lang et al. (2004).

6

Sampling II: Theory

DISTRIBUTIONS

At the end of this chapter, you should understand why it's possible to estimate *very accurately, most of the time,* the average age of the 228 million adults in the United States by talking to just 1,600 of them. And you should understand why you can also do this *pretty accurately, much of the time,* by talking to just 400 of them. Sampling theory is partly about **distributions**, which come in a variety of shapes. Figure 6.1 shows what is known as the **normal distribution**.

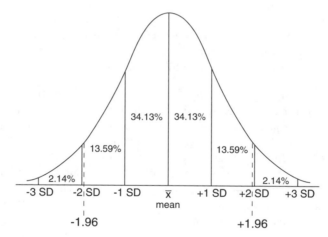

FIGURE 6.1.
The normal curve and the first, second, and third standard deviations.

THE NORMAL CURVE AND *Z*-SCORES

The so-called normal distribution is generated by a formula that can be found in many intro statistics texts. The distribution has a mean of 0 and a **standard deviation** of 1. The standard deviation is a measure of how much the scores in a distribution vary from the mean score. The larger the standard deviation, the more dispersion around the mean. Here's the formula for the standard deviation, or *sd*. (We will take up the *sd* again in chapter 20. The *sd* is the square root of the variance, which we'll take up in chapter 21.)

$$sd = \sqrt{\frac{\Sigma \, (x - \bar{x})^2}{n - 1}}$$

Formula 6.1

130

The symbol $\bar{x}$ in formula 6.1 is read "x-bar" and is used to signify the mean of a *sample*. The mean of a *population* (the parameter we want to estimate), is symbolized by μ (the Greek lower-case letter "mu," pronounced "myoo"). The standard deviation of a population is symbolized by σ (the Greek lower-case letter "sigma"), and the standard deviation of a sample is written as *SD* or *sd* or *s*. Read formula 6.1 as follows: The standard deviation is the square root of the sum of all the squared differences between every score in a set of scores and the mean, divided by the number of scores minus 1.

The standard deviation of a sampling distribution of means is the **standard error** of the mean, or *SEM*. The formula for calculating *SEM* is:

$$SEM \ \frac{sd}{\sqrt{n}} \qquad\qquad \textbf{Formula 6.2}$$

where *n* is the sample size. In other words, the standard error of the mean gives us an idea of how much a sample mean varies from the mean of the population that we're trying to estimate.

Suppose that in a sample of 100 merchants in a small town in Malaysia, you find that the average income is RM12,600 (about $3,500 in 2009 U.S. dollars), with a standard deviation of RM4,000 (RM is the symbol for the Malaysian Ringgit). The standard error of the mean is:

$$12,600 \ \pm \ \frac{4000}{\sqrt{100}} \ = \ 12,600 \ \pm \ 400$$

Do the calculation:

$$12,600 \ + \ 400 \ = \ 13,000$$
$$12,600 \ - \ 400 \ = \ 12,200$$

In normal distributions—that is, distributions that have a mean of 0 and a standard deviation of 1—exactly 34.135% of the area under the curve (the white space between the curve and the baseline) is contained in between the perpendicular line that represents the mean in the middle of the curve in figure 6.1 and the line that rises from the baseline at 1 standard deviation above and 1 standard deviation below the mean.

Appendix A is a table of *z*-scores, or **standard scores.** These scores are the number of standard deviations from the mean in a normal distribution, in increments of 1/100th of a standard deviation. For each *z*-score, beginning with 0.00 standard deviations (the mean) and on up to 3.09 standard deviations (on either side of the mean), appendix A shows the *percentage of the physical area under the curve of a normal distribution*. That percentage represents the percentage of cases that fall within any number of standard deviations above and below the mean in a normally distributed set of cases.

We see from appendix A that 34.13% of the area under the curve is one standard deviation above the mean and another 34.13% is one standard deviation below the mean. Thus, 68.26% of all scores in a normal distribution fall within one standard deviation of the mean. We also see from appendix A that 95.44% of all scores in a normal distribution fall within two standard deviations and that 99.7% fall within three standard deviations.

Look again at figure 6.1. You can see why so many cases are contained within 1 *sd* above and below the mean: The normal curve is tallest and fattest around the mean and much more of the area under the curve is encompassed in the first *sd* from the mean than is encompassed between the first and second *sd* from the mean.

If 95.44% of the area under a normal curve falls within two *sd* from the mean, and if 99.7% fall within 3 *sd*, then exactly 95% (a nice, round number) should fall within slightly less than two and exactly 99% should fall within slightly less than three standard deviations. And indeed, from appendix A, we see that 1.96 standard deviations above and below the mean account for 95% of all scores in a normal distribution and that 2.58 *sd* account for 99% of all scores. This, too, is shown in figure 6.1.

The normal distribution is an idealized form. In practice, many variables are not distributed in the perfectly symmetric shape we see in figure 6.1. Figure 6.2 shows some other shapes for distributions. Figure 6.2a shows a **bimodal distribution**. Suppose the *x*-axis in figure 6.2a is age, and the *y*-axis is the percentage of people who respond "yes" to the question "Did you like the beer commercial shown during the Superbowl yesterday?" The bimodal distribution shows that people in their 20s and people in their 60s liked the commercial, but others didn't.

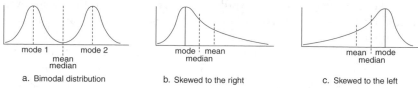

FIGURE 6.2.
Bimodal and skewed distributions.

Figure 6.2b and figure 6.2c are **skewed distributions**. A distribution can be skewed positively (with a long tail going off to the right) or negatively (with the tail going off to the left). Figures 6.2b and 6.2c look like the distributions of scores in two very different university courses. In figure 6.2b, most students got low grades, and there is a long tail of students who got high grades. In figure 6.2c, most students got relatively high grades, and there is a long tail of students who got lower grades.

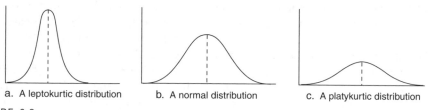

FIGURE 6.3.
Three symmetric distributions including the normal distribution.

The normal distribution is symmetric, but not all symmetric distributions are normal. Figure 6.3 shows three variations of a **symmetric distribution**—that is, distributions for which the mean and the median are the same. The one on the left is **leptokurtic** (from Greek, meaning "thin bulge") and the one on the right is **platykurtic** (meaning "flat bulge"). The curve in the middle is the famous bell-shaped, normal distribution. In a leptokurtic, symmetric distribution, the standard deviation is less than 1.0; and in a platykurtic, symmetric distribution, the standard deviation is greater than 1.0. The physical distance between marriage partners (whether among tribal people or urbanites) usually forms a leptokurtic distribution. People tend to marry people who live near them, and there are fewer and fewer marriages as the distance between partners increases (Sheets 1982). By contrast, we expect the distribution of height and weight of athletes in the

National Basketball Association to be more platykurtic across teams since coaches are all recruiting players of more-or-less similar build.

The shape of a distribution—normal, skewed, bimodal, and so on—contains a lot of information about what is going on, but it doesn't tell us *why* things turned out the way they did. A sample with a bimodal or highly skewed distribution is a hint that you might be dealing with more than one population or culture.

THE CENTRAL LIMIT THEOREM

The fact that many variables are not normally distributed would make sampling a hazardous business, were it not for the **central limit theorem**. According to this theorem, if you take many samples of a population, and *if the samples are big enough*, then:

1. The mean and the standard deviation of the sample means will usually approximate the true mean and standard deviation of the population. (You'll understand why this is so a bit later in the chapter, when we discuss confidence intervals.)
2. The distribution of sample means will approximate a normal distribution.

We can demonstrate both parts of the central limit theorem with some examples.

Part 1 of the Central Limit Theorem

Table 6.1 shows the per capita gross domestic product (PCGDP) for the 50 poorest countries in the world in 2007.

Here is a random sample of five of those countries: Uzbekistan, Senegal, Guinea, Rwanda, and Liberia. Consider these five as a **population** of units of analysis. In 2007, these countries had an annual per capita GDP, respectively of $704, $908, $452, $354, and $195 (U.S. dollars). These five numbers sum to $2,613 and their average, 2613/5, is $522.60.

There are 10 possible samples of two elements in any population of five elements. All 10 samples for the five countries in our example are shown in the left-hand column of table 6.2. The middle column shows the mean for each sample. This list of means is the **sampling distribution**. And the right-hand column shows the **cumulative mean**.

Notice that the mean of the means for all 10 samples of two elements—that is, the mean of the **sampling distribution**—is $522.60, which is *exactly the actual mean* per capita GDP of the five countries in the population. In fact, it must be: *The mean of all possible samples of size 2 is equal to the parameter that we're trying to estimate.*

Figure 6.4 (left) is a **frequency polygon** that shows the distribution of the five actual GDP values. A frequency polygon is just a histogram with lines connecting the tops of the bars so that the shape of the distribution is emphasized. Compare the shape of this distribution to the one in figure 6.4 (right) showing the distribution of the 10 sample means for the five GDP values we're dealing with here. That distribution looks more like the shape of the normal curve: It's got that telltale bulge in the middle.

Part 2 of the Central Limit Theorem

Figure 6.5 shows the distribution of the 50 data points for GDP in table 6.1. The range is quite broad, from $118 to $978 per year per person, and the shape of the distribution is multimodal.

The actual mean of the data in table 6.1—that is, the parameter we want to estimate—is $533.28. There are 2,118,760 samples of size 5 that can be taken from 50 ele-

Table 6.1 Per Capita Gross Domestic Product (PCGDP) in U.S. Dollars for the 50 Poorest Countries in the World, 2007

Country	PCGDP	Country	PCGDP
Burundi	118	Burkina Faso	483
DR-Congo	151	Mali	554
Zimbabwe	159	Tajikistan	555
Liberia	195	Comoros	556
Ethiopia	201	Cambodia	598
Guinea-Bissau	211	Haiti	612
Malawi	257	Benin	618
Eritrea	271	N. Korea	618
Niger	289	Ghana	647
Somalia	291	Chad	692
Sierra Leone	330	Kyrgyzstan	704
Afghanistan	345	Uzbekistan	704
Rwanda	354	Laos	711
Mozambique	362	Kiribati	762
Tanzania	368	Kenya	786
Gambia	377	Lesotho	797
Madagascar	377	Viet Nam	815
Myanmar	379	Mauritania	874
Togo	386	Senegal	908
Timor-Leste	393	Sao Tome and Principe	912
Central African Rep.	394	Papua New Guinea	953
Uganda	403	Yemen	967
Nepal	419	Zambia	974
Bangladesh	428	India	976
Guinea	452	Solomon Islands	978

SOURCE: United Nations, Dept. of Economic and Social Affairs, Economic and Social Development. http://unstats.un.org/unsd/demographic/products/socind/inc-eco.htm.

Table 6.2 All Samples of Two from Five Elements

Sample	Mean	Cumulative mean
Uzbekistan and Senegal	$(704 + 908)/2 = 806.0$	806.0
Uzbekistan and Guinea	$(704 + 452)/2 = 578.0$	1,384.0
Uzbekistan and Rwanda	$(704 + 354)/2 = 529.0$	1,913.0
Uzbekistan and Liberia	$(704 + 195)/2 = 449.5$	2,362.5
Senegal and Guinea	$(908 + 452)/2 = 680.0$	3,042.5
Senegal and Rwanda	$(908 + 354)/2 = 631.0$	3,673.5
Senegal and Liberia	$(908 + 195)/2 = 551.5$	4,225.0
Guinea and Rwanda	$(452 + 354)/2 = 403.0$	4,628.0
Guinea and Liberia	$(452 + 195)/2 = 323.5$	4,951.5
Liberia and Rwanda	$(195 + 354)/2 = 274.5$	5,226.0
	$\bar{x} = 5,226/10 = 522.6$	

ments. Table 6.3 shows the means from 10 samples of five countries chosen at random from the data in table 6.1.

Even in this small set of 10 samples, the mean is $504.72—quite close to the actual mean of $533.28. Figure 6.6 (left) shows the distribution of these samples. It has the look of a normal distribution straining to happen. Figure 6.6 (right) shows 20 samples of five from the 50 countries in table 6.1. The strain toward the normal curve is unmistakable and the mean of those 20 samples is $505.18.

The problem is that in real research, we don't get to take 10 or 20 samples. We have

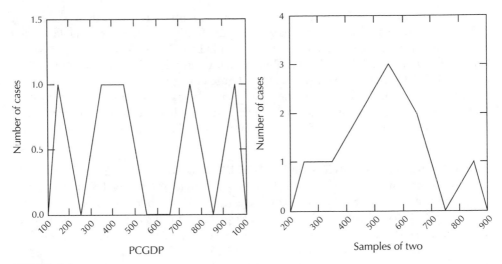

FIGURE 6.4.
Five cases and the distribution of samples of size 2 from those cases.

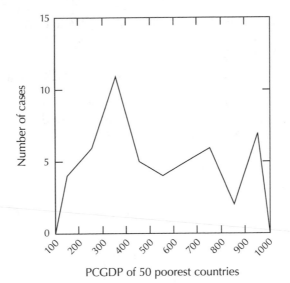

FIGURE 6.5.
The distribution of the 50 data points for GDP in table 6.1.

Table 6.3   10 Means from Samples of Size 5 Taken from the 50 Elements in Table 6.1

522.60	652.80
434.40	461.20
586.20	489.20
468.20	458.60
465.00	509.00

Mean = 504.72
Standard Deviation = 67.51

to make do with one. The first sample of five elements that I took had a mean of $522.60—pretty close to the actual mean of $533.28. But it's very clear from table 6.3 that any one sample of five elements from table 6.1 could be off by a lot. They range, after all, from $434.40 to $652.80. That's a very big spread, when the real average we're trying to estimate is $533.28. Still, as you can see from figure 6.6, as we add samples, the mean of the samples gets closer and closer to the parameter we're trying to estimate and the distribution of the means of the samples looks more and more like the normal distribution.

We are much closer to answering the question: How big does a sample have to be?

THE STANDARD ERROR AND CONFIDENCE INTERVALS

In the hypothetical example on page 131 we took a sample of 100 merchants in a Malaysian town and found that the mean income was RM12,600, standard error 400. We know from figure 6.1 that 68.26% of all samples of size 100 from this population will produce an estimate that is between 1 standard error above and 1 standard error below the mean—that is, between RM12,200 and RM13,000. The 68.26% **confidence interval**, then, is $400.

We also know from figure 6.1 that 95.44% of all samples of size 100 will produce an estimate of 2 standard errors, or between RM13,400 and RM11,800. The 95.44% confidence interval, then, is RM800. If we do the sums for the example, we see that the 95% confidence limits are:

$$RM12,600 \pm 1.96(RM400) = RM11,816 \text{ to } RM13,384$$

and the 99% confidence limits are:

$$RM12,600 \pm 2.58(RM400) = RM11,568 \text{ to } RM13,632$$

Our "confidence" in these 95% or 99% estimates comes from the power of a random sample and the fact that—by the central limit theorem—*sampling distributions are known to be normal irrespective of the distribution of the variable whose mean we are estimating.*

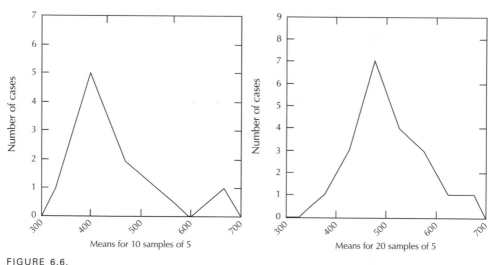

FIGURE 6.6.
Visualizing the central limit theorem: The distribution of sample means approximates a normal distribution. Means for 10 (left) and 20 (right) samples of 5 from the 50 GDP values in table 6.1.

What Confidence Limits *Are* and What They *Aren't*

If you say that the 95% confidence limits for the estimated mean income are RM11,816–13,384, this does *not* mean that there is a 95% chance that the true mean, μ, lies somewhere in that range. The true mean may or may not lie within that range and we have no way to tell. What we can say, however, is that:

1. If we take a very large number of suitably large random samples from the population (we'll get to what "suitably large" means in a minute); and
2. If we calculate the mean, $\bar{x}$, and the standard error, SE, for each sample; and
3. If we then calculate the confidence intervals for each sample mean, based on ± 1.96 SE; then
4. 95% of these confidence intervals will contain the true mean, μ.

Calculating Sample Size for Estimating Means

Now we are *really* close to answering the question about sample size. Suppose we want to get the standard error down to RM200 instead of RM400. We need to solve the following equation:

$$SE \frac{sd}{\sqrt{n}} = 4000 / \sqrt{n} = 200$$

Solving for n:

$$\sqrt{n} = \frac{4000}{200} = 20 \qquad n = 20^2 = 400$$

In other words, to reduce the standard error of the mean from RM400 to RM200, we have to increase the sample size from 100 to 400 people.

Suppose we increase the sample to 400 and we still get a mean of RM12,600 and a standard deviation of RM4000. The standard error of the mean would then be RM200, and we could estimate, with 95% confidence, that the true mean of the population was between RM12,208 and 12,992. With just 100 people in the sample, the 95% confidence limits were RM11,816–13,384. As the standard error goes down, we get narrower—that is, more precise—confidence limits.

Let's carry this forward another step. If we wanted to get the standard error down to RM100 and the 95% confidence interval down to RM200 from RM400, we would need a sample of 1,600 people. There is a pattern here. To cut the 95% confidence interval *in half*, from RM800 to RM400, we had to *quadruple* the sample size from 100 to 400. To cut the interval *in half again*, to RM200, we'd need to *quadruple* the sample size again, from 400 to 1,600.

There is another pattern, too. If we want to increase our confidence from 95% to 99% that the true mean of the population is within a particular confidence interval, we can raise the multiplier in formula 6.2 from roughly 2 standard deviations to roughly 3. Using the confidence interval of RM400, we would calculate:

$$\sqrt{n} = 3\left(\frac{4000}{400}\right) = 30 \qquad n = 30^2 = 900$$

We need 900 people, not 400, to be about 99% confident that our sample mean is within RM400, plus or minus, of the parameter.

SMALL SAMPLES: THE *t*-DISTRIBUTION

In anthropology, even doing surveys, we often have no choice about the matter and have to use small samples.

What we need is a distribution that is a bit more forgiving than the normal distribution. Fortunately, just such a distribution was discovered by W. S. Gossett, an employee of the Guinness brewery in Ireland. Writing under the pseudonym of "Student," Gossett described the distribution known as Student's *t*. It is based on a distribution that takes into account the fact that statistics calculated on small samples vary more than do statistics calculated on large samples and so have a bigger chance of misestimating the parameter of a continuous variable.

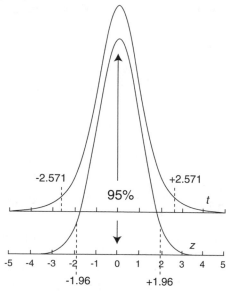

FIGURE 6.7.
Variability in a *t* distribution and a normal distribution.

The *t* distribution is found in appendix B. Figure 6.7 shows graphically the difference in the two distributions. In a normal distribution, plus or minus 1.96 *sd* covers 95% of all sample means. In a *t*-distribution, with 5 degrees of freedom, it takes 2.571 *sd* to cover 95% of all sample means.

The confidence interval for small samples, using the *t* distribution is given in formula 6.3:

$$\text{Confidence Interval} = \bar{x} \pm (t_{\alpha/2})\left[\frac{sd}{\sqrt{n}}\right] \qquad \textbf{Formula 6.3}$$

where alpha (α) is the confidence interval you want. If you want to be 95% confident, then α = .05. Since half the scores fall above the mean and half below, we divide alpha by two and get .025.

Look up what's called the **critical value** of *t* in appendix B. In the column for .025, we see that the value is 2.571 with 5 degrees of freedom. Degrees of freedom are one less than the size of the sample, so for a sample of six we need a *t* statistic of >2.571 to attain 95% confidence. (The concept of degrees of freedom is described further in chapter 20 in the section on t-tests. And keep in mind that we're interested in the **modulus**, or absolute value of t. A value of -2.571 is just as statistically significant as a value of $+2.571$.)

Thus, with small samples—which, for practical purposes, means less than 30 units of analysis—we use appendix B (for t) instead of appendix A (for z) to determine the confidence limits around the mean of our estimate. You can see from appendix B that for large samples—30 or more—the difference between the t and the z statistics is negligible. (The t-value of 2.042 for 30 degrees of freedom—which means a sample of 31—is very close to 1.96.)

The Catch

Suppose that instead of estimating the income of a population with a sample of 100, we use a sample of 10 and get the same result—RM12,600 and a standard deviation of RM4000. For a sample this size, we use the t distribution. With 9 degrees of freedom and an alpha value of .025, we have a t value of 2.262. For a normal curve, 95% of all scores fall within 1.96 standard errors of the mean. The corresponding t value is 2.262 standard errors. Substituting in the formula, we get:

$$RM12,600 \pm 2.262 \left(\frac{RM400}{\sqrt{10}} \right) = RM9,739 \text{ to } 15,461$$

But there's a catch. With a large sample (greater than 30), we know from the central limit theorem that the sampling distribution will be normal even if the population isn't. Using the t distribution with a small sample, we can calculate the confidence interval around the mean of our sample *only under the assumption that the population is normally distributed.*

In fact, looking back at figure 6.5, we know that the distribution of the real data is not perfectly normal. It is somewhat skewed (more about skewed distributions in chapter 20). In real research, we'd never take a sample from a set of just 50 data points—we'd do our calculations on the full set of the actual data. When we take samples, it's because we don't know what the distribution of the data looks like. And that's why sample size counts.

CALCULATING SAMPLE SIZE FOR ESTIMATING PROPORTIONS

And now for proportions. What we've learned so far about estimating the mean of continuous variables (like income and percentages) is applicable to the estimation of proportions as well.

In April 2009, the ABC News/Washington Post poll reported that 41% of Americans over 18 years of age said they had one or more guns in their home. The poll included 1,072 respondents and had, as the media say, a "margin of sampling error of plus-or-minus three percentage points." The point estimate of 41% means that 440 of the 1,072 people polled said that they had at least one gun in their house.

We can calculate the confidence interval around this point estimate. From the central limit theorem, we know that whatever the true proportion of people is who keep a gun in their home, the estimates of that proportion will be normally distributed if we take a large number of samples of 1,072 people each. The formula for determining the 95% confidence limits of a point estimator is:

$$P(\text{the true proportion}) = \pm 1.96 \sqrt{PQ / n} \qquad \textbf{Formula 6.4}$$

We use an italicized letter, P, to indicate the true proportion. Our estimate is the regular upper-case P and Q is 1–P. Table 6.4 shows what happens to the square root of PQ as the true value of P goes up from 10% to 90% of the population.

Table 6.4 Relation of P and Q and $\sqrt{PQ}$

If the value of P is really	Then PQ is	and $\sqrt{PQ}$ is
.10 or .90	.09	.30
.20 or .80	.16	.40
.30 or .70	.21	.46
.40 or .60	.24	.49
.50	.25	.50

We can use our own estimate of P in the equation for the confidence limits. Substituting .41 for P and .59 (1–.41) for Q, we get:

$$P = P \pm 1.96 \sqrt{(.41)(.59)/1072} = .02944$$

which, with rounding error, is the familiar "plus or minus three percentage points." This means that we are 95% confident that the true proportion of adults in the United States who had at least one gun in their home (or at least said they did) at the time this poll was conducted was between 38% and 44%.

Suppose we want to estimate P to within plus-or-minus 2 percentage points instead of 3 and we still want to maintain the 95% confidence level. We substitute in the formula as follows:

$$P = P \pm 1.96 \sqrt{(.41)(.59) / n} = .02$$

and we solve for n:

$$n = 1.96^2(.41)(.59)/.02^2$$
$$n = (3.842)(.41)(.59)/.0004 = 2,324$$

Generalizing, then, the formula for "sample size when estimating proportions in a large population" is:

$$n = z^2(P)(Q)/(\text{confidence interval})^2 \qquad \textbf{Formula 6.5}$$

where z is the area under the normal curve that corresponds to the confidence level we choose. When the confidence level is 95%, then z is 1.96. When the confidence level is 99%, then z is 2.58. And so on.

If we start out fresh and have no prior estimate of P, we follow table 6.4 and set P and Q to .5 each. This maximizes the size of the sample for any given confidence interval or confidence level. If we want a sample that produces an estimate of a proportion with a confidence interval of 2 percentage points and we want to be 95% confident in that estimate, we calculate:

$$n(\text{sample size}) = (1.96)^2(.5)(.5)/(.02)^2 = 2,401$$

In time allocation studies, we estimate the proportion of various behaviors by observing a sample of behaviors. We'll deal with this in chapter 14, on methods of direct observation (see especially table 14.2).

Estimating Proportions in Samples for Smaller Populations

This general formula, 6.5, is *independent of the size of the population.* Florida has a population of about 18 million. A sample of 400 is .000022 of 18 million; a sample of 2,402 is .00013 of 18 million. Both proportions are microscopic. A random, representative sample of 400 from a population of 1 million gets you the same confidence level and the same confidence interval as you get with a sample of 400 from a population of 18 million.

Often, though, we want to take samples from relatively small populations. The key word here is "relatively." When formula 6.4 or 6.5 calls for a sample that turns out to be 5% or more of the total population, we apply the **finite population correction**. The formula (from Cochran 1977) is:

$$n' = \frac{n}{1 + (n - 1 / N)} \qquad \textbf{Formula 6.6}$$

where n is the sample size calculated from formula 6.5; n' (read: n-prime) is the new value for the sample size; and N is the size of the total population from which n is being drawn.

Here's an example. Suppose you are sampling the 540 resident adult men in a Mexican village to determine how many have ever worked illegally in the United States. How many of those men do you need to interview to ensure a 95% probability sample, with a 5% confidence interval? Answer: Because we have no idea what the percentage is that we're trying to estimate, we set P and Q at .5 each in formula 6.4. Solving for n (sample size), we get:

$$n = (1.96)^2(.5)(.5)/(.05)^2 = 384.16$$

which we round up to 385. Then we apply the finite population correction:

$$n' = \frac{385}{1 + (384/540)} = 225$$

This is still a hefty percentage of the 540 people in the population, but it's a lot smaller than the 385 called for by the standard formula (box 6.1).

BOX 6.1

SETTLING FOR BIGGER CONFIDENCE INTERVALS

If we were willing to settle for a 10% confidence interval, we'd need only 82 people in this example, but the trade-off would be substantial. If 65 out of 225, or 29%, reported that they had worked illegally in the United States, we would be 68% confident that from 24% to 34% really did, and 95% confident that 19% to 39% did. But if 24 out of 82 (the same 29%) reported having worked illegally in the United States, we'd be 68% confident that the true figure was between 19% and 39%, and 95% confident that it was between 9% and 49%. With a spread like that, you wouldn't want to bet much on the sample statistic of 29%.

If it weren't for ethnography, this would be a major problem in taking samples from small populations—the kind we often study in anthropology. If you've been doing ethnography in a community of 540 people for 6 months, though, you may feel comfortable taking a confidence interval of 10% because you are personally (not statistically) confident that your intuition about the group will help you interpret the results of a small sample.

Another Catch

All of this discussion has been about estimating single parameters, whether proportions or means. You will often want to measure the interaction among several variables at once. Suppose you study a population of wealthy, middle-class, and poor people in India. That's three kinds of people. Now add two sexes, male and female (that makes six kinds of people) and two religions, Hindu and Muslim (that makes 12 kinds). If you want to know how all those independent variables combine to predict, say, average number of children desired, the sampling strategy gets more complicated.

Representative sampling is one of the trickiest parts of social research. I recommend strongly that you consult an expert in sampling if you are going to do complex tests on your data (**Further Reading:** sampling theory and sample design).

FURTHER READING

Sampling theory and sample design: Jaeger (1984); Kish (1965); Levy and Lemeshow (1999); Sudman (1976).

7

Sampling III: Nonprobability Samples and Choosing Informants

If your objective is to estimate a parameter or a proportion from a sample to a larger population, and your research calls for the collection of data about attributes of individuals (whether those individuals are people or organizations or episodes of a sitcom), then the rule is simple: Collect data from a sufficiently large, randomly selected, unbiased sample. If you know that you *ought* to use an unbiased sample and you have the means to *get* an unbiased sample and you still choose to use a nonprobability sample, then expect to take a lot of flak.

There are, however, three quite different circumstances under which nonprobability samples are exactly what are called for:

1. Nonprobability samples are always appropriate for labor-intensive, in-depth studies of a few cases. Most studies of narratives are based on fewer than 50 cases, so every case has to count. This means choosing cases on purpose, not randomly. In-depth research on sensitive topics requires nonprobability sampling. It can take months of participant observation fieldwork before you can collect narratives about topics like sexual and reproductive history or bad experiences with mental illness or use of illegal drugs.

   Come to think of it, just about everything is a sensitive topic when you dig deeply enough. Sexual history is an obviously sensitive topic, but so is the management of household finances when you get into how people really allocate their resources. People love to talk about their lives, but when you get into the details of a life history, you quickly touch a lot of nerves. Really in-depth research requires informed informants, not just responsive respondents—that is, people whom you choose on purpose, not randomly.

2. Nonprobability samples are also appropriate for large surveys when, despite our best efforts, we just can't get a probability sample. In these cases, use a nonprobability sample and *document the bias*. That's all there is to it. No need to agonize about it.

3. And, as I said at the beginning of chapter 5, when you are collecting cultural data, as contrasted with data about individuals, then expert informants, not randomly selected respondents, are what you really need. Think of the difference between asking someone "How old was your child when you first gave him an egg to eat?" versus "At what age do children here first eat eggs?" I deal with the problem of selecting cultural experts (people who are likely to really know when most mothers introduce eggs around here) later in this chapter.

The major nonprobability sampling methods are: **quota sampling**, **purposive sampling** (also called **judgment sampling**), **convenience sampling**, and **chain-referral (snowball) sampling**. A special kind of mixed method, that combines elements of probability and nonprobability sampling, is the **case control design** (see box 4.6).

QUOTA SAMPLING

Quota sampling is stratified sampling without random selection. It is used widely in election polls as well as in studies that rely on qualitative data, like in-depth interviews.

The key to quota sampling is the development of a **sampling design**, or **sampling grid.** Suppose you are studying the lived experiences of labor migrants to the United States who are back home in their community in Mexico. You want to compare the experiences of (1) people who spent time on jobs in the United States but were caught by the U.S. Border Patrol and deported with those of (2) people who managed to stay on their jobs until they'd accumulated enough money to return on their own. You also want to compare the experiences of Indians and Mestizos and of men and women. That's three binary independent variables: deported/not deported; Indian/Mestizo; male/female. Figure 7.1 shows that there are eight cells in this design. If you want at least five informants in each cell, you'll need to do 40 interviews.

Mexicans who have worked in the United States and returned home							
Deported				Returned voluntarily			
Mestizo		Indian		Mestizo		Indian	
Male	Female	Male	Female	Male	Female	Male	Female

FIGURE 7.1.
Quota sampling grid with three binary independent variables.

Tinsley et al. (2002) interviewed 437 elderly users of Lincoln Park in Chicago. They selected quota samples of about 50 men and 50 women from each of the four major ethnic groups in the area, Blacks, Whites, Hispanics, and Asian Americans. Besides gender and ethnicity, Tinsley et al. stratified on place and time. They divided the park into three zones (north, south, and middle) and three time periods (6 A.M. to 10 A.M., 11 A.M. to 3 P.M., and 4 P.M. to 8 P.M.). There were, then, nine zone-time strata in which interviewers selected respondents. The interviewers were also told to make sure they got some weekday and some weekend users of the park.

When it's done right, quota samples often do a good job of reflecting the population parameters of interest. In other words, quota sampling is an art that often approximates the results of probability sampling at less cost and less hassle than strict probability sampling (box 7.1).

Quota samples are biased toward people you can find easily—which means, for example, that they're biased against really poor and really rich people and against single people who aren't home as much (Marsh and Scarborough 1990)—so quota sampling is dangerous when it comes to making predictions about close election outcomes—or estimating any population parameter, for that matter, if you need precise results.

On the other hand, quota sampling is appropriate in the study of cultural domains. If you want to know how junior sports—Little League Baseball, Pop Warner football, Youth Soccer, junior and senior high school football—function in small communities across the United States, you'd ask people who have children playing those sports. There will be some intracultural variation, but open-ended interviews with four or five really knowl-

BOX 7.1

FAMOUS POLLING DEBACLES FROM QUOTA
SAMPLES

In 1948, pollsters predicted, on the basis of quota sampling, that Thomas Dewey would beat Harry Truman in the U.S. presidential election. The *Chicago Tribune* was so confident in those predictions that they printed an edition announcing Dewey's victory—while the votes were being counted that would make Truman president.

Skip to 1992. In the general election in Britain that year, four different polls published on the day of the election put the Liberal Party, on average, about 1 point ahead of the Conservative Party. All the polls were based on quota sampling. The Conservatives won by 8 points. In fact, from 1992 to 1997, political polls using quota samples in Britain systematically overestimated the support for the Liberals (Curtice and Sparrow 1997). A similar polling debacle happened in the 2002 presidential election in France. Twelve polls predicted that Jacques Chirac and Lionel Jospin would defeat the far-right candidate, Jean-Marie Le Pen in the first round of voting and face each other in a run-off. No one predicted that Le Pen would trounce Jospin and face Chirac in the run-off (Durand et al. 2004).

edgeable people will produce the relevant cultural data—including data on the range of ideas that people have about these institutions (**Further Reading:** quota sampling).

PURPOSIVE OR JUDGMENT SAMPLING

In purposive sampling, you decide the purpose you want informants (or communities) to serve, and you go out to find some. This is somewhat like quota sampling, except that there is no overall sampling design that tells you how many of each type of informant you need for a study. You take what you can get.

I used purposive sampling in my study of the Kalymnian (Greek) sponge-fishing industry (1987). I knew I had to interview sponge merchants, boat owners, and divers, but my first interviews taught me that I had to interview people whom I had never considered: men who used to be divers but who had quit, gone to Australia as labor migrants, and returned to the island. It was very easy to find those returned migrants: Everyone on Kalymnos either had one in their family or knew people who did.

There are many good reasons for using purposive samples. They are used widely in (1) **pilot studies**, (2) **intensive case** studies, (3) **critical case** studies, and (4) studies of **hard-to-find populations**.

1. Pilot studies. These are studies done before running a larger study. In 1999, Katherine Browne, Carla Freeman, and Zobeida Bonilla began a comparative ethnographic study of women entrepreneurs in Martinique, Barbados, and Puerto Rico—that is, in the French-, English-, and Spanish-speaking Caribbean. In a large, multisite study like this, it pays to spend time on pilot research. Each member of the team did 30 in-depth interviews with women who were engaged in a wide range of enterprises, who were of

different ages, and who came from one- and two-parent homes. This helped the team develop their research instruments and provided the baseline for the larger project (Browne 2001).

And speaking of instruments, when you do surveys to test hypotheses, make sure that you test all your scales with a pilot sample. More about all this in chapter 11, on scales.

2. In intensive case studies, the object is often to identify and describe a cultural phenomenon. Dickerson et al. (2000) studied the experiences of American Indian graduate nursing students and cultural barriers that might lead the students to drop out of their training. Dickerson et al. found and interviewed 11 students who were enrolled in an advanced nurse practitioner program. Samples don't get much more purposive than this, and they don't get much more appropriate, either.

Life history research and qualitative research on special populations (drug addicts, trial lawyers, shamans) rely on judgment sampling. Barroso (1997), for example, studied a purposive sample of 14 men and six women in the Tampa, Florida, area, all of whom had lived with AIDS for at least 3 years.

Finally, researchers don't usually pull research sites—villages, tribal encampments, hospitals, school systems—out of a hat. They rely on their judgment to find one that reflects the things they are interested in.

3. Critical case studies. These are done in all fields of science and have long been the basis, by deduction, for the development of theory. Freud based his theory of psychosexual development on a few critical cases from his practice. Steward based his theory of multilineal evolution on a few critical cases from archeology. Political scientists study cases like the Orange Revolution in Ukraine for clues about the transition from autocracy to democracy (McFaul 2007).

Choosing key informants in ethnographic research is a form of critical-case sampling. It would be pointless to select a handful of people randomly from a population and try to turn them into trusted key informants.

4. We almost always have to rely on purposive sampling in the study of hard-to-find populations.

Think about locating and interviewing refugees from Somalia and Ethiopia living in a large American city. Many of these people experienced torture and don't exactly welcome researchers who want to ask them a lot of questions. This was the problem facing researchers in Minneapolis (see Jaranson et al. 2004; Spring et al. 2003). The study design called for a quota sample of 1,200 respondents, including 300 Oromo women, 300 Oromo men, 300 Somali women, and 300 Somali men. The study team recruited male and female interviewers from the community—people who shared ethnicity, language, and religion with the people they were trying to locate and interview. The project team sent out fliers, placed announcements in church bulletins, and made presentations at meetings of Oromo and Somali organizations. The interviewers also used their own social networks to locate potential respondents. Over 25 months, the team built trust in the community and wound with 1,134 of the 1,200 interviews called for in the study.

Kimberly Mahaffy (1996) was interested in how lesbian Christians deal with the cognitive dissonance that comes from being rejected by mainstream Christian churches. Mahaffy sent letters to gay Christian organizations, asking them to put an ad for potential respondents in their newsletters. She sent flyers to women's bookstores and to lesbian support groups, asking for potential respondents to get in touch with her.

Eventually, Mahaffy got 163 completed questionnaires from women who fit the criteria she had established for her research, including 44 from women who self-identified as born-again or evangelical Christians. Mahaffy could not possibly have gotten an unbiased sample of lesbian Christians, but the corpus of data that she collected from her respondents had all the information she needed to answer her research questions (**Further Reading:** purposive sampling).

CONVENIENCE OR HAPHAZARD SAMPLING

Convenience sampling is a glorified term for grabbing whoever will stand still long enough to answer your questions. Sometimes, convenience samples are all that are available, and you just have to make do. Studies of the homeless are usually done with convenience samples, for obvious reasons, as are studies of people who are in intensive care units in hospitals. All samples represent *something*. The trick is to make them representative of what *you* want them to be. That's what turns a convenience sample into a purposive one.

Al-Krenawi and Wiesel-Lev (1999) wanted to understand the emotions of Israeli Bedouin women who had experienced genital mutilation. They interviewed a convenience sample of 12 women who had been through the ritual and 12 who had not but had either seen it first-hand or had heard about women in their own extended families going through it. We wouldn't put much stock in the fact that a specific *percentage* of the women reported sexual problems or relationship problems with various members of their family, but the *list* of problems is very instructive because it is the basis for more in-depth research.

If you want to estimate a parameter, then you know what you have to do: Get a random, representative sample. If you want to know the percentage of adult men in a matrilateral, cross-cousin society who have actually married their biological mother's-brother's-sister (MBZ), you'll either have to count them all or take a random, unbiased sample of sufficient size to be able to make that generalization.

Key informants will tell you that the rule is broken regularly, but not by how much. A convenience sample of women who gather at the village well each day will tell you the range of options for men who don't have a biological MBZ, but not how many choose each option. And if you want to know the effect of a new road on some peasants and you only interview people who come to town on the road, you'll miss all the people who live too far off the road for it to do them any good (**Further Reading:** convenience sampling).

CHAIN REFERRAL, OR NETWORK SAMPLING: THE SNOWBALL AND RDS METHODS

Snowball and **respondent-driven sampling** (RDS) (also known, generically, as **chain referral** methods) are two network sampling methods for studying hard-to-find or hard-to-study populations. Populations can be hard to find and study for at least four reasons: (1) they contain very few members who are scattered over a large area (think strict vegans in rural Georgia, or bilingual deaf children in Texas who are fluent in signing English and Spanish); and/or (2) they are stigmatized and reclusive (HIV-positive people who never show up at clinics until they are sick with AIDS) or even actively hiding (transgendered people who have been physically attacked, men who have battered their female partners);

and/or (3) they are people who really have something to hide (Richardson [1988], for example, used snowball sampling to locate single or divorced women who were in long-term relationships with married men); and/or (4) they are members of an elite group (surgeons, professional athletes) and don't care about your need for data.

Charles Kadushin (1968) laid out the snowball method in his study of elites in modern, complex societies, but elites can just as well be "people in this village whose opinions really count" or "wood carvers in this district whose work is respected" or "native curers who see more than 10 patients a month." Using key informants and/or documents, you locate one or two people in a population. Then you ask those people to (1) list others in the population and (2) recommend someone from the list whom you might interview. You get handed from informant to informant and the sampling frame grows with each interview. Eventually, the sampling frame becomes saturated—that is, no new names are offered. Ostrander (1980) used snowball sampling in her study of class consciousness among upper-class women in a midwestern U.S. city. She selected her first informant by looking for someone who had graduated from an elite women's college, was listed in the social register, was active in upper-class clubs—and who would talk to her. At the end of the interview, she asked the informant to "suggest another woman of your social group, with a background like yours, who might be willing to talk to me."

Thomas Weisner has been following 205 counterculture women and their families since 1974. Weisner built this sample by recruiting women in California who were in their third trimester of pregnancy. He used snowball sampling, but to ensure that participants came from all over the state and represented various kinds of families, he used no more than two referrals from any one source (Weisner 2002:277) (box 7.2).

BOX 7.2

SOMETIMES YOU JUST HAVE TO START OVER

David Griffith and his colleagues used *two* snowball samples in their study of food preferences in Moberly, Missouri. They chose an initial "seed" household in a middle-income neighborhood and asked a man in the house to name three people in town with whom he interacted on a regular basis. The first person cited by the informant lived in a lower-income neighborhood across town. That person, in turn, named other people who were in the lower-income bracket.

After a while, the researchers realized that, though they'd started with a middle-income informant who had children at home, they were getting mostly lower-income, elderly people in the snowball sample. So they started again, this time with a seed from an elite, upper-middle-income neighborhood. By the time they got through, Griffith et al. had a well-balanced sample of 30 informants with whom they did in-depth interviews (reported in J. C. Johnson 1990:78).

Respondent-Driven Sampling

Snowball sampling is popular and fun to do, but it does not produce a statistically representative sample in a large population. In a small community, like practitioners of alternative medicine in a town, the members are likely to be in contact with one another.

Here, snowball sampling is an effective way to build an exhaustive sampling frame from which you can select people at random to interview—or elect to interview all of them. In large communities, though—like all the native curers in a city such as Nairobi—the members who are well known have a better chance of being named in a snowball procedure than members who are less well known. And in large populations, people who have large networks name more people than do people who have small networks. For large populations, then, snowball sampling can produce useful nonprobability samples, but every person does not have the same chance of being included.

Douglas Heckathorn (1997) developed respondent-driven sampling to deal with this problem. Like snowball sampling, RDS begins with a few informants who act as seeds. The informants are paid for being interviewed and are then asked to recruit up to three members of their networks into the study. To move this process along, Heckathorn paid each of his seed informants $10 (this might be $50 today, but you get the idea) and he gave them three coupons. Anyone who came to Heckathorn to be interviewed and who had one of those coupons was paid the same $10. (He upped the bounty to $15 for referring a female drug injector because they were harder to find.) Those informants, in turn, got several coupons and recruited others into the study.

There are two improvements to snowball sampling here. (1) The people whom an informant names in a snowball interview may not want you even to know about their existence, much less be anxious to grant you an interview. In respondent-driven sampling, the initial members of the sample are volunteers as are the people they recruit. (2) When it's done right, the RDS method produces samples that are less biased than are traditional snowball samples (Salganik and Heckathorn 2004) (**Further Reading:** chain referral, snowball, and RDS sampling) (box 7.3).

BOX 7.3

GAMING THE RDS

RDS is now widely used in the study of injection drug users and other populations at high risk for HIV/AIDS. Scott (2008) interviewed 70 injection drug users in Chicago who had participated in the full entire RDS sequence: They had received $20 for completing an interview and had collected $30 more for bringing in three associates (at $10 each) who had also completed an interview. Forty-eight of the 70 had sold at least one of their coupons to someone else because they could not trust three people in their network to complete the interview. This may introduce some distortion to the samples, but RDS remains the best available method for locating and studying populations at risk for HIV/AIDS.

CHOOSING INFORMANTS

Across the social sciences, you'll see references to research participants as "respondents," or "subjects," or "informants." These terms tend to be used by sociologists, psychologists, and anthropologists, respectively. Respondents respond to survey questions, subjects are the subject of some experiment, and informants . . . well, informants tell you *what they think you need to know* about their culture.

There are two kinds of informants: **key informants** and **specialized informants**. Key informants are people who know a lot about their culture and are, for reasons of their own, willing to share all their knowledge with you. When you do long-term ethnography, you develop close relationships with a few key informants—relationships that can last a lifetime. You don't choose these people. They and you choose each other, over time.

Specialized informants have particular competence in some cultural domain. If you want to know the rules of Balinese cockfighting, or how many cows must be given to a Lumasaba bride's parents, or when to genuflect in a Roman Catholic Mass, or what herb tea to give children for diarrhea, you need to talk to people who can speak knowledgeably about those things.

KEY INFORMANTS

Good key informants are people whom you can talk to you easily, who understand the information you need, and who are glad to give it to you or get it for you. Pelto and Pelto (1978:72) advocate training informants "to conceptualize cultural data in the frame of reference" that you, the researcher, use.

In some cases, you may want to just listen. But when you run into a really great informant, I see no reason to hold back. Teach the informant about the analytic categories you're developing and ask whether the categories are correct. In other words, encourage the informant to become the ethnographer.

I've worked with Jesús Salinas since 1962. In 1971, I was about to write an ethnography of his culture, the Ñähñu of central Mexico, when he mentioned that he'd be interested in writing an ethnography himself. I dropped my project and taught him to read and write Ñähñu. Over the next 15 years, Salinas produced four volumes about the Ñähñu people—volumes that I translated and from which I learned many things that I'd never have learned had I written the ethnography myself. For example, Ñähñu men engage in rhyming duels, much like the "dozens" of African Americans. I wouldn't have thought to ask about those duels because I had never witnessed one (see Bernard and Salinas Pedraza 1989).

Just as Salinas has influenced my thinking about Mexican Indian life, Salinas's ethnography was heavily influenced by his association with me. We've discussed and analyzed parts of Ñähñu culture over the years and we've even argued over interpretation of observed facts. (More about all this in the section on native ethnography in chapter 18, plus a different perspective by Harry Wolcott [2008].)

Finding Key Informants

One of the most famous key informants in the ethnographic literature is Doc in William Foote Whyte's *Street Corner Society* (1981 [1943]). Whyte studied "Cornerville," an Italian American neighborhood in a place he called "Eastern City." (Cornerville was the North End of Boston.) Whyte asked some social workers if they knew anyone who could help Whyte with his study. One social worker told Whyte to come to her office and meet a man whom she thought could do the job. When Whyte showed up, the social worker introduced him to Doc and then left the room. Whyte nervously explained his predicament, and Doc asked him "Do you want to see the high life or the low life?" (Whyte 1989:72).

Whyte couldn't believe his luck. He told Doc he wanted to see all he could, learn as much as possible about life in the neighborhood. Doc told him:

Any nights you want to see anything, I'll take you around. I can take you to the joints—the gambling joints. I can take you around to the street corners. Just remember that you're my friend. That's all they need to know. I know these places and if I tell them you're my friend, nobody will bother you. You just tell me what you want to see, and we'll arrange it. . . . When you want some information, I'll ask for it, and you listen. When you want to find out their philosophy of life, I'll start an argument and get it for you. (Whyte 1989:72)

Doc was straight up; he told Whyte to rely on him and to ask him anything, and Doc was good to his word all through Whyte's 3 years of fieldwork. Doc introduced Whyte to the boys on the corner; Doc hung out with Whyte and spoke up for Whyte when people questioned Whyte's presence. Doc was just spectacular.

Or was he? Boelen (1992) visited Cornerville 25 times between 1970 and 1989, sometimes for a few days, other times for several months. She tracked down and interviewed everyone she could find from *Street Corner Society*. Doc had died in 1967, but she interviewed his two sons in 1970 (then in their late teens and early 20s). She asked them what Doc's opinion of Whyte's book had been and reports the elder son saying: "My father considered the book untrue from the very beginning to the end, a total fantasy" (Boelen 1992:29).

Whyte (1996a, 1996b) refuted Boelen's report, as did another of Whyte's key informants (Orlando 1992). We'll never know the whole truth. Whyte certainly made mistakes, but the same can be said for all ethnographers. For some scholars, mistakes invalidate a positivist stance in ethnography. For others, it does not (box 7.4).

BOX 7.4

DOC MAY BE FAMOUS, BUT HE'S NOT UNIQUE

He's not even rare. All successful ethnographers will tell you that they eventually came to rely on one or two key people in their fieldwork. What was rare about Doc is how quickly and easily Whyte teamed up with him. It's not easy to find informants like Doc. When Jeffrey Johnson began fieldwork in a North Carolina fishing community, he went to the local marine extension agent and asked for the agent's help. The agent, happy to oblige, told Johnson about a fisherman whom he thought could help Johnson get off on the right foot.

It turned out that the fisherman was a transplanted northerner; he had a pension from the Navy; he was an activist Republican in a thoroughly Democratic community; and he kept his fishing boat in an isolated moorage, far from the village harbor. He was, in fact, maximally different from the typical local fisherman. The agent had meant well, of course (J. C. Johnson 1990:56).

In fact, the first informants with whom you develop a working relationship in the field may be "deviant" members of their culture. Agar (1980b:86) reports that during his fieldwork in India, he was taken on by the *naik*, or headman of the village. The *naik*, it turned out, had *inherited* the role, but he was not respected in the village and did not preside over village meetings. This did not mean that the *naik* knew nothing about village affairs and customs; he was what Agar called a "solid insider," and yet somewhat of an outcast—a "marginal native," just like the ethnographer was trying to be (Freilich 1977). If you think about it, Agar said, you should wonder about the kind of person who would befriend an ethnographer.

In my own fieldwork (at sea, in Mexican villages, on Greek islands, in rural communities in the United States, and in modern American bureaucracies), I have consistently found the best informants to be people who are cynical about their own culture. They may not be outcasts (in fact, they are always solid insiders), but they say they *feel* somewhat marginal to their culture, by virtue of their intellectualizing of and disenchantment with their culture. They are always observant, reflective, and articulate. In other words, they invariably have all the qualities that I would like to have myself.

Don't choose key ethnographic informants too quickly. Allow yourself to go awash in data for a while and play the field. When you have several prospects, check on their roles and statuses in the community. Be sure that the key informants you select don't prevent you from gaining access to other important informants (i.e., people who won't talk to you when they find out you're so-and-so's friend). Good ethnography is, at its best, a good story, so find trustworthy informants who are observant, reflective, and articulate— who know how to tell good stories—and stay with them. In the end, ethnographic fieldwork stands or falls on building mutually supportive relations with a few key people.

Informants Sometimes Lie

Don't be surprised if informants lie to you. Jeffrey Johnson, a skilled boat builder, worked in an Alaskan boatyard as part of his field study of a fishing community. At one point in his fieldwork, two other ethnographers showed up, both women, to conduct some interviews with the men in the boatyard. "The two anthropologists had no idea I was one of *them*," Johnson reports,

> since I was dressed in carpenter's overalls, with all the official paraphernalia—hammer, tape measure, etc. I was sufficiently close to overhear the interview and, knowing the men being interviewed, recognized quite a few blatant lies. In fact, during the course of one interview, a captain would occasionally wink at me as he told a whopper of a lie. (personal communication)

This is not an isolated incident. A Comox Indian woman spent 2 hours narrating a text for Franz Boas. The text turned out to be nothing but a string of questions and answers. Boas didn't speak Comox well enough to know that he was being duped, but when he found out he noted it in his diary (Rohner 1969:61). And Margaret Mead's adolescent informants probably lied to her about their sex lives—more about that in chapter 12.

In 1938, Melville Herskovits published his massive, two-volume work on the ancient West African kingdom of Dahomey (today Benin). According to Herskovits, there was an annual census and the data from these efforts were used in administering the state. The counting involved the delivery of sacks of pebbles from around the kingdom to the palace at Abomey, with each pebble representing a person. Roger Sandall (1999) has shown that the informant who told Herskovits about this elaborate accounting system may have made it all up.

This sort of thing can happen to anyone who does participant observation ethnography, but some cultures are more tolerant of lying than are others. Nachman (1984) found that the most articulate informants among the Nissan of New Guinea were great truth tellers and accomplished liars at the same time. Among the Nissan, says Nachman, people expect big men to give speeches and to "manipulate others and to create socially acceptable meanings," even if that means telling outright lies (Nachman 1984:552 and see Sala-mone 1977).

SELECTING CULTURALLY SPECIALIZED INFORMANTS

The search for formal and systematic ways to select focused ethnographic informants—people who can help you learn about particular areas of a culture—has been going on for a very long time. In 1957, Marc-Adelard Tremblay was involved in a Cornell University survey research project on poverty in Nova Scotia. He wanted to use ethnographic informants to help the team's researchers design a useful questionnaire, so he made a list of some roles in the community he was studying—things like sawmill owners, doctors, farmers, bankers—and chose informants who could talk to him knowledgeably about things in their area of expertise. Tremblay had no external test to tell him whether the informants he selected were, in fact, the most competent in their areas of expertise, but he felt that on-the-spot clues made the selection of informants valid (Tremblay 1957).

Michael Robbins and his colleagues studied acculturation and modernization among the Baganda of Uganda, using a more formal method to select informants who might be competent on this topic (Robbins et al. 1969). First, they ran a survey of households in a rural sector, asking about things that would indicate respondents' exposure to Western culture. Then they used the results of the survey to select appropriate informants.

Robbins et al. had 80 variables in the survey that had something to do with acculturation and they ran a factor analysis to find out which variables package together. We'll look a bit more at factor analysis in chapter 22. For now, think of factor analysis as a way to reduce those 80 variables to just a handful of underlying variables around which individual variables cluster. It turned out that 14 of the original 80 variables clustered together in one factor. Among those original variables were: being under 40 years of age, drinking European beer, speaking and reading English, having a Western job, and living in a house that has concrete floors and walls.

Robbins et al. called this cluster the "acculturation factor." They chose informants who had high scores on this factor and interviewed them about acculturation. Robbins et al. reversed Tremblay's method. Tremblay used key informants to help him build a survey instrument; Robbins et al. used a survey to find key informants.

Poggie's Study of Ciudad Industrial

In any given domain of culture, some people are more competent than others. In our culture, some people know a lot about the history of baseball; some people can name the actors in every sitcom since the beginning of television in the 1940s. Some people are experts on medicinal plants; others are experts on cars and trucks. John Poggie (1972) did an early study of informant competence. He selected one informant in each of seven Mexican communities. The communities ranged in size from 350 to 3,000 inhabitants. The informants were village or town presidents, or judges, or (in the case of agricultural communities) the local commissioners of communal land. Poggie asked these informants questions about life in the communities, and he compared the answers with data from a high-quality social survey.

For example, Poggie asked the seven informants: "How many men in this town are workers in Ciudad Industrial?" (Ciudad Industrial is a fictitious name of a city that attracted many labor migrants from the communities that Poggie studied.) In his survey, Poggie asked respondents if they had ever worked in Ciudad Industrial. The correlation between the answers given by Poggie's expert informants and the data obtained from the survey was .90.

Table 7.1 Agreement between Informants and Survey Data in Seven Villages

Questions asked of informants	Correlation with questionnaire data
Number of men from this town who are workers in Ciudad Industrial	0.90
Percentage of houses made of adobe	0.71
Percentage of households that have radios	0.52
Percentage of people who eat eggs regularly	0.33
Percentage of people who would like to live in Ciudad Industrial	0.23
Percentage of people who eat bread daily	0.14
Percentage of people who sleep in beds	0.05

SOURCE: J. J. Poggie, "Toward Quality Control in Key Informant Data," *Human Organization*, Vol. 31, pp. 26–29, 1972. Reprinted with permission of the Society for Applied Anthropology.

Poggie also asked: "What percentage of the houses here are made of adobe?" This time, the correlation between the informants and the survey was only .71. Table 7.1 shows the seven questions Poggie asked, and how well his informants did when their answers were compared to the survey.

Overall, informants produced answers most like those in the survey when they were asked to respond to questions about things that are publicly observable. The survey data are not necessarily more *accurate* than the informants' data. But as the questions require informants to talk about things inside people's homes (such as what percentage of people eat eggs), or about what people think (what percentage of people would *like* to work in Ciudad Industrial), informants' answers look less and less like those of the survey.

Poggie concluded that "There is little reason to believe that trust and rapport would improve the reliability and precision concerning what percentage sleep in beds, who would like to live in the new industrial city, or what percentage eat bread daily" (Poggie 1972:29). (For more on selecting informants who have high competence in specialized domains, see the discussion of consensus analysis in chapter 16.)

SAMPLE SIZE IN NONPROBABILITY SAMPLING

There is growing evidence that 10–20 knowledgeable people are enough to uncover and understand the core categories in any well-defined cultural domain or study of lived experience. Morse (1994) recommended a minimum of six interviews for phenomenological studies and 30–50 interviews for ethnographic studies and grounded theory studies. The data from two recent studies support Morse's experience-based guess.

M. G. Morgan et al. (2002:76) did in-depth interviews with four different samples of people about various risks in the environment. As they coded the interviews for concepts, Morgan et al. plotted the number of new concepts in each interview across the four samples. In all four cases, the first few interviews produce a lot of new data, but by 20 interviews, hardly any new information is retrieved.

Guest et al. (2006) interviewed 30 sex workers in Ghana and another 30 in Nigeria. They coded the transcripts in batches of six, working first on the interview from Ghana and then on the ones from Nigeria, and plotted the number of new themes uncovered in the coding. Of the 114 themes identified in the entire corpus, 80 turn up in the first six interviews in both Ghana and Nigeria. Another 20 themes turned up in the second batch of six interviews. Only 5 new themes were added to the codebook to accommodate the 30 interviews from Nigeria.

And, as we'll see in tables 16.13 and 16.14 (when we get to consensus analysis), Weller and Romney (1988:77) showed that just 10–13 knowledgeable informants are needed to understand the contents of a well-defined cultural domain. This is all very good news for ethnographers (and see Handwerker 2001:93–96).

AND FINALLY . . .

Particularly in ethnographic research, you learn in the field, as you go, to select the units of analysis (people, court records, whatever) that will provide the information you need. This is what Russell Belk et al. (1988) did in their detailed ethnographic study of buyers and sellers at a swap meet. When you study a process, like bargaining over goods, and you're doing the research in the field, in real time (not under simulated conditions in a lab), then selecting informants who meet certain criteria is the right thing to do.

The credibility of research results comes from the power of the methods used in measurement and sampling. Good measurement is the key to internal validity and representative sampling is the key to external validity. Well-done nonprobability sampling is actually part of good measurement. It contributes to credibility by contributing to internal validity. When someone reads a research report based on really good measurement of a nonprobability sample, they come away thinking, "Yep, I believe those conclusions about the people who were studied in that piece of research."

That's plenty. If you want the credibility of your conclusions to extend beyond the group of people (or countries, or organizations, or comic books) you studied, then either: (1) Repeat the study one or more times with nonprobability samples; or (2) Use a probability sample. Remember: Every sample represents something. An unbiased sample represents a population with a known probability of error. A nonprobability sample lacks this one feature. For a very, very large number of research questions, this is simply not a problem.

FURTHER READING

Quota sampling: Alaimo et al. (2008); Berinsky (2006); Méjean et al. (2009); Morrow et al. (2007); Weinberger (1973).

Purposive sampling: Auerswald et al. (2004); Topp et al. (2004).

Convenience sampling: Hultsch (2002); Pruchno et al. (2008); Sousa et al. (2004).

Chain referral, snowball and respondent driven sampling: Draus et al. (2005); Heckathorn (2002); Heckathorn and Jeffri (2001); Heckathorn and Wejnert (2008); Kendall et al. (2008); Malekinejad et al. (2008); J. L. Martin and Dean (1993); Penrod et al. (2003); Sudman and Kalton (1986).

Interviewing I: Unstructured and Semistructured

THE BIG PICTURE

The concept of "interviewing" covers a lot of ground, from totally unstructured interactions, through semistructured situations, to highly formal interactions with respondents. Interviewing is done on the phone, in person, by mail and—more and more—by computer or on the Internet. This chapter is about unstructured and semistructured face-to-face interviewing, including the management of focus groups.

Unstructured interviewing goes on all the time and just about anywhere—in homes, walking along a road, weeding a millet field, hanging out in bars, or waiting for a bus. **Semistructured**, or **in-depth interviewing** is a scheduled activity. A semistructured interview is open ended, but follows a general script and covers a list of topics.

There is a vast literature on how to conduct effective interviews: how to gain rapport, how to get people to open up, how to introduce an interview, and how to end one. You can't learn to interview by reading about it, but after you read this chapter and practice some of the techniques described, you should be well on your way to becoming an effective interviewer. You should also have a pretty good idea of how much more there is to learn, and be on your way to exploring the literature.

INTERVIEW CONTROL

There is a continuum of interview situations based on the **amount of control** we try to exercise over people's responses (Dohrenwend and Richardson 1965; Gorden 1987; Spradley 1979). These *different types* of interviews produce *different types* of data that are useful for *different types* of research projects and that appeal to *different types* of researchers. For convenience, I divide the continuum of interviews into four large chunks.

1. Informal Interviewing

At one end there is **informal interviewing**, characterized by a total lack of structure or control. The researcher just tries to remember conversations heard during the course of a day in the field. This requires constant jotting and daily sessions in which you sit at a computer, typing away, unburdening your memory, and developing field notes. Informal interviewing is the method of choice at the beginning of participant observation fieldwork, when you're settling in. It is also used throughout ethnographic fieldwork to build greater rapport and to uncover new topics of interest that might have been overlooked.

When it comes to interviewing, never mistake the adjective "informal" for "lightweight." This is hard, hard work. You have to remember a lot; you have to duck into private corners a lot (so you can jot things down); and you have to use a lot of deception (to keep people from knowing that you're really at work, studying them). Informal interviewing can get pretty tiring.

Still, in some kinds of research, informal interviewing is all you've got. Mark Connolly (1990) studied *gamines*, or street children, in Guatemala City, Guatemala, and Bogotá, Colombia. These children live, eat, and sleep on the street. Hanging out and talking informally with these children was an appropriate way to do this research. Informal ethnography can also be combined with more structured methods, when circumstances allow it. In fact, Rachel Baker (1996a, 1996b) was able to collect anthropometric data on street children in Kathmandu, Nepal, while doing informal ethnography.

2. Unstructured Interviewing

Next comes **unstructured interviewing**, one of the two types covered in this chapter. There is nothing at all informal about unstructured interviewing, and nothing deceptive, either. You sit down with another person and hold an interview. Period. Both of you know what you're doing, and there is no shared feeling that you're just engaged in pleasant chitchat.

Unstructured interviews are based on a clear plan that you keep constantly in mind, but are also characterized by a minimum of control over the people's responses. The idea is to get people to open up and let them express themselves in their own terms, and at their own pace. A lot of what is called **ethnographic interviewing** is unstructured. Unstructured interviewing is used in situations where you have lots and lots of time—like when you are doing long-term fieldwork and can interview people on many separate occasions (box 8.1).

BOX 8.1

PAYING INFORMANTS

Should anthropologists pay their informants? If so, how much? I'm a firm believer in paying for people's time, but there are exceptions. If you are studying people who are worth millions of dollars, paying them is inappropriate. You can't possibly pay them enough to compensate them financially for their time. It's better to make a donation to a charity that they support. This will vary from case to case, but the general rule, for me at least, is that if you want to interview people formally—sit down with them, voice recorder on the table and/or notebook in hand—they should be paid at least the local rate for their time. With key informants, the rule for me is that there's always a culturally appropriate way—money, job training, buying cement for a new school—to compensate people for their contribution to your career.

---

3. Semistructured Interviewing

In situations where you won't get more than one chance to interview someone, **semistructured interviewing** is best. It has much of the freewheeling quality of unstructured interviewing and requires all the same skills, but semistructured interviewing is based on the use of an **interview guide**. This is a written list of questions and topics that need to be covered in a particular order.

This is the kind of interview that most people write about—the kind done in professional surveys. The interviewer maintains discretion to follow leads, but the interview guide is a set of clear instructions—instructions like this one: "Probe to see if informants (men and women alike) who have daughters have different values about dowry and about premarital sex than do people who have only sons."

Formal, written guides are an absolute must if you are sending out several interviewers to collect data. But even if you do all the interviewing on a project yourself, you should build a guide and follow it if you want reliable, comparable qualitative data.

Semistructured interviewing works very well in projects where you are dealing with high-level bureaucrats and elite members of a community—people who are accustomed to efficient use of their time. It demonstrates that you are fully in control of what you want from an interview but leaves both you and your respondent to follow new leads. It shows that you are prepared and competent but that you are not trying to exercise excessive control.

4. Structured Interviewing

Finally, in fully **structured interviews**, people are asked to respond to as nearly identical a set of stimuli as possible. One variety of structured interviews involves use of an **interview schedule**—an explicit set of instructions to interviewers who administer questionnaires orally. Instructions might read: "If the informant says that she or he has at least one daughter over 10 years of age, then ask questions 26b and 26c. Otherwise, go on to question 27."

Self-administered questionnaires are a kind of structured interview. Other structured interviewing techniques include pile sorting, frame elicitation, triad sorting, and tasks that require informants to rate or rank order a list of things. I'll deal with these in chapter 10.

UNSTRUCTURED INTERVIEWING

Unstructured interviewing is truly versatile. It is used equally by scholars who identify with the hermeneutic tradition and by those who identify with the positivist tradition. It is used in studies that require only textual data and in studies that require both textual and numerical data. Ethnographers may use it to develop formal guides for semistructured interviews, or to learn what questions to include, in the native language, on a highly structured questionnaire (see Werner and Schoepfle [1987] for a good discussion of this). I say that ethnographers *may* use unstructured interviewing in developing structured interview schedules because unstructured interviewing also stands on its own.

When you want to know about the **lived experience** of fellow human beings—what it's like to survive hand-to-hand combat, how you get through each day when you have a child dying of leukemia, how it feels to make it across the border into Texas from Mexico only to be deported 24 hours later—you just can't beat unstructured interviewing.

Unstructured interviewing is excellent for building initial rapport with people, before moving to more formal interviews, and it's perfect for talking to informants who would not tolerate a more formal interview. The personal rapport you build with close informants in long-term fieldwork can make highly structured interviewing—and even semistructured interviewing—feel somehow unnatural. In fact, really structured interviewing can get in the way of your ability to communicate freely with key informants.

But not always. Some people want very much to talk about their lives, but they really don't like the unstructured interview format. I once asked a fisherman in Greece if I could have a few minutes of his time to discuss the economics of small-scale fishing. I was about 5 minutes into the interview, treading lightly—you know, trying not to get too quickly into his finances, even though that's exactly what I wanted to know about—when he interrupted me: "Why don't you just get to the point?" he asked. "You want to know how I decide where to fish, and whether I use a share system or a wage system to split the profits, and how I find buyers for my catch, and things like that, right?" He had heard from other fishermen that these were some of the topics I was interviewing people about. No unstructured interviews for him; he was a busy man and wanted to get right to it.

A Case Study of Unstructured Interviewing

Once you learn the art of probing (which I'll discuss in a bit), unstructured interviewing can be used for studying sensitive issues, like sexuality, racial or ethnic prejudice, or hot political topics. I find it particularly useful in studying conflict. In 1972–1973, I went to sea on two different oceanographic research vessels (Bernard and Killworth 1973, 1974). In both cases, there was an almost palpable tension between the scientific personnel and the crew of the ship. Through both informal and unstructured interviewing on land between cruises, I was able to establish that the conflict was predictable and regular. Let me give you an idea of how complex the situation was.

In 1972–1973, it cost $5,000 a day to run a major research vessel, not including the cost of the science. (That would be about $26,000 today.) The way oceanography works, at least in the United States, the chief scientist on a research cruise has to pay for both ship time and for the cost of any experiments he or she wants to run. To do this, oceanographers compete for grants from institutions like the U.S. Office of Naval Research, NASA, and the National Science Foundation.

The spending of so much money is validated by publishing significant results in prominent journals. It's a tough, competitive game and one that leads scientists to use every minute of their ship time. As one set of scientists comes ashore after a month at sea, the next set is on the dock waiting to set up their experiments and haul anchor.

The crew, consequently, might only get 24 or 48 hours shore leave between voyages. That can cause some pretty serious resentment by ships' crews against scientists. And that can lead to disaster. I found many documented instances of sabotage of expensive research by crew members who were, as one of them said, "sick and tired of being treated like goddamn bus drivers." In one incident, involving a British research vessel, a freezer filled with Antarctic shrimp, representing 2 years of data collection, went overboard during the night. In another, the crew and scientists from a U.S. Navy oceanographic research ship got into a brawl while in port (*Science* 1972:1346).

The structural problem I uncovered began at the top. Scientists whom I interviewed felt they had the right to take the vessels wherever they wanted to go, within prudence and reason, in search of answers to questions they had set up in their proposals. The captains of the ships believed (correctly) that *they* had the last word on maneuvering their ships at sea. Scientists, said the captains, sometimes went beyond prudence and reason in what they demanded of the vessels.

For example, a scientist might ask the captain to take a ship out of port in dangerous weather because ship time is so precious. This conflict between crew and scientists has been known—and pretty much ignored—since Charles Darwin sailed with HMS *Beagle* and it will certainly play a role in the productivity of long-term space station operations.

Unraveling this conflict at sea required participant observation and unstructured (as well as informal) interviewing with many people. No other strategy for data collection would have worked. At sea, people live for weeks, or even months, in close quarters, and there is a common need to maintain good relations for the organization to function well.

It would have been inappropriate for me to have used highly structured interviews about the source of tension between the crew and the scientists. Better to steer the interviews around to the issue of interest and to let informants teach me what I needed to know. In the end, no analysis was better than that offered by one engine room mechanic who told me, "These scientist types are so damn hungry for data, they'd run the ship aground looking for interesting rocks if we let them."

Getting Started

There are some important steps to take when you start interviewing someone for the first time. First of all, assure people of anonymity and confidentiality. Explain that you simply want to know what *they* think, and what *their* observations are. If you are interviewing someone whom you have come to know over a period of time, explain why you think their opinions and observations on a particular topic are important. If you are interviewing someone chosen from a random sample, and whom you are unlikely to see again, explain how they were chosen and why it is important that you have their cooperation to maintain representativeness.

If people say that they really don't know enough to be part of your study, assure them that their participation is crucial and that you are truly interested in what they have to say (and you'd better mean it or you'll never pull it off). Tell everyone you interview that you are trying to learn from *them*. Encourage them to interrupt you during the interview with anything they think is important. And always ask for permission to *record* personal interviews *and to take notes*. This is vital. If you can't take notes, then, in most cases, the value of an interview plummets. (See below, on using a recorder and taking notes.)

Keep in mind that people who are being interviewed know that you are shopping for information. There is no point in trying to hide this. If you are open and honest about your intentions, and if you are genuinely interested in what people have to say, many people will help you.

This is not always true, though. When Colin Turnbull went out to study the Ik in Uganda, he found a group of people who had apparently lost interest in life and in exchanging human kindnesses. The Ik had been brutalized, decimated, and left by the government to fend for themselves on a barren reservation. They weren't impressed with the fact that Turnbull wanted to study their culture. In fact, they weren't much interested in anything Turnbull was up to and were anything but friendly (Turnbull 1972).

Letting the Informant or Respondent Lead

If you can carry on "unthreatening, self-controlled, supportive, polite, and cordial interaction in everyday life," then interviewing will come easy to you, and informants will feel comfortable responding to your questions (Lofland 1976:90). But no matter how supportive you are as a person, an interview is never really like a casual, unthreatening conversation in everyday life. In casual conversations, people take more or less balanced turns (Spradley 1979) and there is no feeling that somehow the discussion has to stay on track or follow some theme (see also Hyman and Cobb 1975; Merton et al. 1956). In unstructured interviewing, you keep the conversation focused on a topic, while giving the respondent room to define the content of the discussion.

The rule is: Get people on to a topic of interest and get out of the way. Let the informant provide information that he or she thinks is important.

During my research on the Kalymnian sponge fishermen in Greece, I spent a lot of time at Procopis Kambouris's *taverna*. (A Greek *taverna* is a particular kind of restaurant.) Procopis's was a favorite of the sponge fishermen. Procopis was a superb cook, he made his own wine every year from grapes that he selected himself, and he was as good a teller of sea stories as he was a listener to those of his clientele. At Procopis's *taverna*, I was able to collect the work histories of sponge fishermen—when they'd begun their careers, the training they'd gotten, the jobs they'd held, and so on. The atmosphere was relaxed (plenty of retsina wine and good things to eat), and conversation was easy.

As a participant observer, I developed a sense of camaraderie with the regulars, and we exchanged sea stories with a lot of flourish. Still, no one at Procopis's ever made the mistake of thinking that I was there just for the camaraderie. They knew that I was writing about their lives and that I had lots of questions to ask. They also knew immediately when I switched from the role of participant observer to that of ethnographic interviewer.

One night, I slipped into just such an interview/conversation with Savas Ergas. He was 64 years old at the time and was planning to make one last 6-month voyage as a sponge diver during the coming season in 1965. I began to interview Savas on his work history at about 7:30 in the evening, and we closed Procopis's place at about 3 in the morning. During the course of the evening, several other men joined and left the group at various times, as they would on any night of conversation at Procopis's. Savas had lots of stories to tell (he was a living legend and he played well to a crowd), and we had to continue the interview a few days later, over several more liters of retsina.

At one point on that second night, Savas told me (almost offhandedly) that he had spent more than a year of his life walking the bottom of the Mediterranean. I asked him how he knew this, and he challenged me to document it. Savas had decided that there was something important that I needed to know and he maneuvered the interview around to make sure I learned it.

This led to about 3 hours of painstaking work. We counted the number of seasons he'd been to sea over a 46-year career (he remembered that he hadn't worked at all during 1943 because of "something to do with the war"). We figured conservatively the number of days he'd spent at sea, the average number of dives per trip, and the average depth and time per dive. We joked about the tendency of divers to exaggerate their exploits and about how fragile human memory is when it comes to this kind of detail.

It was difficult to stay on the subject, because Savas was such a good raconteur and a perceptive analyst of Kalymnian life. The interview meandered off on interesting tangents, but after a while, either Savas or I would steer it back to the issue at hand. In the end, discounting heavily for both exaggeration and faulty recall, we reckoned that he'd spent at least 10,000 hours—about a year and a fourth, counting each day as a full 24 hours—under water and had walked the distance between Alexandria and Tunis at least three times.

The exact numbers really didn't matter. What did matter was that Savas Ergas had a really good sense of what *he* thought I needed to know about the life of a sponge diver. It was I, the interviewer, who defined the focus of the interview; but it was Savas, the respondent, who determined the content. And was I ever glad he did.

PROBING

The key to successful interviewing is learning how to probe effectively—that is, to stimulate a respondent to produce more information, without injecting yourself so much into the interaction that you only get a reflection of yourself in the data. Suppose you ask, "Have you ever been away from the village to work?" and the informant says, "Yes." The next question (the probe) is: "Like where?" Suppose the answer is, "Oh, several different places." The correct response is not, "Pachuca? Querétaro? Mexico City?" but, "Like where? Could you name some of the places where you've gone to get work?"

There are many kinds of probes that you can use in an interview. (In what follows, I draw on the important work by Briggs [1986], Dohrenwend and Richardson [1965], Gorden [1987], Hyman and Cobb [1975], Kahn and Cannell [1957], Kluckhohn [1945], Merton et al. [1956], Reed and Stimson [1985], Warwick and Lininger [1975], Whyte [1960], Whyte and Whyte [1984], and on my own experience and that of my students.)

The Silent Probe

The most difficult technique to learn is the **silent probe**, which consists of just remaining quiet and waiting for an informant to continue. The silence may be accompanied by a nod or by a mumbled "uh-huh" as you focus on your note pad. The silent probe sometimes produces more information than does direct questioning. At least at the beginning of an interview, informants look to you for guidance as to whether or not they're on the right track. They want to know whether they're "giving you what you want." Most of the time, especially in unstructured interviews, you want the informant to define the relevant information.

Some informants are more glib than others and require very little prodding to keep up the flow of information. Others are more reflective and take their time. Inexperienced interviewers tend to jump in with verbal probes as soon as an informant goes silent. Meanwhile, the informant may be just reflecting, gathering thoughts, and preparing to say something important. You can kill those moments (and there are a lot of them) with your interruptions.

Glibness can be a matter of *cultural*, not just personal style. Gordon Streib reports that he had to adjust his own interviewing style radically when he left New York City to study the Navajo in the 1950s (Streib 1952). Streib, a New Yorker himself, had done studies based on semistructured interviews with subway workers in New York. Those workers maintained a fast, hard-driving pace during the interviews—a pace with which Streib, as a member of the culture, was comfortable.

But that style was entirely inappropriate with the Navajo, who were uniformly more reflective than the subway workers (Streib, personal communication). In other words, the silent probe is sometimes not a "probe" at all; being quiet and waiting for an informant to continue may simply be appropriate cultural behavior.

On the other hand, the silent probe is a high-risk technique, which is why beginners avoid it. If an informant is genuinely at the end of a thought and you don't provide further guidance, your silence can become awkward. You may even lose your credibility as an interviewer. The silent probe takes practice to use effectively. But it's worth the effort.

The Echo Probe

Another kind of probe consists of simply repeating the last thing someone has said, and asking them to continue. This **echo probe** is particularly useful when an informant is describing a process, or an event. "I see. The goat's throat is cut and the blood is drained into a pan for cooking with the meat. Then what happens?" This probe is neutral and doesn't redirect the interview. It shows that you understand what's been said so far and encourages the informant to continue with the narrative. If you use the echo probe too often, though, you'll hear an exasperated informant asking, "Why do you keep repeating what I just said?"

The Uh-huh Probe

You can encourage an informant to continue with a narrative by just making affirmative comments, like "Uh-huh," or "Yes, I see," or "Right, uh-huh," and so on. Matarazzo (1964) showed how powerful this **neutral probe** can be. He did a series of identical, semistructured, 45-minute interviews with a group of informants. He broke each interview into three 15-minute chunks. During the second chunk, the interviewer was told to make affirmative noises, like "uh-huh," whenever the informant was speaking. Informant responses during those chunks were about a third longer than during the first and third periods. If you use the uh-huh or the silent probe, be sure to stay engaged and look directly at your informants.

The Tell-Me-More Probe

This may be the most common form of probe among experienced interviewers. Respondents give you an answer, and you probe for more by saying: "Could you tell me more about that?" Other variations include "Why exactly do you say that?" and "Why exactly do you feel that way?" You have to be careful about using stock probes like these. As Converse and Schuman point out (1974:50), if you get into a rut and repeat these probes like a robot, don't be surprised to hear someone finishing up a nice long discourse by saying, "Yeah, yeah, and why *exactly* do I feel like that?" (I can guarantee personally that the mortification factor only allows this sort of thing to happen once. The memory of the experience lasts a lifetime.)

The Long Question Probe

Another way to induce longer and more continuous responses is by making your questions longer. Instead of asking, "How do you plant a home garden?" ask, "What are all the things you have to do to actually get a home garden going?" When I interviewed sponge divers on Kalymnos, instead of asking them, "What is it like to make a dive into very deep water?" I said, "Tell me about diving into really deep water. What do you do to get ready and how do you descend and ascend? What's it like down there?"

Later in the interview or on another occasion, I would home in on special topics. But to break the ice and get the interview flowing, there is nothing quite as useful as what Spradley (1979) called the **grand tour question**.

This does not mean that asking longer questions or using neutral probes necessarily produces *better* responses. They do, however, produce *more* responses, and, in general, more is better. Furthermore, the more you can keep an informant talking, the more you can express interest in what they are saying and the more you build rapport. This is especially important in the first interview you do with someone whose trust you want to build (see Spradley 1979:80). There is still a lot to be learned about how various kinds of probes affect what informants tell us.

Threatening questions—those asking for sensitive information—should be short but preceded by a long, rambling run-up: "We're interested in the various things that people do these days in order to keep from getting diseases when they have sex. Some people do different kinds of things, and some people do nothing special. Do you ever use condoms?" If the respondents says, "Yes," or "No," or "Sometimes," *then* you can launch that series of questions about why, why not, when, with whom, and so on. The wording of sensitive questions should be supportive and nonjudgmental. (See below for more on threatening questions.)

Probing by Leading

After all this, you may be cautious about being really directive in an interview. Don't be. Many researchers caution against "leading" an informant. Lofland (1976), for example, warns against questions like, "Don't you think that . . . ?" and suggests asking, "What do you think about . . . ?" He is, of course, correct. On the other hand, any question an interviewer asks leads an informant. You might as well learn to do it well.

Consider this leading question that I asked a Ñähñu Indian: "Right. I understand. The compadre is *supposed* to pay for the music for the baptism fiesta. But what happens if the compadre doesn't have the money? Who pays then?" This kind of question can stop the flow of an informant's narrative stone dead. It can also produce more information than the informant would otherwise have provided. At the time, I thought the informant was being overly "normative." That is, I thought he was stating an ideal behavioral custom (having a compadre pay for the music at a fiesta) as if it were never violated.

It turned out that all he was doing was relying on his own cultural competence— "abbreviating," as Spradley (1979:79) called it. The informant took for granted that the anthropologist knew the "obvious" answer: If the compadre didn't have enough money, well, then there might not be any music.

My interruption reminded the informant that I just wasn't up to his level of cultural competence; I needed him to be more explicit. He went on to explain other things that he considered obvious but that I would not have even known to ask about. Someone who has committed himself to pay for the music at a fiesta might borrow money from *another* compadre to fulfill the obligation. In that case, he wouldn't tell the person who was throwing the fiesta. That might make the host feel bad, like he was forcing his compadre to go into debt.

In this interview, in fact, the informant eventually became irritated with me because I asked so many things that he considered obvious. He wanted to abbreviate a lot and to provide a more general summary; I wanted details. I backed off and asked a different informant for the details. I have since learned to start some probes with "This may seem obvious, but . . ." (box 8.2).

BOX 8.2

LISTEN FOR WHAT'S LEFT OUT

Informants abbreviate all the time, and this means that you have to listen carefully for what's *left out*, not just what's *in* the interview narrative. Laurie Price (1987) collected tales of misfortune from very poor people in Quito, Ecuador. In one story, Maria talks about her crippled 6-year-old daughter. As Price tells it, Maria does not mention that, for months, she carried her daughter every day "down a 200-step flight of public stairs and 4 blocks to the nearest bus stop so the girl could go to physical therapy" (p. 318). The child's father, it turns out, drives a bus that he parks every night next to their house, but during the Herculean effort to help the daughter, the father never pitches in or rearranges his schedule. "Such efforts are the unmarked case for mothers," says Price (p. 319).

Directive probes (leading questions) may be based on what an informant has just finished saying, or may be based on something an informant told you an hour ago or a week ago. As you progress in long-term research, you come to have a much greater appreciation for what you really want from an interview. It is perfectly legitimate to use the information you've already collected to focus your subsequent interviews.

This leads researchers from informal to unstructured to semistructured interviews and even to completely structured interviews like questionnaires. When you feel as though you have learned something important about a group and its culture, the next step to test that knowledge—to see if it is idiosyncratic to a particular informant or subgroup in the culture or if it can be reproduced in many informants.

Baiting: The Phased-Assertion Probe

A particularly effective probing technique is called **phased assertion** (Kirk and Miller 1986), or **baiting** (Agar 1996:142). This is when you act like you already know something to get people to open up.

I used this technique in a study of how Ñähñu Indian parents felt about their children learning to read and write Ñähñu. Bilingual (Spanish-Indian) education in Mexico is a politically sensitive issue (Heath 1972), and when I started asking about it a lot of people were reluctant to talk freely.

In the course of informal interviewing, I learned from a schoolteacher in one village that some fathers had come to complain about the teacher trying to get the children to read and write Ñähñu. The fathers, it seems, were afraid that studying Ñähñu would get in the way of their children becoming fluent in Spanish. Once I heard this story, I began to drop hints that I knew the reason parents were against children learning to read and write Ñähñu. As I did this, the parents opened up and confirmed what I'd found out.

Every journalist (and gossip monger) knows this technique well. As you learn a piece of a puzzle from one informant, you use it with the next informant to get more information, and so on. The more you seem to know, the more comfortable people feel about talking to you and the less people feel they are actually divulging anything. *They* are not the ones who are giving away the "secrets" of the group.

Phased assertion also prompts some informants to jump in and correct you if they think you know a little but that you've "got it all wrong." In some cases, I've purposely made wrong assertions to provoke a correcting response.

Verbal Respondents

Some people try to tell you *too much*. They are the kind of people who just love to have an audience. You ask them one little question and off they go on one tangent after another, until you become exasperated. Converse and Schuman (1974:46) recommend "gentle inattention"—putting down your pen, looking away, leafing through your papers. Nigel King (1994:23) recommends saying something like: "That's very interesting. Could we go back to what you were saying earlier about . . ."

You may, however, have to be a bit more obvious. New interviewers, in particular, may be reluctant to cut off informants, afraid that doing so is poor interviewing technique. In fact, as William Foote Whyte notes, informants who want to talk your ear off are probably used to being interrupted. It's the only way their friends get a word in edgewise. But you need to learn how to cut people off without rancor. "Don't interrupt *accidentally* . . . ," Whyte said, "learn to interrupt *gracefully*" (1960:353, emphasis his). Each situation is somewhat different; you learn as you go in this business.

Nonverbal Respondents

One of the really tough things you run into is someone telling you "I don't know" in answer to lots of questions. In qualitative research projects, where you choose respondents precisely because you think they know something of interest, the "don't know" refrain can be especially frustrating. Converse and Schuman (1974:49) distinguish four kinds of don't-know response: (1) I don't know (and frankly I don't care); (2) I don't know (and it's none of your business); (3) I don't know (actually, I do know, but you wouldn't be interested in what I have to say about that); and (4) I don't know (and I wish you'd change the subject because this line of questioning makes me really uncomfortable). There is also the "(I wish I could help you but) I really don't know."

Sometimes you can get beyond this, sometimes you can't. You have to face the fact that not everyone who volunteers to be interviewed is a good respondent. If you probe those people for information when they say, "I don't know," you tempt them to make something up just to satisfy you, as Sanchez and Morchio (1992) found. Sometimes, you just have to take the "don't know" for an answer and cut your losses by going on to someone else (box 8.3).

LEARNING TO INTERVIEW

It's impossible to eliminate reactivity and subjectivity in interviewing, but like any other craft, you get better and better at interviewing the more you practice. It helps a lot to practice in front of others and to have an experienced interviewer monitor and criticize your performance. Even without such help, however, you can improve your interviewing technique just by paying careful attention to what you're doing. Harry Wolcott (1995) offers excellent advice on this score: Pay as much attention to your own words as you do to the words of your respondents (p. 102).

Wolcott also advises: Keep interviews focused on a few big issues (1995:112). More good advice from one of the most accomplished ethnographers around. Here's a guaranteed way to wreck rapport and ruin an interview: An informant asks you, "Why do you ask? What does that have to do with what we're talking about?" You tell her: "Well, it just seemed like an interesting question—you know, something I thought might be useful somehow down the road in the analysis."

Here you are, asking people to give you their time and tell you about their lives and you're treating that time with little respect. If you can't imagine giving a satisfactory answer to the question: "Why did you ask *that*?" then leave *that* out.

Do *not* use your friends as practice informants. You cannot learn to interview with friends because there are role expectations that get in the way. Just when you're really rolling, and getting into probing deeply on some topic that you both know about, they are likely to laugh at you or tell you to knock it off.

Practice interviews should *not* be just for practice. They should be done on topics you're really interested in and with people who are likely to know a lot about those topics. Every interview you do should be conducted as professionally as possible and should produce useful data (with plenty of notes that you can code, file, and cross-file).

The Importance of Language

Most anthropologists (and an increasing number of sociologists and social psychologists) do research outside their own country. If you are planning to go abroad for research, find people from the culture you are going to study and interview them on some topic of interest. If you are going to Turkey to study women's roles, then find Turkish students at your university and interview them on some related topic.

It is often possible to hire spouses of foreign students for these kinds of "practice" interviews. I put "practice" in quotes to emphasize again that these interviews should

BOX 8.3

THE ETHICS OF PROBING

Are these tricks of the trade ethical? Peter Collings (2009) asked Inuit hunters: "Name all of the people you share country food with." The response was usually a very short list, so, when informants stopped listing names, Collings would ask "What about your x? Surely you share food with your x," where x was a category of relative in Innuinaqtun, the local language. This, said Collings, reminded people that he had command of the kinship terminology and that he knew his informant had an x. Later in the interview, Collings would refer to one of the people whom the informant had named and say "So-and-so is your older brother," using the Innuinaqtun term. "Just as the fieldworker is studying the community," says Collings, "so, too, is the community studying the fieldworker" to find out if he or she is culturally competent (pp. 149–50). By demonstrating cultural competence, Collings argues, phased assertion helps establish rapport—at least where he works (p. 139).

Still, getting people to open up creates responsibilities for your informants. First, there is no ethical imperative in social research more important than seeing to it that you do not harm innocent people who have provided you with information in good faith. Not all respondents are innocents, though. Some people commit wartime atrocities. Some practice infanticide. Some are HIV-positive and, out of bitterness, are purposely infecting others. Do you protect them all? Are any of these examples more troublesome to you than others? These are not extreme cases, thrown in here to prepare you for the worst, "just in case." They are the sorts of ethical dilemmas that field researchers confront all the time.

Second, the better you get at making people open up, the more responsible you become that they don't later suffer some emotional distress for having done so. Informants who divulge *too* quickly what they believe to be secret information can later come to have real regrets and even loss of self-esteem. They may suffer anxiety over how much they can trust you to protect them in the community.

It is sometimes better to stop an informant from divulging privileged information in the first or second interview and to wait until both of you have built a mutually trusting relationship. If you sense that an informant is uncomfortable with having spoken too quickly about a sensitive topic, end the interview with light conversation and reassurances about your discretion. Soon after, look up the informant and engage in light conversation again, with no probing or other interviewing techniques involved. This will also provide reassurance of trust.

Remember: The first ethical decision you make in research is whether to collect certain kinds of information at all. Once that decision is made, *you* are responsible for what is done with that information, and *you* must protect people from becoming emotionally burdened for having talked to you.

produce real data of real interest to you. If you are studying a language that you'll need for research, these practice interviews will help you sharpen your skills at interviewing in that language.

Even if you are going off to the interior of the Amazon, this doesn't let you off the hook. It is unlikely that you'll find native speakers of Yanomami on your campus, but you cannot use this as an excuse to wait until you're out in the field to learn general interviewing skills. Interviewing skills are honed by practice. Among the most constructive things you can do in preparing for field research is to practice conducting unstructured and semistructured interviewing. Learn to interview in Portuguese or Spanish (depending on whether the Yanomami you are going to visit live in the Brazilian or Venezuelan Amazon) before heading for the field and you'll be way ahead. (See the section on language in chapter 12 for more on using interpreters.)

Pacing the Study

Two of the biggest problems faced by researchers who rely heavily on semistructured interviews are boredom and fatigue. Even small projects may require 30–40 interviews to generate sufficient data to be worthwhile. Most field researchers collect their own interview data, and asking the same questions over and over again can get pretty old. Gorden (1987) studied 30 interviewers who worked for 12 days doing about two tape-recorded interviews per day. Each interview was from 1 to 2 hours long.

The first interview on each day, over all interviewers, averaged about 30 pages of transcription. The second averaged only 25 pages. Furthermore, the first interviews, on average, got shorter and shorter during the 12-day period of the study. In other words, on any given day, boredom made the second interview shorter, and over the 12 days boredom (and possibly fatigue) took its toll on the first interviews of each day.

Even anthropologists who spend a year in the field may have focused bouts of interviewing on a particular topic. Plan each project, or subproject, in advance and calculate the number of interviews you are going to get. Pace yourself. Spread the project out if possible, and don't try to bring in all your interview data in the shortest possible time— unless you're studying reactions to a hot issue, in which case, spreading things out can create a serious history confound (see chapter 4).

Here's the tradeoff: The longer a project takes, the less likely that the first interviews and the last interviews will be valid indicators of the same things. In long-term, participant observation fieldwork (6 months to a year), I recommend going back to your early informants and interviewing them a second time. See whether their observations and attitudes have changed, and if so, why.

PRESENTATION OF SELF

How should you present yourself in an interview? As a friend? As a professional? As someone who is sympathetic or as someone who is nonjudgmental? It depends on the nature of the project. When the object is to collect comparable data across respondents, then it makes no difference whether you're collecting words or numbers—cordial-but-nonjudgmental is the way to go.

That's sometimes tough to do. You're interviewing someone on a project about what people can do to help the environment, and your respondent says: "All those eco-Nazis want is to make room for more owls. They don't give a damn about real people's jobs." (Yes, that happened on one of my projects.) That's when you find out whether you can probe without injecting your feelings into the interview. Professional interviewers (the folks who collect the data for the General Social Survey, for example) learn to maintain their equilibrium and move on (see Converse and Schuman 1974).

Some situations are so painful, however, that it's impossible to maintain a neutral facade. Gene Shelley interviewed 72 people in Atlanta, Georgia, who were HIV-positive (Shelley et al. 1995). Here's a typical comment by one of Shelly's informants: "I have a lot of trouble watching all my friends die. Sometimes my whole body shuts down inside. I don't want to know people who are going to die. Some of my friends, there are three or four people a week in the obits. We all watch the obits."

How would *you* respond? Do you say: "Uh-huh. Tell me more about that"? Do you let silence take over and force the respondent to go on? Do you say something sympathetic? Shelley reports that she treated each interview as a unique situation and responded as her intuition told her to respond—sometimes more clinically, sometimes less, depending on her judgment of what the respondent needed her to say. Good advice.

On Just Being Yourself

In 1964, when we were working on the island of Kalymnos, my wife Carole would take our 2-month-old baby for daily walks in a carriage. Older women would peek into the baby carriage and make disapproving noises when they saw our daughter sleeping on her stomach. Then they would reach into the carriage and turn the baby over, explaining forcefully that the baby would get the evil eye if we continued to let her sleep on her stomach.

Carole had read the latest edition of *The Commonsense Book of Baby and Child Care* (the classic "baby book" by Dr. Benjamin Spock). We carried two copies of the book with us—in case one fell out of a boat or something—and Carole was convinced by Dr. Spock's writings that babies who sleep on their backs risk choking on their own mucous or vomit. Since then, medical opinion—and all the baby books that young parents read nowadays—have flip-flopped about this issue several times. At the time, though, not wanting to offend anyone, Carole listened politely and tried to act nonjudgmental.

One day, enough was enough. Carole told off a woman who intervened and that was that. From then on, women were more eager to discuss child-rearing practices in general. When we let our baby crawl around on the floor and didn't bundle her up when we took her out for walks, Greek mothers were unhesitant in telling us that they disapproved. The more we challenged them, the more they challenged us. There was no rancor involved, and we learned a lot more than if Carole had just kept on listening politely and had said nothing. This was informal interviewing in the context of long-term participant observation. If we had offended anyone, there would have been time and opportunity to make amends—or at least come to an understanding about cultural differences.

Little Things Mean a Lot

Little things are important in interviewing, so pay attention to them. How you dress and where you hold an interview, for example, tell your respondent a lot about you and what you expect. The "interviewing dress code" is: Use common sense. Proper dress depends on the venue. Showing up with a backpack or an attaché case, wearing jeans or a business suit—these are choices that should be pretty easy to make once you've made the commitment to accommodate your dress to different circumstances.

Same goes for venue. I've held interviews in bars, in business offices, in government offices, on ferry boats, on beaches, in homes. . . . I can't give you a rule for selecting the single *right* place for an interview, since there may be several right places. But some places are just plain wrong for certain interviews. Here again, common sense goes a long way (**Further Reading:** interviewing).

USING A VOICE RECORDER

Don't rely on your memory in interviewing; use a voice recorder in all structured and semistructured interviews, except where people specifically ask you not to. If you sense some reluctance about the recorder, leave it on the table and don't turn it on right away. Start the interview with chitchat and when things get warmed up, say something like "This is really interesting. I don't want to trust my memory on something as important as this; do you mind if I record it?" Charles Kadushin (personal communication) hands people a microphone with a shut-off switch. Rarely, he says, do respondents actually use the switch, but giving people control over the interview shows that you take them very seriously.

Sometimes you'll be recording an interview and things will be going along just fine and you'll sense that a respondent is backing off from some sensitive topic. Just reach over to the recorder and ask the respondent if she or he would like you to turn it off. Harry Wolcott (1995:114) recommends leaving the recorder on, if possible, when the formal part of an interview ends. Even though you've finished, Wolcott points out, your respondent may have more to say.

Recording Equipment

For simple recording and transcribing of interviews, in a language you understand well, you can get away with a basic audio recorder for under $50. (But buy two of them. When you skimp on equipment costs, and don't have a spare, this almost guarantees that you'll need one at the most inconvenient moment.) Basic recorders, with 256mb of flash memory hold about 150 hours of voice recording. You can also use your iPod as a digital audio recorder with a plug-in microphone. A gigabyte of disk space holds about 400 hours of voice recordings, so an 80-gigabyte iPod has plenty of room for both music and interviews.

Whatever kind of work you do, remember to upload your data regularly to a computer and to store your data in several places—CDs, external hard drives, or online. And if you are in an isolated field site and don't have reliable power, take along a solar battery charger so you can get your data offline and onto a CD.

Some of the better voice recorders come with up to four built-in microphones that capture 360-degree sound. If you use a low-end recorder, then use a good, separate microphone. Some people like wearing a lavalier microphone—the kind you clip to a person's lapel or shirt collar—but many people find them intrusive. I prefer omnidirectional microphones because they pick up voices from anywhere in a room. Sometimes, people get rolling on a topic and they want to get up and pace the room as they talk. Want to kill a really great interview? Tell somebody who's on a roll to please sit down and speak directly into the mike. Good microphones come with stands that keep the head from resting on any surface, like a table. Surfaces pick up and introduce background noise into any recording. If you don't have a really good stand for the mike, you can make one easily with some rubbery foam (the kind they use in making mattresses).

Test your recorder before every interview. And do the testing at home. There's only one thing worse than a recorder that doesn't run at all. It's one that runs but doesn't record. Then your informant is sure to say at the end of the interview: "Let's run that back and see how it came out!" (Yes, that happened to me. But only once. And it needn't happen to anyone who reads this.)

Pay attention to the battery indicator. Want another foolproof way to kill an exciting interview? Ask the informant to "please hold that thought" while you change batteries. When batteries get slightly low, throw them out or recharge them. If you are working in places that have unstable current, you'll rely on batteries to ensure recording fidelity. Just make sure that you start out with fresh batteries for each interview. (You can save a lot of battery life by using house current for all playback, fast forward, and rewind operations—reserving the batteries *only* for recording.) If you prefer household current for recording, then carry along a couple of long extension cords so you have a choice of where to set up for the interview. (See Ives [1995] for more good tips.)

In voice activation mode, the recorder only turns off during long pauses—while an informant is thinking, for example. Holly Williams (personal communication) recommends not using the voice activation feature for interviews. She finds that the long breaks without any sound make transcribing easier. You don't have to shut the machine off and turn it on as many times while you're typing.

Transcribers and VR software

It takes 6–8 hours to transcribe 1 hour of a recorded interview, depending on how closely you transcribe (getting all the "uhs" and "ers" and throat clearings, or just capturing the main elements of speech), how clear the recording is, and how proficient you are in the language and in typing. If you have to transcribe interviews yourself, there are several choices for equipment. Transcription software lets you control the recorder (start, stop, move forward and backward) using the keyboard. Transcriber machines let you do this using a foot pedal. This lets you listen to a couple of seconds of recording at a time, type everything into the computer, and then move on to the next chunk. The technology lets you go back and repeat chunks, all while keeping your hands on the keyboard.

With voice recognition (VR) software, you listen to an interview through a set of headphones and repeat the words—both your questions and your informant's responses—out loud, in your own voice. The software listens to your voice and types out the words across the screen. You go over each sentence to correct mistakes (tell it that the word "bloat" should be "float" for instance) and to format the text (tell it where to put punctuation and paragraph breaks). The process is slow at first, but the software learns over time to recognize inflections in your voice, and it makes fewer and fewer mistakes as weeks go by. It also learns all the special vocabulary you throw at it. The built-in vocabularies of current VRS systems are enormous—something like 300,000 words—but, though they may be ready to recognize polygamy, for example, you'll have to teach it polygyny or fraternal polyandry and words from the language of your field site. So, if you say, "Juanita sold eight *huipiles* at the market this week," you'll have to spell out "Juanita" and "*huipiles*" so the software can add these words to its vocabulary.

As the software gets trained, the process moves up to 95%–98% accuracy at about 100–120 words per minute. With a 2%–5% error rate, you still have to go over every line of your work to correct it, but the total time for transcribing interviews can be reduced by half or more. (More about VR software in appendix E) (**Further Reading:** transcription).

Recording Is Not a Substitute for Taking Notes

Finally, never substitute recording for note taking. Take notes during the interview *about* the interview. Did the informant seem nervous or evasive? Were there a lot of interruptions? What were the physical surroundings like? How much probing did you have to do? Take notes on the contents of the interview, even though you get every word on the machine.

A few informants will let you use a recorder but will balk at your taking notes. Don't assume, however, that informants will be offended if you take notes. Ask them. Most of the time, all you do by avoiding note taking is lose a lot of data. Informants are under no illusions about what you're doing. You're interviewing them. You might as well take notes and get people used to it, if you can.

FOCUS GROUPS

Focus groups are recruited to discuss a particular topic—anything from people's feelings about brands of beer to their experience in toilet training their children. The method derives from work by Paul Lazarsfeld and Robert Merton in 1941 at Columbia University's Office of Radio Research. A group of people listened to a recorded radio program that was supposed to raise public morale prior to America's entry into World War II. The listeners were told to push a red button whenever they heard something that made them react negatively and to push a green button when they heard something that made them react positively. The reactions were recorded automatically by a primitive polygraph-like apparatus. When the program was over, an interviewer talked to the group of listeners to find out why they had felt positively or negatively about each message they'd reacted to (Merton 1987) (box 8.4).

BOX 8.4

NOT ALL GROUP INTERVIEWS ARE *FOCUS GROUP* INTERVIEWS

Sometimes, you just find yourself in an interview situation with a lot of people. You're interviewing someone and other people just come up and insert themselves into the conversation. This happens spontaneously all the time in long-term fieldwork in small communities, where people all know one another. Rachel Baker (1996a, 1996b), for example, studied homeless boys in Kathmandu. When she interviewed boys in temples or junkyards, others might come by and be welcomed into the conversation-interview situation. If you insist on privacy, you might find yourself with no interview at all. Better to take advantage of the situation and just let the information flow. Just be sure to take notes on who's there, who's dominant, who's just listening, and so on, in any group interview.

The commercial potential of Lazarsfeld and Merton's pioneering work was immediately clear. The method of real-time recording of people's reactions, combined with focused interviewing of a group, is today a mainstay in advertising research and product design. MCI, the now defunct long-distance phone company, used focus groups to develop their advertising when they were just starting out. They found that customers didn't blame AT&T for the high cost of their long-distance phone bills; they blamed themselves for talking too long on long-distance calls. MCI came out with the advertising slogan: "You're not talking too much, just spending too much." The rest, as they say, is history (Krueger 1994:33).

Why Are Focus Groups So Popular?

The focus group method was a commercial success from the 1950s on, but it lay dormant in academic circles for more than 20 years. This is probably because the method is virtually devoid of statistics. Beginning in the late 1970s, however, interest among social researchers of all kinds boomed as researchers came to understand the benefits of combining qualitative and quantitative methods.

Focus groups do not replace surveys, but rather complement them. You can convene a focus group to discuss questions for a survey. Do the questions seem arrogant to respondents? Appropriate? Naive? A focus group can discuss the wording of a particular question or offer advice on how the whole questionnaire comes off to respondents. And you can convene a focus group to help interpret the results of a survey. But focus groups are not just adjuncts to surveys. They are widely used to find out *why* people feel as they do about something or the steps people go through in making decisions.

Two Cases of Focus Groups

Knodel et al. (1984), for example, used focus groups to study the fertility transition in Thailand. They held separate group sessions for married men under 35 and married women under 30 who wanted three or fewer children. They also held separate sessions for men and women over 50 who had at least five children. This gave them four separate groups. In all cases, the participants had no more than an elementary school education.

Knodel et al. repeated this four-group design in six parts of Thailand to cover the religious and ethnic diversity of the country. The focus of each group discussion was on the number of children people wanted and why.

Thailand was going through fertility transition in the 1980s, and the focus group study illuminated the reasons for the transition. "Time and again," these researchers report, "when participants were asked why the younger generation wants smaller families than the older generation had, they responded that nowadays everything is expensive" (Knodel et al. 1984:302).

People also said that all children, girls as well as boys, needed education to get the jobs that would pay for the more expensive, monetized lifestyle to which people were then becoming accustomed. It is, certainly, easier to pay for the education of fewer children. These consistent responses are what you'd expect in a society undergoing fertility transition.

Ruth Wilson et al. (1993) used focus groups in their study of acute respiratory illness (ARI) in Swaziland. They interviewed 33 individual mothers, 13 traditional healers, and 17 health care providers. They also ran 33 focus groups: 16 male groups and 17 female groups. The groups had from 4 to 15 participants, with an average of 7.

Each individual respondent and each group was presented with two hypothetical cases. Wilson et al. asked their respondents to diagnose each case and to suggest treatments. Here are the cases:

Case 1. A mother has a 1-year-old baby girl with the following signs: coughing, fever, sore throat, running or blocked nose, and red or teary eyes. When you ask the mother, she tells you that the child can breast-feed well but is not actively playing.

Case 2. A 10-month-old baby was brought to a health center with the following signs: rapid/difficult breathing, chest indrawing, fever for one day, sunken eyes, coughing for three days. The mother tells you that the child does not have diarrhea but has a poor appetite.

Many useful comparisons were possible with the data from this study. For example, mothers attributed the illness in Case 2 mostly to the weather, heredity, or the child's home environment. The male focus groups diagnosed the child in Case 2 as having asthma, fever, indigestion, malnutrition, or worms.

Wilson et al. (1993) acknowledge that a large number of individual interviews make it easier to estimate the degree of error in a set of interviews. However, they conclude that the focus groups provided valid data on the terminology and practices related to ARI in Swaziland. Wilson and her coworkers did, after all, have 240 respondents in their focus groups; they had data from in-depth interviews of all categories of persons involved in treating children's ARI; and they had plenty of participant observation in Swaziland to back them up.

Note some very important things about these studies. First, neither of them was based on a *single focus group* but on *a series of focus groups*. Second, in both studies, the groups were homogeneous with respect to certain independent variables—gender, number of children desired or produced, ethnicity—just as we saw with respect to experimental and sampling design. Finally, in the study by Knodel et al., the 24 groups were chosen to represent a subgroup in a factorial design—again just as we saw with experiments in chapter 4 and with sampling design in chapter 5. In other words, these focus group studies were designed to provide not only in-depth data about the reasons behind people's behavior, but data that could be systematically compared across groups.

Are Focus Groups Valid?

Ward et al. (1991) compared focus group and survey data from three studies of voluntary sterilization (tubal ligation or vasectomy) in Guatemala, Honduras, and Zaire. Ward et al. report that, "Overall, for 28% of the variables the results were similar" in the focus group and survey data. "For 42% the results were similar but focus groups provided additional detail; for 17% the results were similar, but the survey provided more detail. And in only 12% of the variables were the results dissimilar" (p. 273).

In the Guatemala study, 97% of the women surveyed reported no regrets with their decision to have a tubal ligation. The "vast majority" of women in the focus groups also reported no regrets. This was counted as a "similar result." Ten percent of the women surveyed reported having had a tubal ligation for health reasons. In the focus groups, too, just a few women reported health factors in their decision to have the operation, but they provided more detail and context, citing such things as complications from previous pregnancies.

This is an example of where the focus group and survey provide similar results, but where the focus group offers more detail. Data from the focus groups and the survey confirm that women heard about the operation from similar sources, but the survey shows that 40% of the women heard about it from a sterilized woman, 26% heard about it from a health professional, and so on. Here, the survey provides more detail, though both methods produce similar conclusions.

Gillespie (1992) compared the results of four focus groups with data from a survey of the same population and found that results were dissimilar in 18% of the variables. The bottom line: Focus groups—like participant observation, in-depth interviews, and other systematic qualitative methods—should be used for the collection of data about content and process and not for estimating population parameters of personal attributes. The belief that a woman has or does not have a right to an abortion is a personal attribute, like gender, age, annual income, or religion. If you want to estimate the proportion of people in a population who believe that a woman has a right to an abortion, then focus groups are not the method of choice.

A proportion is a number, and if you want a good number—a valid one, a useful one—you need a method that produces exactly that. A survey, based on a representative sample, is the method of choice here. But if you want information about content—about *why* people think a woman should or should not have the right to an abortion—then that's just the sort of thing a focus group can illuminate.

RUNNING A FOCUS GROUP

The group moderator gets people talking about whatever issue is under discussion. Leading a focus group requires the combined skills of an ethnographer, a survey researcher, and a therapist. You have to watch out for people who want to show off and close them down without coming on too strongly. You have to watch out for shy people and draw them out, without being intimidating. Tips on how to do all this, and a lot more, are in *The Focus Group Kit*, a series of six how-to books (D. L. Morgan and Krueger 1998). Don't even think about getting into focus group management without going through this kit (box 8.5).

BOX 8.5

COMPOSITION OF A FOCUS GROUP

Focus groups typically have 6–12 members, plus a moderator. Seven or 8 people is a popular size. If a group is too small, it can be dominated by 1 or 2 loudmouths; if it gets beyond 10 or 12, it gets tough to manage. Smaller groups are better when you're trying to get really in-depth discussions going about sensitive issues (D. L. Morgan 1997). Of course, this assumes that the group is run by a skilled moderator who knows how to get people to open up and how keep them opened up.

The participants in a focus group should be more or less homogeneous and, in general, should not know one another. Richard Krueger, a very experienced focus group moderator, says that "familiarity tends to inhibit disclosure" (1994:18). It's easy to open up more when you get into a discussion with people whom you are unlikely ever to see again (sort of like what happens on long air flights). Obviously, what "homogeneous" means depends on what you're trying to learn. If you want to know why a smaller percentage of middle-class African American women over 40 get mammograms than do their white counterparts, then you need a group of middle-class African American women who are over 40.

In a focus group about sensitive issues like abortion or drug use, the leader works at getting the group to gel and getting members to feel that they are part of an understanding cohort of people. If the group is run by an accomplished leader, one or more members will eventually feel comfortable about divulging sensitive information about themselves. Once the ice is broken, others will feel less threatened and will join in. Moderators should not be known to the members of a focus group, and focus group members should not be employees of a moderator. Hierarchy is not conducive to openness.

In running a focus group, remember that people will disclose more in groups that are supportive and nonjudgmental. Tell people that there are no right or wrong answers to the questions you will ask and emphasize that you've invited people who are similar in their backgrounds and social characteristics. This, too, helps people open up (Krueger 1994:113).

Above all, don't lead too much and don't put words in people's mouths. In studying nutritional habits, don't ask a focus group why they eat or don't eat certain foods; do ask them to talk about what kinds of foods they like and dislike and why. In studying risky sexual behavior, don't ask, "Do you use condoms whenever you visit a prostitute?"; do ask people to talk about their experience with prostitutes and exactly what kind of sexual practices they prefer. Your job is to keep the discussion on the topic. Eventually, people will hit on the nutritional habits or the sexual acts that interest you, and you can pick up the thread from there.

Analyzing Data from Focus Groups

You can analyze focus group data with the same techniques you would use on any corpus of text: field notes, life histories, open-ended interviews, and so on. As with all large chunks of text, you have two choices for very different kinds of analysis. You can do formal content analysis, or you can do qualitative analysis. See chapters 18 and 19 for more about this.

As with in-depth interviews, it's best to record (or videotape) focus groups. This is a bit tricky, though, because any audio of a focus group, whether digital or tape, is hard to understand and transcribe if two or more people talk at once. A good moderator keeps people talking one at a time. Don't hide the recorder or the microphones. Someone is sure to ask if they're being recorded, and when you tell them, "Yes"—which you must do—they're sure to wonder why they had to ask.

If you are just trying to confirm some ideas or to get a general notion of how people feel about a topic, you can simply take notes from the audio and work with your notes. Most focus groups, however, are transcribed. The real power of focus groups is that they produce ethnographically rich data. Only transcription captures a significant part of that richness. But be prepared to work with a lot of information. Any single hour-and-a-half focus group can easily produce 50 pages or more of text.

Many focus groups have two staff members: a moderator and a person who does nothing but jot down the name of each person who speaks and the first few words they say. This makes it easier for a transcriber to identify the voices. If you can't afford this, or if you feel that people would be uncomfortable with someone taking down their names, you can call on people by name, or mention their name when you respond to them. Things can get rolling in a focus group (that's what you want), and you'll have a tough time transcribing the audio if you don't know who's talking (**Further Reading:** focus groups).

RESPONSE EFFECTS

Response effects are measurable differences in the responses of people being interviewed that are predictable from characteristics of the interviewers and those being interviewed— like whether the sex or race or age of interviewer and of the respondent are the same or different—and dozens of other things (box 8.6).

As early as 1929, Stuart Rice showed that the political orientation of interviewers can effect what they report people told them. Rice was doing a study of derelicts in flop houses

BOX 8.6

THE EXPECTANCY EFFECT

In 1966, Robert Rosenthal and Lenore Jacobson (1968) conducted an experiment. At the beginning of the school year, they told some teachers at a school that the children they were about to get had tested out as "spurters." That is, according to tests, they said, those particular children were expected to make significant gains in their academic scores during the coming year. Sure enough, those children did improve dramatically—which was really interesting, because Rosenthal and Jacobson had matched the "spurter" children and teachers at random.

This experiment showed the power of the **expectancy effect**, or "the tendency for experimenters to obtain results they expect, not simply because they have correctly anticipated nature's response but rather because they have helped to shape that response through their expectations" (Rosenthal and Rubin 1978:377).

Strictly speaking, the expectancy effect is not a response effect at all. But for fieldworkers, it is an important effect to keep in mind. If you are studying a small community, or a neighborhood in a city, or a hospital or clinic for a year or more, interacting daily with a few key informants, your own behavior can affect theirs in subtle (and not so subtle) ways, and vice versa. Don't be surprised if you find your own behavior changing over time in relation to key informants.

and he noticed that the men contacted by one interviewer consistently said that their down-and-out status was the result of alcohol; the men contacted by the other interviewer blamed social and economic conditions and lack of jobs. It turned out that the first interviewer was a prohibitionist and the second was a socialist (cited in Cannell and Kahn 1968:549). Katz (1942) found that middle-class interviewers got more politically conservative answers in general from lower-class respondents than did lower-class interviewers, and Robinson and Rhode (1946) found that interviewers who looked non-Jewish and had non-Jewish-sounding names were almost *four times more likely* to get anti-Semitic answers to questions about Jews than were interviewers who were Jewish looking and who had Jewish-sounding names.

Since these pioneering efforts, hundreds of studies have been conducted on the impact of things like race, sex, age, and accent of both the interviewer and the informant; features of the environment where the interview takes place (like whether the interview is done in private or in the presence of a third party); the nature of the task that people are asked to perform (like whether the respondent is asked to write out an answer, in text, or to just circle a number on a form); the mode of the interview (like comparing face-to-face, telephone, and Internet interviews about the same topic).

Sex-of-interviewer effects have been the focus of many studies. Hyman and Cobb (1975), for example, found that female interviewers who took their cars in for repairs themselves (as opposed to having their husbands do it) were more likely to have female respondents who reported getting their own cars repaired. Zehner (1970) found that when women in the United States were asked by women interviewers about premarital sex, they were more inhibited than if they were asked by men. Male respondents' answers were not affected by the gender of the interviewer. McCombie and Anarfi (2002) found the same sex-of-interviewer effect 30 years later in Ghana: Young men (15–18 year olds) were equally likely to tell male or female interviewers that they had had sex, but young women were more likely to divulge this to male interviewers than to female interviewers. In the Tamang Family Research Project in Nepal, William Axinn (1991) found that women were simply better than men as interviewers: The female interviewers had significantly fewer "don't know" responses than did the male interviewers. Axinn supposes this might be because the survey dealt with marital and fertility histories. In a multi-year study in Kenya of women's networks and their AIDS-related behavior, Alex Weinreb (2006) found that the most reliable data were collected by female-*insider* interviewers—that is, women from the local area who were trained to be interviewers for the project— compared to the *stranger*-interviewers who were brought in from the outside (box 8.7).

The Deference Effect

When people tell you what they think you want to know, so as not to offend you, that's called the **deference effect**. Aunger (1992, 2004) may have experienced this in Zaire (see box 8.7). In fact, it happens all the time, and researchers have long been aware of the problem. In 1958, Lenski and Leggett embedded two contradictory questions in a face-to-face interview, half an hour apart. Respondents were asked whether they agreed or disagreed with the following two statements: (1) It's hardly fair to bring children into the world, the way things look for the future; (2) Children born today have a wonderful future to look forward to. Just 5% of Whites agreed with *both* statements compared to 20% of African Americans. Lenski and Leggett concluded that this was the deference effect in action: Blacks were four times more likely than Whites to agree to anything, even contradictory statements, because the interviewers were almost all white and of higher perceived status than the respondents (Lenski and Leggett 1960).

In the National Black Election Study, 872 African Americans were polled before and after the 1984 presidential election. Since interviewers were assigned randomly to respondents, some people were interviewed by a white person before the election and an African American after the election. And vice versa: Some people were interviewed by an African American before the election and a white person on the second wave. When African American interviewers in the preelection polls were replaced by white interviewers in the postelection surveys, African Americans were more likely to say that Blacks don't have the power to change things, that Blacks can't make a difference in local or national elections, that Blacks cannot form their own political party, and that Whites are not responsible for keeping Blacks down—very powerful evidence of a race-of-interviewer effect (D. W. Davis 1997) (box 8.8).

Reese et al. (1986:563) tested the deference effect in a telephone survey of Anglo and Mexican American respondents. When asked specifically about their cultural preference, 58% of Hispanic respondents said they preferred Mexican American culture over other cultures, irrespective of whether the interviewer was Anglo or Hispanic. Just 9% of Anglo respondents said they preferred Mexican American culture when asked by Anglo interviewers, but 23% said they preferred Mexican American culture when asked by Hispanic interviewers.

Questions about gender and gender roles produce deference effects, too. When you ask people in the United States how most couples actually divide child care, men are more likely than women to say that men and women share this responsibility—if the interviewer is a man (Kane and McCaulay 1993:11). Do women have too much influence, just

BOX 8.7

THE INSIDER-INTERVIEW EFFECT IN THE ITURI
FOREST

Robert Aunger (1992, 2004:145–62) studied three groups of people in the Ituri
forest of Zaire. The Lese and Budu are horticultural, and the Efe are foragers.
Aunger wanted to know if they shared the same food avoidances. He and three
assistants, two Lese men and one Budu man, interviewed a total of 65 people.
Each of the respondents was interviewed twice and was asked the same 140
questions about a list of foods.

Aunger identified two types of errors in his data: forgetting and mistakes. If
informants said in the first interview that they did not avoid a particular food
but said in the second interview that they did avoid the food, Aunger counted
the error as forgetfulness. If informants reported in interview two a different
type of avoidance for a food than they'd reported in interview one, then Aunger
counted this as a mistake.

Even with some missing data, Aunger had over 8,000 pairs of responses in
his data (65 *pairs* of interviews, each with up to 140 responses), so he was able
to look for the causes of discrepancies between interview one and interview
two. About 67% of the forgetfulness errors and about 79% of the mistake errors
were correlated with characteristics of informants (gender, ethnic group, age,
and so on). However, about a quarter of the variability in what informants
answered to the same question at two different times was due to characteristics
of the interviewers (ethnic group, gender, native language, etc.), and about 12%
of variability in forgetting was explained by interviewer experience. As the interviewers interviewed more and more informants, the informants were less likely
to report "no avoidance" on interview one and some avoidance on interview
two for a specific food. In other words, interviewers got better and better with
practice at drawing out informants on their food avoidances.

Of the four interviewers, though, the two Lese and the Budu got much better,
while the anthropologist made very little progress. Was this because of Aunger's interviewing style, or because informants generally told the anthropologist
different things than they told local interviewers, or because there is something
special about informants in the Ituri forest? We'll know when we add variables
to Aunger's study and repeat it in many cultures, including our own (**Further
Reading:** response effects).

the right amount of influence, or too little influence in today's society? When asked *this*
question by a male interviewer, men are more likely to say that women have *too much*
influence; when asked the same question by a female interviewer, men are more likely to
say that women have *too little* influence. And similarly for women: When asked by a
female interviewer, women are more likely to say that men have *too much* influence than
when asked by a male interviewer (Kane and Macaulay 1993:14–15).

Lueptow et al. (1990) found that women gave more liberal responses to female interviewers than to male interviewers on questions about gender roles. Men's attitudes about
gender roles were, for the most part, unaffected by the gender of the interviewer—except

> **BOX 8.8**
>
> ## BARACK OBAMA AND THE BRADLEY EFFECT
>
> In 1982, Tom Bradley, the mayor of Los Angeles, ran against George Deukmejian for the office of governor of California. Bradley was ahead in the polls for the governorship of California right up to election day—and lost. Some voters had told pollsters that they were for Bradley, who is black, and then voted for Deukejian, who is white. The so-called Bradley effect was at work in 1989, when Douglas Wilder, an African American, ran against Marshall Coleman, who is white, for the governorship of Virginia. Preelection polls showed that Wilder was far ahead, but in the end, he won by only a slim margin. White voters were more likely to claim Wilder as their choice if the interviewer was African American than if the interviewer was white (Finkel et al. 1991). Barack Obama is widely credited with ending the Bradley Effect, but he lost the 2008 New Hampshire primary to Hillary Clinton by three points after being ahead in the polls by eight points—right up to election day (Kohut 2008).

that highly educated men gave the *most* liberal responses about gender roles to female interviewers. "It appears," said Lueptow et al., "that educated respondents of both sexes are shifting their answers toward the socially desirable positions they think are held by female interviewers" (p. 38). Attitudes about gender roles sure are adaptable. That was in 1990. In 2008, about 26% of the American public was "angry or upset" at the prospect of a woman president, even though, at the time almost 90% of Americans told pollsters that they would vote for a qualified woman foir president (Streb et al. 2008:77).

Questions that aren't race related, by the way, are not affected much by the race or the ethnicity of either the interviewer or the respondent. Still, whenever you have multiple interviewers, keep track of the race, ethnicity, and gender of the interviewer and test for response effects. Identifying sources of bias is better than not identifying them, even if you can't eliminate them (**Further Reading:** the deference effect).

The Social Desirability Effect

When people tell you what they think will make them look good, especially according to prevailing standards of behavior and thought, that's the social desirability effect. Hadaway et al. (1998) went to a large Protestant church and found 115 people in attendance at the Sunday school. On Monday morning, when Hadaway et al. polled the whole church membership, 181 people claimed to have been in Sunday school the previous day. Headcount experiments like this one typically produce estimates of church attendance that are 55%–59% of what people report (T. W. Smith 1998).

The social desirability effect is influenced by the way you ask the question. Major surveys, like the Gallup Poll, ask something like: "How often do you attend religious services?" Then they give the people choices like "once a week, once a month, seldom, never." Presser and Stinson (1998) asked people on Monday to list everything they had done did from "midnight Saturday to midnight last night." When they asked the question this way, 29% of respondents said that they had gone to church. Asking "How often do you go to church?" produced estimates of 37%–45%. This is a 28%–50% *difference* in reported behavior and is statistically very significant (**Further Reading:** social desirability effect).

The Third-Party-Present Effect

We sort of take it for granted that interviews are private conversations, conducted one on one, but in fact, many face-to-face interviews have at least one third party in the room, often the spouse or partner of the person being interviewed. Does this affect how people respond to questions? As with other response effects, the answer is yes, sometimes. Zipp and Toth (2002), for example, analyzed data from a household survey in Britain and found that when the spouses are interviewed together, they are much more likely to agree about many things—like who does what around the house—than when they are interviewed separately. Apparently, people listen to each other's answers and modify their own answers accordingly, which puts on a nice, unified face about their relationship.

As you'd expect, there is a social desirablity effect when a third party is present. Casterline and Chidambaram (1984) examined data from 24 developing countries in the World Fertility Study and found that women in those countries are less likely to admit using contraception when a third party is present at the interview. Anthropologists face this situation a lot: trying to get people to talk about sensitive topics and assuring them of privacy, but unable to find the privacy for an interview.

On the other hand, Aquilino (1993) found that when their spouse is in the room, people report more marital conflict than when they are interviewed alone. They are also more likely to report that they and their spouse lived together before marriage if their spouse is in the room. Perhaps, as Mitchell (1965) suggested 45 years ago, people own up more to sensitive things like this when they know it will be obvious to their spouse that they are lying. Seems like a good thing to test (**Further Reading:** third-party-present effect).

Threatening Questions

In general, if you are asking someone a nonthreatening question, like whether they have a library card, then response effects are minimal. But if you ask people about their alcohol consumption, or whether they ever shoplifted when they were children, or whether they have family members who have had mental illness, or how many sexual partners they've had, then response effects are really important. One key finding on this problem is, intuitively, that disclosure of information about socially undesirable behavior increases with the perception people have of their anonymity (Tourangeau and Yan 2007). So, people open up more on questionnaires about illegal or embarrassing behavior that are self-administered than in surveys conducted face-to-face, and still more when they think that a survey is truly anonymous. (See the section on the randomized response technique and the section on computerized interviews in chapter 9.)

Asking about other people increases reports about socially undesirable behavior. Katz and Naré (2002) asked 1,973 single Muslim women between the ages of 15 and 24 in Dakar, Senegal, if they had ever been pregnant. Three percent of the women said they had. But 25% of the same women said that at least one of their *three closest friends* had been pregnant—more than eight times what they reported about themselves. (See Sudman et al. [1977:147–51] on the three-closest-friends technique.)

Asking the interviewers on a project to record their interviews produces a higher response rate, particularly to sensitive questions about things like sexual behavior. Apparently, when interviewers know that their work can be scrutinized (from the recordings), they probe more and get informants to open up more (Billiet and Loosveldt 1988).

And if you give people choices that include a big number of any behavior, you'll probably get reports of more of that behavior. Tourangeau and Smith (1996) asked men and women: "During the last 12 months, that is, since August/September 1993, how many men [women], if any, have you had intercourse with?" Some people were asked simply to tell the interviewer a number. Others were asked to choose one of the following: 0, 1, 2, 3, 4, 5 or more. And still others were asked to choose one of the following: 1–4, 5–9, 10–49, 50–99, 100 or more. People reported more sex partners when given high-end choices than when given low-end choices or an open-ended question (Tourangeau and Smith 1996:292). In Germany, people reported watching more television when they were given choices that included a big number of hours (Schwarz et al. 1985).

You might be surprised, though, at what counts as a threatening question. R. A. Peterson (1984) asked 1,324 people one of the following questions: (1) How old are you? (2) What is your age? (3) In what year were you born? or (4) Are you 18–24 years of age, 25–34, 35–49, 50–64, 65 or older? Then Peterson got the true ages for all the respondents from reliable records. There was no significant difference in the accuracy of the answers obtained with the four questions, but almost 10% of respondents refused to answer question 1, while only 1% refused to answer question 4, and this difference *is* significant (**Further Reading:** asking threatening questions).

ACCURACY

Even when people tell you what they think is the absolute truth, there is still the question of whether the information they give you is accurate.

A lot of research—ethnographic and survey research alike—is about mapping opinions and attitudes. When people tell you that they *approve of* how the chief is handling negotiations for their village's resettlement, or when they tell you that they *prefer* a particular brand of beer to some other brand, they're talking about internal states. You pretty much have to take their word for such things.

But when we ask people to tell us about their actual behavior (How many times did you take your baby to the clinic last month? How many times last year did you visit your mother's village?), or about their environmental circumstances (How many hectares of land do you have in maize? How many meters is it from your house to the well?), we can't just assume informant accuracy (box 8.9).

We see reports of behavior in our local newspapers all the time: College students today are binge drinking more than they did 5 years ago. Americans are going to church less often than they did a decade ago.

In back of *findings* like these are *questions* like these:

Circle one answer:
How many times last month did you consume five or more beers or other alcoholic drinks in a single day?

> Never
> Once
> Twice
> Three times
> More than three times

How often do you go to church?

> Never
> Occasionally—once a month or less
> About once a week
> More than once a week

BOX 8.9

DIETARY RECALL

Studies of diet and human nutrition mostly rely on informants to recall what they've eaten over the past 24 hours or what they usually eat for various meals. They often produce dreadfully inaccurate results.

C. J. Smith et al. (1996) compared the responses of 575 Pima and Papago Indians (in Arizona) to a 24-hour recall instrument about food intake with responses to a very detailed survey called the Quantitative Food Frequency questionnaire. In the QFF, interviewers probe for a list of regularly consumed foods in a community. Smith et al. also assessed the energy expenditure of 21 people in the research group using the doubly labeled water technique. The DLW technique involves giving people special water to drink—water with isotopes that can be tracked in blood and urine samples—and then testing, over time, their actual intake of nutrients.

The correlation, across the 21 participants, between the energy intake measured by the DLW technique and the energy intake estimated by the informants' responses to the QFF, was 0.48. This correlation is statistically significant, but it means that just 23% (0.48^2) of the variation in actual energy intake across the 21 people was accounted for by their responses to a very detailed interview about their food consumption. And the correlation of actual energy intake with estimates from the 24-hour recall data was much worse.

R. K. Johnson et al. (1996) also found no useful relation between individual 24-hour recall measurements of energy intake among children in Vermont and measurements of those same children by the DLW technique. But, in the all-is-not-lost department, Johnson et al. found that averaging the data for energy intake across *three* 24-hour recalls in 14 days (on day 1, day 8, and day 14) produced results that were very similar to those produced by the DLW technique. So, people hover around giving accurate answers to a question about calorie intake and if you get at least three answers for three time windows and take the average, you may get a useful result (**Further Reading**: measuring food intake and physical activity).

La Pierre Discovers the Problem

We've known for a long time that we should be suspicious of this kind of data. From 1930 to 1932, Richard La Pierre, accompanied by a Chinese couple, crisscrossed the United States, twice, by car. The threesome covered about 10,000 miles, stopping at 184 restaurants and 66 hotels. And they kept records. There was a lot of prejudice against Chinese in those days, but they were not refused service in a single restaurant and just one hotel turned them away (La Pierre 1934).

Six months after the experiment ended, La Pierre sent a questionnaire to each of the 250 establishments where the group had stopped. One of the things he asked was: "Will you accept members of the Chinese race as guests?" Ninety-two percent—230 out of 250—replied "No."

By today's standards, La Pierre's experiment was crude. He could have surveyed a control group—a second set of 250 establishments that they hadn't patronized but that were in the same towns where they'd stopped. With self-administered questionnaires, he couldn't be sure that the people who answered the survey (and who claimed that they wouldn't serve Chinese) were the same ones who had actually served the threesome. And La Pierre didn't mention in his survey that the Chinese couple would be accompanied by a white man.

Still, La Pierre's experiment was terrific for its time. It made clear that what people say they do (or would do) is not a proxy for what they actually do or will do (see Deutscher 1973). This basic finding shows up in what you might think were the most unlikely places: In the 1961 census of Addis Ababa, Ethiopia, 23% of the women underreported the *number of their children*. Apparently, people there didn't count babies who die before reaching the age of 2 (Pausewang 1973:65). People in the United States often omit newborns when they fill out the Decennial Census form (Dillman et al. 2009b:225), and in China today, if a child dies soon after birth, couples may decide to report neither the birth nor the death and instead try to conceive again as quickly as possible. And, under the one-child policy, the births of female babies may not be reported at all because of the desire by couples to have a son (Merli and Rafferty 2000:110).

Why People Are Inaccurate Reporters of Their Own Behavior

People are inaccurate reporters of their own behavior for many reasons. Here are four:

1. Once people agree to be interviewed, they have a personal stake in the process and usually try to answer all your questions—whether they understand what you're after or not.
2. Human memory is fragile, although it's clearly easier to remember some things than others.

Cannell et al. (1961) found that the ability to remember a stay in the hospital is related to the length of the stay, the severity of the illness that lands you there, and whether or not surgery is involved. It's also strongly related to the length of time since discharge. Cannell and Fowler (1965) found that people report accurately 90% of all overnight hospital stays that happened 6 months or less before being interviewed.

It's easy for people to remember a rare event, like surgery, that occurred recently. But, as Sudman and Schwarz (1989) point out, if you ask people to think about some common behavior going back months at a time, they probably use estimation rules. When Sudman and Schwartz asked people "How many [sticks] [cans] of deodorant did you buy in the last 6 months?" they started thinking: "Well, I usually buy deodorant about twice a month in the summer, and about once a month the rest of the year. It's now October, so I suppose I must have bought 10 deodorants over the last 6 months." And then they say, "10," and that's what you write down.

3. Interviews are social encounters. People manipulate those encounters to whatever they think is their advantage.

Adolescent boys tend to exaggerate, and adolescent girls tend to minimize, reports of their own sexual experience (see Catania et al. 1996).

4. People can't count a lot of behaviors, so they use rules of inference.

In some situations, they invoke D'Andrade's "what goes with what" rule (1974) and report what they *suppose* must have happened, rather than what they actually saw. Freeman et al. (1987) asked people in their department to report on who attended a particular colloquium. People who were *usually* at the department colloquium were mentioned as having attended the particular colloquium—even by those who hadn't attended (and see Shweder and D'Andrade 1980).

Reducing Errors: Jogging Informants' Memories

Loftus and Marburger (1983) found that landmarks help reduce forward telescoping—where people report that something happened 1 month ago when it really happened 2 months ago (backward telescoping is rare). The title of their article says it all: "Since the Eruption of Mt. St. Helens, Has Anyone Beaten You Up? Improving the Accuracy of Retrospective Reports with Landmark Events." Means et al. (1989) asked people to recall landmark events in their lives going back 18 months from the time of the interview.

Once the list of personal landmark events was established, people were better able to recall hospitalizations and other health-related events. In the field, as you do life history interviews, try to establish personal milestones for each informant—like their first hunting kill or their clitoridectomy or, for older informants, burying their parents or becoming grandparents—and ask them to report on what has happened since each landmark.

Aided recall increases the number of events recalled, but also appears to increase the telescoping effect (Bradburn 1983:309). In studies where you interview people more than once, you can correct for telescoping by reminding them what they said last time in answer to a question and then asking them about their behavior since their last report.

Event history and **life history calendars** are effective aids to recall and are particularly useful in societies where there are no written records. Leslie et al. (1999:375–78), for example, developed an event calendar for the Ngisonyoka section of the South Turkana pastoralists in northwestern Kenya. The Turkana name their seasons rather than their years. Based on many interviews between 1983 and 1984, Leslie et al. were able to build up a list of 143 major events associated with seasons between 1905 and 1992. Events include things like "no hump" in 1961 (it was so dry that the camels' humps shrank), "bulls" in 1942 (when their bulls were taken to pay a poll tax), and "rescue" in 1978 (when rains came). This painstaking work has made it possible for many researchers to gather demographic and other life history data from the Ngisonyoka Turkana. William Axinn and colleagues (1999:252) also used multiple event cues in Nepal and, like Leslie et al., report that this was particularly helpful for older informants (**Further Reading:** event- and life-history calendars).

If you are working in an industrialized environment with literate informant, you can ask people to review their credit card statements and long-distance phone bills and to remember events, places, and people associated with each credit or phone event. College transcripts help people think about what they were doing and the people they met along the way. Still . . . Horn (1960) asked people to report their bank balance. Of those who did not consult their bankbooks, just 31% reported correctly. Those who consulted their records didn't do that much better. Only 47% reported correctly (reported in Bradburn 1983:309).

It's different, of course, in nonindustrialized societies. When Elliot Fratkin (2004:19) asked Ariaal warriors in northern Kenya how many cattle they owned, the answer was always "many." Veterinary studies showed that the herds of the Samburu (a group closely related to the Ariaal) were two-thirds female and that 50% of those cattle were lactating at any time. A household with 6 nursing calves, Fratkin calculated, would have, on average, 12 cows and 4 female calves, plus 8 male cattle.

Informant accuracy remains a major problem. Gary Wells and colleagues (2003) showed a video of a staged crime to 253 students. Then they showed the students a photo lineup of six people and asked the students to pick out the culprit. Every single student picked one of the six photos, but there was a small problem: The culprit wasn't in the six photos. We need a lot more research about the rules of inference that people use when they respond to questions about where they've been, who they were with, and what they were doing (**Further Reading:** informant accuracy).

FURTHER READING

Transcription: Bailey (2008); Bucholtz (2000); Du Bois (1991); Duranti (2006); Maloney and Paolisso (2001); Matheson (2007); McLellan et al. (2003); Ochs (1979).

Interviewing: Graham (2000); Gubrium and Holstein (2002); Kvale and Brinkman (2009); McCracken (1988); Mishler (1986); Rubin (2005); Seidman (2006); Wengraf (2001).

Focus groups: Krueger (1994); Morgan (1997); Morgan and Krueger (1998); Sayles et al. (2007); Stewart and Shamdasani (1990); Vaughn et al. (1996).

Response effects: Borgers et al. (2004); Bradburn (1983); Cannell et al. (1979); Christian et al. (2009); Javeline (1999); Johnson and Delameter (1976); Schaeffer and Presser (2003); Schuman and Presser (1979, 1981); Schwarz (1999); Schwarz et al. (1991); Singer et al. (1983); Sudman and Bradburn (1974); Tourangeau et al. (2000).

Deference effect: Dotinga et al. (2005); Krysan and Couper (2003).

Social desirability effect: DeMaio (1984); Kreuter et al. (2008); Phillips and Clancy (1972); Press and Townsley (1998); W. W. Smith (2006); van de Mortel (2008).

Third-party present effect: Aquilino (1997); Aquilino et al. (2000); Blair (1979); Boeije (2004); Bradburn (1979); Hartmann (1994); Pollner and Adams (1997); T. W. Smith (1997).

Asking threatening questions: Bradburn et al. (1978); Bradburn, Sudman et al. (1979); Catania et al. (1996); Gribble et al. (1999); Hewitt (2002); Johnston and Walton (1995); Makkai and McAllister (1992); Mooney and Gramling (1991); Wiederman et al. (1994).

Event- and life-history calendars: Belli (1998); Caspi et al. (1996); Freedman et al. (1988); Glassner and van der Vaart (2009); Kessler and Wethington (1991); Martyn and Belli (2002); Yoshihama et al. (2005).

Measuring food intake and physical activity: Graham (2003); Hebert et al. (2002); Hill and Davies (2001); Leenders et al. (2000); Pelto et al. (1989); Prince et al. (2008); Quandt and Rittenbaugh (1986); Schoenberg (1997, 2000); Subar et al. (2003).

Informant accuracy: see **Further Reading**, chapter 2.

Interviewing II: Questionnaires

This is the first of two chapters about **structured interviews**. In a structured interview, each informant or respondent is exposed to the same stimuli. The stimuli are often questions, but they may also be carefully constructed vignettes, lists of words, stacks of photos, clips of music or video, a table full of physical artifacts, or a garden full of plants. The idea in structured interviewing is always the same: to control the input that triggers people's responses so that their output can be reliably compared.

I'll cover two broad categories of methods for structured interviewing: **questionnaires** and a range of methods used in cognitive anthropology, particularly **cultural domain analysis**.

We begin in this chapter with questionnaires and survey research. There are some lessons about how to write good questions and how to build and administer questionnaires that are unique to surveys conducted on the Internet—like exactly where to position the don't-know option in scalar questions (you know, from agree to disagree, etc.) on the screen (Christian et al. 2009; and see Dillman, Smyth, and Christian 2009 on web survey design). The major lessons, though, on how to ask questions in surveys apply to all formats. This chapter focuses on those lessons.

QUESTIONNAIRES AND SURVEY RESEARCH

Survey research goes back over 200 years (take a look at John Howard's monumental 1973 [1792] survey of British prisons), but it really took off in the mid-1930s when quota sampling was first applied to voting behavior studies and to helping advertisers target consumer messages. Over the years, government agencies in all industrialized countries have developed an insatiable appetite for information about various "target populations" (poor people, users of public housing, users of private health care, etc.). Japan developed an indigenous survey research industry soon after World War II, and India, South Korea, Jamaica, Greece, Mexico, and many other countries have since developed their own survey research capabilities (box 9.1).

THE COMPUTER REVOLUTION IN SURVEY RESEARCH

There are four methods for collecting questionnaire data: (1) personal, **face-to-face** interviews, (2) **self-administered** questionnaires, (3) **telephone** interviews, and (4) **online interviews**. All of these methods can be assisted by, or fully automated with, computers.

The computer revolution in survey research began in the 1970s with the development of software for CATI, or "computer-assisted telephone interviewing." With CATI software, you program a set of survey questions and then let the computer do the dialing. Interviewers sit at their computers, wearing telephone headsets, and when a respondent

> **BOX 9.1**
>
> ### ANTHROPOLOGY AND SURVEYS
>
> Anthropologists are finding more and more that good survey technique can add a lot of value to ethnography. In the 1970s, Sylvia Scribner and Michael Cole studied literacy among the Vai of Liberia. Some Vai are literate in English, others are literate in Arabic, and some adult Vai men use an indigenous script for writing letters. As part of their project, Scriber and Cole ran a survey with 650 respondents. Michael Smith, the cultural anthropologist on their team, was skeptical about using this method with the Vai. He wrote the project leaders about his experience in administering the survey there:
>
> > I was surprised when I first saw how long it [the questionnaire] was. I didn't think that anyone would sit down for long enough to answer it, or, if they did, that they would answer it seriously. . . . Well, I was wrong—and it fascinates me why the Vai should, in the busiest season of the year—during two of the worst farming years one could have picked . . . spend a lot of time answering questions which had little to do with the essential business at hand. . . . Not only did the majority of people eventually come, but when they got there they answered with great deliberation. How many times does one remember someone saying, "I don't know, but I'll come back and tell you when I've checked with so-and-so." (Scribner and Cole 1981:47)

agrees to be interviewed, they read the questions from the screen. With the kind of fixed-choice questions that are typical in surveys, interviewers only have to click a box on the screen to put in the respondent's answer to each question. For open-ended questions, respondents talk and the interviewer types in the response.

CASI stands for "computer-assisted self-administered interview." People sit at a computer and answer questions on their own, just like they would if they received a questionnaire in the mail. People can come to a central place to take a CASI survey or you can send them a disk in the mail that they can plug into their own computer (Van Hattum and de Leeuw 1999) . . . or you can set up the survey on the web and people can take it from any Internet connection. With Internet cafés now in the most out-of-the-way places, we can continue to interview our informants between trips to the field (box 9.2).

People take quickly to computer-based interviews and often find them to be a lot of fun. Fun is good because it cuts down on fatigue. Fatigue is bad because it sends respondents into robot mode and they stop thinking about their answers (Barnes et al. 1995; O'Brien and Dugdale 1978). I ran a computer-based interview in 1988 in a study comparing the social networks of people in Mexico City and Jacksonville, Florida. One member of our team, Christopher McCarty, programmed a laptop to ask respondents in both cities about their acquaintanceship networks. Few people in Jacksonville and almost no one in Mexico City had ever seen a computer, much less one of those clunky lug-ables that passed for laptops back then. But our respondents said they enjoyed the experience. "Wow, this is like some kind of computer game," one respondent said.

The technology is wildly better now and fieldworkers are running computer-assisted interview surveys all over the world. Hewett et al. (2004) used A-CASI technology—for "audio, computer-assisted, self-administered interview"—in a study of 1,293 adolescents

BOX 9.2

INTERNET-BASED SURVEYS

Internet surveys are easy to build (there's lots of interactive software out there for it) and easy to analyze (typically, the results come to you on a spreadsheet that you can pop into your favorite stats program). In theory, they should also be easy to administer (you just send people a URL that they can click), but it can be tough getting people to actually take an Internet survey. In 2000, my colleagues and I ran an Internet survey of people who had purchased a new car in the last 2 years or were in the market for a car now. There's no sampling frame of such people, so we ran a national, RDD (random-digit-dialing) screening survey. We offered people who were eligible and who said they had access the Internet $25 to participate in the survey. If they agreed, we gave them the URL of the survey and a PIN. We made 11,006 calls and contacted 2,176 people. That's about right for RDD surveys. (The rest of the numbers either didn't answer, or were businesses, or there was only a child at home, etc.) Of the 2,176 people we contacted, 910 (45%) were eligible for the web survey. Of them, 136 went to the survey site and entered their PIN, and of them, 68 completed the survey.

The data from those 68 people were excellent, but it took an awful lot of work for a purposive (nonrepresentative) sample of 68 people. At the time, 45% of adults Americans had access to the Internet (SAUS 2000: table 913). Today, that number is 83% (SAUS 2009: table 1120), but it's still hard to motivate people to take most web surveys.

When people are motivated, though, web surveys can reach respondents in hard-to-reach groups. To study gay Latino men, Ross et al. (2004) placed about 47 million banner ads on gay-themed websites inviting potential respondents for a university-sponsored study. The ads produced about 33,000 clicks, 1,742 men who started the survey, and 1,026 men who finished it. Those 1,026 men were obviously not a random representative sample, but Internet surveys aren't always meant for getting that kind of data. (For more on increasing response rates to Internet and mixed mode surveys, see Dillman et al. 2009.)

in rural and urban Kenya about very sensitive issues, like sexual behavior, drug and alcohol use, and abortion. With A-CASI, the respondent listens to the questions through headphones and types in his or her answers. The computer—a digitized voice—asks the questions, waits for the answers, and moves on. In the Kenya study, Hewett et al. used yes/no and multiple choice questions and had people punch in their responses on an external keypad. The research team had to replace a few keypads and they had some cases of battery failure, but overall, they report that the computers worked well, that only 2% of the respondents had trouble with the equipment (even though most of them had never seen a computer) and that people liked the format (Hewett et al. (2004:322–24).

This doesn't mean that computers are going to replace live interviewers any time soon. Computers-as-interviewers are fine when the questions are clear and people don't need a lot of extra information. Suppose you ask: "Did you go to the doctor last week?" and the informant responds: "What do you mean by doctor?" She may have gone to a free-standing clinic and seen a nurse practitioner or a physician's assistant. She probably wants to know if this counts as "going to the doctor" (box 9.3) (**Further Reading:** computer-based interviews).

BOX 9.3

CAPI AND MCAPI

CAPI software supports "computer-assisted personal interviewing." MCAPI (mobile CAPI) is particularly good for anthropologists. You build your interview on a laptop or a handheld computer. The computer prompts you (not the respondent) with each question, suggests probes, and lets you enter the data as you go. CAPI and MCAPI make it easier for you to enter and manage the data. Easier is better, and not just because it saves time. It also reduces errors in the data. When you write down data by hand in the field, you are bound to make some errors. When you input those data into a computer, you're bound to make some more errors. The fewer times you have to handle and transfer data, the better. Clarence Gravlee (2002a) used this method to collect data on lifestyle and blood pressure from 100 people in Puerto Rico. His interviews had 268 multiple choice, yes/no, and open-ended questions, and took over an hour to conduct, but when he got home each night from his fieldwork, he had the day's data in the computer.

ADVANTAGES AND DISADVANTAGES OF SURVEY FORMATS

Each major data-collection method—face-to-face, self-administered, telephone, and online interviews—has its advantages and disadvantages. Your choice of a method will depend on your own calculus of things like cost, convenience, and the nature of the questions you are asking.

Personal, Face-to-Face Interviews

Advantages of Face-to Face Interviews

1. They can be used with people who could not otherwise provide information—respondents who are illiterate or nonliterate, blind, bedridden, or very old, for example.
2. If a respondent doesn't understand a question in a personal interview, you can fill in, and, if you sense that the respondent is not answering fully, you can probe for more complete data.

Conventional wisdom in survey research is that each respondent has to hear exactly the same question. In practice, this means not engaging in conversation with people who ask for more information about a particular item on a survey. Not responding to requests for more information might mean sacrificing validity for reliability. There is now evidence that a more conversational style produces more accurate data, especially when respondents really need to get clarifications on unclear concepts (Krosnick 1999; Schober and Conrad 1997).

So, carry a notebook that tells you exactly how to respond when people ask you to clarify an unfamiliar term. If you use more than one interviewer, be sure each of them carries a copy of the same notebook. Good interview schedules are pretested to eliminate terms that are unfamiliar to intended respondents. Still, there is always someone who asks: "What do you mean by 'income'?" or "How much is 'a lot'?"

3. You can use several different data collection techniques with the same respondent in a face-to-face survey interview. Part of the interview can consist of open-ended questions; another part may require the use of visual aids, such as graphs or cue cards; and in still another, you might hand the respondent a self-administered questionnaire booklet and stand by to help clarify potentially ambiguous items. This is a useful technique for asking really sensitive questions in a face-to-face interview.

4. Personal interviews at home can be much longer than telephone or self-administered questionnaires. A 1-hour-long personal interview is relatively easy, and even 2- and 3-hour interviews are common. It is next to impossible to get respondents to devote 2 hours to filling out a questionnaire that shows up in the mail, unless you are prepared to pay well for their time; and it requires exceptional skill to keep a telephone interview going for more than 20 minutes, unless respondents are personally interested in the topic (Holbrook et al. 2003). Note, though, that **street-intercept** or **mall-intercept** interviews (where you interview people on the fly), although face to face, usually have to be very quick.

5. Face-to-face respondents get one question at a time and can't flip through the questionnaire to see what's coming. If you design an interview to start with general questions (how people feel about using new technologies at work, for example) and move on to specific questions (how people feel about using a particular new technology), then you really don't want people flipping ahead.

6. With face-to-face interviews, you know who answers the questions.

Disadvantages of Face-to-Face Interviews

1. They are intrusive and **reactive**. It takes a lot of skill to administer a questionnaire without subtly telling the respondent how you hope he or she will answer your questions. Other methods of administration of questionnaires may be impersonal, but that's not necessarily bad, especially if you've done the ethnography and have developed a set of fixed-choice questions for a questionnaire. Furthermore, the problem of reactivity increases when more than one interviewer is involved in a project. Making it easy for interviewers to deliver the same questions to all respondents is a plus.

2. Personal interviews are costly in both time and money. If you are working alone, without assistants, in an area that lacks good roads, don't plan on doing more than 150–200 face-to-face interviews in a year. If you're working in major cities in Europe or North America you can do more, but it gets really, really tough to maintain a consistent, positive attitude long before you get to the 200th interview. With mailed and telephone questionnaires, you can survey thousands of respondents.

    In addition to the time spent in interviewing people, locating respondents in a representative sample may require going back several times. In urban research especially, count on making up to half a dozen callbacks to get the really hard-to-find respondents.

    It's important to make all those callbacks to land the hard-to-get interviews. Survey researchers sometimes use the **sampling by convenient replacement** technique—going next door or down the block and picking up a replacement for an interviewee who happens not to be home when you show up. As I mentioned in chapter 5, this homogenizes your sample and makes it less and less representative of all the variation in the population you're studying.

3. Personal interview surveys conducted by lone researchers over a long period of time run the risk of being overtaken by events. A war breaks out, a volcano erupts, or the government decides to cancel elections and imprison the opposition. It sounds dramatic, but these sorts of things are actually quite common across the world. Far less dramatic events can make the responses of the last 100 people you interview radically different from those of the first 100 to the same questions. If you conduct a questionnaire survey over a long period of time in the field, it is a good idea to reinterview your first few respondents and check the stability (reliability) of their reports.

Interviewer-Absent Self-Administered Questionnaires

Advantages of Self-Administered Questionnaires

1. Mailed questionnaires (whether on paper or on disk) puts the post office to work for you in finding respondents. If you cannot use the mail (because sampling frames are unavailable, or because you cannot expect people to respond, or because you are in a country where mail service is unreliable), you can use cluster and area sampling (see chapter 5), combined with the **drop-and-collect** technique. This involves leaving a questionnaire with a respondent and going back later to pick it up. Ibeh and Brock (2004) used this in their study of company managers in Nigeria. The standard response rate for mailed questionnaires to busy executives in sub-Saharan Africa is around 36%. Using the drop-and-collect technique, Ibeh and Brock achieved a nearly 60% response rate. With both mailed surveys and the drop-and-collect method, self-administered questionnaires allow a single researcher to gather data from a large, representative sample of respondents, at relatively low cost per datum.

2. All respondents get the same questions with a self-administered questionnaire. There is no worry about interviewer bias or response effects, based on features of the interviewer. As we saw in chapter 8, questions about sexual behavior (including family planning) and about attitudes toward women or men or members of particular ethnic/ racial groups are particularly susceptible to this problem. The perceived sexual orientation of the interviewer, for example, affects how supportive respondents are of homosexuality (Kemph and Kasser 1996).

3. You can ask more complex questions with a self-administered paper questionnaire than you can in a personal interview. Questions that involve a long list of response categories or that require a lot of background data are hard to follow orally, but are often interesting to respondents if worded right on paper.

    For really complex questions, you're better off with CASI because respondents don't have to think about any convoluted instructions at all—instructions like: "Have you ever had hepatitis? If not, then skip to question 42." Later, after the respondent finishes a series of questions about her bout with hepatitis, the questionnaire says: "Now return to question 40." With CASI, the computer does all the work and the respondent can focus on responding.

4. You can ask long **batteries** of otherwise boring questions on self-administered questionnaires that you just couldn't get away with in a personal interview. Look at figure 9.1. Imagine trying to ask someone to sit still while you recited, say, 30 items and asked for their response. CASI is much better at this.

5. In self-administered interviews, people aren't trying to impress anyone, and anonymity

Here is a list of things that people say they'd like to see in their high school.
For each item, check how you feel <u>this</u> high school is doing.

	WELL	OK	POORLY	DON'T KNOW
1. High-quality instruction	——	——	——	——
2. Good pay for teachers	——	——	——	——
3. Good mix of sports and academics	——	——	——	——
4. Preparation for college entrance exams	——	——	——	——
5. Safety	——	——	——	——
6. Music program	——	——	——	——
7. Good textbooks	——	——	——	——

FIGURE 9.1.
A battery item in a questionnaire. Batteries can consist of many items.

provides a sense of security, which produces more reports of things like premarital
sexual experiences, constipation, arrest records, alcohol dependency, interpersonal violence, and so on. L. Peterson et al. (1996) randomly assigned two groups of 57 Swedish
Army veterans to fill out the Beck's Depression Inventory (Beck et al. 1961). One group
used the pencil-and-paper version; the other used a computer-based version. Those
who used the computer-based version had significantly higher mean scores on really
sensitive questions about depression (**Further Reading:** mode effects).

This does *not* mean that *more* reporting of behavior means more *accurate* reporting.
We know better than that. But, as I've said before, more is usually better than less. If
Chicanos report spending 12 hours per week in conversation with their families at home,
and Anglos (as white, non–Hispanic Americans are known in the American Southwest)
report spending 4 hours, I wouldn't want to bet that Chicanos *really* spend 12 hours, on
average, or that Anglos *really* spend 4 hours, on average, talking to their families. But I'd
find the fact that Chicanos reported spending three times as much time talking with their
families pretty interesting.

Disadvantages of Self-Administered Questionnaires
1. You have no control over how people interpret questions on a self-administered instrument, whether the questionnaire is delivered on paper or on a home computer or over
   the Internet. There is always the danger that, no matter how much background work
   you do, no matter how hard you try to produce culturally correct questions, respondents will be forced into making culturally inappropriate choices in closed-ended questionnaires. If the questionnaire is self-administered, you can't answer people's
   questions about what a particular item means.
2. If you are not working in a highly industrialized nation, or if you are not prepared to
   use Dillman's Tailored Design Method (discussed below), you are likely to see response
   rates of 20%–30% from mailed questionnaires and even worse from Internet surveys.
   It is entirely reasonable to analyze the data statistically and to offer conclusions about
   the correlations among variables for those who responded to your survey. But low

response means you can't draw conclusions about larger populations. CASI and audio CASI studies are based on real visits with people, in the field. Response rates for those forms of self-administered questionnaires can be very high. In that study that Hewett et al. did in Kenya, they had a response rate of over 80% (2004:328).

3. Even if a mailed questionnaire is returned, you can't be sure that the respondent who received it is the person who filled it out, and the same is true for Internet and e-mail questionnaires.

4. Mailed questionnaires are prone to serious sampling problems. Sampling frames of addresses are almost always flawed, sometimes very badly. If you use a phone book to select a sample, you miss all those people who don't have phones or who choose not to list their numbers or who just have cell phones. Face-to-face administration of questionnaires is often based on an area cluster sample, with random selection of households within each cluster. This is a much more powerful sampling design than most mailed questionnaire surveys can muster.

5. In some cases, you may want respondents to answer a question without their knowing what's coming next. This is impossible in a self-administered paper questionnaire, but it's not a problem in CASI and audio CASI studies.

6. Self-administered paper and CASI questionnaires are simply not useful for studying nonliterate or illiterate populations, or people who can't use a keyboard.

Telephone Interviews

Advantages of Telephone Interviews

1. Telephone interviews are inexpensive and convenient to do. By the 1970s, answers to many different kinds of questions asked over the phone in the United States were found to be as valid as those to questions asked in person or through the mail (Dillman 1978). Today, telephone interviewing is the most widely used method of gathering survey data across the industrialized nations.

2. Phone interviews have the impersonal quality of self-administered questionnaires and the personal quality of face-to-face interviews. So, telephone surveys are unintimidating (like self-administered questionnaires), but allow interviewers to probe or to answer questions dealing with ambiguity of items (just like they can in personal interviews).

3. Using **random digit dialing** (RDD), you can reach almost everyone who has a phone, including cell phones. In the highly industrialized countries, that means you can reach almost everybody. One survey found that 28% of completed interviews using RDD were with people who had unlisted phone numbers (Taylor 1997:424). There are huge regional differences, though, in the availability of telephones (see below).

4. It is relatively easy to monitor the quality of telephone interviewers' work by having them come to a central place to conduct their operation. But if you don't monitor the performance of telephone interviewers, you invite cheating. (See below, in the section on the disadvantages of telephone interviewing.)

5. There is no reaction to the *appearance* of the interviewer in telephone surveys, although respondents *do* react to accents and speech patterns of interviewers.

   Oskenberg et al. (1986) found that telephone interviewers who had the lowest refusal rates had higher-pitched, louder, and clearer voices. And, as with all types of interviews, there are gender-of-interviewer and race-of-interviewer effects in telephone interviews, too. Respondents try to figure out the race or ethnicity of the interviewer and then tailor responses accordingly. (See the section on response effects in chapter 8.)

6. Telephone interviewing is safe. You can talk on the phone to people who live in urban neighborhoods where many professional interviewers (most of whom are women) would prefer not to go. Telephones also get you past doormen and other people who run interference for the rich.

Disadvantages of Telephone Interviewing

1. If you are doing research in Haiti or Bolivia or elsewhere in the developing world, telephone surveys are out of the question, except for some urban centers, and then only if your research is about relatively well-off people. About 97% of all households in the United States have telephones (Belinfante 2009). This makes *national* surveys a cinch to do and highly reliable. But the distribution of telephones is uneven, which makes some *local* surveys impossible to do by phone. On the Rosebud Sioux Reservation—an area of about 5,000 square kilometers and home to about ten thousand tribal members—telephone penetration is about 75% (FCC 2007).

2. Telephone interviewing using RDD is convenient, but it's no lazy way out: It can take 1,000 calls to get 200–300 interviews—and that's starting with a list of working home phone numbers.

   People are getting tired of phone surveys and are opting out (Morin 2004). In a careful study in 2003, the contact rate (the number of people you can actually talk to in a sample of working home phone numbers) was 79% (down from 90% 6 years earlier) and the refusal rate among people contacted was 66%. All in all, the final response rate was about 25% (Keeter et al. 2006). This biases the outcome for some questions, but the good news is that it doesn't produce consistent bias in the results of surveys (Groves 2006). You can always get nearly 100% study sample completion by replacing refusers with people who will cooperate. (If you do that, make an extra effort to get at least some of the refusers to respond so you can test whether cooperators are a biased sample [box 9.4].)

BOX 9.4

SAMPLES OF PHONE NUMBERS

There are companies that sell telephone numbers for surveys. The numbers are chosen to represent businesses or residences and to represent the varying saturation of phone service in different calling areas. Even the best sample of phone numbers, though, may not be enough to keep you out of trouble. During the 1984 U.S. presidential election, Ronald Reagan's tracking poll used a list of registered voters, Republicans and Democrats alike. The poll showed Reagan comfortably ahead of his rival, Walter Mondale, except on Friday nights. Registered Republicans, it turned out, being wealthier than their counterparts among Democrats, were out Friday nights more than Democrats were, and simply weren't available to answer the phone (Begley et al. 1992:38).

---

3. Telephone interviews must be relatively short, or people will hang up. There is some evidence that once people agree to give you their time in a telephone interview, you

can keep them on the line for a remarkably long time (up to an hour) by developing special "phone personality" traits. Generally, however, you should not plan a telephone interview that lasts for more than 20 minutes.

4. And finally, this: It has long been known that, in an unknown percentage of occasions, hired interviewers willfully falsify data (Boyd and Westfall 1955). When an interviewer who is paid by the completed interview finds a respondent not at home, the temptation is to fill in the interview and get on to the next respondent. It's particularly easy for interviewers to cheat in telephone surveys—from failing to probe, to interviewing unqualified respondents, to fabricating an item response, and even to fabricating whole interviews. Kiecker and Nelson (1996) hired 33 survey research companies to do eight interviews each, ostensibly as "mop-up" for a larger national market survey. The eight respondents were plants—graduate students of drama, for whom this must have been quite a gig—and were the same eight for each of the surveys. Of the 33 interviewers studied, 10 fabricated an entire interview, 32 fabricated at least one item response, and all 33 failed to record responses verbatim.

You can eliminate most cheating by training and monitoring phone interviewers. Presser and Zhao (1992) monitored 40 trained telephone interviewers at the Maryland Survey Research Center. For the 5,619 questions monitored, interviewers read the questions exactly as worded on the survey 91% of the time. Training works.

Still, no matter how much you train interviewers . . . . Johnstone et al. (1992) studied 48 telephone interviews done entirely by women and found that female respondents elicited more sympathy, while male respondents elicited more joking. Men, say Johnstone et al., may be less comfortable than women are with being interviewed by women and wind up trying to subvert the interview by turning it into teasing or banter.

WHEN TO USE WHAT

There is no perfect data-collection method. However, mailed or dropped-off questionnaires are preferable to personal interviews when three conditions are met: (1) You are dealing with literate respondents; (2) You are confident of getting a high response rate (at least 70%); and (3) The questions you want to ask do not require a face-to-face interview or the use of visual aids such as cue cards, charts, and the like. Under these circumstances, you get much more information for your time and money than from the other methods of questionnaire administration.

When you really need complete interviews—answers to all or nearly all the questions in a particular survey—then face-to-face interviews are the way to go. Caserta et al. (1985) interviewed recently bereaved respondents about adjustment to widowhood. They interviewed 192 respondents—104 in person, at home, and 88 by mailed questionnaire. Both groups got identical questions. On average, 82% of those interviewed at home 3–4 weeks after losing their husband or wife answered any given question. Just 68% of those who responded to the mailed questionnaire answered any given question. As Caserta et al. explain, the physical presence of the interviewer helped establish the rapport needed for asking sensitive and personal questions about the painful experience of bereavement (Caserta et al. 1985:640). (Use a hand-held computer and mobile-CAPI software to make sure you ask everyone the same questions. See above, page 190.)

If you are working in a highly industrialized country, and if a very high proportion of the population you are studying has their own telephones, then consider doing a phone survey whenever a self-administered questionnaire would otherwise be appropriate.

If you are working alone or in places where the mails and the phone system are inefficient for data collection, the drop-and-collect technique is a good alternative (see above, page 192).

Finally, there is no rule against using more than one type of interview. Mauritius, an island nation in the Indian Ocean, is an ethnically complex society. Chinese, Creoles, Franco-Mauritians, Hindus, Muslims, and other groups make up a population of about a million. Ari Nave (1997) was interested in how Mauritians maintain their ethnic group boundaries, particularly through their choices of whom to marry. A government office on Mauritius maintains a list of all people over 18 on Mauritius, so it was relatively easy for Nave to get a random sample of the population.

Contacting the sample was another matter. Nave got back just 347 out 930 mailed questionnaires, but he was able to interview another 296 by telephone and face to face, for a total of 643, or 69% of his original sample—a respectable completion rate.

USING INTERVIEWERS

Large surveys routinely employ lots of interviewers. In field research, multiple interviewers may not be worth the cost. If you can collect 100 interviews yourself and maintain careful quality control in your interview technique, then hiring one more interviewer would probably not improve your research by enough to warrant both spending the extra money and worrying about quality control. Recall that for estimating population proportions or means, you have to quadruple the sample size to halve the sampling error. If you can't afford to hire three more interviewers (beside yourself), and to train them carefully so that they at least introduce the *same* bias to every interview as you do, you're better off running the survey yourself and saving the money for other things.

This only goes for surveys in which you interview a random sample of respondents to estimate a population parameter. If you are studying the experiences of a group of people, or are after cultural data (as in "How are things usually done around here?"), then getting more interviews is better than getting fewer, whether you collect the data yourself or have it collected by others.

Training Interviewers

If you hire interviewers, be sure to train them—and monitor them throughout the research. A colleague used a doctoral student as an interviewer in a project in Atlanta. The senior researcher trained the student but listened to the interview tapes that came in. At one point, the interviewer asked a respondent: "How many years of education do you have?" "Four," said the respondent. "Oh," said the student researcher, "you mean you have 4 years of education?" "No," said the informant, bristling and insulted, "I've had 4 years of education beyond high school." The informant was affluent; the interview was conducted in his upper-middle-class house; he had already told the interviewer that he was in a high-tech occupation. So monitor interviewers.

If you hire a *team* of interviewers, you have one extra chore besides monitoring their work. You need to get them to act as a team. Be sure, for example, that they all use the same probes to the various questions on the interview schedule. Especially with open-ended questions, be sure to do random spot checks, *during the survey*, of how interviewers are coding the answers they get. The act of spot-checking keeps coders alert. When you find discrepancies in the way interviewers code responses, bring the group together and discuss the problem openly.

Narratives are coded after the interview. If you use of team of coders, be sure to train them together and get their **interrater reliability** coefficient up to at least .70. In other words, make sure that your interviewers use the same theme tags to code each piece of text. For details on how to do this, see the section on **Cohen's Kappa** in chapter 19.

Carey et al. (1996) studied the beliefs of 51 newly arrived Vietnamese refugees in upstate New York about tuberculosis. The interviews consisted of 32 open-ended questions on beliefs about symptoms, prevention, treatment, and the social consequences of having TB. The two interviewers in this study were bilingual refugees who participated in a 3-day workshop to build their interview skills. They were told about the rationale for open-ended questions and about techniques for getting respondents to open up and provide full answers to the questions. The training included a *written manual* (this is very important) to which the interviewers could refer during the actual study. After the workshop, the trainees did 12 practice interviews with Vietnamese adults who were not in the study.

William Axinn ran the Tamang Family Research Project, a comparative study of villages in Nepal (Axinn 1991). Axinn and his coworkers trained a group of interviewers using the *Interviewer's Manual* from the Survey Research Center at the University of Michigan (University of Michigan 1976). That manual contains the distilled wisdom of hundreds of interviewer training exercises in the United States, and Axinn found the manual useful in training Nepalese interviewers, too.

Axinn recruited 32 potential interviewers. After a week of training (5 days at 8 hours a day, and 2 days of supervised field practice), the 16 best interviewers were selected, 10 men and 6 women. The researchers hired more interviewers than they needed and after 3 months, 4 of the interviewers were fired. "The firing of interviewers who clearly failed to follow protocols," said Axinn et al., "had a considerable positive effect on the morale of interviewers who had worked hard to follow our rules" (1991:200). No one has accused Axinn of overstatement.

Whom to Hire

In general, when hiring interviewers, look for professional interviewers first. Next, look for people who are mature enough to accept the need for rigorous training and who can work as part of a team. If need be, look for interviewers who can handle the possibility of going into some rough neighborhoods and who can answer the many questions that respondents will come up with in the course of the survey.

If you are running a survey based on personal interviews in a developing country, consider hiring college students, and even college graduates, in the social sciences. "Social sciences," by the way, does not mean the humanities. In Peru, Donald Warwick and Charles Lininger found that "some students from the humanities . . . were reluctant to accept the 'rigidities' of survey interviewing." Those students felt that "As educated individuals, they should be allowed to administer the questionnaire as they saw fit in each situation" (Warwick and Lininger 1975:222).

I would not use anyone who had that kind of attitude as an interviewer. But undergraduate social science students in the developing world may have real research experience since most of them aren't going on for graduate training. Students who are experienced interviewers have a lot to contribute to the design and content of questionnaires. Remember, you are dealing with colleagues who will be justly resentful if you treat them merely as employees of your study. By the same token, college students in developing nations are likely to be members of the elite who may find it tough to establish rapport with peasant farmers or the urban poor (Hursh-César and Roy 1976:308).

Make It Easy for Interviewers to Do Their Job

If you use interviewers, be sure to make the questionnaire booklet easy to use. Leave enough space for interviewers to write in the answers to open-ended questions—but not too much space. Big spaces are an invitation to some interviewers to develop needlessly long answers (Warwick and Lininger 1975:152).

Also, use two different type faces for questions and answers; put instructions to interviewers in capital letters and questions for respondents in normal type. Figure 9.2 is an example:

5. INTERVIEWER: CHECK ONE OF THE FOLLOWING

☐ R HAS LIVED IN CHICAGO MORE THAN FIVE YEARS.
   SKIP TO QUESTION 7.

☐ R HAS LIVED IN CHICAGO LESS THAN FIVE YEARS.
   ASK QUESTION 6 AND CONTINUE WITH QUESTION 7.

6. Could you tell me where you were living five years ago?

7. Where were you born?

FIGURE 9.2.
Using two different type faces in a survey instrument.
SOURCE: Adapted from D. P. Warwick and C. A. Lininger. *The Sample Survey: Theory and Practice*, New York: McGraw-Hill, 1975, p. 153.

CLOSED- VERSUS OPEN-ENDED QUESTIONS

The most often-asked question about survey research is whether **fixed-choice** (also called **closed-ended**) or **open-ended** items are better. The answer is that the two formats produce different kinds of data, and it's your call when to use what. A problem with fixed-choice questions is that people focus on the choices they have. If they'd like to offer a response other than those in front of them, they won't do it (Krosnick 1999:544). Daniel Hruschka and colleagues (2004) asked 227 Zimbawean women who were in HIV counseling two questions about how they negotiated the use of condoms. The first question was open-ended:

Think back to when you discussed male condom use with [main male partner] since [the last counseling session]. What exactly did you ask/tell him? Tell me in your own words.

The second question—which was asked immediately after the first—was fixed choice:

Now I'm going to read you a list of things some women tell their partners to try and convince them to use male condoms. Tell me for each one whether you told your partner this to convince him to use male condoms.

1. Told him that she was worried about getting HIV/AIDS.
2. Told him that she is worried about giving HIV/AIDS to him.
3. Reminded him that many of his friends or relatives have already died of HIV/AIDS and that this makes her believe that anyone can get it and pass it on through sex.
4. Told him that if she gets sick with HIV/AIDS, she may no longer be able to take care of him and her children.
5. Told him she wants to use male condoms to prevent pregnancy.

6. Told him about the study and that the study staff wanted you to ask him to use male condoms.

7. Showed him a brochure from the Ministry of Health/National AIDS Control Program everyone in Zimbabwe to use condoms.

The seven items for the fixed-choice question were developed from focus groups with staff at the University of Zimbabwe and in consultation with nurses and other women in the community (Hruschka et al. 2004:188–89). One of the themes extracted from the open-ended responses was: Emphasizing that HIV is everywhere. Women who reported using that negotiation technique were about 300% more likely to report 100% condom use by their partners over the previous 2 months. None of the seven items in the fixed-choice question predicted reported 100% condom use (Hruschka et al. 2004:196).

Schuman and Presser (1981:89) asked a sample of people this question: "Please look at this card and tell me which thing you would most prefer in a job." The card had five items listed: (1) high income, (2) no danger of being fired, (3) working hours are short—lots of free time, (4) chances for advancement, and (5) the work is important and gives a feeling of accomplishment. Then they asked a different sample the open-ended question: "What would you most prefer in a job?" About 17% of the respondents to the fixed-choice question chose "chances for advancement," and over 59% chose "important work." Under 2% of the respondents who were asked the open-ended question mentioned "chances for advancement," and just 21% said anything about "important" or "challenging" or "fulfilling" work.

When the questions get really threatening, fixed-choice questions are generally not a good idea. Masturbation, alcohol consumption, and drug use are reported with 50%–100% greater frequency in response to open-ended questions (Bradburn 1983:299). Apparently, people are least threatened when they can offer their own answers to open-ended questions on a self-administered questionnaire, rather than being forced to choose among a set of fixed alternatives (e.g., once a month, once a week, once a day, several times a day), and are most threatened by a face-to-face interviewer (Blair et al. 1977; Tourangeau and Smith 1996; Tourangeau and Yan 2007).

On the other hand, Ivis et al. (1997) found that at least one pretty embarrassing question was better asked in a fixed-choice format—and over the phone, at that. People in their survey were asked: "How often in the last 12 months have you had five or more drinks on one occasion?" Then, later in the interview, they were asked the same question, but were given nine fixed choices: (1) every day; (2) about once every other day; . . . (9) never in the last year. The fixed-choice format produced significantly more positive responses. The anonymity of telephone surveys provides a certain comfort level where people feel free to open up on sensitive topics. And notice that the anonymity of telephone surveys lets the *interviewer*, as well as the respondent, off the hook. You can ask people things you might be squeamish about if the interview were face to face, and respondents feel that they can divulge very personal matters to disembodied voices on the phone.

Overall, because closed-ended items are so efficient, most survey researchers prefer them to open-ended questions and use them whenever possible. There is no rule, however, that prevents you from mixing question types. Many survey researchers use the open-ended format for really intimidating questions and the fixed-choice format for everything else, even on the phone. Even if there are no intimidating questions in a survey, it's a good idea to stick in a few open-ended items. The open-ended questions break the monotony for the respondent, as do tasks that require referring to visual aids (like a graph).

The responses to fixed-choice questions are unambiguous for purposes of analysis. Be sure to take full advantage of this and **precode fixed-choice** items on a questionnaire. Put the codes right on the instrument so that typing the data into the computer is as easy (and as error free) as possible.

It's worth repeating that when you do computer-assisted interviews in the field (CAPI, mobile-CAPI, CASI, audio-CASI) you cut down on data entry error. The fewer times you have to touch data, the fewer opportunities there are to stick errors in them. I particularly like the fact that we can combine fixed-choice and open-ended questions on a hand-held computer for fieldwork.

QUESTION WORDING AND FORMAT

There are some well-understood rules that all survey researchers follow in constructing questionnaire items. Here are 15 of them.

1. *Be unambiguous.* If respondents can interpret a question differently from the meaning you have in mind, they will. In my view, this is the source of most response error in fixed-choice questionnaires.

Even a simple question like "How often do you visit a doctor?" can be ambiguous. Are acupuncturists, chiropractors, chiropodists, and public clinics all doctors? If you think they are, you'd better tell people that, or you leave it up to them to decide. In some parts of the southwestern United States, people may be visiting native curers and herbalists. Are those practitioners doctors? In Mexico, many community clinics are staffed by nurses. Does "going to the doctor" include a visit to one of those clinics?

Here's how Cannell et al. (1989) recommend asking about doctor visits in the last year:

Have you been a patient in the hospital overnight in the past 12 months since July 1st 1987?
(Not counting when you were in a hospital overnight.) During the past 12 months since July 1st, 1987, how many times did you actually see any medical doctor about your own health?
During the past 12 months since July 1st 1987, were there any times when you didn't actually see the doctor but saw a nurse or other medical assistant working for the doctor?
During the past 12 months since July 1st 1987, did you get any medical advice, prescriptions, or results of tests over the telephone from a medical doctor, nurse, or medical assistant working for a doctor? (Cannell et al. 1989, appendix A:1)

If you ask: "How long have you lived in Mexico City?" does "Mexico City" include the 19 million people who live in the urban sprawl, or just the 9 million who live in the Federal District? And how "near" is "near Nairobi"?

Words like "lunch," "community," "people," and hundreds of other innocent lexical items have lurking ambiguities associated with them, and phrases like "family planning" will cause all kinds of mischief. Half the respondents in the 1985 General Social Survey were asked if they agreed that there was too little spending for "assistance to the poor," and half were asked if there was too little spending for "welfare." A whopping 65% agreed with the first wording; just 19% agreed with the second (T. W. Smith 1987:77).

Even the word "you," as Payne pointed out (1951), can be ambiguous. Ask a nurse at the clinic "How many patients did you see last week?" and you might get a response like: "Who do you mean, me or the clinic?" If the nurse is filling out a self-administered questionnaire, she'll have to decide for herself what you had in mind. Maybe she'll get it right; maybe she won't.

2. *Use a vocabulary that your respondents understand, but don't be condescending.* This is a difficult balance to achieve. If you're studying a narrow population (sugar cane cutters, midwives, leather workers), then proper ethnography and pretesting with a few knowledgeable informants will help ensure appropriate wording of questions.

But if you are studying a more general population, even in a small town of just 3,000 people, then things are very different. Some respondents will require a low-level vocabulary; others will find that vocabulary insulting. This is one of the reasons often cited for doing personal interviews: You want the opportunity to phrase your questions differently for different segments of the population. Realize, however, that this poses risks in terms of reliability of response data.

3. *Remember that respondents must know enough to respond to your questions.* You'd be surprised at how often questionnaires are distributed to people who are totally unequipped to answer them. I get questionnaires in the mail and by e-mail all the time, asking for information I simply don't have.

Most people can't recall with any acceptable accuracy how long they spent in the hospital last year, how many miles they drive each week, or how much they've cut back on their use of air conditioning. They *can* recall whether they own a television, have *ever* been to Cairo, or voted in the recent elections. And they can tell you whether they *think* they got a fair price for the land they vacated when the dam was built or *believe* the local member of parliament is doing a better job than her predecessor at giving equal time to rich people and poor people who come to her with complaints.

4. Make sure there's a *clear purpose for every question* you ask in a survey. When I say "clear purpose," I mean clear to respondents, not just to you. And once you're on a topic, stay on it and finish it. Respondents can get frustrated, confused, and annoyed at the tactic of switching topics and then coming back to a topic that they've already dealt with on a questionnaire. Some researchers do exactly this just to ask the same question in more than one way and to check respondent reliability. This underestimates the intelligence of respondents and is asking for trouble—I have known respondents to sabotage questionnaires that they found insulting to their intelligence.

You can (and should) ask questions that are related to one another at different places in a questionnaire, so long as each question makes sense in terms of its placement in the overall instrument. For example, if you are interviewing labor migrants, you'll probably want to get a labor history—by asking where the respondent has worked during the past few years. Later, in a section on family economics, you might ask whether a respondent has ever sent remittances and from where.

As you move from one topic to another, put in a transition paragraph that makes each shift logical to the respondent. For example, you might say: "Now that we have learned something about the kinds of food you like, we'd like to know about. . . ." The exact wording of these transition paragraphs should be varied throughout a questionnaire.

5. Pay careful attention to **contingencies** and **filter questions**. Many question topics contain several contingencies. Suppose you ask someone if they are married. If they answer

"no," then you probably want to ask whether they've ever been married. You may want to know whether they have children, irrespective of whether they are married or have ever been married. You may want to know what people think is the ideal family size, irrespective of whether they've been married, plan to be married, have children, or plan to have children.

You can see that the contingencies can get very complex. The best way to ensure that all contingencies are accounted for is to build a **contingency flow chart** like that shown in figure 9.3 (Sirken 1972; Sudman and Bradburn 1982).

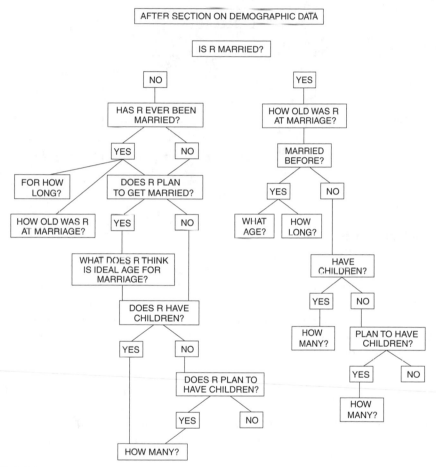

FIGURE 9.3.
Flow chart of filter questions for part of a questionnaire.

6. *Use clear scales.* There are some commonly used scales in survey research—things like: Excellent-Good-Fair-Poor; Approve-Disapprove; Oppose-Favor; For-Against; Good-Bad; Agree-Disagree; Better-Worse-About the Same; etc. Just because these are well known, however, does not mean that they are clear and unambiguous to respondents.

To cut down on the ambiguities associated with these kinds of scales, explain the meaning of each potentially ambiguous scale when you introduce it. With self-administered questionnaires, use 5 scale points rather than 3, if you can. For example, use Strongly Approve, Approve, Neutral, Disapprove, Strongly Disapprove, rather than Approve, Neutral, Disapprove. This will give people the opportunity to make finer-grained choices. If your sample is large enough, you can distinguish during analysis among respondents who answer, say, "strongly approve" versus "approve" on some item. For smaller samples, you can aggregate the data into three categories for analysis.

Self-administered questionnaires allow the use of 7-point scales, like the semantic differential scale shown in figure 9.4, and even longer scales. Telephone interviews often rely on 3-point scales.

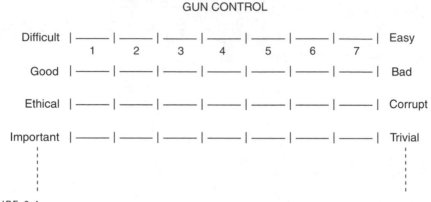

FIGURE 9.4.
A seven-point semantic differential scale.

Notice that the semantic differential scale in figure 9.4 has word anchors at both ends and numbers in the middle, not words. In this kind of scale, we want to let people interpret the dimension indicated by the anchors. In typical rating scales (you know, the 3- and 5-point scales you see in questionnaires), we want to remove ambiguity, so we label all the points in words—like Strongly Agree, Agree, Neutral, Disagree, Strongly Disagree (Peters and McCormick 1966. Much more on how to construct scales in chapter 11.)

7. Try to *package questions in self-administered questionnaires*, as shown earlier in figure 9.1. This is a way to get a lot of data quickly and easily, and, if done properly, it will prevent respondents from getting bored with a survey. For example, you might say "Please indicate how close you feel to each of the persons on this chart" and provide the respondent with a list of relatives (mother, father, sister, brother, etc.) and a scale (Very Close, Close, Neutral, Distant, Very Distant, etc.).

Be sure to make scales unambiguous. If you are asking how often people think they do something, don't say "Regularly" when you mean "More than Once a Month," and limit the list of activities to no more than seven. Then introduce a question with a totally different format, to break up the monotony and to keep the respondent interested.

Packaging is best done in self-administered questionnaires. If you use these kinds of lists in a face-to-face interview, you'll have to repeat the scale for at least the first three items or activities you name, or until the respondent gets the pattern down. This can get very tiring for both interviewers and respondents.

8. If you want respondents to check just one response, then be sure to *make the possible responses to a question exhaustive and mutually exclusive*. This may mean including a "don't know" option.

Here is an example (taken from a questionnaire I received) of what *not* to do:

How do you perceive communication between your department and other departments in the university? [check one]

☐ There is much communication
☐ There is sufficient communication
☐ There is little communication
☐ There is no communication
☐ No basis for perception

The "no basis for perception" response took care of making the item exhaustive. The problem for me on this item was that I wanted to check both "little communication" and "sufficient communication." For me, at least, these two categories were not mutually exclusive—I didn't think there was a lot of communication, and I wasn't at all bothered by that—but the author of the survey asked me to "check one" (box 9.5).

BOX 9.5

THE DON'T-KNOW OPTION

You can always make questionnaire items exhaustive by giving respondents the option of saying some variant of "don't know"—like "no basis for perception." Some researchers feel that this just gives respondents a lazy way out—that people need to be made to work a bit. If there is a good chance that some of your respondents really won't have the information you ask for, then I think the "don't know" option is too important to leave out. In consumer preference surveys, though, where you actually give someone a taste of a cracker and ask them to tell you if they like it, the "don't know" option is a bad idea.

---

9. *Keep questions short.* Many questions require a preamble to set up a time frame or otherwise make clear what you are asking an informant to think about in answering a question. For example:

These next questions are about what your children are doing these days. You said that you have two daughters and a son. Where is your older daughter living? Your younger daughter? Your son?

These next questions are about your travels to sell *huipiles* in the last year. Since October 2005, how many times have you been to Chichicastenango to sell your *huipiles*?

Questions that are likely to intimidate respondents should have long preambles to lessen the intimidation effect. The questions themselves, however, should contain as few words as possible.

10. *Provide alternatives*, if appropriate. Suppose people are being asked to move off their land to make way for a new highway. The government offers to compensate people

for the land, but people are suspicious that the government won't evaluate fairly how much compensation landowners are entitled to. If you take a survey and ask "Should the government offer people compensation for their land?" respondents can answer yes or no for very different reasons. Instead, let people check whether they agree or disagree with a set of alternatives, like: "The government should offer people compensation for their land" and "An independent board should determine how much people get for their land."

11. *Avoid loaded questions*. Any question that begins "Don't you agree that . . ." is a **loaded question**. Sheatsley (1983) points out, however, that asking loaded questions is a technique you can use to your advantage, on occasion, just as leading or baiting informants can be used in unstructured interviewing. A famous example comes from Kinsey's landmark study of sexual behavior of American men (Kinsey et al. 1948). Kinsey asked men "How old were you the first time you masturbated?" This made respondents feel that the interviewer already *knew* about the fact of masturbation and was only in search of additional information.

12. *Don't use* **double-barreled** questions. Here is one I found on a questionnaire: "When did you leave home and go to work on your own for the first time?" There is no reason to assume that someone had to leave home to go to work, or that they necessarily went to work if they left home.

Here is another bad question:

> Please indicate if you agree or disagree with the following statement:
>   Marijuana is no more harmful than tobacco or alcohol, so the personal use of marijuana should be legal.

A respondent can agree (or disagree) with the first part of the statement—the assertion that marijuana is no more harmful than tobacco or alcohol—and may agree or disagree with the second part. If respondents answer "yes" or "no," how do you know if they are indicating agreement with both parts of it or just one part? Which part? How can you tell? You can't. That's why it's a bad question.

13. *Don't take emotional stands in the wording of questions*. Here's an example of the sort of question you see on surveys all the time—and that you should never ask: "Should the legislature raise the drinking age to 21 in order to reduce the carnage among teens on our highways?"

14. When asking for opinions *on controversial issues, specify the referent situation* as much as possible. Instead of asking: "Do you approve of abortion?" ask: "Under what conditions do you approve of abortion?" Then give the respondent as exhaustive a list of circumstances as possible to check—including the option of "under no circumstances." If the circumstances are not exclusive (rape and incest are not necessarily exclusive, for example), then let respondents check as many circumstances as they think appropriate.

15. *Don't put false premises into questions*. I once formulated the following question for a survey in Greece: "Is it better for a woman to have a house and cash as a dowry, or for her to have an education and a job that she can bring to the marriage?" This question was based on a lot of ethnographic work in a community, during which I learned that many families were sinking their resources into getting women educated and into jobs and offering this to eligible bachelors as a substitute for traditional material dowries.

My question, however, was based on the false premise that all families respected the custom of dowry. The question did not allow respondents to state a third alternative—namely, that they didn't think dowry was a custom that ought to be maintained in any form, traditional or modern. In fact, many families were deciding to reject the dowry custom altogether—something that I missed for some time. Pretest questions to avoid this problem.

PRETESTING AND LEARNING FROM MISTAKES

There is no way to emphasize sufficiently the importance of **pretesting** any survey instrument. No matter how much you do to prepare a culturally appropriate questionnaire, it is absolutely guaranteed that you will have forgotten something important or that you will have poorly worded one or more vital element. These glitches can only be identified by pretesting.

If you are building a self-administered questionnaire, bring in a dozen or more pretest respondents and sit with them as they fill out the entire instrument (Sheatsley 1983). Encourage them to ask questions about each item. Your pretest respondents will make you painfully aware of just how much you took for granted, no matter how much ethnographic research you did or how many focus groups you ran before making up a questionnaire. There is no gurantee, by the way, that a dozen pretest respondents are enough. If you're still learning a lot after a dozen pretest respondents, then bring in some more.

For face-to-face interviews, do your pretesting under the conditions you will experience when the survey is underway for real. If respondents are going to come to your office, then pretest the instrument in your office. If you are going to respondents' homes, then go to their homes for the pretest (box 9.6).

Never use any of the respondents in a pretest for the main survey. If you are working in a small community, where each respondent is precious (and you don't want to use up any of them on a pretest), take the survey instrument to another community and pretest it there. This will also prevent the pretest respondents in a small community from gossiping about the survey before it actually gets underway. A "small community," by the way, can be "the 27 students from Taiwan at your university" or all the residents of an Indonesian rice-farming village.

If you have a team of face-to-face interviewers, make sure they all take part in the pretest—and be sure to do some of the pretesting yourself. After the pretests, bring the interviewers together for a discussion on how to improve the survey instrument. Ask them if people found some questions hard to answer—or even refused to answer. Ask them if they would change the wording of any of the questions. Check all this yourself by watching a couple of interviews done by people on your team and note when informants ask questions and how the interviewers respond. That way, you can train interviewers to respond in the same way to questions from informants.

As you conduct the actual survey, ask people to tell you what they think of the study and of the interview they've just been through. At the end of the study, bring all the interviewers back together for an evaluation of the project. If it is wise to learn from mistakes, then the first thing to do is find out what the mistakes are. If you give them a chance, your respondents and your interviewers will tell you.

TRANSLATION AND BACK TRANSLATION

If you are trying to write good survey questions in a language other than your own, the best practice is the method of back translation (Brislin 1970; Werner and Campbell 1970).

BOX 9.6

COGNITIVE INTERVIEWING

Use **cognitive testing** (also called **thinkaloud**) in pretesting questions (Willis 2005). In this method, people think out loud as they decide on how to answer each question in a survey. There are three alternative outcomes when with the thinkaloud technique: (1) People understand the question just as you intended them to; (2) People understand the question very well, but not the way you intended them to; and (3) People don't understand the question at all. Edwards et al. (2005) used this method to pretest a 28-question survey on the use of condoms by women sex workers in Mombassa, Kenya. The result was a survey with culturally appropriate vocabulary for various types of sex clients.

Don Dillman and his colleagues at the Washington State University survey research center begin thinkaloud interviews with two questions: (1) How many residences have you lived in since you were born? (2) How many windows are in your home? On the first question, some people think of cities where they've live, while others try to think of individual residences. On the second, questions come up, like: "Is a sliding glass door a window?" These questions help respondents understand what the interview is really about: learning where the ambiguities are in questions (Dillman, Smyth, and Christian 2009:221–23) (**Further Reading**: thinkaloud and cognitive interviews).

First, write any questionnaire in *your* native language. Then have the questionnaire translated by a bilingual person who is a native speaker of the language you a working in. Work closely with the translator, so that she or he can fully understand the subtleties you want to convey in your questionnaire items.

Next, ask another bilingual person, who is a native speaker of *your* language, to translate the questionnaire back into that language. This back translation should be almost identical to the original questionnaire you wrote. If it isn't, then something was lost in one of the two translations. You'd better find out which one it was and correct the problem.

Beck and Gable (2000) developed a scale for screening postpartum women for depression and then translated the scale into Spanish (Beck and Gable 2003). One item on the original scale was "I felt like my emotions were on a roller coaster." The first translator offered two options for this: "Sentí un sube y baja emocional" and "Sentí un desequilibrio emocional." The second translator translated these as "I felt like my emotions were up and down" and "I felt emotional instability" (Beck and Gable 2003:69). Not exactly the same feeling as "I felt like my emotions were on a roller coaster," but close. Do you go with one of the two Spanish translations offered? Which one? Or do you keep looking for something better in Spanish?" The answer is that you sit down with both translators, talk it through, and come to a consensus (box 9.7).

You can use back translation to check the content of open-ended interviews, but be warned: This is tough work. Daniel Reboussin (1995) interviewed Diola women who had come from southwestern Senegal to Dakar in search of work. All the women used French at work, but they preferred Diola for interviews. Reboussin, who speaks French, spoke very little Diola, so he worked with an interpreter—a man named Antoine Badji—to develop an interview schedule in French, which Badji translated into Diola.

BOX 9.7

ON-THE-FLY TRANSLATION

For all its rough edges, on-the-fly translation is probably just fine for a lot of research. Since 1984, the Demographic and Health Survey (DHS) has been conducted in 75 countries across the developing world to provide data on reproductive health. Each survey is meticulously translated into local (not just national) languages. In Kenya, for example, the DHS is produced in 10 local languages, as well as in English and Swahili. Interviewers are assigned to regions where their native language is dominant. There is always some population mixing, so interviewers get a chunk of survey materials in their own language as well as a chunk in Swahili, the national language. The problem is, lots of people don't speak Swahili. So, when a Luo interviewer runs out of interviews in Luo and has to interview a Luo speaker who doesn't speak Swahili, she has to translate the questions, from a Swahili interview, on the fly. This on-the-fly translation happened in 23% of the 7,480 interviews in the 1998 DHS. Weinreb and Sana (2009) found that this made no statistical difference in the univariate data for 22 out of 24 variables in the survey, from household characteristics to reports about use of contraceptives.

During the interviews, Badji asked questions in Diola and Reboussin audiotaped the responses. After each interview, Badji translated each tape (orally) into French. Reboussin transcribed the French translations, translating into English as he went. Then he read his English transcriptions *back* to Badji, translating (orally) into French as he read. That way, Badji could confirm or disconfirm Reboussin's understanding of Badji's French rendering of the tapes.

As I said, this was tough work. It took Reboussin and Badji 17 weeks to conduct 30 interviews and get them all down into English.

THE RESPONSE RATE PROBLEM

Mailed questionnaires can be very effective, but there is one problem with them that all survey researchers watch for: getting enough of them back. In 1936, the *Literary Digest* sent out 10 million straw poll ballots in an attempt to predict the winner of the presidential election. They got back 2.3 million ballots and predicted Alf Landon over Franklin Delano Roosevelt in a landslide. Roosevelt got 61% of the vote.

You'd think that 2.3 million ballots would be enough for anyone, but two things caused the *Digest* debacle. First, they selected their sample from automobile registries and telephone books. In 1936, this favored richer people who were more likely to be Republican. Second, the 2.3 million ballots were only 23% of the 10 million sent out. The low response rate biased the results in favor of the Republican challenger since those who didn't respond tended to be poorer and less inclined to participate in surveys (Squire 1988).

How to Adjust for Nonresponse

Skip to 1991. The American Anthropological Association sent questionnaires to a sample of 1,229 members. The sample was stratified into several cohorts who had received their Ph.D. degrees beginning in 1971–1972 and ending in 1989–1990. The 1989–1990 cohort comprised 306 then-recent Ph.D.s. The idea was to find out what kinds of jobs those anthropologists had.

The AAA got back 840 completed questionnaires, or 68% of the 1,229, and 41% of those responding from the 1989–1990 cohort said they had academic jobs (American Anthropological Association 1991). The AAA didn't report the response rate by cohort, but suppose that 68% of the 1989–1990 cohort—the same percentage as applies to the overall survey—sent back their questionnaires. That's 208 out of 306 responses. The 41% who said they had academic jobs would be 85 of the 208 respondents; the other 123 had nonacademic jobs.

Suppose that everyone who didn't respond (32%, or 98 out of 306) got nonacademic jobs. (Maybe that's why they didn't bother to respond.) In that case, 98 + 123 = 221 out of the 306 people in the cohort, or 72% got nonacademic jobs that year—not the 59% (100%–41%) as reported in the survey.

It's unlikely that *all* the nonresponders were in nonacademic jobs. To handle the problem of nonresponse, the AAA might have run down a random grab of 10 of the nonresponders and interviewed them by telephone. Suppose that 7 said they had nonacademic jobs. You'll recall from chapter 6 on sampling theory that the formula for determining the 95% confidence limits of a point estimator is:

$$P(\text{the true proportion}) = 1.96 \; \sqrt{PQ / n} \qquad \textbf{Formula 9.1}$$

which means that

$$1.96 \; \sqrt{(.7)(.3) / 10} = .28$$

The probable answer for the 10 holdouts is .70 ± .28. Somewhere between 42% and 98% of the 98 nonresponders from the 1989–1990 cohort probably had nonacademic jobs. In other words, 123 of the responders, plus anywhere from 41 to 96 of the nonresponders had nonacademic jobs, which means that between 164 and 216 of the 306 people in the cohort, or 54% to 71%, probably had nonacademic jobs.

Low response rate can be a disaster. People who are quick to fill out and return mailed questionnaires tend to have higher incomes and consequently tend to be more educated than people who respond later. Any dependent variables that co-vary with income and education, then, will be seriously distorted if you get back only 50% of your questionnaires. And what's worse, there is no accurate way to measure nonresponse bias. With a lot of nonresponse, all you know is that you've got bias but you don't know how to take it into account.

IMPROVING RESPONSE RATES: DILLMAN'S TOTAL DESIGN METHOD

For convenience and cost effectiveness, mailed surveys are still an excellent way to collect a lot of data on a representative sample of respondents. And if you're studying hard-to-get people (like physicians or university deans), mailed surveys are the best way to go. The way to increase response rates in mailed surveys is to use Don Dillman's Tailored Design Method (Dillman 1978; Dillman, Smyth, and Christian 2009).

Professional mailed surveys on consumer behavior and political attitudes done in the United States, following Dillman's method achieve a return rate of 50% to 70% (Dillman, Smyth, and Christian 2009:236). What happens when you ask people really threatening questions? In the Netherlands, Nederhof (1985) conducted a mail survey on attitudes toward suicide and achieved a 65% response rate. Pretty impressive. Outside of North

America and northern Europe, Jussaume and Yamada (1990) achieved a response rate of 56% in Kobe, Japan, and de Rada (2001) had a response rate of 61% in mostly rural Navarra Province in Spain.

Dillman's method is very subtle and has many well-tested components. Full instructions are in Dillman's book (Dillman, Smyth, and Christian 2009), but here is an overview of the main steps.

STEPS IN DILLMAN'S METHOD

1. **Professionalism**: Mailed questionnaires must look thoroughly professional. Jaded, hard-bitten, oversurveyed people simply don't respond to amateurish work. Print questionnaires in booklets on standard-size paper: 8.5″ × 11″ in the United States and analogous size (like A4) in the rest of the world. Dillman recommends using white paper. Fox et al. (1988) reported good results with light green paper, but Beebe et al. (2007), in a controlled field test, found that white paper and smaller booklet size had the best response rate.

You must be thinking: "Controlled tests of *paper color*?" Absolutely. It's because social scientists have done their homework on these little things that a response rate of 70% is achievable—provided you're willing to spend the time and money it takes to look after all the little things. Read on and you'll see how small-but-important those "little things" are.

2. **Front and back covers**: Don't put any questions on either the front or back covers of the booklet. The front cover should contain a title that provokes the respondent's interest, the name and address of the survey's sponsor, and some kind of eye-catching graphic design or photo. By "provoking interest," I don't mean "threatening." A title like "The Greenville Air Quality Survey" is fine. "Polluted Air Is Killing Us" isn't.

Be careful in the use of photos—they contain an enormous amount of information, and you never know how respondents will interpret the information. If a respondent thinks a photo contains an editorial message (for or against some pet political position), then the survey booklet goes straight into the trash. If you don't have an appropriate photo, then use a graphic design.

The back cover should have eye-catching photos or designs, and a *brief* note thanking the respondent and inviting open-ended comments about the questionnaire. Nothing else.

3. **Question order**: Be sure that the first question is directly related to the topic of the study (as determined from the title on the front of the booklet); that it is interesting and easy to answer; and that it is nonthreatening. Once someone starts a questionnaire or an interview, they are likely to finish it. Introduce threatening questions well into the instrument, but don't cluster them all together.

Put general socioeconomic and demographic questions at the end of a questionnaire. These seemingly innocuous questions are threatening to many respondents who fear being identified (Sudman and Bradburn 1982). Once someone has filled out a questionnaire, they are unlikely to balk at stating their age, income, religion, occupation, etc.

4. **Formatting**: Mailed surveys have to look good and be easily readable or they get tossed out. Use bolded letters for instructions to respondents and plain text questions themselves and line answers up vertically rather than horizontally, if possible.

Q26. During the past five years how much better or worse has Kinshasa become as a place to live?

☐ A lot better
☐ Somewhat better
☐ No change
☐ Somewhat worse
☐ A lot worse
☐ Not sure

Never allow a question to break at the end of a page and continue on another page.

5. **Length**: Keep mailed questionnaires down to 12 pages, with no more than 125 questions—that's three sheets of 11″ × 17″ folded in half and printed on both sides. Beyond that, response rates drop (Dillman 1978).

It is tempting to save printing and mailing costs and to try to get more questions into a few pages by reducing the amount of white space in a self-administered questionnaire. Don't do it. Respondents are never fooled into thinking that a thin-but-crowded questionnaire is anything other than what it seems to be: a long questionnaire that has been forced into fewer pages and is going to be hard to work through.

Use lots of open space in building schedules for personal interviews, too. Artificially short, crowded instruments only result in interviewers missing items and possibly in annoying respondents (imagine yourself sitting for 15 minutes in an interview before the interviewer flips the first page of an interview schedule).

6. **The cover letter**: A one-page cover letter should explain, in the briefest possible terms, the nature of the study, how the respondent was selected, who should fill out the questionnaire (the respondent or the members of the household), who is funding the survey, and why it is important for the respondent to send back the questionnaire. ("Your response to this questionnaire is very important. We need your response because. . . .")

The one thing that increases response rate more than any other is university sponsorship (Fox et al. 1988). University sponsorship, though, is not enough. If you want a response rate that is not subject to bias, be sure to address the cover letter directly and personally to the respondent—no "Dear Respondent" allowed, unless you only have addresses, without names—and sign it using a blue ballpoint pen. Ballpoints make an indentation that respondents can see—yes, some people do hold those letters up to the light to check. This marks the letter as having been individually signed. In Japan, Jussaume and Yamada (1990) signed all their letters with an *inkan*, or personal seal, and they wrote the address by hand on the envelope to show that they were serious.

The cover letter must guarantee confidentiality and must explain the presence of an identification number (if there is one) on the questionnaire. Some survey topics are so sensitive that respondents will balk at seeing an identification number on the questionnaire, even if you guarantee anonymity. In this case, Fowler (1984) recommends eliminating the identification number (thus making the questionnaire truly anonymous) and telling the respondents that they simply cannot be identified.

If you do this, enclose a printed postcard with the respondent's name on it and ask the respondent to mail back the postcard *separately* from the questionnaire. Explain that this will notify you that the respondent has sent in the questionnaire so that you won't have to send the respondent any reminders later on. Fowler (1984) found that people hardly ever send back the postcard without also sending back the questionnaire.

7. **Packaging**: Package the questionnaire, cover letter, and reply envelope and postcard in another envelope for mailing to the respondent. Print the respondent's name and address on the mailing envelope. Avoid mailing labels, unless the envelope is too big to fit in your printer. Use first-class postage on the mailing envelope and on the reply envelope. Some people respond better to real stamps, especially bright commemorative stamps, than to metered—even first-class metered—postage (Hensley 1974).

8. **Incentives**: What about incentives to complete a survey? Here, the research is unambiguous: money talks and a prepaid incentive works better than a promise of one (Church 1993; Dillman et al. 2009:275; Warriner et al. 1996). Mizes et al. (1984) found that offering respondents $1 to complete and return a questionnaire resulted in significantly increased returns, but offering respondents $5 did not produce a sufficiently greater return to warrant using this tactic. In 1984, $5 was close to the value of many respondents' time for filling out a questionnaire. This makes responding to a survey more like a strictly economic exchange and, as Dillman pointed out, makes it easier for people to turn down (1978:16).

In other words, despite inflation (the $5 in 1984 would be about $11 now) there is a Goldilocks solution to the problem of how much money to send people as an incentive to fill out and return a survey. If you send people too much money or too little, they may throw the survey away. If you send them just the right amount, they are likely to fill out the survey and return it. Today, except for special populations (like physicians) incentives between $1 and $5 are the norm in the United States.

9. **Contact and follow-up**: This is crucial. Send a letter, by first-class mail, to each respondent explaining the survey and informing the respondent that a questionnaire will be coming along soon. You can send people an e-mail message to tell them that a letter is coming, or you can follow up with an e-mail to ask if people have questions, but don't skimp on sending real invitation letters through the mail (Converse et al. 2008). The pre-notice letter should arrive just a few days to a week before the actual survey shows up. A postcard thank-you/reminder to all potential respondents should arrive a week after sending out the questionnaire. The card thanks the recipient if they've already sent the survey back (and it's crossing the postcard in the mail) and reminds them to fill out the survey if they haven't yet done so. Don't wait until the response rate drops before sending out reminders. Some people hold on to a questionnaire for a while before deciding to fill it out or throw it away. A reminder after 1 week stimulates response among this segment of respondents (Dillman, Smyth, and Christian 2009:250).

Send a second cover letter and questionnaire to everyone who has not responded 3 weeks later, and include another copy of the questionnaire. There is no incentive sent with this packet and the tone of the letter is more urgent. For example: "We really need everyone's cooperation in order to make sure that the result represents people in your area." Finally, 4 or 5 weeks after the postcard, send another cover letter and copy of the questionnaire, but this time send it by courier (FedEx, UPS) or special delivery from the post office.

Does All This Really Make a Difference?

Yes, it does. Thurman et al. (1993) were interested in the attitudes and self-reported behaviors of people who admit to drunk driving. Using Dillman's TDM, they sent out questionnaires to a national sample of 1,310 and got back 765, or 58%. Not bad for a first pass, since you can generally expect about 25% to 30% from the first wave. Unfortunately, for lack of time and money, Thurman et al. couldn't follow through with all the extra mailings.

Of the 765 respondents, 237 said they were nondrinkers. This left 525 eligible questionnaires for analysis. Of the 525 respondents who said they were consumers of alcohol, 133 admitted driving while drunk in the past year. Those 133 respondents provided data of intrinsic interest, but the 765 people who responded from the nationally representative sample of 1,310 may be a biased sample on which to base any generalizations. I say "may be" a biased sample because there is no way to tell. And that's the problem.

The bottom line: The last interview you get in any survey—whether you're sending out questionnaires, doing a phone survey, or contacting respondents for face-to-face interviews—is always the most costly and it's almost always worth it. If you really care about representative data, you won't think of all the chasing around you have to do for the last interviews in a set as a nuisance but as a necessary expense of data collection. And you'll prepare for it in advance by establishing a realistic budget of both time and money.

CROSS-SECTIONAL AND LONGITUDINAL STUDIES

Most surveys are **cross-sectional**. The idea is to measure some variables at a single time. Of course, people's attitudes and reported behaviors change over time, and you never know if a single sample is truly representative of the population. Many surveys are conducted again and again to monitor changes and to ensure against picking a bad sample. Multiple cross-sectional polls use a **longitudinal design**. The daily—even hourly— tracking polls in U.S. presidential elections are an extreme example, but in many industrialized countries some questions have been asked of representative samples for many years.

The Gallup Poll, for example, has been asking Americans for about 70 years to list "the most important problem facing this country today." The data track the concerns of Americans about unemployment, the quality of education, drugs, street crime, the federal deficit, taxes, health care costs, poverty, racism, AIDS, abortion. . . . There are not many surprises in the data (people in the United States are more worried about the economy in recessions, less worried when the economy is clicking along) but data from the Gallup Poll, and others like it, are important because they were collected with the same instrument. People were asked the same question again and again over the years. After several generations of effort, longitudinal survey data have become a treasured resource in the highly industrialized nations.

Longitudinal studies by anthropologists are rare and are also great treasures. Beginning in 1961, Robert Edgerton studied a sample of 48 mildly retarded people in California who had been released from a state mental institution (Edgerton 1967). This was full-blown participant observation: hanging out, following people around, doing in-depth interviews, taking field notes. Edgerton was able to interview 30 of the same people in 1975 (Edgerton and Bercovici 1976) and 15 members of the sample in 1982 (Edgerton et al. 1984). Edgerton last interviewed "Richard" in 1988, just before Richard died at age 68 (Edgerton and Ward 1991). As a result, we know more about how the mildly retarded get through life— how they make ends meet; how they deal (or don't deal) with personal hygiene; how they get people to do things for them, like write letters; how people take advantage of them financially—than we could learn from any cross-sectional study.

Two of the best-known longitudinal studies in anthropology are the Tzintzuntzan project in Mexico and the Gwembe Tonga project in Zambia.

George Foster first went to Tzintzuntzan in 1945 to train some anthropology students from ENAH, Mexico's National School of Anthropology and History (Foster 2002:254). Since then, either he or some other anthropologist has visited the community of 3,600 people almost every year. Foster's students, Robert V. Kemper and Stanley Brandes, began going to Tzintzuntzan in 1967 and a third generation of students has already completed four doctoral dissertations there (Cahn 2002; Kemper, personal communication) and two books (Cahn 2003; Torres Sarmiento 2002). Six comprehensive censuses were taken in Tzintzuntzan from 1945 to 2000 and a seventh got underway in 2010. The latest census involves locating and interviewing thousands of migrants from Tzintzuntan across Mexico and the United States. The archive of the Tzintzuntzan project includes digital records of Foster's 20,000 pages of field notes. (For more on this project and on data sources, see http://eclectic.ss.uci.edu/~drwhite/tzintzun/TziDocument@tion.htm.)

The Gwembe Tonga Project began with visits in 1956 by Elizabeth Colson and Thayer Scudder. Some 57,000 Gwembe Tonga were being resettled to make way for the lake that would form in back of the Kariba dam on the Zambezi River, and Scudder and Colson were studying the effects of that resettlement. In 1962–1963, they realized the "long-term possibilities involved in a study of continuity and change among a people who, having been forcibly resettled in connection with a major dam, were soon to be incorporated with the independent nation of Zambia," as the colonial period came to an end (Scudder and Colson 2002:200). Colson and Scudder continued their work and began recruiting colleagues into the project, including Lisa Cliggett, who now manages the project (Cliggett 2002; Kemper and Royce 2002:192). The last full census was done in 2000–2002 and the data from two of the four original sending villages are updated regularly (Lisa Cliggett, e-mail, August 26, 2009). Like the Tzintzuntzán project, the Gwembe project has incorporated indigenous members on the team

Neither of these important projects started out as longitudinal studies. They just went on and on and on. The field notes and other data from these projects grow in importance every year, as more information is added to the corpus. All cross-sectional studies, including Master's and Ph.D. projects, should be designed as if they were the start of a lifetime of research. You never know (**Further Reading:** longitudinal research in anthropology).

Panel Studies

If the results from two successive samples are very different, you don't know if it's because people's attitudes or reported behaviors have changed, or the two samples are very different, or both. The powerful **panel design** deals with this. In a panel study, you *interview the same people* again and again. Panel studies are like true experiments: Participants are tracked for their exposure or lack of exposure to a series of interventions in the real world.

Perhaps the most well-known panel study of all time is the Framingham Heart Study. In 1948, medical researchers began tracking 5,209 men and women between 30 and 62 years old from one small town—Framingham, Massachusetts. In 1971, as the original

panel began to die off, another 5,124 panelists were added—this time, the original panelists' adult children and their spouses. Every 2 years, all the panelists go in for a complete
medical check-up. This study has identified and nailed down the major risk factors for
heart disease, which include behaviors (exercise, smoking) and inner states (attitudes,
stress) that anthropologists, as well as epidemiologists, are interested in. Basic information
about the Framingham study is available from the National Heart, Lung, and Blood Institute at http://www.framinghamheartstudy.org/index.html.

An important panel study in sociology is the Wisconsin Longitudinal Survey, which
has followed 10,317 people in Wisconsin since they graduated from high school in 1957.
The graduates were contacted in 1964 and again in 1975. In 1992–1993, the researchers
tracked the 9,741 survivors of the original 10,317 and interviewed 87% of them by phone
for an hour. The team did another round of interviews in 2004–2005 and they are planning another wave for 2022, when the Wisconsin high school class of 1957 will be 83
years old (Hauser 2005). The nonsensitive data from the WLS are available at http://
www.ssc.wisc.edu/wlsresearch, and the sensitive data (about, for example, sexual preference, addiction, mental health, or criminal behavior) are available to qualified researchers
at http://www.ssc.wisc.edu/cdha/data/data.html.

Panel studies are rare in cultural anthropology but the few that exist make clear how
important this kind of data is for tracking change over time (see Gravlee et al. [2009] for
a review). The Tsimane' Indian Panel Study (TAPS), begun in 1999, follows the effects of
market exposure on the Tsimane' Indians in villages along the Maniqui River in the
Bolivian Amazon (http://www.tsimane.org). Villages vary in how close they are to the
market town of San Borja—and hence experience more or less market exposure—so, with
panel data, the team can assess changes over time in things like farming practices, nutritional status, and ethnobotanical knowledge. For example, Godoy et al. (2007) found that
the Tsimane' protected their children's food consumption during lean economic times.
Vadez et al. (2008) showed the dramatic effect on deforestation caused by increased rice
cultivation by the Tsimane'. Contrary to expectations, though, neither walking time to
San Borja nor the presence of a permanent road had any effect on deforestation.

Panel studies can be done quickly—even within the year or two of most anthropological fieldwork. Amber Wutich (2009) studied the effects of water scarcity on social interaction in an urban squatter settlement in Cochabamba, Bolivia. After a couple of months
of in-depth interviewing, she and several assistants began a five-wave panel study of random sample of 72 (out of 415) households. They interviewed people in each household
every 2 months for 10 months and found that there was significant variation in the size
of personal network across the five waves. As predicted by theory, just as the dry season
began, people tried harder to mobilize their networks to get more water. Then, as the dry
season advanced, people withdrew from their networks. They knew it was useless and
couldn't afford the risk that they'd have to reciprocate if they did score some water. And
then, as the dry season ended, people went back to their old social interaction pattern
(box 9.8).

Attrition

People drop out between successive waves of panel surveys. If this happens, and the
results of successive waves are very different, you can't tell if that's because of (1) the
special character of the drop out population, (2) real changes in the variables you're
studying, or (3) both. For example, if dropouts tend to be male or poor, your results in
successive waves will overrepresent the experiences of those who are female or affluent. If
you run a panel study, consult a statistician about how to test for the effects of attrition.

Respondent mortality is not always a problem. Roger Trent and I did a panel study of

BOX 9.8

USING ETHNOGRAPHIC DATA IN PANEL STUDIES

Anderson-Fye (2004) studied the body image and eating behavior of 16 adolescent girls in San Andrés, Belize. She began her work with the usual year-in-the-field stint (1996–1997), but went back in each of the next 5 years for several months and did in-depth interviews with each of her informants. While in high-school, the girls showed satisfaction with their body shape and image, but over time, 4 of the 16 developed attitudes or behaviors, or both, characteristic of eating disorders. For example, one of Anderson-Fye's informants, Kara, was happy with her body image, but wound up taking pills and exercising in an effort to be skinny. It turned out that her parents ran a gift shop that catered to American tourists and instructed Kara to be "thin, pretty and friendly" because, as they told Anderson-Fye, those were traits valued by Americans (p. 579). Ethnographic panel data made it possible for Anderson-Fye to track the emergence of these attitudes and behaviors and to tie them to likely causes.

riders on the Morgantown, West Virginia's "People Mover," an automated transport system that was meant to be a kind of horizontal elevator. You get on a little railway car (they carry only 8 seated and 12 standing passengers), push a button, and the car takes you to your stop—a block away or 8 miles across town. The system was brought on line a piece at a time between 1975 and 1980. Trent and I were tracking public support as the system went more places and became more useful (Trent and Bernard 1985). We established a panel of 216 potential users of the system when the system opened in 1975 and reinterviewed the members of that panel in 1976 and 1980 as more and more pieces of the system were added.

All 216 original members of the panel were available during the second wave and 189 were available for the third wave of the survey. Note, though, that people who were unavailable had moved out of Morgantown and were no longer potential users of the system. What counted in this case was maintaining a panel large enough to represent the attitudes of people in Morgantown about the People Mover system. The respondents who stayed in the panel still represented the people whose experiences we hoped to learn about (**Further Reading:** panel attrition).

SOME SPECIALIZED SURVEY TECHNIQUES

Factorial Surveys

In a **factorial survey** (Rossi and Berk 1997; Rossi and Nock 1982), people are presented with **vignettes** that describe hypothetical social situations and are asked for their judgments about those situations. The General Social Survey (http://www.norc.uchicago.org/GSS+Website) is a face-to-face survey of about adults in the United States. From 1972 to 1993, it was an annual survey of 1,500 people. Since 1994, it is run every other year on two samples of 1,500 people). Figure 9.5 shows a vignette that was in the 1992 GSS.

There are 10 variables in this vignette (number of children, marital status of the mother, how much savings the family has, the total income of the family, etc.), with 1,036,800 possible combinations. That seems just about right to me. The calculus for any

Amount already received by this family								Average U.S. family income				
X								X				

| 0 | 50 | 100 | 150 | 200 | 250 | 300 | 350 | 400 | 450 | 500 | 550 | 600 |

FIGURE 9.5.

An example of a vignette from a factorial survey.

SOURCE: "The Dimensions of Poverty: Public Perceptions of the Deserving Poor" by J. A. Will, 1993, *Social Science Research*, p. 322. Reprinted with permission of Academic Press.

individual's opinion about how much money to award the deserving poor on welfare is really that complicated. Now, each of the 1,500 respondents in the GSS saw seven vignettes each, so the survey captured:

$$(1,500 \text{ people}) (7 \text{ vignettes}) (10 \text{ variables}) = 105,000$$

combinations, or a sample of about 10% of all the factors that probably go into people's opinion on this issue.

The results of that survey were very interesting. Respondents awarded people who were looking for work a lot more than they awarded people who weren't looking for work. But mothers only got an extra $6 per week for seeking work, while fathers got over $12. And if mothers were unemployed because they wouldn't take minimum-wage jobs, they had their allotments reduced by $20 per week, on average, compared to what people were willing to give mothers who were working full time. (For comparison, it took about $270 in 2010 to buy what $100 bought in 1986.)

The factorial survey combines the validity of randomized experiments with the reliability of survey research (**Further Reading:** factorial surveys and vignettes).

Time Budgets and Diaries

Time budget surveys have been done all over the world to track how ordinary human beings spend most of their days (Szalai 1972). The idea is to learn about the sequence, duration, and frequency of behaviors and about the contexts in which behaviors take place. Some researchers ask respondents to keep diaries; others conduct "yesterday interviews," in which respondents are asked to go over the last 24 hours and talk about everything they did. Some researchers combine these methods, collecting diaries from respondents and then following up with a personal interview.

Perhaps the earliest time budget in anthropology was done by Audrey Richards between 1930 and 1934 during 2.5 years of fieldwork among the Bemba of Zambia (it was Northern Rhodesia back then). Richards went across the country, spending from 3 to 6 weeks in a series of villages. She pitched her tent in the middle of each village so she could watch people's activities and in two of those villages, Kasaka and Kapamba, she kept daily calendars of all the adults, both men and women (Richards 1939:10–11). Richards asked several informants to estimate how long they took to accomplish various tasks—planting a garden, chasing locusts, cutting trees. Then she averaged what people told her and got a rough estimate for each task. Then she applied those figures to her observations of people in the two villages where she kept records of the daily activities (Richards 939:395 and appendix E).

In 1992, Elizabeth Harrison recruited 16 farmers in two villages of Luapula Province of Zambia to keep records for 4 months of their daily activities. The diaries reveal that the technology for producing cassava meal hadn't changed since Richards's day (E. Harrison

2000:59). They also showed how long seemingly ordinary things can take. Here is Abraham Kasongo, one of Harrison's informants, describing his trip to Kalaba, the capital of the province, to get millet so his mother could brew beer. Kalaba is 8 kilometers away and Kasongo is going by bicycle:

22nd July 1992
Morning I go watering the seeds after watering I came back and wash my body and go to my father's house to get the biscley and start the journey to Kalaba to get the millet. I found the one who has been given the money is not around I start waiting for him around 14 hrs he came and give me millet I go where the people in the village where drinking the coll me and I join them around 15 hrs I start caming back I found my wife is not around I go to my father's house and put millet then I show my father the fish for sale and the piace is K200.00 he take the fish and I start caming back straight to the house. I found my wife priparing fire and start cooking Nshima [the staple food, made from cassava. HRB] with dry vegetables we eat and I go to see Eliza we tolked antill I cam back to slip becouse I was tired I just go straight to slip. (E. Harrison 2000:62)

Discursive diaries, in other words, are like any other qualitative data: They make the process clear and bring out subtleties in behavioral complexes that time budgets can obscure. And, just as with any other survey method, getting both the qualitative and quantitative is better than one kind of data alone.

Susan Shaw's study of family activities in Canada is typical of the use of time budgets in modern societies (1992). Shaw studied 46 middle- and working-class couples who had children living at home. All the fathers were employed full time and among the mothers, 12 were employed full time, 9 were employed part time, and 25 were full-time homemakers. Both parents kept time diaries for 1 day during the week and for 1 day on a weekend. Then, Shaw interviewed the parents separately, for 1 to 2 hours in their homes. For each activity that they had mentioned, parents were asked if they considered the activity to be work or leisure, and why.

Shaw calculated the amount of time that each parent reported spending with their children—playing with them, reading to them, and so on. The rather dramatic results are in table 9.1. For these Canadian families, at least, the more that women work outside the home, the more time fathers spend with their children.

Table 9.1   Average Amount of Time Fathers and Mothers Report Spending with Children, by the Mother's Employment Status

Mother's employment status	N	Time with children per day (in minutes)	
		Mothers	Fathers
Employed full-time	12	97	71
Employed part-time	9	144	52
Full-time homemaker	25	241	23
Total	46		

SOURCE: "Dereifying Family Leisure: An Examination of Women's and Men's Everyday Experiences and Perceptions of Family Time" by S. Shaw, 1992, *Leisure Sciences,* p. 279. Reproduced by permission of Taylor and Francis.

Diaries and time-budget interviews, particularly with the aid of checklists, appear to be more accurate than 24-hour recall of activities. But no matter what you call them, time budgets and diaries are still methods for collecting self-reports of behavior. They may be *less* inaccurate than simply asking people to tell you what they did over the past day or week, but they are not perfect. A lot of work remains to be done on testing the accuracy of activity diaries against data from direct observation. In chapter 14, we'll look at methods for direct observation and measurement of behavior (**Further Reading:** time budgets and time diaries).

Randomized Response

Randomized response is a technique for estimating the amount of some socially negative behavior in a population—things like shoplifting, extramarital sex, child abuse, being hospitalized for emotional problems, and so on. The technique was introduced by Warner in 1965 and is particularly well described by B. Williams (1978:73). It is a simple, fun, and interesting tool. Here's how it works.

First, you formulate two questions, A and B, that can be answered "yes" or "no." One question, A, is the question of interest (say, "Have you ever shoplifted?"). The possible answers to this question (either "yes" or "no") do not have known probabilities of occurring. That is what you want to find out.

The other question, B, must be innocuous and the possible answers (again "yes" or "no") must have known probabilities of occurring. For example, if you ask a someone to toss a fair coin and ask, "Did you toss a heads?" then the probability that they answer "yes" or "no" is 50%. If the chances of being born in any given month were equal, then you could ask respondents: "Were you born in April, May, or June?" and the probability of getting a "yes" would be 25%. Unfortunately, births are seasonal, so the coin-toss question is preferable.

Let's assume you use the coin toss for question B. You ask someone to toss the coin and to note the result *without letting you see it*. Next, have them pick a card, from a deck of 10 cards, where each card is marked with a single integer from 1 to 10. The respondent *does not tell you what number he or she picked*, either. The genuine secrecy associated with this procedure makes people feel secure about answering question A (the sensitive question) truthfully.

Next, hand the respondent a card with the two questions, marked A and B, written out. Tell them that if they picked a number between one and four from the deck of 10 cards, they should answer question A. If they picked a number between 5 and 10, they should answer question B.

That's all there is to it. You now have the following: (1) Each respondent knows they answered "yes" or "no" and which question they answered; and (2) You know *only* that a respondent said "yes" or "no" but not which question, A or B, was being answered.

If you run through this process with a sufficiently large, representative sample of a population, and if people cooperate and answer all questions truthfully, then you can calculate the percentage of the population that answered "yes" to question A. Here's the formula:

$$P_{A\,or\,B} = [(P_{A+} \times P_A) + (P_{B+} \times P_B)] \qquad \textbf{Formula 9.2}$$

The percentage of people who answer "yes" to *either* A or B = (the percentage of people who answer "yes" to question A) times (the percentage of times that question A is asked) plus (the percentage of people who answered "yes" to question B) times (the percentage of times question B is asked).

The only unknown in this equation is the percentage of people who answered "yes" to question A, the sensitive question. We know, from our data, the percentages of "yes" answers to *either* question. Suppose that 33% of all respondents said "yes" to *something*. Since respondents answered question A only if they chose a number from 1 to 4, then A was answered 40% of the time and B was answered 60% of the time. Whenever B was answered, there was a 50% chance of it being answered "yes" because that's the chance of getting a heads on the toss of a fair coin. The problem now reads:

$$.33 = A(.40) + .50(.60) \text{ or}$$
$$.33 = .40A + .30$$

which means that $A = .08$. That is, given the parameters specified in this experiment, if 33% of the sample says "yes" to either question, then 8% of the sample answered "yes" to question A.

There are two problems associated with this technique. First, no matter what you say or do, some people will not believe that you can't identify them and will therefore not tell the truth. Bradburn, Sudman et al. (1979) report that 35% of known offenders would not admit to having been convicted of drunken driving in a randomized response survey. Second, like all survey techniques, randomized response depends on large, representative samples. Because the technique is time consuming to administer, this makes getting large, representative samples difficult.

BOX 9.9

THE LIST EXPERIMENT

The list experiment was developed by Kuklinski et al. (1997) to unobtrusively measure socially undesirable attitudes. In this technique (which is closely related to the randomized response technique), two randomly selected samples of people called the baseline group and the test group—are told:

> Now I'm going to read you four [five] things that sometimes make people angry or upset. After I read all four [five] statements, just tell me how many of them upset you. I don't want to know which ones, just how many.

Then, the interviewer reads four statements to the baseline group and five to the test group. The four statements that get read to both groups are about:

> One: the way gasoline prices keep going up.
> Two: professional athletes getting million-plus salaries.
> Three: requiring seat belts be used when driving.
> Four: large corporations polluting the environment.

The test group gets a fifth statement, like "a black family moving in next door" (Kuklinski et al. 1997), or "a Jewish candidate running for vice president" (J. G. Kane et al. 2004), or "a woman serving as president" (Streb et al. 2008).

If both groups are chosen at random, then average number of items that make people angry should be more-or-less the same in both groups. If the number is bigger for the people in the test group, it must be because of the extra statement. So, if the average number of items that make people angry in the baseline group is 2.5 and the average number in the test group is 3.0, the percentage of people who are angered by the extra item is (3.0 − 2.5 × 100) = .50, or 50%.

Still, the evidence is mounting that for sensitive questions—Did you smoke dope in the last week? Have you ever bought a term paper? Have you stolen anything from your employer?—when you want the truth, the randomized response method is worth the effort. Every time I read in the newspaper that self-reported drug use among adolescents has dropped by such-and-such and amount since whenever-the-last-self-report-survey-was-done, I think about how easy it is for those data to be utter nonsense. And I wonder why the randomized response technique isn't more widely used (**Further Reading:** randomized response) (box 9.9).

MIXED METHODS

Finally, this: With all the great techniques out there for collecting systematic data, there is nothing to stop you from using several methods, even wildly different methods like narratives, questionnaires, and randomized response, in the same study. By now, you know that there is no need to choose between qualitative and quantitative data. Whether you are doing exploratory or confirmatory research, a sensible mix of methods—methods that match the needs of the research—is what you're after.

Furthermore, there is no formula for how to mix methods. You'll use ethnography to develop good questions for a questionnaire, but you'll also use ethnography to interpret and flesh out the results from questionnaires. Ethnography can tell you what parameters you want to estimate, but you need survey data to actually estimate parameters. Ethnography tells you that patrilateral cross-cousin marriage is preferred, but it takes a survey to find out how often the rule is obeyed or ignored. And then it takes more ethnography to find out how people rationalize ignoring the culturally preference. Researchers who are comfortable with both words and numbers routinely move back and forth, without giving it a moment's thought.

Today, mixed methods is becoming the norm rather than something interesting to talk about. Not a moment too soon, either (**Further Reading:** mixed methods).

FURTHER READING

Computer-based interviews: CASI: de Leeuw et al. (2003). A-CASI: Aquilino et al. (2000); Arasteh et al. (2004); Brown et al. (2008); Couper et al. (2003); Gravlee et al. (2006); Greene (2001); Harmon et al. (2009); Mensch et al. (2008); Newman et al. (2002); Potdar and Koenig (2005). CAPI and MCAPI: Childs and Landreth (2006); T. W. Smith (2008).
Mode effects: Aquilino (1994); Bradburn (1983); de Leeuw et al. (1995); Dillman and Christian (2005); Dillman et al. (2009); Gerich (2008); Heerwegh (2009); Hochstim (1967); Monteiro et al. (2008); Tourangeau and Smith (1996).
Thinkaloud and cognitive interviews: Beatty and Willis (2007); Conrad and Blair (2009); Jobe et al. (1996); Mavhu et al. (2008); Willis (2010).
Longitudinal research in anthropology: Hutchinson (1996); Johansen and White (2002).
Panel attrition: Ahern and Le Brocque (2005); Fitzgerald et al. (1998); Rubin (1976); Thomas et al. (2001); Tourangeau and Ye (2009); Twisk and de Vente (2002).
Factorial surveys and vignettes: Gölge et al. (2003); Jasso (1998, 2008); Wallender (2009).
Time budgets and time diaries: Budlender (2007); Esquivel et al. (2008).
Randomized response: Clark and Desharnais (1998); Lara et al. (2004); Lensveldt-Mulders et al. (2005); Nordlund et al. (1994); Scheers and Dayton (1987).
Mixed methods: Creswell (2009); Creswell and Plano-Clark (2007); Morse and Niehaus (2009); Pearce (2002); Tashakkori and Teddlie (2003); Yoshikawa et al. (2008).

10

Interviewing III: Cultural Domains

Cultural domain analysis is the late-model version of **ethnoscience**, a movement in anthropology of the 1950s and 1960s (Sturtevant 1964). The goal of ethnoscience was to understand cultural systems of classification—that is, how people in a group think about lists of things that somehow go together. These can be lists of physical, observable things—plants, colors, animals, symptoms of illness—or conceptual things—occupations, roles, emotions. (For seminal work on modern cultural domain analysis, see Borgatti 1993/1994, 1999 and Weller and Romney 1988).

The spectrum of colors, for example, has a single physical reality that you can see on a machine. Some peoples across the world, however—Xhosa, Navajo, Ñähñu—identify the colors across the physical spectrum of green and blue with a single gloss. In Ñähñu, for example, the word is *nk'ami* and in Navajo it's *dootl'izh*. Linguists and cognitive scientists who study this phenomenon call this color "grue" (see, e.g., Davies et al. 1994; Gammack and Denby 2006; and Kim 1985).

This does *not* mean that people who have a word for grue fail to *see* the difference between things that are the color of grass and things that are the color of a clear sky. They just *label* chunks of the physical spectrum of colors differently than we do and use adjectival modifiers of grue to express color differences within the blue-green spectrum. In Navajo, turquoise is *yáago dootl'izh*, or "sky grue," and green is *tádlidgo dootl'izh*, or "water skum grue" (Oswald Werner, personal communication). If this seems exotic to you, get a chart of, say, 100 lipstick colors or house paint colors and ask people at your university to name the colors. On average, women will probably recognize (and name) more colors than men will; and art majors of both sexes will name more colors than, say, engineering majors will.

KINSHIP AND OTHER DOMAINS

This concern for understanding cultural differences in how people cut the natural world goes a long way back in anthropology—all the way to the early interest in kinship. Lewis Henry Morgan (1997 [1870]) studied systems of kinship nomenclature. His work made clear that if someone says, "This is my sister," you can't assume that they have the same mother and father. Lots of different people can be called "sister," depending on the kinship system. And in his work with the Murray Islanders (in the Torres Straits between Australia and Papua New Guinea) and then later with the Todas of southern India, W.H.R. Rivers developed the genealogical method—those ego-centered graphs for organizing kinship data that we take for granted today—as a way to elicit accurately and systematically the inventory of kin terms in a language (Rivers 1910, 1968 [1914]).

Anthropologists also noticed very early that, although kinship systems *could* be unique to each culture—which would mean that each system required a separate set of rules—they simply weren't. Alfred Kroeber showed in 1909 that just eight features were needed to distinguish kinship terms in any system: (1) whether the speaker and the kin referred to were of the same or different generations; (2) the relative age people who are of the same generation—older or younger brother, for example; (3) whether the person referred to is a collateral or a lineal relative; (4) whether the person referred to is an affinal or consanguineal relative; (5) whether the relative is male or female; (6) whether the speaker is male or female; (7) whether the person who links the speaker and the relative is male or female; and (8) whether the person who links the speaker and the relative is alive or dead.

Now, if you first choose whether to use or not use any of those eight features and then choose among the two alternatives to each feature, you can concoct $3^8 = 6,561$ kinds of kinship systems. But, although there are some rare exceptions (the bilineal Yakö of Nigeria, the ambilineal Gilbert Islanders), most of the world's kinship systems are of one those familiar types you studied in Anthropology 101—the Hawaiian, Sudanese, Omaha, Eskimo, Crow, and Iroquois types. Early anthropologists found it pretty interesting that the world's real kinship systems comprised just a tiny set of the possibilities, and to this day, a small, hardy band of anthropologists continues to study the elements of these systems and how those elements are associated with particular political, economic, or environmental conditions (Kronenfeld 2009; White and Schweizer 1998) (**Further Reading:** kinship studies).

An interest in classifying kinship systems led to methods for discovering sets of terms in other domains, like kinds of foods, things to do on the weekend, kinds of crime, bad names for ethnic groups, dirty words, names for illnesses, etc. Note that none of these is about people's preferences. If we ask people which of two political candidates they favor in an election, we might also ask them about their income, their ethnicity, their age, and so on. Then we look for packages of variables about the people that predict their preference for a candidate. In cultural domain analysis, we're interested in the items that comprise the domain—the illnesses, the edible plants, the jobs that women and men do, etc.—and how those items are related to each other in people's minds (Borgatti 1999; Spradley 1979) (box 10.1). (More about building folk taxonomies in chapter 17.)

The methods for collecting data about the content and structure of cultural domains include *free lists*, *sentence frames*, *triad tests*, *pile sorts*, and *paired comparisons*. All of these methods produce a lot of data very quickly and some of them (particularly free lists and pile sorts) are even fun for people to do. And, with software, like ANTHROPAC (Borgatti 1992a) and UCINET (Borgatti et al. 2002), it's easy to analyze these data. We'll return to analyzing these kinds of data in chapter 16 (**Further Reading:** data collection for domain analysis).

FREE LISTING

Free listing is a deceptively simple, but powerful technique. Data from short, open-ended questions on surveys can be coded to produce lists, as can transcriptions of ethnographic interviews and focus groups. In free listing, however, we tell people: "List all the X you can think of," where X might be things they do on weekends, brands of cars, things people do when they get a cold, ways to avoid pregnancy, places in the community frequented by commercial sex workers, and so on.

The object is to get informants to list as many items as they can in a domain, so you need to probe and not just settle for whatever people say. Brewer et al. (2002:112) found that **semantic cueing** increased the recall of items in a free list by over 40%. Tell infor-

BOX 10.1

HOW SPRADLEY LEARNED TO NAVIGATE THE
POLICE DEPARTMENT

Cultural domains are everywhere. Spradley (1979) reported that he once called
the St. Paul, Minnesota, police department and said he needed to find the case
number of a robbery that had been committed at his house. Two bicycles had
been stolen from his garage in the middle of the night, while he was asleep.
The police had investigated, but Spradley's insurance company needed the case
number to process the claim. When Spradley told the police that he needed the
case number for a "robbery," they quite naturally transferred his call to the
robbery unit. But the people there couldn't help him because, according to their
rules, robberies involve a face-to-face encounter between the criminal and the
victim and the criminal uses a gun.

Spradley was transferred to burglary, but they couldn't help him either
because, they said, theft of bicycles is handled by the juvenile division in St.
Paul. Eventually, Spradley got his case number, but, he said, if he had understood the police culture, he "would have begun with a simple question: What
part of the police department has records of bicycles stolen from a garage when
no one is present?" (1979:142). In other words, if he'd known taxonomy for the
cultural domain of crimes, he'd have asked the right question and gotten taken
care of right away.

mants to: "Think of all the kinds of X [the domain] that are like Y," where Y is that first
item on their initial list. If the informant responds with more items, you take it another
step: "Try to remember other types of X like Y and tell me any new ones that you haven't
already said." Do this until the informant says there are no more items like Y. Then you
repeat the exercise for the second item on the informant's initial list; and the third; and
so on (box 10.2).

You'd be surprised at how much you can learn from a humble set of free lists. Henley
(1969) asked 21 students at Johns Hopkins University to name as many animals as they
could in 10 minutes. She found an enormous variety of expertise when it comes to naming
animals. In just this small group of informants (which didn't even represent the population of Johns Hopkins University, much less that of Baltimore or the United States), the
lists ranged in length from 21 to 110, with a median of 55.

In fact, those 21 people named 423 different animals, and 175 were mentioned just
once. The most popular animals for this group of informants were: dog, lion, cat, horse,
and tiger, all of which were named by more than 90% of informants. Only 29 animals
were listed by more than half the informants, but 90% of those were mammals. By contrast, among the 175 animals named only once, just 27% were mammals.

But there's more. Previous research had shown that the 12 most commonly talked
about animals in American speech are: bear, cat, cow, deer, dog, goat, horse, lion, mouse,
pig, rabbit, and sheep. There are $n(n-1)/2$, or 66 possible unique pairs of 12 animals
(dog-cat, dog-deer, horse-lion, mouse-pig, etc.). Henley examined each informant's list
of animals, and found the difference in the order of listing for each of the 66 pairs.

BOX 10.2

OTHER PROBES

Brewer tested three other kinds of probes for free lists: redundant questioning, nonspecific prompting, and alphabetic cueing. Here's the redundant question that Brewer and his colleagues asked a group of IV-drug users:

> Think of all the different kinds of drugs or substances people use to get high, feel good, or think and feel differently. These drugs are sometimes called recreational drugs or street drugs. Tell me the names of all the kinds of these drugs you can remember. Please keep trying to recall if you think there are more kinds of drugs you might be able to remember. (Brewer et al. 2002:347; and see Brewer and Garrett 2001)

In nonspecific prompting you ask people "What other kinds of X are there?" after they've responded to your original question. You keep asking this question until people say they can't think of any more Xs. And in alphabetic cueing, you ask informants "what kinds of X are there that begin with the letter A?" . . . "With the letter B?" And so on.

That is, if an informant mentioned goats 12th on her list, and bears 32nd, then the distance between goats and bears, for that informant, was $32 - 12 = 20$. Henley standardized these distances (that is, she divided each distance by the length of an informant's list and multiplied by 100) and calculated the average distance, over all the informants, for each of the 66 pairs of animals.

The lowest mean distance was between sheep and goats (1.8). If you named sheep, then the next thing you named was probably goats; and if you named goats, then next thing you named was probably sheep. Most speakers of English (and other Western languages, for that matter) have heard the expression: "That'll separate the sheep from the goats." This part of Western culture was originally a metaphor for distinguishing the righteous from the wicked and then became a metaphor for separating the strong from the weak. The first meaning was mentioned in the Old Testament (Ezekiel 34:17), and then again around 600 years later in the New Testament (Matthew 25:31–33).

Henley's respondents were neither shepherds nor students of Western scriptural lore, but they all knew that sheep and goats somehow "go together." Free lists tell you *what goes with what*, but you need to dig to understand *why*. Cats and dogs were only 2 units apart in Henley's free lists—no surprise there, right?—while cats and deer were 56 units apart. Deer, in fact, are related to all the other animals on the list by at least 40 units of distance, except for rabbits, which are only 20 units away from deer.

Robert Trotter (1981) asked 378 Mexican Americans to name the *remedios caseros*, or home remedies, they knew, and what illnesses each remedy was for. Informants listed a total of 510 remedies for treating 198 illnesses. However, the 25 most frequently mentioned remedies—about 5% of the 510—made up about 41% of all the cases; and the 70 most frequently mentioned illnesses—about 14%—made up 84% of the cases.

Trotter's free-list data reveal a lot about Mexican American perceptions of illness and home cures. He was able to count which ailments were reported more frequently by men and which by women; which ailments were reported more frequently by older people and which by younger people; which by those born in Mexico and which by those born in the United States; and so on.

Informants who are very knowledgeable about the contents of a cultural domain usually provide longer lists than others. Some items will be mentioned over and over again, but eventually, if you keep asking people to list things, you get a lot of repeat items and all the new items are unique—that is, mentioned by only one informant. This happens pretty quickly (by the time you've interviewed 15 or 20 informants) with domains like names of ethnic groups, which are pretty well formed. With fuzzy domains, like "things that mothers do," you might still be eliciting new items after interviewing 30 or 40 people. Long lists don't necessarily mean that people know a lot about the things they name. In fact, in modern societies, people can often name a lot more things than they can recognize in the real world (see box 10.3).

BOX 10.3

LOOSE TALK

John Gatewood (1983) asked 40 adult Pennsylvanians to name all the trees they could think of. Then he asked them to check the trees on their list that they thought they could recognize in the wild. Thirty-seven of them listed "oak," 34 listed "pine," 33 listed "maple," and 31 listed "birch." I suspect that the list of trees and what people say they could recognize would look rather different in, say Wyoming or Mississippi. We could test that.

Thirty-one of the 34 who listed "pine" said they could recognize a pine. Twenty-seven people listed "orange," but only four people said they could recognize an orange tree without oranges hanging all over it. On average, the Pennsylvanians in Gatewood's sample said they could recognize half of the trees they listed, a phenomenon that Gatewood calls **loose talk**. He thinks that many Americans can name a lot more things than they can recognize in nature.

Does this loose talk phenomenon vary by gender? Suppose, Gatewood says, we ask Americans from a variety of subcultures and occupations to list other things besides trees. Would the 50% recognition rate hold? Gatewood and a group of students at Lehigh University asked 54 university students, half women and half men, to list all the musical instruments, fabrics, hand tools and trees they could think of. Then the informants were asked to check off the items in each of their lists that they thought they would recognize in a natural setting.

Gatewood chose musical instruments with the idea that there would be no gender difference in the number of items listed or recognized; he thought that women might name more kinds of fabrics than would men and that men would name more kinds of hand tools than would women. He chose the domain of trees to see if his earlier findings would replicate. All the hypotheses were supported (Gatewood 1984).

A. Kimball Romney and Roy D'Andrade asked 105 American high school students to "list all the names for kinds of relatives and family members you can think of in English" (1964:155). They were able to do a large number of analyses on these data. For example, they studied the order and frequency of recall of certain terms, and the productiveness of modifiers, such as "step-," "half-," "-in-law," "grand-," "great," and so on. They assumed that the nearer to the beginning of a list a kin term occurs, the more salient it is for that particular informant. By taking the average position in all the lists for each kin term, they were able to derive a rank order list of kin terms, according to the variable's saliency.

They also assumed that more salient terms occur more frequently. So, for example, "mother" occurs in 93% of all lists and is the first term mentioned on most lists. At the other end of the spectrum is "grandson," which was only mentioned by 17% of the 105 informants, and was, on average, the 15th, or last term to be listed. They found that the terms "son" and "daughter" occur on only about 30% of the lists. But remember, these informants were all high school students, all of whom *were* sons and daughters, but none of whom *had* sons or daughters. It would be interesting to repeat Romney and D'Andrade's experiment on many different American populations. We could then test the saliency of English kin terms on the many subpopulations.

Finally, free listing can be used to find out where to concentrate effort in applied research, especially in rapid assessment. Researchers interested in high-risk sexual behavior, for example, use the free-list technique to understand domains like "ways to have sex" (Schensul et al. 1994) and "reasons to have sex" (Flores et al. 1998).

Monárrez-Espino et al. (2004) worked on a food aid program for at-risk Tarahumara infants in Mexico. A government agency had developed a basket of nutritional foods for distribution to Tarahumara mothers, but many of the foods (like canned sardines) were culturally unacceptable. Free listing of foods helped set things right.

In a project on which I consulted, interviewers asked people on the North Carolina coast how they viewed the possibility of offshore oil drilling. One of the questions was: "What are the things that make life good around here?" This question cropped up after some informal interviews in seven small, seaside towns. People kept saying "What a nice little town this is" and "What a shame it would be if things changed around here." Informants had no difficulty with the question, and after just 20 interviews, the researchers had a list of over 50 "things that make life good around here." The researchers chose the 20 items mentioned by at least 12 informants and explored the meaning of those items further (ICMR 1993).

The humble free list has many uses. Use it a lot (**Further Reading:** free lists).

THE TRUE-FALSE/YES-NO AND SENTENCE FRAME TECHNIQUES

Another common technique in cultural domain analysis is called the **sentence frame** or **frame elicitation** method. Linda Garro (1986) used the frame elicitation method to compare the knowledge of curers and noncurers in Pichátaro, Mexico. She used a list of 18 illness terms and 22 causes, based on prior research in Pichátaro (Young 1978). The frames were questions, like "can _____ come from _____?" Garro substituted names of illnesses in the first blank, and things like "anger," "cold," "overeating," and so on in the second blank. (ANTHROPAC has a routine for building questionnaires of this type.) This produced an 18×22 yes-no matrix for each of the informants. The matrices could then be added together and submitted to analysis by multidimensional scaling (see chapter 16).

James Boster and Jeffrey Johnson (1989) used the frame-substitution method in their study of how recreational fishermen in the United States categorize ocean fish. They asked 120 fishermen to consider 62 belief frames, scan down a list of 43 fish (tarpon, silver perch, Spanish mackerel, etc.), and pick out the fish that fit each frame. Here are a few of the belief frames:

The meat from   _____ is oily tasting.
It is hard to clean _____ .
I prefer to catch   _____ .

That's $43 \times 62 = 2,666$ judgments by each of 120 informants, but informants were usually able to do the task in about half an hour (Johnson, personal communication). The 62 frames, by the way, came straight out of ethnographic interviews where informants were asked to list fish and to talk about the characteristics of those fish.

Gillian Sankoff (1971) studied land tenure and kinship among the Buang, a mountain people of northeastern New Guinea. The most important unit of social organization among the Buang is the *dgwa*, a kind of descent group, like a clan. Sankoff wanted to figure out the very complicated system by which men in the village of Mambump identified with various *dgwa* and with various named garden plots.

The Buang system was apparently too complex for bureaucrats to fathom, so, to save administrators a lot of trouble, the men of Mambump had years earlier devised a simplified system that they presented to outsiders. Instead of claiming that they had ties with one or more of five different *dgwa*, they each decided which of the two largest *dgwa* they would belong to, and that was as much as the New Guinea administration knew.

To unravel the complex system of land tenure and descent, Sankoff made a list of all 47 men in the village and all 140 yam plots that they had used over the recent past. Sankoff asked each man to go through the list of men and identify which *dgwa* each man belonged to. If a man belonged to more than one, then Sankoff got that information, too. She also asked her informants to identify which *dgwa* each of the 140 garden plots belonged to.

As you might imagine, there was considerable variability in the data. Only a few men were uniformly placed into one of the five *dgwa* by their peers. But by analyzing the matrices of *dgwa* membership and land use, Sankoff was able to determine the core members and peripheral members of the various *dgwa*.

She was also able to ask important questions about intracultural variability. She looked at the variation in cognitive models among the Buang for how land use and membership in descent groups were related. Sankoff's analysis was an important milestone in our understanding of the measurable differences between individual culture versus shared culture. It supported Goodenough's notion (1965) that cognitive models are based on shared assumptions, but that ultimately they are best construed as properties of individuals.

Techniques like true-false and yes-no tests that generate nominal data are easy to construct, especially with ANTHROPAC, and can be administered to a large number of informants. Frame elicitation in general, however, can be boring, both to the informant and to the researcher alike. Imagine, for example, a list of 25 animals (mice, dogs, antelopes . . .), and 25 attributes (ferocious, edible, nocturnal . . .).

The structured interview that results from such a test involves a total of 625 (25×25) questions to which an informant must respond—questions like "Is an antelope edible?" "Is a dog nocturnal?" "Is a mouse ferocious?" People can get pretty exasperated with this kind of foolishness, so be careful to choose domains, items, and attributes that make sense to people when you do frame elicitations and true-false tests (**Further Reading:** sentence frames).

TRIAD TESTS

In a **triad test**, you show people three things and tell them to "Choose the one that doesn't fit" or "Choose the two that seem to go together best," or "Choose the two that are the same." The "things" can be photographs, dried plants, or 3×5 cards with names of people on them. (Respondents often ask "What do you mean by things being 'the same' or 'fitting together'?" Tell them that you are interested in what *they* think that means.) By doing this for all triples from a list of things or concepts, you can explore differences in cognition among individuals, and among cultures and subcultures.

Suppose you ask speakers of English to "choose the item that is least like the other two" in each of the following triads:

DOLPHIN   MOOSE   WHALE
SHARK   DOLPHIN   MOOSE

All three items in the first triad are mammals, but two of them are sea mammals. Some native speakers of English will choose "dolphin" as the odd item out because "whales and moose are both big mammals and the dolphin is smaller." In my experience, though, most people will choose "moose" as the most different because "whales and dolphins are both sea animals." In the second triad, many of the same people who chose "moose" in the first triad will choose "shark" because moose and dolphins are both mammals and sharks are not.

But some people who chose "moose" in triad 1 will choose "moose" again because sharks and dolphins are sea creatures, while moose are not. Giving people a judiciously chosen set of triad stimuli can help you understand interindividual similarities and differences in how people think about the items in a cultural domain (box 10.4).

Lieberman and Dressler (1977) used triad tests to examine intracultural variation in ethnomedical beliefs on the Caribbean island of St. Lucia. They wanted to know if cognition of disease terms varied with bilingual proficiency. They used 52 bilingual English-Patois speakers, and 10 monolingual Patois speakers. From ethnographic interviewing and cross-checking against various informants, they isolated nine disease terms that were important to St. Lucians.

Here's the formula for finding the number of triads in a list of n items:

$$\frac{n(n-1)(n-2)}{6}$$ **Formula 10.1**

In this case, $n = 9$ (the number of disease terms), so there are 84 possible triads.

Lieberman and Dressler gave each of the 52 bilingual informants two triad tests, a week apart: one in Patois and one in English. (Naturally, they randomized the order of the items within each triad and randomized the order of presentation of the triads to informants.) They also measured how bilingual their informants were, using a standard test. The 10 monolingual Patois informants were simply given the triad test.

The researchers counted the number of times that each possible pair of terms was chosen as most alike among the 84 triads. (There are $n \times n - 1/2$ pairs or $9 \times 8/2 = 36$ pairs). They divided the total by seven (the maximum number of times that any pair appears in the 84 triads). This produced a similarity coefficient, varying between 0.0 and 1.0, for each possible pair of disease terms. The larger the coefficient for a pair of terms, the closer in meaning the two terms are. The researchers were then able to analyze these data among English-dominant, Patois-dominant, and monolingual Patois speakers. (I'll show you how to analyze triad test data in chapter 16.)

BOX 10.4

TRIAD TESTS AND COGNITIVE SCIENCE

The triads test was developed in psychology (see Kelly 1955; Torgerson 1958) and has long been used in studies of cognition. Romney and D'Andrade (1964) presented people with triads of American kinship terms and asked them to choose the term that was most *dissimilar* in each triad. For example, when they presented informants with the triad "father, son, nephew," 67% selected "nephew" as the most different of the three items. Twenty-two percent chose "father" and only 2% chose "son." Romney and D'Andrade asked people to explain *why* they'd selected each item on a triad. For the triad "grandson, brother, father," for example, one informant said that a "grandson is most different because he is moved down further" (p. 161). There's a lot of cultural wisdom in that statement.

By studying which pairs of kinship terms their informants chose most often as being as similar, Romney and D'Andrade were able to isolate some of the salient components of the American kinship system (components such as male vs. female, ascending vs. descending generation, etc.). They were able to do this, at least, for the group of informants they used. Repeating their tests on other populations of Americans, or on the same population over time, would yield interesting comparisons.

It turned out that when Patois- and English-dominant informants took the triad test in English, their cognitive models of similarities among diseases was similar. When Patois-dominant speakers took the Patois-language triad test, however, their cognitive model was similar to that of monolingual Patois informants.

This is a very interesting finding. It means that Patois-dominant bilinguals manage to hold on to two distinct psychological models about diseases and switch back and forth between them, depending on what language they are speaking. By contrast, the English-dominant group displayed a similar cognitive model of disease terms, irrespective of the language in which they are tested.

The Balanced Incomplete Block Design for Triad Tests

Typically, the terms that go into a triad test are generated by a free list, and typically the list is much too long for a triad test. As you can see from formula 10.1, with just 9 terms, there are 84 stimuli in a triad test containing nine items. But with 15 items, just 6 more, the number of decisions an informant has to make jumps to 455. At 20 items, it's a mind-numbing 1,140.

Free lists of illnesses, ways to prevent pregnancy, advantages of breast-feeding, places to go on vacation, and so on easily produce 60 items or more. Even a selected, abbreviated list may be 20 items.

This led Michael Burton and Sara Nerlove (1976) to develop the **balanced incomplete block design**, or BIB, for the triad test. BIBs take advantage of the fact that there is a lot of redundancy in a triad test. Suppose you have just four items, 1, 2, 3, 4 and you ask informants to tell you something about *pairs* of these items (e.g., if the items were vegetables, you might ask "Which of these two is less expensive?" or "Which of these two is more nutritious?" or "Which of these two is easier to cook?"). There are exactly six pairs of four items (1–2, 1–3, 1–4, 2–3, 2–4, 3–4), and the informant sees each pair just once.

But suppose that instead of pairs you show the informant triads and ask which two out of each triple are most similar. There are just four triads in four items (1–2–3, 1–2–4, 2–3–4, 1–3–4), but each item appears $(n-1)(n-2)/2$ times, and each pair appears $n-2$ times. For four items, there are $n(n-1)/2 = 6$ pairs; each pair appears twice in four triads, and each item on the list appears three times.

It is all this redundancy that reduces the number of triads needed in a triads test. In a complete set of 84 triads for 9 items, each pair of items appears $n-2$, or seven times. If you have each pair appear just once (called a **lambda 1 design**), instead of seven times, then, instead of 84 triads, only 12 are needed. If you have each pair to appear twice (a lambda 2 design), then 24 triads are needed. For analysis, a lambda 2 design is much better than a lambda 1. Table 10.1 shows the lambda 2 design for 9 items and 10 items.

Table 10.1   Balanced Incomplete Block Designs for Triad Tests Involving 9 and 10 Items

For 9 items, 24 triads are needed, as follows:		For 10 items, 30 triads are needed, as follows:	
Items		Items	
1, 5, 9	1, 2, 3	1, 2, 3	6, 8, 9
2, 3, 8	4, 5, 6	2, 5, 8	7, 10, 3
4, 6, 7	7, 8, 9	3, 7, 4	8, 1, 10
2, 6, 9	1, 4, 7	4, 1, 6	9, 5, 2
1, 3, 4	2, 5, 9	5, 8, 7	10, 6, 7
5, 7, 8	3, 6, 8	6, 4, 9	1, 3, 5
3, 7, 9	1, 6, 9	7, 9, 1	2, 7, 6
2, 4, 5	2, 4, 8	8, 10, 2	3, 8, 9
1, 6, 8	3, 5, 7	9, 3, 10	4, 2, 10
4, 8, 9	1, 5, 8	10, 6, 5	5, 6, 3
3, 5, 6	2, 6, 8	1, 2, 4	6, 1, 8
1, 2, 7	3, 4, 9	2, 3, 6	7, 9, 2
		2, 4, 8	8, 4, 7
		4, 9, 5	9, 10, 1
		5, 7, 1	10, 5, 4

SOURCE: Reprinted from *Social Science Research*, Vol. 5, M. L. Burton and S. B. Nerlove, "Balanced Design for Triad Tests," p. 5, © 1976. Reprinted by permission of Academic Press.

For 10 items, a lambda 2 design requires 30 triads; for 13 items, it requires 52 triads; for 15 items, 70 triads; for 19 items, 114 triads; and for 25 items, 200 triads. Unfortunately, there is no easy formula for choosing *which* triads in a large set to select for a BIB. Fortunately, Burton and Nerlove (1976) worked out various lambda BIB designs for up to 21 items and Borgatti has incorporated BIB designs into ANTHROPAC (1992a). You simply tell ANTHROPAC the list of items you have, select a design, and tell it the number of informants you want to interview. ANTHROPAC then prints out a randomized triad test, one for each informant. (Randomizing the order in which the triads appear to informants eliminates "order-effects"—possible biases that come from responding to a list of stimuli in a particular order.)

Boster et al. (1987) used a triad test in their study of the social network of an office. There were 16 employees, so there were 16 "items" in the cultural domain ("the list of all the people who work here" is a perfectly good domain). A lambda 2 test with 16 items has 80 distinct triads. Informants were asked to "judge which of three actors was the most different from the other two."

Triad tests are easy to create with ANTHROPAC, easy to administer, and easy to score, but they can only be used when you have relatively few items in a cultural domain. In literate societies, most informants can respond to 200 triads in less than half an hour, but it can be a really boring exercise, and boring your informants is a really bad idea. I find that informants can easily handle lambda 2 triad tests with up to 15 items and 70 triads. But I also find that people generally prefer—even like—to do pile sorts (**Further Reading:** triad tasks).

FREE PILE SORTS

In 1966, John Brim put the names of 58 American English role terms (mother, gangster, stockbroker, etc.) on slips of paper. He asked 108 high school students in San Mateo, California, to spread the slips out on their desks and to "put the terms together which you feel belong together" (Burton and Romney 1975:400). This simple, compelling method for collecting data about what-goes-with-what was introduced to anthropology by Michael Burton, who analyzed Brim's data using multidimensional scaling and hierarchical clustering. These powerful tools were brand new at the time and are used today across the social sciences (Burton 1968, 1972). (We'll get back to MDS and clustering in chapter 16 on how to analyze data in cultural domains.)

I've used **free pile sorts** to study the social structure of institutions such as prisons, ships at sea, and bureaucracies, and also to map the cognitively defined social organization of small communities. I simply hand people a deck of cards, each of which contains the name of one of the people in the institution, and ask informants to sort the cards into piles, according to their own criteria. The results tell me how people in the various components of an organization (managers, production workers, advertising people; or guards, counselors, prisoners; or seamen, deck officers, engine room personnel; or men and women in a small Greek village) think about the social structure of the group. Instead of what goes with what, I learn who goes with whom. Then I ask informants to explain *why* people appear in the same pile. This produces a wealth of information about the cognitively defined social structure of a group.

Administering a Pile Sort

Informants often ask two questions when asked to do a pile sort: (1) "What do you mean by 'belong together'?" and (2) "Can I put something in more than one pile?" The answer to the first question is "There are no right or wrong answers. We want to learn what *you* think about these things."

The easy answer to the second question is "No," because there is one card per item and a card can only be in one pile at a time. This answer cuts off a lot of information, however, because people can think of items in a cultural domain along several dimensions at once. For example, in a pile sort of consumer electronics, someone might want to put DVD recorders in one pile with TVs (for the obvious association) and in another pile with camcorders (for another obvious association), but might not want to put camcorders and TVs in the same pile. One way to handle this problem is to have duplicate cards that you can give to people when they want to put an item into more than one pile, but be warned that this can complicate analysis of the data. An alternative is to ask the informant to do **multiple free pile sorts** of the same set of items (box 10.5).

The P-3 Game

In a series of papers, John Roberts and his coworkers used pile sorts and rating tasks to study how people perceive various kinds of behaviors in games (see, for example,

BOX 10.5

PILE SORTS WITH OBJECTS

Pile sorts don't have to be done with cards. James Boster (1987) studied the structure of the domain of birds among the Aguaruna Jívaro of Peru. He paid people to bring him specimens of birds and he had the birds stuffed. He built a huge table out in the open, laid the birds on the table, and asked the Aguaruna to sort the birds into groups.

Carl Kendall led a team project in El Progreso, Honduras, to study beliefs about dengue fever (Kendall et al. 1990). Part of their study involved a pile sort of the nine most common flying insects in the region. They mounted specimens of the insects in little boxes and asked people to group the insects in terms of "those that are similar." Some fieldworkers have used photographs of objects as stimuli for a pile sort.

Borgatti (1999:133), however, points out that physical stimuli, like images or objects, make people focus on form rather than function. In fact, when asked to sort drawings of fish, fishermen in North Carolina sorted on shape—the long thin ones, the ones with a big dorsal fin, the small roundish ones (Boster and Johnson 1989). "In contrast," says Borgatti (1999:133), "sorting *names* of fish allows hidden attributes to affect the sorting"—things like taste or how much of a struggle fish put up. "If you are after shared cultural beliefs," says Borgatti, "I recommend keeping the stimulus as abstract as possible" (1992b:6).

Roberts and Chick 1979; Roberts and Nattrass 1980). One "game," studied by Roberts et al. (1980), is pretty serious: searching for foreign submarines in a P-3 airplane. The P-3 is a four-engine, turboprop, low-wing aircraft that can stay in the air for a long time and cover large patches of ocean. It is also used for search-and-rescue missions. Making errors in flying the P-3 can result in career damage and embarrassment, at least, and injury or death, at worst.

Through extensive, unstructured interviews with Navy P-3 pilots, Roberts et al. isolated 60 named flying errors. (This is the equivalent of extracting a free list from your interviews.) Here are a few of the errors: flying into a known thunderstorm area; taking off with the trim tabs set improperly; allowing the prop wash to cause damage to other aircraft; inducing an autofeather by rapid movement of power level controls. Roberts et al. asked 52 pilots to do a free pile sort of the 60 errors and to rate each error on a 7-point scale of "seriousness."

They also asked the pilots to rank a subset of 13 errors on four criteria: (1) how much each error would "rattle" a pilot; (2) how badly each error would damage a pilot's career; (3) how embarrassing each error would be to commit; and (4) how much "fun" it would be to commit each error. Flying into a thunderstorm on purpose, for example, could be very damaging to a pilot's career, and extremely embarrassing if he had to abort the mission and turn back in the middle (when Roberts et al. did their research in the 1970s, all P-3 pilots were men). But if the mission was successful, then taking the risk of committing a very dangerous error would be a lot of fun for pilots who are, as Roberts called them, "high self-testers" (personal communication).

Inexperienced pilots rated "inducing an autofeather" as more serious than did highly experienced pilots. Inducing an autofeather is more embarrassing than it is dangerous and it's the sort of error that experienced pilots just don't make. On the other hand, as the number of air hours increased, so did pilots' view of the seriousness of "failure to use all available navigational aids to determine position." Roberts et al. suggested that inexperienced pilots might not have had enough training to assess the seriousness of this error correctly (**Further Reading:** pile sorts).

The Lumper-Splitter Problem

In the free pile sort method, people are told that they can make as many piles as they like, so long as they don't make a separate pile for each item or lump all the items into one pile. Like the triad test, the free pile sort presents people with a common set of stimuli, but there's a crucial difference: With free pile sorts, people can group the items together as they see fit. The result is that some people will make many piles, others will make few, and this causes the **lumper-splitter** problem (Weller and Romney 1988:22).

In a pile sort of animals, for example, some informants will put all the following together: giraffe, elephant, rhinoceros, zebra, wildebeest. They'll explain that these are the "African animals." Others will put giraffe, elephant, and rhino in one pile, and the zebra and wildebeest in another, explaining that one is the "large African animal" pile and the other is the "medium-sized African animal pile."

Although they can't put *every* item in its own pile, lots of people put *some* items in singleton piles, explaining that each item is unique and doesn't go with the others. It's fine to ask informants why they made each pile of items, but wait until they finish the sorting task so you don't interfere with their concentration. And don't hover over informants. Find an excuse to walk away for a couple of minutes after they get the hang of it.

Because triad tests present each respondent with exactly the same stimuli, you can compare the data across individuals. Free pile sorts tell you what the structure of the data looks like for a group of people—sort of group cognition—but you can't compare the data from individuals. On the other hand, with pile sorts, you can have as many as 50 or 60 items. All methods have their advantages and disadvantages.

RANKINGS AND PAIRED COMPARISONS

Rank ordering produces interval-level data, while ratings ("on a scale of 1-to-5, how much do you like . . . ?") produce ordinal-level data. Not all behaviors or concepts are easy to rank and there are lots of times when ratings are the best you can do, but when you can get rank-ordered data you shouldn't pass up the opportunity. Eugene Hammel (1962) asked people in a Peruvian village to rank order the people they knew in terms of prestige. By comparing the lists from different informants, Hammel was able to determine that the men he tested all had a similar view of the social hierarchy. Occupations can easily be rank ordered on the basis of prestige, or lucrativeness.

Or even accessibility. The instructions to respondents would be "Here is a list of occupations. Please rank them in order, from most likely to least likely that your daughter will have this occupation." Then ask respondents to do the same thing for their sons. (Be sure to assign people randomly to doing the task for sons or daughters first.) Then compare the average ranking of accessibility against some independent variables and test for intracultural differences among ethnic groups, genders, age groups, and income groups.

Weller and Dungy (1986) studied breast-feeding among Hispanic and Anglo women in southern California. They asked 55 informants for a free list of positive and negative aspects of breast- and bottle-feeding. Then they selected the 20 most frequently mentioned items in this domain and converted the items to neutral, similarly worded statements. A few examples: "A way that doesn't tie you down, so you are free to do more things"; "A way that your baby feels full and satisfied"; "A way that allows you to feel closer to your baby."

Next, Weller and Dungy asked 195 women to rank the 20 statements. The women were asked which statement was most important to them in selecting a method of feeding their baby, which was the next most important to them, and so on. In the analysis, Weller and Dungy were able to relate the average rank order for Hispanics and for Anglos to independent variables like age and education.

Paired Comparisons

The method of **paired comparisons** is an alternative way to get rank orderings of a list of items in a domain. For any set of things, there are $n(n-1)/2$ pairs of those things. Suppose you have a list of five colors: red, green, yellow, blue, and brown. Figure 10.1 shows the paired comparison test to find out an informant's rank-ordered preference for these five colors. In this case, the question would be: "Look at each pair of colors and, for each pair, tell me which one you like more."

In each of the following pairs of colors, please circle the one you like best:

RED	GREEN
RED	YELLOW
RED	BLUE
RED	BROWN
GREEN	YELLOW
GREEN	BLUE
GREEN	BROWN
YELLOW	BLUE
YELLOW	BROWN
BLUE	BROWN

FIGURE 10.1.
A paired comparison test for rank-ordered data.

You might say: "Here are two animals. Which one is the more _____?," where the blank is filled in by "vicious," or "wild," or "smarter," or some other descriptor.

You could ask informants to choose "the food in this pair that is better for you," or "the crime in this pair that you're most afraid of."

I've presented the pairs in figure 10.1 in such a way that you can easily see how the 10 of them exhausts the possibilities for five items. When you present a paired comparison test to an informant, be sure to scramble the order of the pairs to guard against **order effects**—that is, where something about the order of the items in a list influences the choices that informants make.

To find the rank order of the list for each informant, you simply count up how many times each item in a list "wins"—that is, how many times it was circled. If you are studying illnesses and cancer is on the list, and if the question is "which of these pairs of illnesses is more life threatening," you expect to find it circled each time it is paired with another illness—except, perhaps, when it is paired with AIDS. Because this is so predictable, it's not very interesting. It gets really interesting when you have illnesses like diabetes and high blood pressure in your list and you compare the average rank ordering among various ethnic groups.

The paired comparison technique has a lot going for it. People make one judgment at a time, so it's much easier on them than asking them to rank order a list of items by staring at all the items at once. Also, you can use paired comparisons with nonliterate informants by reading the list of pairs to them, one at a time, and recording their answers.

Like triad tests, paired comparisons can only be used with a relatively short list of items in a domain, unless you apply balanced incomplete block designs. With 20 items in a paired comparison task, for example, informants have to make 190 judgments (**Further Reading:** rankings and paired comparisons).

There is one more method for studying the attributes of things: rating scales. This one is so important, it deserves a chapter of its own . . . next.

FURTHER READING

Kinship studies: Alexander (1976); Dousset (2008); Houseman and White (1998); Kronenfeld (2004); Leach (1945); Lehman (1992); Read (2001).

Methods of data collection for domain analysis: de Munck and Sobo (1998); Handwerker (2001); J. C. Johnson and Weller (2002); Weller and Romney (1988).

Free lists: Ross and Medin (2005); Ryan et al. (2000); K. D. Smith et al. (2007); Thompson and Juan (2006); Verma et al. (2001).

Sentence frames: D'Andrade et al. (1972); Frake (1964); Hruschka et al. (2008); Metzger and Williams (1966).

Triad tasks: Durrenberger and Erem (2005); Furlow (2003); Nyamongo (2002); Ross et al. (2005).

Pile sorts: Collins (2006); Longfield (2004); Roberts et al. (1986).

Rankings and paired comparisons: Chavez et al. (1995); Durrenberger (2003); Erickson (1997); Kozak et al. (2008); Thurstone (1927).

Scales and Scaling

This chapter is about building and using **composite measures**. I'll cover four kinds of composite measures: (1) **indexes**, (2) **Guttman scales**, (3) **Likert scales**, and (4) **semantic differential scales**. At the end of the chapter, I'll cover a few other interesting scales. First, though, some basic concepts of scaling.

SIMPLE SCALES: SINGLE INDICATORS

A scale is a device for assigning units of analysis to categories of a variable. The assignment is usually done with numbers, and questions are used a lot as scaling devices. Here are three typical scaling questions:

1. "How old are you?"
   You can use this question to assign individuals to categories of the variable "age." In other words, you can *scale* people by age. The number that this first question produces has ratio properties (someone who is 50 is twice as old as someone who is 25).
2. "How satisfied are you with your classes this semester? Are you satisfied, neutral, or unsatisfied?"
   You can use *this* question to assign people to one of three categories of the variable "satisfied." That is, you can *scale* them according to how satisfied they are with their classes. Suppose we let satisfied = 3, neutral = 2, and unsatisfied = 1. Someone who is assigned the number 3 is *more* satisfied than someone who is assigned the number 1. We don't know if that means 3 times more satisfied, or 10 times, or just marginally more satisfied, so this scaling device produces numbers that have ordinal properties.
3. "Do you consider yourself to be Protestant, Catholic, Jewish, Muslim, some other religion? Or do you consider yourself as having no religion?"
   This scaling device lets you assign individuals to—that is, *scale them* by—categories of the variable "religious affiliation." Let Protestant = 1, Catholic = 2, Jewish = 3, Muslim = 4, and no religion = 5. The numbers produced by *this* device have nominal properties. You can't add them up and find the average religion.

These three questions have different content (they tap different concepts), and produce numbers with different properties, but they have two very important things in common: (1) All three questions are devices for scaling people; and (2) In all three cases, the respondent is the principal source of measurement error.

When you use your own judgment to assign units of analysis to categories of a scaling device, *you* are the major source of measurement error. In other words, if you assign individuals by your own observation to the category "male" or "female," then any mistakes you make in that assignment (in scaling people by sex) are *yours*.

COMPLEX SCALES: MULTIPLE INDICATORS

So, a single question on a questionnaire is technically a scale if it lets you assign the people you're studying to categories of a variable. A lot of really interesting variables however, are complex and can't easily be assessed with single indicators. What single question could you ask an ethnic Chinese shopkeeper in Jakarta to measure how assimilated they were to Indonesian national culture? Could you measure the amount of stress people are experiencing by asking them a single question? We try to measure complex variables like these with complex instruments—that is, instruments that are made up of several indicators. These complex instruments are what people commonly call scales.

A classic concept in all of social research is "socioeconomic status," or SES. Sociologists and psychologists often measure it by combining measures of income, education, and occupational prestige. Each of these measures is, by itself, an operationalization of the concept SES, but none of the measures captures the complexity of the idea of socioeconomic status. Each indicator captures a piece of the concept, and together the indicators produce a single measurement of SES (**Further Reading:** measuring SES).

Some variables are best measured by single indicators and, by Ockham's razor, we would never use a complex scale to measure something when a simple scale will do. So: The function of **single-indicator scales** is to assign units of analysis to categories of a variable. The function of **composite measures**, or complex scales, is exactly the same, but they are used when single indicators won't do the job.

INDEXES

The most common composite measure is a **cumulative index**. Indexes are made up of several items, all of which either count the same or are weighted. The Dow-Jones Industrial Average is an index of the prices of 30 stocks that are traded on the New York Stock Exchange. The U.S. Consumer Price Index is a measure of how much it costs to buy a fixed set of consumer items in the United States. We use indexes to measure people's health risks: the risk of contracting HIV, of getting lung cancer, of having a heart attack, of giving birth to an underweight baby, of becoming an alcoholic, of suffering from depression, and on and on.

And we use indexes with a vengeance to measure cognitive and physical functions. Children in the industrial societies of the world begin taking intelligence tests, achievement tests, and tests of physical fitness from the first day they enter school—or even before that. Achievement indexes—like the SAT, ACT, and GRE—affect so many people in the United States that there's a thriving industry devoted to helping children and adolescents do well on them.

Indexes can be **criterion referenced** or **norm referenced**. If you've ever taken a test where the only way to get an "A" was to get at least 90%, you've had your knowledge of some subject assessed by a criterion-referenced index. If you've ever taken a test where getting an "A" required that you score in the top 10% of the class—even if the highest grade in the class were 70%—then you've had your knowledge of some subject assessed by a norm-referenced index.

Standardized tests (whether of achievement, or of performance, or of personality traits) are usually norm referenced: Your score is compared to the norms that have been established by thousands of people who took the test before you.

How Indexes Work

Multiple-choice exams are cumulative indexes. The idea is that asking just one question about the material in a course would not be a good indicator of students' knowledge of the material. Instead, students typically are asked a bunch of multiple-choice questions.

Taken together, the reasoning goes, all the questions measure how well a student has mastered a body of material. If you take a test that has 60 multiple-choice questions and you get 45 correct, you get 45 points, one for each correct answer. That number, 45 (or 75% of 60 questions), is a cumulative index of how well you did on the test.

Note that in a cumulative index, it makes no difference *which* items are assigned to you. In a test of just 10 questions, for example, there are obviously just 10 ways to get one right—but there are 45 ways to get two right, 120 ways to get three right. . . . Students can get the same score of 80% on a test of 100 questions and miss entirely different sets of 20 questions. This makes cumulative indexes **robust**—that is, they provide many ways to get at an underlying variable (in the case of an exam, the underlying variable is knowledge of the material).

On the other hand, stringing together a series of items to form an index doesn't guarantee that the composite measure will be useful—any more than stringing together a series of multiple-choice questions will fairly assess a student's knowledge of, say, anthropology.

We pretend that: (1) Knowledge is a **unidimensional** variable; (2) A fair set of questions is chosen to represent knowledge of some subject; and, therefore (3) A cumulative index is a fair test of the knowledge of that subject. We know that the system is imperfect, but we pretend in order to get on with life.

We don't have to pretend. When it comes to scaling units of analysis on complex constructs—like scaling countries on the construct of freedom or people on the construct of political conservatism—we can test the unidimensionality of an index with a technique called **Guttman scaling**.

GUTTMAN SCALES

In a **Guttman scale**, as compared to a cumulative index, the measurements for the items have a *particular pattern indicating that the items measure a unidimensional variable.* To understand the pattern we're looking for, consider the following three questions:

1. How much is 124 plus 14?
2. How much is 1/2 + 1/3 + 1/5 + 2/11?
3. If 3X = 133, then how much is X?

If you know the answer to question 3, you probably know the answer to questions 1 and 2. If you know the answer to question 2, but not to 3, it's still safe to assume that you know the answer to question 1. This means that, in general, *knowledge about basic math* is a unidimensional variable.

Now consider a highland, Aymara-speaking Bolivian village. As part of your study, you need to measure the level of acculturation of each person. That is, you want to assign a single number to each person—a number that represents how acculturated to nonindigenous, national Bolivian culture each person is. After some time in the community, you come to understand that there are three key points of acculturation: dress, language, and housing. As Indians acculturate, they dress in Western clothes, learn to speak Spanish fluently (in addition to or instead of Aymara), and build Western-style houses.

From your ethnographic work, you reason that people need significant wealth to afford a Western-style house, with all the imported materials that building one entails. People who have wealth participate in the national economy, which means that they must be fluent in Spanish. Anyone, however, can afford to adopt Western-style clothes, especially used clothing. According to your theory, Western dress is the easiest item to adopt; Spanish comes next; and then comes Western houses.

To test whether the indicators you've identified form a unidimensional, or Guttman scale, set up a table like table 11.1. It's not pretty.

Table 11.1   An Index That Scales with a Guttman Coefficient of Reproducibility <0.90

Informant	Western clothes	Fluent Spanish	Western house
1	+	+	+
2	+	+	+
3	+	+	+
4	+	+	−
5	+	+	
6	+	+	−
7	+	−	−
8	−	−	−
9	−	−	
10	−	+	−
11	−	+	−
12	−	+	−
13	−	−	+
14	−	−	+
15	−	−	+
16	+	−	+

Persons 1, 2, and 3 scored positive on all three items. They each get 3 points. The next three (4, 5, and 6) wear Western clothes and speak fluent Spanish, but live in indigenous-style houses. They each get 2 points. Person 7 wears Western clothes, but does not speak fluent Spanish, and does not live in a Western-style house. This informant gets 1 point on the acculturation index. Persons 8 and 9 have no acculturation points. They wear traditional dress, speak little Spanish, and live in traditional homes. So far so good.

The next three (10, 11, 12) speak fluent Spanish but wear traditional dress and live in traditional houses. The next three (13, 14, 15) live in Western-style homes but wear traditional dress and are not fluent in Spanish. Finally, person 16 wears Western clothes and lives in a Western house, but is not fluent in Spanish.

If we had data from only the first nine respondents, the data would form a perfect Guttman scale. For those first nine respondents, in other words, the three behaviors are indicators of a unidimensional variable, acculturation.

The Coefficient of Reproducibility

Unfortunately, we've got those other seven people to deal with. For whatever reasons, informants 10–16 do not conform to the pattern produced by the data from informants 1–9. The data for persons 10–16 are "errors" in the sense that their data diminish the extent to which the index of acculturation forms a perfect scale. To test how closely any set of index data reproduces a perfect scale, apply Guttman's **coefficient of reproducibility**, or CR. The formula for Guttman's CR is:

$$1 - \frac{\text{number of errors}}{\text{number of entries}} \qquad \textbf{Formula 11.1}$$

Given the pattern in table 11.1 (and from our hypothesis about the order in which people adopt the three indicators of acculturation), we don't expect to see those minus signs in column 1 for respondents 10, 11, and 12. If the data scaled according to our hypothesis, then anyone who speaks fluent Spanish and lives in a traditional house should wear Western-style clothes, as is the case with informants 4, 5, and 6. *Those* informants have a score of 2. It would take three corrections to make cases 10, 11, and 12 conform to the hypothesis (you'd have to replace the minus signs in column one with pluses for respondents 10, 11, and 12), so we count cases 10, 11, and 12 as having one error each.

We don't expect to see the plus signs in column 3 for informants 13, 14, and 15. If our hypothesis were correct, anyone who has a plus in column 3 should have all pluses and a score of 3 on acculturation. If we give respondents 13, 14, and 15 a scale score of 3 (for living in a Western-style house), then those three cases would be responsible for *six* errors—you'd have to stick in two pluses for each of the cases to make them come out according to the hypothesis. Yes, you could make it just three, not six errors, by sticking a minus sign in column 3. Some researchers use this scoring method, but I prefer the more conservative method of scoring more errors. It keeps you on your toes.

Finally, we don't expect that minus sign in column 2 of respondent 16's data. That case creates just one error (you only need to put in one plus to make it come out right). All together, that makes $3 + 6 + 1 = 10$ errors in the attempt to reproduce a perfect scale. For table 11.1, the CR is

$$1 - (10/48) = .79$$

which is to say that the data come within 21% of scaling perfectly. By convention, a coefficient of reproducibility of .90 or greater is accepted as a significant approximation of a perfect scale (Guttman 1950). I'm willing to settle for around .85, especially with the conservative method for scoring errors, but .79 just isn't up to it, so these data fail the Guttman test for unidimensionality.

Some Examples of a Guttman Scale

Robert Carneiro (1962, 1970) had an idea that cultural evolution is orderly and cumulative. If he is right, then cultures evolve by adding certain traits in an orderly way and should show a Guttman-scale-like pattern. Carneiro coded 100 cultures for 354 traits and looked at the pattern. Table 11.2a shows a sample of 12 societies and 11 traits. When you collect data on cases, you don't know what (if any) pattern will emerge, so you pretty much grab cases and code them for traits in random order. The 12 societies and traits in table 11.2a are in random order.

The first thing to do is arrange the pluses and minuses in their "best" possible order—the order that conforms most to the perfect Guttman scale—and compute the CR. We look for the trait that occurs most frequently (the one with the most pluses across the row) and place that one at the bottom of the matrix. The most frequently occurring trait is the existence of special religious practitioners. Then we look for the next most frequent trait and put it on the next to the bottom row of the matrix. We keep doing this until we rearrange the data to take advantage of whatever underlying pattern is hiding in the matrix. The best arrangement of the pluses and minuses in table 11.2a is shown in table 11.2b. Now we can count up the "errors" in the matrix and compute Guttman's coefficient of reproducibility. For these 12 societies and 11 traits, the coefficient is a perfect 1.0 (box 11.1).

DeWalt (1979) used Guttman scaling to test an index of material style of life in a Mexican farming community. He scored 54 informants on whether they possessed eight material items (a radio, a stove, a sewing machine, etc.) and achieved a CR of .95. My hunch is that DeWalt's material-style-of-life scale has its analog in nearly all societies. The particular list of items that DeWalt used in rural Mexico may not scale in a middle-class

Table 11.2a   Carneiro's Matrix Showing the Presence (+) or Absence (−) of 11 Culture Traits among 12 Societies. The Order of Both the Traits and the Societies Is Random

Society	1	2	3	4	5	6	7	8	9	10	11	12
Political leader has considerable authority	+	+	−	−	+	−	−	+	−	+	−	−
Sumptuary laws	−	−	−	−	+	−	−	+	−	−	−	−
Headman, chief, or king	+	+	−	−	+	+	+	+	−	+	+	+
Surplus of food regularly produced	+	+	−	−	+	−	−	+	−	+	−	+
Trade between communities	+	+	−	+	+	+	+	+	−	+	+	+
Ruler grants audiences	−	+	−	−	+	−	−	+	−	+	−	−
Special religious practitioners	+	+	−	+	+	+	+	+	−	+	+	+
Paved streets	−	−	−	−	−	−	−	+	−	−	−	−
Agriculture provides ≥75% of subsistence	+	+	−	−	+	−	+	+	−	+	−	+
Full-time service specialists	−	+	−	−	+	−	−	+	−	−	−	−
Settlements ≥100 persons	+	+	−	−	+	+	+	+	−	+	−	+

Societies: 1 Iroquois, 2 Marquesans, 3 Tasmanians, 4 Yahgan, 5 Dahomey, 6, Mundurucú, 7 Ao Naga, 8 Inca, 9 Semang, 10 Tanala, 11 Vedda, 12 Bontoc

SOURCE: *A Handbook of Method in Cultural Anthropology* by Raoul Naroll and Ronald Cohen, eds., copyright © 1970 by Raoul Naroll and Ronald Cohen. Used by permission of Doubleday, a division of Random House, Inc.

neighborhood of Ulan Bator, but *some* list of material items *will* scale there. You just have to find them.

The way to do this is to code every household in your study for the presence or absence of a list of material items. The particular list could emerge from participant observation or from informal interviews. Then you'd use ANTHROPAC to sort out the matrix, drop some material items, and build the material index that has a CR of 0.90 or better. Greg Guest (2000) did this in his study of 203 households in an Ecuadorian fishing village. He gave each household a score from 1 to 7, depending how many material items they had. That score correlated significantly with the education level of the head of each household.

Table 11.2b   The Data in Table 11.2a Rearranged: The Data Form a Perfect Guttman Scale

Society	1	2	3	4	5	6	7	8	9	10	11	12
Paved streets	−	−	−	−	−	−	−	−	−	−	−	+
Sumptuary laws	−	−	−	−	−	−	−	−	−	−	+	+
Full-time service specialists	−	−	−	−	−	−	−	−	−	+	+	+
Ruler grants audiences	−	−	−	−	−	−	−	−	+	+	+	+
Political leader has considerable authority	−	−	−	−	−	−	−	+	+	+	+	+
Surplus of food regularly produced	−	−	−	−	−	−	+	+	+	+	+	+
Agriculture provides ≥75% of subsistence	−	−	−	−	−	+	+	+	+	+	+	+
Settlements ≥100 persons	−	−	−	−	+	+	+	+	+	+	+	+
Headman, chief, or king	−	−	−	+	+	+	+	+	+	+	+	+
Trade between communities	−	−	+	+	+	+	+	+	+	+	+	+
Special religious practitioners	−	+	+	+	+	+	+	+	+	+	+	+

Societies: 1 Tasmanians, 2 Semang, 3 Yahgan, 4 Vedda, 5 Mundurucú, 6 Ao Naga, 7 Bontoc, 8 Iroquis, 9 Tanala, 10 Marquesans, 11 Dahomey, 12 Inca

---

BOX 11.1

DATA SCALE, VARIABLES DON'T

Given enough items that you think represent a unidimensionl variable, you can usually find a few items that will form a neat Guttman scale. Carneiro coded 100 societies for 354 traits and selected the data that showed the desired pattern. A high coefficient of reproducibility, then, is a necessary but insufficient condition for declaring that (1) a variable is unidimensional, and (2) you've got a scale that measures it. In other words, *only data scale, not variables*. If the items in a cumulative index form a Guttman scale with 0.90 CR or better, we can say that, *for the sample we've tested*, the concept measured by the index is unidimensional—that the items are a composite measure of one and only one underlying concept.

By the way, when Carneiro did this work in the 1960s, it was heroic work. Today, ANTHROPAC (Borgatti 1992a) has a routine for looking at big matrices of pluses and minuses, rearranging the entries into the best pattern, calculating the CR, and showing you which units of analysis and traits to drop to find the optimal solution to the problem.

(We'll get to correlation and statistical significance in chapter 21). Since we expect a correlation between wealth and education, this adds construct validity to Guest's scale.

Careful, though. Oliver Kortendick tried to develop a Guttman scale of wealth in a village in Papua New Guinea. The idea of property ownership may not have existed in that culture prior to contact with Europeans and Australians in the mid-20th century. It was well understood when Kortendick got there, but some things, like cars, were too expensive for anyone there to possess on their own. So villagers bought and owned those items collectively (Kortendick, personal communication).

Indexes That Don't Scale

Indexes that do not scale can still be useful in comparing populations. Dennis Werner (1985) studied psychosomatic stress among Brazilian farmers who were facing the uncertainty of having their lands flooded by a major dam. He used a 20-item stress index developed by Berry (1976).

Because the index did not constitute a unidimensional scale, Werner could not differentiate among his *informants* (in terms of the amount of stress they were under) as precisely as DeWalt could differentiate among *his* informants (in terms of their quality of life). But farmers in Werner's sample gave a stress response to an average of 9.13 questions on the 20-item test, while Berry had found that Canadian farmers gave stress responses on an average of 1.79 questions. It is very unlikely that a difference of such magnitude between two *populations* would occur by chance (**Further Reading:** Guttman scales).

LIKERT SCALES

Perhaps the most commonly used form of scaling is attributed to Rensis Likert (1932). Likert introduced the ever-popular 5-point scale that we talked about in chapter 9, on questionnaire construction. Recall that a typical question might read as follows:

Please consider the following statements carefully. After each statement, check the answer that most reflects your opinion. Would you say you agree a lot with the statement, agree a little, are neutral, disagree a little, or disagree a lot with each statement? Ok, here's the first statement:

When I need credit to bring my bananas to market, I can just go the agricultural bank in Ralundat and they give it to me.

- ☐ Agree a lot
- ☐ Agree
- ☐ Neutral
- ☐ Disagree a little
- ☐ Disagree a lot

The 5-point scale might become 3 points or 7 points, and the Agree-Disagree scale may become Approve-Disapprove, Favor-Oppose, or Excellent-Bad, but the principle is the same. These are all **Likert-type** scales.

I say "Likert-type scales" rather than just "Likert scales" because Likert did more than just introduce a format. He was interested in measuring internal states of people (attitudes, emotions, orientations) and he realized that most internal states are multidimensional. You hear a lot of talk these days about conservatives and liberals, but the concept of political orientation is very complex. A person who is liberal on matters of domestic policy—favoring government-supported health care, for example—may be conservative on matters of foreign political policy—against involvement in any foreign military actions. Someone who is liberal on matters of foreign economic policy—favoring economic aid for all democracies that ask for it—may be conservative on matters of personal behavior—against same-sex marriage, for example.

The liberal-conservative dimension on matters of personal behavior is also complicated. There's no way to assign people to a category of this variable by asking one question. People can have live-and-let-live attitudes about sexual preference and extramarital sex and be against a woman's right to an abortion on demand.

Of course, there are packaging effects. People who are conservative on one dimension of political orientation are *likely* to be conservative on other dimensions, and people who are liberal on one kind of personal behavior are *likely* to be liberal on others. Still, no single question lets you scale people in general on a variable as complex as "attitude toward personal behavior," let alone "political orientation." That's why we need composite scales.

Steps in Building a Likert Scale

Likert's method was to take a long list of possible scaling items for a concept and find the subsets that measured the various dimensions. If the concept were unidimensional, then one subset would do. If it were multidimensional, then several subsets would be needed. Here are the steps in building and testing a **Likert scale**.

1. Identify and label the variable you want to measure. This is generally done by induction—that is, from your own experience (Spector 1992:13). After you work in some area of research for a while, you'll develop some ideas about the variables you want to measure. The people you talk to in focus groups, for example, may impress you with the idea that "people are afraid of crime around here," and you decide to scale people on the variable "fear of crime."

Or you may observe that some people seem to have a black belt in shopping, and others would rather have root canal surgery than set foot in a mall. The task is then to scale (measure) people on a variable you might call "shopping orientation," with all its multidimensionality. You may need a subscale for "shopping while on vacation," another for "car shopping," and another for "shopping for clothing that I really need." (The other way to identify variables is by deduction; see box 1.1).

2. Write a long list of indicator questions or statements. This is usually another exercise in induction. Ideas for the indicators can come from reading the literature on whatever research problem has captured you, from personal experience, from ethnography, from reading newspapers, from interviews with experts.

Free lists are a particularly good way to get at indicators for some variables. If you want to build a scaling device for the concept of "attitudes toward growing old," you could start by asking a large group of people to "list things that you associate with growing old" and then you could build the questions or statements in a Likert scale around the items in the list.

Be sure to use both negative and positive indicators. If you have a statement like "Life in Xakalornga has improved since the missionaries came," then you need a negatively worded statement for balance like "The missionaries have caused a lot of problems in our community." People who agree with positive statements about missionaries should disagree with negative ones.

And don't make the indicator items extreme. Here's a badly worded item: "The coming of the missionaries is the most terrible thing that has ever happened here." Let people tell *you* where they stand by giving them a range of response choices (strongly agree–strongly disagree). Don't bludgeon people with such strongly worded scale items that they feel forced to reduce the strength of their response.

In wording items, all the cautions from chapter 9 on questionnaire design apply: Remember who your respondents are and use *their* language. Make the items as short and as uncomplicated as possible. No double negatives. No double-barreled items. Here is a terrible item:

On a scale of 1 to 5, how much do you agree or disagree with the following statement: "Everyone should speak Hindi and give up their tribal language."

People can agree or disagree with both parts of this statement, or agree with one part and disagree with the other.

When you get through, you should have four or five times the number of items as you think you'll need in your final scale. If you want a scale of, say, six items, use 25 or 30 items in the first test (DeVellis 2003:66).

3. Determine the type and number of response categories. Some popular response categories are agree-disagree, favor-oppose, helpful–not helpful, many-none, like me–not like me, true-untrue, suitable-unsuitable, always-never, and so on. Most Likert scale items have an odd number of response choices: three, five, or seven. The idea is to give people a range of choices that includes a midpoint. The midpoint usually carries the idea of neutrality—neither agree nor disagree, for example. An even number of response choices forces informants to "take a stand"; an odd number of choices lets informants "sit on the fence."

There is no best format. But if you ever want to combine responses into just two categories (yes-no, agree-disagree, like me–not like me), then it's better to have an even number of choices. Otherwise, you have to decide whether the neutral responses get collapsed with the positive answers or the negative answers—or thrown out as missing data.

4. Test your item pool on some respondents. Ideally, you need at least 100—or even 200—respondents to test an initial pool of items (Spector 1992:29). This will ensure that: (1) You capture the full variation in responses to all your items; and (2) The response variability represents the variability in the general population to which you eventually want to apply your scale.
5. Conduct an **item analysis** to find the items that form a unidimensional scale of the variable you're trying to measure. More on item analysis coming up next.
6. Use your scale in your study and run the item analysis again to make sure that the scale is holding up. If the scale does hold up, then look for relations between the scale scores and the scores of other variables for persons in your study.

Item Analysis

This is the key to building scales. The idea is to find out which, among the many items you're testing, need to be kept and which should be thrown away. The set of items that you keep should tap a single social or psychological dimension. In other words, the scale should be unidimensional.

In the next few pages, I'm going to walk through the logic of building scales that are unidimensional. Read these pages very carefully. At the end of this section, I'll advocate using **factor analysis** to do the item analysis quickly, easily, and reliably. No fair, though, using factor analysis for scale construction until you understand the logic of scale construction itself.

There are three steps to doing an item analysis and finding a subset of items that constitute a unidimensional scale: (1) scoring the items, (2a) taking the **interitem correlation** and (2b) **Cronbach's alpha**, and (3) **taking the item-total correlation**.

1. Scoring the Items

The first thing to do is make sure that all the items are properly scored. Assume that we're trying to find items for a scale that measures the strength of support for training in research methods among anthropology students. Here are two potential scale items:

Training in statistics should be required for all undergraduate students of anthropology.

1	2	3	4	5
Strongly disagree	Disagree	Neutral	Agree	Strongly agree

Anthropology undergraduates don't need training in statistics.

1	2	3	4	5
Strongly disagree	Disagree	Neutral	Agree	Strongly agree

You can let the big and small numbers stand for any direction you want, but you must be consistent. Suppose we let the bigger numbers (4 and 5) represent support for training in statistics and let the smaller numbers (1 and 2) represent lack of support for that concept. Those who circle "strongly agree" on the first item get a 5 for that item. Those who circle "strongly agree" on the second item get scored as 1.

2a. Taking the Interitem Correlation

Next, test to see which items contribute to measuring the construct you're trying to get at, and which don't. This involves two calculations: the intercorrelation of the items and the correlation of the item scores with the total scores for each informant. Table 11.3 shows the scores for three people on three items, where the items are scored from 1 to 5.

Table 11.3   The Scores for Three People on Three Likert Scale Items

	Item		
Person	1	2	3
1	1	3	5
2	5	2	2
3	4	1	3

Table 11.4   The Data from the Three Pairs of Items in Table 11.3

Pair 1		Diff	Pair 2		Diff	Pair 3		Diff
1	3	2	1	5	4	3	5	2
5	2	3	5	2	3	2	2	0
4	1	3	4	3	1	1	3	2
Σ_d (Sum of the diffs.)		8			8			4
Σ_d / Max$_d$		0.67			0.67			0.33
$1 - (\Sigma_d / Max_d)$		0.33			0.33			0.67

To find the interitem correlation, we would look at all pairs of columns. There are three possible pairs of columns for a three-item matrix. These are shown in table 11.4.

A simple measure of how much these pairs of numbers are alike or unalike involves, first, adding up their *actual differences*, Σ_d, and then dividing this by the total *possible differences*, MAX$_d$.

In the first pair, the actual difference between 1 and 3 is 2; the difference between 5 and 2 is 3; the difference between 4 and 1 is 3. The sum of the differences is $\Sigma_d = 2 + 3 + 3 = 8$.

For each item, there could be as much as 4 points difference—in Pair 1, someone could have answered 1 to item 1 and 5 to item 2, for example. So for three items, the total possible difference, MAX$_d$, would be $4 \times 3 = 12$. The actual *difference* is 8 out of a possible 12 points, so items 1 and 2 are $8/12 = 0.67$ *different*, which means that these two items are $1 - \Sigma_d / MAX_d = 0.33$ *alike*. Items 1 and 3 are also 0.33 alike, and items 2 and 3 are 0.67 alike.

Items that measure the same underlying construct should be related to one another. If I answer "strongly agree" to the statement "Training in statistics should be required for all undergraduate students of anthropology," then (if I'm consistent in my attitude and if the items that tap my attitude are properly worded) I should strongly disagree with the statement that "anthropology undergraduates don't need training in statistics." If everyone who answers "strongly agree" to the first statement answers "strongly disagree" to the second, then the items are perfectly correlated.

2b. Cronbach's Alpha

Cronbach's alpha is a statistical test of how well the items in a scale are correlated with one another. One of the methods for testing the unidimensionality of a scale is called the **split-half reliability** test. If a scale of, say, 10 items, were unidimensional, all the items would be measuring parts of the same underlying concept. In that case, any five items should produce scores that are more or less like the scores of any other five items. This is shown in table 11.5.

Table 11.5   The Schematic for the Split-Half Reliability Test

Person	Split A: Score on items 1–5	Split B: Score on items 6–10
1	X_1	Y_1
2	X_2	Y_2
3	X_3	Y_3
.	.	.
.	.	.
N	X_n	Y_n
	Total for A	Total for B

Split Halves and the Combinations Rule

There are many ways to split a group of items into halves and each split will give you a different set of totals. Here's the formula for selecting n elements from a set of N elements, paying no attention to the ordering of the elements:

$$\frac{N!}{n!(N-n)!} \qquad \text{Formula 11.2}$$

If you have 10 respondents, then there are $10!/5!(10-5)! = 252$ ways to split them into halves of five each. For 20 items, there are 184,756 possible splits of 10 each. Cronbach's **coefficient alpha** provides a way to get the average of all these split-half calculations directly. The formula for Cronbach's alpha is:

$$\alpha = \frac{N\rho}{1 + \rho(N-1)} \qquad \text{Formula 11.3}$$

where ρ (the Greek letter *rho*) is the average interitem correlation—that is, the average correlation among all pairs of items being tested.

By convention, a good set of scale items should have a Cronbach's alpha of 0.80 or higher. Be warned, though, that if you have a long list of scale items, the chances are good of getting a high alpha coefficient. An interitem correlation of just .29 produces an alpha of .80 in a set of 10 items (DeVellis 2003:98).

Eventually, you want an alpha coefficient of 0.80 or higher for a *short* list of items, all of which hang together and measure the same thing. Cronbach's alpha will tell you if your scale hangs together, but it won't tell you which items to throw away and which to keep. To do that, you need to identify the items that do not discriminate between people who score high and people who score low on the total set of items.

3. Finding the Item-Total Correlation

First, find the total score for each person. Add up each respondent's scores across all the items. Table 11.6 shows what it would look like if you tested 50 items on 200 people (each x is a score for one person on one item).

Table 11.6   Finding the Item-Total Correlation

Person	Item 1	Item 2	Item 3	.	.	Item 50
1	x	x	x	.	.	x
2	x	x	x	.	.	x
3	x	x	x	.	.	x
.	.	.	.	.	.	.
.	.	.	.	.	.	.
200	x	x	x	.	.	x

For 50 items, scored from 1 to 5, each person could get a score as low as 50 (by getting a score of 1 on each item) or as high as 250 (by getting a score of 5 on each item). In practice, of course, each person in a survey will get a total score somewhere in between.

A rough and ready way to find the items that discriminate well among respondents is to divide the respondents into two groups, the 25% with the highest total scores and the 25% with the lowest total scores. Look for the items that the two groups have in common. Those items are *not discriminating* among informants with regard to the concept being tested. Items that fail, for example, to discriminate between people who strongly favor training in methods (the top 25%) and people who don't (the bottom 25%) are not good items for scaling people in this construct. Throw those items out.

There is a more formal way to find the items that discriminate well among respondents and the items that don't. This is the **item-total correlation**. Table 11.7 shows the data you need for this:

Table 11.7   The Data for the Interim Correlation

Person	Total score	Item 1	Item 2	Item 3	.	.	Item 50
1	x	x	x	x	.	.	x
2	x	x	x	x	.	.	x
3	x	x	x	x	.	.	x
.	.	.	.	.	.	.	.
.	.	.	.	.	.	.	.
N	x	x	x	x	.	.	x

With 50 items, the total score gives you an idea of where each person stands on the concept you're trying to measure. If the interitem correlation were perfect, then every item would be contributing equally to our understanding of where each respondent stands. Naturally, some items do better than others. The ones that don't contribute a lot will correlate poorly with the total score for each person. Keep the items that have the highest correlation with the total scores.

You can use any statistical analysis package to find the interitem correlations, Cronbach's alpha, and the item-total correlations for a set of preliminary scale items. Your goal is to get rid of items that detract from a high interitem correlation and to keep the alpha coefficient above 0.80. (For an excellent step-by-step explanation of item analysis, see Spector 1992:43–46.)

TESTING FOR UNIDIMENSIONALITY WITH FACTOR ANALYSIS

Factor analysis is a technique for data reduction. If you have 30 items in a pool of potential scale items, and responses from a sample of people to those pool items, factor analysis lets you reduce the 30 items to a smaller set—say, 5 or 6. Each item is given a score, called its **factor loading**. This tells you how much each item "belongs" to each of the underlying factors. (See chapter 22 for a brief introduction to factor analysis and Comrey [1992] for more coverage.)

If a scale is unidimensional, there will be a single, overwhelming factor that underlies all the variables (items) and all the items will "load high" on that single factor. If a scale is multidimensional, then there will be a series of factors that underlie sets of variables. Scale developers get a large pool of potential scale items (at least 40) and ask a lot of people (at least 200) to respond to the items. Then they run the factor analysis and select those items that load high on the factor or factors (the underlying concept or concepts) they are trying to understand (box 11.2).

BOX 11.2

HOW SCALES ARE DEVELOPED

If you want to see what professional scale developers do, consult any of the following: Klonoff and Landrine (2000) (a scale for measuring acculturation among African Americans), Staats et al. (1996) (a scale measuring commitment to pets), Sin and Yau (2004) (a scale for measuring female role orientation in China), and Simpson and Gangstad (1991) (a scale that measures willingness to engage in uncommitted sexual relations).

You may not develop major scales for others to use but what you *should* do is test the unidimensionality of any composite measure you develop for your own field data, using factor analysis—once you understand the principles of scale development that I've laid out here. Examples of scales developed by anthropologists include one to measure depression in old people (Gatz and Hurwicz 1990) in the United States and one to measure domestic cooperation in Barbados (Handwerker 1996a). I'll walk you through Handwerker's scale in chapter 22 when we get to factor analysis.

VISUAL PROPS AS SCALES
Several scales have been developed over the years with visual props. Four of them are the semantic differential, the ladder of life, the happiness stick, and the faces scale.

Semantic Differential
I've always liked the **semantic differential scaling** method. It was developed in the 1950s by Charles Osgood and his associates at the University of Illinois and has become an important research tool in cognitive studies, including psychology, anthropology, and sociology (Osgood et al. 1957; Snider and Osgood 1969). It has also been used by thousands of researchers across the social sciences, and with good reason: The semantic differential test is easy to construct and easy to administer.

Osgood was interested in how people interpret things—inanimate things (like artifacts or monuments), animate things (like persons or the self), behaviors (like incest, or buying a new car, or shooting a deer), and intangible concepts (like gun control or literacy). This is exactly what Likert scales are designed to test, but instead of asking people to rate questionnaire items about things, Osgood tested people's feelings differently: He gave them a **target item** and a list of **paired adjectives** about the target. The adjective pairs could come from reading of the literature or from focus groups or from ethnographic interviews. Target items can be ideas (land reform, socialism, aggression), behaviors (smoking, running, collecting ground nuts), objects (the mall, a courtroom, horses), environmental conditions (rain, drought, jungle) . . . almost anything.

Figure 11.1 is an example of a semantic differential test. The target is "having a cold." If you were taking this test right now, you'd be asked to place a check on each line, depending on your reaction to each pair of adjectives.

FIGURE 11.1.
A semantic differential scale to test how people feel about the concept of having a cold. The dimensions in this scale are useful for measuring how people feel about many different things.

With a Likert scale, you ask people a series of questions that get at the target concept. In a semantic differential scale, you name the target concept and ask people to rate their feelings toward it on a series of variables. The semantic differential is usually a 7-point scale, as I've indicated in the first adjective pair in figure 11.1. Your score on this test would be the sum of all your answers to the 13 adjective pairs.

Osgood and his associates did hundreds of replications of this test, using hundreds of adjective pairs, in 26 different cultures. Their analyses showed that in every culture, just three major kinds of adjectives account for most of the variation in people's responses: **adjectives of evaluation** (good-bad, difficult-easy), **adjectives of potency** (strong-weak, dominant-submissive, etc.), and **adjectives of activity** (fast-slow, active-inactive, sedentary-mobile, etc.).

As the target changes, you have to make sure that the adjective pairs make sense. The adjective pair ethical-corrupt works for some targets, but you probably wouldn't use it for having a cold.

Vincke et al. (2001) used the semantic differential scale to explore the meaning of 25 sex acts among gay men in Flanders, Belgium. Their informants scaled each act (anal insertive sex, anal receptive sex, insertive fellatio, receptive fellatio, interfemoral sex, and so on) on six paired dimensions: unsatisfying/satisfying, stimulating/dull, interesting/boring, emotional/unemotional, healthy/unhealthy, and safety/danger. Vincke et al. then compared results on the semantic differential for men who practiced safe sex (with one partner or with a condom) and men who practiced unsafe sex (multiple partners and without a condom) to see which sex acts were more gratifying for high-risk-taking and low-risk-taking men (**Further Reading:** semantic differential).

Cantril's Ladder of Life

The scale shown in figure 11.2 is Hadley Cantril's (1965) **ladder of life**. People are asked to list their concerns in life (financial success, healthy children, freedom from war,

FIGURE 11.2.
The ladder of life.
SOURCE: H. Cantril, *The Pattern of Human Concerns*. Copyright © 1965 by Rutgers, The State University. Reprinted by permission of Rutgers University Press.

and so on). Then they are shown the ladder and are told that the bottom rung represents the worst-possible situation and the top rung represents the best. For each of their concerns they are asked to point out where they are on the ladder right now, where they were 5 years ago, and where they think they'll be 5 years from now. Note that the ladder of life is a **self-anchoring scale**. Respondents are asked to explain, in their own terms, what the top and bottom rungs of the ladder mean to them.

Visual props like this are particularly useful for interviewing nonliterate or semiliterate people. Hansen and McSpadden (1993) used the ladder-of-life technique in their studies of Zambian and Ethiopian refugees in Zambia and the United States. In Zambia, Hansen actually constructed a small wooden ladder and found that the method worked well. McSpadden used several methods to explore how Ethiopian refugees adjusted to life in the United States. Even when other methods failed, McSpadden found that the ladder of life method got people to talk about their experiences, fears, and hopes.

Keith et al. (1994) used a modified version of the ladder of life in their study of aging in seven cultures. In five of the sites (two in the United States, one in Hong Kong, and two in Ireland) where most informants were literate, they used a six-rung ladder instead of Cantril's 10-run variety. In Hong Kong, people were comfortable placing themselves *between* but not *on* rungs, so the team redesigned the ladder into a flight of stairs. Among the Herero and !Kung of Botswana, where many people were not literate, they replaced the ladder with the five fingers of the interviewer's hand (Keith et al. 1994:xxx, 113).

Be careful to tell people exactly what you want when you use any kind of visual prop. M. Jones and Nies (1996) used Cantril's ladder to measure the importance of exercise to elderly African American women. At least Jones and Nies *thought* that's what they were measuring. The mean for the ladder rating was about 9 on a scale of 1–10. Respondents thought they were being asked *how important exercise is*, not how important exercise is *to them, personally*. The researchers failed to explain properly to their respondents what the ladder was supposed to measure, and even devout couch potatoes are going to tell you that exercise is important if you ask them the general question (**Further Reading:** ladder of life).

The Happiness Stick

Schwarzwalder et al. (2008) surveyed 1,624 people over 40 in villages around Kongwa town, in Tanzania about problems with vision. (The team gave near-vision glasses to those who needed them—a really good incentive to participate in the survey.) The survey involved Likert-like questions with response categories like "very happy" to "very unhappy" or "very satisfied" to "very unsatisfied," or "no difficulty at all" to "completely unable" to do some everyday task that involved vision—things like sorting rice, using hand tools, reading, or recognizing faces.

Schwarzwalder et al. convened a group of their interviewers, with representatives from the various tribal groups, religions, and languages of the region. The group determined that five colors—white, yellow, green, red, and black—could stand in for the five values on any of the different scales, with white being positive, green being neutral or average, and black being negative. Schwarzwalder et al. gave each interviewer a mahogany rod they called the **happiness stick** (a translation from the local language). The rod was painted white, yellow, green, red, and black, in equal parts, and people indicated their response to each question by pointing to a color on the stick (Schwarzwalder et al. 2008:183).

Visual Props: The Faces Scale

Another interesting device is the **faces scale** shown in figure 11.3. It's a 7-point (or 5-point, or 9-point) scale with stylized faces that change from joy to gloom.

This technique was developed by Kunin in 1955 to measure job satisfaction and has been used widely for this ever since. It's a really good device for capturing people's feelings

FIGURE 11.3.
The faces scale.
SOURCE: F. M. Andrews and S. B. Withey, *Social Indicators of Well-Being: Americans' Perceptions of Life Quality*, appendix A, p. 13. Copyright © 1976. Reprinted by permission of Plenum Publishing Corporation.

about a wide variety of things—health care, personal safety, consumer items (brands of beer, titles of current movies), and so on. People are told: "Here are some faces expressing various feelings. Which face comes closest to how you feel about x?" Try using this scale with names of well-known political figures or music artists just to get a feel for how interesting it is.

Physicians and psychologists use this scale as a prop when they ask patients to describe pain. It's particularly good when working with children (Gulur et al. 2009; Wong and Baker 1988), but it's effective with adults as well (A. Harrison 1993) and, like the ladder of life and the semantic differential, has been used in many populations, in one form or another (**Further Reading** faces scale).

There is some evidence that the meaning of the faces in figure 11.3 is nearly universal (Ekman 1993), but Oliver Kortendick used the faces scale in his research on social networks in Papua New Guinea, and people did not respond well to the task. It seems that the face farthest to the right, which almost everyone in Europe, North America, and Latin America interprets as "unhappy" was interpreted in Papua New Guinea as "hostility" and "aggression"—two emotions that were simply not talked about openly in the village where Kortendick did his work (personal communication).

AND FINALLY

There are thousands of published scales. Whatever you're interested in, the chances are good that someone has developed and tested a scale to measure it. Scales are not automatically portable—a scale that measures stress among Barbadian women may not measure stress among Ghanaian men—but it makes sense to seek out any published scales on variables you're studying. You may be able to adapt the scales to your needs, or you may get ideas for building and testing an alternative scale. Just because scales are not perfectly transportable across time and cultures doesn't mean those scales are useless to you (**Further Reading:** scales and scaling).

FURTHER READING

Measuring SES: Cirino et al. (2002); Ensminger and Fothergill (2003); Oakes and Rossi (2003).

Guttman scaling: Goodenough (1963); Graves et al. (1969); Liao and Tu (2006); Maitra and Schensul (2002); Wutich and Ragsdale (2008).

Semantic differential: Arnold-Cathalifaud et al. (2008); Montiel and Boehnke (2000); Turnage (2008).

Ladder of life: Gallicchio et al. (2009); Suhail and Cochrane (1997).

Faces scale: Pasero (1997); Suhail and Chaudhry (2004).

Scales and scaling: Beere (1990); Coombs (1964); Dunn-Rankin (2004); D. C. Miller and Salkind (2002); Netemeyer et al. (2003); Nunnally and Bernstein (1994); Torgerson (1958).

12

Participant Observation

Participant observation fieldwork is the foundation of cultural anthropology. It involves getting close to people and making them feel comfortable enough with your presence so that you can observe and record information about their lives. If this sounds a bit crass, I mean it to come out that way. Only by confronting the truth about participant observation—that it involves a deception and impression management—can we hope to conduct ourselves ethically in fieldwork. Much more about this later.

Participant observation is both a humanistic method and a scientific one. It produces the kind of experiential knowledge that lets you talk convincingly, from the gut, about what it feels like to plant a garden in the high Andes or dance all night in a street rave in Seattle.

It also produces effective, positivistic knowledge—the kind that can move the levers of the world if it gets into the right hands. Nancy Scheper-Hughes (1992), for example, developed a nomothetic theory, based on participant observation, that accounts for the tragedy of very high infant mortality in northeast Brazil and the direct involvement of mothers in their infants' deaths. Anyone who hopes to develop a program to lower the incidence of infant mortality in that part of the world will have to read Scheper-Hughes's analysis (box 12.1).

Romancing the Methods

It used to be that the skills for doing fieldwork were mysterious and unteachable, something you just learned, out there in the field. In the 1930s, John Whiting and some of his fellow anthropology students at Yale University asked their professor, Leslie Spier, for a seminar on methods. "This was a subject to discuss casually at breakfast," Whiting recalls Spier telling him, not something worthy of a seminar (Whiting 1982:156). Tell this story to seasoned anthropologists at a convention today, and it's a good bet they'll come back with a story of their own just like it.

It's fine for anthropologists to romanticize fieldwork—vulcanologists and oceanographers do it, too, by the way—particularly about fieldwork in places that take several days to get to, where the local language has no literary tradition, and where the chances are nontrivial of coming down with a serious illness. Research really is harder to do in some places than in others. But anthropologists are more likely these days to study the impact of television in culture in Brazil (Kottak 2009), the meaning of hair styles among African American women (Dione Rosado 2007), the everyday culture of the English (Fox 2004), the formation of Croatian identity in Croatia and in Toronto (Winland 2007), how basic training in the U. S. Army transforms young people into soldiers (Bornmann 2009), consumer behavior (Sherry 1995), gay culture (Boellstorff 2007), or life on the mean

BOX 12.1

PARTICIPANT OBSERVATION AND APPLIED ANTHROPOLOGY

Participant observation has long been used in product applications research, where the object is to solve a human problem. One area of applied anthropology that's getting a lot of attention is product development. Panasonic thought it had a winning idea in 1995 for an electric razor that women could use in the shower—but none of the women they observed using the shavers during home visits took it into the shower. The women (who were in bathing suits) all said that (1) they didn't believe a razor could be waterproof and (2) they were afraid of dropping the razor in the shower and cracking the porcelain. The shiny, smooth material used in making the razor was interpreted in Japan as an indicator of quality but was interpreted by American women as an indicator of fragility. And thus the Panasonic Lady Shaver was rebuilt for the American market with a then-new kind of rubbery material that looked (and was) non-slip and waterproof (Rosenthal and Capper 2006:228).

streets of big cities (Bourgois 1995; Fleisher 1998) than they are to study isolated tribal or peasant peoples. It would take a real inventory to find out how much more likely, but in Hume and Mulcock's (2004) collection of 17 self-reflective studies of anthropologists about their fieldwork, just three cases deal with work in isolated communities (**Further Reading:** street ethnography).

And although participant observation in small, isolated communities has some special characteristics, the techniques and skills that are required seem to me to be pretty much the same everywhere.

WHAT *IS* PARTICIPANT OBSERVATION?

Participant observation usually involves fieldwork, but not all fieldwork is participant observation. Gomes do Espirito Santo and Etheredge (2002) interviewed 1,083 male clients of female sex workers and collected saliva specimens (to test for HIV) during 38 nights of fieldwork in Dakar, Senegal. The data collection involved a team of six fieldworkers, and the lead researcher was with the team throughout the 3.5 months that it took to collect the data. This was serious fieldwork, but hardly participant observation.

So much for what participant observation isn't. Here's what it is: Participant observation is one of those **strategic methods** I talked about in chapter 1—like experiments, surveys, or archival research. It puts you where the action is and lets you collect data . . . any kind of data you want, narratives or numbers. It has been used for generations by positivists and interpretivists alike.

A lot of the data collected by participant observers are qualitative: field notes taken about things you see and hear in natural settings; photographs of the content of people's houses; audio recordings of people telling folk tales; video of people making canoes, getting married, having an argument; transcriptions of taped, open-ended interviews, and so on.

But lots of data collected by participant observers are quantitative and are based on methods like direct observation, questionnaires, and pile sorts. Whether you consider yourself an interpretivist or a positivist, participant observation gets you in the door so you can collect life histories, attend rituals, and talk to people about sensitive topics.

Participant observation involves going out and staying out, learning a new language (or a new dialect of a language you already know), and experiencing the lives of the people you are studying as much as you can. Participant observation is about stalking culture in the wild—establishing rapport and learning to act so that people go about their business as usual when you show up. If you are a successful participant observer, you will know when to laugh at what people think is funny, and when people laugh at what you say, it will be because you *meant* it to be a joke.

Participant observation involves immersing yourself in a culture and learning to remove yourself every day from that immersion so you can intellectualize what you've seen and heard, put it into perspective, and write about it convincingly. When it's done right, participant observation turns fieldworkers into instruments of data collection and data analysis.

The implication is that *better* fieldworkers are *better* data collectors and *better* data analyzers. And the implication of *that* is that participant observation is not an attitude or an epistemological commitment or a way of life. It's a craft. As with all crafts, becoming a skilled artisan at participant observation takes practice.

SOME BACKGROUND AND HISTORY

Bronislaw Malinowski (1884–1942) didn't invent participant observation, but he is widely credited with developing it as a serious method of social research. A British social anthropologist (born in Poland), Malinowski went out to study the people of the Trobriand Islands, in the Indian Ocean, just before World War I. At the time, the Trobriand Islands were a German possession, so when the war broke out, Malinowski was interned and could not return to England for 3 years. He made the best of the situation, though. Here is Malinowski describing his methods:

> Soon after I had established myself in Omarkana, Trobriand Islands, I began to take part, in a way, in the village life, to look forward to the important or festive events, to take personal interest in the gossip and the developments of the village occurrences; to wake up every morning to a new day, presenting itself to me more or less as it does to the natives. . . . As I went on my morning walk through the village, I could see intimate details of family life, of toilet, cooking, taking of meals; I could see the arrangements for the day's work, people starting on their errands, or groups of men and women busy at some manufacturing tasks.
>
> Quarrels, jokes, family scenes, events usually trivial, sometimes dramatic but always significant, form the atmosphere of my daily life, as well as of theirs. It must be remembered that the natives saw me constantly every day, they ceased to be interested or alarmed, or made self-conscious by my presence, and I ceased to be a disturbing element in the tribal life which I was to study, altering it by my very approach, as always happens with a newcomer to every savage community. In fact, as they knew that I would thrust my nose into everything, even where a well-mannered native would not dream of intruding, they finished by regarding me as a part and parcel of their life, a necessary evil or nuisance, mitigated by donations of tobacco. (1961 [1922]:7–8)

Ignore the patronizing rhetoric about the "savage community" and "donations of tobacco." (I've learned to live with this part of our history in anthropology. Knowing that all of us, in every age, look quaint, politically incorrect, or just plain hopeless to those who come later has made it easier.) Focus instead on the amazing, progressive (for that time) method that Malinowski advocated: Spend lots and lots of time in studying a culture, learn the language, hang out, do all the everyday things that everyone else does, become inconspicuous by sheer tenaciousness, and stay aware of what's really going on. Apart from the colonialist rhetoric, Malinowski's discussion of participant observation is as resonant today as it was almost a century ago (box 12.2).

BOX 12.2

NOTES AND QUERIES . . .

By the time Malinowski went to the Trobriands, *Notes and Queries on Anthropology*—the fieldwork manual produced by the Royal Anthropological Institute of Great Britain and Ireland—was in its fourth edition. The first edition came out in 1874 and the last edition (the sixth) was reprinted five times until 1971.

Forty years later, that final edition of *Notes and Queries* is still must reading for anyone interested in learning about anthropological field methods. Once again, ignore the fragments of paternalistic colonialism—"a sporting rifle and a shotgun are . . . of great assistance in many districts where the natives may welcome extra meat in the shape of game killed by their visitor" (Royal Anthropological Institute 1951:29)—and *Notes and Queries* is full of useful, late-model advice about how to conduct a census, how to take impressions of engraved objects, and what questions to ask about sexual orientation, infanticide, food production, warfare, art. . . . The book is just a treasure.

We make the most consistent use of participant observation in anthropology, but the method has very, very deep roots in sociology. Beatrice Webb was doing participant observation—complete with note taking and informant interviewing—in the 1880s and she wrote trenchantly about the method in her memoir (Webb 1926). Just about then, the long tradition in sociology of urban ethnography—the "Chicago School"—began at the University of Chicago under the direction of Robert Park and Ernest Burgess (see Park et al. 1925). One of Park's students was his son-in-law, Robert Redfield, the anthropologist who pioneered community studies in Mexico.

Just back from lengthy fieldwork with Aborigine peoples in Australia, another young anthropologist, William Lloyd Warner, was also influenced by Park. Warner launched one of the most famous American community-study projects of all time, the Yankee City series (Warner 1963; Warner and Hunt 1941). (Yankee City was the pseudonym for Newburyport, Massachusetts.) In 1929, sociologists Robert and Helen Lynd published the first of many ethnographies about Middletown. (Middletown was the pseudonym for Muncie, Indiana.)

Some of the classic ethnographies that came out of the early Chicago School include Harvey Zorbaugh's *The Gold Coast and the Slum* (1929) and Clifford Shaw's *The Jack Roller* (1930). In *The Jack Roller*, a 22-year-old named Stanley talks about what it was like to grow up as a delinquent in early 20th-century Chicago. It still makes great reading.

Becker et al.'s *Boys in White* (1961)—about the student culture of medical school in the 1950s—should be required reading, even today, for anyone trying to understand the culture of medicine in the United States. The ethnography tradition in sociology continues in the pages of the *Journal of Contemporary Ethnography*, which began in 1972 under the title *Urban Life and Culture* (**Further Reading:** Chicago School of ethnography).

Participant observation today is everywhere—in political science, management, education, nursing, criminology, social psychology—and one of the terrific results of all this is a growing body of literature about participant observation itself. There are highly focused studies, full of practical advice, and there are poignant discussions of the overall *experience* of fieldwork. For large doses of both, see Wolcott (1995), Agar (1996), and Handwerker (2001). There's still plenty of mystery and romance in participant observation, but you don't have to go out unprepared (**Further Reading:** participant observation fieldwork).

FIELDWORK ROLES

Fieldwork can involve three very different roles: (1) **complete participant**, (2) **participant observer**, and (3) **complete observer**. The first role involves deception—becoming a member of a group without letting on that you're there to do research. The third role involves following people around and recording their behavior with little if any interaction. This is part of direct observation, which we'll take up in chapter 14.

By far, most ethnographic research is based on the second role, that of the participant observer. Participant observers can be insiders who observe and record some aspects of life around them (in which case, they're **observing participants**), or they can be outsiders who participate in some aspects of life around them and record what they can (in which case, they're **participating observers**).

In 1965, I went to sea with a group of Greek sponge fishermen in the Mediterranean. I lived in close quarters with them, ate the same awful food as they did, and generally participated in their life—as an outsider. I didn't dive for sponges, but I spent most of my waking hours studying the behavior and the conversation of the men who did. The divers were curious about what I was writing in my notebooks, but they went about their business and just let me take notes, time their dives, and shoot movies (Bernard 1987). I was a **participating observer**.

Similarly, when I went to sea in 1972 and 1973 with oceanographic research vessels, I was part of the scientific crew, there to watch how oceanographic scientists, technicians, and mariners interacted and how this interaction affected the process of gathering oceanographic data. There, too, I was a participating observer (Bernard and Killworth 1973).

Circumstances can sometimes overtake the role of mere participating observer. In 1979, El Salvador was in civil war. Thousands fled to Honduras where they were sheltered in refugee camps near the border. Phillipe Bourgois went to one of those camps to initiate what he hoped would be his doctoral research in anthropology. Some refugees there offered to show him their home villages and Bourgois crossed with them, illegally, into El Salvador for what he thought would be a 48-hour visit. Instead, Bourgois was trapped, along with about a thousand peasants, for 2 weeks, as the Salvadoran military bombed, shelled, and strafed a 40-square-kilometer area in search of rebels (Bourgois 1990). Perforce, Bourgois became an **observing participant.**

John Van Maanen played both of these roles, one after the other, in his dissertation research on how rookie cops in a California city become street-wise. There was nothing accidental about this, either. First, Van Maanen went through the 3-month training course at the police academy. Everyone at the academy knew why he was there, but he was a full participant in the training. He was an observing participant. Then, for 4 months, Van Maanen rode 8 to 10 hours a day in the back of a patrol car as an participant observer (Van Maanen 1973). His first role not only gave Van Maanen the credibility he needed for his second role to be successful; it also gave him a deep appreciation of what he was observing in his second role.

Researchers at the U.S. Federal Bureau of Prisons asked Mark Fleisher (1989) to do an ethnographic study of job pressures on guards in a maximum-security federal penitentiary in California. It costs a lot to train a guard—a correctional officer, or CO in the jargon of the profession—and there was an unacceptably high rate of them leaving the job after a year or two. Could Fleisher look into the problem?

Fleisher said he'd be glad to do the research and asked when he could start "walking the mainline"—that is, accompanying the COs on their rounds through the prison. He was told that he'd be given an office at the prison and that the guards would come to his office to be interviewed. Fleisher said he was sorry, but he was an anthropologist, he was doing participant observation, and he'd have to have the run of the prison. Sorry, they said back, only sworn correctional officers can walk the prison halls. So, swear me in, said Fleisher, and off he went to training camp for 6 weeks to become a sworn federal correctional officer. *Then* he began his year-long study of the United States Penitentiary at Lompoc, California. In other words, he became an observing participant in the culture he was studying. Like Van Maanen, Fleisher never hid what he was doing. When he went to USP-Lompoc, Fleisher told everyone that he was an anthropologist doing a study of prison life.

Barbara Marriott (1991) studied how the wives of U.S. Navy male officers contributed to their husbands' careers. Marriott was herself the wife of a retired captain. She was able to bring the empathy of 30 years' full participation to her study. She, too, took the role of observing participant and, like Fleisher, she told her informants exactly what she was doing.

Holly Williams (1995) spent 14 years as a nurse, ministering to the needs of children who had cancer. When Williams did her doctoral dissertation, on how the parents of those young patients coped with the trauma, she started as a credible insider, as someone whom the parents could trust with their worst fears and their hopes against all hope. Williams was a complete participant who became an observing participant by telling the people whom she was studying exactly what she was up to and enlisting their help with the research (box 12.3).

HOW MUCH TIME DOES IT TAKE?

Anthropological field research traditionally takes a year or more because it takes that long to get a feel for the full round of people's lives. It can take that long just to settle in, learn a new language, gain rapport, and be in a position to ask good questions and get good answers.

A lot of participant observation studies, however, are done in a matter of weeks or a few months. Norman Conti (2009) was a participant observer during a 21-week course at a police academy, documenting how recruits develop their occupational culture. Gretchen Purser (2009) spent 5 months studying the hiring of illegal immigrant day laborers. She divided her time each week between a street corner that had become a shape-up venue and a not-for-profit agency about a mile away that brought day laborers and potential employers together.

At the extreme low end, it is possible to do useful participant observation in just a few days. Assuming that you've wasted as much time in Laundromats as I did when I was a student, you could conduct a reasonable participant observation study of one such place in a week. You'd begin by bringing in a load of wash and paying careful attention to what's going on around you.

BOX 12.3

GOING NATIVE

Some fieldworkers start out as participating observers and find that they are drawn completely into their informants' lives. In 1975, Kenneth Good went to study the Yanomami in the Venezuelan Amazon. He planned on living with the Yanomami for 15 months, but he stayed on for nearly 13 years. "To my great surprise," says Good, "I had found among them a way of life that, while dangerous and harsh, was also filled with camaraderie, compassion, and a thousand daily lessons in communal harmony" (Good 1991:ix). Good learned the language and became a nomadic hunter and gatherer. He was adopted into a lineage and given a wife. (Good and his wife, Yárima, tried living in the United States, but after a few years, Yárima returned to the Yanomami.)

Marlene Dobkin de Rios did fieldwork in Peru and married the son of a Peruvian folk healer whose practice she studied (Dobkin de Rios 1981). And Jean Gearing (1995) is another anthropologist who married her closest informant on the island of St. Vincent.

Does going native mean loss of objectivity? Perhaps, but not necessarily. In the industrialized countries of the West, we *expect* immigrants to go native. We expect them to become fluent in the local language, to make sure that their children become fully acculturated, to participate in the economy and politics of the nation, and so on. If some of them become anthropologists, no one questions whether their immigrant background produces a lack of objectivity. Since total objectivity is, by definition, a myth, I'd worry more about producing credible data and strong analysis and less about whether going native is good or bad.

After two or three nights of observation, you'd be ready to tell other patrons that you were conducting research and that you'd appreciate their letting you interview them. The reason you could do this is because you already speak the native language and have already picked up the nuances of etiquette from previous experience. Participant observation would help you intellectualize what you already know.

In general, though, participant observation is not for the impatient. Gerald Berreman studied life in Sirkanda, a Pahari-speaking village in north India. Berreman's interpreter-assistant, Sharma, was a Hindu Brahmin who neither ate meat nor drank alcohol. As a result, villagers did neither around Berreman or his assistant. Three months into the research, Sharma fell ill and Berreman hired Mohammed, a young Muslim schoolteacher to fill in.

When the villagers found out that Mohammed ate meat and drank alcohol, things broke wide open and Berreman found out that there were frequent intercaste meat and liquor parties. When villagers found out that the occasional drink of locally made liquor was served at Berreman's house, "access to information of many kinds increased proportionately" (Berreman 1962:10). Even then, it still took Berreman 6 months in Sirkanda before people felt comfortable performing animal sacrifices when he was around (Berreman 1962:20).

And don't think that long term is only for foreign fieldwork. It took Daniel Wolf 3 years just to get into the Rebels, a brotherhood of outlaw bikers, and another couple of years riding with them before he had the data for his doctoral dissertation (Wolf 1991).

The amount of time you spend in the field can make a big difference in what you learn. Raoul Naroll (1962) found that anthropologists who stayed in the field for at least a year were more likely to report on sensitive issues like witchcraft, sexuality, political feuds, etc. Back in chapter 3, I mentioned David Price's study of water theft among farmers in Egypt's Fayoum Oasis. You might have wondered then how in the world he was able to do that study. Each farmer had a water allotment—a certain day each week and a certain amount of time during which water could flow to his fields. Price lived with these farmers for 8 months before they began telling him privately that they occasionally diverted water to their own fields from those of others (1995:106). Ethnographers who have done very long-term participant observation—that is, a series of studies over decades—find that they eventually get data about social change that is simply not possible to get in any other way (Kemper and Royce 2002).

My wife Carole and I spent May 2000 on Kalymnos, the Greek island where I did my doctoral fieldwork in 1964–65. We'd been visiting that island steadily for 40 years, but something qualitatively different happened in 2000. I couldn't quite put my finger on it, but by the end of the month I realized that people were talking to me about grandchildren. The ones who had grandchildren were chiding me—very good-naturedly, but chiding nonetheless—for not having any grandchildren yet. The ones who didn't have grandchildren were in commiseration mode. They wanted someone with whom to share their annoyance that "Kids these days are in no hurry to make families" and that "All kids want today . . . especially girls . . . is to have careers."

This launched lengthy conversations about how "everything had changed" since we had been our children's ages and about how life in Greece was getting to be more and more like Europe (which is what many Greeks call Germany, France, and the rest of the fully industrialized nations of the European Union), and even like the United States. I suppose there were other ways I could have gotten people into give-and-take conversations—about culture change, gender roles, globalization, modernization, and other big topics—but the grandchildren deficit was a terrific opener in 2000. It wasn't just age. These conversations were the result of the rapport that comes with having common history with people.

Here's history. In 1964, Carole and I brought our then 2-month-old daughter with us. Some of the same people who joked with me in 2000 about not having grandchildren had said to me in 1964: "Don't worry, next time you'll have a son." I recall having been really, really annoyed at the time, but writing it down as data. A couple of years later, I sent friends on Kalymnos the announcement of our second child—another girl. I got back kidding remarks like "Congratulations! Keep on trying. . . . Still plenty of time to have a boy!" Those were data, too. And when I told people that Carole and I had decided to stop at two, some of them offered mock condolences: "Oh, now you're really in for it! You'll have to get dowries for *two* girls without any sons to help." Now *those* are data!

Skip to 2004, when our daughter, son-in-law, and new granddaughter Zoë came to Kalymnos for Zoë's first birthday. There is a saying in Greek that "the child of your child is twice your child." You can imagine all the conversations, late into the night, about that. More data. By 2009, the grandchildren deficit had been resolved for many of my cohort, but not for all. By this time, people in their late 60s and early 70s were talking openly about things that could not have been imagined 40 years earlier, like: Who will take care of old people if there are no granddaughters?

Bottom line: You can do highly focused participant observation research in your own language, to answer specific questions about your own culture, in a short time. How do middle-class, second-generation Mexican American women make decisions on which of several brands of pinto beans to select when they go grocery shopping? If you are a middle-class Mexican American woman, you can probably find the answer to that question, using participant observation, in a few weeks, because you have a wealth of personal experience to draw on.

But if you're starting out fresh, and not as a member of the culture you're studying, count on taking 3 months or more, under the best conditions, to be accepted as a participant observer—that is, as someone who has learned enough to learn. And count on taking a lifetime to learn some things.

Rapid Assessment

Applied researchers don't always have the luxury of doing long-term participant observation fieldwork. In fact, applied work—like needs assessment in nutrition, education, and agricultural development—often has to be done in a few weeks. This doesn't leave much time for building rapport, and applied anthropologists have developed **rapid ethnographic assessment** procedures, including **participatory rapid assessment**. These methods are now used by anthropologists in long-term fieldwork.

In **participatory mapping**, for example, people draw maps of their villages and locate key places on the maps. Robert Chambers, a pioneer in PRA, spent 2 full days in 1974 trying to map the wells in an Indian village. Fifteen years later, he tells us, in 1989, one of his colleagues asked people in another Indian village to map their wells. The job was done in 25 minutes and the villagers noted which wells had water and which were dry (Chambers 2006). In **participatory transects**, a technique that Chambers borrowed from wildlife biology, you walk through an area systematically, with key informants, observing and asking for explanations of everything you see along the transect. Chambers also engages people in group discussions of key events in a village's history and asks them to identify clusters of households according to wealth. In other words, as an applied anthropologist, Chambers is called on to do rapid assessment of rural village needs, and he takes the people fully into his confidence as research partners. This method is just as effective in organizations as in small villages.

Applied medical anthropologists also use rapid assessment methods. The focused ethnographic study method, or FES, was developed by Sandy Gove (a physician) and Gretel Pelto (an anthropologist) for the World Health Organization to study acute respiratory illness (ARI) in children. The FES manual gives detailed instructions to fieldworkers for running a rapid ethnographic study of ARI in a community (Gove and Pelto 1994; WHO 1993).

Many ARI episodes turn out to be what physicians call pneumonia, but that is not necessarily what mothers call the illness. Researchers ask mothers to talk about recent ARI events in their households. Mothers also free list the symptoms, causes, and cures for ARI and do pile sorts of illnesses to reveal the folk taxonomy of illness and where ARI fits into that taxonomy. There is also a matching exercise, in which mothers pair locally defined symptoms (fever, sore throat, headache . . .) with locally defined causes (bad water, evil eye, germs . . .), cures (give rice water, rub the belly, take child to the doctor . . .), and illnesses.

The FES method also uses vignettes, or scenarios, much like those developed by Peter Rossi for the factorial survey (see chapter 9). Mothers are presented with cases in which variables are changed systematically ("Your child wakes up with [mild] [strong] fever. He complains that he has [a headache] [stomach ache]," and so on) and are asked to talk about how they would handle the case.

All this evidence—the free narratives, the pile sorts, the vignettes, etc.—is used in understanding the emic part of ARI, the local explanatory model for the illness.

Researchers also identify etic factors that make it easy or hard for mothers to get medical care for children who have pneumonia. These are things like the distance to a clinic, availability of transportation, number of young children at home, availability to mothers of people with whom they can leave their children for a while, and so on.

The key to high-quality, quick ethnography, according to Handwerker (2001), is to go into a study with a clear question and to limit your study to five focus variables. If the research is exploratory, you just have to make a reasonable guess as to what variables might be important and hope for the best. Most rapid assessment studies, however, are applied research, which usually means that you can take advantage of earlier, long-term studies to narrow your focus.

For example, Edwins Laban Moogi Gwako (1997) spent over a year testing the effects of eight independent variables on Maragoli women's agricultural productivity in western Kenya. At the end of his doctoral research, he found that just two variables—women's land tenure security and the total value of their household wealth—accounted for 46% of the variance in productivity of plots worked by women. None of the other variables—household size, a woman's age, whether a woman's husband lived at home, and so on—had any effect on the dependent variable.

If you were doing a rapid assessment of women's agricultural productivity elsewhere in east Africa, you would take advantage of Laban Moogi Gwako's work and limit the variables you tested to perhaps four or five—the two that he found were important and perhaps two or three others. You can study this same problem for a lifetime, and the more time you spend, the more you'll understand the subtleties and complexities of the problem. But the point here is that if you have a clear question and a few, clearly defined variables, you can produce quality work in a lot less time than you might imagine (**Further Reading:** rapid ethnographic assessment).

VALIDITY—AGAIN

There are at least five reasons for insisting on participant observation in the conduct of scientific research about cultural groups.

1. Participant observation opens thing up and makes it possible to collect all kinds of data. Participant observation fieldworkers have witnessed births, interviewed violent men in maximum-security prisons, stood in fields noting the behavior of farmers, trekked with hunters through the Amazon forest in search of game, and pored over records of marriages, births, and deaths in village churches and mosques around the world.

It is impossible to imagine a complete stranger walking into a birthing room and being welcomed to watch and record the event or being allowed to examine any community's vital records at whim. It is impossible, in fact, to imagine a stranger doing *any* of the things I just mentioned or the thousands of other intrusive acts of data collection that fieldworkers engage in all the time. What makes it all possible is participant observation.

2. Participant observation reduces the problem of **reactivity**—of people changing their behavior when they know that they are being studied. As you become less and less of

a curiosity, people take less and less interest in your comings and goings. They go about their business and let you do such bizarre things as conduct interviews, administer questionnaires, and even walk around with a stopwatch, clipboard, and camera.

Phillipe Bourgois (1995) spent 4 years living in El Barrio (the local name for Spanish Harlem) in New York City. It took him a while, but eventually he was able to keep his tape recorder running for interviews about dealing crack cocaine and even when groups of men bragged about their involvement in gang rapes.

Margaret Graham (2003) weighed every gram of every food prepared for 75 people eating over 600 meals in 15 households in the Peruvian Andes. This was completely alien to her informants, but after 5 months of intimate participant observation, those 15 families allowed her to visit them several times, with an assistant and a food scale.

In other words: Presence builds trust. Trust lowers reactivity. Lower reactivity means higher validity of data. Nothing is guaranteed in fieldwork, though. Graham's informants gave her permission to come weigh their food, but the act of doing so turned out to be more alienating than either she or her informants had anticipated. By local rules of hospitality, people had to invite Graham to eat with them during the three visits she made to their homes—but Graham couldn't accept any food, lest doing so bias her study of the nutritional intake of her informants. Graham discussed the awkward situation openly with her informants, and made spot checks of some families a few days after each weighing episode to make sure that people were eating the same kinds and portions of food as Graham had witnessed (Graham 2003:154).

And when Margaret LeCompte told children at a school that she was writing a book about them, they started acting out in "ways they felt would make good copy" by mimicking characters on popular TV programs (LeCompte et al. 1993).

3. Participant observation helps you ask sensible questions, in the native language. Have you ever gotten a questionnaire in the mail and said to yourself: "What a dumb set of questions"? If a social scientist who is a member of your own culture can make up what you consider to be "dumb" questions, imagine the risk *you* take in making up a questionnaire in a culture very different from your own! Remember, it's just as important to ask sensible questions in a face-to-face interview as it is on a survey instrument.

4. Participant observation gives you an intuitive understanding of what's going on in a culture and allows you to speak with confidence about the meaning of data. Participant observation lets you make strong statements about cultural facts that you've collected. It extends both the internal and the external validity of what you learn from interviewing and watching people. In short, participant observation helps you understand the *meaning* of your observations (box 12.4).

5. Many research problems simply cannot be addressed adequately by anything except participant observation. If you want to understand how a local court works, you can't very well disguise yourself and sit in the courtroom unnoticed. The judge would soon spot you as a stranger, and after a few days you would have to explain yourself. It is better to explain yourself at the beginning and get permission to act as a participant observer. In this case, your participation consists of acting like any other local person who might sit in on the court's proceedings. After a few days, or weeks, you would have a pretty good idea of how the court worked: what kinds of crimes are adjudicated, what kinds of penalties are meted out, and so forth. You might develop some specific hypotheses from your qualitative notes—hypotheses regarding covariations between

BOX 12.4

THE MEANING OF DATA

In 1957, N. K. Sarkar and S. J. Tambiah published a classic study, based on questionnaire data, about economic and social disintegration in a Sri Lankan village. They concluded that about two-thirds of the villagers were landless. The British anthropologist, Edmund Leach, did not accept that finding (Leach 1967). He had done participant observation fieldwork in the area and knew that the villagers practiced patrilocal residence after marriage. By local custom, a young man might receive *use* of some of his father's land even though legal ownership might not pass to the son until the father's death.

In assessing land ownership, Sarkar and Tambiah asked whether a "household" had any land, and if so, how much. They defined an independent household as a unit that cooked rice in its own pot. Unfortunately, all married women in the village had their own rice pots. So Sarkar and Tambiah wound up estimating the number of independent households as very high and the number of those households that owned land as very low. Based on these data, they concluded that there was gross inequality in land ownership and that this characterized a "disintegrating village" (the title of their book).

Don't conclude from Leach's critique that questionnaires are "bad," while participant observation is "good." I can't say often enough that participant observation makes it possible to collect quantitative survey data or qualitative interview data from some sample of a population. Qualitative and quantitative data inform each other and produce insight and understanding in a way that cannot be duplicated by either approach alone. Whatever data collection methods you choose, participant observation maximizes your chances for making valid statements.

severity of punishment and independent variables other than severity of crime. Then you could test those hypotheses on a sample of courts.

Think this is unrealistic? Try going down to your local traffic court and see whether defendants' dress or manner of speech predict variations in fines for the same infraction. The point is, getting a general understanding of how any social institution or organization works—the local justice system, a hospital, a ship, or an entire community—is best achieved through participant observation.

ENTERING THE FIELD
Perhaps the most difficult part of actually doing participant observation fieldwork is making an entry. There are five rules to follow.

1. There is no reason to select a site that is difficult to enter when equally good sites are available that are easy to enter (see chapter 3). In many cases, you *will* have a choice—among equally good villages in a region, or among school districts, hospitals, or cell blocks. When you have a choice, take the field site that promises to provide easiest access to data.

2. Go into the field with plenty of written documentation about yourself and your project. You'll need formal letters of introduction—at a minimum, from your university,
   or from your client if you are doing applied work on a contract. Letters from universities should spell out your affiliation, who is funding you, and how long you will be at
   the field site.

Be sure that those letters are in the language spoken where you will be working, and
that they are signed by the highest academic authorities possible.

Letters of introduction should not go into detail about your research. Keep a separate
document handy in which you describe your proposed work and present it to gatekeepers
who ask for it, along with your letters of introduction.

Of course, if you study an outlaw biker gang, like Daniel Wolf did, forget about letters
of introduction (Wolf 1991). On the other hand, Johnny Moore was president of an
outlaw biker gang in Mississippi before he teamed up with sociologist Columbus Hopper
to study biker gangs (Hopper and Moore 1983). Moore had "courtesy cards" from biker
gangs across the country that served as letters of introduction (Hopper and Moore
1990:385).

3. Don't try to wing it, unless you absolutely have to. There is nothing to be said for
   "getting in on your own." Use personal contacts to help you make your entry into a
   field site.

When I went to Kalymnos, Greece, in 1964, I carried with me a list of people to look
up. I collected the list from people in the Greek American community of Tarpon Springs,
Florida, who had relatives on Kalymnos. When I went to Washington, DC, to study how
decision-makers in the bureaucracy used (or didn't use) scientific information, I had
letters of introduction from colleagues at Scripps Institution of Oceanography (where I
was working at the time).

If you are studying any hierarchically organized community (hospitals, police departments, universities, school systems, etc.), it is usually best to start at the top and work
down. Find out the names of the people who are the gatekeepers and see them first.
Assure them that you will maintain strict confidentiality and that no one in your study
will be personally identifiable.

In some cases, though, starting at the top can backfire. If there are warring factions in
a community or organization, and if you gain entry to the group at the top of *one* of
those factions, you will be asked to side with that faction.

Another danger is that top administrators of institutions may try to enlist you as a
kind of spy. They may offer to facilitate your work if you will report back to them on
what you find out about specific individuals. This is absolutely off limits in research. If
that's the price of doing a study, you're better off choosing another institution. In the 2
years I spent doing research on communication structures in federal prisons, no one ever
asked me to report on the activities of specific inmates. But other researchers have
reported experiencing this kind of pressure, so it's worth keeping in mind (**Further Reading:** gatekeepers).

4. Think through in advance what you will say when ordinary people (not just gatekeepers) ask you: What are you doing here? Who sent you? Who's funding you? What good
   is your research and who will it benefit? Why do you want to learn about people here?

How long will you be here? How do I know you aren't a spy for _____ ?
(where the blank is filled in by whoever people are afraid of).

The rules for presentation of self are simple: Be honest, be brief, and be absolutely consistent. In participant observation, if you try to play any role other than yourself, you'll just get worn out (D. J. Jones 1973).

But understand that not everyone will be thrilled about your role as a researcher. Terry Williams studied cocaine use in after-hours clubs in New York. It was "gay night" in one bar he went to. Williams started a conversation with a man whose sleeves were fully rolled, exposing tattoos on both arms. The man offered to buy William a drink. Was this Williams's first time at the bar? Williams said he'd been there before, that he was a researcher, and that he just wanted to talk. The man turned to his friends and exploded: "Hey, get a load of this one. He wants to do research on us. You scum bag! What do we look like, pal? Fucking guinea pigs?" (T. Williams 1996:30).

After that experience, Williams became, as he said, "more selective" in whom he told about his real purpose in those after-hours clubs.

5. Spend time getting to know the physical and social layout of your field site. It doesn't matter if you're working in a rural village, an urban enclave, or a hospital. Walk it and write notes about how it *feels* to you. Is it crowded? Do the buildings or furniture seem old or poorly kept? Are there any distinctive odors?

You'd be surprised how much information comes from asking people about little things like these. I can still smell the distinctive blend of diesel fuel and taco sauce that's characteristic of so many bus depots in rural Mexico. Asking people about those smells opened up long conversations about what it's like for poor people, who don't own cars, to travel in Mexico and all the family and business reasons they have for traveling. If something in your environment makes a strong sensory impression, write it down.

A really good early activity in any participant observation project is to make maps and charts—kinship charts of families, chain-of-command charts in organizations, maps of offices or villages or whatever physical space you're studying, charts of who sits where at meetings, and so on.

For making maps, take a GPS (global positioning system) device to the field with you. GPS devices that are accurate to within 3 meters or less are available for under $200 (see appendix E for more). What a GPS does is track your path via satellite, so that if you can walk the perimeter of an area, you can map it and mark its longitude and latitude accurately. Eri Sugita (2006) studied the relation between the washing of hands by the mothers of young children and the rate of diarrheal disease among those children in Bugobero, Uganda. Sugita used a GPS device to map the position of every well and every spring in Bugobero. Then she walked to each of the water sources from each of the 51 households in her study and, wearing a pedometer, measured the travel distance to the nearest source of clean water.

Another good thing to do is to take a census of the group you're studying as soon as you can. When she began her fieldwork on the demography and fertility in a Mexican village, Julia Pauli (2000) did a complete census of 165 households. She recorded the names of all the people who were considered to be members of the household, whether they were living there or not (a lot of folks were away, working as migrant laborer). She recorded their sex, age, religion, level of education, marital status, occupation, place of birth, and where each person was living right then. Then, for each of the 225 women who had given birth at least once, she recorded the name, sex, birth date, education, current occupation, marital status, and current residence of each child.

Pauli gave each person in a household their own, unique identification number and she gave each child of each woman in a household an I.D. number—whether the child was living at home, away working, or married and living in a separate household in the village. In the course of her census, she would eventually run into those married children living in other households. But because each person kept his or her unique I.D. number, Pauli was able to link all those born in the village to their natal homes. In other words, Pauli used the data from her straightforward demographic survey to build a kinship network of the village.

A census of a village or a hospital gives you the opportunity to walk around a community and to talk with most of its members at least once. It lets you be seen by others and it gives you an opportunity to answer questions, as well as to ask them. It allows you to get information that official censuses don't retrieve. And it can be a way to gain rapport in a community. But it can also backfire if people are afraid you might be a spy. Michael Agar reports that he was branded as a Pakistani spy when he went to India, so his village census was useless (1980b).

THE SKILLS OF A PARTICIPANT OBSERVER

To a certain extent, participant observation must be learned in the field. The strength of participant observation is that you, as a researcher, become the instrument for data collection and analysis through your own experience. Consequently, you have to experience participant observation to get good at it. Nevertheless, there are a number of skills that you can develop before you go into the field.

Learning the Language

Unless you are a full participant in the culture you're studying, being a participant observer makes you a freak. Here's how anthropologists looked to Vine Deloria (1969:78), a Sioux writer:

> Anthropologists can readily be identified on the reservations. Go into any crowd of people. Pick out a tall gaunt white man wearing Bermuda shorts, a World War II Army Air Force flying jacket, an Australian bush hat, tennis shoes, and packing a large knapsack incorrectly strapped on his back. He will invariably have a thin, sexy wife with stringy hair, an I. Q. of 191, and a vocabulary in which even the prepositions have eleven syllables. . . . This creature is an anthropologist.

Now, four decades later, it's more likely to be the anthropologist's husband who jabbers in 11-syllable words, but the point is still the same. The most important thing you can do to stop being a freak is to speak the language of the people you're studying—and speak it well. Franz Boas was adamant about this. "Nobody," he said, "would expect authoritative accounts of the civilization of China or Japan from a man who does not speak the languages readily, and who has not mastered their literatures" (1911:56). And yet, "the best kept secret of anthropology," says Robbins Burling, "is the linguistic incompetence of ethnological fieldworkers" (2000 [1984]:v).

That secret is actually not so much well kept as ignored. In 1933, Paul Radin, one of Franz Boas's students, complained that Margaret Mead's work on Samoa was superficial because she wasn't fluent in Samoan (Radin 1966 [1933]:179). Sixty-six years later, Derek Freeman (1999) showed that Mead was probably duped by at least some of her adolescent informants about the extent of their sexual experience because she didn't know the local language.

In fact, Mead talked quite explicitly about her use of interpreters. It was not necessary, said Mead, for fieldworkers to become what she called *virtuosos* in a native language. It was enough simply to *use* a native language, as she put it, without actually speaking it fluently:

> If one knows how to exclaim "how beautiful!" of an offering, "how fat!" of a baby, "how big!" of a just shot pig; if one can say "my foot's asleep" or "my back itches" as one sits in a closely pack native group with whom one is as yet unable to hold a sustained conversation; if one can ask the simple questions: "Is that your child?" "Is your father living?" "Are the mosquitoes biting you?" or even utter culturally appropriate squeals and monosyllables which accompany fright at a scorpion, or startle at a loud noise, it is easy to establish rapport with people who depend upon affective contact for reassurance. (Mead 1939:198)

Robert Lowie would have none of it. A people's ethos, he said, is never directly observed. "It can be inferred only from their self-revelations," and this, indeed, requires the dreaded virtuosity that Mead had dismissed (Lowie 1940:84–87). The "horse-and-buggy ethnographers," said Lowie, in a direct response to Mead in the *American Anthropologist*, accepted virtuosity—that is, a thorough knowledge of the language in which one does fieldwork—on principle. "The new, stream-lined ethnographers," he taunted, rejected this as superfluous (Lowie 1940:87). Lowie was careful to say that a thorough knowledge of a field language did not mean native proficiency. And, of course, Mead understood the benefits of being proficient in a field language. But she also understood that a lot of ethnography gets done through interpreters or through contact languages, like French, English, and pidgins . . . the not-so-well kept secret in anthropology (**Further Reading:** using interpreters).

Still . . . according to Brislin et al. (1973:70), Samoa is one of those cultures where "it is considered acceptable to deceive and to 'put on' outsiders. Interviewers are likely to hear ridiculous answers, not given in a spirit of hostility but rather sport." Brislin et al. call this the **sucker bias** and warn fieldworkers to watch out for it. Presumably, knowing the local language fluently is one way to become alert to and avoid this problem.

And remember Raoul Naroll's finding that anthropologists who spent at least a year in the field were more likely to report on witchcraft? He also found that anthropologists who spoke the local language were more likely to report data about witchcraft than were those who didn't. Fluency in the local language doesn't just improve your rapport, it increases the probability that people will tell you about sensitive things, like witchcraft and that even if people try to put one over on you, you'll know about it (Naroll 1962:89–90).

When it comes to doing effective participant observation, learning a new jargon in your own language is just as important as learning a foreign language. Peggy Sullivan and Kirk Elifson studied the Free Holiness church, a rural group of Pentecostals whose rituals include the handling of poisonous snakes (rattles, cottonmouths, copperheads, and water moccasins). They had to learn an entirely new vocabulary:

> Terms and expressions like "annointment," "tongues," "shouting," and "carried away in the Lord" began having meaning for us. We learned informally and often contextually through conversation and by listening to sermons and testimonials. The development of our understanding of the new language was gradual and probably was at its greatest depth when we were most submerged in the church and its culture. . . . We simplified

our language style and eliminated our use of profanity. We realized, for example, that one badly placed "damn" could destroy trust that we had built up over months of hard work. (Sullivan and Elifson 1996:36)

How to Learn a New Language

In my experience, the way to learn a new language is to learn a few words and to say them brilliantly. Yes, study the grammar and vocabulary, but the key to learning a new language—and to using it effectively in ethnography—is saying things right, even just a handful of things. This means capturing not just the pronunciation of words, but also the intonation, the use of your hands, and other nonverbal cues that show you are really, really serious about the language and are trying to look and sound as much like a native as possible. Michael Herzfeld (2009b) reports that when he did his first summer's fieldwork in Bangkok, he couldn't get ordinary people in the street to respond to him in Thai. People just stared at him. On his second trip, a Thai person asked *him* for directions on the street. What had changed? Despite his white Western face, a street vendor told him, he had Thai gestures and *looked* Thai (p. 141).

When you say the equivalent of "Hey, hiya doin'" instead of the equivalent of "Hello, how are you today?" with just the right intonation in any language—Zulu or French or Arabic—people will think you know more than you do. They'll come right back at you with a flurry of words, and you'll be lost. Fine. Tell them to slow down—again, in that great accent and body language you're cultivating.

Consider the alternative: You announce to people, with the first, badly accented, stilted words out of your mouth, that you know next to nothing about the language and that they should therefore speak to you with that in mind. When you talk to someone who is not a native speaker of your language, you make an automatic assessment of how large their vocabulary is and how fluent they are. You adjust both the speed of your speech and your vocabulary to ensure comprehension. That's what Zulu and Arabic speakers will do with you, too. The trick is to act in a way that gets people into pushing your limits of fluency and into teaching you cultural insider words and phrases.

The real key to learning a language is to acquire vocabulary. People will usually figure out what you want to say if you butcher the grammar a bit, but they need nouns and verbs to even begin the effort. This requires studying lists of words every day and using as many new words every day as you can engineer into a conversation. Try to stick at least one conspicuously idiomatic word or phrase into your conversation every day That will not only nail down some insider vocabulary, it will stimulate everyone around you to give you more of the same.

A good fraction of any culture is in the idioms and especially in the metaphors (more about metaphors in chapter 19). To understand how powerful this can be, imagine you are hired to tutor a student from Nepal who wants to learn English. You point to some clouds and say "clouds" and she responds by saying "clouds." You say "very good" and she says "no brainer." You can certainly pick up the learning pace after that kind of response.

As you articulate more and more insider phrases like a native, people will increase the rate at which they teach you by raising the level of their discourse with you. They may even compete to teach you the subtleties of their language and culture. When I was learning Greek in 1960 on a Greek merchant ship, the sailors took delight in seeing to it that my vocabulary of obscenities was up to their standards and that my usage of that vocabulary was suitably robust.

To prepare for my doctoral fieldwork in 1964–65, I studied Greek at the University of

Illinois. By the end of 1965, after a year on the island of Kalymnos, my accent, manner-isms, and vocabulary were more Kalymnian than Athenian. When I went to teach at the University of Athens in 1969, my colleagues there were delighted that I wanted to teach in Greek, but they were conflicted about my accent. How to reconcile the fact that an educated foreigner spoke reasonably fluent Greek with what they took to be a rural, working-class accent? It didn't compute, but they were very forgiving. After all, I *was* a foreigner, and the fact that I was making an attempt to speak the local language counted for a lot.

So, if you are going off to do fieldwork in a foreign language, try to find an intensive summer course in the country where that language is spoken. Not only will you learn the language (and the local dialect of that language), you'll make personal contacts, find out what the problems are in selecting a research site, and discover how to tie your study to the interests of local scholars. You can study French in France, but you can also study it in Montreal, Martinique, or Madagascar. You can study Spanish in Spain, but you can also study it in Mexico, Bolivia, or Paraguay.

You'd be amazed at the range of language courses available at universities these days: Ulithi, Aymara, Quechua, Nahuatl, Swahili, Turkish, Amharic, Basque, Eskimo, Navajo, Zulu, Hausa, Amoy. . . . If the language you need is not offered in a formal course, try to find an individual speaker of the language (the husband or wife of a foreign student) who would be willing to tutor you in a self-paced course. There are self-paced courses in hundreds of languages available today, with lots of auditory material on disks or online.

There are, of course, many languages for which there are no published materials, except perhaps for a dictionary or part of the Judeo-Christian Bible. For those languages, you need to learn how to reduce them to writing quickly so that you can get on with learning them and with fieldwork. To learn how to reduce *any* language to writing, see the tutorial by Oswald Werner (2000a, 2000b, 2001, 2002a, 2002b) (**Further Reading:** language and fieldwork) (box 12.5).

BOX 12.5

WHEN NOT TO MIMIC

The key to understanding the culture of loggers, lawyers, bureaucrats, school-teachers, or ethnic groups is to become intimately familiar with their vocabu-lary. Words are where the cultural action is. My rule about mimicking pronunciation changes, though, if you are studying an ethnic or occupational subculture in your own society and the people in that subculture speak a differ-ent dialect of your native language. In this situation, mimicking the local pro-nunciation will just make you look silly. Even worse, people may think you're ridiculing them.

Building Explicit Awareness

Another important skill in participant observation is what Spradley (1980:55) called **explicit awareness** of the little details in life. Try this experiment: The next time you see someone look at their watch, go right up to them and ask them the time. Chances are they'll look again because when they looked the first time they were not *explicitly aware* of what they saw. Tell them that you are a student conducting a study and ask them to chat with you for a few minutes about how they tell time.

Many people who wear analog watches look at the *relative positions* of the hands, and not at the numbers on the dial. They subtract the current time (the position of the hands now) from the time they have to be somewhere (the image of what the position of the hands will look like at some time in the future), and calculate whether the difference is anything to worry about. They never have to become explicitly aware of the fact that it is 3:10 P.M. People who wear digital watches may be handling the process somewhat differently. We could test that.

Kronenfeld et al. (1972) reported an experiment in which informants leaving several different restaurants were asked what the waiters and waitresses (as they were called in those gender-differentiated days) were wearing and what kind of music was playing. Informants agreed much more about what the waiters were wearing than about what the waitresses were wearing. The hitch: None of the restaurants had waiters, only waitresses.

Informants also provided more detail about the kind of music in restaurants that did not have music than they provided for restaurants that did have music. Kronenfeld et al. speculated that, in the absence of real memories about things they'd seen or heard, informants turned to cultural norms for what must have been there (i.e., "what goes with what") (D'Andrade 1973).

You can test this yourself. Pick out a large lecture hall where a male professor is not wearing a tie. Ask a group of students on their way out of a lecture hall what color tie their professor was wearing. Or observe a busy store clerk for an hour and count the number of sales she rings up. Then ask her to estimate the number of sales she handled during that hour.

You can build your skills at becoming explicitly aware of ordinary things. Get a group of colleagues together and write separate, detailed descriptions of the most mundane, ordinary things you can think of: making a bed, doing laundry, building a sandwich, shaving (face, legs, underarms), picking out produce at the supermarket, and the like. Then discuss one another's descriptions and see how many details others saw that you didn't and vice versa. If you work carefully at this exercise, you'll develop a lot of respect for how complex, and how important, the details of ordinary life are. If you want to see the level of detail you're shooting for here, read Anthony F. C. Wallace's little classic "Driving to Work" (1965). Wallace had made the 17-mile drive from his home to the University of Pennsylvania about 500 times when he drew a map of it, wrote out the details, and extracted a set of rules for his behavior. He was driving a 1962 Volkswagen Beetle in those days. It had 12 major mechanical controls (from the ignition switch to the windshield wiper—yes, there was just one of them, and you had to pull a switch on the instrument panel with your right hand to get it started), all of which had to be handled correctly to get him from home to work safely every day.

Building Memory

Even when we are explicitly aware of things we see, there is no guarantee that we'll remember them long enough to write them down. Building your ability to remember things you see and hear is crucial to successful participant observation research.

Try this exercise: Walk past a store window at a normal pace. When you get beyond it and can't see it any longer, write down all the things that were in the window. Go back and check. Do it again with another window. You'll notice an improvement in your ability to remember little things almost immediately. You'll start to create mnemonic devices for remembering more of what you see. Keep up this exercise until you are satisfied that you can't get any better at it.

Here's another one. Go to a church service other than one you're used to. Take along two colleagues. When you leave, write up what you each think you saw, in as much detail as you can muster and compare what you've written. Go back to the church and keep doing this exercise until all of you are satisfied that (1) you are all seeing and writing down the same things and (2) you have reached the limits of your ability to recall complex behavioral scenes.

Try this same exercise by going to a church service with which you *are* familiar and take along several colleagues who are *not*. Again, compare your notes with theirs, and keep going back and taking notes until you and they are seeing and noting the same things. You can do this with any repeated scene that's familiar to you: a bowling alley, a fast-food restaurant, etc. Remember, training your ability to see things *reliably* does not guarantee that you'll see thing *accurately*. But reliability is a necessary but insufficient condition for accuracy. Unless you become at least a reliable instrument of data gathering, you don't stand much of a chance of making valid observations.

Bogdan (1972:41) offers some practical suggestions for remembering details in participant observation. If, for some reason, you can't take notes during an interview or at some event, and you are trying to remember what was said, *don't talk to anyone* before you get your thoughts down on paper. Talking to people reinforces some things you heard and saw at the expense of other things.

Also, when you sit down to write, try to remember things in historical sequence, as they occurred throughout the day. As you write up your notes you will invariably remember some particularly important detail that just pops into memory out of sequence. When that happens, jot it down on a separate piece of paper (or tuck it away in a separate little note file on your word processor) and come back to it later, when your notes reach that point in the sequence of the day.

Another useful device is to draw a map—even a rough sketch will do—of the physical space where you spent time observing and talking to people that day. As you move around the map, you will dredge up details of events and conversations. In essence, let yourself walk through your experience. You can practice all these memory-building skills now and be much better prepared if you decide to do long-term fieldwork later.

Maintaining Naïveté

Try also to develop your skill at being a novice—at being someone who genuinely wants to learn a new culture. This may mean working hard at suspending judgment about some things. David Fetterman made a trip across the Sinai Desert with a group of Bedouins. One of the Bedouins, says Fetterman,

> shared his jacket with me to protect me from the heat. I thanked him, of course, because I appreciated the gesture and did not want to insult him. But I smelled like a camel for the rest of the day in the dry desert heat. I thought I didn't need the jacket. . . . I later learned that without his jacket I would have suffered from sunstroke. . . . An inexperienced traveler does not always notice when the temperature climbs above 130 degrees Fahrenheit. By slowing down the evaporation rate, the jacket helped me retain water. (1989:33)

Maintaining your naïveté will come naturally in a culture that's unfamiliar to you, but it's a bit harder to do in your own culture. Most of what you do "naturally" is so automatic that you don't know how to intellectualize it.

If you are like many middle-class Americans, your eating habits can be characterized by the word "grazing"—that is, eating small amounts of food at many, irregular times during the course of a typical day, rather than sitting down for meals at fixed times. Would you have used that kind of word to describe your own eating behavior? Other members of your own culture are often better informants than you are about that culture, and if you really let people teach you, they will.

If you look carefully, though, you'll be surprised at how heterogeneous your culture is and how many parts of it you really know nothing about. Find some part of your own culture that you don't control—an occupational culture, like long-haul trucking, or a hobby culture, like amateur radio—and try to learn it. That's what you did as a child. This time, try to intellectualize the experience. Take notes on what you learn about *how to learn*, on what it's like being a novice, and how you think you can best take advantage of the learner's role. Your imagination will suggest a lot of other nooks and crannies of our culture that you can explore as a thoroughly untutored novice.

When Not to Be Naive

The role of naive novice is not *always* the best one to play. Humility is inappropriate when you are dealing with a culture whose members stand a lot to lose by your incompetence. Michael Agar (1973, 1980a) did field research on the life of heroine addicts in New York City. His informants made it plain that Agar's ignorance of their lives wasn't cute or interesting to them.

Even with the best of intentions, Agar could have given his informants away to the police by just by being stupid. Under such circumstances, you shouldn't expect your informants to take you under their wing and teach you how to appreciate their customs. Agar had to learn a lot, and very quickly, to gain credibility with his informants.

There are situations where your expertise is just what's required to build rapport with people. Anthropologists have typed documents for illiterate people in the field and have used other skills (from coaching basketball to dispensing antibiotics) to help people and to gain their confidence and respect. If you are studying highly educated people, you may have to prove that you know a fair amount about research methods before they will deal with you. Agar (1980b:58) once studied an alternative lifestyle commune and was asked by a biochemist who was living there: "Who are you going to use as a control group?" In my study of ocean scientists (Bernard 1974), several informants asked me what computer programs I was going to use to do a factor analysis of my data.

Building Writing Skills

The ability to write comfortably, clearly, and often is one of the most important skills you can develop as a participant observer. Ethnographers who are not comfortable as writers produce few field notes and little published work. If you have any doubts about your ability to pound out thousands of words, day in and day out, then try to build that skill now, before you go into the field for an extended period.

The way to build that skill is to team up with one or more colleagues who are also trying to build their expository writing ability. Set concrete and regular writing tasks for yourselves and criticize one another's work on matters of clarity and style. There is nothing trivial about this kind of exercise. If you think you need it, do it.

Good writing skills will carry you through participant observation fieldwork, writing a dissertation and, finally, writing for publication. Don't be afraid to write clearly and compellingly. The worst that can happen is that someone will criticize you for "popularizing" your material. I think ethnographers should be criticized if they take the exciting material of real people's lives and turn it into deadly dull reading.

Hanging Out, Gaining Rapport

It may sound silly, but just **hanging out** is a skill, and until you learn it you can't do your best work as a participant observer. Remember what I said at the beginning of this chapter: Participant observation is *a strategic* method that lets you learn what you want to learn and apply all the data collection methods that you may want to apply.

When you enter a new field situation, the temptation is to ask a lot of questions to learn as much as possible as quickly as possible. There are many things that people can't or won't tell you in answer to questions. If you ask people too quickly about the sources of their wealth, you are likely to get incomplete data. If you ask too quickly about sexual liaisons, you may get thoroughly unreliable responses.

Hanging out builds trust, or **rapport**, and trust results in ordinary conversation and ordinary behavior in your presence. Once you know, from hanging out, exactly what you want to know more about, and once people trust you not to betray their confidence, you'll be surprised at the direct questions you can ask.

In his study of Cornerville (Boston's heavily Italian American neighborhood called North End), William Foote Whyte wondered whether "just hanging on the street corner was an active enough process to be dignified by the term 'research.' Perhaps I should ask these men questions," he thought. He soon realized that "one has to learn when to question and when not to question as well as what questions to ask" (1989:78).

Philip Kilbride studied child abuse in Kenya. He did a survey and focused ethnographic interviews, but "by far the most significant event in my research happened as a byproduct of participatory 'hanging out,' being always in search of case material." While visiting informants one day, Kilbride and his wife saw a crowd gathering at a local secondary school. It turned out that a young mother had thrown her baby into a pit latrine at the school. The Kilbrides offered financial assistance to the young mother and her family in exchange for "involving ourselves in their . . . misfortune." The event that the Kilbrides had witnessed became the focus for a lot of their research activities in the succeeding months (Kilbride 1992:190).

The Ethical Dilemma of Rapport

Face it: "Gaining rapport" is a euphemism for impression management, one of the "darker arts" of fieldwork, in Harry Wolcott's apt phrase (2005:chap. 6). E. E. Evans-Pritchard, the great British anthropologist, made clear in 1937 how manipulative the craft of ethnography really is. He was doing fieldwork with the Azande of Sudan and wanted to study their rich tradition of witchcraft. Even with his long-term fieldwork and command of the Azande language, Evans-Pritchard couldn't get people to open up about witchcraft, so he decided to "win the good will of one or two practitioners and to persuade them to divulge their secrets in strict confidence" (1958 [1937]:151). Strict confidence? He was planning on writing a book about all this.

Progress was slow, and although he felt that he could have "eventually wormed out all their secrets" he hit on another idea: His personal servant, Kamanga, was initiated into the local group of practitioners and "became a practising witch-doctor" under the tutelage of a man named Badobo (Evans-Pritchard 1958 [1937]:151). With Badobo's full knowledge, Kamanga reported every step of his training to his employer. In turn, Evans-Pritchard used the information "to draw out of their shells rival practitioners by playing on their jealousy and vanity."

Badobo knew that anything he told Kamanga would be tested with rival witch doctors. Badobo couldn't lie to Kamanga, but he could certainly withhold the most secret material. Evans-Pritchard analyzed the situation carefully and pressed on. Once an ethnographer is "armed with preliminary knowledge," he said, "nothing can prevent him from driving deeper and deeper the wedge if he is interested and persistent" (Evans-Pritchard 1958 [1937]:152).

Still, Kamanga's training was so slow that Evans-Pritchard nearly abandoned his inquiry into witchcraft. Providence intervened. A celebrated witch doctor, named Bögwözu, showed up from another district and Evans-Pritchard offered him a very high wage if he'd take over Kamanga's training. Evans-Pritchard explained to Bögwözu that he was "tired of Badobo's wiliness and extortion," and that he expected his generosity to result in Kamanga learning all the tricks of the witch doctor's trade (Evans-Pritchard 1958 [1937]:152).

But the really cunning part of Evans-Pritchard's scheme was that he continued to pay Badobo to tutor Kamanga. He *knew* that Badobo would be jealous of Bögwözu and would strive harder to teach Kamanga more about witch-doctoring. Here is Evans-Pritchard going on about his deceit and the benefits of this tactic for ethnographers:

> The rivalry between these two practitioners grew into bitter and ill-concealed hostility. Bögwözu gave me information about medicines and magical rites to prove that his rival was ignorant of the one or incapable in the performance of the other. Badobo became alert and showed himself no less eager to demonstrate his knowledge of magic to both Kamanga and to myself. They vied with each other to gain ascendancy among the local practitioners. Kamanga and I reaped a full harvest in this quarrel, not only from the protagonists themselves but also from other witch-doctors in the neighborhood, and even from interested laymen. (Evans-Pritchard 1958 [1937]:153)

Objectivity

Finally, **objectivity** is a skill, like language fluency, and you can build it if you work at it. Some people build more of it, others less. More is better.

If an objective measurement is one made by a robot—that is, a machine that is not prone to the kind of measurement error that comes from having opinions and memories—then no human being can ever be completely objective. We can't rid ourselves of our experiences, and I don't know anyone who thinks it would be a good idea even to try.

We can, however, become aware of our experiences, our opinions, our values. We can hold our field observations up to a cold light and ask whether we've seen what we wanted to see, or what is really out there. The goal is not for us, as humans, to become objective machines; it is for us to achieve objective—that is, accurate—knowledge by transcending our biases. No fair pointing out that this is impossible. It *is* impossible to do completely, but it's not impossible to do at all. Priests, social workers, clinical psychologists, and counselors suspend their own biases all the time, more or less, in order to listen hard and give sensible advice to their clients.

Colin Turnbull held objective knowledge as something to be pulled from the thicket of subjective experience. Fieldwork, said Turnbull, involves a self-conscious review of one's own ideas and values—one's self, for want of any more descriptive term. During fieldwork you "reach inside," he observed, and give up the "old, narrow, limited self, discovering the new self that is right and proper in the new context." We use the field experience, he said, "to know ourselves more deeply by conscious subjectivity." In this way, he concluded, "the ultimate goal of objectivity is much more likely to be reached and our understanding of other cultures that much more profound" (Turnbull 1986:27). When he was studying the Ik of Uganda, he saw parents goad small children into touching fire and then laughing at the result. It took everything he had, he once told me, to transcend his biases, but he managed (see Turnbull 1972).

Many phenomenologists see objective knowledge as the goal of participant observation. Danny Jorgensen, for example, advocates complete immersion and **becoming the phenomenon** you study. "Becoming the phenomenon," Jorgensen says, "is a participant observational strategy for penetrating to and gaining experience of a form of human life. It is an objective approach insofar as it results in the accurate, detailed description of the insiders' experience of life" (Jorgensen 1989:63). In fact, many ethnographers have become cab drivers, exotic dancers, jazz musicians, or members of satanic cults, to do participant observation fieldwork.

If you use this strategy of full immersion, Jorgensen says, you must be able to switch back and forth between the insiders' view and that of an analyst. To do that—to maintain your objective, analytic abilities—Jorgensen suggests finding a colleague with whom you can talk things over regularly. That is, give yourself an outlet for discussing the theoretical, methodological, and emotional issues that inevitably come up in full participation field research. It's good advice.

Objectivity and Neutrality

Objectivity does not mean (and has never meant) **value neutrality**. No one asks Cultural Survival, Inc. to be neutral in documenting the violent obscenities against indigenous peoples of the world. No one asks Amnesty International to be neutral in its effort to document state-sanctioned torture. We recognize that the power of the documentation is in its objectivity, in its chilling irrefutability, not in its neutrality.

Claire Sterk, an ethnographer from the Netherlands, has studied prostitutes and intravenous drug users in mostly African American communities in New York City and Newark, New Jersey. Sterk was a trusted friend and counselor to many of the women with whom she worked. In one 2-month period in the late 1980s, she attended the funeral of seven women she knew who had died of AIDS. She felt that "every researcher is affected by the work he or she does. One cannot remain neutral and uninvolved; even as an outsider, the researcher is part of the community" (Sterk 1989:99, 1999).

Laurie Krieger, an American woman doing fieldwork in Cairo, studied physical punishment against women. She learned that wife beatings were less violent than she had imagined and that the act still sickened her. Her reaction brought out a lot of information from women who were recent recipients of their husbands' wrath. "I found out," she says, "that the biased outlook of an American woman and a trained anthropologist was not always disadvantageous, as long as I was aware of and able to control the expression of my biases" (Krieger 1986:120).

At the end of his second year of research on street life in El Barrio, Phillipe Bourgois's friends and informants began telling him about their experiences as gang rapists. Bourgois's informants were in their mid- to late 20s then, and the stories they told were of things they'd done as very young adolescents, more than a decade earlier. Still, Bourgois says, he felt betrayed by people whom he had come to like and respect. Their "childhood stories of violently forced sex," he says, "spun me into a personal depression and a research crisis" (1995:205).

In *any* long-term field study, be prepared for some serious tests of your ability to remain a dispassionate observer. Hortense Powdermaker (1966) was once confronted with the problem of knowing that a lynch mob was preparing to go after a particular black man. She was powerless to stop the mob and fearful for her own safety.

I have never grown accustomed to seeing people ridicule the handicapped, though I see it every time I'm in rural Mexico and Greece, and I recall with horror the death of a young man on one of the sponge diving boats I sailed with in Greece. I knew the rules of safe diving that could have prevented that death; so did all the divers and the captains of the vessels. They ignored those rules at terrible cost. I wanted desperately to *do* something, but there was nothing anyone could do. My lecturing them at sea about their unsafe diving practices would not have changed their behavior. That behavior was driven, as I explained in chapter 2, by structural forces and the technology—the boats, the diving equipment—of their occupation. By suspending active judgment of their behavior, I was able to record it. "Suspending active judgment" does not mean that I eliminated my bias or that my feelings about their behavior changed. It meant only that I kept the bias to myself while I was recording their dives (box 12.6).

BOX 12.6

OBJECTIVITY AND INDIGENOUS RESEARCH

Objectivity gets its biggest test in **indigenous research**—that is, when you study your own culture. Barbara Meyerhoff worked in Mexico when she was a graduate student. Later, in the early 1970s, when she became interested in ethnicity and aging, she decided to study elderly Chicanos. The people she approached kept putting her off, asking her "Why work with us? Why don't you study your own kind?" Meyerhoff was Jewish. She had never thought about studying her own kind, but she launched a study of poor, elderly Jews who were on public assistance. She agonized about what she was doing and, as she tells it, never resolved whether it was anthropology or a personal quest.

Many of the people she studied were survivors of the Holocaust. "How, then, could anyone look at them dispassionately? How could I feel anything but awe and appreciation for their mere presence? . . . Since neutrality was impossible and idealization undesirable, I decided on striving for balance" (Meyerhoff 1989:90).

There is no final answer on whether it's good or bad to study your own culture. Plenty of people have done it, and plenty of people have written about what it's like to do it. On the plus side, you'll know the language and you'll be less likely to suffer from culture shock. On the minus side, it's harder to recognize cultural patterns that you live every day and you're likely to take a lot of things for granted that an outsider would pick up right away.

If you are going to study your own culture, start by reading the experiences of others who have done it so you'll know what you're facing in the field (**Further Reading:** studying your own culture).

GENDER, PARENTING, AND OTHER PERSONAL CHARACTERISTICS

By the 1930s, Margaret Mead had already made clear the importance of gender as a variable in data collection (see Mead 1986). Gender has at least two consequences: (1) it limits your access to certain information, and (2) it influences how you perceive others.

In all cultures, you can't ask people certain questions because you're a [woman] [man]. You can't go into certain areas and situations because you're a [woman] [man]. You can't watch this or report on that because you're a [woman] [man]. Even the culture of social scientists is affected: Your credibility is diminished or enhanced with your colleagues when you talk about a certain subject because you're a [woman] [man] (Altorki and El-Solh 1988; Golde 1986; Scheper-Hughes 1983; Warren 1988; Whitehead and Conaway 1986).

Sara Quandt, Beverly Morris, and Kathleen DeWalt spent months investigating the nutritional strategies of the elderly in two rural Kentucky counties (Quandt et al. 1997). According to DeWalt, the three women researchers spent months, interviewing key informants, and never turned up a word about the use of alcohol. "One day," says DeWalt:

> the research team traveled to Central County with Jorge Uquillas, an Ecuadorian sociologist who had expressed an interest in visiting the Kentucky field sites. One of the informants they visited was Mr. B, a natural storyteller who had spoken at length about life of the poor during the past 60 years. Although he had been a great source of information about use of wild foods and recipes for cooking game he had never spoken of drinking or moonshine production.
>
> Within a few minutes of entering his home on this day, he looked at Jorge Uquillas, and said "Are you a drinking man?" (Beverly whipped out the tape recorder and switched it on.) Over the next hour or so, Mr. B talked about community values concerning alcohol use, the problems of drunks and how they were dealt with in the community, and provided a number of stories about moonshine in Central County. The presence of another man gave Mr. B the opportunity to talk about issues he found interesting, but felt would have been inappropriate to discuss with women. (DeWalt et al. 1998:280)

On the other hand, feminist scholars have made it clear that gender is a negotiated idea. What you can and can't do if you are a man or a woman is more fixed in some cultures than in others, and in all cultures there is lots of individual variation in gender roles. Although men or women may be "expected" to be this way or that way in any given place, the variation in male and female attitudes and behaviors within a culture can be tremendous.

All participant observers confront their personal limitations and the limitations imposed on them by the culture they study. When she worked at the Thule relocation camp for Japanese Americans during World War II, Rosalie Wax did not join any of the women's groups or organizations. Looking back after more than 40 years, Wax concluded that this was just poor judgment.

> I was a university student and a researcher. I was not yet ready to accept myself as a total person, and this limited my perspective and my understanding. Those of us who instruct future field workers should encourage them to understand and value their full range of being, because only then can they cope intelligently with the range of experience they will encounter in the field. (Wax 1986:148)

Besides gender, we have learned that being a parent helps you talk to people about certain areas of life and get more information than if you were not a parent. My wife and I arrived on the island of Kalymnos, Greece, in 1964 with a 2-month-old baby. As Joan Cassell says, children are a "guarantee of good intentions" (1987:260), and wherever we went, the baby was the conversation opener. But be warned: Taking children into the field can place them at risk. (More on health risks below. And for more about the effects of fieldwork on children who accompany researchers, see Butler and Turner 1987.)

Being divorced has its costs. Nancie González found that being a divorced mother of two young sons in the Dominican Republic was just too much. "Had I to do it again," she says, "I would invent widowhood with appropriate rings and photographs" (1986:92).

Even height may make a difference: Alan Jacobs once told me he thought he did better fieldwork with the Maasai because he's 6′ 5″ than he would have if he'd been, say, an average-sized 5′10″.

Personal characteristics make a difference in fieldwork. Being old or young lets you into certain things and shuts you out of others. Being wealthy lets you talk to certain people about certain subjects and makes others avoid you. Being gregarious makes some people open up to you and makes others shy away. There is no way to eliminate the "personal equation" in participant observation fieldwork, or in any other scientific data-gathering exercise for that matter, without sending robots out to do the work. Even then, the robots would have their own problems. In all sciences, the personal equation (the influence of the observer on the data) is a matter of serious concern and study (Romney 1989).

SEX AND FIELDWORK

It is unreasonable to assume that single, adult fieldworkers are all celibate, yet the literature on field methods was nearly silent on this topic for many years. When Evans-Pritchard was a student, just about to head off for Central Africa, he asked his major professor for advice. "Seligman told me to take ten grains of quinine every night and keep off women" (Evans-Pritchard 1973:1). As far as I know, that's the last we heard from Evans-Pritchard on the subject.

Colin Turnbull (1986) tells us about his affair with a young Mbuti woman, and Dona Davis (1986) discusses her relationship with an engineer who visited the Newfoundland village where she was doing research on menopause. In Turnbull's case, he had graduated from being an asexual child in Mbuti culture to being a youth and was expected to have sexual relations. In Davis's case, she was expected not to have sexual relations, but she also learned that she was not bound by the expectation. In fact, Davis says that "being paired off" made women more comfortable with her because she was "simply breaking a rule everyone else broke" (1986:254).

Proscriptions against sex in fieldwork are silly, because they don't work. But understand that this is one area that people everywhere take very seriously. The rule on sexual behavior in the field is this: Do nothing that you can't live with, both professionally and personally. This means that you have to be even more conscious of any fallout, for you and for your partner, than you would in your own community. Eventually, you will be going home. How will that affect your partner's status? (**Further Reading:** sex and fieldwork).

SURVIVING FIELDWORK

The title of this section is the title of an important book by Nancy Howell (1990). Even 20 years on, anyone who does fieldwork in developing nations should read this book. Howell surveyed 204 anthropologists about illnesses and accidents in the field, and the results are sobering. The maxim that "anthropologists are otherwise sensible people who don't believe in the germ theory of disease" (Rappaport 1990) is apparently correct.

Through the 1980s, 100% of anthropologists who did fieldwork in south Asia reported being exposed to malaria, and 41% reported contracting the disease. Eighty-seven percent of anthropologists who worked in Africa reported exposure, and 31% reported having had malaria. Seventy percent of anthropologists who work in south Asia reported having had some liver disease.

Among all anthropologists, 13% reported having had hepatitis A. I was hospitalized for 6 weeks for hepatitis A in 1968 and spent most of another year recovering. Glynn Isaac died of hepatitis B at age 47 in 1985 after a long career of archeological fieldwork in Africa. Typhoid fever is also common among anthropologists, as are amoebic dysentery, giardia, ascariasis, hookworm, and other infectious diseases.

Accidents have injured or killed many fieldworkers. Fei Xiaotong, a student of Malinowski's, was caught in a tiger trap in China in 1935. The injury left him an invalid for 6 months. His wife died in her attempt to go for help. Michelle Zimbalist Rosaldo was killed in a fall in the Philippines in 1981. Thomas Zwickler, a graduate student at the University of Pennsylvania, was killed by a bus on a rural road in India in 1985. He was riding a bicycle when he was struck. Kim Hill was accidentally hit by an arrow while out with an Ache hunting party in Paraguay in 1982 (Howell 1990).

Five members of a Russian-American team of researchers on social change in the Arctic died in 1995 when their *umiak* (a traditional, walrus-hided Eskimo boat) was overturned by a whale (see Broadbent 1995). The researchers included three Americans (two anthropologists—Steven McNabb and Richard Condon—and a psychiatrist—William Richards), two Russians (one anthropologist—Alexander Pika—and the chief Eskimo ethnographic consultant to the project—Boris Mumikhpykak). Nine Eskimo villagers also perished in that accident. I've had my own unpleasant brushes with fate and I know many others who have had very, very close calls.

What can you do about the risks? Get every inoculation you need before you leave, not just the ones that are required by the country you are entering. Check your county health office for the latest information from the Centers for Disease Control about illnesses prevalent in the area you're going to. If you go into an area that is known to be malarial, take a full supply of antimalarial drugs with you so you don't run out while you're out in the field.

When people pass around a gourd full of *chicha* (beer made from corn) or *pulque* (beer made from cactus sap) or palm wine, decline politely and explain yourself if you have to. You'll probably insult a few people, and your protests won't always get you off the hook, but even if you only lower the number of times you are exposed to disease, you lower your risk of contracting disease.

After being very sick in the field in Mexico, I learned to carry a supply of bottled beer with me when I was visiting a house where I was sure to be given a gourd full of local brew. The gift of bottled beer was appreciated and it headed off the embarrassment of having to turn down a drink I'd rather not have. It also made clear that I'm not a teetotaler. If you *are* a teetotaler, you've got a ready-made get-out.

If you do fieldwork in a remote area, consult with physicians at your university hospital for information on the latest blood-substitute technology. If you are in an accident in a remote area and need blood, a nonperishable blood substitute can buy you time until you can get to a clean blood supply. Some fieldworkers carry a supply of sealed hypodermic needles with them in case they need an injection. Don't go anywhere without medical insurance and don't go to developing countries without evacuation insurance. It costs $60,000 or more to evacuate a person by jet from central Africa to Paris or Frankfurt. It costs about $60 a month for insurance to cover it.

Fieldwork in remote areas isn't for everyone, but if you're going to do it, you might as well do it as safely as possible. Candice Bradley is a Type-I diabetic who did long-term fieldwork in western Kenya. She took her insulin, glucagon, blood-testing equipment, and needles with her. She arranged her schedule around the predictable, daily fluctuations in her blood-sugar level. She trained people on how to cook for her and she laid in large stocks of diet drinks so that she could function in the relentless heat without raising her blood sugars (Bradley 1997:4–7).

With all this, Bradley still had close calls—near blackouts from hypoglycemia—but her close calls are no more frequent than those experienced by other field researchers who work in similarly remote areas. The rewards of foreign fieldwork can be very great, but so are the risks, even under the best conditions (**Further Reading:** dangerous fieldwork).

THE STAGES OF PARTICIPANT OBSERVATION

In what follows, I will draw on three sources of data: (1) a review of the literature on field research; (2) conversations with colleagues during the last 40 years, specifically about their experiences in the field; and (3) 5 years of work, with the late Michael Kenny, directing National Science Foundation field schools in cultural anthropology and linguistics.

During our work with the field schools (1967–1971), Kenny and I developed an outline of **researcher response** in participant observation fieldwork. Those field schools were 10 weeks long and were held each summer in central Mexico, except for one that we held in the interior of the Pacific Northwest. In Mexico, students were assigned to Ñähñu-speaking communities in the vicinity of Ixmiquilpan, Mexico. In the Northwest field school, students were assigned to small logging and mining communities in the Idaho panhandle. In Mexico, a few students did urban ethnography in the regional capital of Pachuca; in the Northwest field school, a few students did urban ethnography in Spokane, Washington.

What Kenny and I found so striking was that the stages we identified in the 10-week field experiences of our students were the same across all these places. Even more interesting—to us, anyway—was that the experiences our students had during those 10-week stints as participant observers apparently had exact analogs in our own experiences with year-long fieldwork.

1. Initial Contact

During the initial contact period, many long-term fieldworkers report experiencing a kind of euphoria as they begin to move about in a new culture. It shouldn't come as any surprise that people who are attracted to the idea of living in a new culture are delighted when they begin to do so.

But not always. Here is Napoleon Chagnon's recollection of his first encounter with the Yanomami: "I looked up and gasped when I saw a dozen burly, naked, sweaty, hideous men staring at us down the shafts of their drawn arrows! . . . had there been a diplomatic way out, I would have ended my fieldwork then and there" (Chagnon 1983:10–11).

The desire to bolt and run is more common than we have admitted in the past. Charles Wagley, who would become one of our discipline's most accomplished ethnographers, made his first field trip in 1937. A local political chief in Totonicapán, Guatemala, invited Wagley to tea in a parlor overlooking the town square. The chief's wife and two daughters joined them. While they were having their tea, two of the chief's aides came in and hustled everyone off to another room. The chief explained the hurried move to Wagley:

> He had forgotten that an execution by firing squad of two Indians, "nothing but vagrants who had robbed in the market," was to take place at five P.M. just below the parlor. He knew that I would understand the feelings of ladies and the grave problem of

trying to keep order among brutes. I returned to my ugly pensión in shock and spent a night without sleep. I would have liked to have returned as fast as possible to New York. (Wagley 1983:6)

Finally, listen to Rosalie Wax describe her encounter with the Arizona Japanese internment camp that she studied during World War II. When she arrived in Phoenix it was 110°. Later that day, after a bus ride and a 20-mile ride in a GI truck, across a dusty landscape that "looked like the skin of some cosmic reptile," with a Japanese American who wouldn't talk to her, Wax arrived at the Gila camp. By then it was 120°. She was driven to staff quarters, which was an army barracks divided into tiny cells, and abandoned to find her cell by a process of elimination.

It contained four dingy and dilapidated articles of furniture: an iron double bedstead, a dirty mattress (which took up half the room), a chest of drawers, and a tiny writing table—and it was hotter than the hinges of Hades. . . . I sat down on the hot mattress, took a deep breath, and cried. . . . Like some lost two-year-old, I only knew that I was miserable. After a while, I found the room at the end of the barrack that contained two toilets and a couple of wash basins. I washed my face and told myself I would feel better the next day. I was wrong. (Wax 1971:67)

2. Culture Shock

Even among fieldworkers who have a pleasant experience during their initial contact period (and many do), almost all report experiencing some form of depression and shock soon thereafter—usually within a few weeks. (The term "culture shock," by the way, was introduced in 1960 by an anthropologist, Kalervo Oberg.) One kind of shock comes as the novelty of the field site wears off and there is this nasty feeling that research has to get done. Some researchers (especially those on their first field trip) may also experience feelings of anxiety about their ability to collect good data.

A good response at this stage is to do highly task-oriented work: making maps, taking censuses, doing household inventories, collecting genealogies, and so on. Another useful response is to make clinical, methodological field notes about your feelings and responses in doing participant observation fieldwork.

Another kind of shock is to the culture itself. **Culture shock** is an uncomfortable stress response and must be taken very seriously. In extreme cases of culture shock, nothing seems right. You may find yourself very upset at a lack of clean toilet facilities, or people's eating habits, or their child-rearing practices. The prospect of having to put up with the local food for a year or more may become frightening. You find yourself focusing on little annoyances—something as simple as the fact that light switches go side to side rather than up and down may upset you.

This last example is not fanciful, by the way. It happened to a colleague of mine. When I first went to work with the Ñähñu in 1962, men would greet me by sticking out their right hand. When I tried to grab their hand and shake it, they deftly slid their hand to my right so that the back of their right hand touched the back of my right hand. I became infuriated that men didn't shake hands the way "they're supposed to." You may find yourself blaming everyone in the culture, or the culture itself, for the fact that your informants don't keep appointments for interviews or don't keep them "on time."

Culture shock commonly involves a feeling that people really don't want you around (which may, in fact, be the case). You feel lonely and wish you could find someone with whom to speak your native language. Even with a spouse in the field, the strain of using another language day after day and concentrating hard so that you can collect data in that language can be emotionally wearing.

A common personal problem in field research is not being able to get any privacy. Many people across the world find the Anglo-Saxon notion of privacy grotesque. When we first went out to the island of Kalymnos in Greece in 1964, Carole and I rented quarters with a family. The idea was that we'd be better able to learn about family dynamics that way. Women of the household were annoyed and hurt when my wife asked for a little time to be alone. When I came home at the end of each day's work, I could never just go to my family's room, shut the door, and talk to Carole about my day, or hers, or our new baby's. If I didn't share everything with the family we lived with during waking hours, they felt rejected.

After about 2 months of this, we had to move out and find a house of our own. My access to data about intimate family dynamics was curtailed. But it was worth it because I felt that I'd have had to abort the whole trip if I had to continue living in what my wife and I felt was a glass bowl all the time. As it turns out, there is no word for the concept of privacy in Greek. The closest gloss translates as "being alone," and connotes loneliness.

I suspect that this problem is common to all English-speaking researchers who work in developing countries. Here's what M. N. Srinivas, himself from India, wrote about his work in the rural village of Ramapura, near Mysore:

> I was never left alone. I had to fight hard even to get two or three hours absolutely to myself in a week or two. My favorite recreation was walking to the nearby village of Kere where I had some old friends, or to Hogur which had a weekly market. But my friends in Ramapura wanted to accompany me on my walks. They were puzzled by my liking for solitary walks. Why should one walk when one could catch a bus, or ride on bicycles with friends. I had to plan and plot to give them the slip to go out by myself. On my return, however, I was certain to be asked why I had not taken them with me. They would have put off their work and joined me. (They meant it.) I suffered from social claustrophobia as long as I was in the village and sometimes the feeling became so intense that I just had to get out. (1979:23)

Culture shock subsides as researchers settle in to the business of gathering data on a daily basis, but it doesn't go away because the sources of annoyance don't go away.

Unless you are one of the very rare people who truly go native in another culture, you will cope with culture shock, not eliminate it. You will remain conscious of things annoying you, but you won't feel like they are crippling your ability to work. Like Srinivas, when things get too intense, you'll have the good sense to leave the field site for a bit rather than try to stick it out (**Further Reading:** culture shock).

3. Discovering the Obvious

In the next phase of participant observation, researchers settle into collecting data on a more or less systematic basis (see Kirk and Miller 1986). This is sometimes accompanied by an interesting personal response—a sense of discovery, where you feel as if informants are finally letting you in on the "good stuff" about their culture. Much of this "good stuff" will later turn out to be commonplace. You may "discover," for example, that women have more power in the community than meets the eye or that there are two systems for dispute settlement—one embodied in formal law and one that works through informal mechanisms.

Sometimes, a concomitant to this feeling of discovery is a feeling of being in control of dangerous information and a sense of urgency about protecting informants' identities. You may find yourself going back over your field notes, looking for places that you might have lapsed and identified an informant, and making appropriate changes. You may worry about those copies of field notes you have already sent home and even become a little worried about how well you can trust your major professor to maintain the privacy of those notes.

This is the stage of fieldwork when you hear anthropologists start talking about "their" village, and how people are, at last, "letting them in" to the secrets of the culture. The feeling has its counterpart among all long-term participant observers. It often spurs researchers to collect more and more data; to accept every invitation, by every informant, to every event; to fill the days with observation and to fill the nights with writing up field notes. Days off become unthinkable, and the sense of discovery becomes more and more intense.

This is the time to take a real break.

4. The Break

The mid-fieldwork break, which usually comes after 3 or 4 months, is a crucial part of the overall participant observation experience for long-term researchers. It's an opportunity to get some distance, both physical and emotional, from the field site. It gives you a chance to put things into perspective, think about what you've got so far, and what you need to get in the time remaining. Use this time to collect data from regional or national statistical services; to visit with colleagues at the local university and discuss your findings; to visit other communities in other parts of the country. And be sure to leave some time to just take a vacation, without thinking about research at all.

Your informants also need a break from you. "Anthropologists are uncomfortable intruders no matter how close their rapport," wrote Charles Wagley. "A short respite is mutually beneficial. One returns with objectivity and human warmth restored. The anthropologist returns as an old friend" who has gone away and returned, and has thereby demonstrated his or her genuine interest in a community (Wagley 1983:13). Everyone needs a break.

5. Focusing

After the break, you will have a better idea of exactly what kinds of data you are lacking, and your sense of problem will also come more sharply into focus. The reason to have a formally prepared design statement *before* you go to the field is to tell you what you should be looking for. Nevertheless, even the most focused research design will have to be modified in the field. In some cases, you may find yourself making radical changes in your design, based on what you find when you get to the field and spend several months actually collecting data.

There is nothing wrong or unusual about this, but new researchers sometimes experience anxiety over making any major changes. The important thing at this stage is to focus the research and use your time effectively rather than agonizing over how to save components of your original design, if that design turns out to be truly unworkable.

6. Exhaustion, the Second Break, and Frantic Activity

After 7 or 8 months, some participant observers start to think that they have exhausted their informants, both literally and figuratively. That is, they may become embarrassed about continuing to ask informants for more information. Or they may make the supreme mistake of believing that their informants have no more to tell them. The reason this is such a mistake, of course, is that the store of cultural knowledge in any culturally competent person is enormous—far more than anyone could hope to extract in a year or two.

At this point, another break is usually a good idea. You'll get another opportunity to take stock, order your priorities for the time remaining, and see both how much you've done and how little. The realization that, in fact, informants have a great deal more to teach them, and that they have precious little time left in the field, sends many investigators into a frenetic burst of activity during this stage.

7. Leaving the Field

The last stage of participant observation is leaving the field. Don't neglect this part of the process. Let people know that you are leaving and tell them how much you appreciate their help. The ritual of leaving a place in a culturally appropriate way will make it possible for you to go back and even to send others.

Participant observation is an intensely intimate and personal experience. People who began as your informants may become your friends as well. In the best of cases, you come to trust that they will not deceive you about their culture, and they come to trust you not to betray them—that is, not to use your intimate knowledge of their lives to hurt them. (You can imagine the worst of cases.) There is often a legitimate expectation on both sides that the relationship may be permanent, not just a 1-year fling.

For many long-term participant observation researchers, there is no final leaving of "the field." I've been working with some people, on and off, for 45 years. Like many anthropologists who work in Latin America, I'm godparent to a child of my closest research collaborator. From time to time, people from Mexico or from Greece will call my house on the phone, just to say "hi" and to keep the relationship going.

Or their children, who happen to be doing graduate work at a university in the United States, will call and send their parents' regards. They'll remind you of some little event they remember when they were 7 or 8 and you came to their parents' house to do some interviewing and you spilled your coffee all over yourself as you fumbled with your tape recorder. People remember the darndest things. You'd better be ready when it happens.

THE FRONT-EDGE: COMBINING METHODS

More and more researchers these days, across the social sciences, have learned what a powerful method powerful participant observation is at all stages of the research process. The method stands on its own, but it is also increasingly part of a mixed-method strategy, as researchers combine qualitative and quantitative data to answer questions of interest.

Laura Miller (1997) used a mix of ethnographic and survey methods to study gender harassment in the U.S. Army. Keeping women out of jobs that have been traditionally reserved for men is *gender* harassment; asking women for sex in return for a shot at one of those jobs is *sexual* harassment. (Gender harassment need not involve sexual harassment, or vice versa.)

Miller spent nearly 2 years collecting data at eight army posts and at two training centers in the United States where war games are played out on simulated battlefields. She lived in Somalia with U.S. Army personnel for 10 days, in Macedonia for a week, and in Haiti for 6 days during active military operations in those countries. Within the context of participant observation, she did unstructured interviewing, in-depth interviewing, and group interviewing. Her group interviews were spontaneous: over dinner with a group of high-ranking officers; sitting on her bunk at night, talking to her roommates; in vehicles, bouncing between research sites, with the driver, guide, protocol officer, translator, and guard (Miller, personal communication).

It turns out that "forms of gender harsassment" in the U.S. Army is one of those cultural domains that people recognize and think about, but for which people have no ready list in their heads. You can't just ask people: "List the kinds of gender harassment." From her ethnographic interviews, though, Miller was able to derive what she felt was just such a list, including:

1. *resistance* to authority (hostile enlisted men ignore orders from women officers);
2. *constant scrutiny* (men pick up on every mistake that women make and use those mistakes to criticize the abilities of women in general);
3. *gossip and rumors* (women who date many men are labeled "sluts," women who don't date at all are labeled "dykes," and any woman can easily be unjustly accused of "sleeping her way to the top");
4. *outright sabotage* of women's tools and equipment on work details; and
5. *indirect threats* against women's safety (talking about how women would be vulnerable to rape if they were to go into combat).

This list emerges from qualitative research—hanging out, talking to people and gaining their trust, and generally letting people know that you're in for the long haul with them. If you are trying to develop programs to correct things that are wrong with a program, then this list, derived entirely from participant observation, is enough. An education program to counter gender harassment against women in the U.S. Army must include something about each of the problems that Miller identified.

Although ethnographic methods are enough to *identify* the problems and processes— the what and the how of culture—ethnography can't tell you *how much* each problem and process counts. Yes, enlisted army men can and do sabotage army women's tools and equipment on occasion. How often? Ethnography can't help with that one. Yes, men do sometimes resist the authority of women officers. How often? Ethnography can't help there, either.

Fortunately, Miller also collected questionnaire data—from a quota sample of 4,100 men and women, Whites and Blacks, officers and enlisted personnel. In those data, 19% of enlisted men and 18% of male noncommissioned officers (like sergeants) said that women should be treated exactly like men and should serve in the combat units just like men, but just 6% of enlisted women and 4% of female noncommissioned officers agreed with this sentiment. You might conclude, Miller says, that men are more supportive than women are of equality for women in combat roles. Some men with whom Miller spoke, however, said that women should be given the right to serve in combat *so that, once and for all, everyone will see that women can't cut it.*

Are men really what Miller called "hostile proponents" of equality for women? Could that be why the statistics show so many more men in favor of women serving in combat units? Miller went back to her questionnaire data: About 20% of men in her survey said that women should be assigned to combat units just like men were—but almost to a man they also said that putting women into combat units would reduce the military's effectiveness.

In other words, the numerical analysis showed that Miller's concept of "hostile proponent of equality" was correct. This subtle concept advances our understanding considerably of how gender harassment against women works in the U.S. Army.

Did you notice the constant feedback between ethnographic and survey data here?

The ethnography produced ideas for policy recommendations and for the content for a questionnaire. The questionnaire data illuminated and validated many of the things that the ethnographer learned during participant observation. Those same survey data produced anomalies—things that didn't quite fit with the ethnographer's intuition. More ethnography turned up an explanation for the anomalies. And so on. Ethnographic and survey data combined produce more insight than either does alone.

FURTHER READING

Street ethnography: Agar (1973); Connolly and Ennew (1996); Fleisher (1995); Gigengack (2000); Kane and Mason (2001); Lambert et al. (1995); Weppner (1977).

Chicago School of ethnography: Abbot (1997); Bulmer (1984); Lofland (1983).

Participant observation fieldwork: A. Anderson (2003); Atkinson et al. (2001); Behar (1996); Bogdan (1972); Burawoy (1991); DeWalt and DeWalt (2002); Fenno (1990); Fine and Sandstrom (1988); Gummerson (2000); Kirk and Miller (1986); Lofland (1976); Schatz (2009); C. D. Smith and Kornblum (1996); Spradley (1980); Stocking (1983); Woods (1986).

Rapid ethnographic assessment: Baker (1996a, 1996b); Beebe (2001); Bentley et al. (1988); D'Antona et al. (2008). For more on the focused ethnographic study method, see Hudelson (1994); G. H. Pelto (1992); P. J. Pelto (1994); Scrimshaw and Gleason (1992); Scrimshaw and Hurtado (1987); Trotter et al. (2001).

Gatekeepers: Harrington (2003); Kawulich (in press); Maginn (2007); Rashid (2007); Sanghera and Thapar-Björkert (2008); Wanat (2008).

Using interpreters: Borchgrevink (2003); Hsieh (2008); Jentsch (1998).

Language and fieldwork: Herzfeld (1983, 2009a); Owusu (1978); Werner (1994); Winchatz (2006).

Studying your own culture; indigenous research: Altorki and El-Sohl (1988); Fahim (1982); Messerschmidt (1981); Stephenson and Greer (1981); Zaman (2008).

Sex and fieldwork: Kulick and Willson (1995); Lewin and Leap (1996); Markowitz and Ashkenazi (1999).

Dangerous fieldwork: Belousov et al. (2007); Lee (1995); Lee-Treweek and Linkogle (2000); Nordstrom and Robben (1995); Sampson and Thomas (2003).

Culture shock: Bochner (2000); Furnham and Bochner (1986); Mumford (1998).

13

Field Notes and Database Management

Those who want to use qualitative methods because they seem easier
than statistics are in for a rude awakening.

—Taylor and Bogdan 1984:53

Anthropologists collect many kinds of data. Some collect survey data; others collect audio and video recordings or networks or caches of personal letters. . . . But all anthropologists take field notes. In this chapter, I focus on how to write field notes and how to handle other kinds of material—like newspaper clippings and photos—that we accumulate during fieldwork. The lessons about coding and analyzing field notes apply just as well to transcripts of interviews and to other textual data, which we'll take up in chapter 19.

ABOUT FIELD NOTES

Plan to spend 2–3 hours every working day of a participant observation study writing up field notes, working on your diary, and coding interviews and notes. Ralph Bolton asked 34 anthropologists about their field note practices; they reported spending anywhere from 1.5 hours to 7 hours a day on write-up (1984:132).

Remember that it takes twice as long to write up notes *about* a recorded interview as it does to conduct an interview in the first place. You have to listen to a recorded interview at least once before you can write up the essential notes from it, and then it takes as long again to get the notes down. If you need full transcriptions of interviews, plan to spend around 6 hours for each hour of interview, assuming that the recording is clear, the interview is in your own language, and you have a transcribing machine with a foot pedal. You can cut transcription time in half by using voice recognition software (more about this back in chapter 8, and see appendix E).

Every colleague with whom I've ever discussed this agrees that it's best to set aside a time each day for working on your notes. And don't sleep on your notes. It's easy to forget material that you want in your notes if you don't write them up in the afternoon or evening each day. The same goes for your own thoughts and impressions of events. If you don't write them up every day, while they are fresh, you'll forget them.

This means that you shouldn't get embroiled in a lot of activities that prevent you from writing up field notes. There are plenty of exceptions to this rule. Here's one. You are studying how families create culture by telling and retelling certain stories. You sit down to write up the day's field notes and you get a call from a key informant who tells you to come right on over to meet her father who is leaving on a trip in the morning and wants to tell you himself the story she had told you earlier about his experience as a refugee during World War II. You couldn't possibly turn that one down. But remember, it's easy to let doing anything except writing notes become the norm rather than the exception.

Create many small notes rather than one long, running commentary. Make many separate note files, rather than adding to the same humongous file day after day. You can have one file for each day, or you can have files for each interview or each event you attend.

There are two radically different styles when it comes to writing field notes. Some people like to immerse themselves completely in the local culture and concentrate on the experience. They write up field notes when and as they find the time. Most ethnographers advocate writing up field notes every day, while you are still capable of retrieving detail about the day's events and interactions. I've done both and, like Miles and Huberman (1994), I'm convinced that obsessiveness about writing field notes is the way to go.

HOW TO WRITE FIELD NOTES

The method I present here for making and coding field notes was developed and tested by the late Michael Kenny and me, between 1967 and 1971, when we ran those NSF-supported field schools in cultural anthropology that I described in chapter 12. Kenny and I relied initially on our own experience with field notes, and we borrowed freely from the experience of many colleagues. The method we developed—involving jottings, a diary, a daily log, and three kinds of formal notes—was used by 40 field-school participants in the United States and in Mexico and by others since then.

Two things can be said about the method I'm going to lay out here: (1) It works; and (2) It's not the only way to do things. If you do field research, you'll develop your own style of writing notes and you'll add your own little tricks as you go along. Still, the method described here will help you work systematically at taking field notes and it will allow you to search through them quickly and easily to look for relations in your data. I wish I had used this method when I was doing my own M.A. and Ph.D. fieldwork—and I wish that computers and database management systems had been available then, too.

FOUR TYPES OF FIELD NOTES

You'll write four kinds of notes in fieldwork: **jottings**, a diary, a log, and field notes proper.

Jottings

Field jottings—what Roger Sanjek calls **scratch notes** (1990:96)—are what get you through the day. Human memory is a very poor recording device, especially for the kind of details that make the difference between good and so-so ethnographic research. Keep a note pad with you at all times and make field jottings on the spot. This applies to both formal and informal interviews in bars and cafés, in homes and on the street.

It also applies to things that just strike you as you are walking along. Jottings will provide you with the trigger you need to recall a lot of details that you don't have time to write down while you're observing events or listening to an informant. Even a few key words will jog your memory later. Remember: *If you don't write it down, it's gone.*

Clearly, there are times when you just can't take notes. Morris Freilich did research in the 1950s with the Mohawks in Brooklyn, New York, and on the Caughnanaga Reservation, 10 miles south of Montreal. He did a lot of participant observation in a bar and, as Freilich tells it, every time he pulled out a notebook his audience became hostile. So,

Freilich kept a small notebook in his hip pocket and would periodically duck into the men's room at the bar to scribble a few jottings (Freilich 1977:159).

William Sturtevant used stubby little pencils to take furtive notes; he found the technique so useful, he published a note about it in the *American Anthropologist* (1959). When Hortense Powdermaker did her research on race relations in Mississippi in 1932, she took surreptitious notes on sermons at African American churches. "My pocketbook was large," she said, "and the notebook in it was small" (1966:175).

Every fieldworker runs into situations where it's impossible to take notes. It is always appropriate to be sensitive to people's feelings, and it is sometimes a good idea to just listen attentively and leave your notebook in your pocket. You'd be surprised, though, how few of these situations there are. Don't talk yourself into not jotting down a few notes on the incorrect assumption that people won't like it if you do.

The key is to take up the role of researcher immediately when you arrive at your field site, whether that site is a peasant village in a developing nation or a corporate office in Chicago. Let people know from the first day you arrive that you are there to study their way of life. Don't try to become an inconspicuous participant rather than what you really are: an observer who wants to participate as much as possible. Participant observation means that you try to *experience* the life of your informants to the extent possible; it doesn't mean that you try to melt into the background and *become* a fully accepted member of a culture other than your own.

It's usually impossible to do that anyway. After decades of coming and going in Indian villages in Mexico, I still stick out like a sore thumb and never became the slightest bit inconspicuous. Be honest with people and keep your note pad out as much of the time as possible. Ask your informants for their permission to take notes while you are talking with them. If people don't want you to take notes, they'll tell you.

Or they may tell you to take notes when you don't want to. Paul Killworth studied the social organization of the British Army. Because notebooks are, as he says, "part of Army uniform," he was able to go anywhere with his notebook in hand and take notes freely. But if he put his notebook aside for more than a few minutes, soldiers would ask him if he was getting lazy. "More than one relaxing moment," he says, "was stopped by someone demanding that I write something down" (1997:5).

Or they may ask to see your notes. A student researcher in one of our field schools worked in a logging camp in Idaho. He would write up his notes at night from the jottings he took all day. Each morning at 6:00 A.M. he nailed the day's sheaf of notes (along with a pen on a string) to a tree for everyone to look at. Some of the men took the time to scribble helpful (or amusing or rude) comments on the notes. If you use this technique, watch out for the CNN effect. That's when people tell you things they want to tell everyone because they know you're going to broadcast whatever they say. This is a disaster if you're trying to make everybody around you feel confident that you're not going to blab about them.

Even when people get accustomed to your constant jottings, you can overdo it. Emerson et al. (1995:23) cite the following field note from an ethnographer who was studying divorce negotiations:

> On one occasion when finishing up a debriefing . . . [the mediator] began to apply some eye make-up while I was finishing writing down some observations. She flashed me a mock disgusted look and said, "Are you writing *this* down too!" indicating the activity with her eye pencil.

The Diary

Notes are based on observations that will form the basis of your publications. A diary, on the other hand, is personal. It's a place where you can run and hide when things get tough. You absolutely need a diary in any ethnography project. It will help you deal with loneliness, fear, and other emotions that make fieldwork difficult.

A diary chronicles how you feel and how you perceive your relations with others around you. If you are really angry at someone, you should write about it—in your diary. Jot down emotional highs and lows while they're happening, if you can, and write them up in your diary at the end of the day. During data analysis, your diary will become an important professional document. It will give you information that will help you interpret your field notes and will make you aware of your personal biases.

Dennis McGilvray (1989) did fieldwork in Akkaraipattu, Sri Lanka in 1969–71. Here is an excerpt from his diary:

> January 7, 1970. Akkaraipattu. A miserable night indeed. Slight fever, humidity, and mosquitoes. Abuthahir doesn't come at 5:00 A.M. as he promised. But at 6:00 A.M., just as I was finally getting to sleep, he came to slaughter the cow to inaugurate the house. The whole spectacle was quite bloody and aroused deep sympathy from me for the poor cow. A mob of 75 children plus various old adults assemble to watch the butchering and to watch me. Mainly me. What little appetite I had soon vanished, and I basically felt sick, but nonetheless I had to endure endless questions and invasions of my morning bathing and shaving ritual. It seems that word of my camera, typewriter, and tape recorder has spread for miles around. And everyone also knows I am getting a jeep, and they all want reservations for rides. In a more healthy state, I would be able to tolerate the speechless scrutiny of my every action, but this morning I came close to blowing my lid.
>
> February 18, 1970. Akkaraipattu. For the first time, really, since being in Akk, I would love to have a drink. Just a nice highball with ice, nothing too powerful. I am weary. It was another of those days when people grab me by the tongue and won't let go. It's what I need to learn Tamil, I know, but it is often mindwracking and definitely like brainwashing. Right now, after everyone has finally gone and I am alone at last, I wish I could take a hot bath and crawl into a soft cool bed (dry, too) with clean sheets. But I can't: everything, my sleeping bag included, is slightly damp from the rain. The mosquitoes and sundry bugs are waiting for me, and the bed still has no mattress so I sleep on planks. What a drag. I still feel as if I am not well-enough coordinated in studying Tamil: it is all just bits and pieces. "The Tamil Chef," latest installment. Samitamby, my Barber neighbor, hailed me to the back fence again for another culinary delicacy. This time it was tortoise eggs and a bunch of green leaves. 'Vitamin A and calcium!' he exhorted, brandishing the clump of leaves. Palani (my Tamil cook), under strong pressure from Samitamby, laced every item for lunch with these damn leaves, which have zero taste whatsoever. As for the eggs, I tried the omelet but couldn't take the boiled eggs: they are still soft when cooked and look like rancid cheese fon[due] inside . . . .

Franz Boas got engaged to Marie Krackowizer in May 1883, just 3 weeks before beginning his first field trip. It was a grueling 15 months on Baffin Island and at sea. Boas missed German society terribly and, although he couldn't mail the letters, he wrote about 500 pages to his fiancée. Here is an excerpt from his diary:

> December 16, north of Pangnirtung. My dear sweetheart. . . . Do you know how I pass these long evenings? I have a copy of Kant with me, which I am studying, so that I shall not be so completely uneducated when I return. Life here really makes one dull and stupid. . . . I have to blush when I remember that during our meal tonight I thought

how good a pudding with plum sauce would taste. But you have no idea what an effect privations and hunger, real hunger, have on a person. Maybe Mr. Kant is a good antidote! The contrast is almost unbelievable when I remember that a year ago I was in society and observed all the rules of good taste, and tonight I sit in this snow hut with Wilhelm and an Eskimo eating a piece of raw, frozen seal meat which had first to be hacked up with an axe, and greedily gulping my coffee. Is that not as great a contradiction as one can think of? (Cole 1983:29)

When Malinowski was trapped in the Trobriand Islands during World War I, he too, missed his fiancée and European society and occasionally lashed out at the Trobrianders in his diary (Malinowski 1967:253–54). Fieldwork in another culture is an intense experience, but don't think that you have to be stranded in Sri Lanka or the Arctic or Melanesia for things to get intense.

Your diary will give you an outlet for writing things that you don't want to become part of a public record. Publication of Malinowski's and Boas's diaries have helped make all fieldworkers aware that they are not alone in their frailties and self-doubts.

The Log

A log is a running account of how you plan to spend your time, how you actually spend your time, and how much money you spent. A good log is the key to doing systematic fieldwork and to collecting both qualitative and quantitative data on a systematic basis.

A field log should be kept in bound books of blank, lined pages. Some of my students have been able to use PDAs with schedule-planning apps for their logs, but there's something to be said for a big, clunky logbook, at least 6″ × 8″ in size so that you can see at a glance what your agenda is as you have that first cup of coffee in the morning.

Each day of fieldwork, whether you're out for a year or a week, should be represented by a double page of the log. The pages on the left should list what you *plan* to do on any given day. The facing pages will recount what you *actually* do each day.

Begin your log on pages 2 and 3. Put the date on the top of the even-numbered page to the left. Then, go through the entire notebook and put the successive dates on the even-numbered pages. By doing this in advance, even the days on which you "do nothing," or are away from your field site, will have double log pages devoted to them.

The first day or two that you make a log you will use only the right-hand pages where you keep track of where you go, who you see, and what you spend. Some people like to carry their logs around with them. Others prefer to jot down the names of the people they run into or interview, and enter the information into their logs when they write up their notes in the evening. Keep a file of 25-word profiles on as many people you meet as you can.

You can start by jotting profiles on index cards (one for each person you meet) and then moving the profile to your computer when you write your field notes. Before you go into any second or third interview, look up the key biographical information you have about the person (PDAs are perfect for this sort of thing). During the first couple of minutes of the interview, work in a comment that shows you remember some of those key bio-facts. You'll be surprised how far that'll take you.

Jot down the times that you eat and what you eat, and write down who you eat with and how much you spend on all meals away from your house. You'd be surprised at how much you learn from this, too.

After a day or two, you will begin to use the left-hand sheets of the log. As you go through any given day, you will think of many things that you want to know but can't resolve on the spot. Write those things down in your jot book or in your log. When you write up your field notes, think about who you need to interview, or what you need to observe, regarding each of the things you wondered about that day.

Right then and there, open your log and commit yourself to finding each thing out at a particular time on a particular day. If finding something out requires that you talk to a particular person, then put that person's name in the log, too. If you don't know the person to talk to, then put down the name of someone whom you think can steer you to the right person.

Suppose you're studying a school system. It's April 5 and you are talking to MJR, a fifth-grade teacher. She tells you that since the military government took over, children have to study politics for 2 hours every day and she doesn't like it. Write a note to yourself in your log to ask mothers of some of the children about this issue and to interview the school principal.

Later on, when you are writing up your notes, you may decide not to interview the principal until after you have accumulated more data about how mothers in the community feel about the new curriculum. On the left-hand page for April 23 you note: "target date for interview with school principal." On the left-hand page of April 10 you note: "make appointment for interview on 23rd with school principal." For April 6 you note: "need interviews with mothers about new curriculum."

As soon as it comes to you that you need to know how many kilowatt hours of electricity were burned in a village, or the difference in price between fish sold off a boat and the same fish sold in the local market, commit yourself *in your log to a specific time* when you will try to get answers to your questions. Whether the question you think of requires a formal appointment, or a direct, personal observation, or an informal interview in a bar, write the question down in one of the left-hand pages of your log.

Don't worry if the planned activity log you create for yourself winds up looking nothing like the activities you actually engage in from day to day. Frankly, you'll be lucky to do half the things you think of to do, much less do them when you want to. The important thing is to fill those left-hand pages, as far out into the future as you can, with specific information that you need and specific tasks you need to perform to get that information.

This is not just because you want to use your time effectively, but because the process of building a log forces you to think hard about the questions you really want to answer in your research and the data you really need. You will start any field research project knowing some of the questions you are interested in. But those questions may change; you may add some and drop others—or your entire emphasis may shift.

The right-hand pages of the log are for recording what you actually accomplish each day. As I said, you'll be appalled at first at how little resemblance the left-hand and the right-hand pages have to one another. You'll get over it. Just keep reminding yourself that good fieldwork does not depend on the punctuality of informants or on your ability to do all the things you want to do. It depends on your systematic work over a period of time. If some informants do not show up for appointments (and often they won't), you can evaluate whether or not you really need the data you thought you were going to get from them. If you do need the data, put a note on the left-hand page for that same day, or for the next day, to contact the informant and reschedule the appointment.

If you still have no luck, you may have to decide whether it's worth more of your time to track down a particular person or a particular piece of information. Your log will tell you how much time you've spent on it already and will make the decision easier. There's plenty of time for everything when you think you've got months stretching ahead of you.

But you only have a finite amount of time in any fieldwork project to get useful data, and the time goes very quickly.

FIELD NOTES

And now, about field notes. . . . Let's face it: After a hard day trekking all over [town] [the village] [the jungle] [the desert] interviewing people, hanging out, and recording behavior, it's hard to sit down and write up field notes. Sometimes, it's downright intimidating. We know this much about field notes for sure: The faster you write up your observations, the more detail you can get down. More is better. Much more is much better (except, of course, when data are systematically biased, in which case more is decidedly worse) (box 13.1).

BOX 13.1

SOLAR CHARGING FIELD COMPUTERS

If you're doing fieldwork in an area without electricity, the choices are: Take notes by hand or use solar chargers for your computer. Laptops, and even notebook computers, require a lot of power, which makes solar charging tough. Batteries for PDAs can be charged from portable solar cells. With wireless keyboards and lots of apps, PDAs are becoming more useful as replacements for laptops in fieldwork.

You can't be too paranoid about backing up your notes. E-mail copies of them to a couple of trusted friends or colleagues (encrypt the notes if you need to), or send them CDs if you don't have any access to the Internet. Ask them to print a copy of your notes for you, so you've got a hard copy somewhere in case your computer is stolen *and* all your backup disks are destroyed in a fire at the same time. Think this can't happen? Think again. Trees are a renewable resource. Make paper backups. And upload your notes to an Internet server for good measure.

There are three kinds of field notes: **methodological notes**, descriptive notes, and analytic notes.

Methodological Notes

Methodological notes deal with technique in collecting data. If you work out a better way to keep a log than I've described here, don't just *use* your new technique; write it up in your field notes and publish a paper about your technique so others can benefit from your experience. (See appendix E for a list of professional journals that publish articles on research methods in the social and behavioral sciences.) If you find yourself spending too much time with marginal people in the culture, make a note of it, and discuss how that came to be. You'll discover little tricks of the trade, like the "uh-huh" technique discussed in chapter 8. (Remember that one? It's where you learn how and when to grunt encouragingly to keep an interview going.) Write up notes about your discoveries. Mark all these notes with a big "M" at the top—M for "method."

Methodological notes are also about your own growth as an instrument of data collection. Collecting data is always awkward when you begin a field project, but it gets easier as you become more comfortable in a new culture. During this critical period of adjustment, you should intellectualize what you're learning about doing fieldwork by taking methodological notes.

When I first arrived in Greece in 1960, I was invited to dinner at "around 7 P.M." When I arrived at around 7:15 (what I thought was a polite 15 minutes late), I was embarrassed to find that my host was still taking a bath. I should have known that he really meant "around 8 P.M." when he said "around 7." My methodological note for the occasion simply stated that I should not show up for dinner before 8 P.M. in the future.

Some weeks later, I figured out the general rules for timing of evening activities, including cocktails, dinner, and late-night desserts in the open squares of Athens. Robert Levine has studied the psychology of time by asking people around the world things like "How long would you wait for someone who was late for a lunch appointment?" On average, Brazilians say they'd wait 62 minutes. On average, says Levine, "Americans would need to be back at their office two minutes *before*" the late Brazilian lunch was just getting underway (Levine 1997:136).

When I began fieldwork with the Ñähñu people of central Mexico in 1962, I was offered *pulque* everywhere I went. I tried to refuse politely; I couldn't stand the stuff. But people were very insistent and seemed offended if I didn't accept the drink. Things were particularly awkward when I showed up at someone's house and there were other guests there. Everyone enjoyed *pulque* but me, and most of the time people were too poor to have beer around to offer me.

At that time, I wrote a note that people "felt obliged by custom to offer *pulque* to guests." I was dead wrong. As I eventually learned, people were testing me to see if I was affiliated with the Summer Institute of Linguistics (SIL), an evangelical missionary group (and nondrinkers of alcohol) that had its regional headquarters in the area where I was working.

The SIL is comprised of many excellent linguists who produce books and articles on the grammar of the nonwritten languages of the world and translations of the Bible into those languages. There was serious friction between the Indians who had converted to Protestantism and those who remained Catholic. It was important for me to disassociate myself from the SIL, so my methodological note discussed the importance of conspicuously consuming alcohol and tobacco to identify myself as an anthropologist and not as a missionary.

Nine years later, in 1971, I still couldn't stand *pulque*—and I was sure that drinking out of those common gourds that were passed around was what sent me to the hospital in 1968. I started carrying a couple of six packs of beer in the car and offering it to people who offered me *pulque*. This worked and the methods lesson was clear: Beer kept my reputation of independence from the SIL intact and was universally accepted because beer was costly, and prestigious, compared to *pulque*.

Eight years later, in 1979, I read that William Partridge had a similar predicament during his work in Colombia (Kimball and Partridge 1979:55). Everywhere Partridge went, it seems, people offered him beer, even at 7:00 A.M. He needed an acceptable excuse, he said, to avoid spending all his waking hours getting drunk.

After a few months in the field, Partridge found that telling people "*Estoy tomando una pastilla*" ("I'm taking a pill") did the trick. Locally, the pill referred to in this phrase was used in treating venereal disease. Everyone knew that you didn't drink alcohol while you were taking this pill, and the excuse was perfect for adding a little virility boost to

Partridge's reputation. Partridge used his knowledge of local culture to get out of a tough situation.

Methodological notes, then, have to do with the conduct of field inquiry itself. You will want to make methodological notes especially when you do something silly that breaks a cultural norm. If you are feeling particularly sheepish, you might want to write those feelings into your diary where no one else will see what you've written, but you don't want to waste the opportunity to make a straightforward methodological note on such occasions, as well.

Descriptive Notes

Descriptive notes are the meat and potatoes of fieldwork. Most notes are descriptive and are from two sources: watching and listening. Interviews with informants produce acres of notes, especially if you use a recorder and later write down large chunks of what people say or even transcribe the interviews completely. Observations of processes, like feeding children, building a house, making beer, and so on, also produce a lot of notes. Descriptive field notes may contain birth records that you've copied out of a local church registry; or they may consist of summary descriptions of a village plaza, or an urban shopping mall, or any environmental features that you think are important.

The best way to learn to write descriptive field notes is to practice doing it with others who are also trying to learn. Get together with one or more partners and observe a process that's unfamiliar to all of you. It could be a church service other than one you've seen before, or it could be an occupational process that you've not witnessed. (I remember the first time I saw plasterers hang ceilings: They do it on stilts.)

Whatever you observe, try to capture in field notes the details of the behavior and the environment. Try to get down "what's going on." Then ask informants who are watching the ceremony or process to explain what's going on and try to get notes down on their explanation. Later, get together with your research partner(s) and discuss your notes with one another. You'll find that two or three people see much more than just one sees. You might also find that you and your partners saw the same things but wrote down different subsets of the same information.

Analytic Notes

You will write up fewer analytic notes than any other kind. This is where you lay out your ideas about how you think the culture you are studying is organized. Analytic notes can be about relatively minor things. When I finally figured out the rules for showing up on time for evening functions in Greece, that was worth an analytic note. And when I understood the rules that governed the naming of children, that was worth an analytic note, too.

As I said in chapter 2, in the section on theory, it took me almost a year to figure out why the casualty rate among Kalymnian sponge divers was going up, while the worldwide demand for natural sponges was going down. When it finally made sense, I sat down and wrote a long, long analytic field note about it. After thinking about the problem for many years, I finally understood why bilingual education in Mexico does not result in the preservation of Indian languages (it's a long story; see Bernard 1992). As the ideas developed, I wrote them up in a series of notes.

Analytic notes are the product of a lot of time and effort and may go on for several pages. They are often the basis for published papers or for chapters in dissertations and books. They will be the product of your understanding and that will come about through your organizing and working with descriptive and methodological notes over a period of time. Don't expect to write a great many analytic notes, but write them all your life, even (especially) after you are out of the field.

CODING FIELD NOTES

Gene Shelley (1992) studied people who suffer from end-stage kidney disease. Most patients are on hemodialysis. Some are on peritoneal dialysis. The "hemo" patients go to a dialysis center, several times a week, while the "pero" patients perform a dialysis (called continuous ambulatory peritoneal dialysis, or CAPD) on themselves several times a day.

Figure 13.1 shows three descriptive notes from Shelley's research. First, there's a delimiter (she used the dollar sign) that marks the beginning of each note. This lets you pack all the notes together in one big file so a word processor or text analysis program knows where notes begin and end. Next is a unique number that identifies the note in a continuing sequence, starting with 0001. Next is the date.

Then come some numbers that refer to theme codes. In note 3, this is preceded by a location indicator. Finally, at the end of the codes at the top of each field note, there's a cryptic indicator of the person to whom Shelley attributes the information—except for note 3, which was based on observation (box 13.2).

Theme Codes: The OCM

Shelley used a modified version of the *Outline of Cultural Materials*, or OCM, to code her field notes. The OCM was developed originally by G. P. Murdock in 1950 as a way to index and organize ethnographic materials in the Human Relations Area Files (more about HRAF and the OCM in the section on content analysis in chapter 19). The OCM has gone through several editions over the years, and the latest edition is available online at http://www.yale.edu/hraf/outline.htm (Murdock et al. 2004 [1961]).

There are 91 big cultural domains in the OCM, in blocks of 10, from 10 to 91. Block 58, for example, covers marriage with codes for nuptials (585), divorce (586), and so on. Other major domains are things like kinship, entertainment, social stratification, war, health, sex, and religious practices. Every project is unique, so you'll need codes that aren't in the OCM, but you can add decimals (or words) and extend the codes forever. Table 13.1 shows Shelley's adaptation of the OCM code 757 (medical therapy):

Don't be put off by the lengthiness of the OCM coding list. That is its strength. Lots of anthropologists have used the OCM over the years to code their field notes and other materials. George Foster coded his 50 years of notes on the Mexican community of Tzintzuntzán using the OCM, and Robert V. Kemper uses it to code the data that he's collecting on the same community (George Foster, personal communication; Kemper 2002:289). John Honigman used it in his fieldwork on Canadian Indians; the 37 field researchers in Clyde Kluckhohn's Comparative Study of Values in Five Cultures Project all used the OCM to code their notes, as did the fieldworkers on the Cornell University team project studying a village in India (Sanjek 1990:108, 232, 331). You'll only use a fraction of the codes on any given project, but once you start using it in the field, you'll quickly find yourself building supplemental coding schemes to fit your particular needs.

Figure 13.2 shows how Gordon Gibson (of the Smithsonian) used the OCM to code a series of ethnographic films on the Himba, a cattle-herding society in Namibia (in Kreiss and Stockton 1980:287). The film coded in figure 13.2 is about a wedding, so each piece is coded 585, the OCM code for nuptials. Where the hut is seen, the code for dwellings (342) is inserted. Where the film shows people eating meat, the codes 262 (diet) and 264

$ 615 8-16-89: 757.3; Dr. H

Dr. H explains that in peritoneal dialysis you exchange 2 liters of fluid several times a day (based on body size). Women do it about 3 times and men about 4 times because of larger body size. People mostly do a "dwell" for about 8 hours overnight while they sleep (fluid is inflowed into peritoneal cavity and allowed to sit there overnight). Then they do peritoneal dialysis when they wake up and another time or two during the day. Peritoneal dialysis patients are pretty close to being healthy. They have to take medication but you cannot tell them from healthy people, he says.

$ 742 8-30-89: 57.3, 757.5; Nurse Ralph B.

CAPD training takes about a week to 10 days. During this time, the patient comes in every day and receives training. Ralph thinks that when the whole family comes in for the training, the patients do better. They have about 20 CAPD patients right now. Ralph said there are 3 types of CAPD patients: (1) those patients who are already on hemo and in pretty good shape, usually well-motivated. (2) those who are late getting started and are in trouble (medically) and are hurriedly trying to learn the procedure. (It takes 2 weeks to get a catheter inserted and then have it heal. Since this surgery is viewed as "elective surgery," it can be bumped and rescheduled.) Only after surgery and healing can the training take place. (3) those who have lost a kidney which was transplanted. They are just waiting for another kidney and they view CAPD as temporary and are not that motivated to learn it because they think they won't be on it long.

$ 876 12-6-89: Waiting Room 571; 580; 580.7; 580.1; 264; 12;

While waiting to talk to Dr. H, I sat in the hemodialysis waiting room. I watched and listed to patients (and waiting family) who were waiting to get on the dialysis machines. They were talking about how sometimes the staff is rough with them when putting the needles in to get the vein access. One guy said the needle went once "right into his bone." Another guy said "the girl had to try 7 times" to get his blood and he was about to hit her. (The nurse said at the time, "I know this hurts.") Another woman threatened physical harm to technicians who draw blood roughly. One patient mentioned that sometimes they have to get different vein access sites (i.e., the groin or the top of the foot). They were all talking, not always to anyone in particular (but sometimes they were). They were talking in a way so that everyone in the room could be in the conversation if they wanted to.

FIGURE 13.1.

Field notes from Gene Shelley's study of kidney disease patients (1992). Reproduced by permission.

(eating) are inserted. In the frame at 11:45:10, the code for visiting (574) appears, and in the two earlier frames, the code for childhood activities (857) is inserted. When Gibson did this work in the 1970s, the database was held on a mainframe. Today, you would just watch an ethnographic film on your computer and enter codes as you go.

Many people find the use of number codes distracting. Matthew Miles and Michael Huberman (1994), authors of a wonderful book on qualitative data analysis, advocated

BOX 13.2

CODING VERSUS INDEXING

I want to make clear the three different uses of the word "code." When I say: "Use codes for places and informant names," the word "code" means an *encryption device*. The object is to hide information, not dispense it. When William Partridge interviewed cannabis growers in Colombia, he identified the texts by a letter code and kept the only copy of his notes in a locked trunk (Kimball and Partridge 1979:174). You don't have to be interviewing cannabis growers to be paranoid about keeping your informants' identity secret. You never know what seemingly innocuous information might embarrass or hurt someone if your data fall into the wrong hands.

When I say: "Code your notes for the themes you develop in your analysis," the word "code" means an *indexing device*. Suppose you do 100 interviews with women about their birthing experience. If you stick the code PAIN into the text whenever a woman mentions anything about pain or about feeling hurt, you'd be using the code PAIN as an indexing device—that is, as a way to find your way back to all the places in the text where anything about pain is mentioned. It's just like an index to a book. It says that "sampling" is on page 237 and sure enough, when you go to page 237, you find you're reading about sampling.

The third meaning of the word "code" is a *measurement device*. Suppose you make judgments about the amount of pain—by counting words like "agony" as indicating more pain than words like "distress" or by looking at the content and meaning of the text and counting "It was painful, but I got through it" as indicating less pain than "I prayed I would die." You might use codes like LO-PAIN, MID-PAIN, or HI-PAIN and in this case, you'd be using codes for more than nominal measurement.

the use of words or mnemonics that look like the original concept. Like many researchers, they find that mnemonic codes (like ECO for economics, DIV for divorce, and so on) are easier to remember than numbers. Figure 13.3 shows an example of how to do this.

Another value of using your own codes is that they develop naturally from your study and you'll find it easy to remember them as you code your notes each day. Strauss and

Table 13.1   Shelley's (1992) Adaptation of the OCM Code 757 on Medical Therapy

757.1	Transplantation
757.2	Hemodialysis
757.3	CAPD (peritoneal dialysis)
757.4	Home dialysis
757.5	Adjustment to dialysis
757.6	Compliance with medical regime
757.7	Machinery involved in dialysis
757.8	Medicines
757.9	Medical test results
757.91	HIV test results

13 GIBSON (film)		E-5 (1961) 1969 HIMBA	
11:09:29	Picture	Bride and companion walk toward hut, then bride and unmarried girl drop to their knees and crawl into hut. People are seen sitting in front of hut as the two disappear inside.	585* 342
	Sound	The bride and their companions solemnly return to the hut in Vesenga's village where she has been staying, and she and the unmarried girl enter the hut.	
11:29:30	Picture	People sitting and standing near hut.	585*
	Sound	Women and children of the village, and those visiting, from other villages, have gathered to sit near the bride.	342 574 857
11:42:22	Picture	Boys seated eating meat.	585*
	Sound	Young boys eat together.	262 857
11:45:10	Picture	Meat in basket and men seated, eating. A man standing and eating meat off a bone, places the bone on a bush. The groom is seated, his arms folded on his knees. He takes a piece of meat from a pail on the ground between his feet.	585* 264 574
	Sound	The bridegroom and his friends are still seated by the bower, where they are finishing.	

FIGURE 13.2.

Gibson's coding of the Himba films.

SOURCE: L. Kreiss and E. Stockton, "Using the Outline of Cultural Materials as a Basis for Indexing the Content of Ethnographic Films," *Behavior Science Research*, Vol. 15, pp. 281–93, 1980.

Corbin (1990:68) recommend **in vivo** codes as names for things. In vivo codes are catchy phrases or words used by informants. In his study of Alaskan fishermen, Jeffrey Johnson heard people talking about a "clown." The word turned out to be a terrific label for a type of person found in many organizations. The term emerged in vivo from the mouths of Johnson's informants. (More on in vivo coding in chapter 19).

If you use your own coding scheme, or if you modify an existing scheme (like the OCM), be sure to write up a verbose codebook in case you forget what "A5" or "EMP" or whatever-cute-abbreviations-you-dreamed-up-at-the-time-you-did-th e-coding mean.

And don't get too picky when you make up your own codes. Coding is supposed to be data reduction, not data proliferation. Mathew Miles was involved in a big ethnographic project to evaluate six schools. All the researchers developed their own codes and the code list quickly grew to 202 categories of actors, processes, organizational forms, and

---

412 MA XOR 101210 MIG WOM ECO

This is note number 412. It's about an informant named MA in these notes, and she is from a village you label XOR. The date is October 12, 2010, and the note is about migration from her village in search of work. The note is coded using abbreviations for themes as being about migration (MIG), about women (WOM), and about economics (ECO).

FIGURE 13.3.

Coding field notes with mnemonics.

efforts. Each of the six researchers insisted that his or her field site was unique and that the highly specialized codes were all necessary. It became impossible for anyone to use the unwieldy system, and they just stopped coding altogether (Miles 1983:123).

The important thing is not which coding scheme you use, it's that you code your notes and do it consistently. In most projects, the coding scheme takes shape as the notes are written. The scheme is revised a lot before it becomes stable. Some anthropologists, even those who use the OCM, wait a month or more, to see how their field notes are shaping up, before they think about how to code the notes.

ANALYZING FIELD NOTES

Until about 1980, field notes were all written on cards or sheets of paper and then hand-marked with codes indicating themes. Some people still like to write field notes on paper, but most fieldworkers type up their notes on a computer or PDA and then use a text analysis program to code those notes. Text analysis programs don't analyze anything, but they do take a lot of the drudgery out of coding and they make it easier to analyze your notes (box 13.3).

BOX 13.3

USING A WORD PROCESSOR TO CODE AND RETRIEVE FIELD NOTES

If all you want to do is find and retrieve notes about particular topics whenever you want, then a word processor is all you need. Just create a symbol that will never be used for anything except codes—perhaps the ampersand followed by a backslash, &\ Then use that symbol to tag material in your notes. For example, you might tuck the phrase "&\marriage" into your notes as an indicator that you're talking about marriage "about here." Then, when you want to look for chunks of text that deal with marriage, you just look for the code &\marriage.

Tucking tags like this into your notes lets you mark text that is about marriage, even though the word "marriage" might not be mentioned (as might be the case, say, in a description of a wedding ceremony).

You can also use the font features (bold, italics, color) of a word processor to code your notes. You'd be surprised at what you can do with a simple word processor. For more, see Ryan (2004) and La Pelle (2004). Lots more about finding and coding themes in texts in chapter 19.

I think it's best to start analyzing with the ocular scan method, or eyeballing. In this low-tech method, you go through your notes, reading them, one at a time. You live with them, read them over and over again, and eventually get a feel for what's in them. This is followed by the interocular percussion test, in which patterns jump out and hit you between the eyes. For some, nothing is more fun or efficient at this early stage of analysis than pawing through a sheaf of printed notes, moving them around on the floor, putting them into piles, and thinking about them. For others, printing notes is a waste of time and trees. They like to read through their notes on a screen and code on the fly. There is no single best way to analyze field notes. Figure out what you like and stay with it.

For me, a text analysis program is the way to go. You can ask questions like: "Find every note in which I used the word *woman* but only if I also used the word *migration* within three lines of the word *woman*." If you code your notes with themes, you can look for any combination of those, too. The mechanics are simple. The important thing is to decide what the themes are then to use those themes in coding your notes. We'll get the problem of finding themes in chapter 19.

DATABASE MANAGEMENT

What do you do if you have physical things, like photos or news clippings, rather than notes? Local newspapers are a great source of data about communities, but once you start clipping all the interesting stories, you quickly wind up with hundreds of pieces. And the same goes for photos. They are full of information, but—especially with digital photos—it's easy to accumulate a huge number of them.

Database management is the way to handle these kinds of data. Number your clippings or photos, starting with 00001, and set up a database using any of the popular programs, like Microsoft Access® or FileMaker Pro®. The records of the database will be the numbered items, from 1 to *n*. The fields of the database will include things like the name of the informant associated with each item, the place where you collected it, the date, and the topics associated with it, and so on. Some items may get one or two topical codes; others may need 10, so build at least 10 code spaces into the database.

When you ask the database "Which clippings are about palm oil?" or "Which photos are about old men in the plaza?" or "Which are about market sellers *and* about meat *and* about servants making purchases for others?" you'll get back answers like: "The information you want is on records 113, 334, 376, 819, 820, and 1,168."

Once you get accustomed to setting up databases, you'll wonder how you ever got along without them.

14

Direct and Indirect Observation

You can observe a lot by just watching.

—Yogi Berra 1964, cited in Berra and Garagiola 1998

Interviewing is a great way to learn about attitudes and values. And it's a great way to find out what people think they do. When you want to know what people *actually do*, however, there is no substitute for watching them or studying the physical traces their behavior leaves behind. This chapter is about **direct observation** (watching people and recording their behavior on the spot) and **indirect observation** (the archeology of human behavior).

There are two big strategies for direct observation of behavior. You can be blatant about it and **reactive**, or you can be unobtrusive and **nonreactive**. In reactive observation, people know that you are watching them and may play to their audience—you. You can wind up with data about what people want you to see and learn little about what people do when you're not around. In unobtrusive observation, you study people's behavior *without their knowing it*. This stops people from playing to an audience, but it raises tough ethical questions. We'll get to some of those problems later in this chapter.

We begin with the two most important methods for direct observation, **continuous monitoring** and **spot sampling** of behavior. Then we take up unobtrusive observation (and the ethical issues associated it), and, finally, indirect observation.

CM—CONTINUOUS MONITORING

In continuous monitoring, or CM, or **focal follows**, you watch a person, or group of people, and record their behavior as faithfully as possible. The technique was developed in the field of management by Charles Babbage, the 19th-century mathematician who invented the computer. He studied the behavior of workers in a factory and determined that a pound of number 11 straight pins (5,546 of them) should take exactly 7.6892 hours to make (Niebel 1982:4; original: Babbage 1835:184).

CM is widely used in assessing the quality of human interactions—between, for example, adolescent girls and their mothers (Baril et al. 2009), workers and employers (Sproull 1981), the police and civilians (Sykes and Brent 1983), clinical professors and young physicians (Graffam et al. 2008) (**Further Reading:** continuous monitoring).

CM is the core method of **ethology** (Hutt and Hutt 1970; Lorenz 1981). Most ethologists study nonhuman animals (everything from moths to fish to chimpanzees), but Darwin (1998 [1872]) used direct observation of facial expressions to study emotions in humans and animals—an area of interest ever since (Ekman 1973, 1980; Leeland 2008). CM is a mainstay in behavioral psychology for assessing anxieties and phobias (Harb et al. 2003), and it has been used to study how people eat (Stunkard and Kaplan 1977; Zive et al. 1998) and how people use architectural space (Bechtel 1977). CM is a staple method in the study of how hunters and fishermen make a living (Aswani 2005; Bird et al. 2009; Hawkes et al. 1991; Koster 2007) and how children learn to hunt and forage (Hewlett and Lamb 2005). CM is one of the all-around varsity methods (**Further Reading:** ethology and human ethology).

ETHOGRAMS

It is standard practice in ethology to develop an **ethogram**, or list of behaviors, for a species being studied. It's painstaking work. Lee and Brewis (2009) spent a summer doing pilot research to develop a list of 37 behaviors associated with foraging by children in a Mexican shantytown. Then they followed 20 children for a total of 15 hours each (watching each child for three blocks of about 5 hours at a time) coding for everything in their list of behaviors. The codes included things like begging, getting a gift of food from a peer, and getting money through informal employment. Some of the behaviors were: being in school, doing chores inside the house, and being en route to or from school or work and household. Figure 14.1 shows a part of one of their observations.

12:00	Father gives Carlos 1 peso
12:15	Leaves to play kites with friends, on way to the bakery where he works informally
12:34	Given a bakery basket to carry to the next neighborhood to sell door-to-door
13:09	Forages a medium orange from a neighborhood tree, and eats it while carrying the bread door-to-door (does not eat any of the bread)
13:20	Returns basket to baker, and is paid 4.5 pesos
13:29	Returns home, watches television
14:04	Gives his father 50 centavos
14:05	Goes to corner store alone, and uses remaining 5 pesos to purchase flavored corn chips (120 grams) and Tic-Tac candy (16 gram pack)
14:09	Shares chips and candy with his nephew (age 5 years) and friend (11 years), until all is eaten
14:30	Returns home

FIGURE 14.1.
Sequence of activities of "Carlos," age 11, Thursday, July 15, 2004 (a sunny day).
SOURCE: Lee and Brewis (2009:441).

Kneidinger et al. (2001) studied touching behavior in 119 mostly white, male baseball players and 52 mostly white, female softball players in six major universities in the southeastern United States. Kneidinger et al. developed an ethogram of 37 touching behaviors before they even launched their main study. The touching behaviors included things like tapping gloves, high fives, butt slaps, and chest grabs ("one participant grabs the front of the other participant's shirt").

The main study involved watching and recording 1,961 touching behaviors across 99 innings of baseball for the men and 1,593 touching behaviors across 63 innings of softball for the women. Among the interesting results: Men and women touched each other the same amount after winning games, but women touched each other more than men touched each other after losing games (Kneidinger et al. 2001:52).

CONTINUOUS MONITORING IN ANTHROPOLOGY

CM has a long and noble history in anthropology. When Eliot Chapple was still a student at Harvard in the 1930s, he built a device he called the "interaction chronograph" for recording on a rolling sheet of paper the minute features (facial expressions, gestures) of human interaction. The interaction chronograph is, as far as I can tell, the unheralded forerunner of the hand-held computer recording systems used for continuous monitoring in ethology, psychology, and anthropology today (Chapple 1940; Chapple and Donald 1947).

In 1949, John Roberts and a Zuni interpreter took turns sitting in one of the rooms of a Zuni house, simply dictating their observations into a tape recorder. (That recorder, by the way, was the size of a suitcase and weighed 30 pounds.) This went on for 5 days and produced data for a 75,000-word book, rich in detail about everyday Zuni life. Figure 14.2 shows some excerpts from Roberts's work.

People let Roberts park in their homes for 5 days because Roberts was a participant

---

0940

E1DaE1S09 is dressed in blue denim overalls and blue denim shirt. FaSiSoSo is wearing a cotton shirt, heavy trousers, jacket and oxfords. The girls are wearing dresses, socks, and shoes. 2Da24 has on a blouse, skirt, green socks, and oxfords.

0941-(FaSiSo37D)

YoDaSo1 came into SCR from ESCR carrying a little toy in his hand.

0945-(FaSiSo37d)

I intended going to the buck herd today to take out my bucks (rams). I was going to bring them down to Zuni to feed them to get them in good shape—but there is no time to go over there today. I think I will go tomorrow.

AdE1So27A went into ESCR, ENCR, and SER, but he had nothing to report.

Mo61 is still in SER shelling corn.

0950

Mo61 walks back into WNCR to build a fire in the WNCR cooking stove.

AdE1So27A says that she is going to make hominy with the stew.

3Da22 is mounting turquoise on sticks for grinding.

YoDaSo1 came into SCR a few moments ago with a homemade cardboard horse which had been cut out by YoDaHu22.

2Da2Da3 followed YoDaSo1.

This house is full of activity and the children are running back and forth. They are not playing outside today because the weather is poor.

E1Da28 is mounting turquoise on sticks in preparation for grinding. She has a fire going in WR, which is a very large room to heat.

FIGURE 14.2.

Excerpts from Roberts's observations of a Zuni household. Persons and things are identified by shorthand notation. For example, 2Da2Da3 is the family's second daughter who is 3 years old. Sequence begins at 9:40 A.M. and ends at 10:00 A.M.

SOURCE: J. M. Roberts, *Zuni Daily Life.* © 1965 [orig. 1956], HRAF Press. Reproduced with permission.

Table 14.1   Nutritional Behavior of Four Pilagá Indian Children

Behavior	Yorodaikolik (4 years)	Tanpani (8–9 years)	Naicho (6 years)	Deniki (15 months)
Given food	9	7	27	42
Deprived of food	7	0	2	4
Deprivation followed by restitution	1	0	1	2
Attempt made to deprive of food	2	1	1	4
Gives food	8	7	1	3
Withholds food	6	5	2	3
Deprives others of food	2	6	1	0
Attempts to deprive others of food	1	5	0	1
Receives part of a whole	0	1	0	4
Punished while eating	0	0	0	3
Total observations of each child from which these are taken	190	207	238	208

SOURCE: I. N. Mensh and J. Henry. 1953. Direct Observation and Psychological Tests in Anthropological Field Work. *American Anthropologist* 55(4): 466. http://www.anthrosource.net.

observer of Zuni life and had gained his informants' confidence. Even earlier, in 1936–37, Jules and Zunia Henry did fieldwork among the Pilagá Indians of Argentina. Among the data they collected was a set of direct observations of children. Table 14.1 shows the data from observations made on four children for 10 kinds of behaviors associated with eating and food sharing.

The data in table 14.1 were extracted from 843 observations of children's behavior. Here are two of those observations from the original data:

The three children of Diwa'i are feeding peacefully together. Deniki, the baby, waves his hand for food and mother gives him a small piece of palm dipped in fat. After eating a second piece he is given the breast.

Deniki, Nacho, and Soroi are together. Deniki is holding a dish with a very small quantity of cooked fruit in it. Soroi says, "Share it with me," and takes one fruit out of the dish. Naicho immediately snatches another one away violently, but not before Deniki has already taken one out, which he then offers to Naicho, appearing not to comprehend her action. (Mensh and Henry 1953:467)

The Zapotec Children Study

Douglas Fry used CM to study aggressive play among Zapotec children. From 1981 to 1983, Fry did 18 months of participant observation fieldwork in La Paz and San Andrés, two small Zapotec-speaking villages just 4 miles apart in the Valley of Oaxaca, Mexico. During the last 5 months of his research, Fry did direct, continuous monitoring of 24 children (3–8 years old) in each village. Before that, he visited almost all the households in the villages several times so that children had become accustomed to him when he began his intensive observation.

Fry describes his data collection procedures clearly:

The formal focal sampling observations were conducted between May and September of 1983. They represent each day of the week and encompass the daylight hour. Most observations (84%) were conducted within family compounds, although children were also observed in the streets, town squares, school yards, fields, and hills. I alternated sampling between the two communities on a weekly to biweekly basis. A total of 588 observations were conducted, resulting in an average of approximately 12 observations for each focal child (M = 12.25, *SD* = 6.21). On average, each focal child was observed for just over 3 hours (M = 3.13 hours, *SD* = 1.39 hours), resulting in a total of 150 hours of observation time for the entire sample. [It is common in scientific papers to report means and standard deviations; hence the M and *SD* figures in this paragraph. HRB]

Focal observations were narrated into a tape recorder carried in a small backpack or recorded on paper using a shorthand system. I recorded a running commentary of the behaviors engaged in by the focal child, using behavior elements defined in the previously developed ethogram. I moved with a focal child in order to maintain continuous visual contact (Altmann 1974), but did not remain so close as to interfere with actions or unduly attract the child's attention. Whenever a focal child engaged in any type of antagonistic behavior, the specifics of the interaction were noted, including identity of the interactant(s) and any facial expressions or gestures. For instance, interactions such as the following were recorded: Focal boy punches, pushes sister of 3 year old while laughing (sister does nothing in response). (Fry 1990:326–27)

Fry developed his ethogram of Zapotec children by watching them in public places before beginning his study of focal individuals. Based on 150 hours of focal child observation, Fry's data contain 764 episodes of what he calls "play aggression" and 85 episodes of "serious aggression."

Play aggression is a punch, kick, tackle, etc., accompanied by smiles, laughs, and play-faces. Serious aggression acts are episodes accompanied by low frowns, bared teeth, fixated gazes, and crying. Fry found that when girls initiated serious aggression, it was almost always with other girls (93% of cases). But when boys initiated serious aggression, it was just as likely to be with girls as with other boys (**Further Reading:** studying children under natural conditions) (box 14.1).

BOX 14.1

DIRECT OBSERVATION VERSUS SELF-REPORTS

Pearson (1990) used CM to study how Samoans in Western Samoa, American Samoa, and Honolulu used energy. Pearson had the idea that, as Samoans moved to Honolulu and became more urbanized, there would be changes in lifestyle and that these changes would show up in their energy intake and expenditure. Pearson asked people to recall their activities over the past 24 hours, and then, to check the **24-hour recall** data, he and a female assistant monitored 47 men and 43 women.

The team did 825 hours of observation and had their subjects in direct view 92% of the time. The estimates of energy expenditure from direct observation of the 47 men were 33%–80% lower than the estimates from the recall data. For women, the estimates were 27%–53% lower. Women had better recall of their activities, but men and women were both way off the mark, particularly in recalling their light-to-moderate work of the previous day. Pearson's work makes it clear that, when it comes to measuring energy expenditure, recall is not a good substitute for observation.

The Shopping Study

Martin Murtaugh (1985) used CM to study the use of arithmetic by grocery shoppers. He recruited 24 adults in Orange County, California. Accompanied by two observers, each informant wore a tape recorder while shopping at a supermarket. As the informants went about their shopping, they talked into the tape recorder about how they were deciding which product to buy, what size to choose, and so on.

One observer mapped the shopper's route through the store and recorded the prices and amounts of everything purchased. The other researcher kept up a running interview with the shopper, probing for details. Murtagh was aware of the potential for reactivity in his study. But he was interested in understanding the way people thought through ordinary, everyday arithmetic problems, and his experiment was a good way to generate those problems under natural conditions.

Many CM researchers record their own observations orally. It's less tedious than writing; it lets you focus your eyes on what's going on; it lets you record details later that might be left out of a on-the-spot written description; it avoids the limitations of a check list; and it lets you get information about context as well as about the behavior you're studying. Moreover, you can easily transcribe your recorded observations, once you've got your voice recognition software trained (see above, chapter 8, and appendix E).

But there are trade-offs. If you want measurements from qualitative data (like running commentaries on tape), you have to code them. That is, you have to listen to the recordings, over and over again, and decide what behaviors to code for each of the people you observe. Coding on the spot (by using a behavioral checklist or by inputting codes into a handheld computer) produces immediate quantitative data. You can't code *and* talk into a recorder at the same time, so you need to decide what kind of data you need and why you need them before you choose a method.

If you are trying to understand a behavioral *process*, then focus on qualitative data. If you need measurements of *how much* or *how often* people engage in this or that behavior, then focus on quantitative data. And, as always, who says you can't do both?

CODING CONTINUOUS MONITORING DATA

Go to a shopping mall and record the interaction behavior of 30 mother-child pairs for 2 minutes each. Record carefully the number of children each mother has and her interaction with each child. Try to find out whether interaction patterns are predictable from: (1) the number of children a mother has to cope with; (2) the ages of the children; (3) the socioeconomic class or ethnicity of the family; or (4) some other factors.

This exercise is instructive, if not humbling. It's a real challenge to code for socioeconomic class and ethnicity when you can't talk to the people you observe. Do this with at least one colleague so you can both check the reliability of your coding.

In hypothesis-testing research, where you already know a lot about the people you are studying, you go out to observe armed with a coding scheme worked out in advance. The idea is to record any instances of behavior that conform to the items in the scheme. This allows you to see if your hunches are correct about conditions under which certain behaviors occur. In some studies, you might be interested in noting instances of aggressive versus submissive behavior. In other cases, those variables might be irrelevant.

Coding Schemes

Just as with attitude scales and surveys (in chapters 9 and 11), there's no point in reinventing the wheel. Over the years, researchers have developed coding schemes for using direct observation in many different situations—in studies of interactions between married couples, in studies of teacher effectiveness, in worker-management negotiations, and so on. If others have developed and tested a good system for coding behaviors of interest to you, use it. Don't feel that it's somehow more prestigious or morally better for you to make up everything from scratch. Knowledge grows when researchers can compare their data to the data others have collected using the same or similar instruments.

Figure 14.3 shows the basic coding scheme for **interaction process analysis,** a system developed 60 years ago by Robert F. Bales in his research on communications in small groups (Bales 1950).

PROBLEM AREAS   OBSERVATION CATEGORIES

Positive Reactions A	1	Shows solidarity, raises other's status, gives help, rewards
	2	Shows tension release, jokes, laughs, shows satisfaction
	3	Agrees, shows passive acceptance, understands, concurs, complies
Attempted Answers B	4	Gives suggestions, direction, implying autonomy for other
	5	Gives opinion, evaluation, analysis, expresses feelings, wishes
	6	Gives orientation, information, repeats, clarifies, confirms
Questions C	7	Asks for orientation, information, repetition, confirmation
	8	Asks for opinion, evaluation, analysis, expression of feeling
	9	Asks for suggestions, direction, possible ways of action
Negative Reactions D	10	Disagrees, shows passive rejection, formality, withholds help
	11	Shows tension, asks for help, withdraws out of field
	12	Shows antagonism, deflates other's status, defends or asserts self

FIGURE 14.3.
Categories for direct observation.
SOURCE: SOURCE: R. F. Bales, "Some Uniformities of Behavior in Small Social Systems." In *Social Interaction Systems: Theory and Measurement,* p. 165. New Brunswick, NJ: Transaction Publishers, 2000.

Despite its age, the Bales coding scheme continues to be used in the study of classrooms (Koivusaari 2002) and work teams (Nam et al. 2009)—in fact, in any situation where people interact with one another.

Stewart (1984) audiotaped 140 doctor-patient interactions in the offices of 24 family physicians and assessed the interactions with Bales's interaction process analysis. Ten days later, Stewart interviewed the patients at their homes to assess satisfaction and compliance. That is, were the patients satisfied with the care they'd gotten and were they taking the pills they'd been told to take? Sure enough, when physicians are coded as engaging in many patient-centered behaviors, patients report higher compliance and satisfaction.

One of the best things about the interaction process analysis system is that any act of communication can be identified as being one of those 12 categories in figure 14.3, and the 12 categories are recognizable in many cultures around the world. A more detailed outline for coding interpersonal relations was developed by Bales and Cohen (1979). A complete course on how to use their system is available in their book, aptly titled *SYMLOG*, which stands for "systematic multiple level observation of groups" (box 14.2).

BOX 14.2

DOING CONTINUOUS MONITORING IS HARDER
THAN IT SOUNDS

Make no mistake about this: Continuous monitoring is tough to do. It takes several months of intensive training for observers to become adept at using complex coding schemes. In the 1920s, Rudolf von Laban developed a system of 114 signs with which to record dance or any other set of human movements (see Lange 1975). If you are trying to understand the meaning of complex human body movement, you've got to start with some way to record the basic data, like any other text. Brenda Farnell used Laban's script (known as **labanotation**) in her meticulous research on Plains Indian sign language (1995) and has written extensively about how the system can be used in the anthropological study of human movement in general (Farnell 1994, 1996; Farnell and Graham 1998).

These days, behavioral coding in psychology and ethology is being done with hand-held computers and software that lets you program any key to mean "initiates conversation," "reciprocates affect," or whatever. (See Ice [2004] and Koster [2006] for details about using this technology and see appendix E.) As it becomes easier for fieldworkers to observe and code behavior at the same time, I think we'll see renewed interest in continuous monitoring and in the use of complex coding schemes like labanotation.

One of the problems in the use of direct observation is the need for reliable coding by several researchers of the same data. We'll take up measures of intercoder reliability in chapter 19 on text analysis. The problem of testing intercoder reliability is the same, whether you're coding text or behavior.

COMPARATIVE RESEARCH—THE SIX CULTURE STUDY
Broad, general coding schemes are particularly useful for comparative research. Whether you're comparing sessions of psychotherapy groups, interaction sessions in laboratory experiments, or the natural behavior of people in field studies, using a common coding scheme really pays off because you can make direct comparisons across cases and look for generalizations.

The most important comparative study of children ever was run by Beatrice and John Whiting between 1954 and 1956. In the Six Culture Project, field researchers spent from 6 to 14 months in Okinawa, Kenya, Mexico, the Philippines, New England, and India. They made a total of some 3,000 5-minute (continuous monitoring) observations on 67 girls and 67 boys between the ages of 3 and 11.

Observations were limited to just 5 minutes because they were so intense, produced so much data, and required so much concentration and effort that researchers would have become fatigued and lost a lot of data in longer sessions. The investigators wrote out, in clear sentences, everything they saw children doing during the observation periods. They also recorded data about the physical environment and others with whom children were interacting.

The data were sent from the field to Harvard University for coding according to a scheme of 12 behavior categories that had been worked out in research going back some 15 years before the Six Culture Study began. The behavioral categories included: seeks help, seeks attention, seeks dominance, suggests, offers support, offers help, acts socially, touches, reprimands, assaults sociably, assaults not sociably, symbolic aggression (frightens, insults, threatens with gesture, challenges to compete). (Full details on the use of the Whiting scheme are published in Whiting et al. [1966]. See Whiting and Whiting [1973] for a discussion of their methods for observing and recording behavior.)

On average, every 10th observation was coded by two people, and these pairs of "coding partners" were rotated so that coders could not slip into a comfortable pattern with one another. Coders achieved 87% agreement on children's actions; that is, given a list of 12 kinds of things a child might be doing, coders agreed 87% of the time. They also agreed 75% of the time on the act that precipitated a child's actions and 80% of the time on the effects of a child's actions (Whiting and Whiting 1975:55).

The database from the Six Culture Study consists of approximately 20,000 recorded acts, for 134 children, or about 150 acts per child, on average.

Very strong conclusions can be drawn from this kind of robust database. For example, Whiting and Whiting (1975:179) note that nurturance, responsibility, success, authority, and casual intimacy "are types of behavior that are differentially preferred by different cultures." They conclude that "these values are apparently transmitted to the child before the age of six." They found no difference in amount of nurturant behavior among boys and girls 3–5 years of age. After that, however, nurturant behavior by girls increases rapidly with age, while boys' scores on this trait remain stable.

By contrast, reprimanding behavior starts out low for both boys and girls and increases with age equally for both sexes, across six cultures. The older the children get, the more likely they are to reprimand anyone who deviates from newly learned cultural rules. "Throughout the world," the Whitings conclude, "two of the dominant personality traits of children between seven and eleven are self-righteousness and bossiness" (1975:184). Anyone who grew up with an older sibling already knows that, but the Whitings' demonstration of this cross-cultural fact is a major scientific achievement.

USING VIDEO FOR CONTINUOUS MONITORING

Even with a fixed coding scheme, an observer in a CM situation has to decide among alternatives when noting behavior—whether someone is acting aggressively, or just engaging in rough play, for example. Recording behavior on film or video lets several analysts study the behavior stream and decide at leisure how to code it. It also makes your data available for coding by others, now and in the future. (Human ethologists, like Irenäus

Eibl-Eiblsfeldt [1989], have amassed hundreds of miles of film and videotape of ordinary people doing ordinary things across the world.)

In the 1970s, Marvin Harris and his students installed videotape cameras in the public rooms of several households in New York City. Families gave their permission, of course, and were guaranteed legal control over the cameras during the study and of the videotapes after the cameras were removed. Teams of observers monitored the equipment from remote locations. Later, the continuous verbal and nonverbal data were coded to study regularities in interpersonal relations in families.

Anna Lou Dehavenon (1978), for example, studied two black and two white families for 3 weeks and coded their nonverbal behavior for such things as compliance with requests and the distribution and consumption of foods in the households. Dehavenon's data showed that the amount of authoritarianism in the four families correlated perfectly with income differences. The lower the family income, the more superordinate behavior in the home (1978:3).

One would hypothesize, from participant observation alone, that this was the case. But *testing* this kind of hypothesis requires the sort of quantified data that straightforward, direct observation provides. (See Sharff [1979] and Reiss [1985] for two more studies of households using the Harris videotapes.)

By the 1980s, anthropologists were using video in studies of consumer behavior. Observers at Planmetrics, a marketing research firm, videotaped 70 volunteer parents, for over 200 hours, as the volunteers diapered their babies. The research was done on contract with Kimberly-Clark, manufacturer of "Huggies," a brand of disposable diapers. The cameras were not hidden, and after a while people just went about their business as usual, according to Steven Barnett, the anthropologist who led the study.

Close observation showed that many parents could not tell whether their babies needed a diaper change, so the researchers recommended that the diapers contain an exterior chemical strip that changed color when the baby was wet. The observers also noticed that parents were powdering their babies' legs and that parents were treating the red marks left by the diaper gathers as if the marks were diaper rash. The firm recommended that the gathers be redesigned so that there would be no more red marks (Kilman 1985; Lewin 1986). Today, video is used routinely in research on product design and use (Wasson 2000) (box 14.3).

CM and Reactivity

Finally, there are two ways to lower reactivity in continuous monitoring. One of them is participant observation. Once you've built up rapport and trust in a field situation, people are less likely to change their behavior when you're around. Even if they do change their behavior, you're more likely to notice the change and take that into account.

The second way to lower reactivity is training. We can't eliminate observer bias entirely, but lots and lots of evidence shows that training helps make people better—more reliable and more accurate—observers (Hartmann and Wood 1990; Kent et al. 1977). We do the best we can. Just because a "perfectly aseptic environment is impossible," Clifford Geertz (1973:30) reminds us (paraphrasing the economist Robert Solow 1970:101), doesn't mean we "might as well conduct surgery in a sewer."

Joel Gittelsohn and his coworkers (1997) tested the effects of participant observation and training on reactivity in their study of child-care practices in rural Nepal. Over the course of a year, 10 trained fieldworkers observed behavior in 160 households. Each home was visited seven times. Except for a 3–4 hour break in the middle of the day, the fieldworkers observed a focal child, 2–5 years of age, and all the caregivers of that child, from 6:00 A.M. until 8:00 P.M. This study, then, involved both children and adults.

The observers coded for over 40 activities, including health-related behaviors, feeding activities, and various kinds of social interactions (punishment, affection, and so on). The rate of some behaviors changed a lot over the course of the year. On average, across 1,101 observations, the number of times per day that a caregiver served food to a child without asking the child if he or she wanted it fell by half.

The observers also coded *each time they were interrupted* by one of the people whom they were observing (and what the interruption was about: e.g., light conversation, being asked for favors or medicine). This allowed Gittelsohn et al. to track reactivity across the seven household visits. Reactivity was noticeable during the first visit and then fell off dramatically. This study shows clearly that: (1) reactivity exists, and (2) it goes away quickly when indigenous observers stay on the job over time (Gittelsohn et al. 1997).

SPOT SAMPLING AND TIME ALLOCATION STUDIES

Instantaneous spot sampling, or **time sampling**, was developed in behavioral psychology in the 1920s and is widely used in ethology today. In **time allocation** (TA) studies, which are based on time sampling, an observer appears at randomly selected places, and at randomly selected times, and records what people are doing when they are first seen (Gross 1984).

The idea behind the TA method is simple and appealing: If you sample a sufficiently large number of representative acts, you can use the percentage of *times* people are seen doing things (working, playing, resting, eating) as a proxy for the percentage of *time* they spend in those activities.

Charles Erasmus used spot sampling in his study of a Mayo Indian community in northern Mexico (1955). As Erasmus and his wife went about the village, investigating "various topics of ethnographic interest," they took notes of what people were doing at the moment they encountered them. They did not use a representative sampling strategy but they were very systematic in their recording of data.

Individual charts were made for each man, woman, and child in the village, and on those charts were noted the page numbers from the field log where the activity descriptions were to be found. These page numbers were recorded on the charts according to the hours of the day when the observations were made. Thus, the individual charts served as indexes to the field log as well as a means of making sure that equal attention was being given to all families at all hours of the day. Periodic examination of the charts showed which households and which hours of the day were being neglected, so that visits about the community could be planned to compensate for these discrepancies. (Erasmus 1955:325)

It's difficult to top this research for sheer elegance of design and the power of the data it produced. In the 3 months from July to September 1948, the Erasmuses made about 5,000 observations on 2,500 active adults, 2,000 children, and 500 elders in the community. From those observations, Erasmus demonstrated that men in the village he studied spent about the same time at work each day as did semiskilled workers in Washington, DC. At the time, Melville Herskovits was trying to combat the racist notion that primitive and peasant peoples are lazy and unwilling to exert themselves. Herskovits's assertion was vindicated by Erasmus's TA research.

Reactivity in TA Research

In CM, getting around the reactivity problem involves staying with the program long enough to get people accustomed to your being around. Eventually, people just get plain tired of trying to manage your impression and they act naturally.

In TA research, the trick is to catch a glimpse of people in their natural activities before they see you coming on the scene—before they have a chance to modify their behavior.

Richard Scaglion (1986) did a TA survey of the residents of Upper Neligum, a Samakundi Abelam village in the Prince Alexander Mountains of East Sepik Province in Papua New Guinea. "It is not easy," he says, "for an anthropologist in the field to come upon an Abelam unawares. Since I did not want to record 'greeting anthropologist' as a frequent activity when people were first observed, I often had to reconstruct what they were doing immediately before I arrived" (p. 540).

Monique Borgerhoff-Mulder and Tim Caro (1985) coded the observer's judgment of whether people saw the observer first, or vice versa, and compared that to whether the Kipsigis (in Kenya) they were studying were observed to be active or idle. People were coded as being idle significantly more often when they spied the observer coming before the observer saw them.

Did people become idle when they saw an observer approaching? Or was it easier for idle people to see an observer before the observer saw them? Borgerhoff-Mulder and Caro found that people who were idle were sitting or lying down much more often than were people who were active. People at rest may be more attentive to their surroundings than those who are working and would be judged more often to have seen the researcher approaching.

SAMPLING PROBLEMS

There are five questions to ask when drawing a sample for a TA study:

1. Who do I watch?
2. Where do I go to watch them?
3. When do I go there?
4. How often do I go there?
5. How long do I spend watching people when I get there? (Gross 1984)

Allen Johnson's study (1975) of the Machiguenga is instructive. The Machiguenga are horticulturalists in the Peruvian Amazon. They live along streams, in small groups of related families, with each group comprising from about 10 to 30 people, and subsist primarily from slash-and-burn gardens. They supplement their diet with fish, grubs, wild fruits, and occasional monkeys from the surrounding tropical forest. Johnson spent 14 months studying the Machiguenga in the community of Shimaa.

Johnson's strategy for selecting people to study was simple: Because all travel was on foot, he decided to sample all the households within 45 minutes of his own residence. This produced a convenience sample of 13 households totaling 105 persons. The Machiguenga live along streams, so each time Johnson went out he walked either upstream or downstream, stopping at a selected household along the route. He selected the hour of the day to go out and the houses to vist at random.

Thus, Johnson used a nonrandom sample of all Machiguenga households, but he randomized the times that he visited any household in his sample. This sampling strategy sacrificed some external validity, but it was high on internal validity. Johnson could not claim that his sample of households *statistically* represented all Machiguenga households. His 14 months of experience in the field, however, makes his claim for the representativeness of his data credible.

That is, if Johnson's data on time allocation in those 13 households seem to *him* to reflect time allocation in Machiguenga households generally, then they probably do. But we can't be sure. Fortunately, randomizing his visits to the 13 households, and making a lot of observations (3,945 of them, over 134 different days during the 14-month fieldwork period), gives Johnson's results a lot of *internal* validity. So, even if you're skeptical of the external validity of Johnson's study, you could repeat it (in Shimaa or in some other Machiguenga community) and see whether you got the same results.

Regina Smith Oboler (1985) did a TA study among the Nandi of Kenya. She was interested in differences in the activities of adult men and women. The Nandi, Oboler said, "conceptualize the division of labor as sex segregated. Is this true in practice as well? Do men and women spend their time in substantially different or similar types of activities?" (p. 203).

Oboler selected 11 households, comprising 117 people, for her TA study. Her sample was not random. "Selecting a random sample," she said, "even for one *kokwet* (neighborhood) would have made observations impossibly difficult in terms of travel time" (Oboler 1985:204). Instead, Oboler chose a sample of households that were matched to social and demographic characteristics of the total population and within half an hour walking distance from the compound where she lived.

Oboler divided the daylight hours of the week into 175 equal time periods and gave each period (about 2 hours) a unique three-digit number. Then, she chose time periods at random from the list of 175 numbers to visit each household. She visited each household four times a week (on different days of the week) during 2 weeks each month and made nearly 1,500 observations on those households during her 9 months in the field.

Oboler found that, for her sample of observations, adult men spend around 38% of their time "in activities that might reasonably be considered 'work' by most commonly used definitions of that term" (Oboler 1985:205). Women in her sample spent over 60% of their time working.

Sampling Table for TA Studies

Table 14.2 shows the number of spot observations necessary to estimate the frequency of an activity to within a fractional accuracy. It also tells you how many observations you need if you want to see an activity at least once with 95% probability.

Table 14.2 Number of Observations Needed to Estimate the Frequency of an Activity to within a Fractional Accuracy

True frequency of activity	Number of observations needed to see the activity at a particular fraction of accuracy							To see activities at least once with 95% probability
f	0.05	0.10	0.15	0.20	0.30	0.40	0.50	
0.01	152127	38032	16903	9508	4226	2377	1521	299
0.02	75295	18824	8366	4706	2092	1176	753	149
0.03	49685	12421	5521	3105	1380	776	497	99
0.04	36879	9220	4098	2305	1024	576	369	74
0.05	29198	7299	3244	1825	811	456	292	59
0.06	24074	6019	2675	1505	669	376	241	49
0.07	20415	5104	2268	1276	567	319	204	42
0.08	17671	4418	1963	1104	491	276	177	36
0.09	15537	3884	1726	971	432	243	155	32
0.10	13830	3457	1537	864	384	216	138	29
0.15	8708	2177	968	544	242	136	87	19
0.20	6147	1537	683	384	171	96	61	14
0.25	4610	1152	512	288	128	72	46	11
0.30	3585	896	398	224	100	56	36	9
0.40	2305	576	256	144	64	36	23	6
0.50	1537	384	171	96	43	24	15	5

SOURCE: H. R. Bernard and P. D. Killworth, "Sampling in Time Allocation Research," *Ethnology*, Vol. 32, p. 211. Copyright © 1993. Reprinted with permission.

Here's how to read the table. Suppose people spend about 5% of their time eating. This is shown in the first column as a frequency, f, of 0.05. If you want to estimate the frequency of the activity to within 20%, look across to the column in the center part of table 14.2 under 0.20. If you have 1,825 observations, and your data say that people eat 5% of the time, then you can safely say that the true percentage of time spent eating is between 4% and 6%. (Twenty percent of 5% is 1%; 5%, plus or minus 1%, is 4%–6%. For the formula used to derive the numbers in table 14.2, see Bernard and Killworth 1993.)

Suppose you do a study of the daily activities of families in a community and your data show that men eat 4% of the time and women eat 6% of the time. If you have 300 observations, then the error bounds of the two estimates overlap considerably (about 0.02–0.06 for the men and 0.04–0.08 for the women).

You need about 1,800 observations to tell whether 0.06 is really bigger than 0.04 comparing across groups. It's the same for other activities: If women are seen at leisure 20% of their time and caring for children 25% of their time, then, as table 14.2 shows, you need 1,066 observations to tell if women really spend more time caring for children than they do at leisure.

Oboler had 1,500 observations. It is clear from table 14.2 that her findings about men's and women's leisure and work time are not accidents. An activity seen in a sample of just 256 observations to occur 40% of the time can be estimated actually to occur between 40%, plus or minus 15% of 40%, or between 34% and 46%. Since men are seen working 38% of the time and about half of Oboler's 1,500 observations were of men, her finding is solid.

Nighttime Sampling

Most time allocation studies are done during the daylight hours, between 6 A.M. and 7–8 P.M. In Johnson's case, this was explicitly because "travel after dark is hazardous, and because visiting at night is not encouraged by the Machiguenga" (Johnson 1975:303).

Of course, we know that life doesn't stop when the sun goes down. Kenneth Good spent 13 years with the Yanomami in the Venezuelan Amazon. The Yanomami, Good reports, sit around at night and plan the next day's hunt—not in whispers, but in full volume. When the mood strikes, a Yanomami man might sit in his hammock and give a speech, to everyone within earshot. "A Yanomami night," says Good, "was like another day. . . . Like the Yanomami, I'd spend eleven hours in my hammock at night to get seven or eight hours of actual sleep" (Good 1991:41–42).

Richard Scaglion (1986) did nighttime spot observations in his study of the Abelam in New Guinea. In 1983, when Scaglion did his study, there were 350 people in the village, living in 100 households. Scaglion randomly selected 2 households each day, and visited them at randomly selected times, throughout the day *and night*.

Scaglion didn't get much sleep during the month that he did this work, but his findings were worth the sacrifice. He coded his 153 observations into 13 categories of activities: sleeping, gardening, idle, cooking and food preparation, ritual, visiting, eating, hunting, construction, personal hygiene, child care, cleansing and washing, and craftwork. Only 74% of Abelam activities *during nighttime hours* were coded as "sleeping." Seven of the nine observations that he coded as "ritual" occurred after dark. Half of all observations coded as "hunting" occurred at night, and six out of eight observations coded as "visiting" were nocturnal.

Had he done his TA study only during the day, Scaglion would have overestimated the amount of time that Abelam people spend gardening by about a fourth. His data show that gardening takes up about 26% of the Abelam's daylight hours, but only 20% of their total waking time in each 24-hour period.

It may not always be possible to conduct TA studies at night. Johnson, you'll remember, made a point of the fact that the Machiguenga discourage nighttime visiting. Scaglion, on the other hand, worked among a people who "go visiting at unusual hours, even when their prospective host is likely to be sleeping."

Scaglion, in fact, rather enjoyed showing up at people's houses during odd hours in 1983. He had done his doctoral research in the same village in 1974–75. In those days, he says, "I was still quite a novelty. . . . I was frequently awakened by hearing '*Minoa, mine kwak*?' ('Hey, you, are you sleeping?'). This study allowed me to return old favors by visiting people in the late night hours to be sure *they* were sleeping" (Scaglion 1986:539) (**Further Reading:** time allocation studies).

Coding and Recording Time Allocation Data

Sampling is one of two problems in TA research. The other is measurement. How do we know that when Oboler recorded that someone was "working," we would have recorded the same thing? If you were with Johnson when he recorded that someone was engaged in "hygiene behavior," would you have agreed with his assessment? Every time? You see the problem.

It gets even more thorny. Suppose you work out a coding scheme that everyone agrees with. And suppose you train other observers to see just what you see. (Rogoff [1978] achieved a phenomenal 98% interobserver agreement in her study of 9 year olds in Guatemala.) Or, if you are doing the research all by yourself, suppose you are absolutely consistent in recording behaviors (i.e., you never code someone lying in a hammock as sleeping when they're just lounging around awake).

Even if all these reliability problems are taken care of, what about observation validity? What do you do, for example, when you see people engaged in multiple behaviors? A woman might be holding a baby and stirring a pot at the same time. Do you code her as engaged in child care or in cooking? (Gross 1984:542). If someone saw that you were lying down reading and you were studying for an exam, should they record that you were working or relaxing?

Do you record all behaviors? Do you mark one behavior as primary? This last question has important implications for data analysis. There are only so many minutes in a day, and the percentage of people's time that they allocate to activities has to add up to 100%. If you code multiple activities as equally important, then there will be more than 100% of the day accounted for. Most TA researchers use their intuition, based on participant observation, to decide which of the multiple simultaneous activities they witness to record as the primary one and which as secondary.

The best solution is to record *all* possible behaviors you observe in the order of their primacy, according to your best judgment at the time of observation. Use a check sheet to record behaviors. Use a separate check sheet for each observation you make. This can mean printing up 1,000 sheets for a TA study, and hauling them home later. You can save yourself a lot of work by using a hand-held computer with the equivalent of an electronic check sheet installed that lets you watch behavior and code it on the spot (see appendix E) (box 14.4).

BOX 14.4

ON BEING PROPERLY PARANOID ABOUT LOSING DATA

Saving work is one of two good reasons to use hand-held computers to record observational data. The other good reason to give up paper check sheets if you can is that, eventually, you have to type in the data anyway, transferring them from paper to computer so you can run statistical analyses. Each time you record behavioral data—as you watch it and as you transfer it from paper to computer—there is a chance of error. That's just how it is. So eliminating one step in the data management process cuts down on errors in data.

If you must hand-code your original observations, enter the data into a laptop while you're still in the field as a precaution against loss of the original data sheets. Be paranoid about data. Those horror stories you've heard about lost data? They're true. (Read M. N. Srinivas's account [1979:xiii] of how he lost all three copies of his field notes, compiled over a period of 18 years, in a fire at Stanford.)

EXPERIENCE SAMPLING

In **experience sampling** (ES), people respond at random times during a day or a week to questions about what they're doing, or who they're with, or what they're feeling at the moment. Some researchers ask informants to carry around a beeper and, when the beeper goes off, to jot an entry into a diary or talk about their actions, feelings, and surroundings into a small digital recorder. Some researchers ask informants to respond to a telephone interviewer (Kubey et al. 1996), and some researchers ask informants to fill out a form on an Internet-enabled cell phone or PDA (Foo et al. 2009; Wenze et al. 2007).

ES offers two big advantages. First, it combines the power of random spot checks with the relative ease of having people report on their own behavior. Csikszentmihalyi and Larson (1987) demonstrated the reliability of ES in a number of studies. Validity is another matter, but when people record or talk about what they're doing and how they're feeling on the spot, this should lessen the inherent inaccuracy of recall data. The second advantage is that, working on your own, you can only be in one place at a time, but with those beepers or cell phones, you can collect spot-observation data from lots of people at once.

In anthropology, Garry Chick used ES in his study (1994) of a small machine-tool company in Pennsylvania. Chick wanted to test Marx's theory that automation would eliminate the need for skilled labor by turning complex tasks into a series of routine steps that could be performed by drones. Drones should find their work boring, unsatisfying, and unimportant.

There were 11 machinists, all men, in the small shop. Four of them worked on traditional, manually controlled lathes in turning out machine tools. Three worked only on a newly installed, computer-controlled lathe (you program it to do a job and then you more-or-less stand by while it executes your instructions). And four worked on both types of lathes, depending on the job.

Each man was beeped 30 times—six times a day over a 5-day week—and at each beep, he stopped what he was doing within 10 minutes and filled out a 2-minute questionnaire. (Each man kept a spiral-bound booklet of questionnaires handy in the shop.) There should have been 330 questionnaires (11 men filling out 30 each), but one man was beeped while he was in the bathroom and one was beeped while he was filling out a questionnaire (having been beeped 2 minutes before). That's what happens when you collect data at random points, but random means random and no tinkering with it.

For each of the experience samples, workers indicated what they were doing. If they were operating a machine (or more than one), they indicated which one(s). Then they answered 14 attitude questions. Here they are:

On a scale from 1–10, where 1 means "definitely not" and 10 means "definitely yes," what I was doing:
  1. was enjoyable.
  2. was interesting.
  3. was complex/technical.
  4. was fun.
  5. was under my control.
  6. was monotonous.
  7. was machine paced.
  8. was tricky.
  9. held my attention.

On a scale from 1–10, where 1 means "definitely not" and 10 means "definitely yes," at the time I was signaled, I was:
  10. pressed for time.
  11. working on my own.
  12. thinking about things other than work.
  13. doing something that I felt was important.
  14. doing something that required a lot of skill.

The results were mixed. The men found working on the computer-controlled machines more interesting, more satisfying, and more important than working on the manual machines, and they found programming the computer-controlled machines even more interesting than running them. But these machinists also felt more in control when they worked on manual lathes.

If you use self-administered questionnaires, you need literate informants to do experience sampling. But, as Chick says, "with more and more anthropological research in modern and modernizing societies, experience sampling can be a valuable addition to the anthropologist's tool kit" (1994:6). And if you give people little voice recorders, you may be able to use the ES method with nonliterate populations (**Further Reading:** experience sampling).

COMBINING CONTINUOUS MONITORING AND SPOT SAMPLING

The difference between CM and spot sampling is analogous to the difference between ethnography and survey research. With ethnography, you get information about process; with survey research, you get data that let you estimate parameters for a population. Spot sampling is used in TA research precisely because the goal is to estimate parameters—like how much time, on average, women spend cooking, or men spend throwing pots, or children spend laid up ill at home. If you want to know the ingredients of *mafongo* (a dish native to Puerto Rico) and the order in which they are added, you have to watch continuously as someone makes it. (Making it yourself, as part of participant observation, produces embodied knowledge, yet a third kind of information.)

Robin O'Brian (1998) combined CM and spot sampling in her study of Mayan craftswomen in Chiapas, Mexico. The women sold their crafts to tourists at a local market. Several times a week, O'Brian went through the market (entering from a randomly selected spot each time) and coded what every woman craft seller was doing, using a check sheet adapted from A. Johnson et al.'s (1987) standardized time allocation activity codes.

O'Brian also did continuous monitoring for 3 hours of 15 women, and these two kinds of data produced more information than either kind alone. Her aggregate, spot-sampling data showed that the women spent 82% of their time waiting for tourists to buy something. The women weren't just sitting around, though. They spent 17% of their waiting time producing more crafts (doing macramé or embroidery or hand-spinning wool) and another 17% eating, cleaning children, or nursing. The CM data showed that women were interrupted in their productive activities 36% of their waiting time (that is, 36% of 82%, or 30% of their entire day) and that the interruptions were as likely to be responding to their children's needs as they were to be selling to tourists.

PLUSES AND MINUSES OF DIRECT OBSERVATION

On balance, direct observation provides much more accurate results about behavior than do reports of behavior. Ricci et al. (1995) studied 40 people in Kalama, a peri-urban village about 15 miles north of Cairo. One day, a set of trained observers watched the 40 participants for 2.5 hours. The observers noted whether people were engaged in any of 17 activities and how long each person spent at each activity.

The next day, the participants were asked to recall, sequentially, what they had done the entire day before, and how long they had spent at each activity. The interviewers did not mention any of the 17 activities, but they tried to improve respondent recall by asking about activities before and after locally significant time markers, like call to prayer. Ten of the 40 were toddlers, so Ricci et al. focused on the recall data of the 24 adults and the six school-age children.

Ricci et al. were very forgiving in their analysis. Informants were scored as being correct if they could recall an activity at all and say correctly whether it had been done in the morning or afternoon observation period (9:00–11:30 A.M. or 12:30–3:00 P.M.). Ricci et al. scored only errors of omission (leaving out activities) and threw out errors of commission (inventing activities that had not been observed).

And informants *still* got it wrong—a lot. Across men and women, across agricultural and nonagricultural households, informants got it wrong, on average, 56% of the time. Five of the 6 women who had been observed breast-feeding failed to report that activity the next day; 13 of the 15 women who had been observed washing clothes failed to report that activity the next day.

If you want to know whether, say, caring for animals happens more often than, say, gathering fuel, self-reports might be enough. But if you want to know *how often* those behaviors actually occur, then nothing short of direct observation will do.

I don't want to give the impression, however, that direct observation data are automatically accurate. Lots of things can clobber the accuracy of directly observed behavior. Observers may be biased by their own expectations of what they are looking for or by expectations about the behavior of women or men or any ethnic group (Kent et al. 1977; Repp et al. 1988).

You may feel awkward about walking around with a clipboard (and perhaps a stopwatch) and writing down what people are doing—or with beeping people and asking them to interrupt what they're doing to help you get some data. This is a reasonable concern, and direct observation is not for everyone. It's not a detached method, like sending out questionnaires and waiting for data to be delivered to your doorstep.

It is not a fun method, either. Hanging out, participating in normal daily activities with people, and writing up field notes at night is more enjoyable than monitoring and recording what people are doing.

But many fieldworkers find that direct observation allows them to address issues that are not easily studied by any other method. Grace Marquis (1990) studied a shantytown in Lima, Peru. Children in households that kept chickens were at higher risk for getting diarrhea than were other children. The chickens left feces in the homes, and the feces contained an organism that causes diarrhea. Continuous monitoring showed that children touched the chicken droppings and, inevitably, touched their mouths with their hands. It was hard, tedious work, but the payoff was serious.

Direct observation is time consuming, but random spot-checking of behavior is a very cost effective and productive way to use *some* of your time in any field project. When you're studying a group that has clear boundaries (a village, a hospital, a school), you can get very fine-grained data about people's behavior from a TA study, based on random spot checks. More importantly, as you can see from table 14.2, with proper sampling you can generalize to large populations (whole school districts, an entire aircraft manufacturing plant, even cities) from spot checks of behavior, in ways that no other method allows.

You may be concerned that a strictly observational approach to gathering data about human behavior fails to capture the *meaning* of data for the actors. This, too, is a legitimate concern. A classic example is Geertz's (1973:6–7) observation that a wink can be the result of getting a speck of dust in your eye or a conscious act of conspiracy. And that's just a wink. People can engage in any of thousands of behaviors (skipping a class, wearing a tie, having their navel pierced . . .) for many, many different reasons. Knowing the meaning of behavior to others is essential to understanding it ourselves.

On the other hand, one of our most important goals in science is to constantly challenge our own ideas about what things mean. That's how theories develop, are knocked down, and gain in their power to explain things. Why shouldn't we also challenge the theories—the explanations—that the people we study give us for their own behavior?

Ask people who are coming out of a church, for example, why they just spent 2 hours there. Some common responses include "to worship God," "to be a better person," "to teach our children good values." Hardly anyone says "to dress up and look good in front of other people," "to meet potential golf partners for later this Sunday afternoon," or "to maximize my ability to meet potential mates whose ethnic and social backgrounds are compatible with my own." Yet, we know that these last three reasons are what *some* people would say if they thought others wouldn't disapprove.

Finally, you may have some qualms about the ethics of obtrusive observation. It cannot be said too often that *every single data collection act* in the field has an ethical component, and a fieldworker is obliged every single time to think through the ethical implications of data collection acts. Personally, I have less difficulty with the potential ethical problems of obtrusive, reactive observation than I do with any other data collection method, including participant observation. In obtrusive observation, people actually *see* you (or a camera) taking down their behavior, and they can ask you to stop. Nothing is hidden.

In participant observation, we try to put people at ease, make them forget we're really listening hard to what they're telling us, and get them to "open up." We ask people to take us into their confidence, and we are handed the responsibility for not abusing that confidence.

But the method that presents the *most* ethical problems is unobtrusive, *non*reactive direct observation.

UNOBTRUSIVE OBSERVATION

Disguised field observation is the ultimate in participant observation—you join, or pretend to join, some group and secretly record data about people in the group.

In 1960, John H. Griffin, a white journalist went through some drug treatment to temporarily turn his skin black. He traveled the southern United States for about a month, taking notes on how he was treated. His book, *Black Like Me* (1961) was a real shocker. It galvanized a lot of support by Whites in the North for the then fledgling Civil Rights movement. Clearly, Griffin engaged in premeditated deception in gathering the data for his book. But Griffin was a journalist; scientists don't deceive their informants, right?

Pseudopatients and Simulated Clients

Wrong. Samuel Sarkodie, an M.A. student in medical sociology at the University of Legon, in Ghana, spent 3 days in a rural hospital in 1994 as a pseudopatient with a false case of malaria. The hospital staff were in on the study—they had been recruited by Sarkodie's supervisor, Sjaak van der Geest, a Dutch anthropologist who works in Ghana—and Sarkodie wrote a detailed report for the hospital. Presumably, the report was helpful, but Sarkodie's fellow patients were duped (van der Geest and Sarkodie 1998).

Twenty years earlier, David Rosenhan recruited seven confederates who, like him, checked themselves into mental hospitals and took surreptitious notes about how they were treated. They gave false names and occupations (they couldn't very well mention their real occupations since three of them were psychologists and one was a psychiatrist), and reported hearing voices. One was diagnosed as manic-depressive, and the rest as schizophrenics, and all were admitted for treatment.

This was tough work. The pseudopatients were not allowed to divulge what they were up to just because they were tired of (or exasperated with) the experiment. The only way out was to be diagnosed by the hospital staff as ready for release. It took between 1 week and 7 weeks of confinement to achieve this, and when they were released, the pseudopatients were all diagnosed with "schizophrenia in remission" or as "asymptomatic" or as "improved" (Rosenhan 1973, 1975).

Rosenhan's field experiment made clear the power of labeling: Once you are diagnosed as insane, people treat you as insane. Period. Some of the genuine inmates at the hospitals saw through the charade, but none of the staff ever did (box 14.5).

BOX 14.5

ARE THESE PSEUDOPATIENT STUDIES ETHICAL?

The simulated client method has been used in dozens of studies to evaluate the performance of physicians, pharmacists, family-planning clinics, and other health care providers in developing nations. (See Madden et al. [1997] for a review of these studies.) And fake clients—men and women, black, white, and Hispanic—are sent out by U.S. government agencies regularly to apply for jobs, to rent apartments, or to buy homes and to uncover discrimination (Sharpe 1998). The U.S. Supreme Court has ruled that this practice is legal in the pursuit of fair housing (Ayres 1991:823), and the Equal Employment Opportunity Commission uses data from these field experiments to sue offending businesses.

People across the political spectrum have quite different ideas about whether this is just a dose of the same medicine that offenders dish out (which seems fair), or entrapment (which seems foul). Does this mean that ethics are simply a matter of political orientation and opinion? In the abstract, most people answer this question with a strong "no." When things get concrete—when the fortunes and reputations of real people are at stake—the answer becomes less clear (van den Borne 2007).

But if you think deceiving landlords or Realtors or the staff of mental hospitals is something, read on (**Further Reading:** pseudopatients and simulated clients).

The Tearoom Trade Study

Without telling people that he was studying them, Laud Humphreys (1975) observed hundreds of homosexual acts among men in St. Louis, Missouri. Humphreys's study produced very important results. The men involved in this tearoom trade, as it is called, came from all walks of life, and many were married and living otherwise straight lives. Humphreys made it clear that he did not engage in homosexual acts himself, but played the role of the "watch queen," or lookout, warning his informants when someone approached the restroom. This deception and unobtrusive observation, however, did not cause the storm of criticism that accompanied the first publication of Humphreys's work in 1970.

That was caused by Humphreys having taken his research a step further. He jotted down the license plate numbers of the men who used the restroom for quick, impersonal sex and got their names and addresses from motor vehicle records. He waited a year after doing his observational work, and then, on the pretext that they had been randomly selected for inclusion in a general health survey, he interviewed 100 of his research subjects in their homes.

Humphreys was careful to change his car, his hairstyle, and his dress. According to him, his informants did not recognize him as the man who had once played watch queen for them in public toilets. *This* is what made Humphreys's research the focus of another debate, which is still going on, about the ethics of nonreactive field observation.

Five years after the initial study was published, Humphreys himself said that he had made a mistake. He had endangered the social, emotional, and economic lives of people he studied. Had his files been subpoenaed, he could not have claimed immunity. He decided at the time that he would go to jail rather than hurt his informants (Humphreys 1975).

Humphreys was an ordained Episcopal priest who had held a parish for more than a decade before going to graduate school. He was active in the Civil Rights movement in the early 1960s and spent time in jail for committing crimes of conscience. His credentials as an ethical person, conscious of his responsibilities to others, were in good order. Everyone associated with him agreed that Humphreys was totally committed to protecting his informants.

But listen to what Arlene Kaplan Daniels had to say about all this, in a letter to Myron Glazer, a sociologist and ethnographer:

> In my opinion, no one in the society deserves to be trusted with hot, incriminating data. Let me repeat, *no one.* . . . We should not have to rely on the individual strength of conscience which may be required. Psychiatrists, for example, are notorious gossipers [about their patients]. . . . O. K., so they mainly just tell one another. But they *sometimes* tell wives, people at parties, you and me. [Daniels had done participant observation research on psychiatrists.] And few of them would hold up under systematic pressure from government or whatever to get them to tell. . . . The issue is not that a few brave souls *do* resist. The issue is rather what to do about the few who will not. . . . There is *nothing* in our training—any more than in the training of psychiatrists, no matter what they say—to prepare us to take up these burdens. (quoted in Glazer 1975:219–20; emphasis in original)

Researchers who conduct the kinds of studies that Humphreys did invoke several arguments to justify the use of deception.

1. It is impossible to study such things as homosexual encounters in public restrooms in any other way.
2. Disguised field observation is a technique that is available only to researchers who are physically and linguistically indistinguishable from the people they are studying. To use this technique, you must be a member of the larger culture. There is, therefore, no real ethical question involved, other than whether you, as an individual, feel comfortable doing this kind of research.
3. Public places, like restrooms, are, simply, public. The counterargument is that people have a right to expect that their behavior in public toilets will not be recorded, period. (Koocher 1977)

Sechrest and Phillips (1979) take a middle ground. They say that "public behavior should be observable by any means that protect what might be called 'assumed' privacy, the privacy that one might expect from being at a distance from others or of being screened from usual views" (p. 14). Casual observation is fine, but the use of telescopes, listening devices, or peepholes would be unethical.

My own position is that the decision to use deception is up to you, provided that the *risks of detection are your own risks and no one else's*. When Jack Weatherford (1986) took a job as manager of a porn shop in Washington, DC, the people who came to the store to watch the movies or connect with prostitutes didn't know they were being studied by a participant observer, but neither were they in any danger that their identities would be divulged. And similarly, when Wendy Chapkis became a licensed massage therapist and became a participant observer in her secret research on prostitution (1997), she assumed risks, but the risks were hers. If detection risks harm to others, then don't even consider disguised participant observation. Recognize, too, that it may not be possible to foresee the potential harm that you might do using disguised observation. This is what leads scholars like Kai Erikson (1967, 1996) to the conclusion that research that requires deception is never justified (**Further Reading:** deception in participant observation).

GRADES OF DECEPTION

But is all deception equally deceitful? Aren't there **grades of deception**? In the 1960s, Edward Hall and others (Hall 1963, 1966; Watson and Graves 1966) showed how people in different cultures use different "body language" to communicate—that is, they stand at different angles to one another, or at different distances when engaging in serious versus casual conversation. Hall called this different use of space **proxemics**. He noted that people learn this proxemic behavior as part of their early cultural learning and he hypothesized that subcultural variations in spatial orientation often leads to breakdowns in communication, isolation of minorities, and so on.

This seminal observation by an anthropologist set off a flurry of research that continues to this day (for a review, see Farnell 1999). Early on, Aiello and Jones (1971) studied the proxemic behavior of middle-class white and lower-class Puerto Rican and black schoolchildren. They trained a group of elementary schoolteachers to observe and code the distance and orientation of pairs of children to one another during recess periods (**Further Reading:** proxemics).

Sure enough, there were clear cultural and gender differences. White children stand much farther apart in ordinary interaction than do either black or Puerto Rican children. The point here is that the teachers were natural participants in the system. The researchers trained these natural participants to be observers to cut out any reactivity that outsiders might have caused in doing the observation (box 14.6).

Levine (1997) used casual, unobtrusive observation to study the walking speed of people in different size cities, and Rotton et al. (1990) tested whether people walk faster in a climate-controlled mall or in an open-air shopping. Contrary to popular wisdom, heat didn't slow down urban shoppers of either sex. And Sykes et al. (1993) sat unobtrusively in bars, counting the number of drinks people consumed. Confirming popular wisdom, people drink faster and spend less time in bars when they are in groups of two or more than when they're alone.

I don't consider these field studies of shoppers, children, pedestrians, and drinkers in bars to be unethical. The people being studied were observed in the course of their ordinary activities, out in the open, in truly public places. Despite making unobtrusive observations or taking surreptitious pictures, the deception involved was passive—it didn't involve "taking in" the subjects of the research, making them believe one thing to get them to do another. I don't think that any real invasion of privacy occurred.

BOX 14.6

LOWERING REACTIVITY IN DIRECT OBSERVATION
RESEARCH

For his master's degree, Mark House studied shoppers in Nizhny Novgorod, a city on the Volga River about 400 miles east of Moscow in the Volga region. As he followed shoppers around, House held his little tape recorder to his ear, as if he were talking on a cell phone, and dictated notes. Shawn Scherer (1974) studied pairs of children in a schoolyard in Toronto. He used only lower-class black and lower-class white children in his study, to control for socioeconomic effects. Scherer adapted techniques from photogrammetry (making surveys by using photographs). He mounted a camera in a park adjacent to the schoolyard. Using a telephoto lens, he took unobtrusive shots of pairs of children who were at least 30 meters away.

This got rid of the reactivity problem. Then Scherer devised a clever way to measure the average distance between two children and did his analysis on the quantitative data. Scherer found no significant differences in the distance between pairs of white or black children.

The Micturition Study

You can't say that about the work of Middlemist et al. (1976). They wanted to measure the length of time it takes for men to begin urinating, how long men continue to urinate, and whether these things are affected by how close men stand to each other in public toilets. (*Why* they wanted to know these things is another story.)

At first, the researchers pretended to be combing their hair at the sink in a public toilet at a university. They tracked the time between the sound of a fly being unzipped and urine hitting the water in the urinal as the time for onset, then they noted how long it took for the sound of urine to stop hitting the water in the urinal and counted this as the duration of each event. They noted whether subjects were standing alone, next to someone, or one or two urinals away from someone.

In general, the closer the man being watched stood to another man, the longer it took him to begin urinating and the shorter the duration of the event. This confirmed laboratory research showing that social stress inhibits relaxation of the urethral sphincter in men, thus inhibiting flow of urine.

Middlemist et al. decided to control the independent variable—how far away another man was from each subject. They placed "BEING CLEANED" signs on some urinals and forced unsuspecting men to use a particular urinal in a public toilet. Then a confederate stood next to the subject, or one urinal away, or did not appear at all. The observer hid in a toilet stall next to the urinals and made the measurements. The problem was, the observer couldn't hear flies unzipping and urine hitting the water from inside the stall—so the researchers used a periscopic prism, trained on the area of interest, to make the observations directly.

Personally, I doubt that many people would have objected to the study if Middlemist and his colleagues had just lurked in the restroom and done simple, unobtrusive observation. But when they contrived to make men urinate in a specific place, when they contrived to manipulate the dependent variable (urination time), and, above all, when they got that periscope into the act, that changed matters. This is a clear case of invasion of privacy by researchers, in my view.

In a severe critique of the research, Koocher (1977:120) said that "at the very least, the design seems laughable and trivial." Middlemist et al. (1977:123) defended themselves, saying that "we believe . . . that the pilot observation and the experiment together constitute an example of well-controlled field research, adequate to test the null hypothesis that closeness has no effect" on the duration of urination among men in public restrooms. Actually, Middlemist et al.'s study *design* was anything but trivial. In fact, it was quite elegant. And the results of their research have been cited many times in articles on the stress of crowding—like why many people prefer to stand in commuter trains rather than sit in middle seats between other passengers (Evans and Wener 2007)—and on paruresis, an anxiety disorder that inhibits urination in the presence of, or anticipated presence of others (Boschen 2008). Whether the research was ethical is another matter.

Passive Deception

Passive deception involves no experimental manipulation of informants to get them to act in certain ways. Humphreys's first, strictly observational study (not the one where he used a pretext to interview people in their homes) involved passive deception. He made his observations in public places where he had every right to be in the first place. He took no names down, and there were no data that could be traced to any particular individual. Humphreys observed felonies, and that makes the case more complex. But in my opinion, he had the right to observe others in public places, irrespective of whether those observed believed that they would or would not be observed. What he did with his observations—following people up by tracking them through their license plates—is, like Middlemist et al.'s periscope, another matter.

Anthropologists use passive deception all the time. I have spent hours pretending to be a shopper in department stores and have observed mothers who are disciplining their children. I have played the role of a strolling tourist on Mexican beaches (an easy role to play since that was exactly what I was) and recorded how American and Mexican families occupied beach space. I have surreptitiously clocked the time it takes for people who were walking along the streets of Athens (Greece), New York City, Gainesville (Florida), and Ixmiquilpan (Mexico) to cover 10 meters of sidewalk at various times of the day. I have stood in crowded outdoor bazaars in Mexico, watching and recording differences between Indians and non-Indians in the amount and kinds of produce purchased.

I have never felt the slightest ethical qualm about having made these observations. In my opinion, passive deception is ethically aseptic. Ultimately, however, the responsibility for the choice of method, and for the practical, human consequences of using a particular method, rests with you, the individual researcher. You can't foist off that responsibility on "the profession," or on some "code of ethics."

Are you disturbed by the fact that Humphreys did his research at all, or only by the fact that he came close to compromising his informants? As you answer that question for yourself, you'll have a better idea of where *you* stand on the issue of disguised field observation. (For more on the ethics of deception, see **Further Reading**, chapter 4.)

BEHAVIOR TRACE STUDIES

Think of trace studies as behavioral archeology. Do people in different cultures really have a different sense of time? Levine and Bartlett (1984) went to 12 cities in six countries and noted the time on 15 randomly chosen bank clocks in each city. Then they measured the difference between the time shown on the clocks and the time reported by the local telephone company in each city. The most accurate public clocks were Japanese—off by an average of just 34 seconds. U.S. clocks were next (off by an average of 54 seconds), followed by the clocks in Taiwan, England, and Italy (71 sec., 72 sec., and 90 sec., respectively). Indonesia came in last, at 189 sec.

Here you have hard, archeological evidence of clock-setting behavior across six countries. Real people had set those 15 clocks in each city, and real people were responsible for making sure that the clocks were adjusted from time to time. Levine and Bartlett looked at whether differences in the average deviation of the clocks from the real time predicted differences in the rate of heart disease.

They don't. The country with the lowest rate of heart disease, Japan, has the most accurate clocks and the fastest overall pace of life (as measured by several other indicators). Apparently, according to Levine and Bartlett, it's possible in some cultures to be hard *working* without being hard *driving*.

Sechrest and Flores (1969) recorded and analyzed bathroom graffiti in a sample of men's public toilets in Manilla and Chicago. They wanted to examine attitudes toward sexuality in the two cultures. The results were striking. There was no difference in the percentage of graffiti in the two cities that dealt with heterosexual themes. But fully 42% of the Chicago graffiti dealt with homosexuality, whereas only 2% of the Manilla graffiti did, showing a clear difference in the two cultures regarding level of concern with homosexuality.

Gould and Potter (1984) did a survey of used-up (not smashed-up) automobiles in five Providence, Rhode Island, junkyards. They calculated that the average use-life of American-made cars is 10.56 years, irrespective of how many times cars change hands. This is a good deal longer than most Americans would guess. Gould also compared use-life against initial cost and found that paying more for a car doesn't affect how long it will last. Interesting and useful findings.

In their classic book on *Unobtrusive Measures*, Webb et al. (1966) identified a class of measures based on erosion. Administrators of Chicago's Museum of Science and Industry had found that the vinyl tiles around an exhibit showing live, hatching chicks needed to be replaced about every 6 weeks. The tiles around other exhibits lasted for years without having to be replaced. Webb et al. (p. 37) suggested that this erosion measure (the rate of wear on vinyl tiles) might be a proxy for a direct measure of the popularity of exhibits. The faster the tiles wear out, the more popular the exhibit (box 14.7).

The Garbage Project

The Garbage Project was founded in 1973 by archeologist William Rathje at the University of Arizona. For over 25 years, Rathje and his associates studied consumer behavior patterns in Tucson, Arizona, by analyzing the garbage from a representative sample of residents. It was a great effort at applying trace measures.

In 1988, about 6,000 residents of Tucson were sent flyers, explaining that they were selected to be part of a study of recycling behavior. Their garbage would be studied, the flyer explained, and confidentiality was assured, but if they didn't want to be part of the study, residents could send in a card and they would be removed from the list. About 200 people returned the cards and opted out of the study (Wilson Hughes, personal communication). (And see Hughes [1984] for a detailed review of the methodology of the Garbage Project.)

By studying the detritus of ordinary people, researchers on the Garbage Project learned

WEIGHING THE EVIDENCE

Dean Archer and Lynn Erlich (1985) had a hypothesis that sensational crimes (with a lot of press coverage) result in increased sales of handguns. The police would not allow them to see the handgun applications, so they asked a member of the police staff to put the permits into envelopes, by month, for 3 months before and 3 months after a particular sensational crime. Then they weighed the envelopes and converted the weight to handgun applications. To do this, they got a chunk of blank applications and found out how many applications there were per ounce.

The technique is very reliable. The correlation between the estimates of researchers and the actual weights of the envelopes was .99, and in a controlled experiment, researchers were able to tell the difference of just one sheet of paper in 15 out of 18 tries. Real data can be messy, though. Lots of handgun applications have addenda attached, for example. Still, the correlation between researchers' estimates and the true number of handgun applications across 6 months was .94.

As Archer and Erlich suggest, the weight method can be used to study confidential records when you want to know only aggregate outcomes—about things like drunk driving arrests, the influx of psychiatric patients to a clinic, the number of grievance filings in a company, the number of abortion referrals, and the number of complaints against agencies—and don't need data about individuals.

interesting things about food consumption and waste among Americans. Squash is the favored baby food among Hispanics in the United States, and 35% of all food from chicken take-out restaurants is thrown away (Rathje 1992). You can accurately estimate the population of an area by weighing only the plastic trash. Children, it turns out, generate as much plastic trash as adults do (Edmondson 1988).

Early in the Garbage Project, researchers expected that people would not waste much beef during a shortage, but exactly the opposite happened in 1973. Two things were shown to be responsible for this finding. First, as the shortage took hold, the price of beef rose, and people started buying cheaper cuts. Some residents did not know how to prepare those cuts properly, and this created more waste; others found that they didn't like the cheaper cuts and threw out more than they usually would have; and cheaper cuts have more waste fat to throw out to begin with. Second, as the price continued to rise, people started buying greater quantities of beef, perhaps as a hedge against further price hikes. Inevitably, some of the increased purchases spoiled from lack of proper storage (Rathje 1984:17).

Rathje found the same pattern of consumer behavior during the sugar shortage of 1975. He reasoned that whenever people changed their food-buying and -consuming habits drastically, there would be at least a short-term increase in food loss. Conversely, when people use foods and ingredients that are familiar to them they waste less in both preparation and consumption.

This led Rathje to compare the food loss rate among Mexican Americans and Anglos in Tucson and Milwaukee. "The final results of Mexican-American cooking," Rathje said, "can be extremely varied—chimichangas, burros, enchiladas, tacos, and more—but the basic set of ingredients are very few compared to standard Anglo fare. Thus, Mexican-American households should throw out less food than Anglo households" (Rathje 1984:17–18). In fact, this is exactly what Rathje found in both Tucson and Milwaukee.

Beside Tucson and Milwaukee, studies of fresh household garbage have been done in New Orleans, Marin County (California), Mexico City, and Sydney (Australia).

Pros and Cons of Trace Studies

The most important advantage of trace studies is that they are nonreactive, so long as the people you are studying are kept in the dark about what you are doing. What happens when people are told that their garbage is being monitored? Ritenbaugh and Harrison (1984) compared data from an experimental group (people who were told that their garbage was being monitored) and a control group (people who were not told). There was no difference in the refuse disposal behavior of the experimental and control groups—with one important exception. The number of empty bottles of alcoholic drinks that showed up was significantly lower when people knew that their garbage was being monitored.

Where did the extra bottles go? Buried in the backyard? Stuffed in the trash cans of neighbors who were not in the sample? It remains a mystery.

In addition to being nonreactive, behavioral trace studies yield enormous amounts of data that can be standardized, quantified, and compared across groups and over time (Rathje 1979). Moreover, traces reflect many behaviors more accurately than informant reports of those behaviors.

In 1986, as part of a contract with the Heinz Corporation, Rathje and his colleagues asked women in the Tucson area if they had used any store-bought baby food in the past week. Uniformly, the Hispanic mothers insisted that they had not used any such product. You can guess the rest: They had as many baby-food jars in their garbage as did the Anglo households—and this, despite that fact that 45% of the Hispanic women in Tucson at the time were working outside the home (Rathje and Murphy 1992). Those women were caught in a bind: They didn't have time to prepare home-made baby food, but they couldn't admit this to a stranger asking questions.

Trace studies like the Garbage Project have plenty of problems, however. Early in the project, it became apparent that garbage disposals were going to be a serious problem. The researchers constructed a subsample of 32 households, some of which had disposals, some of which did not. They studied these 32 households for 5 weeks and developed a "garbage disposal correction factor" (Rathje 1984:16).

As the project went on, researchers learned that some families were recycling all their aluminum cans, and others were throwing theirs in the trash. This made it difficult to compare households regarding their consumption of soft drinks and beer. Some families had compost heaps that they used as fertilizer for their vegetable gardens. This distorted the refuse count for those families. Garbage Project researchers had to develop correction factors for all of these biases, too (see G. G. Harrison 1976).

As with much unobtrusive research, the Garbage Project raised some difficult ethical problems. To protect the privacy of the households in the study, no addresses or names of household members were recorded. All personal items, such as photographs and letters, were thrown out without being examined. The hundreds of student sorters who worked on the project signed pledges not to save anything from the refuse they examined. All the sampling, sorting, and data analysis procedures were approved by the Human Subjects Research Committee of the University of Arizona.

The Garbage Project received consistent coverage in the press, both nationally and locally in Tucson. In 1984, after 10 years of work, Hughes reported that "no public concern over the issue of personal privacy has been expressed, and community response has been supportive" (Hughes 1984:42). With proper safeguards, trace measures generate lots of useful data about human behavior.

ARCHIVAL RESEARCH

One of the great advantages to doing archival research is that it is truly nonreactive. Whether you're studying archival records of births, migrations, visits to a hospital, or purchases of hybrid seed, people can't change their behavior after the fact. The original data might have been collected reactively, but that's one reason why historians demand such critical examination of sources.

Another advantage of doing what Caroline Brettell calls "fieldwork in the archives" (1998) is that you can study things using archival data that would be too politically "hot" to study any other way. And archival research is inexpensive. Be on the lookout for interesting archival materials: government reports, personal diaries or photo collections, industrial data, medical records, school records, wills, deeds, records of court cases, tax rolls, and land-holding records.

Cultural Processes

Archival resources can be particularly useful in studying cultural processes through time. June Helm (1980) found that between 1829 and 1891, traders at the Hudson's Bay Company posts of the upper Mackenzie Delta had surveyed the Indians who traded at their stores. On the basis of those data, Helm concluded that, before 1850, the Indians of the area had practiced female infanticide. After 1850, missionaries were successful in stopping infanticide. Nancy Howell (1981), a demographer, subjected Helm's data to a sophisticated statistical analysis and corroborated Helm's conclusion.

Daniel Swan and Gregory Campbell (1989) studied the population records of 1877 to 1907 for the Osage reserve. They were able to show that from 1877 to 1887, the full bloods declined at 6.4% a year and the mixed bloods increased at 7.3% a year. This had great consequences for the Osage because the full bloods and mixed bloods had formed voting blocs on economic issues. In particular, the full bloods resisted turning the reserve land into private property. Whites who married into the tribe fraudulently claimed tribal mixed-blood status. The mixed bloods were in favor of the private property measures.

Using fashion magazines going back to 1844, Alfred Kroeber made eight separate measurement of women's clothing in the United States and France (Kroeber 1919). He measured things like the diameter of the skirt at the hem, the diameter of the waist, the depth of decolletage (measured from the mouth to the middle of the corsage edge in front), and so on. After analyzing the data, Kroeber claimed to have found "an underlying pulsation in the width of civilized women's skirts, which is symmetrical and extends in its up and down beat over a full century; and an analogous rhythm in skirt length, but with a period of only about a third the duration" (p. 257). Kroeber offered his finding as evidence for long-cycle behavior in civilization.

Allport and Hartman (1931) criticized Kroeber for having been insufficiently critical of his sources. They found, for example, that the range in width of skirts for one year, 1886, was greater than the range Kroeber reported for 1859–1864 and that some years had very few cases on which to base measurements. If the data are suspect, Allport and Hartman concluded, then so are the regularities Kroeber claimed to have found (1931:342–43).

Richardson scoured the archives of fashion and extended the database from 1605–1936 (Richardson and Kroeber 1940). Before making measurements for all the new years included in the study, Richardson redid Kroeber's measurements for 1844–1846 and for 1919 and assured herself that she was coding each plate the same way Kroeber had done in 1919 (Richardson and Kroeber 1940).

Lowe and Lowe (1982) reanalyzed the Richardson-Kroeber data for the 150 years from 1787–1936, using all the firepower of modern statistics and computers. You'll be pleased to know that Kroeber's first analysis was vindicated: Stylistic change in women's dress is in stable equilibrium (changing with patterned regularity), and is driven by "inertia, cultural continuity, a rule system of aesthetic proportions, and an inherently unpredictable element" (Lowe and Lowe 1982:521).

Mulcahy and Herbert (1990) added data for the years 1937–1982 and found more variability in those 46 years than in the 150 years before 1937. For example, a plot of the moving average for skirt width from 1811–1926 has the same shape as the plot for 1926–1976. In other words, the cycle of skirt length had been cut by more than half in 1976.

The Problem with Archival Data

Kroeber's early work is being vindicated, but Allport and Hartman's critique was right on target in 1931. You can't be too critical of your sources. Archival data may appear clean, especially if they come packaged on computer files and are coded and ready to be analyzed. But they may be riddled with error. Consider carefully all the possible sources of bias (informant error, observer error, etc.) that might have been at work in the setting down of the data. Ask how, why, and under what conditions a particular set of archival data was collected. Ask who collected the data and what biases she or he might have had.

No data are free of error. In some parts of Mexico, the number of consensual unions is greater than the number of formal marriages, making court records about marriages problematic. In the United States, on the other hand, crime statistics are notoriously untrustworthy. Many crimes go unreported, and those that are reported may not be recorded at all, or may be recorded in the wrong category. In some countries, rural people may wait as long as 6 months to report a birth, and a significant fraction of their children may die within that period. (See Naroll [1962] and Handlin [1979] for discussions of data quality control in archival research.) It is almost always better to understand distortion in data than to throw them out. (For more on archival research in anthropology, see Brettell 1998.)

FURTHER READING

Continuous monitoring: Algase et al. (1997); Black and Reiss (1967); Chadsey-Rusch and Gonzalez (1988); Drury (1990); Frank et al. (1997); Guilmet (1979); LeCompte (1978); LeCompte et al. (1993); Longabaugh (1980); McCall (1978); Reiss (1971).

Ethology and human ethology: Atzwanger et al. (1997); Burkhardt (2005); Chisholm (1983); Eibl-Eiblsfeldt (1989); Houck and Drikamer (1996); Lehner (1996); P. Martin and Bateson (1993).

Studying children's behavior under natural conditions: Fine and Sandstrom (1988); McIver et al. (2009); Meehan (2009); Pellegrini (1996).

Time allocation studies: Bock (2002); Bove et al. (2000); Gurven and Kaplan (2006); Hames (1992); Umezaki et al. (2002).

Experience sampling: Hektner et al. (2007); Scollon et al. (2005). See Kahneman et al. (2004) for a method that duplicates experience sampling through direct interviews rather than with beeper interrupts.

Pseudopatients and simulated clients: Chalker et al. (2004); Katz and Naré (2002); Marsh et al. (2004); Tuladhar et al. (1998); Viberg et al. (2009).

Deception in participant observation: Brymer (1998); Bulmer (1991); Cassell (1982); Lauder (2003); Lugosi (2006); Rynkiewick and Spradley (1976).

Proxemics: Ardener (1981); Høgh-Olesen (2008); Kendon (1981); Kenner and Katsimaglis (1993); Low and Lawrence-Zúñiga (2003).

15

Introduction to Qualitative and Quantitative Analysis

This is the first of eight chapters about analyzing data. In this chapter, we begin with the basics—what analysis is and how to use matrices, tables, and flow charts to present the results of data analysis. Then we move on to two chapters on analyzing data in cognitive anthropology, two chapters on text analysis, and three chapters about statistics. You'll notice as we go through these chapters that some of them very quantitative in orientation, some are qualitative, and some are a blend of qualitative and quantitative approaches. It's fair to say that there are qualitative and quantitative data and that these different types of data need to be analyzed with different methods. But, in my view, forcing people in the social sciences to choose between qualitative and quantitative approaches results in trained incapacity.

QUALITATIVE, QUANTITATIVE

By a quirk of English grammar, the phrase "qualitative data analysis" is delightfully ambiguous. Unless someone spells it out in lots of words, you never know if the phrase means "the qualitative analysis of data" or the "analysis of qualitative data." And the same goes for "quantitative data analysis." Figure 15.1 lays out the possibilities.

Analysis	Data	
	Qualitative	Quantitative
Qualitative	a) Interpretive text studies. Hermeneutics, Grounded Theory	b) Search for and presentation of meaning in results of quantitative processing
Qualitative	c) Turning words into numbers. Classic Content Analysis, Word Counts, Free Lists, Pile Sorts, etc.	d) Statistical and mathematical analysis of numeric data

FIGURE 15.1.
Qualitative-quantitative data analysis.
SOURCE: H. R. Bernard. 1996. "Qualitative Data, Quantitative Analysis." *Cultural Anthropology Methods Journal*, Vol. 8, pp. 9–11. Sage Publications. Used by permission.

Cell *a* is the *qualitative analysis of qualitative data.* Interpretive studies of texts are of this kind. You focus on and name themes in texts. You tell the story, as you see it, of how the themes are related to one another and how characteristics of the speaker or speakers account for the existence of certain themes and the absence of others. You may deconstruct the text, look for hidden subtexts, and, in general, try to let your audience know—using the power of good rhetoric—the deeper meaning or the multiple meanings of the text.

Looking diagonally from cell *a*, cell *d* refers to numerical or statistical analysis of numerical data. Lots of useful data about human behavior come to us as numbers. Direct observation of behavior, village censuses, time allocation studies, close-ended questions in surveys—all produce numerical data.

Cell *b* is the qualitative analysis of quantitative data. This can involve the search for patterns using visualization methods, like multidimensional scaling and hierarchical clustering. (We'll get to these methods next, in chapter 16.) Cell *b* is also about the search for, and the presentation of, *meaning* in the results of quantitative data processing. It's what quantitative analysts do after they get through doing the work in cell *d*. Without the work in cell *b*, cell *d* studies are sterile and superficial.

Which leaves cell *c*, the quantitative analysis of qualitative data. This involves turning the data from words or images into numbers. Scholars in communications, for example, tag a set of television ads from Mexico and the United States to test whether consumers are portrayed as older in one country than in the other. Political scientists code the rhetoric of a presidential debate to look for patterns and predictors of policies. Archeologists code a set of artifacts to produce emergent categories or styles or to test whether some intrusive artifacts can be traced to a source.

Most quantitative analysis in the social sciences involves reducing people (as observed directly or through their texts) to numbers; most qualitative analysis involves reducing people to words—*your* words about the meaning of *their* words or actions or artifacts. I say "most" because a lot of analysis these days, qualitative and quantitative, involves visualization of data: not just looking for patterns in data, but showing the patterns as maps, networks, and matrices.

It's pretty obvious, I think, that each kind of data—qualitative and quantitative—and each kind of data reduction—qualitative and quantitative—is useful for answering certain kinds of questions. Skilled researchers can do it all.

WHAT'S ANALYSIS?

Analysis is the search for patterns in data and for ideas that help explain why those patterns are there in the first place. The way I see it, analysis is ultimately all qualitative. It starts before you collect data—you have to have some ideas about what you're going to study—and it continues throughout any research effort. As you develop ideas, you test them against your observations: Your observations may then modify your ideas, which then need to be tested again, and so on. Don't look for closure in the process. If you're doing it right, it never stops (box 15.1).

Don't worry about getting ideas. Once you have data in your hands, words or numbers, your hardest job will be to sort through all the ideas you get and decide which ones to test. And don't worry about seeing patterns in your data or about not being able to come up with causal explanations for things you see. It can happen very fast, often in a matter of hours or days after starting any research project, so be suspicious of your pet ideas and continually check yourself to make sure you're not inventing or at least not embellishing patterns.

Seeing patterns that aren't there happens all the time in research, qualitative or quanti-

DATA PROCESSING AND DATA ANALYSIS

Most methods for quantitative analysis—things like factor analysis, cluster analysis, regression analysis, and so on—are really methods for data *processing* and for finding patterns in data. Interpreting those patterns is up to you. Interpretation—telling us what findings mean, linking your findings to the findings of other research —starts with ideas in your head and comes out in words on paper. It's a pretty qualitative exercise.

tative, just from eagerness and observer expectations. If you are highly self-critical, your tendency to see patterns everywhere will diminish as the research progresses.

The Constant Validity Check

The problem can also get worse, though, if you accept uncritically the folk analyses of articulate or prestigious informants. It's important to seek the emic perspective and to document folk analyses (Lofland 1971), but as your interviews and field notes pile up, try consciously to switch back and forth between the emic and etic perspectives. Check yourself from either buying into folk explanations or rejecting them without considering their possible validity. It's not hard to do this, it's just hard to remember to do it systematically. Here are some guidelines.

1. If you are interviewing people, look for consistencies and inconsistencies among knowledgeable informants and find out why those informants disagree about important things.
2. Whenever possible, check people's reports of behavior or of environmental conditions against more objective evidence. If you were a journalist and submitted a story based on informants' reports without checking the facts, you'd never get it past your editor's desk. I see no reason not to hold anthropologists to the standard that journalists face every day.
3. Be open to negative evidence rather than annoyed when it pops up. When you run into a case that doesn't fit your theory, ask yourself whether it's the result of: (a) normal **intracultural variation**, (b) your lack of knowledge about the range of appropriate behavior, or (c) a genuinely unusual case.
4. As you come to understand how something works, seek out alternative explanations from key informants and from colleagues, and listen to them carefully. American folk culture, for example, holds that women left home for the work force because of something called "feminism" and "women's liberation." That's a popular emic explanation.

    An alternative explanation is that feminist values and orientations are supported, if not caused, by women being *driven* out of their homes and into the workforce by the hyperinflation during the 1970s that drove down the purchasing power of their husbands' incomes (Margolis 1984). Both the emic, folk explanation and the etic explanations are interesting for different reasons.
5. Try to fit extreme cases into your theory, and if the cases won't fit, don't be too quick

to throw them out. It is always easier to throw out cases than it is to reexamine your own ideas, but the easy way out is hardly ever the right way in research.

DATA MATRICES

One of the most important concepts in all data analysis—whether we're working with quantitative or qualitative data—is the **data matrix**. There are two basic kinds of data matrices: **profile matrices** and **proximity matrices**. Figure 15.2 shows what these two kinds of matrices look like.

Respondent	Age	Sex	Education	Natal Household Size	Current Household Size	Ethnicity
1	27	2	3	6	4	3
2	31	1	2	3	2	1
3	.	.	.	.	.	.
4	.	.	.	.	.	.
.	.	.	.	.	.	.
.	.	.	.	.	.	.
.	.	.	.	.	.	.
.	.	.	.	.	.	.

a.   Profile matrix of persons by variables

	Age	Sex	Education	Natal Household Size	Current Household Size	Ethnicity
Age	——					
Sex		——				
Education			——			
Natal Household Size				——		
Current Household Size					——	
Ethnicity						——

b.   Proximity matrix of the variables (columns) in figure 15.1a

FIGURE 15.2.
Two kinds of matrices: Profiles and Proximities.

Profile Matrices

Across the social sciences, most data analysis is about *how properties of things are related to one another*. We ask, for example, "Is the ability to hunt related to the number of wives a man has?" "Is having an independent source of income related to women's total fertility?" "Are remittances from labor migrants related to the achievement in school of children left behind?" "Is the per capita gross national product of a nation related to the probability that it will go to war with its neighbors?"

This is called **profile analysis.** You start with series of *things*—units of analysis—and you measure a series of *variables* for each of those things. This produces a profile matrix, or, simply, a data matrix. *A data matrix is a table of cases and their associated variables.* Figure 15.2(a) shows the shape of a profile matrix. Each unit of analysis—each row—is *profiled* by a particular set of measurements on some variables—the columns.

The units of analysis in a profile matrix are often respondents to a questionnaire, but they can be dowry records, folk tales, interview texts, churches—even time periods (1980, 1981, 1982, . . . 1991).

Proximity Matrices

Profile matrices contain *measurements of variables for a set of items*. Proximity matrices contain *measurements of relations, or proximities, between items*. If the measurements in a proximity matrix tell *how close things are to each other* then you have a **similarity matrix**. If the measurements in a proximity matrix tell *how far apart things are from each other*, then you have a **dissimilarity matrix** (box 15.2).

Figure 15.2b shows a similarity matrix of variables. Imagine the list of variable names stretching several feet to the right, off the right-hand margin of the page, and several feet down, off the lower margin. That is what would happen if you had, say, 100 variables about each of your respondents. For each and every pair of variables in the matrix of data, you could ask: Are these variables related?

We'll need the concept of a proximity matrix for all kinds of analyses coming up in the chapters that follow.

PRESENTING RESULTS IN MATRICES AND TABLES

An important part of all analysis, qualitative and quantitative, is the production of visual displays. Laying out your data in table or matrix form and drawing your theories out in the form of a flow chart or map helps you understand what you have and helps you communicate your ideas to others (Miles and Huberman 1994). Learning to build and use qualitative data matrices and flow charts requires practice, but you can get started by studying examples published in research journals.

Donna Birdwell-Pheasant (1984), for example, wanted to understand how differences in interpersonal relations change over time in the village of Chunox, Belize. She questioned 216 people about their relations with members of their families over the years, and simulated a longitudinal study with data from a cross-sectional sample. She checked the retrospective data with other information gathered by questionnaires, direct observations, and semistructured interviews. Table 15.1 shows the analytic framework that emerged from Birdwell-Pheasant's work.

Birdwell-Pheasant identified five kinds of relations: absent, attenuated, coordinate, subordinate, and superordinate. These represent the rows of the matrix in table 15.1. The columns in the matrix are the four major types of family relations: ascending generation (parents, aunts, uncles, etc.), siblings, spouse, and descending generation (children, nephews, and nieces, etc.).

Birdwell-Pheasant then went through her data and "examined all the available data on Juana Fulana and decided whether, in 1971, she had a coordinate or subordinate relation-

Table 15.1 Birdwell-Pheasant's Matrix of Criteria for Assigning Values to Major Relationships between People in Her Study

Values of relationships	Major Types of Relationships			
	Ascending generation	*Siblings*	*Spouse*	*Descending generation*
Absent	parents deceased, migrated permanently, or estranged	only child; siblings deceased, migrated permanently, or estranged	single or widowed; spouse migrated or permanently estranged	no mature offspring; all offspring deceased, or migrated permanently, or estranged
Attenuated	does not live with parents or participate in work group with parent; does visit and/or exchange food	does not live with siblings or participate in work groups with them; does visit and/or exchange food	separation, but without final termination of union; e.g., temporary migration	offspring do not live with parents or participate in work group with them; do visit and/or exchange food
Coordinate	participates in work group with parents, sharing decision-making authority	participates in work group with siblings under parents' authority; or works with siblings only, sharing decision making	married; in charge of own sex-specific domain with minimal interference from partner	participates in a work group with offspring, sharing decision-making authority
Subordinate	participates in work group with parent; parent makes decisions	participates in work group of siblings; other sibling(s) make decisions	individual's normal control within sex-specific domain is interfered with by spouse	dependent, elderly parent, unable to work
Superordinate	makes decisions for dependent, elderly parent who is unable to work	participates in work group with siblings; makes decisions for group	interferes with spouse's normal controls within sex-specific domain	heads work group that includes one or more mature offspring; makes decisions for group

SOURCE: D. Birdwell-Pheasant, "Personal Power Careers and the Development of Domestic Structure in a Small Community" *American Ethnologist* 11(4), 1985. Reproduced by permission of the American Anthropological Association. Not for further reproduction.

ship with her mother (e.g., did she have her own kitchen? her own wash house?)." (In Latin America, Juan Fulano and Juana Fulana are the male and female equivalents of "so-and-so"—as in "Is so-and-so married?")

Birdwell-Pheasant repeated the process, for *each* of her 216 informants, for *each* of the four relations in table 15.1, and for *each* of the years 1965, 1971, 1973, 1975, and 1977. This required 216(4)(5) = 4,320 decisions. Birdwell-Pheasant didn't have data on all possible informant-by-year-by-relation combinations, but by the time she was through, she had a database of 742 "power readings" of family relations over time and was able to make some very strong statements about patterns of domestic structure over time in Chunox. This is an excellent example of the use of qualitative data to develop a theory and the conversion of qualitative data to a set of numbers for testing that theory.

Stephen Fjellman and Hugh Gladwin (1985) studied the family histories of Haitian migrants to the United States. Fjellman and Gladwin found an elegant way to present a lot of information about those histories in a simple chart. Table 15.2 shows one chart for a family of four people in 1982.

Table 15.2   Family History of Haitian Migrants to Miami

Year	Jeanne	Anna (mother)	Lucie (sister)	Charles (brother)	Marc (adopted son)	Helen (aunt)	Hughes & Valerie (cousins)	Number in household
1968	+							1
1971	+	+	+	+				4
1975	+	+	+	+	+			5
1976	+	+	−	−	+			3
1978	+	+	−	+	+		*	4
1979	+	+	−	+	+	+	*	5
1982	+	+	−	−	+	+	*	4

SOURCE: S. M. Fjellman and H. Gladwin, "Haitian Family Patterns of Migration to South Florida" *Human Organization*, Vol. 44, p. 307, 1985. Reprinted with permission from the Society for Applied Anthropology.

This Haitian American family began in 1968 when Jeanne's father sent her to Brooklyn, New York, to go to high school. The single plus sign for 1968 shows the founding of the family by Jeanne. Jeanne's father died in 1971, and her mother, sister, and brother joined her in New York. Jeanne adopted Marc in 1975, and in 1976 she and her mother moved with Marc to Miami. Lucie and Charles remained together in New York. The two minus signs in the row for 1976 indicate that Jeanne's sister and brother were no longer part of the household founded by Jeanne.

Two years later, in 1978, Lucie got married and Charles joined Jeanne's household in Miami. Also in 1978, Jeanne began saving money and applying for visas to bring her cousins Hughes and Valerie to Miami. The asterisks show that these two people are in the process of joining the household. In 1979, Anna's sister, Helen joined the family, and in 1982 Charles went back to New York to live again with Lucie.

There is a lot of information in this chart, but the detail is gone. We don't know *why* Jeanne went to the United States in 1968; we don't know *why* Charles left Jeanne's household in 1976 or *why* he rejoined the group in 1978. Fjellman and Gladwin present seven of these family history charts in their article and they provide the historical detail in vignettes below each chart. Their purpose in reducing all the historical detail to a set of pluses and minuses, however, is to allow us to see the *patterns* of family growth, development, and decay.

PRESENTING RESULTS: CAUSAL FLOW CHARTS

Causal maps represent theories about how things work. They are visual representations of ideas that emerge from studying data, seeing patterns, and coming to conclusions about what causes what. Causal maps do not have to have numbers attached to them, although that is where causal modeling eventually leads. After all, it is better to know *how much* one thing causes another than to know simply that one thing *does* cause another. With or without numbers, though, causal models are best expressed as a **flow chart**.

A causal flow chart consists of a set of boxes connected by a set of arrows. The boxes contain descriptions of states (like being the youngest child, or owning a tractor, or being Catholic, or feeling angry), and the arrows tell you how one state leads to another. The simplest causal map is a visual representation of the relation between two variables

$$A \rightarrow B$$

which reads: "A leads to or causes B."

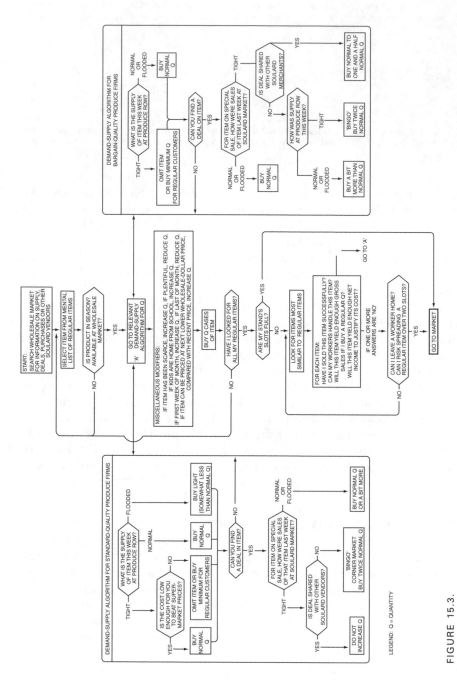

FIGURE 15.3.

Plattner's model for how merchants in the Soulard Market in St. Louis decide what and how much produce to buy.

SOURCE: S. Plattner, "Economic Decision Making in a Public Marketplace." *American Ethnologist*, Vol. 9, p. 404, 1982. Reproduced by permission of the American Anthropological Association. Not for further reproduction.

Real life is usually much, much more complicated than that. Look at figure 15.3. It is Stuart Plattner's **algorithm**, based on intensive interviews and participant observation at produce markets in St. Louis, for how merchants decide what stock to buy. *An algorithm is a set of ordered rules that tell you how to solve a problem*—like "find the average of a list of numbers," or, in this case, "determine the decisions of produce merchants." (The capital letter Q in figure 15.3 stands for "quantity.")

Read the flow chart from top to bottom and left to right, following the arrows. At the beginning of each week, the merchants seek information on the supply and cost of produce items. After that, the algorithm gets complicated. Plattner notes that the model may seem "too complex to represent the decision process of plain folks at the marketplace." However, Plattner says, the chart "still omits consideration of an enormous amount of knowledge pertaining to qualities of produce at various seasons from various shipping areas" (Plattner 1982:405).

Now, on to the nuts and bolts of data analysis.

16

Cognitive Anthropology I: Analyzing Cultural Domains

In chapter 10, I introduced you to five methods for collecting systematic data about cultural domains: free lists, sentence frames, triad tests, pile sorts, and paired comparisons. In this chapter, I'll show you how to analyze these kinds of data. In the next chapter, I'll show you three more methods that are grounded in cognitive anthropology: componential analysis, folk taxonomies, and ethnographic decision modeling. We begin with free lists (box 16.1).

ANALYZING FREE LISTS

Gery Ryan and I asked 34 people: "Please write down the names all the fruits you can think of" (Bernard and Ryan 2010:167). Because free list data are texts, they have to be cleaned up before you can analyze them. Only 10 people listed grapes, but another 22 (for a total of 32 out of 34 people) listed grape (in the singular). Before counting up the frequency for each item in the free lists, we had to combine all mentions of grapes and grape. It doesn't matter whether you change grapes into grape or vice versa, so long as you make all the required changes.

It takes some work to clean up the spelling in free lists. In our data, three people listed bananna (wrong spelling), and 27 people listed banana (right spelling); three people listed avacado (wrong), one listed avocato (wrong), and six people listed avocado (right). Cantaloupe was hopeless, as was pomegranate. We got eight cantaloupe (the preferred spelling in the dictionary), six cantelope, two cantelopes, and three canteloupe. We got 17 listings for guava and one for guayaba, which happens to be the Spanish term for guava. We got 10 listings for passion fruit and one for passion-fruit, with a hyphen (when computers list word frequencies, they see those two listings as different).

Once the data were cleaned, we plotted how often each fruit was mentioned. The result is the scree plot in figure 16.1. ("Scree" refers to the rocks that pile up at the base of a cliff and the telltale L-shape of the scree.)

The shape of the curve in figure 16.1 is typical for a well-defined domain, like fruits: The 34 informants named a total of 147 different fruits, but 88 of those fruits were named by just one person (prickly pear and quince, for example) and almost everyone named a few items (apple and orange, for example). Compare that to the results for lists of "things that mothers do." For this domain, our 34 informants named 554 items, of which 515 were named by just one person and only a handful (love, clean, cook) were named by five or more people.

The difference is that fruits (and animals, and names of racial/ethnic groups, and emo-

---

BOX 16.1

ABOUT SKILLS IN DATA ANALYSIS

We could begin our tour of data analysis anywhere, with any kind of data, because all data analysis, whether we're talking about the qualitative or quantitative kind, requires the same set of big skills. Here's a list of those big skills: (1) logical reasoning; (2) ways to test the results of logical reasoning. That's it. That's the whole list of big skills. All the other skills (and there are hundreds of them) are in one of the two big-skill categories.

The ability to engage in constant comparison, for example, is a really nice skill to develop. It's part of the logical-reasoning set of tools and it means being able to hold some ideas in your head so you can compare them to new ones that emerge as you analyze data. For qualitative data, this means holding on to themes in some narratives and comparing them to new themes that pop into your head as you read the narratives a second and a third and a fourth time. For quantitative data, constant comparison means looking for patterns in many small findings as you run, say, correlations or chi-squared tests to examine hypotheses about what goes with what.

The point is, any skills you learn about how to analyze any data—qualitative or quantitative—are going to serve you well as you work with more and different kinds of data. In fact, having lots of skills in analyzing data will make you fearless about collecting different kinds of data. Once you master multidimensional scaling and cluster analysis, for example—two methods of analysis we'll cover in this chapter—you'll be able to analyze network data and once you can do that, you can do semantic network analysis, which will dramatically extend your capacity to analyze text, and . . . you get the idea (appendix E).

---

tions) are very well defined, but things that mothers do (and things that people might do on a weekend, and things that you can do to stay healthy) are much less well-defined cultural domains. Many of the most interesting domains are things that people don't have easy lists for.

Measuring the Salience of Free-List Items

Gery Ryan and I asked 42 American adolescents (20 boys and 22 girls) to list things they were worried about concerning their health (Bernard and Ryan 2010:170). Table 16.1 shows the results.

Over three-quarters of the informants (76.2%) mentioned sexually transmitted diseases (STDs), and over a third (35.7%) specifically mentioned HIV/AIDS. This is what we expect from adolescents but, surprisingly, nearly half (45.2%) of the informants (all under age 20) were worried about cancer—a worry usually associated with older people.

When we explored this, we found that just 6 of the 20 boys in our sample (30%) had mentioned cancer, compared to 13 of the 22 girls (59%). And when the boys mentioned cancer at all, they ranked it fifth, on average, of the illnesses they were worried about, compared to second for the girls. The girls, it turned out, were very worried about breast cancer, but when the data from both genders were combined, this wasn't noticeable.

The frequency of items in a set of free lists is one indicator of the importance—or

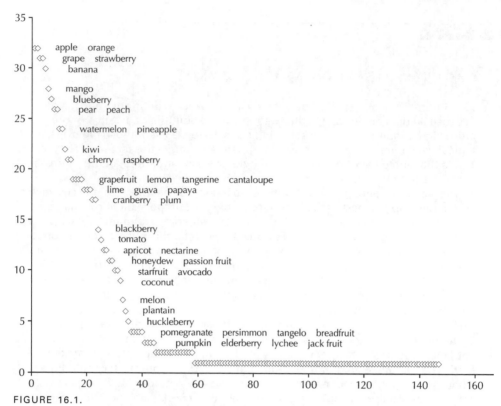

FIGURE 16.1.

Scree plot of free list of 143 fruits from 34 informants.

SOURCE: H. R. Bernard and G. W. Ryan, *Analyzing Qualitative Data: Systematic Approaches*. Los Angeles: Sage Publications. 2010. p. 169. Used by permission.

Table 16.1   Free List Results from 42 Adolescents about Their Health Concerns

	Total Sample (N = 42)		Girls (n = 22)			Boys (n = 20)			Difference women% – men%
	Freq.	%	Rank	Freq.	%	Rank	Freq.	%	
Cold/Flu	12	28.6	3	10	45.5	9	2	10.0	35.5
Cancer	19	45.2	2	13	59.1	5	6	30.0	29.1
Eating Disorders	10	23.8	4	8	36.4	9	2	10.0	26.4
HIV/AIDS	15	35.7	3	10	45.5	6	5	25.0	20.5
Mono	10	23.8	5	7	31.8	8	3	15.0	16.8
Stress	8	19.0	7	5	22.7	8	3	15.0	7.7
Weight-Obesity	10	23.8	6	6	27.3	7	4	20.0	7.3
Skin-related	13	31.0	5	7	31.8	5	6	30.0	1.8
Hygiene	8	19.0	8	4	18.2	7	4	20.0	− 1.8
Disease	8	19.0	8	4	18.2	7	4	20.0	− 1.8
Eating Right	7	16.7	9	3	13.6	7	4	20.0	− 6.4
STDs	32	76.2	1	16	72.7	1	16	80.0	− 7.3
Fitness	12	28.6	7	5	22.7	4	7	35.0	− 12.3
Drug Abuse	9	21.4	9	3	13.6	5	6	30.0	− 16.4
Alcohol-related	16	38.1	6	6	27.3	2	10	50.0	− 22.7
Smoking-related	11	26.2	9	3	13.6	3	8	40.0	− 26.4

SOURCE: H. R. Bernard and G. W. Ryan, *Analyzing Qualitative Data: Systematic Approaches*. Los Angeles: Sage Publications. 2010. p. 171. Used by permission.

salience—of those items to informants. Another indicator is how early, on average, an item gets mentioned. If you ask native speakers of American English to list animals, you'll find that (1) cat and dog are mentioned a lot, and (2) they are mentioned early (Henley 1969). In fact, those two animals are typically the first two animals that get mentioned.

Charismatic megafauna—elephants, whales, lions, and so on—also get mentioned a lot, but usually after the common household animals get named. Thus, in addition to frequency, we can measure the average rank that each item appears in a set of lists. Free listing, however, produces lists of varying length. It's one thing to name elephants fifth in a list of 30 animals and quite another to name elephants fifth in a list of 10 animals, and several methods for taking these factors into account are available.

Smith's S (J. J. Smith and Borgatti 1997) takes into account both the frequency of an item and how early in each list is mentioned and is a popular measure of item cognitive salience. It is also "highly correlated with simple frequency" (Borgatti 1999:149) and so, for most analyses, simple frequency counts of free list data are all that's needed. ANTHROPAC software (Borgatti 1992a) makes short work of free lists (see appendix E) (**Further Reading**: measuring salience. See **Further Reading** on free lists in chapter 10.)

Selecting Items from a Free List for Further Study

Researchers use scree plots to choose a set of items to study in more depth. For example, by counting the dots in figure 16.1, we see that (1) 14 fruits were mentioned by 20 or more of our 34 informants, and (2) 58 items were mentioned by at least two of our informants. All the other fruits were mentioned just once.

How many items should we choose from these data as representing the contents of the domain? There is no formal rule here, but a good general rule is to select items that are mentioned by at least 10% of your informants. If you have 40 informants, then choose items that were mentioned by at least four of them. If this still produces too many items, then move up to 15% of informants or more.

There is nothing forcing you to take every item that's mentioned a lot, especially if you already know something about the domain you're studying. If you want to study, say, 40 items in depth, you can choose some that are mentioned frequently and others that are mentioned less frequently—or even by no one at all.

An item mentioned once is usually not a good candidate to include for further work on the structure of the domain. The whole idea of a cultural domain, as contrasted with an individual cognitive domain is that the content is shared (Borgatti 1999). On the other hand, we often want to know where a particular item fits within a cultural domain.

Once we have identified the items in a cultural domain, the next step is to examine how the items are related to each other. To do this, we ask informants to make similarity judgments—to tell us what goes with what. Pile sorts are an effective method for collecting these judgments.

ANALYZING PILE SORT DATA

Begin a pile sort task by writing the name of each item on a single card (index cards work nicely). Label the back of each card with the number from 1 to n (where n is the total number of items in the domain). Spread the cards out randomly on a large table with the item-side up and the number-side down. (Be sure to shuffle the deck between informants.) Ask informants to sort the cards into piles according to which items they think belong together.

Figure 16.2 shows the pile sort data for one male informant who sorted the names of

1. Apple

2. Orange

3. Papaya

4. Mango

5. Peach

6. Blueberry

7. Watermelon

8. Pineapple

9. Pear

10. Strawberry

11. Lemon

12. Cantaloupe

13. Grapefruit

14. Plum

15. Banana

16. Avocado

17. Fig

18. Cherry

One Person's Sorting of 18 Fruits:

Pile #1: 2, 11, 13

Pile #2: 1, 5, 9, 14, 17, 18

Pile #3: 3, 4, 8, 15, 16

Pile #4: 6, 10

Pile #5: 7, 12

FIGURE 16.2.

Pile sort data from one person for 18 fruits.

SOURCE: H. R. Bernard and G. W. Ryan, *Analyzing Qualitative Data: Systematic Approaches*. Los Angeles: Sage Publications. 2010. p. 173. Used by permission.

18 fruits. It also shows the format for recording the pile sort data. Pile #1 contained items 2, 11, and 13. In other words, this informant put the cards for orange, lemon, and grapefruit into one pile.

Table 16.2 shows the data from figure 16.2 in the form of a similarity matrix, similar to the one you saw in chapter 15.

When the informant put items 2, 11, and 13 (orange, lemon, grapefruit) into a pile, he did so because he thought the items were similar. To indicate this, there is a 1 in the matrix where items 2 and 11 intersect; another 1 in the cell where items 2 and 13 intersect; and another 1 in the cell where 11 and 13 intersect.

Similarly for Pile #2: There is a 1 in the 1-5 cell, the 1-9 cell, the 1-14 cell, and so on. There are 0s in all the cells that represent no similarity of a pair of items (for this informant) and 1s down the diagonal (since items are similar to themselves). Notice that if 11 is similar to 13, then 13 is similar to 11, so this particular matrix is also symmetric. In a

Table 16.2 Similarity Matrix from One Person's Pile Sorting of the 18 Fruits

		1 AP	2 OR	3 PA	4 MA	5 PE	6 BL	7 WA	8 PI	9 PE	10 ST	11 LE	12 CA	13 GR	14 PL	15 BA	16 AV	17 FI	18 CH
1	APPLE	1	0	0	0	1	0	0	0	1	0	0	0	0	1	0	0	1	1
2	ORANGE	0	1	0	0	0	0	0	0	0	0	1	0	1	0	0	0	1	0
3	PAPAYA	0	0	1	1	0	0	0	1	0	0	0	0	0	0	1	1	0	0
4	MANGO	0	0	1	1	0	0	0	1	0	0	0	0	0	0	1	1	0	0
5	PEACH	1	0	0	0	1	0	0	1	1	1	0	0	0	1	0	0	1	1
6	BLUEBERRY	0	0	0	0	0	1	0	0	0	1	0	0	0	0	0	0	0	0
7	WATERMELON	0	0	0	0	0	0	1	0	0	0	0	0	0	0	0	0	0	0
8	PINEAPPLE	0	0	1	1	1	0	0	1	0	0	0	0	0	0	1	1	0	0
9	PEAR	1	0	0	0	1	0	0	0	1	0	0	0	0	1	0	0	1	1
10	STRAWBERRY	0	0	0	0	1	1	0	0	0	1	0	0	0	0	0	0	0	0
11	LEMON	0	1	0	0	0	0	0	0	0	0	1	0	1	0	0	0	0	0
12	CANTALOUPE	0	0	0	0	0	0	0	0	0	0	0	1	0	0	0	0	0	0
13	GRAPEFRUIT	0	1	0	0	0	0	0	0	0	0	1	0	1	0	0	0	0	0
14	PLUM	1	0	0	0	1	0	0	0	1	0	0	0	0	1	0	0	1	1
15	BANANA	0	0	1	1	0	0	0	1	0	0	0	0	0	0	1	1	0	0
16	AVOCADO	0	0	1	1	0	0	0	1	0	0	0	0	0	0	1	1	0	0
17	FIG	1	1	0	0	1	0	0	0	1	0	0	0	0	1	0	0	1	1
18	CHERRY	1	0	0	0	1	0	0	0	1	0	0	0	0	1	0	0	1	1

symmetric matrix, the bottom and top halves (above and below the diagonal of 1s) are identical (box 16.2).

BOX 16.2

GETTING PILE-SORT DATA INTO A COMPUTER

ANTHROPAC is a DOS program, but it's still the easiest way I know to import pile sort data into a computer for analysis. Once you have pile sort data into a computer, you can use any major statistical package to analyze the matrices. I use UCINET, a windows program, because it shares files with ANTHROPAC. Any data you import with ANTHROPAC is available to UCINET for analysis. UCINET also can export data as an Excel file, so you can use the data in your favorite statistics program.

ANALYZING PILE SORT DATA: MDS

If you examine it carefully, you'll see that, despite the 1s and 0s, there is not a shred of math in table 16.2. It contains nothing more than the information in the bottom half of figure 16.2, displayed as 1s and 0s, and there is nothing numerical about those 1s and 0s. They simply stand for oranges and papayas and so on. But by substituting 1s and 0s for the names of the items, we can use software to look for patterns in the informant's pile sort data.

Figure 16.3 is a multidimensional scaling, or MDS, of these data. MDS is one of several visualizations methods now widely used in all the sciences—methods that look for patterns in numerical data and display those patterns graphically. The MDS in figure 16.3 shows the pattern in table 16.2. That is, it shows how one informant sees the similarities among the 18 fruits.

Look carefully at table 16.2. There are 1s in the cells 2-11, 2-13, and 11-13. This is because the informant put orange (2), lemon (11), and grapefruit (13) in one pile and nothing else in that pile. This behavior is presented graphically in figure 16.3 with the orange-lemon-grapefruit cluster shown separated from other clusters.

How MDS Works

You'll sometimes see **multidimensional scaling** called **smallest-space analysis**. That's because MDS programs work out the best spatial representation of a set of objects that are represented by a set of similarities. Suppose, for example, that you measure the distance, in miles, among three cities, A, B, and C. The matrix for these cities is in the inside box of table 16.3.

Clearly, cities A and C are closer to one another than are A and B, or B and C. You can represent this with a triangle, as in figure 16.4a.

In other words, we can place points A, B, and C on a plane in some position relative to each other. The distance between A and B is longer than that between A and C (reflecting the difference between 40 and 50 miles); and the distance between B and C is longer than that between A and C (reflecting the difference between 40 and 80 miles).

A rule in graph theory says that you can plot the relations among any set of relations

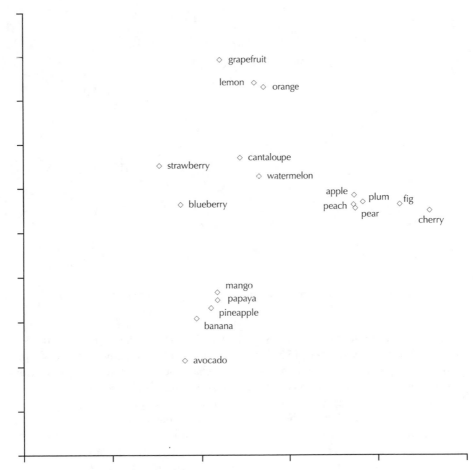

FIGURE 16.3.
Two-dimensional MDS for 18 fruits sorted by one informant.

in *n*–1 dimensions, where *n* is the number relations. With three cities, there are three relations: AB, AC, and BC, so it's easy to plot all the distances in proper proportion to one another in a two-dimensional graph. In fact, figure 16.4a contains precisely the same information as the inside box of table 16.3, but in graphic form. You can see in figure 16.4a that the physical distance (in inches) between B and C is twice that of A and C.

If we add a fourth city, things get considerably more complicated. With four items,

Table 16.3   **Matrix of Distances among Four Cities**

	A	*B*	*C*	*D*
A	X	50	40	110
B		X	80	45
C			X	115
D				X

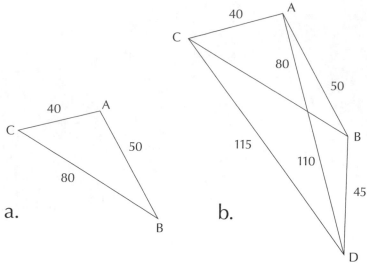

FIGURE 16.4.
Two-dimensional plot of the distance among three cities (a) and among four cities (b).

there are six relations to cope with: AB, AC, AD, BC, BD, and CD. These relations are shown in the large box of table 16.3. We can plot the relations among these six pairs perfectly in a graph of $n - 1 = 5$ dimensions, but what would we do with a 5-dimensional graph? Instead, we try 2 dimensions and see if the distortion is acceptable.

MDS programs produce a statistic that measures this distortion, or "stress," as it's called, which tells us how far off the graph is from one that would be perfectly proportional. The lower the stress, the better the solution. Table 16.4 shows the road distance, in miles, between all pairs of nine cities in the United States. Most researchers will accept a stress of <0.15 in an MDS graph. The MDS graph produced from the set of relations in table 16.4, and shown in figure 16.5, has a stress of about zero because table 16.4 contains metric data—reasonably accurate measures of a physical reality. In this case, it's distance between points on a map (box 16.3).

Table 16.4   Distances between Nine U.S. Cities (in Miles)

	BOS	NY	DC	MIA	CHI	SEA	SF	LA	DEN
Boston	0								
NY	206	0							
DC	429	233	0						
Miami	1504	1308	1075	0					
Chicago	963	802	671	1329	0				
Seattle	2976	2815	2684	3273	2013	0			
SF	3095	2934	2799	3053	2142	808	0		
LA	2979	2786	2631	2687	2054	1131	379	0	
Denver	1949	1771	1616	2037	996	1037	1235	1059	0

SOURCE: *Anthropac 4.0* and *Anthropac 4.0 Methods Guide,* by S. P. Borgatti, 1992a, 1992b. Reprinted with permission of the author.

Figure 16.5 looks suspiciously like a map of the United States. All nine cities are placed in proper juxtaposition to one another, but the map looks sort of upside-down and backward. If we could only flip the map over from left to right and from bottom to top. . . . Multidimensional scaling programs are notoriously unconcerned with details like this. So

BOX 16.3

TWO KINDS OF PROXIMITIES

The numbers in table 16.4 are dissimilarities, not similarities. Recall from chapter 15 that in a similarity matrix, bigger numbers mean that pairs of things are closer to each other—more like each other—and smaller numbers mean that things are farther apart—less like each other. In a dissimilarity matrix, bigger numbers means that pairs of things are farther apart—less like each other—and smaller numbers mean that things are closer to each other—more like each other. And recall, too, that similarity and dissimilarity matrices are known collectively as proximity matrices because they tell you how close or far apart things are.

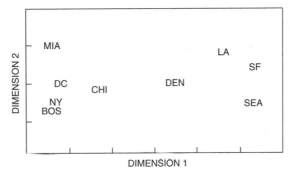

FIGURE 16.5.
Two-dimensional MDS solution for the numbers in table 16.4.

long as they get the juxtaposition right, they're finished. Figure 16.5 shows that the program got it right. (Obviously, you can rotate any MDS graph through some angle about any axis and it will still have the same meaning. Think about a map of the surface of the Earth from the perspective of someone who is looking out from 100 miles inside the Earth. It would be the same map that you're accustomed to, but flipped.)

This means that you can use MDS to create outline maps of your own. To map a village, you would measure the distance between all pairs of some set of points, like a church, a well, a school, and so on. A set of 10 points means 45 pairs and 45 measurements. The more pairs of points you measure the more accurate the map will be, but, as you can see from figure 16.5, even a set of nine points (and 36 measurements) gets you a basic outline map of the United States (**Further Reading:** multidimensional scaling).

Interpreting MDS Graphs

It's convenient to think of the MDS graph in figure 16.3 as a sort of mental map. That is, it represents what the informant was thinking when he pile sorted those fruits. I say "sort of mental map" because MDS graphs of pile-sort data are not one-to-one maps of what's going on inside people's heads. We treat them, however, as a rough proxy for what people were thinking when they made piles of cards or words or whatever.

356

Looking at figure 16.3, it looks like there's a citrus cluster, a berry cluster, a melon cluster, a fruit tree cluster, and a tropical cluster. We can check our intuition about these clusters by running a **cluster analysis**, shown in figure 16.6.

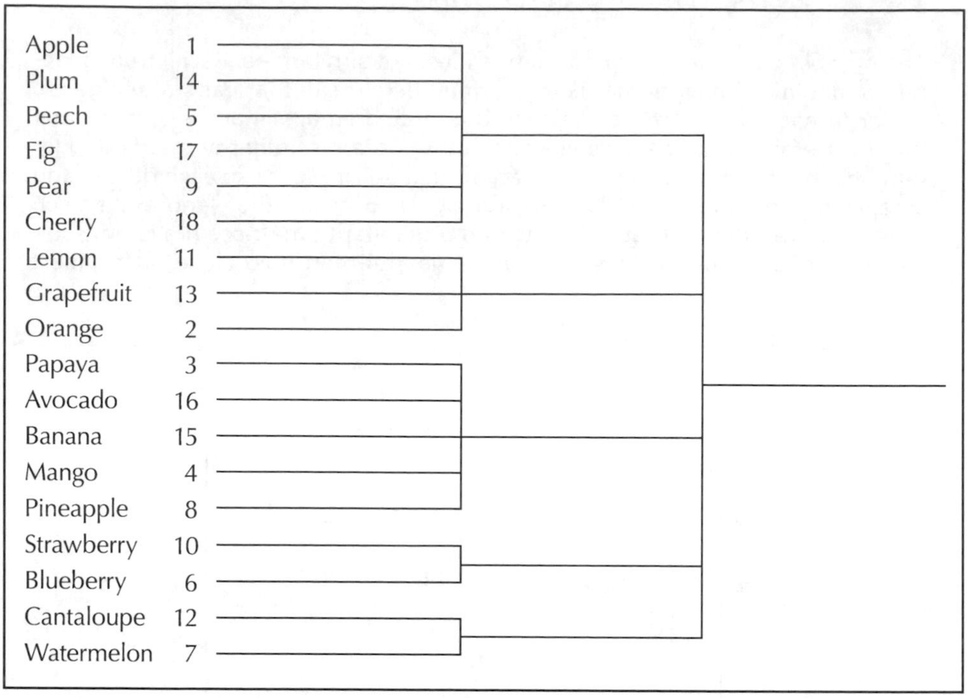

FIGURE 16.6.
Cluster analysis of 18 fruits from one pile sort.
SOURCE: H. R. Bernard and G. W. Ryan, *Analyzing Qualitative Data: Systematic Approaches*. Los Angeles: Sage Publications. 2010. p. 177. Used by permission.

Read figure 16.6 as follows: At the first level of clustering, the informant put #7 (watermelon) and #12 (cantaloupe) together, and he put #6 (blueberry) and #10 (strawberry) together. These two clusters together form a cluster at the second level. And the same goes for the other clusters: They come together at the second level and all form one big cluster.

Because there is just one informant, there can only be two levels. The first level is the level at which the informant made the separate piles. The second is the entire set of fruits. I've taken you through what looks like a trivial exercise to show you how to read the cluster diagram (or dendrogram) and the MDS picture. As we'll see next, things get more interesting when we add informants (box 16.4).

Analyzing Pile Sort Data: Aggregate Matrices

To test whether this pattern holds up, Ryan and I asked five more informants to do the pile sort exercise (Bernard and Ryan 2010:179). Each informant's data produce an individual similarity matrix of 1s and 0s, like the matrix shown in table 16.2. Table 16.5 shows the aggregate similarity matrix for the six informants.

To produce table 16.5, just stack the six individual matrices on top of one another, count the number of 1s down the column for each cell, and divide by six. (This is all done

BOX 16.4

DIMENSIONS AND CLUSTERS IN MDS

Susan Weller (1983) asked 24 Guatemalan women—some urban, some rural—to do a pile sort of 27 illness names. Figure 16.7 shows the MDS graph of the illnesses for Weller's urban sample.

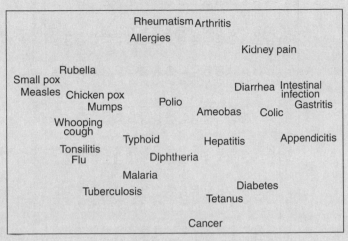

FIGURE 16.7.

MDS representation of 27 illnesses for urban Guatemalan women.

Source: S. Weller, "New Data on Intracultural Variability: The Hot-Cold Concept of Medicine and Illness," *Human Organization*, Vol. 42, pp. 249–57. © 1983. Reprinted with permission of the Society for Applied Anthropology.

When you interpret an MDS graph, look for **arrays**, or **dimensions** as well as for clusters. There is a clump on the right that might be called "gastrointestinal disorders." On the left there is a clump of "childhood disorders." Those, at least, are the labels that struck Weller as appropriate. I agree with her intuition about this. What do *you* think?

How about the arrays, or dimensions? To me, it looks like informants distinguish between chronic and acute illnesses (from top to bottom in figure 16.7) and between infectious and noninfectious illnesses (from left to right). But remember: Interpretation of numerical results is always a brazen, flat-out qualitative exercise, a Rorschach test for social scientists—which is why I like it so much. Use every technique you can think of in data analysis, and let your experience guide your interpretation. Interpretation of results is where data analysis in all science ultimately becomes a humanistic activity.

instantly with a computer program, like ANTHROPAC or UCINET.) That tells you the percentage of people who put each pair of fruits together in a pile. Because there are six informants here, the numbers in the cells of table 16.5 can be 0.00 (none out of six), 0.17 (one out of six), 0.33 (two out of six), 0.50 (three out of six), 0.67 (four out of six), 0.83 (five out of six), and 1.00 (six out of six).

Table 16.5 Aggregate Similarity Matrix from Six Pile Sorts of the 18 Fruits in Figure 16.2

	ap	or	pap	man	pea	blu	wat	pin	per	str	lem	can	gpf	plu	ban	avc	fig	chr
Apple	1.00	0.00	0.00	0.00	0.83	0.00	0.17	0.00	0.83	0.00	0.00	0.00	0.00	0.83	0.17	0.00	0.17	0.33
Orange	0.00	1.00	0.17	0.17	0.00	0.00	0.17	0.17	0.00	0.00	0.83	0.17	1.00	0.00	0.00	0.17	0.00	0.00
Papaya	0.00	0.17	1.00	0.67	0.17	0.00	0.17	0.50	0.17	0.00	0.00	0.17	0.17	0.17	0.33	0.67	0.17	0.00
Mango	0.00	0.17	0.67	1.00	0.00	0.00	0.17	0.50	0.00	0.00	0.00	0.33	0.17	0.00	0.33	0.67	0.00	0.00
Peach	0.83	0.00	0.17	0.00	1.00	0.00	0.00	0.00	1.00	0.00	0.00	0.00	0.00	1.00	0.17	0.17	0.17	0.33
Blueberry	0.00	0.00	0.00	0.00	0.00	1.00	0.00	0.00	0.00	0.83	0.00	0.00	0.00	0.00	0.00	0.00	0.50	0.67
Watermelon	0.17	0.17	0.17	0.17	0.00	0.00	1.00	0.17	0.00	0.00	0.00	0.83	0.17	0.00	0.00	0.17	0.00	0.00
Pineapple	0.00	0.17	0.50	0.50	0.00	0.00	0.17	1.00	0.00	0.00	0.00	0.17	0.17	0.00	0.50	0.50	0.00	0.00
Pear	0.83	0.00	0.17	0.00	1.00	0.00	0.17	0.00	1.00	0.00	0.00	0.17	0.17	1.00	0.17	0.17	0.17	0.33
Strawberry	0.00	0.00	0.00	0.00	0.00	0.83	0.00	0.00	0.00	1.00	0.00	0.00	0.00	0.00	0.00	0.00	0.50	0.50
Lemon	0.00	0.83	0.00	0.00	0.00	0.00	0.00	0.00	0.00	0.00	1.00	0.00	0.83	0.00	0.00	0.00	0.00	0.00
Cantaloupe	0.00	0.17	0.17	0.33	0.00	0.00	0.83	0.17	0.00	0.00	0.00	1.00	0.17	0.00	0.00	0.17	0.00	0.00
Grapefruit	0.00	1.00	0.17	0.17	0.00	0.00	0.17	0.17	0.00	0.00	0.83	0.17	1.00	0.00	0.00	0.17	0.00	0.00
Plum	0.83	0.00	0.17	0.00	1.00	0.00	0.00	0.00	1.00	0.00	0.00	0.00	0.00	1.00	0.17	0.17	0.17	0.33
Banana	0.17	0.00	0.33	0.33	0.17	0.00	0.00	0.50	0.17	0.00	0.00	0.00	0.00	0.17	1.00	0.33	0.00	0.00
Avocado	0.00	0.17	0.67	0.67	0.17	0.00	0.17	0.50	0.17	0.00	0.00	0.17	0.17	0.17	0.33	1.00	0.00	0.00
Fig	0.17	0.00	0.00	0.00	0.17	0.50	0.17	0.00	0.17	0.50	0.00	0.00	0.00	0.17	0.00	0.00	1.00	0.50
Cherry	0.33	0.00	0.00	0.00	0.33	0.67	0.00	0.00	0.33	0.50	0.00	0.00	0.00	0.33	0.00	0.00	0.50	1.00

SOURCE: H. R. Bernard and G. W. Ryan, *Analyzing Qualitative Data: Systematic Approaches*. Los Angeles: Sage Publications. 2010. p. 179. Used by permission.

For example, reading across the top row in table 16.5, we see that five out of six informants (83%) put apple and pear in the same pile. Reading across the third row, we see that four out of six people (67%) put papaya and mango in the same pile. And so on. Just like table 16.2, table 16.5 is symmetric (check it and see for yourself).

Cluster Analysis and Pile Sort Data

Figure 16.8 shows the MDS plot of the data in table 16.5. It looks pretty much like figure 16.3, but there are some differences. Averaging across the six informants, figs and cherries now appear to be in a separate cluster and to be a bridge between the berry group (strawberries and blueberries) and the major tree-fruit group (apples, plums, peaches, and pears). Furthermore, banana, which was in the tropical fruit cluster for our first informant, now appears to be a bridge between the tropical fruit cluster (mangos, papayas, pineapples, and avocados) and the traditional tree fruit cluster (apples, plums, peaches, and pears (box 16.5).

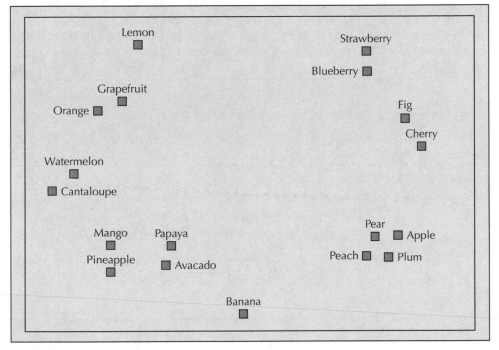

FIGURE 16.8.
Multidimensional scaling of the data in table 16.5.
SOURCE: H. R. Bernard and G. W. Ryan, *Analyzing Qualitative Data: Systematic Approaches*. Los Angeles: Sage Publications. 2010. p. 181. Used by permission.

The cluster analysis on the data in table 16.5 is shown in figure 16.9. It confirms that, despite some expected intracultural variation, these informants saw cherries and figs as related to strawberries and blueberries and saw all four of these fruits as more closely related to apples, plums, peaches, and pears than to all the other fruits.

How Cluster Analysis Works

Consider the following example from de Ghett (1978:121):

1   3   7   9   14   20   21   25

BOX 16.5

CLUSTERS AND BRIDGES

What does it mean to say that "figs and cherries appear to be a bridge between the berry group and major tree-fruit group" or that "banana appears to be a bridge between tropical fruits and traditional tree fruits"?

When we interviewed people about why they put various fruits together, some people who put figs and cherries with apples and pears said "These all grow on trees." People who put figs and/or cherries into other piles said things like "Figs are more exotic, but not like mangoes" or "Cherries grow on trees, but they are small and clumpy." Some informants said that banana was a tropical fruit and "went with papaya," but others said it was unique and belonged in a group by itself. One person said it belonged with apples and pears "because you can mix them together to make fruit salad."

Always ask people to explain their pile choices. Later, when you see figs and cherries in an MDS graph lying between a berries cluster and traditional tree-fruit cluster, you'll have some basis for interpreting the graph.

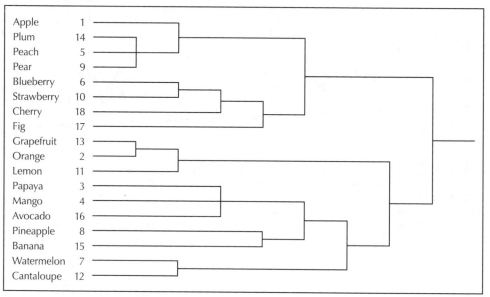

FIGURE 16.9.
Cluster analysis of the data in table 16.5.
SOURCE: H. R. Bernard and G. W. Ryan, *Analyzing Qualitative Data: Systematic Approaches*. Los Angeles: Sage Publications. 2010. p. 182. Used by permission.

This set of numbers has no meaning at all, so we can concentrate on the method of clustering them, without any interpretation getting in the way. When we get through with this example, we'll move on to a set of numbers that does have meaning. The distance between 1 and 3 is 2. The distance between 21 and 25 is 4. So, in a numerical sense, 1 and 3 are twice as similar to one another as 21 and 25 are to one another. Table 16.6 shows the dissimilarity matrix for these numbers.

Table 16.6   Dissimilarity Matrix for Clustering

	1	3	7	9	14	20	21	25
1	0							
3	2	0						
7	6	4	0					
9	8	6	2	0				
14	13	11	7	5	0			
20	19	17	13	11	6	0		
21	20	18	14	12	7	1	0	
25	24	22	18	16	11	5	4	0

SOURCE: V. J. de Ghett, "Hierarchical Cluster Analysis" *Quantitative Ethology,* ed. by P. W. Colgan. 1978. Reprinted by permission of John Wiley & Sons, Inc.

There are several ways to find clusters in this matrix. Two of them are called **single-link** or **closest-neighbor analysis** and **complete-link** or **farthest-neighbor analysis** (there are others, but I won't go into them here). In single-link clustering, we use only the numbers adjacent to the diagonal: 2, 4, 2, 5, 6, 1, 4. The two clustering solutions (done with UCINET) are shown in figure 16.10.

In the single-link solution, the two closest neighbors are 20 and 21. They are exactly one unit of distance apart, and there is a 1 adjacent to the diagonal of the original matrix where 20 and 21 come together. In figure 16.10a, 20 and 21 are shown joined at level 1. The numbers 1,3 and the numbers 7,9 are the next closest neighbors. They are both two units apart. Figure 16.10a shows them joined at level 2.

Once a pair is joined, it is considered a unit. The pairs 1,3 and 7,9 are joined together at level 4 because they are four units apart (the nearest neighbor to the pair 1,3 is 7, which is four units from 3). The pair 21,25 are also four units apart. However, 20,21 are already joined, so 25 joins this pair at level 4. The connections are built up to form a tree.

Figure 16.10b shows the complete-link (or farthest neighbor) clustering solution for the data in table 16.6. In complete-link clustering, all the numbers in table 16.6 are used. Once again, the pair 20,21 is joined at level 1 because the pair is just one unit apart. The pairs 1,3 and 7,9 join at level 2.

a. SINGLE LINK

	1	3	7	9	14	20	21	25
Level								
1						x	x	x
2	x	x	x		x	x	x	
4	x	x	x	x	x	x		

b. COMPLETE LINK

	1	3	7	9	14	20	21	25
Level								
1						x	x	x
2	x	x	x		x	x	x	
5	x	x	x		x	x	x	
7	x	x	x		x	x	x	x
13	x	x	x	x	x	x	x	x
24	x	x	x	x	x	x	x	x

FIGURE 16.10.
Cluster analysis of the data in table 16.6.

Up to this point, the complete-link and single-link solutions are identical. At the next level, though, things change. The neighbors of 20,21 are 14 and 25. The farthest neighbor from 14 to 20,21 is 21. The distance is seven units. The farthest neighbor from 25 to 20,21 is 20. The distance is five units. Since five is less than seven, 25 joins 20,21 at level 5. But the two pairs 1,3 and 7,9 are not joined at this level.

The only number not yet joined to some other number is 14. It is compared to its farthest neighbors in the adjacent clusters: 14 is 11 units away from 25 (which is now part of the 20,21,25 cluster) and it's seven units away from the 7,9 cluster. So, at level 7, 14 is joined to 7,9. The same game is played out with all the clusters to form the tree in figure 16.10b.

Clusters of Cities

The complete-link method tends to create more discrete clusters; the single-link method tends to clump things together more. The method you choose determines the results you get. Look at figure 16.11a and b to see what happens when we use the single-link and complete link clustering methods on the data in table 16.4.

```
              a. SINGLE LINK                                    b. COMPLETE LINK
          S                       C                                          C  S
          E            B          H   D                            B         H  E            D
      M   A            O          I   E                        M   O         I  A            E
      I   T            S          C   N                        I   S         C  T            N
      A   T            T          A   V                        A   T         A  T            V
      M   L   S   L    O   N   D  G   E                        M   O   N   D  G  L   S   L   E
      I   E   F   A    N   Y   C  O   R                        I   N   Y   C  O  E   F   A   R
Level                                               Level
206               x x x                             206       x x x
233               x x x x x                         379       x x x              x x x
379       x x x   x x x x x                         429       x x x x x          x x x
671       x x x   x x x x x x x                     963       x x x x x x x      x x x
808   x x x x x   x x x x x x x                     1037      x x x x x x x      x x x x x
996   x x x x x   x x x x x x x x x x               1235      x x x x x x x      x x x x x x x
1037  x x x x x x x x x x x x x x x x               1504      x x x x x x x x x  x x x x x x x
1075 x x x x x x x x x x x x x x x x x              3273      x x x x x x x x x x x x x x x x x x
```

FIGURE 16.11.
Complete link and single link solutions for the data in table 16.4.

To me, the complete-link method seems better with these data. Denver "belongs" with San Francisco and Los Angeles more than it belongs with Boston and New York. But that may be my own bias. Coming from New York, I think of Denver as a western U.S. city, but I've heard people from San Francisco talk about "going *back east* to Denver for the weekend" (**Further Reading:** cluster analysis).

A REAL RESEARCH EXAMPLE: GREEN BEHAVIOR AND ELECTRIC CARS IN THE UNITED STATES

Now that you know how MDS and cluster analysis work, let's walk through an example from real research. In the mid-1990s, under a contract from a U.S. automobile manufacturer, Gery Ryan, Steve Borgatti, and I studied the domain of green behaviors in the United States—that is, things people believe they can do to help the environment (Bernard et al. 2009). Using free lists, we generated 85 "things people can to do help the environment." Then, 44 people pile-sorted those 85 items. The results (MDS) are shown in figure 16.12.

With all the labels for the behaviors, it's hard to see the pattern, but if we cut the labels down to three- and four-letter abbreviations and run a cluster analysis, a strong pattern emerges. Figure 16.13 contains the exact same information as figure 16.12 but with named

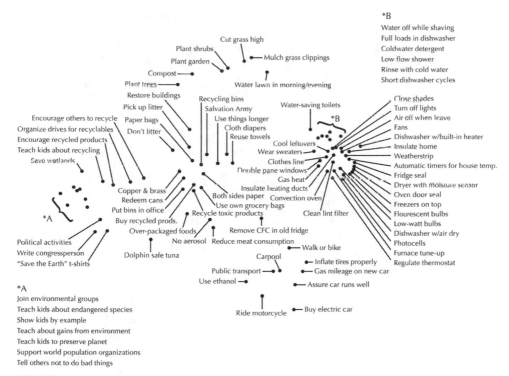

FIGURE 16.12.

MDS of 85 green behaviors.

SOURCE: H. R. Bernard, G. Ryan, and S. Borgatti. "Green Cognition and Behavior: A Cultural Domain Analysis." In *Networks, Resources and Economic Action. Ethnographic Case Studies in Honor of Hartmut Lang*, p. 200. C. Greiner and W. Kokot, eds. Berlin: Dietrich Reimer Verlag.

circles around the clusters. The cluster analysis told us where to draw the circles, but the names for those clusters of green behaviors—"household," "lawn and garden," "recycling," "advocacy," "transportation"—are the result of our analysis.

I said earlier that you can insert items into a domain analysis even if nobody mentions it in free lists. See the label "Elec" in the transportation cluster? It stands for "buy an electric car." When we did this research, in 1996, electric and hybrid cars were still in the design stage. Our client wanted to know where Americans might place the behavior of "buying an electric car" within the domain of green behaviors, so we stuck that item into the pile sort task of the study, even though none of our informants mentioned this behavior in the free list of "things people can do for the environment."

ANALYZING TRIAD DATA

Triad tests produce similarity matrices and these can also be analyzed using MDS and clustering. Recall from chapter 10 how triad tests work. Figure 16.14 shows the instructions and first 10 lines of a typical triad test. In this case, the domain is a list of 15 emotions: love, anger, disgust, shame, fear, anguish, envy, anxious, tired, happy, sad, lonely, bored, hate, and excitement. The data come from a class project where we interviewed 40 people and used a lambda-2 design. In a complete design with 15 items, there are $n(n-1)(n-2)/6 = 455$ triads, but that's because every pair of items shows up $(n-2) = 13$ times. We used a lambda-2, balanced incomplete block design, or BIBD (see chapter 10 for details on BIBDs). In a lambda-2 BIBD, each pair of items shows up twice and this cuts the number of triads down to just 70. Since each pair of items shows up twice, each

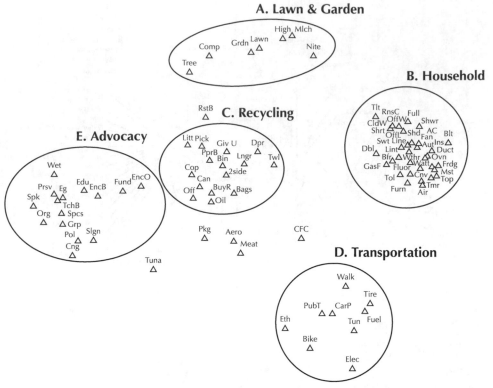

FIGURE 16.13.
Redrawing of figure 16.12 showing the results of a cluster analysis for 85 green behaviors.
SOURCE: H. R. Bernard, G. Ryan, and S. Borgatti. "Green Cognition and Behavior: A Cultural Domain Analysis." In *Networks, Resources and Economic Action. Ethnographic Case Studies in Honor of Hartmut Lang*, p. 202. C. Greiner and W. Kokot, eds. Berlin: Dietrich Reimer Verlag.

cell in the item-by-item similarity matrix for each informant can contain just three numbers: 0.00, 0.50, or 1.00.

Figure 16.15 shows the individual similarity matrices from two informants who took the triad test about emotions. Looking across the first row of Matrix #1, we see a 0.00 in the first cell for love-love, and then zeros down the diagonal since the matrix is symmetric. Next, we see that both times the informant saw the pair love-anger, she circled one of them, making the other member of the love-anger pair similar to the third item in that triad. The same thing happened for love-disgust and love-shame. When she saw the pair love-fear, though, she circled one of them once and she circled the third item in the triad once. That is, half the time she kept the pair together (as similar) and half the time she kept them apart (as dissimilar, compared to a third item), so there's a 0.50 in that cell. She did the same thing for love-hate. She kept the pairs love-happy and love-excitement together both times they showed up in the triad test, and we see 1.00 in those cells.

Compare this to informant #2. He also kept the love-happy and love excitement pairs together both times they show up in his triad test, but he never kept love-fear together; he kept love-envy together once; and he kept love-hate together twice.

To aggregate the 40 individual matrices from this triad test, we stack them on top of each other (software does this for us), sum down each cell and divide by 40 to get an average similarity for each pair of items. Figure 16.16 shows this aggregate similarity matrix.

Thank you for participating in this study. On the next page, you will find a set of three words on each line. For each set, please mark the item that is MOST DIFFERENT from the other two. For example, for the set

CHERRY   APPLE   DOG

you would circle DOG, since cherries and apples are very similar, at least when compared to dogs. Here is another example:

DOG   CAT   ROCK

In this case, you would probably circle ROCK. Please give an answer for EVERY set of three, even if you are not sure of the answer. DO NOT SKIP ANY SETS: If you don't know the answer, just guess. Thank you.

ANGER	SAD	ENVY
BORED	ANGUISH	SAD
LONELY	FEAR	ENVY
SAD	LOVE	ANGUISH
ANXIOUS	HATE	HAPPY
TIRED	ANXIOUS	BORED
HATE	LOVE	ANGUISH
ANGER	LOVE	HAPPY
FEAR	LOVE	ANXIOUS
TIRED	HAPPY	LONELY

FIGURE 16.14.
Instructions for a triad test.

```
Matrix #1:
                    1    2    3    4    5    6    7    8    9   10   11   12   13   14   15
                  LOVE ANGR DISG SHAM FEAR ANGU ENVY ANXI TIRE HAPP SAD  LONE BORE HATE EXCI
                  ---- ---- ---- ---- ---- ---- ---- ---- ---- ---- ---- ---- ---- ---- ----
 1        LOVE    0.00 0.00 0.00 0.00 0.50 0.00 0.00 0.00 0.00 1.00 0.00 0.00 0.00 0.50 1.00
 2       ANGER    0.00 0.00 1.00 0.00 0.50 0.50 0.00 0.50 0.00 0.00 0.00 0.00 0.00 1.00 0.00
 3     DISGUST    0.00 1.00 0.00 1.00 1.00 1.00 0.50 1.00 0.00 0.00 0.50 0.00 0.00 1.00 0.00
 4       SHAME    0.00 0.00 1.00 0.00 0.50 1.00 1.00 0.00 1.00 0.00 0.00 0.50 0.00 0.50 0.00
 5        FEAR    0.50 0.50 1.00 0.50 0.00 0.50 1.00 1.00 0.00 0.00 0.00 0.50 0.00 1.00 0.00
 6     ANGUISH    0.00 0.50 1.00 1.00 0.50 0.00 1.00 1.00 0.00 0.00 1.00 0.00 0.00 0.50 0.00
 7        ENVY    0.00 0.00 0.50 1.00 1.00 1.00 0.00 0.50 0.00 0.00 0.50 0.50 0.50 0.50 0.00
 8     ANXIOUS    0.00 0.50 1.00 0.00 1.00 1.00 0.50 0.00 0.00 0.00 0.00 0.00 0.00 0.00 0.50
 9       TIRED    0.00 0.00 0.00 1.00 0.00 0.00 0.00 0.00 0.00 0.00 1.00 0.50 1.00 0.00 0.00
10       HAPPY    1.00 0.00 0.00 0.00 0.00 0.00 0.00 0.00 0.00 0.00 0.50 0.00 0.00 0.50 1.00
11         SAD    0.00 0.00 0.50 0.00 0.00 1.00 0.50 0.00 1.00 0.50 0.00 1.00 0.50 0.50 0.00
12      LONELY    0.00 0.00 0.00 0.50 0.50 0.00 0.50 0.00 0.50 0.00 1.00 0.00 0.50 0.00 0.00
13       BORED    0.00 0.00 0.00 0.00 0.00 0.00 0.50 0.00 1.00 0.00 0.50 0.50 0.00 0.00 0.50
14        HATE    0.50 1.00 1.00 0.50 1.00 0.50 0.50 0.00 0.00 0.50 0.50 0.00 0.00 0.00 0.00
15  EXCITEMENT    1.00 0.00 0.00 0.00 0.00 0.00 0.00 0.50 0.00 1.00 0.00 0.00 0.50 0.00 0.00


Matrix #2:
                    1    2    3    4    5    6    7    8    9   10   11   12   13   14   15
                  LOVE ANGR DISG SHAM FEAR ANGU ENVY ANXI TIRE HAPP SAD  LONE BORE HATE EXCI
                  ---- ---- ---- ---- ---- ---- ---- ---- ---- ---- ---- ---- ---- ---- ----
 1        LOVE    0.00 0.00 0.00 0.00 0.00 0.00 0.50 0.00 0.00 1.00 0.00 0.00 0.00 1.00 1.00
 2       ANGER    0.00 0.00 1.00 0.00 1.00 0.50 1.00 0.50 0.00 0.00 0.00 0.00 0.00 1.00 0.00
 3     DISGUST    0.00 1.00 0.00 1.00 1.00 1.00 1.00 0.00 0.00 0.00 0.50 0.00 0.00 0.50 0.00
 4       SHAME    0.00 0.00 1.00 0.00 0.00 0.50 0.00 1.00 1.00 0.00 1.00 0.00 0.00 0.50 0.00
 5        FEAR    0.00 1.00 1.00 0.00 0.00 1.00 1.00 0.50 0.00 0.00 0.50 0.50 0.00 1.00 0.00
 6     ANGUISH    0.00 0.50 1.00 0.50 1.00 0.00 1.00 1.00 0.00 0.00 1.00 0.00 0.00 0.50 0.00
 7        ENVY    0.50 1.00 1.00 0.00 1.00 1.00 0.00 0.50 0.00 0.00 0.00 0.50 0.00 0.50 0.00
 8     ANXIOUS    0.00 0.50 1.00 1.00 0.50 1.00 0.50 0.00 0.50 0.00 0.50 0.00 0.00 0.50 0.50
 9       TIRED    0.00 0.00 0.00 1.00 0.00 0.00 0.00 0.50 0.00 0.00 1.00 0.50 0.50 0.00 0.00
10       HAPPY    1.00 0.00 0.00 0.00 0.00 0.00 0.00 0.00 0.00 0.00 0.00 0.00 0.00 0.00 1.00
11         SAD    0.00 0.00 0.50 1.00 0.50 1.00 0.00 0.50 1.00 0.00 0.00 1.00 0.00 0.00 0.00
12      LONELY    0.00 0.00 0.00 0.00 0.50 0.00 0.50 0.00 0.50 0.00 1.00 0.00 0.50 0.00 0.00
13       BORED    0.00 0.00 0.00 0.00 0.00 0.00 0.00 0.00 0.50 0.00 0.00 0.50 0.00 0.00 0.00
14        HATE    1.00 1.00 0.50 0.50 1.00 0.50 0.50 0.50 0.00 0.00 0.00 0.00 0.00 0.00 0.50
15  EXCITEMENT    1.00 0.00 0.00 0.00 0.00 0.00 0.00 0.50 0.00 1.00 0.00 0.00 0.00 0.50 0.00
```

FIGURE 16.15.
Two matrices from a triad test.

```
Aggregate Proximity Matrix

                    1    2    3    4    5    6    7    8    9   10   11   12   13   14   15
                  LOVE ANGR DISG SHAM FEAR ANGU ENVY ANXI TIRE HAPP SAD  LONE BORE HATE EXCI
                  ---- ---- ---- ---- ---- ---- ---- ---- ---- ---- ---- ---- ---- ---- ----
 1        LOVE    0.00 0.09 0.08 0.21 0.10 0.08 0.35 0.16 0.10 0.82 0.20 0.14 0.08 0.41 0.74
 2       ANGER    0.09 0.00 0.85 0.19 0.59 0.64 0.46 0.32 0.00 0.17 0.40 0.09 0.04 0.95 0.11
 3     DISGUST    0.08 0.85 0.00 0.76 0.76 0.66 0.55 0.63 0.08 0.08 0.38 0.08 0.14 0.70 0.13
 4       SHAME    0.21 0.19 0.76 0.00 0.22 0.75 0.51 0.38 0.57 0.10 0.57 0.39 0.09 0.47 0.06
 5        FEAR    0.10 0.59 0.76 0.22 0.00 0.57 0.40 0.71 0.05 0.11 0.55 0.59 0.08 0.86 0.21
 6     ANGUISH    0.08 0.64 0.66 0.75 0.57 0.00 0.85 0.47 0.20 0.10 0.70 0.31 0.08 0.69 0.09
 7        ENVY    0.35 0.46 0.55 0.51 0.40 0.85 0.00 0.44 0.06 0.08 0.08 0.30 0.28 0.47 0.11
 8     ANXIOUS    0.16 0.32 0.63 0.38 0.71 0.47 0.44 0.00 0.16 0.29 0.30 0.17 0.20 0.39 0.40
 9       TIRED    0.10 0.00 0.08 0.57 0.05 0.20 0.06 0.16 0.00 0.14 0.63 0.44 0.73 0.04 0.13
10       HAPPY    0.82 0.17 0.08 0.10 0.11 0.10 0.08 0.29 0.14 0.00 0.34 0.09 0.04 0.08 0.85
11         SAD    0.20 0.40 0.38 0.57 0.55 0.70 0.08 0.30 0.63 0.34 0.00 0.71 0.31 0.24 0.19
12      LONELY    0.14 0.09 0.08 0.39 0.59 0.31 0.30 0.17 0.44 0.09 0.71 0.00 0.59 0.06 0.06
13       BORED    0.08 0.04 0.14 0.09 0.08 0.08 0.28 0.20 0.73 0.04 0.31 0.59 0.00 0.14 0.19
14        HATE    0.41 0.95 0.70 0.47 0.86 0.69 0.47 0.39 0.04 0.08 0.24 0.06 0.14 0.00 0.28
15  EXCITEMENT    0.74 0.11 0.13 0.06 0.21 0.09 0.11 0.40 0.13 0.85 0.19 0.06 0.19 0.28 0.00
```

FIGURE 16.16.
Aggregate proximity matrix for triads: 40 informants, 15 emotions.

Reading across the first line, we see that 82% of the time, these 40 informants put love and happy together but they put love and bored together only 8% of the time. Reading down the second column, we see that informants put hate and anger together 95% of the time but never put anger and tired together.

Figure 16.17 shows the multidimensional scaling, in two dimensions, for the aggregate similarity matrix in figure 16.16.

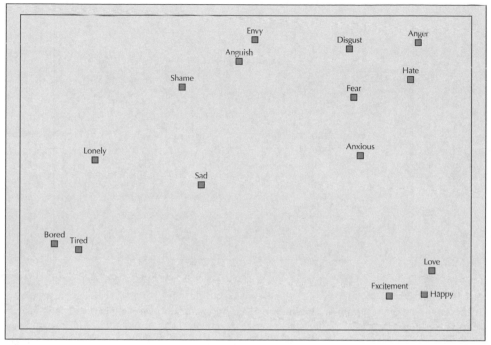

FIGURE 16.17.
MDS in two dimensions of the data in figure 16.16.

Moore et al. (1999) studied these same emotions, using a triad test, in Japanese speakers, Chinese speakers, and American English speakers. Figure 16.18 shows the shared model for these emotion terms in all three languages. (Moore et al. used correspondence analysis to produce the display in figure 16.18. Correspondence analysis is another method for visualizing relations among sets of items.) Naturally, there is some part of the model that is unique to each language and some part that is unique to each individual. But what stands out to me is the overlap—the sharing of the model in figures 16.17 and 16.18. Using triad tests, pile sorts, and other systematic methods lets you make these kinds of comparisons (**Further Reading:** triad tests and see **Further Reading**, chapter 10).

ANALYZING SENTENCE FRAMES
John Young and Linda Garro (1994 [1981]) studied illness beliefs and illness behaviors in two communities in Mexico. In the 1970s, when Young and Garro did their work there, the people of Uricho had good access to Western medicine—good roads, nearby clinics with medical staff, etc.—and the people of Pichátaro had little access. In fact, the people of Pichátaro went to Western doctors half as much as did the people of Uricho. Young and Garro wanted to test whether this difference in behavior was reflected in a different set of beliefs about the causes and symptoms of illness.

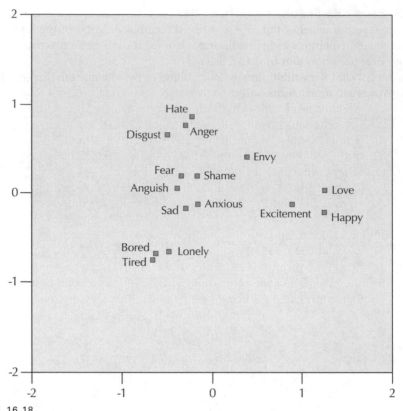

FIGURE 16.18.

A shared model of the semantic structure of 15 emotions for Chinese, English, and Japanese.
SOURCE: A. Kimball Romney et al., "Cultural Universals: Measuring the Semantic Structure of Emotion Terms in English and Japanese." *PNAS*, Vol. 94, pp. 5489–94, 1997. National Academy of Sciences USA.

One of the methods they used for this test was frame substitution. Tables 16.7 and 16.8 show the illnesses and sentence frames in their research with 20 informants. Each informant was asked 396 (18 × 22) questions: Can dysentery come from anger? (illness 5, frame 1) Does dysentery come from walking about without shoes? (illness 5, frame 19) Can you get fever sores from eating lots of cold things? (illness 17, frame 12) . . . and so on.

Table 16.9 shows the format for the profile matrix that would result from each informant's responses. Each illness could have from 0 to 22 properties (causes or symptoms) and there are 18(17)/2 = 153 pairs of the 18 illnesses. Each time an informant said that a pair of illnesses had the same cause or symptom, that pair of illnesses got a point. There were 20 informants, so each pair of illnesses could have from 0 to (20 × 22) = 440 points.

The MDS for the two 18 × 18 similarity matrices (one for Pichátaro and one for Uricho) that result from all this is shown in figures 16.19a and 16.19b. The circles indicate the clusters found by cluster analysis of the same data. Recall that any MDS can be rotated 360 degrees in any plane with no loss of information. Bottom line: Young and Garro got the same results about illness *beliefs* in both villages, even though the people in one village had better access to Western medicine and took advantage of that access (**Further Reading:** sentence frames).

Table 16.7   Illness Terms Used in Term-Frame Interviews

1. *Enfermedad de corazón*	"Heart illness"
2. *Empacho*	"Blocked digestion"
3. *Cólico*	"Colic"; sharp stomach pains
4. *Mollera caida*	"Fallen fontanel"; displacement of a section of the top of the skull
5. *Disenteria*	"Dysentery"
6. *Calor subido*	"Risen heat"
7. *Gripa*	"Grippe"; cold, flu
8. *Desposiciones*	"Diarrhea"
9. *Sofoca del estómago*	"Bloated stomach"
10. *Latido*	"Palpitations"; brought on by eating delay
11. *Broncomonia*	"Bronchopneumonia"
12. *Anginus*	Swollen glands in the neck
13. *Bilis*	"Bile"; illness resulting from a fright or other strong emotional experience
14. *Punzadas*	Sharp headache around the temples
15. *Pulmonia*	"Pneumonia"
16. *Mal de ojo*	"Evil eye"; also *erátikua* or *tzitíparata*
17. *Fogazo*	"Fever sores"
18. *Bronquitis*	"Bronchitis"

SOURCE: J. C. Young and L. Y. Garro, "Variation in the Choice of Treatment in Two Mexican C Communities," *Social Science and Medicine*, Vol. 16, pp. 1453–63, table 3, 1982.

Table 16.8   Belief Frames Used in Term-Frame Interviews

1. Can [X] come from anger? (¿Puede venir [X] por un coraje?)
2. Does [X] come from the "heat"? (¿Viene [X] por el calor?)
3. Are there pains in the chest with [X]? (¿Hay dolores en el pecho con [X]?)
4. When you leave a warm place and enter into the cold air, can you get [X]? (¿Cúando sale de un lugar caliente y entra en el aire frio, se puede agarrar [X]?)
5. Can you get [X] from eating lots of "hot" things? (¿Se puede agarrar [X] por comer muchas cosas calientes?)
6. Does [X] come from an "air"? (¿Viene [X] por un aire?)
7. With [X] does the head hurt? (¿Con [X] duele la cabeza?)
8. Can you cure [X] with folk remedies? (¿Puede curar [X] con remedios caseros?)
9. Does [X] come from germs? (¿Viene [X] por los microbios?)
10. Does [X] come from not eating "by the hours"? (¿Viene [X] por no comer a las horas?)
11. With [X] do you lose your appetite? (¿Con [X] se quita la hambre?)
12. Can you get [X] from eating lots of "cold" things? (¿Se puede agarrar [X] por comer muchas cosas frescas?)
13. With [X] is there a temperature? (¿Con [X] hay calentura?)
14. When you get wet, can you get [X]? (¿Cúando se moja uno, se puede agarrar [X]?)
15. With [X] is there pain in the stomach? (¿Con hay dolar en el estómago?)
16. Does [X] come from the "cold"? (¿Viene [X] por el frio?)
17. Does [X] come by contagion from other people? (¿Viene [X] por contagio de otras personas?)
18. Can [X] come from witchcraft? (¿Puede venir [X] por la brujeria?)
19. Does [X] come from walking about without shoes? (¿Viene [X] por pisar sin zapatos?)
20. When you have [X], do you have to take "hot" remedies to be cured? (¿Cúando uno tiene [X] tiene que tomar cosas calientes para curarse?)
21. Can you cure [X] with "doctors'" remedies? (¿Puede curar [X] con remedies médicos?)
22. Can [X] come from a fright? (¿Puede venir [X] por un susto?)

SOURCE: J. C. Young and L. Y. Garro, "Variation in the Choice of Treatment in Two Mexican C Communities," *Social Science and Medicine*, Vol. 16, pp. 1453–63, table 4, 1982.
Note: Spanish frames reflect local usage.

Table 16.9 Profile Matrix for One Informant's Responses to the 396 Questions in Young and Garro's Test of Illness Beliefs

	1	2	3	4	5	6	7	8	9	10	11	12	13	14	15	16	17	18
1																		
2																		
3																		
4																		
5																		
6																		
7																		
8																		
9																		
10																		
11																		
12																		
13																		
14																		
15																		
16																		
17																		
18																		
19																		
20																		
21																		
22																		

ANALYZING PAIRED COMPARISONS

Pile sorts, sentence frames, and triad tests all help us understand the semantic structure of items in a cultural domain. We also want to understand how people evaluate the items in a domain on a particular attribute. The most common way to evaluate items on an attribute is with a rating scale, like the one in figure 16.20. Ratings are fine when you have lots of items, but they produce a lot of ties because people can give the same rating number to many items. With rank-ordered data, there are no ties: You can only put one item first, one second, and so on. If you have 15 or fewer items in a domain, then try to get rank-ordered data.

One way to do that is to spread a set of cards out on a table, each with the name of an item, and ask people to pick up their top ranked one (most good-natured dog; most scary illness; most difficult musical instrument to play) . . . then the next most, and the next most, and so on. If people have a hard time with this, then paired comparisons is the answer.

In paired comparisons, people are shown all pairs of items in a list, one pair at a time, and are asked to evaluate each pair, separately, on an attribute. Instead of asking "On a scale of 1 to 5, please rate these emotions on their intensity," we would ask "For each pair of emotions, circle the one that you think has more intensity." For the studies of 15 emotions, there would be $n(n - 1) / 2 = 15(14) / 2 = 105$ pairs: anxious-bored, hate-fear, disgust-excitement, tired-shame, etc., etc.

Each item in a set appears $n - 1$ times in the set of all pairs, so in the case of the 15 emotions, informants would see hate, for example, paired with each of the other 14 emotions. This gives each emotion 14 chances to win—to be circled as having higher intensity, in this case. The number of times an item wins in this game is its rank order. Ranking data can be analyzed with various statistical methods, *including the cultural consensus model* (**Further Reading:** paired comparisons. Also see **Further Reading**, chapter 10).

CULTURAL CONSENSUS ANALYSIS

Historically, anthropologists described cultures in terms of norms—the Navajo are matrilocal, the Yakö practice double descent—but a landmark paper in 1975 by Pelto and Pelto made clear that intracultural variation—based on things like gender, age, economic status, occupational specialization, and so on—was the norm. Some cultural knowledge, like the names of the months, is widely shared but much cultural knowledge is distributed unevenly. We hear, for example, that women know more about fashion than men do in the United States and that men know more about cars than women do. We hear that young people in the Amazon village where we're working aren't learning the names and uses of medicinal plants as much as their elders did. How can we test if knowledge in particular cultural domains varies by gender or age? **Cultural consensus analysis** gives us a way to measure the extent to which people agree about the contents of a cultural domain—to measure domain-specific cultural competence.

CULTURAL COMPETENCE

Consensus analysis is based on a long and distinguished intellectual history on the power of collective wisdom, going back to a paper by the Marquis de Condorcet (1785) on the probability of a jury reaching a correct decision (Batchelder and Romney 1986) in legal cases as opposed to relying on the judgment of a single person. In 1907, Francis Galton attended a fair in Plymouth, England where 800 people guessed the weight of an ox. The ox weighed 1,198 pounds. The spread of guesses went from 1,074 to 1,293 pounds but the mean was 1,196 pounds (Galton 1907a, 1907b)—almost dead on.

And Robyn Dawes (1977) asked 25 male members of the faculty in psychology at the University of Oregon to rate the height of all other 24 colleagues using five scales, like those I discussed in chapter 11: semantic differential (from short to tall), Likert-like (extremely short to extremely tall), and so on. The first factor scores for the five scales—the score on the underlying variable with which all the scales were associated—correlated .98 with the actual height of the men. The title of Dawes's article was "Suppose We Measured Height with Rating Scales Instead of Rulers?" Well, the answer is: As long as you take the average of a bunch of people on those scales, you can lose the rulers and do pretty well. (For a review of collective wisdom, see Surowiecki 2004.)

James Boster (1985, 1986) walked 58 Aguaruna Jívaro women (in Peru) through a garden that had 61 varieties of manioc. He asked the women *waji mama aita*? ("What kind of manioc is this?") and calculated the likelihood that all possible pairs of women agreed on the name of a plant. Boster had planted the garden himself, so he *knew* the true identification of each plant. Sure enough, *the more women agreed* on the identification of a plant, *the more likely they were to know* what the plant actually was. In other words, people who know a lot about—are highly competent in—a cultural domain tend to agree

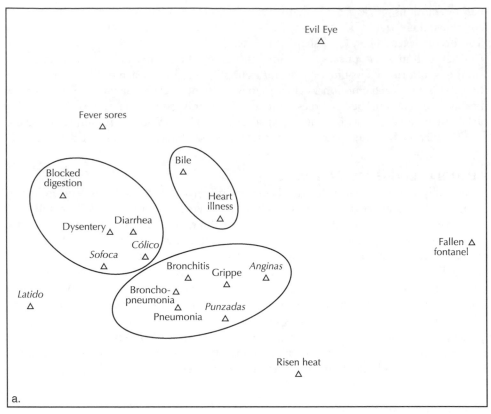

FIGURE 16.19a.

MDS of Pichátaro term-frame data.

SOURCE: J. C. Young and L. Y. Garro, "Variation in the Choice of Treatment in Two Mexican C Communities," *Social Science and Medicine*, Vol. 16, pp. 1453–63, figure 2, 1982.

with each other about the content of the domain and people who know little tend to disagree.

When Agreement Equals Knowledge: Equation 1

Romney et al. (1986) took all this a step further by showing exactly how, and under what conditions, agreement among a set of people equals knowledge. (For details of the proof, see the original article by Romney et al. [1986] and see Borgatti and Carboni [2007] and Weller [2007] for particularly clear explanations of the theory.) Weller (2007) is a key resource for instructions on how to run consensus analysis and how to interpret the results. In brief, there are two equations: one expressing the probability that a person answers a question correctly and one expressing the probability that two people agree on the answer to a question. The first equation comes from classical test theory—the kind that produces all those standardized tests you've taken all your life.

$$m_i = d_i + 1 - d_i/L \qquad \textbf{Formula 16.1}$$

Adjusting for Guessing

This equation says that the probability of getting the answer to a question right (m_i) is the probability that you know the answer (d_i) plus the probability ($1 - d_i/L$) that you

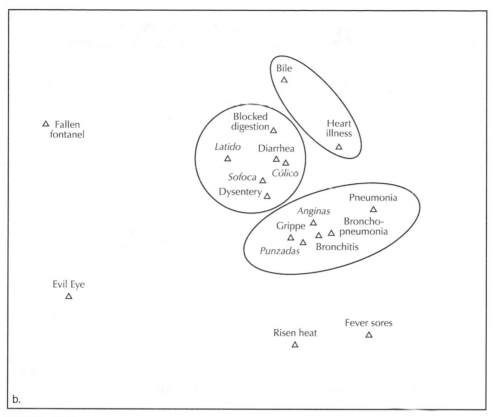

FIGURE 16.19b.

MDS of Uricho term-frame data.

SOURCE: J. C. Young and L. Y. Garro, "Variation in the Choice of Treatment in Two Mexican C Communities," *Social Science and Medicine*, Vol. 16, pp. 1453–63, figure 3, 1982.

guess right if you don't know the answer, and where *L* is the number of choices available for guessing. In a true-false question, for example, there is a .50 probability of guessing the right answer at random. In a question with three answers, the probability of guessing right is .33. In a test where each question has five answers, it's .20. The formula for adjusting a test score for guessing is

$$K = [S - 1/L]/[1 - 1/L]$$ **Formula 16.2**

where K = actual knowledge, S is the original test score, and L is the number of choices available when a student has to guess the answer (see Borgatti 1997; Weller 2007).

Table 16.10 shows the answers by one student to 25 multiple choice questions on one of my Introduction to Anthropology exams. The questions on this exam each had five possible answers, so the student made 25 choices of a number between 1 and 5. To find out how well the student did on the whole exam, we count up the number of matches between the student's vector of numbers and the vector that represents the correct answers and we divide by the total number of questions. This student got 19 matches, or $19/25 = .76$.

The student's adjusted knowledge score would be:

$$K = [.76 - .20]/[1 - .20] = .70.$$

Please rate the following emotions in terms of their intensity, where "1" indicates the least amount of intensity, and where "5" indicates the greatest amount of intensity.

ANXIOUS	1____	2____	3____	4____	5____
ENVY	1____	2____	3____	4____	5____
LONELY	1____	2____	3____	4____	5____
BORED	1____	2____	3____	4____	5____
ANGUISH	1____	2____	3____	4____	5____
HATE	1____	2____	3____	4____	5____
DISGUST	1____	2____	3____	4____	5____
FEAR	1____	2____	3____	4____	5____
EXCITEMENT	1____	2____	3____	4____	5____
SHAME	1____	2____	3____	4____	5____
TIRED	1____	2____	3____	4____	5____
LOVE	1____	2____	3____	4____	5____
ANGER	1____	2____	3____	4____	5____
SAD	1____	2____	3____	4____	5____
HAPPY	1____	2____	3____	4____	5____

FIGURE 16.20.
An example of a rating scale.

Table 16.10   Grading a Test with an Answer Key for 25 Multiple-Choice Questions

Questions

1	2	3	4	5	6	7	8	9	10	11	12	13	14	15	16	17	18	19	20	21	22	23	24	25

Answers

3	3	2	3	2	1	4	3	2	2	5	5	2	2	5	5	1	3	1	4	2	1	5	4	1

Answer key

3	3	2	2	2	4	4	3	2	2	5	4	2	1	5	2	1	3	1	4	3	1	5	4	1

In other words, d_i for this student—the probability that she actually *knows* the answer to any question on the test—is .70.

When Agreement Equals Knowledge: Equation 2

The second equation in the consensus model is the probability that two people, i and j, agree on the answer to a question. There are four ways for this to happen: (1) i and j both know the answer with probability d; (2) i knows the answer and j guesses correctly; (3) j knows the answer and i guesses correctly; and (4) neither i nor j know the answer but they make the same guess, which may or may not be the correct one. The combined probability here is:

$$m_{ij} = d_i d_j + \frac{1 - d_i d_j}{L}$$ **Formula 16.3**

which, as Borgatti and Carboni (2007:454) say, in a marvelous understatement, is "pleasingly analogous to" the first equation.

Assumptions of the Model

In other words, under certain conditions, "we can estimate the amount of knowledge of each person by knowing only the pattern of agreement among persons in the group" (Borgatti and Carboni 2007:455). Here are the conditions:

1. Informants share a common culture and there is a culturally correct answer to any question you ask them. The culturally correct answer might be incorrect from an outsider's perspective (as often happens when we compare folk knowledge about illnesses or plants or climate to scientific knowledge). Any variation you find among informants is the result of *individual* differences in their knowledge, not the result of being members of subcultures.
2. Informants give their answers to your test questions independently of one another. Consensus analysis is not for focus-group data.
3. All the questions in your test come from the same cultural domain and are more-or-less of equal difficulty. No fair asking about the uses of medicinal plants and the rules of kinship in the same test.

Running Consensus Analysis

If these assumptions are met, we can run a factor analysis of the corrected-for-guessing, people-by-question matrix. The results tell us if our informants share a single culture about the domain we're testing and, if they do, what their knowledge of that domain is and how knowledge varies among them.

Factor analysis, remember, is a set of statistical techniques for reducing a data matrix to a set of underlying variables. It is used in the development of attitude scales to look for packages of specific items (like how you feel about gun control or abortion or single-sex marriage) that measure different aspects of big, underlying variables (like rightish or leftish political orientation).

In consensus analysis, it is used to test whether there is a single, underlying component of shared knowledge or culture. If there is, then there will be one major factor—knowledge of the domain—and each person's score on that factor is their competence in the domain. One major factor—a single culture—is indicated when (1) the first factor is large relative to the second (you'll know this if the first eigenvalue in the factor analysis is at least three times the size of the second), and (2) no informant has a negative score on the first factor since (if there is a single culture, people shouldn't have negative knowledge of it).

If the ratio of the first to the second eigenvalue is less than 3-to-1 or if there are negative scores on the first factor, then there may be more than one culture in the group of informants who took the test. For example, men and women may represent different cultural subgroups for some domains, as might members of different ethnic or religious groups. You can test this by running a consensus analysis on the subgroups separately.

There are two other possibilities. First, one group of people may be competent in a domain while another group knows little about it. For example, Romney et al. (1987) asked 26 undergraduates (13 men and 13 women) about the effectiveness of 15 kinds of birth control. Seven of the men had negative scores on the first factor of the analysis, so Romney et al. ran the analysis separately on the men and the women. For the women, the ratio of the first to the second eigenvalue was more than 4-to-1, so there was one big underlying factor (knowledge about the effectiveness of birth control methods) and the women's factor scores were all positive. For the men, the ratio was about 1-to-1, and six of the 13 had negative scores on the first factor. In other words, for those 13 men, it wasn't just that they didn't share a culture about the domain, they had little or no knowledge of the domain at all.

Another possibility is that you've got a shaman, or the equivalent, in your sample. If you run a consensus analysis and find one or two negative first-factor (knowledge) scores out of a large sample, it may be that you've included people whose knowledge about the domain is so specialized it doesn't jibe with that of others in the mainstream. It is to the advantage of shamans everywhere, whether their knowledge is about curing illness or making money on the stock market, to protect that knowledge by keeping it maximally different from mainstream knowledge. Use consensus analysis to find highly knowledge-able informants but never pass up the chance to interview a shaman.

Retrieving the Answer Key to a Test

If there is a single culture—if there is one major factor representing knowledge of the domain and if there are no negative scores on that factor—then informant scores on the first factor represent their knowledge about—their competence in—the domain. And because of the relationship between formulas 16.1 and 16.3—that is, the relation between agreement and knowledge—we can retrieve the answer key to the set of questions on the test by looking at the most common answers—that wisdom-of-crowds thing again—and by giving more weight to the answers of the high scorers on the test when the crowd is split on the answers to a particular culture.

I tested this, using UCINET (Borgatti et al. 2002) on data from a 1995 intro class in anthropology. There were 168 students in the class and the exam had 60 questions. Recall that the ratio of the first eigenvalue to the second should be at least 3-to-1 to conclude that there is a consensus. In this case, the ratio was more than 20-to-1, so there was, indeed, one big underlying factor associated with the answers that students gave to the questions on the test. Because the purpose of the test was to gauge students' knowledge of the material, the factor can be interpreted as knowledge, and each student's score on that big factor can be interpreted as his or her score on the test.

Figure 16.21 shows the correlation between the first factor score for each student and the score that each student actually got on the test. The correlation is 0.96—almost per-fect. It's so close, in fact, that had I lost the answer key, I could have given every student his or her factor score as the grade for the test with no impact on the final grade for the course. And this is no fluke: Borgatti and Carboni (2007:458) ran this analysis on a test of 91 students in an organizational behavior class and got a 0.95 correlation—again, almost perfect.

The answer key for my test that was derived from the analysis was also almost perfect. Taking the majority answers to the 60 questions and adjusting for guessing, the analysis got 58 right. Here are the two questions that it missed:

"Natural selection" selects for:
(1) reproductive success.
(2) survival of the fittest.
(3) survival of the species.
(4) adaptive radiation.
(5) random mutations.

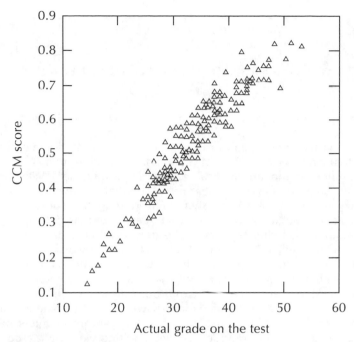

FIGURE 16.21.
Plot of raw grades and scores from a cultural consensus analysis on an Intro to Anthropology test. The correlation is 0.96.

The first hominid to live in regions with cold winters was:

(1) Homo erectus.
(2) Homo hablis.
(3) Homo sapiens neandertalensis.
(4) archaic Homo sapiens.
(5) Australopithecus afarensis.

For the first question, 70 students picked (1), reproductive success (the correct answer), but 79 students picked (2), survival of the fittest. For the second question, 49 students picked (1), Homo erectus (the correct answer) but 90 students picked (3), Homo sapiens neandertalensis. (In those days, Neanderthals were still classified as a subspecies of modern humans. Today, some anthropologists would classify them as a separate species.) Popular culture—about Neanderthal Man and about the phrase "survival of the fittest"—was just too powerful to be overcome fully by some anthropology lectures (box 16.6).

What this means is that if you can retrieve an etically correct answer key, you can apply the model (cautiously, always cautiously . . . see box 16.6) to tests of emic data—like people's ideas about who hangs out with whom in an organization or what people think are good ways to cure a cold, avoid getting AIDS, take care of a baby, etc. It still takes knowledge of the local culture to fully understand the distribution of knowledge about a cultural domain. But when we ask people during fieldwork to tell us the uses of various plants or to list the sacred sites in a village or to rate the social status of others in a community, we don't want to know only their opinions. We want to know the uses of the

BOX 16.6

CULTURAL CONSENSUS AND MULTIPLE ANSWER
KEYS

Hruschka et al. (2008) used frame elicitation in interviews with women in Matlab, Bangladesh, about the causes and symptoms of postpartum hemorrhage.
Of the 149 in their sample, 98 were lay women, 37 were traditional birth attendants (TBAs), and 14 were skilled birth attendants (SBAs)—that is, women who
had been trained in modern medical techniques for midwifery. When Hruschka
et al. ran the data through consensus analysis, the ratio of the first to the second
eigenvalue was nearly 6-to-1 and there were no negative competencies. This
indicated a single cultural model. But when they picked the data apart, *none* of
the SBAs agreed with the statement "*alga* (evil spirits) is a cause of excessive,
life-threatening bleeding," whereas 84% of TBAs and 78% of lay women agreed.
This turned out to indicate a pattern: The SBAs agreed among themselves about
many of the items in the cultural knowledge test; the lay women and the TBAs
agreed among themselves; and the two groups disagreed. In other words, the
two groups of women were drawing their answers to test questions from different answer keys. Hruschka et al. point out that "anthropologists have long
observed this possibility in modern society," citing work by Margaret Mead
(1940) and Fredrik Barth (2002).

plants and the location of the sacred sites and the social status of people. We never had
an answer key to tell whether informants were reporting this information accurately. Now
we do.

MAKING UP QUESTIONS FOR A FORMAL CONSENSUS TEST

A really important part of running a formal consensus analysis is building good test
items. This takes work. Start with systematic and in-depth interviews with knowledgeable
informants about the domain you're investigating and do a close analysis of those qualitative data so that you can create sensible questions—that is, questions that reflect the
content of the domain. We expect professors who make up course exams to know the
material cold, and you should expect no less of yourself when you make up questions for
a formal consensus analysis. About half the questions should be positive (true, yes, agree)
and about half should be negative (false, no, disagree).

Jeffrey Johnson and David Griffith (1996) studied what people in North Carolina know
about the link between seafood safety and coastal pollution using the formal cultural
consensus model. First, they asked some expert informants to free-list (1) the kinds of
pollution along the Atlantic coast (examples included acid rain, chemical runoff as the
result of coastal erosion, and so on); (2) the species (clams, crabs, tuna) that might be
affected by the various types of pollution; and (3) problems that might arise, like diseases
in fish. From these data, Johnson and Griffith identified 12 types of pollution, 11 causes
of pollution, and 10 species. Next, they asked a convenience sample of commercial fishermen and local residents of various ethnic backgrounds to (1) pile sort the types of

pollution; (2) link each pollutant to the problems they cause; and (3) identify the species that each pollutant affected the most.

Johnson and Griffith asked the informants to explain why they made all these linkages and transcribed the results. Then, three coders went through the transcripts, tagging statements about the how seafood, pollutants and various risks to health and the environment were related. There were 53 statements identified by at least two of the three coders. The researchers turned these into a true-false knowledge test, with half the statements positive (true) and half being negative. For example, "heavy metals cause sores on both fish and people" is true (positive), but "heavy metals are necessary nutrients for both fish and people" is false (negative). Finally, they gave the test to 142 people in the area including: (1) a representative sample of 132 people, stratified by residence (rural-urban), income (high and low), and ethnicity (white and black); (2) 10 students from their university; and (3) 10 marine scientists. They analyzed the 142(people)-by-53(statement) matrix using the formal consensus model. The first eigenvalue in the analysis of the agreement matrix was over seven times bigger than the second. Those 142 people, despite coming from such different backgrounds, drew from a single culture in answering the 53 questions on the test about seafood and pollution.

Fine-grained analysis, though, turned up some interesting differences. The consensus was that the following statement was true: "Much of the pollution dumped into coastal and ocean waters has no effect on the flavor or seafood." The scientists, however, disagreed.

The Informal Model: Pile Sorts, Triad Tests, and Rank Ordered Data

When you have ordinal or ratio or rank-ordered data, including data from pile sorts and triad tests, use the informal model of consensus analysis (Weller 2007) (box 16.7).

BOX 16.7

LUMPERS AND SPLITTERS

Be careful, though: With free pile sorts, some people make just a few piles and others make many. Lumpers and splitters are technically not responding to the same cues when you ask them to sort items freely into piles. This means you can test whether there is a single culture—whether most people see the relations among a set of items in a pile sort similarly—and you can look for informants who are most representative of the culture, but you wouldn't put much stock in individual factor scores or use those scores as input into any other analysis.

In this model, you create a people-by-people similarity matrix from the original people-by-item test and factor the similarity matrix. You can do this in most statistical packages, but ANTHROPAC and UCINET will do it automatically. Here's an example.

Adam Kiš (2007) found that people in the village of Njolomole, Malawi had stopped going to every funeral because, with AIDS, there were just too many to go to. Kiš asked 23 people to: "Name all of the reasons you can think of for attending a funeral." He listed the 12 reasons cited most often on a piece of paper and asked 30 people: "If there were too many funerals in your village so that you could not attend each one, which of the following reasons would be the most important in helping you decide which funerals to attend?" Then he asked people to mark the next most important reason, and the next, and so on down the list. Table 16.11 shows his data.

These are rank-ordered data, so the informal consensus model is appropriate. To do this, correlate all pairs of rows in table 16.11 and turn it into a 30-by-30, people-by-people similarity matrix (any statistical package will do). The result for the first 10 rows is shown in table 16.12.

Read table 16.12 as follows: Informants 4 and 9 are highly and positively correlated (0.741); informants 6 and 2 are hardly correlated at all (0.070); informants 2 and 3 are weakly and negatively correlated (−0.364); and so on. The negative correlation for informants 2 and 3 means that they tended to rank the reasons for going to a funeral in some opposite ways. For example, looking across rows 2 and 3 of table 16.11, informant 2 ranked HEL (helping the family of the deceased with funeral preparations) last on his list, and informant 3 ranked it third.

Next, factor analyze the 30-by-30 matrix of informant agreements using a variant of factor analysis called minimal residuals (or MINRES) or maximum likelihood (ML). I did this with SYSTAT, but you can use SPSS or any major statistical package. The results are in figure 16.22. The first factor is large, relative to the second (the ratio is 3.157), which means that there is a single culture at work, despite the differences in the way people ranked their reasons for going to a funeral. There is a nice range of scores—from 0.07 (for informant 2) to 0.92 (for informant 30)—and there are no negative scores, but some people (like informants 10, 11, 22, 25, and 30) are clearly more knowledgeable about the shared reasons for going to a funeral than others are.

Kiš interviewed these knowledgeable informants in depth and asked them why reciprocity (attending someone's funeral so that his or her family will attend your family's funerals) was the runaway most-important reason given and why carrying the coffin and partaking of the traditional funeral feast were ranked so low. It turned out that carrying coffins was only for young men and his sample of 30 informants did not have that many young men in it. If he'd had more young men in his sample, this might have resulted in a higher overall ranking of eating as a reason for attending a funeral, since coffin bearers get generous portions of food.

Selecting Domain-Specific Informants

This brings up a really interesting use of consensus analysis: selecting domain-specific informants. Table 16.13, from Weller and Romney (1988), shows the number of informants you need to produce valid and reliable data about particular cultural domains, given that the three conditions of the model are more-or-less met. (I say "more-or-less" because the model is very robust, which means that it produces very similar answers even when its conditions are more-or-less, not perfectly, met.) Just 10 informants, with an average competence of .7 have a 99% probability of answering each question on a true-false test correctly, with a confidence level of .95. Only 13 informants, with a relatively low average competence of .5 are needed if you want a 90% probability of answering each question on a test correctly, with a confidence level of .95.

And, as table 16.14 shows, when you have interval level data, if you interview 10 informants whose responses correlate .49, then the aggregate of their answers are likely to correlate .95 with the true answers. Consensus analysis, shows that: (1) Only a relatively small sample of informants are needed for studying particular cultural domains; and (2)

Table 16.11 Rankings of 12 Reasons for Attending a Funeral (1 = Most Important, 12 = Least Important)

Informant	Reason											
	REC	SOR	HEL	CUS	REL	EAT	FRI	GIF	CON	GOO	CHU	COF
1	4	1	2	7	6	12	11	8	5	10	3	9
2	1	5	12	4	11	7	3	2	8	9	10	6
3	4	5	3	9	2	12	11	8	6	2	10	7
4	3	4	2	10	5	12	6	7	1	11	9	8
5	2	11	3	10	4	12	5	6	1	7	8	9
6	3	8	9	2	7	12	10	6	5	1	4	1
7	1	8	10	6	5	12	7	4	2	9	3	11
8	3	7	5	8	1	9	2	11	4	10	6	12
9	3	2	4	11	1	12	8	5	7	10	9	6
10	1	5	3	2	10	12	11	8	4	7	6	9
11	2	4	7	1	5	12	11	6	3	8	9	10
12	1	2	4	6	9	12	8	5	7	3	10	11
13	3	4	1	5	11	9	7	6	8	2	12	10
14	4	10	2	6	1	12	7	9	3	8	5	11
15	2	5	3	1	11	12	10	9	4	6	8	7
16	5	3	6	4	11	12	8	7	1	2	9	10
17	7	4	8	6	9	12	10	3	5	1	2	11
18	1	8	3	6	5	12	4	11	2	7	9	10
19	5	4	1	8	9	12	3	7	10	11	2	6
20	1	10	2	11	8	12	5	4	6	3	9	7
21	2	5	8	7	6	12	1	11	4	9	3	10
22	3	4	2	1	6	12	7	9	5	11	8	10
23	1	3	5	11	7	12	10	2	4	6	8	9
24	12	10	5	8	1	11	2	7	3	4	6	9
25	2	1	7	3	4	12	8	10	5	9	6	11
26	1	7	3	2	5	9	8	6	4	10	12	11
27	1	4	2	9	5	12	8	3	11	7	6	10
28	1	7	4	2	5	12	9	11	10	8	3	6
29	3	4	9	5	1	12	2	8	6	10	7	11
30	1	2	4	6	5	12	11	7	3	7	9	10

The list of reasons are: REC = reciprocity (attending a specific person's funeral so that his or her family members will attend your family's funerals), SOR = sorrow, HEL = to help the family of the deceased with funeral preparations, CUS = going out of custom, REL = going because ego is a relative of the deceased, EAT = to eat the requisite funeral feast, FRI = attending because ego is a friend of the deceased, GIF = to bring gifts to the family of the deceased, CON = to console the family of the deceased, GOO = to say good-bye to the deceased, CHU = going because ego is a member of the same church as the deceased, COF = to carry the coffin.

SOURCE: A. Kiš, *NAPA Bulletin 27* pp. 129–140, 2007. Table 1, p. 134. Used by permission.

Table 16.12 Correlation Matrix for the First 10 Rows of Table 16.11

	1	2	3	4	5	6	7	8	9	10
1	1.000	-0.231	0.399	0.650	0.273	0.245	0.406	0.336	0.601	0.699
2	-0.231	1.000	-0.364	-0.028	-0.098	0.070	0.273	-0.147	-0.007	0.105
3	0.399	-0.364	1.000	0.420	0.462	0.378	0.084	0.175	0.587	0.364
4	0.650	-0.028	0.420	1.000	0.748	-0.049	0.441	0.601	0.741	0.455
5	0.273	-0.098	0.462	0.748	1.000	0.245	0.587	0.622	0.448	0.336
6	0.245	0.070	0.378	-0.049	0.245	1.000	0.608	0.042	-0.112	0.622
7	0.406	0.273	0.084	0.441	0.587	0.608	1.000	0.483	0.280	0.469
8	0.336	-0.147	0.175	0.601	0.622	0.042	0.483	1.000	0.406	0.140
9	0.601	-0.007	0.587	0.741	0.448	-0.112	0.280	0.406	1.000	0.196
10	0.699	0.105	0.364	0.455	0.336	0.622	0.469	0.140	0.196	1.000

FACTOR ANALYSIS

Method of extraction: Maximum likelihood
Method of rotation: NONE
Minimum eigenvalue to retain: 1.0

EIGENVALUES

FACTOR	VALUE	PERCENT	CUM %	RATIO
1:	12.709	42.4	42.4	3.157
2:	4.026	13.4	55.8	1.444
3:	2.788	9.3	65.1	1.177
4:	2.368	7.9	73.0	1.253
5:	1.889	6.3	79.3	1.038
6:	1.820	6.1	85.3	1.295
7:	1.405	4.7	90.0	1.181
8:	1.190	4.0	94.0	1.254

Individual scores on the first factor:

1	0.750	11	0.815	21	0.506
2	0.070	12	0.774	22	0.826
3	0.589	13	0.514	23	0.712
4	0.756	14	0.707	24	0.090
5	0.645	15	0.722	25	0.824
6	0.539	16	0.633	26	0.739
7	0.633	17	0.380	27	0.666
8	0.542	18	0.803	28	0.577
9	0.594	19	0.365	29	0.606
10	0.820	20	0.501	30	0.922

FIGURE 16.22.
Factor analysis of the complete 30 × 30 matrix implied by table 16.12.

Table 16.13 Minimal Number of Informants Needed to Classify a Desired Proportion of Questions with a Specified Confidence Level for Different Levels of Cultural Competence

Proportion of questions	Average level of cultural competence				
	.5	.6	.7	.8	.9
.95 confidence level					
0.80	9	7	4	4	4
0.85	11	7	4	4	4
0.90	13	9	6	4	4
0.95	17	11	6	6	4
0.99	29	19	10	8	4
.99 confidence level					
0.80	15	10	5	4	4
0.85	15	10	7	5	4
0.90	21	12	7	5	4
0.95	23	14	9	7	4
0.99	>30	20	13	8	6

SOURCE: S. C. Weller and A. K. Romney, *Systematic Data Collection*, p. 77. © 1988. Reprinted by permission of Sage Publications.

There will be variation in knowledge among informants who are competent in a cultural domain.

Consensus analysis is great for finding top people who can talk about well-defined areas of cultural knowledge. But if you are doing general descriptive ethnography and you're looking for all-around good informants, consensus analysis is *not* a substitute for

Table 16.14 Agreement among Individuals and Estimated Validity of Aggregating
Their Responses for Different Samples

Agreement	Validity				
	0.80	0.85	0.90	0.95	0.99
0.16	10	14	22	49	257
0.25	5	8	13	28	148
0.36	3	5	8	17	87
0.49	2	3	4	10	51

SOURCE: S. C. Weller and A. K. Romney, *Systematic Data Collection*, p. 77. © 1988. Reprinted by permission of Sage Publications.

the time-honored way that ethnographers have always chosen key informants: luck, intuition, and hard work by both parties to achieve a working relationship based on trust (**Further Reading:** consensus analysis).

Cultural Consonance

An important development in the use of consensus analysis is the cultural consonance model by William Dressler and his colleagues (Dressler, Baliero et al. 2007; Dressler et al. 1996) and the application of the consonance model to the study of lifestyle and health. Here, lifestyle is defined as *having things* and *doing things* that one needs to have and do so as to have a good life as an X, where X is whatever people you're working with. Material things might be anything from a bicycle to a Ferrari, while behavioral things might be anything from visiting the district capital at least once a year to only flying first class, depending on where you're working.

To get a material-style-of-life scale, you need a list of, material goods and leisure activities. The list can come from inventorying homes, from open-ended interviews about leisure, from free lists, from the *Style* section of the local newspaper. . . . You can create a Guttman scale of the items, as Pollnac et al. (1975) and DeWalt (1979) did, or you can ask people, as Dressler does (1996) to rate each item from 1-to-3 for its importance to living a good life (1 = not at all important, 2 = somewhat important, and 3 = very important). If you have 20 or fewer items, you can ask people to rank order them in terms of importance. A trick here is to ask people to divide the items first into three piles (unimportant to very important) and then to rank the items within each pile. This is easier for people to do than to rank order a lot of items in one go.

The informants-by-lifestyle-items matrix can then be analyzed to see if the pattern of responses indicates a cultural consensus about what it takes to be living well. Dressler did this in Brazil and found that 22 of 39 material and behavioral items were considered somewhat important or very important for an ideal lifestyle. Then, in a later survey, Dressler asked what percentage of those 22 culturally important things people owned. He calls this measure "cultural consonance"—the fit between what people do and what the cultural consensus says they ought to do. It turns out that cultural consonance in lifestyle accounts for a significant amount of the variation in blood pressure and other health outcomes.

The consensus model is a major contribution to social science. Besides cultural consonance, it is being used in studies comparing of folk and scientific ecological and medical knowledge (Byron 2003; Chavez et al. 1995; Ross and Medin 2005; Torres 2005), acculturation (Ross et al. 2006), and many other areas (**Further Reading:** consensus analysis).

FURTHER READING

Measuring salience: J. J. Smith et al. (1995); Sutrop (2001); Thompson and Juan (2006).
Multidimensional scaling: Bolton and Vincke (1996); Kruskal and Wish (1978); Romney et al. (1972); Schweizer (1980); Shepard et al. (1972); Sturrock and Rocha (2000); Weisner (1973).
Cluster analysis: Aldenderfer and Blashfield (1984); Doreian (2004).
Sentence frames: Hruschka et al. (2008).
Consensus analysis: Caulkins (2001); de Munck et al. (2002); Furlow (2003); Garro (2000); Handwerker (2002); Harvey and Bird (2004); Jaskyte and Dressler (2004); M. L. Miller et al. (2004); Reyes-Garcia, Byon et al. (2003); Reyes-García, Godoy et al. (2003); Swora (2003).

17

Cognitive Anthropology II: Decision Modeling, Taxonomies, and Componential Analysis

This chapter is about three more methods that come from cognitive anthropology: decision modeling, taxonomic analysis, and componential analysis. These methods all have two things in common: They are entirely qualitative and they are based on systematic logic. You'll see the same properties in some of the methods for analyzing text, like analytic induction and grounded theory. All together, these methods make clear that qualitative doesn't mean wimpy.

ETHNOGRAPHIC DECISION MODELS

Ethnographic decision models (EDMs) predict the choices that people make under specific circumstances. Any recurring decision—to buy or not to buy a car, to use or not use a condom during sex, to take a sick child to the doctor—can be modeled with this method. The method was developed by Christina Gladwin (1989) and is based on asking questions, sorting out some logical rules about how the questions have to be ordered, and laying out the order in a picture (like a tree diagram) or in writing.

As with all cognitive research methods, we don't know if EDMs just predict behavior or if they also reflect the way people think about things. The jury is still out on that one. But EDMs get the prediction right 80%–90% of the time and that's as good as it gets in the social sciences.

How to Build EDMs

There are four main steps in doing decision modeling: (1) Select a specific behavioral choice to model and elicit decision criteria from a convenience sample of respondents. (2) Further elaborate and verify the decision criteria on a purposive, heterogeneous sample of informants. (3) Use the ethnographic data from step 1 and the survey data from step 2 to build a hierarchical decision model. (4) Test the model on an independent and, if possible, representative sample from the same population. We'll take these in turn.

Step 1. First, decide on the decision you are studying and what the alternatives are in that decision. EDMs are not limited to binary decisions but are easiest to build for questions about behaviors that can be answered yes or no. I'll use the decision "to make your 8 A.M. class or not" as an example. The alternatives are yes and no.

Step 2. A grand tour ethnographic question like "Tell me about why people go to class

386

or skip 8 A.M. classes" will get you a lot of information about the alternatives and the reasons for the alternatives, especially from expert informants. The major alternatives are: Get up and go to class, get up and do something else, sleep in. The "get up and do something else" alternative consists of a list: lounge around, watch old soaps on the tube, study for an exam later in the day, and so on.

Step 3. To make your ethnographic knowledge about the decision more formal—that is, to build an EDM—track down Alex, a respondent who has an 8 A.M. class and ask: "Did you make your 8 A.M. class today?" When he answers, ask him: "Why [did you] [didn't you] go to that class?" Suppose he says, "I went to class today because I *always* go to class unless I'm sick." Ask him: "Were you sick this morning?" Record his answer and draw a **tree diagram** (also called a **dendrogram**), like the one in figure 17.1, to represent his decision.

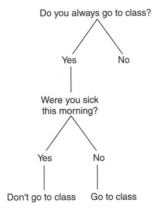

FIGURE 17.1.
An ethnographic decision model after interviewing one informant (Alex).

Figure 17.1 accounts perfectly for Alex's decision. It has to; it contains nothing more than the information from the ethnographic interview with Alex.

Now go to your second respondent, Sheila, who says that yes, she went to her 8 A.M. class. Why? "It's a really tough class," she says, "If I miss one of those classes, I'll never catch up."

Every reason for your respondents' decisions becomes a question you can ask. Use what you learned from your interview with Alex and ask Sheila: "Do you *always* go to class?" Sheila says that she sometimes skips early classes if those classes are really easy and she needs to study for an exam in another class later in the day. Ask her: "Were you sick this morning?" If she says, "no," draw the diagram in figure 17.2.

Your third respondent, Brad, says that no, he didn't go to class this morning; no, he doesn't always go to class; yes, he skips class when he's sick; no, he wasn't sick this morning; no, he didn't have an exam later in the day; no, his 8 A.M. class isn't tough; but he was out very late last night and just didn't feel like going to class this morning. Figure 17.3 combines all the information we have for Alex, Sheila, and Brad.

In fact, we don't know if Sheila was out late last night, and if she had been, whether that would have affected her decision to go to class early this morning. We can find out by going back and asking Sheila the new question. We could also go back and ask Alex if he had an exam later in the day and if he'd been out late last night.

But we won't. In practice, it is very difficult to go back to informants and ask them all

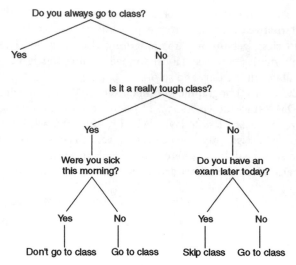

FIGURE 17.2.
An ethnographic decision model after interviewing two informants (Alex and Sheila).

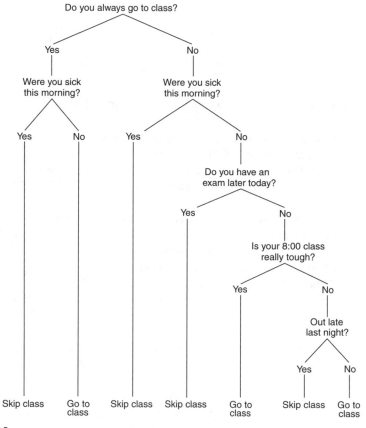

FIGURE 17.3.
An ethnographic decision model after interviewing three informants (Alex, Sheila, and Brad).

the questions you accumulate from EDM interviews. Instead, the usual practice is to build a composite diagram, like the one in figure 17.3, and push on. We also won't ask Brad what he *would* have done if he'd had a really tough 8:00 A.M. class and had been out late the night before. In building EDMs, *we deal only with people's reports of their actual, most recent behavior.*

Eventually, you'll stop getting new decisions, reasons, and constraints. Building a model for the decision on a single campus to attend or not attend early classes probably won't require more than 20 informants. Building an EDM that accounts for this decision on two very different campuses—say, a small, private college and a huge state school—may take twice that many informants. As the culture gets more heterogeneous, the sample size needed to find a stable decision model goes up. Accounting for the decisions of students in New York City and Sussex, England, will require more interviews. Add Mexico City and the number may double again. Add Cameroon. . . .

Step 4. Figure 17.3 may account for all the decisions of your next several informants, but eventually you'll run into an informant who says she doesn't always go to class, she wasn't sick this morning, she doesn't have a tough class at 8 A.M., she wasn't out late last night, and she still didn't make her early class today. Why? Because she just didn't feel like it.

If you add enough constraints, you can always build a model to account for every decision of every respondent. But what's the use of a model with 20 different sets of ordered reasons that accounts for the decisions of 20 informants? You might as well just ask every informant to explain his or her actions. The trick is to model the decisions of, say, 18 out of 20 informants (90% prediction) with just a handful of ordered rules. So, when you stop getting new reasons or constraints from EDM interviews, try building a model that accounts for at least 80% of the decisions with the fewest number of rules. Then—and here's the important part—test your model against an entirely new group of informants (box 17.1).

BOX 17.1

THE INTERVIEW FOR THE SECOND GROUP OF INFORMANTS IS DIFFERENT

It's different because you do ask them all the questions in your model (that is, you probe for all the reasons and constraints for the decision that your first group taught you), and then you guess what their decision was. In our example, you'd interview 20 or 30 new informants, all of whom have 8 A.M. classes, and you'd ask each one: Do you always go to class? Were you sick this morning? Were you out late last night? and so on, exhausting all the questions from your model. If your model works, you'll be able to *predict* the decisions of the second group from their answers to the model's questions.

Testing an EDM on a National Sample

Gery Ryan, Steve Borgatti, and I built a decision model for this question: "Think about the last time you had an empty can in your hand—juice, iced tea, soda, beer, whatever.

What did you do with it?" (Ryan and Bernard 2006). We interviewed a convenience sample of 70 people in California, North Dakota, and Florida and asked them 31 questions about the event, but we were able to predict 90% of reported decisions with just the questions in figure 17.4.

Read figure 17.4 as follows: Start by asking whether the informant at home when they made the most recent decision about what to do with that can. If they were at home, then ask if they recycle other products besides cans. If they were, then guess that they claimed to have recycled the can. This will result in two errors. That is two out of 23 people in this condition claim not to have recycled. Read the rest of figure 17.4 similarly. The whole model gets 63 out of 70, or 90% right—and that's 77% better than assigning people a result (recycle or not) randomly.

Figure 17.5 shows what happened when Ryan and I tested our ethnographic model in a nationally representative telephone survey of 386 people in the United States. We got 84.5% right, and that was 59% better than chance. It may not work for everything, but on this model, the ethnographic model was a proxy for a national model of the decision on what to do with an empty can.

REPRESENTING COMPLICATED MODELS WITH TABLES AND IF-THEN CHARTS

Young and Garro's EDM: Decision Tables

James Young and Linda Garro studied how Tarascan people in Pichátaro, Mexico, choose one of four ways to treat an illness: Use a home remedy, go to a native curer, see a *practicante* (a local, nonphysician practitioner of modern medicine), or go to a physician (see Garro 1986; Young 1980; Young and Garro 1982, 1994 [1981]). From their ethnographic work, Young and Garro believed that the decision to use one or another of these treatments depended on four factors:

1. how serious an illness was perceived to be (gravity);
2. whether a home remedy for the illness was known;
3. whether the informant had confidence in the general efficacy of a mode of treatment for a particular illness; and
4. accessibility (in terms of cost and transportation) of a particular mode of treatment.

The choice situations emerged from structured interviews with eight men and seven women who were asked:

> If you or another person in your household were ill, when—for what reasons—would you [consult] [use] _____ instead of [consulting] [using] _____? (Young and Garro 1994 [1981]:132)

Young and Garro used this question frame to elicit responses about all six possible pairs of treatment alternatives: home remedy vs. a physician, curer vs. home remedy, and so on. To check the validity of the statements made in the interviews, Young and Garro collected case histories of actual illnesses and their treatments from each of the 15 informants.

Next, the researchers completed interviews with 20 informants using a series of "What if . . ." questions to generate decisions, under various combinations of circumstances, regarding the selection of treatments for illnesses. For example, informants were asked:

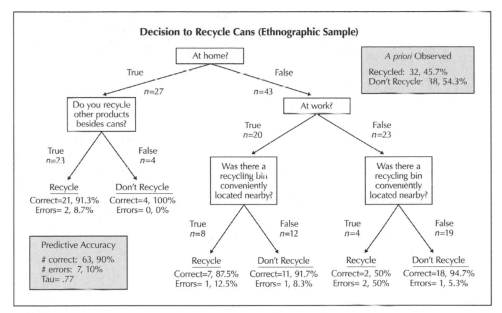

FIGURE 17.4.

Ethnographic decision model for recycling cans.

SOURCE: G.W. Ryan and H. R. Bernard, "Testing an Ethnographic Decision Tree Model on a National Sample: Recycling Beverage Cans," *Human Organization*, Vol. 65, pp. 103–14, 2006. Reprinted with permission of the Society for Applied Anthropology.

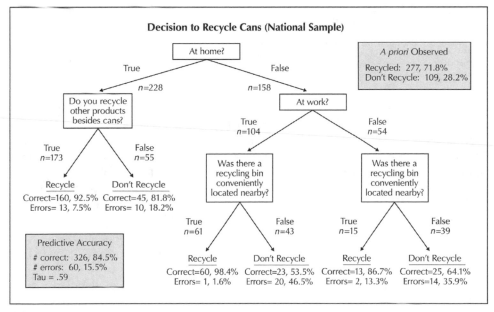

FIGURE 17.5.

National test of an ethnographic decision model.

SOURCE: G. W. Ryan and H. R. Bernard, "Testing an Ethnographic Decision Tree Model on a National Sample: Recycling Beverage Cans," *Human Organization*, Vol. 65, pp. 103–14, 2006. Reprinted with permission of the Society for Applied Anthropology.

Let's say there is a person who has a very grave illness. In this family, money is scarce—sure, they're eating, but there is just not anything left over. They have had this illness in the family before, and they now know of the remedy that benefited the illness on the previous occasion. What do you think they are going to do? (Young and Garro 1994 [1981]:137)

This vignette combines the condition of a serious illness (level 3 on gravity in tables 17.1 and 17.2), with lack of accessibility (no money), and a known remedy that can be applied at home. Young and Garro used the three levels of gravity, two possible conditions of knowing a remedy (yes and no), and two possible conditions of accessibility (yes and no) in making up the vignettes, which meant that they had to make up eight of them. Each vignette was presented to each informant for a response. Tables 17.1 and 17.2 show the **decision tables** for Young and Garro's data.

Table 17.1   Young and Garro's Decision Table Showing How Pichatareños Choose an Initial Method of Treating an Illness

Rules:	1	2	3	4	5	6	7	8	9
Conditions									
gravity[a]	1	1	1	2	2	2	3	3	3
known home remedy[b]	Y	N	N	Y	N				
faith[c]		F	M	(F)	F	M	F	M	(M)
accessibility[d]								N	Y
Choices									
self-treatment	X			X					
curer		X			X		X		
practicante			X			X		X	
physician									X

a. 1 = nonserious, 2 = moderately serious, 3 = grave
b. Y = yes, N = no
c. F = favors folk treatment, M = favors medical treatment
d. Y = money and transportation available, N = either money or transportation not available
SOURCE: Reprinted by permission of Waveland Press, Inc., from J. C. Young and L. C. Garro, *Medical Choice in a Mexican Village*, 1981 (reissued 1994), p. 154. All rights reserved.

From these qualitative data, collected in structured interviews, Young and Garro developed their decision model, for the initial choice of treatment. The model, containing nine decision rules, is shown in table 17.1. Rule number 1, for example, says that if the illness is not serious and there is a known home remedy, then treat the illness yourself. Rule number 9 says that for grave illnesses there is an implicit understanding that physicians are better (hence the M in parentheses), so if there is money, then go to a physician.

Rule number 9 also says that for the few cases of very grave illnesses where physicians are commonly thought not to be effective, apply rule number 7 and go to a curer. The blank spaces in the top part of table 17.1 indicate irrelevant conditions. In rule number 1, for example, there is no question about accessibility for home remedies because they cost little or nothing and everyone has access to them.

Sometimes the treatment selected for an illness doesn't work and another decision has to be made. Table 17.2, with 11 decision rules, shows Young and Garro's analysis of this second stage of decision making. Their entire two-stage model is based on their sense of emerging patterns in the data they collected about decision-making. The question, of course, is: Does it work?

Young and Garro tested their model against 444 treatment choices gathered from 62

Table 17.2   Young and Garro's Decision Table Showing How Pichatareños Choose a Method of Treating an Illness When Their First Choice Doesn't Work

Rules:	1	2	3	4	5	6	7	8	9	10	11
Conditions											
preceding choice[a]	ST	ST	ST	ST	C-P	C-P	C	P	Dr	Dr	Dr
current gravity[b]		1–2	3	3	1	2–3	2–3	2–3			
faith[c]	F	M	M	(M)							M
accessibility[d]			N	Y		Y	N	N		N	Y
Choices											
self-treatment					X						
curer	X							X	X	X	
practicante		X	X				X				
physician				X		X					X

a. ST = self-treatment, C = curer, P = *practicante*, Dr = physician
b. 1 = nonserious, 2 = moderately serious, 3 = grave
c. F = favors folk treatment, M = favors medical treatment
d. Y = money and transportation available, N = either money or transportation not currently available
SOURCE: Reprinted by permission of Waveland Press, Inc., from J. C. Young and L. C. Garro, *Medical Choice in a Mexican Village*, 1981 (reissued 1994), p. 156. All rights reserved.

households over a 6-month period. To make the test fair, none of the informants in the test were among those whose data were used in developing the model. Table 17.3 shows the results of the test. There were 157 cases covered by rule number 1 from table 17.1 (first-stage decision), and in every single case informants did what the rule predicted. In table 17.3, errors (informants' choices that are not predicted by the model) are in parentheses, so informants did what rule number 6 predicted 20 out of 29 times.

Overall, for the first stage, Young and Garro's decision rules predict about 94% of informants' reported behavior. After removing the cases covered by rules 1 and 4 (which account for half the cases in the data, but which could be dismissed as common-sense, routine decisions and not in need of any pretentious "analysis"), their model still predicts almost 83% of reported behavior. Even for the second stage, after first-stage decisions fail to result in a cure, and decisions get more complex and tougher to predict, the model predicts an impressive 84% of reported behavior.

Ryan and Martínez's EDM: IF-THEN Charts

Gery Ryan and Homero Martínez (1996) built an EDM for how mothers in San José, Mexico, treated children who have diarrhea. Ryan and Martínez knew, from living in the village, that mothers there use seven different treatments in treating their children's diarrhea. Five of the treatments consist of giving the child one or more of the following: (1) tea, (2) homemade rice water, (3) medication from the pharmacy (their informants told them "If you can say it, you can buy it"), (4) a carbonated beverage, or (5) a commercially produced oral rehydration solution. The other two treatments are: (6) manipulating the child's body (massaging the child's body, pinching the child's back) or (7) taking the child to the doctor.

Ryan and Martínez asked 17 mothers in San José who had children under age 5 what they did the last time their children had diarrhea. Then they went systematically through the treatments, asking each mother why she had used X instead of A, X instead of B, X instead of C, and so on down through the list.

Mothers in San José listed the following factors for choosing one treatment over another:

Table 17.3   Test Results of Young and Garro's Decision Model of How Pichatareños Choose a Treatment Method When They Are Ill

Table	Rule	Self-treatment	Curer	Practicante	Physician	Totals	Percentage correct
				Treatment Method Chosen			
18.1	1	157				157	
	2		4			4	
	3			5		5	
	4	67			(1)	68	
	5		8			8	
	6	(2)		20	(7)	29	
	7		8			8	
	8		(2)	4	(2)	8	
	9			(2)	11	13	
				Subtotal		300	94.7%
18.2	1		19			19	
	2		(1)	28	(6)	35	
	3		(3)	6		9	
	4			(2)	22	24	
	5	3	(1)			4	
	6	(2)	(2)	(1)	24	29	
	7	(1)		3	(2)	6	
	8		2	(1)		3	
	9	(1)	7			8	
	10					0	
	11				7	7	
				Subtotal		144	84.0%
				Total		444	91.2%

duration of the episode
perceived cause (from worms, from *empacho*, from food, etc.)
whether there was mucous in the stool
whether there was blood in the stool
whether the stools smelled bad
whether the stools were frequent or not
whether the stools were loose or not
whether the child had fever
color of the stool
whether the child had a dry mouth
whether the child had dry eyes
whether the child was vomiting
whether the child had swollen glands

Table 17.4 shows the data from the 17 women in Ryan and Martínez's original sample and the decision to take the child to the doctor. Read the table like this: Mother #1 said that her child's last episode of diarrhea lasted 2 days and was caused by bad food. The stools contained mucous, but did not contain blood. The stools smelled bad, were frequent, and were loose. The child had fever, the stools were yellow. The child had dry

Table 17.4 Decisions to Take a Child to the Doctor in San José, Mexico

mother	doctor	days	cause	muc.	blood	smell	freq	loose	fever	color	mouth	eyes	vomit	gland
1	N	2	C	Y	N	Y	Y	Y	Y	A	Y	Y	N	N
2	N	20	E	Y	N	Y	Y	Y	N	A	Y	Y	N	N
3	Y	8	T	N	N	Y	Y	Y	Y	N	Y	Y	N	N
4	Y	8	C	Y	N	Y	N	Y	Y	V	.	.	Y	Y
5	N	3	P	Y	N	Y	Y	Y	Y	A	Y	Y	N	Y
6	N	3	L	N	N	Y	Y	Y	N	B	Y	Y	N	N
7	Y	8	D	Y	N	Y	Y	Y	N	A	Y	Y	N	N
8	N	1	D	N	N	Y	Y	Y	N	A	.	.	N	N
9	N	.	C	Y	N	N	Y	Y	N	B	Y	Y	N	N
10	N	3	O	N	N	Y	Y	Y	N	A	Y	Y	N	N
11	N	2	C	N	N	N	N	N	N	A	.	.	N	N
12	N	.	C	N	N	Y	Y	Y	N	A	Y	Y	N	N
13	N	4	C	N	N	Y	N	N	N	A	Y	Y	N	N
14	Y	4	E	N	N	Y	Y	Y	Y	V	Y	.	N	N
15	Y	3	I	Y	Y	Y	Y	Y	Y	A	Y	Y	Y	N
16	N	2	C	Y	N	N	Y	Y	N	V	Y	Y	N	N
17	N	7	E	N	N	N	Y	Y	N	A	N	N	N	N

Cause	Color
C = food D = teething	A = yellow
L = worms T = dirt	V = green
E = empacho P = parasites	B = white
I = indigestion O = other	N = black

SOURCE: G. W. Ryan and H. Martínez, "Can We Predict What Mothers Do? Modeling Childhood Diarrhea in Rural Mexico," *Human Organization*, Vol. 55, pp. 47–57, 1996. Reprinted with permission of the Society for Applied Anthropology.

mouth and dry eyes, but was not vomiting and did not have swollen glands. In the end, Mother #1 did not take her child to the doctor. (The codes for cause and color are from Spanish; see the legend just below the table.)

Table 17.4 makes it clear that mothers took their children to the doctor if the child had blood in the stool, had swollen glands, or was vomiting, or if the diarrhea had lasted *more than* 7 days. None of the other factors played a part in the final decision to take the child to the doctor.

But remember: There were seven different treatments, and mothers often try several treatments in any given episode. Ryan and Martínez looked at the pattern of circumstances for all seven treatments and built a model that accounted for the treatment decisions made by the 17 mothers. Their model had just six rules and three constraints.

Figure 17.6 shows the model as a series of IF-THEN statements. Notice the constraints: For a woman to choose a modern medication, she has to know about it and it has to be easy to get and cheap. The constraints to the rules are derived from ethnographic interviews. So was the observation that mothers distinguished between curative and palliative treatments—treatments that stop diarrhea and treatments that simply make the child feel better until the episode is over. The model **postdicted** (accounted for) 89% of the treatments that the 17 mothers had reported.

Next, Ryan and Martínez tested their model. They interviewed 20 more mothers, but this time they asked each woman every question in the model. In other words, they asked each woman: "In your child's last episode of diarrhea, did the stools have blood in them? Did the child have swollen glands? What caused the diarrhea?" and so on. The IF-THEN model in figure 17.6 accounted for 84% of the *second* group's treatment decisions (**Further Reading:** ethnographic decision models).

Rule 1
IF   Child has blood stools OR child has swollen glands OR child is vomiting
THEN   take child to doctor.

Rule 2
IF   diarrhea is caused by *empacho*
THEN   give physical treatment.

Rule 3
IF   previous rules do not apply OR there is no cure with *empacho* treatment
THEN   give the highest preferred curing treatment that meets
                 constraints.

Rule 4
IF   previous treatment did not stop diarrhea
THEN   compare the two highest preferred treatments of remaining options.

Rule 4.1
IF   one is a curing remedy AND meets its constraints
THEN   give this treatment.

Rule 4.2
IF   both or neither are curing remedies AND each meets its respective constraints
THEN   give the highest-ranked preference.

Rule 5
IF   the previous treatment did not stop the diarrhea AND
            the episode is less than 1 week
THEN   repeat rule 4.

Rule 6
IF   the episode has lasted more than 1 week
THEN   take the child to a doctor.

Constraints
IF   you know how to make ORS (oral rehydration solution) AND
            your child will drink ORS
THEN   give ORS.
IF   you know a medication that works for diarrhea AND
            you have it in the house
THEN   give the pill or liquid medication.
IF   you know a medication that works for diarrhea AND
            it is cheap AND
            it is easy to obtain
THEN   give the pill or liquid medication.

FIGURE 17.6.
Ryan and Martínez's decision model as a series of IF-THEN rules.
SOURCE: G. W. Ryan and H. Martínez, "Can We Predict What Mothers Do? Modeling Childhood Diarrhea in Rural Mexico," *Human Organization*, Vol. 55, pp. 47–57, 1996. Reprinted with permission of the Society for Applied Anthropology.

FOLK TAXONOMIES

There are about 6,000 languages spoken in the world today. Speakers of all those languages name things in the natural world. In 1914, Henderson and Harrington published a monograph on the ethnozoology of the Tewa Indians of New Mexico. Scholars ever since have been interested in understanding the variety of ways in which people organize their knowledge of the natural world.

In the 1950s, anthropologists began systematically producing **folk taxonomies**—that is, hierarchical, taxonomic graphs to represent how people organize their knowledge of plants and animals. These ethnobotanical and ethnozoological taxonomies don't necessarily mirror scientific taxonomies, but the whole point of what became known as **ethnoscience** is to understand cultural knowledge on its own terms.

Scientific taxonomies for plants and animals recognize six primary levels of distinction (phylum, class, order, family, genus, and species) and lots of in-between levels as well (infraorder, superorder, subclass, etc., etc.), but folk taxonomies of plants and animals across the world are generally limited to five or, at most, six levels. Figure 17.7 (from D'Andrade 1995) shows part of the folk taxonomy of *creatures* for native speakers of English.

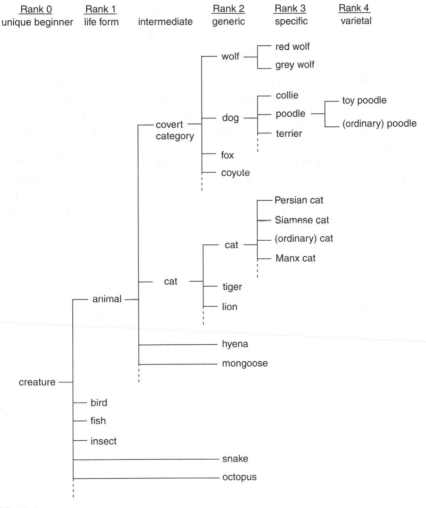

FIGURE 17.7.

Partial taxonomy for *creatures* in English.

SOURCE: R. G. D'Andrade, *The Development of Cognitive Anthropology*, p. 99. © 1995 Cambridge University Press. Reprinted by permission.

Covert Categories

There are six culturally appropriate levels of hierarchical distinction identified in figure 17.7: (1) First, there is the unique beginner, a single label that identifies the cultural domain. (2) Next comes a relatively small set of life forms (animals, fish, insects, etc.). (3) Then there is an intermediate level, which includes **covert categories**, if any exist in a particular taxonomy. Folk genera (level 4), folk species (level 5), and folk varieties (level 6) round out the picture.

There is a covert, unnamed category in figure 17.7 comprising wolves, foxes, dogs, coyotes, and some other things (the dashed line extending down from coyote, indicates that the covert category contains more than what's listed in the figure). In a scientific taxonomy, foxes are not in the same genus with dogs and wolves. The latter are in the genus *Canis*, while foxes are in the genus *Vulpes*. Many speakers of English, however, classify foxes and wolves in the category of "things in the dog family," or "canines," and a folk taxonomy of English animal terms respects that.

The intermediate category of "cat" is not covert. How can you tell? As D'Andrade says, you can say "Look at that cat!" if you're talking about a tiger, but it's weird to say "Look at that dog" if you're pointing to a fox, so "cat" is a named intermediate category and "dog" isn't.

Two more things about figure 17.7. Note how we use words for generic animals in English that would be at the species level in a scientific taxonomy (wolf, coyote, and dog are all members of the genus *Canis*, species *lupus*, *latrans*, and *familiaris*, respectively), and how the species level in the folk taxonomy comprises names for subspecies in a scientific taxonomy.

Also, look at how D'Andrade has placed octopus and snake and snake in figure 17.7. The horizontal lines show that D'Andrade has classified these creatures as **nonaffiliated generics**. They might be classified as life forms, but, as D'Andrade points out, there are many nonaffiliated generics in the ocean, including clams, lobsters, seahorses, jellyfish, and octopi.

Cultural Domains and Folk Taxonomies

It was quickly recognized that folk taxonomies could be developed for *any* **cultural domain**, not just for ethnobotanical and ethnozoological knowledge, and that we use folk taxonomies all the time to order our experience and guide our behavior.

Take someone to a supermarket—one they've never been to before—and ask them to find peanut butter. Follow them as they make their way around the store and get them to talk about what they think they're doing. Here's a typical response:

> Well, let's see, milk and eggs are over there by that wall, and the meat's usually next to that, and the canned goods are kind of in the middle, with the soaps and paper towels and stuff on the other side, so we'll go right in here, in the middle. No, this is the soap aisle, so let's go over to the right. . . . Sure, here's the coffee, so it's got to be on this aisle or the next, with cans of things like ravioli.

Any competent member of U.S. or Canadian culture will find the peanut butter in a hurry, but not everything is so clear. Shredded coconut and walnuts are often shelved with flour in the United States because they are used in baking, but other nuts—cashews and peanuts, for example—may be shelved somewhere else, like with the snacks. Lychee nuts (a Chinese dessert food) and matzohs (unleavened bread boards eaten primarily by Jews) are sometimes shelved in U.S. supermarkets together under "ethnic foods," but may be shelved in separate "Oriental foods" and "Jewish foods" sections if local populations of those groups are sufficiently large.

How to Make a Taxonomy: Pile Sorts

Pile sorting is an efficient method for generating **taxonomic trees** (Werner and Fenton 1973). Simply hand informants the familiar pack of cards, each of which contains some term in a cultural domain. Informants sort the cards into piles, according to whatever criterion makes sense to them. After the first sorting, informants are handed each pile and asked to go through the exercise again. They keep doing this until they say that they cannot subdivide piles any further. At each sorting level, informants are asked if there is a word or phrase that describes each pile.

Perchonock and Werner (1969) used this technique in their study of Navajo animal categories. After an informant finished doing a pile sort of animal terms, Perchonock and Werner built a branching tree diagram, like the one in figure 17.8. They would ask the informant to make up sentences or phrases that expressed some relation between the nodes. They found that informants intuitively grasped the idea of tree representations for taxonomies.

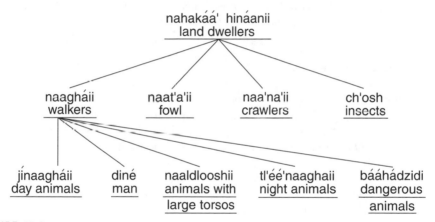

FIGURE 17.8.

Part of the Navajo animal kingdom, derived from a pile sort.

SOURCE: N. Perchonock and O. Werner, "Navaho Systems of Classification: Some Implications for Ethnoscience." *Ethnology*, Vol. 8, pp. 229–42. Copyright © 1969. Reprinted by permission.

How to Make a Taxonomy: Lists and Frames

In building a folk taxonomy, many researchers combine the free-list and frame elicitation techniques I described in chapter 10. Start with the frame:

What kinds of _____ are there?

where the blank is "cars," "trees," "saddles," "snow," "soldiers"—whatever you're interested in understanding. This frame is used again and again, until an informant says that the question is silly.

For example, suppose you asked a native speaker of American English "What kinds of foods are there?" You might get a list like: pasta, meat, fish, fruits, vegetables, snacks. . . ."

(You'll probably get a slightly different set of labels if you ask a native speaker of British English this same question.)

Next, you ask: "What kinds of pasta [meats] [fish] [etc.] are there?" The answer for meats might be: beef, lamb, chicken, pork, venison. . . .

So you extend the search: "What kinds of beef [lamb] [chicken] [etc.] are there?" For some people, at least, you'll find that beef is divided into steak, chops, hamburger, and so on, and that chicken is divided into dark meat and white meat. But if you ask "What kinds of steaks are there?" you might be told: "There are no kinds; they just are what they are." If you're dealing with a real steak lover, you might be told about Porterhouse, T-bone, rib eye, Delmonico, filet mignon, and so on.

Once you have a list of lexical items in a domain, and once you've got the basic divisions down, the next step is to find out about overlaps. Some foods, like peanuts, get classified as snacks and as protein sources by different people—or even by the same person at different times.

The point is, although the Food and Drug Administration may have codified foods in the United States, there is no codified set of folk rules for a taxonomy of foods in U.S. culture. The only way to map this is to construct folk taxonomies from information provided by a number of people and to get an idea of the range of variation and areas of consistency in how people think about this domain. You can learn about the possible overlaps in folk categories by using the substitution frames:

Is _____ a kind of_____ ?
Is _____ a part of _____ ?

Once you have a list of terms in a domain, and a list of categories, you can use this substitution frame for all possible combinations. Are marshmallows a kind of meat? A kind of fish? A kind of snack? This can get really tedious, but discovering **levels of contrast**—that *magenta* is a kind of *red*, that *cashews* are a kind of *nut*, that *alto* is a kind of *sax*, or that *ice cream* is a kind of *dessert*—just takes plain hard work. Unless you're a child, in which case all this discovery is just plain fun.

A common way to display folk taxonomies is with a branching tree diagram. Figure 17.9 shows a tree diagram for part of a folk taxonomy of passenger cars. I elicited this taxonomy in Morgantown, West Virginia, from Jack in 1976.

Things to Look for in Folk Taxonomies

There are five points to make about the taxonomy shown in figure 17.9:

1. Interinformant variation is common in folk taxonomies. That is, different people may use different words to refer to the same category of things. Sometimes, in fact, terms can be almost idiosyncratic. Jack distinguished among what he called "regular cars," "station wagons," and "vans." The term "regular cars" is not one your normally see in automobile ads, or hear from a salesperson on a car lot.
2. Category labels do not necessarily have to be simple lexical items, but may be complex phrases. The category labeled "4-wheel drive" vehicles in figure 17.9 was sometimes called "off-road vehicles" in 1976, or even "vehicles you can go camping in or tow a horse trailer with." Jack said that Jeep station wagons were both wagons *and* 4-wheel-drive cars you can go camping in.
3. Labels change over time. By the 1990s, those cars that Jack had called "vehicles you can go camping in or tow a horse trailer with" were being called "utes" by some

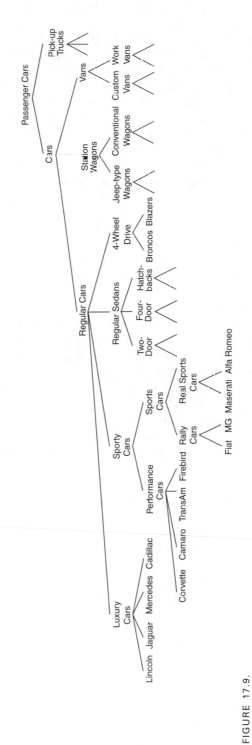

FIGURE 17.9.
Part of Jack's taxonomy of cars and trucks.

people—short for "sport utility vehicle." Today, the term widely used is SUV, though small SUVs are sometimes called "cute utes."

4. There are those covert categories I mentioned—categories for which people have no label at all, or at least not one they find easily accessible. Some people insist that Corvettes, Camaros, Maseratis, and MGs are part of a single category, which they find difficult to name (one informant suggested "sporty cars" as a label). Others, like Jack, separate "performance cars" from "sports cars" and even subdivide sports cars into "true sports cars" and "rally cars." Be on the lookout for unlabeled categories (that is, unlabeled nodes in a branching tree diagram) in any folk taxonomy.

5. Even when there are consistent labels for categories, the categories may represent multiple dimensions, each of which has its own levels of contrast. For example, many native speakers of American English recognize a category of "foreign cars" that cuts across the taxonomy in figure 17.9. There are foreign sports cars, foreign luxury cars, and foreign regular cars.

Folk taxonomies can be very, very complex. One way to get at the complexity is through multidimensional scaling (see chapter 16). Another is a technique known as componential analysis (**Further Reading:** folk taxonomies).

COMPONENTIAL ANALYSIS

Componential analysis is a formal, qualitative technique for studying meaning. There are two objectives: (1) to specify the conditions under which a native speaker of a language will call something (like a plant, a kinsman, a car) by a particular term and (2) to understand the cognitive process by which native speakers decide which of several possible terms they should apply to a particular thing.

The first objective is descriptive, but the second is a kind of **causal analysis** and is what the developers of the technique had in mind in the 1950s and 1960s (see Conklin 1955; Frake 1962; Goodenough 1956; Wallace 1962). Charles Frake, for example, described componential analysis as a step toward "the analysis of terminological systems in a way which reveals the conceptual principles that generate them" (1962:74). This created a lot of criticism, but more on that later.

Componential analysis is based on the principle of **distinctive features** in phonology, the branch of linguistics devoted to the study of the sounds of a language. To understand the principle, think about the difference in the sounds represented by P and B in English. Both are made by twisting your mouth into the same shape. This is a *feature* of the P and B sounds called "bilabial" or "two-lipped."

Another feature is that they are both "stops." That is, they are made by stopping the flow of air for an instant as it moves up from your lungs and releasing the flow suddenly. An S sound, by contrast, also requires that you restrict the air flow, but not completely. You kind of let the air slip by in a hiss. The only difference between a P and a B sound is that the P is voiceless while the B is voiced—you vibrate your vocal cords while making a P.

If you add up all the phonological features of the words "bit" and "pit," the only feature that differentiates them is voicing on the first sound in each word. The "pitness" of a pit and the "bitness" of a bit are clearly not in the voicelessness or voicedness of the sounds P and B, but any native speaker of English will distinguish the two words, and their meanings, and can trace the difference between them to that little feature of voicing if you push them a bit.

There is a unique little bundle of features that define each of the consonantal sounds in English. The only difference between the words "mad" and "bad" is that the bilabial sound M is nasal, and not a stop. These distinctive features carry meaning for native speakers of a language.

This principle can be adapted to the study of other domains of culture. Any two "things" (sounds, kinship terms, names of plants, names of animals, etc.) can be distinguished by exactly one binary feature that either occurs (+) or doesn't occur (− +).

Table 17.5   A Componential Analysis of Four Things with Two Features

	Feature 1	Feature 2
Thing 1	+	+
Thing 2	+	−
Thing 3	−	+
Thing 4	−	−

Table 17.5 shows that with two features you can distinguish four things: Thing 1 can be (+ +), thing 2 can be (+ −), thing 3 can be (− +), and thing 4 can be (− −). Each bundle of features is different and defines each of the four things. With three binary features, you can distinguish eight things; with four, 16; with five, 32; and so on.

When componential analysis was introduced into cultural anthropology, it was applied to the set of English kinship terms (Goodenough 1956) and it continues to be used for understanding kinship systems (Pericliev and Valdez-Perez 1998). A daughter in English, for example, is a *consanguineal, female, descending generation* person. So is a niece, but a niece is *through a sibling or a spouse.*

Table 17.6 shows the distinctive feature principle applied to a list of 22 barnyard animals. (This example was first suggested by Hjelmslev 1961:70.) Stallions are adult male horses and foals are baby horses. Notice that there is no column in table 17.6 labeled "male" and no column labeled "juvenile." A parsimonious set of features for distinguishing among these animals does not require all that information. A stallion is a nonfemale, gendered (that is, not neutered), adult horse. Any horse that is not female and gendered and not an adult must be a colt. A barrow is a neutered, adult hog, and a wether is a neutered, adult sheep.

Actually, if we wanted the most parsimonious set of features we would drop one of the last four columns in table 17.6. Those columns identify the general class of animals— horses, cattle, sheep, and swine—to which each named animal belongs. If the domain of barnyard animals comprised *just* those four classes, then a not-horse, not-cattle, not-sheep animal *must* be a swine. I've left all four animal classes in table 17.6 because there are other classes of barnyard animals not yet represented (chickens, rabbits, goats, etc.).

Componential analysis can be applied to any domain of a language where you are interested in understanding the semantic features that make up the domain. Table 17.7 shows a componential analysis of seven cars, using three features elicited from Jack (he of the taxonomy shown in figure 17.9).

A Corvette is an expensive car, not very practical, and not foreign; a Mercedes is an expensive, practical, foreign car; and so on. Each of the seven cars is uniquely defined by the three features Jack mentioned (box 17.2).

PROBLEMS WITH COMPONENTIAL ANALYSIS

There are two problems with componential analysis. First of all, it seems a bit shallow to say that a Corvette is an expensive, impractical, American car and nothing more, or

Table 17.6   A Componential Analysis of 17 Barnyard Animals

	Female	Neuter	Adult	Horses	Cattle	Sheep	Swine
Cow	+	−	+	−	+	−	−
Bull	−	−	+	−	+	−	−
Steer	−	+	+	−	+	−	−
Calf	−	+	−	−	+	−	−
Heifer	+	−	−	−	+	−	−
Mare	+	−	+	+	−	−	−
Stallion	−	−	+	+	−	−	−
Gelding	−	+	+	+	−	−	−
Foal	−	+	−	+	−	−	−
Filly	+	−	−	+	−	−	−
Colt	−	−	−	+	−	−	−
Sow	+	−	+	−	−	−	+
Boar	−	−	+	−	−	−	+
Barrow	−	+	+	−	−	−	+
Piglet	−	+	−	−	−	−	+
Gilt	+	−	−	−	−	−	+
Shoat	−	−	−	−	−	−	+
Sheep	−	−	+	−	−	+	−
Ram	−	−	+	−	−	+	−
Ewe	+	−	+	−	−	+	−
Wether	−	+	+	−	−	+	−
Lamb	−	−	−	−	−	+	−

that a Mercedes is an expensive, practical, foreign car and nothing more. You can get so caught up in finding the minimal analytic combination of features in this type of analysis that you forget you're interested in the meaning that people assign to different objects in a domain. On the other hand, if you know the most parsimonious set of distinctive features for an item in a domain, you can predict how someone will label new things in the domain that they haven't encountered before.

The second problem with componential analysis is the same one we run into with all cognitive research methods: We have no idea if it reflects how people actually think. This problem was raised early in the development of cognitive studies by Robbins Burling (1964), who noted that, in a folk taxonomy of trees, he could not tell the essential cognitive difference between hemlock and spruce. "Is it gross size, type of needle, form of bark, or what?" If an ethnographer could not answer this question, Burling observed, then no componential analysis could claim to be "more than an exercise of the analyst's imagination" (p. 27).

Of course, this same critique could apply to any social research that "imputes the

Table 17.7   Minimal Componential Analysis for Seven Cars, According to Jack

	Expensive	Practical	Foreign
Corvette	+	−	−
Firebird	−	−	−
MG	−	−	+
Maserati	+	−	+
Mercedes	+	+	+
Jeep	−	+	−
Dodge Van	+	+	−

BOX 17.2

COMPONENTIAL ANALYSIS FROM ETHNOGRAPHY

James Faris (1968) studied the lexicon of social events in Cat Harbour, a small fishing community on the northeast coast of Newfoundland. During his research, Faris asked about the different kinds of social events and learned that some were classified as "occasions" and others were not. The occasions included weddings, funerals, birthdays, scoffs, and events at which mummers could be present. The nonoccasions included meetings of fishermen (called "union meetings"), church services, christenings, teas, banquets, socials, concerts, suppers, and evening gatherings of men (p. 120). To understand what separated occasions from nonoccasions, Faris looked at the features of the events. Some were fun, others not. Some were public, others limited to a few families. All occasions involve serving food, but so do some of the nonoccasions.

By systematically examining the features of each social event and the meaning of each event to the people of Cat Harbour, Faris solved the puzzle. All of the so-called occasions involved approved deviation from the rules of everyday behavior. Scoffs, for example, involve a few couples who get together to dance, play cards, and eat a meal to which they all contribute. The men (and occasionally, the women) drink, and there is a lot of sexual banter—something that would not be tolerated in other situations. All the ingredients for the scoff, or dinner, are stolen. Under any other circumstance, this would not be tolerated, but one is allowed to "buck" (a euphemism for stealing) the makings of a scoff from neighbors and friends. A scoff, Faris tells us, is "an occasion of sanctioned license, a legitimization of behavior and action normally considered 'sin'" (p. 228).

Likewise, weddings involved dancing "jigs and reels with heavy sexual overtone" and men drinking to excess. "After having heard from several persons of the evils of sexual license and excessive drink," Faris says, "I observed these same people participating with gusto in these activities at a 'wedding'—only to be told again by them the following day of the evils of sexual license and excessive drinking" (p. 228). At funerals, the mourners are removed from everyday roles, and birthdays are excuses for scoffs. At Christmas, people dress in costumes and masks and go around to houses where they are fed food and alcohol. Men may dress as women and women as men. All in all, Faris concluded, the feature that distinguished the so-called occasions from other social events was the sanctioned deviance.

presence of something inside people" (like values and attitudes) and must be balanced with a positive perspective on what *can* be done (Hymes 1964:119).

In fact, what can be done is impressive, intuitively compelling analysis of the meanings that people attach to terms in their languages: Decision analysis allows us to predict which of several behavioral options people will take, under specific circumstances; taxonomic analysis lets us predict which class of things some new thing will be assigned to; componential analysis lets us predict what classification label will be assigned to some object.

These methods produce effective knowledge that finds application in practical fields like health care delivery and advertising (**Further Reading:** componential analysis).

FURTHER READING

Ethnographic decision models: K. A. Beck (2005); Gladwin (1976, 1980, 1983); Hurwicz (1995); Morera and Gladwin (2006); Quinn (1978); Ruiz-Caseres and Heymann (2009).

Folk taxonomies: Atran (1998); Begossi et al. (2008); Berlin et al. (1968, 1973); Brown et al. (1975); Frake (1961); Tyler (1969); Werner and Schoepfle (1987).

Componential analysis: Hedican (1986); Kendall (1983); Rushforth (1982).

Text Analysis I: Interpretive Analysis, Narrative Analysis, Performance Analysis, and Conversation Analysis

There is growing interest these days in the analysis of texts. Little wonder. Most of the recoverable information about human thought and behavior in complex societies is naturally occurring text: books, magazines, and newspapers, diaries, property transactions, recipes, correspondence, song lyrics, billboards . . .

And there's more—lots and lots more. *Artifacts* (clay pots, houses, toys, clothing, computers, furniture) and *images* (family photo albums and videos, slasher films, sitcoms) are texts. *Behaviors* (making beer, laying out a garden, dressing the dead for funerals) and *events* (church ceremonies, homecoming games, blind dates) are texts. All these things come to us raw, in qualitative form. We can study them raw or we can code them—turn them into variables—and study the relations among the variables. Both approaches produce insight and understanding.

Enormous corpora of texts are available online—all U.S. Supreme Court opinions, the great works of the major world religions, all of Shakespeare's writings, every surviving ancient Greek and Latin text, 160 years of the *New York Times*, to name just a few—with more and more added all the time. Ethnographic texts on a culture-area probability sample of 60 societies around the world are available on line from the Human Relations Area Files (more on HRAF in chapter 19 when we get to content analysis).

Scholars of social change have long relied on longitudinal survey data—the Gallup Poll (continually collected data since 1935) and the General Social Survey (almost every year since 1972) are just two of the hundreds of data sets available for time series analysis. But longitudinal qualitative data are also plentiful. For a window on American popular culture, for example, take a look at the themes dealt with in country music and in *Superman* comics over the years. Or look at sitcoms and product ads from the 1950s and the 2000s.

In the 1950s, for example, Lucille Ball created a furor when she got pregnant and dared to continue making episodes of the *I Love Lucy* show. Now think about any episode of *Two and a Half Men* or *30 Rock*. Or scan some of the recent episodes of popular soap operas and compare them to episodes from 50 years ago. Today's sitcoms and soaps contain many more sexual innuendos.

How many more? If you really wanted to measure that, you could code two representative samples of sitcoms and soaps, one from the 1950s and another from the past 10 years, and compare the codes statistically. That's content analysis.

Interpretivists, on the other hand, might be more interested in understanding the meaning across time of concepts like "flirtation," "deceit," "betrayal," "sensuality," and "love," or the narrative mechanisms by which any of these concepts is displayed or responded to by various characters.

Text analysis is for positivists and interpretivists alike and there is no single method for doing it. Some of the traditions of text analysis include: (1) **interpretive analysis**, (2) **narrative analysis**, (3) **performance analysis**, (4) **conversation analysis**, (5) **schema analysis**, (6) **grounded theory**, (7) **content analysis**, and (8) **analytic induction**. I deal with the first four of these methods in this chapter and with the other four in chapter 19. The first four methods rely mostly on the intuition and erudition of the analyst, while the last four make increasing use of computer programs. Whatever your taste in methods—super-qualitative or super-quantitative, super-inductive or super-deductive—there's something for everyone in text analysis.

Before we get to text *analysis*, though, I want to tell you about the great tradition of text *collection* in anthropology.

TEXT ARE US

Anthropologists have been big producers and collectors of texts, right from the beginning of the discipline. In 1881, Adolph Bastian argued that, with indigenous cultures of the world disappearing fast, "our guiding principle . . . in anthropology, prehistory, or ethnology should be to collect everything" (Bastian 1881:217; cited in Bunzl 1996:48).

For Franz Boas, Bastian's young colleague at the Berlin Museum, that meant collecting texts, and more texts, about the indigenous cultures of the world, *in the native languages* of those cultures. Boas trained his students (Kroeber, Lowie, Sapir, etc.) to collect verbatim text in as many indigenous American languages as they could reach.

This was really tough to do before voice recorders were invented, but that first generation of American anthropologists persevered and made use of every new technology they could to produce texts and more texts. In 1936, Margaret Mead and Gregory Bateson hauled heavy movie cameras to Bali and, with cinematographer Jane Belo (1960), shot hundreds of hours of cinéma verité of Balinese dances and rituals—a treasure trove of fundamental ethnographic data that's available today for analysis and reanalysis (http://www.loc.gov/avconservation/packard/).

Boas practiced what he preached. He collected huge volumes of texts in several American Indian and Eskimo languages (Boas 1917, 1928a, 1928b). In the summer of 1888, while doing fieldwork in British Columbia, Boas met George Hunt. Hunt's father was a fur trader from Scotland and his mother was Tlingit, but Hunt grew up in Fort Rupert and became fluent in Kwakwala, the language of the Kwakiutl. Hunt lived as a Kwakiutl, married a Kwakiutl woman, and participated fully in the ceremonial life of the tribe. After Boas returned to New York, he and Hunt corresponded for 5 years and then, in 1893, Boas brought Hunt and several other Kwakiutl to the World's Fair in Chicago. It was there that Boas trained Hunt to write Kwakwala phonetically.

Hunt returned to British Columbia and Boas returned to New York. But from then on, for 40 years, Boas kept in touch with Hunt by mail, asking Hunt for information about this or that aspect of Kwakiutl culture. By the time Hunt died in 1933, he had produced 5,650 pages of Kwakiutl text. Boas relied on this rich corpus of descriptive ethnography for most of his reports about Kwakiutl life (Rohner 1966; see Boas 1910a, 1935–1943; Boas and Hunt 1902–1905, 1906). In fact, of Boas's 5,000 pages of published work, 4,000 pages are unannotated translations of Kwakiutl language texts (Berman 1996:216) and there are thousands more pages in the Boas archives (at the American

Philosophical Society in Philadelphia) that remain unpublished, waiting to be analyzed by another generation of scholars.

Native Ethnography

This was the first of what would become a tradition called **native ethnography**. It was carried forward by several of Boas's students, including Edward Sapir, whose first job after completing his Ph.D. under Boas's direction was at the Canadian Geological Survey, in Ottawa. One of the ethnographers who worked under his direction there was Marius Barbeau. In 1914, Barbeau went to the Northwest Coast to work with the Tsimshian and hired William Beynon as his interpreter. Beynon was 26 at the time, and only recently arrived from Victoria, but he spoke fluent Tsimshian (his mother was Tsimshian and his father was Welsh) (M. Anderson and Halpin 2000:4).

Barbeau wrote to Sapir that his new informant could recite Tsimshian myths and write them down in English at the same time. Sapir advised Barbeau to teach Beynon to write Tsimshian, as Sapir had taught his own informant to write Nootka, so that Beynon could work even more independently. "There is," said Sapir, "no absolute reason why every bit of material that one utilizes in his work should have been personally obtained" (Sapir's letter to Barbeau, February 1, 1915; quoted in Anderson and Halpin 2000:5–6.) This was the start of Beynon's career as a professional informant. By the time he died in 1958, Beynon had sent Barbeau 54 Canadian government–issued notebooks of 50 pages each, filled with Tsimshian texts and with observations of Tsimshian daily life and ceremonies (Anderson and Halpin 2000:7).

Beynon never published a monograph based on his ethnographic notebooks, but four of his notebooks, detailing the ceremonies in 1945 surrounding the raising of five totem poles, were rescued from the archives and published verbatim (Anderson and Halpin 2000).

Another of Boas's students, Paul Radin, however, took the method of native ethnography further. Radin studied the language and culture of the Winnebago Indians and, following his mentor's lead, trained Sam Blowsnake to write in Winnebago. Blowsnake started writing his autobiography. After one day, he came to Radin, worried about what white people might think when they read it (Blowsnake confesses in the narrative to murdering a Potowatami). Radin reassured him, and Blowsnake polished off the manuscript in 2 days. Relying on a bilingual Winnebago-English interpreter, Radin translated and published the manuscript in 1920 as *Crashing Thunder: The Autobiography of a Winnebago Indian* (Radin 1983 [1920]).

Radin's insistence that he "in no way influenced [Crashing Thunder], either directly or indirectly in any way" seems disingenuous today. And including that part about murdering a Potawatami was poor professional judgment, by today's standards. But *Crashing Thunder* is, in my view, a milestone in the history of anthropology. Since then, the method of native ethnography has been greatly extended.

Fadwa El Guindi, for example, worked in the 1960s and 1970s with Abel Hernández Jiménez, on a native ethnography of the Zapotec people of Oaxaca. One of El Guindi's colleagues, Harvey Rosenbaum, taught Hernández linguistics while El Guindi taught him anthropology (El Guindi 2004:141). El Guindi used open-ended interviewing to get Hernández to discuss four rituals: a baptism, a child's funeral, a wedding, and an adult's funeral. After each discussion (which covered things like the ordering of events in each ritual, who participates, and the meaning of ritual objects), Hernández wrote up his description of one of the rituals, and El Guindi collected parallel data on her own to compare with those of her colleague (El Guindi and Hernández Jiménez 1986:25).

El Guindi (2004:chap. 4) observes that some classic work in visual anthropology should also be counted as native ethnography. From 1963 to 1965, for example, Asen Balicki worked with Itimanguerk, a Netsilik Inuit hunter, producing a monumental film record of indigenous Netsilik culture: nearly 50 miles of film, including nine finished films totaling nearly 11 hours (Balicki 1989; El Guindi 2004:129–34). And in 1966, Sol Worth and John Adair gave 16-mm movie cameras to seven Navajo men and women to learn about Navajo life "through Navajo eyes"—the title of the book describing this famous project (El Guindi 2004:140–46; Worth and Adair 1970, 1972).

Ignacio Bizarro Ujpán has been the long-term informant and friend of anthropologist James Sexton. Between 1972 and 1974, at Sexton's urging, Bizarro wrote his autobiography in Spanish. He also began a diary in 1972, which he kept for 5 years. Sexton edited the diary, removing repetitive events and what he felt was trivial material detailing "the kinds of meals he [Bizarro] ate each day, the saying of his nightly prayers, his daily work routine, how well he slept, and common illnesses like colds and headaches" (Sexton 1981:4).

Sexton supplemented the diary with taped interviews. In his method, he inserts his questions in italics into Bizarro's narrative, to show "what kind of information Ignacio volunteered and how much of it is material I solicited from my own perspective." This partnership has gone on for decades (see Bizarro Ujpán [1981, 1985, 1992, 2001] and Sexton and Bizarro Ujpán 1999) and continues today (**Further Reading:** native ethnography).

The Ñähñu Native Ethnography

My own contribution to this tradition of native ethnography has been in collaboration with Jesús Salinas Pedraza, a Ñähñu teacher from the Mezquital Valley in central Mexico. Jesús and I met in 1962 when I went to the Mezquital to study Ñähñu for my M.A. In 1971, I told him that I was thinking of writing an ethnography of the Ñähñu. He said that he might like to write one himself, and so for the next 16 years, he wrote, and I translated and annotated, a four-volume, 232,000-word book on Ñähñu culture in Ñähñu (Bernard and Salinas Pedraza 1989; Salinas Pedraza 1984; Salinas Pedraza and Bernard 1978).

Just as I had developed a writing system for Ñähñu and had taught Jesús to intellectualize about the phonology of his language, I supposed that I would teach him to take field notes about ceremonies and to write about all the details of everyday life. As I said in 1989, in the introduction to the Ñähñu ethnography:

> I saw him writing up a bunch of raw facts and me guiding him in the analysis of those facts, as we teased out the underlying meaning of the texts produced by his unschooled efforts. I saw myself guiding Jesús, monitoring and supervising his work, and seeing to it that the ethnography he would produce would meet the high standards of modern anthropology. I wanted to be able to say that, as the professional anthropologist of this team, I had laid academic hands on Jesús's work and that the result was much better for it. (Bernard and Salinas Pedraza 1989:24)

I was soon disabused of these illusions. Jesús Salinas wrote his 232,000-word ethnography of the Ñähñu with very little active coaching from me.

Wolcott's Critique of Native Ethnography

Very little active coaching, but still. . . . Harry Wolcott (2008:163–169) offers two incisive critiques of the Ñähñu native ethnography project: (1) that I had more influence on Jesús Salinas's writing of the Ñähñu ethnography than I imagined in 1989, and (2) that the Ñähñu ethnography is not really an ethnography because Jesús Salinas is not really an ethnographer.

Wolcott is right about the first point. As he points out, early on in the Ñähñu ethnography project, I presented Salinas with a Spanish-language version of the *Outline of Cultural Materials*, the detailed codebook developed by George Peter Murdock to categorize ethnographic materials on cultures of the world (Murdock 1971). This reflected my own training and was hardly a totally hands-off approach to the content of Jesús's work.

In fact, my influence extended far beyond just advocating that Salinas pay attention to the categories of the OCM. By the time we completed the translation of the Ñähñu native ethnography in 1988, Jesús and I had known one another for 26 years. I had asked him countless questions about Ñähñu culture before we ever got started on the project and countless more as we sat, elbow to elbow, translating the ethnography from Ñähñu into English (we worked through Spanish as an intermediary language). I forced him to think out loud about things that he might otherwise never have contemplated consciously. In the end, the content of the Ñähñu native ethnography was the result of constant negotiation, constant interaction between Jesús Salinas and me.

On the other hand, Jesús was not chained to the OCM and he went far beyond simply addressing my questions. He wrote about things that I could not have asked about, simply because of my ignorance of Ñähñu culture. I made plain that I was interested in the uses of plants, but he wrote about plants that I didn't know existed.

I asked him to begin the Ñähñu ethnography with a chapter on the setting and explained that this was about the geography, the climate, the flora and fauna, and so on. Again, this was straight out of my own training, and Jesús followed my instructions, but the result was nothing like anything I *would* have written, because it was nothing I *could* have written. As the ethnography begins, Jesús walks the reader through the Mezquital Valley, naming the mountains and describing the villages in great detail: which villages produce lime for tortillas, which produce charcoal, and so on. He asked me if he could include information on the weather and the seasons and the winds and what effect they all had on people, plants, and animals. I could not even have formulated the questions in Ñähñu to retrieve that kind of information.

Others may choose to pursue the method of native ethnography differently, but I would do it the same way again. I would provide a framework and a long list of topics (the OCM, for example). I wouldn't tell the native ethnographer what content to provide, but, as I did with Jesús, I would ask plenty of questions, based on my own knowledge of the local culture—and on the holes I recognize in that knowledge. I believe strongly that we need more, much more, of this kind of work in anthropology.

Wolcott's second critique—that the Ñähñu ethnography is not really an ethnography because Jesús Salinas is not really an ethnographer—raises a really interesting question: Who gets to be called an ethnographer? One school of thought is captured in Paul Bohannan's aphorism that "without an ethnographer there is no ethnography" (1995:157). Wolcott quotes this maxim to lead off his penetrating discussion of insider and outsider ethnography (Wolcott 2008:137). In this perspective, Jesús Salinas's work is "the stuff out of which ethnography is made," but it is "not quite 'ethnographic enough'" (2008:168). Just as it is the rare ethnographer who can master the details of a culture the way Salinas masters his, says Wolcott, "it would be an even rarer 'native' who would have an intuitive grasp of ethnography" (2008:168).

In my view, this makes far too much of interpretation and not nearly enough of

description. Here is Salinas, the ethnographer, presenting a description of one insect—
illustrating what Wolcott (2008:168) identifies, correctly, as crushing detail:

> 1163. The nigua. These are the same size and have the same characteristics as squirrel
> and cat fleas. The nigua also jumps and turns up everywhere. One can see them in the
> feet of pigs. The feet are cut open by the fleas which deposit their eggs between the toes.
> The eggs are in a large, white ball in the pig's flesh. 1164. This is cured by putting on
> criolina so that the foot of the animal suppurates and the flea egg-balls runn out. This
> flea also affects people's feet; they go between the toes. At first, they just itch; though
> one knows it itches, one may think it's just any old flea. 1165. But after three days, the
> itching gets worse, and it begins to suppurate and it grows worse and worse. When it
> gets like this it is opened up with a needle and a ball comes out, filled with eggs. 1166.
> A hole remains where the ball is taken out, as if a piece of flesh were removed. One
> must burn the ball so that the fleas won't be born. It is said that if it is thrown on the
> ground, the heat from the earth will hatch the eggs. 1167. So that they won't hatch, the
> balls are removed from people's feet and thrown into the fire to burn up. If one allows
> the swelling on the feet to burst by itself, then it hurts even more. 1167. Niguas lay their
> eggs in the webbing between the toes. Of course, this happens to people who don't wear
> huaraches; niguas are an affliction of those who go barefoot. Sometimes it causes just
> itching and other times it itches and hurts. (Bernard and Salinas 1989:209)

And here is Salinas, the storyteller, talking about religion and playing, what Wolcott says
is "the docent, giving us a carefully arranged tour" (2008:169):

> 1136. Right next to San Clemente is another small village called El Nogal. This commu-
> nity belongs to Orizabita and only has 17 full citizens. All together, among the men,
> women, and children, there are 55 people there. There is no church of either of the two
> religions. The people of San Clemente tried to impose Protestantism on the people of
> El Nogal, but the people of El Nogal did not like that religion. Because of that, and
> because of other things that they did to them, the people of El Nogal abandoned Protes-
> tantism, became even stronger believers in Catholicism, and opted to follow their
> pueblo, which is Orizabita. [Bernard and Salinas 1989:533]

There were, to be sure, complaints over the years that Boas's work was nothing more
than a mountain of raw facts. Leslie White complained that Boas's Kwakiutl texts were
not intelligible because they were without commentary (White 1963:55), and George Peter
Murdock mocked Boas's "five-foot shelf" of monographs about the Kwakiutl as contributing little to understanding the social structure of the Kwakiutl (Murdock 1949:xiv, n.
5).

From my perspective, ethnography has not outlived the positivist, descriptive function
it had for Boas and his students, and the goal of native ethnography is the same today as
it was in Boas's time: Get it down and get it right, in the natives' own languages. "Getting
it right" is a goal, not a given, so we keep trying to improve the method. One thing we
can do is to provide training (even more than I offered Jesús Salinas) in what scholars
of culture are interested in knowing. Another is to provide extensive commentary and
explanations of the native-language materials (as I did in the Ñähñu native ethnography
[Bernard and Salinas Pedraza 1989]).

More important than commentary or explanation, however, is the ineluctable presence
of those 232,000 words of Ñähñu that Salinas produced about Ñähñu culture. Many of
the languages in which Boas's students collected ethnographic texts are no longer spoken,
or will soon die out. The texts collected by the Boasians for 50 years, though, are a pre-

cious resource for all scholars interested in the diversity of human culture. Debates about -isms—structuralism, materialism, postmodernism—come and go, but texts are forever (box 18.1).

BOX 18.1

IS AN *N* OF 1 REALLY SCIENCE?

Salinas's native ethnography is one person's report of selected aspects of Ñähñu culture. What if other Ñähñu don't agree with Salinas on key issues? What if other Ñähñu think that Salinas focused too much on the flora and fauna of the Mezquital Valley and ignored other elements of the culture? Well, all ethnographies are written by *someone*. Why shouldn't other Ñähñu disagree with Salinas about his take on key issues? "Why not," Jesús once asked me, "invite a group of Ñähñu to read the Ñähñu version of the ethnography and offer new interpretations?" I can hardly wait.

Other Kinds of Native Ethnography

The term "native ethnography" covers a lot of ground. At one end of the spectrum are the works of George Hunt, Jesús Salinas, Crashing Thunder, Abel Hernández Jiménez, and Ignacio Bizarro Ujpán, written entirely in a the nonliterary, indigenous language of the native ethnographer.

At the other end are the works of indigenous people who have become professional anthropologists and who write about their own culture in one of the major literary languages of the world, like English, Japanese, French, Spanish, etc. Included here are the works of scholars like Jomo Kenyatta (1938) and Victor Uchendu (1965), who wrote ethnographies of the Gikuyu (in Kenya) and Igbo (in Nigeria), respectively. Both were bilingual speakers of English and their tribal language; both were trained as anthropologists; and both wrote in English. Kenyatta studied with Bronislaw Malinowski at the London School of Economics in the 1930s. Uchendu's ethnography of the Igbo was written as his M.A. thesis in anthropology when he was a student at Northwestern University (1965).

Another genre comprises autobiographies by speakers of nonliterary languages who were not trained as ethnographers but who wrote in a major literary language. Between 1964 and 1968, Refugio Savala, a Yaqui poet, wrote his richly detailed autobiography in English (Savala 1980). In his narrative, Savala tries to describe Yaqui culture in general by showing his family's participation in it (Sands 1980).

Other examples of this genre for North American Indians include *The Middle Five: Indian Schoolboys of the Omaha Tribe* by Francis La Flesche (1963 [1900]) about life at a boarding school; *Wah'Kon-Tah: The Osage and the White Man's Road*, by John Joseph Mathews (1968 [1932]) about life under a particular Indian agent on the Osage Reservation in the late 1800s; and *The Way to Rainy Mountain* by N. Scott Momaday (1969), in which Momaday, who holds a Ph.D. in English from Stanford, tells of his attempt to seek his identity as a Kiowa from his grandmother and from other elders with whom he consulted.

Yet another genre of native ethnography comprises the "as told to" autobiographies. One famous example is *Black Elk Speaks*. John Neihardt, an epic poet from Nebraska, met Black Elk, an Oglala Sioux, in 1930. A year later, Neihardt and his daughters went to Black Elk's home on the Pine Ridge Reservation. Black Elk spoke in Sioux and his words were translated by his son Ben, who had studied at Carlisle University.

Neihardt says that it was his own function "to translate the old man's story, not only in the factual sense—for it was not the facts that mattered most—but rather to recreate in English the mood and manner of the old man's narrative" (Neihardt 1972 [1932]:xii).

Other examples of this genre for North American Indians include the as-told-to autobiography of Don Talayesva, a Hopi (Simmons 1942); of John Lame Deer, a Miniconjou Sioux (Lame Deer and Erdoes 1972); of Two Leggings, a Crow (Nabokov 1967); and of Left Handed, a Navajo (Dyk 1938; Dyk and Dyk 1980). Here is Ruth Dyk, telling us how the story of Left Handed was actually recorded. "Since Left Handed did not know English he told his story in Navajo, and it was translated bit by bit by Philip Davis, a Navajo. Left Handed would speak a minute or two, Philip would translate, and my husband would write down the translation" (Dyk and Dyk 1980:xvii).

Roger Keesing recorded the life story of 'Elota, a Big Man of the Kwaio in the Solomon Islands (Keesing 1978). The 15 recording sessions took place over a 4-month period of time. Keesing translated the tapes and provides a sketch of Kwaio culture and history. Andrew Strathern recorded and translated the life history of Ongka, a Big Man of the Kawelka in Papua New Guinea (Strathern 1979). At first, Strathern prompted Ongka, but he soon left the Big Man alone with the tape recorder. "I would return to the room from time to time to change the cassette over," reports Strathern, "and would find him fully engrossed, gesturing and smiling into the microphone" (p. x).

During two field trips to Botswana in 1971 and 1975, Marjorie Shostak collected 30 hours of taped interviews with Nisa, a !Kung woman. Nisa was about 50 in 1971—an advanced age for a !Kung woman at that time. She spoke only in !Kung, and Shostak's English translation ran to hundreds of typewritten pages (Shostak 1981:42–43). Shostak edited the tapes—in some cases, brings parts of stories together to create continuous chronological narrative—to produce Nisa's moving autobiography.

Mountain Wolf Woman was the sister of Crashing Thunder. Her autobiography was recorded in Ann Arbor, Michigan, in 1958, at the home of Nancy Lurie. Over a period of 5 weeks, during which Mountain Wolf Woman lived with the Luries, she told her story in Winnebago, and Lurie recorded it on tape. Then, using the Winnebago tapes as a guide, and a second tape recorder, Mountain Wolf Woman told her story again, in English (Lurie 1961).

Lurie and Mountain Wolf Woman translated the Winnebago tape together, and Mountain Wolf Woman's grand-niece, Frances Thundercloud Wentz, helped Lurie produce the final, detailed translation. Lurie is critically aware of her influence on the final product: "The final preparation of an acceptable English narrative from a literary and scholarly point of view required decisions for which I must take full responsibility." These decisions, said Lurie, include "choice of tenses, equivalents of idiomatic expressions, insertion of words necessary for clarification, and the like" (Lurie 1961:95).

Lurie also recorded comments that Mountain Wolf Woman made during the 5-week stay and inserted some of these comments into the final published narrative. She had them set in italics to show where she had added text from materials other than the original tapes.

All of these different kinds of native ethnographies offer glimpses—some more descriptive, some more interpretive—into the lived experience of people in other cultures. But all of them depend first on the collection of mountains of texts.

And now, on to text analysis.

INTERPRETIVE ANALYSIS

In **interpretive analysis**, the hermeneutic method is extended to the study of all kinds of texts, including jokes, sermons, songs, and even actions. Modern hermeneutics in social science, you'll recall from chapter 1, is an outgrowth of the Western tradition of biblical exegesis. In that tradition, the books of the Bible were assumed to contain eternal truths, put there by an omnipotent creator through some emissaries—prophets, writers of the gospels, and the like. The object of interpretation is to understand the meaning of the original words, given all the conditions of the present.

In the late 19th century, Wilhelm Dilthey (1989 [1883]) argued that this method of text interpretation was central to the human sciences. A century later, Paul Ricoeur (1979:73) argued that human behavior itself could be treated as an interpretable text. In anthropology, the person most associated with this tradition is Clifford Geertz (1972:26), who famously called culture "an assemblage of texts" that were available to be interpreted—that is, to be understood as those who acted them out understood them and to be related to larger social forces. Today, this interpretive method is widely practiced in anthropology. Here are two examples:

(1) Michael Herzfeld (1977) studied renditions of the *khelidonisma*, or swallow song, sung in modern Greece as part of the welcoming of spring. Herzfeld collected texts of the song from ancient, medieval, and modern historical sources and recorded texts of current-day renditions in several locations across Greece. His purpose was to show that inconsistencies in the texts come not from "some putative irrationality in the processes of oral tradition" but are, in fact, reflections of structural principles that underlie the rite of passage for welcoming spring in rural Greece. To make his point, Herzfeld looked for anomalies across renditions—like "March, my good March" in one song compared to "March, terrible March" in another. Herzfeld claims that the word "good" is used ironically in Greek where the referent is a source of anxiety.

Is March a subject of symbolic anxiety for Greek villagers? Yes, says, Herzfeld, it is, and we can tell that it is because of widely observed practices like avoidance of certain activities during the *drimata* (the first 3 days of March). Herzfeld supports his analysis by referring to the *drimes*, a word that denotes the first 3 days of August, which are associated with malevolent spirits. Since March is the transition from winter to summer and August is the transition from summer to winter, Herzfeld concludes that there is symbolic danger associated with these mediating months. He finds support for this analysis in the fact that February is never referred to with an unequivocally good epithet.

This is interpretive analysis—the search for meanings and their interconnection in the expression of culture. The method requires deep involvement with the culture, including an intimate familiarity with the language, so that the symbolic referents emerge during the study of those expressions. You can't see the connections among symbols if you don't know what the symbols are and what they are supposed to mean. Herzfeld used his intimate knowledge of Greek language and culture to make the connection between the *khelidonisma* poems and the structural principle of danger in months of transition.

(2) James Fernández (1967) recorded and transcribed the sermons of two African cult leaders, Ekang Engono of Koungoulou, Kango, Gabon, and William Richmond of Sydenham, Durban, South Africa. Engono preached in Make (a dialect of Fang) and

Richmond preached in Zulu. The sermon by Richmond is 45 pages of text, but the one by Engono is quite short. Here it is in its entirely:

> The Ngombi is Fang. The Ngombi is something to take great care of. The Ngombi is the fruit that is full of juice, it is something that can act badly, can feel badly, can cause irritation and trouble. It is better that it should be irritating, that it should burst open. The man who knows well the Fang Ngombi, he has his treasure in the land of the dead. Men must not steal iron because it comes from the forge, it is a man's brother, it is the equivalent of man. The blood of the nursing mother is the food of the afterbirth. We don't know the miracle of the spirit. The Ngombi leaves this on earth with us. We are unfortunate because man does not know the significance of eboka. We are the destroyers of the earth. Our destruction makes noise to God. The miracle is between our thighs. Listen to the words of the wind; listen to the words of the Fang Ngombi, listen to the words of the village. They are of great meaning to you. The widow can not cause trouble through her chatter unless she and another like her marry the same husband. The man without witchcraft is an Angel, he is a dove, hence the ancestors said the poor man is one of two things. He is either worn out or he is without witchcraft.

Fernández interprets each of the esoteric images in the sermon—the Ngombi, the iron, the miracle between the thighs, the blood of the nursing mother, the chatter of the widow—showing how they are components of Engono's general exhortation to his flock to protect marriage and pregnancy. The Ngombi, for example, is a sacred harp, the sound of which (for the members of this cult) is the voice of the goddess of fecundity, and gifts of iron were traditional for bride price.

But this is not just an exercise in interpretation of esoteric images. Fernández notes that in 1960, when he recorded the sermon, the Fang had experienced a dramatic, 40-year decline in fertility, the consequence of an epidemic of venereal disease. In fact, the existence of the cult was in response to this decline.

This, too, is interpretive analysis. Fernández used his intimate knowledge of Fang language and culture to show how the otherwise-esoteric contents of a brief sermon addressed societal problems. Fernández translates the sermon into the language and world view of his reader, filling in the gaps and making explicit some linkages that are only implicit in the text (**Further Reading:** interpretive analysis).

NARRATIVE ANALYSIS

Human beings are natural story tellers. You can ask people anything about their personal experience, from the extraordinary—like what it's like to survive hand-to-hand combat—to the mundane—like how they make breakfast, and you'll get a narrative. **Narrative analysis** is the search for regularities in how people, within and across cultures, tell stories.

One major genre of narratives involves recounting an event: What happened? How did it happen? Why did it happen? What was the result? The object is to discover themes and recurring structures. Robert Rubinstein, for example, asked 103 middle-class, married women in Philadelphia, ages 40–62, to describe how they reacted to the recent death of their widowed mothers. In the lengthy interviews, one question that Rubinstein asked was: "Can you tell me the story of your mother's death? What happened? How did she die?" (1995:259).

The stories of these women ranged from short, chronological sequences (mostly from women who had light or no care-giving duties during their mother's terminal illness or whose mother died suddenly or who lived at least 2 hours away from their mother by car) to long, complex stories about their mothers' illness and death (mostly from women who had heavy care-giving responsibilities and whose mother's terminal illness lasted more than 6 months).

Despite the differences in story length, Rubinstein (1995) found strong structural regularities. Most informants began their stories with what Rubinstein calls a "medical preamble" (p. 262) and a "narrative of decline element" (p. 263):

> And she even began to notice, you know, something wasn't quite right. All the testing they had done, they said, you know, her mental ability isn't that impaired. And I kinda laughed because in January they had said that she was kinda, like, not too bad for a woman who had seen multiple decline in systems. And I kinda laughed because I wanted to come [back for testing] this year. And they said, "Well, bring her back next year and we'll, you know, assess her. This will be a relative point from which we can determine how gradual her decline is becoming." [So] I call them a year later to say she's dead.

Most women "medicalized the stories of their mothers' deaths" (Rubinstein 1995:263), with details about visits to emergency rooms and about decisions to have surgery, for example. Most informants also mentioned their mother's personality traits:

> So, we didn't push her to move in [with me]. You know, we let her make the decision. And then in May she, uh, we closed up her apartment. She never actually went back and she liked it that way. Yeah, she liked leaving there when she was able to walk [out]. [There's some people for whom] it's almost an insult to their dignity and their independence to be seen that way [starting to physically slide downhill], you know to end up being carted out in a wheel chair. You know, people were noticing that she [mother] wasn't herself, and she was a pretty forceful individual, very dominant, very independent, very outspoken, and her mental abilities had begun to slip a little, but her physical decline was becoming more noticeable. (p. 268)

Notice the transcription. The author selectively uses "kinda" instead of "kind of" to convey the conversational tone of the story, but he also inserts brackets to indicate things that were implied, but not said, in the narrative. There is only the barest attempt to include the kind of detailed information about false starts and tokens (like umm and uhh) that are required in transcriptions for conversation analysis (coming up in chapter 19).

Finally, if women were present at their mother's death, they often described the death scene. Here are two contrasting scenes that Rubinstein (1995) counts as similar parts of these narratives:

> 1. . . . And she kept on talking. And a lot of it was about things from the past. But whatever it was, even when my brother and sister got there, we couldn't, umm, none of us got through to her. Her eyes were just moving around . . . and she even suffered to the very end, I mean, in her own way. It wasn't a peaceful death, really. (p. 270)

> 2. Most of the family was there, and my mother was having more difficulty breathing and I had her in my arms trying to talk to her, reassuring her that I loved her and one thing and another. And she died. . . . Yes, right in my arms, which was a beautiful way to die. It was like my mother's gift of peace to me, knowing that I could not have been any closer. (p. 271)

Rubinstein's analysis, in the best tradition of narrative analysis, focuses on the stories themselves, on the themes—like the medicalization of death, the impossible dilemmas that arise in deciding on medical care for the terminally ill, the emotional pain for daughters of not being able to find the "mother-who-was" in mothers who were demented—and on how themes are combined and ordered in predictable ways (**Further Reading**: narrative analysis).

PERFORMANCE ANALYSIS: ETHNOPOETICS

Performance analysis involves the search for regularities in the delivery of highly stylized narratives, like folk tales, sermons, and political speeches. **Ethnopoetics** is performance analysis applied to oral literature.

In 1977, Dell Hymes reported that "the narratives of the Chinookan peoples of Oregon and Washington can be shown to be organized in terms of lines, verses, stanzas, scenes, and what many call acts." Hymes felt that this discovery might be relevant to many indigenous languages of the Americas (1977:431). That turned out to be an understatement.

Chinookan is a family of American Indian languages from the northwest coast of North America. Shoalwater Chinook and Kathlamet Chinook are two mutually unintelligible languages (related in the way French and Spanish are both Romance languages), but Franz Boas had run into an informant who was fluent in both Shoalwater and Kathlamet and had collected texts in both languages between 1890 and 1894. Hymes examined those texts as well as texts from Clackamas Chinook (collected in 1930 and 1931 by Melville Jacobs) and in Wasco-Wishram Chinook (collected by Sapir in 1905, by Hymes in the 1950s, and by Michael Silverstein in the 1960s and 1970s).

What Hymes found was that features of Chinook that might have seemed idiosyncratic to the speakers of those three Chinook languages—Shoalwater, Kathlamet, and Clackamas Chinook—were actually "part of a common fabric of performance style," so that the three languages "share a common form of poetic organization" (Hymes 1977:431) (box 18.2).

BOX 18.2

A THEORY OF ETHNOPOETICS

Hymes's discovery was truly important. It made clear once and for all that Native American texts have something to contribute to a general theory of poetics and literature. Hymes discovered the existence of verses, by recognizing repetition within a block of text. "Covariation between form and meaning," said Hymes, "between units with a recurrent Chinookan pattern of narrative organization, is the key" (1977:438).

In some texts, Hymes found recurrent linguistic elements that made the task easy. Linguists who have worked with precisely recorded texts in Native American languages have noticed the recurrence of elements like "Now," "Then," "Now then," and "Now again" at the beginning of sentences. These kinds of things often signal the separation of verses. The trick is to recognize them and the method is to look for "abstract features that co-occur with the use of initial particle pairs in the narratives" of other speakers who use initial particle pairs. The method, then, is a form of controlled comparison (1977:439).

In a series of articles and books (1976, 1977, 1980a, 1980b, 1981), Hymes showed that most Native American texts of narrative performance (going back to the early texts collected by Boas and his students and continuing in today's narrative performance by American Indians as well) are organized into verses and stanzas that are aggregated into groups of either fives and threes or fours and twos. Boas and his students organized the narratives of American Indians into lines.

According to Virginia Hymes, this hid from view "a vast world of poetry waiting to be released by those of us with some knowledge of the languages" (1987:65). Dell Hymes's method, according to Virginia Hymes, involves "working back and forth between content and form, between organization at the level of the whole narrative and at the level of the details of lines within a single verse or even words within a line" (1987:67–68). Gradually, an analysis emerges that reflects the analyst's understanding of the larger narrative tradition and of the particular narrator.

This emergent analysis doesn't happen miraculously. It is, Virginia Hymes reminds us, only through close work with many narratives by many narrators that you develop an understanding of the narrative devices that people use in a particular language and the many ways they use those little devices (1987).

But all this depends on having texts—lots of them, like those that Boas and his students left us—marked for features like voice quality, loudness, pausing, intonation, stress, and nonphonemic vowel length (Hymes 1977:452–53).

Tedlock's Study of the *Popol Vuh*

Dennis Tedlock (1987) showed the exegetical power that linguistic methods can bring to the text analysis. He had translated the *Popol Vuh*, a 16th-century Quiché Maya manuscript that had been written out by Francisco Ximénez, a missionary of the time. The *Popol Vuh* is one of those big epics, like the *Iliad* or *Beowulf* that were meant to be recited aloud. Is it possible, Tedlock asked, to analyze the text and figure out how to narrate it today as performers would have done in ancient times?

In doing his translation of the *Popol Vuh*, Tedlock (1987) had relied on Andrés Xiloj, a modern speaker of Quiché. Xiloj had not been trained to read Maya, but he was literate in Spanish and made the transition very quickly. "When he was given his first chance to look at the Popol Vuh text, he produced a pair of spectacles and began reading aloud, word by word" (p. 145).

Like many medieval manuscripts in Europe, Ximénez's rendition of the *Popol Vuh* was more or less an undifferentiated mass of text with almost no punctuation. In other words, Tedlock had no clues about how a performer of the narrative 400 years ago might have varied his timing, emphasized this or that segment, used different intonations, and so forth.

Tedlock's (1987) solution was to study stylized oral narratives (not just casual speech) of modern speakers of the Quiché. He recorded speeches, prayers, songs, and stories and looked for phrases and patterns in the wording that had analogs in the *Popol Vuh* (p. 147). He devised special punctuation symbols for marking pauses, accelerations, verse endings, and so on and applied them to the *Popl Vuh*. It's in the use of those written marks that we see Tedlock's analysis—his understanding of how a performance went.

Tedlock then made systematic comparison across other ancient texts to look for recurrent sound patterns that signify variations in meaning. (Think of how we use rising intonation at the end of sentences in English to signify a question and how some people in our society use the same intonation in declarative sentences at the beginning of phone conversations when the object is to jar someone's memory, as in: "Hi, this is Mary? I was in your intro class last semester?") What Tedlock found was that Quiché verse has the same structure as ancient Middle Eastern texts—texts that, he points out, predate Homer. In fact, Tedlock concluded it is the same structure found in all living oral traditions that have not yet been influenced by writing (1987:146; and see Tedlock 1977).

Sherzer's Study of Kuna Chants

Joel Sherzer (1994) presents a detailed analysis of a 2-hour performance that he recorded in 1970 of a traditional San Blas Kuna chant (the Kuna are an indigenous people from Panama). The chant was rendered by Chief Olopinikwa and recorded on tape. Like many linguistic anthropologists, Sherzer had taught an assistant, Alberto Campos, to use a phonetic transcription system. After the chant, Sherzer asked Campos to transcribe and translate the tape. Campos put Kuna and Spanish on left- and right-facing pages (p. 907).

Another chief responded to Olopinikwa, usually with some utterance like "So it is." Sherzer noticed that Campos left those responses out of the translation, but it was just those responses that turned out to be markers for verse endings in the chant. And Campos left out words like "Thus" at the beginning of a verse and phrases like "it is said, so I pronounce" spoken by the narrator at the end of a verse. These phrases also contribute to the line and verse structure of the chant. Campos, in other words, edited the chant to give Sherzer the essentials, but it was the seemingly inessential things—those little framing phrases—that defined cultural competence in performance of the narrative (1994:908).

A key method of text analysis in ethnopoetics is text presentation. As Sherzer discovered, verse breaks in Kuna narratives are determined by regular turn-taking between narrating chief and responding chief. In presenting Chief Olopinikwa's performance in print, Sherzer begins each line of the main narrative flush left and indents the lines of the responding chief.

A few years earlier, in his presentation of *The Hot Pepper Story*, Sherzer (1990:178) used a highly literal translation. In the original text, there are many repetitions of a small number of words and themes. Sherzer felt that a liberal translation would fail to capture the poetics of performance, so in his commentary he describes the thematic elements in the text but uses the device of literalness in the translation to draw the reader's attention to those elements (**Further Reading:** performance analysis and ethnopoetics).

TRANSLATIONS AS TEXTS

Translations are texts in their own right and can be analyzed just as original texts can. William Hanks (1988) reviewed Munroe Edmonson's (1986) translation of *The Book of Chilam Balam of Chumayel*. Edmonson had translated and annotated the original Mayan corpus into 5,514 lines of text, changing the format of presentation in the process. In the original, the lines had run clear across the page, but Edmonson presented the text in short lines to emphasize what he considered to be the verse structure. Hanks analyzed not only the Mayan text but the literary style that Edmonson used in his presentation. This method is well known from generations of work on literary criticism applied to translations (Rose 1997) and on linguistics applied to translation. (See Nida [1975] AND Nida and Taber [1969] for the classic work here.)

In translating Ñähñu (Otomí) parables, folk tales, and jokes, Jesús Salinas and I presented a fully literal translation and a fully liberal translation, in addition to a transcription of the Ñähñu (Bernard and Salinas Pedraza 1976). Figure 18.1 is a piece of the text from that effort:

At the time, I felt that I couldn't show some of the characteristics of the original,

Ñähñu
1. n'a zi ñ'oho rc zi memapa sä maa rä za 'mefi. 2. i'mu n'a rä tuya rä zi mane.
3. i geetwu rä besinu ko rä 'mehñä nu'ä rä zi ñoho. 4. nde handätho nu'ä rä zi
tiiya eenbi ko nu'ä rä 'mohñä'ä rä zi ñ'oho di pa rä 'memapa. 5. i maa rä zi
'mefi'ä rä zi ñ'oho mi südi. 6. bi m'efa'ä rä zi 'mehñä bi hñätsä rä ñhuni. 7. di
ge'ä bos yaa maa bi 'wini'ä rä däme. 8. 'ne bi pengi pa 'mu rä ngu nu'ä rä
'mehñä pa 'wingyä mbo'oni nu rä nguu.

Literal English Translation
1. a little man the little laborer has gone to his little work. 2. and there is a
the old lady his little *comadre*. 3. and nearby his neighbor with his wife this
the little man. 4. well, she sees only this the little old lady that is to say with
this his wife this the little man he goes to the laborer. 5. and he went to the
little work the little man in the morning. 6. she went after the little women
she brought his meal. 7. from this well already she goes to give to eat to her
husband. 8. then she goes back to stay in her house this the woman to give
to eat to her animals this her house.

Free English Translation
1. Once there was a nice little *peon* who went to work. 2. His *comadre* lived
near this man and his wife, and she could see what the wife was doing. The
man would go to work and his wife would follow him later and bring his meal.
8. Then she would go back to her home and feed her animals.

FIGURE 18.1.
Excerpt from Ñähñu stories.
SOURCE: H. R. Bernard and J. Salinas Pedrazas. "Otomí Parables, Folktales, and Jokes." *International Journal of American Linguistics*, Native American Text Series, 1(2): I, 1976. The University of Chicago Press. All rights reserved. Reprinted with permission.

idiomatic Ñähñu in a free, idiomatic English translation, so I suggested to Salinas that we present both, along with a literal translation from Ñähñu to English. That way, readers could decide for themselves if my idiomatic translation from Ñähñu to English made sense. (The original publication, in fact, was marked for tone and for pauses, which I've left out here.) Later, in translating Salinas's four-volume ethnography of the Ñähñu, I didn't have the luxury of including either the Ñähñu or a literal translation, and so I settled on a middle course: The English is idiomatic and grammatical but I tried deliberately to reflect Salinas's style (see Bernard and Salinas Pedraza 1989).

We're still experimenting with methods for presenting texts of indigenous performance that capture the subtleties of performance. We can't know for sure if a particular presentation actually captures the regular features of narrative, but the same could be said for any interpretive effort in which anthropologists try to understand and present to an audience the meaning of cultural utterances and practices. Tedlock's work with Andrés Xiloj, Sherzer's with Alberto Campos, and my work with Jesús Salinas are experiments in method to understand the grammar of narrative performance. And speaking of grammars beyond the sentence . . .

DISCOURSE ANALYSIS

Conversation analysis is part of discourse analysis—the study of naturally occurring, language in use. Scholars of discourse analysis, like Brenda Farnell and Laura Graham (1998:412), see discursive practices—all the little things that make our utterances uniquely our own—as concrete manifestations both of the culture we share with others and of our very selves. What we do in traditional ethnography, according to Joel Sherzer and Greg Urban (1986:1), is distill discourse into a description of a culture. What we ought to be observing—and describing—they say, is ordinary discourse itself, since culture emerges from the constant interaction and negotiation between people (box 18.3).

BOX 18.3

HOW JAPANESE CHILDREN LEARN TO BOW CORRECTLY

Here's an example of how much of culture can be encapsulated in an ordinary discourse event. I went to Japan for 4 months in 1991 to work at the National Museum of Ethnology in Osaka. I didn't speak Japanese, so I was limited to studying things that I could observe directly and about which I could hold discussions, in English, with my colleagues at the museum. I noticed that many Japanese bowed when they said good-bye to someone on the telephone and I became interested in the cultural artifact of bowing.

I rode the bus to work every day. Most regular riders of the buses in Osaka buy blocks of tickets in advance, at a discount. When people leave the bus, they drop one of their fare tickets into a hopper next to the driver. As the bus rolled to a stop one day, a boy of about 5 implored his mother to let him drop off her ticket as they left the bus. The mother gave him the ticket, left the bus, and watched from the sidewalk as the toddler dropped off the ticket and scampered, grinning, down the bus's stairs to her.

The mother gave the child a stern look and said something that I couldn't hear. The child scampered back up the stairs, faced the driver, and bowed deeply from the waist. "*Arigato gozaimashitááá*," said the boy to the driver, with heavy, lengthened emphasis on the final syllable. The driver bowed slightly and acknowledged the boy, saying "*Doozu*," while smiling at the mother who waited at the bottom of the stairs for her son.

It turns out that the child was mimicking, in phrase and diction, the formal way that an adult man might say thank you with great emphasis in Japanese. Had I been able to tape that one small discourse event, I'm sure that there would have been enough exegesis by my Japanese colleagues at the museum to have produced a book on socialization of men and women into the ways of bowing and of saying thanks.

Formal **discourse analysis** involves taping of actual interactions and careful coding and interpretation. Howard Waitzkin and his colleagues (1994:32) taped 336 encounters involving older patients and primary-care internists. (The physicians included some in private practice, some who worked in a teaching hospital, and some who worked both in private practice and in hospital outpatient departments.)

Waitzkin et al. randomly chose 50 of these encounters for intensive study. They had each of the 50 encounters transcribed, verbatim—with all the "uhs," pauses, and whatnot that occur in real discourse—and two research assistants checked the accuracy of the transcriptions against the original tape.

During the interpretation phase, research assistants read the transcripts and noted the ones that dealt with aging, work, gender roles, family life, leisure, substance use, and socioemotional problems—all areas in which the researchers were interested at the time. The assistants read through the transcripts and tagged instances where either the doctors or the patients "made statements that conveyed ideological content or expressed messages of social control" (Waitzkin et al. 1994:328).

To illustrate their interpretive approach to discourse analysis, Waitzkin et al. go through two texts in detail. They use the same method as that used in biblical exegesis: A chunk of text is laid out, followed by commentary involving all the wisdom and understanding that the commentators can bring to the effort. For example, Waitzkin et al. produce this snippet of interaction between a doctor (D) and his patient (P), an elderly woman who has come in for a follow-up of her heart disease:

> P: Well I should—now I've got birthday cards to buy. I've got seven or eight birthdays this week—month. Instead of that I'm just gonna write 'em and wish them a happy birthday. Just a little note, my grandchildren.
> D: Mm hmm.
> P: But I'm not gonna bother. I just can't do it all, Dr.—
> D: Well.
> P: I called my daughters, her birthday was just, today's the third.
> D: Yeah.
> P: My daughter's birthday in Princeton was the uh first, and I called her up and talked with her. I don't know what time it'll cost me, but then, my telephone is my only connection.

Waitzkin et al. comment:

> At no other time in the encounter does the patient refer to her own family, nor does the doctor ask. The patient does her best to maintain contact, even though she does not mention anything that she receives in the way of day-to-day support. Compounding these problems of social support and incipient isolation, the patient recently has moved from a home that she occupied for 59 years. [Waitzkin et al. 1994:330–31]

When they get through presenting their running commentary on the encounter, Waitzkin et al. interpret the discourse:

> This encounter shows structural elements that appear beneath the surface details of patient-doctor communication. . . . Contextual issues affecting the patient include social isolation; loss of home, possessions, family, and community; limited resources to preserve independent function; financial insecurity; and physical deterioration associated with the process of dying. . . . After the medical encounter, the patient returns to the same contextual problems that trouble her, consenting to social conditions that confront the elderly in this society.
>   That such structural features should characterize an encounter like this one becomes rather disconcerting, since the communication otherwise seems so admirable. . . . The doctor manifests patience and compassion as he encourages a wide-ranging discussion of socioemotional concerns that extend far beyond the technical details of the patient's physical disorders. Yet the discourse does nothing to improve the most troubling features of the patient's situation. To expect differently would require redefining much of what medicine aims to do. (Waitzkin et al. 1993:335–36)

Waitzkin et al. make clear that alternative readings of the same passage are possible and advocate, as part of their method, the systematic archiving, in publicly available places, of texts on which analysis is conducted. When the project was over, Waitzkin filed the transcripts with University Microfilms International so that other researchers could use the data for later analysis.

Conversation Analysis

Conversation analysis is the search for the grammar of ordinary discourse, or **talk-in-interaction**. It is the study of how people take turns in ordinary discourse—who talks first (and next, and next), who interrupts, who waits for a turn.

If you listen carefully to ordinary conversations between equals, you'll hear a lot of sentence fragments, false starts, interruptions, overlaps (simultaneous speech), and repeating of words and phrases. It may sound messy at first, but as students of conversation have learned, there is order in all that seeming chaos as participants respond to each other (even in strong disagreements and shouting matches) and take turns (Goodwin 1981:55).

The rules of turn-taking are, like the rules of grammar that govern the formation of sentences, known to native speakers of any language. But unlike the other rules of grammar, the rules for taking turns are flexible, and allow turn-taking to be negotiated, on the fly, by participants in a conversation. At the molecular level, then, every conversation is unique, but the study of many conversational exchanges can expose the general rules, within and across cultures, that govern how conversations start, evolve, and end.

Transcriptions

To identify turns and other features of conversations, you need detailed records of actual talk-in-interaction. The tactic for signaling the intention to take a turn or to repair a broken turn sequence may be words or they may be prosodic features of speech (intonation, length of vowels, stress, and so on), or they may be breaths, tokens (like er, ummm, eh), or even gestures or gazes. Coding schemes have been devised for marking all these different features.

The system most widely used for transcribing speech was developed by Gail Jefferson Conventions for recording gestures and gazes were developed by Charles Goodwin (1994). Table 18.1 provides the common conventions for transcribing conversations (**Further Reading:** transcription).

Taking Turns

Harvey Sacks and his colleagues, Emmanuel Schegloff and Gail Jefferson, are widely credited for developing the systematic study of order in conversations (Jefferson 1973; Sacks et al. 1974; Schegloff 1972; Schegloff and Sacks 1973). Among the basic rules they discovered are that the person who is speaking may (but does not have to) identify the next speaker to take a turn (Sacks et al. 1974). This is done with conversational devices—like "so what do you think, Jack?"—or with gazes or body language (Goodwin 1986, 1994). If the person speaking does not select the next speaker, then any other person in the conversation can self-select to take a turn.

Alternatively, the next speaker may jump in before a speaker has completed a turn, by anticipating the end of a turn—a supportive gesture—or by interrupting and trying to take away the speaker's turn by force—a hostile gesture. Big gaps occur so rarely in real conversations because speakers anticipate the end of turns so well. For example:

1. A: What a cute *nose.*
2. B: All babies ha—
3. A: [No they don't

Table 18.1 Conventions for Transcribing Conversations

Symbol	Definition
:	Indicates length. More colons indicate more length.
>text<	Speech between angle brackets is faster than normal speech.
(text)	Text in parentheses means that the transcriber had doubts about it.
( )	Parens with no text means that transcriber could not make it out at all.
(1.6)	Numbers in parens indicate pauses, in seconds and tenths of a second.
(.)	A period in parens indicates an untimed and quick pause.
((text))	Double parens contain comments by the researcher about people's gestures, gazes, and so on. Often in italics.
[ ]	Square brackets indicate where one person interrupts another or talks simultaneously.
–	An en-dash (longer than a hyphen) indicates an abrupt end in the middle of a word.
?	A question mark indicates rising intonation. It does not necessarily mean that a question is being asked.
.	A period indicates falling intonation. It does not necessarily mean the end of a sentence.
=	The equal sign indicates that a person takes a turn immediately as the previous turn ends.
°text°	Text between degree symbols is quieter than the rest of the text.
TEXT	Text in caps is louder than the rest of the text.
<u>Text</u>	Underlining means that the text is emphasized.
.hh and hh	These indicate inhaled (with period first) and exhaled (no period) breaths, as often occurs in natural conversation.

SOURCE: Adapted from *Issues in the Transcription of Naturally Occurring Talk. Caricature versus Capturing Pronunciation Particulars*, by G. Jefferson, 1983. Tilburg Papers on Language and Literature. Tilburg, Netherlands: University of Tilburg. http://www.liso.ucsb.edu/Jefferson/Caricature.pdf (accessed February 9, 2010).

A takes a turn; B jumps in immediately; and then A says, "no they don't" just as the syllable "ba" in "baby" registers. There are no gaps because the end of the second turn, by B, is predictable to A.

If the turn-taking runs out of steam in a conversation, either because it becomes unpredictable or the content gets used up, and no one jumps in to take a turn at the appropriate time, then the current speaker may (but does not have to) continue talking. If none of these things happen, then there will be a gap in the conversation. Gaps don't usually last very long if the rules of conversation are followed.

Of course, the rules are often broken in real conversations. People often do interrupt each other unsupportively and don't wait to take their turns. People who get interrupted don't always push on, trying to finish their turn, but relinquish their turn instead, without finishing. People usually recognize when the preferred order of turn-taking has not been adhered to and engage in what are called repair tactics. For example, Sacks et al. (1974) noted that when two people start talking over each other, one of them might just stop and let the other finish.

1. A: [It's not like we—
2. B: [Some people are—
3. B: Sorry.
4. A: No, g'head
5. B: hhhh I wus jus gonna say that some people aren't innerested in sports at all.
6. A: [Right

This is a simple repair tactic that doesn't involve any serious content. Other repair tactics can be more complex. The result of this repair sequence could have come out differently. But in the study of hundreds of natural conversations between equals, we can uncover the rules governing how people open and close conversations, how they repair mistakes (when they break the rules of turn-taking, for example), and how they segue from one theme to another.

The turn-taking sequence can be suspended, as for example, in the telling of jokes and stories. If I say, "Did you hear the one about? . . ." and you say, "No, tell me," then this suspends turn-taking until you're finished with the joke. If you interrupt me in the middle of telling the joke, this breaks the rule for this conversation element. And the same thing goes for story telling. If I say, "I was on the flight from Hell coming back from Detroit last week" and you respond by saying "What happened?" then I get to tell you the story all the way through. Certain kinds of interruptions are permitted, but sidetracking me completely from the story is not permitted.

Here, again, though, we find the rule broken all the time. And when sidetracking happens, one of several repair sequences might kick in. "Sorry, I got you off track. Then what happened?" is a repair sequence. We've all experienced the pain of never getting back to a story from which we were sidetracked in a conversation. When that happens, we might think badly of the person who did it, or we might shrug it off—depending on the context and what's at stake. If you're in a job interview and the interviewer sidetracks you, you'd probably think twice about insisting that the interviewer let you finish the story you were telling.

Adjacency Pairs

Among the first things that conversation analysts noticed when they started looking carefully at conversations was ordered pairs of expressions, like questions and greetings (Schegloff and Sacks 1973). Once the first part of a pair occurs, the second part is expected.

Sacks (1992:3) noticed that workers at a psychiatric hospital's emergency telephone line greeted callers by saying something like, "Hello. This is Mr. Smith. May I help you?" Most of the time, the response was "Hello, this is Mr. Brown," but on one occasion, the caller responded, "I can't hear you." When the worker repeated his greeting, "This is Mr. *Smith*," with an emphasis on Smith, the caller responded "Smith." In this case, the rule for an adjacency pair was not really being broken. It was being negotiated by both parties, on the fly, during the conversation. Mr. Smith, the suicide prevention worker, was trying to get the caller to give his name, and the caller was trying *not* to give his name.

If conversations are dynamic things, with constant negotiation, then, to understand the rules of conversations, you can't interview people about the rules of, say, greetings. You have to study real conversations in which greetings occur.

Here is an example of an adjacency pair—a question-answer pair—that's broken up between its parts.

1. A: Is it good? The Szechuan pork?
2. B: Y'like spicy, uh—
3. A: [Yeah
4. B: It's kinda, y'know, hot.
5. A: *Great*
6. B: Yeah, me too.

There is a lot going on here. A asks B if a particular dish is good. This is the first part of a question pair, which calls for an answer. B responds with another question, which creates a new expectation for an answer. A anticipates this and answers "yeah" (line 3) before B finishes her thought (which presumably was "y'like spicy, uh, food?").

B doesn't want to give up her turn just yet, so she completes the thought, in line 4. This gives A the opportunity to reaffirm that she does, in fact, like spicy food (that her "yeah" in line 3 was not just an acknowledgment of B's question) before she answers the first one. A reaffirms her "yeah" response with "great" in line 5. The segment ends with B agreeing that she, too, likes spicy food.

Looking at this segment, it seems like the first adjacency pair, the question about whether the Szechuan pork is good, has never been answered. But it has. The answer is implied in the inserted question in line 2 and the retesting in line 4, all of which is a shorthand for: "Yes, if you like spicy food, then the Szechuan pork is good; otherwise it isn't" (**Further Reading:** conversation analysis).

If this seems complicated, it's because it is. It's very, very complicated. Yet, every native speaker of English understands every piece of this analysis because: (1) The segment of conversation is rule based; (2) We understand the rules; and (c) We understand that the outcome is the result of cooperation by both speakers, A and B, as they attend to each other's words, draw on cultural knowledge that they share, and build a conversation dynamically. In this case, two people, in a conversation among equals, have worked together to build a particular outcome.

And if you think this is complicated, just add more speakers. With two people in a conversation, A and B, there are two pairs of people—AB (as seen from A's perspective) and BA (as seen from B's perspective)—figuring out each other's motives and behaviors and negotiating their way through the interaction. With three people in a conversation (A, B, and C), there are six pairs (AB, BA, AC, CA, BC, CB) doing the negotiating. With six people, there are 30 such pairs. Deborah Tannen (2005) analyzed 2 hours and 40 minutes of conversation among six friends at a Thanksgiving dinner. The analysis alone is a 170-page book, and that doesn't include the hundreds of pages of transcripts (box 18.4).

BOX 18.4

SPECIAL RULES FOR SPECIAL KINDS OF CONVERSATIONS

Some conversations require special rules so that they don't break up, like dinner parties do, into lots of smaller conversations. Pilots and air traffic controllers around the world wait for each other to finish a thought before taking the next turn. Juries have special rules for turn taking, with a leader (or foreperson) who ensures that the cultural rules for these formal conversations (written down nowhere, but widely understood) are followed. Among other things, the rules require that no one gets completely drowned and sidelined, unless they deserve to be (by first breaking the cultural rules themselves and trying to dominate). (See Manzo [1996] for a detailed analysis of turn-taking by a jury.)

We turn next to methods that involve coding a corpus of text for themes and analyzing the themes for patterns.

FURTHER READING

Native ethnography: Firbank (2008); Fournillier (2007); Narayan (1993); Rudolph (1997); Sharma (2006).

Interpretive analysis: Garot (2004); Mann (2007); Rabelo and Souza (2003); Segre (1988); Yakali-Çamoglu (2007)

Narrative analysis: Bridger and Maines (1998); Griffin (1993); Özyildirim (2009); Riessman (1993).

Performance and ethnopoetics: Blommaert (2006); Fabian (1990); Pratt and Wieder (1993); Webster (2008).

Transcription: Atkinson and Heritage (1984); Psathas (1979); Psathas and Anderson (1990).

Conversation analysis: Drew and Heritage (2006); Markee (2000); Psathas (1995); Sacks et al. (1974); ten Have (1999).

Text Analysis II: Schema Analysis, Grounded Theory, Content Analysis, and Analytic Induction

Unlike the methods in chapter 18, the methods in this chapter rely more on coding text for themes and then analyzing the themes for patterns. **Schema analysis** and **grounded theory** are mostly in the inductive tradition of social science, while **content analysis** and **analytic induction** are mostly in the deductive tradition. I say "mostly" because even the choice of what to study comes from some theoretical position, so right off the bat, the inductive-deductive divide is a bit arbitrary.

All of the methods in this chapter are supported by software. More about this as we move along. First, let's talk about coding text for themes.

Coding Themes

Coding turns free-flowing texts into a set of nominal variables (what statisticians mean, by the way, when they use the phrase "qualitative data"). In a set of texts about the experience of divorce, people do or do not talk about what to do about pension funds; they do or do not talk about how their children are taking it; they do or do not talk about their relations with their former in-laws; and so on.

Where do you stop? There is practically no end to the number of themes you can isolate for any text. When I was in high school, my physics teacher put a bottle of Coca-Cola on his desk and challenged our class to come up with interesting ways to describe that bottle. Each day for weeks that bottle sat on his desk as new physics lessons were reeled off, and each day new suggestions for describing that bottle were dropped on the desk on the way out of class.

I don't remember how many descriptors we came up with, but there were dozens. Some were pretty lame (pour the contents into a beaker and see if the boiling point was higher or lower than that of sea water) and some were pretty imaginative (cut off the bottom and test its magnifying power), but the point was to show us that there was no end to the number of things we could describe (measure) about that Coke bottle, and the point sank in. I remember it every time I try to code a text (box 19.1).

How to Find Themes

When you start to work with a corpus of written text, just read it and if you see something that you think might be important, highlight it, either with markers or on a

BOX 19.1

INDUCTIVE AND DEDUCTIVE CODING

Grounded-theory research is mostly based on **inductive** or **"open" coding**. The idea is to become grounded in the data and to allow understanding to emerge from close study of the texts. That's why Barney Glaser and Anslem Strauss (1967), the originators of this approach, called it the *discovery* of grounded theory.

Content analysis (which we'll take up in a bit) is mostly based on deductive coding. In doing deductive analysis of text, you start with a hypothesis *before* you start coding. The idea is to test whether your hypothesis is correct. Inductive research is what you do when you're in the exploratory and discovery phase of *any* research project, whether your data are words or numbers. Deductive research is what you do in the confirmatory stage of any research project—no matter what kind of data you have. There is no point in talking about which is better. They're both terrific if you use them to answer appropriate questions.

computer. Some of the words and phrases you highlight will turn into names for themes. In fact, Corbin and Strauss (2008:65) recommend explicitly using actual phrases from your text—the words of real people—to name themes, a technique they call **in vivo** coding.

Willms et al. (1990) and Miles and Huberman (1994) suggest starting with some general themes derived from reading the literature and adding more themes and subthemes as you go. This is somewhere between inductive and deductive coding. You have a general idea of what you're after and you know what at least some of the big themes are, but you're still in a discovery mode, so you let new themes emerge from the texts as you go along.

Look for repetitions. "Anyone who has listened to long stretches of talk," says Roy D'Andrade, "knows how frequently people circle through the same network of ideas" (1991:287). In my study of how ocean scientists interact with the people in Washington, DC, who are responsible for ocean policy (Bernard 1974), I kept hearing the word "brokers." Scientists and policymakers alike used this word to describe people whom they trusted to act as go-betweens, so "broker" became one of the code themes for my work.

Look for unusual terms or common words that are used in unusual ways. James Spradley (1972) recorded conversations among homeless men (they were called tramps in those days) at informal gatherings, meals, and card games. Spradley kept hearing the men talk about "making a flop," which was their jargon for finding place to sleep each night. Spradley went through his material and isolated everything he could find about flops: ways to make a flop, kinds of people who bother you when you flop, and so on. Then Spradley went back to his informants and asked them for more information about each of these subthemes.

And, said Spradley (1979:199–201), look for evidence of social conflict, cultural contradictions, informal methods of social control, things that people do in managing impersonal social relationships, methods by which people acquire and maintain achieved and ascribed status, and information about how people solve problems. Each of these arenas is likely to yield major themes in cultures.

More Techniques for Finding Themes

Other techniques for finding themes include pile sorting, making word counts, and producing **key-word-in-context** (KWIC) tables. To use the pile-sorting method—what Lincoln and Guba (1985:347–49) call cutting and sorting—look for real quotes from the interviews you do with informants that represent what you think are important topics in the data. Cut out each quote (making sure to leave some of the context in which the quote occurs) and paste it onto a 3 × 5 index card. On the back of the card, note who said it and where it appeared in the text. Then, lay out the cards on a big table, sort them into piles of similar quotes, and *name each pile*. These are the themes (Ryan and Bernard 2003:94).

You can check your reliability by asking several friends or colleagues (the more the better) to sort the cards into piles of "what goes with what." Sayles et al. (2007) analyzed 300 pages of transcripts from seven focus groups about the experience of stigma among people living with HIV. First, they read the transcripts and picked out 500 statements that represented what they thought were themes. Next, they printed the statements on slips of paper and sorted the slips into piles of more general themes, or domains. Then, other team members went through the material and decided, by consensus, if each of the slips belonged in its original pile or in one of the other piles—or a brand new pile.

Ryan (1995) used the pile-sort method to find themes in his study of household health-care in Njinikom, Cameroon. As they did the pile sort, coder discussed with one another their reasons for putting items together or separating them. Ryan recorded the discussion and used the data to help identify the themes in his data.

Word lists and the **KWIC technique** are extensions of the philosophy behind in vivo coding in grounded theory: If you want to understand what people are talking about, look closely at the words they use. The method has a very, very long history. The classic KWIC method is a **concordance**, which is a list of every substantive word in a text with its associated sentence. Concordances have been done on sacred texts from many religions and on famous works of literature from Euripides (Allen and Italie 1954), to Beowulf (Bessinger and Smith 1969), to Dylan Thomas (Farringdon and Farringdon 1980). These days, KWIC lists are generated by asking a computer to find all the places in a text where a particular word or phrase appears and printing it out in the context of some number of words (say, 30) before and after it. You (and others) can sort these instances into piles of similar meaning to assemble a set of themes.

Ryan and Weisner (1996) told fathers and mothers of adolescents: "Describe your children. In your own words, just tell us about them." In looking for themes in these rich texts, Ryan and Weisner did a word count. Mothers were more like than fathers to use words like as "friends," and "creative," and "honest"; fathers were more likely than were mothers to use words like "school," "student," and "independent." These counts became clues about the themes that Ryan and Weisner eventually used in coding the texts.

No matter how you actually *do* inductive coding—whether you start with paper and highlighters or use a computer to paw through your texts; whether you use in vivo codes, or use numbers, or make up little mnemonics of your own; whether you have some big themes in mind to start or let all the themes emerge from your reading—by the time you identify the themes and refine them to the point where they can be applied to an entire corpus of texts, a lot of interpretive analysis has already been done. Miles and Huberman say simply: "Coding is analysis" (1994:56).

Kurasaki's and Nyamongo's Codebooks

Kurasaki (1997) studied the ethnic identity of *sansei*, third-generation Japanese Americans. She interviewed 20 people and used a grounded-theory approach to do her analysis. She started with seven major themes: (1) a sense of history and roots, (2) values and ways of doing things, (3) biculturality, (4) sense of belonging, (5) sense of alienation, (6) self-concept, and (7) worldview. As the analysis progressed, she split the major themes into subthemes. So, for example, she split the first theme into: (1) sense of having a Japanese heritage and (2) sense of having a Japanese American social history.

As the coding progressed further, she eventually decided to combine two of the major themes (sense of belonging and sense of alienation) and wound up with six major themes and a total of 18 themes. Kurasaki assigned her own numerical codes to each of the themes—1.1 for the first subtheme in macrotheme 1, 7.2 for the second subtheme in macrotheme 7, and so on—and used those numbers to actually code her transcribed interviews. Her codebook is shown in table 19.1.

Table 19.1   Kurasaki's Coding Scheme for Her Study of Ethnic Identity among *Sansei* in California

First-order category	Second-order category	Numeric code
Sense of history and roots	Sense of having a Japanese heritage	1.1
	Sense of having a Japanese American social history	1.2
Values and ways of doing things	Japanese American values and attitudes	2.1
	Practice of Japanese customs	2.2
	Japanese way of doing things	2.3
	Japanese American interpersonal or communication styles	2.4
	Japanese language proficiency	2.5
Biculturality	Integration or bicultural competence	3.1
	Bicultural conflict or confusion	3.2
Sense of belonging	Sense of a global ethnic or racial community	4.1
	Sense of interpersonal connectedness with same ethnicity or race of others	4.2
	Sense of intellectual connectedness with other ethnic or racial minorities	4.3
	Searching for a sense of community	4.4
Sense of alienation	Sense of alienation from ascribed ethnic or racial group	5.1
Self-concept	Sense of comfort with one's ethnic or racial self	6.1
	Searching for a sense of comfort with one's ethnic or racial self	6.2
Worldview	Social consciousness	7.1
	Sense of oppression	7.2

SOURCE: "Ethnic Identity and Its Development among Third-Generation Japanese Americans" by K. S. Kurasaki, 1997. Ph.D. diss., Department of Psychology, DePaul University.

Nyamongo (1998) did semistructured interviews with 35 Gusii people in Kenya about how they responded to various symptoms associated with malaria. In addition to using a grounded-theory approach to develop the theme codes, Nyamongo wanted to do statistical analysis of his data. Table 19.2 shows his codebook. (Nyamongo did all the interviewing in Gusii—a language spoken by about two million people in Kenya—and all the interviews were transcribed in Gusii, but he coded the transcripts using English themes and English-looking mnemonics.)

Table 19.2   Nyamongo's (1998) Codebook: How Gusii Respond to Malaria

Column	Code	Variable description and variable values
1–3	RESP_ID	Informant number, from 001–035
4–11	NAME	Name of the informant
12–13	AGE	Age in years as reported by the informant.
14–18	GENDER	1 = female, 2 = male
19–32	OCC	Occupation of the informant. This is a nominal variable. The possible entries are housewife (1), farmer (2), retired worker (3), security guard (4), teacher (5), student (6), artisan (7), village elder (8), and n.a. if the informant reported no occupation.
33	SES	Socioeconomic status is an ordinal variable measured by presence of the following in the homestead: 1 = grass-thatched house, 2 = iron-sheet-roofed, dirt-floor house, 3 = iron-sheet-roofed, cemented-floor house, 4 = semipermanent house, 5 = permanent house, 9 = information not available
.		
.		
41	CAUSE1	Mosquito is mentioned by informant as the cause of malaria: 1 = yes, 0 = no
42	CAUSE2	Eating sugarcane, ripe bananas, and roast green maize are mentioned by informant as the cause of malaria: 1 = yes, 0 = no
43	CAUSE3	Causes other than CAUSE1 and CAUSE2 are given: 1 = yes, 0 = no
.		
.		
48	CTRL1	What should be done to reduce malaria cases? 1 = keep compound clean, 0 = other
49	CTRL2	What should be done to reduce malaria cases? 1 = take medicine for prophylaxis, 0 = other
50	CTRL3	What should be done to reduce malaria cases? 1 = use net or spray or burn coil, 0 = other
51	CTRL4	What should be done to reduce malaria cases? 1 = nothing can be done, 0 = other
52	DIAG	Diagnosis of illness by the informant: 1 = malaria, 0 = other illness
53	FACTOR1	Does cost influence whether people use home management or hospital-based care? 1 = yes, 0 = no
54	FACTOR2	Does duration of sickness influence whether people use home management or hospital-based care? 1 = yes, 0 = no
.		
.		
55	FACTOR3	Is intensity (severity) a factor influencing whether people use home management or hospital-based care? 1 = yes, 0 = no
56	HELP1	Type of support given to informant by family or friends: 1 = buying medicine, 0 = other
.		
.		
75	SYM1	The informant mentions headache as a symptom: 1 = yes, 0 = no
.		
.		
80	SYM14	The informant mentions child has unusual cries as a symptom: 1 = yes, 0 = no
81	SYM15	Other—if not one of SYM1 through SYM14: 1 = yes, 0 = no

Table 19.2 (Continued)

Column	Code	Variable description and variable values
91	TREAT11	Did the informant report using pills bought over the counter as the first treatment resort? 1 = yes, 0 = no
.		
.		
96	TREAT21	Second treatment resort: The values are the same as for TREAT11, column 91
.		
.		
119	WITCH	The informant mentions that witchcraft may be implicated if patient has malaria: 1 = yes, 0 = no
120	YESDIAG	Does the coder think the informant made the right diagnosis based on the informant's stated symptoms? 1 = yes, 0 = no
121	COST	Cost of receiving treatment from private health care provider in Kenyan shillings, from 0001–9999, 9999 = information not available

SOURCE: Nyamongo 1998. Data reproduced by permission of the author.

Notice the difference between Nyamongo's and Kurasaki's codebooks. In addition to some basic information about each respondent (in columns 1–33), Nyamongo coded for 24 themes. Those 24 themes, however, were nominal variables. He coded occupation, for example, as one of eight possible types. And notice that he used words, not numbers for those occupations, and that one possible entry was "information not available" (columns 19–32, 33, 121).

The code SYM1, in column 75, stands for "symptom #1" and refers to whether or not an informant mentioned headache in his or her narrative as a symptom of malaria. Nyamongo coded for whether people mentioned any of 14 symptoms, and he added a 15th code, SYM15 (in column 81) for "other." When you break up a list of things into a series of yes/no, present/absent variables, like Nyamongo did with CAUSE and SYM and so on, it turns nominal variables into a series of **dummy variables**. Thus, Nyamongo's codebook has a total of 88 theme *variables* (including all the dummy variables), even though he coded for just 24 *themes* (like symptoms, treatments, and so on).

Table 19.3 Part of the Data Matrix from Nyamongo's Analysis of 35 Gusii Texts

Person	Age	Sex	Occupation	SES	...	CTRL1	...	CAUSE1	...	HELP1	...	WITCH	...
1	48	M	retired worker	2		1		1		0		0	
2	58	M	farmer	1		0		1		0		1	
3	68	M	clan elder	1		1		1		0		1	
.			.	.		.		.		.		.	
.			.	.		.		.		.		.	
.			.	.		.		.		.		.	
33	54	F	teacher	2		1		1		0		0	
34	57	F	artisan	2		0		0		0		0	
35	26	F	housewife	1		1		1		0		1	

Table 19.3 shows a piece of the **data matrix** produced by Nyamongo's coding of the 35 narratives (**Further Reading:** codebooks).

We turn now to methods of analysis that rely on having discovered themes in text. We begin with grounded theory.

GROUNDED THEORY

Human experience is endlessly interesting because it is endlessly unique. On the other hand, we also know that human experience is patterned. Discovering pattern in human experience requires close, inductive examination of unique cases plus the application of deductive reasoning. **Grounded-theory** is a set of systematic techniques for doing this. The method was developed by two sociologists, Barney Glaser and Anslem Strauss, in a seminal book titled *The Discovery of Grounded Theory: Strategies for Qualitative Research* (1967). As the title implies, the aim is to discover theories—causal explanations—grounded in empirical data, about how things work.

The original method of grounded theory was in the positivist tradition of social science. Glaser (2002) remained committed to the original, mostly inductive approach, while Strauss—first in 1987 on his own and then with Julie Corbin (Corbin and Strauss 2008; Strauss and Corbin 1998)—allowed for more use of deduction. And, in an influential series of books and articles, Kathy Charmaz (1995, 2000, 2002) has developed an alternative method, called constructivist grounded theory. This brand of the method—in which informants and researchers create data together, interactively, during an interview—is in the interpretivist tradition of the social science.

Whichever tradition you favor, there are three steps in grounded theory: Coding the texts for themes; linking themes into theoretical models; and displaying and validating the models (box 19.2).

BOX 19.2

THEORETICAL SAMPLING

For a true grounded-theory study, begin coding with the first interview and use **theoretical sampling** to select informants. That is, select cases for study as concepts emerge (Glaser and Strauss 1967:45–77; Strauss and Corbin 1998:205–12). This method of sampling is well known to ethnographers. In grounded theory, coding, sampling, and theory building are all done together and you stay focused on one topic. A lot of research today that flies under the banner of grounded theory is actually the application of the method after a set of texts has been collected and does not involve theoretical sampling.

Linking Themes and Building Conceptual Models by Memoing

Once you have a *set of themes* coded in a *set of texts*, the next step is to identify *how themes are linked to each other* in a theoretical model (Miles and Huberman 1994:134–37). **Memoing** is the key to doing this. In memoing, you continually write down your thoughts about what you're reading. These thoughts become information on which to develop theory. Memoing is taking "field notes" on observations about texts. The observations can be about the themes that you see emerging or your ideas about how the themes are connected. The important thing is, just as with ethnographic field notes, to get your thoughts down as you have them (Corbin and Strauss 2008:117–41).

Once a model starts to take shape, start shopping for negative cases—ones that don't fit the pattern. Suppose you comb through a set of narratives from women in the labor market. Some women say that they got upset with their last job and quit. You find that most of the women who did this have husbands who earn a pretty good living. Now you have a take-this-job-and-shove-it category. Is there a case in which a woman says "You know, I'd be outta this crummy job in a minute if I didn't have two kids at home to take care of"? Don't wait for that case to come to you. Go looking for it. This is theoretical sampling.

Negative cases either disconfirm parts of a model or suggest new connections that need to be made. In either case, negative cases need to be accommodated when you present your results (**Further Reading:** negative case analysis).

Kearney et al.'s Study of Pregnant Women Who Use Crack

So, how do you actually build theoretical models and what do they look like? Here's a step-by-step example.

Margaret Kearney and her colleagues (1995) interviewed 60 women who reported using crack cocaine an average of at least once weekly during pregnancy. The semistructured interviews lasted from 1 to 3 hours and covered childhood, relationships, life context, previous pregnancies, and actions during the current pregnancy related to drug use, prenatal care, and self-care. Kearney et al. coded and analyzed the transcripts as they went. As new topics emerged, investigators asked about the topics in subsequent interviews. In this way, they linked data collection and data analysis in one continuous effort.

Kearney et al. coded the data first for the general topics they used to guide the interviews. Later, they would use these codes to search for and retrieve examples of text related to various interview topics. Next, team members reread each transcript searching for examples of social psychological themes in the women's narratives. Each time they found an example, they asked: "What is this an example of?" The answers suggested substantive categories that were refined with each new transcript.

Kearney et al. looked at how substantive categories were related. They recorded their ideas about these interactions in the forms of memos and developed a preliminary model. With each subsequent transcript, they looked for negative cases and pieces of data that challenged their emerging model. They adjusted the model to include the full range of variation that emerged in the transcripts.

To begin with, Kearney et al. identified five major categories, which they called: VALUE, HOPE, RISK, HARM REDUCTION, and STIGMA MANAGEMENT. (Capital letters are often used for code names in grounded-theory research, just as in statistical research.) Women valued their pregnancy and the baby-to-be in relation to their own life priorities (VALUE); women expressed varying degrees of hope that their pregnancies would end well and that they could be good mothers (HOPE) and they were aware that cocaine use posed risks to their fetus but they perceived that risk differently (RISK). Women tried in various ways to minimize the risk to the fetus (HARM REDUCTION) and they used various stratagems to reduce social rejection and derision (STIGMA MANAGEMENT).

By the time they had coded 20 interviews, Kearney et al. realized that the categories HARM REDUCTION and STIGMA MANAGEMENT were components of a more fundamental category that they labeled EVADING HARM. After about 30 interviews had been coded, they identified and labeled an overarching psychological process they called SALVAGING SELF that incorporated all five of the major categories. By the time they'd done 40 interviews, Kearney et al. felt they had reached **theoretical saturation**, which means that they were not discovering new categories or relations among categories. Just to make sure, they conducted another 20 interviews and confirmed the saturation.

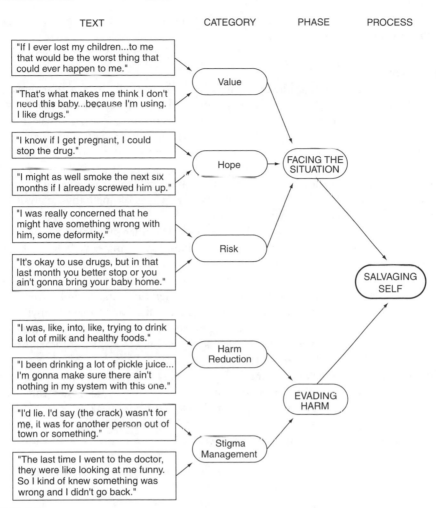

FIGURE 19.1.

The relation of themes/categories in Kearney et al.'s analysis of how pregnant drug users viewed their own behavior.

SOURCE: M. H. Kearney et al., "Salvaging Self—A Grounded Theory of Pregnancy on Crack Cocaine." *Nursing Research*, Vol. 44, pp. 208–13. © 1995, Lippincott Williams & Wilkins. Reprinted with permission.

Figure 19.1 shows the graphic model that Kearney et al. produced to represent their understanding of how the process worked. Kearney et al. described in rich detail each of the major categories that they discovered, but notice how each of the substantive themes in their model is succinctly defined by a quote from a respondent.

When the steps of the grounded-theory approach are followed, models or theories are produced that are, indeed, *grounded* in the text. These models, however, are not the final product of the grounded-theory approach. In their original formulation, Glaser and Strauss (1967) emphasized that the building of grounded-theory models is a step in the research process. The next is to confirm the validity of a model by testing it on an independent sample of data. Kearney et al. checked the validity of their model by presenting it to knowledgeable respondents (pregnant drug users), to members of the project staff, and to health and social service professionals who were familiar with the population (**Further Reading:** grounded theory).

Using Exemplar Quotes

Besides displaying models, one of the most important methods in text analysis is the presentation of direct quotes from respondents—quotes that lead the reader to understand quickly what it took you months or years to figure out. You choose segments of text—verbatim quotes from respondents—as exemplars of concepts and theories or as exemplars of exceptions to your theories (those superimportant negative cases).

This technique looks easy, but it's not. You have to choose the exemplars very carefully because your choices constitute your analysis, as far as the reader is concerned, and you have to avoid what Lofland (1971) called the two great sins of qualitative analysis to use the exemplar quote technique effectively.

The first sin, excessive analysis, involves the all-too-familiar practice of jargony writing and the avoidance of plain English to say plain things. If you analyze a batch of data and conclude that something simple is going on, don't be afraid to say so. There is absolutely nothing of scientific value to be gained from making straightforward things complicated.

Compare these two sentences: (1) "The more generations that people from various ethnic groups are in the United States, the less likely they are to speak anything but English." (2) "Over an expanding number of generations, people of ethnic heritage in the United States become, probabilistically, less likely to adhere to their traditional linguistic symbol systems." The best word to describe the second sentence is "yucky."

The second sin consists of avoiding doing any analysis on your own—being so gun-shy of theory and jargon that you simply fill up your papers and books with lengthy quotes from people and offer no analysis at all. Data do not speak for themselves. I've been in rooms full of data and never heard a sound. You have to develop your ideas (your analysis) about what's going on, state those ideas clearly, and illustrate them with selected quotes from your respondents.

Katherine Newman (1986), for example, collected life history material from 30 white, middle-class American women, ages 26–57, who had suffered severe losses of income as a result of divorce. Newman discovered and labeled two groups of women, according to her informants' own accounts of which period in their lives had the greatest effect on how they viewed the world. Women whose adolescent and early married years were in the 1960s and early 1970s seemed to be very different from "women of the Depression" who were born between 1930 and 1940.

These women had grown up in two very different socioeconomic and political environments; the differences in those environments had a profound effect on the shaping of people's subjective, interpretive, and symbolic views of the world, and, according to Newman's analysis, this accounted for differences in how her informants responded to the economic loss of divorce. Newman illustrated her analytic finding with quotes from her informants.

One woman said:

> I grew up in the '30s on a farm in Minnesota, but my family lost the farm during the Depression. Dad became a mechanic for the WPA, after that, but we moved around a lot. I remember that we never had any fresh fruits or vegetables during that whole time. At school there were soup lines and food handouts. . . . You know, I've been there. I've seen some hard times and it wasn't pleasant. Sometimes when I get low on money now, I get very nervous remembering those times.

By contrast, "women of the '60s" felt the economic loss of divorce but tended to stress the value of having to be more self-reliant and the importance of friends, education, and personal autonomy over dependence on material things. Newman illustrated this sentiment with quotes like the following:

> Money destroyed my marriage. All my husband wanted was to accumulate more real estate. We had no emotional relationship. Everything was bent toward things. Money to me now is this ugly thing.

Newman found differences in the way women in the two age cohorts dealt with kin support after divorce, the way they related to men in general, and a number of other things that emerged as patterns in her data. For each observation of a patterned difference in response to life after divorce, Newman used selected quotes from her informants to make the point.

Here's another example, from the study I did with Ashton-Vouyoucalos (1976) on Greek labor migrants. Everyone in the population we were studying had spent 5 years or more in West Germany and had returned to Greece to reestablish their lives. We were interested in how these returned migrants felt about the Greece they returned to, compared with the Germany they left.

Before doing a survey, however, we collected life histories from 15 people, selected because of their range of experiences. Those 15 returned migrants were certainly no random sample, but the consistency of their volunteered observations of differences between the two cultures was striking. Once we noticed the pattern emerging, we laid out the data in tabular form, as shown in table 19.4. The survey instrument that we eventually built reflected the concerns of our informants.

In reporting our findings, Ashton-Vouyoucalos and I referred to the summary table and illustrated each component with selected quotes from our informants. The issue of gossip, for example (under "negative aspects of Greece" in table 19.4), was addressed by Despina, a 28-year-old woman from Thrace. Despina was happy to be back in Greece, but she said:

> Look, here you have a friend you visit. Sooner or later you'll wear or do something she doesn't like. We have this habit of gossiping. She'll gossip behind your back. Even if it's your sister. In Germany, they don't have that, at least. Not about what you wear or what you eat. Nothing like that. That's what I liked.

By the way, the translation of Despina's comment has been doctored to make it sound a bit more seamless than it did in the original. I've seen thousands of really interesting quotes in ethnographic reports, and common sense says that most of them were fixed up a bit. I don't see anything wrong with this. In fact, I'm grateful to writers who do it. Unexpurgated speech is terrible to read. It's full of false starts, run-ons, fragments, pauses, filler syllables (like "uh" and "y'know"), and whole sentences whose sole purpose is to give speakers a second or two while they think of what to say next. Of course, if you are doing conversation analysis, you need *all* the detail. But if you're doing whole text analysis and you don't edit that stuff, you'll bore your readers to death.

We turn next to schema analysis—the discovery of cultural models.

SCHEMAS, MODELS, AND METAPHORS
Schema analysis combines elements of anthropological linguistics and cognitive psychology in the examination of text. For example, we hear sentences every day that we've never

Table 19.4   Summary of Repatriates' Ambivalent Statements about Greece

Negative aspects of Greece

Economic

1. Wages are low.
2. Few jobs are available, especially for persons with specialized skills.
3. Working conditions are poor.
4. Inflation is high, especially in the prices of imported goods.

Sociocultural

1. People in general (but especially public servants) are abrupt and rude.
2. The roads are covered with rubbish.
3. Everyone, even friends and relatives, gossips about each other and tries to keep each other down.
4. People of the opposite sex cannot interact easily and comfortably.

Political

1. The government is insecure and might collapse with ensuing chaos or a return to dictatorship.
2. Fear of actual war with Turkey creates a climate of insecurity.

Negative aspects of Germany

Economic

1. Economic opportunities are limited because a foreigner cannot easily open up a private business.
2. People are reluctant to rent good housing at decent prices to migrant workers.

Sociocultural

1. One feels in exile from one's home and kin.
2. Life is limited to house and factory.
3. The weather seems bitterly cold and this furthers the sense of isolation.
4. Migrants are viewed as second-class citizens.
5. Children may be left behind in Greece, to the sometimes inadequate care of grandparents.
6. Lack of fluency in German puts Greek workers at a disadvantage.
7. Parents must eventually choose between sending their children to German schools (where they will grow away from their parents) or to inadequate Greek schools in German cities.
8. Factory routines are rigid, monotonous, and inhuman and sometimes the machinery is dangerous.

Political

1. Migrants have no political voice in Germany or in their home country while they are abroad.

SOURCE: "Return Migration to Greece" by H. R. Bernard and S. Ashton-Vouyoucalos, 1976, *Journal of the Steward Anthropological Society* 8:31–51. Table reproduced with permission from the *Journal of the Steward Anthropological Society.*

heard before and somehow we manage to decode them. We don't have a list of sentences in our heads. Instead, we learn a list of rules for making words and for putting words together into sentences.

Some rules are phonological. Consider this sentence: "He worked for two bosses at the same time." We don't pronounce the word "bosses" as if it were "bossiss" (where the iss rhymes with the second syllable in "practice"). That would violate the phonological rule that demands voicing of sibilants (like the final s in "bosses") after vowels like the ə, or schwa (the second vowel in "bosses"). When you add voice to the s sound, it becomes a z sound.

Some rules are syntactic. We don't say "He is writing book" because that violates the English syntactic rule that requires an article (either "the" or "a") before the noun "book."

And some rules are semantic. We don't say "busy, purple forests dream indignantly" because, even though the syntax is correct, that would violate semantic rules about the kinds of things that can be busy or purple or that can dream. It is, however, the prerogative—even the mandate—of poets to concoct new images by violating just these rules.

Phonology, syntax, and semantics are increasingly complex sets of rules for building sensible utterance. Schema analysis takes this rule-based explanation of behavior a step further. Everyday life—to say nothing of special situations, like major rituals—is just too complex for people to deal with one scene at a time. There must, the reasoning goes, be some rules—a grammar—that help us make sense of so much information. These rules comprise schemas (Casson 1983:430).

Schemas, or **scripts**, as Schank and Abelson (1977) called them, enable culturally skilled people to fill in the details of a story. We often hear things like "Fred lost his data because he forgot to save his work." We know that Fred's forgetting to save his work didn't actually *cause* him to lose his data. A whole set of links are left out, but they are easily filled in by listeners who have the background to do so.

When you buy a car, you expect to bargain on the price, but when you order food in a restaurant you expect to pay the price on the menu. You know that you are supposed to tip in certain kinds of restaurants and that you don't tip at fast-food counters. When someone you hardly know says, "Hi, how's it going?" they don't expect you to stop and give them a complete run-down on how your life is going these days. If you did launch into a peroration about your life, you'd be acting outside the prevailing schema—breaking frame, as Erving Goffman put it (1974). When people do that, we react viscerally and wonder "How the heck did they get in here with all the sane people?"

When many people in a society share a schema, then the schema is cultural. How can we learn about cultural schemas? Most anthropologists do this by analyzing narratives. Willett Kempton (1987), for example, asked people to tell him about how they adjusted the thermostats for the furnaces in their homes. He found that Americans have two quite different schemas for how thermostats work. Some people hold to a feedback theory: The thermostat senses the temperature and turns the furnace on or off to keep the room at some desired temperature. This theory produces set-it-and-forget-it behavior. You set the thermostat at some temperature and let the system do its job. Other people hold to a valve theory. You set the thermostat at some much higher temperature than what you really want. This forces the furnace to pour out lots of heat, fast. When the temperature is where you want it, you turn the dial down. The first theory is etically correct and the second is etically incorrect, but the second is widely held and is responsible for a lot of wasted energy. (People who push the elevator button over and over again probably subscribe to a valve theory. We could test that.)

Three Examples of Schema Analysis

The American marriage schema

Naomi Quinn interviewed 11 American couples about marriage. The couples came from different parts of the country. Some were recently married; others were married a long time. And they represented various occupations, education levels, and ethnic and religious groups. Each of the 22 people were interviewed separately for 15 to 16 hours, and the interviews were transcribed.

Quinn has analyzed this body of text to discover the concepts underlying American marriage and to show how these concepts are tied together—how they form a cultural schema, shared by people from different backgrounds about what constitutes success and failure in marriage (Quinn 1982, 1987, 1992, 1996, 1997).

Quinn's method is to look for metaphors in rhetoric—as proxies for themes—and to deduce the schemas, or underlying principles, that could produce those metaphors. For instance, Quinn's informants often compared marriages (their own and those of others) to manufactured and durable products ("It was put together pretty good") and to journeys ("We made it up as we went along; it was a sort of do-it-yourself project"). And when people were surprised at the breakup of a marriage, they would say things like "That marriage was like the Rock of Gibraltar" or "It was nailed in cement." People use these metaphors because they assume that their listeners know that cement and the Rock of Gibraltar are things that last forever.

The method of looking at metaphors as indicators of schemas was developed by George Lakoff and Mark Johnson (2003 [1980]), but Quinn goes further. She reasons that if schemas are what make it possible for people to fill in around the bare bones of a metaphor, then the metaphors must be surface phenomena and cannot themselves be the basis for shared understanding. She tries to understand how metaphors group together and finds that the hundreds of metaphors in her enormous corpus of text all fit into just eight classes: lastingness, sharedness, compatibility, mutual benefit, difficulty, effort, success (or failure), and risk of failure.

The classes of metaphors, the underlying concepts, are linked together in a schema that guides the discourse of ordinary Americans about marriage. Here is Quinn's understanding of that schema:

> Marriages are ideally lasting, shared and mutually beneficial. . . . Benefit is a matter of fulfillment. . . . Fulfillment and, more specifically, the compatibility it requires, are difficult to realize but this difficulty can be overcome, and compatibility and fulfillment achieved, with effort. Lasting marriages in which difficulty has been overcome by effort are regarded as successful ones. Incompatibility, lack of benefit, and the resulting marital difficulty, if not overcome, put a marriage at risk of failure. (Quinn 1997:164)

The Trobriand Land Dispute Schema

Edwin Hutchins (1980) recorded and transcribed a formal dispute in the Trobriand Islands, in which two men, Motobasi and Kailima, make speeches to an open court in their village. In these speeches, both men claim the right to cultivate a particular garden plot.

Motobasi, it seems, has sent one of his followers to cut a garden. Kailimila disputes Motobasi's right to cut the garden. Motobasi says:

> It is easy for me to take up this garden and cut it. I was cutting it when my younger brothers said "you have recently come. You shall not touch these things. These are our things because we *pokala*'ed previously." But as you know, this was a woman's garden, Ilawokuvamalasi's garden. My older brother cut it by himself. When he died, he gave it to his sister. (Hutchins 1980:68)

To win the case, Motobasi will have to refute the statements of his younger brothers who tell him "You shall not touch these things." To understand Motobasi's logic, we need to know that *pokala* is the giving of something by someone of inferior status to someone of superior status "in the hope, but without the promise, that something will be returned" (Hutchins 1980:25–26) and that Trobriand society is divided into matrilineal descent groups.

Motobasi's claim on the garden depends on his listeners filling in around the edges. He hopes that his matrilineal claim, through his sister, will trump his younger brothers' claim through *poloka*. Eventually, the fact that Motobasi could not specify the person whom the brothers had *pokala*'ed will prejudice his case.

The most important finding in Hutchins's account, though, is not that the Trobrianders have a schema for dealing with property disputes and that their schema—with its matrilineal clans and *poloka* exchange, and so on—is very different from our own. Hutchins shows that, within their schema, the Trobrianders use the same logic as we would use in coming to a decision in a dispute. This implies that the rules of logic are universal and it lays to waste the idea that technologically primitive peoples are not up to the abstract logic that Westerners are so proud of inventing (Hutchins 1980:128).

The Mexican Folktale Schema

Holly Mathews (1992) collected 60 tellings of *La Llorona* (the weeping woman), a morality tale told across Mexico. Here is one telling, which Mathews says is typical:

> La Llorona was a bad woman who married a good man. They had children and all was well. Then one day she went crazy and began to walk the streets. Everyone knew but her husband. When he found out he beat her. She had much shame. The next day she walked into the river and drowned herself. And now she knows no rest and must forever wander the streets wailing in the night. And that is why women must never leave their families to walk the streets looking for men. If they are not careful they will end up like La Llorona. (p. 128)

In another telling, La Llorona kills herself because her husband becomes a drunk and loses all their money. In yet another, she kills herself because her husband is seen going with other women and La Llorona, in disbelief, finally catches him paying off a woman in the streets.

Mathews found that men and women tended to emphasize different things in the story, but the woman always winds up killing herself, no matter who tells it. The morality tale succeeds in shaping people's behavior, she says, because the motives of the characters in the story conform to a schema, shared by men an women alike, about how men and women see each other's fundamental nature (Mathews 1992:129).

Men, according to Mathews's understanding of the cultural model in rural Mexico, view women as sexually uncontrolled. Unless they are controlled, or control themselves, their true nature will emerge and they will begin (as the story says) to "walk the streets" in search of sexual gratification. Men, for their part, are viewed by women as sexually insatiable. Men are driven, like animals, to satisfy their desires, even at the expense of family obligations. In her grammar of the La Llorona tales, Mathews shows that women have no recourse but to kill themselves when they cannot make their marriages work.

Mathews goes beyond identifying the schema and tries to explain where the schema comes from. Most marriages in the village where Mathews did her research (in the state of Oaxaca) are arranged by parents and involve some exchange of resources between the families. Once resources like land are exchanged there's no turning back, which means that parents can't, or won't take back a daughter if she wants out of a marriage. Then, as Mathews explains, the only way a woman can end her marriage is suicide (1992:150). And that, Mathews, says, is why suicide is part of virtually all tellings of the La Llorona tale (**Further Reading:** schema analysis, mental models, metaphor analysis).

CONTENT ANALYSIS

Content analysis is a set of methods for systematically coding and analyzing qualitative data. These methods are used across the social sciences and the humanities to explore explicit and covert meanings in text—also called **manifest** and **latent content**—and for testing hypotheses about texts. Whether the research task is exploratory or confirmatory, content analysis is usually quantitative analysis (box 19.3).

BOX 19.3

HOW CONTENT ANALYSIS BECAME ADMISSIBLE IN
COURT

When the Nazis came to power in the 1930s, the U.S. Government Communications Commission began monitoring short-wave radio broadcasts from Germany. Analysts established 14 major propaganda themes in the Nazi media. In
1942, the U.S. Department of Justice accused William Dudley Pelley of sedition,
claiming that Pelley was publishing pro-Nazi propaganda while the United
States was at war with Germany.

The government asked independent coders to classify 1,240 items in Pelley's
publications as belonging or not belonging to one of those 14 Nazi propaganda
themes. Harold Lasswell, a political scientist and expert in propaganda analysis,
testified that 1,195 of the items (96.4%) "were consistent with and suggested
copying from the German propaganda themes" (*United States v. Pelley* 1942).
Pelley was convicted. The conviction was upheld by the U.S. Circuit Court of
Appeals, and the admissibility in court of evidence based on this simple method
of content analysis was established (Goldsen 1947).

Content analysis doesn't have to be complicated to be effective. Maxine Margolis
(1984) did ethnohistorical research on the changing images of women in the United
States. She used the *Ladies Home Journal*, from 1889 to 1980, as an archival database, and
asked a simple question: Do ads in the *Ladies' Home Journal* for household products show
homemakers or servants using those products?

From historical data, Margolis knew that the large pool of cheap servant labor in U.S.
cities—labor that had been driven there by the Industrial Revolution—was in decline by
about 1900. The readers of the *Ladies' Home Journal* in those days were middle-class
women who were accustomed to employing household servants. Margolis's counts
showed clearly the transformation of the middle-class homemaker from an employer of
servants to a direct user of household products.

Margolis took a random sample of her database (2 years per decade of the magazine,
and 2 months per year, for a total of 36 magazines), but she did not have to devise a
complex tagging scheme. She simply looked for the presence or absence of a single, major
message. It is very unlikely that Margolis could have made a mistake in coding the ads
she examined. Servants are either portrayed in the ad, or they aren't. So, by defining a
nominal variable, and one that is easily recognized, Margolis was able to do a content
analysis that added an interesting dimension to her historical ethnographic work on
changing images of middle-class urban women.

"Texts" don't have to be made of words for content analysis. The Codex Borgia is
one of just a few surviving books from ancient Mesoamerica. Written in pictographs, it
documents, in beautiful, gory detail, the ceremonies and gods associated with each day of
the 260 days in the ancient Mesoamerican ritual calendar. There were three great civilizations in ancient Mexico: one centered in Teotihuacán, in the central valley; one in Oaxaca,
centered in Monte Alban; and the Mayan civilization, which occupied a huge area from
southern Mexico to Honduras. The Codex Borgia was painted in Mixtec style—that is,

the style from Oaxaca—but the iconography of the Borgia is widely regarded as Nahua— that is, from the central valley. Which raises the question: Who painted the Borgia? It couldn't have been a Maya, but was it a Nahua or a Mixtec?

John Paddock (1985) noticed that while the focus of the Codex Borgia is on the gods and their associated ceremonies, that of another Mixtec document, the Codex Nuttall, is on events associated with noble families. But both codices have something in common: really gory depictions of human sacrifice—the kind that involved bending the victim over a large, round rock, so that his feet and head were lower than his chest, and then extracting his heart with a flint blade (Paddock 1985:362).

Paddock coded and counted. There are 126 scenes of sacrifice per 100 pages in the Borgia versus 19 per 100 in the Nuttall. In fact, says Paddock, "Borgia *drags* in blood where it is only remotely appropriate" (Paddock 1985:66) and appears to celebrate human sacrifice, whereas the other Mixtec codices seem to deplore it. What's going on?

The Nahua-speaking peoples (the last of whom were the Aztecs) probably came to the Valley of Mexico around 600 A.D., toward the end of the Teotihuacán civilization. Comparing the art of Teotihuancán and that of the Mayans, Paddock notes the absence in Teotihuacán period art, anywhere in Mexico, of violent military scenes. The spread of the Teotihuacán civilization appears to have been the result more of trade than of conquest.

Tezcatlipoca is a fearsome, bloodthirsty god, and a central deity in Borgia, but he doesn't appear in Oaxaca until after the Aztec invasion in the mid-15th century C.E. Paddock argues that the patron of the Codex Borgia was a Nahua high priest at a large, wealthy center who had a Mixtec painter in his employ and who told the Mixtec painter what to put into the codex. "If the painter was too dainty with the blood," says Paddock, he would be corrected. If he showed it too prominently for the patron's taste, he would hear about that" (Paddock 1985:378). And if he knew what was good for him—if he wanted to stay alive—he did exactly what his patron asked of him.

Content analysis is easily applied to film. Cowan and O'Brien (1990) wanted to know, for example, whether men or women in slasher films were more likely to be survivors, and what other personal characteristics accounted for those who got axed and those who lived. The corpus of text in this case was 56 slasher movies.

These movies contained a total of 474 victims, who were coded for gender and survival. Conventional wisdom about slasher films holds that victims are mostly women and slashers are mostly men. Although slashers in these films were, in fact, mostly men, it turned out that victims were equally likely to be women or men. Surviving as a female slasher victim, however, was strongly associated with the absence of sexual behavior and with being less physically attractive than nonsurviving women. The male nonsurvivors were cynical, egotistical, and dictatorial. Cowan and O'Brien conclude that, in slasher films, sexually pure women survive and that "unmitigated masculinity" ends in death (1990:195).

The methodological issues associated with content analysis are all evident here. Does the sample of 56 films used by Cowan and O'Brien justify generalizing to slasher films in general? Did the coders who worked on the project make correct judgments in deciding things like the physical attractiveness of female victims or the personality and behavioral characteristics of the male victims? These two issues in particular, sampling and coding, are at the heart of content analysis. (For content analysis of young adults' reactions to slasher films, see Nolan and Ryan 2000.)

Sampling in Content Analysis

There are two components to sampling in content analysis. The first is identifying the *corpus* of texts; the second is identifying the units of analysis *within* the texts. If you collect

40 or 50 life histories, then you naturally analyze the whole corpus. But when the units of data run into the hundreds or even thousands—like all television commercials that ran during prime time in August 2005; all front-page stories of the *New York Times* from 1851 to 2005; all campaign speeches by John Kerry and George W. Bush during the 2004 presidential campaign—then a representative sample of records must be made.

Gilly (1988) did a cross-cultural study of gender roles in advertising. She videotaped a sample of 12 hours of programming in Los Angeles (United States), Monterrey (Mexico), and Brisbane (Australia), from 8 A.M. to 4 P.M. on Tuesday and from 7 P.M. to 11 P.M. on Wednesday. To control for seasonal variation between the hemispheres, the U.S. and Mexico samples were taken in September 1984 and the Australia sample was taken in February 1985. There were 617 commercials: 275 from the United States, 204 from Mexico, and 138 from Australia.

Because of her research question, Gilly used only adult men and women who were on camera for at least 3 seconds or who had at least one line of dialog. There were 169 women and 132 men in the U.S. ads; 120 women and 102 men in the Mexican ads; and 52 women and 49 men in the Australian ads.

Text analysis—particularly nonquantitative analysis—is often based on purposive sampling. Trost (1986) thought the relationship between teenagers and their families might be affected by five different dichotomous variables. To test this idea, he intentionally selected five cases from each of the 32 possible combinations of the five variables and conducted 160 interviews.

Nonquantitative studies in content analysis may also be based on extreme or deviant cases, cases that illustrate maximum variety on variables, cases that are somehow typical of a phenomenon, or cases that confirm or disconfirm a hypothesis. Even a single case may be enough to display something of substantive importance, but Morse (1994) suggests using at least six participants in studies where you're trying to understand the essence of experience and carrying out 30–50 interviews for ethnographies and grounded theory studies.

Once a sample of texts is established, the next step is to identify the basic, nonoverlapping units of analysis. This is called **unitizing** (Krippendorf 2004a) or **segmenting** (Tesch 1990). The units may be entire texts (books, interviews, responses to an open-ended question on a survey) or segments (words, word-senses, sentences, themes, paragraphs). If you want to compare across texts—to see *whether or not* certain themes occur—the whole text (representing a respondent or an organization) is the appropriate unit of analysis. When the idea is to compare the *number of times a theme occurs* across a set of texts, then you need to break the text down into smaller chunks, each of which reflects a theme.

Coding in Content Analysis

With a set of texts in hand, the next steps are to develop a codebook and actually code the text to produce a text-by-theme matrix. Consider Elizabeth Hirschman's work (1987) on how people sell themselves to one another in personal ads. From her reading of the literature on resource theory, Hirschman thought that she would find 10 kinds of resources in personal ads: love, physical characteristics, educational status, intellectual status, occupational status, entertainment services (nonsexual), money status, demographic information (age, marital status, residence), ethnic characteristics, and personality info (not including sexual or emotional characteristics).

Hirschman formulated and tested specific hypotheses about which resources men and women would offer and seek in personal ads. She selected 20 test ads at random from the *New York Magazine* and *The Washingtonian* and checked that the 10 kinds of resources were, in fact, observable in the ads. Sexual traits and services were less than 1% of all resources coded. This was 1983–1984, but even then, ads with explicit references to sexual traits and services were more common in other periodicals than in *The Washingtonian* and *New York Magazine*.

Hirschman next gave 10 men and 11 women the list of resource categories and a list of 100 actual resources ("young," "attractive," "fun loving," "divorced," "32-year-old," etc.) gleaned from the 20 test ads. She asked the 21 respondents to match the 100 resources with the resource category that seemed most appropriate. This exercise demonstrated that the resource items were **exhaustive** and **mutually exclusive**: No resource items were left over, and all of them could be categorized into only 1 of the 10 resource categories.

When she was confident her codebook worked, Hirschman tested her hypotheses. She sampled approximately 100 female-placed ads and 100 male-placed ads from each magazine—a total of 400 ads. A male and a female coder, working independently (and unaware of the hypotheses of the study), coded 3,782 resource items taken from the 400 ads as belonging to 1 of the 10 resource categories. The coding took 3 weeks. This is not easy work.

Hirschman was concerned with **intercoder reliability**—that is, making sure that coders saw the same thing when they coded those ads. She gave the data to a third coder who identified discrepancies between the first two coders. Of 3,782 resource items coded, there were discrepancies (theme contrasts) on 636 (16.8%), and one of the coders failed to code 480 items (12.7%). Hirschman resolved the theme contrasts herself. She checked the omissions against the ads to see if the coder who had made an assignment had done so because the resource was, in fact, in the ad. This was always the case, so the 480 resource items omitted by one coder were counted as if they had been assigned to the ad by both coders.

The results? Men were more likely than women to *offer* monetary resources; women were more likely than men to *seek* monetary resources. Women were more likely than men to offer physical attractiveness. Washington, DC, and New York City are supposed to be hip places, yet the way men and women wrote their own personal ads in 1983–1984 conformed utterly to traditional gender role expectations. In 1998, a sample of 380 Internet personal ads showed that men continued to seek a particular kind of body in women whereas women continued to offer a particular kind of body and, although men and women alike mentioned their financial status, women still were more likely to explicitly seek someone who is financially secure. Gil-Burman et al. (2002), though, found evidence of what may be a major shift in Spain: Men of all ages sought physical attractiveness in women; women under 40 sought physical attractiveness in men (**Further Reading:** content analysis).

INTERCODER RELIABILITY

It is quite common in content analysis to have more than one coder mark up a set of texts. The idea is to see whether the constructs being investigated are shared—whether multiple coders reckon that the same constructs apply to the same chunks of text. There is a simple way to measure agreement between a pair of coders: you just line up their codes and calculate the percentage of agreement. This is shown in table 19.5 for two coders who have coded 20 texts for a single theme, using a binary code, 1 or 0.

Both coders have a 0 for texts 1, 4, 5, 7, and 10, and both coders have a 1 for text 2. These two coders agree a total of 6 times out of 10—5 times that the theme, whatever it is, does not appear in the texts, and 1 time that the theme does appear. On 4 out of 10

Table 19.5   Measuring Simple Agreement between Two Coders on a Single Theme

	Units of Analysis (documents/observations)									
	1	2	3	4	5	6	7	8	9	10
Coder 1	0	1	0	0	0	0	0	0	1	0
Coder 2	0	1	1	0	0	1	0	1	0	0

texts, the coders disagree. On text 9, for example, coder 1 saw the theme in the text, but coder 2 didn't. Overall, these two coders agree 60% of the time.

The total observed agreement, though, is not a good measure of intercoder reliability because people can agree that a theme is present or absent in a text just by chance. To adjust for this possibility, many researchers use a statistic called **Cohen's kappa** (Cohen 1960), or k.

Cohen's kappa

Kappa is a statistic that measures *how much better than chance* is the agreement between a pair of coders on the presence or absence of binary (yes/no) themes in texts. Here is the formula for kappa:

$$k = \frac{\text{Observed} - \text{Chance}}{1 - \text{chance}} \qquad \textbf{Formula 19.1}$$

When k is 1.0, there is perfect agreement between coders. When k is zero, agreement is what might be expected by chance. When k is negative, the observed level of agreement is less than what you'd expect by chance. And when k is positive, the observed level of agreement is greater than what you'd expect by chance. Table 19.6 shows the data in table 19.5 rearranged so that we can calculate kappa.

Table 19.6   The Coder-by-Coder Agreement Matrix for the Data in Table 19.5

		Coder 2		
		Yes	No	Coder 1 totals
Coder 1	Yes	1 (a)	1 (b)	2
	No	3 (c)	5 (d)	8
	Coder 2 totals	4	6	10 (n)

The *observed agreement* between Coder 1 and Coder 2 is:

$$\frac{(a+d)}{n}$$

Here, Coder 1 and Coder 2 agreed that the theme was present in the text once (cell a) and they agreed that the theme was absent five times (cell d), for a total of 6, or 60% of the 10 texts.

The probability that Coder 1 and Coder 2 agree by chance is:

$$\frac{a+b}{n} \times \frac{a+c}{n} + \frac{c+d}{n} \times \frac{b+d}{n}$$

Here, the probability that Coder 1 and Coder 2 agreed by chance is $.08 + .48 = .56$. Using formula 19.1, we calculate kappa:

$$k = \frac{.6 - .56}{1 - .56} = .0909$$

In other words, the 60% observed agreement between the two coders for the data in table 19.5 is about 9% better than we'd expect by chance. Whether we're talking about agreement between two people who are coding a text or two people who are coding behavior in a time allocation study, 9% better than chance is nothing to write home about.

Carey et al. (1996) asked 51 newly arrived Vietnamese refugees in New York State 32 open-ended questions about tuberculosis. Topics included knowledge and beliefs about TB symptoms and causes as well as beliefs about susceptibility to the disease, prognosis for those who contract the disease, skin-testing procedures, and prevention and treatment methods. The researchers read the responses and built a code list based simply on their own judgment. The initial codebook contained 171 codes.

Then Carey et al. broke the text into 1,632 segments. Each segment was the response by 1 of the 51 respondents to 1 of the 32 questions. Two coders independently coded 320 of the segments, marking as many of the themes as they thought appeared in each segment. Segments were counted as reliably coded if both coders used the same codes on it. If one coder left off a code or assigned an additional code, then this was considered a coding disagreement.

On their first try, only 144 (45%) out of 320 responses were coded the same by both coders. The coders discussed their disagreements and found that some of the 171 codes were redundant, some were vaguely defined, and some were not mutually exclusive. In some cases, coders simply had different understandings of what a code meant. When these problems were resolved, a new, streamlined codebook was issued, with only 152 themes, and the coders marked up the data again. This time they were in agreement 88.1% of the time.

To see if this apparently strong agreement was a fluke, Carey et al. tested intercoder reliability with kappa. The coders agreed perfectly ($k = 1.0$) on 126 out of the 152 codes that they'd applied to the 320 sample segments. Only 17 (11.2%) of the codes had final k values ≥ 0.89. As senior investigator, Carey resolved any remaining intercoder discrepancies himself (Carey et al. 1996).

How much intercoder agreement is enough? As with so much in real life, the correct answer, I think, is: It depends. It depends, for example, on the level of inference required. If you have texts from single mothers about their efforts to juggle home and work, it's easier to code for the theme "works full time" (a low-inference theme) than it is to code for the theme "enjoys her job" (a high-inference theme).

It also depends on what's at stake. X-rays are texts, after all, and I'd like a pretty high level of intercoder agreement if a group of physicians were deciding on whether a particular anomaly meant my going in for surgery or not. In text analysis, the standards are still evolving. Many researchers are satisfied with kappa values of around .70; others like to shoot for .80 and higher (Gottschalk and Bechtel 1993; Krippendorf 2004b) (**Further Reading:** interrater reliability).

HRAF: CROSS-CULTURAL CONTENT ANALYSIS

In the 1940s, George Peter Murdock, Clellan S. Ford, and other behavioral scientists at Yale led the effort to organize an interuniversity, nonprofit organization that is now the Human Relations Area Files (HRAF) at Yale University. HRAF is now the world's largest archive of ethnography, with about a million pages of text, collected from some 8,000 books and articles, on almost 400 cultural groups around the world. The archive is grow-ing at about 40,000 pages a year more than half the material is available and searchable on the Internet through the 400-plus libraries at institutions that subscribe. (Go to: http://www.yale.edu/hraf and see appendix E for more.)

Pages of the HRAF database are indexed by professional anthropologists, following the *Outline of Cultural Materials*, or OCM. This is a massive indexing system that was devel-oped by Murdock and others (2004 [1961]) to organize and classify material about cul-tures and societies of the world. The OCM is used by cross-cultural researchers to find ethnographic data for testing hypotheses about human behavior across cultures, and some anthropologists use it to code their field notes (see chapter 13).

There are 82 main domains in the OCM, in blocks of 10, from 10 to 91. Block 16, for example, is about demography. Within this block there are eight subdomains labeled 161, 162, . . . 168. These domains cover specific topics like mortality (code 165), external migration (code 167), and so on. Block 58 covers the family with codes for nuptials (585), termination of marriage (586), etc. Other major blocks of codes are for domains like kinship, entertainment, social stratification, war, health and welfare, sickness, sex, reli-gious practices. . . .

HRAF turns the ethnographic literature into a database for content analysis and cross-cultural tests of hypotheses because you can search the archive for every reference to any of the codes across the more than 400 cultures that are covered.

Doing Cross-Cultural Text-Based Research

There are five steps in doing an HRAF study (Otterbein 1969):

1. State a hypothesis that requires cross-cultural data.
2. Draw a representative sample of the world's cultures.
3. Find the appropriate OCM codes in the sample.
4. Code the variables according to whatever conceptual scheme you've developed in forming your hypothesis.
5. Run the appropriate statistical tests and see if your hypothesis is confirmed.

Sampling and Galton's Problem

In 1889, Edward Tylor gave a paper at the Royal Society in London in which he tried to relate, among other things, marital residence (matrilocal, patrilocal, etc.) to customs of kin avoidance. Francis Galton asked: Weren't some of the societies that Mr. Tylor was using in his analysis related to one another? Wouldn't that negate using them each as an independent example of the same variable?"

This became known as **Galton's Problem.** One way to deal with it is to use the Stan-dard Cross-Cultural Sample of 186 societies (Murdock and White 1969) or the HRAF Probability Sample of 60 societies (HRAF 1967) as your sample. These samples were developed so that the societies would be independent of one another, linguistically and culturally.

Another way is to treat the relation between pairs of societies as an independent vari-able—that is, to measure how close they are linguistically, culturally, or geographically—and to use that variable as a predictor of whatever hypothesis you're testing (Dow and Eff 2008; Dow et al. 1984).

Or you can, as Carol and Melvin Ember suggest (2001:89), choose a simple random sample from the 400 societies that are currently described in the HRAF archives. If you use the 60-society sample as your corpus, you can run your test on 30 societies and then compare your results to the other 30. If you get the same answers twice, you can be much more confident about them than if you get them just once.

CODING IN HRAF

If a piece of an ethnography is coded as 682, this means that it is about offenses against life. It does not tell you what the offense is. It may be killing someone by accidentally setting fire to their house; it may be paying a sorcerer to cast a deadly spell on someone who subsequently dies; it may be a revenge or honor killing; or it may be an inappropriate act in battle. The only way to tell is to read the material and convert the primary ethnographic material into usable codes for statistical analysis. You might use 1 = war, 2 = rape, 3 = use of witchcraft, and so on, depending on your particular research problem.

In a classic study, Landauer and Whiting (1964) tested the association between stress (both physical and emotional) in infancy and height. Psychologists had found in lab experiments that stroking rat pups (a very stressful thing to do to a baby rat) led to longer adult rats. Do humans respond as rats do to physical and emotional stress in infancy? Landauer and Whiting tested this on two samples of societies across the world for which sufficient data were available.

The dependent variable here is mean adult male height and the independent variable is the presence of piercing (lips, nose, scarification, circumcision) or molding (of arms or legs or head) during the first 24 months of life. Table 19.7 shows the result.

Table 19.7   The Results of Landauer and Whiting's Study

	Piercing or molding present during first 24 months	
Study 1 (35 societies)	Present (n = 17)	Absent (n = 18)
Mean height	65.18 inches	62.69 inches
	t = 3.72, p < .002	
Study 2 (30 societies)	Present (n = 19)	Absent (n = 11)
Mean height	66.05 inches	63.41 inches
	t = 4.68, p < .001	

SOURCE: T. K. Landauer and J. W. M. Whiting, "Infantile Stimulation and Adult Stature of Human Males," *American Anthropologist*, Vol. 66, no. 5, pp. 1007–28, 1964.

Landauer and Whiting knew they had to be very cautious about interpreting the results shown in table 19.7 because correlation does not, by itself, imply cause. It could be that parents who put their infants through this kind of stress give those children more food or better medical care, which supports growth. Or it could be that boys who are stressed during infancy become more aggressive and only the tallest survive. "This," said Landauer and Whiting, "is the problem with correlational research" (1964:1018).

Still, they were able to control for, and rule out, variations in sunlight (and hence in the body's production of vitamin D) and variations in population genetics—two factors that are well known to cause variations in height. More importantly, they took an idea from the lab (where internal validity is strong because of the controlled conditions of the experiment) and tested it in the field. Yes, the experiments were on lab animals, but the experiments on rats were about manipulation (all that stroking) of endocrines that are known to control growth. Why not, they asked, test this across species, as well as across cultures?

The key to this research is not the data about adult height. It's the coding of the ethnographic, textual data about piercing, molding, scarring, circumcising, and so on. In the end, in content analysis as in all research, *you* have to make the measurements.

Over the years, as researchers have used HRAF, they've read through the primary materials and coded variables that were germane to their particular studies. Barry and Schlegel (1980) edited a book containing published codes for several hundred variables on the 186-society sample developed by Murdock and White (1969). The *World Cultures Journal* (WCJ) has published most of the codes in Barry and Schlegel on diskette and continues to publish codes from cross-cultural studies (http://eclectic.ss.uci.edu/~drwhite/worldcul/world.htm), and codes for 300 variables have been published on disk by HRAF Press for a 60-society sample (box 19.4).

BOX 19.4

PUBLISHING CODES

Coding is painstaking work. Carol and Melvin Ember (2002) were interested in the relationship between various aspects of child rearing (If corporal punishment is present in a society, is it usually the mother or the father who does it? Are fathers usually present or absence in infants' lives? How much does the father care for infants?) and the amount of interpersonal viollence in societies by adult men. Some of the codes they used on child-rearing practices had been published elsewhere, but it took the Embers 4 years to code the variables for frequency of war and interpersonal aggression in the 186-society sample, so, like most cross-cultural researchers, they published those codes (Ember and Ember 1992).

Testing hypotheses on published codes contributes to theory in anthropology. Using published codes, Barber (1998) found that the frequency of male homosexual activity was low in hunting and gathering societies and increased with the complexity of agricultural production. Ethnographic reports of male homosexuality were also more likely for societies in which women did not control their own sexuality—a well-known correlate of increased reliance on complex agriculture.

Other Problems

Information is not always where you expect it to be in HRAF. There is no code in the OCM for family violence, so when David Levinson (1989) did the research for his book on this topic, he asked the coders at HRAF how *they* would code it. They said that they would classify family violence under code 593 (family relations) or code 578 (in-group antagonisms).

Levinson scoured HRAF for references to those codes, and did, in fact, find a lot of material. He coded whether or not a society was reported to exhibit family violence, what kind of violence was reported (child abuse, abuse of the elderly, etc.), and how severe the violence was. Later, while he was browsing through the files, Levinson noticed that wife beating—clearly, a form of family violence—was usually coded under 684, sex and marital offenses. Wife beating, it turns out, is reported for many societies only in cases of adultery or suspicion of adultery, and hence, under code 684 (Levinson, personal communication). The lesson for conducting cross-cultural research is pretty clear: There is no substitute for reading the ethnographies and looking for new clues on how to code variables.

There is also no substitute for good data. The quality of ethnographic data depends crucially on the skill of the person who collected and recorded those data. Ethnographers may be biased in recording their data. Even if they are not biased, they may have the misfortune to interview incompetent informants—or even people who just lied. William Divale (1976), for example, tested the long-standing idea that women have higher status as societal complexity increases. He correlated two independent measures of female status with societal complexity across a representative sample of cultures and found—against all expectations—that the higher the complexity of the society, the *lower* the status of women.

Divale recalculated the correlation using only ethnographies written by people who had spent at least a year in the field and who spoke the native language fluently. When he did this, he found high female status reported at all levels of societal complexity, with low status reported primarily among less-complex societies. The unexpected relation between female status and societal complexity vanished (**Further Reading:** cross-cultural hypothesis testing).

ANALYTIC INDUCTION

Analytic induction is a formal, qualitative method for building up causal explanations of phenomena from a close examination of cases. The method involves the following steps: (1) Define a phenomenon that requires explanation and propose an explanation. (2) Examine a single case to see if the explanation fits. (3) If it does, then examine another case. An explanation is accepted until a new case falsifies it.

When you find a case that doesn't fit, then, under the rules of analytic induction, the alternatives are to change the explanation to include the new case or redefine the phenomenon to exclude the nuisance case. Ideally, the process continues until a universal explanation for all known cases of a phenomenon is attained. (Explaining cases by declaring them all unique is not an option of the method. That's a convenient way out, but it doesn't get us anywhere.)

Charles Ragin (1987, 1994) formalized the logic of analytic induction, using an approach based on **Boolean logic**. Boolean variables are dichotomous: true or false, present or absent, and so on. This seems simple enough, but it's going to get very complicated, very quickly, so pay attention. Remember, there is no math in this. It's entirely qualitative. In fact, Ragin (1994) calls his Boolean method of induction **qualitative comparative analysis**, or QCA.

Suppose you have four dichotomous variables, including three independent, or causal, variables, and one independent, or outcome, variable. With one dichotomous variable, A, there are two possibilities: A and not-A. With two dichotomous variables, A and B, there are four possibilities: A and B, A and not-B, not-A and B, not-A and not-B. With three dichotomous variables, there are eight possibilities; with four there are 16 . . . and so on.

We've seen all this before—in the discussion about factorial designs of experiments (chapter 4); in the discussion of how to use the number of subgroups to figure out sample size (chapter 5); in the discussion of how to determine the number of focus groups you need in any particular study (chapter 8); and in the discussion of factorial questionnaires (chapter 9). The same principle is involved.

Thomas Schweizer (1991, 1996) applied this Boolean logic in his analysis of conflict

454

CHAPTER 19

and social status in Chen Village, China. In the 1950s, the village began to prosper with the application of technology to agriculture. The Great Leap Forward and the Cultural Revolution of the 1960s, however, reversed the village's fortunes. Chan et al. (1984) reconstructed the recent history of Chen Village, focusing on the political fortunes of key actors there.

Schweizer coded the Chan et al. text for whether each of 13 people in the village experienced an increase or a decrease in status after each of 14 events (such as the Great Leap Forward, land reform and collectivization, the collapse of Red Brigade leadership, and an event known locally as "the great betrothal dispute"). Schweizer wound up with a 13-actor-by-14-event matrix, where a 1 in a cell meant that an actor had success in a particular event and a 0 meant a loss of status in the village.

When Schweizer looked at this actor-by-event matrix he found that, over time, nine of the actors consistently won or consistently lost. That means that for nine of the villagers, there was just one outcome, a win or a loss. But four of the actors lost *sometimes* and won other times. For each of these four people, there could be a win or a loss, which means there are eight possible outcomes.

In total, then, Schweizer needed to account for 17 unique combinations of actors and outcomes. He partitioned the 17 unique cases according to three binary independent variables (whether a villager was originally from a city or had been raised in the village, whether a villager had a proletarian or a nonproletarian background, and whether a villager had ties to people outside the village or not) and one dependent variable (whether the person was an overall success). There are a total of four variables. Table 19.8 shows the 16 outcomes that are possible with four binary variables, and the number of actual cases, out of 17, for each of those outcomes.

Table 19.8 The Outcome of 17 Cases from Schweizer's (1996) Text Analysis

Success	External ties	Proletarian background	Urban origin	No. of cases
0	0	0	0	2
0	0	0	1	2
0	0	1	0	1
0	0	1	1	0
0	1	0	0	0
0	1	0	1	0
0	1	1	0	2
0	1	1	1	0
1	0	0	0	1
1	0	0	1	3
1	0	1	0	0
1	0	1	1	0
1	1	0	0	0
1	1	0	1	1
1	1	1	0	4
1	1	1	1	1

By setting up the logical possibilities in table 19.8, Schweizer was able to test several hypotheses about success and failure in Chen Village. You can see, for example, that just two people who were originally from a city (people who had been sent to the village to work during the Cultural Revolution) turned out to be failures, but five people from the city turned out to be successful. People from an urban background have an advantage, but you can also see from table 19.8 that it's not enough. To ensure success, you should come from a proletarian family OR have good external ties (which provide access to information and power at the regional level).

Failure is predicted even better: If an actor has failed in the Chen Village disputes, then he or she is of rural origin (comes from the village) OR comes from a nonproletarian family AND has no ties to authorities beyond the village. The Boolean formula for this statement is:

$$Lack\ of\ success \rightarrow nonurban\ v\ (nonproletarian\ and\ lack\ of\ ties)$$

The substantive conclusions from this analysis are intuitively appealing: In a communist revolutionary environment, it pays over the years to have friends in high places; people from urban areas are more likely to have those ties; and it helps to have been born into a politically correct (that is, proletarian) family.

Analytic induction helps identify the simplest model that logically explains the data. Like classic content analysis and cognitive mapping, human coders have to read and code the text into an event-by-variable matrix. The object of the analysis, however, is not to show the relations between all codes, but to *find the minimal set of logical relations* among the concepts that accounts for a single dependent variable.

With three binary independent variables (as in Schweizer's data), two **logical operators** (OR and AND), and three implications ("if A then B," "if B then A," and "if A, then and only then, B"), there are 30 multivariate hypotheses: 18 when all three independent variables are used, plus 12 when two variables are used. With more variables, the analysis becomes much more difficult, but there are now computer programs that test all possible multivariate hypotheses and find the optimal solution (see appendix E).

These are not easy analyses to do, and some people I talk to about this kind of work wonder how qualitative analysis ever got so complicated. It just goes to show that qualitative doesn't mean wimpy (**Further Reading:** qualitative comparative analysis) (box 19.5).

COMPUTERS AND TEXT ANALYSIS

Finally . . . anyone who collects mountains of text will want to take advantage of modern text analysis software. Don't take the phrase "text analysis software" literally. Computer programs do a lot, but in the end, *you* do the analysis; *you* make the connections and formulate hypotheses to test; *you* draw conclusions and point them out to your readers.

The two broad approaches in text analysis—inductive, hypothesis-generating research and deductive, hypothesis-testing research—are reflected in the available software. Programs for automated content analysis are based on the concept of a computerized, contextual dictionary. You feed the program a piece of text; the program looks up each word in the dictionary and runs through a series of disambiguation rules to see what the words mean—for example, whether the word "concrete" is a noun (stuff you pave your driveway with) or an adjective, as in "I need a concrete example of this or I won't believe it."

Work on automated text analysis began in the 1960s. Philip Stone and others (1966) developed a program for doing automated content analysis called the *General Inquirer*. They tested it on 66 suicide notes—33 written by men who had actually taken their own lives, and 33 written by men who were asked to produce simulated suicide notes. The program parsed the texts and picked the actual suicide notes 91% of the time (Ogilvie et al. 1966). The latest version of the system (which runs with a dictionary called the Harvard IV-4) has a 13,000-word dictionary and over 6,000 rules. It can tell whether the word "broke" means "fractured," or "destitute," or "stopped functioning," or (when paired with "out") "escaped" (Rosenberg et al. 1990:303). (For more about the *General Inquirer*, see appendix E.)

About the same time, Nicholas Colby (1966) developed a special-purpose dictionary for Zuni and Navajo texts. From his ethnographic work, Colby had the impression that

BOX 19.5

THE BOOLEAN LOGIC IN SCHWEIZER'S ANALYSIS

Here are the details of the Boolean logic of Schweizer's analysis (Schweizer 1996). Three possible hypotheses can be derived from two binary variables: "If A then B," "If B then A," and "If A, then and only then, B." In the first hypothesis, A is a sufficient condition to B and B is necessary to A. This hypothesis is falsified by all cases having A and not B. In the second hypothesis, B is a sufficient condition to A and A is necessary to B. The second hypothesis is falsified by all cases of B and not A. These two hypotheses are **implications** or **conditional statements**. The third hypothesis (an **equivalence** or **biconditional statement**) is the strongest: Whenever you see A, you also see B and vice versa; the absence of A implies the absence of B and vice versa. This hypothesis is falsified by all cases of A and not B, and all cases of B and not A.

Applied to the data from Chen Village, the strong hypothesis is falsified by many cases, but the sufficient condition hypotheses (urban origin implies success; proletarian background implies success; having external ties implies success) are true in 86% of the cases (this is an average of the three sufficient condition hypotheses). The necessary condition hypotheses (success implies urban origin; success implies proletarian background; success implies external ties) are true in just 73% of cases (again, an average). (There are seven disconfirming cases in 51 possible outcomes of the 12 **sufficient condition** possibilities—4 possible outcomes for each of three independent variables and one dependent variable. There are 14 disconfirming cases in 51 possible outcomes of the 12 **necessary condition** possibilities.) To improve on this, Schweizer tested multivariate hypotheses, using the logical operators OR and AND (Schweizer 1996).

the Navajo regarded their homes as havens and places of relaxation but that the Zuni viewed their homes as places of discord and tension. To test this idea, Colby developed two groups of words, one group associated with relaxation (words like assist, comfort, affection, happy, and play) and one associated with tension (words like discomfort, difficult, sad, battle, and anger). He then had the computer look at the 35 sentences that contained the word "home" *and* one of the words in the two word groups. Navajos were more than twice as likely as the Zuni to use relaxation words when talking about home than they were to use tension words; the Zuni were almost twice as likely as the Navajo to use tension words when they talked about their home.

Over the years, computer-assisted content analysis has developed into a major industry. When you hear "This call may be monitored for quality assurance purposes," it's likely that the conversation will be turned into text that will be submitted to a high-end data-mining program for analysis.

Most content analysis, however, is not based on computerized dictionaries. It's based on the tried-and-true method of coding a set of texts for themes, producing a text-by-theme profile matrix, and then analyzing that matrix with statistical tools. Most text analysis packages today support this kind of work. You code themes on the fly, as you read the text on the screen, and the program produces the text-by-theme matrix for you. Then, you import the matrix into your favorite stats package (SPSS®, SAS®, SYSTAT®, etc.) and run all the appropriate tests (about which, more in chapters 20, 21, and 22).

Programs for doing grounded-theory-type research are also widely available. No program does everything, so do your homework before deciding on what to buy. A good place to start is the CAQDAS Networking Project (http://caqdas.soc.surrey.ac.uk). CAQDAS (pronounced cactus—really) stands for computer-assisted qualitative data analysis software. The CAQDAS site is continually updated with information on tools for analyzing qualitative data. Those tools are getting more sophisticated, with more features added all the time. Were transcription not such a nuisance, social science would have focused long ago on the wealth of qualitative data that describe life and history across the globe. But with voice-recognition software coming on strong (see chapter 8), and transcription becoming less and less intimidating, all forms of text analysis —narrative analysis, discourse analysis, grounded theory, content analysis—will become more and more attractive.

Text analysis is only just beginning to come into its own. It's going to be very exciting.

FURTHER READING

Codebooks: Dey (1993); Miles and Huberman (1994).

Negative case analysis: Becker (1998); Dey (1993); Lincoln and Guba (1985); Miles and Huberman (1994); Strauss and Corbin (1990).

Grounded theory: Bryant and Charmaz (2007); Churchill et al. (2007); Ekins (1997); Glaser (1992); Strauss and Corbin (1997); Van Vliet (2008).

Schema analysis: Brewer (1999, 2000); D'Andrade (1991); D'Andrade and Strauss (1992); Holland and Quinn (1987); Izquierdo and Johnson (2007); Nishida (1999); Paolisso (2007); Shore (2009); Strauss and Quinn (1997).

Mental models: Bang et al. (2007); Bennardo (2002); Gentner and Stevens (1983); Johnson-Laird (1983); Ross (2002); Wierzbicka (2004).

Metaphor analysis: Bennardo (2008); Dunn (2004); Ignatow (2004); Lakoff and Kövecses (1987); Rees et al. (2007); Santa Ana (1999).

Content analysis: Krippendorf (2004a); Parekh and Berisin (2001); Sousa Campos et al. (2002); Yancey and Yancey (1997).

Interrater reliability: Krippendorf (2004b); Kurasaki (2000); Popping and Roberts (2009); Ryan (1999).

Cross-cultural hypothesis testing: Ember (2007); Jankowiak and Fischer (1995); Levinson (1978, 1990); Rohner et al. (1973); Sanderson and Roberts (2008).

QCA qualitative comparative analysis: Haworth-Hoeppner (2000); Ragin (1998); Roscigno and Hodson (2004); Vink and Van Vliet (2009).

Univariate Analysis

The next three chapters deal with methods for analyzing quantitative data. We begin with descriptive and inferential univariate analysis. Then, in chapters 21 and 22, we move on to bivariate and multivariate analysis.

Descriptive analysis involves understanding data through graphic displays, through tables, and through summary statistics. Descriptive analysis is about the data you have in hand. **Inferential analysis** involves making inferences about the world beyond the data you have in hand.

When you say that the average age of people in a village is 44.6 years, that's a descriptive analytic statement. When you say that there is a 95% probability that the true mean of the population from which you drew a sample of people is between 42.5 and 47.5 years, that's an inferential statement: You are inferring something about a population from data in a sample.

In **univariate analysis**, we examine variables precisely and in detail and get to know the data intimately. **Bivariate analysis** involves looking at associations between pairs of variables and trying to understand how those associations work. **Multivariate analysis** involves, among other things, understanding the effects of more than one independent variable at a time on a dependent variable.

Suppose you're interested in the causes of variation in the income of women. You measure income as the dependent variable and some independent variables like: age, marital status, employment history, number of children, ages of children, education, and so on. The first thing to do is examine carefully the properties of all the variables. That's the univariate part of the analysis.

Next, you'd look at the association between each independent variable and the dependent variable. You'd also look at the association between pairs of independent variables. That's the bivariate part. Finally, you'd look at the simultaneous effect of the independent variables on the dependent variable or variables. That's the multivariate part.

Each part helps us answer questions about how things work.

CODING AND CODEBOOKS FOR QUANTITATIVE DATA

Quantitative data processing depends crucially on having a useful **codebook**. A codebook for quantitative data spells out exactly how to transform observations into numbers that can be manipulated statistically and searched for patterns.

A good codebook is worth a lot in data analysis and it's worth more every year. It tells you (and others) what you have in your data—what variables you've studied, what you've called those variables, and how you've stored information about them. You simply can't analyze quantitative data without a good, clear codebook.

458

Just as important, neither can anyone else. You can't share your data with other researchers unless you give them a codebook they can use. Six months after you finish anything but the simplest projects (those with only half a dozen or fewer variables), even *you* won't recognize your own data without a codebook. And if you want to reanalyze your data several years after a project has ended, or compare data you (or someone else) collected in 2005 with data you collect now, you won't be able to do so unless you have a good codebook handy.

Coding

The first rule for coding quantitative data is: Don't analyze while you're coding. This rule is the exact opposite of the rule that applies to inductive coding of qualitative data. In that case, coding text *is* analysis—thinking about what each piece of text means, developing hypotheses about the people who are described, boiling the text down to a series of mnemonics.

It's different with a set of numbers. Suppose you ask 400 randomly selected people, aged 20–70, how old they are. You could get as many as 51 different ages, and you'll probably get at least 20 different ages.

I've seen many researchers code this kind of data into four or five categories—such as 20–29, 30–39, 40–49, 50 and older—before seeing what they've got. Recall from chapter 2 that this just throws away the interval-level power of data about age. You can always tell the computer to package data about age (or income, or any interval-level variable) into a set of ordinal chunks. But if you actually code the data into ordinal chunks to begin with, you can never go back.

Here's a concrete example of something that's a little more complex than age. Gene Shelley studied the strength of ties between friends and acquaintances (Shelley et al. 1990). Every other day for a month, she called 20 informants on the phone to talk about things they'd learned in the previous 2 days about their friends and acquaintances. People mentioned things like "So-and-so told me she was pregnant," "So-and-so's father called and told me my friend made his first jump in parachute school," and so on. Shelley asked people to estimate how long it had been between the time something happened to one of their friends/acquaintances and the time they (the informants) heard about it. This estimated time was the major dependent variable in the research.

There were 20 informants, who submitted to 15 interviews each, and in each interview almost every informant was able to name several events of interest. Thus, there were over 1,000 data records (one for each event remembered by an informant). The length of time estimated by informants between an event happening to someone they knew and their hearing about it ranged from "immediately," to "10 years," with dozens of different time periods in between ("about 5 minutes," "two and a half months," etc.).

The temptation was to make up about five codes, like $1 = 5$ minutes or less, $2 = 6$ minutes to 19 minutes, $3 = 20$ minutes to an hour, and so on. But how do you decide what the right breaks are? Shelley decided to code everything in *days* or *fractions of days* (1 minute is .0007 days; 10 years is 3,650 days, without worrying about leap years) (Shelley et al. 1990). Shelley didn't throw away data by turning a ratio-level variable (minutes) into an ordinal variable (arbitrary chunks of time).

Here's another example, using a nominal variable. Suppose you are studying the personal histories of 200 Mexican men who have had experience as illegal labor migrants to the United States. If you ask them to name the towns in which they have worked, you might get a list of 300 communities—100 more than you have informants! The temptation would be to collapse the list of 300 communities into a shorter list, using some kind of scheme. You might code them as Southeast, Southwest except California, California,

Midwest, Northwest, mid-Atlantic, and so on. Once again, you'd be making the error of doing your analysis in the coding.

Once you've got all the data entered into a computer, you can print them, lay them out, stare at them, and start making some decisions about how to "package" them for statistical analysis. You might decide to label each of the 300 communities in the list according to its population size, or according to its ethnic and racial composition (more than 20% Spanish surname, for example), or its distance in kilometers from the Mexican-U.S. border. All those pieces of information are available from the U.S. Census and other sources online. But if you collapse the list into a set of categories during coding, then your option to add codes about the communities is closed off.

Building Codebooks

Table 20.1 shows the codebook for a street-intercept survey that some colleagues and I ran in Mexico City (Bernard et al. 1989). At the time, we were just beginning to develop what became known as the network scale-up method for estimating the size of populations that you can't count. In this case, the population we wanted to estimate was the number of people who had died in the 1985 Mexico City earthquake. The codebook in table 20.1 contains three essential pieces of information:

1. A short name for each variable.
2. A full, clear description of each variable.
3. A list of the possible values that each variable can take.

I will discuss these in turn.

1. *Short name.* Make variable names as obvious as possible and keep them short. It is customary to begin each **data record** (that is, each line of data) with a **unique identifier** and to list that identifier as the first variable in a codebook. This usually means the informant number. We called the first variable here INTNUM, which was the interview number in the street-intercept project.

Here are some examples of common variable names you'll see in social research: AGE, INCOME, EDUC, HOUSETYP (house type), OWNCAR (does the informant own a car?), MIGRATE (does the informant have plans to migrate?), PQOL (perceived quality of life). Of course, each project is different and will contain variables that are specific to the research. Some examples that I've seen in articles or reports are VISNAI (has the informant ever visited Nairobi?), BIRTHCON (what is the informant's position on birth control?), and DISTH20 (how far is the household from potable water?).

2. *Variable description.* Be as clever as you like with variable names; just be sure to include a chatty description of each variable in the codebook so you'll know what all those clever names mean a year later. Leave nothing to the imagination of the user of a codebook (and that includes you). For example, "age of informant, to the nearest year, and reported by the informant," is much better than "age of informant."

Some variables require a lot of description. Consider this helpful codebook description of a variable: "Perceived Quality of Life. This was measured using an index consisting of the six items that follow. Each item is scored separately, but the items can be added to form an index. Because each item is scored from 1 to 5, the index of perceived quality of life can vary from 6 to 30 for any informant."

If you are using an established index or scale or data collection technique, then name it (i.e., "the Bogardus social distance scale") and provide a citation to the source (Bogardus 1933). If you have adapted a published technique to meet your particular needs, then mention that in your codebook, too. For example, "I have used the Fischer method of

Table 20.1   Codebook for Mexico City Network Study, January 15, 1987

Variable name	Variable description	Values
INTNUM	Interview number.	0001B2400
ZONE	Number of the zone of the city, from on a map of Mexico City where interview was conducted.	1B120
CLAZONE	Socioeconomic class of the zone of the city, as determined by the interviewers.	1 = Lower Class, 2 = Middle Class, 3 = Upper Class
SEX	The sex of the respondent.	1 = Male, 2 = Female
CLASRESP	Socioeconomic class of the respondent, as determined by the interviewers.	1 = Lower Class, 2 = Middle Class, 3 = Upper Class
AGE	Age of respondent, self-reported, in years.	15–99
SCHOOL	Number of years respondent spent in school.	0–25
DFLIVE	Number of years respondent has lived in Mexico City (D.F., or Distrito Federal)	0–99
OCCN	Occupation.	1 = Housewife, 2 = Regular Employment, 3 = Retired, 4 = Unemployed, 5 = Other
DOC	Does the respondent know a physician who works in the public hospitals?	1 = Yes, 2 = No
YESDOC	Does the interviewer think the respondent really does know a physician in the public hospitals?	1 = Yes, 2 = No
QUAKE	Does the respondent know someone who died in the 1985 earthquake?	1 = Yes, 2 = No
YESQUAKE	Does the interviewer think the respondent really does know someone who died in the 1985 earthquake?	1 = Yes, 2 = No
HOWLONG	How many days did it take before the respondent learned that someone he or she knew had died in the quake?	1 = 0B15 days, 2 = 15B30 days, 3 = 31B45 days, 4 = 46B60 days, 5 = 61+ days
MAIL	Does the respondent know someone who works for the postal authority?	1 = Yes, 2 = No
YESMAIL	Does the interviewer think the respondent really does know someone who works for the postal authority?	1 = Yes, 2 = No
ROBBED	Does the respondent know someone who was robbed in the street in 1986?	1 = Yes, 2 = No
YESROB	Does the interviewer think the respondent really does know someone who was robbed in the street in 1986?	1 = Yes, 2 = No
BUS100	Does the respondent know someone who is a bus driver on Route 100? (This is the name of the job of public bus driver in Mexico City.)	1 = Yes, 2 = No
YESBUS	Does the interviewer think the respondent really does know someone who is a bus driver on Route 100?	1 = Yes, 2 = No
PESERO	Does the respondent know someone who drives a *pesero* in Mexico City? (These are private cars and Volkswagen minibuses that operate along established routes as privately owned, public conveyances.)	1 = Yes, 2 = No
YESPES	Does the interviewer think the respondent really does know someone who drives a *pesero* in Mexico City?	1 = Yes, 2 = No
PRIEST	Does the respondent know a Catholic priest in Mexico City?	1 = Yes, 2 = No
YESPRIES	Does the interviewer think the respondent really does know someone who is a Catholic priest in Mexico City?	1 = Yes, 2 = No
VENDOR	Does the respondent know someone who works as a street vendor in the underground economy?	1 = Yes, 2 = No
YESVEND	Does the interviewer think the respondent really does know someone who works as a street vendor in the underground economy?	1 = Yes, 2 = No
TV	Does the respondent know someone who works for Televisa, the television company in Mexico City?	1 = Yes, 2 = No
YESTV	Does the interviewer think the respondent really does know someone who works for Televisa, the television company in Mexico City?	1 = Yes, 2 = No
WIND	Does the respondent know someone who makes his living cleaning car windshields at stoplights in Mexico City and asking for tips?	1 = Yes, 2 = No
YESWIND	Does the interviewer think the respondent really does know someone who makes his living cleaning car windshields at stoplights in Mexico City and asking for tips?	1 = Yes, 2 = No
RAPE	Does the respondent know someone who was raped in the street in 1986?	1 = Yes, 2 = No
YESRAPE	Does the interviewer think the respondent really does know someone who was raped in the street in 1986?	1 = Yes, 2 = No
INTID	Identity of the interviewer.	1 = Eileen, 2 = Isabel, 3 = Alejandro, 4 = Juan, 5 = Maria, 6 = Jorge
KNOW	How many people does the respondent think he or she knows?	1 = 0B100, 2 = 101B500, 3 = 501B1000, 4 = 1001B1500, 5 > 1500

generating social networks (Fischer 1982) but have adapted it in translation for use with the Kipsigis."

Later, you or another researcher can compare the relevant items on your survey instrument with those in the published index. And always file a copy of any survey instrument with your codebook.

3. *Variable values.* Specify the values that each variable can take and what each value means. Marital status, for example, is often coded as 1 = married, 2 = divorced, 3 = separated, 4 = widowed, 5 = never married, 6 = unknown. Religion might be coded as 1 = Shintoist, 2 = Buddhist, 3 = Hindu, 4 = Tribal, 5 = Others, 6 = Unknown.

Notice in table 20.1 that I violated my own rule, in *two* places, about not analyzing data until you have them. See those variables HOWLONG and KNOW? The codes for these variables were set during a brainstorming session in Mexico with the interview team after they'd done a few test interviews on the street. It turned out that people just couldn't answer those two questions (How many days was it before you learned that this person had died in the quake? How many people do you think you know, all told?) by giving a number, so the team came up with some chunks (31–45 days, 501–1,000 people, etc.) that they thought were reasonable.

And remember to mark **string variables** (also called **character variables**) in your codebook. String variables are alphabetic characters and have no numerical properties. If you have the name of the interviewer as a variable (in case you want to check for interviewer response effects), that name is a string of characters.

Cleaning Data

No matter how careful you are, you're going to make mistakes in coding and entering data into a computer. Even if you code behavioral data in the field directly into a handheld computer, believe me, you'll make mistakes. Everyone does. The trick is to catch the mistakes.

The best way to catch coding and data entry errors is with a data editor, like Excel® or the spreadsheet in full-featured statistical analysis packages (see appendix E). Suppose you have a variable called NUMCHILD, or "number of children." If you suspect that none of your informants have more than 10 children, you can tell the editor to "find the cases in the column for NUMCHILD where the entry is greater than 10." If the program finds such cases, you can decide whether the entry is an error or if it just means the informant has a lot of kids. Similarly, if an informant says that she has never had children, you want to make sure that the variable for number of grandchildren is also 0.

You can move columns of numbers around with a data editor. When you enter data, you often don't know which variables to put together. Later, as you become more familiar with your data, you'll want to move columns around so you can eyeball the data matrix and look for mistakes and incompatibilities. Once you have your data into the computer and cleaned, you're ready to start analyzing them (**Further Reading:** cleaning data).

RAW DATA

The first thing to do, before you try any fancy statistical operations on your data, is lay them out and get a feel for them. How many cases are there of people over 70? What is the average number of children in each household? How many people in your sample have extreme views on some key attitude questions?

Table 20.2 shows the raw data for five variables and 30 respondents. These data come from a telephone survey that Gery Ryan, Stephen Borgatti, and I did of 609 adults in the United States (Bernard et al. 2009). Part of the survey was about people's attitudes toward

Table 20.2 30 Records from Bernard et al.'s Study of Green Attitudes

RESP	GENDER	REDUCE	GUNGHO	AGE	EDUC
1	2	5	1	46	18
2	2	4	2	56	12
3	1	4	3	25	18
4	1	5	4	24	12
5	1	4	2	60	5
6	1	2	4	51	18
7	1	2	4	53	14
8	2	5	4	25	13
9	1	2	4	21	15
10	2	4	4	67	13
11	2	2	1	34	16
12	1	5	3	47	18
13	1	4	1	35	12
14	2	4	3	67	12
15	1	4	4	20	12
16	2	4	2	24	15
17	1	5	2	38	16
18	2	5	2	53	14
19	1	4	2	38	12
20	2	4	3	31	14
21	1	5	4	54	15
22	2	5	4	52	14
23	1	4	2	37	14
24	1	2	1	53	14
25	1	5	5	49	18
26	1	3	3	46	16
27	2	5	4	78	14
28	2	5	2	41	12
29	1	4	2	57	12
30	1	4	4	69	10

environmental activism. (The 30 respondents in table 20.2 are a random sample of the 609.)

The first variable, gender, is a nominal, or **qualitative variable**. The respondents were men and women over the age of 18, selected randomly from across the 48 continental states of the United States. Men were coded as 1 (GENDER = male); women were coded as 2 (GENDER = female). In statistics, qualitative description entails assigning numbers to classes of things. Those numbers, though—like 1 for male and 2 for female—are just substitute names for "male" and "female." They are not quantities. The average of the 1s and 2s in the column for GENDER in table 20.2 is 1.4, but that's no more helpful than knowing the average telephone number in New York City.

The second two variables are items that Kempton et al. (1995) used in their study of environmental values in America. My colleagues and I wanted to see if we could replicate their results. These ordinal variables are responses, on a scale of 1 to 5, to two statements:

Americans are going to have to drastically reduce their level of consumption over the next few years.
    <1> strongly disagree
    <2> disagree
    <3> neutral
    <4> agree
    <5> strongly agree

Environmentalists wouldn't be so gung-ho if it were their jobs that were threatened.
<1> strongly disagree
<2> disagree
<3> neutral
<4> agree
<5> strongly agree

I've labeled the responses to the two items REDUCE and GUNGHO in table 20.2. Notice that these two items are sort of opposites. The more you agree with REDUCE, the *stronger* your support for environmentalist issues is likely to be. But the more you agree with GUNGHO, the *weaker* your support for environmentalist issues is likely to be. If we want bigger numbers, like 4 and 5, always to stand for support of environmentalism and smaller numbers, like 1 and 2, always to stand for lack of support, then we have to transform the data for GUNGHO so that they run in the same direction as the data for REDUCE. We can easily do that in any statistics package.

This is a very important part of univariate analysis—getting the data into the computer in just the right form.

Variables 4 and 5, AGE (the respondent's age) and EDUC (the respondent's level of education), are interval. (They are really ratio variables, but recall from chapter 2 that ratio variables are conventionally referred to as "interval.") For AGE, we simply asked respondents "How old are you?" Here is the question from the survey that produced the data for EDUC:

What is the highest grade of school or year in college you yourself completed?

None	0
Elementary	01
Elementary	02
Elementary	03
Elementary	04
Elementary	05
Elementary	06
Elementary	07
Elementary	08
High School	09
High School	10
High School	11
High School	12
College—one year	13
College—two years	14
College—three years	15
College—four years	16
Some Graduate School	17
Graduate/Prof. Degree	18

FREQUENCY DISTRIBUTIONS

Tables 20.3a–e show the raw data from table 20.2 transformed into a set of **frequency distributions**. I used SYSTAT® to produce tables 20.3a–e, but any program will do.

Using a Distribution Table

One thing to look for in a frequency distribution is variability. If a variable has no variability, then it is simply not of any further interest. If everyone in this sample of

Table 20.3a Frequency Table of the Variable GENDER

Count	Cum. count	Percent	Cum. percent	Variable GENDER
18	18	60	60	Male
12	30	40	100	Female

Table 20.3b Frequency Table of the Variable AGE

Count	Cum. count	Percent	Cum. percent	Variable AGE
1	1	3.3	3.3	20
1	2	3.3	6.7	21
2	4	6.7	13.3	24
2	6	6.7	20.0	25
1	7	3.3	23.3	31
1	8	3.3	26.7	34
1	9	3.3	30.0	35
1	10	3.3	33.3	37
2	12	6.7	40.0	38
1	13	3.3	43.3	41
2	15	6.7	50.0	46
1	16	3.3	53.3	47
1	17	3.3	56.7	49
1	18	3.3	60.0	51
1	19	3.3	63.3	52
3	22	10.0	73.3	53
1	23	3.3	76.7	54
1	24	3.3	80.0	56
1	25	3.3	83.3	57
1	26	3.3	86.7	60
2	28	6.7	93.3	67
1	29	3.3	96.7	69
1	30	3.3	100.0	78

Table 20.3c Frequency Table of the Variable EDUC

Count	Cum. count	Percent	Cum. percent	Variable EDUC
1	1	3.3	3.3	5
1	2	3.3	6.7	10
8	10	26.7	33.3	12
2	12	6.7	40.0	13
7	19	23.3	63.3	14
3	22	10.0	73.3	15
3	25	10.0	83.3	16
5	30	16.7	100.0	18

Table 20.3d Frequency Table of the Variable REDUCE

Count	Cum. count	Percent	Cum. percent	Variable REDUCE
5	5	16.7	16.7	2
1	6	3.3	20.0	3
13	19	43.3	63.3	4
11	30	36.7	100.0	5

Table 20.3e Frequency Table of the Variable GUNGHO

Count	Cum. count	Percent	Cum. percent	Variable GUNGHO
4	4	13.3	13.3	1
9	13	30.0	43.3	2
5	18	16.7	60.0	3
11	29	36.7	96.7	4
1	30	3.3	100.0	5

respondents were the same gender, for instance, we wouldn't use GENDER in any further analysis. Looking carefully at the frequency distribution is your first line of defense against wasting a lot of time on variables that don't vary.

We see from table 20.3a that 60% of the sample are men. Table 20.3b shows that age is pretty evenly distributed. Table 20.3c shows that two-thirds of the sample (20 out of 30) had more than a high school education and that 5 of the 30 had graduate degrees. Most people (24 out of 30) agreed or strongly agreed with the statement that Americans are going to have to reduce consumption drastically in the coming years (table 20.3d).

People were pretty evenly split, though, on whether environmentalists would be so gung-ho if their jobs were threatened (table 20.3e): 13 people either disagreed or strongly disagreed with that sentiment, and 12 people either agreed or strongly agreed (5 were neutral).

Frequency distributions give you hints about how to collapse variables. With 609 respondents in the full survey, we had plenty of responses to all possible answers for the question about reducing consumption. But with a sample of just 30 responses in table 20.2 above, we didn't get anyone who said they strongly disagreed with the statement that Americans are going to have to drastically reduce their consumption in the coming years.

You can see this in the far right-hand column of table 20.3d. If all we had were these 30 cases, we'd want to create a three-category variable—disagree, neutral, and agree—by collapsing the data for REDUCE into (1) the 5 people who answered 2 (disagree); (2) the 1 person who answered 3 (neutral); and (3) the 24 people who answered 4 or 5 (agree and strongly agree).

It's not always obvious how to group data. In fact, it's often better not to. Look at table 20.3c. Only 2 people in our sample of 30 had less than 12 years of education. We could conveniently group those 2 people into a category called "less than high school." There is a bulge of 8 people who had 12 years of education (they completed high school), but then we see just 2 people who reported 1 year of college and 7 people who reported 2 years of college. That bulge of 7 respondents might be people who went to a community college. We might group those two sets of people into a category called "up to 2 years of college."

Those three people in table 20.3c who reported 4 years of college form an obvious class ("finished college"), and so do the five people who reported having a graduate or professional degree that required more than 4 years of college. But what do we do with those three people who reported 3 years of college? We could lump them together with the three respondents who finished college, but we could also lump them with the nine people who reported 1 or 2 years of college.

The problem is, we don't have any iron-clad decision rule that tells us how to lump data into categories. We don't want to maintain a separate category of just three respondents (the people who reported 3 years of college), but we don't know if they "belong" (in some socially important sense) with those who had some college or with those who completed college.

I recommend *not* grouping interval-level data unless you really have to. No matter which decision you make about those three people who reported 3 years of college in table 20.3c, you're turning an interval-level variable (years of education) into an ordinal-level variable (less than high school, high school, etc.). As you saw with earlier, with the variables HOWLONG and KNOW in the Mexico City study, there are times when this is a good idea, but trading interval for ordinal measurement means throwing away data. You need a really good reason to do that.

MEASURES OF CENTRAL TENDENCY

Once we have the data laid out and a feel for what's in there, we can start describing the variables. The first thing to do is get some overall measure of the "typical" value for each variable. This is called a measure of **central tendency**.

The three most widely used measures of central tendency are the **mode**, the **median**, and the **mean**. All these get packaged together in everyday speech as some kind of "average," but we have to be more precise in data analysis. Each measure of central tendency carries important information about the values of a variable.

Here are the definitions for each of these measures of central tendency:

1. *The mode is the attribute of a variable that occurs most frequently.* The mode can be found for nominal-, ordinal-, and interval-level variables, but it is the only measure of central tendency available for nominal variables.
2. *The median is the midpoint in a distribution above and below which there are an equal number of scores in a distribution.* The median can be found for ordinal- and interval-level variables.
3. *The mean, or the average, is the sum of the individual scores in a distribution, divided by the number of scores.* The mean can be found for ordinal- and interval-level variables.

CENTRAL TENDENCY: THE MODE

The mode is the attribute of a variable that occurs most frequently. Technically, the mode is not calculated; it is observed. You find it by simply looking at the data and seeing which attribute of a variable occurs the most. In table 20.3b, we see that the modal value for education is 12 years (there are 8 out of 30 cases). This tells us that finishing high school is the most common level of education in our sample of 30 respondents.

All variables (nominal, ordinal, and interval) have modal values, but nominal variables can *only* have modal values. In table 20.3a, for example, we see that there are 18 men (GENDER = 1) and 12 women (GENDER = 2). The mode for gender, then, is male for this sample of 30 (box 20.1). (The mode, by the way, was female for the full survey of 609 respondents. When you work with small samples, fluctuations of this magnitude are normal.)

Many distributions have more than one mode, and bimodal distributions are quite common. In a rural community that has experienced a lot of out-migration, for example, the age structure is likely to be bimodal: There are young people hanging around who aren't old enough to leave and old people who can't find work in the city because of their age.

Using the Mode

The mode is often said to be the weakest measure of central tendency, but it's very useful when you want to make a statement about a prominent qualitative attribute of a

BOX 20.1

REPORTING THE MODE

The mode can also be reported in terms of percentages or as ratios. With 12 women and 18 men, women are 12/30 = .40 of our sample and the ratio of men to women is 18/12 = 1.5, while the ratio of women to men is 12/18 = .67. Reporting that "there were 1.5 men for every woman in this survey" is the same as saying that "60% of the respondents were men." Reporting that "there were .67 women for every man in this survey" is the same as saying that "40% of the respondents were women."

group. "More people profess to be Buddhist in this prefecture of Japan than profess any other religion" is such a statement.

The mode is also a good common-sense alternative to the sometimes unrealistic quality of the mean. Saying that "the modal family size is 4 people" makes a lot more sense than saying that "the average family size is 3.81 people"—even if both statements are true.

CENTRAL TENDENCY: THE MEDIAN

The median is the point in a distribution above and below which there are an equal number of scores in a distribution. If you've ever taken a standardized test like the ACT, SAT, or GRE and scored in 86th percentile, then 14% of the scores were higher than yours (.86 + .14 = 1.0).

Ten percent of scores in a list are below the 10th percentile and 90% are above it. The 25th percentile is called the **first quartile** and the 75th percentile is the **third quartile**. The difference between the values for the 25th and 75th percentiles is known as the **interquartile range** and is a measure of dispersion for ordinal and interval-level variables. (More on measures of dispersion later.)

The median is the 50th percentile. It can be used with ranked or ordinal data and with interval- or ratio-level data. For an *odd number* of unique observations on a variable, the median score is $(n + 1)/2$, where n is the number of cases in a distribution and the scores are arranged in order.

Suppose we ask nine people to tell us how many brothers and sisters they have, and we get the following answers:

$$0 \quad 0 \quad 1 \quad 1 \quad 1 \quad 1 \quad 2 \quad 2 \quad 3$$

The median observation is 1 because it is the middle score—there are four scores on either side of it, $(n + 1)/2 = 5$, and we see that the median is the fifth case in the series, once the data are arranged in order.

Often as not, of course, as with the data on those 30 respondents from the green survey shown in table 20.2, you'll have an *even number* of cases. Then the median is the average of $n/2$ and $(n/2 + 1)$, or the midpoint between the *two* middle observations, once the data are arranged in order. I asked 16 undergraduate students "How long do you think you'll live?" Here are the responses:

$$70 \quad 73 \quad 75 \quad 75 \quad 79 \quad 80 \quad 80 \quad 83 \quad 85 \quad 86 \quad 86 \quad 87 \quad 87 \quad 90 \quad 95 \quad 96$$

$n/2 = 8$ and $n/2 + 1 = 9$, so the median is 84, midway between the two middle observations, 83 and 85. (By the way, if the two middle observations had been, say, 83, then the midpoint between them would be 83.)

The Median of Grouped Data

A lot of data are reported in intervals, or groups. For example, some people are uncomfortable with a straightforward question like "How much money do you make?" so researchers often ask something like:

Now we'd like to get an idea of about how much you earn each year. Do you earn:
(1) less than $10,000 per year?
(2) $10,000 or more but less than $20,000 per year?
(3) $20,000 or more but less than $30,000 per year?
(4) $30,000 or more but less than $40,000 per year?
(5) $40,000 or more but less than $50,000 per year?

and so on. This produces **grouped data**. In table 20.3b, the two middle scores for AGE are 46 and 47, so the median is 46.5. Table 20.4 shows the data on AGE from table 20.3b, grouped into 10-year intervals. To find the median in grouped data, use the formula for finding any percentile score in a distribution of grouped data:

$$PS = L + i \left\{ \frac{n - C}{f} \right\}$$ **Formula 20.1**

where:

PS   is the percentile score you want to calculate;
L   is the true lower limit of the interval in which the percentile score lies;
n is the case number that represents the percentile score;
C   is the cumulative frequency of the cases up to the interval *before* the one in which the percentile score lies;
i is the interval size; and
f is the count, or *frequency*, of the interval in which the median lies.

Table 20.4   Frequency Table of the Grouped Variable AGE

Count	Cum. count	Variable AGE
6	6	20–29
6	12	30–39
5	17	40–49
8	25	50–59
5	30	60+

In applying formula 20.1 to the data in table 20.4, the first thing to do is calculate n. There are 30 cases and we are looking for the score at the 50th percentile (the median), so n is $(30)(.50) = 15$. We are looking, in other words, for a number *above which* there are 15 cases and *below which* there are 15 cases. Looking at the data in table 20.4, we see that there are 12 cases up to 39 years of age and 17 cases up to 49 years of age. So, C is 12, and the median case lies somewhere in the 40–49 range.

The true lower limit, L, of this interval is 39.5 (midway between 39 and 40, the boundary of the two groups), and the interval, i, is 10 years. Putting all this into the formula, we get:

$$PS = 39.5 + \left\{ 10 \frac{15 - 12}{5} \right\} = 39.5 + 10(.6) = 45.5$$

So, the median age for the grouped data on 30 people is 45.5 years. Notice that: (1) The median for the *ungrouped* data on AGE in table 20.3b is 46.5, so in grouping the data we lose some accuracy in our calculation; and (2) None of the respondents in table 20.3b actually reported a median age of 45.5 or 46.5.

I've given you this grand tour of the median as a specific percentile score because I want you to understand the conceptual basis for this statistic. I'm going to do the same thing for all the statistical procedures I introduce here and in the next two chapters. Once you understand the concepts behind these statistics (the median, the standard deviation, z-scores, chi-square, t-tests, and regression), you should do all future calculations by computer. It's not just easier to calculate statistics by computer—it's more accurate. You're less likely to make mistakes in recording data on a computer and when you do make mistakes (I make them all the time), it's easier to find and fix them. Just think of how easy it is to find spelling errors in a document when you use a word processor.

CENTRAL TENDENCY: THE MEAN

The **arithmetic mean**, or the average, is the *sum of the individual scores in a distribution, divided by the number of scores*. The formula for calculating the mean is:

$$\bar{x} = \Sigma \ x/n \qquad \text{Formula 20.2}$$

where $\bar{x}$ (read: x-bar) is the mean, $\Sigma \ x$ means "sum all the values of x" and n is the number of values of x. To calculate the mean, or average age of the 30 respondents whose data are shown in table 20.2, we add up the 30 ages and divide by 30. The mean age of these 30 respondents is 45.033 years. (We use $\bar{x}$ when we refer to the mean of a sample of data; we use the Greek letter μ when we refer to the mean of an entire population.)

The formula for calculating the *mean of a frequency distribution* is:

$$\bar{x} = \Sigma \ fx/n \qquad \text{Formula 20.3}$$

where $\Sigma \ fx$ is the sum of the attributes of the variable times their frequencies.

Table 20.5 shows the calculation of the mean age for the frequency distribution shown in table 20.3b.

Calculating the Mean of Grouped Data

Table 20.6 shows the calculation of the mean for the grouped data on AGE in table 20.4. When variable attributes are presented in ranges, as in the case here, we take the midpoint of the range.

Note the problem in taking the mean of the grouped data in table 20.6. If you go back to table 20.3b, you'll see that all six of the people who are between 20 and 29 are really between 20 and 25. Counting them all as being 25 (the midpoint between 20 and 29) distorts the mean.

Also, there are five people over 60 in this data set: one who is 60, two who are 67, and one each who are 69 and 78. *Their* average age is 68.2, but they are all counted as being just 60 + in table 20.4. In calculating the mean for these grouped data, I've assigned the

Table 20.5   Calculating the Mean for the Data in Table 20.3b

Count (f)	AGE (x)	fx
1	20	20
1	21	21
2	24	48
2	25	50
1	31	31
1	34	34
1	35	35
1	37	37
2	38	76
1	41	41
2	46	92
1	47	47
1	49	49
1	51	51
1	52	52
3	53	159
1	54	54
1	56	56
1	57	57
1	60	60
2	67	134
1	69	69
1	78	78

$$\sum fx = 1{,}351$$

$$\sum fx/n = 1{,}351/30 = 45.033$$

Table 20.6   Calculating the Mean for the Frequency Table of the Grouped Variable AGE

AGE range	Midpoint (x)	f	fx
20–29	25	6	150
30–39	35	6	210
40–49	45	5	225
50–59	55	8	440
60 +	65	5	325

$$n = 30 \qquad \sum fx = 1{,}350$$
$$\bar{x} = 1{,}350/30$$
$$= 45.00$$

midpoint to be 65, *as if the range were 60–69*, even though the actual range is 60–78, and the real midpoint of the 60 + category is

$$(60 + 67 + 67 + 69 + 78)/5 = 68.2$$

If you have grouped data, however, it will usually be because the data were collected in grouped form to begin with. In that case, there is no way to know what the real range or the real midpoint is for the 60+ category, so we have to assign a midpoint that conforms to the midpoints of the other ranges. Applying the midpoint for all the other classes, the midpoint for the 60+ category would be 65, which is what I've done in table 20.6.

You can see the result of all this distortion: The grouped data have a mean of 45.00, while the ungrouped data have a calculated mean of 45.033. In this case, the difference is teeny, but it won't always be that way. If you collect data in groups about interval variables like age, you can never go back and see how much you've distorted things. So, to repeat: It's always better to collect interval data at the interval level, if you can, rather than in grouped form. You can group the data later, during the analysis, but you can't "ungroup" them if you collect data in grouped form to begin with.

A Mathematical Feature of the Mean

The arithmetic mean has an important feature: *The sum of the deviations from the mean of all the scores in a distribution is zero.* While the median and the mean are both midpoints in sets of scores, the mean is the point in a distribution at which the two halves balance each other out. You can see this in table 20.7, which shows data from 10 countries on the percentage of women over the age of 15 who are illiterate. This feature of the mean figures prominently in the calculation of variance, which is coming up in the section on measures of dispersion.

Table 20.7 Data on Female Illiteracy in 10 Countries (from Table 20.8) Showing How the Sum of the Deviations from the Mean of a Distribution Is Zero

Country	FEMILLIT	Score − Mean $x - \bar{x}$
El Salvador	18.6	18.6 − 13.9 = 4.7
Iran	20.7	20.7 − 13.9 = 6.8
Latvia	0.2	0.2 − 13.9 = −13.7
Namibia	11.1	11.1 − 13.9 = −2.8
Panama	6.6	6.6 − 13.9 = −7.3
Slovenia	0.3	0.3 − 13.9 = −13.6
Suriname	7.4	7.4 − 13.9 = −6.5
Armenia	1.4	1.4 − 13.9 = −12.5
Chad	48.5	48.5 − 13.9 = 34.6
Ghana	24.2	24.2 − 13.9 = 10.3
	$\sum x = 139$ $\bar{x} = 139/10 = 13.9$	$\sum (x - \bar{x}) = 0.00$

Scores below the mean:	Scores above the mean:
−13.7	4.7
−2.8	6.8
−7.3	34.6
−13.6	10.3
−6.5	−12.5
Total deviation below the mean = −56.4	Total deviation above the mean = 56.4

The data in table 20.7 are a random sample of the data in table 20.8. That table shows some **social indicators** for 50 randomly selected countries around the world. We'll be using the data in table 20.8 as we go along in the next two chapters (box 20.2).

SHAPE: VISUALIZING DISTRIBUTIONS

A really good first cut at understanding whether data are normal or skewed is to lay them out graphically. This is easy to do with any of the full-featured statistics programs out there these days. I'll show you six ways to lay out your data: bar graphs and pie charts for nominal and ordinal variables; stem-and-leaf plots, box-and-whisker plots, histograms, and frequency polygons for interval variables.

Table 20.8 Some Social Indicators for 50 Randomly Selected Countries

Country	LEXMALE	LEXFEM	INFMORT	MFRATIO	TFR	FEMILLIT	PCGDP
Albania	74.2	80.4	14.2	97	1.85	14.7	3,451
Argentina	72.5	80.0	12.0	96	2.16	2.4	7,705
Armenia	71.3	77.7	22.2	87	1.79	1.4	2,651
Austria	78.2	83.2	4.1	95	1.41		44,087
Bahamas	72.3	78.1	7.9	96	1.95	3.02	1,087
Brunei	75.5	80.5	5.3	107	1.95	7.8	38,417
Cameroon	52.0	53.4	79.8	100	4.20	23.1	1,044
Cape Verde	69.6	74.9	21.4	92	2.52	24.7	3,235
Chad	48.7	51.3	129.9	99	5.78	48.5	692
Chile	76.2	82.3	6.5	98	1.89	2.9	7,884
China	72.3	75.9	20.4	108	1.79	14.1	3,915
Congo	53.5	55.5	77.5	100	3.92	14.1	2,666
Ecuador	72.9	78.9	17.6	100	2.38	6.9	3,700
El Salvador	67.5	77.0	17.5	89	2.22	18.6	4,005
Equatorial Guinea	50.9	53.3	90.9	98	5.08	14.3	8917
Gambia	55.7	59.2	72.2	98	4.64	58.4	442
Ghana	57.1	59.0	67.0	103	4.00	24.2	675
Hungary	69.2	77.4	6.0	90	1.42	0.8	13,413
Iran	71.1	74.1	24.2	103	1.74	20.7	4,966
Ireland	78.1	82.9	4.2	100	1.92		46,826
Japan	80.1	87.2	3.1	95	1.27		37,052
Kenya	56.3	57.5	57.2	100	4.54	13.5	994
Laos	65.3	68.4	41.3	100	3.19	36.2	904
Latvia	68.7	78.1	8.3	85	1.48	0.2	11,300
Lesotho	46.9	46.6	60.7	89	3.05	3.6	591
Liberia	58.7	61.5	87.7	99	4.69	52.3	216
Maldives	71.5	74.9	18.1	102	1.94	1.8	4,054
Mongolia	65.1	71.2	37.3	98	1.92	1.1	1,584
Namibia	61.6	62.5	27.2	97	3.07	11.1	3,682
Nepal	67.2	69.0	35.8	99	2.66	64.0	443
Netherlands	78.5	82.6	4.3	98	1.77		44,122
Nicaragua	71.5	77.8	18.1	98	2.55	29.9	1,041
Pakistan	67.6	68.3	57.4	106	3.58	63.0	1,029
Panama	73.8	79.1	15.7	102	2.41	6.6	7,613
Poland	72.3	80.4	6.2	93	1.29	0.3	10,790
Romania	70.3	77.2	12.9	95	1.35	1.5	7,782
Samoa	69.8	76.0	19.5	109	3.55	1.1	3,189
Senegal	55.5	58.8	55.7	98	4.50	61.9	1,003
Slovenia	75.4	82.6	3.6	95	1.47	0.3	24,613
South Africa	51.8	53.8	37.3	97	2.42	11.7	5,014
Spain	78.6	84.7	3.8	97	1.56	2.0	29,898
Sri Lanka	71.3	78.6	14.2	797	2.22	7.9	1,776
Sudan	58.3	61.4	61.9	101	3.70	40.6	1,512
Suriname	66.5	73.7	20.5	100	2.29	7.4	6,546
Switzerland	80.2	84.7	3.9	95	1.49		60,805
Tanzania	57.4	59.1	55.2	99	5.30	20.9	563
Togo	62.3	65.7	65.7	98	3.87	43.0	394
United Arab Emir.	77.3	79.5	9.0	205	1.88	14.4	46,601
Uruguay	73.7	80.7	11.5	93	2.03	1.3	9,320
Zambia	48.7	50.0	78.4	100	5.34	18.8	1,175

LEXMALE and LEXFEM are the life expectancies, at birth, for children born during 2010–2015. SOURCE: United Nations Department of Economic and Social Affairs/Population Division, Population Estimates and Projections Section. http://esa.un.org/unpp/index.asp?panel=2.

INFMORT is the number of children who die, per 1,000 born, during the first year of life. SOURCE: United Nations Department of Economic and Social Affairs/Population Division 35 *World Population Prospects: The 2008 Revision.* Table A18, for 2010–2015. http://www.un.org/esa/population/publications/wpp2008/wpp2008_highlights.pdf.

MFRATIO is the number of males per 100 females in , 2010–2015. SOURCE: United Nations Department of Economic and Social Affairs/Population Division 35 *World Population Prospects: The 2008 Revision.* Table A1. http://www.un.org/esa/population/publications/wpp2008/wpp2008_highlights.pdf.

TFR, or total fertility rate, is an estimate of the number of children a girl born during 2010–2015 will bear if current fertility patterns holds and she lives through her entire child-bearing years. SOURCE: United Nations Department of Economic and Social Affairs/Population Division 35 *World Population Prospects: The 2008 Revision.* Table A15. http://www.un.org/esa/population/publications/wpp2008/wpp2008_highlights.pdf.

FEMILLIT is the percentages of women, >15 years of age who are illiterate. SOURCE: UNESCO Institute for Statistics, assessment of July 2002, supplemented by UNESCO Statistical Yearbook 1999. http://www.un.org/Depts/unsd/social/literacy.htm. Data file "Illiteracy rate and illiterate population, 15 years and older" at: http://www.uis.unesco.org/ev.php?ID=5794_201&ID2=DO_TOPIC.

PCGDP is the per capita gross domestic product in 2010. SOURCE: International Monetary Fund. World Economic Outlook Database, April 2009. http://www.imf.org/external/pubs/ft/weo/2009/01/weodata/index.aspx.

THE OUTLIER PROBLEM

The mean is one of the all-time great statistics, but it has one very important drawback: In small samples, it's heavily influenced by special cases, called **outliers**, and even in large samples, it's heavily influenced by big gaps in the distribution of cases. The median, however, is not as strongly affected by extreme scores. In table 20.8, for example, the mean per capita GDP is $10,908, while the median is just $3,808. Take out Liberia (with $216 PCGDP) and Switzerland (with $68,805) and the mean drops 7.5% to $10,091, while the median remains at $3,808.

When interval data (like life expectancy) are normally distributed, the mean is the best indicator of central tendency. When interval data are highly skewed (as is often the case with income), the median may be a better indicator of central tendency. You absolutely must get a feel for the **shape of distributions** to understand what's going on.

Bar Graphs and Pie Charts

Bar graphs and **pie charts** are two popular ways to graph the distribution of nominal and ordinal variables. Figure 20.1 shows bar graphs for two of the variables in table 20.2: GENDER and GUNGHO. Figure 20.2 shows the pie charts for the same variables. Notice that in the bar charts, the bars don't touch one another. This indicates that the data are nominal or ordinal and not continuous.

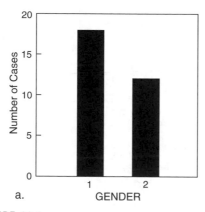
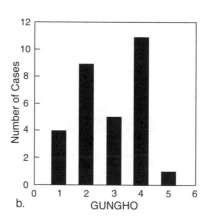

FIGURE 20.1.
Bar charts for the variables GENDER and GUNGHO in table 20.2.

The categories of the variables are shown along the horizontal axis of the bar graph. The horizontal, or x-axis, is also called the **abscissa**. The number of each category is shown on the left vertical axis. The vertical, or y-axis, is also called the **ordinate**. You can show the percent of each category on the y-axis instead.

In figure 20.1a, men are labeled 1 and women are labeled 2. Notice that it makes no

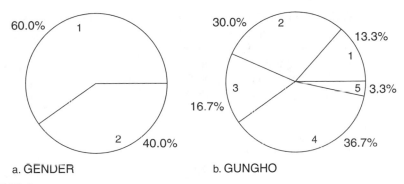

FIGURE 20.2.
Pie charts for the variables GENDER and GUNGHO in table 20.2.

difference whether we put the bar for men or the bar for the women on the left or the right when we graph GENDER. There is no order implied in the attributes of a nominal variable. When we graph ordinal variables, however, like GUNGHO, the order of the bars becomes important.

Stem-and-Leaf Plots

I like to start visualizing interval data by running **stem-and-leaf plots** and **box plots**. Figure 20.3 shows a stem-and-leaf plot for the variable MFRATIO in table 20.8.

Inspection of table 20.8 confirms that the lowest value for this variable is 85 men per 100 women (in Latvia). The "stem" in the stem-and-leaf plot is 85, and the 0 next to it is the "leaf." There are two cases of 93 men per 100 women (Poland and Uruguay), so there are two 0s after the 93 stem. The M in figure 20.3 stands for the median, or the 50th percentile (it's 98), and the Hs indicate the lower hinge and the upper hinge, or the 25th and the 75th percentiles. The two cases below 89 and the three cases above 107 are techni-cally considered outliers. This variable looks like it's pretty normally distributed, with a hump of cases in the middle of the distribution and tails going off in both directions.

Distributions Again

We can check to see if the variable is, in fact, normally distributed or skewed by evalu-ating the distribution. That's where box plots come in.

Just as a refresher, back in chapter 6, on sampling theory, we looked at some basic *shapes* of distributions: skewed to the right, skewed to the left, bimodal, and normal. I have shown them again in figure 20.4, but this time notice the mode, the median, and the mean:

1. the mode, the median, and the mean are the same in the normal distribution;
2. the mean is pulled to the left of the median in negatively skewed distributions;
3. the mean is pulled to the right of the median in positively skewed distributions; and
4. some distributions are bimodal, or even multimodal. In these cases, you need to calcu-late two or more means and medians because the global mean and median give you a distorted understanding of the distribution.

Box-and-Whisker Plots

Stem-and-leaf plots give you exact values for the median, the hinges of the interquartile range, and the cases in the tails of a distribution. Box-and-whisker plots (or, simply, **box**

Stem and Leaf Plot of variable: MFRATIO, N = 50
              Minimum: 85.000
              Lower hinge: 95.000
              Median: 98.000
              Upper hinge: 100.000
              Maximum: 205.000

              85   0
              87   0
* * * Outside Values * * *
              89   00
              90   0
              92
              93   00
              95H   00000
              96   00
              97   00000
              98M   00000000
              99   0000
              100H   00000000
              101   0
              102   00
              103   00
              106   0
              107   0
* * * Outside Values * * *
              108   0
              109   0
              205   0

FIGURE 20.3.
Stem-and-leaf plot for the variable MFRATIO in table 20.8.

plots) throw out the details and show you just the shape of a distribution. Together, the quantitative data from a stem-and-leaf plot and the purely qualitative image of a box plot give you a lot of useful information.

Figure 20.5 shows the box plots for MFRATIO (with and without the one enormous outlier), TFR, and PCGDP. The boxes themselves show you the interquartile range—the middle 50% of the cases. The vertical line that marks off the box at the left is the 25th percentile (the lower hinge) of the plot; the vertical line that marks off the box at the right is the 75th percentile (the upper hinge).

The vertical line inside the box is the median, or the 50th percentile. Fifty percent of the cases in the distribution fall to the right of the median line and 50% fall to the left.

The whiskers in box plots extend *one-and-a-half times the interquartile range* from the lower and upper hinges of the box, or about 2.7 standard deviations from the mean when data are normally distributed. Cases outside that range are *outliers* and are marked by an asterisk. Cases that are more than *three times the interquartile range* from the hinges are *extreme outliers* and are marked by a little circle.

The box plot for MFRATIO (figure 20.5a) shows that, in 50% of the countries of the world, the interquartile range is a very, very narrow band, with very, very short whiskers,

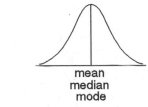

mean
median
mode

a. Normal distribution

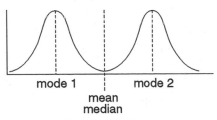

mode 1   mode 2
mean
median

b. Bimodal distribution

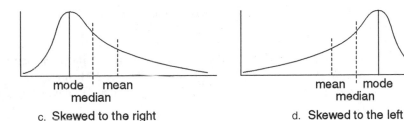

mode ' mean   mean ' mode
median   median

c. Skewed to the right   d. Skewed to the left

FIGURE 20.4.
Some basic types of distributions.

a few outliers, and one extreme outlier. In fact, the interquartile range for this variable is between 95 and 100 men per 100 women. The mean is 99.9 and the median is 98.0—and skewed to the left.

Figure 20.5b shows MFRATIO with the extreme outlier excluded. Now the mean and the median for this variable are almost identical (97.8 and 98.0) and the distribution looks more-or-less normal. This is *not* a case for throwing out outliers. It *is* a case for examining every variable in your data set to get a feel for the distributions as the first step in analysis.

Figure 20.5c shows that 50% of the countries in the world had a very low per capita gross national product. There is almost no whisker to the left of the box, indicating that only a very few countries were below the interquartile range. There is a long whisker to the right of the box, as well as three outliers (asterisks) and three extreme outliers (circles). The circle farthest to the right is Switzerland, with over $68,000 in per capita GNP. To put this in perspective, Liechtenstein had the world's highest PCGDP in 2010, at around $85,000. The United States was tenth, at $47,500 and Zimbabwe was at the bottom, at around $200 (https://www.cia.gov/library/publications/the-world-factbook/rank order/ 2004rank.html). The shape of the box-and-whisker plot in figure 20.5c reflects the fact that the world's population is divided between the haves and the have-nots.

Finally, figure 20.5d shows that total fertility in 2010 ranged from about 1.3 and about 5.8, and that there were no outliers (that is, no cases beyond the whiskers). This is another

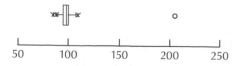

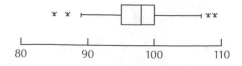

a. MFRATIO (all values)

b. MFRATIO (excluding the extreme outlier)

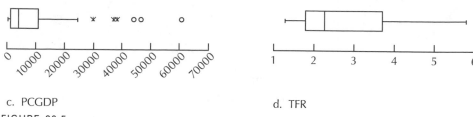

c. PCGDP

d. TFR

FIGURE 20.5.

Box-and-whisker plots for three social indicators of 50 countries (from table 20.8).

variable that looks like it might be normally distributed, but notice that the median (the midline in the box) is off center to the left. The mean for TFR is 2.74, higher than the median, which is 2.26. We need more information. We'll get it with the next set of data visualizations.

Histograms and Frequency Polygons

Two other graphic methods are useful in univariate analysis: **histograms** and **frequency polygons.** Frequency polygons are line drawings made by connecting the tops of the bars of a histogram and displaying the result without the bars. What you get with both graphs is pure shape—less information than you get with box plots or stem-and-leaf plots but easily interpreted. Figure 20.6 shows the histograms and frequency polygons for TFR, MFRATIO, and PCGDP.

These visualizations for MFRATIO nail down what we know from the box-plot of that variable: Most countries are in a narrow range, but a few are real outliers. The histogram/polygon for PCGDP removes all doubt about the shape of this variable: It is skewed to the right, with most countries at the bottom and a long tail of countries to the right.

And we can now see that the variable TFR is distributed bimodally. Countries across the world tend to have either low TFR (22 have a TFR of 2 or below) or high TFR (18 have a TFR of 3 and up), with just 10 countries in the middle range, between 2 and 3.

Bimodal Distributions

Obviously, if we calculate the median or mean for a bimodal variable, we won't get a realistic picture of the central tendency in the data. To understand TFR better, I divided the data into cases at or above the median of 2.26 and cases below it. Then I calculated the means and medians for each of the two sets of data and ran the frequency polygons.

Figure 20.7a shows the frequency polygon for the cases up to the median; figure 20.7b shows the polygon for the cases above the median. Now it looks as though we may have

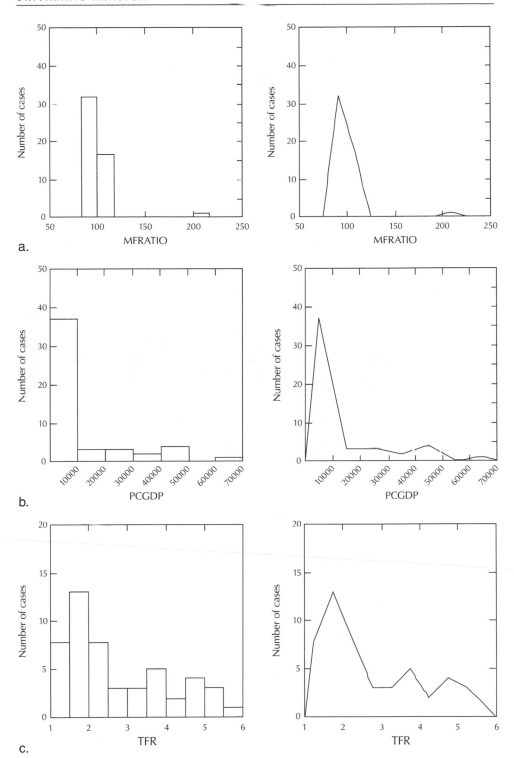

FIGURE 20.6.
Histograms (left) and frequency polygons (right) for MFRATIO, TFR, and PCGDP in table 20.8.

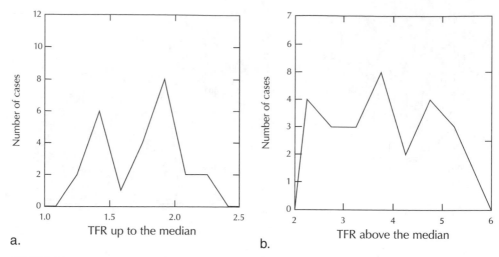

FIGURE 20.7.

Frequency polygons for TFR (in table 20.8) above the median (a) and below the median (b).

a multimodal distribution. This might be the result of sampling error. I tested this by running the same analysis on the 195 countries of the world for which we have data on TFR. The frequency polygon for this analysis is shown in figure 20.8. Compare the shape of this graph to the one for TFR on the lower right in figure 20.6. This tells us that (1) the results we got by analyzing the 50-country sample are a good reflection of the data from which the sample was drawn, and (2) TFR really is bimodal.

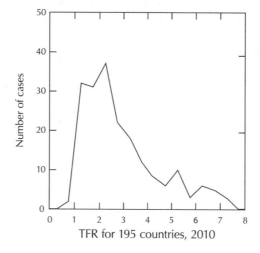

FIGURE 20.8.

Frequency polygon for TFR for 195 countries of the world, 2010.

SOURCE: UN Department of Economic and Social Affairs, Population Division (2007). United Nations World Population Prospects: 2006 Revision, table A15. http://www.un.org/esa/population/publications/wpp2006/WPP2006_Highlights_rev.pdf.

Bimodal and multimodal distributions are everywhere. Figure 20.9 shows the frequency polygon for LEXFEM, female life expectancy in table 20.8. This is no sampling

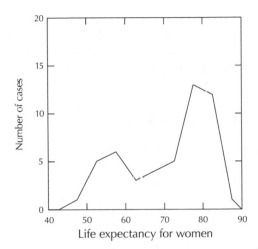

FIGURE 20.9.
Frequency polygon for LEXFEM in table 20.8.

artifact, either. The bulge on the right covers countries in which women can expect to live, on average, about 80 years. The bulge on the left covers countries in which women can expect to live, on average, just 61 years.

The moral is: Examine the frequency distribution for each of your variables. For interval and ordinal variables, find out if the distributions around the mean or median are symmetrical. If the distributions *are* symmetrical, then the mean is the measure of choice for central tendency. If the distributions are skewed, then the median is the measure of choice. And if the distributions are bimodal (or multimodal), then do a much closer examination and find out what's going on.

MEASURES OF DISPERSION I: RANGE AND INTERQUARTILE RANGE

After central tendency and shape, the next thing we want to know about data is something about how homogeneous or heterogeneous they are—that is, something about their **dispersion** or variation The concept of dispersion is easily seen in the following example. Here are the ages of two groups of five people:

| Group 1: | 35 | 35 | 35 | 35 | 35 |
| Group 2: | 35 | 75 | 15 | 15 | 35 |

Both groups have an average age of 35, but one of them obviously has a lot more variation than the other. Consider MFRATIO in table 20.8. The mean number of males to 100 females in the world was 99.9 in 2010. One measure of variation in this mean across the 50 countries in our sample is the range. Inspecting the column for MFRATIO in table 20.8, we see that Latvia had the lowest ratio, with 85 males for every 100 females, and the United Arab Emirates (UAE) had the highest ratio, with 205. The range, then, is $205 - 85 = 120$. The range is a useful statistic, but it is affected strongly by extreme scores. Without the UAE, the range is 24, a drop of nearly 80%.

The **interquartile range** avoids extreme scores, either high or low. The 75th percentile for MFRATIO is 100 and the 25th percentile is 95, so the interquartile range is $100 - 95$

= 5. This tightens the range of scores, but sometimes it *is* the extreme scores that are of interest. The interquartile range of freshmen SAT scores at major universities tells you about the middle 50% of the incoming class. It doesn't tell you if the university is recruiting athletes whose SAT scores are in the bottom 25%, the middle 50%, or the top 25% of scores at those universities (see Klein 1999).

MEASURES OF DISPERSION II: VARIANCE AND THE STANDARD DEVIATION

The best-known and most-useful measure of dispersion for a sample of interval data is the **standard deviation**, usually written just *s* or *sd*. The *sd* is a *measure of how much, on average, the scores in a distribution deviate from the mean score*. It is gives you a feel for how homogeneous or heterogeneous a population is. (We use *s* or *sd* for the standard deviation of a *sample*; we use the lowercase Greek sigma, σ, for the standard deviation of a population.)

The *sd* is calculated from the **variance**, written s^2, which is the *average squared deviation from the mean* of the measures in a set of data. To find the variance in a distribution: (1) Subtract each observation from the mean of the set of observations; (2) Square the difference, thus getting rid of negative numbers; (3) Sum the differences; and (4) Divide that sum by the sample size. Here is the formula for calculating the variance:

$$s^2 = \frac{\Sigma (x - \bar{x})^2}{n - 1}$$
 Formula 20.4

where s^2 is the variance, *x* represents the raw scores in a distribution of interval-level observations, $\bar{x}$ is the mean of the distribution of raw scores, and *n* is the total number of observations.

Notice that we need to square the difference of each observation from the mean and *then* take the square root later. As we saw in calculating the mean, $\Sigma (x - \bar{x}) = 0$. That is, the simple sum of all the deviations from the mean is zero. Squaring each $x - \bar{x}$ gets rid of the negative numbers.

Variance describes in a single statistic how homogeneous or heterogeneous a set of data is, and by extension, how similar or different are the units of analysis described by those data. Consider the set of scores in table 20.2 on the variable called REDUCE. These scores show people's support for the idea that "Americans are going to have to drastically reduce their consumption over the next few years." Suppose that for each level of education, you could predict the level of support for that attitudinal item about cutting back on consumption. If you could do this in 100% of all cases, then you would speak of "explaining all the variance" in the dependent variable.

I've never encountered this strength of association between two variables in the social sciences, but some things come pretty close, and in any event, the principle is what's important.

The standard deviation, s, is the square root of the variance, s^2. The formula for the standard deviation is:

$$s = \sqrt{\frac{\Sigma (x - \bar{x})^2}{n - 1}}$$
 Formula 20.5

Table 20.9 shows how to calculate the standard deviation for the data on female illiteracy in table 20.7. The sum of the $(x - \bar{x})^2$ is 2,008.86 and $n = 10$.

Substituting in the formula for standard deviation, we get:

Table 20.9   How to Calculate the Standard Deviation for the Data on Female Illiteracy in Table 20.7

COUNTRY	FEMILLIT	Score – Mean $x - \bar{x}$	
El Salvador	18.6	$(18.6 - 13.9)^2 =$	22.09
Iran	20.7	$(20.7 - 13.9)^2 =$	46.24
Latvia	0.2	$(0.20 - 13.9)^2 =$	187.69
Namibia	11.1	$(11.1 - 13.9)^2 =$	7.84
Panama	6.6	$(6.6 - 13.9)^2 =$	53.29
Slovenia	0.3	$(0.3 - 13.9)^2 =$	184.96
Suriname	7.4	$(7.4 - 13.9)^2 =$	42.25
Armenia	1.4	$(1.4 - 13.9)^2 =$	156.25
Chad	48.5	$(48.5 - 13.9)^2 =$	1,197.16
Ghana	24.2	$(24.2 - 13.9)^2 =$	109.09
		$\sum (x - \bar{x})^2 = 2,008.86/9$	
		$s = \sqrt{2008.86} = 14.94$	

$$s = \sqrt{\frac{2008.86}{9}} = 14.94$$

If we were reporting these data, we would say that "the average percentage of adult female illiteracy is 13.9 with *sd* 14.9."

For grouped data, we take the midpoint of each interval as the raw score and use formula 20.6 to calculate the standard deviation:

$$s = \sqrt{\frac{\sum f(x - \bar{x})^2}{n - 1}} \qquad \textbf{Formula 20.6}$$

Table 20.10 shows the procedure for calculating the standard deviation for the grouped data in table 20.4. We know from table 20.6 that $\bar{x} = 45$ for the data in table 20.4.

Table 20.10   Calculating the Standard Deviation for the Grouped Data in Table 20.4

AGE X	f	Midpoint x	$x - \bar{x}$		$(x - \bar{x})^2$	$f(x - \bar{x})^2$
20–29	6	25	$25 - 45 =$	-20	400	2,400
30–39	6	35	$35 - 45 =$	10	100	600
40–49	5	45	$45 - 45 =$	0	0	0
50–59	8	55	$55 - 45 =$	10	100	800
60+	5	65	$65 - 45 =$	20	400	2,000
	$\sum x = 30$		$\sum(x - \bar{x}) = 0$		$\sum f(x - \bar{x})^2 = 5,800$	

Substituting in formula 20.6 for *sd*, we get:

$$s = \sqrt{\frac{5,800}{29}} = 14.14$$

and we report that "the mean age is 45.00, *sd* 14.14." For comparison, the mean age and *sd* of the 30 ages (the ungrouped data) in table 20.3b are 45.033 and 15.52. Close, but not dead on.

Are these numbers describing ages and percentages of illiteracy large, or small, or about normal? There is no way to tell except by comparison across cases. By themselves, numbers like means and standard deviations simply describe a set of data. But in comparative perspective, they help us produce theory; that is, they help us develop ideas about what causes things, and what those things, in turn, cause. We'll compare cases when we get to bivariate analysis in the chapter coming up next (**Further Reading:** exploring data).

THE LOGIC OF HYPOTHESIS TESTING

One thing we can do, however, is test whether the *mean of a sample of data*, $\bar{x}$, *is likely to represent the mean of the population*, μ, from which the sample was drawn. We'll test whether the mean of FEMILLIT in table 20.7 is likely to represent the mean of the population of the 50 countries in table 20.8. To do this, we will use the logic of **hypothesis testing**. This logic is used very widely—not just in the social sciences, but in all probabilistic sciences, like meteorology and genetics.

The key to this logic is the statement that we can test whether the mean of the sample *is likely to represent* the mean of the population. Here's how the logic works.

1. First, we set up a **null hypothesis**, written H_0, which states that there is no difference between the sample mean and the mean of the population from which the sample was drawn.
2. Then we set up the **research hypothesis** (also called the **alternative hypothesis**), written H_1, which states that, in fact, the sample mean and the mean of the population from which the sample was drawn are different.
3. Next, we decide whether the research hypothesis is only about **magnitude** or is **directional.** If H_1 is only about magnitude—that is, it's **nondirectional**—then it can be stated just as it was in (2) above: The sample mean and the mean of the population from which the sample was drawn are different. Period.

If H_1 is directional, then it has to be stated differently: The sample mean is [bigger than] [smaller than] the mean of the population from which the sample was drawn. This decision determines whether we will use a **one-tailed** or a **two-tailed** test of the null hypothesis.

To understand the concept of one- and two-tailed tests, suppose you have a bell curve that represents the distribution of means from many samples of a population. Sample means are like any other variable. Each sample has a mean, and if you took thousands of samples from a population you'd get a distribution of means (or proportions). Some would be large, some small, and some exactly the same as the true mean of the population. The distribution would be normal and form a bell curve like the one in figure 20.4 and in figure 6.1.

The unlikely means (the very large ones and the very small ones) show up in the narrow area under the tails of the curve, while the likely means (the ones closer to the true mean of the population) show up in the fat, middle part. In research, the question you want to answer is whether the means of variables from one, particular sample (the one *you've* got) probably represent the tails or the middle part of the curve.

Hypothesis tests are two tailed when you are interested only in whether the magnitude of some statistic is significant (i.e., whether you would have expected that magnitude by chance). When the direction of a statistic is not important, then a two-tailed test is called for.

As we'll see in chapter 21, however, when you predict that one of two means will be higher than the other another (like two tests taken a month apart), you would use a one-tailed test. After all, you'd be asking only whether the mean was likely to fall in one tail of the normal distribution. Look at appendix A carefully. Scores significant at the .10 level for a two-tailed test are significant at the .05 level for a one-tailed test.

4. Finally, we determine the **alpha level**, written α, which is the **level of significance** for the hypothesis test. Typically, alpha is set at the .05 level or at the .01 level of significance What this means is that if a mean or a proportion from a sample is likely to occur more than alpha—say, more than 5% of the time—then we *fail to reject the null hypothesis*.

And conversely: If the mean or a proportion of a sample is likely to occur by chance less than alpha, then we *reject the null hypothesis*. Alpha defines the **critical region** of a sampling distribution—that is, the fraction of the sampling distribution small enough to reject the null hypothesis.

In neither case do we prove the research hypothesis, H_1. We either reject or fail to reject the null hypothesis. Failing to reject the null hypothesis is the best we can do, since, in a probabilistic science, we can't ever really prove any research hypothesis beyond any possibility of being wrong (box 20.3).

BOX 20.3

ON BEING SIGNIFICANT

By custom—and only by custom—researchers generally accept as statistically significant any outcome that is not likely to occur by chance more than 5 times in 100 tries. This *p* value, or probability value, is called the .05 level of significance. A *p* of .01 is usually considered very significant, and .001 is often labeled highly significant.

Many researchers use asterisks instead of *p* values in their writing to cut down on number clutter. A single asterisk signifies a *p* of .05, a double asterisk signifies a value of .01 or less, and a triple asterisk signifies a value of .001 or less. If you read: "Men were more likely than women** to report dissatisfaction with local schoolteacher training," you'll know that the double asterisk means that the difference between men and women on this variable was significant at the .01 level or better.

And remember: Statistical significance is one thing, but substantive significance is another matter entirely. In exploratory research, you might be satisfied with a .10 level of significance. In evaluating the side effects of a medical treatment, you might demand a .001 level—or an even more stringent test of significance.

Type I and Type II Errors

There is one more piece to the logic of hypothesis testing. The choice of an alpha level lays us open to making one of two kinds of error—called, conveniently, **Type I errors** and **Type II errors.**

If we reject the null hypothesis when it's really true, that's a Type I error. If we fail to reject the null hypothesis when it is, in fact, false, that's a Type II error.

Suppose the government of a small Caribbean island wants to increase tourism. To do this, somebody suggests implementing a program to teach restaurant workers to wash their hands after going to the bathroom and before returning to work. The idea is to lower the incidence of food-related disease and instill confidence among potential tourists. The program is implemented in a small number of restaurants as a pilot study and you get to evaluate the results.

The null hypothesis is that the average amount of food-borne disease will be the same in restaurants that don't implement the program and in restaurants that do. The data show that H_0 is false at the .05 level of significance. This is great news. The program works. But suppose you reject the null hypothesis when it's really true—the program really is useless. Your Type I error (accepting H_0 when it's false) sets off a flurry of activity: The Ministry of Health requires restaurant owners to shell out for the program. And for what?

The obvious way to guard against this Type I error is to raise the bar and set alpha at, say, .01. That way, a Type I error would be made once in 100 tries, not 5 times in 100. But you see immediately the cost of this little ploy: It increases dramatically the probability of making a Type II error—not rejecting H_0 when we should do exactly that. In this case— where H_0 being false means that the program works but you don't detect that—the result is that you place people at greater risk of food-borne disease.

In a probabilistic science, we are always in danger of making one or the other of these errors. Do we try to avoid one kind more than the other? It depends on what's at stake. A Type I error at the .01 level for an HIV test means that 1 person out of 100 is declared HIV-free when they are really HIV-positive. How big a sample do you need to get that error level down to one out of a thousand? This is the kind of question answered by **power analysis**, which we'll look at in chapter 21.

SO, WHAT ABOUT THE MEAN OF FEMILLIT?

As you know from chapter 6, statistics (like the mean) vary from sample to sample and how much they vary depends on: (1) the size of the sample and (2) the amount of actual variation in the population from which you take your sample. The average amount of error we make in estimating a parameter from sample statistics is called the **standard error**, or *SE*, of the statistic. The standard error of the mean, *SEM*, is the standard deviation, *sd*, divided by the square root of the sample size, *n*:

$$SEM = \frac{sd}{\sqrt{n}}$$
Formula 20.7

We can calculate the *SEM* for the sample of 10 countries on the variable FEMILLIT. From table 20.9, we know that $\bar{x} = 13.9\%$ and $sd = 14.94$, so:

$$SEM = \frac{14.94}{\sqrt{10}} = 4.72$$

Now, knowing the *SEM*, we can ask whether the mean of the sample of 10 cases in table 20.7 (13.9%) can be distinguished statistically from the mean of the population of countries in table 20.8. Since this is a small sample, we can test this using a Student's *t* distribution, which I introduced in chapter 6. We have data on the percentage of adult female illiteracy for 45 of the 50 countries in table 20.8, and the mean for *those* data is 18.16%. The formula for calculating *t*, when the parameter, μ, is known, is:

$$t = \frac{\bar{x} - \mu}{SEM}$$
Formula 20.8

So, for the sample of 10 countries on FEMILLIT,

$$t = (13.9 - 18.16)/4.72 = -0.996$$

We can test whether the value of t is statistically significant by referring to the t table in appendix B. To use appendix B, we need to know: (1) how many degrees of freedom we have and (2) whether we want a one- or a two-tailed test (box 20.4).

BOX 20.4

DEGREES OF FREEDOM

To understand the concept of degrees of freedom, suppose I give you a jar filled with thousands of beans numbered from 1 to 9 and ask you to pick two that sum to 10. If you pick a 4 on the first draw, then you must pick a 6 on the next; if you pick a 5 on the first draw, then you must pick another 5; and so on. This is an example of one degree of freedom, because after the first draw you have no degrees of freedom left.

Suppose, instead, that I ask you to pick four beans that sum to 25. In this example, you have three degrees of freedom. No matter what you pick on the first draw, there are lots of combinations you can pick on the next three draws and still have the beans sum to 25. But if you pick a 6, a 9, and a 7 on the first *three* draws, then you must pick a 3 on the last draw. You've run out of degrees of freedom.

For a one-sample, or univariate t-test, the degrees of freedom, or *df*, is simply $n-1$. For the sample of 10 representing FEMILLIT there are $10-1 = 9$ degrees of freedom.

Testing the Value of *t*

We'll use a two-tailed test for the problem here because we are only interested in whether our sample mean, 13.9, is significantly *different from*, the population mean of 18.16. Thus, the null hypothesis is that 13.9% could be found just by chance if we drew this sample of 10 countries from a population of countries where the mean is 18.16%.

Looking at the values in appendix B, we see that any t value above 2.262 is statistically significant at the .05 level with 9 degrees of freedom for a two-tailed test. With a t of .996 (we only look at the absolute value and ignore the minus sign), we can not reject the null hypothesis. The true mean percentage of female illiteracy rates across the 50 countries of the world is statistically indistinguishable from 13.9%.

Testing the Mean of Large Samples

Another way to see this is to apply what we learned about the normal distribution in chapter 6. We know that in any normal distribution for a large population, 68.26% of the statistics for estimating parameters will fall within one standard error of the actual parameter; 95% of the estimates will fall between the mean and 1.96 standard errors; and 99% of the estimates will fall between the mean and 2.58 standard errors.

In table 20.2, I showed you a sample of the data from the study that Ryan, Borgatti, and I did on attitudes about environmental activism (Bernard at al. 2009). In that study, we interviewed a random sample of 609 adults from across the United States. The mean age of respondents in our sample was 44.21, *sd* 15.75. Only 591 respondents agreed to tell us their age, so the standard error of the mean is:

$$15.75 \; / \; \sqrt{591} \; = \; 0.648$$

Because we have a large sample, we can calculate the 95% confidence limits using the z distribution in appendix A:

$$44.21 \pm 1.96(0.648) =$$
$$44.21 - 1.27 = 42.94 \text{ and } 44.21 + 1.27 = 45.48$$

In other words, we expect that 95% of all samples of 591 taken from the millions of adults in the United States will fall between 42.94 and 45.48. As we saw in chapter 6, these numbers are the 95% **confidence limits** of the mean. As it happens, we know from the U.S. Census Bureau that the real average age of the adult (over-18) population in the United States in 1997 (when the survey was done) was 44.98.

Thus: (1) the sample statistic ($\bar{x} = 44.21\%$) and (2) the parameter ($\mu = 44.98\%$) *both* fall within the 95% confidence limits, and we *can not reject the null hypothesis* that our sample comes from a population whose average age is equal to 44.98%.

MORE ABOUT z-SCORES

As we saw also in chapter 6 on sampling, every real score in a distribution has a z-score, also called a **standard score**. A z-score tells you how far, in standard deviations, a real score is from the mean of the distribution. The formula for finding a z-score is:

$$z = \frac{(\text{raw score} - \bar{x})}{SD}$$

Formula 20.9

To find the z-scores of the data on FEMILLIT in table 20.7, subtract 13.9 (the mean) from each raw score and divide the result by 14.94 (the sd). Table 20.11 shows these z-scores.

Table 20.11   z-Scores for the Data on FEMILLIT in Table 20.7

Country	Score − Mean $x - \bar{x}$	z-Score
El Salvador	18.6 − 13.9 = 4.7	4.7/14.9 = 0.3154
Iran	20.7 − 13.9 = 6.8	6.8/14.9 = 0.4564
Latvia	0.2 − 13.9 = −13.7	−13.7/14.9 = −0.9195
Namibia	11.1 − 13.9 = −2.8	−2.8/14.9 = −0.1879
Panama	6.6 − 13.9 = −7.3	−7.3/14.9 = −0.4899
Slovenia	0.3 − 13.9 = −13.6	−13.6/14.9 = −0.9128
Suriname	7.4 − 13.9 = −6.5	−6.5/14.9 = −0.4362
Armenia	1.4 − 13.9 = −12.5	−12.5/14.9 = −0.8389
Chad	48.5 − 13.9 = 34.6	34.6/14.9 = 2.3221
Ghana	24.2 − 13.9 = 10.3	10.3/14.9 = 0.6913

Why Use Standard Scores?

There are several advantages to using standard scores rather than raw scores. First of all, although raw scores are always in specialized units (percentages of people, kilos of meat, hours of time, etc.), standard scores measure the difference, in standard deviations, between a raw score and the mean of the set of scores. A z-score close to 0 means that the raw score was close to the average. A z-score that is close to plus-or-minus 1 means that the raw score was about 1 sd from the mean, and so on.

What this means, in practice, is that when you standardize a set of scores, you create a scale that lets you make comparisons *within* chunks of your data.

For example, we see from table 20.11 that the female illiteracy rates for Ghana and

Chad are 24.2% and 48.5%, respectively. One of these raw numbers is about double the other. This tells us something, but the z-score tells us more. The percentage of female illiteracy in Ghana is almost twice the mean of 13.9 for these 10 countries but it's only about .69 standard deviations above the mean. The percentage for Chad is about 3.5 times the mean, but it is 2.32 sd above the mean. Ghana's score on this indicator of human development is within striking distance of the world mean, but Chad's is way out on the right-hand tail of the distribution.

A second advantage of standard scores over raw measurements is that standard scores are independent of the units in which the original measurements are made. This means that you can compare the relative position of cases across different variables.

Medical anthropologists measure variables called "weight-for-length" and "length for age" in the study of nutritional status of infants across cultures. Linda Hodge and Darna Dufour (1991) studied the growth and development of Shipibo Indian children in Peru. They weighed and measured 149 infants, from newborns to 36 months in age.

By converting all measurements for height and weight to z-scores, they were able to compare their measurements of the Shipibo babies against standards set by the World Health Organization (Frisancho 1990) for healthy babies. The result: By the time Shipibo children are 12 months old, 77% of boys and 42% of girls have z-scores of -2 or more on *length-for-age*. In other words, by a year old, Shipibo babies are more than 2 sd under the mean for babies who, by this measure, are healthy.

By contrast, only around 10% of Shipibo babies (both sexes) have z-scores of -2 or worse on *weight-for-length*. By a year, then, most Shipibo babies are clinically "stunted" but they are not clinically "wasted." This does not mean that Shipibo babies are small but healthy. Infant mortality is as high as 50% in some villages, and the z-scores on all three measures are similar to scores found in many developing countries where children suffer from malnutrition (box 20.5).

BOX 20.5

ON SCORING 1.96 ON THE SATS

z-scores do have one disadvantage: They can be downright unintuitive. Imagine trying to explain to people who have no background in statistics why you are proud of having scored a 1.96 on the SAT. Getting a z-score of 1.96 means that you scored almost 2 sd above the average and that only 2.5% of all the people who took the test scored higher than you did. If you got a z-score of $-.50$ on the SAT, that would mean that about a third of all test takers scored lower than you did. That's not too bad, but try explaining why you're not upset about getting a minus score on any test.

This is why **T-scores** (with a capital *T*—not to be confused with Student's *t*) were invented. The mean of a set of z-scores is always 0 and its standard deviation is always 1. *T*-scores are linear transformations of z-scores. For the SAT and GRE, the mean is set at 500 and the standard deviation is set at 100. A score of 400 on these tests, then, is one standard deviation below the mean; a score of 740 is 2.4 sd above the mean (Friedenberg 1995:85).

THE UNIVARIATE CHI-SQUARE TEST

Finally, **chi-square** (often written χ^2) is an important part of univariate analysis. It is a test of whether the distribution of a series of counts is likely to be a chance event. The formula for χ^2 is:

$$\chi^2 = \sum \frac{(O-E)^2}{E} \qquad \text{Formula 20.10}$$

where O represents the observed number of cases and E represents the number of cases you'd expect, *ceteris paribus*, or "all other things being equal."

Suppose that among 14 families there are a total of 42 children. If children were distributed equally among the 14 families, we'd expect each family to have three of them. Table 20.2 shows what we would expect and what we might find in an actual set of data. The χ^2 value for this distribution is 30.65.

Table 20.12   Chi-Square for a Univariate Distribution

Expected number of children per family

Family #

1	2	3	4	5	6	7	8	9	10	11	12	13	14	Total
3	3	3	3	3	3	3	3	3	3	3	3	3	3	42

Observed number of children per family

Family #

1	2	3	4	5	6	7	8	9	10	11	12	13	14	Total
0	0	5	5	5	6	6	0	0	3	1	0	6	5	42

(observed − expected)²

9	9	4	4	4	9	9	9	9	0	4	9	9	4

$\dfrac{\text{(observed − expected)}^2}{\text{expected}}$

3	3	1.33	1.33	1.33	3	3	3	3	0	1.33	3	3	1.33

$$\chi^2 = \sum \frac{\text{(observed − expected)}^2}{\text{Expected}} = 3 + 3 + 1.33 + 1.33 + \ldots 1.33 = 30.65$$

Finding the Significance of χ^2

To determine whether this value of χ^2 is statistically significant, first calculate the degrees of freedom (abbreviated *df*) for the problem. For a univariate table:

$$df = \text{the number of cells, minus one}$$
$$\text{or } 14 - 1 = 13 \text{ in this case.}$$

Next, go to appendix C, which is the distribution for χ^2, and read down the left-hand margin to 13 *df* and across to find the *critical value* of χ^2 for any given level of significance. The levels of significance are listed across the top of the table. The greater the significance of a χ^2 value, the less likely it is that the distribution you are testing is the result of chance.

Considering the χ^2 value for the problem in table 20.12, the results look pretty significant. With 13 df, a χ^2 value of 22.362 is significant at the .05 level; a χ^2 value of 27.688 is significant at the .01 level; and a χ^2 value of 34.528 is significant at the .001 level.

With a χ^2 of 30.65, we can say that the distribution of the number of children across the 14 families is statistically significant at better than the .01 level, but not at the .001 level.

Statistical significance here means only that the distribution of number of children for these 14 families is not likely to be a chance event. Perhaps half the families happen to be at the end of their fertility careers and half are just starting. Perhaps half the families are members of a high-fertility ethnic group and half are not. The *substantive* significance of these data requires interpretation, based on your knowledge of what's going on, on the ground.

Univariate numerical analysis—frequencies, means, distributions, and so on—and univariate graphical analysis—histograms, box plots, frequency polygons, and so on—tell us a lot. Begin all analysis this way and let all your data and your experience guide you in their interpretation. It is not always possible, however, to simply scan your data and use univariate, descriptive statistics to understand the subtle relations that they harbor. That will require more complex techniques, which we'll take up in the next two chapters.

FURTHER READING

Cleaning data: Dijkers and Creighton (1994); Karmaker and Kwek (2007); Van den Broeck et al. (2005).

Exploring data: Hartwig and Dearing (1979); Pryjmachuk and Richards (2007); Tukey (1977).

Bivariate Analysis: Testing Relations

This chapter is about describing relations between pairs of variables—**covariations**—and testing the significance of those relations.

The *qualitative* concept of covariation creeps into ordinary conversation all the time: "If kids weren't exposed to so much TV violence, there would be less crime." Ethnographers also use the concept of covariation in statements like: "Most women said they really wanted fewer pregnancies, but claimed that this wasn't possible so long as the men required them to produce at least two fully grown sons to work the land." Here, the number of pregnancies is said to covary with the number of sons husbands say they need for agricultural labor.

The concept of *statistical* covariation, however, is more precise. There are two primary and two secondary things we want to know about a statistical relation between two variables:

The primary questions are these:

1. How big is it? That is, how much better could we predict the score of a dependent variable in our sample if we knew the score of some independent variable? Correlation coefficients answer this question.
2. Is the covariation due to chance, or is it statistically significant? In other words, is it likely to exist in the overall population to which we want to generalize? Statistical tests answer this question.

For many problems, we also want to know:

3. What is its direction? Is it positive or negative?
4. What is its shape? Is it linear or nonlinear?

Answers to these questions about *qualities* of a relationship come best from looking at graphs.

Testing for **statistical significance** is a mechanical affair—you look up, in a table, whether a statistic showing covariation between two variables is, or is not statistically significant. I'll discuss how to do this for several of the commonly used statistics that I introduce below. Statistical significance, however, does not necessarily mean substantive or theoretical importance. Interpreting the substantive and theoretical importance of statistical significance is anything but mechanical. It requires thinking. And that's *your* job.

THE *t*-TEST: COMPARING TWO MEANS

We begin our exploration of bivariate analysis with the two-sample *t*-test. In chapter 20, we saw how to use the one-sample *t*-test to evaluate the probability that the mean of a sample reflects the mean of the population from which the sample was drawn. The two-sample *t*-test evaluates whether the means of two independent groups differ on some variable. Table 21.1 shows some data that Penn Handwerker collected in 1978 from American and Liberian college students on how many children those students wanted.

Table 21.1 Number of Children Wanted (CW) by College Students in the United States and in Liberia

#	CW	Region	Sex	#	CW	Region	Sex	#	CW	Region	Sex
1	1	USA	M	29	0	USA	F	57	12	WA	M
2	3	USA	M	30	0	USA	F	58	12	WA	M
3	3	USA	M	31	0	USA	F	59	8	WA	M
4	3	USA	M	32	0	USA	F	60	6	WA	M
5	3	USA	M	33	1	USA	F	61	4	WA	M
6	3	USA	M	34	1	USA	F	62	4	WA	M
7	2	USA	M	35	2	USA	F	63	2	WA	M
8	2	USA	M	36	2	USA	F	64	3	WA	M
9	2	USA	M	37	2	USA	F	65	3	WA	M
10	2	USA	M	38	2	USA	F	66	4	WA	M
11	2	USA	M	39	2	USA	F	67	4	WA	M
12	2	USA	M	40	2	USA	F	68	4	WA	M
13	1	USA	M	41	2	USA	F	69	4	WA	M
14	6	USA	M	42	2	USA	F	70	3	WA	F
15	1	USA	M	43	2	USA	F	71	3	WA	F
16	1	USA	M	44	6	WA	M	72	3	WA	F
17	4	USA	M	45	4	WA	M	73	3	WA	F
18	0	USA	M	46	4	WA	M	74	7	WA	F
19	5	USA	F	47	4	WA	M	75	2	WA	F
20	4	USA	F	48	5	WA	M	76	4	WA	F
21	4	USA	F	49	5	WA	M	77	6	WA	F
22	4	USA	F	50	5	WA	M	78	4	WA	F
23	3	USA	F	51	5	WA	M	79	4	WA	F
24	2	USA	F	52	5	WA	M	80	4	WA	F
25	3	USA	F	53	7	WA	M	81	4	WA	F
26	0	USA	F	54	12	WA	M	82	4	WA	F
27	2	USA	F	55	6	WA	M	83	4	WA	F
28	0	USA	F	56	6	WA	M	84	4	WA	F

SOURCE: *Data Analysis with MYSTAT* by H. R. Bernard and W. P. Handerwerker, 1995. McGraw-Hill. Reproduced with permission of The McGraw-Hill Companies.

Table 21.2 shows the relevant statistics for the data in table 21.1. (I generated these with SYSTAT®, but you can use any statistics package.)

There are 43 American students and 41 Liberian students. The Americans wanted, on average, 2.047 children, 1.396 *sd*, *SEM* 0.213. The Liberians wanted, on average, 4.951 children, 2.387 *sd*, *SEM* 0.373.

Table 21.2 Descriptive Statistics for Data in Table 21.1

	CW-USA	CW-Liberia
N of cases	43	41
Minimum	0	2
Maximum	6	12
Mean	2.047	4.951
95% CI Upper	2.476	5.705
95% CI Lower	1.617	4.198
Standard Error	0.213	0.373
Standard Deviation	1.396	2.387

The null hypothesis, H_0, is that these two means, 2.047 and 4.951, come from random samples of the *same* population—that there is no difference, except for sampling error, between the two means. Stated another way, these two means come from random samples of two populations with identical averages. The research hypothesis, H_1, is that these two means, 2.047 and 4.951, come from random samples of truly different populations.

The formula for calculating t for two independent samples is:

$$t = \frac{\bar{x}_1 - \bar{x}_2}{\sqrt{s^2 \left(\frac{1}{n_1} + \frac{1}{n_2}\right)}}$$

Formula 21.1

That is, t is the difference between the means of the samples, divided by the fraction of the standard deviation, μ, of the total population, that comes from each of the two separate populations from which the samples were drawn. (Remember, we use Roman letters, like s, for sample statistics, and Greek letters, like μ, for parameters.) Since the standard deviation is the square root of the variance, we need to know the variance, μ^2, of the **parent population**.

The parent population is the general population from which the two samples were pulled. Our best guess at μ^2 is to pool the variances from the two samples:

$$s^2 = \frac{(n_1 - 1)\, s_1^{\,2} + (n_2 - 1)s_2^{\,2}}{n_1 + n_2 - 2}$$

Formula 21.2

which is very messy, but just a lot of arithmetic. For the data on the two groups of students, the **pooled variance** is:

$$s^2 = \frac{(43 - 1)1.396^2 + (41 - 1)2.387^2}{43 + 41 - 2} = \frac{81.85 + 227.91}{82} = 3.778$$

Now we can solve for t:

$$t = \frac{2.047 - 4.951}{\sqrt{3.778(.0477)}} = \frac{-2.904}{\sqrt{.180}} = \frac{-2.904}{.4243} = -6.844$$

Testing the Value of t

We can evaluate the statistical significance of t using appendix B. Recall from chapter 20 that we need to calculate the degrees of freedom and decide whether we want a one- or a two-tailed test to find the critical region for rejecting the null hypothesis. For a two-sample t-test, the degrees of freedom equals:

$$(n_1 + n_2) - 2$$

so there are $43 + 41 - 2 = 82$ degrees of freedom in this particular problem (box 21.1).

We'll use a two-tailed test for the problem here because we are only interested in the magnitude of the difference between the means, not its direction or sign (plus or minus). We are only interested here, then, in the **absolute value** of t, 6.844.

Looking at the values in appendix B, we see that any t-value above 3.291 is significant for a two-tailed test at the .001 level. Assuming that our samples represent the populations of American students and Liberian students, we'd expect the observed difference in the means of how many children they want to occur by chance less than once every thousand times we run this survey.

BOX 21.1

ONE- AND TWO-TAILED TESTS

To recap from chapter 20, if you test the possibility that one mean will be higher than another, then you need a one-tailed test. After all, you're only asking whether the mean is likely to fall in one tail of the t-distribution (see figure 6.7). With a one-tailed test, a finding of no difference (the null hypothesis) is equivalent to finding that you predicted the wrong mean to be the one that was higher. If you want to test only whether the two means are different (and not that one will be higher than the other), then you need a two-tailed test. In appendix B, as in appendix A, scores significant at the .10 level for a two-tailed test are significant at the .05 level for a one-tailed test; scores significant at the .05 level for a two-tailed test are significant at the .025 level for a one-tailed test, and so on.

ANALYSIS OF VARIANCE

A t-test measures the difference between two means. Analysis of variance, or ANOVA, is a technique that applies to a set of two or more means. Table 21.3 shows the scores for four groups of states in the United States (not including Washington, DC) on the percent-

Table 21.3 Percentage of Teenage Births in the 50 U.S. States

Northeast			Midwest			South			West	
	x_1	x_1^2		x_2	x_2^2		x_3	x_3^2		x_4	x_4^2
NY	7.0	49.00	KS	10.3	106.09	FL	10.9	118.81	NM	15.7	246.49
VT	7.6	57.76	SD	9.8	96.04	AR	14.6	213.16	OR	8.9	79.21
NJ	6.4	40.96	WI	8.7	75.69	KY	12.9	166.41	ID	9.1	82.81
PA	9.3	86.49	IA	8.7	75.69	LA	13.7	187.69	HI	8.5	72.25
MA	6.4	40.96	IN	11.2	125.44	MD	8.9	79.21	NV	10.8	116.64
NH	6.6	43.56	OH	11.0	121.00	MS	17.1	292.41	CO	9.7	94.09
ME	8.4	70.56	ND	8.0	64.00	AL	13.6	184.96	UT	6.9	47.61
CT	6.9	47.61	MI	10.1	102.01	DE	10.4	108.16	CA	9.5	90.25
RI	9.7	94.09	MN	7.1	50.41	GA	12.2	148.84	WY	11.8	139.24
			MO	11.0	121.00	OK	13.9	193.21	WA	8.4	70.56
			NE	8.6	73.96	VA	8.6	73.96	AZ	12.7	161.29
			IL	10.1	102.01	NC	11.7	136.98	AK	10.1	102.01
						WV	12.5	156.25	MT	9.7	94.09
						TN	13.2	172.24			
						SC	13.4	179.56			
						TX	13.5	182.25			

$\sum x_1 = 68.3$ $\sum x_2 = 114$ $\sum x_3 = 201.1$ $\sum x_4 = 133.4$

$\sum x_1^2 = 530.99$ $\sum x_2^2 = 1{,}113.34$ $\sum x_3^2 = 2{,}594.01$ $\sum x_4^2 = 1{,}431.51$

$n = 9$ $n = 12$ $n = 16$ $n = 13$

$\bar{x}_1 = 7.59$ $\bar{x} = 9.58$ $\bar{x} = 12.57$ $\bar{x} = 10.26$

$s_1^2 = 1.584$ $s_2^2 = 1.838$ $s_3^2 = 4.562$ $s_4^2 = 5.211$

SOURCE: U.S. Census Bureau, *Statistical Abstract of the United States, 2010*. Washington, DC, 2009, table 89, http://www.census.gov/compendia/statab/2010/tables/10s0089.pdf.

age of teenage births in 2007. Each group of states has a **mean percentage** of teenage births. The question we want to answer is: Are the differences among the means significantly different, at say, the .05 level?

To answer this question we will calculate the ratio of the **between-group variance**, $s_{between}^2$, to the **within-group variance**, s_{within}^2. The between-group and within-group variances sum to the **total variance**, s^2. We already know, from chapter 20, the formula for the total variance. Here it is again:

$$S^2 = \frac{\Sigma\,(x - \bar{x})^2}{n - 1}$$

Formula 21.3

where x represents the raw scores in a distribution of interval-level observations, $\bar{x}$ is the mean of the distribution of raw scores, and n is the total number of observations. So, to find the variance in a distribution: (1) subtract each observation from the mean of the set of observations; (2) square the difference (thus getting rid of negative numbers); (3) sum the squared differences (this is called the **sum of the squares**); and (4) divide that sum by the sample size, minus 1.

The variance is calculated from the sum of the squares, $\Sigma\,(x - \bar{x})^2$. Here is the formula for calculating the sum of the square directly from the data in table 21.3:

$$\Sigma\,x^2 - \frac{(\Sigma\,x)^2}{n}$$

Formula 21.4

At the bottom of table 21.3, I've calculated the four separate, or within-group, variances, using formula 21.3 above. Applying formula 21.4, the total sums of squares for the data in table 21.3 is:

$$530.99 + 1{,}122.30 + 2{,}596.01 + 1{,}396.54 - \frac{(68.3 + 115 + 201.1 + 131.8)^2}{50}$$

$$= 5{,}645.84 - \frac{266{,}462.24}{50} = 5{,}645.84 - 5{,}329.24 = 316.60$$

The formula for calculating the sum of the squares between groups is:

$$\Sigma\,\frac{(\Sigma\,x_{1...2...n})^2}{n_{1...2...n}} - \frac{(\Sigma\,x_{total})^2}{n_{total}}$$

Formula 21.5

Thus, the between-group sum of the squares is:

$$(68.3^2 / 9) + (115^2 / 12) + (20.1.1^2 / 16) + (131.8^2 / 13) - 8{,}367.005 =$$
$$518.32 + 1{,}102.08 + 2{,}527.58 + 1{,}336.25 - 5{,}329.24 = 154.99$$

And since:

within-group sum of squares =
total sum of squares − between-group sum of squares

the within-group sums of square is:

$$316.60 - 154.99 = 161.61$$

We can now calculate $s_{between}^2$, the between-group variance, and $s_{between}^2$, the within-group variance.

$$s_{between}^2 = \frac{\text{total between-group sums of squares}}{\text{the degrees of freedom between groups}}$$

and

$$s_{within}^2 = \frac{\text{total within-group sums of squares}}{\text{the degrees of freedom within groups}}$$

We compute the degrees of freedom between groups and the degrees of freedom within groups as follows:

$$df \text{ between groups} = \text{the number of groups} - 1$$
$$df \text{ within groups} = n - \text{the number of groups}$$

So, for the data in table 21.3, the df between groups is $4 - 1 = 3$, and the df within groups is $50 - 4 = 46$. Then:

$$\text{the between-group variance} = 154.99/3 = 51.66$$

and

$$\text{the within-group variance} = 161.61/46 = 3.51$$

We now have all the information we need to calculate the **F-ratio**, which is:

$$\frac{s_{between}^2}{s_{within}^2}$$

(The F statistic was named for Sir Ronald Fisher, who developed the idea for the ratio of the between-group and the within-group variances as a general method for comparing the relative size of means across many groups.) We calculate the ratio of the variances:

$$F = 51.66/3.51 = 14.78$$

(See box 21.2.)

BOX 21.2

ROUNDING ERROR VERSUS COMPUTER CALCULATIONS

If you run the ANOVA on a computer, using SYSTAT®or SPSS®, etc., you'll get a slightly different answer: 14.70. The difference (0.08) is due to rounding in all the calculations we just did. Computer programs may hold on to 12 decimal places all the way through before returning an answer. In doing these calculations by hand, I've rounded each step of the way to just two decimal places. Rounding error doesn't affect the results of the ANOVA calculations in this particular example because the value of the F statistic is so big. But when the value of the F statistic is below 5, then a difference of .08 either way can lead to errors of interpretation.

The moral is: Learn how to do these calculations by hand, once. Then, use a computer program to do the drudge work for you, once you know what you're doing.

Well, is 14.78 a statistically significant number? To find out, we go to appendix D, which shows the values of F for the .05 and the .01 level of significance. The values for the between-group *df* are shown across the top of appendix D, and the values for the within-group *df* are shown along the left side. Looking across the top of the table, we find the column for the between-group *df*. We come down that column to the value of the within-group *df*. In other words, we look down the column labeled 3 and come down to the row for 46.

There is no row for exactly 46 degrees of freedom for the within-group value, so we use the nearest value, which is for 40 *df*. We see that any F value greater than 2.84 is statistically significant at the .01 (that is, the 1%) level. The F value we got for the data in table 21.3 was a colossal 14.78. As it turns out, this is statistically significant beyond the .001 level.

Examples of ANOVA

Camilla Harshbarger (1986) tested the productivity—measured in average-bushels-per-hectare—of 44 coffee farmers in Costa Rica as a function of which credit bank they used or if they used no credit at all. This is the sort of problem that calls for ANOVA because Harshbarger had four different means—one for each of the three credit sources and one for farmers who chose not to use credit. The ANOVA showed that there was no significant difference in productivity in Harshbarger's sample, no matter where they got credit, or even if they didn't use credit.

Carole Jenkins (1981) surveyed 750 children in Belize for protein-calorie malnutrition (PCM). She had four means—one for each of the four ethnic groups (Creole, Mestizo, Black Carib, and Maya) in her research area. An analysis of variance showed that there was a very strong relationship between ethnic group and the likelihood of suffering from childhood PCM.

Sokolovsky et al. (1978) compared the average number of first-order relations and the average number of multiplex relations among three groups of psychiatric patients who were released to live in a hotel in midtown New York City. (First-order relations are primary relations with others; multiplex relations contain more than one kind of content, such as relations based on visiting and on who to borrow money from, for example.)

One group of patients had a history of schizophrenia with residual symptoms; a second group had a history of schizophrenia without residual symptoms; and the third group had no psychotic history. An ANOVA showed clearly that the average network size (both first-order and multiplex networks) was different among the three groups. From these data (and from field observation and in-depth interviews), Sokolovsky was able to draw strong conclusions about the ability of members of the three groups to cope with deinstitutionalization.

Whenever you observe three or more groups (age cohorts, members of different cultures or ethnic groups, people from different communities) and count anything (e.g., some behavior over a specific period of time, or the number of particular kinds of contacts they make, or the number of kilograms of fish they catch), then ANOVA is the analytic method of choice. If you are interested in the causes of morbidity, for example, you could collect data on the number of sick days among people in various social groups over a given period of time. Other dependent variables in which anthropologists are interested, and which are amenable to ANOVA, are things like blood pressure, number of minutes per day spent in various activities, number of grams of nutrients consumed per day, and scores on tests of knowledge about various cultural domains (plants, animals, diseases), to name just a few (box 21.3).

BOX 21.3

A FAMILY OF ANOVA TECHNIQUES

When there is one dependent variable (such as a test score) and one independent variable (a single intervention like the reading program), then no matter how many groups or tests are involved, a **one-way ANOVA** is needed. If more than one independent variable is involved (say, several competing new housing programs, and several socioeconomic backgrounds), and there is a single dependent variable (a reading test score), then **multiple-way ANOVA**, or **MANOVA**, is called for. When two or more dependent variables are correlated with one another, then **analysis of covariance**, or **ANCOVA** techniques are used.

DIRECTION AND SHAPE OF COVARIATIONS

As you can tell from my discussion of box plots and frequency polygons and such in chapter 20, I like to look at things like shape and direction—qualitative things—in connection with numerical results.

For example, the amount of cholesterol you have in your blood and the probability that you will die of a heart attack at any given age are **positive covariants**: The *more* cholesterol, the *higher* the probability.

By contrast, *the more education* you have, *the lower the probability that you smoke cigarettes*. Education and the probability of smoking cigarettes are **negative covariants**.

Some shapes and directions of bivariate relations are shown in the four **scatterplots** (also called **scattergrams**) of figure 21.1. Figure 21.1a is a plot of violent crimes and physicians per 100,000 people in each of the 50 states in the United States (not including Washington, DC). The dots are scattered haphazardly, and it's pretty obvious that there is *no relation* between these two variables.

Linear and Nonlinear Relations

Figure 21.1b shows the correlation between LEXFEM (life expectancy for women) and INFMORT (infant mortality) in table 20.8. This is a clear case of a **linear and negative relation** between two variables: The higher the score on one variable, the lower the score tends to be on the other. We see in figure 21.1b that in countries where women's life expectancy is high, infant mortality tends to be low, and vice versa.

By convention, the values of dependent variables are plotted on the Y axis, or **abscissa** of a scatterplot, and the values of independent variables are plotted on the X axis, or **ordinate**. Notice that in this case, it is not really clear which is the dependent and which is the independent variable. The relation between the two variables in figure 21.1b is strong and clear, but recall from chapter 2 that we need much more than a strong correlation to understand cause and effect.

Figure 21.1c shows the positive correlation between TFR and FEMILLIT in table 20.8 This is a clear case of a **linear and positive relation**: The higher the score on one variable, the higher the score tends to be on the other. So, the higher the percentage of female illiteracy, the higher the total fertility rate across the sample of countries.

Figure 21.1d is a plot of INFMORT and PCDGP in table 20.8. The dots in figure 21.1d

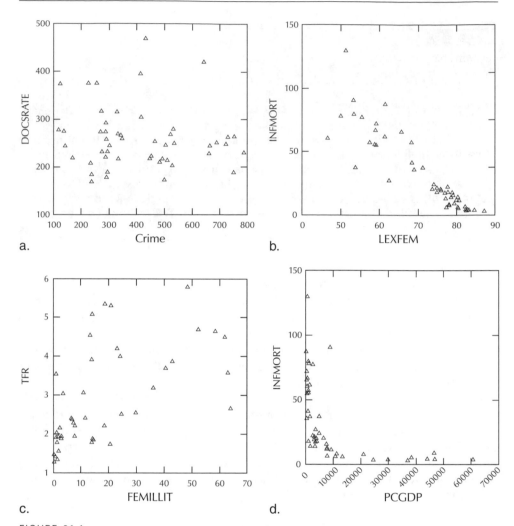

FIGURE 21.1.

Scatterplots of bivariate relations.

SOURCE: Figure 21.1a, U.S. Census Bureau, *Statistical Abstract of the United States, 2010*. Washington, DC, 2009, tables 159 and 297, http://www.census.gov/compendia/statab. Figures 21.1b–d, see sources for table 20.8.

are not scattered around randomly—*something* is clearly going on between these two variables. As the per capita GDP rises, the rate of infant mortality falls, but the *shape* of the relation is **nonlinear**.

Nonlinear relations are very common in the real world. The relation between age and the number of people one knows has a peaked shape, like an upside-down V. Early in life, the number of friends, kin, and acquaintances is small, but that number grows as you get older. This relation is linear and positive. The longer you live, the more people you get to know.

Up to a point. If you live long enough, a lot of the people you know start dying, and your network shrinks. There is a strong, negative relation between age and number of people in your network after age 70.

CROSS-TABS OF NOMINAL VARIABLES

Now that we've looked at shape and direction, let's get down to actually looking for relations between variables. We begin with nominal variables and move on to ordinal and then interval variables.

Table 21.4 shows an example of a 2 × 2 (read: two-by-two) **cross-tabulation table**, or **cross-tab**, of two nominal variables: family types (two parents with children and single parents) and race (black and white) in the United States in 2008. A 2 × 2 table is also called a **four-fold table**. Any table comparing data on two variables is called a **bivariate table**, but not all bivariate tables are 2 × 2, since variables can take more than just two values.

Table 21.4   A 2 × 2 Table of Household Type by Race in the United States in 2008 (in thousands)

	White	African American	Row totals
Two parents	22,857 (75.1%)	2,256 (40.3%)	25,113
Single parent	7,594 (24.9%)	3,347 (59.7%)	10,941
Column totals	30,451 (100%)	5,603 (100%)	36,054

SOURCE: U.S. Census Bureau, *Statistical Abstract of the United States, 2010*. Washington, DC, 2009, table 67, http://www.census.gov/compendia/statab/2010/tables/10s0067.pdf.

Conventions for Displaying Bivariate Tables

There are some easy-to-follow conventions for displaying tables like these. Table 21.4 is a complete table. The numbers at the margins—down the right-hand column and along the bottom row—are called, unsurprisingly, the **marginals**. The sum of the marginals down the right-hand side and the sum of the marginals across the bottom are identical, and the number in the lower-right-hand corner (36,054) is the total frequency of elements in the table.

I prefer to keep tables uncluttered and to show only the percentages in each cell and the *n* for each column. You get a better understanding of what's going on from percentages than from raw numbers in a table like this, and the interested reader can always calculate the *n* for each cell.

In bivariate tables, no matter what size (2 × 2, 3 × 2, or larger tables), the convention is to put the dependent variables in the rows and the independent variable in the columns. Then there's an easy rule to follow in reading a table: *percentage down the columns and interpret across the rows.* There are, of course, exceptions—they are, after all, conventions and not laws. When the independent variable has too many categories to fit on a narrow page, it makes sense to show the independent variables in the rows.

Percentaging down table 21.4, we see that 75.1% of white households with children had two parents in 2008, and 24.9% were headed by single parents. In black households with children, the percentages are 40.3% and 59.7%, respectively. *Interpreting across*, we see that 75.1% of white households with children had two parents in 2008 compared to 40.3% for black households. Among single-parent households, 24.9% were white and 59.7% were black. Interpreting the numbers in a cross-tab forces you to think about explanations. The probability of a child having two parents was much higher for white children in 2008 than it was for black children—about two-and-a-half times higher, in fact.

What's going on? As I explained in chapter 2, association between two variables does not, by itself, imply cause—no matter how strong the association. The dependent variable in table 21.4 is obviously family type. Nobody's skin color (which is, at bottom, what the so-called race variable is about in the United States) depends on whether they are a member of a two-parent or a one-parent family.

And clearly—and I mean absolutely, positively, no-fooling, clearly—being black did not cause anyone, not one single person, to be part of a single-parent household. Being a black man in the United States, however, means a high probability of attending poorly funded schools, and poor schooling produces severe disadvantage in the labor market. When men in the United States don't provide financial support, poor women are likely to turn to welfare.

Historically, welfare systems have punished women who have a live-in husband by lowering the women's allotments. Some women respond by maintaining single-parent households and some fraction of African American, single-parent families are caused by this sequence of events. There are, then, several **intervening** and **antecedent variables** that link being counted as black by the U.S. Census and being part of a single-parent household. (See figure 2.4 about intervening and antecedent variables.)

Some of the most interesting puzzles about human life involve understanding the role of intervening and antecedent variables—and figuring out which is which. Middle-aged men who drink at least six cups of coffee a day are more likely to have a heart attack than are men who don't drink coffee at all. Men who drink a lot of coffee, however, consume more alcohol, more saturated fats, and more cholesterol than men who don't drink coffee. The heavy coffee drinkers are less likely to exercise, more likely to smoke, and more likely to be impatient, aggravated people (the famous Type A personality). The jury is still out on how all these factors are related, but lots of researchers are trying to disentangle this problem (Ketterer and Maercklein 1991; Riksen et al. 2009).

Here's another one. Interethnic marriage often increases when tribal peoples move from rural villages to cities. One effect of this is that unilineal systems are under pressure to become bilateral over time. Is it just the lack of prospective mates from one's own ethnic group that causes this? Or is there something inherently unstable about unilineal kinship systems under urban conditions (see Clignet 1966; Feldman 1994)?

LAMBDA AND THE PRE PRINCIPLE

Table 21.5 is a hypothetical 2×2 table showing the breakdown, by gender, of adult monolingual Indians and adult bilingual Indian/Spanish speakers in a Mexican village.

Table 21.5 Monolingual and Bilingual Speakers, by Gender, in a Mexican Village, 1962

	Men	Women	Row totals
Bilingual	61 (82%)	24 (36%)	85
Monolingual	13 (18%)	42 (64%)	55
Column totals	74	66	140

old error = 55

new error = 13 + 24 = 37

$$\lambda = \frac{55 - 37}{55} = .33$$

I've included the marginals and the *n*s in the cells to make it easier to do the calculation here.

Reading across table 21.5, we see that 82% of the men were bilingual, compared to 36% of the women. Clearly, gender is related to whether someone is a bilingual Indian/ Spanish speaker or whether he or she is monolingual in the Indian language only.

Suppose that for the 140 persons in table 21.5 you were asked to guess whether they were bilingual or monolingual, but you didn't know their gender. The mode for the dependent variable in this table is "bilingual" (85 bilinguals compared to 55 monolinguals), so you should guess that everybody is bilingual. If you did that, you'd make 55 mistakes out of the 140 choices, for an error rate of 55/140, or 39%. We'll call this the **old error**.

Suppose, though, that you have all the data in table 21.5—you know the mode for gender as well as for bilingual status. Your best guess now would be that every man is bilingual and every woman is monolingual. You'd still make some mistakes, but fewer than if you just guessed that everyone is bilingual.

How many fewer? When you guess that every male is bilingual, you make exactly 13 mistakes, and when you guess that every female is monolingual, you make 24 mistakes, for a total of 37 out of 140 or 37/140 = 26%. This is the **new error**. The difference between the old error (39%) and the new error (26%), divided by the old error is the **proportionate reduction of error**, or **PRE**. Thus,

$$PRE = \frac{55 - 37}{55} = .33$$

This PRE measure of association for nominal variables is called **lambda**, written either λ or *L*. Like all PRE measures of association, lambda has the nice quality of being intuitively and directly interpretable. A λ of .33 means that if you know the scores on an independent variable, you can guess the scores on the dependent variable 33% more of the time than if you didn't know anything about the independent variable.

CHI-SQUARE

While λ demonstrates the intuitively compelling PRE principle, there are problems with it. There is no way to test whether any value of lambda shows a particularly strong or weak relationship between variables; it can take different values depending on whether you set up the dependent variable in the rows or the columns; and it can be very low, even when there is an intuitively clear association between nominal variables. Lambda for table 21.4, for example, is just 0.10—that is, if you guess that all white families with children in the United States have two parents and that all black families have one parent, you make 10% fewer errors than if you guess that all families have two parents.

With bivariate data on nominal variables, many researchers use χ^2 (chi-square). **Chi-square** tells you whether or not a relation exists between or among variables and it tells you the probability that a relation is the result of chance. But it is *not* a PRE measure of correlation, so it doesn't tell you the *strength* of association among variables.

The principal use of χ^2, then, is for testing the null hypothesis that there is no relation between two nominal variables. If, after a really good faith effort, we fail to accept the null hypothesis, we can reject it. Using this approach, we never prove anything using statistical tests like χ^2. We just fail to disprove things. As it turns out, that's quite a lot.

CALCULATING χ^2

The formula for calculating χ^2 for a bivariate table is the same as the one we saw in chapter 20 for a univariate distribution. Here it is again:

$$\chi^2 = \sum \frac{(O-E)^2}{E}$$ Formula 21.6

where O represents the observed number of cases in a particular cell of a bivariate table, and E represents the number of cases you'd expect for that cell *if there were no relation* between the variables in that cell.

For each cell in a bivariate table, simply subtract the expected frequency from the observed and square the difference. Then divide by the expected frequency and sum the calculations for all the cells. Clearly, if all the observed frequencies equal all the expected frequencies, then χ^2 will be zero; that is, there will be no relation between the variables.

Although χ^2 can be zero, it can never have a negative value. The more the Os differ from the Es (i.e., something nonrandom is going on), the bigger χ^2 gets.

Calculating the Expected Frequencies for χ^2 in Bivariate Tables

Chi-square is calculated on raw frequencies, not on percentages in tables. The expected frequencies are calculated *for each cell* with the formula:

$$F_e = \frac{(R_t)(C_t)}{n}$$ Formula 21.7

where F_e is the expected frequency for a particular cell in a table; (R_t) is the frequency total for the row in which that cell is located; (C_t) is the frequency total for the column in which that cell is located; and n is the total sample size (the lower-right-hand marginal).

The test for χ^2 can be applied to any size bivariate table. Table 21.6 shows a hypotheti-

Table 21.6   A Hypothetical Census of Religious Belief in Four Groups of Native Americans

Tribe	Catholic	Protestant	Native American Church	Total
			Religion	
Observed frequencies				
1	150	104	86	340
2	175	268	316	759
3	197	118	206	521
4	68	214	109	391
Total	590	704	717	2,011
Expected frequencies				
1	99.75	119.03	121.22	
2	222.68	265.71	270.61	
3	152.85	182.39	185.76	
4	114.71	136.88	139.41	

cal census of observed adherents, in four Native American tribes, of three competing religions, and the expected number of adherents to each religion. Reading across the top of the table, in tribe #1, there are 150 Catholics, 104 Protestants, and 86 members of the Native American Church. For Tribe #1, we expect:

$$\frac{(340)(590)}{2,011} = 99.75$$

Catholics (the cell in the upper-left-hand corner of table 21.6). We expect 119.03 Protestants and 121.22 members of the Native American Church for Tribe #1, and so on.

Chi-square for this table is a walloping 162.08. To determine the *df* for a bivariate χ^2 table, we calculate:

$$df = (r - 1)(c - 1)$$ **Formula 21.8**

which means: Multiply the number of rows, minus one, by the number of columns, minus one. For table 21.6, there are:

$$(4 - 1 \text{ rows})(3 - 1 \text{ columns}) = 6df$$

Without even looking it up in appendix C (the χ^2 distribution), it's clear that the competing religions are not evenly distributed across the groups. If you had collected these data, you'd now be faced with the problem of interpreting them—that is, telling the story of how the various religions gain adherents at the expense of the others in various places.

Suppose that instead of a census, we take a 10% random sample of the groups—one that turns out to reflect almost perfectly the religious preferences of the population. The results, and the expected frequencies, would look like table 21.7.

Table 21.7 Observed and Expected Frequencies for a 10% Sample of the Data in Table 21.6

	Religion			
Tribe	Catholic	Protestant	Native American Church	Total
Observed frequencies				
1	15	10	9	34
2	18	27	32	77
3	20	12	21	53
4	7	21	11	39
Total	60	70	73	203
Expected frequencies				
1	10.04926	11.72414	121.22	
2	22.75862	26.55172	270.61	
3	15.66502	18.27586	185.76	
4	11.52709	11.52709	139.41	

Chi-square for table 21.7 is 15.44—still significant at the .02 level, but if we'd taken a 5% sample, χ^2 would be around 7 or 8, and with six degrees of freedom it would no longer be statistically significant, even at the .10 level. Sample size makes a real difference here.

THE SPECIAL CASE OF THE 2 × 2 TABLE

When you have a 2 × 2 cross-tab of nominal data, there is an easy formula to follow for computing χ^2. Here it is:

$$\chi^2 = \frac{n(|ad - bc| - n/2)^2}{(a + b)(c + d)(a + c)(b + d)}$$ **Formula 21.9**

where *a*, *b*, *c*, and *d* are the individual cells shown in figure 21.2, and *n* is the total of all the cells (the lower-right-hand marginal). The four sums in the denominator are the sums of the two rows and the two columns in figure 21.2.

Marlene Dobkin de Rios (1981) studied the clientele of a Peruvian folk healer. She

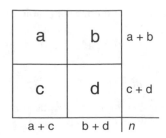

FIGURE 21.2.
The cells in a 2 × 2 table.

suspected that women clients were more likely to have had personal experience with witchcraft (or to have a close family member who has had personal contact with witchcraft) than were men clients. Table 21.8 shows Dobkin de Rios's data and the calculation of χ^2 directly from the cell frequencies, using formula 21.9. Dobkin de Rios's suspicion is certainly supported by these data.

Table 21.8   Dobkin de Rios's Data on Experience with Witchcraft by Gender

	Women clients	Men clients	Row totals
Personal experience with witchcraft	63	12	75
No personal experience with witchcraft	5	15	20
Column totals	68	27	95

χ^2 using formula 20.9

$$\chi^2 = \frac{95(945 - 60)^2}{(75)(20)(68)(27)} = \frac{74,406,375}{2,754,000} = 27.02 \quad p < .001$$

SOURCE: Reprinted from *Social Science and Medicine,* Vol. 15B, M. Dobkin de Rios "Socioeconomic Characteristics of an Amazon Urban Healer's Clientele," pp. 51–63, © 1981, with permission of Elsevier.

THE ODDS RATIO

The **odds ratio**, while also not a PRE statistic, is a measure of the relation between nominal variables. In table 21.8, among those who report having personal experience with witchcraft the odds are 5.25-to-1 that it's a woman (63/12 = 5.25). Among those who report not having had personal experience with witchcraft, the odds are one-third (5/15 = .33) that it's a man.

For 2 × 2 tables, the two primary odds are a/c and b/d. The odds ratio is

$$\frac{a\,/\,c}{b\,/\,d} \qquad\qquad \textbf{Formula 21.10}$$

which can be collapsed to simply *ad/bc*. The odds ratio for is table 21.8 is:

$$945/60 = 15.75$$

If the ratio of *a/c* were the same as the ratio of *b/d*, then the odds ratio would be 1. The degree to which the odds ratio is not 1 is a measure of association between the variables. In this case, the ratio of *a/c* is more than 15 times bigger than the ratio of *b/d*.

This means that women clients are that much more likely than men clients to have had personal experience with witchcraft.

FISHER'S EXACT TEST

Notice that there are only five cases in one of the cells in table 21.8—women who report no personal experience with witchcraft. When there are fewer than five cases *expected* in any cell, χ^2 can be distorted and there is a danger of drawing the wrong conclusion from the data.

There are, however, $68(20)/95 = 14.32$ cases *expected* of women who report not having any personal experience with witchcraft. The fact that only five cases actually turned up in this cell is thus strong evidence, not a cause for worry.

When the expected number of frequencies for any cell in a 2×2 table is less than 5, **use Fisher's exact probability test**. Here's an example.

Table 21.9   Data on the Number of Girlfriends by Height

	≤161.85	>161.85 cm	Column totals
≤ 4 girlfriends	7	2	9
[expected]	[4.8]	[4.2]	
> 4 girlfriends	1	5	6
[expected]	[3.2]	[2.8]	
Row totals	8	7	15

SOURCE: T. Gregor, "Short People." Reprinted from *Natural History*, Vol. 88, no. 2, pp. 14–21. Copyright © Natural History Magazine, Inc., 1979. Reproduced by permission.

Table 21.9 shows data from Thomas Gregor's study (1979) of height and social success among the Mehinaku of the Brazilian Amazon. The median height of 15 unmarried, adult men in the tribe was 161.85 cm (just under 5'4"). The median number of girlfriends that each man had was four. The independent variable in table 21.9, then, is height, measured as equal to or less than the median, or greater than the median. The dependent variable is the number of girlfriends, measured as equal to or less than the median, or greater than the median.

Of the eight men who were at or below median height, seven had four or fewer girlfriends. Of the seven men who were above median height, five had more than four girlfriends. The *expected* values for each cell are shown in brackets in table 21.9.

The cells have expected values of less than 5, so we apply Fisher's exact text. There are thousands of ways to throw the expected cases (5, 3, 4, 3) into four cells, but there are fewer ways to do it if you have to make the right-hand marginals add up to the observed values. Given a set of fixed marginals in a 2×2 table, the probability of seeing any distribution of cases is:

$$p = \frac{(a + b)!(c + d)!(a + c)!(b + d)!}{n!a!b!c!d!}$$

Formula 21.11

where a, b, c, and d are the actual contents of the four cells in the 2×2 table (see figure 21.2 above) and n is the total number of cases. An exclamation point signifies the factorial of a number, or the product of a sequence of numbers. So, 4! is four-factorial, or $4 \times 3 \times 2 \times 1 = 24$. Calculators can't handle the factorials of large numbers, but you can do the needed calculations on a spreadsheet when you have the relatively small numbers involved in a Fisher's exact test and full-featured statistical packages all have Fisher's exact test built in.

The exact probability of observing the particular distribution of cases in table 21.9 is:

$$p = \frac{(362,880)(720)(40,320)(5,040)}{(1,307,674,368,000)(5,040)(2)(1)(120)} = 0.033566434$$

For a one-tailed test of the null hypothesis, we need to add this probability to the probability of finding any other distributions that are more extreme than the one in the actual data. There is one configuration of these data that is more extreme: $a = 8$, $b = 0$, $c = 1$, and $d = 6$ (where a, b, c, and d are the cells in figure 21.2). The exact probability of that distribution is 0.001398601. For a one-tailed test, we add these probabilities:

$$0.033566434 + 0.001398601 = 0.034965$$

For a two-tailed test, the probability is .041. (It's not just double the one-tailed probability because the distribution of the elements in table 21.9 is uneven, but it's easy to calculate using any major stats package.) There is a strong hint in these data that men who are above median height have more girlfriends than are men who are below median height in this tribe. But the case is tentative and awaits further tests on larger samples.

GAMMA: THE ALL-PURPOSE PRE MEASURE OF ASSOCIATION FOR ORDINAL VARIABLES

Once you understand the PRE principle, a lot of things in statistics fall into place. Kempton et al. (1995) surveyed intentionally selected samples of people in the United States whom they thought would show pro- and anti-environmentalist attitudes. (Members of the Sierra Club, for example, are people you'd anticipate would be pro-environmental activism and loggers are people you'd think would be against that kind of activity.) Here are two questions from Kempton et al.'s study:

You shouldn't force people to change their lifestyle for the sake of the environment.
1. Disagree   2. Neutral   3. Agree

Environmentalists wouldn't be so gung-ho if it were their jobs that were threatened.
1. Disagree   2. Neutral   3. Agree

Gery Ryan, Stephen Borgatti, and I used these items in a survey we ran (Bernard et al. 2009), and table 21.10 shows the results. Notice that these items are reverse scored, so that a higher number indicates support for environmentalism.

Table 21.10   Distribution of Responses on Two Ecological Attitude Items

Force change in lifestyle	Gung-ho			
	Disagree	Neutral	Agree	Row totals
Disagree	16	7	61	84
Neutral	7	7	7	21
Agree	13	4	27	44
Column totals	36	18	95	149

If the two variables were perfectly related, then every respondent who agreed with one statement would agree with the other; every respondent who disagreed with one statement would disagree with the other; and so on. Things never work out so neatly, but if you knew the **proportion of matching pairs** among your respondents, you'd have a PRE measure of association for ordinal variables. The measure would tell you how much more correctly you could guess the rank of one ordinal variable for each respondent if you knew the score for the other ordinal variable in a bivariate distribution.

What we would like is a PRE measure of association that tells us whether knowing the ranking of pairs of people on one variable increases our ability to predict their ranking on a second variable, and by how much. To do this, we need to understand the ways in which pairs of ranks can be distributed. This will not appear obvious at first, but bear with me.

The number of possible pairs of observations (on any given unit of analysis) is

$$\text{No. of pairs of observations} = \frac{n(n - 1)}{2} \qquad \textbf{Formula 21.12}$$

where n is the sample size. There are $(149)(148)/2 = 11,026$ pairs of observations in table 21.10.

There are several ways that pairs of observations can be distributed if they are ranked on two ordinal variables.

1. They can be ranked in the same order on *both* variables. We'll call these "same."
2. They can be ranked in the opposite order on both variables. We'll call these "opposite."
3. They can be tied on either the independent or dependent variables, or on both. We'll call these "ties."

In fact, in almost all bivariate tables comparing ordinal variables, there are going to be a lot of pairs with tied values on both variables. **Gamma**, written G, is a useful measure of association between two ordinal variables because it *ignores* all the tied pairs. The formula for G is:

$$G = \frac{\text{No. of same-ranked pairs } - \text{ No. of opposite-ranked pairs}}{\text{No. of same-ranked pairs } + \text{ No. of opposite-ranked pairs}} \qquad \textbf{Formula 21.13}$$

G is an intuitive statistic; it ranges from -1.0 (for a perfect negative association) to $+1.0$ (for a perfect positive association), through 0 in the middle for complete independence of two variables.

If there are just two ordinal ranks in a measure, and if the number of opposite-ranked pairs is 0, then G would equal 1. Suppose we measure income and education in a Malaysian community ordinally, such that: (1) Anyone with less than a high school diploma is counted as having low education, and anyone with at least a high school diploma is counted as having high education; and (2) Anyone with an income of less than RM28,300 a year is counted as having low income, whereas anyone with at least RM28,300 a year is counted as having high income. (RM is the symbol for the Malaysian ringgit. RM28,300, or about $8,200 U.S. dollars, was the average per capita GDP in Malaysia in 2008.)

Now suppose that *no one* who had at least a high school diploma earned less than RM28,300 a year. There would be no pair of observations, then, in which low income and high education (an opposite pair) co-occurred.

If the number of same-ranked pairs is zero, then G would equal $+1.0$. Suppose that *no one* who had high education also had a high income. This would be a perfect negative association, and G would be -1.0. Both $+1.0$ and -1.0 are perfect correlations.

Calculating the Pairs for *G*

The number of same-ranked pairs in a bivariate table is calculated by multiplying each cell by the sum of all cells *below it and to its right*. The number of opposite-ranked pairs is calculated by multiplying each cell by the sum of all cells *below it and to its left*. This is diagramed in figure 21.3.

In Table 21.10, the number of same-ranked pairs is:		The number of opposite-ranked pairs is:	
16 (7 + 7 + 4 + 27)	= 720	61 (7 + 7 + 13 + 4)	= 1,891
+ 7 (7 + 27)	= 238	+ 7 (7 + 13)	= 140
+ 7 (4 + 27)	= 217	+ 7 (4 + 13)	= 119
+ 7 (27)	= 189	+ 7 (13)	= 91
Total	1,364	Total	2,241

FIGURE 21.3.
Calculating gamma.

G for table 21.10, then, is:

$$G = \frac{1,364 - 2,241}{1,364 + 2,241} = \frac{-877}{3,605} = -0.24$$

G tells us that the variables are associated negatively—people who agree with either of the statements tend to disagree with the other, and vice versa—but it also tells us that the association is relatively weak.

IS *G* SIGNIFICANT?

How weak? If you have more than 50 elements in your sample, you can test for the probability that *G* is due to sampling error using a procedure developed by Goodman and Kruskal (1963). A useful presentation of the procedure is given by Loether and McTavish (1993:598, 609). First, *G* must be converted to a *z*-score, or standard score. The formula for converting *G* to a *z*-score is:

$$z = (G - \gamma) \sqrt{(n_s + n_o) / 2n(1 - G^2)} \qquad \textbf{Formula 21.14}$$

where *G* is the *sample* gamma, γ is the gamma for the *population*, n is the size of your sample, n_s is the number of same-ranked pairs, and n_o is the number of opposite-ranked pairs.

As usual, we proceed from the null hypothesis and assume that γ for the entire population is zero—that is, that there really is no association between the variables we are studying. If we can reject that hypothesis, then we can assume that the *G* value for our sample probably approximates the *G* value, γ, for the population. Using the data from figure 21.3 and the *G* value for table 21.10:

$$z = (-.24 - 0) \sqrt{\frac{1,364 + 2,241}{2(149)(1 - (-.24^2))}} = -0.86$$

You'll recall that appendix A—the *z*-score table—lists the proportions of area under a normal curve that are described by various *z*-score values. To test the significance of *G*, look for the *z*-score in column 1 of the table. Column 2 shows the area under a normal curve between the mean (assumed to be zero for a normal curve) and the *z*-score. We're interested in column 3, which shows the area under the curve that is *not* accounted for by the *z*-score.

A z-score of -0.86 accounts for all but .1949 of the area under a normal curve. This means that we can *not* reject the null hypothesis. The G score of -0.24 is not sufficiently strong to confirm that there is a significant association between responses to the two attitudinal questions about environmental activism.

KENDALL'S T_b

Some researchers prefer a statistic called **Kendall's** T_b (also written τ_b and pronounced tau-b) instead of gamma for bivariate tables of ordinal data because G ignores tied pairs in the data. The formula for T_b is:

$$t_b = \frac{n_s - n_o}{\sqrt{(n_s + n_o + n_{td})(n_s + n_o + n_{ti})}} \qquad \textbf{Formula 21.15}$$

where n_s is the number of same-ranked pairs, n_o is the number of opposite-ranked pairs, n_{td} is the number of pairs tied on the dependent variable, and n_{ti} is the number of pairs tied on the independent variable. The formula for calculating the tied pairs is:

$$n_{td} = \Sigma\, R(R - 1)/2 \qquad n_{ti} = \Sigma\, C(C - 1)/2 \qquad \textbf{Formula 21.16}$$

where R refers to the row marginals (the dependent variable) and C refers to the column marginals (the independent variable). In table 21.10:

$$n_{td} = [84(83) + 21(20) + 44(43)]/2 = 4,642$$
$$n_{ti} = [36(35) + 18(17) + 95(94)]/2 = 5,248$$

We already have the numerator for T_b in this case (we calculated the number of same-ranked and opposite-ranked pairs in figure 21.3), so:

$$t_b = \frac{1,364 - 2,241}{\sqrt{(1,364 + 2,241 + 4,462)(1,364 + 2,241 + 5,248)}} = -0.10$$

This confirms the weak, negative association we saw from the results of the G test. Kendall's T_b will usually be smaller than G because G ignores tied pairs, while T_b uses almost all the data (it ignores the relatively few pairs that are tied on both variables).

YULE'S Q: *G* FOR 2 × 2 TABLES

Yule's Q is the equivalent of G for 2 × 2 tables of ordinal variables, like high versus low prestige, salary, education, religiosity, and so on. Yule's Q can be calculated on frequencies or on percentages. The formula is:

$$Q = \frac{ad - bc}{ad + bc} \qquad \textbf{Formula 21.17}$$

Yule's Q is an easy-to-use statistic. A good rule of thumb for interpreting Q is given by J. A. Davis (1971): When Q is 0, the interpretation is naturally that there is no association between the variables. When Q ranges from 0 to -0.29, or from 0 to $+0.29$, you can interpret this as a negligible or small association. Davis interprets a Q value of ± 0.30 to ± 0.49 as a "moderate" association; a value of ± 0.50 to ± 0.69 as a "substantial" association; and a value of ± 0.79 or more as a "very strong" association.

Rutledge (1990) was interested in the effect of one- or two-parent families on children's relations with their mothers and fathers. She surveyed African American, college-aged women, mostly from Chicago. One of the questions she asked was: "When you were growing up, how close were you to your father? Were you considerably close, moderately close, or not close at all?" I've collapsed Rutledge's data into two response categories, close and not close, in table 21.11.

Table 21.11 Family Structure and Self-Reported Closeness to Parents

Close to father?	Two parents	One parent	Total
Yes	135	36	171
No	13	31	44
Total	148	67	215

SOURCE: E. M. Rutledge, "Black Parent-Child Relations: Some Correlates," *Journal of Comparative Family Studies,* Vol. 21, pp. 369–78, 1990. Abstracted from data in table 2. Reprinted by permission.

Here is the calculation of Yule's Q for these data:

$$Q = \frac{(135)(31) - (36)(13)}{(135)(31) + (36)(13)} = \frac{4,185 - 468}{4,185 + 468} = 0.80$$

Yule's Q for these data is .80. Most of the women ($135/148 = .91$) who come from two-parent homes are close to their fathers, compared to fewer than half who come from one-parent homes ($31/67 = .46$) are not. The reason is obvious: Overwhelmingly, one-parent homes are headed by mothers, not by fathers.

WHAT TO USE FOR NOMINAL AND ORDINAL VARIABLES
In general:

1. Use χ^2 to see how often you could expect to find the differences you see in the table just by chance. Calculate odds ratios to measure the strength of relationships.
2. Use G (or tau, or—in the case of 2 × 2 tables—Yule's Q) to measure the association between two ordinal variables.

In actual practice, ordinal variables with seven ranks are treated if they were interval variables. In fact, many researchers treat ordinals with just five ranks as if they were intervals, because association between interval-level variables can be analyzed by the most powerful statistics—which brings us to correlation and regression.

CORRELATION: THE POWERHOUSE STATISTIC FOR COVARIATION
When at least one of the variables in a bivariate relation is interval or ratio level, we use a measure of correlation: **Spearman's *r*,** written r_s when the data are rank ordered; **Pearson's product moment correlation**, written simply as *r*, to measure the strength of linear relations; or **eta squared** (eta is the Greek letter η, pronounced either eat-a or ate-a) to measure the strength of certain kinds of nonlinear relations. (Go back to the section on "shape of relation" at the beginning of this chapter if you have any doubts about the concept of a nonlinear relation.)

SPEARMAN'S *r*
Table 21.12 shows some data collected by Allyn Stearman (1989:224). She measured the amount of game meat taken, over 56 days, by 16 Yuquí hunters in the Bolivian Amazon.

These data are arranged in rank order of meat taken. So, Alejandro is the winner, with 226 kilos of meat during the 56-day observation period. Lorenzo and Jonatán are tied for

Table 21.12 Ranking of Yuquí Hunters by Game Taken

Name	Kilos of meat	Kilos of fish
Alejandro	226.00	53.75
Jaime	185.50	101.00
Leonardo	152.50	8.50
Humberto	144.75	120.50
Daniel	78.00	119.50
Joel	74.50	34.25
Jorge	59.50	23.00
Timoteo	51.00	1.50
Tomás	51.00	123.80
Lucas	46.00	107.50
Guillermo	45.75	190.25
Victor	29.50	38.25
Manuel	14.50	28.50
Benjamin	10.00	128.00
Jonatán	0.00	198.00
Lorenzo	0.00	279.00

SOURCE: A. M. Stearman, "Yuquí Foragers in the Bolivian Amazon: Subsistence Strategies, Prestige and Leadership in an Acculturating Society," *Journal of Anthropological Research,* Vol. 45, pp. 219–44. Reproduced by permission of the *Journal of Anthropological Research* © 1989.

last. We can use Spearman's *r* to test the extent to which a hunter's take of fish matches his take of meat. Just looking at the data, we suspect the correlation is negative. That is, it appears that hunters who take a lot of meat are not focusing on fish and vice versa. Here is the formula for Spearman's *r*:

$$r_s = 1 - \frac{6\Sigma d^2}{n(n^2 - 1)}$$ **Formula 21.18**

where *d* is the difference between the ranks on all pairs of objects. Table 21.13 shows the computation of d^2 for the data on these hunters.

For these hunters, at least, there is a moderate negative correlation between their success in hunting meat and their success in hunting fish.

PEARSON'S *r*

Pearson's *r* measures how much changes in one variable correspond with equivalent changes in the other variables. It can also be used as a measure of association between an interval and an ordinal variable, or between an interval and a **dummy variable.** (Dummy variables are nominal variables coded as 1 or 0, present or absent. See chapter 19 on text analysis.) The square of Pearson's *r* is a PRE measure of association for linear relations between interval variables. **R-squared** tells us how much better we could predict the scores of a dependent variable, if we knew the scores of some independent variable.

Table 21.14 shows data for two interval variables for a random sample of 10 of the 50 countries in table 20.8: (1) infant mortality and (2) life expectancy for women.

To give you an idea of where we're going with this example, the correlation between INFMORT and TFR across the 50 countries in table 20.8 is around 0.91, and this is reflected in the sample of 10 countries for which the correlation is *r* = 0.81.

Now, suppose you had to predict the TFR for each of the 10 countries in table 21.14 *without knowing anything about the infant mortality rate for those countries.* Your best guess—your lowest prediction error—would be the mean, 2.63 children per woman. You

Table 21.13   Computing Spearman's Rank Order Correlation Coefficient for the Data in Table 21.12

Hunter	Rank for meat	Rank for fish	Difference in the ranks	d^2
Alejandro	1	10	−9	81
Jaime	2	9	−7	49
Leonardo	3	15	−12	144
Humberto	4	6	−2	4
Daniel	5	7	−2	4
Joel	6	12	−6	36
Jorge	7	14	−7	49
Timoteo	8	16	−8	64
Tomás	9	5	4	16
Lucas	10	8	2	4
Guillermo	11	2	9	81
Victor	12	11	1	1
Manuel	13	13	0	0
Benjamín	14	4	10	100
Jonatán	15	3	12	144
Lorenzo	16	1	15	225
				total d^2 1,002

$$r_s = 1 - \frac{6(1002)}{16(16^2 - 1)} = 1 - 6012/4080 = -.474$$

Table 21.14   Infant Mortality by TFR for 10 Countries from Table 20.8

Country	INFMORT x	TFR y
Armenia	22.2	1.79
Chad	129.9	5.78
El Salvador	17.5	2.22
Ghana	67.0	4.00
Iran	24.2	1.74
Latvia	8.3	1.48
Namibia	27.2	3.07
Panama	15.7	2.41
Slovenia	3.6	1.47
Suriname	20.5	2.29
Mean of x = 25.49	Mean of y = 2.63	

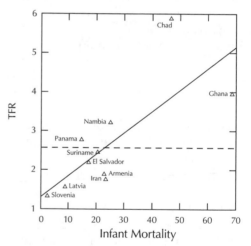

FIGURE 21.4.
A plot of the data in table 21.14. The dotted line is the mean of TFR. The solid line is drawn from the regression equation $y = 1.018 + .051x$.

can see this in figure 21.4 where I've plotted the distribution of TFR and INFMORT for the 10 countries in table 21.14.

The Sums of the Squared Distances to the Mean

Each dot in figure 21.4 is physically distant from the dotted mean line by a certain amount. The sum of the squares of these distances to the mean line is the smallest sum possible (that is, the smallest cumulative prediction error you could make), given that you *only* know the mean of the dependent variable. The distances from the dots *above* the line to the mean are positive; the distances from the dots *below* the line to the mean are negative. The sum of the actual distances is zero. Squaring the distances gets rid of the negative numbers.

But suppose you *do* know the data in table 21.14 regarding the infant mortality rate for each of those 10 countries. Can you reduce the prediction error in guessing the TFR for those countries? Could you draw another line through figure 21.4 that "fits" the dots better and reduces the sum of the distances from the dots to the line?

You bet you can. The solid line that runs diagonally through the graph in figure 21.4 minimizes the prediction error for these data. This line is called the **best fitting line**, or the **least squares line**, or the **regression line**. When you understand how this regression line is derived, you'll understand how correlation works.

REGRESSION

The formula for the regression line is

$$y = a + bx \qquad \qquad \textbf{Formula 21.19}$$

where y is the variable value of the dependent variable, a and b are some constants (which you'll learn how to derive in a moment), and x is the variable value of the independent variable. The constant, a, is computed as:

$$a = \bar{y} - b\bar{x} \qquad \qquad \textbf{Formula 21.20}$$

and b is computed as

$$b = \frac{n(\Sigma\ xy) - (\Sigma\ x)(\Sigma\ y)}{n(\Sigma\ x^2) - (\Sigma\ x)^2} \qquad \qquad \textbf{Formula 21.21}$$

Table 21.15 shows the data needed for finding the regression equation for the raw data in table 21.14. At the bottom of table 21.15 you'll find a shortcut formula (formula 21.22) for calculating Pearson's r directly from the data in the table.

The constant b is:

$$b = \frac{10(856.04) - (254.9)(26.25)}{10(9,733.85) - (254.90)^2} = \frac{1,805.55}{32,364.49} = 0.056$$

and the constant a is then:

$$a = 2.63 - .056(25.49) = 1.20$$

The regression equation for any pair of scores on infant mortality (x) and TFR (y), then, is:

$$y = a + bx = 1.20 + .056(x)$$

Drawing the Regression Line

To draw the regression line in figure 21.4, find the expected y coordinate for two of the actual data points on the independent variable, x. Choose the x values that are farthest apart to maximize the accuracy of the line. For table 21.16, choose Slovenia and Chad:

1. For Slovenia, the expected TFR is:

$$y = 1.20 + .056(3.6) = 1.40$$

Table 21.15 Computation of Pearson's *r* Directly from Data in Table 20.14

Country	INFMORT x	TFR y	xy	x^2	y^2
Armenia	22.2	1.79	39.74	492.84	3.20
Chad	48.7	5.78	281.49	2,371.69	33.41
El Salvador	17.5	2.22	38.85	306.25	4.93
Ghana	67.0	4.00	268.00	4,489.00	16.00
Iran	24.2	1.74	42.11	585.64	3.03
Latvia	8.3	1.48	12.28	68.89	2.19
Namibia	27.2	3.07	83.50	739.84	9.43
Panama	15.7	2.41	37.84	246.49	5.81
Slovenia	3.6	1.47	5.29	12.96	2.16
Suriname	20.5	2.29	46.95	420.25	5.24
Total	254.90	26.25	856.04	9,733.85	85.40

$n = 10$ $\bar{x} = 25.49$ $\bar{y} = 2.63$

$$r_{xy} = \frac{n\sum xy - \sum x \sum y}{\sqrt{\left[n\sum x^2 - \left(\sum x\right)^2 \right]\left[n\sum y^2 - \left(\sum y\right)^2 \right]}}$$

Formula 21.22

$$r = \frac{8560.4 - 6,691.13}{\sqrt{(96,938.5 - 64,974.01)(854.00 - 689.06)}} = 0.81$$

2. For Chad, the expected number of infant deaths per 1,000 live births is:

$$y = 1.20 + .056(48.7) = 3.97$$

Put a dot on figure 21.4 at the intersection of

$$x = 3.6, y = 1.40$$

and

$$x = 48.7, y = 3.97$$

and connect the dots. That's the regression line.

The squared deviations (the distances from any dot to the line, squared) add up to less than they would for any other line we could draw through that graph. That's why the regression line is also called the **best fitting** or the **least squares** line.

Suppose we want to predict the dependent variable *y* (TFR) when the independent variable *x* (INFMORT) is 3.8, as it is in the Czech Republic. In that case,

$$y = 1.20 + .056(3.8) = 1.41$$

or 1.41 total births during the lifetime of women in the Czech Republic. In other words, the regression equation lets us estimate the TFR for infant mortality levels that are not represented in our sample. The actual TFR for the Czech Republic was 1.24 in 2009. Even a small, random sample of 10 countries does pretty well in helping us make these kinds of predictions.

HOW REGRESSION WORKS

To give you an absolutely clear idea of how the regression formula works, table 21.16 shows all the predictions along the regression line for the data in table 21.14.

Table 21.16   Regression Predictions for the Dependent Variable in Table 21.14

For the country of	Where the infant mortality rate in 2008 was	Predict that the TFR will be	And compare that to the actual TFR in table 20.8
Armenia	22.2	1.20 + .056(22.2) = 2.44	1.79
Chad	48.7	1.20 + .056(48.7) = 3.93	5.78
Ghana	67.0	1.20 + .056(67.0) = 4.95	4.00
El Salvador	17.5	1.20 + .056(17.5) = 2.18	2.22
Iran	24.2	1.20 + .056(24.2) = 2.56	1.74
Latvia	8.3	1.20 + .056(8.3) = 1.66	1.48
Namibia	27.2	1.20 + .056(27.2) = 2.72	3.07
Panama	15.7	1.20 + .056(15.7) = 2.08	2.41
Slovenia	3.6	1.20 + .056(3.6) = 1.40	1.47
Suriname	20.5	1.20 + .056(20.5) = 2.35	2.29

We now have two predictors of TFR: (1) the mean TFR, which is our best guess when we have no data about some independent variable like infant mortality, and (2) the values produced by the regression equation when we *do* have information about something like infant mortality.

Each of these predictors produces a certain amount of error, or *variance*, which is the difference between the predicted number for the dependent variable and the actual measurement. This is also called the **residual**—that is, what's left over after making your prediction using the regression equation. (To anticipate the discussion of multiple regression in chapter 22: The idea in multiple regression is to use two or more independent variables in order to reduce the size of the residuals.)

You'll recall from chapter 20, in the section on variance and the standard deviation, that in the case of the mean, the total variance is the average of the squared deviations of the observations from the mean, $\{\Sigma (x - \bar{x})^2 / n\}$. In the case of the regression line predictors, the variance is the sum of the squared deviations from the regression line. Table 21.17 compares these two sets of errors, or variances, for the data in table 21.14.

Table 21.17   Comparison of the Error Produced by Guessing the Mean TFR in Table 21.14 and the Error Produced by Applying the Regression Equation for Each Guess

Country	TFR y	Old error $(y - \bar{y})^2$	Prediction using the regression equation	New error $(y - $ the prediction using the regression equation$)^2$
Armenia	1.79	0.71	2.44	0.42
Chad	5.78	9.23	3.93	3.42
El Salvador	2.22	0.17	2.18	0.002
Ghana	4.00	1.88	4.95	0.90
Iran	1.74	0.79	2.56	0.67
Latvia	1.48	1.32	1.66	0.03
Namibia	3.07	0.19	2.72	0.12
Panama	2.41	0.05	2.08	0.11
Slovenia	1.47	1.35	1.40	0.005
Suriname	2.29	0.12	2.35	0.004
		$\Sigma = 15.81$		$\Sigma = 5.68$

We now have all the information we need for a true PRE measure of association between two interval variables. Recall the formula for a PRE measure: the old error minus the new error, divided by the old error. For our example in table 21.14:

$$\text{PRE} = \frac{15.81 - 5.68}{15.81} = 0.64$$

In other words: The proportionate reduction of error in guessing the TFR in table 21.14—given that you know the distribution of informant mortality rates and can apply a regression equation—compared to just guessing the mean of TFR is 0.64, or 64%.

This quantity is usually referred to as **r-squared** (written r^2), or the amount of variance accounted for by the independent variable. It is also called the **coefficient of determination** because it tells us how much of the variance in the dependent variable is predictable from (determined by) the scores of the independent variable. The Pearson product moment correlation, written as r, is the square root of this measure, or, in this instance, 0.80. (We calculated r in table 21.15 by applying formula 21.22 and got $r = 0.81$. The difference is rounding error when we do these calculations by hand. You won't get this error when you use a computer to do the calculations.)

CALCULATING r AND r^2

I've given you this grand tour of regression and correlation because I want you to see that Pearson's r is not a direct PRE measure of association; its *square*, r^2, is.

So, what's better, Pearson's r or r^2 for describing the relation between interval variables? Pearson's r is easy to compute from raw data and it varies from -1.0 to $+1.0$, so it has direction and an intuitive interpretation of magnitude. Mathematically, of course, r has to be at least as big (and almost always bigger) than r^2. By contrast, r^2 is a humbling statistic. A correlation of 0.30 looks impressive until you square it and see that it explains just 9% of the variance in what you're studying.

The good news is that if you double a correlation coefficient, you quadruple the variance accounted for. For example, if you get an r of 0.25, you've accounted for 6.25% of the variance, or error, in predicting the score of a dependent variable from a corresponding score on an independent variable. An r of 0.50 is twice as big as an r of 0.25, but four times as good, because 0.50^2 means that you've accounted for 25% of the variance.

Accounting for Variance

What does "accounting for variance" mean? It simply means being able to make a better prediction with an independent variable than we could without one. Recall from chapter 20 that the total amount of variance in an observed set of scores is the sum of the squared deviations from the mean, divided by $n - 1$. This is shown in formula 21.23.

$$\text{Variance} = \frac{\Sigma (x - \bar{x})^2}{n - 1} \qquad \textbf{Formula 21.23}$$

Well, if the correlation between the two variables in table 21.14 is $r = 0.81$, and its square is $r^2 = 0.66$, then we can say "we have accounted for 66% of the variance." I'll define what we mean by this.

The mean TFR for the 10 countries in table 21.15 is 2.63, and the total variance (sum of squares in table 21.17) is 15.81. When we predict TFR, using the regression formula from the infant mortality rate, the variance in the predicted scores will be

$$(1 - .64)15.81 = 5.69$$

Except for rounding error, this is the total "new error" in table 21.17 and this is what it means to say that "about 64% of the variance in TFR is [accounted for] [determined by] [predicted by] the infant mortality rate across 10 countries."

By the way, in case you're wondering, the correlation between infant mortality and TFR across the 50 countries in table 20.8 is 0.91 and the correlation between these two variables across all countries of the world is 0.82.

TESTING THE SIGNIFICANCE OF *r*

Just as with *G*, it is possible to test whether or not any value of Pearson's *r* is the result of sampling error, or reflects a real covariation in the larger population. In the case of *r*, the null hypothesis is that, within certain confidence limits, we should predict that the real coefficient of correlation in the population of interest is actually zero. In other words, there is no relation between the two variables.

We need to be particularly sensitive to the possible lack of significance of sample statistics when we deal with small samples—which is a lot of the time, it turns out. To simplify testing the confidence limits of *r*, I have constructed table 21.18, which you can use to get a ball-park reading on the significance of Pearson's *r*. The top half of table 21.18 shows the 95% confidence limits for representative samples of 30, 50, 100, 400, and 1,000, where

Table 21.18   Confidence Limits for Pearson's *r* for Various Sample Sizes

Pearson's *r*	Sample size				
	30	50	100	400	1,000
0.1	ns	ns	ns	ns	.04–.16
0.2	ns	ns	.004–.40	.10–.29	.14–.26
0.3	ns	.02–.54	.11–.47	.21–.39	.24–.35
0.4	.06–.67	.14–.61	.21–.55	.32–.48	.35–.45
0.5	.17–.73	.25–.68	.31–.63	.42–.57	.45–.54
0.6	.31–.79	.39–.75	.45–.71	.53–.66	.56–.64
0.7	.45–.85	.52–.82	.59–.79	.65–.75	.67–.73
0.8	.62–.90	.67–.88	.72–.86	.76–.83	.78–.82
0.9	.80–.95	.83–.94	.85–.93	.88–.92	.89–.91

Top half of table: 95% confidence limits

Pearson's *r*	30	50	100	400	1,000
0.1	ns	ns	ns	ns	.02–.18
0.2	ns	ns	ns	.07–.32	.12–.27
0.3	ns	ns	.05–.51	.18–.41	.23–.45
0.4	ns	.05–.80	.16–.59	.28–.50	.33–.46
0.5	.05–.75	.17–.72	.28–.67	.40–.59	.44–.56
0.6	.20–.83	.31–.79	.41–.74	.51–.68	.55–.65
0.7	.35–.88	.46–.85	.55–.81	.63–.76	.66–.74
0.8	.54–.92	.62–.90	.69–.88	.75–.84	.77–.83
0.9	.75–.96	.80–.95	.84–.94	.87–.92	.88–.91

Bottom half of table: 99% confidence limits

the Pearson's *r* values are .1, .2, .3, etc. The bottom half of table 21.18 shows the 99% confidence limits.

Reading the top half of table 21.18, we see that at the 95% level the confidence limits for a correlation of 0.20 in a random sample of 1,000 are 0.14 and 0.26. This means that in fewer than 5 tests in 100 would we expect to find the correlation smaller than 0.14 or larger than 0.26. In other words, we are 95% confident that the true *r* for the population (written ρ, which is the Greek letter rho) is somewhere between 0.14 and 0.26.

By contrast, the 95% confidence limits for an r of 0.30 in a random sample of 30 is not significant at all; the true correlation could be 0, and our sample statistic of 0.30 could be the result of sampling error.

The 95% confidence limits for an r of 0.40 in a random sample of 30 is statistically significant. We can be 95% certain that the true correlation in the population (ρ) is no less than 0.05 and no larger than 0.67. This is a statistically significant finding, but not much to go on insofar as external validity is concerned. You'll notice that with large samples (like 1,000), even very small correlations are significant at the .01 level (box 21.4).

BOX 21.4

STATISTICAL SIGNIFICANCE

On the other hand, just because a statistical value is significant doesn't mean that it's important or useful in understanding how the world works. Looking at the lower half of table 21.18, we see that even an r value of 0.40 is statistically insignificant when the sample is as small as 30. If you look at the spread in the confidence limits for both halves of table 21.18, you will notice something very interesting: A sample of 1,000 offers *some* advantage over a sample of 400 for bivariate tests, but the difference is small and the costs of the larger sample could be very high, especially if you're collecting all your own data.

Recall from chapter 6, on sampling, that to halve the confidence interval you have to quadruple the sample size. Where the unit cost of data is high—as in research based on direct observation of behavior or on face-to-face interviews—the point of diminishing returns on sample size is reached quickly. Where the unit cost of data is low—as it is with mailed questionnaires or with telephone surveys—a larger sample is worth trying for.

NONLINEAR RELATIONS

And now for something different. All the examples I've used so far have been for linear relations where the best-fitting "curve" on a bivariate scatterplot is a straight line. A lot of really interesting relations, however, are **nonlinear**.

Smits et al. (1998) measured the strength of association between the educational level of spouses in 65 countries and how that relates to industrialization. Figure 21.5 shows what they found. It's the relation between per capita energy consumption (a measure of industrialization and hence of economic development) and the amount of educational homogamy in those 65 countries. (Homogamy means marrying someone who is similar to you, so educational homogamy means marrying someone who has the same level of education as you do.) The relation between the two variables is very clear: It's an inverted U.

You might think that the relation between these two variables would be linear—people of similar education would be attracted to each other—but it isn't. Here's how Smits et al. reckon the inverted U happens: People in nonindustrialized countries rely mostly on agriculture, so family background (which determines wealth) tends to be the main criterion for selecting mates. As industrialization takes off, education becomes more and more

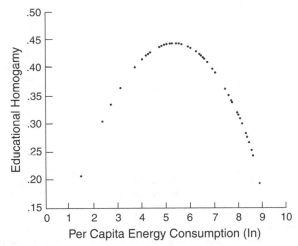

FIGURE 21.5.

The relation between per capita energy consumption and educational homogamy is nonlinear.
SOURCE: J. Smits et al., "Educational Homogamy in 65 Countries: An Explanation of Differences in Openness Using Country-Level Explanatory Variables." *American Sociological Review*, Vol. 63, pp. 264–85. © 1998 by the American Sociological Association. Reprinted with permission.

important and family background becomes less important for building wealth. Educated people seek each other out to maximize their life chances.

Eventually, though, when countries are highly industrialized, education is widespread, people have high wages, and there are social security systems. People in *those* countries don't have to rely on their children for support in old age, so romantic love becomes the dominant force in mate selection and the level of educational homogamy drops like a stone.

Here's another one. Beginning with −5° F and continuing up to 75° F, the mean number of assaults rises steadily with the average daily temperature in U.S. cities. Then it begins to drop. Figure 21.6, from Cohn and Rotton (1997), shows the dramatic pattern. The reasons for this pattern are very complex (and controversial), but it is clear from figure 21.6 that a simple, linear correlation is inadequate to describe what's going on.

If you get a very weak r or r^2 for two variables that you believe, from theory or from field research, are strongly related, then draw a scatterplot and check it out. Scatterplots are available in all the major statistical packages and they are, as you saw in figure 21.1, packed with information. For sheer intuitive power, there is nothing like them.

Figure 21.7a, for example, is the same plot we saw in figure 21.1d of infant mortality and per capita gross domestic product in 2010 for the 50 countries in table 20.8. I've repeated the figure here because I want you to see it next to figure 21.7b, which is a plot of infant mortality and the **natural logarithm** of PCGDP.

The correlation between the original variables in figure 21.7a is −0.53. This indicates a moderate, negative relation, but the scatterplot clearly shows that the relation is not linear. Transforming each value of PCGDP into its natural logarithm has the effect of making the distribution more normal, but it changes the interpretation of the graph.

In figure 21.7b, the correlation is now a strong −0.74, but we know from figure 21.7a that the relation between raw PCGDP and infant mortality is not linear. Countries at the bottom, with around $200 dollars in per capita domestic product, have to raise their

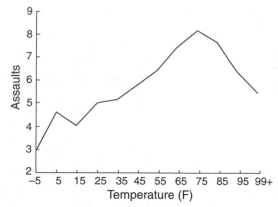

FIGURE 21.6.

The relationship between temperature and the rate of assault is nonlinear.

SOURCE: E. G. Cohn and J. Rotton, "Assault as a Function of Time and Temperature: A Moderator-Variable Time-Series Analysis." *Journal of Personality and Social Psychology,* Vol. 72, pp. 1322–34. © 1997 by the American Psychological Association. Reprinted with permission.

PCGDP more than 13 times to cut their infant mortality rate in half, but countries with a PCGDP of $10,000 have to raise this figure less than four times to achieve the same result. At around $19,000 per year, it takes less than a doubling of PCGDP to halve the infant mortality rate. On the other hand, there's a big difference—in absolute terms—between halving the infant mortality rate in rich versus poor countries. Cutting infant mortality in half for countries at the bottom end means reducing the number of deaths from about 60 to 30 per 1,000 babies born, while halving the infant mortality of countries

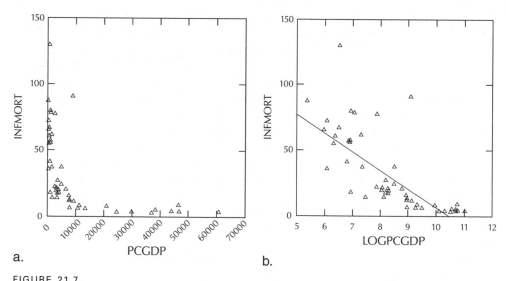

FIGURE 21.7.

Transforming variables. (*a:* Infant mortality by per capita gross domestic product for 50 countries in table 20.8. *b:* Infant mortality by the log of per capita gross domestic product for 50 countries in table 20.8.)

that have at least $20,000 in per capita GDP means the difference between about 30 and 15 infant deaths per 1,000 babies born each year.

If a scatterplot looks anything like figure 21.7a, consider transforming the data into their logarithms. If a scatterplot looks like the shapes in figures 21.5 or 21.6, then consider using eta-squared, a statistic for nonlinear regression.

CALCULATING ETA-SQUARED

Eta-squared, written η^2 or eta², is a PRE measure that tells you how much better you could do if you predicted the separate means for *chunks* of your data than if you predicted the mean for all your data. Figure 21.8 graphs the hypothetical data in table 21.19. These data show, for a sample of 20 people, ages 12–89, their "number of close friends and acquaintances."

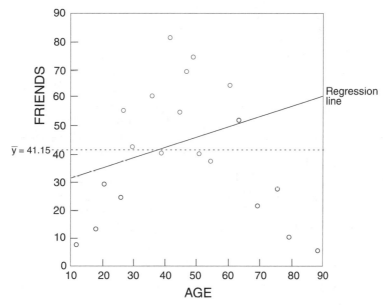

FIGURE 21.8.
Number of friends by age.

The dots in figure 21.8 are the data points from table 21.19. Respondent #10, for example, is 45 years of age and was found to have approximately 55 friends and acquaintances. The horizontal dashed line in figure 21.8 marked $\bar{y}$ is the global average for these data, 41.15.

Clearly: (1) The global average is not of much use in predicting the dependent variable; (2) Knowing a person's age *is* helpful in predicting the size of his or her social network; but (3) The linear regression equation is hardly any better than the global mean at reducing error in predicting the dependent variable. You can see this by comparing the mean line and the regression line (the slightly diagonal line running from upper left to lower right in figure 21.8). They are not that different.

What that regression line depicts is the correlation between age and size of network, which is a puny -0.099. But if we inspect the data visually, we find that there are a couple of natural "breaks." It looks like there's a break in the late 20s, and another somewhere in the 60s. We'll break these data into three age chunks from 12 to 26, 27 to 61, and 64

Table 21.19 Hypothetical Data on Number of Friends by Age

Person	Age	Number of friends	
1	12	8	
2	18	14	$\bar{y}_1 = 19.25$
3	21	30	
4	26	25	
5	27	56	
6	30	43	
7	36	61	
8	39	41	
9	42	82	$\bar{y}_2 = 57.00$
10	45	55	
11	47	70	
12	49	75	
13	51	41	
14	55	38	
15	61	65	
16	64	52	
17	70	22	
18	76	28	$\bar{y}_3 = 23.80$
19	80	11	
20	89	6	
		$\bar{y} = 41.15$	

to 89, take separate means for each chunk, and see what happens. I have marked the three chunks and their separate means on table 21.19.

Like r, which must be squared to find the variance accounted for, η^2 is a measure of this and is calculated from the following formula:

$$\eta^2 = 1 - \frac{\Sigma(y - \bar{y}_c)^2}{\Sigma(y - \bar{y})^2} \qquad \textbf{Formula 21.24}$$

where $\bar{y}_c$ is the average for each chunk and y is the overall average for your dependent variable. For table 21.19, η^2 is:

$$\eta^2 = 1 - \frac{3,871.55}{10,058.55} = 0.62$$

which is the proportionate reduction of error in predicting the number of friends people have from the three separate averages of their age, rather than from the global average of their age. This shows a pretty strong relation between the two variables, despite the very weak Pearson's r.

STATISTICAL SIGNIFICANCE, THE SHOTGUN APPROACH, AND OTHER ISSUES

To finish this chapter, I want to deal with four thorny issues in social science data analysis: (1) measurement and statistical assumptions, (2) significance tests, (3) eliminating the outliers, and (4) the shotgun method of analysis.

Measurement and Statistical Assumptions

By now you are comfortable with the idea of nominal, ordinal, and interval-level measurement. This seminal notion was introduced into social science in a classic article by

S. S. Stevens in 1946. Stevens said that statistics like t and r, because of certain assumptions that they made, required interval-level data, and this became an almost magical prescription.

Thirty-four years later, Gaito (1980) surveyed the (by then voluminous) mathematical statistics literature and found no support for the idea that measurement properties have anything to do with the selection of statistical procedures. Social scientists, said Gaito, confuse measurement (which focuses on the meaning of numbers) with statistics (which doesn't care about meaning at all) (p. 566). So, treating ordinal variables as if they were interval, for purposes of statistical analysis, is almost always a safe thing to do, especially with five or more ordinal categories (Boyle 1970; Labovitz 1971a).

The important thing is measurement, not statistics. As I pointed out in chapter 2, many concepts, such as gender, race, and class are much more subtle and complex than we give them credit for. Instead of measuring them qualitatively (remember that assignment of something to a nominal category is a qualitative act of measurement), we ought to be thinking hard about how to measure them ordinally.

Emile Durkheim was an astute theorist. He noted that the division of labor became more complex as the complexity of social organization increased (Durkheim 1933 [1893]). But he, like other theorists of his day, divided the world of social organization into a series of dichotomous categories (*Gemeinschaft* vs. *Gesellschaft*, or mechanical vs. organic solidarity).

Today, social theorists want to know how degrees of differences in aspects of social organization (like the division of labor in society) are related to social complexity. This requires some hard thinking about how to measure these two variables with more subtlety. The meaning of the measurements is crucial (**Further Reading:** measurement in anthropology).

Eliminating the Outliers

Another controversial practice in data analysis is called "eliminating the outliers," which means removing extreme values from data analysis. If there are clear indications of measurement error (a person with a score of 600 on a 300-point test turns up in your sample), you can throw out the data that are in error. The problem comes when outliers (so-called freak cases) are eliminated just to smooth out data—to achieve better fits of regression lines to data. A single wealthy household might be ignored in calculating the average household income in a community on the theory that it's a "freak case." But what if it isn't a freak case? What if it represents a small, but substantively significant proportion of cases in the community? Eliminating it only prevents the discovery of that fact.

Trivially, you can always achieve a perfect fit to a set of data if you reduce it to just two points. After all, two points are always connected by a straight line. But is creating a good fit what you're after? Don't you really want to understand what makes the data messy in the first place? In general, you cannot achieve understanding of messiness by cleaning things up. Still, as in all aspects of research, be ready to break this rule, too, when you think you'll learn something by doing so.

Figure 21.9a shows the relation between the number of violent crimes per 100,000 people and the average annual pay for people in the 50 U.S. states and Washington, DC, in 2007. Figure 21.9b shows exactly the same thing, but without including the data from Washington, DC. The correlation between the two variables *with* DC in the picture is 0.28. When we leave out the data for DC, the correlation sinks to 0.06.

That's because the violent crime rate in Washington, DC, was an appalling 1,414 per

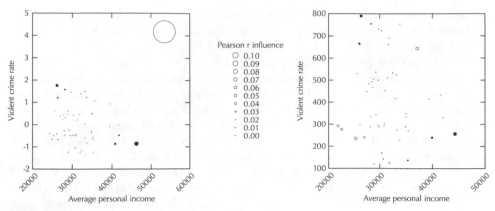

FIGURE 21.9.

The effects of outliers. Violent crimes in the United States (*left:* for all states and Washington, DC; *right:* for all states, without Washington, DC), per 100,000 population, by average annual pay, 2008.

SOURCE: U.S. Census Bureau, *Statistical Abstract of the United States, 2010.* Washington, DC, 2009, tables 297 and 665, http://www.census.gov/compendia/statab.

100,000 population in 2008, and the average annual pay there was $62,484. For the 50 states in the United States, the next highest violent crime rate, in Florida, was half that of DC, and the next highest average pay, in Connecticut, was just 12% lower than that in DC.

The sizes of the dots in figure 21.9 indicate the influence each data point has on the correlation—that is, how much the correlation would change if you took each data point out of the calculation. That huge circle in the upper-right-hand corner of figure 21.9b is DC. Now, *that's* an outlier.

What to do with outliers? Try using the median to describe the central tendency rather than eliminating cases. Or report the results of your analysis with and without outliers, as I just did with figure 21.9.

Tests of Significance

This is a hot topic in social science. Fifty years ago, researchers began arguing that statistical **tests of significance** are virtually useless (Rozeboom 1960) and the debate has raged on ever since (see Ziliak and McCloskey [2008] for a review) (**Further Reading:** significance tests).

I wouldn't go that far. Consider the hypothesis that the universe is expanding. As Wainer (1999) points out, being able to reject the hull hypothesis at $p < .05$ would be quite a contribution. Will Dr. X be denied tenure a year from now? Lots of people, says Wainer, would be happy to know that they could reject the null hypothesis at, say, $p < .001$.

It's true that if you don't have a representative sample, then a test of statistical significance doesn't allow you to generalize beyond your particular sample of data. On the other hand, if you get significant results on a nonrandom sample, at least you can rule out the operation of random properties *in your sample* (Blalock 1979:238–39).

Use tests of significance but remember that they aren't magical and that the .01 and .05 levels of significance, although tribal customs, are not sacred. They are simply conventions that have developed for convenience over the years. Greenwald et al. (1996:181–82) offer some useful advice about reporting *p* values.

1. In many situations, it's enough to use simple asterisks in your prose to indicate statistical significance. But if you need to report p values, then do so with an $=$ sign, not with a $<$ or $>$ sign. If a p value is .042, don't report it as $p <.05$ ("the probability is less than .05"). Just report it as $p = .042$ and be done with it. Probability, just like the confidence we have in probabilistic results, is a continuous variable. Why cut out all that information with arbitrary cutoffs?

2. A single p value of .05 is as an indicator of a relation, but is not convincing support for a hypothesis. By tradition, researchers almost never report probabilities that are greater than .05. Five *repeated results* of $p = .06$, or even .10, are more convincing than a single result of $p = .05$ that something's really going on.

The Bonferroni Correction

If you want to be especially cautious in reporting correlations, you can apply a test known as the **Bonferroni correction**. There are two kinds of spurious correlation. One happens when the correlation between two variables is caused by a third, independent, variable. Another occurs when two variables covary because of sheer accident. It happens all the time. In fact, it occurs with a known probability.

Take a random sample of, say, 30 variables in the world, measure them, and correlate all possible pairs of those variables. (There are $n(n - 1)/2 = 435$ pairs of 30 anything.) According to the Bonferroni rule, you should get a correlation, significant at the $p = <.05$ level, in 5% of all cases—in 22 out of 435 pairs—just by chance. So, if you build a matrix with 435 pairs of correlations and find that 20 of them are significant at the .05 level or better, you can't be sure that this is not simply a random event.

You *always* have to explain why any two variables are correlated, since correlation, by itself, never implies cause and effect. But when you go fishing for significant correlations in a big matrix of them, and find fewer than you'd expect by chance alone, things are even tougher.

How tough? Pick a level of significance for reporting findings in your data—say, .05. If you have 30 variables in your analysis, and 435 tests of covariations in your matrix, divide .05 by 435 = .0001. If you report these correlations as significant at the 5% level (the level you chose originally), then, according to the Bonferroni rule, your report will be valid (see Kirk 1982; Koopmans 1981). This is a very, very conservative test, but it will prevent you from making those dreaded Type I errors, and reporting significant relations that aren't really there.

On the other hand, this will increase your chance of making Type II errors—rejecting some seemingly insignificant relations when they really *are* important. You might fail to show, for example, that certain types of exposure are related to contracting a particular disease, and this would have negative public health consequences. There's no free lunch.

Consider the study by Dressler (1980). He studied a sample of 40 people in the Caribbean island of St. Lucia, all of whom had high blood pressure. Dressler measured nine variables having to do with his respondents' ethnomedical beliefs and their compliance with a physician-prescribed treatment regimen. He reported the entire matrix of $(9 \times 8)/2 = 36$ correlations, 13 of which were significant at the 5% level or better.

Dressler might have expected just $36 \times .05 = 1.8$ such correlations by chance. Three of the 13 correlations were significant at the .001 level. According to the Bonferroni rule, correlations at the $.05/36 = .0014$ level would be reportable at the .05 level as valid. Under the circumstances, however (13 significant correlations with only about two expected by chance), Dressler was quite justified in reporting all his findings and was not being overly conservative.

I feel that if you are doing fieldwork, and using small data sets, you should be comfortable with tests of significance at the $p < .10$ level, especially if you can repeat your finding in independent tests. Two or three repeated experiments that produce similar results in the same direction at the .10 level of significance are more convincing evidence of something going on than is one experiment that just barely pans out at the .05 level.

On the other hand, you can always find significant covariations in your data if you lower alpha (the level of significance) enough, so be careful. Remember, you're using statistics to get hints about things that are going on in your data. I cannot repeat often enough the rule that real analysis (building explanations and suggesting plausible mechanisms that make sense out of covariations) is what you do *after* you do statistics.

I also can't stress enough the difference between **statistical significance** and **practical significance**. If you have a large enough *n* (in the thousands), you will surely find significant statistical relations in your data. Each of those relations may account for a small amount of the variance in what you're interested in understanding, but that doesn't mean that the relations are of practical use.

Lots of research across the world shows a strong correlation between instruction about the dangers of unprotected sex and an increase in knowledge about HIV/AIDS, but not necessarily any changes in risky sexual behavior. Instruction in the use of contraceptives produces an increase in knowledge about reproductive health, but not necessarily a decrease in fertility.

Even when an increase in knowledge does produce desired changes in behavior, the practical significance of this information may be set aside by political realities. If you start early enough, teaching children about the dangers of smoking apparently produces a reduction in smoking. Suppose you come up with a curriculum that costs $60,000 to implement in a school district of 2,000 students and that produces an aggregate reduction of 10% in smoking behavior and that the 10% is a statistically significant reduction. Will the school board shell out this money? The statistical level of significance in the results may play *some* role in the board's decision, but I'll bet that other things will weigh even more heavily in their deliberations.

Statistical Power

The **power** of a statistical test is the probability of *correctly accepting your research hypothesis*. If you're thinking: "You mean it's the probability of taking 'yes' for an answer?" then you're right on track. As you know, the traditional way to conduct research is to: (1) formulate a hypothesis; (2) turn the hypothesis around into a null hypothesis; and then (3) try as hard as we can to prove the null hypothesis.

This is *not* perverse. All of us positivists out here know that it's impossible to absolutely, positively, prove any hypothesis to be forever unfalsifiably true. So we do the next best thing. We try our very best to disprove our best ideas (our research hypotheses) and hope that we fail, leaving us with the right to say that our best guess is that we were right to begin with.

What this means in the real life of researchers is that statistical power is the probability of avoiding *both* Type I *and* Type II errors: rejecting the null hypothesis when it's really true (Type I error) or accepting a null hypothesis when it's really false (Type II error).

This probability depends on two things: (1) the minimum size of the difference between two outcomes that you will accept as a *real* difference and (2) the size of the sample. So, to achieve a given amount of statistical power in any experiment or survey, you need to calculate the size of the sample required, given the minimum size of the difference between two outcomes—the effect size—that you will accept as a real difference (Cohen 1988; Kraemer and Thiemann 1987).

This is a very important and subtle issue. Suppose you ask 100 men and 100 women, matched for socioeconomic status, race, and religion, to take the Attitudes Toward Women Scale (AWS). The null hypothesis is that there is no difference between the mean scores of the men and the mean scores of the women on this scale. How big a difference do you need between the mean of the men and the mean of the women on this scale to reject the null hypothesis and conclude that, in fact, the difference is real—that men and women really differ on their attitudes toward women as expressed in the AWS?

The answer depends on the power of the test of the difference in the means. Suppose you analyze the difference between the two means with a t-test, and suppose that the test is significant at the .05 level. Statistical power is the probability that you are wrong to report this result as an indicator that you can reject the null hypothesis.

The result, at the $p = .05$ level, indicates that the difference you detected between the mean for the men and the mean for the women would be expected to occur by chance fewer than 5 times in 100 runs of the same experiment. It does *not* indicate that you are $1 - p$, or 95% confident that you have correctly rejected the null hypothesis. The power of the finding of $p = .05$ depends on the size of the sample and on the size of the difference that you expected to find before you did the study.

In the case of the AWS, there are 40 years of data available. These data make it easy to say how big a difference you expect to find if the men and women in your sample are really different in their responses to the AWS. Many surveys, especially those done in foreign fieldwork, are done without this kind of information available. You can offer a theory to explain the results from one experiment or survey. But you can't turn around and use those same data to *test* your theory. As replications accumulate for questions of importance in the social sciences, the question of statistical power becomes more and more important.

So, what's the right amount of statistical power to shoot for? Cohen (1992) recommends that researchers plan their work—that is, set the effect size they recognize as important, set the level of statistical significance they want to achieve (.05, for example, or .01), and calculate the sample size—to achieve a power of .80.

A power value of .80 would be an 80% chance of recognizing that our original hypothesis is really true and a 20% chance of rejecting our hypothesis when it's really true. If you shoot for a power level of much lower than .80, says Cohen, you run too high a risk of making a Type II error.

On the other hand, power ratings much higher than .80 might require such large ns that researchers couldn't afford them (Cohen 1992:156). If you want 90% power for a .01 (1%) two-tailed test of, say, the difference between two Pearson's rs, then, you'd need 364 participants (respondents, subjects) to detect a difference of .20 between the scores of the two groups. If you were willing to settle for 80% power and a .05 (5%) two-tailed test, then the number of participants drops to 192. (To find the sample size needed for any given level of power, see Kraemer and Theimann 1987:105–12.)

The Shotgun Approach

A closely related issue concerns "shotgunning." This involves constructing a correlation matrix of all combinations of variables in a study and then relying on tests of significance to reach substantive conclusions.

Kunitz et al. (1981) studied the determinants of hospital utilization and surgery in 18 communities on the Navajo Indian Reservation during the 1970s. They measured 21 variables in each community, including 17 independent variables (the average education of adults, the percentage of men and women who worked full time, the average age of men and women, the percentage of income from welfare, the percentage of homes that had bathrooms, the percentage of families living in traditional hogans, etc.) and 4 dependent variables (the rate of hospital use and the rates for the three most common types of surgery). Table 21.20 shows the correlation matrix of all 21 variables in this study.

There are $n(n-1)/2$ pairs in any list of items, so, for a symmetric matrix of 21 items there are 210 possible correlations. Kunitz et al. point out in the footnote to their matrix that, for $n = 18$, the .05 level of probability corresponds to $r = 0.46$ and the .01 level corresponds to $r = 0.56$. By the Bonferroni correction, they could have expected:

$$[(21 \times 20)/2](.05) = 10.5$$

correlations significant at the 0.05 level and

$$[(21 \times 20)/2](.01) = 2.1$$

correlations significant at the .01 level by chance. There are 73 correlations significant at the .05 level in table 21.20, and 42 of those correlations are significant at the .01 level.

Kunitz et al. examined these correlations and were struck by the strong association of the hysterectomy rate to all the variables that appear to measure acculturation. I'm struck by it, too. This interesting finding was not the result of deduction and testing; it was the result of shotgunning. The finding is not proof of anything, but it sure seems like a strong clue to me. I'd want to follow this up with research on how acculturation affects the kind of medical care that women receive and whether all those hysterectomies are necessary.

THE PROBLEM WITH THE SHOTGUN APPROACH

The problem with shotgunning is that you might be fooled into thinking that *statistically* significant correlations are also *substantively* significant. This is a real danger, and it should not be minimized (Labovitz 1972). It results from two problems.

1. You have to be very careful about choosing a statistical measure of association, depending on how the variables were measured in the first place. A significant correlation in a matrix may be an artifact of the statistical technique used and not be of any substantive importance. Running a big correlation matrix of all your variables may produce some statistically significant results that would be insignificant if the proper test had been applied.
2. There is a known probability that any correlation in a matrix might be the result of chance. The number of expected significant correlations in a matrix is equal to the level of significance you choose, times the number of variables. If you are looking for covariations that are significant at the 5% level, then you only need 20 tests of covariation to find one such covariation by chance. If you are looking for covariations that are significant at the 1% level, you should expect to find one, by chance, in every 100 tries. In a matrix of 100 variables with 4,950 correlations, you might find around 50 significant correlations at the 1% level by chance.

This does not mean that 50 correlations at the 1% level in such a matrix *are* the result of chance. They just *might* be. There could be 100 or more significant correlations in a symmetric matrix of 100 variables. If 50 of them (4950/100) might be the result of chance, how can you decide which 50 they are? You can't. You can never know for sure whether

Table 21.20   Correlation Matrix of All 21 Variables in Kunitz et al.'s Study of Hospital Use on the Navajo Reservation

	1	2	3	4	5	6	7	8	9	10	11	12	13	14	15	16	17	18	19	20
1 Near hospital																				
2 Near surgery	.67																			
3 Wage work	-.24	-.09																		
4 Welfare	.52	.46	-.54																	
5 Education of men	-.42	-.43	.73	-.49																
6 Education of women	.01	-.21	.67	-.32	.81															
7 Hogans	.07	.37	-.26	.72	-.28	-.40														
8 Bathrooms	-.44	-.57	.63	.63	.70	.64	-.47													
9 Household size	.01	-.16	-.48	.24	-.34	-.07	.04	.12												
10 Working women	-.35	-.36	.68	-.65	.65	.57	-.48	.62	-.22											
11 Working men	-.24	-.18	.73	-.37	.73	.63	-.16	.41	-.45	.45										
12 Vehicles	.34	-.08	.40	-.17	.22	.52	-.53	.29	-.06	.31	.40									
13 Median income	-.45	-.51	.66	-.60	.67	.60	-.38	.79	-.07	.83	.48	.27								
14 Per capita income	-.25	-.20	.68	-.46	.61	.40	-.15	.29	-.68	.48	.51	.30	.47							
15 Age of women	-.23	-.03	-.47	-.15	-.36	-.66	-.02	-.46	-.30	-.37	-.32	-.56	-.43	-.04						
16 Age of men	.28	.15	-.77	.31	-.60	-.55	.01	-.67	.06	-.51	-.68	-.35	-.63	-.45	.60					
17 Age of patients	.13	.47	.13	-.14	-.21	-.15	-.18	-.22	-.36	-.04	-.26	-.15	-.26	-0.2	.29	.32				
18 Hysterectomies	-.41	-.48	.62	-.55	.57	.46	-.23	.75	-.09	.45	.46	.39	.62	.59	-.37	-.62	0.28			
19 Appendectomies	-.31	-.40	.32	-.14	.44	.33	.16	.51	.13	.07	.27	.01	.42	.35	-.31	-.49	-.56	-.62		
20 Cholesystectomies	-.23	-.70	.15	-.43	.35	.34	-.46	.68	.22	.19	.12	.31	.40	.14	-.17	-.17	-.35	.70	.49	
21 Hospital rate	-.49	.24	.02	-.26	.02	-.25	-.09	.16	-.19	-.04	-.34	-.33	.01	.22	.43	0.16	.45	.17	.10	.18

N = 18   0.46, p = .05   0.56, p = 0.01

SOURCE: S. J. Kunitz et al., "Determinants of Hospital Utilization and Surgery on the Navajo Indian Reservation, 1972–1978," *Social Science and Medicine* 15B, pp. 71–79 © 1981. Reprinted with permission from Elsevier.

any particular correlation is the result of chance. You simply have to be careful in your interpretation of *every* correlation in a matrix.

Use the shotgun. Be as cavalier as you can in looking for statistically significant covariations, but be very conservative in interpreting their substantive importance. Correlations are hints to you that something is going on between two variables. Just keep in mind that the leap from correlation to cause is often across a wide chasm.

If you look at table 21.18 again, you can see just how risky things can be. A correlation of 0.60 is significant at the 1% level of confidence with a sample as small as 30. Notice, however, that the correlation in the population is 99% certain to fall between 0.20 and 0.83, which is a pretty wide spread. You wouldn't want to build too big a theory around a correlation that just might be down around the 0.20 level, accounting for just 4% of the variance in what you're interested in!

Remember these rules:

1. Not all significant findings at the 5% level of confidence are equally important. A very weak correlation of .10 in a sample of a million people would be statistically significant, even if it were substantively trivial. By contrast, in small samples, substantively important relations may show up as statistically insignificant.
2. Don't settle for just one correlation that supports a pet theory; insist on several, and be on the lookout for artifactual correlations.

Fifty years ago, before statistical packages were available, it was a real pain to run any statistical tests. It made a lot of sense to think hard about which of the thousands of possible tests one really wanted to run by hand on an adding machine. Computers have eliminated the drudge work in data analysis, but they haven't eliminated the need to think critically about your results. If anything, computers have made it more important than ever to be self-conscious about the interpretation of statistical findings. But if you *are* self-conscious about this issue, and dedicated to thinking critically about your data, then I believe you should take full advantage of the power of the computer to produce a mountain of correlational hints that you can follow up.

Finally, by all means, use your intuition in interpreting correlations; common sense and your personal experience in research are powerful tools for data analysis. If you find a correlation between the number of times that men have been arrested for drug dealing and the number of younger siblings they have, you'd suspect that this correlation might be just a chance artifact.

On the other hand, maybe it isn't. There is just as much danger in relying slavishly on personal intuition and common sense as there is in placing ultimate faith in computers. What appears silly to you may, in fact, be an important signal in your data. The world is filled with self-evident truths that aren't true and self-evident falsehoods that aren't false. The role of science, based on solid technique and the application of intuition, is to sort those things out.

FURTHER READING

Measurement in anthropology: Burton (1973); Dressler et al. (2005).
Significance tests: Armstrong (2007); Carver (1978, 1993); Cohen (1994); Labovitz (1971b).

22

Multivariate Analysis

Most of the really interesting dependent variables in the social world—things like personality type, amount of risk-taking behavior, level of wealth accumulation, attitudes toward women or men—appear to be caused by a large number of independent variables, many of which are dependent variables themselves. The goal of multivariate analysis is to test hypotheses about *how* variables are related, based on a theory of causation. This is called **causal modeling**.

Multivariate analysis involves an array of statistical procedures—things like multiple regression, partial regression, factor analysis, and so on. I'll introduce you to the conceptual basis of some of these methods here. I hope that this will give you an idea of the range of tools available and enough information so you can read and understand research articles in which these techniques are used. I also hope that this will arouse your curiosity enough so that you'll study these methods in more advanced classes. This is the fun part.

ELABORATION: CONTROLLING FOR INDEPENDENT VARIABLES

We begin with the **elaboration method** developed by Paul Lazarsfeld and his colleagues (1972) for analyzing data from surveys (see especially Rosenberg 1968). This method involves teasing out the complexities in a bivariate relation by **controlling for** the effects of a third (antecedent or intervening) variable.

It's going to take you a while to get through the next half-dozen pages on the elaboration method. The writing is clear and there's nothing more complicated than a chi-square (χ^2), so they're not tough going. They're just plain tedious. Bear with me though. Eventually, you'll give a computer a list of independent variables, specify a dependent variable, and let the machine do the heavy lifting. But the next few pages will give you an appreciation of what a multivariate analysis does. They will also give you the skills you need to conduct a multivariate analysis in the field, while your thoughts are fresh and you still have time to collect any data you find you need. So be patient, pay close attention to the tables, and stay with it.

BUILDING TABLES

Suppose you are working in Peru and you suspect that Indians who move to Lima are no better off than Indians who remain in the villages. The Indians claim that they are seeking better jobs and better opportunities for their children, but you think that they are not getting what they came to the city to find. You conduct a survey of 250 village residents from a particular region and 250 migrants who have gone to the city from the same region. Table 22.1 shows the relation between residence and accumulated wealth status for your sample.

Table 22.1 Wealth by Residence for a Sample of 500 Peruvian Indians (Hypothetical Data)

Wealth	Rural	Urban	Row totals
Not poor	84	91	175
Poor	166	159	325
Column totals	250	250	500

$\chi^2 = .56$ ns (not significant)

Chi-square for this table is not significant. Assuming that you have measured wealth status using an appropriate index for both the urban and village environments, residence appears to make no difference in wealth accumulation among these informants.

Table 22.2, however, shows that after 5 years or more in the city, 68% (28/41) were no longer poor by local standards. In fact, the odds of emerging from poverty increase steadily over time. There is no guarantee, but the Indians' perception that urban migration works in their favor is substantially correct from these data. Thus, controlling for time allows the significant bivariate relation between wealth and urban residence to emerge.

Table 22.2 Wealth by Time in the City for Urban Migrants

Wealth	<1 year	1–3 years	3–5 years	>5 years	Row totals
Not poor	6	20	37	28	91
Poor	77	50	19	13	159
Column totals	83	70	56	41	250

$\chi^2 = 63.35$, $p < .001$

Although time is an important factor in understanding *what's* going on, it doesn't tell us anything about *how* the process works. We know from many studies that education is related positively to wealth. Table 22.3 shows the breakdown for the entire sample of 500, including the rural stay-at-homes and the urban migrants.

Table 22.3 Wealth by Education for the Entire Sample

Wealth	Did not complete 8th grade	Completed 8th grade	Row totals
Not poor	62	113	175
Poor	179	146	325
Column totals	241	259	500

$\chi^2 = 17.59$, $p < .001$, OR = 2.24

Chi-square is highly significant, and the odds ratio for this table is OR = 2.24. The odds of being poor for those who haven't completed 8 years of school are about two-and-a-quarter times those of people who have completed the eighth grade.

Table 22.4 breaks down education by residence. Chi-square for this table is also highly significant, and the odds ratio is 2.34. In other words, urbanites are more likely (two-and-a-third times more likely, in fact) to complete *secundaria*, or the eighth grade. This, it appears, leads to greater wealth.

We can test this hypothesis by producing a single cross-tab of wealth by education, controlling for residence. This is done in table 22.5, which really consists of two separate tables, each of which can be analyzed statistically. (Place the control variables above the independent variable when constructing multivariate tables.)

Table 22.4 Education by Residence

Education	Rural	Urban	Row totals
Completed 8th grade	100	159	259
Did not complete 8th grade	150	91	241
Column totals	250	250	500

$\chi^2 = 27.88$, $p < .001$, OR $= 2.62$

Table 22.5 Wealth by Education, Controlling for Residence

	Rural			Urban		
	≥8th grade	<8th grade	Row totals	≥8th grade	<8th grade	Row totals
Not poor	50	34	84	63	28	91
Poor	50	116	166	96	63	159
Column totals	100	150	250	159	91	250

$\chi^2 = 20.09$, $p < .001$, OR $= 3.41$ $\chi^2 = 1.96$ ns (not significant)

Things are a bit more complex than we imagined at first. Education makes a difference in the odds of escaping poverty, but only among rural people. What's going on here? To find out, we continue to elaborate the analysis, looking at other variables and how they may be magnifying or suppressing relationships.

As you add variables, of course, the number of tables required goes up, *as does the required sample size.* Adding a third variable, residence, to the analysis of wealth by education, requires two additional tables: residence by wealth and residence by education. Adding family size to the model, we need *three* additional tables. Tables 22.6, 22.7, and 22.8 show the breakdown for family size by education, wealth by family size, and family size by residence.

Table 22.6 Family Size by Education

	≥8th grade	<8th grade	Row totals
≤ 3 children	170	129	299
> 3 children	89	112	201
Column totals	259	241	500

$\chi^2 = 7.62$, $p < .01$, OR $= 1.65$

Table 22.7 Family Size by Wealth

	>3 children	≤3 children	Row totals
Not poor	84	91	175
Poor	215	110	325
Column totals	299	201	500

$\chi^2 = 15.59$, $p < .001$, OR $= 2.12$

In table 22.6, we see that people with more education tend to have smaller families. In table 22.7, we see that poor families tend to have more children. And in table 22.8, we see

Table 22.8   Family Size by Residence

	Rural	Urban	Row totals
>3 children	167	132	299
≤3 children	83	118	201
Column totals	250	250	500

$\chi^2 = 10.19$, $p < .001$, OR = 1.80

that rural people tend to have more children. It appears from these tables that economic status may be related more strongly to family size than to education or to residence.

To disentangle things, we look at the original relationship between wealth and residence, controlling for family size. Table 22.9 shows that when we do that, the effect of residence on economic status remains insignificant for rural people, but it makes a big difference for urban residents. When we look at the relationship between wealth and education in table 22.10, we see that the influence of education on wealth is insignificant for large families, but is highly significant for small families.

Table 22.9   Wealth by Residence, Controlling for Family Size

	Rural			Urban		
	Number of children		Row totals	Number of children		Row totals
	>3	≤3		>3	≤3	
Not poor	54	30	84	30	61	91
Poor	113	53	166	102	57	159
Column totals	167	83	250	132	117	250

$\chi^2 = .36$ ns (not significant) $\chi^2 = 22.58$, OR = 3.64

Table 22.10   Wealth by Education, Controlling for Family Size

	>3 children			≤3 children		
	Education		Row totals	Education		Row totals
	≥8 years	<8 years		≥8 years	<8 years	
Not poor	54	30	84	59	32	91
Poor	116	99	215	30	80	110
Column totals	170	129	299	89	112	201

$\chi^2 = 2.63$ ns (not significant) $\chi^2 = 24.48$, OR = 4.92

To get the full picture, we now produce table 22.11, which shows the bivariate relationship between wealth status and education, now controlling for *both* family size and residence simultaneously.

READING A COMPLEX TABLE
Reading across table 22.11, we see that among urban families with at least an eighth-grade education and three or fewer children, 43 out of 59, or 73%, are above the poverty line. Among urban families with at least an eighth-grade education and more than three children, only 20% (20/100) are above the poverty line. Among rural families with at least an

Table 22.11 Wealth by Education, Controlling for Family Size and Residence

| | Rural | | | | | Urban | | | | |
| | >3 children | | ≤3 children | | | >3 children | | ≤3 children | | |
	≥8th grade	<8th grade	≥8th grade	<8th grade	Row totals	≥8th grade	<8th grade	≥8th grade	<8th grade	Row totals
Not poor	34	20	16	14	84	20	10	43	18	91
Poor	36	77	14	39	166	80	22	16	41	159
Column totals	70	97	30	53	250	100	32	59	59	250

eighth-grade education and with three or fewer children, 53% are above the poverty line. Among rural people with at least an eighth-grade education and more than three children, 49% are above the poverty line.

In other words, for rural people, education appears to be the key to rising above poverty. So long as they increase their education, they are about as likely (49% vs. 53%) to increase their economic status, whether or not they limit natality.

For urban migrants, the picture is different. We saw from table 22.2 that the longer the urban migrants remained in the city, the greater the likelihood that they would rise above poverty. Now we know that unless they lower their natality *and* increase their education, the poverty-stricken villagers in our sample are probably better off staying home and not migrating to the city. If the urban migrants in our sample (all of whom started out as poor villagers) fail to limit natality, they lose the advantage that education would otherwise bring them. Rural people keep this advantage, irrespective of family size.

Explaining this finding is up to you. That's what theory is all about. A causal connection between variables requires a mechanism that explains how things work. (See chapter 2 if you need to go over the issue of covariation and causality.) In this instance, we might conjecture that rural people have lower overall expenses, especially if they own their own land and homes. They usually have extended families that cut down the cost of child care and that provide no-interest loans during emergencies. They grow much of their own food. And having more children may help them farm more land and cut down on expenses.

Urban people get more education, and this gets them better paying jobs. But if they have many mouths to feed, and if they have to pay rent, and if they lack the financial support of kin close by, then these factors may vitiate any advantage their education might otherwise bring.

TAKING THE ELABORATION ANOTHER STEP

We can look for clues that support or challenge our theory by elaborating the model still further, this time using family size as the dependent variable. Table 22.12 shows the result of cross-tabulating family size by education, controlling for residence.

Chi-square for the left half of this table is insignificant, but for the right half it is highly significant. Rural informants with less than an eighth-grade education are more likely than urban informants with less than an eighth-grade education to have more than three children (65% versus 35%). Among rural informants, in fact, level of education has little or no effect on family size (70% of those with higher education have large families vs. 65% of those with lower education).

Among urban informants, education is strongly associated with family size. More-educated urban informants are more likely than less-educated informants to have more

Table 22.12   Family Size by Education, Controlling for Residence

	Rural			Urban		
	≥8th grade	<8th grade	Row totals	≥8th grade	<8th grade	Row totals
>3 children	70	97	167	100	32	132
≤3 children	30	53	83	59	59	118
Column totals	100	150	250	159	91	250
	$\chi^2 = .77$ ns (not significant)			$\chi^2 = 17.86$, $p < .001$, OR = 3.13		

than three children, according to these data. This throws new light on the subject, and begs to be explained. We know that higher education without small families does not produce an increase in economic status for these poor migrants. We know, too, that most people, whether urban or rural, keep having large families, although large families are less prevalent among urbanites than among rural residents (132 out of 250 vs. 167 out of 250).

To understand this case still further, consider table 22.13, which cross-tabulates family size by wealth, controlling for both education and residence. This table shows that neither

Table 22.13   Family Size by Wealth, Controlling for Education and Residence

	Rural					Urban				
	≥8th grade		<8th grade		Row totals	≥8th grade		<8th grade		Row totals
	Poor	Not poor	Poor	Not poor		Poor	Not poor	Poor	Not poor	
>3 children	34	36	20	77	167	20	80	10	22	132
≤3 children	16	14	14	39	83	43	16	18	41	118
Column totals	50	50	34	116	250	63	96	28	63	250

wealth nor education influences family size among rural informants. For urban residents, however, the story is quite different. As expected, those urban informants who have both increased their education and increased their wealth have small families.

Go through table 22.13 carefully and make the appropriate comparisons across the rows and between the two halves. Compare also the results of this table with those of table 22.11, in which wealth status was the dependent variable.

From these tables, we can now hazard a guess about how these variables interact. We can draw a **conceptual model** of the whole process we've been looking at. It's in figure 22.1.

Most people in our sample are poor. Sixty-six percent of rural informants (166/250) and 64% of urban informants (159/250) are below the poverty line by our measurements. Among rural informants, education provides an edge in the struggle against poverty, irrespective of family size, but for urban migrants, education only provides an edge in the context of lowered family size.

Among those who remain in the villages, then, education may lead either to accumulation of wealth through better job opportunities, or it may have no effect. The chances are better, though, that it leads to wealth. Once this occurs, it leads to control of fertility. Among urban informants, education leads either to control of natality or not. If not, then education has practically no effect on the economic status of poor migrants. If it leads to lowered natality, then it may lead, over time, to a favorable change in economic status.

We can check this model by going back to our data on wealth status by number of

FOR RURAL INFORMANTS	FOR URBAN INFORMANTS
EDUCATION	EDUCATION
↓	↓
WEALTH ACCUMULATION	LOWER FAMILY SIZE
↓	↓
LOWER FAMILY SIZE	WEALTH ACCUMULATION

FIGURE 22.1.
Model of how wealth, education, and family size interact in urban and rural environments for informants in tables 21.11 and 21.13.

years in the city to see if those migrants who are economically successful over time have both increased their education *and* lowered their natality. Plausible assumptions about time ordering of variables are crucial in building causal models. Knowing, for example, that wealthy villagers never move to the city rules out some alternative explanations for the data presented here.

You get the picture. The elaboration method can produce subtle results, but it is quite straightforward to use and depends only on your imagination, on simple arithmetic (percentages), and on basic bivariate statistics.

PARTIAL CORRELATION

Of course, I haven't proven anything by all this laying out of tables. Don't misunderstand me. Elaboration tables are a great start—they test whether your ideas about some antecedent or intervening variables are plausible by showing what *could* be going on—but they don't tell you *how things work* or *how much* those antecedent or intervening variables are contributing to a correlation you want to understand. For that, we need something a bit more . . . well, elaborate. Partial correlation is a direct way to control for the effects of a third (or fourth or fifth . . .) variable on a relationship between two variables.

Here's an interesting case. Across the 50 states in the United States, there is a stunning correlation ($r = .778$) between the percentage of live births to teenage mothers (15–19 years of age) and the number of motor vehicle deaths per hundred million miles driven. States that have a high rate of road carnage have a high rate of births to teenagers, and vice versa.

This one's a real puzzle. Obviously, there's no *direct* relation between these two variables. There's no way that the volume of highway slaughter causes the number of teenage mothers (or vice versa), so we look for something that might cause both of them.

I have a hunch that these two variables are correlated because they are both the consequence of the fact that certain regions of the country are poorer than others. I know from my own experience, and from having read a lot of research reports, that the western and southern states are poorer, overall, than are the industrial and farming states of the Northeast and the Midwest. My hunch is that poorer states will have fewer miles of paved road per million people, poorer roads overall, and older vehicles. All this might lead to more deaths per miles driven.

Table 22.14 shows the **zero order correlation** among three variables: motor vehicle deaths per hundred million miles driven (it's labeled MVD in table 22.14); the percentage

Table 22.14 Correlation Matrix for Three Variables

	Variable 1 MVD	Variable 2 TEENBIRTH	Variable 3 INCOME
MVD	1.00		
TEENBIRTH	.778	1.00	
INCOME	−.662	−.700	1.00

SOURCE: MVD for 1995, Table 1018, *Statistical Abstract of the United States* (1997). TEENBIRTH for 1996, Table 98, *Statistical Abstract of the United States* (1997). INCOME for 1996, Table 706, *Statistical Abstract of the United States* (1997).

of live births to young women 15–19 years of age (TEENBIRTH); and average personal income (INCOME). Zero-order correlations do not take into account the influence of other variables.

We can use the formula for partial correlation to test directly what effect, if any, income has on the correlation between TEENBIRTH and MVD. The formula for partial correlation is:

$$r_{12 \cdot 3} = \frac{r_{12} - [r_{32}r_{13}]}{[\sqrt{1 - r_{32}^2}] \, [\sqrt{1 - r_{13}^2}]} \qquad \textbf{Formula 22.1}$$

where $r_{12 \cdot 3}$ = means "the correlation between variable 1 (MVD) and variable 2 (TEEN-BIRTH), *controlling* for variable 3 (INCOME) is . . ."

Table 22.15 Calculating the Partial Correlations for the Entries in Table 22.14

Pairs	Pearson's r	r^2	$1 - r^2$	$\sqrt{1 - r^2}$
r_{12} (MVD and TEENBIRTH)	.778	0.60528	0.39472	0.628264
r_{13} (MVD and INCOME)	−.662	0.43824	0.56176	0.749504
r_{32} (TEENBIRTH and INCOME)	−.700	0.49	0.51	0.714143

Table 22.15 shows the calculation of the partial correlations for the entries in table 22.14. So, the partial correlation between MVD and TEENBIRTH, controlling for INCOME is:

$$\frac{.778 - [(.700)(-.662)]}{(.714143)(.749504)} = \frac{.3146}{.535253} = .5877594$$

which we can round off to .59. (Remember, we have to use a *lot* of decimal places during the calculations in order to keep the rounding error in check. When we get through with the calculations we can round off to two or three decimal places.) In other words, when we **partial out** the effect of income, the correlation between MVD and TEENBIRTH drops from about 0.78 to about 0.59. That's because income is correlated with motor vehicle deaths ($r = -0.662$) *and* with teenage births ($r = -0.700$).

If a partial correlation of 0.59 between the rate of motor vehicle deaths and the rate of teenage births still seems high, then perhaps other variables are at work. You can "partial out" the effects of two or more variables at once, but as you take on more variables, the formula naturally gets more complicated.

A simple correlation is referred to as a **zero-order correlation**. Formula 22.1 is for a **first-order correlation**. The formula for a **second-order correlation** (controlling for two variables at the same time) is:

$$r_{12 \cdot 34} = \frac{r_{12 \cdot 3} - [r_{14 \cdot 3}\, r_{24 \cdot 3}]}{[\sqrt{1 - r^2_{14 \cdot 3}}]\,[\sqrt{1 - r^2_{24 \cdot 3}}]} \qquad \textbf{Formula 22.2}$$

You can also work out and test a model of how several independent variables influence a dependent variable all at once. This is the task of multiple regression, which we'll take up next. (For more on partial correlation, see Gujarati 2003.)

MULTIPLE REGRESSION

Partial correlation tells us how much a third (or fourth . . .) variable contributes to the relation between two variables. **Multiple regression** puts all the information about a series of variables together into a single equation that takes account of the interrelationships among independent variables. The result of multiple regression is a statistic called **multiple-R**, which is the combined correlation of a set of independent variables with the dependent variable, taking into account the fact that each of the independent variables might be correlated with each of the *other* independent variables.

What's really interesting is R^2. Recall from chapter 21 that r^2—the square of the Pearson product moment correlation coefficient—is the amount of variance in the dependent variable accounted for by the independent variable in a simple regression. R^2, or **multiple-R squared**, is the amount of variance in the dependent variable accounted for by two or more independent variables simultaneously.

Now, if the predictors of a dependent variable were all uncorrelated with each other, we could just add together the pieces of the variance in the dependent variable accounted for by each of the independent variables. That is, it would be nice if $R^2 = r_1^2 + r_2^2 + r_3^2 + \ldots$

It's a real nuisance, but independent variables *are* correlated with one another. This interdependence among independent variables is called **multicollinearity**, which we'll get to later. What we need is a method for figuring out how much variance in a dependent variable is accounted for by a series of independent variables after taking into account all of the overlap in variances accounted for across the independent variables. That's what multiple regression does.

The Multiple Regression Equation

We covered basic regression in chapter 21, but just to bring you back up to speed, remember that in simple regression we use an equation that expresses how an independent variable is related to a dependent variable. On the left-hand side of the equation, we have the unknown score for y, the dependent variable. On the right-hand side, we have the y-intercept, called a. It's the score for y if the dependent variable were zero. We have another coefficient, called b, that tells by *how much* to multiply the score on the independent variable for each unit change in that variable.

The general form of the equation (from chapter 21, formula 21.19) is:

$$y = a + bx$$

which means that the dependent variable, y, equals some constant plus another constant times the independent variable, x. So, for example, a regression equation like:

Starting Annual Income $= \$22,000 + (\$4,000 \times \text{Years of College})$

predicts that, on average, people with a high school education will start out earning $22,000 a year; people with 1 year of college will earn $26,000; and so on. A person with

9 years of university education (say, someone who has a Ph.D.) would be predicted to start at $58,000:

$$\text{Starting Annual Income} = \$22,000 + (\$4,000 \times 9) = \$58,000$$

Suppose that the average starting salary for someone who has a Ph.D. is $75,000. Several things could account for the discrepancy between our prediction and the reality. Sampling problems, of course, could be the culprit. Or it could be that there is just a lot of variability in starting salaries of people who have the Ph.D. English teachers who go to work in small, liberal arts colleges might start at $45,000 and people who have a Ph.D. in finance and who go to work for major brokerage companies might start at $150,000.

No amount of fixing the sample will do anything to get rid of the variance of starting salaries. In fact, the better the sample, the better it will reflect the enormous variance in those salaries.

In simple regression, if starting salary and years of education are related variables, we want to know "How accurately can we predict a person's starting salary if we know how many years of education they have beyond high school?" In multiple regression, we build more complex equations that tell us how much each of *several* independent variables contributes to predicting the score of a single dependent variable.

A typical question for a multiple regression analysis might be "How well can we predict a person's starting salary if we know how many years of college they have, *and* their major, *and* their gender, *and* their age, *and* their ethnic background?" Each of those independent variables contributes something to predicting a person's starting salary after high school.

The regression equation for two independent variables, called x_1 and x_2, and one dependent variable, called y, is:

$$y = a + b_1x_1 + b_2x_2 \qquad \textbf{Formula 22.3}$$

which means that we need to find a separate constant—one called b_1 and one called b_2—by which to multiply each of the two independent variables. The general formula for multiple regression is:

$$y = a + b_1x_1 + b_2x_2 \ldots b_nx_n \qquad \textbf{Formula 22.4}$$

(See box 22.1.)

BOX 22.1

MULTIPLE REGRESSION IS ALSO A PRE MEASURE

Recall that simple regression yields a PRE measure, r^2. It tells you how much better you can predict a series of measures of a dependent variable than you could by just guessing the mean for every measurement. Multiple regression is also a PRE measure. It, too, tells you how much better you can predict measures of a dependent variable than you could if you guessed the mean—but using all the information available in a series of independent variables.

The key to regression are those **b** coefficients, or **weights**, in formula 22.4. We want coefficients that, when multiplied by the independent variables, produce the best possible prediction of the dependent variable—that is, we want predictions that result in the smallest possible **residuals**. Those coefficients, by the way, are not existential constants. Remember that samples yield *statistics*, which only *estimate* parameters. Your statistics change with every sample you take and with the number of independent variables in the equation.

The MVD-TEENBIRTH Puzzle

Let's try to solve the puzzle of the relation between teenage births and the rate of motor vehicle deaths. We can take a stab at this using multiple regression by trying to predict the rate of teenage births *without* the data from motor vehicle deaths.

From our previous analyses with elaboration tables and with partial correlation, we already had an idea that income might have something to do with the rate of teen births. We know from the literature (Handwerker 1998) that poverty is associated with violence and with teenage pregnancy, and that this is true across ethnic groups, so I've added a variable on violent crimes that I think might be a proxy for the amount of violence against persons in each of the states.

Table 22.16   Correlation Matrix for Variables Associated with the Percentage of Teenage Births in the United States

	TEENBIRTH	INCOME	VIOLRATE	MVD
TEENBIRTH	1.00			
INCOME	−.700	1.00		
VIOLRATE	.340	.190	1.00	
MVD	.778	−.662	.245	1.00

Table 22.16 shows the correlation matrix for the four variables: TEENBIRTH (the percentage of births to teenagers in the 50 U.S. states during 1996); INCOME (the mean per capita income for each of the 50 states during 1996); VIOLRATE (the rate of violent crime—rape, murder, assault, and robbery—per 100,000 population in the 50 states in 1995); and MVD (the number of motor vehicle deaths per 100 million vehicle miles in each of the 50 states in 1995).

We see right away that the mean per capita income predicts the rate of births to teenagers ($r = -.700$) almost as well as does the rate of motor vehicle deaths ($r = .778$), and that mean income *also* predicts the rate of motor vehicle deaths rather well ($r = -.662$).

This is a clue about what might be going on: An antecedent variable, the level of income, might be responsible for the rate of motor vehicle deaths *and* the rate of teenage births. (By the way, did you notice that the strong correlations above were *negative*? The greater the mean income in the state, the lower the rate of teenage births and the lower the rate of motor vehicle deaths. Remember, correlations can vary from -1.0 to $+1.0$ and the strength of the correlation has nothing to do with its direction.)

And one more thing: The rate of violent crimes against people is moderately correlated with the rate of teenage births ($r = .340$), but is only weakly correlated with the mean income ($r = .190$) and with the rate of motor vehicle deaths ($r = .245$).

The task for multiple regression is to see how the independent variables predict the dependent variable *together*. If the correlation between mean per capita income and the rate of births to teenagers is $-.700$, that means that the independent variable accounts for 49% ($-.700^2$) of the variance in the dependent variable. And if the correlation between the rate of violent crimes and the rate of births to teenagers is .340, then the independent variable accounts for 11.56% ($.340^2$) of the variance in the dependent variable.

We can't just add these variances-accounted-for together, though, because the two independent variables are related to each other—each of the independent variables accounts for some variance in the other.

Table 22.17   Multiple Regression Output from SYSTAT®

Dep Var: TEENBIRTH   *N*: 50   Multiple-R: 0.850   Squared multiple-R: 0.722
Adjusted squared multiple-R: 0.710   Standard error of estimate: 1.829

Effect	Coefficient	Std Error	Std Coef	Tolerance	t	p (2 Tail)
CONSTANT	28.096	1.822	0.0	.	15.423	0.000
VIOLRATE	0.006	0.001	0.491	0.964	6.269	0.000
INCOME	− 0.001	0.000	− 0.793	0.964	− 10.130	0.000

Table 22.17 shows what the output looks like from SYSTAT® when I asked the program to calculate the multiple correlation, R, for INCOME and VIOLRATE on TEENBIRTH.

Table 22.17 tells us that the regression equation is:

$$\text{TEENBIRTH} = 28.096 + (.006 \times \text{VIOLRATE}) + (-.001 \times \text{INCOME})$$

For example, the violence rate for Wisconsin was 281 crimes per 100,000 residents in 1995 and the average income in Wisconsin was $21,184 in 1996. The regression equation predicts that the teenage birthrate for Wisconsin will be 8.6. The actual rate was 10.6 in 1996. The mean rate of teenage births for the 50 U.S. states was 12.9. The multiple regression, then, makes a better prediction than the mean: The difference between 10.6 and 12.9 is 2.3, while the difference between 8.6 and 10.6 is 2.0.

If you work out all the differences between the predictions from the *multiple* regression equation and the predictions from the *simple* regression equation involving *just* the effect of income on teenage births, the difference in the predictions will be the difference between accounting for 49% of the variance versus accounting for 72.2% of the variance in the dependent variable.

Details of the Regression Equation

In this example, *y* is TEENBIRTH, x_1 is INCOME, and x_2 is VIOLRATE. $R^2_{1 \cdot 23}$ is the variance in TEENBIRTH (the 1 in the subscript) accounted for by *both* INCOME and VIOLRATE (the 2 and 3 in the subscript). This relation is:

$$R^2_{1 \cdot 23} = r^2_{12} + r^2_{1(3 \cdot 2)}$$

which we can read as follows: The total variance in TEENBIRTH equals the variance accounted for by INCOME, plus the variance accounted for by VIOLRATE once the effect of INCOME has been accounted for. Calculating $R^2_{1 \cdot 23}$, then:

$$R^2_{1 \cdot 23} = r_{13} - (r_{12})(r_{32}) = .340 - (-.700)(.19) = .473$$

Taking the partial contribution of this relation to the dependent variable:

$$\frac{.473}{\sqrt{1-.19^2}} = .481776$$

The contribution of this correlation to the variance of TEENBIRTH is $.481776^2$, or $.23211$. INCOME accounts for 49% of the variance in TEENBIRTH. Adding contributions, we get $.49 + .23211$, or 72.2%, which is the squared multiple-R in table 22.17.

There are three coefficients in the regression equation: a, b_1, and b_2. These are the coefficients in formula 22.3. Each of the b coefficients is the product of the standardized regression coefficient for each independent variable with the ratio of the standard deviation of the independent variable to the standard deviation of the dependent variable.

The standardized coefficient for the relation between x_1 (TEENBIRTH) and x_2 (INCOME) is:

$$b(x_1 x_2) = \frac{r_{12} - (r_{13})(r_{23})}{1 - (r_{23})^2}$$

for INCOME $(x_2), b = -.793$
for VIOLRATE $(x_3), b = -.491$

These figures are given in table 22.17 as the "Std. Coef," or **standardized coefficients**.

The SD for the mean of INCOME is:	3,074.969
The SD for the mean of TEENBIRTH is:	3.399
The SD for the mean of VIOLRATE is:	269.225

Thus:

$$b_1 = (-.793)(3074.969) / 3.399 = -.001$$

and:

$$b_2 = (.491)(269.225) / 3.399 = .006$$

These figures, b_1 and b_2, are given in table 22.17 as the "Coefficients," and are the **unstandardized regression coefficients**. The method for calculating the value for a in the multiple regression equation is beyond the scope of this book. (For more about deriving multiple regression equations, consult Pedhazur [1997] or Gujarati [2003].)

But there's more. If we add up the variances accounted for by the zero-order correlations of INCOME and VIOLRATE on TEENBIRTH, we get 49% + 11.56% = 60.56%. According to the results in table 22.17, however, the income in a state and the rate of violent crimes *together* account for 72.2% of the variance in teenage births. In other words, the two variables acting together account for *more* than they do separately, and this is the case despite the fact that the independent variables are moderately correlated ($r = .340$) with each other.

In fact, INCOME explains 43.82% of the variance in motor vehicle deaths ($r = -.662$ and r^2 is $.4382$) and VIOLRATE explains 6% of the variance in motor vehicle deaths ($r = .245$ and r^2 is $.0600$). *Together*, though, INCOME and VIOLRATE have a multiple-R of $.762$ and an R^2 of $.581$. Here again, the two variables explain more variance working together than they explain working separately.

In other words, it's the complex association of per capita income *and* the level of violence that explains so much variance in *both* the rate of teenage births and the rate of motor vehicle deaths. It turns out that lots of things are best explained by a series of variables acting together (box 22.2).

EXAMPLES OF MULTIPLE REGRESSION

Graves and Lave (1972) modeled the starting wage of Navajo men who moved from the reservation in the 1960s to Denver. Graves and Lave started with 19 variables that they

CAUTION: AUTOMATED REGRESSION NOW
AVAILABLE EVERYWHERE

All of the major programs for statistical analysis today produce what is called a **stepwise multiple regression.** You specify a dependent variable and a series of independent variables that you suspect play some part in determining the scores of the dependent variable.

The program looks for the independent variable that correlates best with the dependent variable and then adds in the variables one at a time, accounting for more and more variance, until all the specified variables are analyzed, or until variables fail to enter because incremental explained variance is lower than a preset value, say, 1%. (There are even programs that test all possible path analysis equations . . . more on path analysis in a bit.)

Stepwise multiple regression is another one of those controversial hot topics in data analysis. Some people feel strongly that it is mindless and keeps you from making your own decisions about what causes what in a complex set of variables. It's rather like the significance test controversy and the shotgun controversy I discussed in chapter 21.

My take on it is the same: Learn to use all the tools and make your own decisions about the meaning of your findings. It's *your* responsibility to do the data processing and it's *your* responsibility to determine the meaning of your findings. Don't let robots take over any of your responsibilities. And don't be afraid to use all the hot new tools, either.

thought might relate in some way to starting wage—things like age, marital status, father's occupation, proficiency in English, prior urban experience, and internal versus external control (feeling that you do or don't control what happens to you), and so on. Using stepwise multiple regression, Graves and Lave eliminated variables (like English proficiency, which vanished when they controlled for education) and settled on the following equation:

STARTING WAGE $= .87 + .10$EDUC $+ .08$VT $+ .13$PW $+ .17$MARSTAT $+ .11$FO

where EDUC is the number of years of education beyond 10 (education only made a difference in starting wage after the 10th year), VT is the level of vocational training (skilled, like carpentry, vs. semiskilled, like house painting), PW is the highest premigration wage a man earned on the reservation, MARSTAT is marital status (married or unmarried), and FO is father's occupation (whether the migrant's father was a wage laborer or not—many Navajos in those days were sheep herders).

The equation says: Start with 87 cents an hour (remember, this was mid-1960s); add 10 cents an hour for every year of education beyond 10; add 8 cents if the man had strong vocational skills; add 13 cents for each dollar the man had earned in his best job before migrating (in those days, the median premigration wage was $1.50 an hour), add 17 cents if the man is married, and add 11 cents if his father had worked for wages.

R^2 for this equation is .54, which means that the equation accounts for 54% of the variance in starting wage.

Now that you know how it works, here are two more examples of multiple regression. John Poggie (1979) was interested in whether the beliefs of Puerto Rican fishermen about the causes of success in fishing were related to their actual success in fishing. He measured success by asking six key informants to rank 50 fishermen on this variable. Because his research was exploratory, he had a wide range of independent variables, three of which he guessed were related to fishing success: the fishermen's expressed orientation toward delaying gratification (measured with a standard scale), their boat size, and their years of experience at the trade.

The deferred gratification measure accounted for 15% of the variance in the dependent variable; years of experience accounted for another 10%; and boat size accounted for 8%. Together, these variables accounted for 33% of the variance in the success variable.

Mwango (1986) studied the decision by farmers in Malawi to devote part of their land to growing new cash crops (tobacco and hybrid maize) rather than planting only the traditional crop, called "maize of the ancestors." His units of analysis were individual farms; his dependent variable was the ratio of land planted in tobacco and hybrid maize to the total land under plow. And his eight independent variables were: the total cultivated land area, in hectares; the number of years a farmer was experienced in using fertilizers; whether the farming household usually brewed maize beer for sale; whether farmers owned any cattle at all; whether farmers had had any training in animal husbandry practices from the local extension agents; whether the family had an improved house (this required an index consisting of items such as a tin roof, cement floor, glass windows, and so on); whether the farmer owned a bicycle; and whether the farmer owned a plow and oxcart. These independent variables together accounted for 48% of the variance in the dependent variable.

On Explaining Just a Little of Something

In social science research, multiple regression (including path analysis, which is coming up next) typically accounts for between 30% and 50% of the variance in any dependent variable, using between two and eight independent variables. Like the equation from Graves and Lave (1972) above, you'll see plenty of regression equations with individual variables that explain 10% or less of what people are trying to understand. Does accounting for 10% of the variance in what you're interested in seem feeble? Consider:

1. In 2006, the average white male baby had a life expectancy at birth of 75.7 years in the United States, or 27,648 days. The life expectancy at birth for the average African American male baby was 69.7 years, or 25,457 days. The *difference* is 2,191 days. (In 1970, the figures were 67.1 years vs. 60.0 years, or a difference of 3,593 days.)
2. There were approximately 2.2 million births in Mexico in 2007, and around 43,500 infant deaths—that is, about 19.6 infant deaths per 1,000 live births. Compare these figures to the United States, where there were 4.3 million births in the same year and approximately 27,000 infant deaths, or about 6.2 per 1,000 live births. If the infant mortality rate in Mexico were the same as that in the United States, the number of infant deaths would be about 13,500 instead of 43,500. The *difference* would be 30,000 infant deaths.

Suppose you could account for just 10% of the *difference* in longevity among white and African American men in the United States (219 days) or 10% of the *difference* between the United States and Mexico in infant deaths (3,000 babies). Would that be worth doing? In my view, the most important contribution a social scientist can make to ameliorating a social problem is to be right about what causes it, and "accounting for variance" is part of causal modeling.

PATH ANALYSIS

Path analysis is a particular application of multiple regression. In multiple regression, we know (1) which independent variables help to predict some dependent variable and (2) how much variance in the dependent variable is explained by each independent variable. But multiple regression is an inductive technique: It does not tell us which are the antecedent variables, which are the intervening variables, and so on.

Path analysis is the application of multiple regression for testing conceptual models of multivariate relations—that is, for testing specific theories about how the independent variables in a multiple regression equation may be influencing each other—and how this ultimately leads to the dependent variable outcome.

The method was developed by the geneticist Sewall Wright in 1921 and became very popular in the social sciences in the 1960s (see Duncan 1966). It fell out of favor for a while (isn't it nice to know that even in statistics there are fads and fashions?), but it's making a strong comeback as full-featured statistics packages become more widely available.

I rather like the method because it depends crucially on the researcher's best guess about how a system of variables really works. It is, in other words, a nice combination of quantitative and qualitative methods. Here's an example.

Thomas (1981) studied leadership in Niwan Witz, a Mayan village. He was interested in understanding what causes some people to emerge as leaders, while others remain followers. From existing theory, Thomas thought that there should be a relation among leadership, material wealth, and social resources. He measured these complex variables for all the household heads in Niwan Witz (using well-established methods) and tested his hypothesis using Pearson's r. Pearson correlations showed that, indeed, in Niwan Witz leadership is strongly and positively related to material wealth and control of social resources.

Because the initial hypothesis was supported, Thomas used multiple regression to look at the relation of leadership to *both* types of resources. He found that 56% of the variance in leadership was explained by just three variables in his survey: wealth (accounting for 46%), family size (accounting for 6%), and number of close friends (accounting for 4%). But, since multiple regression does not, as Thomas said, "specify the causal structure among the independent variables" (1981:132), he turned to path analysis.

From prior literature, Thomas conceptualized the relation among these three variables as shown in figure 22.2. He felt that leadership, L, was caused by all three of the independent variables he had tested, that family size (fs) influenced both wealth (w) *and* the size of one's friendship network (fr), and that wealth was a factor in determining the number of one's friends.

The **path coefficients** in figure 22.2 are **standardized values**: They show the influence of the independent variables on the dependent variables in terms of standard deviations. The path coefficients in figure 22.2, then, show that "a one standard deviation increase in wealth produces a .662 standard deviation increase in leadership; a one standard deviation increase in family size results in a .468 standard deviation increase in leadership; and so on" (Thomas 1981:133). (For details about how path coefficients are determined, consult a textbook in multivariate analysis, like Kelloway 1998.)

Four things are clear from figure 22.2: (1) Among the variables tested, wealth is the most important cause of leadership in individuals. (2) Family size has a moderate causal

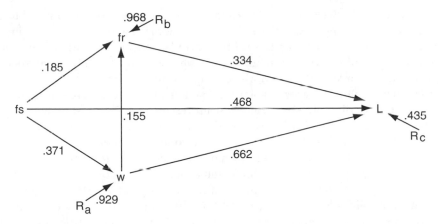

FIGURE 22.2.

Path analysis of effects of wealth, friendship, and family size on leadership in Niwan Witz.

SOURCE: J. S. Thomas, "The Socioeconomic Determinants of Leadership in a Tojalabal Maya Community." *American Ethnologist*, Vol. 8, pp. 127–38, 1981. Reproduced by permission of the American Anthropological Association. Not for further reproduction.

influence on wealth (making wealth a dependent, as well as an independent variable in this system). (3) The size of a person's friendship network is only weakly related to either family size or wealth. (4) The combined direct and indirect effects of family size, wealth, and friendship network on leadership account for 56.5% (1 − .435) of the variance in leadership scores for the household heads of Niwan Witz.

Thomas concludes from this descriptive analysis that if you want to become a leader in the Mayan village of Niwan Witz, you need wealth, and the best way to get that is to start by having a large family.

Path analysis lets you test a particular theory about the relations among a system of variables, but it doesn't produce the theory; that's *your* job. In the case of Niwan Witz, for example, Thomas specified that he wanted his path analysis to test a particular model in which wealth causes leadership. The results were strong, leading Thomas to reject the null hypothesis that there really is no causal relation between wealth and leadership. But even the strong results that Thomas got don't prove anything. In fact, Thomas noted that an alternative theory is plausible. It might be that leadership in individuals (wherever they get it from) causes them to get wealthy rather than the other way around.

Path analysis often serves as reality therapy for social scientists. It's fun to build conceptual models—to think through a problem and hypothesize how variables are linked to each other—but our models are often much more complicated than they need to be. Path analysis can help us out of this fix. We can test several plausible theories and see which is most powerful. But in the end, you're left out there, all by yourself, defending your theory on the basis of whatever data are available right now.

MULTICOLLINEARITY

Multivariate models are subject to a problem that simply can't exist when you have one independent variable: Independent variables can be correlated. In fact, when two variables both strongly predict a third, you'd expect the first two to be correlated. This **multicollinearity** means that you may not be able to tell the influence of one independent variable *free from the influence of the independent variables with which it is correlated.*

One way to avoid this problem is to conduct true experiments and nothing but true experiments. By assigning research participants randomly to control and experimental groups, we ensure that any correlation between independent variables is the result of chance. Nice work if you can get it, but most of what we want to study in anthropology requires fieldwork or survey research where things get messy.

Fortunately, multicollinearity distorts the findings of multiple regression only occasionally, and multicollinearity problems show up very clearly. The most dramatic sign of a multicollinearity problem is when your statistical program tells you that it cannot solve the equation. Some statistical programs calculate a **condition index** that diagnoses multicollinearity. A condition index between 10 and 30 signals moderate to strong multicollinearity, and an index over 30 signals a severe multicollinearity problem (Gujarati 1995).

But basic regression output shows the most common sign of a multicollinearity problem: Low probabilities for zero-order correlations between a series of independent variables and one dependent variable remain low in multivariate models when the variables are entered separately, but the probabilities for all the variables rise when you put them in the model together.

For example, an old puzzle, going all the way back to Durkheim (1951 [1897]), that remains of continuing interest is how to account for different rates of suicide across political units (countries, provinces, counties, cities). Table 22.18 shows the zero-order

Table 22.18   Zero-Order Correlations of Four Variables That Appear to Be Related

	SUICIDE	BTU	INCOME	OVER65
SUICIDE	1.00			
BTU	0.437	1.00		
INCOME	−0.520	−0.330	1.00	
OVER65	−0.367	−0.454	0.093	1.00

SOURCE: SUICIDE in 1994, Table 132, *Statistical Abstract of the United States* (1995). BTU in 1994, Table 925, *Statistical Abstract of the United States* (1997). INCOME in 1995, Table 698, *Statistical Abstract of the United States*. OVER 65 in 1995, Table 34, *Statistical Abstract of the United States* (1996).

correlations among four variables for the 50 states of the United States plus Washington, DC. SUICIDE is the number of deaths by suicide, per 100,000 in 1994; BTU is the average energy consumption, per person, in millions of BTUs in 1995; INCOME is the average personal income in 1995; and OVER65 is the percentage of people who were over 65 in 1996.

Notice that the rate of suicide (the ninth-leading cause of death in the United States) is correlated with each of the three independent variables. The higher the level of energy consumption (i.e., the worse the weather), the higher the rate of suicide. The higher the average personal income, the lower the rate of suicide. And the higher the proportion of old people, the *lower* the rate of suicide. (Suicide is the third-leading cause of death, after accidents and homicide, among Americans 15–24 years of age, but is hardly a factor among the elderly.)

Furthermore, each of these zero-order correlations is statistically very significant. Table 22.19 shows the regression between each of these independent variables separately and the rate of suicide. The *p*-value in each case is very low, indicating a highly significant statistical relation.

Table 22.20 shows what happens when we use multiple regression to check for spurious relations. If we put INCOME and BTU into the regression together, both variables remain statistically significant. If we put INCOME and OVER65 into the regression, both vari-

Table 22.19 Separate Regressions of Three Independent Variables with SUICIDE

Dep Var: SUICIDE   N: 51   Multiple R: 0.520   Squared multiple R: 0.270
Adjusted squared multiple R: 0.255   Standard error of estimate: 3.112

Effect	Coefficient	Std Error	Std Coef	Tolerance	t	p (2 Tail)
CONSTANT	24.789	2.799	0.000	.	8.856	0.000
INCOME	−0.001	0.000	−0.520	1.000	−4.257	0.000

Dep Var: SUICIDE   N: 51   Multiple R: 0.437   Squared multiple R: 0.191
Adjusted squared multiple R: 0.174   Standard error of estimate: 3.277

Effect	Coefficient	Std Error	Std Coef	Tolerance	t	p (2 Tail)
CONSTANT	9.309	1.184	0.000	.	7.860	0.000
BTU	0.010	0.003	0.437	1.000	3.397	0.001

Dep Var: SUICIDE   N: 51   Multiple R: 0.372   Squared multiple R: 0.139
Adjusted squared multiple R: 0.121   Standard error of estimate: 3.381

Effect	Coefficient	Std Error	Std Coef	Tolerance	t	p (2 Tail)
CONSTANT	21.509	3.061	0.000	.	7.026	0.000
OVER65	−0.667	0.238	−0.372	1.000	−2.807	0.007

Table 22.20 Regressions of the Three Pairs of Independent Variables with SUICIDE

Dep Var: SUICIDE   N: 51   Multiple R: 0.591   Squared multiple R: 0.349
Adjusted squared multiple R: 0.322   Standard error of estimate: 2.969

Effect	Coefficient	Std Error	Std Coef	Tolerance	t	p (2 Tail)
CONSTANT	20.038	3.318	0.000	.	6.038	0.000
INCOME	−0.000	0.000	−0.421	0.891	−3.417	0.001
BTU	0.007	0.003	0.298	0.891	2.413	0.020

Dep Var: SUICIDE   N: 51   Multiple R: 0.610   Squared multiple R: 0.372
Adjusted squared multiple R: 0.346   Standard error of estimate: 2.915

Effect	Coefficient	Std Error	Std Coef	Tolerance	t	p (2 Tail)
CONSTANT	31.282	3.502	0.000	.	8.933	0.000
INCOME	−0.001	0.000	−0.490	0.991	−4.264	0.000
OVER65	−0.564	0.202	−0.321	0.991	−2.798	0.007

ables remain significant. Thus, both BTU and OVER65 show effects on suicide rates that are independent of the effects of INCOME.

But look what happens when we enter all three independent variables into the regression. Table 22.21 shows the result: INCOME *remains* statistically significant, but *neither* BTU *nor* OVER65 are.

If BTU remained statistically significant while OVER65 did not, we could conclude that OVER65 had no effect on suicide independently of INCOME and BTU. Likewise, if OVER65 remained statistically significant while BTU did not, we could conclude that BTU had no effect on suicide independently of INCOME and OVER65. In this instance, however, we can only conclude that we have a multicollinearity problem that obscures our findings. We can't tell if either BTU or OVER65 has effects on suicide independently

Table 22.21 Regression of All Three Independent Variables and SUICIDE

Dep Var: SUICIDE   *N*: 51   Multiple R: 0.630   Squared multiple R: 0.397
Adjusted squared multiple R: 0.358   Standard error of estimate: 2.889

Effect	Coefficient	Std Error	Std Coef	Tolerance	t	p (2 Tail)
CONSTANT	26.898	4.806	0.000	.	5.597	0.000
INCOME	−0.000	0.000	−0.434	0.889	−3.613	0.001
BTU	0.004	0.003	0.183	0.714	1.362	0.180
OVER65	−0.439	0.228	−0.245	0.793	−1.927	0.060

of INCOME. (In fact, the condition index for this regression is 27, which indicates strong to severe multicollinearity.)

FACTOR ANALYSIS

Factor analysis is based on the simple and compelling idea that if things we observe are correlated with each other, they must have some underlying variable in common. Factor analysis refers to a set of techniques for identifying and interpreting those underlying variables.

For example, people in the United States who are in favor of gun control are likely (but not guaranteed) to be in favor of: (1) a woman's right to an abortion, (2) participation by the U.S. military in overseas peacekeeping missions of the United Nations, and (3) affirmative action in college admissions. People who are against gun control are likely to favor: (1) restrictions on abortion, (2) less involvement of the United States in UN peacekeeping missions, and (3) curbs on affirmative action.

Of course, people are free to mix and match their opinions on any of these issues, but overall, there is a strong association of opinions across these issues. Factor analysis assumes that this association is the result of an underlying, hypothetical variable, a general attitude orientation. We can use a set of statistical techniques to identify both the existence and the content of this underlying variable. Naming the variable is a strictly qualitative exercise.

Many studies have demonstrated the existence of an underlying value orientation usually called "liberal versus conservative." Liberals and conservatives exhibit packages of attitudes about things like personal freedom (as with the right to own a hand gun or the right to an abortion), about foreign policy (as with involvement in peacekeeping missions), and about domestic policies (as with affirmative action).

This idea of multidimensional supervariables that underlie a set of observations was first articulated in 1904 by Charles E. Spearman (he for whom Spearman's rank-order correlation coefficient is named—see chapter 21). Spearman noticed that the scores of students on various exams (classics, French, English, math, etc.) were correlated. He suggested that the exam scores were correlated with each other because they were all correlated with an underlying factor, which he labeled g, for general intelligence.

The single-factor theory of intelligence has been repudiated and defended over the years and continues to be the focus of scholarly and political debate, but the idea of factors—multidimensional variables—that underlie and give rise to a set of correlated events is one of the most important developments in all the social sciences.

The data for factor analysis are often attitude items, like the kind you see in Likert scales, but can just as well be about artifacts (movies, songs, buildings, cars, brands of beer . . .), people (movie stars, politicians, fashion models, criminals, classical musicians . . .), or even countries. Factor analysis is used across the social sciences in data reduction—to explore large data sets with dozens or even hundreds of variables in order to extract a few variables that tell a big story.

In political science, for example, Lieske (1993) partitioned the 3,164 counties in the United States into 10 distinctive regional subcultures by looking for common, underlying factors in the correlations among 45 racial, ethnic, religious, and social structural variables. In social psychology, Stein et al. (1991) used factor analysis to test the influence of ethnicity, socioeconomic status, and various anxieties as barriers to the use of mammography among white, African American, and Hispanic women. Factor analysis confirmed the influence of five kinds of anxiety: fear of radiation, fear of pain, embarrassment about breast exams, anxiety about what might be found, and concerns about cost.

Factor Analysis and Scales

As I mentioned in chapter 11, factor analysis is widely across the social sciences in building reliable, compact scales for measuring social and psychological variables. Suppose, for example, you are interested in attitudes toward gender role changes among women. You suspect that the underlying forces of role changes are related to premarital sexuality, working outside the home, and the development of an independent social and economic life among women. You make up 50 attitudinal items and collect data on those items from a sample of respondents.

Factor analysis will help you decide whether the 50 items you made up really test for the underlying forces you think are at work. If they do, then you could use a few benchmark items—the ones that "load high" on the factors—and this would save you from having to ask every respondent about all 50 items you made up. You would still get the information you need—or much of it, anyway. How much? The amount would depend on how much variance in the correlation matrix each of your factors accounted for.

The notion of variance is very important here. Factors account for chunks of variance—the amount of dispersion or correlation in a correlation matrix. Factors are extracted from a correlation matrix in the order of the amount of variance that they explain in the matrix. Some factors explain a lot of variance; others may be very weak and are discarded by researchers as not being useful. In a dense matrix, only one or a few factors may be needed to account for a lot of variance, while in a dispersed matrix, many factors may be needed.

The most common statistical solution for identifying the underlying factors in a correlation matrix is called the **orthogonal solution**. In orthogonal factor analyses, factors are found that have as little correlation with each other as possible. Other solutions that result in intercorrelated factors are also possible (the various solutions are options that you can select in all the major statistical packages, like SAS®, SYSTAT®, and SPSS®). Some researchers say that these solutions, although messier than orthogonal solutions, are more like real life.

So-called **factor loadings** are the correlations between the factors and the variables that are subsumed by, or appear to be components of, factors. All the old variables "load" on each new factor. The idea is to establish some cutoff below which you would not feel comfortable accepting that an old variable "loaded onto" a factor. Many researchers use 0.50 as the cutoff, and look at loadings of 0.30–49 as worth considering. Some researchers insist that a variable should load at least 0.60 before accepting it as an unambiguous component of a factor and look at variables that load between 0.30 and 0.59 as worth considering.

Once you have a list of variables that load high on a factor (irrespective of sign, plus or minus), you look at the list and decide what the factor *means*. An example should make all this a lot clearer.

Handwerker's Domestic Cooperation Scale

Penn Handwerker (1996a, 1998) used factor analysis to test whether the construct of "domestic cooperation" on Barbados was unidimensional. He asked a random sample of 428 Barbadian women whether their husband or boyfriend helped with any of the following: cooking, washing clothes, washing dishes, bathing children, taking children places, and caring for children. To put these items of domestic cooperation in context, he also asked each woman whether her husband or boyfriend was *expected* to treat her as an equal and whether her husband or boyfriend *did, in fact*, treat her as an equal.

Table 22.22 is a schematic of Handwerker's data matrix. The eight variables are labeled COOK, WASH, DISH, BATHE, TAKE, CARE, EQUAL1, and EQUAL2. Table 22.22 is a profile matrix (see figure 15.2a), but factor analysis is done on a similarity matrix (see figure 15.2b). If Handwerker had asked the women: "On a scale of 1–5, how much does your husband or boyfriend help you with the cooking," the entries in table 22.22 would have been 1–5. With that kind of data, a factor analysis program would turn the profile matrix into a similarity matrix by calculating Pearson's r for all possible pairs of columns. But Handwerker asked the women Yes/No questions (that's why table 21.22 contains only 0s and 1s).

Table 22.22 Schematic of Handwerker's Profile Matrix

ID	COOK	WASH	DISH	BATH	TAKE	CARE	EQUAL1	EQUAL2
1	1	0	1	1	1	0	1	0
2	0	1	0	0	1	0	1	1
3	1	0	0	0	1	1	1	0
.								
.								
.								
438	1	1	0	1	1	0	1	1

SOURCE: W. P. Handwerker, adapted from "Constructing Likert Scales: Testing the Validity and Reliability of Single Measures of Multidimensional Variables," *Cultural Anthropology Methods Journal*, Vol. 8, no. 1, p. 2, 1996a. Reprinted by permission of Sage Publications.

One way to turn a 1/0 profile matrix into a similarity matrix is to calculate the percentage of matches for all possible pairs of columns. That is, when two columns have a 1 or a 0 in the same row, count that as a hit. When two columns have different entries in the same row, count that as a miss. Then, count up all the hits and divide by 428 (the number of possible hits for 428 respondents).

This results in what's called a **simple matching coefficient**. (There are other kinds of matching coefficients, but I won't go into them here.) The result is an 8 × 8 similarity matrix. Table 22.23 shows the results of Handwerker's factor analysis of that matrix.

In reading the output from factor analysis, we look for items that load high on each factor. For me, that means loadings of at least .60. From table 22.23, it's clear that the domain of "domestic cooperation" is *not* unidimensional. In fact, it has three dimensions. Interpreting the results in table 22.23, it seemed to Handwerker that Factor 1 had something to do with "household chores." He labeled that factor "Domestic." Factor 2, he thought, comprised "chores associated with children," so he labeled it "Children." In open-ended interviews, Barbadian women interpreted the third factor as being about affection and empowerment within families, so Handwerker labeled it "Affection."

Table 22.23   Factor Loadings for Handwerker's Data

Variable	Factor 1 Domestic	Factor 2 Children	Factor 3 Affection
COOK	**0.893**	0.232	0.161
WASH	**0.895**	0.121	0.058
DISH	**0.824**	0.329	0.191
BATHE	**0.795**	0.324	0.194
TAKE	0.291	**0.929**	0.159
CARE	0.307	**0.922**	0.175
EQUAL1	0.188	0.203	**0.734**
EQUAL2	0.091	0.066	**0.854**
Explained Variance	39.15	25.516	17.841

SOURCE: W. P. Handwerker, "Constructing Likert Scales: Testing the Validity and Reliability of Single Measures of Multidimensional Variables," *Cultural Anthropology Methods Journal*, Vol. 8, no. 1, p. 2, 1996a. Reprinted with permission of Sage Publications.

Over the next few years, Handwerker had the opportunity to refine and test his scale on two more Caribbean islands, Antigua and St. Lucia. He dropped EQUAL1 because it was redundant with EQUAL2 and he dropped the question about "caring for children in other ways" (CARE) because respondents told him that it was ambiguous.

Handwerker also added four new questions—things that had come up in open-ended interviews as important to women: (1) Does your partner take responsibility for the children for an evening or an afternoon when you have something to do? (2) Does your partner take time off from work to share responsibility for children who are sick? (3) Does your partner talk with you and respect your opinion? (4) Does your partner spend his free time with you?

Table 22.24 shows the results for Antigua and St. Lucia. There are at least four things to notice about table 22.24:

Table 22.24   Handwerker's Data from Antigua and St. Lucia

Variable	Antigua			St. Lucia		
	Domestic	Children	Affection	Domestic	Children	Affection
COOK	**0.793**	0.317	0.106	**0.783**	0.182	0.161
WASH	**0.845**	0.163	0.090	**0.818**	0.056	0.018
DISH	**0.791**	0.320	0.203	**0.781**	0.197	0.173
BATHE	0.493	**0.654**	0.207	**0.695**	0.584	0.090
TAKE	0.271	**0.738**	0.289	0.246	**0.790**	0.196
TIME	0.253	**0.820**	0.258	0.228	**0.833**	0.061
SICK	0.210	**0.786**	0.151	0.121	**0.742**	−.067
FREET	0.100	0.299	**0.802**	−.010	**0.691**	0.319
EQUAL	0.147	0.155	**0.898**	0.177	0.117	**0.883**
TALK	0.142	0.200	**0.883**	0.113	0.112	**0.909**
Explained variance	26.460	26.459	25.051	24.188	27.905	18.191

SOURCE: W. P. Handwerker, "Constructing Likert Scales: Testing the Validity and Reliability of Single Measures of Multidimensional Variables," 1996a, *Cultural Anthropology Methods Journal*, Vol. 8, no. 1, p. 3, 1996a. Reprinted with permission of Sage Publications.

1. Despite the subtraction of some variables and the addition of others, the results from all three islands are very stable. COOK, WASH, and DISH are components of a single large factor across all three Caribbean countries.
2. Although BATHE loads high on the domestic chore factor across all three islands, it

also loads high on the children factor for two of the islands. This item should be dropped in the future because it does not reliably distinguish the two factors.

3. FREET loads on the children factor for St. Lucia, but it loads on the affection factor for Antigua. It turns out that Handwerker's assistant changed the wording for the FREET question slightly when she did the interviews on Antigua. Instead of asking: "Does your partner spend his free time with you?" she asked "Does your partner spend his free time with you or with your children?" (Handwerker 1996a:3). That little change apparently made enough of a difference in the responses to change the factor loading.

4. Across all three replications, the three factors in tables 22.23 and 22.24 account for 70%–80% of the variance in the original data matrix. That is, about three-fourths to four-fifths of the variance in the original data is accounted for by just three underlying variables (the three factors) rather than the full list of original variables. For women across the Caribbean, the construct of domestic cooperation is multidimensional and comprised of three subconstructs: sharing of everyday domestic chores, sharing of responsibilities for children, and affection from men as defined by being treated as an equal.

DISCRIMINANT FUNCTION ANALYSIS

Discriminant function analysis (DFA) is used to classify cases into categorical variables from ordinal and interval variables. For example, we may want to classify which of two (or more) groups an individual belongs to: male or female; those who have been labor migrants versus those who have not; those who are high, middle, or low income; those in favor of something and those who are not; and so on.

DFA is a statistical method developed for handling this problem. It has been around for a long time (Fisher 1936) but, like most multivariate techniques, DFA has become more popular since user-friendly computer programs have made it easier to do.

Lambros Comitas and I used DFA in our study of two groups of people in Athens, Greece: those who had returned from having spent at least 5 years in West Germany as labor migrants and those who had never been out of Greece. We were trying to understand how the experience abroad might have affected the attitudes of Greek men and women about traditional gender roles (Bernard and Comitas 1978). Our sample consisted of 400 persons: 100 male migrants, 100 female migrants, 100 male nonmigrants, and 100 female nonmigrants. Using DFA, we were able to predict with 70% accuracy whether an informant had been a migrant on the basis of just five variables.

There are some things you need to be careful about in using DFA, however. Notice that our sample in the Athens study consisted of half migrants and half nonmigrants. That was because we used a disproportionate, stratified sampling design to ensure adequate representation of returned migrants in the study. Given our sample, we could have guessed whether one of our informants was a migrant with 50% accuracy, without any information about the informant at all.

Only a very small fraction of the population of Athens consists of former long-term labor migrants to West Germany. The chances of stopping an Athenian at random on the street and grabbing one of those returned labor migrants was less than 5% in 1977 when we did the study.

Suppose that, armed with the results of the DFA that Comitas and I did, I asked random Athenians five questions, the answers to which allow me to predict 70% of the time whether any respondent had been a long-term labor migrant to West Germany. No matter what the answers were to those questions, I'd be better off predicting that the random Athenian was *not* a returned migrant. I'd be right more than 95% of the time.

Furthermore, why not just ask the random survey respondent straight out: "Are you a returned long-term labor migrant from West Germany?" With such an innocuous question, presumably I'd have gotten a correct answer at least as often as our 70% prediction based on knowing five pieces of information.

DFA is a powerful classification device, but it is not really a prediction device. Still, many problems (like the one Comitas and I studied) are essentially about understanding things so you can classify them correctly. Livingstone and Lunt (1993) surveyed 217 people in Oxford, England, and divided them into six types, based on whether or not people were in debt, whether or not people had savings, and people who live exactly within their income (with neither savings nor debt). DFA, using a variety of variables (age, class, education, income, expenses, attitudes toward debt, etc.) correctly classified almost 95% of the cases into one of the six groups that Livingstone and Lunt had identified.

Gans and Wood (1985) used DFA technique for classifying Samoan women as "traditional" or "modern" with respect to their ideal family size. If women stated that they wanted three or fewer children, Gans and Wood placed them in a category they labeled "modern." Women who said they wanted four or more children were labeled "traditional." DFA showed that just six of the many variables that Gans and Wood had collected allowed them to classify correctly which category a woman belonged to in 75% of all cases. The variables were such things as age, owning a car, level of education, etc.

It would have been ridiculous for Gans and Wood to have asked women straight out: "Are you traditional or modern when it comes to the number of children you'd like?" DFA (combined with on-the-ground ethnography) gave them a good picture of the variables that go into Samoan women's desired family size.

Similarly, Comitas and I were able to describe the attitudinal components of gender role changes by using DFA, and our prediction rate of 70% was significantly better than the 50% we'd have gotten by chance, given our sampling design. If you're careful about how you interpret the results of a discriminant function analysis, it can be a really important addition to your statistical tool kit.

AND FINALLY . . .

In a world of thousands of variables and millions of combinations of variables, how do you decide what to test? There is no magic formula. My advice is to follow every hunch you get. Some researchers insist that you have a good theoretical reason for including variables in your design and that you have a theory-driven reason to test for relations among variables once you have data. They point out that anyone can make up an explanation for any relation or lack of relation after seeing a table of data or a correlation coefficient.

This is very good advice, but I think it's a bit too restrictive, for three reasons:

1. I think that data analysis should be lots of fun, and it can't be unless it's based on following your hunches. Most relations are easy to explain, and peculiar relations beg for theories to explain them. You just have to be very careful not to conjure up support for every statistically significant relation, merely because it happens to turn up. There is a delicate balance between being clever enough to explain an unexpected finding and just plain reaching too far. As usual, there is no substitute for thinking hard about your data.

2. It is really up to you during research design to be as clever as you can in thinking up

variables to test. You're entitled to include some variables in your research just because you think they might come in handy. Just don't overdo it. There is nothing more tedious than an interview that drones on for hours without any obvious point other than that the researcher is gathering data on as many variables as possible.

3. The source of ideas has no necessary effect on their usefulness. You can get ideas from an existing theory or from browsing through data tables—or from talking about research problems with your friends. The important thing is not *how* you get a hunch, it's *whether you can test* your hunches and create plausible explanations for whatever findings come out of those tests. If others disagree with your explanations, then let them demonstrate that you are wrong, either by reanalyzing your data or by producing new data. But stumbling onto a significant relation between some variables does nothing to invalidate the relation.

So, when you design your research, try to think about the kinds of variables that might be useful in testing your hunches. Use the principles in chapter 3 and consider internal state variables (e.g., attitudes, values, beliefs); external state variables (e.g., age, height, gender, race, health status, occupation, wealth status); physical and cultural environmental variables (e.g., rainfall, socioeconomic class of a neighborhood); and time or space variables (Have attitudes changed over time? Do the people in one community behave differently from those in another otherwise similar community?).

In applied research, important variables are the ones that let you target a policy—that is, focus intervention efforts on subpopulations of interest (the rural elderly, victims of violent crime, overachieving third graders, etc.)—or that are more amenable to policy manipulation (knowledge is far more manipulable than attitudes or behavior, for example). No matter what the purposes of your research, or how you design it, the two principle rules of data analysis are:

1. If you have an idea, test it.
2. You can't test it if you don't have data on it.

Don't be afraid to play and have a good time with data analysis. If you hang around people who use complex statistical tools in their research, you'll hear them talking about "massaging" their data, "teasing out signals" from their data, and "separating the signals from the noise." These are not the sorts of phrases used by people who are bored with what they're doing.

Enjoy.

APPENDIX A

Table of Areas under a Normal Curve

(A) z	(B) area between mean and z	(C) area beyond z	(A) z	(B) area between mean and z	(C) area beyond z	(A) z	(B) area between mean and z	(C) area beyond z
0.00	.0000	.5000	0.37	.1554	.3446	0.80	.2881	.2119
0.01	.0040	.4960	0.41	.1591	.3409	0.81	.2910	.2090
0.02	.0080	.4920	0.42	.1628	.3372	0.82	.2939	.2061
0.03	.0120	.4880	0.43	.1664	.3336	0.83	.2967	.2033
0.04	.0160	.4840	0.44	.1700	.3300	0.04	.2995	.2005
0.05	.0199	.4801	0.45	.1736	.3264	0.85	.3023	.1977
0.06	.0239	.4761	0.46	.1772	.3228	0.86	.3051	.1949
0.07	.0279	.4721	0.47	.1808	.3192	0.87	.3078	.1922
0.08	.0319	.4681	0.48	.1844	.3156	0.88	.3106	.1894
0.09	.0359	.4641	0.49	.1879	.3121	0.89	.3133	.1867
0.10	.0398	.4602	0.50	.1915	.3085	0.90	.3159	.1841
0.11	.0438	.4562	0.51	.1950	.3050	0.91	.3186	.1814
0.12	.0478	.4522	0.52	.1985	.3015	0.92	.3212	.1788
0.13	.0517	.4483	0.53	.2019	.2981	0.93	.3238	.1762
0.14	.0557	.4443	0.54	.2054	.2946	0.94	.3264	.1736
0.15	.0596	.4404	0.55	.2088	.2912	0.95	.3289	.1711
0.16	.0636	.4364	0.56	.2123	.2877	0.96	.3315	.1685
0.17	.0675	.4325	0.57	.2157	.2843	0.97	.3340	.1660
0.18	.0714	.4286	0.58	.2190	.2810	0.98	.3365	.1635
0.19	.0753	.4247	0.59	.2224	.2776	0.99	.3389	.1611
0.20	.0793	.4207	0.60	.2257	.2743	1.00	.3413	.1587
0.21	.0832	.4168	0.61	.2291	.2709	1.01	.3438	.1562
0.22	.0871	.4129	0.62	.2324	.2676	1.02	.3461	.1539
0.23	.0910	.4090	0.63	.2357	.2643	1.03	.3485	.1515
0.24	.0948	.4052	0.64	.2389	.2611	1.04	.3508	.1492
0.25	.0987	.4013	0.65	.2422	.2578	1.05	.3531	.1469
0.26	.1026	.3974	0.66	.2454	.2546	1.06	.3554	.1446
0.27	.1064	.3936	0.67	.2486	.2514	1.07	.3577	.1423
0.28	.1103	.3897	0.68	.2517	.2483	1.08	.3599	.1401
0.29	.1141	.3859	0.69	.2549	.2451	1.09	.3621	.1379
0.30	.1179	.3821	0.70	.2580	.2420	1.10	.3643	.1357
0.31	.1217	.3783	0.71	.2611	.2389	1.11	.3665	.1335
0.32	.1255	.3745	0.72	.2642	.2358	1.12	.3686	.1314
0.33	.1293	.3707	0.73	.2673	.2327	1.13	.3708	.1292
0.34	.1331	.3669	0.74	.2704	.2296	1.14	.3729	.1271
0.35	.1368	.3632	0.75	.2734	.2266	1.15	.3749	.1251
0.36	.1406	.3594	0.76	.2764	.2236	1.16	.3770	.1230
0.37	.1443	.3557	0.77	.2794	.2206	1.17	.3790	.1210
0.38	.1480	.3520	0.78	.2823	.2177	1.18	.3810	.1190
0.39	.1517	.3483	0.79	.2852	.2148	1.19	.3830	.1170
1.20	.3849	.1151	1.61	.4463	.0537	2.02	.4783	.0217
1.21	.3869	.1131	1.62	.4474	.0526	2.03	.4788	.0212
1.22	.3888	.1112	1.63	.4484	.0516	2.04	.4793	.0207
1.23	.3907	.1093	1.64	.4495	.0505	2.05	.4798	.0202
1.24	.3925	.1075	1.65	.4505	.0495	2.06	.4803	.0197
1.25	.3944	.1056	1.66	.4515	.0485	2.07	.4808	.0192
1.26	.3962	.1038	1.67	.4525	.0475	2.08	.4812	.0188
1.27	.3980	.1020	1.68	.4535	.0465	2.09	.4817	.0183
1.28	.3997	.1003	1.69	.4545	.0455	2.10	.4821	.0179
1.29	.4015	.0985	1.70	.4554	.0446	2.11	.4826	.0174
1.30	.4032	.0968	1.71	.4564	.0436	2.12	.4830	.0170
1.31	.4049	.0951	1.72	.4573	.0427	2.13	.4834	.0166
1.32	.4066	.0934	1.73	.4582	.0418	2.14	.4838	.0162
1.33	.4082	.0918	1.74	.4591	.0409	2.15	.4842	.0158
1.34	.4099	.0901	1.75	.4599	.0401	2.16	.4846	.0154

(A) z	(B) area between mean and z	(C) area beyond z	(A) z	(B) area between mean and z	(C) area beyond z	(A) z	(B) area between mean and z	(C) area beyond z
1.35	.4115	.0885	1.76	.4608	.0392	2.17	.4850	.0150
1.36	.4131	.0869	1.77	.4616	.0384	2.18	.4854	.0146
1.37	.4147	.0853	1.78	.4625	.0375	2.19	.4857	.0143
1.38	.4162	.0838	1.79	.4633	.0367	2.20	.4861	.0139
1.39	.4177	.0823	1.80	.4641	.0359	2.21	.4864	.0136
1.40	.4192	.0808	1.81	.4649	.0351	2.22	.4868	.0132
1.41	.4207	.0793	1.82	.4656	.0344	2.23	.4871	.0129
1.42	.4222	.0778	1.83	.4664	.0336	2.24	.4875	.0125
1.43	.4236	.0764	1.84	.4671	.0329	2.25	.4878	.0122
1.44	.4251	.0749	1.85	.4678	.0322	2.26	.4881	.0119
1.45	.4265	.0735	1.86	.4686	.0314	2.27	.4884	.0116
1.46	.4279	.0721	1.87	.4693	.0307	2.28	.4887	.0113
1.47	.4292	.0708	1.88	.4699	.0301	2.29	.4890	.0110
1.48	.4306	.0694	1.89	.4706	.0294	2.30	.4893	.0107
1.49	.4319	.0681	1.90	.4713	.0287	2.31	.4896	.0104
1.50	.4332	.0668	1.91	.4719	.0281	2.32	.4898	.0102
1.51	.4345	.0655	1.92	.4726	.0274	2.33	.4901	.0099
1.52	.4357	.0643	1.93	.4732	.0268	2.34	.4904	.0096
1.53	.4370	.0630	1.94	.4738	.0262	2.35	.4906	.0094
1.54	.4382	.0618	1.95	.4744	.0256	2.36	.4909	.0091
1.55	.4394	.0606	1.96	.4750	.0250	2.37	.4911	.0089
1.56	.4406	.0594	1.97	.4756	.0244	2.38	.4913	.0087
1.57	.4418	.0582	1.98	.4761	.0239	2.39	.4916	.0084
1.58	.4429	.0571	1.99	.4767	.0233	2.40	.4918	.0082
1.59	.4441	.0559	2.00	.4772	.0228	2.41	.4920	.0080
1.60	.4452	.0548	2.01	.4778	.0222	2.42	.4922	.0078
2.43	.4925	.0075	2.74	.4969	.0031	3.05	.4989	.0011
2.44	.4927	.0073	2.75	.4970	.0030	3.06	.4989	.0011
2.45	.4929	.0071	2.76	.4971	.0029	3.07	.4989	.0011
2.46	.4931	.0069	2.77	.4972	.0028	3.08	.4990	.0010
2.47	.4932	.0068	2.78	.4973	.0027	3.09	.4990	.0010
2.48	.4934	.0066	2.79	.4974	.0026	3.10	.4990	.0010
2.49	.4936	.0064	2.80	.4974	.0026	3.11	.4991	.0009
2.50	.4938	.0062	2.81	.4975	.0025	3.12	.4991	.0009
2.51	.4940	.0060	2.82	.4976	.0024	3.13	.4991	.0009
2.52	.4941	.0059	2.83	.4977	.0023	3.14	.4992	.0008
2.53	.4943	.0057	2.84	.4977	.0023	3.15	.4992	.0008
2.54	.4945	.0055	2.85	.4978	.0022	3.16	.4992	.0008
2.55	.4946	.0054	2.86	.4979	.0021	3.17	.4992	.0008
2.56	.4948	.0052	2.87	.4979	.0021	3.18	.4993	.0007
2.57	.4949	.0051	2.88	.4980	.0020	3.19	.4993	.0007
2.58	.4951	.0049	2.89	.4981	.0019	3.20	.4993	.0007
2.59	.4952	.0048	2.90	.4981	.0019	3.21	.4993	.0007
2.60	.4953	.0047	2.91	.4982	.0018	3.22	.4994	.0006
2.61	.4955	.0045	2.92	.4982	.0018	3.23	.4994	.0006
2.62	.4956	.0044	2.93	.4983	.0017	3.24	.4994	.0006
2.63	.4957	.0043	2.94	.4984	.0016	3.25	.4994	.0006
2.64	.4959	.0041	2.95	.4984	.0016	3.30	.4995	.0005
2.65	.4960	.0040	2.96	.4985	.0015	3.35	.4996	.0004
2.66	.4961	.0039	2.97	.4985	.0015	3.40	.4997	.0003
2.67	.4962	.0038	2.98	.4986	.0014	3.45	.4997	.0003
2.68	.4963	.0037	2.99	.4986	.0014	3.50	.4998	.0002
2.69	.4964	.0036	3.00	.4987	.0013	3.60	.4998	.0002
2.70	.4965	.0035	3.01	.4987	.0013	3.70	.4999	.0001
2.71	.4966	.0034	3.02	.4987	.0013	3.80	.4999	.0001
2.72	.4967	.0033	3.03	.4988	.0012	3.90	.49995	.00005
2.73	.4968	.0032	3.04	.4988	.0012	4.00	.49997	.00003

SOURCE: *Statistical Tables and Formulas,* Table 1, p. 3. New York: John Wiley, 1981. Reprinted by permission of A. Hald.

APPENDIX B

Student's *t* Distribution

	Level of significance for one-tailed test					
	.10	.05	.025	.01	.005	.0005
	Level of significance for two-tailed test					
df	.20	.10	.05	.02	.01	.001
1	3.078	6.314	12.706	31.821	63.657	636.619
2	1.886	2.920	4.303	6.965	9.925	31.598
3	1.638	2.353	3.182	4.541	5.841	12.941
4	1.533	2.132	2.776	3.747	4.604	8.610
5	1.476	2.015	2.571	3.365	4.032	6.859
6	1.440	1.943	2.447	3.143	3.707	5.959
7	1.415	1.895	2.365	2.998	3.499	5.405
8	1.397	1.860	2.306	2.896	3.355	5.041
9	1.383	1.833	2.262	2.821	3.250	4.781
10	1.372	1.812	2.228	2.764	3.169	4.587
11	1.363	1.796	2.201	2.718	3.106	4.437
12	1.356	1.782	2.179	2.681	3.055	4.318
13	1.350	1.771	2.160	2.650	3.012	4.221
14	1.345	1.761	2.145	2.624	2.977	4.140
15	1.341	1.753	2.131	2.602	2.947	4.073
16	1.337	1.746	2.120	2.583	2.921	4.015
17	1.333	1.740	2.110	2.567	2.898	3.965
18	1.330	1.734	2.101	2.552	2.878	3.922
19	1.328	1.729	2.093	2.539	2.861	3.883
20	1.325	1.725	2.086	2.528	2.845	3.850
21	1.323	1.721	2.080	2.518	2.831	3.819
22	1.321	1.717	2.074	2.508	2.819	3.792
23	1.319	1.714	2.069	2.500	2.807	3.767
24	1.318	1.711	2.064	2.492	2.797	3.745
25	1.316	1.708	2.060	2.485	2.787	3.725
26	1.315	1.706	2.056	2.479	2.779	3.707
27	1.314	1.703	2.052	2.473	2.771	3.690
28	1.313	1.701	2.048	2.467	2.763	3.674
29	1.311	1.699	2.045	2.462	2.756	3.659
30	1.310	1.697	2.042	2.457	2.750	3.646
40	1.303	1.684	2.021	2.423	2.704	3.551
60	1.296	1.671	2.000	2.390	2.660	3.460
120	1.289	1.658	1.980	2.358	2.617	3.373
∞	1.282	1.645	1.960	2.326	2.567	3.291

SOURCE: *Statistical Tables for Biological, Agricultural and Medical Research,* R. A. Fisher and F. Yates, Pearson Education Limited. © 1963 R. A. Fisher and F. Yates. Printed and published in Great Britain by Oliver & Boyd Ltd., Edinburgh. Reprinted by permission.

APPENDIX C
Chi-Square Distribution Table

df	.99	.95	.90	.80	.70	.50
			Probabilities			
1	.000157	.00393	.0158	.0642	.148	.455
2	.0201	.103	.211	.446	.713	1.386
3	.115	.352	.584	1.005	1.424	2.366
4	.297	.711	1.064	1.649	2.195	3.357
5	.554	1.145	1.610	2.343	3.000	4.351
6	.872	1.635	2.204	3.070	3.828	5.348
7	1.239	2.167	2.833	3.822	4.671	6.346
8	1.646	2.733	3.490	4.594	5.527	7.344
9	2.088	3.325	4.168	5.380	6.393	8.343
10	2.558	3.940	4.865	6.179	7.267	9.342
11	3.053	4.575	5.578	6.989	8.148	10.341
12	3.571	5.226	6.304	7.807	9.034	11.340
13	4.107	5.892	7.042	8.634	9.926	12.340
14	4.660	6.571	7.790	9.467	10.821	13.339
15	5.229	7.261	8.547	10.307	11.721	14.339
16	5.812	7.962	9.312	11.152	12.624	15.338
17	6.408	8.672	10.085	12.002	13.531	16.338
18	7.015	9.390	10.865	12.857	14.440	17.338
19	7.633	10.117	11.651	13.716	15.352	18.338
20	8.260	10.851	12.443	14.578	16.266	19.337
21	8.897	11.591	13.240	15.445	17.182	20.337
22	9.542	12.338	14.041	16.314	18.101	21.337
23	10.196	13.091	14.848	17.187	19.021	22.337
24	10.865	13.848	15.659	18.062	19.943	23.337
25	11.524	14.611	16.473	18.940	20.867	24.337
26	12.198	15.379	17.292	19.820	21.792	25.336
27	12.879	16.151	18.114	20.703	22.719	26.336
28	13.565	16.928	18.939	21.588	23.647	27.336
29	14.256	17.708	19.768	22.475	24.577	28.336
30	14.953	18.493	20.599	23.364	25.508	29.336

	Probabilities						
df	.30	.20	.10	.05	.025	.01	.001
1	1.074	1.642	2.706	3.841	5.024	6.635	10.827
2	2.408	3.219	4.605	5.991	7.378	9.210	13.815
3	3.665	4.624	6.251	7.815	9.348	11.345	16.268
4	4.878	5.989	7.779	9.488	11.143	13.277	18.465
5	6.064	7.289	9.236	11.070	12.832	15.086	20.517
6	7.231	8.588	10.645	12.592	14.449	16.812	22.457
7	8.383	9.803	12.017	14.067	16.013	18.475	24.322
8	9.524	11.030	13.362	15.507	17.535	20.090	26.125
9	10.656	12.242	14.684	16.919	19.023	21.666	27.877
10	11.781	13.442	15.987	18.307	20.483	23.209	29.588
11	12.899	14.631	17.275	19.675	21.920	24.725	31.264
12	14.011	15.812	18.549	21.026	23.337	26.217	32.909
13	15.119	16.985	19.812	22.362	24.736	27.688	34.528
14	16.222	18.151	21.064	23.685	26.119	29.141	36.123
15	17.322	19.311	22.307	24.996	27.488	30.578	37.697
16	18.418	20.465	23.542	26.296	28.845	32.000	39.252
17	19.511	21.615	24.769	27.587	30.191	33.409	40.790
18	20.601	22.760	25.989	28.869	31.526	34.805	42.312
19	21.689	23.900	27.204	30.144	32.852	36.191	43.820
20	22.775	25.038	28.412	31.410	34.170	37.566	45.315
21	23.858	26.171	29.615	32.671	35.479	38.932	46.797
22	24.939	27.301	30.813	33.924	36.781	40.289	48.268
23	26.018	28.429	32.007	35.172	38.076	41.638	49.728
24	27.096	29.553	33.196	36.415	39.364	42.980	51.179
25	28.172	30.675	34.382	37.652	40.646	44.314	52.620
26	29.246	31.795	35.563	38.885	41.923	45.642	54.052
27	30.319	32.912	36.741	40.113	43.194	46.963	55.476
28	31.391	34.027	37.916	41.337	44.461	48.278	56.893
29	32.461	35.139	39.087	42.557	45.722	49.588	58.302
30	33.530	36.250	40.256	43.773	46.979	50.892	59.703

SOURCE: *Statistical Tables for Biological, Agricultural and Medical Research,* R. A. Fisher and F. Yates, Pearson Education Limited. © 1963 R. A. Fisher and F. Yates. Printed and published in Great Britain by Oliver & Boyd Ltd., Edinburgh. Reprinted by permission.

APPENDIX D

F Table for the .05 Level of Significance

df_2	Numerator Degrees of Freedom							
df_1	1	2	3	4	5	6	8	10
1	161.4	199.5	215.7	224.6	230.2	234.0	238.9	241.9
2	18.51	19.00	19.16	19.25	19.30	19.33	19.37	19.40
3	10.13	9.55	9.28	9.12	9.01	8.94	8.85	8.79
4	7.71	6.94	6.59	6.39	6.26	6.16	6.04	5.96
5	6.61	5.79	5.41	5.19	5.05	4.95	4.82	4.74
6	5.99	5.14	4.76	4.53	4.39	4.28	4.15	4.06
7	5.59	4.74	4.35	4.12	3.97	3.87	3.73	3.64
8	5.32	4.46	4.07	3.84	3.69	3.58	3.44	3.35
9	5.12	4.26	3.86	3.63	3.48	3.37	3.23	3.14
10	4.96	4.10	3.71	3.48	3.33	3.22	3.07	2.98
11	4.84	3.98	3.59	3.36	3.20	3.09	2.95	2.85
12	4.75	3.89	3.49	3.26	3.11	3.00	2.85	2.75
13	4.67	3.81	3.41	3.18	3.03	2.92	2.77	2.67
14	4.60	3.74	3.34	3.11	2.96	2.85	2.70	2.60
15	4.54	3.68	3.29	3.06	2.90	2.79	2.64	2.54
16	4.49	3.63	3.24	3.01	2.85	2.74	2.59	2.49
17	4.45	3.59	3.20	2.96	2.81	2.70	2.55	2.45
18	4.41	3.55	3.16	2.93	2.77	2.66	2.51	2.41
19	4.38	3.52	3.13	2.90	2.74	2.63	2.48	2.38
20	4.35	3.49	3.10	2.87	2.71	2.60	2.45	2.35
21	4.32	3.47	3.07	2.84	2.68	2.57	2.42	2.32
22	4.30	3.44	3.05	2.82	2.66	2.55	2.40	2.30
23	4.28	3.42	3.03	2.80	2.64	2.53	2.37	2.27
24	4.26	3.40	3.01	2.78	2.62	2.51	2.36	2.25
25	4.24	3.39	2.99	2.76	2.60	2.49	2.34	2.24
26	4.23	3.37	2.98	2.74	2.59	2.47	2.32	2.22
27	4.21	3.35	2.96	2.73	2.57	2.46	2.31	2.20
28	4.20	3.34	2.95	2.71	2.56	2.45	2.29	2.19
29	4.18	3.33	2.93	2.70	2.55	2.43	2.28	2.18
30	4.17	3.32	2.92	2.69	2.53	2.42	2.27	2.16
40	4.08	3.23	2.84	2.61	2.45	2.34	2.18	2.08
60	4.00	3.15	2.76	2.53	2.37	2.25	2.10	1.99
80	3.96	3.11	2.72	2.48	2.33	2.21	2.05	1.95
120	3.92	3.07	2.68	2.45	2.29	2.17	2.02	1.91
∞	3.84	3.00	2.60	2.37	2.21	2.10	1.94	1.83

Degrees of Freedom for the Denominator

				Numerator Degrees of Freedom				
df_1 df_2	12	15	20	30	40	60	120	∞
1	243.9	245.9	248.0	250.1	251.1	252.2	253.3	254.3
2	19.41	19.43	19.45	19.46	19.47	19.48	19.49	19.50
3	8.74	8.70	8.66	8.62	8.59	8.57	8.55	8.53
4	5.91	5.86	5.80	5.75	5.72	5.69	5.66	5.63
5	4.68	4.62	4.56	4.50	4.46	4.43	4.40	4.36
6	4.00	3.94	3.87	3.81	3.77	3.74	3.70	3.67
7	3.57	3.51	3.44	3.38	3.34	3.30	3.27	3.23
8	3.28	3.22	3.15	3.08	3.04	3.01	2.97	2.93
9	3.07	3.01	2.94	2.86	2.83	2.79	2.75	2.71
10	2.91	2.85	2.77	2.70	2.66	2.62	2.58	2.54
11	2.79	2.72	2.65	2.57	2.53	2.49	2.45	2.40
12	2.69	2.62	2.54	2.47	2.43	2.38	2.34	2.30
13	2.60	2.53	2.46	2.38	2.34	2.30	2.25	2.21
14	2.53	2.46	2.39	2.31	2.27	2.22	2.18	2.13
15	2.48	2.40	2.33	2.25	2.20	2.16	2.11	2.07
16	2.42	2.35	2.28	2.19	2.15	2.11	2.06	2.01
17	2.38	2.31	2.23	2.15	2.10	2.06	2.01	1.96
18	2.34	2.27	2.19	2.11	2.06	2.02	1.97	1.92
19	2.31	2.23	2.16	2.07	2.03	1.98	1.93	1.88
20	2.28	2.20	2.12	2.04	1.99	1.95	1.90	1.84
21	2.25	2.18	2.10	2.01	1.96	1.92	1.87	1.81
22	2.23	2.15	2.07	1.98	1.94	1.89	1.84	1.78
23	2.20	2.13	2.05	1.96	1.91	1.86	1.81	1.76
24	2.18	2.11	2.03	1.94	1.89	1.84	1.79	1.73
25	2.16	2.09	2.01	1.92	1.87	1.82	1.77	1.71
26	2.15	2.07	1.99	1.90	1.85	1.80	1.75	1.69
27	2.13	2.06	1.97	1.88	1.84	1.79	1.73	1.67
28	2.12	2.04	1.96	1.87	1.82	1.77	1.71	1.65
29	2.10	2.03	1.94	1.85	1.81	1.75	1.70	1.64
30	2.09	2.01	1.93	1.84	1.79	1.74	1.68	1.62
40	2.00	1.92	1.84	1.74	1.69	1.64	1.58	1.51
60	1.92	1.84	1.75	1.65	1.59	1.53	1.47	1.39
80	1.88	1.80	1.70	1.60	1.54	1.49	1.41	1.32
120	1.83	1.75	1.66	1.55	1.50	1.43	1.35	1.25
∞	1.75	1.67	1.57	1.46	1.39	1.32	1.22	1.00

Degrees of Freedom for the Denominator

Appendix E: Resources for Fieldworkers

CODES OF ETHICS

A Guide to Professional Ethics in Political Science (3rd ed.):
   http://www.apsanet.org/imgtest/ethicsguideweb.pdf
American Sociological Association Code of Ethics:
   http://www.asanet.org/about/ethics.cfm
Code of Ethics of the American Anthropological Association:
   http://www.aaanet.org/committees/ethics/ethcode.htm
Code of Ethics of the International Society of Ethnobiology:
   http://www.ethnobiology.net/ethics.php
Ethical Principles of Psychologists and Code of Conduct:
   http://www.apa.org/ethics/code2002.html
National Association for the Practice of Anthropology. Ethical Guidelines for Practitioners:
   http://practicinganthropology.org/ethical-guidelines
Society for Applied Anthropology. The Statement of Professional and Ethical Responsibilities:
   http://www.sfaa.net/sfaaethic.html

DIRECT OBSERVATION AND SURVEY RESEARCH

For information on using a PDA in the field to input data from direct observation of behavior, see Gravlee et al. (2006). These researchers used *Entryware* MCAPI (mobile computer-assisted personal interview) software from Techneos (www.techneos.com). Ice (2004) used *The Noldus Observer* in her field research. These and other products turn a PDA into a data-entry and data-management device. You program the keys (or use a mouse or stylus as the input device) to record events according to your own codes. This eliminates the need for checklists and coding sheets when you do direct observation, which lets you keep your eyes on the action. Many programs let you build screens for running survey interviews in the field. New products are being developed quickly. To find these, search for software for CAPI (computer-assisted personal interview), MCAPI (mobile CAPI), CASI (computer-assisted self-interview), and ACASI (audio CASI). With ACASI, people hear the interview and respond on a computer rather than read the interview. The advantage is that the interview can be entirely private.

STATISTICS PACKAGES

There are many excellent packages available. Before buying a stat package, find out if your campus has a site license for one or more of the following programs. If you have to buy a program of your own, check the Internet sites for student prices. Here are the URLs for widely used stats packages:

SAS® http://www.sas.com/technologies/analytics/statistics/stat/index.html
SPSS® http://www.spss.com. For students, search for SPSS Grad Pack.
SYSTAT® http://www.systat.com. Students can download MYSTAT, a smaller version of SYSTAT, at no cost: http://www.systat.com/MystatProducts.aspx
WINKS® http://www.texasoft.com
STATA® http://www.stata.com

There are many online courses offered in statistics, including commercial courses and freeware.

VOICE RECOGNITION SOFTWARE

Two popular programs are Dragon's *Naturally Speaking*® http://www.nuance.com /naturallyspeaking and the VR software that comes with Windows 7. For the Mac: http://www.macspeech.com.

ANTHROPAC

This package contains a suite of programs for collecting and analyzing data on cultural domains. There are routines for collecting and analyzing free lists, piles sorts, triads, paired comparisons, and ratings. Tools for analysis include multidimensional scaling, hierarchical clustering, property fitting (PROFIT), factor analysis, correspondence analysis, and quadratic assignment. Except for property fitting, all of these tools for analysis are available in UCINET. Files produced in ANTHROPAC and UCINET are compatible with one another and can be exported from UCINET to Excel. ANTHROPAC is the only program that imports data from free lists, triad tests, and paired comparisons. UCINET and ANTHROPAC are the only programs that run the formal model of consensus analysis. Both programs are available from http://www.analytictech.com.

TEXT ANALYSIS PROGRAMS

For information on many of the programs available, go to http://www.textanalysis.info and to http://caqdas.soc.surrey.ac.uk.

For a tutorial on choosing the right software for you, go to http://caqdas.soc.surrey .ac.uk/PDF/2009ChoosingaCAQDASPackage.pdf.

There is no such thing as a best program. Some are designed especially for video and some will let you treat documents and images alike as text that you can code. Many programs have free, downloadable demos. Try before you buy and remember: If you don't know how to write, a word processor won't help you. If you don't know anything about statistics, a stats package won't help you. In the same way, text analysis software will *facilitate* text analysis, but it won't *do* text analysis. That's a job that only you can do.

Many programs are being developed to do automatic text analysis. For example, see Kathleen Carley's work on AutoMap (http://www.casos.cs.cmu.edu/projects/automap). The *General Inquirer* is still available free (http://www.wjh.harvard.edu/~inquirer). Commercial products will be expensive for a while.

For semantic network analysis, see James Danowski's work on WORDij: http://free wordij.net

For information on workshops and conferences on text analysis, go to:

http://qualquant.net
http://caqdas.soc.surrey.ac.uk
http://www.asu.edu/clas/polisci/cqrm/institute.html
http://www.uofaweb.ualberta.ca/iiqm/Conferences.cfm
http://www.uofaweb.ualberta.ca/iiqm/SummerProgramAndResidency.cfm
http://www.esourceresearch.org/tabid/380/default.aspx

GPS

The Global Positioning System, or GPS, was developed by the Department of Defense in the United States. It relies on a system of satellites with worldwide coverage. A simple GPS unit, for under $200, can access the system and tell you, within 3 meters, your position on the Earth's surface. For more on the GPS, go to: http://www.gps.gov and http://tycho.usno.navy.mil/gps.html.

For reviews of GPS units: http://reviews.cnet.com/gps.

HAND-HELD COMPUTERS—PDAS

This technology has converged with telephone service and with Internet service. For reviews of PDAs and smart phones, go to: http://www.consumerreports.org and http://reviews.cnet.com/cell-phones.

TRANSCRIBING AIDS

Most field researchers have moved to digital recording and transcribing. For reviews of digital recorders and transcribers, http://reviews.cnet.com/1770-5_7-0.html?query = transcriber&tag = srch. There are several transcriber systems available that will handle both audio and video data, including Transana (open source): http://www.transana.org and HyperTranscribe: http://www.researchware.com.

JOURNALS THAT PUBLISH ARTICLES ABOUT RESEARCH METHODS

There are dozens of journals that publish articles on research methods in the social sciences. The journals listed here are devoted *primarily* to research methods.

Qualitative Methods

Forum: Qualitative Sozialforschung
   This journal publishes in English and is free at http://www.qualitative-research.net/index.php/fqs.

Qualitative Research, Qualitative Inquiry, and *Qualitative Health Research*
   These three journals from Sage Publications are devoted to the discussion of and the promotion of qualitative methods in social science. Go to http://www.sagepub.com.

Journal of Contemporary Ethnography
   This is not a methods journal, but I browse it regularly. It began in 1972. Many articles contain information about the methods and techniques used in the research. Go to http://jce.sagepub.com.

Qualitative and Quantitative Methods

Administrative Science Quarterly

ASQ is published by the Johnson Graduate School of Management at Cornell University. The journal has a long history of publishing articles on qualitative research methods, beginning with a now classic special issue in 1979, edited by John Van Maanen. The special issue was published as a book and is a valuable resource (Van Maanen 1983). Go to http://www2.johnson.cornell.edu/publications/asq.

Bulletin de Méthodologie Sociologique

This multidisciplinary quarterly publishes articles in French or English. All articles have abstracts in both English and French. To see the contents of current and back issues, go to: http://bms.sagepub.com.

Field Methods

This interdisciplinary journal is devoted to articles about methods for collecting, analyzing, and presenting data about human thought and human behavior in the natural world. Go to: http://fmx.sagepub.com.

Organizational Research Methods

This journal focuses entirely on research methods for studies of organizations. Go to: http://orm.sagepub.com.

Journal of Mixed Methods Research

This journal started in 2007. The title reflects the recognition, across the social sciences, of the importance of mixing qualitative and quantitative methods in many studies. Go to: http://mmr.sagepub.com.

Quantitative Methods

Public Opinion Quarterly

POQ began in 1937 and is one of the best. It is published by Oxford University Press for the American Association for Public Opinion Research. This is where you go to learn the latest on writing good questionnaires, on techniques for interviewing, on training interviewers, and so on. Go to: http://poq.oxfordjournals.org.

Sociological Methodology

This is a book-length once-a-year publication sponsored by the American Sociological Association and published by Wiley-Blackwell. Go to: http://www.wiley.com/bw/journal.asp?ref=0081-1750.

Sociological Methods and Research

This is a quarterly, interdisciplinary journal that publishes articles by methodologists from across the spectrum of social science. Go to http://smr.sagepub.com.

Psychological Methods

This journal, devoted to methods in research design and measurement, has been published by the American Psychological Association since 1996. Go to http://www.apa.org/pubs/journals/met/index.aspx.

Social Science Research

   SSR is an interdisciplinary journal that publishes papers in all areas of quantitative social research and has many papers on research methods. Go to: http://www.elsevier .com/locate/ssresearch.

World Cultures Journal

   Published since 1985, this journal is devoted to cross-cultural studies—that is, the use of cultures as units of analysis. Go to: http://eclectic.ss.uci.edu/~drwhite/worldcul/ world7.htm.

QCA: QUALITATIVE COMPARATIVE ANALYSIS

The COMPASS site is devoted to small-n analysis and has information about QCA, including programs that do this kind of Boolean analysis. Go to: http://www.compasss .org.

   For information about QCA software, see http://www.compasss.org/pages/resources/ software.html and http://www.u.arizona.edu/~cragin/fsQCA. In addition, ANTHROPAC has a routine for analyzing truth tables.

HUMAN RELATIONS AREA FILES

The main site for HRAF is at: http://www.yale.edu/hraf.

   It has tutorials for doing and for teaching cross-cultural research. It also has the latest (2004) version of the *Outline of Cultural Materials*: http://www.yale.edu/hraf/Ocm_xml/ traditionalOcm.xml.

   An easier-to use version of the OCM is at: http://www.yale.edu/hraf/Ocm_xml/ newOcm.xml.

References

Abbot, A. 1997. Of time and space: The contemporary relevance of the Chicago School. *Social Forces* 75:1149–82.

Abdul-Rahman, M. S. 2003. *Islam: Questions and answers.* Vol. 4, *The Hadeeth and its sciences.* London: MSA Publications Ltd.

Adams, J., and J. Moody. 2007. To tell the truth; Concordance in multiply recorded network data. *Social Networks* 29:44–58.

Adams, S. 1950. Does face validity exist? *Educational and Psychological Measurement* 10:319–28.

Addams, J. 1926. *Twenty years at Hull House.* New York: Macmillan.

Agar, M. 1973. *Ripping and running.* New York: Academic Press.

Agar, M. 1980a. Getting better quality stuff: Methodological competition in an interdisciplinary niche. *Urban Life* 9:34–50.

Agar, M. 1980b. *The professional stranger.* New York: Academic Press.

Agar, M. 1996. *The professional stranger: An informal introduction to ethnography.* 2nd ed. San Diego: Academic Press.

Ahern, K., and R. Le Brocque. 2005. Methodological issues in the effects of attrition: Simple solutions for social scientists. *Field Methods* 17:53–69.

Ahmed, A. M., and M. Hammarstedt. 2008. Discrimination in the rental housing market: A field experiment on the Internet. *Journal of Urban Economics* 64:362–72.

Ahrentzen, S., D. W. Levine, and W. Michelson. 1989. Space, time, and activity in the home: A gender analysis. *Journal of Environmental Psychology* 9:89–101.

Aiello, J. R., and S. E. Jones. 1971. Field study of the proxemic behavior of young school children in three subcultural groups. *Journal of Personality and Social Psychology* 19:351–56.

Alaimo, K., E. Packnett, R. A. Miles, and D. J. Kruger. 2008. Fruit and vegetable intake among urban community gardeners. *Journal of Nutrition Education and Behavior* 40:95–101.

Aldenderfer, M. S., and R. K. Blashfield. 1984. *Cluster analysis.* Beverly Hills, CA: Sage.

Alexander, J. 1976. A study of the cultural domain of "relatives." *American Ethnologist* 3:17–38.

Algase, D. L., B. Kupferschmid, C. A. Beel-Bates, and E. R. A. Beattie. 1997. Estimates of stability of daily wandering behavior among cognitively impaired long-term care residents. *Nursing Research* 46:172–78.

Al-Krenawi A., and R. Wiesel-Lev. 1999. Attitudes toward and perceived psychosocial impact of female circumcision as practiced among the Bedouin-Arabs of the Negev. *Family Process* 38:431–43.

Allen, J. T., and G. Italie. 1954. *A concordance to Euripides.* Berkeley: University of California Press.

Allport, F. H., and D. A. Hartman. 1931. The prediction of cultural change: A problem illustrated in studies by F. Stuart Chapin and A. L. Kroeber. In *Methods in social science*, S. A. Rice, ed., 307–52. Chicago: University of Chicago Press.

Altmann, J. 1974. Observational study of behavior: Sampling methods. *Behaviour* 49:227–67.

Altorki, S., and C. Fawzi El-Solh, eds. 1988. *Arab women in the field: Studying your own society.* Syracuse, NY: Syracuse University Press.

Alvard, M. S. 2004. The ultimatum game, fairness, and cooperation among big game hunters. In *Foundations of human sociality: Ethnography and experiments in 15 small-scale societies*, J. Henrich, R. Boyd, S. Bowles, H. Gintis, E. Fehr, and C. Camerer, eds., 413–35. Oxford: Oxford University Press.

American Anthropological Association (AAA). 1991. 1990 Ph.D. survey results. *Anthropology Newsletter*. Vol. 32:1, 44.

Anderson, A. 2003. *A place on the corner*. Chicago: University of Chicago Press.

Anderson, A. B., and E. S. Anderson. 1983. People and the Palm Forest. (Contract 51–07–79–07 to John Ewel.) Final report to United States Dept. of Agriculture, Forest Service, Consortium for the Study of Man's Relationship with the Global Environment. Washington, DC: USDA. (Also available through NTIS.)

Anderson, M., and M. Halpin, eds. 2000. In *Potlatch at Gitsegukla: William Beynon's 1945 field notebooks*, W. Beynon, ed., 3–52. Vancouver, BC: University of British Columbia Press.

Anderson, S. 2003. Why dowry payments declined with modernization in Europe but are rising in India. *Journal of Political Economy* 111:269–310.

Anderson-Fye, E. P. 2004. A "Coca-Cola" shape: Cultural change, body image, and eating disorders in San Andrés, Belize. *Culture, Medicine, and Psychiatry* 28:561–95.

Anspach, R. R., and N. Mizrachi. 2006. The field worker's fields: Ethics, ethnography and medical sociology. *Sociology of Health and Illness* 28:713–31.

Aquilino, W. S. 1993. Effects of spouse presence during the interview on survey responses concerning marriage. *Public Opinion Quarterly* 57:358–76.

Aquilino, W. S. 1994. Interview mode effects in surveys of drug and alcohol use. *Public Opinion Quarterly* 58:210–40.

Aquilino, W. S. 1997. Privacy effects on self-reported drug use: Interactions with survey mode and respondent characteristics. In *The validity of self-reported drug use: Improving the accuracy of survey estimates*, L. Harrison and A. Hughes, eds., 383–415. Rockville, MD: National Institute on Drug Abuse, Division of Epidemiology and Prevention Research.

Aquilino, W. S., D. L. Wright, and A. J. Supple. 2000. Response effects due to bystander presence in CASI and paper-and-pencil surveys of drug use and alcohol use. *Substance Use and Misuse* 35:845–67. Special issue: *Methodological Issues in the Measurement of Drug Use.*

Arasteh, K., D. C. Des Jarlais, S. R. Friedman, T. E. Perlis, and C. F. Turner. 2004. Audio-computerized self-interviewing for research data collection at drug abuse treatment programs. *Addiction* 99:885–96.

Archer, D., and L. Erlich. 1985. Weighing the evidence: A new method for research on restricted information. *Qualitative Sociology* 8:345–58.

Ardener, S., ed. 1981. *Women and space: Ground rules and social maps*. New York: St. Martin's Press.

Aristotle. Metaphysics. The Internet Classics Archive. Copyright © 1994–2000, D. C. Stevenson, Web Atomics. http://classics.mit.edu/Aristotle/metaphysics.html (accessed February 25, 2009).

Armstrong, J. S. 2007. Significance tests harm forecasting. *International Journal of Forecasting* 23:321–27.

Arnold-Cathalifaud, M., D. Thumala, A. Urquiza, and A. Ojeda. 2008. Young people's images of old age in Chile: Exploratory research. *Educational Gerontology* 34:105–23.

Aronson, E., and J. Mills. 1959. The effect of severity of initiation on liking for a group. *Journal of Abnormal and Social Psychology* 59:177–81.

Arp, W., III, and K. Boeckelman. 1997. Religiosity: A source of black environmentalism and empowerment? *Journal of Black Studies* 28:255–67.

Aswani, S. 2005. Customary sea tenure in Oceania as a case of rights-based fishery management: Does it work? *Reviews in Fish Biology and Fisheries* 15:285–307.

Atkinson, J. M., and J. Heritage, eds. 1984. *Structures of social action: Studies in conversation analysis*. New York: Cambridge University Press.

Atkinson, P., A. Coffey, S. Delamont, J. Lofland, and L. Lofland, eds. 2001. *Handbook of ethnography*. London: Sage.

Atran, S. 1998. Folk biology and the anthropology of science: Cognitive universals and cultural particulars. *Behavioral and Brain Sciences* 21:547–69.

Atzwanger, K., K. Grammer, K. Schäfer, and A. Schmitt, eds. 1997. *New aspects of human ethology*. New York: Plenum Press.

Auerswald, C. L., K. Greene, A. Minnis, I. Doherty, J. Ellen, and N. Padian. 2004. Qualitative assessment of venues for purposive sampling of hard-to-reach youth. An illustration in a Latino community. *Sexually Transmitted Diseases* 31:133–38.

Aunger, R. 1992. Sources of variation in ethnographic interview data: The case of food avoidances in the Ituri forest, Zaire. Paper presented at the annual meeting of the American Anthropological Association, San Francisco, California, December 2–6.

Aunger, R. 2004. *Reflexive ethnographic science*. Walnut Creek, CA: AltaMira.

Auster, C. J., and S. C. Ohm. 2000. Masculinity and femininity in contemporary American society: A reevaluation using the Bem Sex-Role Inventory. *Sex Roles* 43:499–528.

Axinn, W. G. 1991. The influence of interviewer sex on responses to sensitive questions in Nepal. *Social Science Research* 20:303–19.

Axinn, W. G., T. E. Fricke, and A. Thornton. 1991. The microdemographic community-study approach. *Sociological Methods and Research* 20:187–217.

Axinn, W. G., L. D. Pearce, and D. Ghimire. 1999. Innovations in life history calendar applications. *Social Science Research* 28:243–64.

Ayres, I. 1991. Fair driving: Gender and race discrimination in retail car negotiations. *Harvard Law Review* 104:817–72.

Babbage, C. 1835. *On the economy of machinery and manufactures*. 4th ed. London: Charles Knight.

Babbie, E. 1983. *The practice of social research*. 3rd ed. Belmont, CA: Wadsworth.

Bacon, Francis. 1902 [1620]. *Novum organum*, Joseph Devey, ed. New York: American Home Library Company.

Bailey, J. 2008. First steps in qualitative data analysis: Transcribing. *Family Practice* 25:127–31.

Baker, J., M. Levy, and D. Grewal. 1992. An experimental approach to making retail store environmental decisions. *Journal of Retailing* 68:445–60.

Baker, R. 1996a. PRA with street children in Nepal. *PLA Notes* 25:56–60. London: International Institute for Environment and Development.

Baker, R. (with C. Panter-Brick and A. Todd). 1996b. Methods used in research with street children in Nepal. *Childhood* 3:171–93.

Bales, R. F. 1950. *Interaction process analysis. A method for the study of small groups*. Cambridge, MA: Addison-Wesley.

Bales, R. F., and S. P. Cohen. 1979. *SYMLOG: A system for the multiple level observation of groups*. New York: The Free Press.

Balicki, A. 1989. *The Netsilik Eskimo*. Prospect Heights, IL: Waveland.

Banerjee, A., M. Bertrand, S. Datta, and S. Mullainathan. 2009. Labor market discrimination in Delhi: A field experiment. *Journal of Comparative Economics* 37:14–27.

Bang, M., D. L. Medin, and S. Atran. 2007. Cultural mosaics and mental models of nature. *Proceedings of the National Academy of Sciences* 104:13868–74.

Barber, N. 1998. Ecological and psychosocial correlates of male homosexuality: A cross-cultural investigation. *Journal of Cross-Cultural Psychology* 29:387–401.

Barchard, K. A., and J. Williams. 2008. Practical advice for conducting ethical online experiments and questionnaires for United States psychologists. *Behavior Research Methods* 40:1111–28.

Baril, H., J. Danielle, E. Chartrand, and M. Dubé. 2009. Females' quality of relationships in adolescence and friendship support in adulthood. *Canadian Journal of Behavioural Science* 41:161–68.

Barnes, J. H., B. F. Banahan, III, and K. E. Fish. 1995. The response effect of question order in computer-administered questioning in the social sciences. *Social Science Computer Review* 13:47–63.

Barroso, J. 1997. Reconstructing my life: Becoming a long-term survivor of AIDS. *Qualitative Health Research* 7:57–74.

Barry, H., III, and A. Schlegel. 1980. *Cross-cultural samples and codes*. Pittsburgh: University of Pittsburgh Press.

Barth, F. 2002. An anthropology of knowledge. *Current Anthropology* 43:1–18.

Bartlett, F. C. 1937. Psychological methods and anthropological problems. *Africa* 10:401–19.

Basiotis, P. P., S. O. Welsh, F. J. Cronin, J. L. Kelsay, and W. Mertz. 1987. Number of days of food intake records required to estimate individual and group nutrient intakes with defined confidence. *Journal of Nutrition* 117:1638–41.

Batchelder, W. H., and A. K. Romney. 1986. The statistical analysis of a general Condorcet model for dichotomous choice situations. In *Information pooling and decision making*, B. Grofman and G. Owen, eds., 103–12. Greenwich, CT: JAI.

Baugh, J. 1983. *Black street speech: Its history, structure, and survival.* Austin: University of Texas Press.

Beatty, P. C., and G. B. Willis. 2007. Research synthesis: The practice of cognitive interviewing. *Public Opinion Quarterly* 71:287–311.

Beautrais, A. L., P. R. Joyce, and R. T. Mulder. 1998. Youth suicide attempts: A social and demographic profile. *Australian & New Zealand Journal of Psychiatry* 32:349–57.

Bechky, B. A. 2003. Object lessons: Workplace artifacts as representations of occupational jurisdiction. *American Journal of Sociology* 109:720–52.

Bechtel, R. B. 1977. *Enclosing behavior.* Stroudsburg, PA: Dowden, Hutchinson, & Ross.

Beck, A. T., C. H. Ward, M. Mendelson, J. E. Mock, and J. Erbaugh. 1961. An inventory for measuring depression. *Archives of General Psychiatry* 4:561–71.

Beck, C. T., and R. K. Gable. 2000. Postpartum Depression Screening Scale: Development and psychometric testing. *Nursing Research* 49:272–82.

Beck, C. T., and R. K. Gable. 2003. Postpartum Depression Screening Scale: Spanish version. *Nursing Research* 52:296–306.

Beck, K. A. 2005. Ethnographic decision tree modeling: A research method for counseling psychology. *Journal of Counseling Psychology* 52:243–49.

Becker, A. E., R. A. Burwell, Stephen E. Gilman, D. B. Herzog, and P. Hamburg. 2002. Eating behaviors and attitudes following prolonged exposure to television among ethnic Fijian adolescent girls. *British Journal of Psychiatry* 180:509–14.

Becker, H. S. 1998. *Tricks of the trade: How to think about your research while you're doing it.* Chicago: University of Chicago Press.

Becker, H. S., B. Geer, E. C. Hughs, and A. L. Strauss. 1961. *Boys in white. Student culture in medical school.* Chicago: University of Chicago Press.

Beebe, J. 2001. *Rapid assessment: An introduction.* Walnut Creek, CA: AltaMira.

Beebe, T. J., S. M. Stoner, K. J. Anderson, and A. R. Williams. 2007. Selected questionnaire size and color combinations were significantly related to survey response rates. *Journal of Clinical Epidemiology* 60:1184–89.

Beere, C. A. 1990. *Gender roles: A handbook of tests and measures.* New York: Greenwood Press.

Begley, S., H. Fineman, and V. Church. 1992. The science of polling. *Newsweek*, September 28, pp. 38–39.

Begossi, A., M. Clauzet, J. L. Figueiredo, L. Garuana, R. V. Lima, P. F. Lopes, M. Ramires, A. L. Silva, and R. A. M. Silvano. 2008. Are biological species and higher ranking categories real? Fish folk taxonomy on Brazil's Atlantic forest coast and in the Amazon. *Current Anthropology* 49:291–306.

Behar, R. 1996. *The vulnerable observer: Anthropology that breaks your heart.* Boston: Beacon Press.

Belinfante, A. 2009. Telephone subscribership in the United States. Federal Communications Commission Report, August 2009. http://hraunfoss.fcc.gov/edocs_public/attachmatch/DOC -292759A1.pdf (accessed August 23, 2009).

Belk, R. W., J. F. Sherry, Jr., and M. Wallendorf. 1988. A naturalistic inquiry into buyer and seller behavior at a swap meet. *Journal of Consumer Research* 14:449–69.

Belli, R. F. 1998. The structure of autobiographical memory and the event history calendar: Potential improvements in the quality of retrospective reports in surveys. *Memory* 6:383–406.

Belo, J. 1960. *Trance in Bali.* New York: Columbia University Press.

Belousov, K., T. Horlick Jones, M. Bloor, Y. Gilinskiy, V. Golbert, Y. Kostikovsky, M. Levi, and D. Pentsov. 2007. Any port in a storm: Fieldwork difficulties in dangerous and crisis-ridden settings. *Qualitative Research* 7:155–75.

Bem, S. L. 1974. The measurement of psychological androgyny. *Journal of Consulting and Clinical Psychology* 42:155–62.

Bem, S. L. 1979. Theory and measurement of androgyny: A reply to the Pedhazur-Tetenbaum and Locksley-Colten critiques. *Journal of Personality and Social Psychology* 37:1047–54.

Ben-David, J., and T. A. Sullivan. 1975. Sociology of science. *Annual Review of Sociology* 1:203–22.

Bennardo, G. 2002. Map drawing in Tonga, Polynesia: Accessing mental representations of space. *Field Methods* 14:390–417.

Bennardo, G. 2008. Metaphors, source domains, and key words in Tongan speech about social relationships: 'Ofa "love" is giving. *Anthropological Linguistics* 50:174–204.

Bentley, M. E., G. H. Pelto, W. L. Straus, D. A. Schumann, C. Adegbola, E. de la Pena, G. A. Oni, K. H. Brown, and S. L. Huffman. 1988. Rapid ethnographic assessment: Applications in a diarrhea management program. *Social Science and Medicine* 27:107–16.

Berg, D. N., and K. K. Smith, eds. 1988. *The Self in social inquiry: researching methods*. Newbury Park, CA: Sage.

Berinsky, A. J. 2006. American public opinion in the 1930s and 1940s. The analysis of quota-controlled survey data. *Public Opinion Quarterly* 70:499–529.

Berlin, B., D. E. Breedlove, and P. H. Rave. 1968. Covert categories and folk taxonomies. *American Anthropologist* 70:290–99.

Berlin, B., D. E. Breedlove, and P. H. Rave. 1973. General principles of classification and nomenclature in folk biology. *American Anthropologist* 75:214–42.

Berman, J. 1996. "The culture as it appears to the Indian himself": Boas, George Hunt, and the methods of ethnography. In *Volksgeist as method and ethic*, G. W. Stocking, Jr., ed., 215–56. Madison: University of Wisconsin Press.

Bermant, G. 1982. Justifying social research in terms of social benefit. In *Ethical issues in social science research*, T. L. Beauchamp et al., eds., 125–43. Baltimore: The Johns Hopkins University Press.

Bernard, H. R. 1967. Kalymnian sponge diving. *Human Biology* 39:103–30.

Bernard, H. R. 1974. Scientists and policymakers: A case study in the ethnography of communications. *Human Organization* 33:261–75.

Bernard, H. R. 1987. Sponge fishing and technological change in Greece. In *Technology and social change*, 2nd ed., H. R. Bernard and P. J. Pelto, eds., 167–206. Prospect Heights, IL: Waveland.

Bernard, H. R. 1992. Preserving language diversity. *Human Organization* 41:82–88.

Bernard, H. R. 1993. Methods belong to all of us. In *Assessing cultural anthropology*, R. Borofsky, ed., 168–78. New York: McGraw Hill.

Bernard, H. R., and S. Ashton-Vouyoucalos. 1976. Return migration to Greece. *Journal of the Steward Anthropological Society* 8:31–51.

Bernard, H. R., and L. Comitas. 1978. Greek return migration. *Current Anthropology* 19:658–59.

Bernard, H. R., E. Johnsen, P. Killworth, and S. Robinson. 1989. Estimating the size of an average personal network and of an event population. In *The small world*, M. Kochen, ed., 159–75. Norwood, NJ: Ablex.

Bernard, H. R., and P. D. Killworth. 1973. On the social structure of an ocean-going research vessel and other important things. *Social Science Research* 2:145–84.

Bernard, H. R., and P. D. Killworth. 1974. Scientists and crew. *Maritime Studies and Management* 2:112–25.

Bernard, H. R., and P. D. Killworth. 1993. Sampling in time allocation research. *Ethnology* 32:211.

Bernard, H. R., P. D. Killworth, L. Sailer, and D. Kronenfeld. 1984. The problem of informant accuracy: The validity of retrospective data. *Annual Review of Anthropology* 13:495–517.

Bernard, H. R., and P. J. Pelto. 1987. Technology and anthropological theory. In *Technology and social change*, rev. 2nd ed., H. R. Bernard and P. J. Pelto, eds., 359–76. Prospect Heights, IL: Waveland.

Bernard, H. R., and G. W. Ryan. 2010. *Analyzing qualitative data: Systematic approaches*. Thousand Oaks, CA: Sage.

Bernard, H. R., G. Ryan, and S. Borgatti. 2009. Green cognition and behavior: A cultural domain analysis. In *Networks, resources and economic action. Ethnographic case studies in honor of Hartmut Lang*, C. Greiner and W. Kokot, eds., 189–215. Berlin: Dietrich Reimer Verlag.

Bernard, H. R., and J. Salinas Pedraza, eds. 1976. Otomí parables, folktales, and jokes. *International Journal of American Linguistics*, Native American Text Series, Vol. 1, No. 2. Chicago: University of Chicago Press.

Bernard, H. R., and J. Salinas Pedraza. 1989. *Native ethnography: A Mexican Indian describes his culture*. Newbury Park, CA: Sage.

Berra, Y., and J. Garagiola. 1998. *The Yogi book: "I really didn't say everything I said."* New York: Workman Publishing.

Berreman, G. D. 1962. *Behind many masks*. Ithaca, NY: Society for Applied Anthropology.

Berry, J. 1976. *Human ecology and cognitive style*. New York: Wiley.

Bessinger, J. B., and P. H. Smith. 1969. *A concordance to Beowulf*. Ithaca, NY: Cornell University Press.

Bickel, R., S. Weaver, T. Williams, and L. Lange. 1997. Opportunity, community, and teen pregnancy in an Appalachian state. *Journal of Educational Research* 90:175–81.

Billiet, J., and G. Loosveldt. 1988. Improvement of the quality of responses to factual survey questions by interviewer training. *Public Opinion Quarterly* 52:190–211.

Bird, D. W., R. Bliege Bird, and B. F. Codding. 2009. In pursuit of mobile prey: Martu hunting strategies and archaeofaunal interpretation. *American Antiquity* 74:3–29.

Birdwell-Pheasant, D. 1984. Personal power careers and the development of domestic structure in a small community. *American Ethnologist* 11:699–717.

Bizarro Ujpán, I. 1981. *Son of Tecun Uman: A Maya Indian tells his life story*. J. D. Sexton, ed. Tucson: University of Arizona Press.

Bizarro Ujpán, I. 1985. *Campesino: The diary of a Guatemalan Indian*, J. D. Sexton, transl. and ed. Tucson: University of Arizona Press.

Bizarro Ujpán, I. 1992. *Ignacio: The diary of a Maya Indian of Guatemala*, J. D. Sexton, transl. and ed. Philadelphia: University of Pennsylvania Press.

Bizarro Ujpán, I. 2001. *Joseño: Another Mayan voice speaks from Guatemala*, J. D. Sexton, transl. and ed. Albuquerque: University of New Mexico Press.

Black, D., and A. J. Riess, Jr. 1967. Patterns of behavior in police and citizen transactions. In *Studies in crime and law enforcement in major metropolitan areas. Field surveys III. U.S. President's Commission on Law Enforcement and Administration of Justice*. Vol. 2, 1–39. Washington, DC: U.S. Government Printing Office.

Blair, E. 1979. Interviewing in the presence of others. In *Improving interview method and questionnaire design: Response effects to threatening questions in survey research*, N. M. Bradburn and S. Sudman, eds., 134–46. San Francisco: Jossey-Bass.

Blair, E., S. Sudman, N. M. Bradburn, and C. B. Stocking. 1977. How to ask questions about drinking and sex: Response effects in measuring consumer behavior. *Journal of Marketing Research* 14:316–21.

Blalock, H. M., Jr. 1964. *Causal inferences in nonexperimental research*. New York: Norton.

Blalock, H. M., Jr., ed. 1971. *Causal models in the social sciences*. New York: Aldine-Atherton.

Blalock, H. M., Jr. 1979. *Social statistics*. Rev. 2nd ed. New York: McGraw-Hill.

Blass, T. 1999. The Milgram paradigm after 35 years: Some things we no know about obedience to authority. *Journal of Applied Social Psychology* 29:955–78.

Blommaert, J. 2006. Applied ethnopoetics. *Narrative Inquiry* 16:181–90.

Boas, F. 1910a. *Kwakiutl tales*. New York: Columbia University Press.

Boas, F. 1910b. *Changes in bodily form of descendants of immigrants*. United States Immigration Commission, Senate Document 208, 61st Congress. Washington, DC: Government Printing Office.

Boas, F., ed. 1911. *Handbook of American Indian languages*. Washington, DC: Bureau of American Ethnology, Bulletin No. 40.

Boas, F. 1917. *Folk-tales of Salishan and Sahaptin tribes*. Lancaster, PA: American Folk-Lore Society.

Boas, F. 1928a. *Kerasan texts*. New York: The American Ethnological Society.

Boas, F. 1928b. *Bella Bella texts*. New York: Columbia University Press.

Boas, F. 1935–43. *Kwakiutl tales*, New Series. New York: Columbia University Press.

Boas, F., and G. Hunt. 1902–1905. *Kwakiutl texts*. Leiden, The Netherlands: E. J. Brill.

Boas, F., and G. Hunt. 1906. *Kwakiutl texts*, Second Series. *Memoirs of the American Museum of Natural History* 14. New York: G. E. Stechert.

Bochner, S. 1971. The use of unobtrusive measures in cross-cultural attitudes research. In *A question of choice: An Australian Aboriginal dilemma*, R. M. Berndt, ed., 107–15. Nedlands: University of Western Australia Press.

Bochner, S. 1972. An unobtrusive approach to the study of housing discrimination against Aborigines. *Australian Journal of Psychology* 24:335–37.

Bochner, S. 1980. Unobtrusive observation in cross-cultural experimentation. In *Handbook of cross-cultural psychology*, H. C. Triandis and J. W. Berry, eds. Vol. 2, *Methodology*, 319–88. Boston: Allyn & Bacon.

Bochner, S. 2000. Culture shock. In *Encyclopedia of psychology*, A. E. Kazdin, ed. Vol. 2, 410–13. Washington, DC: American Psychological Association.

Bock, J. 2002. Evolutionary demography and intrahousehold time allocation: School attendance and child labor among the Okavango Delta peoples of Botswana. *American Journal of Human Biology* 14:206–21.

Bock, J., and S. E. Johnson. 2004. Subsistence ecology and play among the Okavango Delta peoples of Botswana. *Human Nature* 15:63–81.

Boeije, H. R. 2004. And then there were three: Why third persons are present in interviews and the impact on the data. *Field Methods* 16:3–32.

Boelen, W. A. M. 1992. *Street corner society*. Cornerville revisited. *Journal of Contemporary Ethnography* 21:11–51.

Boellstorff, T. 2007. Queer studies in the house of anthropology. *Annual Review of Anthropology* 36:17–35.

Bogardus, E. S. 1933. A social distance scale. *Sociology and Social Research* 17:265–71.

Bogdan, R. 1972. *Participant observation in organizational settings*. Syracuse, NY: Syracuse University Press.

Bohannan, P. 1995. *How culture works*. New York: Free Press.

Bolton, R. 1984. We all do it, but how? A survey of contemporary fieldnote procedure. In *Final report: Computers in ethnographic research* (Grant NIE–G–78–0062), pp. 119–44. Washington, DC: National Institute of Education (ERIC, No. ED 1. 310/2:248173).

Bolton, R., and J. Vincke. 1996. Risky sex and sexual cognition: The cartography of eros among Flemish gay men. *Journal of Quantitative Anthropology* 6:171–208.

Booth, C., ed. 1902. *Life and labor of the people of London*. New York: Macmillan.

Borchgrevink, A. 2003. Silencing language: Of anthropologists and interpreters. *Ethnography* 4:95–121.

Borgatti, S. P. 1992a. *Anthropac 4.98*. Columbia, SC: Analytic Technologies. http://www.analytictech.com/ (accessed May 13, 2009).

Borgatti, S. P. 1992b. *Anthropac 4.0 methods guide*. Columbia, SC: Analytic Technologies.

Borgatti, S. P. 1993/1994. Cultural domain analysis. *Journal of Quantitative Anthropology* 4:261–78.

Borgatti, S. P. 1997. Consensus analysis. http://www.analytictech.com/borgatti/consensu.htm (accessed March 8, 2010).

Borgatti, S. P. 1999. Elicitation techniques for cultural domain analysis. In *Enhanced ethnographic methods*, J. J. Schensul, M. D. LeCompte, B. K. Natasi, and S. P. Borgatti, eds., 115–51. Walnut Creek, CA: AltaMira.

Borgatti, S. P., and I. Carboni. 2007. On measuring individual knowledge in organizations. *Organizational Research Methods* 10:449–62.

Borgatti, S. P., M. G. Everett, and L. C. Freeman. 2002. *Ucinet for Windows*. Harvard, MA: Analytic Technologies. http://www.analytictech.com/ (accessed December 12, 2009).

Borgerhoff-Mulder, M. B., and T. M. Caro. 1985. The use of quantitative observational techniques in anthropology. *Current Anthropology* 26:323–36.

Borgers, N., J. Hox, and D. Sillel. 2004. Response effects in surveys on children and adolescents: Options, negative wording, and neutral mid-point. *Quality and Quantity* 38:17–33.

Bornmann, J. W. 2009. Becoming soldiers: Army basic training and the negotiation of identity. Ph.D. dissertation, George Washington University.

Borofsky, R. 2005. *Yanomami: The fierce controversy and what we can learn from it.* Berkeley: University of California Press.

Boschen, M. J. 2008. Paruresis (psychogenic inhibition of micturition): Cognitive behavioral formulation and treatment. *Depression and Anxiety* 25:903–12.

Boserup, E. 1970. *Women's role in economic development.* London: Allen & Unwin.

Boster, J. S. 1985. Requiem for the omniscient informant: There's life in the old girl yet. In *Directions in cognitive anthropology*, J. Dougherty, ed., 177–98. Urbana: University of Illinois Press.

Boster, J. S. 1986. Exchange of varieties and information between Aguaruna manioc cultivators. *American Anthropologist* 88:428–36.

Boster, J. S. 1987. Agreement between biological classification systems is not dependent on cultural transmission. *American Anthropologist* 89:914–20.

Boster, J. S., and J. C. Johnson. 1989. Form or function: A comparison of expert and novice judgments of similarity among fish. *American Anthropologist* 91:866–89.

Boster, J. S., J. C. Johnson, and S. C. Weller. 1987. Social position and shared knowledge: Actors' perceptions of status, role, and social structure. *Social Networks* 9:375–87.

Bourgois, P. I. 1990. Confronting anthropological ethics: Ethnographic lessons from Central America. *Journal of Peace Research* 27:43–54.

Bourgois, P. I. 1995. *In search of respect: Selling crack in El Barrio.* New York: Cambridge University Press.

Bove, R. B., C. R. Valeggia, and P. T. Ellison. 2000. Girl helpers and time allocation of nursing women among the Toba of Argentina. *Human Nature* 13:457–72.

Boyd, H. W. Jr., and R. Westfall. 1955. *The Journal of Marketing* 19: 311–24.

Boyle, E., Jr. 1970. Biological patterns in hypertension by race, sex, body weight, and skin color. *Journal of the American Medical Association* 213:1637–43.

Bradburn, N. M. 1983. Response effects. In *Handbook of survey research*, P. H. Rossi, J. D. Wright, and A. B. Anderson, eds., 289–328. New York: Academic Press.

Bradburn, N. M., S. E. Blair, and C. Stocking. 1978. Question threat and response bias. *Public Opinion Quarterly* 42:221–34.

Bradburn, N. M., and S. Sudman et al. 1979. *Improving interview method and questionnaire design: Response effects to threatening questions in survey research.* San Francisco: Jossey-Bass.

Bradley, C. 1997. Doing fieldwork with diabetes. *Cultural Anthropology Methods Journal* 9(2):1–7.

Brettell, C. B. 1998. Fieldwork in the archives: Methods and sources in historical anthropology. In *Handbook of methods in cultural anthropology*, H. R. Bernard, ed., 513–46. Walnut Creek, CA: AltaMira.

Brewer, D. D., and S. B. Garrett. 2001. Evaluation of interviewing techniques to enhance recall of sexual and drug injection partners. *Sexually Transmitted Diseases* 28:666–77.

Brewer, D. D., S. B. Garrett, and G. Rinaldi. 2002. Free-listed items are effective cues for eliciting additional items in semantic domains. *Applied Cognitive Psychology* 16:343–58.

Brewer, W. F. 1999. Schemata. In *The MIT encyclopedia of the cognitive sciences*, R. A. Wilson and F. C. Keil, eds., 729–30. Cambridge, MA: MIT Press.

Brewer, W. F. 2000. Bartlett's concept of the schema and its impact on theories of knowledge representation in contemporary cognitive psychology. In *Bartlett, culture and cognition*, A. Saito, ed., 69–89. Hove, England: Psychology Press.

Bridger, J. C., and D. R. Maines. 1998. Narrative structures and the Catholic Church closings in Detroit. *Qualitative Sociology* 21:319–40.

Bridges, F. S., and N. P. Coady. 1996. Affiliation, urban size, urgency, and cost of responses to lost letters. *Psychological Reports* 79:775–80.

Bridges, F. S., K. B. Keeton, and L. N. Clark. 2002. Responses to lost letters about a 2000 General Election amendment to abolish prohibition of interracial marriages in Alabama. *Psychological Reports* 91:1148–50.

Bridgman, P. W. 1927. *The logic of modern physics*. New York: Macmillan. (Reprinted 1980, New York: Arno.)

Briggs, C. L. 1986. *Learning how to ask: A sociolinguistic appraisal of the role of the interview in social science research*. New York: Cambridge University Press.

Brim, J. A., and D. H. Spain. 1974. *Research design in anthropology: Paradigms and pragmatics in the testing of hypotheses*. New York: Holt, Rinehart, and Winston.

Brislin, R. W. 1970. Back-translation for cross-cultural research. *Journal of Cross-Cultural Psychology* 1:185–216.

Brislin, R. W., W. J. Lonner, and R. M. Thorndike. 1973. *Cross-cultural research methods*. New York: Wiley.

Broadbent, N. 1995. Accident claims lives of researchers in Russian Far East. *Anthropology Newsletter*, November, 39–40.

Brown, C. H., J. Kolar, B. J. Torrey, T. G. Truong-Quang, and P. Volkman. 1975. Some general principles of biological and non-biological folk classification. *American Ethnologist* 3:73–85.

Brown, J. L., P. A. Vanable, and M. D. Eriksen. 2008. Computer-assisted self-interviews: A cost effectiveness analysis. *Behavior Research Methods* 40:1–7.

Browne, K. E. 2001. Female entrepreneurship in the Caribbean: A multisite, pilot investigation of gender and work. *Human Organization* 60:326–42.

Bruwer, J. D., and N. E. Haydam. 1996. Reducing bias in shopping mall-intercept surveys: The time-based systematic sampling method. *South African Journal of Business Management* 27:9–17.

Bryant, A., and K. Charmaz, eds. 2007. *The Sage handbook of grounded theory*. London: Sage.

Bryant, C. 1985. *Positivism in social theory and research*. New York: St. Martin's.

Brymer, R. A. 1998. Hanging out with the good 'ole boys, gangsters, and other disreputable characters: Field research, quantitative research, and exceptional events. In *Doing ethnographic research: Fieldwork settings*, S. Grills, ed., 143–61. Thousand Oaks, CA: Sage.

Bucholtz, M. 2000. The politics of transcription. *Journal of Pragmatics* 32:1439–65.

Budlender, D. 2007. A critical review of selected time use surveys. United Nations Research Institute for Social Development. Gender and Development Programme Paper Number 2. http://www.unrisd.org/ (accessed September 1, 2009).

Bulmer, M. 1984. *The Chicago School of Sociology: Institutionalization, diversity, and the rise of sociological research*. Chicago: University of Chicago Press.

Bulmer, M., ed. 1991. *Social research ethics: An examination of the merits of covert participant observation*. New York: Holmes and Meier.

Bunzl, M. 1996. Franz Boas and the Humboldtian tradition. In *Volksgeist as method and ethic*, G. W. Stocking, Jr., ed., 17–78. Madison: University of Wisconsin Press.

Burawoy, M. 1991. *Ethnography unbound: Power and resistance in the modern metropolis*. Berkeley: University of California Press.

Burger, J. 2009. Replicating Milgram. Would people still obey today? *American Psychologist* 64:1–11.

Burkhardt, R. W. 2005. *Patterns of behavior: Konrad Lorenz, Niko Tinbergen and the founding of ethology*. Chicago: University of Chicago Press.

Burling, R. 1964. Cognition and componential analysis: God's truth or hocus-pocus? *American Anthropologist* 66:20–28.

Burling, R. 2000 [1984]. *Learning a field language*. Prospect Heights, IL: Waveland.

Burton, M. L. 1968. Multidimensional scaling of role terms. Ph.D. dissertation, Stanford University.

Burton, M. L. 1972. Semantic dimensions of occupation names. In *Multidimensional scaling: Applications in the behavioral sciences*, A. K. Romney, R. N. Shepard, and S. B. Nerlove, eds. Vol. 2, *Applications*, 55–72. New York: Seminar Press.

Burton, M. L. 1973. Mathematical anthropology. *Annual Review of Anthropology* 2:189–99.

Burton, M. L., and S. B. Nerlove. 1976. Balanced design for triad tests. *Social Science Research* 5:247–67.

Burton, M. L., and A. K. Romney. 1975. A multidimensional representation of role terms. *American Ethnologist* 2:397–407.

Bush, A. J., and J. F. Hair, Jr. 1985. An assessment of the mall intercept as a data collection method. *Journal of Marketing Research* 22:158–67.

Butler, B., and D. M. Turner. 1987. *Children and anthropological fieldwork.* New York: Plenum.

Byrne, B., M. Harris, J. G. Consorte, and J. Lang. 1995. What's in a name? The consequences of violating Brazilian emic color-race categories in estimates of social well-being. *Journal of Anthropological Research* 41:389–97.

Byron, E. 2003. Market integration and health: The impact of markets and acculturation on the self-perceived morbidity, diet, and nutritional status of the Tsimane' Amerindians of lowland Bolivia. Ph.D. dissertation, University Florida.

Cabassa, L. J. 2003. Measuring acculturation: Where we are and where we need to go. *Hispanic Journal of Behavioral Sciences* 25:127–46.

Cahn, P. S. 2002. Being the third generation in Tzintzuntzan. In *Chronicling cultures: Long-term field research in anthropology,* R. V. Kemper and A. P. Royce, eds., 313–28. Walnut Creek, CA: AltaMira.

Cahn, P. S. 2003. *All religions are good in Tzintzuntzan: Evangelicals in Catholic Mexico.* Austin: University of Texas Press.

Cahnman, W. J. 1948. A note on marriage announcements in the *New York Times. American Sociological Review* 13:96–97.

Calahan, D. 1968. Correlates of respondent accuracy in the Denver validity survey. *Public Opinion Quarterly* 32:607–21.

Calder, N. 1993. *Studies in early Muslim jurisprudence.* New York: Oxford University Press.

Campbell, D. T. 1957. Factors relevant to the validity of experiments in social settings. *Psychological Bulletin* 54:297–312.

Campbell, D. T. 1974. Evolutionary epistemology. In *The library of living philosophers,* P. A. Schlipp, ed. Vol. 14, *The philosophy of Karl Popper,* Book 1, 413–63. La Salle, IL: Open Court Publishing.

Campbell, D. T. 1975. Degrees of freedom and the case study. *Comparative Political Studies* 8:178–93.

Campbell, D. T. 1979. Degrees of freedom and the case study. In *Qualitative and quantitative methods in evaluation research,* T. D. Cook and C. S. Reichart, eds., 49–67. Beverly Hills, CA: Sage.

Campbell, D. T., and R. F. Boruch. 1975. Making the case for randomized assignment to treatments by considering the alternatives: Six ways in which quasi-experimental evaluations in compensatory education tend to underestimate effects. In *Evaluation and experiment: Some critical issues in assessing social programs,* C. A. Bennett and A. A. Lumsdaine, eds., 195–296. New York: Academic Press.

Campbell, D. T., and H. L. Ross. 1968. The Connecticut crackdown on speeding: Time-series data in quasi-experimental analysis. *Law and Society Review* 3:33–53.

Campbell, D. T., and J. C. Stanley. 1966. *Experimental and quasi-experimental designs for research.* Chicago: Rand McNally.

Cannell, C. F., G. Fisher, and T. Bakker. 1961. Reporting of hospitalization in the Health Interview Survey. In *Health statistics.* Series D, No. 4. USDHEW, PHS. Washington, DC: U.S. Government Printing Office.

Cannell, C. F., and F. J. Fowler. 1965. Comparison of hospitalization reporting in three survey procedures. In *Vital and health statistics.* Series 2, No. 8. Washington, DC: U.S. Government Printing Office.

Cannell, C. F., and R. L. Kahn. 1968. Interviewing. In *The handbook of social psychology,* 2nd ed., G. Lindzey and E. Aronson, eds. Vol. 2, *Research methods,* 526–95. Reading, MA: Addison-Wesley.

Cannell, C. F., L. Oksenberg, and J. M. Converse, eds. 1979. *Experiments in interview techniques. Field experiments in health reporting 1971–1977.* Ann Arbor: Institute for Social Research, University of Michigan.

Cannell C. F., L. Oksenberg, G. Kalton, K. Bischoping, and F. J. Fowler. 1989. *New techniques for pretesting survey questions.* Final Report, Grant No. HS 05616. National Center for Health Services Research and Health Care Technology Assessment. Ann Arbor: Survey Research Center, University of Michigan.

Cantril, H. 1965. *The pattern of human concerns.* New Brunswick, NJ: Rutgers University Press.

Cantwell, A.-M., E. Friedlander, and M. L. Tramm, eds. 2000. *Ethics and anthropology: Facing future issues in human biology, globalism, and cultural property.* New York: New York Academy of Sciences.

Caplan, P. J., ed. 2003. *The ethics of anthropology: Debates and dilemmas.* New York: Routledge.

Caplan, P. J., M. Crawford, J. S. Hyde, and J. T. E. Richardson. 1997. *Gender differences in human cognition.* London: Oxford University Press.

Carey, J. W., M. Morgan, and M. J. Oxtoby. 1996. Intercoder agreement in analysis of responses to open-ended interview questions: Examples from tuberculosis research. *Cultural Anthropology Methods Journal* 8(3):1–5.

Carneiro, R. L. 1962. Scale analysis as an instrument for the study of cultural evolution. *Southwestern Journal of Anthropology* 18:149–69.

Carneiro, R. L. 1970. Scale analysis, evolutionary sequences, and the rating of cultures. In *A handbook of method in cultural anthropology,* R. Naroll and R. Cohen, eds., 834–71. Garden City, NY: Natural History Press.

Carrithers, M. 2005. Anthropology as a moral science of possibilities. *Current Anthropology* 46:433–56.

Carver, R. P. 1978. The case against statistical significance testing. *Harvard Educational Review* 48:378–99.

Carver, R. P. 1993. The case against statistical significance testing, revisited. *Journal of Experimental Education* 61:287–92.

Caserta, M. S., D. A. Lund, and M. F. Diamond. 1985. Assessing interviewer effects in a longitudinal study of bereaved elderly adults. *Journal of Gerontology* 40:637–40.

Caspi, A., T. E. Moffitt, A. Thornton, D. Freedman, J. W. Amell, H. Harrington, J. Smeijers, and P. A. Silva. 1996. The life history calendar: Research and clinical assessment method for collecting retrospective event-history data. *International Journal of Methods in Psychiatric Research* 6:101–14.

Cassell, J. 1982. Harm, benefits, wrongs, and rights in fieldwork. In *The ethics of social research: fieldwork, regulation, and publication,* J. E. Sieber, eds., 7–31. New York: Springer-Verlag.

Cassell, J., ed. 1987. *Children in the field.* Philadelphia: Temple University Press.

Cassell, J., and S-E. Jacobs, eds. 1987. *Handbook on ethical issues in anthropology.* Washington, DC: American Anthropological Association. http://www.aaanet.org/committees/ethics/toc.htm (accessed June 13, 2009).

Casson, R. 1983. Schemata in cultural anthropology. *Annual Review of Anthropology* 12:429–62.

Casterline, J. B., and V. C. Chidambaram. 1984. The presence of others during the interview and the reporting of contraceptive knowledge and use. In *Survey analysis for the guidance of family planning programs,* J. A. Ross and R. McNamara, eds., 267–98. Liege, Belgium: Ordina Editions.

Catania, J. A., D. Binson, J. Canchola, L. M. Pollack, W. Hauck, and T. J. Coates. 1996. Effects of interviewer gender, interviewer choice, and item wording on responses to questions concerning sexual behavior. *Public Opinion Quarterly* 60:345–75.

Caulkins, D. D. 2001. Consensus, clines, and edges in Celtic cultures. *Cross-Cultural Research* 35:109–26.

Chadsey-Rusch, J., and P. Gonzalez. 1988. Social ecology of the workplace: Employers' perceptions versus direct observations. *Research in Developmental Disabilities* 9:229–45.

Chagnon, N. 1983. *Yanomamo. The fierce people.* 3rd ed. New York: Holt, Rinehart & Winston.

Chalker, J., S. Ratanawijitrasin, N. T. K Chuc, M. Petzold, and G. Tomson. 2004. Effectiveness of a multi-component intervention on dispensing practices at private pharmacies in Vietnam and Thailand—A randomized controlled trial. *Social Science and Medicine* 60:131–41.

Chambers, R. 2006. Participatory mapping and geographic information systems: Whose map? Who is empowered and who is disempowered? Who gains and who loses? The Electronic Journal on Information Systems in Developing countries 25(2):1–11. http://www.ejisdc.org/ojs2/index.php/ejisdc/article/viewFile/239/ 160 (accessed March 8, 2010).

Chan, A., R. Madsen, and J. Unger. 1984. *Chen Village. The recent history of a peasant community in Mao's China.* Berkeley: University of California Press.

Chan, S. S. C., D. M. K. Chow, E. K. Y. Loh, D. C. N. Wong, K. K. F. Cheng, W. Y. C. Fung, and

P. S. Y. Cheung. 2007. Using a community-based outreach program to improve breast health awareness among women in Hong Kong. *Public Health Nursing* 24:265–73.

Chapkis, W. 1997. *Live sex acts: Women performing erotic labor.* New York: Rutledge.

Chapman, P., R. B. Toma, R. V. Tuveson, and M. Jacob. 1997. Nutrition knowledge among adolescent high school female athletes. *Adolescence* 32:437–46.

Chapple, E. D. 1940. Measuring human relations: An introduction to the study of the interaction of individuals. *Genetic Psychology Monographs* 22:3–47.

Chapple, E. D., and G. Donald, Jr. 1947. An evaluation of department store salespeople by the interaction chronograph. *Journal of Marketing* 12:173–85.

Charmaz K. 1995. Grounded theory. In *Rethinking methods in psychology*, J. A. Smith, R. Harré, and L. van Langenhove, eds., 27–49. London: Sage.

Charmaz, K. 2000. Grounded theory: Objectivist and constructivist methods. In *The handbook of qualitative research*, N. K. Denzin and Y. Lincoln, eds., 507–35. Thousand Oaks, CA: Sage.

Charmaz, K. 2002. Qualitative interviewing and grounded theory analysis. In *Handbook of interview research*, J. F. Gubrium and J. A. Holstein, eds., 675–94. Thousand Oaks, CA: Sage.

Chavez, L. R., F. A. Hubbell, J. M. McMullin, R. G. Martinez, and S. I. Mishra. 1995. Structure and meaning in models of breast and cervical cancer risk factors: A comparison of perceptions among Latinos, Anglo women, and physicians. *Medical Anthropology Quarterly* 9:40–74.

Chick, G. 1994. Experience sampling in anthropological research. *Cultural Anthropology Methods Journal* 6(2): 4–6.

Childs, J. H., and A. Landreth. 2006. Analyzing interviewer/respondent interactions while using a mobile computer-assisted interview device. *Field Methods* 18:335–51.

Chisholm, J. S. 1983. *Navajo infancy: An ethological study of child development.* Hawthorne, NY: Aldine.

Choi, N., and D. R. Fuqua. 2003. The structure of the Bem Sex Role Inventory: A summary report of 23 validation studies. *Educational and Psychological Measurement* 63:872–87.

Chomsky, N. 1957. *Syntactic structures.* 's-Gravenhage, The Netherlands: Mouton.

Chomsky, N. 1959. Review of *Verbal Behavior* by B. F. Skinner. *Language* 35:26–58.

Chomsky, N. 1969. *Deep structure, surface structure, and semantic interpretation.* Bloomington: Indiana University Linguistics Club.

Chomsky, N. 1972. *Language and mind.* New York: Harcourt, Brace, Jovanovich.

Chomsky, N. 1977. Recent contributions to the theory of innate ideas: Summary of oral presentation. In *Philosophy of language*, J. Searle, ed., 121–29. Oxford: Oxford University Press.

Christian, L. M., N. L. Parsons, and D. A. Dillman. 2009. Designing scalar questions for web surveys. *Sociological Methods and Research* 37:393–425.

Church, A. H. 1993. Estimating the effect of incentives on mail survey response rates: A meta-analysis. *Public Opinion Quarterly* 57:62–79.

Churchill, S. L., V. L. Plano Clark, K. Prochaska-Cue, J. W. Creswell, and L. Ontai-Grzebik. 2007. How rural low-income families have fun: A grounded theory study. *Journal of Leisure Research* 39:271–94.

Cialdini, R. B., R. J. Borden, A. Thorne, M. R. Walker, S. Freeman, and L. R. Sloan. 1976. Basking in reflected glory: Three (football) field studies. *Journal of Personality and Social Psychology* 34:366–75.

Cirino, P. T., C. E. Chin, R. A. Sevcik, M. Wolf, M. Lovett, and R. D. Morris. 2002. Measuring socioeconomic status: Reliability and preliminary validity for different approaches. *Assessment* 9:145–55.

Claiborne, W. 1984. Dowry killings show social stress in India. *Washington Post*, September 22, p. A1.

Clark, S. J., and R. A. Desharnais. 1998. Honest answers to embarrassing questions: Detecting cheating in the randomized response model. *Psychological Methods* 3:60–68.

Cliggett, L. 2002. Multigenerations and multidisciplines: Inheriting fifty years of Gwembe Tong research. In *Chronicling cultures: Long-term field research in anthropology*, R. V. Kemper and A. P. Royce, eds., 239–51. Walnut Creek, CA: AltaMira.

Clignet, R. 1966. Urbanization and family structure in the Ivory Coast. *Comparative Studies in Society and History* 8:385–401.

Clignet, R. 1970. *Many wives, many powers: Authority and power in polygynous families.* Evanston, IL: Northwestern University Press.

Coast, E. 2002. Maasai socioeconomic conditions: A cross-border comparison. *Human Ecology* 30:79–105.

Cochran, W. G. 1977. *Sampling techniques.* 2nd ed. New York: Wiley.

Cohen, J. 1960. A coefficient of agreement for nominal scales. *Educational and Psychological Measurement* 20:37–48.

Cohen, J. 1988. *Statistical power analysis for the behavioral sciences.* 2nd ed. Hillsdale, NJ: Lawrence Erlbaum.

Cohen, J. 1992. A power primer. *Psychological Bulletin* 112:155–59.

Cohen, J. 1994. The earth is round ($p < .05$). *American Psychologist* 49:997–1003.

Cohen-Kettenis, P. T., and L. J. G. Gooren. 1999. Transsexualism. A review of etiology, diagnosis and treatment. *Journal of Psychosomatic Research* 46:315–33.

Cohn, E. G., and J. Rotton. 1997. Assault as a function of time and temperature: A moderator-variable time-series analysis. *Journal of Personality and Social Psychology* 72:1322–34.

Colby, B. N. 1966. The analysis of culture content and the patterning of narrative concern in texts. *American Anthropologist* 68:374–88.

Cole, D. 1983. The value of a person lies in his *herzenbildung*: Franz Boas' Baffin Island letter-diary, 1883–1884. In *Observers observed*, G. W. Stocking, Jr., ed., 13–52. Madison: University of Wisconsin Press.

Coleman, B. E. 1999. The impact of group lending in northeast Thailand. *Journal of Development Economics* 60:105–41.

Coleman, J. S. 1966. *Equality of educational opportunity.* Washington, DC: U.S. Dept. of Health, Education, and Welfare, Office of Education/National Center for Education Statistics.

College Board. 2008. SAT Reasoning Test: Mean scores by gender within ethnicity. Table 8. http://professionals.collegeboard.com/profdownload/Total_Group_Report.pdf (accessed March 13, 2009).

Collings, P. 2009. Participant observation and phased assertion as research stragegies in the Canadian Arctic. *Field Methods* 21:133–53.

Collins, C. C. 2006. Cultural models of domestic violence: Perspectives of human service professionals. Ph.D. dissertation, University of Alabama-Birmingham.

Comrey, A. L. 1992. *A first course in factor analysis.* 2nd ed. Hillsdale, NJ: Lawrence Erlbaum.

Comte, A. 1875–77. *System of positive polity.* London: Longmans, Green and Co.

Comte, A. 1877. *Cours de philosophie positive.* Paris : J.-B. Ballière.

Comte, A. 1974. *The positive philosophy.* New York: AMS Press.

Condorcet, M. de. 1785. Essai sur l'application de l'analyse à la probabilité des décisions rendues à la pluralité de voix. Paris: Imprimerie Royale. http://gallica.bnf.fr/ark:/12148/bpt6k417181.image.f4.pagination (accessed November 30, 2009).

Conklin, H. C. 1955. Hanunóo color categories. *Southwestern Journal of Anthropology* 11:339–44.

Connolly, M. 1990. Adrift in the city: A comparative study of children in Bogota, Colombia, and Guatemala City. *Child and Youth Services* 14:129–49.

Connolly, M., and J. Ennew, eds. 1996. Children out of place. Special Issue on working and [*sic*] street children. *Childhood* 3, issue 2.

Conrad, F. G., and J. Blair. 2009. Sources of error in cognitive interviews. *Public Opinion Quarterly* 73:32–55.

Conti, N. 2009. A Visioth system: Shame, honor, and police socialization. *Journal of Contemporary Ethnography* 38:409–32.

Converse, J. M., and H. Schuman. 1974. *Conversations at random. Survey research as the interviewers see it.* New York: Wiley.

Converse, P. D., E. W. Wolfe, X. Huang, and F. L. Oswald. 2008. Response rates for mixed-mode surveys using mail and e-mail/Web. *American Journal of Evaluation* 29:99–107.

Cook, S. W. 1975. A comment on the ethical issues involved in West, Gunn, and Chernicky's "Ubiquitous Watergate": An attributional analysis. *Journal of Personality and Social Psychology* 32:66–68.

Cook, T. D., and D. T. Campbell. 1979. *Quasi-experimentation: Design and analysis issues for field settings.* Chicago: Rand McNally College Publishing.

Cooke, C. A. 2004. Young people's attitudes towards guns in America, Great Britain, and Western Australia. *Aggressive Behavior* 30:93–104.

Coombs, C. H. 1964. *A theory of data.* New York: Wiley.

Corbin, J., and A. Strauss. 2008. *Basics of qualitative research.* 3rd ed. Thousand Oaks, CA: Sage.

Corral-Verdugo, V. 1997. Dual "realities" of conservation behavior: Self-reports vs. observations of re-use and recycling behavior. *Journal of Environmental Psychology* 17:135–45.

Cottingham, J. 1999. *Descartes.* New York: Routledge.

Cotton, E., and C. Byrd-Bredbenner. 2007. Knowledge and psychosocial effects of the film *Super Size Me* on young adults. *Journal of the American Dietetic Association* 107:1197–203.

Couper, M. P., E. Singer, and R. Tourangeau. 2003. Understanding the effects of audio-CASI on self-reports of sensitive behavior. *Public Opinion Quarterly* 67:385–95.

Cowan, G., and M. O'Brien. 1990. Gender and survival vs. death in slasher films—A content analysis. *Sex Roles* 23:187–96.

Crabb, P. B., and D. Bielawski. 1994. The social representation of material culture and gender in children's books. *Sex Roles* 30:69–79.

Creswell, J. W. 2009. *Research design: Qualitative, quantitative, and mixed methods approaches.* 3rd ed. Thousand Oaks, CA: Sage.

Creswell, J. W., and V. L. Plano-Clark. 2007. *Designing and conducting mixed methods research.* Thousand Oaks, CA: Sage.

Cronk, L. 2000. Female-biased parental investment and growth performance among the Mukogodo. In *Adaptation and human behavior: An anthropological perspective*, L. Cronk, N. Chagnon, and W. Irons, eds., 203–21. New York: Aldine de Gruyter.

Cronk, L. 2007. The influence of cultural framing on play in the trust game: A Maasai example. *Evolution and Human Behavior* 28:352–58.

Crume, T. L., C. DiGiuseppe, T. Byers, A. P. Sirotnak, and C. J. Garrett. 2002. Underascertainment of child maltreatment fatalities by death certificates, 1990–1998. *Pediatrics* 110:e18. http://pediatrics.aappublications.org/cgi/reprint/110/2/e18 (accessed June 28, 2009).

Cruz, T. H., S. W. Marshall, J. M. Bowling, and A. Villaveces. 2008. The validity of a proxy acculturation scale among U.S. Hispanics. *Hispanic Journal of Behavioral Sciences* 30:425–46.

Csikszentmihalyi, M., and R. Larson. 1987. Validity and reliability of the experience-sampling method. Special issue: Mental disorders in their natural settings: The application of time allocation and experience-sampling techniques in psychiatry. *Journal of Nervous and Mental Disease* 175:526–36.

Curtice, J., and N. Sparrow. 1997. How accurate are traditional quota opinion polls? *Journal of the Market Research Society* 39:433–48.

Cushman, T. 2004. Anthropology and genocide in the Balkans. An analysis of conceptual practices of power. *Anthropological Theory* 4:5–28

Daley, W. R., A. Karpati, and M. Shelk. 2001. Needs assessment of the displaced population following the August 1999 earthquake in Turkey. *Disasters* 25:67–75.

Daly, M., and M. Wilson. 1988. *Homicide.* New York: Aldine de Gruyter.

Daly, M., and M. Wilson. 1998. *The truth about Cinderella.* New Haven, CT: Yale University Press.

D'Andrade, R. G. 1973. Cultural constructions of reality. In *Cultural illness and health*, L. Nader and T. W. Maretzki, eds., 115–27. Washington, DC: American Anthropological Association.

D'Andrade, R. G. 1974. Memory and the assessment of behavior. In *Measurement in the social sciences*, H. M. Blalock, Jr., ed., 159–86. Chicago: Aldine.

D'Andrade, R. G. 1991. The identification of schemas in naturalistic data. In *Person schemas and maladaptive interpersonal patterns*, M. Horowitz, ed., 279–301. Chicago: University of Chicago Press.

D'Andrade, R. G. 1995. *The development of cognitive anthropology.* Cambridge: Cambridge University Press.

D'Andrade, R. G., N. Quinn, S. B. Nerlove, and A. K. Romney. 1972. Categories of disease in American English and Mexican Spanish. In *Multidimensional scaling,* A. K. Romney, R. Shepard, and S. B. Nerlove, eds. Vol. 2, *Applications,* 9–54. New York: Seminar Press.

D'Andrade, R. G., and C. Strauss, eds. 1992. *Human motives and cultural models.* New York: Cambridge University Press.

D'Antona, A. de O., A. D. Cak, and L. K. Vanwey. 2008. Collecting sketch maps to understand property land use and land cover in large surveys. *Field Methods* 20:66–84.

Darwin, C. 1998 [1872]. *The expression of the emotions in man and animals.* 3rd. ed. New York: Oxford University Press.

Davies, I., C. Davies, and G. Corbett. 1994. The basic colour terms of Ndebele. *African Languages and Cultures* 7:36–48.

Davis, D. L. 1986. Changing self-image: Studying menopausal women in a Newfoundland fishing village. In *Self, sex and gender in cross-cultural fieldwork,* T. L. Whitehead and M. E. Conaway, eds., 240–62. Urbana: University of Illinois Press.

Davis, D. W. 1997. The direction of race of interviewer effects among African-Americans: Donning the black mask. *American Journal of Political Science* 41:309–23.

Davis, J. A. 1971. *Elementary survey analysis.* Englewood Cliffs, NJ: Prentice-Hall.

Davis, K., and S. Weller. 1999. The effectiveness of condoms in reducing heterosexual transmission of HIV. *Family Planning Perspectives* 31:272–79.

Davis, N. Z. 1981. Printing and the people. In *Literacy and social development in the West,* H. J. Graf, eds., 69–95. Cambridge: Cambridge University Press.

Dawes, R. M. 1977. Suppose we measured height with rating scales instead of rulers. *Applied Psychological Measurement* 1:267–73.

de Ghett, V. J. 1978. Hierarchical cluster analysis. In *Quantitative ethology,* P. W. Colgan, ed., 115–44. New York: Wiley.

Dehavenon, A. L. 1978. Superordinate behavior in urban homes: A video analysis of request-compliance and food control behavior in two black and two white families living in New York City. Ph.D. dissertation, Columbia University.

de Leeuw, E., J. Hox, and S. Kef. 2003. Computer-assisted self-interviewing tailored for special populations and topics. *Field Methods* 15:223–51.

de Leeuw, E., J. Hox, and G. Snijkers. 1995. The effect of computer-assisted interviewing on data quality. A review. *Journal of the Market Research Society* 37:325–44.

Dellino, D. 1984. Tourism: Panacea or plight. Impacts on the quality of life on Exuma, Bahamas. Master's thesis, University of Florida.

Deloria, V. 1969. *Custer died for your sins: An Indian manifesto.* New York: Macmillan.

DeMaio, T. J. 1984. Social desirability and survey measurement: A review. In *Surveying subjective phenomena,* C. F. Turner and E. Martin, eds. Vol. 2, 257–82. New York: Russell Sage Foundation.

de Munck, V. C., N. Dudley, and J. Cardinale. 2002. Cultural models of gender in Sri Lanka and the United States. *Ethnology* 41:225–61.

de Munck, V. C., and E. J. Sobo, eds. 1998. *Using methods in the field: A practical introduction and casebook.* Walnut Creek, CA: AltaMira.

de Rada, V. D. 2001. Mail surveys using Dillman's TDM in a southern European country: Spain. *International Journal of Public Opinon Research* 13:159–72.

D'Eramo-Melkus, G. D., G. Spollett, V. Jefferson, D. Chyun, B. Tuohy, T. Robinson, and A. Kaisen. 2004. A culturally competent intervention of education and care for black women with type 2 diabetes. *Applied Nursing Research* 17:10–20.

Derrick, C. G., J. S. A. Miller, and J. M. Andrews. 2008. A fish consumption study of anglers in at at-risk community: A community-based participatory approach to risk reduction. *Public Health Nursing* 25:312–18.

Descartes, R. 1960 [1637]. *Discourse on method; and meditations.* New York: Liberal Arts Press.

Descartes, R. 1993 [1641]. *Discourse on method and meditations on first philosophy,* D. A. Cress, transl. 3rd ed. Indianapolis: Hackett Publishing.

De Smith, M. J., M. F. Goodchild, and P. A. Longley. 2007. *Geospatial analysis: A comprehensive guide to principles, techniques, and software tools*. Leicester, UK: Matador.

Deutscher, I. 1973. *What we say, what we do*. Glenview, IL: Scott Foresman.

DeVellis, R. F. 2003. *Scale development: Theory and applications*. 2nd ed. Newbury Park, CA: Sage.

DeWalt, B. R. 1979. *Modernization in a Mexican ejido*. New York: Cambridge University Press.

DeWalt, K. M., and B. R. DeWalt. 2002. *Participant observation: A guide for fieldworkers*. Walnut Creek, CA: AltaMira.

DeWalt, K. M., B. R. DeWalt, and C. B. Wayland. 1998. Participant observation. In *Handbook of methods in cultural anthropology*, H. R. Bernard, ed., 259–99. Walnut Creek, CA: AltaMira.

Dey, I. 1993. *Qualitative data analysis: A user-friendly guide for social scientists*. London: Routledge & Kegan Paul.

Dickerson, S. S., M. A. Neary, and M. Hyche-Johnson. 2000. Native American graduate nursing students' learning experiences. *Journal of Nursing Scholarship* 32:189–96.

Dijkers, M. P. J. M., and C. L. Creighton. 1994. Data cleaning in occupational therapy research. *Occupational Therapy Journal of Research* 14:144–56.

Dillman, D. A. 1978. *Mail and telephone surveys: The total design method*. New York: Wiley.

Dillman, D. A., and L. M. Christian. 2005. Survey mode as a source of instability in responses across surveys. *Field Methods* 17:30–52.

Dillman, D. A., G. Phelps, R. Totora, K. Swift, J. Kohrell, J. Berck, and B. L. Messer. 2009. Response rate and measurement differences in mixed-mode surveys using mail, telephone, interactive voice response (IVR) and the Internet. *Social Science Research* 38:1–18.

Dillman, D. A., J. D. Smyth, and L. M. Christian. 2009. *Internet, mail, and mixed-mode surveys: The tailored design method*. New York: Wiley.

Dilthey, W. 1989 [1883]. *Introduction to the human sciences*. Princeton, NJ: Princeton University Press.

Dinapoli, P. P. 2009. Early initiation of tobacco use in adolescent girls: Key sociocultural influences. *Applied Nursing Research* 22:126–32.

Dione Rosado, S. 2007. Nappy hair in the diaspora: Exploring the cultural politics of hair among women of African descent. Unpublished doctoral dissertation, University of Florida.

Ditmar, H. 1991. Meanings of material possessions as reflections of identity: Gender and social-material position in society. *Journal of Social Behavior and Personality* 6:165–86.

Divale, W. T. 1976. Female status and cultural evolution: A study in ethnographer bias. *Behavior Science Research* 11:169–212.

Dobkin de Rios, M. 1981. Socioeconomic characteristics of an Amazon urban healer's clientele. *Social Science and Medicine* 15B:51–63.

Dohrenwend, B. S., and S. A. Richardson. 1965. Directiveness and nondirectiveness in research interviewing: A reformulation of the problem. *Psychology Bulletin* 63:475–85.

Doob, A. N., and A. E. Gross. 1968. Status of frustrator as an inhibitor of horn honking responses. *Journal of Social Psychology* 76:213–18.

Dordick, G. A. 1996. More than refuge. *Journal of Contemporary Ethnography* 24:373–404.

Doreian, P. 2004. Cluster analysis. In *The SAGE encyclopedia of social science research methods*, M. Lewis-Beck, A. Bryman, and T. F. Liao, eds., 128–30. Thousand Oaks, CA: Sage.

Dorjahn, V. 1977. Temne household size and composition: Rural changes over time and rural-urban differences. *Ethnology* 16:105–27.

Dorjahn, V. 1988. Changes in Temne polygyny. *Ethnology* 27:367–90.

Dotinga, A. R. J., J. M. van den Eijndem, W. Bosveld, and H. F. L. Garretsen. 2005. The effect of data collection mode and ethnicity of interviewer on response rates and self-reported alcohol use among Turks and Moroccans in the Netherlands: An experimental study. *Alcohol and Alcoholism* 40:242–48.

Doughty, P. 1979. A Latin American specialty in the world context: Urban primacy and cultural colonialism in Peru. *Urban Anthropology* 8:383–98.

Dousset, L. 2008. The "global" versus the "local": Cognitive processes in kin determination in Aboriginal Australia. *Oceania* 78:260–79.

Dow, M. M., M. Burton, D. White, and K. Reitz. 1984. Galton's problem as network autocorrelation. *American Ethnologist* 11:754–70.

Dow, M. M., and E. A. Eff. 2008. Global, regional, and local network autocorrelation in the Standard Cross-Cultural Sample. *Cross-Cultural Research* 42:148–71.

Drake, S. 1978. *Galileo at work: His scientific biography*. Chicago: University of Chicago Press.

Draus, P. J., H. A. Siegal, R. G. Carlson, R. S. Falck, and J. Wang. 2005. Cracking the cornfields: Recruiting illicit stimulant drug users in rural Ohio. *The Sociological Quarterly* 46:165–89.

Dressler, W. W. 1980. Ethnomedical beliefs and patient adherence to a treatment regimen: A St. Lucian example. *Human Organization* 39:88–91.

Dressler, W. W. 1996. Culture and blood pressure: Using consensus analysis to create a measurement. *Cultural Anthropology Methods* 8(3):6–8.

Dressler, W. W., M. C. Balieiro, and J. E. dos Santos. 1997. The cultural construction of social support in Brazil: Associations with health outcomes. *Culture, Medicine and Psychiatry* 21:303–35.

Dressler, W. W., M. C. Balieiro, and J. E. dos Santos. 2002. Cultural consonance and psychological distress. *Paidéia: Cadernos de Psicologia e Educação* 12:5–18.

Dressler, W. W., M. C. Balieiro, R. P. Ribeiro, and J. E. dos Santos. 2007. A prospective study of cultural consonance and depressive symptoms in urban Brazil. *Social Science and Medicine* 65:2058–69.

Dressler, W. W., C. D. Borges, M. C. Balieiro, and J. E. dos Santos. 2005. Measuring cultural consonance: Examples with special reference to measurement theory in anthropology. *Field Methods* 17:331–55.

Dressler, W. W., J. E. dos Santos, and M. C. Balieiro. 1996. Studying diversity and sharing in culture: An example of lifestyle in Brazil. *Journal of Anthropological Research* 52:331–53.

Dressler, W. W., R. P. Ribeiro, M. C. Balieiro, K. S. Oths, and J. E. dos Santos. 2004. Eating, drinking and being depressed: The social, cultural and psychological context of alcohol consumption and nutrition in a Brazilian community. *Social Science and Medicine* 59:709–20.

Drew, P., and J. Heritage, eds. 2006. *Conversation analysis*. Thousand Oaks, CA: Sage.

Drury, C. C. 1990. Methods for direct observation of performance. In *Evaluation of human work: A practical ergonomics methodology*, J. R. Wilson and E. N. Corlett, eds., 35–57. New York: Taylor & Francis.

Du Bois, J. 1991. Transcription design principles for spoken discourse research. *Pragmatics* 1:71–106.

Ducanes, G., and M. Abella. 2008. Labor shortage responses in Japan, Korea, Singapore, Hong Kong, and Malaysia: A review and Evaluation. ILO Asian Regional Programme on Governance of Labour Migration Working Paper No. 2. Bangkok: International Labor Organization. http://digitalcommons.ilr.cornell.edu/cgi/viewcontent.cgi?article=1054&context=intl (accessed December 2, 2010).

Dugger, C. W. 2000. Kerosene, weapon of choice for attacks on wives in India. *New York Times*, December 26, p. A1.

Duncan, O. D. 1966. Path analysis: Sociological examples. *American Journal of Sociology* 72:1–16.

Dunn, C. D. 2004. Cultural models and metaphors for marriage: An analysis of discourse at Japanese wedding receptions. *Ethos* 32:348–73.

Dunn-Rankin, P. 2004. *Scaling methods*. 2nd ed. Mahwah, NJ: Lawrence Erlbaum.

Durand, C., A. Blais, and M. Larochelle. 2004. The polls in the 2002 French presidential election: An autopsy. *Public Opinion Quarterly* 68:602–22.

Duranleau, D. 1999. Random sampling of regional populations: A field test. *Field Methods* 11:61–67.

Duranti, A. 2006. Transcripts, like shadows on a wall. *Mind, Culture and Activity* 13:301–10.

Durkheim, E. 1933 [1893]. *The division of labor in society*, G. Simpson, transl. Glencoe, IL: The Free Press.

Durkheim, E. 1951 [1897]. *Suicide. A study in sociology*. Glencoe, IL: The Free Press.

Durkheim, E. 1958. *Socialism and Saint-Simon*, A. Gouldner, ed., C. Sattler, transl. Yellow Springs, OH: Antioch Press.

Durrenberger, E. P. 2003. Using paired comparisons to measure reciprocity. *Field Methods* 15:271–88.

Durrenberger, E. P., and D. Doukas. 2008. Gospel of wealth, gospel of work: Counterhegemony in the U.S. working class. *American Anthropologist* 110:214–24.

Durrenberger, E. P., and S. Erem. 2005. Checking for relationships across domains measured by triads and paired comparisons. *Field Methods* 17:150–69.

Dyk, W. 1938. *Son of Old Man Hat*. New York: Harcourt Brace.

Dyk, W., and R. Dyk. 1980. *Left Handed; A Navaho autobiography*. New York: Columbia University Press.

Dyl, J., and S. Wapner. 1996. Age and gender differences in the nature, meaning, and function of cherished possessions for children and adolescents. *Journal of Experimental Child Psychology* 62:340–77.

Easlea, B. 1980. *Witch hunting, magic, and the new philosophy*. Atlantic Highlands, NJ: Humanities Press.

Edel, M., and A. Edel. 1968. *Anthropology and Ethics*. Revised ed. Cleveland: Press of Case Western Reserve University.

Edgerton, R. B. 1966. Conceptions of psychosis in four East African societies. *American Anthropologist* 68(Part 1):408–25.

Edgerton, R. B. 1967. *The cloak of competence*. Berkeley: University of California Press.

Edgerton, R. B., and S. Bercovici. 1976. The cloak of competence: Years later. *American Journal of Mental Deficiency* 80:485–97.

Edgerton, R. B., M. Bollinger, and B. Herr. 1984. The cloak of competence: After two decades. *American Journal of Mental Deficiency* 88:345–51.

Edgerton, R. B., and A. Cohen. 1994. Culture and schizophrenia: The DOSMD challenge. *British Journal of Psychiatry* 164:222–31.

Edgerton, R. B., and T. W. Ward. 1991. I gotta put my foot down. Richard T. Jarrett, III. In *"I've seen it all." Lives of older persons with mental retardation in the community*, R. B. Edgerton and M. A. Gaston, eds., 123–49. Baltimore: Paul H. Brookes Publishing.

Edmondson, B. 1988. This survey is garbage (analyzing trash to estimate populations). *American Demographics* 10:13–15.

Edmonson, M. S., transl. and ed. 1986. *Heaven-born Mérida and its destiny: The Book of Chilam Balam of Chumayel*. Austin: University of Texas Press.

Edwards, M., S. Thomsen, and C. Toroitich-Ruto. 2005. Thinking aloud to create better condom-use questions. *Field Methods* 17:183–99.

Eibl-Eiblsfeldt, I. 1989. *Human ethology*. New York: Aldine de Gruyter.

Einarsdóttir, J. 2006. Child survival in affluence and poverty: Ethics and fieldwork experiences from Iceland and Guinea-Bissau. *Field Methods* 18:189–204.

Eisenstein, E. 1979. *The printing press as an agent of change: Communications and cultural transformations in early modern Europe*, 2 vols. Cambridge: Cambridge University Press.

Ekins, R. 1997. *Male femaling: A grounded theory approach to cross-dressing and sex-changing*. New York: Routledge.

Ekman, P., ed. 1973. *Darwin and facial expression. A century of research in review*. New York: Academic Press.

Ekman, P. 1980. *The face of man: Expression of universal emotions in a New Guinea village*. New York: Garland STPM Press.

Ekman, P. 1993. Facial expression and emotion. *American Psychologist* 48:384–92.

El Guindi, F. 2004. *Visual anthropology*. Walnut Creek, CA: AltaMira.

El Guindi, F., and A. Hernández Jiménez. 1986. *The myth of ritual. A native's ethnography of Zapotec life-crisis rituals*. Tucson: University of Arizona Press.

Elliott, B. 2005. *Phenomenology and imagination in Husserl and Heidigger*. New York: Routledge.

Ember, C. R. 2007. Using the HRAF collection of ethnography in conjunction with the standard cross-cultural sample and the ethnographic atlas. *Cross-Cultural Research* 41:396–427.

Ember, C. R., and M. Ember. 1992. Resource unpredictability, mistrust, and war: A cross-cultural study. *Journal of Conflict Resolution* 36:242–62.

Ember, C. R., and M. Ember. 2001. *Cross-cultural research methods*. Walnut Creek, CA: AltaMira.

Ember, C. R., and M. Ember. 2002. Father absence and male aggression. A re-examination of the comparative evidence. *Ethos* 29:296–314.

Emerson, R. M., R. I. Fretz, and L. L. Shaw. 1995. *Writing ethnographic fieldnotes*. Chicago: University of Chicago Press.

Ensminger, M. E., and K. Fothergill. 2003. A decade of measuring SES: What it tells us and where to go from here. In *Socioeconomic status, parenting, and child development*, M. H. Bornstein and R. H. Bradley, eds., 13–27. Mahwah, NJ: Lawrence Erlbaum.

Erasmus, C. J. 1955. Work patterns in a Mayo village. *American Anthropologist* 57:322–33.

Erickson, P. 1997. Contraceptive methods: Do Hispanic adolescents and their family planning care providers think about contraceptives the same way? *Medical Anthropology* 17:65–82.

Erikson, K. T. 1967. A comment on disguised observation in sociology. *Social Problems* 14:366–73.

Erikson, K. T. 1996. A response to Richard Leo. *The American Sociologist* 27:129–30.

Esquivel, V., D. Budlender, N. Folbre, and I. Hirway. 2008. Explorations: Time use surveys in the south. *Feminist Economics* 14:107–52.

Evans, G. W., and R. E. Wener. 2007. Crowding and personal space invasion on the train: Please don't make me sit in the middle. *Journal of Experimental Psychology* 27:90–94.

Evans-Pritchard, E. E. 1958 [1937]. *Witchcraft, oracles, and magic among the Azande*. Oxford: Oxford University Press.

Evans-Pritchard, E. E. 1973. Some reminiscences and reflections on fieldwork. *Journal of the Anthropological Society of Oxford* 4:1–12.

Fabian, J. 1990. *Power and Performance: Ethnographic explorations through proverbial wisdom and theater in Shaba, Zaire*. Madison: University of Wisconsin Press.

Fahim, H. M. 1982. *Indigenous anthropology in non-Western societies: Proceedings of a Burg-Wartenstein symposium*. Durham: University of North Carolina Press.

Faris, J. C. 1968. Validation in ethnographical description: The lexicon of "occasions" in Cat Harbou. *Man*, New Series, 3:112–24.

Farnell, B. 1994. Ethno-graphics and the moving body. *Man* 29:929–74.

Farnell, B. 1995. Do you see what I mean? Plains Indian sign talk and the embodiment of action. Austin: University of Texas Press.

Farnell, B. 1996. Movement notation systems. In *The world's writing systems*, P. T. Daniels and W. Bright, eds., 1–25. New York: Oxford University Press.

Farnell, B. 1999. Moving bodies, acting selves. *Annual Review of Anthropology* 28:341–73.

Farnell, B., and L. R. Graham. 1998. Discourse-centered methods. In *Handbook of methods in cultural anthropology*, H. R. Bernard, ed., 411–57. Walnut Creek, CA: AltaMira.

Farringdon, J. M., and M. G. Farringdon. 1980. *A concordance and word-lists to the poems of Dylan Thomas*. Swansea, England: Ariel House.

Federal Communications Commission (FCC). 2007. List of federally recognized tribal lands and telephone penetration rates. http://wireless.fcc.gov/auctions/data/crossreferences/TL_Telephone_Penetration_Rate_2007.pdf (accessed March 23, 2009).

Feigl, H. 1980. Positivism. In *Encyclopaedia brittanica*, Vol. 14. Chicago: Encyclopaedia Brittanica.

Feigl, H., and A. Blumberg. 1931. Logical positivism: A new movement in European philosophy. *Journal of Philosophy* 28:281–96.

Feinberg, R. 2007. Dialectics of culture: Relativism in popular and anthropological discourse. *Anthropological Quarterly* 80:777–90.

Feldman, K. D. 1994. Socioeconomic structures and mate selection among urban populations in developing regions. *Journal of Comparative Family Studies* 25:329–43.

Feldman, R. E. 1968. Response to compatriot and foreigner who seek assistance. *Journal of Personality and Social Psychology* 10:202–14.

Fenno, R. 1990. *Watching politicians: Essays on participant observation*. Berkeley: Institute of Governmental Studies, University of California.

Fernández, J. 1967. Revitalized words from "the parrot's egg" and "the bull that crashes in the kraal": African cult sermons. In *Essays on the verbal and visual arts. Proceedings of the 1966*

Annual Meeting of the American Ethnological Society, 45–63. Seattle: University of Washington Press.

Festinger, L. A. 1957. *A theory of cognitive dissonance*. Stanford, CA: Stanford University Press.

Fetterman, D. 1989. *Ethnography step by step*. Newbury Park, CA: Sage.

Fine, G. A., and K. L. Sandstrom. 1988. *Knowing children: Participant observation with minors*. Newbury Park, CA: Sage.

Finkel, S. E., T. M. Guterbock, and M. J. Borg. 1991. Race-of-interviewer effects in a preelection poll: Virginia 1989. *Public Opinion Quarterly* 55:313–30.

Finkler, K. 1974. *Estudio comparativo de la economía de dos comunidades de México: El papel de la irrigación*. Mexico City: Instituto Nacional Indigenista.

Finocchiaro, M. A. 2005. *Retrying Galileo, 1633–1992*. Berkeley: University of California Press.

Firbank, O. E. 2008. Unpacking the meaning of quality in Quebec's health-care system: The input of commissions of inquiry. *Health Care Analysis* 16:375–96.

Fischer, C. 1982. *To dwell among friends: Personal networks in town and city*. Chicago: University of Chicago Press.

Fisher, R. A. 1936. The use of multiple measurements in taxonomic problems. *Annals of Eugenics* 7:179–88.

Fitzgerald, J., P. Gottschalk, and R. Moffitt. 1998. An analysis of the impact of sample attrition on the second generation of respondents in the Michigan panel study of income dynamics. *The Journal of Human Resources* 33:300–43.

Fitzpatrick, T. R., S. Alemán, and T. V. Tran. 2008. Factors that contribute to independent activity functioning among a group of Navajo elders. *Research on Aging* 30:318–33.

Fjellman, S. M., and H. Gladwin. 1985. Haitian family patterns of migration to South Florida. *Human Organization* 44:301–12.

Fleisher, M. 1989. *Warehousing violence*. Newbury Park, CA: Sage.

Fleisher, M. 1995. *Beggars and thieves: Lives of urban street criminals*. Madison: University of Wisconsin Press.

Fleisher, M. 1998. *Dead end kids: Gang girls and the boys they know*. Madison: University of Wisconsin Press.

Flores, E., S. L. Eyre, and S. G. Millstein. 1998. Sociocultural beliefs related to sex among Mexican American adolescents. *Hispanic Journal of Behavioral Sciences* 20:60–82.

Fluehr-Lobban, C. 1998. Ethics. In *Handbook of methods in cultural anthropology*, H. R. Bernard, ed., 173–202. Walnut Creek, CA: AltaMira.

Fluehr-Lobban, C. 2002. *Ethics and the profession of anthropology dialogue for ethically conscious practice*. 2nd ed. Walnut Creek, CA: AltaMira.

Fluehr-Lobban, C. 2008. Anthropology and ethics in America's declining imperial age. *Anthropology Today* 24:18–22.

Foo, M-D., M. A. Uy, and R. A. Baron. 2009. How do feelings influence effort? An empirical study of entrepreneurs' affect and venture effort. *Journal of Applied Psychology* 94:1086–94.

Foster, G. 2002. A half-century of field research in Tzintzuntzan, Mexico: A personal view. In *Chronicling cultures: Long-term field research in anthropology*, R. V. Kemper and A. P. Royce, eds., 252–83. Walnut Creek, CA: AltaMira.

Fournillier, J. B. 2007. Trying to return home: A Trinidadian's experience of becoming a "native ethnographer." *Qualitative Inquiry* 15:740–65.

Fowler, F. J. 1984. *Survey research methods*. Newbury Park, CA: Sage.

Fox, K. 2004. *Watching the English*. London: Hodder and Stoughton.

Fox, R. J., M. R. Crask, and J. Kim. 1988. Mail survey response rate. *Public Opinion Quarterly* 52:467–91.

Frake, C. O. 1961. The diagnosis of disease among the Subanum of Mindanao. *American Anthropologist* 63:113–32.

Frake, C. O. 1962. The ethnographic study of cognitive systems. In *Anthropology and human behavior*, 72–85. Washington, DC: Anthropological Society of Washington.

Frake, C. O. 1964. Notes on queries in anthropology. In *Transcultural studies in cognition*, A. K. Romney and R. G. D'Andrade, eds. *American Anthropologist* 66, Part II.

Frank, S. H., K. C. Stange, D. Langa, and M. Workings. 1997. Direct observation of community-based ambulatory encounters involving medical students. *JAMA, The Journal of the American Medical Association* 278:712–16.

Fratkin, E. 2004. *Ariaal pastoralists of Kenya*. Boston: Pearson.

Freedman, D. A. 2001. Ecological inference and the ecological fallacy. In *International encyclopedia of the social and behavioral sciences*, N. J. Smelser and P. B. Baltes, eds. Vol. 6, 4027–30. New York: Elsevier.

Freedman, D., A. Thornton, D. Camburn, D. Alwin, and L. Young-DeMarco. 1988. The life history calendar: A technique for collecting retrospective data. *Sociological Methodology* 18:37–68.

Freeman, D. 1999. *The fateful hoaxing of Margaret Mead: A historical analysis of her Samoan research*. Boulder, CO: Westview.

Freeman, L. C., A. K. Romney, and S. C. Freeman. 1987. Cognitive structure and informant accuracy. *American Anthropologist* 89:310–25.

Freilich, M., ed. 1977. *Marginal natives at work: Anthropologists in the field*. 2nd ed. Cambridge, MA: Schenkman.

Friedenberg, L. 1995. *Psychological testing. Design, analysis, and use*. Needham Heights, MA: Allyn & Bacon.

Frisancho, A. R. 1990. *Anthropometric standards for the assessment of growth and nutritional status*. Ann Arbor: University of Michigan Press.

Fry, D. P. 1990. Play aggression among Zapotec children: Implications for the practice hypothesis. *Aggressive Behavior* 16:321–40.

Furlow, C. 2003. Comparing indicators of knowledge within and between cultural domains. *Field Methods* 15:51–62.

Furnham, A., and S. Bochner. 1986. *Culture shock: Psychological reactions to unfamiliar environments*. London: Methuen.

Gaito, J. 1980. Measurement scales and statistics: Resurgence of an old misconception. *Psychological Bulletin* 87:564–67.

Galilei, Galileo. 1967 [1632]. *Dialogue concerning the two chief world systems, Ptolemaic & Copernican*, S. Drake, transl. Berkeley: University of California Press.

Galilei, Galileo. 1997 [1632]. *Galileo on the world systems: A new abridged translation and guide*, M. A. Finocchiaro, transl. Berkeley: University of California Press.

Gallicchio, L., S. Miller, H. Zacur, and J. A. Flaws. 2009. Race and health-related quality of life in midlife women in Baltimore, Maryland. *Maturitas* 63:67–72.

Galton, F. 1907a. Vox populi. *Nature* 75:450–51.

Galton, F. 1907b. Reply to Hooker. *Nature* 75:509–10.

Gammack, J., and E. Denby. 2006. The true hue of grue. *New Ideas in Psychology* 24:82–97.

Gans, L. P., and C. S. Wood. 1985. Discriminant analysis as a method for differentiating potential acceptors of family planning: Western Samoa. *Human Organization* 44:228–33.

Garot, R. 2004. "You're not a stone": Emotional sensitivity in a bureaucratic setting. *Journal of Contemporary Ethnography* 33:735–66.

Garro, L. C. 1986. Intracultural variation in folk medical knowledge: A comparison between curers and noncurers. *American Anthropologist* 88:351–70.

Garro, L. C. 2000. Remembering what one knows and the construction of the past: A comparison of cultural consensus theory and cultural schema theory. *Ethos* 28:275–319.

Gates, R., and P. Solomon. 1982. Research using the mall intercept: State of the art. *Journal of Advertising Research* 22:43–49.

Gatewood, J. B. 1983. Loose talk: Linguistic competence and recognition ability. *American Anthropologist* 85:378–86.

Gatewood, J. B. 1984. Familiarity, vocabulary size, and recognition ability in four semantic domains. *American Ethnologist* 11:507–27.

Gatz, M., and M. Hurwicz. 1990. Are old people more depressed? Cross-sectional data on Center for Epidemiological Studies Depression Scale factors. *Psychology and Aging* 5:284–90.

Gaulin, S. C., and J. S. Boster. 1990. Dowry as female competition. *American Anthropologist* 92:994–1005.

Gearing, J. 1995. Fear and loving in the West Indies: Research from the heart. In *Taboo: Sex, identity, and erotic subjectivity in anthropological fieldwork*, D. Kulick and M. Willson, eds., 186–218. London: Routledge.

Geertz, C. 1972. Deep play: Notes on the Balinese cockfight. *Daedalus* 101:1–37.

Geertz, C. 1973. *The interpretation of cultures. Selected essays.* New York: Basic Books.

Gentner, D., and A. L. Stevens, eds. 1983. *Mental Models.* Hillsdale, NJ: L. Erlbaum Associates.

Gerard, H. B., and G. C. Mathewson. 1966. The effects of severity of initiation on liking for a group: A replication. *Journal of Experimental Social Psychology* 2:278–87.

Gerich, J. 2008. Real or virtual? Response behavior in video-enhanced, self-administered computer interviews. *Field Methods* 20:356–76.

Gerring, J. 2007. *Case study research: Principles and practices.* New York: Cambridge University Press.

Gigengack, R., ed. 2000. Contemporary street ethnography. Special section of *Focaal Tidschrift voor Anthropologie*, No. 36.

Gil-Burman, C., F. Peláez, and S. Sánchez. 2002. Mate choice differences according to sex and age: An analysis of personal advertisements in Spanish newspapers. *Human Nature* 13:493–508.

Gillespie, R. M. 1992. A test of the external validity of focus group findings using survey research and statistical inference. Ph.D. dissertation, Iowa State University.

Gilly, M. C. 1988. Sex roles in advertising: A comparison of television advertisements in Australia, Mexico, and the United States. *Journal of Marketing* 52:75–85.

Gilovich, T., R. Vallone, and A. Tversky. 1985. The hot hand in basketball—on the misperception of random sequences. *Cognitive Psychology* 17:295–314.

Gil-White, F. J. 2004. Ultimatum game with ethnicity manipulation: Problems faced doing field economic experiments and their solutions. *Field Methods* 16:157–83.

Giorgi, A. 1986. Theoretical justification for the use of descriptions in psychological esearch. In *Qualitative research in psychology: Proceedings of the International Association for Qualitative Research*, P. D. Ashworth, A. Giorgi, and J. J. de Koning, eds., 6–46. Pittsburgh, PA: Duquesne University Press.

Gittelsohn, J., A. V. Shankar, K. P. West, and R. M. Ram. 1997. Estimating reactivity in direct observation studies of health behaviors. *Human Organization* 56:182–89.

Gladwin, C. H. 1976. A view of Plan Puebla: An application of hierarchical decision models. *Journal of Agricultural Economics* 59:881–87.

Gladwin, C. H. 1980. A theory of real life choice: Applications to agricultural decisions. In *Agricultural decision making*, P. Barlett, ed., 45–85. New York: Academic Press.

Gladwin, C. H. 1983. Contributions of decision-tree methodology to a farming systems program. *Human Organization* 42:146–57.

Gladwin, C. H. 1989. *Ethnographic decision tree modeling.* Newbury Park, CA: Sage.

Glantz, S. A., K. W. Kacirk, and C. McCulloch. 2004. Back to the future: Smoking levels in movies in 2002 compared with 1950 levels. *American Journal of Public Health* 94:261–63.

Glaser B. G. 1992. *Basics of grounded theory.* Mill Valley, CA: Sociology Press.

Glaser, B. G. 2002. Constructivist grounded theory? FQS. Forum: *Qualitative Social Research* 3(3). http://www.qualitative-research.net/index.php/fqs/index (accessed March 7, 2010).

Glaser, B. G., and A. Strauss. 1967. *The discovery of grounded theory: Strategies for qualitative research.* New York: Aldine.

Glaser, J. M., and M. Gilens. 1997. Interregional migration and political resocialization: A study of racial attitudes under pressure. *Public Opinion Quarterly* 61:72–96.

Glassner, T., and W. van der Vaart. 2009. Applications of calendar instruments in social surveys: A review. *Quality and Quantity* 43:333–49.

Glazer, M. 1975. Impersonal sex. In *Tearoom trade: Impersonal sex in public places*, L. Humphreys, ed., 213–22. Enl. ed. with a retrospect on ethical issues. Chicago: Aldine.

Godoy, R. 2002. The life cycle, ecological, and economic determinants of spousal leisure sharing: Panel estimations from Tawahka Amerindians, Honduras. *Human Ecology* 30:317–37.

Godoy, R., V. Reyes-García, S. Tanner, W. R. Leonard, T. McDade, and T. W. Huanca. 2008. Can we trust an adult's estimate of parental school attainment? Disentangling social desirability bias and random measurement error. *Field Methods* 20:26–45.

Godoy, R., V. Reyes-García, V. Vadez, W. R. Leonard, and E. Byron. 2007. How well do foragers protect food consumption? Panel evidence from a Native Amazonian society in Bolivia. *Human Ecology* 35:723–32.

Goffman, E. 1974. *Frame analysis*. New York: Harper & Row.

Golde, P., ed. 1986. *Women in the field: Anthropological experiences*. 2nd ed. Berkeley: University of California Press.

Goldman, L. 2002. *Science, reform and politics in Victorian Britain: The Social Science Association, 1857–1886*. New York: Cambridge University Press.

Goldsen, J. M. 1947. Analyzing the contents of mass communication: A step toward inter-group harmony. *International Journal of Opinion & Attitude Research* 1:81–92.

Goldstein, M. C. 1971. Stratification, polyandry, and family structure in central Tibet. *Southwestern Journal of Anthropology* 27:64–74.

Gölge, Z. B., M. F. Yavuz, S. Mudderisoglu, and M. S. Yavuz. 2003. Turkish university students' attitudes toward rape. *Sex Roles* 49:653–61.

Gomes do Espirito Santo, M. E. and G. D. Etheredge. 2002. How to reach clients of female sex workers: A survey "by surprise" in brothels in Dakar, Senegal. *Bulletin of the World Health Organization* 80:709–13.

González, N. S. 1986. The anthropologist as female head of household. In *Self, sex and gender in cross-cultural fieldwork*, T. L. Whitehead and M. E. Conaway, eds., 84–102. Urbana: University of Illinois Press.

González, R. J. 2007. Towards mercenary anthropology? The new U.S. Army counterinsurgency manual *FM 3-24* and the military-anthropology complex. *Anthropology Today* 23:14–19.

Good, K. (with D. Chanoff). 1991. *Into the heart*. New York: Simon & Schuster.

Goodall, C., and O. Appiah. 2008. Adolescents' perceptions of Canadian cigarette package warning labels: Investigating the effects of message framing. *Health Communication* 23:117–27.

Goode, W. J., and P. K. Hatt. 1952. *Methods in social research*. New York: McGraw-Hill.

Goodenough, W. 1956. Componential analysis and the study of meaning. *Language* 32:195–216.

Goodenough, W. 1963. Some applications of Guttman scale analysis to ethnography and culture theory. *Southwestern Journal of Anthropology* 19:235–50.

Goodenough, W. 1965. Rethinking "status" and "role": Toward a general model of the cultural organization of social relationships. In *The relevance of models for social anthropology. Association of Social Anthropology Monographs I*, M. Banton, ed., 1–24. London: Tavistock.

Goodman, L., and W. Kruskal. 1963. Measures of association for cross classifications III: Approximate sampling theory. *Journal of the American Statistical Association* 58:302–22.

Goodwin, C. 1981. *Conversational organization: Interaction between speakers and hearers*. New York: Academic Press.

Goodwin, C. 1986. Gesture as a resource for the organization of mutual orientation. *Semiotica* 62:29–49.

Goodwin, C. 1994. Recording human interaction in natural settings. *Pragmatics* 3:181–209.

Gorden, R. L. 1987. *Interviewing: Strategy, techniques, and tactics*. 4th ed. Chicago: Dorsey Press.

Gordon, D. 1991. Female circumcision and genital operations in Egypt and the Sudan: A dilemma for anthropologists. *Medical Anthropology Quarterly* 5:3–14.

Gordon, S. 1991. *The history and philosophy of social science*. New York: Routledge.

Gorman, D. M., and J. C. Huber, Jr. 2007. Do medical cannabis laws encourage cannabis use? *International Journal of Drug Policy* 18:160–67.

Gottschalk, L. A., and R. J. Bechtel. 1993. *Psychologic and neuropsychiatric assessment. Applying the Gottschalk-Gleser content analysis method to verbal sample analysis using the Gottschalk-Bechtel computer scoring system*. Palo Alto, CA: Mind Garden.

Gould, R. A., and P. B. Potter. 1984. Use-lives of automobiles in America: A preliminary archaeological view. In *Toward an ethnoarchaeology of modern America*, R. A. Gould, ed., 69–93. Brown University: Department of Anthropology, Research Papers in Anthropology (No. 4).

Gove, S., and G. H. Pelto. 1994. Focused ethnographic studies in the WHO programme for the control of acute respiratory infections. *Medical Anthropology* 15:409–24.

Graffam, B., L. Bowers, and K. N. Keene. 2008. Using observations of clinicians' teach practices to build a model of clinical instruction. *Academic Medicine* 83:768–74.

Grafova, I. B., V. A. Freedman, R. Kuman, and J. Rogowski. 2008. Neighborhoods and obesity in later life. *American Journal of Public Health* 98:2065–71.

Graham, B. 2000. *The research interview*. New York: Continuum.

Graham, M. A. 2003. Adaptation of the weighed food record method to households in the Peruvian Andes and ethnographic insights on hunger. *Field Methods* 15:143–60.

Graves, T. D., N. B. Graves, and M. J. Korbin. 1969. Historical inferences from Guttman scales: The return of age-area magic? *Current Anthropology* 10:317–38.

Graves, T. D., and C. A. Lave. 1972. Determinants of urban migrant Indian wages. *Human Organization* 31:47–61.

Gravlee, C. C. 2002a. Mobile computer-assisted personal interviewing with handheld computers: The Entryware System 3.0. *Field Methods* 14:322–36.

Gravlee, C. C. 2002b. Skin color, blood pressure, and the contextual effect of culture in southeastern Puerto Rico. Ph.D. dissertation, University of Florida.

Gravlee, C. C., H. R. Bernard, and W. R. Leonard. 2003a. Heredity, environment, and cranial form: A re-analysis of Boas's immigrant data. *American Anthropologist* 105:125–38.

Gravlee, C. C., H. R. Bernard, and W. R. Leonard. 2003b. Boas's *Changes in Bodily Form*: The immigrant study, cranial plasticity, and Boas's physical anthropology. *American Anthropologist* 105:326–32.

Gravlee, C. C., and W. W. Dressler. 2005. Skin pigmentation, self-perceived color, and arterial blood pressure in Puerto Rico. *American Journal of Human Biology* 17:195–206.

Gravlee, C. W., W. Dressler, and H. R. Bernard. 2005. Skin color, social classification, and blood pressure in Puerto Rico. *American Journal of Public Health* 95:2191–97.

Gravlee, C. C., D. P. Kennedy, R. Godoy, and W. Leonard. 2009. Methods for collecting panel data: What cultural anthropology learn from other disciplines? *Journal of Anthropological Research* 65:453–83.

Gravlee, C. C., S. N. Zenk, S. Woods, Z. Rowe, and A. J. Schulz. 2006. Handheld computers for direct observation of the social and physical environment. *Field Methods* 18:382–97.

Greene, P. D. 2001. Handheld computers as tools for writing and managing field data. *Field Methods* 13:181–97.

Greenwald, A. G., R. González, R. J. Harris, and D. Guthrie. 1996. Effect sizes and *p* values: What should be reported and what should be replicated? *Psychophysiology* 33:175–83.

Gregor, T. 1979. Short people. *Natural History* 88:14–21.

Gregson, S., T. Zhuwau, R. M. Anderson, and S. K. Chandiwana. 1998. Is there evidence for behaviour change in response to AIDS in rural Zimbabwe? *Social Science & Medicine* 46:321–30.

Gribble, J. N., H. G. Miller, and S. M. Rogers. 1999. Interview mode and measurement of sexual behaviors: Methodological issues. *Journal of Sex Research* 36:16–24.

Grieco, E. M., and R. C. Cassidy. 2001. Overview of race and Hispanic origin. Census 2000 Brief C2KBR/01–1. Washington, DC: U.S. Bureau of the Census. March 2001. http://www.census.gov/prod/2001pubs/c2kbr01-1.pdf (accessed March 8, 2010).

Griffin, J. H. 1961. *Black like me*. Boston: Houghton-Mifflin.

Griffin, L. J. 1993. Narrative, event-structure analysis, and causal interpretation in historical sociology. *American Journal of Sociology* 98:1094–133.

Gross, D. R. 1984. Time allocation: A tool for the study of cultural behavior. *Annual Review of Anthropology* 13:519–58.

Gross, D. R. 1992. *Discovering anthropology*. Mountain View, CA: Mayfield.

Groves, R. M. 2006. Nonresponse rates and nonresponse bias in household surveys. *Public Opinion Quarterly* 70:646–75.

Gubrium, J. F., and J. A. Holstein. 2002. *Handbook of interview research: Context and method*. Thousand Oaks, CA: Sage.

Guéguen, N., C. Jacob, H. Le Guellec, T. Morineau, and M. Lourel. 2008. Sound level of environmental music and drinking behavior: A field experiment with beer drinkers. *Alcoholism: Clinical and Experimental Research* 32:1795–98.

Guest, G. 2000. Using Guttman scaling to rank wealth: Integrating quantitative and qualitative data. *Field Methods* 12:346–57.

Guest, G., A. Bunce, and L. Johnson. 2006. How many interviews are enough? An experiment with data saturation and variability. *Field Methods* 18:59–82.

Guilmet, G. M. 1979. Instructor reaction to verbal and nonverbal-visual behavior in the urban classroom. *Anthropology and Education Quarterly* 10:254–66.

Gujarati, D. N. 1995. *Basic econometrics.* 3rd ed. New York: McGraw-Hill.

Gujarati, D. N. 2003. *Basic econometrics.* 4th ed. New York: McGraw-Hill.

Gulur, P., S. W. Rodi, T. A. Washington, J. P. Cravero, G. J. Fanciullo, G. J. McHugo, and J. C. Baird. 2009. Computer face scale for measuring pediatric pain and mood. *The Journal of Pain* 10:173–79.

Gummerson, E. 2000. *Qualitative methods in management research.* 2nd ed. Thousand Oaks, CA: Sage.

Gurven, M., and H. Kaplan. 2006. Determinants of time allocation across the lifespan. A theoretical model and application to the Machiguenga and Piro of Peru. *Human Nature* 17:1–49.

Güth, W., R. Schmittberger, and B. Schwarze. 1982. An experimental analysis of ultimatum bargaining. *Journal of Economic and Behavior Organization* 3:367–88.

Guttman, L. 1950. The basis for scalogram analysis. In *Studies in social psychology in World War II,* S. A. Stouffer et al., eds. Vol. 4, *Measurement and prediction,* 60–90. Princeton, NJ: Princeton University Press.

Hadaway, C. K., P. L. Marler, and M. Chaves. 1993. What the polls don't show: A closer look at U.S. church attendance. *American Sociological Review* 58:741–52.

Hadaway, C. K., P. L. Marler, and M. Chaves. 1998. Overreporting church attendance in America: Evidence that demands the same verdict. *American Sociological Review* 63:122–30.

Hall, E. T. 1963. A system of notation of proxemic behavior. *American Anthropologist* 65:1003–26.

Hall, E. T. 1966. *The hidden dimension.* New York: Doubleday.

Hames, R. 1992. Time allocation. In *Evolutionary ecology and human behavior,* E. A. Smith and B. Winterhalder, eds., 203–35. New York: Aldine de Gruyter.

Hammel, E. A. 1962. Social rank and evolutionary position in a coastal Peruvian village. *Southwestern Journal of Anthropology* 18:199–215.

Handlin, O. 1979. *Truth in history.* Cambridge, MA: Harvard University Press.

Handwerker, W. P. 1989. *Women's power and social revolution: Fertility transition in the West Indies.* Newbury Park, CA: Sage.

Handwerker, W. P. 1993. Simple random samples of regional populations. *Cultural Anthropology Methods Journal* 5(1):12.

Handwerker, W. P. 1996a. Constructing Likert scales: Testing the validity and reliability of single measures of multidimensional variables. *Cultural Anthropology Methods Journal* 8(1):1–6.

Handwerker, W. P. 1996b. Power and gender: Violence and affection experienced by children in Barbados, W. I. *Medical Anthropology* 17:101–28.

Handwerker, W. P. 1998. Why violence? A test of hypotheses representing three discourses on the roots of domestic violence. *Human Organization* 57:200–208.

Handwerker, W. P. 2001. *Quick ethnography: A guide to rapid multi-method research.* Walnut Creek, CA: AltaMira.

Handwerker, W. P. 2002. The construct validity of cultures: Cultural diversity, cultural theory, and a method for ethnography. *American Anthropologist* 104:106–22.

Handwerker, W. P., J. Hatcherson, and J. Herbert. 1997. Sampling guidelines for cultural data. *Cultural Anthropology Methods Journal* 9(1):7–9.

Hanks, W. F. 1988. Grammar, style, and meaning in a Maya manuscript. Review of *Heaven born Mérida and its destiny: The book of Chilam Balam of Chumayel. International Journal of American Linguistics* 54:331–69.

Hanneman, R. A., and M. Riddle. 2005. *Introduction to social network analysis.* Riverside: University of California, Riverside. http://www.faculty.ucr.edu/~hanneman/nettext/ (accessed March 5, 2010).

Hansen, A., and L. A. McSpadden. 1993. Self-anchoring scale, or ladder of life: A method used with diverse refugee populations. Unpublished manuscript.

Harari, H., O. Harari, and R. V. White. 1985. The reaction to rape by American male bystanders. *Journal of Social Psychology* 125:653–58.

Harb, G. C., W. Eng, T. Zaider, and R. G. Heimberg. 2003. Behavioral assessment of public-speaking anxiety using a modified version of the Social Performance Rating Scale. *Behaviour Research and Therapy* 41:1373–80.

Harburg, E., L. Gleibermann, P. Roeper, M. A. Schork, and W. J. Schull. 1978. Skin color, ethnicity and blood pressure I: Detroit blacks. *American Journal of Public Health* 68:1177–83.

Hardesty, D. M., and W. O. Bearden. 2004. The use of expert judges in scale development. Implications for improving face validity of measures of unobservable constructs. *Journal of Business Research* 57:98–107.

Harmon, T., C. F. Turner, S. M. Rogers, E. Eggleston, A. M. Roman, M. A. Villaroel, J. R. Chromy, L. Ganapathi, and S. P. Li. 2009. Impact of T-CASI on survey measurement of subjective phenomena. *Public Opinion Quarterly* 73:255–80.

Harrington, B. 2003. The social psychology of access in ethnographic research. *Journal of Contemporary Ethnography* 32:592–625.

Harris, M. 1968. *The rise of anthropological theory.* New York: Thomas Crowell.

Harris, M., J. G. Consorte, J. Lang, and B. Byrne. 1993. Who are the Whites? Imposed census categories and the racial demography of Brazil. *Social Forces* 72:451–62.

Harrison, A. 1993. Comparing nurses' and patients' pain evaluations: A study of hospitalized patients in Kuwait. *Social Science & Medicine* 36:683–92.

Harrison, E. 2000. Men, women and work in rural Zambia. *European Journal of Development Research* 12:53–71.

Harrison, E. 2006. Unpacking the anti-corruption agenda: Dilemmas for anthropologists. *Oxford Development Studies* 34:15–29.

Harrison, F. V., ed. 1997. *Decolonizing anthropology: Moving further toward an anthropology of liberation.* Arlington, VA: Association of Black Anthropologists, American Anthropological Association.

Harrison, G. G. 1976. Sociocultural correlates of food utilization and waste in a sample of urban households. Ph.D. dissertation, University of Arizona.

Harrower, M. J. 2009. Is the hydraulic hypothesis dead yet? Irrigation and social change in ancient Yemen. *World Archaeology* 41:58–72.

Harshbarger, C. L. 1986. Agricultural credit in San Vito, Costa Rica. Master's thesis, University of Florida.

Harshbarger, C. L. 1995. Farmer-herder conflict and state legitimacy in Cameroon. Ph.D. dissertation, University of Florida.

Hartman, J. J. 1978. Social demographic characteristics of Wichita, Sedwick County. In *Metropolitan Wichita—Past, present, and future,* G. Miller and J. Skaggs, eds., 22–37. Lawrence: Kansas Regents Press.

Hartman, J. J., and J. Hedblom. 1979. *Methods for the social sciences: A handbook for students and non-specialists.* Westport, CT: Greenwood.

Hartmann, D. P., and D. D. Wood. 1990. Observational methods. In *International handbook of behavior modification therapy,* 2nd ed., A. S. Bellack, M. Hersen, and A. E. Kazdin, eds., 107–38. New York: Plenum.

Hartmann, P. 1994. Interviewing when the spouse is present. *International Journal of Public Opinion Research* 6:298–306.

Hartwig, F., and B. E. Dearing. 1979. *Exploratory data analysis.* Beverly Hills, CA: Sage.

Harvey, S. M., and S. T. Bird. 2004. What makes women feel powerful? An exploratory study of relationship power and sexual decision-making with African Americans at risk for HIV/STDs. *Women and Health* 39:1–18.

Hatch, D., and M. Hatch. 1947. Criteria of social status as derived from marriage announcements in the *New York Times*. *American Sociological Review* 12:396–403.

Hauser, R. M. 2005. Survey response in the long run: The Wisconsin Longitudinal Study. *Field Methods* 17:3–29.

Hausman, D. B., and A. Hausman. 1997. *Descartes's legacy: Minds and meaning in early modern philosophy.* Toronto: University of Toronto Press.

Hawkes, K., J. F. O'Connell, N. G. Blurton Jones, O. T. Oftedal, and R. J. Blumenschine. 1991. Hunting income patterns among the Hadza: Big game, common goods, foraging goals and the evolution of the human diet. *Philosophical Transactions: Biological Sciences* 334:243–51.

Haworth-Hoeppner, S. 2000. The critical shapes of body image: The role of culture and family in the production of eating disorders. *Journal of Marriage and the Family* 62:212–27.

Hayek, F. A. von 1952. *The counter-revolution of science.* Glencoe, Il.: The Free Press.

Heath, S. B. 1972. *Telling tongues.* New York: Columbia University Press.

Hebert, J. R., C. B. Ebbeling, C. E. Matthews, T. G. Hurley, Y. S. Ma, S. Drucker, and L. Clemow. 2002. Systematic errors in middle-aged women's estimates of energy intake: Comparing three self-report measures to total energy expenditure from doubly labeled water. *Annals of Epidemiology* 12:577–86.

Heckathorn, D. D. 1997. Respondent-driven sampling: A new approach to the study of hidden populations. *Social Problems* 44:174–99.

Heckathorn, D. D. 2002. Respondent-driven sampling II: Deriving valid population estimates from chain-referral samples of hidden populations. *Social Problems* 49:11–34.

Heckathorn, D. D., and J. Jeffri. 2001. Finding the beat: Using respondent-driven sampling to study jazz musicians. *Poetics* 28:307–29.

Heckathorn, D. D., and C. Wejnert. 2008. Web-based network sampling: Efficiency and efficacy of respondent-driven sampling for online research. *Sociological Methods and Research* 37:105–34.

Hedge, A., and Y. H. Yousif. 1992. Effects of urban size, urgency, and cost on helpfulness: A cross-cultural comparison between the United Kingdom and the Sudan. *Journal of Cross-Cultural Psychology* 23:107–15.

Hedican, E. J. 1986. Sibling terminology and information theory: An hypothesis concerning the growth of folk taxonomy. *Ethnology* 25:229–39.

Heerwegh, D. 2009. Mode differences between face-to-face and web surveys: An experimental investigation of data quality and social desirability effects. *International Journal of Public Opinion Research* 21:111–21.

Hektner, J. M., J. Schmidt, and M. Csikszentmihalyi. 2007. *Experience sampling method: Measuring the quality of everyday life.* Thousand Oaks, CA: Sage.

Helm, J. 1980. Female infanticide, European diseases, and population levels among the Mackenzie Dene. *American Ethnologist* 7:259–85.

Helms, R., and D. Jacobs. 2002. The political context of sentencing: An analysis of community and individual determinants. *Social Forces* 81:577–604.

Henderson, J., and J. P. Harrington. 1914. *Ethnozoology of the Tewa Indians.* Smithsonian Institution, Bureau of American Ethnology, Bulletin 56. Washington, DC: Government Printing Office.

Henley, N. M. 1969. A psychological study of the semantics of animal terms. *Journal of Verbal Learning and Verbal Behavior* 8:176–84.

Henrich, J., R. Boyd, S. Bowles et al. 2005. "Economic man" in cross-cultural perspective: Behavioral experiments in 15 small-scale societies. *Behavioral and Brain Sciences* 28:795–855.

Henry, G. T. 1990. *Practical sampling.* Newbury Park, CA: Sage.

Hensley, W. E. 1974. Increasing response rates by choice of postage stamps. *Public Opinion Quarterly* 38:280–83.

Herrera, C. D. 2001. Ethics, deception, and "those Milgram experiments." *Journal of Applied Philosophy* 18:245–56.

Hertwig, R., and A. Ortmann. 2008. Deception in experiments: Revisiting the arguments in its defense. *Ethics and Behavior* 18:59–92.

Herzfeld, M. 1977. Ritual and textual structures: The advent of spring in rural Greece. In *Text and context,* R. K. Jain, ed., 29–45. Philadelphia: Institute for the Study of Human Issues.

Herzfeld, M. 1983. Looking both ways: The ethnographer in the text. *Semiotica* 46:151–66.

Herzfeld, M. 2009a. *Evicted from eternity: The restructuring of modern Rome*. Chicago: The University of Chicago Press.

Herzfeld, M. 2009b. The cultural politics of gesture. *Ethnography* 10:131–52.

Hewitt, M. 2002. Attitudes toward interview mode and comparability of reporting sexual behavior by personal interview and audio computer-assisted self-interviewing: Analyses of the 1995 National Survey of Family Growth. *Sociological Methods and Research* 31:3–26.

Hewett, P. C., A. S. Erulkar, and B. S. Mensch. 2004. The feasibility of computer-assisted survey interviewing in Africa: Experience from two rural districts in Kenya. *Social Science Computer Review* 22:319–34.

Hewlett, B. S., and M. E. Lamb, eds. 2005. *Hunter-gatherer childhoods*. New Brunswick, NJ: Transaction Publishers.

Hiatt, L. R. 1980. Polyandry in Sri Lanka: A test case for parental investment theory. *Man* 15:583–98.

Hielscher, S., and J. Sommerfeld. 1985. Concepts of illness and the utilization of health-care services in a rural Malian village. *Social Science and Medicine* 21:469–81.

Hill, R. J., and P. S. W. Davies. 2001. The validity of self-reported energy intake as determined using the doubly labelled water technique. *British Journal of Nutrition* 85:415–30.

Hine, C. 2000. *Virtual ethnography*. London: Sage.

Hinton, P. 2002. The "Thailand controversy" revisited. *Australian Journal of Anthropology* 13:155–77.

Hirschman, E. C. 1987. People as products: Analysis of a complex marketing exchange. *Journal of Marketing* 51:98–108.

Hjelmslev, L. 1961. *Prolegomena to a theory of language*, F. J. Whitfield, transl. Revised English ed. Madison: University of Wisconsin Press.

Hochstim, J. R. 1967. A critical comparison of three strategies of collecting data from households. *Journal of the American Statistical Association* 62:976–89.

Hodge, L. G., and D. Dufour. 1991. Cross-sectional growth of young Shipibo Indian children in eastern Peru. *American Journal of Physical Anthropology* 84:35–41.

Hodges, H. A. 1952. *The philosophy of Wilhelm Dilthey*. London: Routledge and Paul.

Hodson, R. 2004. A meta-analysis of workplace ethnographies. Race, gender, and employee attitudes and behaviors. *Journal of Contemporary Ethnography* 33:4–38.

Hoffman, L. L., A. P. Jackson, and S. A. Smith. 2005. Career barriers among Native American Students living on reservations. *Journal of Career Development* 32:31–45.

Høgh-Olesen, H. 2008. Human spatial behavior: The spacing of people, objects and animals in six cross-cultural samples. *Journal of Cognition and Culture* 8:245–80.

Holbrook, A. L., M. C. Green, and J. A. Krosnick. 2003. Telephone versus face-to-face interviewing of national probability samples with long questionnaires. Comparisons of respondent satisficing and social desirability response bias. *Public Opinion Quarterly Volume* 67:79–125.

Holland, D., and N. Quinn. 1987. *Cultural models in language and thought*. Cambridge: Cambridge University Press.

Holland, D., and D. Skinner. 1987. Prestige and intimacy: The cultural models behind Americans' talk about gender types. In *Cultural models in language and thought*, D. Holland and N. Quinn, eds., 78–111. New York: Cambridge University Press.

Hollis, M. 1996. Philosophy of social science. In *The Blackwell companion to philosophy*, N. Bunnin and E. P. Tsui-James, eds., 358–87. Oxford: Blackwell.

Holmes, C. T., and R. L. Keffer. 1995. A computerized method to teach Latin and Greek root words: Effect on verbal SAT scores. *Journal of Educational Research* 89:47–50.

Hopper, C. B., and J. Moore. 1983. Hell on wheels: The outlaw motorcycle gangs. *The Journal of American Culture* 6:58–64.

Hopper, C. B., and J. Moore. 1990. Women in outlaw motorcycle gangs. *Journal of Contemporary Ethnography* 18:363–87.

Horn, W. 1960. Reliability survey: A survey on the reliability of response to an interview survey. *Het PTT-Bedrijf* (The Hague) 10:105–56.

Hornik, J. 1992. Tactile stimulation and consumer response. *Journal of Consumer Research* 19:449–58.

Hornik, J., and S. Ellis. 1988. Strategies to secure compliance for a mall intercept interview. *Public Opinion Quarterly* 52:539–51.

Horowitz, I. L. 1965. The life and death of Project Camelot. *Trans-Action* 3:3–7, 44–47.

Houck, L. D., and L. C. Drickamer, eds. 1996. *Foundations of animal behavior: Classic papers with commentaries.* Chicago: University of Chicago Press.

Houseman, M., and D. R. White. 1998. Taking sides: Marriage networks and Dravidian kinship in Lowland South America. In *Transformations of kinship,* M. Godelier, T. R. Trautmann, and F. E. Tjon Sie Fat, eds., 214–43. Washington, DC: Smithsonian Institution Press.

Howard, J. 1973 [1792]. *Prisons and lazarettos.* Vol. 1. *The state of the prisons in England and Wales: With preliminary observations, and an account of some foreign prisons and hospitals.* Montclair, NJ: Patterson Smith.

Howell, N. 1981. Inferring infanticide from Hudson's Bay Company population data 1829–1934. Working Paper No. 26, Structural Analysis Programme, Department of Sociology, University of Toronto.

Howell, N. 1990. *Surviving fieldwork.* Washington, DC: American Anthropological Association.

HRAF. 1967. The HRAF quality-control sample universe. *Behavior Science Notes* 2:63–69.

Hruschka, D. J., B. Cummings, D. C. St. John, J. Moore, G. Khumalo-Sakutukwa, and J. W. Carey. 2004. Fixed-choice and open-ended response formats: A comparison from HIV prevention research in Zimbabwe. *Field Methods* 16:184–202.

Hruschka, D. J., L. M. Sibley, N. Kalim, and J. K. Edmonds. 2008. When there is more than one answer key: Cultural theories of postpartum hemorrhage in Matlab, Bangladesh. *Field Methods* 20:315–37.

Hsieh, E. 2008. "I am not a robot!" Interpreters' views of their roles in health care settings. *Qualitative Health Research* 18:1367–83.

Hudelson, P. M. 1994. The management of acute respiratory infections in Honduras: A field test of the Focused Ethnographic Study (FES). *Medical Anthropology* 15:435–36.

Hudson, H. F. 2004. *The great betrayal: Fraud in science.* Orlando: Harcourt.

Hughes, W. W. 1984. The method to our madness: The garbage project methodology. In *Household refuse analysis: Theory, method, and applications in social science,* W. L. Rathje and C. K. Ritenbaugh, eds., 41–50. *American Behavioral Scientist* 28(1, entire issue).

Hultsch, D. F., S. W. S. Macdonald, M. A. Hunter, S. B. Maitland, and R. A. Dixon. 2002. Sampling and generalisability in developmental research: Comparison of random and convenience samples of older adults. *International Journal of Behavioral Development* 26:345–59.

Hume, L., and J. Mulcock, eds. 2004. *Anthropologists in the field.* New York: Columbia University Press.

Humphreys, L. 1975. *Tearoom trade: Impersonal sex in public places.* Enl. ed. with a retrospect on ethical issues. Chicago: Aldine.

Hunt, M. M. 1997. *How science takes stock: The story of meta-analysis.* New York: Russell Sage Foundation.

Hursh-César, G., and P. Roy, eds. 1976. *Third World surveys: Survey research in developing nations.* Delhi: Macmillan.

Hurwicz, M-L. 1995. Physicians' norms and health care decisions of elderly Medicare recipients. *Medical Anthropology Quarterly* 9:211–35.

Husserl, E. 1964 [1907]. *The idea of phenomenology,* W. P. Alston and G. Nakhnikian, transl. The Hague: Nijhoff.

Husserl, E. 1999. *The essential Husserl: Basic writings in transcendental phenomenology,* D. Welton, ed. Bloomington: Indiana University Press.

Hutchins, E. 1980. *Culture and inference.* Cambridge, MA: Harvard University Press.

Hutchinson, S. E. 1996. *Nuer dilemmas: Coping with money, war, and the state.* Berkeley: University of California Press.

Hutt, S. J., and C. Hutt. 1970. *Direct observation and measurement of behavior.* Springfield, IL: C. C. Thomas.

Hyman, H. H., and W. J. Cobb. 1975. *Interviewing in social research*. Chicago: University of Chicago Press.

Hymes, D. 1964. Discussion of Burling's paper. *American Anthropologist* 66:116–19.

Hymes, D. 1976. Louis Simpson's "The deserted boy." *Poetics* 5:119–55.

Hymes, D. 1977. Discovering oral performance and measured verse in American Indian narrative. *New Literary History* 8:431–57.

Hymes, D. 1980a. Verse analysis of a Wasco text: Hiram Smith's "At'unaqa." *International Journal of American Linguistics* 46:65–77.

Hymes, D. 1980b. Particle, pause, and pattern in American Indian narrative verse. *American Indian Culture and Research Journal* 4:7–51.

Hymes, D. 1981. *In vain I tried to tell you: Essays in Native American ethnopoetics*. Philadelphia: University of Pennsylvania Press.

Hymes, V. 1987. Warm Springs Sahaptin narrative analysis. In *Native American discourse: Poetics and rhetoric*, J. Sherzer and A. Woodbury, eds., 62–102. Cambridge: Cambridge University Press.

Ibeh, K. I. N., and J. K.-U. Brock. 2004. Conducting survey research among organisational populations in developing countries: Can the drop and collect technique make a difference? *International Journal of Marketing Research* 46:375–83.

Ice, G. 2004. Technological advances in observational data collection: The advantages and limitations of computer-assisted data collection. *Field Methods* 16:352–75.

ICMR. Institute for Coast and Marine Resources and East Carolina University. 1993. Coastal North Carolina socioeconomic study, Vol. 4. Pile sort and data analysis. Final rept. http://www.ntis.gov/search/product.aspx?ABBR = PB95261566 (accessed February 18, 2011).

Ignatow, G. 2004. Speaking together, thinking together? Exploring metaphor and cognition in a shipyard union dispute. *Sociological Forum* 19:405–33.

International Monetary Fund (IMF). 2009. World Economic Outlook Database, April 2009. http://tinyurl.com/c2rwdh (accessed June 21, 2009).

Isaac, R., and A. Shah. 2004. Sex roles and marital adjustment in Indian couples. *International Journal of Social Psychiatry* 50:129–41.

Ives, E. 1995. *The tape-recorded interview. A manual for fieldworkers in folklore and oral history*. 2nd ed. Knoxville: University of Tennessee Press.

Ivis, F. J., S. J. Bondy, and E. M. Adlaf. 1997. The effect of question structure on self-reports of heavy drinking: Closed-ended versus open-ended questions. *Journal of Studies on Alcohol* 58:622–24.

Izquierdo, C., and A. Johnson. 2007. Desire, envy and punishment: A Matsigenka emotion schema in illness narratives and folk stories. *Culture, Medicine, and Psychiatry* 31:419–44.

Jacobs, L. 1995. *The Jewish religion: A companion*. New York: Oxford University Press.

Jacoby, H. 1995. The economics of polygyny in sub-Saharan Africa: Female productivity and the demand for wives in Côte d'Ivoire. *Journal of Political Economy* 103:938–71.

Jaeger, R. M. 1984. *Sampling in education and the social sciences*. New York: Longmans, Green.

Jamieson, P., K. H. Jamieson, and D. Romer. 2003. The responsible reporting of suicide in print journalism. *American Behavioral Scientist* 46:1643–60.

Jankowiak, W. R., and E. F. Fischer. 1995. A cross-cultural perspective on romantic love. *Ethnology* 31:149–55.

Jaranson, J. M., J. Butcher, L. Halcón, D. R. Johnson, C. Robertson, K. Savik, M. Spring, and J. Westermeyer. 2004. Somali and Oromo refugees: Correlates of torture and trauma history. *American Journal of Public Health* 94:591–98.

Jargowsky, P. A. 2005. The ecological fallacy. In *The encyclopedia of social measurement*, K. Kempf-Leonard, ed. Vol. 1, *A–E*, 715–22. Oxford: Elsevier/Academic Press.

Jasanoff, S., G. E. Markle, J. C. Petersen, and T. Pinch. 1995. *The handbook of science and technology studies*. Thousand Oaks, CA: Sage.

Jaskyte, K., and W. W. Dressler. 2004. Studying culture as an integral aggregate variable: Organizational culture and innovation in a group of nonprofit organizations. *Field Methods* 16:265–84.

Jasso, G. 1998. Exploring the justice of punishments: Framing, expressiveness, and the just prison sentence. *Social Justice Research* 11:397–422.

Jasso, G. 2008. Distributive justice and CEO compensation. *Acta Sociologica* 51:123–43.

Javeline, D. 1999. Response effects in polite cultures. *Public Opinion Quarterly* 63:1–28.

Jefferson, G. 1973. A case of precision timing in ordinary conversation: Overlapped tag-positioned address terms in closing sequences. *Semiotica* 9:47–96.

Jefferson, M. 1939. The law of the primate city. *Geographical Review* 29:226–32.

Jenkins, C. 1981. Patterns of growth and malnutrition in Belize. *American Journal of Physical Anthropology* 56:169–78.

Jenkins, J. H., and R. J. Barrett, eds. 2004. *Schizophrenia, culture, and subjectivity: The edge of experience.* New York: Cambridge University Press.

Jentsch, B. 1998. The "interpreter effect": Rendering interpreters visible in cross-cultural research and methodology. *Journal of European Social Policy* 8:275–89.

Jobe, J. B., D. M. Keler, and A. F. Smith. 1996. Cognitive techniques in interviewing older people. In *Answering questions: Methodology for determining cognitive and communicative processes in survey research,* N. Schwarz and S. Sudman, eds., 197–219. San Francisco: Jossey-Bass.

Johansen, U. C., and D. R. White. 2002. Collaborative long-term ethnography and longitudinal social analysis of a nomadic clan in southeastern Turkey. In *Chronicling cultures: Long-term field research in anthropology,* R. V. Kemper and A. P. Royce, eds., 81–98. Walnut Creek, CA: AltaMira.

Johnson, A. 1975. Time allocation in a Machiguenga community. *Ethnology* 14:310–21.

Johnson, A. 1978. *Quantification in anthropology.* Stanford, CA: Stanford University Press.

Johnson, A., and others. 1987. *The time allocation studies checklist.* Los Angeles: UCLA Time Allocation Project. (Also in *Cross-cultural studies of time allocation.* New Haven, CT: Human Relations Area Files.)

Johnson, J. C. 1990. *Selecting ethnographic informants.* Newbury Park, CA: Sage.

Johnson, J. C., and D. C. Griffith. 1996. Pollution, food safety, and the distribution of knowledge. *Human Ecology* 24:87–108.

Johnson, J. C., and S. C. Weller. 2002. Elicitation techniques for interviewing. In *Handbook of interview research,* J. F. Gubrium and J. A. Holstein, eds., 491–514. Thousand Oaks, CA: Sage.

Johnson, R. K., P. Driscoll, and M. I. Goran. 1996. Comparison of multiple-pass 24-hour recall estimates of energy intake with total energy expenditure determined by the doubly labeled water method in young children. *Journal of the American Dietetic Association* 96:1140–44.

Johnson, W. T., and J. D. Delamater. 1976. Response effects in sex surveys. *Public Opinion Quarterly* 40:165–81.

Johnson-Laird, P. N. 1983. *Mental models: Toward a cognitive science of language, inference, and consciousness.* Cambridge, MA: Harvard University Press.

Johnston, J., and C. Walton. 1995. Reducing response effects for sensitive questions: A computer-assisted self-interview with audio. *Social Science Computer Review* 13:304–19.

Johnstone, B., K. Ferrara, and J. M. Bean. 1992. Gender, politeness, and discourse management in same-sex and cross-sex opinion-poll interviews. *Journal of Pragmatics* 18:405–30.

Jones, D. J. 1973. The results of role-playing in anthropological research. *Anthropological Quarterly* 46:30–37.

Jones, M., and M. A. Nies. 1996. The relationship of perceived benefits of and barriers to reported exercise in older African American women. *Public Health Nursing* 13:151–58.

Jones, R. 2008. Soap opera video on handheld computers to reduce young urban women's sex HIV risk. *AIDS and Behavior* 12:876–84.

Joravsky, D. 1970. *The Lysenko affair.* Cambridge, MA: Harvard University Press.

Jordan, B. 1992. *Birth in four cultures: A cross-cultural investigation of childbirth in Yucatan, Holland, Sweden, and the United States.* 4th exp. ed. Revised by R. Davis-Floyd. Prospect Heights, IL: Waveland.

Jordan, B., and A. Henderson. 1993. Interaction analysis: Foundations and practice. Palo Alto, CA: Xerox Palo Alto Research Center and Institute for Research on Learning. Working paper.

Jorgensen, D. 1989. *Participant observation.* Newbury Park, CA: Sage.

Jorgensen, J. G., R. McCleary, and S. McNabb. 1985. Social-indicators in Native village Alaska. *Human Organization* 44:2–17.

Jussaume, R. A., Jr., and Y. Yamada. 1990. A comparison of the viability of mail surveys in Japan and the United States. *Public Opinion Quarterly* 54:219–28.

Kadushin, C. 1968. Power, influence and social circles: A new methodology for studying opinion makers. *American Sociological Review* 33:685–99.

Kahn, R. L., and C. F. Cannell. 1957. *The dynamics of interviewing.* New York: Wiley.

Kahneman, D., A. B. Krueger, and D. A. Schkade. 2004. A survey method for characterizing daily life experience: The day reconstruction method. *Science* 306:1776–80.

Kallan, J. E. 1998. Drug abuse-related mortality in the United States: Patterns and correlates. *American Journal of Drug and Alcohol Abuse* 24:103–17.

Kane, E. W., and L. J. Macaulay. 1993. Interviewer gender and gender attitudes. *Public Opinion Quarterly* 57:1–28.

Kane, J. G., S. C. Craig, and K. D. Wald. 2004. Religion and presidential politics in Florida: A list experiment. *Social Science Quarterly* 85:281–93.

Kane, S., and T. Mason. 2001. AIDS and criminal justice. *Annual Review of Anthropology* 30:457–79.

Karmaker, A., and S. Kwek. 2007. An iterative refinement approach for data cleaning. *Intelligent Data Analysis* 11:547–60.

Kasl, S. V. 1996. The influence of the work environment on cardiovascular health: A historical, conceptual, and methodological perspective. *Journal of Occupational Health Psychology* 1:42–56.

Katsurada, E., and Y. Sugihara. 1999. A preliminary validation of the Bem Sex Role Inventory in Japanese culture. *Journal of Cross-Cultural Psychology* 30:641–45.

Katz, D. 1942. Do interviewers bias polls? *Public Opinion Quarterly* 6:248–68.

Katz, K., and C. Naré. 2002. Reproductive health knowledge and use of services among young adults in Dakar, Senegal. *Journal of Biosocial Science* 34:215–31.

Kawulich, B. In press. Gatekeeping: An ongoing adventure in research. *Field Methods.*

Kearney, M. H., S. Murphy, K. Irwin, and M. Rosenbaum. 1995. Salvaging self—A grounded theory of pregnancy on crack cocaine. *Nursing Research* 44:208–13.

Keating, C. F., D. W. Randall, T. Kendrick, and K. A. Gutshall. 2003. Do baby-faced adults receive more help? The (cross-cultural) case of the lost resume. *Journal of Nonverbal Behavior* 27:89–109.

Keesing, R. M. 1978. *'Elota's story. The life and times of a Solomon Islands big man.* New York: St. Martin's.

Keeter, S., C. Kennedy, M. Dimock, J. Best, and P. Craighillo. 2006. Gauging the impact of growing nonresponse on estimates from a national RDD telephone survey. *Public Opinion Quarterly* 70:759–79.

Keil, J. E., S. H. Sandifer, C. B. Loadholt, and E. Boyle, Jr. 1981. Skin color and education effects on blood pressure. *American Journal of Public Health* 71:532–34.

Keil, J. E., H. A. Tyroler, S. H. Sandifer, and E. Boyle, Jr. 1977. Hypertension: Effects of social class and racial admixture. *American Journal of Public Health* 67:634–39.

Keith, J., C. L. Fry, A. P. Glascock, C. Ikels, J. Dickerson-Putnam, H. Harpending, and P. Draper. 1994. *The aging experience: Diversity and commonality across cultures.* Thousand Oaks, CA: Sage.

Kelloway, E. K. 1998. *Using LISREL for structural equation modeling: A researcher's guide.* Thousand Oaks, CA: Sage.

Kelly, G. A. 1955. *The psychology of personal constructs.* New York: Norton.

Kemper, R. V. 1997. Ethical issues for social anthropologists: A North-American perspective on long-term research in Mexico. *Human Organization* 56:479–83.

Kemper, R. V. 2002. From Student to Steward: Tzintzuntzan as extended community. In *Chronicling cultures: Long-term field research in anthropology,* R. V. Kemper and A. P. Royce, eds., 284–312. Walnut Creek, CA: AltaMira.

Kemper, R. V., and A. P. Royce, eds. 2002. *Chronicling cultures: Long-term field research in anthropology.* Walnut Creek, CA: AltaMira.

Kemph, B. T., and T. Kasser. 1996. Effects of sexual orientation of interviewer on expressed attitudes toward male homosexuality. *The Journal of Social Psychology* 136:401–3.

Kempton, W. 1987. Two theories of home heat control. In *Cultural models in language and thought,* D. Holland and N. Quinn, eds., 222–42. New York: Cambridge University Press.

Kempton, W., J. S. Boster, and J. A. Jartley. 1995. *Environmental values in American culture.* Cambridge, MA: MIT Press.

Kendall, C. 1983. Loose structure of family in Honduras. *Journal of Comparative Family Studies* 16:257–72.

Kendall, C., L. R. F. S. Kerr, G. L. Werneck, M. K. Pontes, L. G. Johnston, and K. Sabin. 2008. An empirical comparison of respondent-driven sampling, time-location sampling, and snowball sampling for behavioral surveillance in men who have sex with men, Fortaleza, Brazil. *AIDS and Behavior* 12(Suppl 1):S97–S104.

Kendall, C., E. Leontsini, E. Gil, F. Cruz, P. Hudelson, and P. Pelto. 1990. Exploratory ethnoentomology. Using ANTHROPAC to design a dengue fever control program. *Cultural Anthropology Methods* 2(2):11–12.

Kendon, A., ed. 1981. *Nonverbal communication, interaction, and gesture: Selections from semiotica.* The Hague: Mouton.

Kenner, A. N., and G. Katsimaglis. 1993. Gender differences in proxemics: Taxi-seat choice. *Psychological Reports* 72:625–26.

Kent, R. N., J. Kanowitz, K. D. O'Leary, and M. Cheiken. 1977. Observer reliability as a function of circumstances of assessment. *Journal of Applied Behavioral Analysis* 10:317–24.

Kenyatta, J. 1938. *Facing Mt. Kenya.* London: Secker & Warburg.

Kerlinger, F. N. 1973. *Foundations of behavioral research.* New York: Holt, Rinehart & Winston.

Kessler, R. C., and E. Wethington. 1991. The reliability of life event reports in a community survey. *Psychological Medicine* 21:723–38.

Ketterer, M. W., and G. H. Maercklein. 1991. Caffeinated beverage use among Type A male patients suspected of CAD/CHD: A mechanism for increased risk? *Stress Medicine* 7:119–24.

Kiecker, P., and J. E. Nelson. 1996. Do interviewers follow telephone instructions? *Journal of the Market Research Society* 38:161–76.

Kilbride, P. L. 1992. Unwanted children as a consequence of delocalization in modern Kenya. In *Anthropological research: Process and application*, J. J. Poggie, B. R. DeWalt, and W. W. Dressler, eds., 185–206. Albany: State University of New York Press.

Kilcullen, D. 2007. Ethics, politics and nonstate warfare. A response to González in this issue. *Anthropology Today* 23:20.

Killworth, P. D., and H. R. Bernard. 1974. CATIJ: A new sociometric technique and its application to a prison living unit. *Human Organization* 33:335–50.

Killworth, P. R. P. 1997. Culture and power in the British army: Hierarchies, boundaries and construction. Ph.D. dissertation, University of Cambridge.

Kilman, L. 1985. Anthropological studies help sell U. S. products. *Pittsburgh Post Gazette*, September 30, p. 15.

Kim, A. I. 1985. Korean color terms: An aspect of semantic fields and related phenomena. *Anthropological Linguistics* 27:425–36.

Kimball, S. T., and W. T. Partridge. 1979. *The craft of community study: Fieldwork dialogues.* Gainesville: University of Florida Press.

King, G. 1997. *A solution to the ecological inference problem: Reconstructing individual behavior from aggregate data.* Princeton, NJ: Princeton University Press.

King, N. 1994. The qualitative research interview. In *Qualitative methods in organizational research: A practical guide*, C. Cassell and G. Symon, eds., 14–36. Thousand Oaks, CA: Sage.

Kinsey, A. C., W. B. Pomeroy, and C. E. Martin. 1948. *Sexual behavior in the human male.* Philadelphia: Saunders.

Kirk, J., and M. Miller. 1986. *Reliability and validity in qualitative research.* Newbury Park, CA: Sage.

Kirk, R. E. 1982. *Experimental design.* 2nd ed. Monterrey, CA: Brooks/Cole.

Kiš, A. D. 2007. An analysis of the impact of AIDS on funeral culture in Malawi. *NAPA Bulletin* 27:129–40.

Kish, L. 1965. *Survey sampling.* New York: J. Wiley.

Klass, G., and L. Crothers. 2000. An experimental evaluation of web-based tutorial quizzes. *Social Science Computer Review* 18:508–15.

Klein, F. C. 1999. On sports: Academic dilemma. *The Wall Street Journal*, April 2, p. W4.

Kleinman, A. 1980. *Patients and healers in the context of culture: An exploration of the borderland between anthropology, medicine, and psychiatry.* Berkeley: University of California Press.

Klonoff, E. A., and H. Landrine. 2000. Revising and improving the African American Acculturation Scale. *Journal of Black Psychology* 26:235–61.

Kluckhohn, K. 1945. The personal document in anthropological science. In *The use of personal documents in history, anthropology, and sociology*, L. Gottschalk, C. Kluckhohn, and R. Angell, eds., 79–176. New York: Social Science Research Council, Bulletin 53.

Knecht, T., and L. M. Martinez. 2009. Humanizing the homeless. Does contact erode stereotypes? *Social Science Research* 38:521–34.

Kneidinger, L. M., T. L. Maple, and S. A. Tross. 2001. Touching behavior in sport: Functional components, analysis of sex differences, and ethological considerations. *Journal of Nonverbal Behavior* 25:43–62.

Knodel, J., N. Havanon, and A. Pramualratana. 1984. Fertility transition in Thailand: A qualitative analysis. *Population and Development Review* 10:297–315.

Kohut, A. 2008. Getting it wrong. *New York Times*, January 10. http://www.nyt.com (accessed August 23, 2009).

Koivusaari, R. 2002. Horizontal and vertical interaction in children's computer-mediated communications. *Educational Psychology* 22:235–47.

Koocher, G. P. 1977. Bathroom behavior and human dignity. *Journal of Personality and Social Psychology* 35:120–21.

Koopmans, L. H. 1981. *An introduction to contemporary statistics.* Boston: Duxbury.

Korn, J. H. 1997. *Illusions of reality: A history of deception in social psychology.* Albany: State University of New York Press.

Koster, J. M. 2006. The use of the Observer 5.0 and a Psion handheld computer in a remote fieldwork setting. *Field Methods* 18:430–36.

Koster, J. M. 2007. Hunting and subsistence among the Mayangna and Miskito of Nicaragua's Bosowas Biosphere Reserve. Unpublished doctoral dissertation, Pennsylvania State University.

Kottak, C. 2009. *Prime-time society: An anthropological analysis of television and culture.* Updated ed. Walnut Creek, CA: Left Coast Press.

Kozak, R. A., W. C. Spetic, H. W. Harshaw, T. C. Maness, and S. R. J. Sheppard. 2008. Public priorities for sustainable forest management in six forest-dependent communities of British Columbia. *Canadian Journal of Forest Research* 38:3071–84.

Kozinets, R. V. 2010. *Netnography: Doing ethnographic research online.* London: Sage.

Kraemer, H. C., and S. Thiemann. 1987. *How many subjects? Statistical power analysis in research.* Newbury Park, CA: Sage.

Kreiss, L., and E. Stockton. 1980. Using the outline of cultural materials as a basis for indexing the content of ethnographic films. *Behavior Science Research* 15:281–93.

Kremer-Sadlik, T., and A. L. Paugh. 2007. Everyday moments: Finding "quality time" in American working families. *Time and Society* 16:287–308.

Kreuter, F., S. Presser, and R. Tourangeau. 2008. Social desirability bias in CATI, IVR, and Web surveys: The effects of mode and question sensitivity. *Public Opinion Quarterly* 72:847–65.

Krieger, L. 1986. Negotiating gender role expectations in Cairo. In *Self, sex and gender in cross-cultural fieldwork*, T. L. Whitehead and M. E. Conaway, eds., 117–28. Urbana: University of Illinois Press.

Krippendorf, K. 2004a. *Content analysis: An introduction to its methodology.* Thousand Oaks, CA: Sage.

Krippendorf, K. 2004b. Reliability in content analysis. Some common misconceptions and recommendations. *Human Communications Research* 30:411–33.

Kroeber, A. L. 1909. Classificatory systems of relationship. *Journal of the Royal Anthropological Institute* 39:77–84.

Kroeber, A. L. 1919. On the principle of order in civilization as exemplified by changes in women's fashions. *American Anthropologist* 21:235–63.

Kronenfeld, D. B. 2004. Definitions of cross versus parallel: Implications for a new typology (an appreciation of A. Kimball Romney). In *Methods of comparison: Studies in honor of A. Kimball Romney*. Thousand Oaks, CA.: Sage. Special Issue, *Cross-Cultural Research* 38:249–69.

Kronenfeld, D. B. 2009. *Fanti kinship and the analysis of kinship terminologies*. Urbana-Champaign: University of Illinois Press.

Kronenfeld, D. B., J. Kronenfeld, and J. E. Kronenfeld. 1972. Toward a science of design for successful food service. *Institutions and Volume Feeding* 70:38–44.

Krosnick, J. A. 1999. Survey research. *Annual Review of Psychology* 50:537–67.

Krueger, R. A. 1994. *Focus groups: A practical guide for applied research*. 2nd ed. Thousand Oaks, CA: Sage.

Kruskal, J. B., and M. Wish. 1978. *Multidimensional scaling*. Beverly Hills, CA: Sage.

Krysan, M., and M. P. Couper. 2003. Race in the live and virtual interview: Racial deference, social desirability, and activation effects in attitude surveys. *Social Psychology Quarterly* 66:364–83.

Kubey, R. W., R. Larson, and M. Csikszentmihalyi. 1996. Experience sampling method: Application to communication research questions. *Journal of Communications* 46:99–120.

Kuklinski, J. H., M. D. Cobb, and M. Gilens. 1997. Racial attitudes and the "New South." *The Journal of Politics* 59:323–49.

Kulick, D., and M. Willson, eds. 1995. *Taboo: Sex, identity, and erotic subjectivity in anthropological fieldwork*. London: Routledge.

Kunin, T. 1955. The construction of a new type of attitude measure. *Personnel Psychology* 8:65–77.

Kunitz, S. J., H. Temkin-Greener, D. Broudy, and M. Haffner. 1981. Determinants of hospital utilization and surgery on the Navajo Indian Reservation, 1972–1978. *Social Science and Medicine* 15B:71–79.

Kunovich, R. S., and R. G. Rashid. 1992. Mirror training in three dimensions for dental students. *Perceptual and Motor Skills* 75:923–28.

Kurasaki, K. S. 1997. Ethnic identity and its development among third-generation Japanese Americans. Ph.D. dissertation, Department of Psychology, DePaul University.

Kurasaki, K. S. 2000. Intercoder reliability for validating conclusions drawn from open ended interview data. *Field Methods* 12:179–94.

Kvale, S., and S. Brinkman. 2009. *InterViews: Learning the craft of qualitative research interviewing*. 2nd ed. Thousand Oaks, CA: Sage.

Laban Moogi Gwako, E. 1997. The effects of women's land tenure security on agricultural productivity among the Maragoli of western Kenya. Ph.D. dissertation, Washington University.

Labov, W. 1972. *Language in the inner city: Studies in the Black English vernacular*. Philadelphia: University of Pennsylvania Press.

Labovitz, S. 1971a. The assignment of numbers to rank order categories. *American Sociological Review* 35:515–24.

Labovitz, S. 1971b. The zone of rejection: Negative thoughts on statistical inference. *Pacific Sociological Review* 14:373–81.

Labovitz, S. 1972. Statistical usage in sociology. *Sociological Methods and Research* 3:14–37.

La Flesche, F. 1963 [1900]. *The middle five: Indian schoolboys of the Omaha Tribe*. Madison: University of Wisconsin Press.

Lagnado, D. A., M. R. Waldmann, Y. Hagmayer, and S. A. Sloman. 2007. Beyond covariation: Cues to causal structure. In *Causal learning. Psychology, philosophy, and computation*, A. Gopnik and L. Schulz, eds., 154–72. New York: Oxford University Press.

Lakoff, G., and Z. Kövecses. 1987. The cognitive model of anger in American English. In *Cultural models in language and thought*, D. Holland and N. Quinn, eds., 195–221. New York: Cambridge University Press.

Lakoff, G., and M. Johnson. 2003 [1980]. *Metaphors we live by*. Chicago: University of Chicago Press.

Lambert, E., R. S. Ashery, and R. H. Needle, eds. 1995. *Qualitative methods in drug abuse and HIV research*. Rockville, MD: National Institute on Drug Abuse, Division of Epidemiology and Prevention Research.

Lame Deer, J., and R. Erdoes. 1972. *Lame Deer, seeker of visions.* New York: Simon & Schuster.

Landauer, T. K., and J. W. M. Whiting. 1964. Infantile stimulation and adult stature of human males. *American Anthropologist* 66:1007–28.

Lang, H., P. Challenor, and P. D. Killworth. 2004. A new addition to the family of space sampling methods. *Field Methods* 16:55–69.

Lange, R., ed. 1975. *Laban's principles of dance and movement notation.* 2nd ed. Boston: Plays.

La Pelle, N. 2004. Simplifying qualitative data analysis using general purpose software tools. *Field Methods* 16:85–108.

Lapham, S. C., J. C'de Baca, G. McMillan, and W. C. Hunt. 2004. Accuracy of alcohol diagnosis among DWI offenders referred for screening. *Drug and Alcohol Dependence* 76:135–41.

La Pierre, R. T. 1934. Attitudes versus actions. *Social Forces* 13:230–37.

Lara, D., J. Strickler, C. D. Olavarrieta, and C. Ellerston. 2004. Measuring induced abortion in Mexico: A comparison of four methodologies. *Sociological Methods and Research* 32:529–58.

Lara-Cantú, M. A., and R. Navarro-Arias. 1987. Self-description of Mexican college students in response to the Bem Sex Role Inventory and other sex role items. *Journal of Cross-Cultural Psychology* 18:331–44.

Laraia, B. A., A. M. Siega-Riz, J. S. Kaufman, and S. J. Jones. 2004. Proximity of supermarkets is positively associated with diet quality index for pregnancy. *Preventive Medicine* 39:869–75.

Lastrucci, C. L. 1963. *The scientific approach.* Cambridge: Schenkman.

Latané, B., and J. M. Darley. 1968. Group inhibition of bystander intervention in emergencies. *Journal of Personality and Social Psychology* 10:215–21.

Lauder, M. 2003. Covert participant observation of a deviant community: Justifying the use of deception. *Journal of Contemporary Religion* 18:185–96.

Laurent, C., K. Seck, N. Coumba, T. Kane, N. Samb, A. Wade, F. Liégeois, S. Mboup, I. Ndoye, and E. Delaporte. 2003. Prevalence of HIV and other sexually transmitted infections, and risk behaviours in unregistered sex workers in Dakar, Senegal. *AIDS* 17:1811–16.

Lazarsfeld, P. F. 1954. *Mathematical thinking in the social sciences.* Glencoe, IL: The Free Press.

Lazarsfeld, P. F. 1982. *The varied sociology of Paul F. Lazarsfeld: Writing.* New York: Columbia University Press.

Lazarsfeld, P. F., A. Pasanella, and M. Rosenberg, eds. 1972. *Continuities in the language of social research.* New York: The Free Press.

Lazarsfeld, P. F., and M. Rosenberg. 1955. *The language of social research.* Glencoe, IL: The Free Press.

Lea, K. L. 1980. Francis Bacon. *Encyclopaedia britannica*, Vol. 2. Chicago: Encyclopaedia Britannica.

Leach, E. R. 1945. Jinghpaw kinship terminology: An experiment in ethnographic algebra. *Journal of the Royal Anthropological Institute of Great Britain and Ireland* 75:59–72.

Leach, E. R. 1967. An anthropologist's reflection on a social survey. In *Anthropologists in the field*, D. C. Jongmans and P. C. Gutkind, eds., 75–88. Assen, The Netherlands: Van Gorcum.

LeCompte, M. D. 1978. Learning to work: The hidden curriculum of the classroom. *Anthropology and Education Quarterly* 9:22–37.

LeCompte, M. D., and J. Preissle (with R. Tesch). 1993. *Ethnography and qualitative design in educational research.* 2nd ed. San Diego: Academic Press.

Lee, R. M. 1995. *Dangerous fieldwork.* London: Sage.

Lee, S., and A. Brewis. 2009. Children's autonomous food acquisition in Mexican shantytowns. *Ecology of Food and Nutrition* 48:435–56.

Leeland, K. B. 2008. *Face recognition: New research.* New York: Nova Science Publishers.

Leenders, N. Y. J. M., W. M. Sherman, and H. N. Nagaraja. 2000. Comparison of four methods of estimating physical activity in adult women. *Medicine and Science in Sports and Exercise* 32:1320–26.

Lees, S. H. 1986. Coping with bureaucracy: Survival strategies in irrigated agriculture. *American Anthropologist* 88:610–22.

Lee-Treweek, G., and Linkogle, S., eds. 2000. *Danger in the field: Risk and ethics in social research.* London: Routledge.

Lehman, F. K. 1992. Relationship between genealogical and terminological structure in kinship. *Journal of Quantitative Anthropology* 4:95–122.

Lehner, P. N., ed. 1996. *Handbook of ethological methods.* 2nd ed. New York: Cambridge University Press.

Leith, L. M. 1988. Choking in sports: Are we our own worst enemies? *International Journal of Sport Psychology* 19:59–64.

Lenski, G. E., and J. C. Leggett. 1960. Caste, class and deference in the research interview. *American Journal of Sociology* 65:463–67.

Lensveldt-Mulders, G. J. L. M., J. J. Hox, P. G. M. van der Heuden, and C. J. M. Maas. 2005. Meta-analysis of randomized response research: Thirty-five years of validation. *Sociological Methods and Research* 33:319–48.

Leslie, P. W., R. Dyson-Hudson, E. A. Lowoto, and J. Munyesi. 1999. Appendix 1. Ngisonyoka event calendar. In *Turkana herders of the dry savanna: Ecology and biobehavioral response of nomads to an uncertain environment,* M. A. Little and P. W. Leslie, eds., 375–78. New York: Oxford University Press.

Lesorogol, C. K. 2007. Bringing norms in. The role of context in experimental dictator games. *Current Anthropology* 48:920–26.

Levine, N. E. 1988. *The dynamics of polyandry: kinship, domesticity, and population on the Tibetan border.* Chicago: University of Chicago Press.

Levine, N. E., and J. B. Silk. 1997. Why polyandry fails: Sources of instability in polyandrous marriages. *Current Anthropology* 38:375–98.

Levine, R. V. 1997. *A geography of time.* New York: Basic Books.

Levine, R. V., and K. Bartlett. 1984. Pace of life, punctuality, and coronary heart disease in six countries. *Journal of Cross-Cultural Psychology* 15:233–55.

Levine, R. V., A. Norenzayan, and K. Philbrick. 2001. Cross-cultural differences in helping strangers. *Journal of Cross-Cultural Psychology* 32:543–60.

Levinson, D., ed. 1978. *A guide to social theory: Worldwide cross-cultural tests.* New Haven, CT: HRAF Press.

Levinson, D. 1989. *Family violence in cross-cultural perspective.* Newbury Park, CA: Sage.

Levinson, D. 1990. Bibliography of substantive worldwide cross-cultural studies. *Behavior Science Research* 24:105–40.

Levy, P. S., and S. Lemeshow. 1999. *Sampling of populations: Methods and applications.* 3rd ed. New York: Wiley.

Levy-Storms, L., and S. P. Wallace. 2003. Use of mammography screening among older Samoan women in Los Angeles County: A diffusion network approach. *Social Science and Medicine* 57:987–1000.

Lewin, E., and W. Leap, eds. 1996. *Out in the field: Reflections of lesbian and gay anthropologists.* Urbana: University of Illinois Press.

Lewin, T. 1986. Cultural consultant: Steve Barnett. Casting an anthropological eye on American consumers. *New York Times,* May 11, p. A6.

Lewis, O. 1961. *The children of Sánchez.* New York: Random House.

Lewis, O. 1965. *La Vida: A Puerto Rican family in the culture of poverty—San Juan and New York.* New York: Random House.

Liao, P-S, and H-H Tu. 2006. Examining the scalability of sexual permissiveness in Taiwan. *Social Indicators Research* 76:207–32.

Lieberman, D., and W. W. Dressler. 1977. Bilingualism and cognition of St. Lucian disease terms. *Medical Anthropology* 1:81–110.

Lieske, J. 1993. Regional subcultures of the United States. *The Journal of Politics* 55:888–913.

Lightcap, J. L., J. A. Kurland, and R. L. Burgess. 1982. Child abuse: A test of some predictions from evolutionary theory. *Ethology and Sociobiology* 3:61–67.

Likert, R. 1932. A technique for the measurement of attitudes. *Archives of Psychology* 22:1–55.

Lincoln, Y. S., and E. G. Guba. 1985. *Naturalistic inquiry.* Beverly Hills, CA: Sage.

Livingstone, S., and P. Lunt. 1993. Savers and borrowers: Strategies of personal financial management. *Human Relations* 46:963–85.

Locke, J. 1996 [1690]. *An essay concerning human understanding*, K. P. Winkler, ed. Abridged. India-napolis: Hackett Publishing.

Loehlin, J. C., J. M. Horn, and J. L. Ernst. 2009. Antecedents of children's adult outcomes in the Texas adoption project. *Journal of Personality* 77:1–22.

Loether, H. J., and D. G. McTavish. 1993. *Descriptive and inferential statistics*. Boston: Allyn & Bacon.

Lofland, J. H. 1971. *Analyzing social settings. A guide to qualitative observation and analysis*. Belmont, CA: Wadsworth.

Lofland, J. H. 1976. *Doing social life*. New York: Wiley.

Lofland, L. H. 1983. Understanding urban life: The Chicago legacy. *Urban Life* 11:491–511.

Loftus, E. F., and W. Marburger. 1983. Since the eruption of Mt. St. Helens, has anyone beaten you up? Improving the accuracy of retrospective reports with landmark events. *Memory and Cognition* 11:114–20.

Longabaugh, R. 1980. The systematic observation of behavior in naturalistic settings. In *Handbook of cross-cultural psychology*, H. C. Triandis and J. W. Berry, eds. Vol. 2, *Methodology*, 57–126. Boston: Allyn & Bacon.

Longfield, K. 2004. Rich fools, spare tyres, and boyfriends: Partner categories, relationship dynamics, and Ivorian women's risk for STIs and HIV. *Culture, Health and Sexuality* 6:483–500.

Loo, R., and K. Thorpe. 1998. Attitudes toward women's roles in society: A replication after 20 years. *Sex Roles* 39:903–12.

Loo, R., and K. Thorpe. 2005. Relationships between attitudes towards women's roles in society, and work and life values. *Social Science Journal* 42:367–74.

Lorenz, K. 1981. *The foundations of ethology*. New York: Springer-Verlag.

Low, S. M., and D. Lawrence-Zúñiga. 2003. *The anthropology of space and place: Locating culture*. Malden, MA: Blackwell.

Lowe, J. W. G., and E. D. Lowe. 1982. Cultural pattern and process: A study of stylistic change in women's dress. *American Anthropologist* 84:521–44.

Lowie, R. H. 1940. Native languages as ethnographic tools. *American Anthropologist* 42:81–89.

Lowrey, T. M., and C. Otnes. 1994. Construction of a meaningful wedding: Differences in the priorities of brides and grooms. In *Gender issues and consumer behavior*, J. A. Costa, ed., 164–83. Thousand Oaks, CA: Sage.

Lucretius Carus, Titus. 1998. *De rerum natura. (On the nature of the universe)*, R. Melville, transl. New York: Oxford University Press.

Lueptow, L. B., S. L. Moser, and B. F. Pendleton. 1990. Gender and response effects in telephone interviews about gender characteristics. *Sex Roles* 22:29–42.

Lugosi, P. 2006. Between overt and covert research: Concealment and disclosure in an ethnographic study of commercial hospitality. *Qualitative Inquiry* 12:541–61.

Lundberg, G. A. 1964. *Foundations of sociology*. New York: David McKay.

Lurie, N. 1961. *Mountain Lone Wolf Woman, Sister of Crashing Thunder: The autobiography of a Winnebago woman*. Ann Arbor: University of Michigan Press.

Lynd, R. S., and H. M. Lynd. 1929. *Middletown. A study in contemporary American culture*. New York: Harcourt, Brace & Co.

MacClancy, J. 2002. *Exotic no more: Anthropology on the front lines*. Chicago: University of Chicago Press.

MacCorquodale, K. 1970. On Chomsky's review of Skinner's *Verbal Behavior*. *Journal of the Experimental Analysis of Behavior* 13:83–99.

Mach, E. 1976. *Knowledge and error: Sketches on the psychology of enquiry*, B. McGuiness, ed., T. J. McCormack and P. Foulkes, transl. Boston: D. Reidel.

Madden, J. M., J. D. Quick, and D. Ross-Degnan. 1997. Undercover careseekers: Simulated clients in the study of health provider behavior in developing countries. *Social Science and Medicine* 45:1465–82.

Madrigal, M., and J. Chen. 2008. Moderating and mediating effects of team identification in regard to causal attributions and summary judgments following a game outcome. *Journal of Sport Management* 22:717–33.

Maginn, P. J. 2007. Negotiating and securing access: Reflections from a study into urban regeneration and community participation in ethnically diverse neighborhoods in London, England. *Field Methods* 19:425–40.

Mahaffy, K. A. 1996. Cognitive dissonance and its resolution: A study of lesbian Christians. *Journal for the Scientific Study of Religion* 35:392–402.

Maitra, S. and S. L. Schensul. 2002. Reflecting diversity and complexity in marital sexual relationships in a low-income community in Mumbai. *Culture, Health, and Sexuality* 4:133–51.

Makkai, T., and I. McAllister. 1992. Measuring social indicators in opinion surveys: A method to improve accuracy on sensitive questions. *Social Indicators Research* 27:169–86.

Makkreel, R. A. 1975. *Dilthey: Philosopher of the human sciences*. Princeton, NJ: Princeton University Press.

Malekinejad, M., L. G. Johnston, C. Kendall, L. R. F. S. Kerr, M. R. Rifkin, and G. W. Rutherford. 2008. Using respondent-driven sampling methodology for HIV biological and surveillance in international settings: A systematic review. *AIDS and Behavior* 12(Suppl 1):S105–S130.

Malinowski, B. 1961 [1922]. *Argonauts of the western Pacific*. New York: Dutton.

Malinowski, B. 1967. *A diary in the strict sense of the term*. New York: Harcourt, Brace & World.

Maloney, R. S., and M. Paolisso. 2001. What can digital audio data do for you? *Field Methods* 13:88–96.

Mann, S. 2007. Understanding farm succession by the objective hermeneutic method. *Sociologia Ruralis* 47:369–83.

Manning, R., M. Levine, and A. Collins. 2007. The Kitty Genovese murder and the social psychology of helping. The parable of the 38 witnesses. *American Psychologist* 62:555–62.

Manzo, J. 1996. Taking turns and taking sides: Opening scene from two jury deliberations. *Social Psychology Quarterly* 59:107–25.

Margolis, M. 1984. *Mothers and such*. Berkeley: University of California Press.

Marini, M. M., and B. Singer. 1988. Causality in the social sciences. *Sociological Methodology* 18:347–409.

Markee, N. 2000. *Conversation analysis*. Mahwah, NJ: Erlbaum Associates.

Markie, P. J. 1986. *Descartes' gambit*. Ithaca, NY: Cornell University Press.

Markowitz, F., and M. Ashkenazi. 1999. *Sex, sexuality, and the anthropologist*. Urbana: University of Illinois Press.

Marlanai, V. 2008. The changing relationship between family size and educational attainment over the course of socioeconomic development: Evidence from Indonesia. *Demography* 45:693–717.

Marquis, G. S. 1990. Fecal contamination of shanty town toddlers in households with non-corralled poultry, Lima, Peru. *American Journal of Public Health* 80:146–50.

Marriott, B. 1991. The use of social networks by naval officers' wives. Ph.D. dissertation, University of Florida.

Marsh, C., and E. Scarborough. 1990. Testing nine hypotheses about quota sampling. *Journal of the Market Research Society* 32:485–506.

Marsh, V. M., W. M. Mutemi, A. Willetts, K. Bayah, S. Were, A. Ross, and K. Marsh. 2004. Improving malaria home treatment by training drug retailers in rural Kenya. *Tropical Medicine and International Health* 9:451–60.

Martin, C., S. D. Anton, H. Walden, C. Arnett, F. L. Greenway, and D. A. Williamson. 2007. Slower eating rate reduces the food intake of men, but not women: Implications for behavioral weight control. *Behaviour Research and Therapy* 45:2349–59.

Martin, J. 1981. Relative deprivation: A theory of distributive injustice for an era of shrinking resources. In *Research in organizational behavior*, L. L. Cummings and B. M. Staw, eds. Vol. 3, 53–107. Greenwich, CT: JAI Press.

Martin, J. L., and L. Dean. 1993. Developing a community sample of gay men for an epidemiological study of AIDS. In *Researching sensitive topics*, C. M. Renzetti and R. M. Lee, eds., 82–100. Newbury Park, CA: Sage.

Martin, P., and P. Bateson. 1993. *Measuring behaviour*. 2nd ed. New York: Cambridge University Press.

Martyn, K. K., and R. F. Belli. 2002. Retrospective data collection using event history calendars. *Nursing Research* 51:270–74.

Matarazzo, J. 1964. Interviewer mm-humm and interviewee speech duration. *Psychotherapy: Theory, Research and Practice* 1:109–14.

Matheson, J. L. 2007. The voice transcription technique: Use of voice recognition software to transcribe digital interview data in qualitative research. *The Qualitative Report* 12:547–60. http://www.nova.edu/ssss/QR/QR12-4/matheson.pdf (accessed December 24, 2008).

Mathews, H. F. 1987. Intracultural variation in beliefs about gender in a Mexican community. *The American Behavioral Scientist* 31:219–33.

Mathews, H. F. 1992. The directive force of morality tales in a Mexican community. In *Human motives and cultural models*, R. G. D'Andrade and C. Strauss, eds., 127–62. New York: Cambridge University Press.

Mathews, J. J. 1968 [1932]. *Wah'Kon-Tah: The Osage and the white man's road*. Norman: University of Oklahoma Press.

Matland, R. E., and D. T. Studlar. 1996. The contagion of women candidates in single-member district and proportional representation electoral systems: Canada and Norway. *Journal of Politics* 58:707–33.

Mavhu, W., L. Langhuag, B. Manyonga, R. Power, and F. Cowan. 2008. What is "sex" exactly? Using cognitive interviewing to improve the validity of sexual behaviour reporting among young people in rural Zimbabwe. *Culture, Health and Sexuality* 10:563–72.

Max-Planck Institute. 2002. The human life table database 2002. http://www.lifetable.de/ (accessed March 8, 2009).

Maxwell, J. A. 2004. Using qualitative methods for causal explanation. *Field Methods* 16:243–64.

McCall, G. 1978. *Observing the law: Field methods in the study of crime and the criminal justice system*. New York: The Free Press.

McCarroll, J. E., A. S. Blank, and K. Hill. 1995. Working with traumatic material: Effects on Holocaust Memorial Museum staff. *American Journal of Orthopsychiatry* 65:66–75.

McCarty, C. 2002. Structure in personal networks. *Journal of Social Structure* 3:1. http://www.cmu.edu/joss/content/articles/volume3/McCarty.html (accessed March 8, 2010).

McCarty, C., C. Collins, E. Lavigne, M. Smith, and P. Schoaff. 2010. *EgoNet*. Sourceforge. http://sourceforge.net/projects/egonet/ (accessed March 5, 2010).

McCombie, S. C., and J. K. Anarfi. 2002. The influence of sex of interviewer on the results of an AIDS survey in Ghana. *Human Organization* 61:51–57.

McCracken, G. 1988. *The long interview*. Newbury Park, CA: Sage.

McDonald, D. D., and R. G. Bridge. 1991. Gender stereotyping and nursing care. *Research in Nursing and Health* 14:373–78.

McDonald, L. 1993. *The early origins of the social sciences*. Montreal: McGill-Queen's University Press.

McDonald, L. 1994. *The women founders of the social sciences*. Ottawa: Carleton University Press.

McFate, M. 2005. Anthropology and counterinsurgency: The strange story of their curious relationship. *Military Review* 85:24–38.

McFaul, M. 2007. Ukraine imports democracy: External influences on the Orange Revolution. *International Security* 32:45–83.

McGilvray, D. 1989. A few selected excerpts from my Sri Lanka diary, 1969–1971. *Field Methods* [*Cam Newsletter*] 1(1):6–7.

McIver, K. L., W. H. Brown, K. A. Pfeiffer, M. Dowda, and R. R. Pate. 2009. Assessing children's physical activity in their homes: The observational system for recording physical activity in children—home. *Journal of Applied Behavior Analysis* 42:1–16.

McKenzie, J. F., M. L. Wood, J. E. Kotecki, J. K. Clark, and R. A. Brey. 1999. Establishing content validity: Using qualitative and quantitative steps. *American Journal of Health Behavior* 23:311–18.

McLellan, E., K. M. MacQueen, and J. L. Neidig. 2003. Beyond the qualitative interview: Data preparation and transcription. *Field Methods* 15:63–84.

McNamara, M. S. 2005. Knowing and doing phenomenology: The implications of the critique of "nursing phenomenology" for a phenomenological inquiry: A discussion paper. *International Journal of Nursing Studies* 42:695–704.

McPhee, S. J., T. T. Nguyen, S. J. Shema, B. Nguyen, C. Somkin, P. Vo, and R. Pasick. 2002. Validation of recall of breast and cervical cancer screening by women in an ethnically diverse population. *Preventive Medicine* 35:463–73.

Mead, M. 1939. Native languages as field-work tools. *American Anthropologist* 41:189–205.

Mead, M. 1940. Social change and cultural surrogates. *Social Psychology of Education* 14:92–109.

Mead, M. 1979. Anthropological contributions to national policies during and immediately after World War II. In *The uses of anthropology*, W. Goldschmidt, ed., 145–57. Washington, DC: American Anthropological Association.

Mead, M. 1986. Fieldwork in Pacific islands, 1925–1967. In *Women in the field: Anthropological experiences*, 2nd ed., P. Golde, ed., 293–332. Berkeley: University of California Press.

Means, B., A. Nigam, M. Zarrow, E. F. Loftus, and M. S. Donaldson. 1989. *Autobiographical memory for health related events*. National Center for Health Statistics, Vital and Health Statistics, Series 6, No. 2. Washington, DC: U.S. Government Printing Office.

Meehan, C. L. 2009. Maternal time allocation in two cooperative childrearing societies. *Human Nature* 20:375–93.

Mehta, R., and R. W. Belk. 1991. Artifacts, identity, and transition: Favorite possessions of Indians and Indian immigrants to the United States. *Journal of Consumer Research* 17:398–411.

Méjean, C., P. Traissac, S. Eymard-Duvenay, F. Delpeuch, and B. Maire. 2009. Influence of acculturation among Tunisian migrants in France and their past/present exposure to the home country on diet and physical activity. *Public Health Nutrition* 12:832–41.

Mensch, B. S., P. C. Hewett, R. Gregory, and S. Helleringer. 2008. Sexual behavior and STI/HIV status among adolescents in rural Malawi: An evaluation of the effect of interview mode on reporting. *Studies in Family Planning* 39:321–44.

Mensh, I. N., and J. Henry. 1953. Direct observation and psychological tests in anthropological field work. *American Anthropologist* 55:461–80.

Merli, M. G., and A. E. Rafferty. 2000. Are births underreported in rural China? Manipulation of statistical records in response to China's population policies. *Demography* 37:109–26.

Merriam, S. B. 2009. *Qualitative research: A guide to design and implementation*. 3rd ed. San Francisco: Jossey-Bass.

Merton, R. K. 1938. Science and the social order. *Philosophy of Science* 5:323–37.

Merton, R. K. 1970. *Science technology and society in seventeenth century England*. New York: Harper and Row.

Merton, R. K. 1973. *The sociology of science: Theoretical and empirical investigations*. Chicago: University of Chicago Press.

Merton, R. K. 1987. The focused interview and focus groups. *Public Opinion Quarterly* 51:550–66.

Merton, R. K., M. Fiske, and P. L. Kendall. 1956. *The focused interview: A manual of problems and procedures*. Glencoe, IL: The Free Press.

Messerschmidt, D. A., ed. 1981. *Anthropologists at home in North America: Methods and issues in the study of one's own society*. New York: Cambridge University Press.

Metzger, D. G., and G. E. Williams. 1966. Procedures and results in the study of native categories: Tseltal firewood. *American Anthropologist* 68:389–407.

Meyerhoff, B. 1989. So what do you want from us here? In *In the field: Readings on the field research experience*, C. D. Smith and W. Kornblum, eds., 83–90. New York: Praeger.

Middlemist, R. D., E. S. Knowles, and C. F. Matter. 1976. Personal space invasion in the lavatory: Suggestive evidence for arousal. *Journal of Personality and Social Psychology* 33:541–46.

Middlemist, R. D., E. S. Knowles, and C. F. Matter. 1977. What to do and what to report: A reply to Koocher. *Journal of Personality and Social Psychology* 35:122–24.

Miles, M. B. 1983. *Qualitative data as an attractive nuisance: The problem of analysis*. Newbury Park, CA: Sage.

Miles, M. B., and A. M. Huberman. 1994. *Qualitative data analysis*. 2nd ed. Thousand Oaks, CA: Sage.

Milgram, S. 1963. Behavioral study of obedience. *Journal of Abnormal and Social Psychology* 67:371–78.

Milgram, S. 1965. Some conditions of obedience and disobedience to authority. *Human Relations* 18:57–76.

Milgram, S. 1967. The small-world problem. *Psychology Today* 1:60–67.

Milgram, S. 1969. The lost-letter technique. *Psychology Today* 3:30–33, 66–68.

Milgram, S. 1974. *Obedience to authority*. New York: Harper & Row.

Milgram, S., L. Mann, and S. Harter. 1965. The lost-letter technique: A tool for social research. *Public Opinion Quarterly* 29:437–38.

Mill, J. S. 1866. *Auguste Comte and positivism*. Philadelphia: Lippincott.

Mill, J. S. 1869. *The subjection of women*. New York: D. Appleton & Co.

Miller, A. S., and T. Nakamura. 1996. On the stability of church attendance patterns during a time of demographic change: 1965–1988. *The Journal for the Scientific Study of Religion* 35:275–84.

Miller, D. C., and N. J. Salkind. 2002. *Handbook of research design and social measurement*. 6th ed. Thousand Oaks, CA: Sage.

Miller, K. W., L. B. Wilder, F. A. Stillman, and D. M. Becker. 1997. The feasibility of a street-intercept survey method in an African-American community. *American Journal of Public Health* 87:655–58.

Miller, L. L. 1997. Not just weapons of the weak: Gender harassment as a form of protest for Army men. *Social Psychology Quarterly* 60:32–51.

Miller, M. L., J. Kaneko, P. Bartram, J. Marks, and D. D. Brewer. 2004. Cultural consensus analysis and environmental anthropology: Yellowfin tuna fishery management in Hawaii. *Cross-Cultural Research* 38:289–314.

Minadeo, R. 1969. *The lyre of science: Form and meaning in Lucretius' De Rerum Natura*. Detroit: Wayne State University Press.

Minton, A. P., and R. L. Rose. 1997. The effects of environmental concern on environmentally friendly consumer behavior: An exploratory study. *Journal of Business Research* 40:37–48.

Mishler, E. G. 1986. *Research interviewing: Context and narrative*. Cambridge, MA: Harvard University Press.

Mishra, S. I., L. R. Chavez, J. R. Magaña, P. Nava, R. Burciaga Valdez, and F. A. Hubbell. 1999. Improving breast cancer control among Latinas: Evaluation of a theory-based educational program. *Health Education and Behavior* 25:653–70.

Mitchell, P. C. 1913. *Thomas Huxley: A sketch of his life and work*. London: Methuen.

Mitchell, R. 1965. Survey materials collected in the developing countries: Sampling, measurement, and interviewing obstacles to intra- and international comparisons. *International Social Science Journal* 17:665–85.

Mizes, J. S., E. L. Fleece, and C. Ross. 1984. Incentives for increasing return rates: Magnitude levels, response bias, and format. *Public Opinion Quarterly* 48:794–800.

Momaday, N. S. 1969. *The way to Rainy Mountain*. Albuquerque: University of New Mexico Press.

Monárrez-Espino, J., T. Greiner, and H. Mártinez. 2004. Rapid qualitative assessment to design a food basket for young Tarahumara children in Mexico. *Scandinavian Journal of Nutrition* 48:4–12.

Montalvo, F. F., and G. E. Codina. 2001. Skin color and Latinos in the United States. *Ethnicities* 1:321–41.

Monteiro, C. A., A. A. Florindo, R. M. Claro, and E. C. Moura. 2008. Validity of indicators of physical activity and sedentariness obtained by telephone survey. *Reviste de Saùde Pública* 42. http://www.scielo.br/pdf/rsp/v42n4/en_6897.pdf (accessed August 23, 2009).

Montgomery, H. 2007. Working with child prostitutes in Thailand: Problems of practice and interpretation. *Childhood* 14:415–30.

Montiel, C. J., and K. Boehnke. 2000. Preferred attributes of effective conflict resolvers in seven societies: Culture, development level, and gender differences. *Journal of Applied Social Psychology* 30:1071–9.

Mooney, L. A., and R. Gramling. 1991. Asking threatening questions and situational framing: The effects of decomposing survey items. *The Sociological Quarterly* 32:289–300.

Moore, C. C., A. K. Romney, T.-L. Hsia, and C. D. Rusch. 1999. The universality of the semantic structure of emotion terms: Methods for the study of inter- and intra-cultural variability. *American Anthropologist* 101:529–46.

Moran, D. 2000. *Introduction to phenomenology*. London: Routledge.

Morera, M. C., and C. H. Gladwin. 2006. Does off-farm work discourage soil conservation? Incentives and disincentives throughout two Honduran hillside communities. *Human Ecology* 34:355–78.

Morgan, D. L. 1997. *Focus groups as qualitative research*. 2nd ed. Thousand Oaks, CA: Sage.

Morgan, D. L., and R. Krueger. 1998. *The focus group kit*, 6 vols. Thousand Oaks, CA: Sage.

Morgan, L. H. 1877. *Ancient society; or, researches in the lines of human progress from savagery, through barbarism to civilization*. New York: H. Holt.

Morgan, L. H. 1997 [1870]. *Systems of consanguinity and affinity of the human family*. Lincoln: University of Nebraska Press.

Morgan, M. G., B. Fischoff, A. Bostrom, and C. J. Atman. 2002. *Risk communication: A mental models approach*. New York: Cambridge University Press.

Morin, R. 2004. Don't ask me: As fewer cooperate on polls, criticism and questions mount. *The Washington Post*, October 28, p. C01.

Morrison, D. L., and R. Clements. 1997. The effect of one partner's job characteristics on the other partner's distress: A serendipitous, but naturalistic, experiment. *Journal of Occupational and Organizational Psychology* 70:307–24.

Morrison, F. J., E. M. Griffith, and J. A. Frazier. 1996. Schooling and the 5 to 7 shift: A natural experiment. In *The five to seven year shift: The age of reason and responsibility*, A. J. Sameroff and M. M. Haith, eds., 161–86. Chicago: University of Chicago Press.

Morrison, M., and T. Morrison. 1995. A meta-analytic assessment of the predictive validity of the quantitative and verbal components of the Graduate Record Examination with graduate grade point average representing the criterion of graduate success. *Educational and Psychological Measurement* 55:309–16.

Morrow, K. M., S. Vargas, R. K. Rosen, A. L. Christensen, L. Salomon, L. Shulman, C. Barroso, and J. L. Fava. 2007. The utility of non-proportional quota sampling for recruiting at-risk women for microbicide research. *AIDS and Behavior* 11:586–95.

Morse, J. M. 1994. Designing funded qualitative research. In *Handbook of qualitative research*, N. K. Denzin and Y. S. Lincoln, eds., 220–35. Thousand Oaks, CA: Sage.

Morse, J. M., and L. Niehaus. 2009. *Mixed method design. Principles and procedures*. Walnut Creek, CA: Left Coast Press.

Mosier, C. I. 1947. A critical examination of the concept of face validity. *Educational and Psychological Measurement* 7:191–205.

Moustakas, C. 1994. *Phenomenological research methods*. Thousand Oaks, CA: Sage Publications.

Mulcahy, F. D., and S. Herbert. 1990. Women's formal evening wear, 1937–1982. *Journal of Social Behavior and Personality* 5:481–96.

Mumford, D. B. 1998. The measurement of culture shock. *Social Psychiatry* 33:149–54.

Murdock, G. P. 1949. *Social structure*. New York: Macmillan Co.

Murdock, G. P. 1971. *Outline of cultural materials*. 4th rev. ed., with modifications. New Haven, CT: Human Relations Area Files, Inc.

Murdock, G. P., C. S. Ford, A. E. Hudson, R. Kennedy, L. W. Simmons, and J. W. Whiting. 2004 [1961]. *Outline of cultural materials*. 5th rev. ed., modified in 2004. New Haven, CT: Human Relations Area Files, Inc.

Murdock, G. P., and D. R. White. 1969. Standard cross-cultural sample. *Ethnology* 8:329–69.

Murphy, G., L. B. Murphy, and T. M. Newcomb. 1937. *Experimental social psychology*. New York: Harper & Brothers.

Murray, T. 1980. Learning to deceive. *The Hastings Center Report* 10:2:11–14.

Murtaugh, M. 1985. The practice of arithmetic by American grocery shoppers. *Anthropology and Education Quarterly* 16:186–92.

Mwango, E. 1986. The sources of variation in farmer adoption of government recommended technologies in the Lilongwe rural development program area of Central Malawi. Master's thesis, University of Florida.

Nabokov, P. 1967. *Two Leggings: The making of a Crow warrior*. New York: Crowell.

Nachman, S. R. 1984. Lies my informants told me. *Journal of Anthropological Research* 40:536–55.

Nachmias, D., and C. Nachmias. 1976. *Research methods in the social sciences*. New York: St. Martin's Press.

Nam, C. B., and M. Boyd. 2004. Occupational status in 2000—Over a century of census-based measurement. *Population Research and Policy Review* 23:327–58.

Nam, C. S., J. B. Lyons, H-S Hwang, and S. Kim. 2009. The process of team communication in multi-cultural contexts: An empirical study using Bales' interaction process analysis (IPA). *International Journal of Industrial Ergonomics* 39:771–82.

Narayan, K. 1993. How native is a "native" anthropologist? *American Anthropologist* 95:671–86.

Naroll, R. 1962. *Data quality control*. New York: The Free Press.

National Cancer Institute. 1997. *Risks of cigarette smoking for women on the rise*. NIH news release. http://www.nih.gov/news/pr/apr97/nci-23.htm (accessed March 8, 2010).

Naumes, W., and M. J. Naumes. 2006. *The art & craft of case writing*. 2nd ed. Armonk, NY: M. E. Sharpe.

Nave, A. 1997. Conducting a survey in a newly developed country. *Cultural Anthropology Methods Journal* 9(2):8–12.

Nederhof, A. J. 1985. A survey on suicide: Using a mail survey to study a highly threatening topic. *Quality and Quantity* 19:293–302.

Neihardt, J. 1972 [1932]. *Black Elk speaks*. New York: Pocket Books.

Netemeyer, R. G., W. O. Bearden, and S. Sughash. 2003. *Scaling procedures: Issues and applications*. Thousand Oaks, CA: Sage.

Nevo, B. 1985. Face validity revisited. *Journal of Educational Measurement* 22:287–93.

Newman, J. C., D. C. Des Jarlais, C. F. Turner, J. Gribble, P. Cooley, and D. Paone. 2002. The differential effects of face-to-face and computer interview modes. *American Journal of Public Health* 92:294–97.

Newman, K. S. 1986. Symbolic dialects and generations of women: Variations in the meaning of post-divorce downward mobility. *American Ethnologist* 13:230–52.

Nida, E. A. 1975. *Language structure and translation: Essays*. Stanford, CA: Stanford University Press.

Nida, E. A., and C. Taber. 1969. *The theory and practice of translation*. Leiden, The Netherlands: E. J. Brill.

Niebel, B. W. 1982. *Motion and time study*. 7th ed. Homewood, IL: Irwin.

Nightingale, F. 1871. *Introductory notes on lying-in institutions*. London: Longmans, Green.

Nisbet, R. A. 1980. *The history of the idea of progress*. New York: Basic Books.

Nishida, H. 1999. Cognitive approach to intercultural communication based on schema theory. *International Journal of Intercultural Relations* 5:753–77.

Nolan, J. M., and G. Ryan. 2000. Fear and loathing at the cineplex: Gender differences in descriptions and perceptions of slasher films. *Sex Roles* 42:39–56.

Nordlund, S., I. Holme, and S. Tamsfoss. 1994. Randomized response estimates for the purchase of smuggled liquor in Norway. *Addiction* 89:401–5.

Nordstrom, C., and A. C. G. M. Robben, eds. 1995. *Fieldwork under fire: Contemporary studies of violence and culture*. Berkeley: University of California Press.

North, A. C., and D. J. Hargreaves. 1999. Can music move people? The effects of musical complexity and silence on waiting time. *Environment and Behavior* 31:136–49.

Norvilitis, J. M., and H. M. Reid. 2002. Evidence for an association between gender-role identity and a measure of executive function. *Psychological Reports* 90:35–45.

Nunnally, J. C., and I. H. Bernstein. 1994. *Psychometric theory*. 3rd ed. New York: McGraw-Hill.

Nyamongo, I. K. 1998. Lay people's responses to illness: An ethnographic study of anti-malaria behavior among the Abagusii of southwestern Kenya. Ph.D. dissertation, University of Florida.

Nyamongo, I. K. 2002. Assessing intracultural variability statistically using data on malaria perceptions in Gusii, Kenya. *Field Methods* 14:148–60.

Oakes, J. M., and P. H. Rossi. 2003. The measurement of SES in health research: Current practice and steps toward a new approach. *Social Science and Medicine* 56:769–84.

Oberg, K. 1960. Culture shock and the problem of adjustment in new cultural environments. *Practical Anthropology* 7:170–79. Reprinted in R. G. Weaver, 2000, *Culture, communication and conflict: readings in intercultural relations*, 175–76. Rev. 2nd ed. Boston: Pearson Publishing.

Oboler, R. S. 1985. *Women, power, and economic change: The Nandi of Kenya.* Stanford, CA: Stanford University Press.

O'Brian, R. 1998. Stationary spot behavior and extended observation: Adapting time allocation to marketplaces. *Cultural Anthropology Methods* 10(3):57–60.

O'Brien, T. O., and V. Dugdale. 1978. Questionnaire administration by computer. *Journal of the Market Research Society* 20:228–37.

Ochs, E. 1979. Transcription as theory. In *Developmental pragmatics*, E. Ochs and B. Schieffelin, eds., 43–72. New York: Academic Press.

O'Connor, A. 2001. *Poverty knowledge: Social science, social policy, and the poor in twentieth-century U.S. history.* Princeton, NJ: Princeton University Press.

Ogburn, W. F. 1930. The folk-ways of a scientific sociology. *Publication of the American Sociological Society* 25:1–10.

Ogilvie, D. M., P. J. Stone, and E. S. Schneidman. 1966. Some characteristics of genuine versus simulated suicide notes. In *The General Inquirer: A computer approach to content analysis*, P. J. Stone, D. C. Dunphy, M. S. Smith, and D. M. Ogilvie, eds., 527–35. Cambridge, MA: MIT Press.

Okaqaki, L., M. K. Helling, and G. E. Bingham. 2009. American Indian college students' ethnic identity and beliefs about education. *Journal of College Student Development* 50:157–76.

Olson, R. G. 1993. *The emergence of the social sciences, 1642–1792.* New York: Twayne Publishers.

Öngen, D. E. 2007. The relationship between sensation seeking and gender role orientation among Turkish university students. *Sex Roles* 57:111–18.

Orlando, R. A. 1992. Boelen may know Holland, Boelen may know Barzini, but Boelen "Doesn't know Diddle about the North End!" *Journal of Contemporary Ethnography* 22:69–79.

Ortberg, J. C., Jr., R. L. Gorsuch, and G. J. Kim. 2001. Changing attitude and moral obligation: Their independent effects on behavior. *Journal for the Scientific Study of Religion* 40:489–96.

Osgood, C. E., D. J. Suci, and P. H. Tannenbaum. 1957. *The measurement of meaning.* Urbana: University of Illinois Press.

Oskenberg, L., L. Coleman, and C. F. Cannell. 1986. Interviewers' voices and refusal rates in telephone surveys. *Public Opinion Quarterly* 50:97–111.

Ostrander, S. A. 1980. Upper-class women: Class consciousness as conduct and meaning. In *Power structure research*, G. W. Domhoff, ed., 73–96. Beverly Hills, CA: Sage.

Oths, K. S. 1994. Health care decisions of households in economic crisis: An example from the Peruvian highlands. *Human Organization* 53:245–54.

Otterbein, K. 1969. Basic steps in conducting a cross-cultural study. *Behavior Science Notes* 4:221–36.

Owusu, M. 1978. Ethnography of Africa: The usefulness of the useless. *American Anthropologist* 80:310–34.

Oyuela-Caycedo, A., and J. J. Vieco Albarracín. 1999. Aproximación cuantitativa a la organización social de los ticuna del trapecio amazónico colombiano. *Revista Colombiana de Antropología* 35:146–79.

Özkan, T., and T. Lajunen. 2006. What causes the differences in driving between young men and women? The effects of gender roles and sex on young drivers' driving behavior and self-assessment of skills. *Transportation Research Part F: Traffic Psychology and Behavior* 9:269–77.

Özyildirim, I. 2009. Narrative analysis: An analysis of oral and written strategies in personal experience narratives. *Journal of Pragmatics* 41:1209–22.

Paddock, J. 1985. Covert content in Codices Borgia and Nuttall. *Ethos* 13:358–80.

Palmer, D. C. 2006. On Chomsky's appraisal of Skinner's *Verbal Behavior*: A half century of misunderstanding. *The Behavior Analyst* 29:253–67.

Paolisso, M. 2007. Taste the traditions: Crabs, crab cakes, and the Chesapeake Bay blue crab fishery. *American Anthropologist* 109:654–55.

Papadopoulos, F. C., E. Petridou, C. E. Frangakis, T. Farmakakis, H. Moller, and G. Rider. 2004. Switching to the Euro: Still hard to swallow. *Archives of Disease in Childhood* 89:382–83.

Paredes, J. A. 1974. The emergence of contemporary Eastern Creek Indian identity. In *Social and cultural identity: Problems of persistence and change. Southern Anthropological Society Proceedings*, No. 8, T. K. Fitzgerald, ed., 63–80. Athens: University of Georgia Press.

Paredes, J. A. 1992. "Practical history" and the Poarch Creeks: A meeting ground for anthropologist and tribal leaders. In *Anthropological research: Process and application*, J. J. Poggie, B. R. DeWalt, and W. W. Dressler, eds., 211–26. Albany: State University of New York Press.

Parekh, R., and E. V. Beresin. 2001. Looking for love? Take a cross-cultural walk through the personals. *Academic Psychiatry* 25:223–33.

Park, R. E., E. W. Burgess, and R. D. McKenzie. 1925. *The city*. Chicago: University of Chicago Press.

Pasero, C. L. 1997. Using the faces scale to assess pain. *American Journal of Nursing* 97:19–20.

Patten, C. A., J. E. Martin, K. J. Filter, and T. D. Wolter. 2002. Utility and accuracy of collateral reports of smoking status among 256 abstinent alcoholic smokers treated for smoking cessation. *Addictive Behaviors* 27:687–96.

Pauli, J. 2000. Das Geplante Kind. Demographischer, Wirtschaftlicher und Sozialer Wandel in einer Mexikanischen Gemeinde. Ph.D. thesis, University of Cologne.

Pausewang, S. 1973. *Methods and concepts of social research in a rural and developing society*. Munich: Weltforum Verlag.

Paxon, H. 2004. *Making modern mothers: Ethics and family planning in urban Greece*. Berkeley: University of California Press.

Payne, S. L. 1951. *The art of asking questions*. Princeton, NJ: Princeton University Press.

Pearce, L. D. 2002. Integrating survey and ethnographic methods for systematic anomalous case analysis. *Sociological Methodology* 32:103–32.

Pearson, J. 1990. Estimation of energy expenditure in Western Samoa, American Samoa, and Honolulu by recall interviews and direct observation. *American Journal of Human Biology* 2:313–26.

Pedhazur, E. J. 1997. *Multiple regression in behavioral research: Explanation and prediction*. 3rd ed. Fort Worth, TX: Harcourt Brace College Publishers.

Pellegrini, A. D. 1996. *Observing children in their natural worlds: A methodological primer*. Mahwah, NJ: Lawrence Erlbaum.

Pels, P. 2008. What has anthropology learned from the anthropology of colonialism? *Social Anthropology* 16:280–99.

Pelto, G. H., P. J. Pelto, and E. Messer, eds. 1989. *Research methods in nutritional anthropology*. Tokyo: The United Nations University.

Pelto, P. J. 1970. *Anthropological research: The structure of inquiry*. New York: Harper and Row.

Pelto, P. J. 1994. Focused ethnographic studies on sexual behavior and AIDS/STDs. *Indian Journal of Social Work* 55:589–601.

Pelto, P. J., and G. H. Pelto. 1975. Intra-cultural diversity: Some theoretical issues. *American Ethnologist* 2:1–18.

Pelto, P. J., and G. H. Pelto. 1978. *Anthropological research: The structure of inquiry*. New York: Cambridge University Press.

Peng, T. K. 2006. Construct validation of the Bem Sex Role Inventory in Taiwan. *Sex Roles* 55:843–51.

Penrod, J., D. B. Preston, R. E. Cain, and M. T. Starks. 2003. A discussion of chain referral as a method of sampling hard-to-reach populations. *Journal of Transcultural Nursing* 14:100–107.

Perchonock, N., and O. Werner. 1969. Navajo systems of classification: Some implications of food. *Ethnology* 8:229–42.

Pericliev, V., and R. E. Valdes-Perez. 1998. Automatic componential analysis of kinship semantics with a proposed structural solution to the problem of multiple models. *Anthropological Linguistics* 40:272–317.

Pescosolido, B. A., and E. R. Wright. 2003. The view from two worlds: The convergence of social network reports between mental health clients and their ties. *Social Science and Medicine* 58:1795–806.

Peters, D. L., and E. J. McCormick. 1966. Comparative reliability of numerically anchored versus job-task anchored rating scales. *Journal of Applied Psychology* 50:92–96.

Peterson, L., V. Johannsson, and S. G. Carlsson. 1996. Computerized testing in a hospital setting: Psychometric and psychological effects. *Computers in Human Behavior* 12:339–50.

Peterson, M., and B. M. Johnstone. 1995. The Atwood Hall health promotion program, Federal Medical Center, Lexington, KY: Effects on drug-involved federal offenders. *Journal of Substance Abuse Treatment* 12:43–48.

Peterson, R. A. 1984. Asking the age question. *Public Opinion Quarterly* 48:379–83.

Petros, Prince of Greece. 1963. *A study of polyandry.* The Hague: Mouton.

Pfeiffer, J., S. Gloyd, and L. Ramirez Li. 2001. Intrahousehold resource allocation and child growth in Mozambique: An ethnographic case–control study. *Social Science and Medicine* 53:83–97.

Phillips, D. L., and K. J. Clancy. 1972. Effects of "social desirability" in survey studies. *American Journal of Sociology* 77:921–40.

Piliavin, I. M., J. Rodin, and J. A. Piliavin. 1969. Good samaritanism: An underground phenomenon? *Journal of Personality and Social Psychology* 13:289–99.

Pinkelton, B. E., E. W. Austin, M. Cohen, Y-C Y. Chen, and E. Fitzgerald. 2008. Effects of peer-led media literacy curriculum on adolescents' knowledge and attitudes towards sexual behavior and media portrayals of sex. *Health Communciation* 23:462–72.

Plattner, S. 1982. Economic decision making in a public marketplace. *American Ethnologist* 9:399–420.

Poggie, J. J. 1972. Toward quality control in key informant data. *Human Organization* 31:23–30.

Poggie, J. J. 1979. Small-scale fishermen's beliefs about success and development: A Puerto Rican case. *Human Organization* 38:6–11.

Pollnac, R. B., C. Gersuny, and J. J. Poggie. 1975. Economic gratification patterns of fishermen and mill workers in New England. *Human Organization* 34:1–7.

Pollner, M., and R. E. Adams. 1997. The effect of spouse presence on appraisals of emotional support and household strain. *Public Opinion Quarterly* 61:615–26.

Popping, R., and C. W. Roberts. 2009. Coding issues in modality analysis. *Field Methods* 21:244–64.

Porter, R., ed. 2003–2006. *The Cambridge history of science.* 7 vols. New York: Cambridge University Press.

Posey, D. A. 2004. *Indigenous knowledge and ethics: A Darrell Posy reader.* New York: Routledge.

Potdar, R., and M. A. Koenig. 2005. Does audio-CASI improve reports of risky behavior? Evidence from a randomized field trial among young urban men in India. *Studies in Family Planning* 36:107–16.

Powdermaker, H. 1966. *Stranger and friend: The way of an anthropologist.* New York: Norton.

Pratt, S., and D. L. Wieder. 1993. The case of saying a few words and talking for another among the Osage people: "Public speaking" as an object of ethnography. *Research on Language and Social Interaction* 26:353–408.

Prebisch, R. 1984. *Power relations and market laws.* Notre Dame, IN: The Helen Kellogg Institute for International Studies, University of Notre Dame.

Prebisch, R. 1994. Latin American periphery in the global system of capitalism. In *Paradigms in economic development: Classic perspectives, critiques, and reflections,* R. Kanth, ed., 165–76. Armonk, NY: M. E. Sharpe.

Press, J. E., and E. Townsley. 1998. Wives' and husbands' housework reporting: Gender, class, and social desirability. *Gender and Society* 12:188–218.

Presser, S., and L. Stinson. 1998. Data collection mode and social desirability bias in self-reported religious attendance. *American Sociological Review* 63:137–45.

Presser, S., and S. Zhao. 1992. Attributes of questions and interviewers as correlates of interviewing performance. *Public Opinion Quarterly* 56:236–40.

Price, D. H. 1993. The evolution of irrigation in Egypt's Fayoum Oasis: State, village and conveyance loss. Ph.D. dissertation, University of Florida.

Price, D. H. 1995. Water theft in Egypt's Fayoum oasis: Emics, etics, and the illegal. In *Science, materialism, and the study of culture,* M. F. Murphy and M. L. Margolis, eds., 96–110. Gainesville: University Press of Florida.

Price, D. H. 2003. Subtle means and enticing carrots. The impact of funding on American Cold War anthropology. *Critique of Anthropology* 23:373–41.

Price, L. 1987. Ecuadorian illness stories. In *Cultural models in language and thought*, D. Holland and N. Quinn, eds., 313–42. Cambridge: Cambridge University Press.

Pridemore, W. A., M. B. Chamlin, and J. K. Cochran. 2007. An interrupted time-series analysis of Durkeim's social deregulation thesis: The case of the Russian Federation. *Justice Quarterly* 24:272–90.

Prince, S. A., K. B. Adamo, M. E. Hamel, J. Hardt, S. C. Gorber, and M. Tremblay. 2008. A comparison of direct versus self-report measures for assessing physical activity in adults: A systematic review. *International Journal of Behavioral Nutrition and Physical Activity* 5, article 56.

Probst, T. M. 2003. Exploring employee outcomes of organizational restructuring. A Solomon four-group study. *Group and Organization Management* 28:416–39.

Pruchno, R. A., J. E. Brill, Y. Shands, J. R. Gordon, M. W. Genderson, M. Rose, and F. Cartwright. 2008. Convenience samples and caregiving research: How generalizable are the findings. *The Gerontologist* 48:820–27.

Pryjmachuk, S., and D. A. Richards. 2007. Look before you leap and don't put all your eggs in one basket: The need for caution and prudence in quantitative data analysis. *Journal of Research in Nursing* 12:43–54.

Psathas, G., ed. 1979. *Everyday language*. New York: Irvington Publishers.

Psathas, G. 1995. *Conversation analysis: The study of talk-in-interaction*. Thousand Oaks, CA: Sage.

Psathas, G., and T. Anderson. 1990. The "practices" of transcription in conversation analysis. *Semiotica* 78:75–99.

Purser, G. 2009. The dignity of job seeking men: Boundary work among immigrant day laborers. *Journal of Contemporary Ethnography* 38:117–39.

Qin, L., and S. Yianjie. 2003. Revision of Bem Sex Role Inventory. *Chinese Mental Health Journal* 17:550–53.

Quandt, S. A., and C. Ritenbaugh. 1986. *Training manual in nutritional anthropology*. Washington, DC: American Anthropological Association.

Quandt, S. A., M. Z. Vitolins, K. M. DeWalt, and G. Roos. 1997. Meal patterns of older adults in rural communities: Life course analysis and implications for undernutrition. *Journal of Applied Gerontology* 16:152–71.

Quételet, A. 1969 [1835]. *Physique sociale, ou, essai sur le développement des facultés de l'homme*. Paris: J.-B. Bailliere et fils. Reprinted in trans. in 1969 from the 1842 ed. as *A treatise on man and the development of his faculties*. Gainesville, FL: Scholars' Facsimiles and Reprints.

Quinn, N. 1978. Do Mfantse fish sellers estimate probabilities in their heads? *American Ethnologist* 5:206–26.

Quinn, N. 1982. "Commitment" in American marriage: A cultural analysis. *American Ethnologist* 9:755–98.

Quinn, N. 1987. Convergent evidence for a cultural model of American marriage. In *Cultural models in language and thought*, N. Quinn and D. Holland, eds., 173–92. Cambridge: Cambridge University Press.

Quinn, N. 1992. The motivational force of self-understanding: Evidence from wives' inner conflicts. In *Human motives and cultural models*, R. G. D'Andrade and C. Stauss, eds., 90–126. New York: Cambridge University Press.

Quinn, N. 1996. Culture and contradiction: The case of Americans reasoning about marriage. *Ethos* 24:391–425.

Quinn, N. 1997. Research on the psychodynamics of shared task solutions. In *A cognitive theory of cultural meaning*, C. Strauss and N. Quinn, eds., 189–209. Cambridge: Cambridge University Press.

Quinnipiac University. 2009 (May 14). Report on the Qunnipiac Poll. http://www.quinnipiac.edu/ x1295.xml?ReleaseID = 1298 (accessed August 5, 2009).

Rabelo, M., and L. Souza. 2003. Temporality and experience. On the meaning of *nervoso* in the trajectory of urban working-class women in Northeast Brazil. *Ethnography* 4:333–61.

Radin, P. 1966 [1933]. *The method and theory of ethnology*. New York: Basic Books.

Radin, P. 1983 [1920]. *Crashing Thunder: The autobiography of a Winnebago Indian*. University of California Publications in American Archaeology and Ethnology, Vol. 16, No. 7. Berkeley: University of California Press.

Rafferty, A. E., ed. 1998. Special Issue on Causality in the Social Sciences, in Honor of Herbert L. Costner. *Sociological Methods and Research* 27(2).

Ragin, C. C. 1987. *The comparative method: Moving beyond qualitative and quantitative strategies*. Berkeley: University of California Press.

Ragin, C. C. 1994. Introduction to qualitative comparative analysis. In *The comparative political economy of the welfare state*, T. Janowski and A. M. Hicks, eds., 299–317. Cambridge: Cambridge University Press.

Ragin, C. C. 1998. The logic of qualitative comparative analysis. *International Review of Social History* 43(suppl. 6):105–24.

Ramirez, J. R., and W. D. Crano. 2003. Deterrence and incapacitation: An interrupted times series of California's three-strikes law. *Journal of Applied Social Psychology* 33:110–44.

Ramírez-Esparza, N., M. R. Mehl, J. Alvarez-Bermúdez, and J. W. Pennebaker. 2009. Are Mexicans more or less social than Americans? Insights from a naturalistic observation study. *Journal of Research in Personality* 43:1–7.

Rappaport, R. 1990. Forward. In *Surviving fieldwork*, N. Howell, ed., vii–viii. Washington, DC: American Anthropological Association.

Rashid, S. F. 2007. Accessing married adolescent women: The realities of ethnographic research in an urban slum environment in Dhaka, Bangladesh. *Field Methods* 19:369–83.

Rathje, W. L. 1979. Trace measures. Garbage and other traces. In *Unobtrusive measurement today*, L. Sechrest, ed., 75–91. San Francisco: Jossey-Bass.

Rathje, W. L. 1984. The garbage decade. In *Household refuse analysis: Theory, method, and applications in social science*, W. L. Rathje and C. K. Ritenbaugh, eds., 9–29. *American Behavioral Scientist* 28(1, entire issue).

Rathje, W. L. 1992. Garbage demographics. *American Demographics* 14:50–54.

Rathje, W. L., and C. Murphy. 1992. Garbage demographics. *American Demographics* 14:50–54.

Read, D. W. 2001. Formal analysis of kinship terminologies and its relationship to what constitutes kinship. *Anthropological Theory* 2:239–67.

Reboussin, D. 1995. From Affiniam-Boutem to Dakar: Migration from the Casamance, life in the urban environment of Dakar and the resulting evolutionary changes in local Diola organizations. Ph.D. dissertation, University of Florida.

Reed, T. W., and R. J. Stimson, eds. 1985. *Survey interviewing. Theory and techniques*. Sydney: Allen & Unwin.

Rees, C. E., L. V. Knight, and C. E. Wilkinson. 2007. Doctors being up there and we being down here: A metaphorical analysis of talk about student/doctor-patient relationships. *Social Science and Medicine* 65:725–37.

Reese, S. D., W. A. Danielson, P. J. Shoemaker, Tsan-Kuo Chang, and Huei-ling Hsu. 1986. Ethnicity-of-interviewer effects among Mexican-American and Anglos. *Public Opinion Quarterly* 50:563–72.

Reiss, A. J., Jr. 1971. *The police and the public*. New Haven, CT: Yale University Press.

Reiss, N. 1985. *Speech act taxonomy as a tool for ethnographic description: An analysis based on videotapes of continuous behavior in two New York households*. Philadelphia: John Benjamins.

Repp, A. C., G. S. Nieminen, E. Olinger, and R. Brusca. 1988. Direct observation: Factors affecting the accuracy of observers. *Exceptional Children* 55:29–36.

Resnik, D. B. 2007. *The price of truth: How money affects the norms of science*. New York: Oxford University Press.

Reyes-García, V., E. Byron, V. Vadez, R. Godoy, L. Apaza, E. Pérez Limache, W. R. Leonard, and D. Wilkie. 2003. Measuring culture as shared knowledge: Do data collection formats matter? Cultural knowledge of plant uses among Tsimane' Amerindians, Bolivia. *Field Methods* 15:1–22.

Reyes-García, V., R. Godoy, V. Vadez, L. Apaza, E. Byron, T. Huanca, W. R. Leonard, E. Pérez, and

D. Wilkie. 2003. Ethnobotanical knowledge shared widely among Tsimane' Amerindians, Bolivia. *Science* 299:1707.

Riach, P. A., and J. Rich. 2004. Deceptive field experiments of discrimination: Are they ethical? *Kyklos* 57:457–70.

Ricci, J. A., N. W. Jerome, N. Megally, and O. Galal. 1995. Assessing the validity of information recall: Results of a time use pilot study in peri-urban Egypt. *Human Organization* 54:304–8.

Richards, A. I. 1939. *Land, labour and diet in northern Rhodesia: An economic study of the Bemba tribe.* London: Oxford University Press.

Richardson, J., and A. L. Kroeber. 1940. Three centuries of women's dress fashions: A quantitative analysis. *Anthropological Records* 5:111–53.

Richardson, L. 1988. Secrecy and status: The social construction of forbidden relationships. *American Sociological Review* 53:209–19.

Rickford, J. R., and R. J. Rickford. 2000. *Spoken soul: The story of black English.* New York: Wiley.

Ricoeur, P. 1979. *Main trends in philosophy / Paul Ricoeur.* New York: Holmes & Meier.

Ricoeur, P. 1981. *Hermeneutics and the human sciences: Essays on language, action, and interpretation.* New York: Cambridge University Press.

Ricoeur, P. 2007. *From text to action.* New ed. Evanston, IL: Northwestern University Press.

Riessman, C. K. 1993. *Narrative analysis.* Newbury Park, CA: Sage.

Riksen, N. P., G. A. Rongen, and P. Smits. 2009. Acute and long-term cardiovascular effects of coffee: Implications for coronary heart disease. *Pharmacology and Therapeutics* 121:185–91.

Rindfleisch, A., J. E. Burroughs, and F. Denton. 1997. Family structure, materialism, and compulsive consumption. *Journal of Consumer Research* 23:312–25.

Ritenbaugh, C. K., and G. G. Harrison. 1984. Reactivity of garbage analysis. In *Household refuse analysis: Theory, method, and applications in social science*, W. L. Rathje and C. K. Rittenbaugh, eds., 51–70. *American Behavioral Scientist* 28(1, entire issue).

Rivers, W. H. R. 1910. The genealogical method of anthropological inquiry. *Sociological Review* 3:1–12.

Rivers, W. H. R. 1968 [1914]. *Kinship and social organization.* New York: Humanities Press.

Robbins, M. C., A. V. Williams, P. L. Kilbride, and R. B. Pollnac. 1969. Factor analysis and case selection in complex societies. *Human Organization* 28:227–34.

Roberts, J. M., and G. E. Chick. 1979. Butler County eight-ball: A behavioral space analysis. In *Sports, games, and play: Social and psychological viewpoints*, J. H. Goldstein, ed., 65–100. Hillsdale, NJ: Lawrence Erlbaum.

Roberts, J. M., T. V. Golder, and G. E. Chick. 1980. Judgment, oversight, and skill: A cultural analysis of P-3 pilot error. *Human Organization* 39:5–21.

Roberts, J. M., and S. Nattrass. 1980. Women and trapshooting: Competence and expression in a game of physical skill with chance. In *Play and culture*, H. B. Schwartzman, ed., 262–90. West Point, NY: Leisure Press.

Roberts, J. M., S. Morita, and L. K. Brown. 1986. Personal categories for Japanese sacred places and gods: Views elicited from a conjugal pair. *American Anthropologist* 88:807–24.

Robinson, D., and S. Rhode. 1946. Two experiments with an anti-Semitism poll. *Journal of Abnormal and Social Psychology* 41:136–44.

Robinson, J. A. 1996. The relationship between personal characteristics and attitudes towards black and white speakers of informal non-standard English. *The Western Journal of Black Studies* 20:211–20.

Robinson, M. B., and C. E. Robinson. 1997. Environmental characteristics associated with residential burglaries of student apartment complexes. *Environment and Behavior* 29:657–75.

Robinson, W. S. 1950. Ecological correlations and the behavior of individuals. *American Sociological Review* 15:351–57.

Rocha, J. M. 2005. Measuring traditional agro-ecological knowledge: An example from peasants in the Peruvian Andes. *Field Methods* 17:356–72.

Rogoff, B. 1978. Spot observation: An introduction and examination. *Quarterly Newsletter of the Institute for Comparative Human Development* 2:21–26.

Rohde, D. 2007. Army enlists anthropology in war zones. *New York Times*, October 5, http://www .nytimes.com/2007/10/05/world/asia/05afghan.html (accessed June 11, 2009).

Rohner, R. 1966. Franz Boas, ethnographer of the Northwest Coast. In *Pioneers of American anthropology*, J. Helm, ed., 149–212. Seattle: University of Washington Press.

Rohner, R. 1969. *The ethnography of Franz Boas.* Chicago: University of Chicago Press.

Rohner, R., B. R. DeWalt, and R. C. Ness. 1973. Ethnographer bias in cross-cultural research. *Behavior Science Notes* 8:275–317.

Romney, A. K. 1989. Quantitative models, science and cumulative knowledge. *Journal of Quantitative Anthropology* 1:153–223.

Romney, A. K., W. H. Batchelder, and S. C. Weller. 1987. Recent applications of cultural consensus theory. *American Behavioral Scientist* 31:163–77.

Romney, A. K., and R. G. D'Andrade, eds. 1964. Cognitive aspects of English kin terms. In *Transcultural studies in cognition. American Anthropologist* 66 (3, part 2, entire issue):146–70.

Romney, A. K., C. C. Moore, and C. D. Rusch. 1997. Cultural universals: Measuring the semantic structure of emotion terms in English and Japanese. *Proceedings of the National Academy of Sciences* 94:5489–95.

Romney, A. K., R. N. Shepard, and S. B. Nerlove, eds. 1972. *Multidimensional scaling.* Vol. 2, *Applications.* New York: Seminar Press.

Romney, A. K., S. C. Weller, and W. H. Batchelder. 1986. Culture as consensus: A theory of culture and informant accuracy. *American Anthropologist* 88:313–38.

Roscigno, V. J., and R. Hodson. 2004. The organizational and social foundations of worker resistance. *American Sociological Review* 69:14–39.

Rose, M. G. 1997. *Translation and literary criticism: Translation as analysis.* Manchester, England: St. Jerome.

Rosenberg, M. 1968. *The logic of survey analysis.* New York: Basic Books.

Rosenberg, S. D., P. P. Schnurr, and T. E. Oxman. 1990. Content analysis: A comparison of manual and computerized systems. *Journal of Personality Assessment* 54:298–310.

Rosenhan, D. L. 1973. On being sane in insane places. *Science* 179:250–58.

Rosenhan, D. L. 1975. The contextual nature of psychiatric diagnosis. *Journal of Abnormal Psychology* 84:462–74.

Rosenthal, R., and L. Jacobson. 1968. *Pygmalion in the classroom.* New York: Holt, Rinehart & Winston.

Rosenthal, R., and D. B. Rubin. 1978. Interpersonal expectancy effects: The first 345 studies. *The Behavioral and Brain Sciences* 3:377–415.

Rosenthal, S. R., and M. Capper. 2006. *Journal of Product Innovation Management* 23:215–37.

Ross, M. W., E. J. Essien, and I. Torres. 2006. Conspiracy beliefs about the origin of HIV/AIDS in four racial/ethnic groups. *Journal of Acquired Immune Deficiency Syndrome* 41:342–44.

Ross, M. W., B. R. S. Rosser, J. Stanton, and J. Konstan. 2004. Characteristics of Latino men who have sex with men on the Internet who complete and drop out of an Internet-based sexual behavior survey. *AIDS Education and Prevention* 16:526–37.

Ross, N. 2002. Cognitive aspects of intergenerational change: Mental models, culture change, and environmental behavior among the Lancandon Maya of southern Mexico. *Human Organization* 61:125–38.

Ross, N., T. Barrientos, and A. Esquit-Choy. 2005. Triad tasks, a multipurpose tool to elicit similarity judgments: The case of Tzotzil Maya plant taxonomy. *Field Methods* 17:269–82.

Ross, N., and D. L. Medin. 2005. Ethnography and experiments: Cultural models and expertise effects elicited with experimental research techniques. *Field Methods* 17:141–49.

Rossi, P. H., and R. Berk. 1997. *Just punishments: Federal guidelines and public views compared.* New York: Aldine de Gruyter.

Rossi, P. H., and S. L. Nock. 1982. *Measuring social judgments: The factorial survey approach.* Newbury Park, CA: Sage.

Rotton, J., and M. Shats. 1996. Effects of state humor, expectancies, and choice on postsurgical mood and self-medication: A field experiment. *Journal of Applied Social Psychology* 26:1775–94.

Rotton, J., M. Shats, and R. Standers. 1990. Temperature and pedestrian tempo. Walking without awareness. *Environment and Behavior* 22:650–74.

Rousseau, J.-J. 1988 [1762]. *On the social contract*, D. A. Cress, trans. and ed. Indianapolis: Hackett Publishing.

Royal Anthropological Institute of Great Britain and Ireland (RAI). 1951. *Notes and queries on anthropology*. 6th ed., rev. London: Routledge & K. Paul.

Rozeboom, W. 1960. The fallacy of the null-hypothesis significance test. *Psychological Bulletin* 67:416–28.

Rubel, A. J., C. W. O'Nell, and R. Collado-Adrdón. 1984. *Susto. A folk illness*. Berkeley: University of California Press.

Rubin, D. B. 1976. Inference and missing data. *Biometrika* 63:581–92.

Rubin, H. J. 2005. *Qualitative interviewing: The art of hearing data*. 2nd ed. Thousand Oaks, CA: Sage.

Rubinstein, R. L. 1995. Narratives of elder parental death: A structural and cultural analysis. *Medical Anthropology Quarterly* 9:257–76.

Rudd, E., E. Morrison, J. Picciano, and M. Nerad. 2008. Social science Ph.D.s five+ years out: Anthropology report. Seattle: University of Washington Graduate School/College of Education. at http://depts.washington.edu/cirgeweb/c/wp-content/uploads/2008/03/anthro-final-03-11-08.pdf (accessed June 12, 2009).

Rudolph, L. I. 1997. Self as Other: Amar Singh's diary as reflexive "native" ethnography. *Modern Asian Studies* 31:143–75.

Ruiz-Caseres, M., and J. Heymann. 2009. Children home alone unsupervised: Modeling parental decisions and associated factors in Botswana, Mexico, and Vietnam. *Child Abuse and Neglect* 33:312–23.

Rushforth, S. 1982. A structural semantic analysis of Bear Lake Athapaskan kinship classification. *American Ethnologist* 9:559–77.

Rutledge, E. M. 1990. Black parent-child relations: Some correlates. *Journal of Comparative Family Studies* 21:369–78.

Ryan, G. W. 1995. Medical decision making among the Kom of Cameroon: Modeling how characteristics of illnesses, patients, caretakers, and compounds affect treatment choice in a rural community. Ph.D. dissertation, University of Florida.

Ryan, G. W. 1999. Measuring the typicality of text: Using multiple coders for more than just reliability and validity checks. *Human Organization* 58:313–22.

Ryan, G. W. 2004. Using a word processor to tag and retrieve blocks of text. *Field Methods* 16:109–30.

Ryan, G. W., and H. R. Bernard. 2000. Data management and analysis methods. In *Handbook of qualitative research*, 2nd ed., N. Denzin and Y. Lincoln, eds., 769–802. Thousand Oaks, CA: Sage.

Ryan, G. W., and H. R. Bernard. 2003. Techniques to identify themes. *Field Methods* 15:85–109.

Ryan, G. W., and H. R. Bernard. 2006. Testing an ethnographic decision tree model on a national sample: Recycling beverage cans. *Human Organization* 65:103–14.

Ryan, G. W., and H. Martínez. 1996. Can we predict what mothers do? Modeling childhood diarrhea in rural Mexico. *Human Organization* 55:47–57.

Ryan, G. W., J. M. Nolan, and P. S. Yoder. 2000. Successive free listing: Using multiple free lists to generate explanatory models. *Field Methods* 12:83–107.

Ryan, G. W., and T. Weisner. 1996. Analyzing words in brief descriptions: Fathers and mothers describe their children. *Cultural Anthropology Methods Journal* 8(3):13–16.

Rynkiewick, M., and J. P. Spradley, eds. 1976. *Ethics and anthropology: Dilemmas in fieldwork*. New York: John Wiley.

Sackett, R. 1996. Time, energy, and the indolent savage. A quantitative cross-cultural test of the primitive affluence hypothesis. Ph.D. dissertation, University of California, Los Angeles.

Sacks, H. 1992. *Lectures on conversation*. Cambridge, MA: Basil Blackwell.

Sacks, H., E. A. Schegloff, and G. Jefferson. 1974. A simplest systematics for the organization of turn-taking conversation. *Language* 50:696–735.

Sahlins, M. 1972. *Stone Age economics.* Chicago: Aldine.

Salamone, F. 1977. The methodological significance of the lying informant. *Anthropological Quarterly* 50:117–24.

Salganik, M. J., and D. D. Heckathorn. 2004. Sampling and estimation in hidden populations using respondent-driven sampling. *Sociological Methodology* 34:193–239.

Salinas Pedraza, J. 1984. *Etnografía del Otomí.* Mexico City: Instituto Nacional Indigenista.

Salinas Pedraza, J., and H. R. Bernard. 1978. *Rc Hnycnhyu. The Otomí.* Vol. 1, *Geography and fauna.* Albuquerque: University of New Mexico Press.

Salmon, M. H. 1997. Ethical considerations in anthropology and archaeology; or, relativism and justice for all. *Journal of Anthropological Research* 53:47–63.

Sampson, H., and M. Thomas. 2003. Risk and responsibility. *Qualitative Research* 3:165–89.

Sanchez, M. E., and G. Morchio. 1992. Probing "Don't Know" answers: Effects on survey estimates and variable relationships. *Public Opinion Quarterly* 56:454–74.

Sandall, R. 1999. Herskovits' last day in Dahomey. *Anthropology Today* 15:18–20.

Sanderson, S. K., and W. W. Roberts. 2008. The evolutionary forms of the religious life: A cross-cultural, quantitative analysis. *American Anthropologist* 110:454–66.

Sands, K. 1980. Preface. In *Autobiography of a Yaqui poet*, R. Savala, ed., vii–ix. Tucson: University of Arizona Press.

Sanghera, G., and S. Thapar-Björkert. 2008. Methodological dilemmas: Gatekeepers and positionality in Bradford. *Ethnic and Racial Studies* 31:543–62.

Sanjek, R. 1990. *Fieldnotes.* Ithaca, NY: Cornell University Press.

Sankoff, G. 1971. Quantitative analysis of sharing and variability in a cognitive model. *Ethnology* 10:389–408.

Santa Ana, O. 1999. "Like an animal I was treated": Anti-immigrant metaphor in U.S. public discourse. *Discourse and Society* 10:191–224.

Sarton, G. 1935. Quételet (1796–1874). *Isis* 23:6–24.

Sarton, G. 1952–1959. *A history of science.* Cambridge, MA: Harvard University Press.

SAUS. 1947. Statistical abstract of the United States. Washington, DC: U.S. Census Bureau. http://www.census.gov/prod/www/abs/statab1901-1950.htm (accessed March 8, 2009).

SAUS. 2000. Statistical abstract of the United States. http://www.census.gov/prod/www/abs/statab1995_2000.html (accessed August 23, 2009).

SAUS. 2004–2005. http://www.census.gov/prod/www/abs/statab2001_2005.html/ (accessed March 5, 2010).

SAUS. 2009. Statistical abstract of the United States. http://www.census.gov/compendia/statab/2009/2009edition.html/ (accessed March 5, 2010).

Savala, R. 1980. *Autobiography of a Yaqui poet.* Tucson: University of Arizona Press.

Sayles, J. N., G. W. Ryan, J. S. Silver, C. A. Sarkisian, and W. E. Cunningham. 2007. Experiences of social stigma and implications for healthcare among a diverse population of HIV positive adults. *Journal of Urban Health: Bulletin of the New York Academy of Medicine.* doi:10.1007/s11524-007-9220-4.

Scaglion, R. 1986. The importance of nighttime observations in time allocation studies. *American Ethnologist* 13:537–45.

Schaeffer, N. C., and S. Presser. 2003. The science of asking questions. *Annual Review of Sociology* 29:65–88.

Schank, R. C., and R. P. Abelson. 1977. *Scripts, plans, goals, and understanding: An inquiry into human knowledge structures.* Hillsdale, NJ: Lawrence Erlbaum.

Schatz, E., ed. 2009. *Political ethnography: What immersion contributes to the study of power.* Chicago: University of Chicago Press.

Scheerer, G. E., S. Smith, and K. Thomas. 2009. "Shopping while black": Examining racial discrimination in a retail setting. *Journal of Applied Social Psychology* 39:1432–44.

Scheers, N. J., and C. M. Dayton. 1987. Improved estimation of academic cheating behavior using the randomized response technique. *Research in Higher Education* 26:61–69.

Schegloff, E. A. 1972. Sequencing in conversational opening. In *Directions in sociolinguistics*, J. Gumpertz, ed., 346–80. New York: Holt, Reinhart and Winston.

Schegloff, E. A., and H. Sacks. 1973. Opening up closings. *Semiotica* 7:289–327.

Schensul, S. L., J. Schensul, G. Oodit, U. Bowan, and S. Ragobur. 1994. Sexual intimacy and changing lifestyles in an era of AIDS. *Reproductive Health Matters* No. 3(May):83–92.

Scheper-Hughes, N. 1983. Introduction: The problem of bias in androcentric and feminist anthropology. In *Confronting problems of bias in feminist anthropology*, N. Scheper-Hughes, ed., 109–16. *Women's Studies* 10 (special issue).

Scheper-Hughes, N. 1992. *Death without weeping. The violence of everyday life in Brazil*. Berkeley: University of California Press.

Scherer, S. E. 1974. Proxemic behavior of primary-school children as a function of the socioeconomic class and subculture. *Journal of Personality and Social Psychology* 29:800–805.

Schiller, F. C. S. 1969 [1903]. *Humanism. Philosophical essays*. Freeport, NY: Books for Libraries Press.

Schlegel, A., and H. Barry, III. 1986. The cultural consequences of female contribution to subsistence. *American Anthropologist* 88:142–50.

Schober, M. F., and F. G. Conrad. 1997. Does conversational interviewing reduce survey measurement error? *Public Opinion Quarterly* 61:576–602.

Schoenberg, N. E. 1997. A convergence of health beliefs: An "ethnography of adherence" of African-American rural elders with hypertension. *Human Organization* 56:174–81.

Schoenberg, N. E. 2000. Patterns, factors, and pathways contributing to nutritional risk among rural African American elders. *Human Organization* 59:235–44.

Schuman, H., and S. Presser. 1979. The open and closed question. *American Sociological Review* 44:692–712.

Schuman, H., and S. Presser. 1981. *Questions and answers in attitude surveys*. San Diego: Academic Press.

Schuster, J. A. 1977. *Descartes and the scientific revolution*. Princeton, NJ: Princeton University Press.

Schutz, A. 1962. *Collected papers I: The problem of social reality*. The Hague: Martinus Nijhoff.

Schwarz, N. 1966. *Cognition and communication: Judgment biases, research methods, and the logic of conversation*. Hillsdale, NJ: Lawrence Erlbaum.

Schwarz, N. 1999. Self-reports. How the questions shape the answers. *American Psychologist* 54:93–105.

Schwarz, N., H.-J. Hippler, B. Deutsch, and F. Strack. 1985. Response scales: Effects of category range on reported behavior and comparative judgments. *Public Opinion Quarterly* 49:388–95.

Schwarz, N., B. Knäuper, H.-J. Hippler, E. Noelle-Neumann, and L. Clark. 1991. Rating scales: Numeric values may change the meaning of scale labels. *Public Opinion Quarterly* 55:570–82.

Schwarzwalder, A. Z. Chilangwa, I. Patel, A. Burke, and M. Lynch. 2008. Testing a tool to scale quality of life indicators in Tanzania. *Field Methods* 20:179–90.

Schweizer, T. 1980. Multidimensional scaling of internal differences in similarity data: The perception of interethnic similarity in Indonesia. *Journal of Anthropological Research* 36:149–73.

Schweizer, T. 1991. The power struggle in a Chinese community, 1950–1980: A social network analysis of the duality of actors and events. *Journal of Quantitative Anthropology* 3:19–44.

Schweizer, T. 1996. Actor and event orderings across time: Lattice representation and Boolean analysis of the political disputes in Chen Village, China. *Social Networks* 18:247–66.

Schweizer, T. 1998. Epistemology: The nature and validation of anthropological knowledge. In *Handbook of methods in cultural anthropology*, H. R. Bernard, ed., 39–87. Walnut Creek, CA: AltaMira.

Science. 1972. The Brawling Bent. March 24, 1346–47.

Scollon, C. N., E. Diener, and S. Oishi. 2005. An experience sampling and cross-cultural investigation of the relation between pleasant and unpleasant affect. *Cognition and Emotion* 19:27–52.

Scott, G. 2008. "They got their program, and I got mine": A cautionary tale concerning the ethical implications of of using respondent-driven sampling to study injection drug users. *International Journal of Drug Policy* 19:42–51.

Scribner, S., and M. Cole. 1981. *The psychology of literacy*. Cambridge, MA: Harvard University Press.

Scrimshaw, N., and G. R. Gleason, eds. 1992. *RAP. Rapid Assessment Procedures. Qualitative methodologies for planning and evaluation of health related programmes.* Boston: International Nutrition Foundation for Developing Countries.

Scrimshaw, S. C. M., and E. Hurtado. 1987. *Rapid assessment procedures for nutrition and primary health care: Anthropological approaches to improving programme effectiveness.* Los Angeles: UCLA Latin American Center Publications, University of California.

Scudder, T., and E. Colson. 2002. Long-term research in Gwembe Valley, Zambia. In *Chronicling cultures: Long-term field research in anthropology,* R. V. Kemper and A. P. Royce, eds., 197–238. Walnut Creek, CA: AltaMira.

Sechrest, L., and L. Flores. 1969. Homosexuality in the Philippines and the United States: The handwriting on the wall. *Journal of Social Psychology* 79:3–12.

Sechrest, L., and M. Phillips. 1979. Unobtrusive measures: An overview. In *Unobtrusive measurement today,* L. Sechrest, ed., 1–17. San Francisco: Jossey-Bass.

Segre, C. 1988. *Introduction to the analysis of the literary text,* John Meddemmen, trans. Bloomington: University of Indiana Press.

Seidman, I. 2006. Interviewing as qualitative research: A guide for researchers in education and the social sciences. 3rd ed. New York: Teachers College Press.

Sexton, J. D., ed. 1981. Background of the story. In *I. Bizarro Ujpán, Son of Tecún Umán: A Maya Indian tells his life story,* 3–20. Tucson: University of Arizona Press.

Sexton, J. D., and I. Bizzaro Ujpán. 1999. *Heart of Heaven, Heart of Earth, and other Mayan folktales.* Washington, DC: Smithsonian Institution Press.

Shadish, W. R., and T. D. Cook. 2008. The renaissance of field experimentation in evaluating interventions. *Annual Review of Psychology* 60:607–29.

Sharff, J. W. 1979. Patterns of authority in two urban Puerto Rican households. Ph.D. dissertation, Columbia University.

Sharma, D. 2006. Performing Nautanki: Popular community folk performances as sites of dialogue and social change. Ph.D. dissertation, Ohio University.

Sharpe, R. 1998. EEOC backs away from filing race-bias suit. *The Wall Street Journal,* June 24, p. A4.

Shaw, C. R. 1930. *The jack-roller. A delinquent boy's own story.* Chicago: University of Chicago Press.

Shaw, S. 1992. Dereifying family leisure: An examination of women's and men's everyday experiences and perceptions of family time. *Leisure Studies* 14:271–86.

Sheatsley, P. B. 1983. Questionnaire construction and item wording. In *Handbook of survey research,* P. H. Rossi, J. D. Wright, and A. B. Anderson, eds., 195–230. New York: Wiley.

Sheets, J. W. 1982. Nonleptokurtic marriage distances on Colonsay and Jura. *Current Anthropology* 23:105–6.

Shelley, G. A. 1992. The social networks of people with end-stage renal disease: Comparing hemodialysis and peritoneal dialysis patients. Ph.D. dissertation, University of Florida.

Shelley, G. A., H. R. Bernard, and P. D. Killworth. 1990. Information flow in social networks. *Journal of Quantitative Anthropology* 2:201–25.

Shelley, G. A., H. R. Bernard, P. D. Killworth, E. C. Johnsen, and C. McCarty. 1995. Who knows your HIV status? What HIV+ patients and their network members know about each other. *Social Networks* 17:189–217.

Shenk, M. K. 2007. Dowry and public policy in contemporary India. The behavioral ecology of a "social evil." *Human Nature* 18:242–63.

Shepard, R. N., A. K. Romney, and S. B. Nerlove. 1972. *Multidimensional scaling: Theory and applications in the behavioral sciences.* Vol 2. *Applications.* New York: Seminar Press.

Sherma, R. D., and A. Sharma, eds. 2008. *Hermeneutics and Hindu thought: Toward a fusion of horizons.* New York: Springer.

Sherratt, Y. 2006. *Continental philosophy of social science: Hermeneutics, genealogy, critical theory.* New York: Cambridge University Press.

Sherry, J. F., Jr. 1995. *Contemporary marketing and consumer behavior: An anthropological sourcebook.* Thousand Oaks, CA: Sage.

Sherzer, J. 1990. *Verbal art in San Blas.* Cambridge: Cambridge University Press.

Sherzer, J. 1994. The Kuna and Columbus: Encounters and confrontations of discourse. *American Anthropologist* 96:902–25.

Sherzer, J., and G. Urban. 1986. Introduction. In *Native South American discourse,* J. Sherzer and G. Urban, eds., 1–14. Berlin: Mouton.

Shore, B. 2009. Making time for family: Schemas for long-term family memory. *Social Indicators Research* 93:95–103.

Shostak, M. 1981. *Nisa: The life and words of a !Kung woman.* Cambridge, MA: Harvard University Press.

Shweder, R., and R. G. D'Andrade. 1980. The systematic distortion hypothesis. In *Fallible judgment in behavioral research,* R. Shweder, ed., 37–58. San Francisco: Jossey-Bass.

Silverman, E. K. 2004. Anthropology and circumcision. *Annual Review of Anthropology* 33:419–45.

Simmons, L. W., ed. 1942. *Sun Chief: The autobiography of a Hopi Indian.* New Haven, CT: Yale University Press.

Simpson, J. A., and S. W. Gangestad. 1991. Individual differences in sociosexuality: Evidence for convergent and discriminant validity. *Journal of Personality and Social Psychology* 60:870–83.

Sin, L. Y. M., and O. H. M. Yau. 2004. Female role orientation of Chinese women: Conceptualization and scale development. *Psychology and Marketing* 21:1033–58.

Singer, E. M., R. Frankel, and M. B. Glassman. 1983. The effect of interviewer characteristics and expectations on response. *Public Opinion Quarterly* 47:68–83.

Sireci, S. G. 1998. The construct of content validity. *Social Indicators Research* 45:83–117.

Sirken, M. G. 1972. *Designing forms for demographic surveys.* Chapel Hill: Laboratories for Population Statistics, Manual Series, No. 3. The Department of Biostatistics, School of Public Health, The Carolina Population Center, University of North Carolina.

Skinner, B. F. 1957. *Verbal behavior.* New York: Appleton-Century-Crofts.

Smith, C. D., and W. Kornblum, eds. 1996. *In the field. Readings on the research experience.* Westport, CT: Praeger.

Smith, C. J., R. G. Nelson, S. A. Hardy, E. M. Manahan, P. H. Bennett, and W. C. Knowler. 1996. Survey of the diet of Pima Indians using quantitative food frequency assessment and 24-hour recall. *Journal of the American Dietetic Association* 96:778–84.

Smith, E. A. 1998. Is Tibetan polyandry adaptive? Methodological and metatheoretical analyses. *Human Nature* 9:225–61.

Smith, J. J., and S. P. Borgatti. 1997. Salience counts—And so does accuracy: Correcting and updating a measure for free-list-item salience. *Journal of Linguistic Anthropology* 7:208–9.

Smith, J. J., L. Furbee, K. Maynard, S. Quick, and L. Ross. 1995. Salience counts: A domain analysis of English color terms. *Journal of Linguistic Anthropology* 5:203–16.

Smith, K. D., S. T. Smith, and J. C. Christopher. 2007. What defines the good person? Cross-cultural comparisons of experts' models with lay prototypes. *Journal of Cross-Cultural Psychology* 38:333–60.

Smith, L. D. 1986. *Behaviorism and logical positivism.* Stanford, CA: Stanford University Press.

Smith, M. L., and G. V. Glass. 1977. Meta-analysis of psychotherapy outcome studies. *American Psychologist* 32:752–60.

Smith, R. 1997. *The Norton history of the human sciences.* New York: W.W. Norton.

Smith, T. W. 1987. That which we call welfare by any other name would smell sweeter. An analysis of the impact of question wording on response patterns. *Public Opinion Quarterly* 51:75–83.

Smith, T. W. 1997. The impact of the presence of others on a respondent's answers to questions. *International Journal of Public Opinion Research* 9:33–47.

Smith, T. W. 1998. A review of church attendance measures. *American Sociological Review* 63:131–36.

Smith, T. W. 2008. An experimental comparison of methods of measuring ethnicity. *Field Methods* 20:171–78.

Smith, W. W. 2006. Social desirability bias and exit survey responses: The case of a First Nations campground in Central Ontario, Canada. *Tourism Management* 28:917–19.

Smits, J., W. Ultee, and J. Lammers. 1998. Educational homogamy in 65 countries: An explanation of differences in openness using country-level explanatory variables. *American Sociological Review* 63:264–85.

Snider, J. G., and C. E. Osgood., eds. 1969. *Semantic differential technique.* Chicago: Aldine.

Soifer, V. 1994. *Lysenko and the tragedy of Soviet science,* L. Gruliow and R. Gruliow, trans. New Brunswick, NJ: Rutgers University Press.

Sokolovsky, J., C. Cohen, D. Berger, and J. Geiger. 1978. Personal networks of ex-mental patients in a Manhattan SRO hotel. *Human Organization* 37:5–15.

Sokolowski, R. 2000. *Introduction to phenomenology.* New York: Cambridge University Press.

Solow, R. M. 1970. Science and ideology in economics. *Public Interest* 21:94–107.

Sousa, V. D., J. A. Zauszniewski, and C. M. Musil. 2004. How to determine whether a convenience sample represents the population. *Applied Nursing Research* 17:130–33.

Sousa Campos, L. de, E. Otta, and J. de Oliveira Siqueira. 2002. Sex differences in mate selection strategies: Content analyses and responses to personal advertisements in Brazil. *Evolution and Human Behavior* 23:395–406.

Spearman, C. 1904. "General intelligence" objectively determined and measured. *American Journal of Psychology* 15:201–93.

Spector, P. E. 1992. *Summated rating scale construction.* Newbury Park, CA: Sage.

Spence, J. T., and R. Helmreich. 1972. Who likes competent women? Competence, sex role congruence of interests, and subjects' attitudes toward women as determinants of interpersonal attraction. *Journal of Applied Social Psychology* 2:197–213.

Spence, J. T., and R. L. Helmreich. 1978. *Masculinity and femininity: Their psychological dimensions, correlates, and antecedents.* Austin: University of Texas Press.

Spiegelberg, H. 1980. *Phenomenology. Encyclopaedia brittanica,* 15th ed., Vol. 14. Chicago: Encyclopaedia Brittanica.

Spradley, J. P. 1972. Adaptive strategies of urban nomads. In *Culture and cognition: Rules, maps, and plans,* J. P. Spradley, ed., 235–78. New York: Chandler.

Spradley, J. P. 1979. *The ethnographic interview.* New York: Holt, Rinehart & Winston.

Spradley, J. P. 1980. *Participant observation.* New York: Holt, Rinehart & Winston.

Spring, M., J. Westermeyer, L. Halcon, K. Savik, C. Robertson, D. R. Johnson, J. N. Butcher, and J. Jaranson. 2003. Sampling in difficult to access refugee and immigrant communities. *Journal of Nervous and Mental Disease* 191:813–19.

Sproull, L. S. 1981. Managing education programs: A micro-behavioral analysis. *Human Organization* 40:113–22.

Squire, P. 1988. Why the 1936 "Literary Digest" poll failed. *Public Opinion Quarterly* 52:125–33.

Srinivas, M. N. 1979. The fieldworker and the field: A village in Karnataka. In *The fieldworker and the field,* M. N. Srinivas, A. M. Shah, and E. A. Ramaswamy, eds., 19–28. Delhi: Oxford University Press.

Srinivasan, S. 2005. Daughters or dowries? The changing nature of dowry practice in South India. *World Development* 33:593–615.

Staats, S., D. Miller, M. J. Carnot, K. Rada, and J. Turner. 1996. The Miller-Rada Commitment to Pets Scale. *Anthrozoos* 9:88–94.

Stearman, A. M. 1989. Yuquí foragers in the Bolivian Amazon: Subsistence strategies, prestige, and leadership in an acculturating society. *Journal of Anthropological Research* 45:219–44.

Stein, J., S. A. Fox, and P. J. Murata. 1991. The influence of ethnicity, socioeconomic status, and psychological barriers on the use of mammography. *Journal of Health and Social Behavior* 32:101–13.

Stein, R. H. 1987. *The synoptic problem.* Grand Rapids, MI: Baker Book House.

Stemmer, N. 1990. Skinner's "Verbal Behavior," Chomsky's review, and mentalism. *Journal of the Experimental Analysis of Behavior* 54:307–16.

Stemmer, N. 2004. Has Chomsky's argument been refuted? A reply to Skinner, Cautilli, and Hantula. *The Behavior Analyst Today* 4:376–82.

Stephenson, J. B., and L. S. Greer. 1981. Ethnographers in their own cultures: Two Appalachian cases. *Human Organization* 30:333–43.

Sterk, C. E. 1989. Prostitution, drug use, and AIDS. In *In the field: Readings on the field research experience,* C. D. Smith and W. Kornblum, eds., 91–100. New York: Praeger.

Sterk, C. E. 1999. *Tricking and tripping: Prostitution in the era of AIDS.* Putnam Valley, NY: Social Change Press.

Stevens, S. S. 1946. On the theory of measurement. *Science* 103:677–80.

Steward, J. H. 1949. Cultural causality and law: A trial formulation of early civilization. *American Anthropologist* 51:1–27.

Steward, J. H. 1955. *Theory of culture change; the methodology of multilinear evolution.* Urbana: University of Illinois Press.

Stewart, D. W., and P. N. Shamdasani. 1990. *Focus groups: Theory and practice.* Newbury Park, CA: Sage.

Stewart, M. A. 1984. What is a successful doctor-patient interview? A study of interactions and outcomes. *Social Science and Medicine* 19:167–75.

Stocking, G. W., Jr. 1983. *Observers observed: Essays on ethnographic fieldwork.* Madison: University of Wisconsin Press.

Stone, P. J., D. C. Dunphy, M. S. Smith, and D. M. Ogilvie. 1966. *The General Inquirer: A computer approach to content analysis.* Cambridge, MA: MIT Press.

Storer, N. W. 1966. *The social system of science.* New York: Holt, Rinehart & Winston.

Storosum, J. G., B. J. van Zwieten, and T. Wohlfarth. 2003. Suicide risk in placebo vs. active treatment in placebo-controlled trials for schizophrenia. *Archives of General Psychiatry* 60:365–68.

Stouffer, S. A., E. A. Suchman, L. C. DeVinney, S. A. Star, and R. M. Williams. 1949. *The American soldier: Adjustment during army life.* Princeton, NJ: Princeton University Press.

Strathern, A. 1979. *Ongka: A self-account by a New Guinea big man.* New York: St. Martin's.

Strauss, A., and J. Corbin. 1990. *Basics of qualitative research. Grounded theory procedures and techniques.* Thousand Oaks, CA: Sage.

Strauss, A., and J. Corbin, eds. 1997. *Grounded theory in practice.* Thousand Oaks, CA: Sage.

Strauss, A., and J. Corbin. 1998. *Basics of qualitative research: Grounded theory procedures and techniques.* 2nd ed. Thousand Oaks, CA: Sage.

Strauss, C., and N. Quinn. 1997. *A cognitive theory of cultural meaning.* New York: Cambridge University Press.

Streb, M. J., B. Burrell, B. Frederick, and M. A. Genovese. 2008. Social desireability effects and support for a female president. *Public Opinion Quarterly* 72:76–89.

Streib, G. F. 1952. Use of survey methods among the Navaho. *American Anthropologist* 54:30–40.

Stunkard, A., and D. Kaplan. 1977. Eating in public places: A review of reports of the direct observation of eating behavior. *International Journal of Obesity* 1:89–101.

Sturrock, K., and J. Rocha. 2000. A multidimensional scaling stress evaluation table. *Field Methods* 12:49–60.

Sturtevant, W. C. 1959. A technique for ethnographic note-taking. *American Anthropologist* 61:677–78.

Sturtevant, W. C. 1964. Studies in ethnoscience. In *Transcultural studies in cognition,* A. K. Romney and R. G. D'Andrade, eds. *American Anthropologist* 66:Part II:99–131.

Subar, A. F., V. Kipnis, R. P. Troiano, D. Midthune, D. A. Schoeller, S. Bingham, C. O. Sharbaugh, J. Tabulsi, S. Runswick, R. Ballard-Barbash, J. Sunshine, and A. Schatzkin. 2003. Using intake biomarkers to evaluate to evaluate the extent of dietary misreporting in a large sample of adults: The OPEN Study. *American Journal of Epidemiology* 158:1–13.

Sudman, S. 1976. *Applied sampling.* New York: Academic Press.

Sudman, S., E. Blair, N. M. Bradburn, and C. Stocking. 1977. Estimates of threatening behavior based on reports of friends. *Public Opinion Quarterly* 41:261–64.

Sudman, S., and N. M. Bradburn. 1974. *Response effects in surveys: Review and synthesis.* Chicago: Aldine.

Sudman, S., and N. M. Bradburn. 1982. *Asking questions.* San Francisco: Jossey-Bass.

Sudman, S., N. M. Bradburn, and N. Schwarz. 1996. *Thinking about answers: The application of cognitive processes to survey methodology.* San Francisco: Jossey-Bass.

Sudman, S., and G. Kalton. 1986. New developments in the sampling of special populations. *Annual Review of Sociology* 12:401–29.

Sudman, S., and N. Schwarz. 1989. Contributions of cognitive psychology to advertising research. *Journal of Advertising Research* 29:43–53.

Sugarman, J. R., G. Brenneman, W. LaRoque, C. W. Warren, and H. I. Goldberg. 1994. The urban Indian oversample in the 1988 National Maternal and Infant Health Survey. *Public Health Reports* 109:243–50.

Sugihara, Y., and E. Katsurada. 2000. Gender-role personality traits in Japanese culture. *Psychology of Women Quarterly* 24:309–18.

Sugihara, Y., and J. A. Warner. 1999. Endorsements by Mexican-Americans of the Bem Sex-Role Inventory: Cross-ethnic comparison. *Psychological Reports* 85:201–11.

Sugita, E. W. 2006. Increasing quantity of water: Perspectives from rural households in Uganda. *Water Policy* 8:529–37.

Suhail, K., and H. R. Chaudhry. 2004. Predictors of subjective well-being in and Eastern Muslim culture. *Journal of Social and Clinical Psychology* 23:359–76.

Suhail, K., and R. Cochrane. 1997. Seasonal changes in affective state in samples of Asian and white women. *Social Psychiatry and Psychiatric Epidemiology* 32:149–57.

Sullivan, P., and K. Elifson. 1996. In the field with snake handlers. In *In the field. Readings on the research experience*, C. D. Smith and W. Kornblum, eds., 33–38. New York: Praeger.

Sundvik, L., and M. Lindeman. 1993. Sex-role identity and discrimination against same-sex employees. *Journal of Occupational and Organizational Psychology* 66:1–11.

Surowiecki, J. 2004. *The wisdom of crowds: Why the many are smarter than the few and how collective wisdom shapes business, economies, societies and nations.* New York: Doubleday.

Sutrop, U. 2001. List task and a cognitive salience index. *Field Methods* 13:263–76.

Swan, D. C., and G. R. Campbell. 1989. Differential reproduction rates and Osage population change, 1877–1907. *Plains Anthropologist* 34(124, pt. 2):61–74.

Swora, M. G. 2003. Using cultural consensus analysis to study sexual risk perception: A report on a pilot study. *Culture, Health, and Sexuality* 5:339–52.

Sykes, R. E., and E. E. Brent. 1983. *Policing: A social behaviorist perspective.* New Brunswick, NJ: Rutgers University Press.

Sykes, R. E., R. D. Rowley, and J. M. Schaefer. 1990. Effects of group participation on drinking behaviors in public bars: An observational survey. *Journal of Social Behavior and Personality* 5(special issue):385–402.

Szalai, A., ed. 1972. *The use of time. Daily activities of urban and suburban populations in twelve countries.* The Hague: Mouton.

Tannen, D. 2005. *Conversational style: Analyzing talk among friends.* New York: Oxford University Press.

Tashakkori, A., and C. Teddlie. 2003. *Handbook of mixed methods in social and behavioral research.* Thousand Oaks, CA: Sage.

Taylor, H. 1997. The very different methods used to conduct telephone surveys of the public. *Journal of the Marketing Research Society* 37:421–32.

Taylor, S. J., and R. Bogdan. 1984. *Introduction to qualitative research methods.* 2nd ed. New York: Wiley.

Tedlock, D. 1977. Toward an oral poetics. *New Literary History* 8:507–19.

Tedlock, D. 1987. Hearing a voice in an ancient text: Quiché Maya poetics in performance. In *Native American discourse: Poetics and rhetoric*, J. Sherzer and A. Woodbury, eds., 140–75. Cambridge: Cambridge University Press.

ten Have, P. 1999. *Doing conversation analysis: A practical guide.* Thousand Oaks, CA: Sage.

Tesch, R. 1990. *Qualitative research: Analysis types and software tools.* New York: Falmer Press.

Tewksbury, R. 2002. Bathhouse intercourse: Structural and behavioral aspects of an erotic oasis. *Deviant Behavior* 23:75–112.

Thaler, R. H. 1988. The ultimatum game. *The Journal of Economic Perspectives* 2:195–206.

Thomas, D., E. Frankenber, and J. P. Smith. 2001. Lost but not forgotten: Attrition and follow-up in the Indonesia family life survey. *The Journal of Human Resources* 36:556–92.

Thomas, J. S. 1981. The economic determinants on leadership on a Tojalabal Maya community. *American Ethnologist* 8:127–38.

Thompson, E. C., and Z. Juan. 2006. Comparative cultural salience: Measures using free-list data. *Field Methods* 18:398–412.

Thurman, Q., S. Jackson, and J. Zhao. 1993. Drunk-driving research and innovation: A factorial survey study of decisions to drink and drive. *Social Science Research* 22:245–64.

Thurstone, L. L. 1927. A law of comparative judgment. *Psychological Review* 34:273–86.

Timm, J. R., ed. 1992. *Texts in context. Traditional hermeneutics in South Asia.* Albany: State University of New York Press.

Tinsley, H. E., D. J. Tinsley, and C. E. Croskeys. 2002. Park usage, social milieu, and psychosocial benefits of park use reported by older urban park users from four ethnic groups. *Leisure Sciences* 24:199–218.

Tooker, E. 1997. Introduction. In *Systems of consanguinity and affinity of the human family*, L. H. Morgan, ed., vii–xx. Lincoln: University of Nebraska Press.

Topp, L., B. Barker, and L. Degenhardt. 2004. The external validity of the results derived from ecstasy users recruited using purposive sampling strategies. *Drug and Alcohol Dependence* 73:33–40.

Torgerson, W. S. 1958. *Theory and methods of scaling.* New York: Wiley.

Torres, V. M. 2005. A cultural model of pregnancy: A comparison between Mexican physicians and working-class women in Tijuana, B.C. *The Social Science Journal* 42:91–96.

Torres Sarmiento, S. 2002. *Making ends meet: Income-generating strategies among Mexican immigrants.* New York: LFB Scholarly Publishing LLC.

Toulmin, S. E. 1980. Philosophy of science. *Encyclopaedia brittanica.* Vol. 16. Chicago: Encyclopaedia Brittanica.

Tourangeau, R., and T. W. Smith. 1996. Asking sensitive questions: The impact of data collection, question format, and question context. *Public Opinion Quarterly* 60:275–304.

Tourangeau, R., L. J. Rips, and K. Rasinksi. 2000. *The psychology of survey response.* New York: Cambridge University Press.

Tourangeau, R., and T. Yan. 2007. Sensitive questions in surveys. *Psychological Bulletin* 133:859–83.

Tourangeau, R., and C. Ye. 2009. The framing of the survey request and panel attrition. *Public Opinion Quarterly* 73:338–48.

Transportation Research Board and Institute of Medicine. 2005. Does the built environment influence physical activity? Examining the evidence. Special Report 282. Washington, DC: Transportation Research Board. http://onlinepubs.trb.org/onlinepubs/sr/sr282.pdf (accessed March 8, 2010).

Tremblay, M. 1957. The key informant technique: A non-ethnographic application. *American Anthropologist* 59:688–701.

Trent, R., and H. R. Bernard. 1985. Local support for an innovative transit system. *Journal of Advanced Transportation Research* 19:237–39.

Trockel, M., A. Wall, S. S. Williams, and J. Reis. 2008. When the party for some becomes a problem for others: The effect of perceived secondhand consequences of drinking behavior on drinking norms. *The Journal of Psychology* 142:57–69.

Trost, J. E. 1986. Statistically nonrepresentative stratified sampling: A sampling technique for qualitative studies. *Qualitative Sociology* 9:54–57.

Trotter, R. T., II. 1981. *Remedios caseros*: Mexican-American home remedies and community health problems. *Social Science and Medicine* 15B:107–14.

Trotter, R. T., II, R. H. Needle, E. Goosby, C. Bates, and M. Singer. 2001. A methodological model for rapid assessment response and evaluation: The RARE program in public health. *Field Methods* 13:137–59.

Tsang, J-A, and W. C. Rowatt. 2007. *International Journal for the Psychology of Religion* 17:99–120.

Tukey, J. W. 1977. *Exploratory data analysis.* Reading, MA: Addison-Wesley Publishing Co.

Tuladhar, S. M., S. S. Acharya, M. Pradhan, J. Pollock, and G. Dallabetta. 1998. The role of pharmacists in HIV/STD prevention: Evaluation of an STD syndromic management intervention in Nepal. *AIDS* 12(Suppl. 2):S81–S87.

Turnage, A. K. 2008. Email flaming behavior and organizational conflict. *Journal of Computer-Mediated Communication* 13:43–59.

Turnbull, C. 1972. *The mountain people.* New York: Simon & Schuster.

Turnbull, C. 1986. Sex and gender: The role of subjectivity in field research. In *Self, sex and gender in cross-cultural fieldwork*, T. L. Whitehead and M. E. Conaway, eds., 17–29. Urbana: University of Illinois Press.

Turner, S. P. 1986. *The search for a methodology of social science.* Boston: D. Reidel Publishing Co.

Tversky, A., and D. Kahneman. 1971. Belief in the law of small numbers. *Psychological Bulletin* 76:105–10.

Twenge, J. M. 1997. Attitudes towards women, 1970–1995. *Psychology of Women Quarterly* 21:35–51.

Twisk, J., and W. de Vente. 2002. Attrition in longitudinal studies: How to deal with missing data. *Journal of Clinical Epidemiology* 55:329–37.

Tyler, S. A., ed. 1969. *Cognitive anthropology.* New York: Holt, Rinehart and Winston.

Uchendu, V. 1965. *The Igbo of Southeastern Nigeria.* New York: Holt, Rinehart & Winston.

Umezaki, M., T. Yamauchi, and R. Ohtsuka. 2002. Time allocation to subsistence activities among the Hulii in rural and urban Papua New Guinea. *Journal of Biosocial Science* 34:133–37.

United States v. Pelley. 1942. Same v. Brown; Same v. Fellowship Press, Inc. Nos. 8086-8088. United States Court of Appeals for the Seventh Circuit. 132 F.2d 170; 1942 U.S. App. LEXIS 2559. December 17, 1942.

University of Michigan. Survey Research Center. 1976. *Interviewer's Manual.* Rev. ed. Ann Arbor: Institute for Social Research, University of Michigan.

U.S. Bureau of the Census. n.d. Statement by William G. Barron Jr. on the current status of results of Census 2000 Accuracy and Coverage Evaluation Survey. CB01-CS.06. http://www.census.gov/Press-Release/www/releases/archives/census_2000/000710.html (accessed March 8, 2010).

Vadez, V., V. Reyes-García, R. Godoy, L. Williams, L. Apaza, E. Byron, T. Huanca, W. R. Leonard, E. Pérez, and D. Wilkie. 2003. Validity of self-reports to measure deforestation: Evidence from the Bolivian highlands. *Field Methods* 15:289–304.

Vadez, V., V. Reyes-García, T. Huanca, and W. R. Leonard. 2008. Cash cropping, farm technologies, and deforestation: What are the connections? A model with empirical data from the Bolivian Amazon. *Human Organization* 67:384–96.

van de Mortel, T. F. 2008. Faking it: Social desirability response bias in self-report research. *Australian Journal of Advanced Nursing* 25:40–48.

van den Borne, F. 2007. Using mystery clients to assess condom negotiation in Malawi: Some ethical concerns. *Studies in Family Planning* 38:322–30.

Van den Broeck, J., S. Argeseanu Cunningham, R. Eeckels, and K. Herbst. 2005. Data cleaning: Detecting, diagnosing, and editing data abnormalities. *PLoS Med* 2:e267.

van der Geest, S., and S. Sarkodie. 1998. The fake patient: A research experiment in a Ghanaian hospital. *Social Science & Medicine* 47:1373–81.

Van Hattum, M. J. C., and E. D. de Leeuw. 1999. A disk-by-mail survey of pupils in primary schools: Data quality and logistics. *Journal of Official Statistics* 15:413–29.

Van Maanen, J. 1973. Observations on the making of a policeman. *Human Organization* 32:407–18.

Van Maanen, J. ed. 1983. *Qualitative methodology.* Beverly Hills, CA: Sage.

Van Vliet, K. J. 2008. Shame and resilience in adulthood: A grounded theory study. *Journal of Counseling Psychology* 55:233–45.

Van Willigen, J., and V. C. Channa. 1991. Law, custom, and crimes against women: The problem of dowry death in India. *Human Organization* 50:369–77.

Vannatta, R. A. 1996. Risk factors related to suicidal behavior among male and female adolescents. *Journal of Youth and Adolescence* 25:149–60.

Vasquez, L. A., E. Garcia-Vasquez, S. A. Bauman, and A. S. Sierra. 1997. Skin color, acculturation, and community interest among Mexican American students: A research note. *Hispanic Journal of Behavioral Sciences* 19:377–86.

Vaughn, S., J. S. Schumm, and J. M. Sinagub. 1996. *Focus group interviews in education and psychology.* Thousand Oaks, CA: Sage.

Verma, R. K., G. Rangaiyan, R. Singh, S. Sharma, and P. J. Pelto. 2001. A study of male sexual health problems in a Mumbai slum population. *Culture, Health, and Sexuality* 3:339–52.

Viberg, N., P. Mujinja, W. Kalala, L. Kumaranayake, S. Vyas, G. Tomson, and C. S. Lundborg. 2009. STI management in Tanzanian private drugstores: Practices and roles of drug sellers. *Sexually Transmitted Infections* 85:300–307.

Vieth, A. Z., K. K. Hagglund, D. L. Clay, and R. G. Frank. 1997. The contribution of hope and affectivity to diabetes-related disability: An exploratory study. *Journal of Clinical Psychology in Medical Settings* 4:65–77.

Villaveces, A., P. Cummings, V. E. Espitia, T. D. Koespell, B. McKnight, and A. L. Kellerman. 2000. Effect of a ban on carrying firearms on homicide rates in 2 Colombian cities. *JAMA* 283(9):1205–9.

Vincke, J., R. Bolton, and P. De Vleeschouwer. 2001. The cognitive structure of the domain of safe and unsafe gay sexual behavior in Belgium. *AIDS CARE* 13:57–70.

Vink, M. P., and O. Van Vliet. 2009. Not quite crisp, not yet fuzzy? Assessing the potentials and pitfalls of multi-value QCA. *Field Methods* 21:265–89.

Virués-Ortega, J. 2006. The case against B. F. Skinner 45 years later: An encounter with N. Chomsky. *The Behavior Analyst* 29:243–51.

Voltaire. 1967 [1738]. *The elements of Sir Isaac Newton's philosophy*, J. Hanna, trans. London: Cass.

Wagley, C. 1983. Learning fieldwork: Guatemala. In *Fieldwork: The human experience*, R. Lawless, V. H. Sutlive, and M. D. Zamora, eds., 1–18. New York: Gordon & Breach.

Wagner, P. 2001. *A history and theory of the social sciences: Not all that is solid melts into air*. Thousand Oaks, CA: Sage.

Wainer, H. 1999. One cheer for null hypothesis significance testing. *Psychological Methods* 4:212–13.

Waitzkin, H., T. Britt, and C. Williams. 1994. Narratives of aging and social problems in medical encounters with older persons. *Journal of Health and Social Behavior* 35:322–48.

Wakin, E. 1992. *Anthropology goes to war: Professional ethics and counterinsurgency in Thailand*. Madison: University of Wisconsin, Center for Southeast Asian Studies.

Walker, I. 2006. Drivers overtaking bicyclists: Objective data on the effects of riding position, helmet use, vehicle type, and apparent gender. *Accident Analysis and Prevention* 39:417–25.

Wallace, A. F. C. 1962. Culture and cognition. *Science* 135:351–57.

Wallace, A. F. C. 1965. Driving to work. In *Context and meaning in cultural anthropology*, M. E. Spiro, ed., 277–96. New York: The Free Press.

Wallender, L. 2009. 25 years of factorial surveys in sociology: A review. *Social Science Research* 38:505–20.

Waltermaurer, E. M., C. A. Ortega, and L.-A. McNutt. 2003. Issues in estimating the prevalence of intimate partner violence: Assessing the impact of abuse status on participation bias. *Journal of Interpersonal Violence* 18:959–74.

Walters, A. S., and M-C. Curran. 1996. "Excuse me, Sir? May I help you and your boyfriend?": Salespersons' differential treatment of homosexual straight encounters. *Journal of Homosexuality* 31:135–52.

Walther, F. J. 2005. Withholding treatment, withdrawing treatment, and palliative care in the neonatal intensive care unit. *Early Human Development* 81:965–72.

Wanat, C. L. 2008. Getting past the gatekeepers: Differences between access and cooperation in public school research. *Field Methods* 20:191–208.

Wang, Y., and J. Heitmeyer. 2006. Consumer attitude toward US versus domestic apparel in Taiwan. *International Journal of Consumer Studies* 30:64–74.

Ward, V. M., J. T. Bertrand, and L. F. Brown. 1991. The comparability of focus group and survey results. *Evaluation Review* 15:266–83.

Warner, J., T. R. Weber, and R. Albanes. 1999. "Girls are retarded when they're stoned." Marijuana and the construction of gender among adolescent females. *Sex Roles* 40:25–43.

Warner, W. L., ed. 1963. *Yankee City*. New Haven, CT: Yale University Press.

Warner, W. L., and P. S. Hunt. 1941. *The social life of a modern community*. New Haven, CT: Yale University Press.

Warren, C. A. B. 1988. *Gender issues in field research*. Newbury Park, CA: Sage.

Warriner, K., J. Goyder, H. Gjertsen, P. Hohner, and K. McSpurren. 1996. Charities, no; lotteries, no; cash, yes. Main effects and interactions in a Canadian incentives experiment. *Public Opinion Quarterly* 60:542–62.

Warwick, D. P., and C. A. Lininger. 1975. *The sample survey: Theory and practice*. New York: McGraw-Hill.

Wasson, C. 2000. Ethnography in the field of design. *Human Organization* 59:377–88.

Watson, O. M., and T. D. Graves. 1966. Quantitative research in proxemic behavior. *American Anthropologist* 68:971–85.

Wax, R. 1971. *Doing fieldwork: Warnings and advice*. Chicago: University of Chicago Press.

Wax, R. 1986. Gender and age in fieldwork and fieldwork education: "Not any good thing is done by one man alone." In *Self, sex and gender in cross-cultural fieldwork*, T. L. Whitehead and M. E. Conaway, eds., 129–50. Urbana: University of Illinois Press.

Weatherford, J. M. 1986. *Porn row*. New York: Arbor House.

Webb, B. 1926. *My apprenticeship*. London: Longmans, Green.

Webb, E. J., D. T. Campbell, R. D. Schwartz, and L. Sechrest. 1966. *Unobtrusive measures: Nonreactive research in the social sciences*. Chicago: Rand McNally.

Webb, S., and B. P. Webb. 1910. *The state and the doctor*. New York: Longmans, Green.

Webster, A. K. 2008. "To all the former cats and stomps of the Navajo Nation": Performance, the individual and cultural poetic traditions. *Language in Society* 37:61–89.

Weinberger, M. 1973. Getting the quota sample right. *Journal of Advertising Research* 13:69–72.

Weinreb, A. 2006. The limitations of stranger-interviewers in rural Kenya. *American Sociological Review* 71:1014–39.

Weinreb, A., and M. Sana. 2009. The effects of questionnaire translation on demographic data and analysis. *Population Research and Policy Review* 28:429–54.

Weisner, T. 1973. The primary sampling unit: A nongeographicl based rural-urban sample. *Ethos* 1:546–59.

Weisner, T. 2002. The American dependency conflict: Continuities and discontinuities in behavior and values of countercultural parents and their children. *Ethos* 29:271–95.

Weller, S. C. 1983. New data on intracultural variability: The hot-cold concept of medicine and illness. *Human Organization* 42:249–57.

Weller, S. C. 2007. Cultural consensus theory: Applications and frequently asked questions. *Field Methods* 19:339–68.

Weller, S. C., and C. I. Dungy. 1986. Personal preferences and ethnic variations among Anglo and Hispanic breast and bottle feeders. *Social Science and Medicine* 23:539–48.

Weller, S. C., and A. K. Romney. 1988. *Structured interviewing*. Newbury Park, CA: Sage.

Wellman, B. 2007. Challenges in collecting personal network data: The nature of personal network analysis. *Field Methods* 19:111–15.

Wells, G. L., E. A. Olson, and S. D. Charman. 2003. Distorted retrospective eyewitness reports as functions of feedback and delay. *Journal of Experimental Psychology: Applied* 9:42–52.

Wengraf, T. 2001. *Qualitative research interviewing: Biographic, narrative, and semistructured methods*. Thousand Oaks, CA: Sage.

Wenze, S. J., K. C. Gunthert, and N. R. Forand. 2007. Influence of dysphoria on positive and negative cognitive reactivity to daily mood fluctuations. *Behaviour Research and Therapy* 45:915–27.

Weppner, R. S., ed. 1977. *Street ethnography: Selected studies of crime and drug use in natural settings*. Beverly Hills, CA: Sage.

Werblow, J. A., H. M. Fox, and A. Henneman. 1978. Nutrition knowledge, attitudes and patterns of women athletes. *Journal of the American Dietetic Association* 73:242–45.

Werner, D. 1985. Psycho-social stress and the construction of a flood-control dam in Santa Catarina, Brazil. *Human Organization* 44:161–66.

Werner, O. 1994. Ethnography and translation. Issues and challenges. *Sartoniana* 7:59–135.

Werner, O. 2000a. How to reduce an unwritten language to writing: I (vowels). *Field Methods* 12:61–71.

Werner, O. 2000b. How to reduce an unwritten language to writing: II (consonants). *Field Methods* 12:239–50.

Werner, O. 2001. How to reduce an unwritten language to writing: III (phonetic similarity, suspicious pairs, and minimal pairs). *Field Methods* 13:97–102.

Werner, O. 2002a. How to reduce an unwritten language to writing: IV. Complementary distribution. *Field Methods* 14:217–27.

Werner, O. 2002b. How to reduce an unwritten language to writing: V. Problems with phonemes. *Field Methods* 14:337–42.

Werner, O., and D. T. Campbell. 1970. Translating, working through interpreters, and the problem of decentering. In *Handbook of method in cultural anthropology*, R. Naroll and R. Cohen, eds., 398–420. New York: Natural History Press.

Werner, O., and J. Fenton. 1973. Method and theory in ethnoscience or ethnoepistemology. In *A handbook of method in cultural anthropology*, R. Naroll and R. Cohen, eds., 537–78. New York: Columbia University Press.

Werner, O., and G. M. Schoepfle. 1987. *Systematic fieldwork.* 2 vols. Newbury Park, CA: Sage.

Wertz, R. T. 1987. Language treatment for aphasia is efficacious, but for whom? *Topics in Language Disorders* 8:1–10.

West, C. T., and M. Vásquez-León. 2008. Misreading the Arizona landscape; Reframing analyses of environmental degradation in southeastern Arizona. *Human Organization* 67:373–83.

West, S. G., S. P. Gunn, and P. Chernicky. 1975. Ubiquitous Watergate: An attributional analysis. *Journal of Personality and Social Psychology* 32:55–65.

White, D. R., and T. Shweizer. 1998. Kinship, property transmission, and stratification in Javanese villages. In *Kinship, networks, and exchange*, T. Shweizer and D. R. White, eds., 36–58. New York: Cambridge University Press.

White, K. R. 1980. Socio-economic status and academic achievement. *Evaluation in Education* 4:79–81.

White, L. A. 1959. *The evolution of culture. The development of civilization to the fall of Rome.* New York: McGraw-Hill.

White, L. A. 1963. *The ethnography and ethnology of Franz Boas.* Austin: The Museum of the University of Texas.

Whitehead, T. L., and M. E. Conaway, eds. 1986. *Self, sex and gender in cross-cultural fieldwork.* Urbana: University of Illinois Press.

Whiting, B. W., and J. W. M. Whiting. 1973. Methods for observing and recording behavior. In *Handbook of method in cultural anthropology*, R. Naroll and R. Cohen, eds., 282–315. New York: Columbia University Press.

Whiting, B. W., and J. W. M. Whiting (with R. Longabaugh). 1975. *Children of six cultures: A psycho-cultural analysis.* Cambridge, MA: Harvard University Press.

Whiting, J. W. M. 1982. Standards for psychocultural research. In *Crisis in anthropology. View from Spring Hill, 1980*, E. A. Hoebel, R. Currier, and S. Kaiser, eds., 155–64. New York: Garland.

Whiting, J. W. M., I. L. Child, and W. W. Lambert et al. 1966. *Field guide for a study of socialization.* New York: Wiley.

WHO. 1993. *Focused ethnographic study of acute respiratory infections.* Division for the Control of Diarrhoeal and Respiratory Diseases, ARI/93.2. Geneva: WHO.

Whyte, W. F. 1960. Interviewing in field research. In *Human organization research*, R. W. Adams and J. J. Preiss, eds., 299–314. Homewood, IL: Dorsey.

Whyte, W. F. 1981 [1943]. *Street corner society: The social structure of an Italian slum.* 3rd ed. Chicago: University of Chicago.

Whyte, W. F. 1984. *Learning from the field: A guide from experience.* Newbury Park, CA: Sage.

Whyte, W. F. 1989. Doing research in Cornerville. In *In the field: Readings on the field research experience*, C. D. Smith and W. Kornblum, eds. 69–82. New York: Praeger.

Whyte, W. F. 1996a. Qualitative sociology and deconstructionism. *Qualitative Inquiry* 2:220–26.

Whyte, W. F. 1996b. Facts, interpretations and ethics in qualitative inquiry. *Qualitative Inquiry* 2:242–44.

Whyte, W. F., and K. K. Whyte. 1984. *Learning from the field: A guide from experience.* Newbury Park, CA: Sage.

Wiederman, M., D. Weis, and E. Algeier. 1994. The effect of question preface on response rates in a telephone survey of sexual experience. *Archives of Sexual Behavior* 23:203–15.

Wierzbicka, A. 2004. The English expression good boy and good girl and cultural models of child rearing. *Culture and Psychology* 10:251–78.

Wiessner, P. 2009. Experimental games and games of life among the Ju/'hoan Bushmen. *Current Anthropology* 50:133–38.

Wilk, R. R. 1990. Household ecology: Decision making and resource flows. In *The ecosystem approach in anthropology. From concept to practice,* E. F. Moran, ed., 323–56. Ann Arbor: University of Michigan Press.

Wilke, J. R. 1992. Supercomputers manage holiday stock. *The Wall Street Journal,* December 23, p. B1:8.

Williams, B. 1978. *A sampler on sampling.* New York: Wiley.

Williams, H. A. 1995. Social support, social networks and coping of parents of children with cancer: Comparing White and African American parents. Ph.D. dissertation, University of Florida.

Williams, T. 1996. Exploring the cocaine culture. In *In the field. Readings on the research experience,* C. D. Smith and W. Kornblum, eds., 27–32. New York: Praeger.

Willis, G. B. 2005. *Cognitive interviewing.* London: Sage.

Willis, G. B., ed. 2010. Advances in cognitive interviewing: Applications to cross-cultural surveys. *Field Methods* 23(2). Special issue on cognitive interviewing.

Willms, D. G., J. A. Best, D. W. Taylor, J. R. Gilbert, D.M.C. Wilson, E. A. Lindsay, and J. Singer. 1990. A systematic approach for using qualitative methods in primary prevention research. *Medical Anthropology Quarterly* 4:391–409.

Wilson, D., J. McMaster, R. Greenspan, L. Mboyi, T. Ncube, and B. Sibanda. 1990. Cross-cultural validation of the Bem Sex Role Inventory in Zimbabwe. *Personality and Individual Differences* 11:651–56.

Wilson, D. S., D. T. O'Brien, and A. Sesma. 2009. Human prosociality from an evolutionary perspective: Variation and correlations at a city-wide scale. *Evolution and Human Behavior* 30:190–200.

Wilson, M. D. 1991. *Descartes.* London: Routledge.

Wilson, R. P., M. Nxumalo, B. Magonga, Jr., G. A. Shelley, K. A. Parker, and Q. Q. Dlamini. 1993. Diagnosis and management of acute respiratory infections by Swazi child caretakers, healers, and health providers, 1990–1991. Joint paper by United States Agency for International Development and U.S. Department of Health and Human Services, Centers for Disease Control and Prevention. http://dec.usaid.gov/index.cfm?p = search.getCitation&CFID = 8363&CFTOKEN = 79619267&rec_no = 82321 (accessed March 8, 2010).

Winchatz, M. R. 2006. Fieldworker or foreigner? Ethnographic interviewing in nonnative languages. *Field Methods* 18:83–97.

Windelband, W. 1998 [1894]. History and natural science. *Theory and Psychology* 8:5–22.

Winland, D. 2007. *We are now a nation. Croats between "home" and "homeland."* Toronto: University of Toronto Press.

Wittfogel, K. A. 1957. *Oriental despotism; a comparative study of total power.* New Haven, CT: Yale University Press.

Wolcott, H. 1995. *The art of fieldwork.* Walnut Creek, CA: AltaMira.

Wolcott, H. 2001. *Writing up qualitative research.* 2nd ed. Thousand Oaks, CA: Sage.

Wolcott, H. 2005. *The art of fieldwork.* 2nd ed. Walnut Creek, CA: AltaMira.

Wolcott, H. 2008. *Ethnography: A way of seeing.* 2nd ed. Walnut Creek, CA: AltaMira.

Wolf, D. R. 1991. High-risk methodology. Reflections on leaving an outlaw society. In *Experiencing fieldwork,* W. B. Shaffir and R. A. Stebbins, eds., 211–23. Newbury Park, CA: Sage.

Wolf, E. R., and J. G. Jorgensen. 1970. Anthropology on the warpath in Thailand. *New York Review of Books,* November 19, pp. 26–35.

Wong D., and C. Baker. 1988. Pain in children: Comparison of assessment scales. *Pediatric Nursing* 14:9–17.

Woods, P. 1986. *Inside schools; ethnography in educational research.* New York: Routledge and Kegan Paul.

Woodside, A. G., and E. J. Wilson. 2002. Respondent accuracy. *Journal of Advertising Research* 45 (September–October):7–18. Special issue: Survey methodology. The web.

Woolhouse, R. S. 1996. Locke. In *The Blackwell companion to philosophy*, N. Bunnin and E. P. Tsui-James, eds., 541–54. Oxford: Blackwell.

Worth, S., and J. Adair. 1970. Navajo filmmakers. *American Anthropologist* 72:9–33.

Worth, S., and J. Adair. 1972. *Through Navajo eyes: An exploration in film communication and anthropology.* Albuquerque: University of New Mexico Press.

Wuthnow, R. 1976. A longitudinal, cross-national indicator of societal religious commitment. *Journal for the Scientific Study of Religion* 16:87–99.

Wutich, A. 2009. Water scarcity and the sustainability of a common pool resource institution in the Andes. *Human Ecology* 37:179–92.

Wutich, A., and K. Ragsdale. 2008. Water insecurity and emotional distress: Coping with supply, access, and seasonal variability of water in a Bolivian squatter settlement. *Social Science and Medicine* 67:2116–25.

Yakali-Çamoglu, D. 2007. Turkish family narratives: The relationships between mothers and daughters-in-law. *Journal of Family History* 32:61–178.

Yancey, G. A., and S. W. Yancey. 1997. Black-white differences in the use of personal advertisements for individuals seeking interracial relationships. *Journal of Black Studies* 27:650–67.

Yarrow, D., A. S. Baron, and M. R. Benaji. 2006. From American city to Japanese village: A cross-cultural investigation of implicit race attitudes. *Child Development* 77:1268–81.

Yildirim, K., A. Akalin-Baskaya, and M. Celebi. 2007. The effects of window proximity, partition height, and gender on perceptions of open-plan offices. *Journal of Environmental Psychology* 26:154–65.

Yin, R. K. 2008. *Case study research: Design and methods.* 4th ed. Thousand Oaks, CA: Sage.

Yoshihama, M., B. Gillespie, A. C. Hammock, R. F. Belli, and R. M. Tolman. 2005. Does the life history calendar method facilitate the recall of intimate partner violence? Comparison of two methods of data collection. *Social Work Research* 29:151–63.

Yoshikawa, H., T. S. Weisner, A. Kalil, and N. Way. 2008. Mixing qualitative and quantitative research in developmental science: Uses and methodological choices. *Developmental Psychology* 44:344–54.

Young, J. C. 1978. Illness categories and action strategies in a Tarascan town. *American Ethnologist* 5:81–97.

Young, J. C. 1980. A model of illness treatment decisions in a Tarascan town. *American Ethnologist* 7:106–31.

Young, J. C., and L. Y. Garro. 1982. Variation in the choice of treatment in two Mexican communities. *Social Science and Medicine* 16:1453–63.

Young, J. C., and L. C. Garro. 1994 [1981]. *Medical choice in a Mexican village.* Prospect Heights, IL: Waveland.

Zahavi, D. 2003. *Husserl's phenomenology.* Stanford, CA: Stanford University Press.

Zaman, S. 2008. Native among the natives. *Journal of Contemporary Ethnography* 37:135–54.

Zehner, R. B. 1970. Sex effects in the interviewing of young adults. *Sociological Focus* 3:75–84.

Zhang, J., J. M. Norvilitis, and S. Jin. 2001. Measuring gender orientation with the Bem Sex Role Inventory in Chinese culture. *Sex Roles* 44:237–51.

Zhu, S-H., S. Wong, H. Tang, C-W. Shi, and M. S. Chen. 2007. High quit ratio among Asian immigrants in California: Implications for population tobacco cessation. *Nicotine and Tobacco Research* 9(suppl. 3):S505–S514.

Zigon, J. 2009. Morality and personal experience: The moral conceptions of a Muscovite man. *Ethos* 37:78–101.

Ziliak, S. T., and D. N. McCloskey. 2008. *The cult of statistical significance: How the standard error costs us jobs, justice, and lives.* Ann Arbor: University of Michigan Press.

Zimmerman, M. A., C. H. Caldwell, and D. H. Bernat. 2002. Discrepancy between self-reported and school-reported grade point average: Correlates with psychosocial outcomes among African American adolescents. *Journal of Applied Social Psychology* 32:86–109.

Zipp, J. F., and J. Toth. 2002. She said, he said, they said: The impact of spousal presence in survey research. *Public Opinion Quarterly* 66:177–208.

Zive, M. M., G. C. Frank-Spohrer, J. F. Sallis, T. L. McKenzie, J. P. Elder, C. C. Berry, S. L. Broyles, and P. R. Nader. 1998. Determinants of dietary intake in a sample of white and Mexican-American children. *Journal of the American Dietetic Association* 98:1282–89.

Znaniecki, F. 1963 [1952]. *Cultural sciences. Their origin and development.* Urbana: University of Illinois Press.

Zorbaugh, H. W. 1929. *The Gold Coast and the slum. A sociological study of Chicago's near North Side.* Chicago: The University of Chicago Press.

Subject Index

Author Index

About the Author

H. Russell Bernard (Ph.D., University of Illinois, 1968) is professor of anthropology, emeritus at the University of Florida and is a member of the National Academy of Sciences. He has taught or done research at Washington State University, West Virginia University, the University of Michigan, the University of Athens, the University of Cologne, the University of Kent, the National Museum of Ethnology (Osaka), and Scripps Institution of Oceanography. Bernard works with indigenous people to develop publishing outlets for works in previously nonwritten languages and does research in social network analysis, particularly on the problem of estimating the size of uncountable populations. His book (with Jésus Salinas Pedraza) *Native Ethnography: A Mexican Indian Describes His Culture* (Sage, 1989) won special mention in the 1990 Chicago Folklore Prize. Other books include *Technology and Social Change* (edited with Pertti Pelto, Waveland, 1983, 2d ed.), four editions of *Research Methods in Anthropology* (Sage, 1988; AltaMira, 1994, 2000, 2006), *Data Analysis with MYSTAT* (McGraw-Hill, 1995, with W. Penn Handwerker), *Handbook of Methods in Cultural Anthropology* (edited, AltaMira, 1998), *Analyzing Qualitative Data: Systematic Approaches* (with Gery Ryan, Sage, 2009), and *Social Research Methods* (Sage, 2000). Bernard received the 2003 Franz Boas Award from the American Anthropological Association for his service to the discipline. He was editor of *Human Organization* (1976–1981) and the *American Anthropologist* (1981–1989), and he founded and edits the journal *Field Methods*. He has worked since 1987 in NSF-supported research methods training programs and serves on the Board of Directors of the Human Relations Area Files.